P9-DYZ-958

International Directory of

COMPANY
HISTORIES

International Directory of

COMPANY HISTORIES

VOLUME 80

Editor

Tina Grant

ST. JAMES PRESS

An imprint of Thomson Gale, a part of The Thomson Corporation

Detroit • New York • San Francisco • New Haven, Conn. • Waterville, Maine • London

International Directory of Company Histories, Volume 80
Tina Grant, Editor

Project Editor
Miranda H. Ferrara

Editorial
Virgil Burton, Donna Craft, Louise Gagné,
Peggy Geeseman, Julie Gough, Linda Hall,
Sonya Hill, Keith Jones, Lynn Pearce, Kristen
Peltonen, Holly Selden, Justine Ventimiglia

Production Technology Specialist
Mike Weaver

Imaging and Multimedia
Leslie Light, Michael Logusz

Composition and Electronic Prepress
Gary Leach, Evi Seoud

Manufacturing
Rhonda Dover

Product Manager
Jennifer Bernardelli

LIBRARY OF CONGRESS CATALOG NUMBER 89-190943

ISBN 1-55862-584-4

This title is also available as an e-book
ISBN 1-55862-628-X

BRITISH LIBRARY CATALOGUING IN PUBLICATION DATA

International directory of company histories, Vol. 80
I. Tina Grant
33.87409

Printed in the United States of America
10 9 8 7 6 5 4 3 2 1

Contents

Preface

The St. James Press series *The International Directory of Company Histories* (*IDCH*) is intended for reference use by students, business people, librarians, historians, economists, investors, job candidates, and others who seek to learn more about the historical development of the world's most important companies. To date, *IDCH* has covered over 7,900 companies in 80 volumes.

INCLUSION CRITERIA

Most companies chosen for inclusion in *IDCH* have achieved a minimum of US$25 million in annual sales and are leading influences in their industries or geographical locations. Companies may be publicly held, private, or nonprofit. State-owned companies that are important in their industries and that may operate much like public or private companies also are included. Wholly owned subsidiaries and divisions are profiled if they meet the requirements for inclusion. Entries on companies that have had major changes since they were last profiled may be selected for updating.

The *IDCH* series highlights 10% private and nonprofit companies, and features updated entries on approximately 50 companies per volume.

ENTRY FORMAT

Each entry begins with the company's legal name; the address of its headquarters; its telephone, toll-free, and fax numbers; and its web site. A statement of public, private, state, or parent ownership follows. A company with a legal name in both English and the language of its headquarters country is listed by the English name, with the native-language name in parentheses.

The company's founding or earliest incorporation date, the number of employees, and the most recent available sales figures follow. Sales figures are given in local currencies with equivalents in U.S. dollars. For some private companies, sales figures are estimates and indicated by the abbreviation *est.* The entry lists the exchanges on which the company's stock is traded and its ticker symbol, as well as the company's NAIC codes.

Entries generally contain a *Company Perspectives* box which provides a short summary of the company's mission, goals, and ideals; a *Key Dates* box highlighting milestones in the company's history; lists of *Principal Subsidiaries*, *Principal Divisions*, *Principal Operating Units*, *Principal Competitors*; and articles for *Further Reading*.

American spelling is used throughout *IDCH*, and the word "billion" is used in its U.S. sense of one thousand million.

Users of the *IDCH* series will notice some changes to the look of the series starting with Volume 77. The pages have been redesigned for better clarity and ease of use; the standards for entry content, however, have not changed.

SOURCES

Entries have been compiled from publicly accessible sources both in print and on the Internet such as general and academic periodicals, books, and annual reports, as well as material supplied by the companies themselves.

CUMULATIVE INDEXES

IDCH contains three indexes: the **Index to Companies**, which provides an alphabetical index to companies discussed in the text as well as to companies profiled, the **Index to Industries**, which allows researchers to locate companies by their principal industry, and the **Geographic Index**, which lists companies alphabetically by the country of their headquarters. The indexes are cumulative and specific instructions for using them are found immediately preceding each index.

SUGGESTIONS WELCOME

Comments and suggestions from users of *IDCH* on any aspect of the product as well as suggestions for companies to be included or updated are cordially invited. Please write:

The Editor
International Directory of Company Histories
St. James Press
27500 Drake Rd.
Farmington Hills, Michigan 48331-3535

St. James Press does not endorse any of the companies or products mentioned in this series. Companies appearing in the *International Directory of Company Histories* were selected without reference to their wishes and have in no way endorsed their entries.

Notes on Contributors

Gerald E. Brennan
Writer and musician based in Germany.

Kimberly Burton
Writer and editor based in Michigan.

M. L. Cohen
Novelist, business writer, and researcher living in Paris.

Ed Dinger
Writer and editor based in Bronx, New York.

Paul R. Greenland
Illinois-based writer and researcher; author of two books and former senior editor of a national business magazine; contributor to *The*

Encyclopedia of Chicago History, *The Encyclopedia of Religion*, and the *Encyclopedia of American Industries*.

Robert Halasz
Former editor in chief of *World Progress* and *Funk & Wagnalls New Encyclopedia Yearbook*; author, *The U.S. Marines* (Millbrook Press, 1993).

Frederick C. Ingram
Writer based in South Carolina.

Brenda Kubiac
Writer based in Michigan.

Carrie Rothburd
Writer and editor specializing in corporate

profiles, academic texts, and academic journal articles.

Kevin Teague
Writer living on the California central coast; author of the novel *The Rise of Charlie Drop*.

Frank Uhle
Ann Arbor-based writer; movie projectionist, disc jockey, and staff member of *Psychotronic Video* magazine.

A. Woodward
Wisconsin-based writer.

List of Abbreviations

¥ Japanese yen

£ United Kingdom pound

$ United States dollar

A.E. Anonimos Eteria (Greece)

A.O. Anonim Ortaklari/Ortakligi (Turkey)

A.S. Anonim Sirketi (Turkey)

A/S Aksjeselskap (Norway)

A/S Aktieselskab (Denmark, Sweden)

AB Aktiebolag (Finland, Sweden)

AB Oy Aktiebolag Osakeyhtiot (Finland)

AED Emirati dirham

AG Aktiengesellschaft (Austria, Germany, Switzerland, Liechtenstein)

ARS Argentine peso

ATS Austrian shilling

AUD Australian dollar

ApS Amparteselskab (Denmark)

Ay Avoinyhtio (Finland)

B.A. Buttengewone Aansprakeiijkheid (The Netherlands)

B.V. Besloten Vennootschap (Belgium, The Netherlands)

BEF Belgian franc

BHD Bahraini dinar

BRL Brazilian real

Bhd. Berhad (Malaysia, Brunei)

C. de R.L. Compania de Responsabilidad Limitada (Spain)

C.A. Compania Anonima (Ecuador, Venezuela)

C.V. Commanditaire Vennootschap (The Netherlands, Belgium)

CAD Canadian dollar

CEO Chief Executive Officer

CFO Chief Financial Officer

CHF Swiss franc

CIO Chief Information Officer

CLP Chilean peso

CNY Chinese yuan

COO Chief Operating Officer

COP Colombian peso

CRL Companhia a Responsabilidao Limitida (Portugal, Spain)

CZK Czech koruna

Co. Company

Corp. Corporation

D&B Dunn & Bradstreet

DEM German deutsche mark

DKK Danish krone

DZD Algerian dinar

EEK Estonian Kroon

EGP Egyptian pound

ESOP Employee Stock Options and Ownership

ESP Spanish peseta

EUR euro

FIM Finnish markka

FRF French franc

G.I.E. Groupement d'Interet Economique (France)

GRD Greek drachma

GmbH Gesellschaft mit beschraenkter Haftung (Austria, Germany, Switzerland)

HKD Hong Kong dollar

HUF Hungarian forint

I/S Interesentselskap (Norway)

I/S Interessentselskab (Denmark)

IDR Indonesian rupiah

IEP Irish pound

ILS new Israeli shekel

INR Indian rupee

IPO Initial Public Offering

ISK Icelandic krona

ITL Italian lira

Inc. Incorporated (United States, Canada)

JMD Jamaican dollar

K/S Kommanditselskab (Denmark)

K/S Kommandittselskap (Norway)

KG Kommanditgesellschaft (Austria, Germany, Switzerland)

KGaA Kommanditgesellschaft auf Aktien (Austria, Germany, Switzerland)

KK Kabushiki Kaisha (Japan)

KPW North Korean won

KRW South Korean won

KWD Kuwaiti dinar

LBO Leveraged Buyout

Lda. Limitada (Spain)

L.L.C. Limited Liability Company (United States)

Ltd. Limited (Various)

Ltda. Limitada (Brazil, Portugal)

Ltee. Limitee (Canada, France)

LUF Luxembourg franc

mbH mit beschraenkter Haftung (Austria, Germany)

MUR Mauritian rupee

MXN Mexican peso

MYR Malaysian ringgit

N.V. Naamloze Vennootschap (Belgium, The Netherlands)

NGN Nigerian naira

NLG Netherlands guilder

NOK Norwegian krone

NZD New Zealand dollar

OAO Otkrytoe Aktsionernoe Obshchestve (Russia)

OMR Omani rial

OOO Obschestvo s Ogranichennoi Otvetstvennostiu (Russia)

Oy Osakeyhtiö (Finland)

PHP Philippine peso

PKR Pakistani rupee

PLC Public Limited Co. (United Kingdom, Ireland)

PLN Polish zloty

PTE Portuguese escudo

Pty. Proprietary (Australia, South Africa, United Kingdom)

QAR Qatari rial

REIT Real Estate Investment Trust

RMB Chinese renminbi

RUB Russian ruble

S.A. Société Anonyme (Belgium, France, Greece, Luxembourg, Switzerland, Arab speaking countries)

S.A. Sociedad Anónima (Latin America, Spain, Mexico)

S.A. Sociedades Anônimas (Brazil, Portugal)

S.A.R.L. Sociedade Anonima de Responsabilidade Limitada (Brazil, Portugal)

S.A.R.L. Société à Responsabilité Limitée (France, Belgium, Luxembourg)

S.A.S. Societá in Accomandita Semplice (Italy)

S.A.S. Societe Anonyme Syrienne (Arab speaking countries)

S.R.L. Sociedad de Responsabilidad Limitada (Spain, Mexico, Latin America)

S.R.L. Società a Responsabilitá Limitata (Italy)

S.R.O. Spolecnost s Rucenim Omezenym (Czechoslovakia

S.p.A. Società per Azioni (Italy)

SAA Societe Anonyme Arabienne

SAR Saudi riyal

SEK Swedish krona

SGD Singapore dollar

Sdn. Bhd. Sendirian Berhad (Malaysia)

Sp. z.o.o. Spólka z ograniczona odpowiedzialnoscia (Poland)

Ste. Societe (France, Belgium, Luxembourg, Switzerland)

THB Thai baht

TND Tunisian dinar

TRL Turkish lira

TWD new Taiwan dollar

VAG Verein der Arbeitgeber (Austria, Germany)

VEB Venezuelan bolivar

VND Vietnamese dong

YK Yugen Kaisha (Japan)

ZAO Zakrytoe Aktsionernoe Obshchestve (Russia)

ZAR South African rand

ZMK Zambian kwacha

The Advisory Board Company

2445 M Street N.W.
Washington, D.C. 20037
U.S.A.
Telephone: (202) 266-5600
Fax: (202) 266-5700
Web site: http://www.advisoryboardcompany.com

Public Company
Founded: 1979 as Research Council of Washington
Employees: 681
Sales: $141.6 (2005)
Stock Exchanges: NASDAQ
Ticker Symbol: ABCO
NAIC: 541611 Administrative Management and General Management Consulting Services

■ ■ ■

The Advisory Board Company is a Washington, D.C.-based public company that provides best practices research and hosts seminars for 2,500 health care industry members, including hospitals, insurers, pharmaceutical companies, and biotech firms. The company gathers information from its membership and beyond to produce daily and weekly news briefs, and generate about 50 major studies and 3,000 customized reports each year. These publications document the best, and sometimes worst, practices in the industry as a way to help members improve their management and ultimately save money. The Advisory Board approach has proven to be a cost-effective alternative to high-priced consulting firms like Boston Consulting Group,

Bain & Company, and McKinsey & Company. Consequently, the firm maintains a yearly membership retention rate of around 85 percent. Through its Web site, Advisory.com, the Advisory Board allows its members to search and download the complete findings of its major research studies, underlying data, case profiles, news stories, and other documents. The firm also offers H*Works, a program that helps hospitals implement the best practices revealed through Advisory Board studies.

ORIGINS VIA A NIXON ADMINISTRATION INTERN

The Advisory Board Company was founded by David G. Bradley, who was born in the nation's capitol, perhaps accounting for his early interest in politics (especially Republican politics from the age of 15). Born in 1953, he was of college age when Richard Nixon was elected president in 1968. While earning a B.A. in political science at Swarthmore, Bradley landed a college internship at the White House during Nixon's first term in office. Bradley also went to work for the Committee to Re-Elect the President, the infamous CREEP of the Watergate scandal that would end in Nixon's resignation from office. Bradley's dream was to run for the United States Senate by the time he was 30, and he viewed a business career as a way to achieve that end. In preparation he earned an MBA from the Harvard School of Business, followed by a law degree from Georgetown University.

In 1979, at the age of 26, he established the Research Council of Washington as a firm that was willing to conduct any type of research for any company in any industry. He initially set up shop in his mother's Watergate apartment with four Princess telephones and four folding card tables. Already he had an exit strategy in mind: build the business, sell it for a few million dollars, and then use his fattened bank account to seek elected office. Executing that plan, however, proved more difficult than anticipated.

It soon became obvious to Bradley that the business model he had designed for the Research Council was too broad and impractical. After four years he was earning about $25,000 a year, barely enough to pay the bills, let alone make him a wealthy senatorial candidate. And even if he tried to sell the company, he was unlikely to find any buyers. He had no choice but to put his dreams on hold and focus all of his attention on building the Research Council, which until this point had enjoyed a modicum of success, doing work for 200 of the Fortune 500 companies. However, the firm had not been able to gain expertise in any particular area, with the possible exception of such esoteric subjects as jet engine sales and the European fountain pen market. In 1983 the firm made a key shift in emphasis by establishing a dedicated financial services research unit, and to reflect this shift in strategy the firm changed its name to The Advisory Board Company. By 1987 its client roster included every major North American retail bank as well as large European banks.

In 1986 the Advisory Board launched a research division dedicated to the health care industry. It enjoyed steady growth over the next decade, building up its membership to include more than 1,500 hospitals and health systems. Nevertheless, the practice would only receive secondary status at the Advisory Board, which focused most of its attention on financial services. Then, in 1993, the firm established a corporate division to serve the research needs of the top executives of the world's largest corporations. The unit's first program, the Corporate Leadership Council, targeted the heads of human resource offices. In a matter of just 18 months, the Advisory Board signed up nearly half of the Fortune 500, a successful debut that further overshadowed the health care division.

As the Advisory Board finally found its footing in the 1980s and early 1990s, Bradley achieved the wealth he had long desired, but by now his political ambitions were moribund. More so, his life was far from glamorous and filled with drudgery. He told the *Columbia Journalism Review*, "My best friend threatened, if he outlives me, to have 'a man of fine research' chiseled onto my tombstone." On a 13-hour flight to Vietnam after turning 40 years old, Bradley had the rare opportunity to devote some time to reflecting on where he was in his life. As he recalled for *Columbia Journalism Review*, "I looked older. I was living in D.C., which had no elected senators. I wasn't a Republican anymore. I was never going to be a senator." Also during the trip, Bradley bought a magazine to read, prompting the thought that perhaps he could fulfill his interest in politics through the media. "If I couldn't take the course, then at least I could audit it," was how he later described his new ambition.

BRADLEY BUYS MAGAZINE: 1997

Bradley soon contacted a magazine broker and attempted to buy his favorite magazine, *The New Republic*, only to find the price tag more than he was willing to pay. Instead, in 1997 he purchased the *National Journal*, which covered all aspects of the federal government. At this juncture, Bradley turned his attention from the Advisory Board, although he continued to own it, and devoted his time to building a small publishing empire, adding the *Atlantic Monthly* in 1999.

To fund his journalistic endeavors, Bradley began to repackage the assets of the Advisory Board and sold off large interests in them through public offerings. In October 1997 the financial services and corporate practice divisions, serving 1,300 clients across ten different research areas, was spun off as the Corporate Executive Board. In 1999 Bradley raised funds for his media aspirations by taking the spin-off company public, netting $142 million.

After the departure of the Corporate Executive Board, Advisory Board became devoted solely to the health care practice, which had been somewhat neglected since 1996 when Advisory Board began focusing most of its attention on the development of the corporate division. Gradually the firm beefed up its best-practices consulting business, offering clients programs on such topics as emergency room reform, nurse recruitment, and heart care trends. *Investor's Business Daily* offered a sketch of The Advisory Board's health care "shared-cost" business model: the company "uses its own customers as suppliers of ideas and solutions to pressing peer issues. ... After arranging study groups among key member organizations, Advisory Board builds research

KEY DATES

■

1979: David G. Bradley forms the Research Council of Washington.

1983: Research Council becomes The Advisory Board Company.

1986: Advisory Board launches its health care practice.

1993: The company launches a corporate practice.

1999: The company's corporate and banking practices are spun off.

2001: Advisory Board is taken public.

2004: Frank J. Williams is named chairman of the board.

programs around key topics of concern. It then distributes the findings to members. The idea is that health care companies will learn from each other."

It was a clever strategy on a number of levels. The material could be used to form multiple programs that could be cross-sold to the same members, and the addition of new members cost virtually nothing. Most importantly, the Advisory Board programs were effective and far less expensive that those developed by big name consulting firms. The firm's excellent retention rate of its members spoke to the quality of its work. Although the average contract was less than $40,000, compared to the $1 million a large consultant might charge, Advisory Board clients usually bought two or three contracts a year. "That's enough to keep Advisory Board cash-rich," according to *Investor's Business Daily.* "Customers pay subscription fees upfront, though the company recognizes the proceeds over 12 months." As a result, the firm received about 80 percent of its cash in the first quarter of the year and had it available for use the rest of the year. As the new Advisory Board gained its footing, revenues inched upward, from $52 million in fiscal 1997 to $55.3 million a year later, $57.8 million in fiscal 1999, and $58.5 million in 2000.

At the start of the new century, however, the business really began to find traction. In April 2000 Advisory Board initiated the launch of seven new programs, rolled out in the ensuing months. To accommodate this expansion the firm also doubled it sales force. Five of the new programs offered best practices installation support for a set fee. Program implementation also formed the basis of a new endeavor in 2000, H*Works, which was dedicated to helping hospitals implement best practice solutions in such areas as patient satisfaction, the

recruitment and retention of nurses, bad debts, and the growth of revenue streams. The Advisory Board Company was well established in the hospital field by now, with 15 of the top 16 hospitals as clients, according to *U.S. News and World Report*, including Duke University Medical Center, Johns Hopkins Hospital, and Massachusetts General Hospital. In the early 2000s the firm began branching out, looking to tap into other potential client bases, such as pharmaceuticals and medical device manufacturers.

ADVISORY BOARD TAKEN PUBLIC: 2001

In 2001 Bradley was ready to duplicate what he had previously done with Corporate Executive Board, and papers were filed to make a $95 million initial public offering of Advisory Board stock. With Credit Suisse First Boston acting as underwriter, the IPO was priced at $19 a share and completed in November 2002. All of the proceeds went to Bradley and other company insiders. Afterwards Bradley continued to hold a 30-percent interest in Advisory Board, a number that would decrease as he continued to liquidate his stake in the business and concentrate on his magazine holdings. Advisory Board stock began trading on the NASDAQ and steadily increased in price, peaking above $35 per share by mid-February before tailing off, then resuming a steady climb above the $50 mark.

Wall Street was optimistic about the future of Advisory Board for obvious reasons. As the Baby Boom generation aged, the health care field, which was already one of the largest sectors of the U.S. economy, was poised to grow at an accelerated clip. Moreover, hospitals, a major client base for the firm, were under increasing pressure to cut costs and spending. The Advisory Board was much cheaper than consulting firms, and the information and data it had to offer addressed both costs savings and revenue enhancement, thus making the firm even more attractive to hospitals feeling an economic pinch.

Leading the company was Frank J. Williams, who joined Advisory Board in September 2000 as an executive vice president. He was named chief executive officer nine months later, and like Bradley, he held an MBA from Harvard Business School. He was also well versed in the health care consulting field, having learned the ropes at Bain & Company. He also worked at Vivra Specialty Partners, a private health care services and technology firm. Before coming to Advisory Board he served as president of MedAmerica OnCall, which offered outsourced services to hospitals, managed care companies, and physicians. In November 2004 Williams became Advisory Board's chairman of the board.

Under Williams, Advisory Board launched three new programs in fiscal 2002. The most significant was the Workforce Management program that helped senior human resource executives address the problem of a nationwide shortage of clinical staff and increased staff turnover. For the year, revenues increased 27 percent to $81 million and net income totaled $10 million. Fiscal 2003 was an even better year for Advisory Board, which enjoyed a record-breaking 89 percent renewal rate of institutional clients and a 24 percent increase in revenues, topping the $100 million threshold. Net income jumped to $14.4 million. The company continued to launch new programs—including the Margin Enhancement, Executive Leadership, and Service Line Management programs—and succeeded in cross-selling them to many of its existing customers.

The major program launch of fiscal 2004 was the Nursing Business Performance Program. This provided a comprehensive program to assist nursing executives in improving staff productivity as well as patient care. Revenues continued to climb in fiscal 2004, reaching $121.8 million, while net income increased to $18.7 million. The upward trend continued in fiscal 2005, as sales grew 16 percent to $141 million and net income increased to $23.3 million. Advisory Board had been involved in the health care field for 20 years, and there was every reason to expect the firm to enjoy long-term sustained growth.

Ed Dinger

PRINCIPAL SUBSIDIARIES

Advisory Board Services, Inc.; Advisory Board Investments, Inc.

PRINCIPAL COMPETITORS

Bain & Company; The Boston Consulting Group Inc.; IMS Health; McKinsey & Company.

FURTHER READING

Adams, Lorraine, Warren Strobel, and Kate O'Brien, "The Magazine of Restoration Washington," *Columbia Journalism Review*, September/October 2002, p. 28.

Alva, Marilyn, "Washington, D.C. Consultant Hits Stride With Unique Strategy," *Investor's Business Daily*, June 24, p. A04.

Kuczynski, Alex, "At Atlantic Monthly, a Tense Staff Sizes Up the New Owner," *New York Times*, September 29, 1999, p. C1.

Much, Marilyn, "Consulting Firm Looks To Ease Hospitals' Pain," *Investor's Business Daily*, May 25, 2005, p. A09.

Sherman, Scott, "Going Long, Going Deep," *Columbia Journalism Review*, November/December 2002, p. 48.

Shinkle, Kirk, "Inexpensive Products, Services Pay Off Here," *Investor's Business Daily*, May 1, 2003, p. A06.

América Móvil, S.A. de C.V.

———————— ■ ————————

Lago Alberto 366
Mexico City, D.F. 11320
Mexico
Telephone: (52) (55) 2581-4411
Fax: (52) (55) 2581-4423
Web site: http://www.americamovil.com.mx

Public Company
Incorporated: 2000
Employees: 23,303
Sales: MXN 182.15 billion ($16.71 billion) (2005)
Stock Exchanges: Mexico City New York NASDAQ
Ticker Symbol: AMXA AMX AMOV
NAIC: 517110 Wired Telecommunications Carrier; 517212 Cellular and Other Wireless Telecommunications; 555112 Offices of Other Holding Companies

■ ■ ■

América Móvil, S.A. de C.V., is the largest provider of wireless communications services in Latin America, based on equity subscribers (that is, based on the company's economic interest in its subsidiaries' subscribers) and is also the largest fixed-line operator in Central America. A Mexican corporation, América Móvil receives about half of its annual revenues from its activities in Mexico, where it operates under the name Telcel, but it also does business in most other Latin American countries and the United States. Carlos Slim Helú, the richest man in Latin America, and certain members of his immediate family, together hold a majority interest in América

Móvil through a holding company, América Telecom, S.A. de C.V., which also holds a controlling interest in Mexico's leading fixed-line telecommunications company, Teléfonos de México, S.A. de C.V. (Telmex). Next to Wal-Mart de México, S.A. de C.V., América Móvil and Telmex are the largest privately held (that is, nongovernment) companies in Mexico, in terms of annual revenue. América Móvil places its subsidiaries under a holding company named Sercotel, S.A. de C.V.

TELCEL BEFORE 2000

América Móvil traces its history, through Telcel, back to the establishment in 1956 of Publicidad Turística, S.A., an affiliate of Telmex—which was then owned by the Mexican government—that published telephone directories. In 1981 the government granted this firm a concession for the installation and operation of a wireless telephone system in Mexico. Publicidad Turística changed its name in 1984 to Radiomóvil Dipsa, S.A. de C.V., and in 1989 this company began operation under the Telcel trademark. Between 1988 and 1990 Telcel expanded its cellular network on its concession, Band B of the frequency spectrum, to cover the Mexico City metropolitan area and the cities of Cuernavaca, Guadalajara, Monterrey, Tijuana, and Toluca, and in 1990, when Telmex was privatized, Telcel began offering cellular services in all regions of Mexico. At the end of 1995 it held 57 percent of the market—a growing market because of frustration with poor service and installation delays by Telmex for fixed-line phones.

Telcel pioneered in the use of prepaid phone cards—called Amigo cards—in 1996 for economically

COMPANY PERSPECTIVES

We intend to capitalize on our position as the leader in wireless telecommunications in Latin America to continue to expand our subscriber base, both by development of our existing businesses and selected strategic acquisitions in the region. We seek to become a leader in each of our markets by providing better coverage and services and benefiting from economies of scale. We closely monitor our costs and expenses, and we will continue to explore alternatives to further improve our operating margins.

minded customers. Parents, for example, were reluctant to give access to mobile phones to children who could not be trusted to ration the time they spent chatting with their friends. These cards were heavily promoted, even by unorthodox means such as vendors in yellow jumpsuits at major road intersections. Telcel introduced a PCS system in Mexico City in 1999 and later extended this service to all regions of Mexico. At the end of the summer of 2000, it had almost 9 million of the almost 12 million cellular-phone subscribers in Mexico. It was also offering voice and data services.

AMÉRICA MÓVIL: 2000-04

Telmex began acquiring subsidiaries outside Mexico in 1999. By the time, a year later, it announced its intention to spin off América Móvil as an independent company for cellular and broadband Internet services, it was the largest mobile-service provider in Latin America, with about ten million subscribers. In addition to its Mexican base, it had, by the end of 2000, telecommunications interests in Argentina, Brazil, Colombia, Ecuador, Guatemala, Puerto Rico, the United States, and Uruguay. After the spinoff was effected, América Móvil was listed on stock exchanges in Mexico City, Madrid, and New York, but Telmex's holding company, Carso Global Telecom S.A. de C.V., retained majority control. A month earlier, Telmex issued $1 billion in five-year bonds to provide the new company with funds to engage in wireless-license auctions in Brazil, and it did not have to assume any of Telmex's debts.

Although Telmex's Telcel holding formed the base of América Móvil, the new company also had other important holdings, such as 49 percent stakes (later sold) in CompUSA Inc. and the Mexican cable-TV provider Empresas Cablevisión, S.A. de C.V. In addi-

tion, it was a partner, along with Bell Canada International Inc. and SBC Communications Inc., in a consortium called Telecom Américas Ltd. This consortium was aimed at developing wireless and broadband operations in South America, and it already owned cellular operations in Brazil and Colombia, broadband wireless services in Venezuela and Argentina, and a Brazilian telephony and broadband-cable unit offering pay television and high-speed Internet access. By June 2002, when Bell Canada International agreed to sell its 39 percent stake in Telecom Américas to América Móvil for possibly as much as $1.9 billion, the consortium was operating four cellular-phone companies in Brazil. (América Móvil also bought SBC's 12 percent stake.) The company won more mobile-phone licenses in Brazil later in 2002, including one covering the coveted metropolitan São Paulo market, making it a formidable rival to European-owned companies in Latin America's most populous country and one underserved in the cellular market, by Mexican standards.

América Móvil's headlong expansion continued unabated into 2003. Unlike its rivals, the company was not interested in just cherry-picking affluent customers. Using its Mexican model, América Móvil was eager to win customers en masse, regardless of how much money they had to spend. Relatively cheap fixed plans offered a given amount of minutes for a given amount of money. When the buyer used up the minutes, the plan automatically converted to an account that allowed further purchase through calling cards. América Móvil also customarily fielded two or three times as many points of sale as its competitors, mostly through third parties. "They believe a bigger net catches more fish," an industry executive explained to *Latin Trade*. "They want to get as many phones into as many hands as possible, so they make sure the phones are everywhere. ...It's simple stuff, and it's ruthlessly executed." América Móvil's expansion also was enhanced by its deep pockets and willingness to buy debt-ridden rivals on the cheap. Then Slim's lieutenants came in to cut costs and make the enterprises profitable, a hallmark of the Mexican tycoon's operations. A big acquisition was the purchase of Brazil's BCP S.A. from Banco Safra S.A. and Bell-South Corporation, for $643 million in cash. This made América Móvil Brazil's second-largest mobile-phone operator.

Before the year was out, América Móvil had spent about $1.2 billion to purchase wireless companies in Argentina, Colombia, Ecuador, Guatemala, and Nicaragua, as well as Brazil, where, in addition to BCP, it bought BSE S.A. for $185 million. The company paid about $417 million for Compañía de Telecomunicaciones de El Salvador (CTE) and $49.6 million for a 49-percent share of Empresa Nicaragüense de Telecomu-

in Brazil, 58 percent in Colombia, 155 percent in Argentina, and 27 percent in Mexico, its most mature market. The company also entered Nicaragua and Honduras for the first time. The value of its stock had more than tripled in two years. At the end of the year, the company had 61.1 million subscribers in 11 countries, of which a substantial majority were prepaid customers. América Móvil also had about 1.9 million fixed lines in El Salvador, Guatemala, and Nicaragua. In Mexico, the company had 28.9 million subscribers. In Brazil, with about 13.7 million subscribers, Telecom Américas (by this time only in Brazil) was operating a network covering the principal cities under the brand name Claro. Other brand names were CTI Móvil in Argentina; Comcel in Colombia; Porta in Ecuador; Personal in El Salvador; and PCS Digital in Guatemala and Nicaragua. The U.S. subsidiary, TracFone Wireless, Inc., was engaged in the sale and distribution of prepaid wireless services and wireless phones throughout the United States, Puerto Rico, and the U.S. Virgin Islands. It had 4.4 million subscribers.

AMÉRICA MÓVIL IN 2005

There was further expansion in 2005. América Móvil agreed, in August, to pay $472 million for Chile's third-largest cell phone company in subscriber terms, Smartcom. It also acquired Telecom Italia Mobile S.p. A.'s Peruvian unit for $503.4 million. América Móvil raised its wireless subscriber base to 93.3 million in 2005, a 53 percent increase over the previous year, and its fixed lines to two million. About 90 percent of its wireless customers were using prepaid-rate plans. The average customer paid $16 a month. Its revenues of MXN 182.15 billion ($16.71 billion) were 31 percent higher than the previous year. Net profit reached MXN 31.64 billion ($2.9 billion), 85 percent higher than in 2004. Net debt ended the year at MXN 55.8 billion ($4.8 billion), MXN 12 billion higher than the previous year. Of the company's 2005 revenues, Mexico accounted for just under half the total. During the year, América Móvil acquired a 20-year license to provide nationwide wireless services in Peru and reached an agreement with Hutchinson Telecommunications International Ltd. to purchase its wireless operations in Paraguay, which were operating under the brand name Porthable.

nicaciones, S.A. (Enitel). To raise money for its acquisitions, América Móvil had issued the largest corporate bond ever in Mexico in 2001. It also used derivatives in Mexico to refinance debt from its Latin American subsidiaries. The company had assumed $3 billion in debt to acquire operations in Brazil and Colombia. The business magazine *LatinFinance* chose América Móvil as its corporation of the year for 2003, citing its "astute acquisitions" and "deft issuance in the local capital markets."

By this time Telcel alone had invested $3 billion to far outstrip the competition in Mexico. Much of this money went to develop GSM, an increasingly popular rival to CDMA, which prevailed in the United States. Created in Europe, where it became the standard, GSM digitalized the signal but was expected to require telecommunications companies to instal more radio bases so that the infrastructure would support the number of simultaneous users. Telcel was also spending money on special corporate platforms such as BlackBerry, services to monitor truck fleets, and integration of e-mail with short messages and specific applications such as access to ERP. The company also was deploying or upgrading GSM networks in nearly all the other countries in which it was operating. By the end of 2004 América Móvil had begun providing many of the voice and data services supported by GSM technology, such as SMS, CSD, high-speed CSD, and GPRS.

América Móvil's rate of growth remained phenomenal in 2004. Its subscriber base grew 34 percent

América Móvil's weakest link was proving to be Brazil. Counting not only acquisition costs but also fees for wireless licenses and infrastructure investments, the company spent almost $5 billion in 2002-03 to launch Claro. However, Claro slipped to third place among wireless providers in 2005 and lost money, the only unprofitable América Móvil holding that year. Although it was still gaining customers, more than 80 percent were prepaid clients spending an average of less than $10 a month.

América Móvil further raised its dominance in Latin America in 2006. It purchased the Dominican Republic subsidiary of Verizon Communications Inc., which was providing fixed-line, wireless, and Internet service, for $2.06 billion. It also bought Verizon's 52 percent interest in Telecomunicaciones de Puerto Rico, the holding company of the leading telecommunications firm on the island, for $939 million. It also joined with Telmex in acquiring Verizon's 28.5-percent stake in the leading Venezuelan fixed-line and wireless provider, Nacional Telefónos de Venezuela C.A., for $676 million.

As of 2005, América Móvil had a complex capital structure. Some 68 percent of its capital was in the form of L shares, but this class of shares had no voting rights. More than three-fourths of these were American Depositary Receipts traded in the United States, with Brandes Investment Partners, LP, and J.P. Morgan Chase & Co. as the principal owners. Another 30 percent of the capital, constituting 93 percent of the voting shares, were AA shares. Almost 70 percent of these were held by América Telecom, whose voting stock was majority-owned by Carlos Slim and certain members of his immediate family. Most of the rest of the AA shares were owned by SBC International. Slim was the chairman of the board of América Móvil. The chief executive officer was Daniel Hajj Aboumrad.

Robert Halasz

PRINCIPAL SUBSIDIARIES

AM Latin America LLC (United States); AM Wireless Uruguay, S.A. (Uruguay); AMOV Perú, S.A. (Peru); Compañía de Telecomunicaciones de El Salvador (CTE) (El Salvador; 96%); Comunicación Celular S.A. (Com-cel) (Colombia); Consorcio Ecuatoriano de Telecomunicaciones, S.A. (CONECEL) (Ecuador); CTI Holdings, S.A. (Argentina); Empresa Nicaragüense de Telecomunicaciones, S.A. (ENITEL) (Nicaragua); Telcel (Radiomóvil Dipsa, S.A. de C.V.) (Mexico); Telecomunicaciones de Guatemala, S.A. (Guatemala); TracFone Wireless, Inc. (United States; 98%).

PRINCIPAL COMPETITORS

Iusacell S.A. de C.V.; NII Holdings Inc.; Telefónica Móviles S.A.; Telecom Italia Mobile, S.p.A.; Tele Norte Leste S.A.

FURTHER READING

Castellanos, Camilla, "Mexico's Mobile Phone Leader Forges Ahead in the Face of Increased Competition," *Business Mexico,* December 2001-January 2002, pp. 49-50.

"Continental Roaming," *Latin Trade,* May 2003, pp. 34-36.

"Divide and Conquer," *Business Latin America,* October 9, 2000, p. 3.

Gori, Graham, "Telmex Completes Spinoff of 2 Big Parts of Business." *New York Times,* February 8, 2001, p. W1.

Guimarães, Camila, "O problema de Slim no Brasil," *Exame,* April 12, 2006, pp. 64-66.

Krause, Reinhardt, "Company Sees Room To Grow In Latin America," *Investor's Business Daily,* March 23, 2005, p. A06.

———, "Mexican Carrier Hustles In Latin America," *Investor's Business Daily,* September 16, 2003, p. A06.

Luhnow, David, "Slim's Mexican Mobile Company is on the Prowl," *Wall Street Journal,* June 12, 2002, p. A16.

Lyons, John, "América Móvil Purchases Units in Chile and Peru," *Wall Street Journal,* August 11, 2005, p. B2.

Malkin, Elisabeth, "Big Mexican Cellphone Company Moves into Brazil." *New York Times,* November 23, 2002, p. C3.

———, "3 Verizon Caribbean Units Sold to Mexican Magnate," *New York Times,* April 4, 2006, p. C13.

Moody, John, "Mexican Cellphone Provider Expanding in Latin America," *New York Times,* September 11, 2003, p. W1.

"Movil Moves Beyond Mexico," *LatinFinance,* February 2004, p. 55.

Arcelor Gent

———————————— ■ ————————————

John Kennedylaan 51
Gent,
Belgium
Telephone: (32) 09 347 31 11
Fax: (32) 09 347 49 07
Web site: http://www.sidmar.be

Wholly Owned Subsidiary of Arcelor S.A.
Incorporated: 1962 as Sidérurgie Maritime
Employees: 5,623
Sales: EUR 2.34 billion ($2.8 billion) (2005)
NAIC: 331111 Iron and Steel Mills; 331221 Cold-Rolled
Steel Shape Manufacturing

■ ■ ■

Arcelor Gent, formerly known as Sidmar N. V., remains one of the largest companies within the Arcelor group, which was formed through the merger of Sidmar's parent company, Arbed, with Arceralia and Usinor in 2002. The Gent works operate within Arcelor's flat carbon steel division, alongside StahlWerke Bremen and EKO Stahl. The Gent plant, located along the Ghent-Terneuzen Canal produces nearly 4.5 million tons of crude steel, more than 4 million tons of hot rolling mill, and nearly 3 million tons of cold rolling mill each year. The largest part—nearly 40 percent—of the group's production goes to the automotive industry. The company is also a major supplier of high grade steel to the home appliance, mechanical engineering, and packaging industries. The original European Union countries comprise Arcelor Gent's primary market,

representing nearly 85 percent of the group's output. In addition, Norway, Switzerland and Turkey add an additional 4 percent to the group's sales, while the markets represented by the EU member countries admitted since 2004 add nearly 3 percent to sales. The company also ships to the North American and Chinese markets, although these remain minimal in the group's overall sales. In 2005, Arcelor Gent posted revenues of EUR 2.34 billion. The company took on its new name in 2006, as Arcelor fought off a takeover offer from India's Mittal Steel with plans to merge with Russia's Severstal.

EVOLUTION OF A BELGIAN STEEL PRODUCER

The development of the Benelux market's leading steel producer, Arbed, which as Arcelor later became one of the world's largest steel concerns, began in Luxembourg in the early 19th century. The earliest part of Arbed came through the establishment of Auguste Metz et Cie by brothers Norbert, Auguste, and Charles Metz in 1838, while another major component of the future steel giant was founded by the Victor Tesch in 1856, called the Société Anonyme des Hauts Fourneaux et Forges de Sarrebruck. Linked through marriage, the Metz and Tesch families joined together in 1871 to create a new company, Forges d'Eich—Le Gallais. Metz et Cie later joined with Mines de Luxembourg in establishing another steel producer, the Société Anonyme des Hauts Fourneaux et Forges de Dudelange in 1886.

By 1911, the two companies, together with their two joint ventures, were merged together into a single company, called Acieries Reunies de Burbach-Eich-

Dudelange, or Arbed, for short. Leading the merger was Emile Mayrisch—whose mother was a grand-niece of Norbert Metz, and who had served as director of the Dudelange works since 1897. Joining Mayrisch, who took the position of managing director of the new Luxembourg-based company, was co-founder Gaston Barbanson, a member of the Tesch family with links to Belgium. Arbed became the single-largest corporation in the duchy of Luxembourg, responsible for a large percentage of its gross national product.

Luxembourg remained under control of Germany until the end of World War I. Following the war, the company found its operations split among the new borders between Luxembourg, France, and Germany as defined in the Treaty of Versailles. In the context of the new geographic and economic situation, Mayrisch initially steered Arbed toward a union with its French steel counterparts, in anticipation of a possible economic treaty between France and Luxembourg, despite the objects of Gaston Barbanson, who preferred to seek partnerships in Belgium. The refusal of an economic treaty by France forced Luxembourg to turn to Belgium for an economic partner, however, and in 1922, the two countries signed a treaty of economic union, ending Mayrisch's hopes to create a Luxembourg-French steel giant.

Instead, Arbed turned to Belgium, establishing its first company there, Clouterie et Tréfilerie des Flandres, a producer of nails and similar products. In the late 1920s, the Arbed subsidiary was given instructions to begin buying up land along the Ghent-Terneuzen canal. Originally constructed in the 1820s, the canal had been deepened in 1911 to accept the passage of larger ships

to the city of Ghent (also known as Gent). With access to a major Belgian industrial market, and the strong transport facilities provided by the waterway, the canal was a promising location for the creation of a steel plant.

Through the 1920s, Arbed acquired property along the canal, and by the early 1930s owned some 210 hectares. Plans for construction of the steel plant were suspended, however, amid the economic turmoil of the 1930s. The outbreak of World War II and the German occupation of Belgium provided a new obstacle to the development of the Belgian steel operations. By 1951, however, Arbed's own production had surpassed its prewar levels for the first time, and demand for steel and steel products was rising steadily amid a general European economic boom. In the mid-1950s, Arbed, together with the Belgian authorities, began talks for developing the company's canal property and establishing a steel mill. Arbed launched preparatory studies for the construction of the mill in the late 1950s.

STRONG DEMAND FOR STEEL FUELS GROWTH OF INDUSTRY IN BELGIUM

By the beginning of the next decade, the project took on fresh impetus when the Flemish authorities agreed to dredge the canal in order to enable the passage of the new generation of 65,000-ton Panamax vessels to Ghent. At the same time, Arbed increased the size of its landholding, to 624 hectares. The following year, Arbed further defined the scope of the project, deciding that the Ghent site would focus on the flat product market. The company also set out plans to construct state-of-the-art blast furnaces, and add both cold and hot rolling mills. Arbed received approval for the project from the European coal and steel industry oversight authority in early 1962. By July that year, a new company had been established, called Sidérurgie Maritime, headquarted in Ghent. Arbed was joined in the new company's shareholding by a number of French and Flemish steel groups. Construction of the steelworks began in 1964, and by March 1966, its cold rolling mill began operation. The commissioning of the company's hot rolling mill came at the end of the same year, while the company's blast furnaces and steel mill were commissioned at the beginning of 1967, marking the full-fledged launch of Sidmar, as the company came to be known. Sidmar commissioned its second furnace in 1968.

Into the early 1970s, the company continued to expand, launching the second phase of its construction. This led to the construction of a coke factory in 1972, and two more production units through the 1970s, including a second cold rolling mill opened in 1971.

KEY DATES

■

1928: Steel company Arbed acquires land along the Ghent-Terneuzen Canal.

1962: With French and Belgian steel group investors, Arbed establishes Sidérurgie Maritime (Sidmar).

1967: The Sidmar works begins full-time production.

1975: The Belgian government acquires a minority share in Sidmar during a crisis in the Belgian steel industry.

1980: The Flemish regional government takes over a minority stake in Sidmar.

1990: Arbed buys out the share of Sidmar that is held by the Luxembourg government.

1992: Sidmar acquires 25 percent of Klöckner Stahl in Germany.

1994: The company acquires majority control of Klöckner, which is renamed Stahlwerke Bremen.

1997: Sidmar acquires Ferrometalli Safem, a steel service center in Italy.

1999: Arbed acquires full control of Sidmar.

2001: Arbed merges with Aceralia and Usinor, creating Arcelor.

2006: Arcelor restructures operations, and Sidmar becomes Arcelor Gent.

CRISIS AND RESTRUCTURING LEAD TO GROWTH

Yet Sidmar's growth was soon threatened by the international economic crisis and the near-collapse of the global steel industry during the 1970s. In Belgium, the troubles in the industry led to the nationalization of much of the country's steel interests. With their own operations in danger, Sidmar's Flemish and French shareholders pulled out of the company during this period, as part of the overall restructuring of the Belgian steel industry. The Belgian government, through the Nationale Maatschappij voor de herstructrering van de Nationale Sectoren (or NMNS) then took over the minority stake in Sidmar, while Arbed remained the company's majority shareholder. In 1980, the NMNS transferred its shareholding to Gimvindus, the holding company of the Vlaamse Regering. The Luxembourg government also acquired a stake in Sidmar. Throughout this period, investments in Sidmar had slowed; by 1981, however, the company had once again begun to expand, notably

with the commissioning of the first continuous rolling mill. The company had also launched a diversification effort in order to reduce its exposure to the cyclical steel industry, establishing its own investment operation, Sidinvest. The company also acquired stakes in ALZ, a stainless steel producer in Belgium, a share of Arbed's Brazilian subsidiary Belgo-Mineira. In 1988, Sidmar's diversification effort led it to acquire automation systems producer Egemin, based in Schoten. By the beginning of the 1990s, however, Sidmar had abandoned its diversification effort and instead refocused itself around its flat steel products operations. This was accompanied by a streamlining of its shareholder, as Arbed bought out the Luxembourg government's 17 percent in the company in 1990.

By then, Sidmar had become the single-largest unit in the international Arbed empire. Sidmar launched a restructuring in 1992, in an effort to drive down its costs amid the turbulent economic climate. The company then launched an expansion drive, targeting acquisitions in the steel sector. This led the company to acquire a 25 percent stake in Germany's Klöckner Stahl. By 1994, Sidmar had acquired majority control of the Germany steelmaker, which was subsequently renamed Stahlwerke Bremen. Sidmar followed this purchase with the establishment of its own sales operation, Sidstahl. In 1997, the company also acquired Ferrometalli Safem, a steel service center in Italy, from the Falck Group. Arcelor Group Flat Steel Producer in the New Century Sidmar launched a new expansion effort at the end of the 1990s, announcing a production capacity expansion backed by a EUR 450 million investment in 1999. As part of that program, the company inaugurated four new hot-dip galvanizing lines at its Ghent works.

In the meantime, Arbed had launched its own expansion drive, buying up a 35 percent stake in Spain's Aceralia in 1997. In 1999, Arbed moved to take fulll control of Sidmar, buying out the stake held by Gimvindus. Now one of Arbed's main subsidiaries, Sidmar relaunched its production capacity expansion. In 2001, for example, the company invested more than $215 million on a new continuous slab caster, as well as the expansion of its blast furnaces. In 2002, Sidmar found itself part of a much larger group after Arbed, Aceralia, and France's Usinor agreed to a three-way merger that created Arcelor, the world's third-largest steel group. Following the integration of the three companies, Arcelor announced the launch of a restructuring of its divisional structure, abandoning its geography-based structure in favor of a operational focus. As part of that restructuring, Sidmar received a new name, Arcelor Gent, in 2006. By then, Arcelor itself had come under pressure, after Indian steel leader Mittal launched a hostile takeover offer. Arcelor fought back, agreeing to a merger with Russia's Severstal in June 2006. The resulting company promised to become the world's largest steel group. Arcelor Gent was expected to remain one of the new group's major subsidiaries.

M. L. Cohen

PRINCIPAL SUBSIDIARIES

Agifep S.A. (Luxembourg); Arcelor S.A.(Luxembourg); Arcelor Finances & Services Belgium N.V.; Bourgeois S.A. (France); Decosteel N.V.; EBT GmbH (Germany); Paul Wurth S.A. (Luxembourg); Shangai Bourgeois Leicong (China); Sidarfin N.V.; Sidlease N.V.; Sidstahl N.V.; Sikel N.V.; Tailor Blank Genk N.V.; Zeeland Participatie B.V. (Netherlands).

PRINCIPAL COMPETITORS

Cargill Inc; Chongqing Special Steel (Group) Company Ltd.; Aceros Chile S.A.; Mittal Steel Temirtau; Indian Iron and Steel Company Ltd.; Nippon Steel Corp; Hitachi Metals Ltd.; Corus Nederland B.V.; ThyssenKrupp Steel AG; MAN AG; Mittal Steel Company N.V.; ACINOX S.A.

FURTHER READING

"Arcelor Facility Restarts after Explosion," *Metal Bulletin*, May 16, 2002, p. 18.

Burgert, Philip, "Arbed Eyes Full Sidmar Control," *American Metal Market*, December 13, 1999, p. 16.

"Electrabel to Build Power Plant for Sidmar," *Europe Energy*, December 20, 2005, p. 303.

"In Store for Sidmar," *Steel Times International*, February 2002, p. 17.

Kohl, Christian, "Sidmar Grows in Galvanizing," *New Steel*, June 1999, p. 66.

————, "Sidmar Spending Aims for Balance," *American Metal Market*, February 7, 2000, p. 12.

"SAP Upgrade for Sidmar," *Steel Times International*, September 2004, p. 6.

"Sidmar Posts 8.3% Increases in Turnover," *American Metal Market*, November 28, 2000, p. 4.

"Sidmar vecht Vlaamse regeling emissierechten aan," *De Tijd*, May 20, 2005.

"Sidmar zet Sidcomet project stop," *De Financieel Economische Tijd*, February 1, 2002.

"Staalgroep Arcelor wil voort investeren in staalkennis Sidmar," *De Tijd*, March 21, 2006.

"Staalvakbonden Sidmar en ALZ kiezen niet tussen Arcelor en Mittal," *De Tijd*, March 11, 2006.

"Vlaanderen werkt aan overlevings strategie Sidmar, *De Tijd*, February 22, 2003.

The Bama Companies, Inc.

———— ■ ————

2727 East 11th Street
Tulsa, Oklahoma 74104
U.S.A.
Telephone: (918) 592-0778
Toll Free: (800) 756-2262
Fax: (918) 732-2950
Web site: http://www.bama.com

Private Company
Incorporated: 1927
Sales: $220 million
Employees: 1,043
NAIC: 311410 Frozen Food Manufacturing; 311810
Commercial Bakeries; 311813 Frozen Cakes, Pies,
and Other Pastries Manufacturing; 311821 Cookie
and Cracker Manufacturing; 311822 Flour Mixes
and Dough Manufacturing from Purchased Flour;
311911 Perishable Prepared Food Manufacturing;
424420 Packaged Frozen Food Merchant
Wholesalers

■ ■ ■

The Bama Companies, Inc., manufacture oven-ready
products for customers in the quick-service and casual
restaurant industry and private label products for retail
in more than 17 countries. The company's three main
products are hand-held pies, biscuits, and pizza crust. Its
four facilities include Bama Pie, Bama Foods, Bama
Frozen Dough, and Beijing Bama. Bama's quality
processes include the company's own proprietary "business opportunity management process," Six Sigma.

1927–84: HOME-MADE PIES FOR RESTAURANT CHAINS

In 1927, Cornillia Alabama Marshall founded the Bama
Pie Company in her Texas kitchen. According to
company lore, "Bama" Marshall's homemade pies were
so delicious that people lined up outside the soda
fountain that sold them, waiting to purchase a slice. In
1937, Bama's son, Paul Marshall, and his wife, Lilah,
moved to Tulsa, Oklahoma, where they started a full-
fledged pie-making business, using Bama's recipes for
mouth-watering pie.

Bama evolved under Paul Marshall's leadership. The
small company that specialized in home-baked pies began
to cater to the needs of the biggest and best-known
restaurant chains in the 1960s. In 1967, McDonald's
added Bama's Fried Apple Pie to its national menu. By
the time Marshall handed over the reins of the family
business to his daughter, Paula Marshall-Chapman, in
1984, Bama Pies had grown into a $33 million-a-year
operation.

As the youngest child in the Marshall family and a
woman, Marshall-Chapman had not been in line to take
over the business. Paul Marshall had, in fact, considered
hiring a non-family executive, as well as selling the
company when it became clear that none of his three
sons wanted to be the next head of business. Then, during what Marshall called a "divine intervention," he realized that his daughter, who had worked for the company
for 17 years and had earned a bachelor of science in
business from Oklahoma City University (OCU) in

COMPANY PERSPECTIVES

Bama's success comes from our ambition is to be our customers' first choice and your supplier of choice. We achieve this through extraordinary vision, leadership, integrity, strategic focus and processes—shared by Bama's over 1,000 team members—with a single mission of "People Helping People Be Successful."

1982, knew how to run the business. Marshall-Chapman went on to earn a doctorate in commercial science from OCU in 1993.

However, the 31-year old Marshall-Chapman was viewed with some suspicion by customers and suppliers of the major food-manufacturing concern. "I was a rookie pregnant CEO," Marshall-Chapman recalled in a 1998 *Snack Food and Wholesale Bakery* article, adding, "Dad retired in September and I was due in May." The company's new chief executive inherited a company selling 75 to 85 percent of its output to McDonald's in the form of apple and cherry pies. However, the hamburger giant was threatening to pull its contract because "McDonald's was getting more complaints from its stores about our pies than any other product," Marshall-Chapman recalled.

McDonald's executives flew to Tulsa, and the two companies came up with a solution to their problem: double the number of inspections at the end of Bama's product lines. Two months later, the company had accumulated $100,000 worth of unacceptable pies. "We were just inspecting errors," according to Marshall-Chapman in the *Snack Food and Wholesale Bakery* article, "And losing money."

1984–94: FOCUS ON QUALITY IMPROVEMENT LEADS TO NATIONAL AND INTERNATIONAL GROWTH

Marshall-Chapman turned to Phil Crosby, whose *Quality is Free* had impressed her, for quality assurance help. Crosby was a proponent of incorporating quality improvement processes into a company's day-to-day operations. Crosby's quality audit of Bama revealed that the company was losing nearly $4 million annually because of waste that ranged from 5 to 25 percent of its business and generated half a truckload, or between 25,000 to 35,000 pounds, of unacceptable products a week.

Determined to make the quality improvement process work, Marshall implemented quality improvement teams in 1986, and within nine months, these teams had driven inventory write-offs down from $300,000 to nothing. The company also began to train employees in quality improvement, shutting down lines to do so. McDonald's QA director helped convince other executives at the hamburger giant's corporate headquarters to support Bama's quality improvement program. By 1989, Bama's quality program was a way of corporate life, and there were control charts in the dip room where pies received their sugar glaze.

Marshall did not stop there. After attending a W. Edwards Deming seminar in 1989, she began introducing Deming's concepts into the organization and implementing the Bama's Blue Flame, or Quality Process. The heart of the flame represented the company's mission, vision, and values, while the flame's internal surface represented its daily work, partnerships, planning, teamwork, and process management. By the early 1990s, Marshall had made reading Deming's philosophies a requirement for Bama management, with all managers also attending a series of Deming classes that Marshall led.

The 1990s saw continuing evolution in the company's quality culture and an 18 percent average annual growth rate between 1990 and 1998. Influenced by Stephen Covey's *Seven Habits of Highly Effective People* and The Baldridge performance excellence model, Bama's quality efforts were paralleled by an aggressive capital expenditures program, which, in turn, responded to new business demands. After being asked to develop a biscuit with a "made-from-scratch" taste for McDonald's in 1990, Bama built a new $38 million, 135,000-square foot facility, the Bama Foods facility, dedicated to biscuit production.

In 1994, the company invested in a second plant, this one to handle frozen pizza dough production. The $20 million investment entailed remodeling an old, 78,000-square foot furniture warehouse. All in all, Bama spent nearly $100 million on new plants and production lines between 1990 and 1994, by which time the company had reduced inventory losses by 90 percent, accident rates by 50 percent, and placement of products on hold by 75 percent. Overall production costs on apple pies dropped about 10 percent.

By 1998, the company's overall scrap rate was between 1.5 and 3 percent, and Bama devoted 10,000 hours each year to training.

At the same time, Bama was expanding globally and in new directions. In 1992, it opened a processing plant in Beijing, a 75,000 square foot facility that cost $15 million to supply apple, pineapple, and bean-curd pies

KEY DATES

1927: The Bama Pie Company is founded in Texas by Cornillia Alabama "Bama" Marshall.

1937: Bama's son Paul Marshall opens a pie-making business in Tulsa, Oklahoma, with his wife Lilah.

1967: Bama's Fried Apple Pie becomes part of the McDonald's fast-food menu nationwide.

1984: Paula Marshall-Chapman takes over the $33 million per year family business from her father.

1986: Marshall-Chapman implements quality improvement teams to reduce errors that threaten the company's business with McDonald's.

1990: After a successful test of a "made-from-scratch" biscuit for McDonald's, Bama builds a facility dedicated to biscuit production for the fast-food chain.

1992: A processing plant is opened in Beijing, China, to supply apple, pineapple, and bean-curd pies to McDonald's restaurants in China and Korea.

1994: Bama wins an award for business excellence from McDonald's.

2000: The company introduces the Bama Pie Heritage Collection of gourmet pies.

2001: Bama opens the Marshall Tech Center for research and development of new and improved products.

2003: Bama expands its flagship facility in Tulsa.

2005: Bama is awarded the McDonald's USA National Quality Supplier Award, the fast-food company's top honor for quality.

to McDonald's restaurants in China and Korea. In 1993, it entered into a joint partnership with McDonald's to explore marketing in China. In 1998, Bama doubled the capacity of Bama Beijing.

1995–2005: BAMA'S SALES RATE OUTPACES THAT OF THE RESTAURANT INDUSTRY

Bama also took steps to refocus on its core products in the late 1990s. In 1997, it stopped selling retail products in grocery stores, and, in 1998, it sold its 27-year old Bama Transportation Co. to ROCOR International of Oklahoma City, which continued to provide ground transportation for the company. Also in 1998, it launched its Culinary Group with one chef on staff to launch new dining products. By 2006, the group had expanded to three full-time chefs and a chef's consortium, consisting of certified master chefs and bakers, to create brandable products for marketing.

Continuing on its path for total quality management, the company began to draw attention for its emphasis on quality throughout the mid- to late-1990s. In 1994, Bama won the Oklahoma Quality Award. In 1996, it won McDonald's top honor for business excellence among its 4,000 global suppliers, the Sweeney award. In 1997, it was named one of Ernst & Young's Entrepreneur of the Year companies. In 1999, Bama initiated the Prometheus strategic planning and execution process, with teams at the corporate, facility, and department level responsible for developing and executing action plans that aligned with organizational priorities and opportunities. The following year, Bama integrated a company-wide Business Opportunity Management Process (BOMP) system to coordinate, manage, and measure new business opportunities and to improve current products and processes.

Two additional undertakings took place in the year 2000, reflecting a shift in The Bama Companies to more specialty items. The company returned to its roots with the introduction of a gourmet pie collection sold exclusively through the company's new online Bama Pie division. The Bama Pie Heritage Collection featured pies that were an inch larger in diameter than the typical nine-inch pie, hand-baked, flash frozen, and boxed. Bama Pie's 500-page web site contained baking tips, interviews with local and national guest chefs, bakeware for sale, and a children's area.

That same year, in a move to meet increased demand for specialty breads nationwide, the company also purchased the family-owned Bavarian bakery in Lawton, which produced 40 to 50 different breads each week. In addition, with an increasing number of restaurants turning to frozen dough that they customized in their own kitchens, Bama invested somewhere between $12 and $13 million in a third dough line at its flagship Frozen Dough facility. The addition allowed it to produce twice as much dough, or another 340,000 pounds, each day.

In 2001 Bama created its Marshall Tech Center to support new product research and development. The 28,000-square foot facility included a product development lab, a chef's kitchen, and a sensory area. Bama launched its Six Sigma initiative in 2001, requiring that all leaders in the organization complete its training. Six Sigma is a data-driven approach to analyzing the causes of and identifying solutions for business problems.

Initially, Bama selected eight managers throughout its business areas—operations, customer service, product development, maintenance, engineering, human resources, training, and finance—to become Six Sigma Black Belts. As part of the Six Sigma initiative, the Bama Training Institutes went to online to facilitate employee access to training The company also moved information about health benefits online and made a policy of encouraging employees to complete college through a tuition reimbursement program.

In 2001, Bama was producing 2 million biscuits and 1.5 million pies daily. It reentered the retail sales market, selling Bama-branded frozen biscuits and pies to a major domestic retailer. An ever-growing customer base and increased demand for new dessert products called for a boost in production capability, and in 2003, the company invested in a $20 million expansion of its flagship facility, which created 100 full-time jobs for Tulsa's flagging economy. The expansion added 42,000 square feet of space and more than 7,000 square feet of renovations. That year, Bama had revenues of $210 million and employed a total of 1,000 employees at its headquarters and four factories. The following year, Bama purchased a 1920s-era building to renovate and consolidate its corporate offices.

By 2004, Bama was steadily gaining in market share with a sales rate that was growing faster than rate of growth of the restaurant industry. In the overall frozen baked goods market, which had remained relatively stable since 1999, Bama's sales had increased 70 percent, from $120 million to $200 million. In the retail market, the company had a sales increase from $9 million in 2001 to $20 million in 2004. New products, which, in 2000, represented fewer than 0.5 percent of sales, accounted for more than 25 percent in 2004.

In acknowledgement of Bama's overall competitiveness and quality management, Congress awarded Bama the Malcolm Baldridge National Quality Award in the manufacturing category in 2004. The Baldridge award was created by Congress in 1988 to enhance competitiveness among United States companies and was awarded annually by the U.S. Department of Commerce. In 2005, the company won McDonald's USA's top honor for quality, the McDonald's USA National Quality Supplier Award.

In fact, Bama's number of products had tripled between 2000 and 2005, and between 1999 and 2006, it enjoyed a 47 percent sales increase. This position allowed Bama to elect to do business only with customers that shared its philosophy of developing long-term relationships and to refuse to take part in annual bidding for contracts. As the nation's largest producer of hand-held fruit pies, Bama looked forward to ongoing growth in years to come.

Carrie Rothburd

PRINCIPAL SUBSIDIARIES

Base Inc.

PRINCIPAL COMPETITORS

Flower Foods; George Weston; SYSCO; ARAMARK; Bimbo; Horizon Food; Interstate Bakeries; Jana's Classics; Maple Leaf Foods; Merkel McDonald.

FURTHER READING

Blossom, Debbie, "Tulsa, Oklahoma-Based Bakery Company Slices into Online Market with Gourmet Pies," *Tulsa World*, October 11, 2000.

———, "Tulsa, Oklahoma, Frozen Bakery Firm Invests $13 Million in Expansion, Test Lab," *Tulsa World*, December 15, 2000.

Daniels, Susan E., "A Recipe for Excellence," *Quality Progress*, June 2005, p. 54.

Droege, Tom, "Tulsa, Oklahoma-based Baker Plans New Headquarters," *Tulsa World*, August 25, 2004.

Oacyniak, Bernard, "Lightin' a Fire," *Snack Food & Wholesale Bakery*, February 1998, p. 20.

Theurmer, Karen E., "Bama Foods Bakes in Beijing: Quality Control and Bean-curd Pies," *World Trade*, March 1998, p. 46.

Bashas' Inc.

— ■ —

22402 South Basha Road
Chandler, Arizona 85248
U.S.A.
Telephone: (480) 895-9350
Toll Free: (800) 755-7292
Web site: http://www.bashas.com

Private Company
Incorporated: 1932
Employees: 14,000
Sales: $2 billion (2004)
NAIC: 445110 Supermarkets and Other Grocery (Except
Convenience) Stores; 452910 Warehouse Clubs and
Superstores

■ ■ ■

Bashas' Inc. operates more than 150 supermarkets and
superstores primarily under the banners Food City,
Bashas' Markets (and its rural counterpart Eddie's
Country Store), and AJ's Fine Foods. Bashas' stores are
located throughout Arizona, with a couple in California
and New Mexico. The company has a handful of stores
operating in Navajo (Diné) and other tribal reservations.
One of the company's supermarket formats, Food City,
is geared for Hispanic communities and accounts for
nearly half of revenues. AJ's Fine Foods touts itself as a
gourmet and specialty supermarket, featuring extensive
wine collections and prepared meals. Bashas' also operates an online grocery shopping operation through its
Groceries On The Go service. The Basha family, who
founded the chain in 1932, owns the company. The

company has a reputation for responsiveness to the
shopping preferences of local communities and is quick
to introduce new products and services.

ORIGINS: FROM LEBANON TO ARIZONA

Owing to its standing as a family-run business, Bashas'
corporate roots stretch back to the arrival of the first
Basha family member in the United States in the 19th
century. In 1884, Tanius Basha left Lebanon for New
York City, where he opened an import and export
wholesale store. Two years later, after his entrepreneurial
efforts had shown promise, Tanius sent for his oldest
son to come to New York to help him with his store.
Najeeb Basha, 16 years old when he arrived in New
York to assist his father, made the city his new home
and mercantilism his new profession. In 1901, he married a fellow Lebanese immigrant named Najeeby Srour,
and together the pair began raising a family from whose
ranks Bashas' would be founded. Najeeby gave birth to
nine children, all girls except for two boys, Ike and Eddie: the founders of Bashas' Inc.

Ike and Eddie Basha spent their childhood
surrounded by the mores of retail trade. Their father left
New York in 1910 to join several members of the Srour
family in Ray, Arizona. There, Najeeb assisted his in-
laws in the operation of a mercantile business. After a
stint working for his wife's family, Najeeb was joined by
his wife and children in Arizona and opened his own
store. The store later burned down, prompting Najeeb
to open a second store during the 1920s, by which time
his children, Ike and Eddie included, were old enough

COMPANY PERSPECTIVES

Thousands of Bashas' members have poured labor and love into the company since its founding. Like any family, the personality of Bashas' is a reflection of the quality of the people who work for and grow with the company. Bashas' has survived the ups and downs of the supermarket industry, increased competition and national economic fluctuations because its members are determined to work together to continually make the company better able to serve our customers. Many members choose to remain with Bashas' for decades, and we think that says a lot about Bashas', and a lot about the people who are at its heart, our members.

to lend a hand in the family business. The store, located in Chandler, Arizona, catered to the rural needs of its community, selling groceries, dry goods, and household goods such as furniture.

CHAIN BEGINNING WITH ONE STORE IN 1932

Ike and Eddie Basha learned the retail trade from their parents at the Chandler store, eventually deciding to enter the business themselves when they were old enough to set out on their own. They opened their own store in 1932, marking the beginning of what would later become the Bashas' chain. For their first store, they drew on the model created by their parents and took it one step further by placing a greater emphasis on serving the specifically rural needs of their customers. Aside from its primary stock of groceries, the Basha brothers' store carried a range of goods, including blankets, axes, and gasoline, presenting itself as the quintessential country store. The format endured for the ensuing two decades.

Although the two Basha brothers demonstrated their independence by becoming entrepreneurs, they by no means cut themselves free from their strong familial bonds. All family members, with Najeeby Basha presiding as family matriarch, were involved in running the first and subsequent stores. The women in the family played crucial roles in the business, with one sister serving as a buyer for the stores, another responsible for administrative matters, and other sisters working in various capacities to ensure the operational success of the business. With the entire family working in support, the stores secured a lasting presence in Arizona, representing

the pillars upon which a legacy of Basha involvement in the grocery business was built.

The success of the first store led to the establishment of additional stores in the Bashas' home state of Arizona. For roughly 20 years, the stores were modeled after the first country store, but by the 1950s a new breed of grocery stores was attracting consumers. Supermarkets, larger and stocked with a more diverse range of merchandise than traditional grocery stores, emerged as the format of the future for grocery retailers, convincing the Basha brothers that the success of their chain called for a revamped merchandising approach. They gradually began replacing their grocery stores with supermarkets, effecting an important strategic transition that positioned their stores to take full advantage of the postwar economic boom period.

EDDIE BASHA, JR., TAKING CONTROL IN 1968

During the pivotal transition from country stores to supermarkets, Bashas' lost the leadership of one of its founders. In 1958, Ike Basha died after a quarter-century of stewarding the fortunes of the family business. His death left his brother Eddie in full control over the enterprise, and he was soon joined by the second generation of Bashas in the business, his son Eddie Basha, Jr. After graduating from Stanford University, the younger Basha joined Bashas', helping his father to lead the company during a period in which expansion of the chain became top priority. The partnership of father and son at the helm continued until 1968, when Eddie Basha, Sr., died. At the time of his death, the Bashas' chain consisted of 17 retail outlets.

For a company whose affairs were governed by a tightly-knit family, the loss of the founding brothers could have marked the beginning of a difficult period, but Bashas' enjoyed a seamless transition from one generation to the next. The ease with which the company passed through this potential sticking point was attributable to the talents of Eddie Basha, Jr. In his early 30s when his father died and he assumed full control over the company, Basha developed into an influential business leader and into a much-admired civic leader. He became renowned for his elaborate pranks and gained widespread notoriety as Arizona's Democratic gubernatorial candidate in 1994, when he ran a "people," not "politics," campaign, deprecatorily referring to himself as the chubby grocer.

Basha lost the race for the governor's seat, but he recorded stirring success in building Bashas' into one of the largest private companies in the United States. His talent for expansion, however, was not fully expressed

KEY DATES

1884: The first Basha family member arrives in the United States.
1910: The Basha family moves to Arizona.
1932: Ike and Eddie Basha, Sr., open their first store.
1968: The death of his father leaves Eddie Basha, Jr., in charge of the company.
1981: Bashas' opens the first Diné Markets at the request of the Navajo Nation.
1993: AJ's Fine Foods and Food City join the company's fold.
1996: The Food City business is bolstered with the acquisition of bankrupt MegaFoods Stores, Inc.
1998: Sales reach an estimated $1 billion.
2001: Bashas' buys 22 Southwest Supermarkets at a bankruptcy auction for conversion to the Food City format.
2005: Bashas' is named "Retailer of the Year"; sales are more than $2 billion.

foot perishables warehouse, built to store the chain's frozen food, meat, and produce. A year later, in December 1992, Bashas' opened a 325,000-square-foot dry grocery facility, replacing the use of a leased facility in Phoenix. The new facilities, located 11 miles from the company's 40-year-old main office, composed Bashas' new distribution operation, which was consolidated with the offices of the buying staff by early 1993. Concurrent with the establishment of a single distribution complex, Bashas' opened its own health- and beauty-care (HBC) depot. Previously, the company had purchased up to 80 percent of its HBC inventory from a distributor named Impact Distributing, but control over its own depot enabled Bashas' to purchase nearly all HBC items directly from manufacturers, giving the company greater control over inventory. In the wake of the March 1993 debut of the HBC depot, sales increased markedly, ignited by the advantages engendered by vertical integration.

Rising sales became the predominant theme at Bashas' during the 1990s, particularly after the company embarked on an acquisition campaign that added several new store banners to its portfolio. Coming off $475 million in sales in 1992, the company made quick use of its new HBC depot and distribution complex by acquiring AJ's Fine Foods, an upscale, specialty chain offering prepared gourmet meals, a large wine collection, and specialty baked goods. Also in 1993, the company acquired a single Food City store in Phoenix. For 50 years, Food City had distinguished itself as a supermarket that catered to the particular needs of the Hispanic community in Phoenix, a tradition that Bashas' continued to observe once it took control of the format. Bashas' operated another format tailored for Hispanics, the company's Mercado store, which operated in southern Arizona.

As expansion moved forward, the company continued to experiment with merchandising mixtures and new services. In 1994, for instance, the company opened its first live video department in a Bashas' Markets—the word "live" designating that the actual videotapes were displayed on the shelves. Designed as a theater-within-the-store, the video department housed 5,000 rental units, or more than twice the number of units available at the company's other stores. Also in 1994, the company began installing two-foot by two-foot floor tiles that bore advertisements from national-brand manufacturers, using a tile system called the In-Floor Advertising Unit, patented by Indoor Media Group. Bashas' units, which secured an added revenue stream by using the advertising tiles, were among the first 100 supermarkets in the country to use the In-Floor Advertising Unit.

By late 1994, Bashas' operated 67 stores in Arizona,

until he entered his 50s. During the intervening years, as the company progressed through the 1970s and 1980s, methodical expansion took place, as Basha experimented with different merchandising mixtures. Like his father and uncle before him, Basha endeavored to create supermarkets that catered to the needs of individual communities, the tastes and desires of which often changed from one location to another. By searching for the most appropriate mixture of goods and services, he created stores specifically tailored to what the company called demographic neighborhoods. The fine-tuning process was never ending, as was the expansion of the chain, which by the end of the 1980s included approximately 45 units.

The size of the company at this point represented a half-century of growth, the product of the combined efforts of Ike, Eddie, Sr., and Eddie, Jr. During the ensuing decade, expansion occurred at a dizzying pace. In ten years' time, Basha more than doubled the size of the company, adding a stable of retail banners to the company's portfolio.

AGGRESSIVE EXPANSION: 1990–99

Before Basha began expanding in earnest, he built the infrastructure to support the company's imminent growth. In 1991, the company opened a 125,000-square-making it the third largest grocery chain in the state. Within two years, the company completed its climb up the state's rankings by completing another acquisition. In October 1996, Bashas' reached an agreement to acquire MegaFoods Stores, Inc. MegaFoods, with 16 discount stores in Arizona, was operating under Chapter 11 bankruptcy protection, having declared bankruptcy in August 1994. At the time of the acquisition announcement, Bashas' had 73 stores in operation, 63 of which operated under the Bashas' Market name. The company's other stores included one Mercado unit, two stores that operated as discount units under the Bargain Basket logo, three Food City units, and four AJ's Fine Foods specialty stores. The acquisition of MegaFoods, completed for $22.6 million on the last day of 1996, lifted the number of the company's stores to 89, making it the largest grocery chain in the state.

Following the completion of the MegaFoods transaction, attention was focused on what to do with the addition of the chain. In March 1998, the company announced that it was dropping the MegaFoods name and converting the units to either the Food City or Mercado format.

By 1999, the conversion work had been completed, marking the end of a fruitful decade for the company. Annual sales had reached an estimated $1 billion, representing a more than 100 percent increase from the total recorded seven years earlier. Expansion had taken the chain out of its home state and into New Mexico and California, elevating the company's stature to that of a regional force. For the future, Bashas' appeared well poised to continue its long record of success. Its close attention to the demands of the communities it served and its willingness to change with the times—the company embraced the lucrative prospects of electronic commerce by offering online grocery shopping through its Groceries On The Go Service—promised to produce positive results in the 21st century.

MORE GROWTH IN 2000 AND BEYOND

Bashas' was in growth mode for all of its concepts, a spokesperson told the *Business Journal of Phoenix* in 2001. It was adding up to ten new stores a year, many of them through acquisitions. Bashas' bought 22 Southwest Supermarkets for $9 million at the defunct chain's bankruptcy auction in November 2001. They were slated for conversion to Food City format. Sales were estimated at $1.6 billion for 2002, when the company had 135 stores.

Bashas' opened a dozen stores in 2004. The company was preparing to bring a supermarket to the underserved downtown Phoenix area. A mixed use project was envisioned to revitalize the city's core.

There was a changing of the guard in 2004. Wayne Manning retired as president and was succeeded by Mike Proulx, formerly senior vice-president of retail operations. Proulx had joined the company in 1966 as a "courtesy clerk." The company also was preparing for the eventual retirement of Chairman and CEO Edward "Eddie" Basha, Jr. His cousin A. N. John "Johnny" Basha, a 20-year veteran of the firm's real estate and development department, was designated his successor and named vice-chairman in 2005.

Progressive Grocer pronounced Bashas its national "Retailer of the Year" in 2005. The trade publication praised the company's investment in its employees, community involvement, and Hispanic-oriented merchandising.

Bashas' had doubled in size in the previous ten years, with a total of 153 stores extending throughout Arizona to Needles, California and Crownpoint, New Mexico. These were serviced from a 700,000-square-foot distribution center in Chandler, Arizona, which began supplying some IGA stores in Arizona and New Mexico in 2003.

The company's $2 billion in sales (nearly half of which came from Food City) ranked it third in Arizona's increasingly competitive grocery market, behind Safeway and Fry's (a unit of The Kroger Co.). Bashas' was the only locally owned supermarket chain in the state. The company had 14,000 employees.

Bashas' was one of the few grocers to experience rising sales. Proulx credited the performance with responsiveness to local market conditions. While its competitors' executives pored over demographic reports at their home offices hundreds of miles away, Bashas' was intimately in touch with the community and capable of tailoring its stores to serve individual neighborhoods.

Prepared meals were becoming ever more important in the grocery business, and Bashas' offerings in this department were a key competitive advantage. According to *Progressive Grocer*, all Bashas' stores had a full kitchen; an executive chef developed an extensive menu featuring items such as coconut-crusted chicken (a bestseller) and boneless stuffed pork loin. About three dozen stores had a stone oven for pizza. At least one site, in the Grayhawk resort town near Scottsdale, had a Taco Grill offering freshly made Mexican food.

The company's newest concepts were a health food supermarket called Ike's Farmer's Market and a miniaturized version of AJ's designed to fit in a condominium tower. Bashas' also was introducing retail health clinics in some of its existing Bashas' and Food City stores in partnership with MediMin Inc.

Jeffrey L. Covell
Updated, Frederick C. Ingram

PRINCIPAL OPERATING UNITS

AJ's Fine Foods; Bashas'; Bashas' Diné Markets; Food City.

PRINCIPAL COMPETITORS

Albertson's Inc.; The Kroger Co.; Safeway Inc.; Wal-Mart Stores, Inc.

FURTHER READING

Alaimo, Dan, "Bashas' to Expand Home Shopping," *Supermarket News*, April 24, 2000, p. 59.

———, "Bashas' to Open First Live Video Department," *Supermarket News*, November 14, 1994, p. 57.

"Arizona Business Hall of Fame Inducts Six Members," *Business Journal—Serving Phoenix & the Valley of the Sun*, May 25, 1992, p. 26.

"Bashas' Buys 22 Southwest Supermarkets," *Business Journal of Phoenix*, November 20, 2001.

"Bashas' Consolidates Its Buying, Distribution Staff in Single Facility," *Supermarket News*, March 22, 1993, p. 6.

"Bashas' Names New President, CFO," *Business Journal of Phoenix*, April 22, 2004.

"Bashas' Opens In-Store Clinics," *Drug Store News*, April 10, 2006, p. 4.

"Chubby Grocer Bags 'Boss' Title," *Business Journal—Serving Phoenix & the Valley of the Sun*, October 21, 1994, p. 1.

Elson, Joel, "Bashas' Art Sales Called Fine," *Supermarket News*, May 1, 1995, p. 57.

———, "Bashas' Finds Depot Benefits Sales of HBC," *Supermarket News*, June 7, 1993, p. 33.

Gentry, Connie Robbins, "A Tale of Two Centers," *Chain Store Age*, June 2001, pp. 100f.

Hernandez, Ruben, "Bashas' Taking New Concept to Downtown Phoenix," *Business Journal of Phoenix*, October 25, 2004.

Hogan, Donna, "Chandler, Ariz.-Based Grocery Chain Gains Ground Among Area Rivals," *Tribune* (Mesa, Ariz.), December 23, 2004.

———, "Home-Grown Grocery; Bashas' Prides Itself on Responding Quickly to Customers and Always Looking Out for 'The Next Big Idea,'" *Tribune* (Mesa, Ariz.), January 1, 2006.

Johnson, Rob, "A Family's Fortunes: A 'Pre-History' of Bashas'," http://www.bashas.com/history.php.

Juarez, Macario, Jr., "Bashas' Buys 22 Southwests," *Arizona Daily Star* (Tucson), November 21, 2001, p. D1.

McTaggart, Jenny, and Stephen Dowdell, "Growing Up Bashas'," *Progressive Grocer*, December 1, 2005, pp. 22ff.

Major, Meg, "Meals in Motion," *Progressive Grocer*, September 15, 2005, pp. 83–85.

Riddle, Judith S., "Sourdough Is Rising: The Bread That Began as a San Francisco Specialty Is Now in Demand in Other Parts of the Country," *Supermarket News*, February 8, 1993, p. 45.

Robertson, Anne, "Supermarket Shuffle Continues," *Business Journal of Phoenix*, November 16, 2001.

Tibbitts, Lisa A., "Double Feature: With Both Sell Through and Rental Going for Them, Supermarkets Have Revenues on Upward Spiral," *Supermarket News*, October 17, 1994, p. 40.

Turcsik, Richard, "Desert Delight," *Progressive Grocer*, May 1, 2002, pp. 52ff.

———, "Floor-Tile Ads Found to Help Raise Volume," *Supermarket News*, July 18, 1994, p. 23.

Zweibach, Elliot, "Bashas' Grows When There Is a Need," *Supermarket News*, February 9, 2004, p. 28.

———, "Bashas' Looks at Wholesale Side," *Supermarket News*, June 9, 2003, p. 4.

———, "Galloping in the Sun; Bashas' Is Part of the Arizona Landscape, Adapting Its Formats to Communities Throughout the State," *Supermarket News*, April 7, 2003, p. 10.

———, "MegaFoods Is Selling Its Arizona Units to Bashas'," *Supermarket News*, October 7, 1996, p. 1.

Ben & Jerry's Homemade, Inc.

———■———

30 Community Drive
South Burlington, Vermont 05403-6828
U.S.A.
Telephone: (802) 846-1543
Fax: (802) 846-1610
Web site: http://www.benjerry.com

Wholly-Owned Subsidiary of Unilever
Incorporated: 1978 as Ben & Jerry's Homemade
Employees: 514
Sales: $300 million (2004 est.)
NAIC: 31152 Ice Cream and Frozen Dessert Manufacturing

■ ■ ■

Ben & Jerry's Homemade, Inc., produces superpremium ice cream, frozen yogurt, and ice cream novelties in rich and original flavors, loaded with big chunks of cookies and candy. The company uses natural ingredients almost exclusively and insists its dairy suppliers not use bovine growth hormone on their herds. Ben & Jerry's is distinguished by a corporate philosophy that stresses social action and progressive ideals in addition to profit-making. Its innovative and creative marketing devices have further expressed this progressive spirit. When confronted with a declining market for superpremium ice cream, the company's founders turned increasingly to professional managers and finally sold out to Unilever, which promised to maintain Ben & Jerry's traditional values while taking the brand to new heights. The Ben & Jerry's retail chain has about 450 shops, but most of the brand's ice cream is sold in supermarkets and convenience stores.

EARTHY ORIGINS

Ben & Jerry's was founded in May 1978, when Ben Cohen and Jerry Greenfield opened an ice cream shop in Burlington, Vermont. Cohen had been teaching crafts, and Greenfield had been working as a lab technician when the two decided that "we wanted to do something that would be more fun," as Greenfield later told *People* magazine. In addition, the two wanted to live in a small college town. In 1977, they moved to Burlington, Vermont, and completed a five dollar correspondence course in ice cream making from Pennsylvania State University. With $12,000 in start-up money, a third of which they borrowed, the two renovated an old gas station on a corner in downtown Burlington and opened Ben & Jerry's Homemade.

The first Ben & Jerry's store sold 12 flavors, made with an old-fashioned rock salt ice cream maker and locally produced milk and cream. Initially, ice cream production ran into some glitches. "I once made a batch of rum raisin that stretched and bounced," Greenfield told *People*. With time, however, the pair's rich, idiosyncratic, chunky offerings such as Dastardly Mash and Heath Bar Crunch gained a loyal following. In the summer of 1978, Ben & Jerry inaugurated the first of the many creative marketing ploys that would help drive the growth of their company when they held a free summer movie festival, projecting films onto a blank wall of their building.

By 1980, Ben & Jerry had begun selling their ice

cream to a number of restaurants in the Burlington area. Ben delivered the products to customers in an old Volkswagen squareback station wagon. On his delivery route, he passed many small grocery and convenience stores and decided that they would be a perfect outlet for their products. In 1980, the pair rented space in an old spool and bobbin factory in Burlington and began packaging their ice cream in pint-size cartons with pictures of themselves on the package. "The image we wanted was grass roots," Cohen later told *People*.

The popularity of Ben & Jerry's products brought the company growth, despite the laissez-faire attitude of its two proprietors. At one point, the two were forced to close the doors of their store for a day to devote themselves to sorting out paperwork. In 1981, Ben & Jerry's expanded its pint-packing operations to more spacious quarters behind a car dealership. Shortly thereafter, the company opened its second retail outlet, a franchise on Route 7 in Shelburne, Vermont.

GOING NATIONAL IN 1982

Despite its exclusively local operations, Ben & Jerry's first gained national attention in 1981 when *Time*

magazine hailed its products as "the best ice cream in the world" in a cover story on ice cream. In the following year, Ben & Jerry's began to expand its distribution beyond the state of Vermont. First, an out-of-state store opened, selling Ben & Jerry's products in Portland, Maine. Then, the company began to sell its pints in the Boston area, distributing their goods to stores through independent channels. At the same time, Ben & Jerry's continued its policy of promoting itself through unique and whimsical activities. In 1983, for instance, the company took part in the construction of the world's largest ice cream sundae in St. Albans, Vermont.

With its continuing expansion, Ben & Jerry's developed a need for tighter financial controls on its operations, and the company's founders brought in a local nightclub owner with business experience to be chief operating officer. As sales grew sharply, Cohen and Greenfield slowly came to realize that their small-scale endeavor had exceeded their expectations. They were not entirely happy about this unexpected success. "When Jerry and I realized we were no longer ice cream men, but businessmen, our first reaction was to sell," Cohen told *People* magazine. "We were afraid that business exploits its workers and the community."

Ultimately, Cohen and Greenfield did decide to keep the company, but they vowed not to allow the growth of their enterprise to overwhelm their ideas of how a business could be a force for positive change in a community. "We decided to adapt the company so we could feel proud to say we were the businessmen of Ben & Jerry's," Cohen concluded. Among the stipulations they made to ensure that their company would be different from other parts of corporate America was a salary cap, limiting the best-paid people in the company to wages just five times higher than those of the lowest-paid employees. As Ben & Jerry's grew, this unusual limitation would complicate the company's high-level staffing.

To finance further growth, Greenfield and Cohen decided to raise capital to expand by selling stock to the public. However, in an effort to maintain a sense of local accountability in the company, they limited the stock offering to residents of Vermont, utilizing a little-known clause of the state law governing stocks and brokering. With the proceeds from this sale of stock, the company began construction of a new plant and corporate headquarters in Waterbury, Vermont, about half an hour away from Burlington.

As Ben & Jerry's products continued to garner attention, its prime competitor in the premium ice cream market, Häagen-Dazs, took steps to protect its own share of the market. In 1984, Pillsbury, Häagen-Dazs's corporate parent, threatened to withhold its products

KEY DATES
∎

1978: Ben Cohen and Jerry Greenfield open their first ice cream shop in Burlington, Vermont.
1982: First out-of-state store opens.
1985: National expansion stepped up; Ben & Jerry's Foundation established.
1988: Ben & Jerry's opens first international shops, in Canada and the Caribbean.
1995: Ben Cohen steps aside to let a professional manager take the CEO position.
2000: Ben & Jerry's acquired by Unilever.

from distributors who also sold Ben & Jerry's ice cream. Ben & Jerry's retaliated by filing suit against Pillsbury, and also by launching a publicity campaign with the slogan "What's the Doughboy Afraid Of?" Pillsbury took steps to restrict distribution again in 1987, when it threatened to stop selling its ice cream to retailers who also sold Ben & Jerry's products. In both cases, legal action brought the restrictive practices to an end. By the end of 1984, sales of Ben & Jerry's products had exceeded $4 million, a figure more than twice as large as the previous year's revenues.

In 1985, Ben & Jerry's expanded distribution of its products dramatically, starting up sales of its pints in New York, New Jersey, Pennsylvania, Virginia, Washington, D.C., Georgia, Florida, and Minnesota. To supply these new markets, the company completed work on a modern manufacturing plant. Among the new offerings that year was New York Super Fudge Chunk, created at the suggestion of a customer from New York City. Throughout 1985, sales of Ben & Jerry's products continued at a break-neck pace. By the end of the year, revenues had reached $9 million, an increase of 143 percent from 1984. As part of their program to remain true to their ideals, Cohen and Greenfield established the Ben & Jerry's Foundation to fund community-oriented projects. In addition to the Foundation's initial capitalization, the two pledged 7.5 percent of the company's annual pre-tax profits to the charity.

FARMING OUT IN 1986

In 1986, facing demand for its products that its one Vermont plant was unable to meet, Ben & Jerry's contracted with Dreyer's Grand Ice Cream, an ice cream company located in the Midwest, to manufacture Ben & Jerry's ice cream in its plants and distribute its products in most markets outside the Northeast. In ad-

dition, the company introduced its newest pint flavor, Coffee Heath Bar Crunch.

To promote this and other flavors, as well as the corporate identity, Ben & Jerry's began conducting tours of its Waterbury, Vermont, plant in 1986. In addition, the company launched its "Cowmobile," a converted mobile home that Cohen and Greenfield set out to drive across the country, distributing free scoops of ice cream as they went. Four months into the trip, the Cowmobile burned to the ground outside Cleveland without causing any injuries, bringing the planned expedition to a premature end. These efforts had pushed company sales to $20 million by the end of 1986, as Ben & Jerry's continued to post a remarkable rate of growth.

Cohen and Greenfield's original plan for a cross country trip was brought to fruition in 1987, when "Cow II" made its maiden voyage, also dispensing free scoops of ice cream along the way. After the October 1987 stock market crash, Cow II appeared on Wall Street to hand out scoops of "That's Life" and "Economic Crunch" ice cream to financial industry workers. Along with these highly topical creations, Ben & Jerry's introduced pints of "Cherry Garcia," named for the long-time lead guitarist of the rock group Grateful Dead. In addition, the company began to market its first ice cream novelty, the Brownie Bar. This product consisted of a square of French Vanilla ice cream, sandwiched between two brownies.

At their manufacturing plant in Vermont, Ben & Jerry's also took steps to keep the company in compliance with its ideal of being a socially responsible enterprise. To reduce its impact on the environment, Ben & Jerry's began using its ice cream waste to feed pigs being raised on a farm in Stowe, Vermont. In addition, to keep plant employees happy, the company instituted a variety of gestures, including Elvis day and Halloween costume celebrations, to break the monotony of life in a factory. By the end of 1987, company revenues had increased again, to reach $32 million.

INTERNATIONAL IN 1988

In 1988, Ben & Jerry's opened its first outlets outside the United States when ice cream shops began operating in Montreal, Quebec, and in St. Maarten in the Caribbean. By the end of the year, more than 80 "scoop shops" were flying the Ben & Jerry's banner across 18 different states. At this time, the company decided to hold back on further franchising to make sure that product quality and service in its existing stores met its standards.

Also in 1988, Ben & Jerry's responded to continuing growth in demand for the company's products by opening its second manufacturing facility in Springfield, Vermont. This plant was used to make ice cream novelties, including the "Peace Pop," a chocolate covered ice cream bar on a stick. The name of this product referred to "One Percent for Peace," a nonprofit group founded in part by Cohen and Greenfield that was dedicated to redirecting national resources towards peace.

Together with their employees, Cohen and Greenfield formulated a three-part statement of mission that was designed to sum up the company's unique corporate philosophy. Relying on a theory of "linked prosperity," the mission statement asserted that Ben & Jerry's had a product mission, a social mission, and an economic mission. The company hoped to use this credo to enhance the lives of individuals and communities through its actions. As part of its philosophy of linked prosperity, Ben & Jerry's introduced several new flavors of ice cream that incorporated ingredients from special sources. Rainforest Crunch, marketed in 1989, used nuts produced by rain forest trees. Chocolate Fudge Brownie, brought out in February 1990, used brownies made at a bakery in New York where formerly unemployed and homeless people worked.

Beginning in the late 1980s, Ben & Jerry's joined the trend toward producing low-fat ice cream and yogurt. Ben & Jerry's Light, introduced in 1989, had reduced levels of fat and cholesterol compared to the regular Ben & Jerry's ice cream but no less fat than other "regular" products then on the market. "It was sort of an oxymoron," the company's chief financial officer admitted to the *Wall Street Journal*. Sales of the products never exceeded about $9 million, and in December 1991 the line was declared a mistake and phased out.

Ben & Jerry's frozen yogurt proved far more successful. Boasting a butterfat content between 1 and 5 percent—as opposed to the 17 percent butterfat levels in the regular ice cream—Ben & Jerry's yogurt was selling in 13 cities around the United States in 1992. Within five months, yogurt sales were accounting for 15 to 18 percent of the company's revenues, and by the end of the year, it had become the leader in the superpremium yogurt market. In addition, Ben & Jerry's introduced a pint version of one of its most popular scoop shop offerings, chocolate chip cookie dough. The company had spent five years finding a way to get the chunks of dough into pints of ice cream without having them stick together and gum up the packaging machines. The product was an immediate hit, and soon became the company's best-selling flavor. Finally, the company began to market its ice cream novelties, Peace Pops and Brownie Bars, in "multi-paks" in supermarkets.

In response to continuing demand for its new products, Ben & Jerry's moved to increase its output in

Vermont. The company added a pint production line at its Springfield plant, and also borrowed space at the St. Albans Cooperative Creamery to open another temporary production facility. To increase its capacity over the long term, Ben & Jerry's broke ground on a third ice cream factory in St. Albans in late 1992. Financed through an additional stock offering, this plant was scheduled to be functional in 1994. In addition, the company completed a new distribution center in Bellows Falls, Vermont. Ben & Jerry's also renewed its co-packing agreement with Dreyer's Grand Ice Cream, Inc., its midwestern partner. By the end of 1992, Ben & Jerry's sales overall had reached $132 million, up from $77 million in 1989.

Further from home, Ben & Jerry's opened two ice cream shops in the Russian cities of Petrozavodsk and Kondopoga. With two Russian partners, the company had spent three years navigating the Soviet bureaucracy and finding supplies for the venture, which Cohen and Greenfield hoped would promote friendship between Russians and Americans. After importing equipment and lining up reliable sources for cream, the company was able to open a combination ice cream plant and parlor, which was blessed by a Russian Orthodox priest on its first day.

As Ben & Jerry's moved into the mid-1990s, it could look back on a streak of extraordinary growth. From one small shop in downtown Burlington, Vermont, it had grown to include a chain of nearly 100 franchised shops and a line of products sold in stores across the country. Company leaders were aware that it was unlikely that this rate of expansion could continue forever, since Ben & Jerry's growth had come in a mature and stable market. With its idiosyncratic corporate culture and its strong track record of introducing innovative flavors that drove ever-stronger sales, however, it appeared that Ben & Jerry's was well positioned to continue its success.

NEW CEO IN 1994

Unfortunately, sales of superpremium ice cream slipped in the mid-1990s, as increasingly health-conscious consumers cut back on calories. Ben & Jerry's posted its first quarterly loss ever at the end of 1994, it slowest season. In addition, software problems crippled the new plant at St. Albans, draining the company's resources.

Ben & Jerry's had just over 500 employees in late 1994 when Ben Cohen announced his retirement as CEO. (He remained chairman.) In order to attract the right caliber of management talent to lead the company, Ben & Jerry's controversially dropped the pay formula that had limited the top salary to just five times the lowest. It launched a "Yo! I'm Your CEO" contest which received 20,000 entries from prospective candidates. However, the new CEO, Robert Holland, Jr., was actually chosen by a professional search firm.

Holland had previously become the first African-American partner at the esteemed management consulting firm McKinsey & Co. He applied his manufacturing expertise to developing a new line of sorbets and resolving the costly equipment problems at St. Albans. Developing new markets, however, was the company's top priority.

Ben & Jerry's continued to look abroad for growth. It had but an 8 percent market share in Great Britain—one-third that of Häagen-Dazs. The company tested the waters in France in late 1995. It soon afterwards began a kind of guerrilla marketing blitz, complete with Cowmobile, aimed at capturing the youngest of the country's ice cream connoisseurs. At home, Ben & Jerry's whipped up hip concoctions honoring the Doonesbury and Dilbert cartoons as well as the Vermont rock band Phish.

After a year and a half on the job, Holland decided that he was not the right person to develop these new markets and new products. Perry Odak was tapped to replace Holland. He had served briefly as COO of U.S. Repeating Arms Co., maker of Winchester rifles. This surprised some, given Ben & Jerry's philanthropic contributions to gun control groups. However, Odak had plenty of the desired consumer marketing experience with such companies as Armour-Dial, Jovan Inc., and Atari.

Ben & Jerry's enjoyed increased sales in the United States and United Kingdom in the late 1990s, when international sales accounted for about 11 percent of the total. The company signed a new Canadian distribution deal in 1998. The next year, it redesigned its U.S. distribution network to become less dependent on Dreyer's, signing on with the newly-created Nestle/Pillsbury joint venture, Ice Cream Partners. The company began using unbleached paperboard pint containers and planned to begin outsourcing its frozen novelties in 2000.

ACQUISITION BY UNILEVER IN 2000

In April 2000, Unilever announced it was buying Ben & Jerry's for $326 million in cash. By coincidence, Unilever announced it was also buying diet food maker Slimfast on the same day. Unilever, which had $45 billion in annual sales, boasted such brands as Lipton Tea, Gordon's fish filets, Wisk detergent, and Dove soap—as well as Breyer's, Good Humor, and Sealtest ice creams. Although Unilever was in the process of cutting 1,200 of its total 1,600 brands worldwide, Unilever offered the

power to take Ben & Jerry's, its only superpremium ice cream, to thousands of new consumers.

The purchase reminded at least one observer of the expensive, disastrous 1994 acquisition of Snapple Beverage by Quaker Oats. Snapple also had a quirky image and grass roots origins, but it withered under its new owner until finally Quaker Oats sold it at a huge loss. However, the Anglo-Dutch corporation promised it would maintain Ben & Jerry's commitment to social causes. Cohen and Greenfield were to retain management roles. Unilever and Meadowbrook Lane Capital had originally planned to help take the company private, until they were outbid in that effort by Dreyer's Grand Ice Cream Co. Interestingly, the man who had persuaded Cohen and Greenfield to sell, Unilever's North American head Richard Goldstein, soon left to become CEO of International Flavors and Fragrances.

Ben & Jerry's officially merged with Unilever in August 2000. The company continued to demonstrate its familiar flair for marketing stunts that summer, firing up two hot air balloons for its Stop & Taste the Ice Cream Tour.

In November 2000, Unilever ice cream executive Yves Couette was designated to replace CEO Odak, who was retiring for personal reasons. (He went on to head Wild Oats Markets Inc.) While Couette, a Frenchman, had two dozen years of experience with Unilever, company founders Ben Cohen and Jerry Greenfield had backed another candidate from Ben & Jerry's own board of directors whom they felt was more in line with the company's social values. The founders' choice was reportedly former Coca-Cola Co. marketing executive Pierre Ferrari.

Sales were less than $250 million in 2000, but Odak predicted Unilever could build Ben & Jerry's into a billion-dollar brand within three years, reported *Business Week*. The company had 800 employees.

In spite of the controversy over the selection of CEO, the company continued to be involved in many progressive initiatives. Ben & Jerry's was maintaining its tradition of donating 7.5 percent of profits to charity. Another point of consistency was the company's insistence on using only dairy products from rBGH-free cows.

A switch to Eco-Pint packaging by 2001 demonstrated a continued commitment to environmental consciousness. These containers were made of unbleached, brown paperboard and were more biodegradable. The Eco-Pints were appropriately used to package one of the company's new products: dirt. The company began pitching compost made from its ice cream waste and other ingredients. It was bundled with sunflower seed packets and marketed at garden centers and online as "Terra Fuela." The product was developed with the Intervale Foundation, a Burlington organization focused on sustainable agriculture.

FACING INDUSTRY CONSOLIDATION IN 2001 AND BEYOND

Dreyer's Grand Ice Cream had been distributing Ben & Jerry's in grocery stores in the Midwest and Northwest. This arrangement was extended nationally, and to convenience stores, in February 2001 under a five-year contract. (Nestlé S.A. announced it was buying a majority of Dreyer's in 2002, strengthening its already considerable position in the ice cream market.)

An increasingly competitive marketplace prompted layoffs in 2002. Administrative positions were cut and two Vermont plants (Bellows Falls and Springfield) were shuttered. However, the St. Albans site was being expanded at a cost of $10 million. There were also redundancies due to Unilever combining Ben & Jerry's sales force with that of Good Humor-Breyers, which it also owned.

The company had long been opposed to synthetic hormones, and it began test marketing a line of ice cream made with organic Vermont milk in 2003. In another new Vermont-related initiative, Ben & Jerry's began opening its first co-branded outlets with the environmentally conscious Green Mountain Coffee chain.

Yves Couette stepped down from the CEO spot at the end of 2004. Under his watch, sales had increased 37 percent since 2001 (when they were $237 million) according to *Workforce Management,* while operating margins tripled. *Advertising Age* cited *Dairy Field* magazine figures stating that convenience store and supermarket sales amounted to $198.8 million in the year ending January 2004; this did not include the 450 retail stores. The trade journal *Dairy Foods* estimated Ben & Jerry's 2004 sales at $272 million, ranking it 53rd in its "Dairy 100" listing. Couette was succeeded by Walt Freese, a former Celestial Seasonings manager who had previously been Ben & Jerry's marketing chief. (The company also had a new chief financial officer to replace one who later pled guilty to embezzlement.)

Ben & Jerry's continued to introduce a handful of new flavors every year. It sometimes turned to the public for ideas; in 2006, the company invited customers to participate in its "Do Us a Flavor Contest" to discover "the next lip-smacking, completely unexpected Ben & Jerry's flavor."

Elizabeth Rourke
Updated, Frederick C. Ingram

PRINCIPAL COMPETITORS

Dreyer's Grand Ice Cream Holdings Inc.; Mrs. Fields Famous Brands, LLC; Nestle S.A.; Blue Bell Creameries LP.

FURTHER READING

Ackerman, Jerry, "$326 Million Sale Makes It Ben, Jerry & Unilever but World's Top Consumer Products Company Says Ice Cream Maker's Good Deeds Won't End," *Boston Globe,* April 13, 2000, pp. C1f.

Alexander, Suzanne, "Life's Just a Bowl of Cherry Garcia for Ben & Jerry's," *Wall Street Journal,* July, 1992.

"Ben & Jerry Cool on New Ice Cream CEO," *Reuters News,* November 20, 2000.

"Ben & Jerry's Cuts 26 Jobs Nationwide," *Associated Press Newswires,* February 8, 2003.

"Ben & Jerry's Has a New Leader," *Associated Press Newswires,* October 29, 2004.

"Ben & Jerry's Looks Toward Life after Holland," *Ice Cream Reporter,* October 20, 1996, pp. 1+.

"Ben & Jerry's Tries Organic Ice Cream," *Associated Press Newswires,* June 4, 2003.

Devaney, Polly, "Ben & Jerry's Gets a Licking," *Brand Strategy,* April 1, 2001, p. 16.

"Dreyer's in Distribution Agreement with Ben & Jerry's," *Dairy Markets Weekly,* October 26, 2000, p. 3.

Duecy, Erica, "Ben & Jerry's, Green Mountain Join Forces to Offer Co-Branded Outlets," *Nation's Restaurant News,* July 12, 2004, pp. 4+.

Finch, Julia, and Jane Martinson, "Unilever Gorges on Ice Cream and Slimming Foods," *Guardian,* April 13, 2000.

"Former Ben & Jerry's CFO Pleads to Embezzlement," *Associated Press Newswires,* September 2, 2005.

Goff, Leslie Jaye, "Summertime Heats Up IT at Ice Cream Maker Ben & Jerry's," *Computerworld,* July 2, 2001, p. 27.

Hays, Constance L., "Ben & Jerry's Deal Takes on Slightly New Flavor," *New York Times,* May 2, 2000, p. C1.

Hubbard, Kim, "For New Age Ice Cream Moguls Ben and Jerry, Making 'Cherry Garcia' and 'Chunky Monkey' Is a Labor of Love," *People,* September 10, 1990.

"Ice Cream Giant Comes Up with Pint of Compost," *BioCycle,* December 1, 2001, p. 8.

Kellaway, Lucy, "New Age Rests in Peace, Man: The Socially Responsible Business Ethic Has Now Become a Self-Interested, Cynical PR Message," *Financial Times,* Inside Track, April 17, 2000, pp. 16+.

Kiger, Patrick J., "Corporate Crunch," *Workforce Management,* April 1, 2005, p. 32+.

Larson, Jane, "Founders of Ben & Jerry's Ice Cream Share Ingredients of Success," *Arizona Republic,* December 9, 1998.

McCormick, Jay, "Ben & Jerry's a la Mode," *Business Week,* May 20, 1996, pp. 22+.

McLaughlin, Tim, "Interview—Ben & Jerry Co-Founder Threatens to Quit," *Reuters News,* December 1, 2000.

Mahoney, Sarah, "It Only Looks Easy; For Ben & Jerry's Walt Freese, Tending An Ice-Cream Icon Means Staying True to Its Core Users," *Advertising Age,* March 1, 2005, p. 13.

Nax, Sanford, "Ben & Jerry Accent Shift in Business Success at Fresno, Calif., Conference," *Knight Ridder Tribune Business News,* February 15, 2001.

Pham, Alex, "Gun Adviser Takes Post at Ben & Jerry's: For Fabled Firm, CEO Reflects Changing Times," *Boston Globe,* January 3, 1997, pp. C1+.

Phillips, David, "Dairy 100: Bigger by the Billions," *Dairyfoods.com,* August 1, 2005.

———, "Vermont's Latest Expansion Makes St. Albans the Largest Plant in Ben & Jerry's Streamlined Operations," *Dairy Foods,* September 2003, pp. 50+.

Rathke, Lisa, "Ben & Jerry's Says Job Cuts Pending at Headquarters," *Associated Press Newswires,* October 15, 2002.

Shao, Maria, "The New Emperor of Ice Cream," *Boston Globe,* Economy Section, February 2, 1995, pp. 35+.

———, "A Scoopful of Credentials: CEO Holland Brings an Activist's Blend to Ben & Jerry's," *Boston Globe,* March 1, 1995, pp. 1+.

Smith, Geoffrey, "A Famous Brand on a Rocky Road: Would Ben & Jerry's Sales Soften Without Ben and Jerry?," *Business Week,* December 11, 2000, p. 54.

Tomkins, Richard, "Takeovers That Lose Their Cool," *Financial Times,* Comment & Analysis, April 15, 2000, pp. 13+.

Tomsho, Robert, Joe Pereira, and John Hechinger, "Ben & Jerry's Founders May Quit Unilever Unit," *Wall Street Journal,* November 21, 2000, p. B14.

"Union Wins Decision over Ben & Jerry's," *Boston Globe,* December 16, 1998, p. C5.

Bluegreen Corporation

———————— ■ ————————

4960 Conference Way North, Suite 100
Boca Raton, Florida 33431
U.S.A.
Telephone: (561) 912-8000
Fax: (561) 912-8100
Web site: http://www.bluegreenonline.com

Public Company
Incorporated: 1976 as Patten Realty Corporation
Employees: 4,076
Sales: $684.2 million (2005)
Stock Exchanges: New York
Ticker Symbol: BXG
NAIC: 237210 Land Subdivision

■ ■ ■

With its headquarters in Boca Raton, Florida, Bluegreen Corporation is a public company providing leisure products and services. Its business is divided between two divisions: Bluegreen Communities and Bluegreen Resorts. Bluegreen Communities markets and sells housing units in upscale residential, lake, and golf communities in several markets, including Atlanta, Dallas, Richmond, and San Antonio. Many of the golf courses associated with the properties are designed by well-known professional golfers, such as Fred Couples, Curtis Strange, and Davis Love III. The Bluegreen Resorts division is involved in the resort timeshare business through a flexible points-based system marketed under the Bluegreen Vacation Club name. Although customers buy vacation points rather than a specific property, they are considered "owners" because they retain an underlying interest in a company resort held in trust for their benefit. Moreover, they must also pay an annual maintenance fee, real estate taxes, and any special assessments. The point system, however, provides them with a great deal of flexibility in planning a vacation. Owners can plan stays at the Bluegreen Vacation Club network of 42 timeshare resorts located in popular destinations, including Florida, the Carolinas, the Gulf Coast, the Smoky Mountains, and Aruba. In addition, owners can arrange through an exchange company to stay at 3,700 affiliated resorts around the world. Vacation points also can be rented, traded, or sold to other parties, carried over from one year to the next, or borrowed from the next year for current use.

BUYING THE FIRST PROPERTY: 1964

Bluegreen was founded in Vermont as Patten Realty by Harry S. Patten. He grew up poor in New Hampshire and gained his initial sales experience selling vacuum cleaners while studying psychology at the University of New Hampshire, and afterward became a sales manager for vacation home developer American Central. In 1964 he struck out on his own, hoping to take advantage of urbanites interested in buying a piece of rural property, as well as rural landowners in need of buyers. Patten took a partner, drew on his savings, put down $15,000 on a piece of Vermont property, and never looked back. He went solo a decade later, incorporating his business in 1976 as Patten Realty Corporation. Patten specialized in selling undeveloped property. Typically he bought a large tract of land from a farmer or timber company, putting down just a token payment, divided the land into parcels, from 5 to 20 acres in size, and once the planning and zoning paperwork was completed, he sold the plots as quickly as possible to realize a handsome profit.

Patten worked out of a 25-room farm estate in Stamford, Vermont, and did not open his first branch office until 1982 in Portland, Maine. Although New England remained his focus, Patten began moving into a dozen other states, including Virginia and Michigan. Business soared and Patten took advantage of his momentum by taking the company public in November 1985, netting $7.2 million. The stock was then listed on the New York Stock Exchange, where it became a high flyer for a time, commanding the attention of as many as eight analysts.

Along the way, however, Patten courted controversy. He became the scourge of environmentalists and preservation-minded locals who regarded his company, in the words of the *Wall Street Journal,* as one that "squirmed through regulatory loopholes and used pushy tactics to subdivide land that should never be developed. Also, detractors say, by swooping in and out of small towns that lack land-use plans, it has avoided scrutiny and sometimes left behind subdivisions that later may strain public services, increase natives' taxes or hinder conservation." Patten Realty also ran afoul of customers, as the company was investigated by several New England states for deceptive sales practices. For example, Patten bought a 1,300-acre mountain in Bennington, Vermont, called Mount Anthony, and then divided it into what were called "spaghetti" lots, parcels that provided as many buyers as possible with a highly desirable view (or in the case of lake property, a piece of the lakefront), but resulted in oddly shaped, undesirable configurations. Moreover, Patten salespeople did not inform people interested in building second homes on the property that septic tanks were not allowed, nor could they drill for water. In reality they were buying little more than a campsite. In 1989 Patten reached a settlement with the states of New York, Vermont, Massachusetts, Maine, and New Hampshire, agreeing to issue refunds to consumers who could prove they were deceived. The company denied any wrongdoing and maintained that it settled in order to avoid lengthy and expensive legal proceedings.

MOVING TO BOCA RATON: 1991

Patten Realty reached its high watermark in 1988 when it generated revenues of $120 million and posted net earnings of $15.1 million. The price of its stock peaked around $19. Then the bottom fell out of the real estate market, especially in the Northeast, leading to $45 million in losses in 1990 and 1991, and the stock fell as low as 38 cents a share before rebounding to the $2 range. The company's reputation was dealt another blow when it became the subject of a piece on *60 Minutes* in March 1991. Harry Patten had a winter home in Florida and decided that a change in scenery, and direction, were in order. In 1991 he put the Stamford estate on the market and moved the company to Boca Raton. The company began selling off its Northeast holdings and turned its attention to the Midwest and Southeast.

It was also in 1991 that George F. Donovan joined the company as an independent director on the board of directors. In October 1993 the board asked him to take charge of the company. Donovan told *Smart Business* in a 2005 profile, "My ultimate response was, 'Yes, I think it makes sense. However, I don't think we can build the kind of company the public market wants—a strong growth company—out of the land development business as it was then constituted.'" Donovan was named president and chief operating officer, and before the year was out he became chief executive officer as well, succeeding Harry Patten, who stayed on as chairman. It hardly came as a surprise that Donovan would steer Patten Realty in the direction of timeshares.

The timeshare idea, or vacation ownership, was pioneered in Europe in the mid-1960s. The concept caught on in the United States in the 1970s as a response to a real estate collapse. Desperate condominium developers, unable to sell their units outright, began selling them piecemeal, dividing the property among a multitude of owners who each used the property for a specified period of time. The new industry saw more than its share of fast operators, which tarnished the image of timeshares, but matters began to improve in the late 1980s when major hotel chains saw an opportunity, became involved, and helped to transform timeshares from a questionable real estate investment into a viable vacation alternative. Boston born, Donovan came to real estate with an unusual background: He graduated from Norwich University with a degree in electrical engineering. His first job was selling IBM mainframe computers to aerospace customers. He then went to

KEY DATES

1964: Founder Harry S. Patten begins buying New England property for subdividing.
1976: Patten Realty Corporation is incorporated.
1985: The company is taken public.
1991: The company relocates from Vermont to Boca Raton, Florida.
1993: George Donovan is named CEO.
1994: The company enters the timeshare industry.
1996: The name is changed to Bluegreen Corporation.
2000: An alliance is formed with Bass Pro Shops.
2004: Sales top the $600 million mark.

work for a new software company serving the securities industry, which in turn merged with a company that eventually became Fairfield Communities, a leader in the retirement community sector. Now involved in real estate instead of computers, Donovan became Fairfield's president in 1979 and changed the company's focus to timeshares. By the time he left Fairfield in 1986, it had become one of the largest timeshare companies in the United States. Over the next several years, Donovan was involved in the development of golf communities in the southeastern United States and the Caribbean.

Under Donovan's leadership, Patten Realty entered the vacation ownership business in 1994 with the purchase of a single resort, MountainLoft at the base of Tennessee's Smoky Mountain National Forest. Bluegreen Resorts and Bluegreen Communities also were formed in 1994. A second Smoky Mountain resort, Laurel Crest, was added a year later. In the meantime, Patten quit the company in December 1994 and by the start of 1995 sold back his stock to the company to sever all ties. Then, in March 1996 his name was removed as well, as the company became known as Bluegreen Corporation.

In 1996 Bluegreen entered the Carolinas, breaking ground on Shore Crest Vacation Villas located in North Myrtle Beach. In September 1997 Bluegreen took a major step forward when it acquired Fort Myers, Florida–based RDI Group Inc. in a $7.5 million deal, picking up several timeshare resorts: Orlando Sunshine resort in Orlando, Florida; Shenandoah Crossing in Gordonsville, Virginia; and Christmas Mountain Village in Wisconsin Dells, Wisconsin. In addition, RDI had management contracts with a number of resorts in the Southeast. The RDI acquisition, as a result, gave Bluegreen critical mass and led to the creation of the Bluegreen Vacation club. It was also in 1997 that Bluegreen

opened its first daily fee golf course, designed by professional golfer Fred Couples, in Southport, North Carolina. This formed the core of Bluegreen Communities, as lots surrounding the golf courses were sold to homeowners, who in turn hired contractors to build custom homes. The concept was extended to lake properties and other upscale neighborhoods in Arizona, Texas, Virginia, North Carolina, Tennessee, and California.

STRONG CLOSE TO THE 20TH CENTURY

Bluegreen enjoyed a strong close to the 1990s. The company recorded sales of $115.9 million in 1997, and enjoyed even greater success in 1998. A pair of new resorts became operational during the course of the year, and the company also acquired a half-interest in resort La Cabana, located on the island of Aruba. As a result of these developments and the integration of the RDI assets, Bluegreen experienced a sharp increase in sales of nearly 70 percent to $187.6 million. The upward trend continued in 1999 when the company expanded its Shore Crest Vacation Villas property in Myrtle Beach and Orlando's Sunshine Resort. In addition, Bluegreen entered the urban timeshare market by acquiring The Lodge Allen Inn, located in Charleston, South Carolina. For the year, sales improved 37.1 percent to $257.7 million, accompanied by record net profits of $17 million.

Bluegreen began the new century by forging an alliance with Springfield, Missouri–based Bass Pro Shops, a leading retailer of hunting, fishing, camping, and other sporting gear, best known for its Outdoor World stores. They were massive facilities that were tourist attractions in their own right, combining a wide selection of goods with amusement features, such as target ranges, fish tanks, restaurants, and video arcades. Donovan was visiting the southwest Missouri area when he met Bass Pro Shops founder Johnny Morris and persuaded him to house a Bluegreen booth in Outdoor World locations to market its properties. It proved to be a highly successful co-branding arrangement that was extended to the Bass Pro catalogs and web site. Despite this and other advances, business was soft in 2000. Revenues dipped slightly and net income fell to $6.8 million.

The terrorist attacks on the United States of September 11, 2001 hurt Bluegreen, but not as much as the rest of the travel industry. Earnings continued to slide to $2.7 million. Business picked up again in 2002, and the company forged another important alliance, this one with Boyne USA Resorts, one of North America's largest upscale resort companies. Bluegreen arranged to market its Vacation Club and other products at two Boyne USA Resorts. Also in 2002, Bluegreen opened two more golf courses in Virginia and North Carolina, the former designed by Curtis Strange and the latter by Davis Love III. In another important development, Bluegreen acquired TakeMeOnVacation, L.L.C., a company that generated sales leads using a permission-based marketing strategy. Its software systems were then used to create a direct marketing business unit, Blue-green Direct. The company's ability to market its products was further enhanced in 2002 when Fort Lauderdale BankAtlantic Bankcorp acquired a 40 percent interest, buying the stock previously owned by a pair of institutional shareholders, Morgan Stanley Dean Witter and Grace Brothers. BankAtlantic also owned Levitt and Sons, founded by the legendary residential developer William Levitt, known for the Levittown suburban projects of New York, Pennsylvania, and New Jersey. The Levitt division would now be used to help promote Bluegreen.

By 2003 Bluegreen had completely recovered from the slump earlier in the decade and for the year posted record results: sales of more than $438 million and net income approaching $26 million. During the year, the company acquired a Daytona Beach, Florida, resort as well as tracts of land in Montana and Michigan on which it planned to build new timeshare resorts. Bluegreen also opened two new communities, one near Houston close to a forest and several small lakes, and the other sur-rounding a golf course and river close to Fort Worth.

Bluegreen enjoyed record-setting years in 2004 and 2005, as revenues topped the $600 million mark in 2004 and reach $684.2 million in 2005. Net income increased from $36.5 million to $46.6 million in 2005.

After a dozen years at the helm, Donovan clearly had delivered on his goal of building a strong growth company.

Ed Dinger

PRINCIPAL DIVISIONS

Bluegreen Communities; Bluegreen Resorts.

PRINCIPAL COMPETITORS

Silverleaf Resorts, Inc.; Starwood Hotels & Resorts Worldwide, Inc.; Sunterra Corporation.

FURTHER READING

Jacobs, Daniel G., "Sharing a Life of Leisure," *Smart Business,* April 2005.

Morgenson, Gretchen, "Old Game, New Twist," *Forbes,* January 12, 1987, p. 44.

———, "Sucker the City Bumpkins," *Forbes,* December 26, 1988, p. 39.

Ostrowski, Jeff, "Bank Bets on Name for Selling Timeshares," *Palm Beach Post,* April 13, 2002, p. 10B.

Perry, Nancy J., "Ex-Hick Sells Sticks, Is Market Pick: Harry Patten," *Fortune,* January 5, 1987, p. 52.

Pounds, Stephen, "Selling Time," *Palm Beach Post,* August 23, 2004, p. 1F.

Sedore, David, "The Comeback Trail," *South Florida Business Journal,* December 9, 1991, p. 1.

Stipp, David, "Rural Ruckus," *Wall Street Journal,* June 24, 1988, p. 1.

Boliden AB

———— ■ ————

Box 44
Stockholm,
Sweden
Telephone: +46 08 610 15 00
Fax: +46 08 31 55 45
Web site: http://www.boliden.com

Public Company
Incorporated: 1925 as Västerbottens Gruvaktiebolag and
Skellefteå Gruvaktiebolag
Employees: 4,530
Sales: SEK 20.44 billion ($2.79 billion) (2005)
Stock Exchanges: Stockholm
Ticker Symbol: BOL
NAIC: 331421 Copper (Except Wire) Rolling, Drawing,
and Extruding; 212221 Gold Ore Mining; 212222
Silver Ore Mining; 212231 Lead Ore and Zinc Ore
Mining; 212234 Copper Ore and Nickel Ore Min-
ing; 331419 Primary Smelting and Refining of
Nonferrous Metals (Except Copper and Aluminum);
331491 Nonferrous Metal (Except Copper and
Aluminum) Rolling, Drawing, and Extruding;
331492 Secondary Smelting, Refining, and Alloying
of Nonferrous Metals (Except Copper and
Aluminum)

■ ■ ■

Boliden AB is one of Europe's leading base metal
concerns. The Sweden-based company is Europe's third-
largest copper producer and the region's second largest
zinc producer. Boliden is also active in other base metals

categories, specifically lead, gold and silver. Boliden
handles all phases of metals production, from exploration, to mine operation and milling, to smelting, refining and recycling—the company is one of the world's
leading metals recyclers. Boliden operates three mines in
Sweden and a fourth mine in Ireland. The company's
refinery operations include four copper smelters in
Sweden and Finland, zinc smelters in Finland, Norway
and Sweden, and marketing subsidiaries in Sweden,
Finland, and the Netherlands. The 'new' Boliden's
takeover of the mining and refining operations of
Finland's steel giant Outokumpu occurred in 2003. As
part of that transaction, Outokumpu became Boliden's
major shareholder, with a 49 percent stake in the
company. Outokumpu reduced its stake in Boliden to
16 percent in 2005. Boliden is listed on the Stockholm
Stock Exchange and is led by President and CEO Jan
Johanssen. In 2005, Boliden posted record sales of SEK
20.441 billion.

GOLD RUSH BEGINNINGS IN THE
TWENTIES

Sweden's metal shortage during World War I led the
government to promote exploration efforts in the
country's northern region. One of the groups that took
up the challenge was Centralgruppen Emissionsbolag, a
holding company set up in 1915 to acquire stakes in
new mining companies and developing mines. By 1920,
Centralgruppen had established its own team of
prospectors and other experts, putting into practice the
new geophysical exploration technologies being
developed at the time. Centralgruppen suffered several
years of losses, but its patience—and that of its backing

bank—was rewarded in 1924 when gold was discovered in Fagelmyren.

In order to exploit the mine, the financially troubled Centralgruppen was taken over by its main bank in 1925. The bank then established two mining companies to work the gold field, which by then had become known as Boliden. The two companies, Västerbottens Gruvaktiebolag and Skellefteå Gruvaktiebolag, began constructing their mines that year, with full scale production launched in 1926. At first, all of the region's production was shipped elsewhere for processing, primarily to Germany.

Västerbottens Gruvaktiebolag and Skellefteå Gruvaktiebolag decided to begin their own processing operation. In 1930, the companies inaugurated their first smelter, on the island of Rönnskär. From the start, the company was involved in production of a range of metals, including copper and silver, in addition to gold. In 1931, Västerbottens Gruvaktiebolag and Skellefteå Gruvaktiebolag were merged into a single operation, Boliden. At the same time, the group received permission from the government to increase its production and processing levels, and the Fagelmyren emerged as one of the major sources of European gold.

While the rest of the world slumped into the Great Depression, Boliden itself prospered, and by the mid-1930s employed some 2,500. Sweden's neutrality during World War II also permitted the company to grow strongly. A new metal shortage—this time of lead—prompted the group to expand its operations, with the opening of a lead mine in nearby Laisvall in 1943. Boliden also added new mines and support facilities in the mineral rich regions of Lainejaur, Ravliden, Kristineberg, Adak and Bjukfors. In support of its growing production, the company built its own cableway at the Kristineberg site, which, at 96 kilometers, became the world's longest cableway. By the end of the decade, Boliden had added a new major gold mine, at Akulla. The increased production led the company to expand production at the Rönnskär smelter in 1949.

DIVERSIFYING IN THE POSTWAR ERA

Boliden continued to expand through the 1950s, notably through its 1957 acquisition of Zinkgruvor, which operated a number of mines, including major sites at Garpenberg and Saxberget. The addition of zinc mining operations led the group to build an electrolysis plant in Rönnskär the following year.

Boliden continued expanding its mining operations, particularly with the exploration of the Udden and Nasliden regions during the 1960s. In 1964, Boliden bought a 50 percent stake in Norzink, a zinc smelter in Norway, marking its first international venture. During the decade, Boliden's attention turned to its increasingly diversified operations. These included the production of chemicals, such as sulfuric acid through subsidiary Supra, and the production of superphosphate fertilizers. In support of its chemicals production, the company built a waste fuming plant in Ronsskar in 1962, then added a sulphuric acid production unit at its main smelter site.

During the 1970s, the company acquired Sala Maskinfabrik, a major producer of equipment for the metals industry. Boliden, which worked in partnership with Germany's Preussag during the 1970s, also began developing its own smelting and production technologies. These included its "Kaldo" flash smelting process for lead production, introduced in 1976. The company formed a marketing group, Boliden Contech, in 1981 in order to sell its technologies to third parties.

Boliden's diversification led it into a number of new areas, including the production of chemicals for the pulp and paper industry, the manufacturing of water systems, transport and terminals operations, and strong international trade presence. In the late 1970s, Boliden began a company-wide restructuring effort, designed to emphasize the international component of its varied operations. This led to the creation of Boliden International, which grouped together six of the company's international trading and consulting companies.

During this time, Boliden's metals operations demonstrated strong growth. The company entered metal recycling, eventually becoming one of the world's largest in this sector, through the acquisition of Denmark's Paul Bersoe & Son in 1976. This business was boosted with the 1981 acquisition of Arv Andersson, which also added electronic scrap recycling. The company's mining interests grew in 1980 with the completion of the Aitik mine expansion.

Yet a downturn in the international metals market led Boliden into financial difficulties by mid-decade, and in 1986 the company posted its first-ever loss. By the end of that year, the company had been taken over

The company entered the market in Spain in 1987, buying up Apirsa, a zinc mining group near Seville. Boliden entered Saudi Arabia two years later, forming a joint venture with Petromin to exploit the gold deposit at Sukhaybarat in 1989. The company also acquired the Black Angel zinc lead mine in Greenland. At the same time, Boliden added production units for the manufacture of copper and brass products in the United Kingdom, Belgium, the Netherlands, as well as in Sweden. In 1991, Boliden and parent Trelleborg established a joint-venture to enter the metals and minerals trading market in Eastern Europe. By 1995, the company had begun to exploit a second site in Spain, at Los Frailes.

THE NEW BOLIDEN IN THE NEW CENTURY

Trelleborg undertook a major restructuring in the mid-1990s, culminating with its sale of 51 percent of Boliden on the stock market. In a move designed to bring the company closer to the center of the international metals market, Boliden's shares were listed on the Toronto Stock Exchange in 1997. Boliden was then reincorporated as Boliden Limited, with its headquarters moved to Toronto. In 1998, Boliden added its first North American operation, acquiring the Westmin mining company in Canada, including its underground mine at Myra Falls. The Westmin purchase also gave Boliden a presence in the Chile copper mining market. By then, the company had also entered Mexico, through two exploration joint ventures with Silver Eagle Resources in the United States, and Mexico's gold and silver producer, Luismin SA.

Yet Boliden's American adventure proved short-lived as the company slipped into an extended period of financial difficulty. By 1999 the company had begun to restructure its holdings, selling off, among others, its share of the Saudi Arabia gold joint venture, and moving its headquarters back to Sweden. By 2001, the company had also transferred its shares to the Stockholm exchange. The "new" Boliden's restructuring continued through much of the first half of the new decade, and included exits from its Canadian and Chilean mining operations, as well as the sale of its 50 percent share of Norzink. In 2001, the company also shut down its Laisvall lead mine.

Into the middle of the decade, Boliden's new strategy called for a tighter focus on its core base metals production, and especially copper and zinc. This included the acquisition of copper tubing products manufacturer HME Nederland, in 2002. In 2003, Boliden took a major step forward, becoming one of Europe's leading copper and zinc producers, when it

---

KEY DATES

1915: Centralgruppen Emissionsbolag is established to acquire stakes in the mining companies and mines in Sweden's northern region.

1924: Gold is discovered in Fagelmyren.

1925: Centralgruppen's bank takes over the company and establishes two mining subsidiaries, Västerbottens Gruvaktiebolag and Skellefteå Gruvaktiebolag.

1931: Västerbottens Gruvaktiebolag and Skellefteå Gruvaktiebolag merge to become Boliden.

1940: Boliden opens new mines in Kristineberg, Lainejaur, Ravliden, Adak and Bjukfors.

1957: The company acquires Sweden's Zinkgruvor, including mines at Garpenberg and Saxberget.

1964: Boliden acquires 50 percent of the Norzink joint venture in Norway.

1981: Boliden International is created.

1986: Boliden acquired by Trelleborg AB, which refocuses the group on metals and mining operations.

1987: Boliden enters Spain, acquiring the Seville-based zinc mining group Apirsa.

1989: The company enters the Saudi Arabia gold mining market through a joint venture with Petromin.

1997: Boliden is spun off as a public company, Boliden Ltd., with headquarters in Toronto and a listing on the Toronto exchange.

1999: Boliden returns to Sweden and transfers its listing to Stockholm Stock Exchange.

2001: Boliden begins selling off international mining and metals holdings to refocus on the Scandinavian region.

2003: Boliden acquires Outokumpu's zinc and copper mining and smelting operations.

---

by Swedish conglomerate Trelleborg. The match was a good one, as Trelleborg itself had its origins in the production of equipment for the metals and mining industries. Under a new president, 32-year-old Kjell Nilsson, Boliden began to streamline its operations back to a core of metals and mining operations. This led Boliden, which had remained largely focused on the Swedish and Scandinavian markets, to begin an international expansion through the late 1980s and into the 1990s.

agreed to acquire the zinc and copper operations of Finland's Outokumpu. The deal also included the transfer of Outokumpu's smelting operations. In exchange, Outokumpu, which was itself refocusing on its stainless steel production, acquired Boliden's fabrication and technology businesses, as well as a 49 percent share of Boliden. Outokumpu later sold down its stake in Boliden, to just 16 percent by 2006.

The Outokumpu acquisition worked wonders for Boliden's financial picture, and by the end of 2005, the company had posted strong revenue and profit growth, achieving record results. Boliden continued to invest in its future, opening a new mine in Kvarnberget, and investigating plans to expand both its copper smelter at Harjavalta and its copper mine in Aitik. After more than 80 years, Boliden remained one of Europe's leading base metals producers.

M. L. Cohen

PRINCIPAL SUBSIDIARIES

Aitiks Gruvaktiebolag; Boliden Bergsöe AB; Boliden Bergsoe AS (Denmark); Boliden B.V. (Netherlands); Boliden Commercial AB; Boliden de Mexico S.A. de C.V.; Boliden France Sarl; Boliden Harjavalta Oy (Finland); Boliden International AB; Boliden Kokkola Oy (Finland); Boliden Ltd. (Canada); Boliden Mineral AB; Boliden Odda A/S (Norway); Boliden Rönnskär AB; Boliden Tara Mines Ltd. (Ireland); Boliden Zinc Commercial BV (Netherlands); Bolidens Gruvaktiebolag; Compania Minera Boliden S.A. de C.V.; Garpenbergs Gruvaktiebolag; Hardanger Byggeselskap A/S (Norway); Mineral Holding Finland Oy; Mineral Holding Norway A/S; Mineral Holding Sweden AB; Nikkel og Olivin A/S (Norway); Tara Mines Holding Ltd. (Ireland).

PRINCIPAL COMPETITORS

MAN AG; Commercial Metals Company; Cerro Wire and Cable Company Inc.; Owl Wire and Cable Inc.; Dover Diversified Inc.; Helwan Non-Ferrous Metals Industries; Hitachi Cable Ltd.; Viohalco S.A.

FURTHER READING

"Boliden Buys Overextended Dutch Tube Maker," *American Metal Market*, January 23, 2002, p. 4.

"Boliden Mines $70m with Sale of Outokumpu Takeover Stake," *Euroweek*, January 23, 2004, p. 33.

Brooks, David, "Boliden Swaps its Myra Falls Mine for 5% Equity Stake in Breakwater," *American Metal Market*, February 18, 2004, p. 5.

———, "Boliden to Increase Copper Output in Finland," *American Metal Market*, December 28, 2005, p. 6.

Brown-Humes, Christopher, "Deal Gives Outokumpu 49% of Boliden," *Financial Times*, September 9, 2003, p. 30.

Burgert, Philip, "Half of Boliden Going Public," *American Metal Market*, February 14, 1997, p. 2.

Casteel, Kyran, "Home and Away," *World Mining Equipment*, November 1997, p. 18.

Grey, Paul Francis, "Outokumpu to Sell Mines, Take 49% Stake in Boliden," *American Metal Market*, September 9, 2003, p. 1.

Kennedy, Alan, "Trelleborg Boliden: Global Expansion Continues," *Mining Magazine*, November 1992, p. 307.

LaRue, Gloria T., "Boliden to Increase Production," *American Metal Market*, November 6, 1996, p. 4.

Salak, John, "Despite Hard Times," *American Metal Market*, January 28, 1987, p. 1.

"Trelleborg Sets Boliden Sale," *American Metal Market*, June 3, 1997, p. 4.

Bolsa Mexicana de Valores, S.A. de C.V.

Avenida Paseo de La Reforma 255
Mexico City, D.F.
Mexico
Telephone: (52) 55 5726-6600
Fax: (52) 55 5726-6805
Web site: http://www.bmv.com.mx

Private Company
Incorporated: 1894 as La Bolsa Nacional, S.A.
Employees: 307
Sales: $1.11 billion (2002 est.)
NAIC: 523210 Securities and Commodity Exchanges

■ ■ ■

La Bolsa Mexicana de Valores, S.A. de C.V., or BMV, is Mexico's stock exchange and is also the place where fixed-income securities are bought and sold. These transactions are effected by registered brokerage houses, which collectively are the owners of the BMV. There is no trading floor; buy and sell orders are transmitted and fulfilled by means of an electronic system. Norms for the operation of the exchange are set down by law, and it functions by concession from the Mexican government.

STRUGGLING EXCHANGES: 1894–1975

The BMV traces its beginning to the establishment in 1894 of La Bolsa Nacional, S.A., in the commercial heart of Mexico City. Another exchange was established the following year under the name Bolsa de México,

S.A., and when the two exchanges merged later in the year, it took the name of the latter. Although previous ad hoc efforts—even including trading on the street—had been marked by lack of regulation, the Bolsa suffered from too many rules. Brokers had to pay a fee on their operations, and share prices were in practice higher than those charged by "coyotes" outside the exchange's doors. When the Bolsa de México closed its doors in 1896 or 1897, share prices were being quoted for only 11 companies, among them three banks, a mortgage lender, a brewery, and a paper manufacturer.

The next stock exchange, Bolsa Privada de México, S.A., was founded in 1907. Like the Bolsa de México, it mostly presided over the buying and selling of shares of mineral companies and charged brokers a fee. This exchange became the Bolsa de Valores de México, S.C.L., in 1908. Activity was stilled by the ensuing revolution and civil war, picked up in 1918 with monetary stabilization, and slowed in the early 1920s. A boom in mineral stocks followed, especially for enterprise engaged in oil exploration, but some of these ventures proved to be fraudulent. The 1929 Wall Street crash had a chilling effect on business, and in 1931 the exchange closed in March and April. It was reorganized in 1933 as the Bolsa de Valores de México, S.A., with 60 shareholders. It became the Bolsa de Valores de México, S.A. de C.V., in 1936.

The Bolsa's growth was inhibited by a lack of guarantees of suitable operation of the market or of a wider legal framework in its operation. A 1946 law established a registry for companies quoted on the exchange, obligating each one to present basic information about its juridical personality and financial situation.

The number of issuers of securities increased greatly during the next decade. At the end of 1959, two years after the Bolsa moved to a new building, it had 61 trading members and was dealing in 757 securities. Fixed-rate investments, not stocks, formed the great majority of the trades. Indeed, only about 5 percent of all securities transactions in Mexico were taking place on the official exchanges. The majority of these transactions were being conducted by the central bank and the development bank—government institutions that bought and sold equities and bonds on their own. The capital of all corporations listed on the Bolsa may have totaled no more than 5 percent of the total capital of all corporations.

In the mid-1960s it was estimated that more than 80 percent of all transactions in listed stocks were still being conducted directly through banks and other financial institutions. However, prices were established by quotes on the Bolsa. A member broker could deal off the exchange if he believed he could get a better price than on the trading floor, but he had to charge the customer the commission prescribed by the Bolsa. This commission varied from 0.5 percent to 1 percent, depending on the size of the transaction, and was paid by both buyer and seller. The going rate for membership on the exchange was about $5,000.

More than 95 percent of total transactions in this period involved fixed-income securities. Among these were debt obligations of Nacional Financiera S.A., the federal government industrial-development bank; mortgage certificates; bonds of privately owned financial institutions; corporate mortgage bonds; debt obligations of the federal government or the states; and corporate debenture bonds. A large number of these securities traded at par at all times.

An affiliate of Mexico's largest private bank, Banco Nacional de México S.A. (Banamex), was the largest brokerage house on the exchange. In second place, by 1966, was Promociones y Corretajes S.A. (Procorsa), which was handling about one-fifth of the Bolsa's stock transactions. Its growth came largely from an aggressive pursuit of small investors, including the formation of some 80 investment clubs in which members usually contributed 400 pesos ($32) per month. There were about 10,000 investors in the market, of which about 6,000 were foreigners, mostly Americans and Swiss.

BOOM-AND-BUST CYCLES: 1975–2000

The next big change came in 1975, when the exchange became the Bolsa Mexicana de Valores and absorbed the smaller ones in Monterrey (established 1950) and Guad-alajara (established 1957). The BMV was now a concessionaire of the Secretaria de Hacienda y Crédito Público (SHCP). A government commission already in place continued to oversee and regulate its operations, but new regulations were introduced to protect investors, and the number of brokerage houses given access to the exchange was reduced to 22. The estimated 10,000 investors in 1970 had grown to nearly 25,000 in 1975.

Another government agency, the Instituto Nacional de Depósito de Valores (INDEVAL), was established in 1978 with functions that included overseeing administration, compensation, liquidation, and transfer of securities. Two other major changes occurred at this time: the introduction of 28-day Cetes treasury bonds—short-term government financing—by the central bank, and of petrobonds, also introduced by the federal government, with payment at maturity based on the price of a stated quantity of petroleum. Also, short-term commercial paper entered the market. The years 1977 to 1979 saw a boom fueled by rising oil prices. The debt crisis that followed the fall of oil prices in the early 1980s resulted in the government nationalizing the banks in 1982, when the volume of shares traded on the BMV fell 35 percent and their value fell 57 percent. The market value of all the companies quoted on the exchange dropped to $850 million, compared to $20 billion in 1979.

The BMV introduced trading in futures in 1983. With the loss of confidence in stock values, trading in shares on the market fell from 8.6 percent of total transactions (in value) in 1981 to only 2.2 percent in 1983. Commercial paper accounted for 9 percent, and the buying and selling of Cetes bonds for 85 percent. The BMV's revenues chiefly came from annual fees imposed on the companies quoted on the exchange, fees from agents and brokerage houses, and a fee charged on Cetes transactions.

Two years later, a destructive earthquake struck Mexico City, but trading was suspended for only two days, resuming in another location until the exchange was able to return to his own quarters. By 1986 another bull market had emerged. The BMV was, in June 1987, described as the world's hottest market, with a 50-stock index that had climbed 320 percent in 1986 and another 109 percent in the first quarter of 1987. However, these paper gains were being made in the face of a no-growth economy, triple-digit inflation, and a huge foreign debt. In the fall—on the heels of panic selling on the New York Stock Exchange—the BMV's stock index fell 75 percent in value during a five-week period, illustrating the perils of participating in what remained a thinly traded market for shares. Many tapped-out investors left for good; their number fell from 403,083 in November

1987 to about 120,000 in 1991. The number of accounts fell from 800,000 in 1987 to 110,000 in 2000.

The BMV moved, in 1990, to its own new 22-story building, attached to a domed annex, on Mexico City's main boulevard, the Paseo de la Reforma. The automatization of the trading floor began in 1991 with the purchase of a system from the Vancouver stock exchange. This was adopted to its needs and put in operation but found to lack sufficient flexibility and replaced by a new platform bought in 1995. Floor trading ended in 1999.

At the end of 1994 197 companies with combined market value of $196 billion were listed on the BMV. Its annual sales were larger than that of the stock exchanges of Italy, Spain, or Belgium. That year foreign companies were allowed to list their securities on the exchange, and it received approval to trade index-linked derivatives. Once again, however, the stock market collapsed, this time because of the debt crisis and flight of capital that resulted in the devaluation of the peso in December 1994 and a subsequent deep recession. To meet the new conditions created by the so-called tequila crisis, the BMV introduced another trading instrument—this time in debt shares. The volume of transactions on the BMV fell 60 percent between 1995 and 1999, and the exchange sold its building, remaining there as a tenant.

THE BMV IN THE 21ST CENTURY

As the 20th century ended, there were 190 publicly traded Mexican enterprises, but only a fraction of their shares were being bought and sold on the BMV. More than 70 percent of the activity in these stocks was taking place on the New York Stock Exchange, where these shares were being traded in the form of American Depositary Receipts. Most Mexican corporate bonds were also being traded abroad rather than on the BMV. Globalization had allowed the owners and officers of major Mexican companies to find the financing they needed in U.S. and European markets. Medium-sized firms were still waiting, in early 2004, for the investing climate to improve before offering stock to the public.

The BMV suffered a blow that year when the Spanish owner of Grupo Financiero BBVA Bancomer S.A., one of Mexico's two biggest financial groups, delisted its stock on the exchange. Citigroup Inc., owner of the other one, Grupo Financiero Banamex S.A., had delisted this stock in 2001. The departure of Banamex and Bancomer left only one major financial group, Grupo Financiero Banorte, S.A. de C.V., on the Mexican stock exchange. Also in 2004, the Swiss owner of the major cement company Apasco S.A. de C.V. withdrew this

stock from the market. These actions left ten companies accounting for more than 60 percent of the BMV's market capitalization. Liquidity was even more concentrated, with five stocks—one of them Bancomer—accounting for half of all stock trading in the first half of 2004. Telefónos de México S.A. de C.V. (Telmex), and América Móvil, S.A. de C.V., both controlled by Carlos Slim Helú, the richest man in Latin America, accounted for 27 percent of the volume. These were the first two stocks on which traded options had become available through the BMV's derivatives market.

By the end of 2005, the BMV was doing much better, supported by Mexico's lower rate of inflation, record foreign-currency reserves, and investment-grade rating for its public debt. The exchange's principal index, a basket of 35 stocks, almost tripled in value between 2003 and 2005, a period during which, in 2004-05, it reached new daily highs more than 100 times. However, these gains masked a familiar shortcoming—the narrow base of trading on the exchange. Five companies controlled by Slim—Telmex, América Móvil, Grupo Carso S.A. de C.V., Grupo Financiero Inbursa, S.A. de C.V. and Impulsora del Desarrollo Económico de América Latina, S.A. de C.V.—accounted for 47 percent of the share volume in 2005. Three other companies—Wal-Mart de México, S.A. de C.V., Cemex S.A. de C.V., and Grupo Televisa S.A.—accounted for another 25 percent. Almost 45 percent of the shares of Mexican companies were owned by foreigners. The BMV's total market capitalization of $141 billion in mid-2004 was still below the peak of $215.3 billion just before the tequila crisis of late 1994.

Guillermo Prieto, president of the BMV since 2001, was seeking to make the exchange a financial supermarket offering investors an array of products. One of those proposed was the Fibra, the Spanish acronym for the asset class known in the United States as the Real Estate Investment Trust, or REIT. Another hopeful sign was the entry into the market of Afores—private pension funds that, beginning in 2005, were allowed to invest indirectly in equities.

In addition to trading in shares of stock, the BMV was trading in warrants; fixed-income debt securities; a variety of government securities, including treasury certificates and development bonds; and corporate securities, such as commercial paper and promissory notes. The BMV was owned by 27 registered brokerage firms in 2004.

Robert Halasz

PRINCIPAL COMPETITORS

NASDAQ; New York Stock Exchange, Inc.

FURTHER READING

Bello, Alberto, "Desde el piso de remates," *Expansión,* January 21, 2004–February 4, 2004, pp. 171-72, 175-77.

"Bolsa's Stock Is Rising," *Euromoney,* June 1987, supplement, pp. 12-13.

Bolsas de Valores en América Latina y El Caribe. Caracas: Instituto Interamericano de Mercados de Capital, 1985, pp. 275-311.

Cien Años de la Bolsa de Valores en México 1894-1994. Mexico City: La Bolsa, 1993.

Eiteman, David K., *Stock Exchanges in Latin America.* Ann Arbor: University of Michigan, 1966, pp. 1-13.

Hakim, Miguel, *The Efficiency of the Mexican Stock Market.* New York: Garland, 1992.

Lara, Tania, "Qué pasa en la Bolsa?," *Expansión,* February 22–March 8, 2006, pp. 67-69.

"Look South for Latin Listings," *Euromoney,* January 1995, p. 14.

"Mexico's Money Men Learn to Lure Capital," *Business Week,* November 26, 1966, pp. 118-19, 121.

Smith, Gene, "It's Fiesta Time for the Bolsa," *Business Week,* November 28, 2005, p. 52.

"Vanishing Point," *LatinFinance,* September 2004, pp. 79-80.

Brillstein-Grey
Entertainment

■

9150 Wilshire Boulevard, Suite 350
Hollywood, California 90212
U.S.A.
Telephone: (310) 275-6135
Fax: (310) 275-6180

Private Company
Incorporated: 1969 as the Brillstein Company
Employees: 60 (2005)
Sales: $53.5 million (2005 est.)
NAIC: 711410 Agents and Managers for Artists, Athletes, Entertainers, and Other Public Figures; 512110 Motion Picture and Video Production

■ ■ ■

Brillstein-Grey Entertainment is one of the top personal management and television production firms in Hollywood. The company's clients include stars Adam Sandler, Jennifer Aniston, and David Spade along with numerous screenwriters and producers, while its successful television division has produced hits like *The Sopranos* and *Just Shoot Me*. Since owner and CEO Brad Grey's departure in 2005 to head Paramount Motion Picture Group, the firm has been owned by members of its management.

ORIGINS

Brillstein-Grey Entertainment traces its roots to 1969, when personal manager Bernie Brillstein founded the Brillstein Co. Born in New York City in 1931, Brillstein had been introduced to show business by a comedian uncle, and after service in the U. S. Air Force he was hired by the famed William Morris Agency, where he worked his way up from the mailroom to the position of agent. Two years after being assigned to the company's Los Angeles office, he struck off on his own to represent clients like comic Norm Crosby and *Sesame Street* puppeteer Jim Henson.

The ambitious Brillstein soon began to dabble in television, and after unsuccessfully pitching an adult spin-off of *Sesame Street* featuring Henson's Muppets, he combined the attributes of comedy/variety hit *Laugh-In* and country-flavored shows like *The Beverly Hillbillies* to create the syndicated country music/comedy series *Hee Haw*. It proved a success, and in 1975 Brillstein was able to sell *The Muppet Show* and client Lorne Michaels' *Saturday Night Live* to syndication and NBC, respectively. With a talent roster that included many of the latter's stars like John Belushi, Dan Aykroyd, and Gilda Radner, Brillstein began producing films with them like *The Blues Brothers* and later *Ghostbusters*. Close friend Belushi died of a drug overdose in early 1982, however, and afterwards the stunned manager came close to quitting the business.

In February of 1984 Brillstein met young manager Brad Grey at an industry convention, and when they ran into each other in Hawaii a short time later Grey proposed an informal partnership where he would learn the production side of the business in exchange for bringing in fresh talent. The Bronx-born, 27-years younger Grey had entered show business in 1979 as a gopher at Harvey Weinstein's University of Buffalo concert promotion firm, and soon broke into talent management by signing then-unknown comic Bob Saget.

KEY DATES

1969: Bernie Brillstein founds the Brillstein Company to manage performers.

1975: Brillstein helps launch *The Muppet Show* and *Saturday Night Live*.

1985: Brad Grey begins working for Brillstein as a talent manager.

1986: Brillstein sells the company's production division to Lorimar-Telepictures.

1988: Brillstein exits Lorimar and takes back ownership of company.

1992: Brad Grey becomes an equal partner; the firm is renamed Brillstein-Grey Entertainment.

1992: A distribution deal is signed with Columbia Pictures Television.

1993: Brillstein-Grey's motion picture division is formed.

1994: A $100 million production agreement is signed with ABC.

1996: Brillstein sells his stake to Grey; a $100 million MCA TV deal is signed.

1999: The company signs a new Columbia TriStar TV production deal; the Garry Shandling lawsuit is settled.

2001: The Sarkes/Kernes management company is acquired.

2002: A TV production agreement is signed with 20th Century Fox.

2004: Margaret Riley Management is acquired.

2005: Brad Grey sells the firm to top partners; a deal is signed with Touchstone TV.

Saget helped him add other upcoming comedians like Garry Shandling, Dennis Miller, and Dana Carvey, and after parting amicably with Weinstein (who had by now founded film company Miramax), Grey moved to Los Angeles. A year after meeting Brillstein he began working for his new mentor's firm, where the pair developed a father-and-son-like relationship.

Managers typically collected 15 percent of their clients' earnings in exchange for promoting them, offering strategic advice, running their business operations, and taking care of travel bookings and other necessities. They were not legally permitted to seek work, which was done by talent agents for a 10 percent cut, but in reality this line was often blurred. Managing alone could be lucrative, but it did not have the same earning power as production, where owned assets like films and TV series could generate huge amounts of revenue from syndication, foreign sales, home video, and other derivations.

In 1986 Bernie Brillstein sold control of the Brillstein Company's production arm to Lorimar-Telepictures for $26 million, while Grey remained in charge of the firm's separate talent unit. Brillstein subsequently took the title of chairman and CEO of Lorimar Film Entertainment, but when Lorimar was sold to Warner Brothers in 1988 he left and regained control of his production business in exchange for ownership of several TV shows and films he'd produced including *Alf, Love Connection*, and *Ghostbusters*. The following year Grey was made partner.

BRILLSTEIN-GREY ENTERTAINMENT FORMED IN 1992

In early 1992 Brillstein split the firm's ownership equally with Grey and it became known as Brillstein-Grey Entertainment, with the pair designated co-chairmen. Soon afterward Grey helped the company negotiate a deal with Columbia Pictures Television Distribution to finance and distribute its television series in exchange for a $20 million advance and a share of the profits.

1992 saw the debut of a much-ballyhooed new late-night talk show starring client Dennis Miller, though it failed to strike a chord with the public and was soon canceled. Greater success came from Garry Shandling's *The Larry Sanders Show* on pay-cable network HBO, which garnered critical acclaim and numerous industry awards.

In July of 1993 Brillstein-Grey created a new motion picture division, which would be run by former Sandollar Productions head Howard Rosenman. It quickly signed a so-called "first look" deal with Columbia Pictures, which would have the right of first refusal on all projects. In December, the firm opened an office in New York.

February of 1994 saw television production company Brillstein-Grey Communications formed in partnership with Capital Cities/ABC, which had reportedly put up over $100 million to fund the venture. It was the first deal of its kind between a network and a management firm, as laws restricting such arrangements had recently been relaxed. Some estimates now put Brillstein-Grey's revenues at $100 million per year from management alone, with another sizable amount coming from production.

BRAD GREY TAKES REINS IN 1995

In October of 1995 Brad Grey was named CEO and chairman of the company while Bernie Brillstein took the title of founding partner. The following spring MCA, Inc., bought a 50 percent stake in Brillstein-Grey Entertainment's television and movie production units for approximately $100 million, giving Brad Grey a significant role as a producer of films and television shows. While the deal was being finalized Grey had bought Brillstein's stake in the firm, and afterwards he would keep sole ownership of management unit Brillstein-Grey Enterprises, whose 100-plus client roster included stars like Brad Pitt, Nicholas Cage, Courteney Cox, Sylvester Stallone, and Christian Slater, as well as writers for hit shows *Frasier, Northern Exposure,* and *Cheers.* In June entertainment lawyer and two-year company veteran Lloyd Braun was named president of the firm, which was now also operating a literary unit whose clients included Elmore Leonard and Martin Amis.

At this time Brillstein-Grey was developing more than 30 film projects and had seven TV series in production including *NewsRadio, The Naked Truth* and *The Larry Sanders Show.* Its expertise producing half-hour situation comedies like these had spurred MCA to seek a deal because such series were the most lucrative for later syndication. The agreement reportedly angered new ABC parent Disney, however, because some programs it co-owned with Brillstein-Grey would now be shown on rival networks like NBC, in at least one case sharing the same time slot. Brillstein-Grey subsequently took back ABC's stake in their joint production deal in exchange for a percentage of the earnings from shows like *Politically Incorrect With Bill Maher.*

In January of 1998 Garry Shandling, who had been dropped as a client two months earlier, sued Brillstein-Grey Entertainment and Brad Grey for $100 million. The comic, who was Grey's second-ever management client and had been a close personal friend, claimed that Grey's dual roles as manager and *Larry Sanders Show* executive producer were a conflict of interest. He also alleged that some of its writers had been diverted by Grey to other series and claimed he had helped bring the firm many of its clients and given it the clout to sign lucrative deals with MCA and ABC. The suit quickly became the talk of Hollywood, with Brillstein labeling the comedian "delusional." In March, Grey filed an $18 million countersuit.

Meanwhile, MCA was selling its own television production arm to Barry Diller's USA Networks, and, as it did not have the contractual right to sell its stake in the production venture with Brillstein-Grey, it was forced to cede this back while keeping half of the profit from shows like *Just Shoot Me* and *NewsRadio.* In the fall the latter program was renewed by NBC only when

Brillstein-Grey allowed the network a share of its future syndication profits, which would come when more episodes were completed. The year also saw company president Lloyd Braun leave to head Buena Vista Television, while Grey's attempt to make a splash on Broadway by producing Paul Simon's musical *The Capeman* fell flat.

THE SOPRANOS DEBUTS IN 1999

In early 1999 a new Mafia drama that Brillstein-Grey had unsuccessfully pitched to most of the broadcast networks premiered on HBO. *The Sopranos* became a major popular and critical success and went on to run for six seasons, generating huge revenues for the firm. May saw the company form a new development and production unit called BGTV in partnership with Columbia TriStar Television Group, which would supply financing and split the profits, though the shows produced would be owned by BGTV.

In July 1999 the lawsuit with Shandling was settled out of court on the eve of a jury trial, with the undisclosed settlement reportedly involving the exchange of rights to TV series. The firm also reached exclusive production agreements in 1999 with Diane Keaton's Blue Relief Productions, Hungry Man TV, and *Friends* co-executive producer Alexa Junge, while in early 2000 a strategic alliance was formed with advertising giant J. Walter Thompson USA to merge advertising content with entertainment and digital communications.

In the fall of 2001 Brillstein-Grey Management absorbed the Sarkes/Kernis management company and its 25 clients, including comedians like Andy Richter, Steven Wright, and Cheri Oteri. Another recently added client was New York mayor Rudolph Giuliani, whose stature had grown after his inspiring response to the September 11, 2001 terrorist attacks. The company had earlier found him a $3 million book deal, and after the attacks it helped produce an HBO special that benefited the families of firefighters and police who were killed.

In May 2002 Brillstein-Grey's TV production unit switched studios yet again when the Columbia deal expired, this time moving to 20th Century Fox. The latter would pay for overhead, administrative support, and deficit financing of broadcast television shows, taking no role in cable programs like *The Sopranos.* In September the company formed a feature film production unit with clients and star couple Brad Pitt and Jennifer Aniston called Plan B Entertainment, at which time the Brad Grey Pictures division was shuttered. The year also saw *Just Shoot Me* sold to syndication for $3 million per episode, bringing the firm half of a $525 million payout.

In 2004 Brillstein-Grey absorbed Margaret Riley Management, whose talent roster included a number of successful screenwriters, directors, and producers. During the year 73-year old Bernie Brillstein published *The Little Stuff Matters Most: 50 Rules From 50 Years of Trying to Make a Living*, his second book. He continued to work full time managing clients like Martin Short, Lorne Michaels, and his very first client, comedian Norm Crosby, who at 77 was still earning more than $500,000 per year.

BRAD GREY LEAVES FOR PARAMOUNT IN 2005

Viacom's Paramount Motion Picture Group had secretly begun courting Brad Grey, and in January of 2005 he was named to succeed departing studio head Sherry Lansing, taking the titles of chairman and CEO in March. Supporters cited his good taste, ability to work with talent, and successful television production record, though his feature film experience was relatively thin.

Because of the conflict of interest his new job would create, Grey agreed to sell Brillstein-Grey to a group of partners led by veterans Cynthia Pett-Dante, Jon Liebman, Marc Gurwitz, and Sandy Wernick. Pett-Dante and Liebman would serve as co-presidents, with the latter named CEO. Grey, who would reportedly take a pay cut to gain the prestige of running a studio, would keep a stake in several television shows he had helped produce including *The Sopranos*. Brad Grey Television subsequently reverted to the name Brillstein-Grey Television, while Plan B, the production company he co-owned with Brad Pitt and Jennifer Aniston, would become the sole property of the now-single Pitt and move from Warner Brothers to Paramount.

In the summer of 2005 the company signed a three-year TV production deal with Touchstone Television and lured Aleen Keshishian and JoAnne Colonna away from The Firm, where they had served as co-heads of its talent division, along with Firm manager Mary Putnam Greene. The trio brought with them clients like Sarah Michelle Gellar, Andy Garcia, Natalie Portman, and Orlando Bloom.

In early 2006 Brillstein-Grey Management head Peter Safran left to form his own company, taking along Sean "Puffy" Combs, David Hyde Pierce, Brooke Shields, and others. The firm also dropped author James Frey from its roster after he admitted that his best-selling memoir *A Million Little Pieces* was filled with exaggerations.

Nearly 40 years after its founding as a one-man operation, Brillstein-Grey Entertainment had become a major player in Hollywood. The firm's management division represented more than 150 clients including household names Adam Sandler, Jennifer Aniston, and Sarah Michelle Gellar, as well as a host of talented screenwriters and producers, while its television production arm had built up an enviable track record with hits like *The Sopranos* and *Just Shoot Me*. Under the leadership of new majority owners Cynthia Pett-Dante and Jon Liebman, the firm looked forward to continued growth.

Frank Uhle

PRINCIPAL SUBSIDIARIES

Brillstein-Grey Management; Brillstein-Grey Television.

PRINCIPAL COMPETITORS

The Firm; Mosaic Media Group; 3 Arts Entertainment, Inc.; CKX, Inc.

FURTHER READING

Block, Alex Ben, "Curtain Falls on the Brad and Bernie Show," *Television Week*, January 10, 2005, p. 8.

Brillstein, Bernie and Rensin, David, *Where Did I Go Right? You're No One in Hollywood Unless Someone Wants You Dead.* New York: Little, Brown & Company, 1999.

Carter, Bill, "ABC in Unusual Venture with Talent Firm," *New York Times*, February 3, 1994, p. 1D.

Collins, Monica, "Bernie Brillstein Manages the Funny Business," *USA Today*, June 29, 1987, p. 3D.

Dunkley, Cathy and Lisa De Moraes, "MCA Turns Grey with 50% Share," *Hollywood Reporter*, May 22, 1996, p. 1.

Fleming, Michael, "Prexies Filling Up Grey Area," *Daily Variety*, August 3, 2005.

Flint, Joe, "Hey Now! Garry Shandling Shocks Hollywood with His $100 Million Suit Against Former Manager Brad Grey," *Entertainment Weekly*, February 6, 1998, p. 16.

Foege, Alec, "Shades of Grey," *Mediaweek*, October 4, 1999, p. 35.

Foreman, Liza, "Grey Area: Can TV Vet Make Films?," *Hollywood Reporter*, January 10, 2005.

Gardner, Chris, "Sarkes, Kernis Join Brillstein-Grey," *Hollywood Reporter*, November 6, 2001, p. 1.

Littleton, Cynthia, "Brad Grey TV Lands at 20th With 3-Year Primetime Pact," *Hollywood Reporter*, May 9, 2002, p. 1.

———, "Dialogue" [Brad Grey Interview], *Hollywood Reporter*, September 13, 2002, p. 1.

———, "Keshishian Partners Up at Brillstein-Grey," *Hollywood Reporter*, July 12, 2005.

Littleton, Cynthia and Nellie Andreeva, "Brillstein-Grey TV Unit to Pact with Touchstone," *Hollywood Reporter*, June 15,

2005.

Parker, Donna, "Rosenman Brings 30 Films to Brillstein-Grey," *Hollywood Reporter*, October 4, 1994, p. 3.

Pulley, Brett, "Hollywood Hit Man," *Forbes*, July 8, 2002, p. 128.

Schleier, Curt, "Master of Creative Solutions," *Investor's Business Daily*, September 24, 2004, p. A3.

Schneider, Michael, "Partners at Last: Brad Grey, Columbia TriStar Hook Up to Create BGTV," *Electronic Media*, May 10, 1999, p. 4.

"Shandling and Ex-Manager Settle Suit," *New York Times*, July 3, 1999, p. B17.

Shapiro, Eben, "Manager's Dual Roles Anger Star Client," *Wall Street Journal*, March 6, 1998, p. B1.

Sharkey, Betsy, "Buying Into a Laugh Factory," *Mediaweek*, June 3, 1996, p. 17.

Weinraub, Bernard, "A Hollywood Odd Couple with a One-Two Punch," *New York Times*, February 20, 1994, p. C8.

———, "Bernie Brillstein: Pulling No Punches in the Dream Factory," *New York Times*, November 8, 1999.

bfi British Film Institute

The British Film Institute

—■—

21 Stephen Street
London, W1T 1LN
United Kingdom
Telephone: (44) (20) 7255 1444
Fax: (44) (20) 7436 2071
Web site: http://www.bfi.org.uk

Non-Profit Organization
Incorporated: 1933
Employees: 450 (2006 est.)
Sales: $56.5 million (2004 est.)
NAIC: 519120 Libraries and Archives; 511120 Periodical Publishers; 511130 Book Publishers; 512120 Motion Picture and Video Distribution; 512131 Motion Picture Theaters (Except Drive-Ins); 512199 Other Motion Picture and Video Industries; 711310 Promoters of Performing Arts, Sports, and Similar Events with Facilities

■ ■ ■

The British Film Institute operates under Royal Charter to promote understanding and appreciation of film and television in United Kingdom. The organization maintains one of the world's largest archives of films, television programs, and related materials; operates the three-screen National Film Theatre and an IMAX large-screen theater; releases classic films to theaters and on video; publishes books and the monthly film journal *Sight & Sound*; and organizes the annual London Film Festival and London Lesbian & Gay Film Festival. Other activities include providing an information service for researchers, sponsoring educational programs, and selling copies of material from its archives to film producers.

EARLY YEARS

The British Film Institute (BFI) was founded in 1933 by the British Board of Trade to promote, study, and help educate about film in the United Kingdom. Its creation had been prompted by a report commissioned several years earlier by the British Institute for Adult Education's Commission of Educational and Cultural Films.

In 1934 the organization received its first annual grant of £5,000 from the Cinematograph Fund of the Privy Council, and it also took over the two-year old quarterly publication *Sight & Sound* and inaugurated the *Monthly Film Bulletin*. During the year staff member Ernest Lindgren started a book and periodical library, which in 1935 began to house films. Within three years the National Film Library's collection had grown to 300 titles, some of which were for lending and others for preservation only. The BFI had by this time also begun sponsoring a summer school and public film screenings.

During World War II the organization's film collection was moved from London to a stable in Rudgwick, Sussex, for safekeeping, and its headquarters in Great Russell Street was damaged during the Nazi blitz. After the war a new location was secured on Shaftesbury Avenue, where the BFI was relocated in 1948.

At this time a study was completed that recommended several changes in the agency's operations, and its educational mission was subsequently shifted to the

COMPANY PERSPECTIVES

Inspired by enthusiasm for the moving image and a spirit of adventure, we will seek to inspire others. We will celebrate creativity and encourage innovation and excellence. We will contribute cutting-edge critical perspectives and champion wide-ranging debate. Engaging people all across the UK, we will extend the beneficial reach of film and television, especially among children, young people and socially and culturally diverse audiences. We will seek new ways to improve media literacy and enrich appreciation and understanding of our past, present and future heritage, while fostering lifelong learning and enjoyment. We want to be amongst the UK's leading cultural advocates as well as an influential friend of film-makers and audiences around the world.

recently formed National Committee for Visual Aids in Education, while artists and technicians were encouraged to attend the new British Film Academy. The BFI would focus on running the National Film Library, providing an informational service documenting British films, and promoting film appreciation on a national and regional basis.

In 1949 Denis Forman was named director of the organization, while *Sight & Sound* became a monthly publication edited by younger film critics like Gavin Lambert and Penelope Houston. In 1950 the BFI began a series of film showings at the Institut Francais, and a year later a facility called the Telekinema was built for the Festival of Britain to show three-dimensional and experimental films. When the temporary exhibition in London's South Bank was about to close, Forman proposed that the Telekinema building be converted into a facility called the National Film Theatre (NFT).

In 1952 the NFT opened with filmmaker Karel Reisz serving as its first programmer, and the BFI's Experimental Film Fund was established to provide assistance to new filmmakers. In 1955 Denis Forman resigned to join the Grenada production company and was replaced by James Quinn, while the organization renamed its film library the National Film Archive, underscoring its efforts to preserve early British films. The following year a free program, "60 Years of Cinema," was presented in conjunction with the *Observer* newspaper and drew 200,000 viewers.

LONDON FILM FESTIVAL DEBUTS IN 1957

In 1957 the BFI built a new NFT auditorium under London's Waterloo Bridge near its existing site. In October the new theater hosted the first London Film Festival, which would go on to become one of the organization's signature offerings.

In 1960 the BFI moved its headquarters to a new location on Dean Street, and took possession of 400,000 donated still photographs from the closed *Picture Show* magazine. The following year a new quarterly magazine, *Contrast*, debuted, marking the organization's expansion of its scope to include television.

The BFI had long been funded by the British Treasury, but in 1965 this task was shifted to the Department of Education and Science, which increased its stipend by one-third. The following year was a busy one as the organization, under director Stanley Reed, bought a new site in Berkhamsted to serve as a preservation center, established its first regional theater in Nottingham, and revived the defunct Experimental Film Fund to promote young filmmakers.

In 1967 the BFI distributed a controversial film called *The War Game,* which the British Broadcasting Corporation (BBC) had refused to show on television. A year later the new National Film Archives facility opened and the John Player lecture series was started at the NFT.

In 1970 BFI added an auditorium to the NFT which enabled it to increase the diversity of screenings offered there. One year later Mamoun Hassan was named head of production for the organization and started a program to sponsor low-budget feature films. Then, in 1973 BFI established two new departments, Film Availability Services and Information & Documentation, as well as a new governing structure that utilized advisory committees for each area of the Institute which were chaired by governors who reported to the organization's director.

NITRATE FILM COPYING PROJECT BEGINS IN 1975

In 1975 the BFI implemented a 24-year plan to duplicate some 200 million feet of nitrate film stock held in its archives. The chemically unstable, highly flammable nitrate film had been the industry standard prior to the 1950s, and the organization wanted to copy its collection (including vast amounts of unique newsreel footage and the negatives to many classic films) onto stable "safety" film to preserve it for future generations.

In 1977 the BFI's information department moved

KEY DATES

1933: British Film Institute (BFI) is founded.
1934: BFI takes over publication of *Sight & Sound* magazine.
1935: National Film Library is established under Ernest Lindgren.
1948: BFI mission revised; organization moves to new headquarters.
1952: National Film Theatre opens; Experimental Film Fund is established.
1957: New theater opens under Waterloo Bridge; first London Film Festival is held.
1961: Scope is widened to include television.
1968: New archive facility opens in Berkhamsted.
1983: Royal Charter granted; *BFI Film and Television Yearbook* is introduced.
1988: Museum of the Moving Image opens.
1990: Connoisseur Video is launched with Argos Films to sell classic movies on videotape.
1999: IMAX theater opens on South Bank; Museum of the Moving Image closes.
2006: A £4.5 million expansion of National Film Theatre is begun.

archives to tape television programs off the air for preservation purposes. With funding from broadcasters Channel 4 and ITV it would record some 60 hours per week for posterity. Two years later a season-long program of films on gay and lesbian issues was held at the NFT, which subsequently became an annual event called the London Lesbian and Gay Film Festival.

In 1987 the BFI's headquarters were moved to a newly-purchased site at Stephen Street in London, while a new conservation center opened near the organization's archives in Berkhamsted. Each was funded in large part by American expatriate billionaire J. Paul Getty II.

MUSEUM OF THE MOVING IMAGE OPENS IN 1988

The year 1988 saw the opening of the Museum of the Moving Image (MOMI) in London's South Bank, which would house a collection of film-related artifacts and interactive displays. It had been funded entirely by private donations from the likes of J. Paul Getty II and shipping magnate Sir Yue Kong Pao.

On November 1, 1988, the BFI used a network of volunteers to record the activities of film production companies, television studios, and at viewers' homes around the United Kingdom, as well as taping all broadcast programs for 24 hours in an event called "One Day in the Life of Television." The year also saw Wilf Stevenson appointed director of the organization to replace the departing Anthony Smith, who took the job of president of Magdalen College at Oxford.

In 1990 the BFI partnered with Argos Films to sell videotapes of classic films through Connoisseur Video. A year later *Sight & Sound* absorbed the *Monthly Film Bulletin* and was made over with an eye toward newsstand sales. The BFI Film Classics book series was inaugurated in 1992 by the firm's publishing department, while the long-running annual *British National Film & Video Catalogue* bibliography was mothballed.

The BFI also expanded its educational offerings during 1992 by starting a graduate program in film and television studies at Birkbeck College; formed the London Film and Video Development Agency to promote production, training, and exhibition in that city; and reached an agreement with French Champagne maker Piper-Heidsieck to create new copies of classic films for a touring exhibition. In November the British government announced a three-year freeze of the organization's annual £15 million grant, after which its distribution/exhibition and production divisions were merged and other costs were cut across the board, including grants to regional theaters and film boards. About half of the BFI's operating budget came from the

to a new location on Charing Cross Road, where the organization's headquarters were soon relocated. The Guardian Lecture Series was begun in 1980 and would be taped for broadcast on the BBC.

In 1981 famed British filmmaker Sir Richard Attenborough was appointed governor chairman of the BFI. The organization was facing a decline in funding at this time, and during the next several years it struggled to maintain a full level of service.

In 1982 the first in a series of co-productions with new public broadcaster Channel Four was released, filmmaker Peter Greenaway's *The Draughtsman's Contract*. The copying of nitrate film was continuing as well, now at the rate of seven million feet per year. The latter consumed more than a quarter of the organization's budget of £8 million.

On the BFI's 50th anniversary in 1983 it was granted a Royal Charter, which attested to its importance as a cultural institution. The organization also granted its first honorary fellowships to legendary filmmakers including David Lean, Satyajit Ray, and Orson Welles, and began publishing an annual directory, the BFI Film and Television Yearbook (later Handbook).

In 1984 the BFI established a video unit at its

government, with the rest coming from donations and proceeds from video sales, publishing, and other income generating operations.

Attendance at the NFT and MOMI were in decline, and during 1993 several key personnel left the theater unit. The year also saw veteran film producer Jeremy Thomas take the job of BFI chairman from Sir Richard Attenborough. In 1994 the organization's stipend from the British government was raised from £15 million to £17.1 million, and the BFI also announced it would begin to add video games to its archive.

In 1996 a new strategic report called BFI 2000 was prepared, which laid out a road map for future growth. Plans included moving the NFT to a new site in London's West End, expanding the MOMI, adding a large-screen IMAX theater, and digitizing and expanding access to the BFI's collections via a fiber optic network to universities and arts centers around the United Kingdom. The plan also called for cutting about a quarter of the organization's staff of 520, which helped its already low employee morale sink further. During the year the London Film Festival's director left and its management was shifted to the NFT.

In October the BFI was awarded £15 million to build the proposed IMAX theater. The organization was facing strong criticism in some quarters for the plan, as well as for emphasizing recent popular films and "cult" titles at the NFT, and tilting the MOMI's focus toward entertainment and children's activities rather than history.

In February 1997 a Heritage Lottery Fund grant of nearly £14 million was awarded to the BFI to boost its efforts to preserve films and television programs. Copying of nitrate film had fallen to three million feet per year, while the archive had grown to include 300,000 titles dating from 1894 to the present.

The year also saw director Wilf Stevenson and chairman Jeremy Thomas depart, to be replaced by industry lobbying group head John Woodward and *Fame* director Alan Parker, respectively. The organization faced another funding crisis when the British government announced it was lowering the BFI's stipend to £15.1 million, after which it cancelled funding for feature film production, ended its U.K. Media Desk sponsorship, and cut 40 of its staff of 487. A simultaneous restructuring created four operational departments: Production, Collections, Education, and Exhibition. Also during this time, a new unit called BFI Films was created to sell copies of footage from the organization's archives, and the Film Café restaurant at the NFT was opened.

BFI COMES UNDER WING OF FILM COUNCIL IN 1998

In 1998 a new administrative body called the British Film Council was formed to oversee the activities of the BFI and sister agencies the British Film Commission and British Screen, funding them with taxpayer and National Lottery monies. Chairman Alan Parker and Director John Woodward were named to run the new umbrella organization the following year, with journalist Joan Bakewell and deputy director Jon Teckman taking their respective places.

In 1999 the BFI's new £20 million IMAX theater debuted while the money-losing MOMI was closed, though plans were announced to reopen it later in a new building. A major new addition to the archives was the recently discovered cache of 800 Mitchell and Kenyon "actuality" films from the turn of the century. The nitrate negatives constituted the best collection of its type ever found, and over the next several years they were copied to safety film and a popular television special about them was aired.

In 2000 the Film Council took over the BFI's film production activities, and in 2001 a £1.2 million lottery grant helped fund BFI Online, which would make many items from the archives available on the Internet. In 2002 the organization was again restructured, this time into three departments: Culture and Education; Development and Communication; and Planning and Resources.

During 2002 Jon Teckman left the director's post, and the BFI announced that the MOMI would not reopen as planned. Its space would be taken over by a library, where some former display items were to be shown. Many donors and former board members were furious with the decision, complaining that the earlier announcement of a temporary MOMI shutdown had been disingenuous and questioning the organization's commitment to its historical and educational mission.

In 2003 a new chairman, *English Patient* director Anthony Minghella, was appointed. He vowed to lead the troubled organization back to a focus on education, while also maintaining the activities of the archives, which still had some 110 million feet of nitrate film to copy. Soon afterwards the BFI announced it would eliminate the regional film program that made prints of classic titles available to independent theaters, leaving the job to the Film Council. In June Amanda Nevill was appointed BFI director and another study was undertaken to determine future priorities.

EXPANSION SCALED BACK, COMMERCIALS ARCHIVE ADDED IN 2004

Completed in early 2004, the review recommended that previously announced plans to build a new £35 million Film Centre on the South Bank be shelved for ten years, with a scaled-down version constructed in the vacant MOMI building instead. In the fall the Coca-Cola Company gave the BFI funding to build and preserve a collection of filmed advertisements, while also donating its own materials and urging other firms to follow suit.

In 2005 the BFI joined with Channel 4, the BBC, and the Open University to launch the Creative Archive Licence Group, which would put archival material on-line for free use by filmmakers and educators. It was subsequently expanded, while the organization also began preparation of an educational film download site called Screenonline.

At the start of 2006 the recommended £4.5 million expansion to the NFT was begun, with completion anticipated by the start of the London Film Festival in October. It would include a new research and study area, a small theater, and a gallery.

More than 70 years after its founding, the British Film Institute continued to perform many of the same duties it had originally been charged with, while seeking to more clearly define its mission for the future. Now under the wing of the Film Council, it was taking a conservative approach to expansion while continuing to preserve and make available its rich film and television archives.

Frank Uhle

PRINCIPAL DIVISIONS

National Film and Television Archive; BFI Publishing; National Film Theatre; BFI London IMAX Cinema; BFI National Library; BFI Education.

PRINCIPAL COMPETITORS

La Cinemateque Francaise; The Library of Congress; Museum of Modern Art; George Eastman House; UCLA Film and Television Archive.

FURTHER READING

Alberge, Dalya, "Buffs Accuse Film Theatre of Mediocrity and Vulgarity," *Times* (London), April 18, 1995.

"BFI Cuts Jobs and Restructures," *Screen Finance*, March 20, 1996, p. 1.

"BFI Gears Up for Film Centenary," *Screen Finance*, January 15, 1992.

"BFI Restructures South Bank to Save 1.5 Million," *Screen Finance*, January 13, 1993, p. 12.

"BFI Told to Improve on NFT and MOMI," *Screen Finance*, November 30, 1994, p. 3.

Dunkley, Cathy, "BFI Protesting $1.65 Mil Cut in Gov't Funding," *Hollywood Reporter*, December 19, 1997, p. 14.

Gibbons, Fiachra, "Minghella Takes On Top Job at British Film Institute," *Guardian*, January 11, 2003, p. 7.

Jury, Louise, "BFI Plans for World's Best Film Centre Are Put on Hold," *Independent*, April 3, 2004, p. 10.

———, "South Bank Focuses on 35M Cinematic Centre," *Independent*, April 3, 2002, p. 5.

———, "Work to Begin on National Film Theatre Extension," *Independent*, December 21, 2005, p. 7.

Leitch, Luke, "14 Million Museum of the Moving Image Will Never Reopen," *Evening Standard*, October 4, 2002.

Malcolm, Derek, "Screen Test for New British Film Institute Chairman," *Guardian*, August 5, 1992, p. 33.

Mallalieu, Ben, "BFI Financial Crisis Worsens," *Hollywood Reporter*, February 8, 1994, p. 11.

Milmo, Cahal, "World's Biggest Film Archive Under Scrutiny as New Chairman Tries to Improve Access," *Independent*, May 7, 2003, p. 5.

"Stanley Reed–Obituary," *Times* (London), May 15, 1996.

Tait, Simon, "When This Director Says 'Cut,' His Staff Asks 'How Many?,'" *Times* (London), January 21, 1993.

"U.K. Opens Film Umbrella," *Hollywood Reporter*, July 28, 1998, p. 53.

Walker, Alexander, "Fear and Loathing at the BFI," *Evening Standard*, July 21, 1997, p. 28A.

Bruster's Real Ice Cream, Inc.

730 Mulberry Street
Bridgewater, Pennsylvania 15009
U.S.A.
Telephone: (724) 774-4250
Fax: (724) 774-0666
Web site: http://www.brustersicecream.com/

Private Company
Founded: 1989
Employees: 1,700 (est.)
Sales: $39 million (2004 est.)
NAIC: 311520 Ice Cream and Frozen Dessert Manufacturing

■ ■ ■

Bruster's Real Ice Cream, Inc., is a Bridgewater, Pennsylvania-based private company that operates and franchises a chain of more than 215 walk-up ice cream stores located in the eastern United States. Half a dozen are company-owned units. Bruster's prides itself on making fresh ice cream at each of its stores and baking its own waffle cones and bowls on the premises. Each Bruster's store offers as many as 38 rotating ice cream flavors from a stock of some 150 recipes. Flavors include Chocolate Lovers Trash, Stick in the Mud, Peanut Butter Puddles, Key Lime Pie, Lemon Meringue Pie, Peanut Butter and Jelly, Purple Dinosaur, and Cotton Candy Explosion. Seasonal flavors like Pumpkin, Caramel Apple, Peach, and Winter Wonder are also available. In addition, Bruster's sells frozen yogurt, shakes, smoothies, Blasts (milkshakes with mixed-in cookies or candy),

sundaes and banana splits, ice cream cakes and pies, low-carb and fat-free ice cream, and hand-packed takeout ice cream available in pints, quarts, and half-gallon containers. Bruster's is also known for its lighthearted promotions, such as free dog and cat sundaes; free cones for children under 40 inches in height; Banana Thursday, when every week customers can bring in their own banana and buy a half-price banana split; and PJ Weekend, a March event when anyone who wears pajamas to the store receives a free single-scoop waffle cone.

ENTREPRENEUR AT HEART

By the time Bruster's founder Bruce Reed opened his first ice cream store in 1989, he was already a successful businessman. He grew up in Chippewa, located northwest of Pittsburgh, and learned about the food service business and entrepreneurship at an early age. In 1947 his father, Jerry, returning home from a stint in the Air Force, became enamored with the drive-in restaurants he saw in Fort Wayne, Indiana. He and his wife, Donna, started a restaurant in nearby Bridgewater called Jerry's Curb Service, an eatery where carhop waitresses served burgers, fries, and milk shakes to customers in their vehicles on trays that clipped to the windows. In the 1960s the eatery introduced its signature menu item, the steak salad: thin steak, fries, and salad dressing, served on a bed of lettuce. Bruce Reed witnessed his parents devotion to the business, telling *SBN Magazine Pittsburgh,* "I was raised by babysitters." As a youngster he developed an interest in business, and was known to sell his Halloween candy rather than eat it. When he was just 14 years old, Reed bought unclaimed soldier duffel bags at the Pittsburgh airport and sold the Army clothing inside. At the age of 16 he developed a passion for a Chevrolet Corvette and learned a major business lesson from an uncle, a used car salesman. According to *SBN Magazine Pittsburgh,* the uncle "drove him to a house that was for sale, pointed to it and said, 'There's your Corvette.' Reed didn't understand at first, but his uncle explained that if he bought the house and converted it into three apartments, he could rent the units and have enough cash flow to buy the car of his dreams." With the help of his parents, who agreed to co-sign a loan, he was able to buy the house for $10,000, rent the apartments, and generate enough cash to meet his $200 monthly car payments.

Reed now envisioned buying another ten buildings, in this way generating $2,000 a month and retiring at a young age. He took a job pumping gas at a local service station, and on the side sold Bestline cleaning products. Along the way he picked up another mentor, an auctioneer who schooled him on the art of deal-making. School did not prove as interesting to Reed, however. He had already failed third grade, and as a self-admitted class clown, he was expelled from school during his junior year. He now went to work for his father, who paid him $125 a week to launch a lunchtime business for the restaurant, which to this point was only open at nights. The youngster not only succeeded in the task, he proved to be a better manager than his father. "Dad was a really great guy," Reed told *QSR,* "and he gave everything away. If you wore a uniform, for instance, you ate for free. I didn't think it was run like a business, so I told him it was either him or me. He said to go ahead and take it over."

For several years the high school dropout ran Jerry's, continued to dabble in real estate, and became involved in a number of other business ventures. Even before he was old enough to drink in Pennsylvania he owned a pair of bars. He also ran a vending machine business and a used furniture store. He was making so much money that instead of a Corvette he now bought a Rolls Royce. However, he grew a little too ambitious in the 1970s, investing heavily in gold futures. His timing was poor. The gold market crashed and he was all but bankrupt. Reed soon bounced back, again enjoying success in real estate, and by the late 1970s he was able to afford to buy a farm, where he began raising Clydesdale horses. Over the next decade he continued to run Jerry's and other small businesses, and invest in real estate.

FINDING FUN AND PROFIT IN ICE CREAM

In the late 1980s Reed's sister, Candy Young, was divorced, and to help her out he decided to launch a small business she could manage. He considered a TCBY franchise, but backed away because he simply did not like the chain's frozen yogurt product. Instead he decided to become a franchisee of Handel's Homemade Ice Cream & Yogurt chain, a popular regional chain founded around the same time as Jerry's. Reed estimated that the shop, which was located near Jerry's Curb Service, would generate about $200,000 in sales that first year. Instead, it did $600,000 in business, and he realized that the homemade ice cream was a concept worth pursing further. He elected not to sign the Handel's franchise agreement and changed the name to Bruster's, a play on his first name. His plan was to offer freshly made ice cream using premium ingredients, served in generous portions in a fun atmosphere.

The first Bruster's operation was so successful that it helped to spur Jerry's business, which increased 21 percent the first year and another 17 percent the second year. Reed explained to *QSR* how Bruster's boosted traffic for Jerry's: "You're standing there with an ice cream cone smelling fresh French fries from next door, or vice versa. I think they played off each other really well." During the summer months, business was so heavy outside Jerry's and Bruster's, that two traffic cops were needed seven nights a week. Jerry's was shut down in 1991 and a new 1,400-square-foot version was built to replace the 600-square-foot restaurant that had been in operation since 1964. As a result sales more than doubled at the revamped drive-in. During this time a second Bruster's store opened as well.

Reed quickly learned that ice cream was very much a seasonal business, with meager sales from Thanksgiving to Valentine's Day, but he found it was still cost effective to keep the stores open year round. To attract customers during the slow season, Bruster's began to conduct store tours so customers could see for themselves the fresh ingredients that were being used and how the product was made on site. In addition, the program promoted Bruster's hand-decorated cakes and pies that customers were more likely to purchase year round. The

KEY DATES

1973: Bruce Reed takes over his father's drive-in restaurant, Jerry's Curb Service.
1989: Reed opens the first Bruster's ice cream store next to Jerry's.
1993: Bruster's begins franchising.
2002: Jim Sahene is named CEO.

stores also began running some of their playful promotions, like giving out dog sundaes with a biscuit inside.

GROWTH THROUGH FRANCHISING

Bruster's added two more units in the early 1990s, and Reed found it increasingly frustrating to run a chain, even a small one. After seeing the manager's position turn over three times during the first year of operation of his fourth unit, he decided to investigate a franchising option. This would allow him to transfer the start-up costs and some of the managerial headaches to others. He hired a consultant named Dave Guido to help him put together a plan and in 1993 they began franchising Bruster's Real Ice Cream shops.

Bruster's added franchisees at a solid clip over the next several years, so that in 2000 it was named by *Entrepreneur* magazine as one of America's top 500 franchise chains. A year later there were 85 franchised units in the chain, to go with five company-owned stores, and it was spreading widely, from New England to Florida. Franchisees were lined up in untouched markets in central Ohio, central Pennsylvania, New Hampshire, Georgia, North Carolina, South Carolina, Tennessee, Ohio, Virginia, Florida, and Maryland. It was at this point Reed believed that a change was in order, well aware of his own limitations. "I'm not really a person who thinks too far ahead when I start something," he told Pittsburgh's *Tribune-Review*. "With me it's: Ready, aim, fire. And then after I get into something, I start to think about what to do next." According to *SBN Magazine Pittsburgh,* he decided "it was time to bring on a CEO with the experience, skill and interest to do the strategic planning and develop the systems and procedural guides needed to more than double the number of Bruster's units by the end of 2003."

Reed found his man in 41-year-old Jim Sahene, former president and chief operating officer of TCBY Systems Inc., who was hired by Reed in February 2002. Sahene was born in the Pittsburgh area and still had many family members there. He left at the age of seven when his father, a U.S. Steel executive, was transferred to run an operation in the Bahamas. Sahene returned to the area as an adult, working for the Sheetz convenience store chain. His tenure with TCBY began in 1986 when he became a store manager in Little Rock, Arkansas, at a time when the TCBY operation, which was launched in 1981, totaled 200 units. Sahene rose through the ranks, making president and COO by 1994. By the start of the 2000s TCBY had grown to 3,000 units. It faced increasing competition, sales began to slip, and a decision was made to sell the business. Sahene left after Mrs. Fields Original Cookies Inc. acquired TCBY in June 2000.

Reed learned that Sahene, who was living in Little Rock running a pair of TCBY franchises he bought, might be available and contacted him about taking over as Bruster's CEO. Reed was unfamiliar with Bruster's but liked what he saw when he flew to Pennsylvania for a visit. He was not hired right away, however. The idiosyncratic Reed made sure that all 12 people at his headquarters had a chance to interview Sahene and agreed that he would fit in.

Once on board, Sahene worked to refine Bruster's strategy and organizing systems as the chain grew at a steady pace: 29 franchises added in 2003, 38 in 2004, and 36 in 2005.

For Sahene it was a second chance to grow a franchise, and hopefully avoid the pitfalls he discovered during his time at TCBY. Moreover, he could apply some lessons learned in the past year and a half on the other side of the divide, operating as a franchisee. For Reed it was a chance to spend more time at his 700-acre farm and pursue other business ideas. "What's nice is," he told *SBN Magazine Pittsburgh,* "as you grow a company, you start hiring people to do what you don't like to do." So at mid-decade, with the growth of the Bruster's franchise operation in Sahene's hands, Reed, with consultant Guido, began to focus on his next big idea: franchising the Jerry's Curb Service concept.

Ed Dinger

PRINCIPAL COMPETITORS

Ben & Jerry's Homemade, Inc.; Handel's Homemade Ice Cream & Yogurt; Friendly Ice Cream Corporation; International Dairy Queen, Inc.

FURTHER READING

Gannon, Joyce. "Bruster's Founder Launches Curbside Jerry's Franchise," *Pittsburgh Post-Gazette,* May 22, 2005.
"Industry Watch, One to Watch: Bruster's Real Ice Cream," *QSR Magazine,* June 2004.

Lindeman, Teresa F., "Bruster's, Eyeing Growth, Scoops Up TCBY Veteran," *Pittsburgh Post-Gazette,* February 6, 2002.

Marano, Ray, "Bruster's Ice Cream Moves Into the Franchising Fast Lane," *SBN Magazine Pittsburgh,* March 2002.

Yeomans, Michael, "Bruster's Builds on Reputation," *Tribune-Review (Pittsburgh, Pa.),* February 6, 2002.

Cantel Medical
Corporation

———————■———————

150 Clove Road, 9th Floor
Little Falls, New Jersey 07424
U.S.A.
Telephone: (973) 890-7220
Fax: (973) 890-7270
Web site: http://www.cantelmedical.com

Public Company
Incorporated: 1952 as Charvoz-Carsen Corporation
Employees: 828
Sales: $197.4 million (2005)
Stock Exchanges: New York
Ticker Symbol: CMN
NAIC: 423450 Medical, Dental, and Hospital Equipment and Supplies Merchant Wholesalers

■ ■ ■

Listed on the New York Stock Exchange, Cantel Medical Corporation provides medical equipment and services in the infection prevention and control market through the activities of six subsidiaries. Minntech Corporation, The Biolab Group, and Mar Cor units concentrate on filtration, water, and disinfection technologies. Operating out of Hauppauge, New York, Crosstex International focuses on the dental office market, manufacturing such products as facemask and shields, barrier films, disinfectants, soaps, lotions, sanitizers, patient bibs, and cotton and gauze items. In addition to its U.S. facilities, Crosstex maintains manufacturing in Georgia, Japan, The Netherlands, and Argentina. Saf-T-Pak Inc. is involved in the safe handling and transportation of infectious and biological specimens, offering specialty packaging products and compliance training services. The final subsidiary, Carsen Group, is a Canadian marketer of medical equipment, including flexible and rigid endoscopes, endoscope disinfection equipment, as well as scientific equipment—primarily microscopes and image analysis hardware and software. Cantel maintains its corporate headquarters in Little Falls, New Jersey.

POSTWAR ROOTS

Cantel grew out of the business established by Walter Carsen in Canada in 1946. Raised in Cologne, Germany, Carsen traveled to London, England, in 1940 at the age of 18 to learn the optical industry. After France was defeated by Nazi Germany in that year, Carsen was interred briefly before being allowed to emigrate to Canada in 1941. He settled in Toronto and soon joined the Canadian Army as an electrical and mechanical engineer. After the war he recognized there would be a demand for 35mm cameras and went into business with almost no funding. In 1949 he forged a relationship with Japan's Olympus Optical Company Ltd. to distribute 35mm cameras and a wide range of other optical products that would one day include endoscopes. W. Carsen Co. was a shoestring affair at first, its founder content to live modestly while he built up the business. He scoured Europe, acquiring the marketing rights to a wide range of optical products, including microscopes, fibre-optic medical instruments, binoculars, and telescopes. By the early 1960s the company was generating annual sales in the $10 million range.

In October 1962 Carsen sold the business to New

Jersey-based Charvoz-Carsen, which had been established in 1952. Carsen then went on to enjoy a second life as a patron of the arts in Canada. Charvoz-Carsen was reincorporated in Delaware in 1963 in preparation for going public. The company evolved into a distributor of audio, optical, drafting, and engineering equipment, and graphic and fine art supplies. In September 1986 the company attempted to diversify further by acquiring Stendig Industries Inc., a well known manufacturer and importer of residential and contract furniture.

Because management hoped to become even more involved in the furniture field, in December 1986 Charvoz-Carsen changed its name to Stendig Industries. The company soon added to its furniture assets, acquiring a controlling interest in Vitra Seating, Inc. and also buying Erwin-Lambert, Inc. in 1987. For the year, Stendig posted sales around $52 million, a sharp increase over the $22 million to $24 million the company generated five years earlier. However it proved to be an unwieldy mix of assets and, more importantly, unprofitable. In April 1988 the company began a reorganization effort that led to the hiring of James P. Reilly as chief executive officer a year later. It was with his arrival that Cantel's business mix began to take shape.

Reilly was born in Vineland, New Jersey, in 1940. After earning an undergraduate degree from St. Joseph's University in Philadelphia in 1962, he went to work for the Price Waterhouse accounting firm in Newark. He left in 1969 to take a job with Metrocare Inc., where he became chief financial officer. He then served stints in top management positions at Hanson Industries in Iselin, New York, and Elmont, New York-based Fasig-Tipton Inc., before becoming president and chief operating officer at North American Watch Company in New York City, where he worked from 1985 until the time he joined Stendig.

NAME CHANGE: 1985

According to *Investor's Business Daily*, Reilly arrived "to find [Stendig] deep in debt and spread across too many businesses. The troubled company was selling high-end furniture, graphic arts services and ergonomic office seating. He liquidated and sold businesses, focusing on Cantel's medical equipment and services business, Carsen

Group." In April 1989 Erwin-Lambeth was sold, and the company's name was changed to Cantel Industries. The company's interest in Vitra was also divested in July of that year. Carsen's most valuable asset was its Canadian distribution agreement with Olympus Optical Co. Thus, Reilly elected to focus on the medical products, including microscopes, but the primary focus was on endoscopes, instruments fitted with a video camera to allow doctors to inspect a patient's colon, intestines, or lungs for polyps and cysts that might turn into cancer. Changing Cantel's business mix was not accomplished overnight, however. The company continued to distribute Olympus cameras and other consumer products during the 1990s, and it did not completely exit the furniture business until Charvoz-Dauphin Office Seating's North American divisions were sold in October 1993, fetching $3 million.

Cantel added to its scientific instrument product lines in 1994, signing a long-term agreement with Germany's Jenopyik Technologie GmbH to distribute laser distance measurement and thermal imaging products. An important turning point in the transformation of Cantel occurred in March 1996 when Minneapolis-based MediVators, Inc. was acquired for $10 million in stock. MediVators sold automated disinfection equipment for endoscopes, and the addition of the company helped Reilly to flesh out Cantel's endoscope business. Moreover, it set the stage for Olympus agreeing to promote and distribute Carsen and Medivators' equipment along with its endoscopes. MediVators'endoscope disinfecting system, the DSD-91, was computer controlled and capable of disinfecting two endoscopes simultaneously. It received Food and Drug Administration approval in March 1994. In addition to disinfection equipment, MediVators also sold medical sharps disposal systems, but this business was discontinued a year later. Cantel then added to its disinfection business in March 1998 by acquiring less expensive single and dual disinfection units from Chris Lutz Medical, Inc.

The changes Reilly made to Cantel's business mix began to bear fruit in the late 1990s. Sales totaled $24.7 million in fiscal 1991 and grew to $34.1 million by fiscal 1995. Revenues reached only $35 million in fiscal 1997, to go with net income of $1.1 million. The addition of disinfection products played a key role in Cantel topping $40 million in sales in fiscal 1998 and the recording of $1.7 million in earnings. Revenues continued to grow in fiscal 1999, reaching $50.1 million.

In 2000 Carsen terminated its consumer products business, selling back its inventories of Olympus consumer products to Olympus, and Cantel Industries changed its name to Cantel Medical Corporation. This

KEY DATES

1946: The W. Carsen Co. is formed by Walter Carsen in Canada.

1952: Charvoz-Carsen Inc. is incorporated in New Jersey.

1962: Charvoz-Carsen acquires the W. Carsen Co.

1986: Charvoz-Carsen becomes Stendig Industries, Inc.

1989: Stendig becomes Cantel Industries, Inc.

1996: MediVators is acquired.

2000: The company's name is changed to Cantel Medical Corporation.

2003: Biolab Equipment Ltd. and Mar Cor Services, Inc., are acquired.

2005: Crosstex International is acquired.

began a period of steady expansion as Cantel further defined itself as a medical products company, one focused on the promising field of infection control. According to *Investor's Business Daily* in a 2001 article, about 5 percent of all patients in the United States fell victim to infections they encountered at hospitals and to treat them, hospitals spent about $4 billion a year: "The result is a war on germs as health care providers battle to improve service and reduce liability and treatment costs. That war is turning industry attention toward systematic, facility-wide disinfection programs." What Cantel wanted to do was to make the case that automating the disinfection process was prudent and cost effective, significantly reducing the chance that germs could spread because hospital personnel might lose focus performing a repetitive task. Cantel hoped to not only build its automated disinfection system for endoscopes, including the addition of the chemical disinfectants themselves, but to also use it as a platform to become involved in other aspects of infection control.

MINNTECH CORPORATION
ACQUIRED 2001

With almost no debt and some $5 million in cash, Cantel was ready in 2001 to take the next step in building its infection control business. In September of that year it acquired Plymouth, Minnesota-based, Minntech Corporation in a $77.9 million stock and cash purchase. Founded in 1974, Minntech made disinfection and reprocessing systems for renal dialysis, and filtration and separation products, such as membranes and chemical sterilants, for medical and non-medical applications. With more than $75 million in sales, Minntech doubled

Cantel's revenues. Moreover, the acquisition marked a sea change in Cantel's business mix. Prior to Minntech, Cantel derived about 80 percent of it sales from capital equipment and the rest from the more profitable, and ongoing sale, of consumables. Within three years, the company saw those numbers nearly reverse themselves, as consumables now accounted for three-quarters of all sales. Also of note in 2001, Carsen made a minor acquisition, paying $405,000 for Technimed Instruments Inc. and Technimed International, providers of hand-held surgical instrumentation and rigid endoscope repair services in Canada.

With Minntech in the fold, Cantel experienced an increase of sales from $49 million in fiscal 2001 to $120 million in fiscal 2002 and $129.3 million in fiscal 2003. Net income increased from $4.4 million in fiscal 2001 to more than $7.9 million in fiscal 2003. During this period, in May 2002, Cantel also gained a coveted listing on the New York Stock Exchange. In August 2003, just after the 2003 fiscal year came to a close on July 31, Cantel was ready for further external growth. On the same day, it completed the acquisition of a pair of companies, Biolab Equipment Ltd., acquired for $7.9 million, and Mar Cor Services Inc., acquired for $8.215 million They were both part of a strategy to get Cantel involved in the water treatment business. Based in Canada and founded in 1969, Biolab specialized in "ultra-pure water," serving the biotechnology, medical, pharmaceutical, research, and semiconductor industries. The Skippack, Pennsylvania-based Mar Cor was founded in 1971 and operated in a dozen U.S. cities, providing water treatment equipment design, project management, installation and maintenance, service deionization, and mixing systems to the medical community. Cantel also made inroads internationally in 2003 by acquiring Dutch company Dyped Medical B.V., the addition of which supplemented Minntech's technological capabilities and provided a endoscope disinfection system that was compliant with European standards.

To sustain its growth and keep its pipeline filled with new products, Cantel completed another acquisition in June 2004, paying $8.5 million for Saf-T-Pak in order to become involved in the specialized medical packaging and training field. The focus of Saf-T-Pak was on the safe transport of blood, tissue, and other infectious and biological materials. It was a small company, based in Edmonton, Canada, and generated just $5 million a year, but it provided Cantel with a base in the fast-growing specialized packaging field. The company estimated that each year in the United States about 1 billion biological specimens were shipped to and from medical offices. Moreover, the U.S. Department of Transportation had recently increased the types of specimens that had to adhere to strict packaging standards, providing even greater opportunities for Cantel to develop another niche revenue stream. The company was not dominant in any particular area, but it was well diversified. In fact, according to *Investor's Business Daily,* "If Cantel was more concentrated on one area, it could come under attack. As it is, no single firm complete with it across all product lines."

With contributions from its four acquisitions, Cantel experienced a 31.5 percent increase in sales to $170 million in fiscal 2004, while net income improved to $10.7 million. The company looked to make larger acquisitions, focusing on companies with sales of at least $25 million—due in large part to the regulations imposed of the new Sarbanes-Oxley Act. The paperwork burden had become so great because of the new law that a small acquisition was simply not worth the trouble. Cantel's next acquisition came in August 2005 with the $77.9 million purchase of Crosstex International. Founded in 1953, Crosstex added a new avenue to pursue in the infection control business: the dental office. Crosstex offered a number of single-use infection-control products, including patient bibs, gloves, face masks, and sterilization items. The addition of Crosstex was especially important because several weeks earlier, Olympus decided to end its $38-million-a-year contract with Carsen to distribute medical and scientific supplies in Canada, electing to handle the business in-house. The announcement dealt a blow to the price of Cantel's stock, which traded above $30 but fell into the teens at this news. The Crosstex acquisition helped to provide something of a rebound to the stock price.

Mantel continued to refine its business mix in 2005. In April of that year it established Mar Cor Purification, combining Mar Cor Services and Biolab with Minntech's water filters and disinfectant products. Cantel enjoyed another strong year in fiscal 2005, as sales approached the $200 million mark and net income totalled $15.5 million. Those numbers were likely to continue to improve in light of the addition of Crosstex and the increasing need for infection control that would result from the growing medical needs of an aging baby boom generation.

Ed Dinger

PRINCIPAL SUBSIDIARIES

Crosstex International; Minntech Corporation; Carsen Group Inc.; Biolab Equipment Ltd; Mar Cor Services, Inc.; Saf-T-Pak Inc.

PRINCIPAL COMPETITORS

American Cystoscope Makers, Inc.; McKesson Medical-Surgical, Inc.; Owens & Minor, Inc.

FURTHER READING

Benesh, Peter, "Medical Suppliers Prefers Buyouts To Buzz," *Investor's Business Daily,* July 23, 2004, p. A05.

Elliott, Alan R., "Hospital Germs Are Big Business For Company," *Investor's Business Daily,* May 30, 2001, p. A08.

Fiedler, Terry, "Minntech Takes Cantel Offer," *Star Tribune,* June 1, 2001, p. 1D.

Kareda, Urjo, "Money Well Spent," *Toronto Life,* September 2000, p. 63.

Lynn, Kathleen, "Cantel Medical Acquires Specialist in Infection Control," *Record (Hackensack, New Jersey),* August 4, 2005.

Much, Marilyn, "Just In Case, It Keeps A Checkbook Handy," *Investor's Business Daily,* January 20, 2005, p. A05.

Celestica Inc.

1150 Eglinton Avenue East
Toronto, Ontario M3C 1H7
Canada
Telephone: (416) 448-5800
Fax: (416) 448-4699
Web site: http://www.celestica.com

Public Company
Incorporated: 1994
Employees: 46,000
Sales: $8.5 billion (2005)
Stock Exchanges: Toronto New York
Ticker Symbol: CLS
NAIC: 334412 Printed Circuit Board Manufacturing

■ ■ ■

Based in Toronto, Ontario, Celestica Inc. is a former IBM unit that has emerged as one of the world's largest electronics manufacturing services (EMS) companies. Serving such major original equipment manufacturers (OEMs) as Cisco Systems, Dell, Hewlett-Packard, IBM, Lucent, Motorola, NEC Corporation, and Sun Microsystems, Celestica manufactures computer motherboards, communications and networking cards, and other complex printed circuit assemblies used in personal computers, servers, workstation, peripherals, and communications devices. In addition, the company offers design services as well as supply chain management, global distribution, and post-sales repair services. Although 80 percent owned by Canada's Onex

Corporation, Celestica is a public company, listed on both the Toronto and New York stock exchanges.

ORIGINS: 1980–1990

The man most responsible for the founding and rise to prominence of Celestica was its long-time Chief Executive Officer Eugene Polistuk. An engineering graduate of the University of Toronto in 1969, he went to work for IBM Canada. "For several years, Polistuk had every reason to be happy with his choice of employed," wrote Barbara Hawkins in a 1994 *Canadian Business* profile. "During the 1970s and much of the 1980s, IBM dominated the computer world like some heavy-footed colossus. Its stock-in-trade was leasing big mainframe computers to large corporate customers." While IBM reigned supreme, Polistuk moved up through the ranks of senior management, holding posts in both Canada and the United States. In 1986 he became the head of IBM Canada's Toronto manufacturing unit, which mostly made boxes to contain IBM components. "It was there," according to Hawkins, "that he caught his first whiff of the troubles that would bedevil IBM in the future. The computer giant was under pressure from smaller, nimbler competitors, which were churning out low-priced microcomputers that in many cases could do exactly the same jobs as massive mainframes." With the tide turning against it, IBM began to reorganize, resulting in a widespread downsizing of the corporation. In both 1986 and 1988, Polistuk was forced to trim his headcount.

In order for his unit to survive, Polistuk believed it had to produce items more critical than a metal case. According to Hawkins, "The Toronto operation turned to building circuit boards, memory products and power supplies—products that could be used in a wide range of IBM computers. It invested almost $300 million over seven years in state-of-the-art machinery." Every IBM division was turning to the unit for components by 1993. Although regarded as one of the few bright spots at IBM, the unit was not spared as the corporate giant continued to struggle to regain its footing. More layoffs and other cost-cutting measures ensued, and IBM Canada's very future became uncertain when the parent company began making the transition from low-margin equipment maker to software and services provider. A spin-off of the operation was an obvious choice, but IBM's track record for such attempts in the past was poor. Hawkins reported, "Polistuk was convinced that his division was a different case entirely. He thought it lean and efficient enough to take on anyone. Indeed, he saw a silver lining in renaming the unit and freeing it from IBM. Such a move would allow it to start marketing its products to IBM's rivals, which were reluctant to deal with Big Blue directly but might be enticed to deal with a supplier who was at arm's length from the company."

CELESTICA FORMED: 1994

IBM was won over by Polistuk's arguments in talks that he initiated in 1992, and so in January 1994 Celestica Inc. was incorporated. Although the long-term vision was to set the company free, it was initially a wholly-owned IBM Canada subsidiary. "But it would have its own marketing staff and control its own finances," wrote Hawkins. "Polistuk would be given a free hand to cut costs, encourage innovation and discover new ways to motivate his 1,600 employees—most of them longtime veterans of IBM's bureaucratic mindset." Part of his strategy to stimulate motivation was to cut wages by 5 percent while instituting a profit-sharing program that amounted to 30 percent of an employee's base pay. Hence, the performers were better recompensed and the dead wood penalized. Moreover, he delegated greater

authority to his top managers, who were essentially given a free hand as long as they met performance goals.

Celestica's timing was fortunate because OEMs were increasingly turning to contract manufacturers to furnish components and assemble them under their own labels. Within the first year Celestica lined up some 40 OEMs as customers. A year earlier the IBM unit generated less than 10 percent of its sales from non-IBM clients, but in its first year Celestica increased that contribution to 30 percent. In order to grow non-IBM sales and realize its full potential, however, Celestica needed to further separate itself from IBM in order to attract companies that were still reluctant to do business with an IBM subsidiary.

It did not take long for Celestica to find a suitor, Onex Corporation, a diversified holding company, eager to buy it away from IBM. Onex was founded by noted Canadian dealmaker Gerry Schwartz and had its hand in a wide range of businesses, including movie production, airline food, parking lots, and auto parts. Onex Vice President Anthony Melman was the point person on the Celestica deal. He began the courtship with Polistuk in a private dining room in a Canadian bank in May 2004. Over the next two years they would have more informal talks and Melman began urging IBM to cut loose Celestica, which was becoming ever more frustrated by its corporate parent's reluctance to let it go. Celestica's success, however, was the prime reason IBM held on to it for so long. Nevertheless, it was obvious that eventually the two had to part ways, and finally in 1996 IBM Canada agreed to sell the business. It hired Nebitt Burns Inc. to conduct a search of potential buyers. There was no shortage of interested parties, which were pared down to about a dozen. After another weeding out step, five remained, including an Onex-led group of investors. The finalists were allowed to review Celestica's financial data. In the end Onex won the prize in October 1996, paying $750 million. For Celestica it was a good fit, since Onex was known to take a hands-off approach and encourage a company's management team to take an entrepreneurial approach to growing their business.

Finally on its own, Celestica quickly moved to expand it contract manufacturing capabilities and add new OEMs through acquisitions. In January 1997 it bought Design to Distribution, a United Kingdom-based company that was one of the largest European contract manufacturers. Other acquisitions would follow in 1997, including Hewlett-Packard's Fort Collins, Colorado, printed-circuit board assembly plant; HP's New Hampshire system-assembly operation; and also its Chelmsford, Massachusetts' system-development business. Furthermore, in October 1997 Celestica acquired

KEY DATES

1986: Eugene Polistuk takes over IBM Canada's manufacturing unit.
1994: Manufacturing unit becomes subsidiary Celestica Inc.
1996: Onex Corporation acquired company.
1998: Celestica taken public.
2004: Polistuk retires.

Ascent Power Technology, adding power-systems manufacturing operations in the United States, Canada, and the United Kingdom. As a result of this diversification, Celestica grew less dependent on its former corporate parent. In 1997 only 25 percent of its business came from IBM.

GOING PUBLIC IN 1998

To recoup some of its investment and provide Celestica with cash to fuel further expansion, Onex made plans to take Celestica public in 1998, inviting 11 top North American investment houses to bid for the business. They included the likes of Morgan Stanley Dean Witter and Merrill Lynch & Co. In the end Onex settled on co-lead underwriters: Morgan Stanley and Canada's RBC Dominion Securities Inc. The initial public offering of stock was completed in July 1998, raising $414 million, the largest IPO in EMS history. The rigors of taking the company public did not, however, prevent Celestica from completing eight acquisitions over the course of 1998, culminating in the purchase of International Manufacturing Services, the addition of which provided entry into Asia. The other acquisitions added operations in Northern California, Mexico, and Ireland, filling out Celestica's global footprint. The company grew in other ways as well in 1998, establishing Customer Gateway Centres, where customers could take advantage of Celestica's design prototyping capabilities and set the table for the launch of new products manufactured by Celestica. The initial Centers were located in Toronto, the United States, and Ireland, with others planned for Central Europe and Asia. When the first year of independence came to a close, Celestica reported revenues of $3.2 billion, a significant increase over the $2 billion generated in 1997 and a major step toward fulfilling a goal of $10 billion in sales by 2001.

Celestica returned to the public market, raising additional capital in 1999 to fund expansion. A March equity offering garnered $251 million, followed by another $225 million in May, and a secondary public offering of stock netted another $488 million in November. The money was used to buy five new facilities, most notably in the Czech Republic. In additional a pair of greenfield facilities were opened in Brazil and Malaysia. When the year came to a close, Celestica reported another strong performance, with sales increasing 63 percent to $5.3 billion. It was now the third largest EMS, but growing at a faster rate than the two market leaders: Solectron Corporation and SCI Systems Inc. The $10 billion mark appeared within reach and the $20 billion level appeared to be attainable in the not too distant future.

Expansion continued in 2000, when Celestica made further acquisitions in the United States, Brazil, and Italy, some of which were bought from IBM. In August 2000 Celestica completed its twentieth acquisition in just three years, buying Lowell, Massachusetts-based contract manufacturer Bull Electronics Inc. The company added capacity to its operations in the Czech Republic, Malaysia, and Mexico, and opened an office in Japan. It also signed a major supply agreement with Motorola, a three-year deal worth more than $1 billion in business. Revenues for 2000 totaled $9.8 billion, but just as the $10 billion target appeared in the company's sights, business conditions soured, creating what Polistuk would call the "perfect tech storm."

The telecommunications sector was hit especially hard and money from the capital market became scared and made it companies reluctant to invest in new equipment. Hence, OEMs were impacted, as were vendors like Celestica. The possibility of a tech correction had been foreseen by Polistuk and his team, and the company had already developed a plan to cut expenses, which was quickly implemented. For a time Celestica was actually able to take advantage of conditions. OEMs began outsourcing even more of their work in an effort to contain costs. As well, some firms were putting some of their manufacturing assets up for sale at attractive prices. Celestica bought a NEC plant in Europe and some Motorola facilities. Also in 2001, Celestica acquired Omni Industries Ltd., a Singapore-based contract manufacturer.

Celestica was fortunate to barely meet its $10 billion goal in 2001, but as poor business conditions persisted in 2002, the company did not fare much better than its customers, who were struggling across the board. Revenues dipped 17 percent to $8.3 billion. Especially hard hit were the company's European operations. Nevertheless, Celestica was able to retire some debt and repurchase shares, something its chief competitors could not accomplish.

Sales continued to drop in 2003, declining 19

percent to $6.7 billion. In January 2004, before the yearend numbers were tallied, Polistuk retired, saying in a statement, "I feel it is time for me to pass the leadership of Celestica on to new and very capable hands so that I may refocus my priorities on family and personal interests." Succeeding him as chairman was Robert L. Crandall, who had been a director since 1998. Taking over as CEO was Stephen W. Delaney, president of the Americas division, who took over on an interim basis before becoming Polistuk's permanent replacement.

Business conditions remained quite challenging in 2004. After reporting a first quarter loss in 2004, Celestica cut its work force about 13 percent. Demand began to rebound in 2004 and as a result sales increased to $8.8 billion in 2004, but business had not yet returned to normal. Celestica continued to cut costs, launching a major restructuring effort in 2005 that included deep staff reductions and the closure or winding down of nine plants. For the year 2005 revenues fell slightly to $8.5 billion. Despite an extended period of challenging years, Celestica appeared to be well positioned, lean and efficient, to take advantage when business conditions ultimately improved.

Ed Dinger

PRINCIPAL SUBSIDIARIES

Celestica (US Holdings) Inc.; Celestica Corporation; Celestica (USA) Inc.

PRINCIPAL COMPETITORS

Flextronics International Ltd.; Sanmina-SCI Corporation; Solectron Corporation.

FURTHER READING

Bernstein, Corinne, "Eugene Polistuk—Calmly Builds CEM Celestica Through Aggressive Expansion," *Electronic Buyers' News,* December 22, 1997, p. 78.

Dunn, Darrell, "Putting Growth Goals On A Grand Scale," *Electronic Buyers' News,* October 19, 1998, p. 68.

Harris, Jonathan, "Home of the Whopper," *Canadian Business,* January 29, 1999, p. 36.

Hawkins, Barbara, "Divide and Conquer," *Canadian Business,* December 1994, p. 113.

Showsmith, John, "IBM Sells Successful Celestica For A Song," *Computing Canada,* October 24, 1996, p. 8.

"Something Blue: Gerry Schwartz Was Smart Enough To Take Celestica Off IBM Canada's Hands. Is He Smart Enough to Make It Run?" *Canadian Business,* January 1996, p. 35.

Wahl, Andrew, "Rising Star," *Canadian Business,* June 11, 2001, p. 34.

CHEP Pty. Ltd.

8517 South Park Circle
Orlando, Florida 32819-9040
U.S.A.
Telephone: (407) 370-2437
Toll Free: (888) 243-7111
Fax: (407) 363-5354
Web site: http://www.chep.com

Division of Brambles Industries Ltd.
Incorporated: 1958 as Commonwealth Handling Equipment Pool Pty. Ltd.
Employees: 7,704
Sales: AUD 3.7 billion ($2.7 billion) (2004/05)
NAIC: 488990 Other Support Activities for Transportation

■ ■ ■

CHEP Pty. Ltd. is the world's largest pallet and container pooling service. Customers including multinational corporations find it easier to lease from among CHEP's 265 million pallets and containers than to maintain, repair, and track their own handling materials. The company prides itself on its environmentally friendly recycling operation. CHEP is owned by Brambles of Australia. CHEP can trace its origins back to the materials handling efforts of the Allies during World War II. The company also provides waste management, information management, and industrial services. Worldwide, CHEP has more than 300,000 customers and more than 440 service centers. The two major components are CHEP Americas, based in Florida, and CHEP Europe, which is based in Weybridge, England.

ALLIED ORIGINS

CHEP Pty. Ltd. is derived from the Allied Materials Handling Standing Committee (AMHSC), part of the Australian government's military logistics operations in World War II. AMHSC was enriched by equipment the Americans left behind after the war. AMHSC was privatized in 1949 and became known as the Commonwealth Handling Equipment Pool (CHEP). It was acquired on April 24, 1958 by Brambles Industries, a venerable Australian conglomerate with an established materials handling business. It was later incorporated as simply CHEP Pty. Ltd.

Shippers of fresh fruits and vegetables embraced CHEP's pallet solutions. CHEP also became a leader in the fast-moving consumer good (FMCG) market. In all of these applications, speed was an important requirement; the standardization offered by CHEP facilitated reliable and fast turnarounds. The group introduced its distinctive blue pallets to markets all over the world.

CHEP expanded into neighboring New Zealand in 1974. This operation was bought out by Mogul Corporation and others in the 1980s. It was owned by NZ Rail at one point. Brambles eventually reacquired control of CHEP New Zealand from Freightways and Owens Group in 1997.

In 1975, Brambles formed a successful joint venture in the United Kingdom with the British automotive and industrial group GKN plc, which would be its frequent partner. Belgium, Holland, and Ireland were added in

COMPANY PERSPECTIVES

With an unprecedented combination of supply chain cost reduction, size, scale, superior technology and global reach, CHEP issues, collects, conditions and reissues more than 265 million pallets and containers from a global network of service centers, helping manufacturers and growers transport their products to distributors and retailers. Combining superior technology, decades of experience and an unmatched asset base, CHEP handles pallet and container supply chain logistics for customers in the consumer goods, produce, meat, home improvement, beverage, raw materials, petro-chemical and automotive industries. CHEP services are based on a unique combination of customer-driven operating solutions, quality products, sophisticated control systems and a well-managed global service center infrastructure, which enables its customers to reduce the need for capital expenditures and concentrate their day-to-day operations on their core business competencies.

1978. GKN formed CHEP South Africa as a wholly owned subsidiary in 1979; at the time, Australian companies were not permitted to invest there. This unit would serve as the basis for expansion throughout neighboring countries in the 1990s.

NEW TERRITORIES BEGINNING IN 1980

CHEP entered Canada and France in 1980. Brambles' partner in Canada was Canadian Pacific, but it was bought out in 1988. GKN acquired a 50 percent holding in CHEP Canada in 1990. During the decade, Germany (1984) and Spain (1988) were added to CHEP's territory. Several other European countries were added in the 1990s.

By the end of the 1980s, CHEP's operations in Australia, Europe, and Canada had a pool of 25 million pallets. The outfit had two large competitors on its home turf, the Australian logistics companies TNT and Mayne Nickless, each of which had tens of thousands of employees and international reach.

IN THE UNITED STATES IN 1990

In 1989, GKN-Brambles Enterprises was formed to take over CHEP Europe as well as the Cleanaway waste management business, another joint enterprise between Brambles and GKN. The formation of the new company was a step toward bringing GKN into the CHEP business in North America, where Brambles already owned CHEP Canada and American Pallet Systems.

The U.S. market was entered in September 1990 as GKN and Brambles launched CHEP USA with an investment of about $140 million (£81 million). According to the *Journal of Commerce,* the American pallet pooling market was perceived as fragmented and disorganized, being controlled by a number of trucking companies. CHEP USA originally started with regional centers in Atlanta, Chicago, Los Angeles, and New Jersey, plus about 80 smaller depots, staffed by about 170 employees. The venture already had a three-year contract with Procter and Gamble, and was initially focusing on the dry grocery business. It expected to have three million pallets in its U.S. pool by 1992. The company introduced collapsible plastic containers for perishables to the U.S. market in late 1996.

In 1994, Brambles stepped into Asia with ventures in Malaysia and Singapore. GKN bought a 50 percent holding in these three years later. CHEP Mexico S.A. de C.V. began operations in 1995 with a single client. It soon grew, however, with the expansion of multinationals such as Sam's Club, into Mexico. Local exporters also were using the service. By 1997, CHEP Mexico had about 600 clients, including distributors and manufacturers.

South American ventures were established in Chile in 1995, Brazil in 1998, and Argentina in 1999. By the end of the 1990s, CHEP also was involved in Switzerland, Scandinavia, Hong Kong, Greece, and other markets.

By the mid-1990s, CHEP was managing 63 million pallets in 15 countries on five continents. It had 169 depots in the United States. CHEP relocated the headquarters for it U.S. operation from Park Ridge, New Jersey, to Orlando, Florida, in 1996, enticed by tax incentives from state and local government.

The business had been courted as a source of high-tech jobs, since it relied on sophisticated database management to track pallet movements. CHEP preferred to focus on administering the pallet flow, subcontracting manufacturing, repair, and warehousing to others. In July 1997, CHEP USA announced that it was building a huge repair facility in Illinois in collaboration with PalEx Inc., a joint venture of three U.S. pallet manufacturers.

CHEP was among those studying ways to produce pallets out of plastic. This would, in theory, confer a

KEY DATES

1958: Brambles Industries acquires CHEP from the Australian government.
1981: CHEP begins operations in France with seven employees.
1990: CHEP USA is launched.
2000: Revenues are $2.3 billion; CHEP has 6,800 employees and operations in more than 30 countries.
2001: GKN's share of CHEP is part of the Brambles Industries plc (BIP) spinoff.
2004: CHEP is split into CHEP Americas and CHEP Europe.

number of advantages over wood, such as reduced weight and cost and the possibility of more precise manufacturing tolerances. Wood pallets (which cost about £10 each, according to the *Financial Times*) remained the standard into the next millennium, however, due to their superior strength and durability, and other qualities. CHEP was overseeing 70 million pallets in two dozen countries by the late 1990s. CHEP accounted for 26 percent of GKN's £3.7 billion in revenues in 1998.

CHEP was managing 150 million pallets by 2000. It had 30 million RTP containers, mainly in the United States and Europe. RTP, or reusable transit packaging, mostly consisted of plastic crates for shipping produce. It was becoming more popular among U.S. retail chains such as Wal-Mart and Kroger. Wal-Mart also was embracing CHEP's pallet pooling system, as was Home Depot. CHEP's annual sales were AUD 2.3 billion, or 32 percent of Brambles' total. CHEP had an operating profit of AUD 563 million, 50 percent of the parent group's total. CHEP had 6,800 employees and operations in more than 30 countries.

CHEP, which had long used bar code scanning to track pallets, was developing a couple of new technologies. RFID (radio frequency identification) chips attached to pallets simplified the process. Another refinement was the CHEPCard system of identification cards and portable readers to monitor movements of customers, drivers, and pallets.

An unusual case involving CHEP USA illustrated some of the perils of the pallet management business. CHEP had to sue a couple of U.S. pallet recycling companies for the return of its pallets. In one case, however, Mock Pallets, one of 700 U.S. recyclers who did business with CHEP, countersued for the cost of storing the 30,000 CHEP pallets it had accumulated over a dozen years under Georgia's unique "naked depositary" law. A court awarded Mock $586,000, equivalent to the cost of new pallets, but CHEP was sure it would be overturned. Meanwhile, CHEP UK prevailed in a separate case involving pallet return.

RESTRUCTURING IN 2001 AND BEYOND

GKN's support services businesses, including its share of the CHEP ventures, were spun off on the London Stock Exchange as Brambles Industries plc (BIP) in 2001. BIP and the Australian Brambles Industries Ltd. were combined as dual listed companies.

Business in the United States got a big boost when Wal-Mart began recommending that its suppliers use CHEP's standardized pallets. In November 2002, the company reported that it was missing 14 million pallets in Europe. The European side of the business then underwent an £85 million restructuring (allotting £45 for pallet recovery) to make it more efficient. Whereas the global economy was slowing, CHEP was mostly involved with items such as groceries that sold in good times or bad. The number of U.S. depots was reduced from 230 to 74 in 2002 and 2003; in the process, however, 2.5 million pallets turned up missing.

In 2004 CHEP was restructured into two components, CHEP Americas and CHEP Europe, whose heads would report to Brambles CEO David Turner. The group aimed to save AUD 15 million ($11 million) a year through the streamlining, which eliminated the position of CHEP International head Victor Mendes, who had led the group since 2002.

In 2005, CHEP had more than 7,500 employees in 38 countries. Sales were AUD 3.7 billion for the fiscal year ended in June. The U.S. reusable plastic container business was sold to Gait Packaging Ltd. in October 2005. The next month, Brambles announced that it planned to do away with the dual listed companies structure, in favor of a single company made up of CHEP and the records management unit Recall.

Frederick C. Ingram

PRINCIPAL OPERATING UNITS

CHEP Americas; CHEP Europe.

PRINCIPAL COMPETITORS

Bache Pallets Ltd.; IFCO Systems.

FURTHER READING

Alderton, Roz, "Brambles' CHEP to Appeal Pallet Ruling in the US," *AAP Newsfeed* (Australia), May 14, 2004.

"Brambles Is Tackling Problems at CHEP Europe: Restructuring to Cost £85 Mln," *AFX European Focus,* November 5, 2002.

Cobbs, Chris, "Retailers Begin Using Tags That Track Merchandise," *Orlando Sentinel,* November 29, 2004.

Felsted, Andrea, "Missing Pallets Raise Memories of Previous Fiasco at Brambles," *Financial Times* (London), February 26, 2004, p. 23.

Haynes, Rhys, "Brambles Sheds US Container Business," *AAP Newsfeed* (Australia), September 20, 2005.

Johnson, Jim, "PalEx, CHEP to Open Ill. Pallet Plant," *Waste News,* July 14, 1997, p. 5.

Kaye, Byron, "Brambles Splits CHEP in Two, Division CEO Leaves," *AAP Newsfeed* (Australia), June 24, 2004.

Leadbeater, Charles, "Expansion in the US for GKN with Joint Venture," *Financial Times* (London), June 29, 1990, p. 22.

Malkani, Gautam, "US Expansion Holds Back Brambles; Support Services Costs Grow As CHEP Pallet Side Grows After Wal-Mart Success," *Financial Times* (London), February 28, 2002, p. 26.

Marsh, Peter, "Plastic Surgery for Pallets: Wood May Soon Be Replaced As the Preferred Material for Making Pallets," *Financial Times* (London), December 18, 1997, p. 14.

Marsh, Virginia, "Brambles Surprises Markets with CHEP Shake-Up," *Financial Times* (London), June 25, 2004, p. 29.

Sherwell, Chris, "Brambles Forms Unit with GKN," *Financial Times* (London), February 21, 1989, p. 31.

Stove, Vincent W., "Australia's Brambles Takes Pallet Rental Business to US," *Journal of Commerce,* August 22, 1990, p. 2B.

"Transport Group Buys Pallet Rental Business," *Dominion* (Wellington), July 10, 1997, p. 16.

Walton, Dorothy, "Quick and Easy; Standardization Streamlines Freight Handling," *Business Mexico,* March 1997.

Chris-Craft Corporation

8161 15th Street East
Sarasota, Florida 24243
U.S.A.
Telephone: (941) 351-4900
Web site: http://www.chriscraft.com

Private Company
Incorporated: 2001 as Chris-Craft Corporation
Employees: 250
Sales: $40 million (2004 est.)
NAIC: 336612 Boat Building

■ ■ ■

Chris-Craft Corporation claims the title of America's oldest manufacturer of recreational boats. The company's brand and boatbuilding operations passed through different owners since the 1960s. One of its owners renamed it Chris-Craft Industries, Inc. but sold the boat business to Outboard Marine Corporation (OMC) in 1981. After the 2000 collapse of OMC, a British investor, Stephen Julius, acquired the Florida boatyard and the famous Chris-Craft brand and set out to restore the American legend.

NAFI FORMED 1928

From the 1960s to the 1990s, the Chris-Craft name was held by Chris-Craft Industries, Inc. which had been founded in 1928 in Detroit as National Automotive Fibers, Inc. (NAFI). NAFI manufactured upholstery, interior trim and carpeting, plastic products, and foam rubber for major Detroit automakers, especially Chrysler,

Ford, and Studebaker-Packard. The company was successful but remained a relatively minor supplier to automotive manufacturers. National Automotive Fibers acquired the Montrose Chemical Company of San Francisco in the 1940s, but it nonetheless remained almost wholly dependent on the auto industry, and its revenues often fluctuated wildly, reflecting the fortunes of the automobile market.

National Automotive Fibers operated during and after World War II with moderate success, but in 1956 its fortunes changed dramatically when the company lost more than $1 million on sales of $46 million. The company, however, attracted the attention of Paul V. Shields, senior partner of the Wall Street investment firm Shields & Co., who had determined that its troubles resulted from overdependence on the auto industry. Shields acquired National Automotive Fibers in a bold takeover move, trimmed it of marginally profitable products, and diversified its operations. While the sales revenues of National Automotive dropped to $23 million in 1957, profits rose to a record $1 million, and by 1960 the firm had accumulated assets of $10 million. By then the company had entered into oil and gas operations as well as television and radio broadcasting. In 1959, to emphasize its new identity as a diverse manufacturer, the company's name was changed to NAFI Corporation.

NAFI BUYS CHRIS-CRAFT IN 1960

NAFI's new financial health provided the means in 1960 to acquire the Chris-Craft Company, a boat manufacturer worth $50 million. Chris-Craft was

COMPANY PERSPECTIVES

Today, the Company remains true to the founding beliefs of the Smith family. The pleasure provided by our latest model, the Speedster, is designed to be just as intense as the experience enjoyed by people like Gar Wood, who raced our first wooden-hulled boats at the beginning of the 20th Century. As we celebrate our 130th year, everything we have learned about building boats will continue to set standards by which all other boats are measured. Whether you're considering a Chris-Craft for the first time or for the 21st time, we welcome you aboard and look forward to providing you with a boat that will transport you in every sense.

privately owned by the descendants of its founders, Christopher Columbus Smith and his brother Henry. During the 1880s the Smiths were backwoodsmen in St. Clair County, Michigan, who depended on duck hunting for a living. The two brothers supplemented their incomes by acting as guides for wealthy businessmen and professionals from Detroit who vacationed in the unspoiled environment of St. Clair County. To the brothers' surprise, the tourists admired the simple, sturdy lines of the Smiths' homemade vessels, and they soon found themselves selling the boats to eager buyers. In 1884 they built a boathouse, and boatbuilding soon supplanted the hunting business.

Fifteen years later business was booming in the Smith boathouse on the St. Clair River in Algonac. From simple duck boats the brothers had expanded their product line to include canoes, rowboats, and even a few sailboats. So successful were they that their business had become the town's major industry. The first gasoline-powered boat on the Great Lakes was a Smith craft, as were the fastest speedboat and the world's first hydroplane. By 1930 the boatbuilding firm was called Chris-Craft Corporation, and at the time of its acquisition by NAFI in 1960, it was the largest manufacturer of small boats in the world. The boatyard had moved to Florida in the mid-1950s.

The acquisition of Chris-Craft involved a great deal of negotiation because the company's president, Harsen Smith, was opposed to the sale. Harsen's objections were rooted in his strong loyalty to the company and the desire to maintain its dynastic heritage. Harsen controlled only about 25 percent of the company,

however, and the rest of the Smith family was in favor of selling. The company's valuation at approximately $50 million came as a huge surprise to the family and afforded them the opportunity to be selective in choosing a buyer.

On January 18, 1960, Joseph Flannery, who was the assistant to NAFI's Shields, happened to encounter Owen Smith, Chris-Craft's majority stockholder, at a boat show in New York. Owen indicated that he was amenable to the sale of Chris-Craft, and a series of high-level negotiations began, with the reluctant Harsen Smith the recipient of competing offers between NAFI and a rival bidder, Brunswick Corporation. Within a month of the meeting between Owen Smith and Flannery, NAFI had arranged a complicated buyout of Chris-Craft, with the sale price of $40 million. The sale was predicated on Shields's willingness to agree to a hands-off management style with Chris-Craft. The 1960s proved to be the most successful period in the boat manufacturing company's history, so successful, in fact, that in 1962 NAFI's stockholders agreed to change the company's name to Chris-Craft Industries, Inc., in order to capitalize on the division's success.

While the success of Chris-Craft's marine operations would eventually decline, the stimulus it injected into the parent company was enormous. Except for the manufacture of carpet fibers, insulation, and chemical products, virtually all identification with the old National Automotive Fibers company had disappeared. Thanks to Shields's diversification strategy, NAFI's annual revenues had long since been stabilized.

DIVERSIFICATION AND GROWTH UNDER NEW LEADERSHIP: 1960–89

Throughout the 1960s the Baldwin-Montrose Chemical Co., Inc., a chemical manufacturing company, had invested increasingly in Chris-Craft, and it eventually became the biggest stockholder. Herbert J. Siegel, chairman of Baldwin-Montrose, led a takeover of Chris-Craft, which was completed in 1968. Siegel then assumed the chairmanship of Chris-Craft.

In 1968 the Chris-Craft headquarters were moved from Oakland, California, where they had been since 1962, to New York. Siegel set about streamlining and reorganizing the company, which consisted of three main operations: the boat division; the fast-growing television broadcasting division, with stations in Los Angeles, Minneapolis-St. Paul, and Portland, Oregon; and the small industrial division, consisting of Montrose Chemical of California, the world's largest producer of DDT until the federal government banned it in 1972, and

KEY DATES

1874: Chris-Craft's boatbuilding tradition begins.

1928: National Automotive Fibers, Inc., is established.

1944: Chris-Craft's landing craft are used in D-Day invasion.

1959: National Automotive Fibers changes its name to NAFI Corporation.

1960: NAFI purchases boat manufacturer Chris-Craft Company.

1962: NAFI changes its name to Chris-Craft Industries, Inc.

1968: Baldwin-Montrose Chemical Co., Inc., takes control of Chris-Craft, and Herbert J. Siegel becomes chairman.

1981: Chris-Craft Industries sells its boat division to Outboard Marine Corporation.

1994: With Viacom Inc., Chris-Craft Industries forms United Paramount Network (UPN).

1997: Chris-Craft Industries sells a 50 percent stake in UPN to Viacom Inc.

2000: Chris-Craft boatyard is shut down in the Outboard Marine Corporation collapse.

2001: Chris-Craft Industries merges into News Corp.; Stephen Julius and Stephen Heese take over the Chris-Craft boat business.

2003: Chris-Craft Corporation is making 600 boats a year; sales are about $30 million.

Chris-Craft Industrial Products, Inc. The combined sales for 1968 were $89 million.

The 1970s and 1980s saw Chris-Craft's continued expansion into television broadcasting. During the 1970s Chris-Craft invested in the Twentieth Century-Fox Film Corporation, building its holdings to 19 percent of the outstanding common stock by 1980. In 1981 Chris-Craft obtained a 19.5 percent ownership of United Television, Inc. Siegel then formed BHC Communications, Inc., as a holding company for United Television. BHC owned and operated all eight of Chris-Craft's television stations and was the parent company of United Television, Inc. To further focus on expansion in broadcasting, the company sold its boat division in 1981, leasing the Chris-Craft name to the buyer.

In 1984 Warner Communications, Inc., in an attempt to avert a hostile takeover by Australian investor Rupert Murdoch, welcomed Chris-Craft's investment in the company. Siegel traded 42.5 percent of BHC for 19 percent of Warner Communications. In 1989, when Time Inc. merged with Warner Communications to form Time-Warner Inc., Chris-Craft's investment garnered $2.3 billion.

In the early 1990s Chris-Craft continued to expand into television broadcasting, acquiring Pinelands, Inc., in August 1992 for $313 million. Pinelands owned WWOR-TV, an independent station that broadcast in a tri-state area that included New York City, the second most important television market in the country. By 1992 the company owned and operated six independent and two network-affiliated television stations, and it had become the nation's sixth largest television broadcaster and the second largest independent television producer in the country. In addition, Chris-Craft's stations reached approximately 20 percent of the households in the United States.

UPN FORMED 1994

Chris-Craft Industries took a significant step in the broadcasting market in 1994 when the company announced the formation of a fifth national network—United Paramount Network—in cooperation with Viacom Inc.'s Paramount Television Group. As part of the agreement, Chris-Craft owned 100 percent of UPN, with Paramount having the option to acquire an equal share through January 15, 1997. The network, targeted toward the young male demographic group, premiered in early 1995 and offered four hours of original prime-time programming per week. The following year original programming was increased to six hours per week.

The new network severely affected Chris-Craft's revenues, and during 1995 and 1996 losses due to the costs of UPN totaled $275.6 million. Although Viacom began to share Chris-Craft's burden in early 1997, when it acquired a 50 percent interest in UPN for $160 million, losses continued to rise. In 1997 UPN losses for Chris-Craft equaled $87.4 million, and the following year the company lost $88.6 million. Despite such dismal figures, Chris-Craft's Siegel continued to support UPN and remained optimistic about the network's potential. Siegel stated in the company's 1998 annual report, "UPN's importance to Chris-Craft as a strategic asset remains undiminished. Now in its fifth year, UPN's development, as expected, has been both expensive and uneven. Nonetheless, our commitment to the network's success is unwavering."

UPN continued to drain Chris-Craft's resources in the late 1990s. During the 1997 season the network's ratings were so poor that UPN dropped to sixth place among the major networks. Although the network increased its original programming from three to five nights, UPN's 1998 ratings fell 39 percent from 1997. One new program that debuted in October 1998 set a record for achieving the lowest first-run broadcast rating during prime time. In early 1999 UPN rallied by introducing a new animated comedy based on the popular cartoon series "Dilbert." Still, ratings for the 1998 season fell by 30 percent. Between 1995 and 1999 UPN racked up losses of more than $500 million. The network shifted its target audience from season to season, beginning with family-oriented programming, switching to programming designed to appeal to urban viewers, and then aiming for young males.

While Chris-Craft Industries focused on its broadcast division, the industrial division carried on. With a series of improvements, including the upgrading of manufacturing equipment, the introduction of new processing control systems, and strategic capital investments, the industrial division flourished in the late 1990s. Operating income increased 77 percent over 1997 and 1998, and the division enjoyed record earnings in 1998. Increased earnings were also attributed to the streamlining of the division, as unprofitable product lines were discontinued, increasing numbers of international alliances were established, and products with lower margins were de-emphasized.

UPN's declines were somewhat offset by earnings from television stations, and Chris-Craft continued to acquire additional stations. In 1998 Chris-Craft acquired television station WHSW in Baltimore and changed its call letters to WUTB. In 1999 the company completed the acquisition of WRBW in Orlando, bringing the total number of Chris-Craft's television stations to ten. Also that year, Viacom announced plans to purchase CBS Corporation for $37 billion. Because the Federal Communications Commission (FCC) prohibited companies from owning two broadcast networks, Viacom's announcement raised questions regarding the future of Chris-Craft and Viacom's joint ownership of UPN. In Viacom and Chris-Craft's original agreement, two options for exiting the partnership had been determined—buying out the other partner or paying for what the partner had invested up to that date and providing funds for the future operation of UPN. Either option would cost Viacom substantial sums of money. Industry analysts agreed that Chris-Craft could emerge the winner and offered other possible scenarios—that Viacom might offer Chris-Craft some of its stations in exchange for severing the partnership or that Chris-Craft might sell Viacom's share to another company.

During the first half of 1999 Chris-Craft's net income dropped by nearly half compared to the same period in 1998, from $13.89 million to $7.47 million. The decline was due in large part to increased UPN losses. Undeterred, Chris-Craft continued to back UPN, expanding its prime-time schedule and developing new programs geared toward young males. A week and a half into the new 1999 season, UPN's ratings were up 20 percent from 1998 ratings, a promising start, and the network was reaching 95 percent of all U.S. households through 186 affiliates. Indeed, Chris-Craft could afford to ride out UPN's shaky and costly beginnings, for the company remained debt-free, with consolidated cash and marketable securities holdings of $1.39 billion as of mid-1999.

Viacom unsuccessfully tried to buy Chris-Craft in the fall of 1999 to complement its pending acquisition of CBS Corporation. Chris-Craft chairman Herbert Siegel rebuffed the offer, and instead sold Viacom Inc. his company's 50 percent interest in UPN for only $5 million. Chris-Craft had sunk hundreds of millions of dollars in the network in the few years since it had been launched, noted the *Wall Street Journal.*

NEW OWNERS FOR CHRIS-CRAFT INDUSTRIES, CHRIS-CRAFT BOATS IN 2001

In 2000, Rupert Murdoch's Australian media conglomerate News Corp. successfully outbid Viacom to acquire Chris-Craft Industries. The addition of Chris-Craft's ten stations made News Corp., which also owned the Fox network, by far the largest television broadcaster in the United States. The cash and stock deal was worth $5.3 billion ($3.7 billion for Chris-Craft Industries and $1.6 billion to buy out minority shareholders in BHC Communications Inc. and United Television Inc.); though pricey, it was considered a strategic victory for Murdoch. The buy attracted a great deal of regulatory scrutiny but was ultimately approved by antitrust regulators. The acquisition closed in July 2001 after News Corp. agreed to trade off a couple of TV stations to satisfy the Federal Communications Commission. Chris-Craft Industries was then merged into News Corp.

Chris-Craft Industries had sold its namesake boatyard in 1981 for $5 million; this was later acquired by Outboard Marine Corporation (OMC) of Illinois for $50 million. John Keim, Chris-Craft president from 1989 to 1994, was credited with leading a turnaround at the boatyard. In 1999 OMC installed yet another new management team at Chris-Craft while investing in new computer-controlled cutting equipment for the upholstery shop, noted the *Sarasota Herald Tribune.* In spite of a substantial backlog at Chris-Craft, OMC declared bankruptcy in 2000, however. Its collapse notoriously put more than 300 people at Chris-Craft out of work before Christmas.

Genmar Holdings Inc., led by Irwin L. Jacobs, who

had unsuccessfully bid against OMC for the old Chris-Craft boatyard in 1981, joined Canada's Bombardier Inc. in acquiring all of OMC's assets for $95 million at a February 2001 auction. Genmar also owned a number of other boat makers.

Stephen M. Julius and his former Harvard business school colleague Stephen F. Heese acquired Chris-Craft's boatyard from Genmar in March 2001. Four months later, notes *Forbes*, Julius bought the Chris-Craft brand name from its new owner, News Corp. for a reported $3 million. Chris-Craft Industries had been making $500,000 to $1 million a year simply by leasing its famous name to OMC, Siegel told *Forbes*.

Julius was chairman of the new Chris-Craft Corporation, while Heese served as president. Julius already had a successful track record in rebuilding luxury boat businesses. His United Kingdom venture group, Stellican Ltd., had sold Italy's Cantieri Riva Spa for $34 million after turning it around. Interestingly, many of Riva's designs were based on Chris-Craft models.

The brand's new owners faced a challenging economy, but by the end of the year had a backlog of 350 orders. At the time, Chris-Craft had 75 employees, 60 of them in production. The product lines were initially trimmed from 16 models to six classic styles, officials told the *Sarasota Herald Tribune*. State and local government helped keep the company in Manatee County, Florida, by providing tax breaks based on employment levels.

Forbes reported that Chris-Craft made $30 million in the 2003-04 fiscal year, with an operating profit of $1 million. According to the *Sarasota Herald-Tribune*, the company was on its way to posting revenues of $40 million for 2004. Its 250 employees were building 600 boats a year. Chris-Craft chairman Julius was also acquiring another American legend: Indian Motorcycles.

Sina Dubovoj
Updated, Mariko Fujinaka; Frederick C. Ingram

PRINCIPAL COMPETITORS

Brunswick Corporation; Cantieri Riva SpA; American Marine Holdings, Inc.; Genmar Holdings, Inc.

FURTHER READING

Alexander, Keith L., "Chris-Craft May Be Big Winner in Viacom-CBS Merger," *USA Today*, September 15, 1999, p. B6.

"BHC Communications (Acquires Pinelands, Inc.)," *Wall Street Journal*, August 24, 1992, p. B4.

Carberry, Sonja, "Boat Maker Christopher Columbus Smith—His Perseverance and Vision Helped Chris-Craft Sink the Competition," *Investor's Business Daily*, January 4, 2000, p. A4.

Coolidge, Alexander, "Chris-Craft Is Hiring; Despite Economy, It Has Orders for 350 Powerboats," *Sarasota Herald Tribune*, October 9, 2001, p. D1.

"FCC Clears a Chris-Craft Unit to Buy WWOR-TV," *New York Times*, August 20, 1992, p. D4.

Graham, Jefferson, "Plummeting UPN Hopes for a Rebound," *USA Today*, October 26, 1998, p. D3.

Gribbins, Joseph, *Chris-Craft: A History 1922–1942*, Marblehead, Massachusetts, 2001.

Lippman, John and Martin Peers, "In Clash of Media Titans, a Surprise from News Corp.—Murdoch Trumps Rival Viacom with $5.3 Billion Purchase of Chris-Craft TV Stations," *Wall Street Journal*, August 14, 2000, p. B1.

"Little Movement in Top 25 (Chris-Craft Increased Its Reach from 11% to 18%)," *Broadcasting & Cable*, March 22, 1993, p. 29.

McQuaid, Kevin, "Revving Up a U.S. Icon," *Sarasota Herald-Tribune*, July 27, 2004, p. A1.

Marsteller, Duane, "Boat Manufacturer to Resume Production at Manatee County, Fla., Plant," *Bradenton Herald*, August 24, 2001.

Morais, Richard C., "In Jacob's Wake," *Forbes*, January 10, 2005, p. 82.

"Paul V. Shields Group Acquires Control of Automotive Fibers," *Wall Street Journal*, September 24, 1956, p. 7.

Peers, Martin, and John R. Wilke, "In CBS Merger with Viacom, a Wild Card," *Wall Street Journal*, September 9, 1999, p. B1.

Rodengen, Jeffrey L., *The Legend of Chris-Craft*, Fort Lauderdale: Write Stuff Syndicate, 1988, 294 pp.

Roman, Monica, and Jenny Hontz, "Viacom Buys Equity Stake in UPN," *Variety*, December 9, 1996, p. 39.

Sauer, Matthew, "New Captains at the Helm; Manatee Boat Builder Chris Craft Steers Toward Profits," *Sarasota Herald Tribune*, May 27, 1999, p. 1D.

Savage, Jack, *Chris-Craft in the 1950s*, Osceola, Wisc.: Haynes, 2002.

Savage, Jack, *Chris-Craft*, Osceola, Wisc.: MBI Pub., c. 2000.

Shen, Jun, "President of Illinois-Based Chris-Craft Boats Resigns," *Knight Ridder/Tribune Business News*, February 9, 1994.

Shopes, Rich, "Latest Sale of Chris-Craft Could Bring Glad Tidings," *Sarasota Herald Tribune*, March 13, 2001, p. D1.

———, "Staying Afloat; The Economy Has Been Choppy, But Boat Manufacturers Already Are Riding a Wave of New Sales," *Sarasota Herald Tribune*, August 12, 2002, p. 10.

Citi Trends, Inc.

102 Fahm Street
Savannah, Georgia 31401
U.S.A.
Telephone: (912) 236-1561
Fax: (912) 443-3674

Public Company
Founded: 1946 as Savannah Wholesale Co.
Employees: 1,800
Sales: $289.8 million (2006)
Stock Exchanges: NASDAQ
Ticker Symbol: CTRN
NAIC: 448140 Family Clothing Stores

■ ■ ■

Citi Trends, Inc., based in Savannah, Georgia, is a company that operates a chain of more than 250 stores selling value-priced, urban-inspired apparel and accessories, mostly catering to African-American family customers, who make up about 70 percent of the customer base. Not only does Citi Trends sell hip-hop jeans and oversized T-shirts to younger customers, it also offers men's, women's, and children's clothing and shoes. The stores, which average over 10,000 square feet of selling space, also offer a small home accessories department, selling giftware, lamps, pictures, mirrors, and figurines with an emphasis on African tribal décor. Citi Trends sells private-label apparel as well as major brands, including Apple Bottoms, Dickies Ecko, FUBU, Members Only, Phat Farm, Baby Phat, Sean Jean, and Rocawear. Stores are found primarily in affordable strip

mall locations close to their target demographic in some 12 Southern and Southwestern states, with the most units, 49, located in Georgia. The fast growing Citi Trends company has also entered Midwestern states like Indiana and Ohio and is looking to Northeastern states, such as New Jersey and Pennsylvania, for further expansion. Taken public in 2005, Citi Trends is listed on the NASDAQ.

POST-WORLD WAR II ROOTS

Citi Trends was founded in Savannah in 1946 as Savannah Wholesale Co., serving retail clothiers through the southeastern states, mostly selling women's undergarments and hosiery. The wholesaler operation proved successful enough that in 1958 it branched out to include retail clothing outlets. They were branded Allied Department Stores, an allusion to the victorious Allies of World War II as well as a reflection of the varied merchandise the stores had to offer. Selling value-priced family apparel, Allied found a ready market and expanded modestly throughout the South over the next 20 years.

In 1978 Savannah Wholesale and the Allied chain were purchased by Michigan General Corp., a Dallas-based diverse conglomerate that also held interests in such areas as homebuilding products, oilfield chemicals, highway safety construction, recreational vehicles, paperback books, retail furniture, and a temporary employment agency for engineers. Combined, Michigan General's dozen subsidiaries generated about $140 million by the early 1980s. However, it proved to be an unwieldy mix of businesses and the company took on too much debt to assemble them effectively. As a result, Michigan General lost money for three straight years and was on the verge of bankruptcy when John Boudreau took over as chief executive officer in 1982. He came to Michigan General with a reputation as a turnaround artist, having successfully revived European Overseas Inn, a company that managed European Holiday Inns.

Boudreau took a special interest in Savannah Wholesale, which included the Allied Chain and several A's Bargain Stores. In three years he grew the number of retail outlets from 23 to 117, located in small rural towns in several Southern states. Boudreau also looked to find a retail outlet for Krestmark, a subsidiary that manufactured aluminum doors and windows. In September 1983 he acquired the Diamond Lumber chain of homebuilding supply centers, which was supposed to be a major component in his turnaround strategy for Michigan General. Boudreau also attempted to bring more focus to Michigan General by divesting some assets. In February 1984 he unloaded six subsidiaries, reaping nearly $20 million. Two core businesses now remained: the clothing stores and homebuilding supplies. He would not, however, be given much of a further chance to implement his plan. The company was taken over by General Felt Industries, a manufacturer of artificial grass and carpeting, and its CEO, Rocco Barbieri, was not pleased with what he found, telling *Dallas Business Courier* that Boudreau "left a lot to be desired in terms of making it a well run organization." In June 1985 Boudreau was relieved of his post, and Barbieri took over.

SOLD TO VARIETY WHOLESALERS: 1989

In the first six months of 1985 Savannah Wholesale lost approximately $2 million and one of Barbieri's first tasks was to restore the subsidiary to profitability. While Savannah Wholesale and the Allied chain were able to limp along for the next few years, Barbieri was not able to restore Michigan General to fiscal health. The company lost $34.6 million in 1985. Under pressure from its senior lender, Michigan General then filed for Chapter 11 bankruptcy protection in April 1987.

Nevertheless, Savannah Wholesale was allowed to continue normal operations. Michigan General emerged from Chapter 11 in April 1988 and bond holders gained 80 percent of the common stock. Savannah Wholesale remained a part of the reorganized company until July 1989 when it was sold to Variety Wholesalers, operator of discount stores.

Variety was a very successful retailer, operating more than 400 budget stores in 13 Southern states. The company grew out of a single five and dime store opened in Angier, North Carolina, in 1932 by John Pope, the son of a dry-goods merchant who spent many hours in his father's store while growing up. He was known to sleep under the counter on Saturday nights when the store remained open until midnight in order to cater to farm families who came into town and often liked to shop after treating themselves to a show. The elder Pope anticipated the shortages that would occur should the United States enter World War II and stockpiled goods, allowing him to take advantage of the war years to establish a small chain of stores in North Carolina. A University of North Carolina graduate in commerce, John Pope, along his brothers, took over the operation in 1949 (and two years later he bought them out). The business was incorporated in 1957 as Variety Wholesalers, Inc.

Pope moved away from the once popular full-price five and dime format, converting his outlets to the variety store format in the 1950s and 1960s. He continued to keep his finger on the pulse of small town consumers, focusing on communities in Southern and Mid-Atlantic states. When dollar stores became popular in 1970s, he followed that trend, and in the 1980s he pursued a mix of formats. Variety Wholesalers began to accelerate its growth in the 1970s as family-owned variety stores and five and dime stores were put up for sale by children of founders who were not interested in pursuing the retail trade. Pope now proved adept at buying the chains on the cheap and imposing on them his cost-conscious way of doing business. In the 1970s he bought dozens of Eagle Stores and McCrory/United Stores, and then in the early 1980s added nearly 200 Value Mart Stores, 145 Super Dollar Stores, and 55 P. H. Rose's variety stores. By this point, Pope was operating some 400 stores under four banners, but the retail landscape was changing once again as small town American retailers had to contend with large discounters, in particular Wal-Mart, who were able to leverage their size to buy goods at advantageous prices and sell them to consumers at prices the competition could not hope to match.

Like many retailers Pope had for years advertised heavily, discounting certain items to bring consumers into his stores to buy high-margin merchandise. But this strategy lost its edge because of the discounters. Many

```
┌─────────────────────────────────────────────┐
│                                               │
│                 KEY DATES                     │
│                      ■                        │
│  ├───────────────────────────────────────┤    │
│                                               │
│   1946:  Savannah Wholesale Co. is formed.    │
│   1958:  Savannah Wholesale launches Allied   │
│          Department Stores.                   │
│   1978:  Savannah/Allied is sold to Michigan  │
│          General Corp.                        │
│   1989:  Variety Wholesalers acquire          │
│          Savannah/Allied.                     │
│   1999:  A management-led buyout of the       │
│          company takes place.                 │
│   2001:  The company becomes Citi Trends.     │
│   2005:  Citi Trends makes its initial public │
│          offering of stock.                   │
│                                               │
└─────────────────────────────────────────────┘
```

customers simply bought the advertised specials and nothing else. A pragmatic man, Pope was not hesitant about closing stores, but he was also willing to take a chance. He converted 15 stores on the verge of closing to a format that eliminated sales items. Instead, merchandise was priced at an everyday threshold price, such as the Super 10 format stores, in which everything retailed at $10 or less. The switch worked, customers returned, and Pope was further able to save on advertising costs to restore some of his competitive edge.

Pope and Variety Wholesalers were once again on the upswing when in 1989 the company acquired Savannah Wholesale and the 106 units that remained in the Allied Department Stores chain. Of those, six stores operated under the Allied Kids Wear banner. The Allied operation was not suited for conversion to a one-price store, however, and Pope indicated that he planned to keep it a separate business to be run out of Savannah. He told the *Daily News Record,* "We see this as a diversification and we believe, with our support in some areas of their operation, Allied will become a profitable growth vehicle."

Savannah Wholesale spent the next decade under the control of Variety Wholesalers, a secondary operation that withered as Pope continued to focus on one-price stores and acquired more fading variety store chains. Allied enjoyed a resurgence in 1997 when a new management team was installed and the stores received a much needed makeover, including store renovations and an updating of merchandise. In keeping with these changes the Allied Department Store name was dropped in favor of Allied Fashion for Less.

With the business rebounding, Variety Wholesalers sold the 85-unit chain to management in April 1999, backed by Hampshire Equity Partners, a New York City investment firm founded in 1990. With this independence, Allied began to expand rapidly, finding its niche by focusing on urban fashions, the family market, and the African-American community. A larger store format was introduced in early 2000 that could accommodate a broader range of merchandise. The new stores took a new name, Citi Trends Fashion For Less, and steadily the older Allied Stores were switched over to the new format.

CITI TRENDS NAME ADOPTED
2001

The company adopted the Citi Trends name in July 2001, and in December of that year there was a change at the top ranks of management when R. Edward Anderson was named chief executive officer. Anderson had been Variety Wholesalers' chief financial officer, having joined that company in 1997 as a result of the acquisition of Rose's Stores Inc. Anderson had spent 20 years with Rose's, ultimately become CEO and chairman of the board. Thus, he was a seasoned retailer. He took over a chain of 123 stores and moved quickly to accelerate its growth. Not only did the number of units increase, but stores began to generate more sales, improving from $800,000 in annual sales per store in fiscal 2001 to around $1.1 million by fiscal 2004. These sales increases were also helped by the introduction in fiscal 2003 of a larger store format, featuring about 10,350 square feet of selling space.

Citi Trends' balance sheet revealed steady improvement, as revenues reached $98 million in fiscal 2002, approached $125 million in fiscal 2003, and totaled $157.2 million in fiscal 2004 and $203.4 million in fiscal 2005 (ending January 29, 2005). Net income during this period increased from $2.5 million to more than $7.3 million, and the Citi Trends chain expanded to 212 units. Hampshire Equity was now ready to cash in some of its investment through an initial public offering of stock in May 2005, managed by CIBC World Markets, Piper Jaffray, SG Cowen & Co., and Wachovia Securities. The offering was well received by investors and Citi Trends was able to receive the top range, $14, of its desired price range. The offering raised almost $54 million. Moreover, the stock continued to rise in value when it began trading on the NASDAQ, gaining more than 75 percent of its initial price in three months.

Hampshire Equity sold 10 percent of its stake in Citi Trends, but still retained a 55 percent controlling interest. The offering also provided Citi Trends with some working capital as it continued to expand, with plans in the works to open stores in Delaware, Kentucky, New Jersey, Pennsylvania, Indiana, Illinois, Michigan, Missouri, and Ohio.

In fiscal 2006 sales increased 42.5 percent to $289.8 million and net income almost doubled to $142 million. More importantly, the revenue increase was not just the result of new store openings: comparable store sales increased an impressive 16.7 percent over the prior year. Explaining Citi Trend's success to *DSN Retailing Today*, Anderson said, "Our value-conscious customer has a strong appetite for current urban fashions at strong value prices." At a conference call with analysts in February 2006, Anderson elaborated on the company's "secret to success." According to *DSN Retailing Today*, "Anderson said it related to having an effective, trend-driven buying team with an ability to focus on key looks for the season rather than specific national labels. 'We view the look as more important than the brand. We know that counterintuitive to what a lot of people believe about urban fashions, but we really believe it's got to be the right look first and the brand second,' Anderson said."

Citi Trends appeared to be in the early stages of its growth. Some analysts estimated that the chain could expand as large as 1,200 stores by 2014. It was highly likely that by then Hampshire Equity would no longer hold a stake, however. In May 2006 Gregory P. Flynn, one of the firm's principals, resigned as chairman of Citi Trends. Hampshire Equity had already further reduced its holdings through a secondary stock offering in January 2006, and it now appeared that the firm was ready to sell the balance.

Ed Dinger

PRINCIPAL COMPETITORS

Burlington Coat Factory Warehouse Corporation; Ross Stores, Inc.; The TJX Companies, Inc.

FURTHER READING

Curl, Eric, "Citi Trends Goes Public," *Savannah Morning News*, May 18, 2005.

Howell, Debbie, "Citi Trends Builds Success Targeting Urban Fashion," *DSN Retailing Today*, February 27, 2006, p. 11.

Lee, Steven H., "Michigan General Exits Chapter 11," *Dallas Morning News*, April 2, 1988, p. 5F.

Lloyd, Brenda, "Variety Acquires Allied/Savannah," *Daily News Record*, July 27, 1989, p. 16.

Rogers, Walter M., "After a Shakeup, Michigan General Moves Its Headquarters Out of Dallas," *Dallas Business Courier*, September 30, 1985, p. 7.

Traugot, Catherine Liden, "Variety is the Spice," *Business, North Carolina*, September 1, 1999, p. 22.

conzzeta
HOLDING

Conzzeta Holding

———————— ■ ————————

Giesshuebelstrasse 45
P.O. Box CH-8045
Zurich,
Switzerland
Telephone: (41) 044 468 24 44
Fax: (41) 044 468 24 81
Web site: http://www.conzzeta.ch

Public Company
Incorporated: 1912 as Zuercher Ziegeleien
Employees: 3,280
Sales: CHF 1.15 billion ($944.3 million) (2005)
Stock Exchanges: Swiss
Ticker Symbol: CZH
NAIC: 212321 Construction Sand and Gravel Mining;
212324 Kaolin and Ball Clay Mining; 315999
Other Apparel Accessories and Other Apparel
Manufacturing; 325510 Paint and Coating
Manufacturing; 326150 Urethane and Other Foam
Product (Except Polystyrene) Manufacturing;
327320 Ready-Mix Concrete Manufacturing;
327420 Gypsum and Gypsum Product
Manufacturing; 333298 All Other Industrial
Machinery Manufacturing; 333515 Cutting Tool
and Machine Tool Accessory Manufacturing;
484110 General Freight Trucking, Local; 493110
General Warehousing and Storage Facilities; 531190
Lessors of Other Real Estate Property

■ ■ ■

Conzzeta Holding is a major Swiss holding company with a focus on five distinct areas. The company's larg- est business unit is Machinery and Systems Engineering, which operates in sheet metal and glass processing, through subsidiary Bystronics, and Automation Systems, through Seckler AG and Cox Automation Systems. These companies combine to generate nearly 62.5 percent of the group's sales of CHF 1.15 billion ($944 million) in 2005. Foam Materials, including cushions, pillows, mat- tresses, insulation materials, filters, soundproofing and other products, operates internationally through subsidiary FoamPartner, and adds 11 percent to group sales. The company's Sporting Goods division, responsible for nearly 13 percent of sales, is represented by the Mammut Sports group, a specialist in outdoor, mountaineering and winter sports equipment. Mam- mut's products include sleeping bags, ropes and climb- ing harnesses, clothing, backpacks, hardware and other equipment, as well as coating materials, such ski waxes and ski maintenance products, which add another 10 percent to group sales. Conzzeta's sporting goods and coatings products are marketed under the Mammut, Toko, Raichle and Ajungilak brands. Conzzeta also operates a real estate division. In 2005, the company sold of the last of its construction materials operations, which had been the group's original market. The group's diversification strategy, originally adopted in the early 1980s, has allowed the group to reduce its reliance on the Swiss market, which is expected to account for less than 20 percent of company sales by the end of 2006. Although Conzzeta is listed on the Swiss Stock Exchange, 73.5 percent of the company's shares, and more than 81 percent of voting rights, are held by the Schmidheiny, Spoerry and Auer families. The company is led by Jacob Schmidheiny and Heinrich M.Lanz.

We invest in successful companies in the areas of Machinery and Systems Engineering as well as Industrial and Consumer Products. In the interests of our customers, employees and shareholders, we take holdings and develop the companies in our Group with a long-term perspective. We invest in companies in order to produce useful products and services, create attractive jobs and generate sound profits. We create a framework that enables our executives and employees to act self-reliantly and develop their full potential. We foster innovation on all levels to help our companies defend and develop their strong market positions. We act with consideration for people and nature, and respect the legal and social framework. We build trust, inside and outside the company, through fairness and reliability. We maintain our strong financial fundamentals so that we can withstand difficult periods with equanimity. That is why we finance our business from our own resources.

DIVERSIFICATION PROGRAM LAUNCHED IN 1980

Conzetta Holding had its origins in the founding of Zuercher Ziegeleien in 1912. That company brought together five existing producers of bricks and building tiles, and later developed into one of Switzerland's leading producers and suppliers of construction materials. The company also became associated with the Schmidheiny family, which had founded the later Holcim cement giant in 1912 as well. Together with two other families, the Spoerrys (later associated with the Mettler-Toldeo group) and another prominent Swiss industrial family, the Auers, the Schmidheiny family remained in control of Zuercher Ziegeleien, and later Conzzeta Holdings, into the 21st century.

Zuercher Ziegeleien's strength in the building materials sector came to haunt the company amid the economic crisis of the late 1970s and early 1980s. Hit hard by the collapse of the construction sector, both in Switzerland and in the international market, Zuercher Ziegeleien decided to adopt a new strategy in 1980 calling for a steady diversification of the company's interests.

The company's first step came that same year, with the purchase of fellow Swiss company Fritz Nauer AG, a producer of foam materials. The Nauer company had

been founded in 1937, initially as a sales agent for natural sponges. By 1943, the company had launched its own manufacturing operations, producing viscose sponges. In 1954, the company added to its range again with the launch of polyurethane foam production, developing into a market leader in that category.

Zuercher Ziegeleien found a new expansion target in 1982, with the purchase of Arova-Lenzburg AG. That acquisition took the company onto new ground, adding the production of mountaineering ropes and other equipment and sporting goods. Arova-Lenzburg had been founded in 1862 when Kaspar Tanner opened a workshop producing technical ropes for the local mountaineering market in Dintikon, a small village in the Aargau canton near Lenzburg. The company went on to expand its production to include a variety of equipment for the mountaineering and rock climbing markets, and by 1971 had purchased Walter Schwarzenbach and its yarn and harness weavery plant in St. Gallen.

Zuercher Ziegeleien added another direction in 1987, purchasing Schmid Rhyner AG and its production of architectural paints. Founded in 1973, that company grew into a major global producer of print finishing products and other architectural paints. In 1988, Zuercher Ziegeleien expanded this division with the acquisition of two more architectural paint producers, Roth & Cie. AG, and Siegfried Keller AG, which, founded in 1901, also added its specialty production of soundproofing paints.

Into the early 1990s, Zuercher Ziegeleien focused on strengthening its newly diversified operations. In 1990, for example, Fritz Nauer acquired Gusag Schaumstoffe AG, adding its production of latex foam and cushions and construction packaging. Two years later, Fritz Nauer bought up rival Reisgies Schaumstoffe, founded in 1952 as a polyurethane foam producer. This purchase enabled Fritz Nauer to expand its operations to include production for the automotive industry. Also in 1992, Zuercher Ziegeleien added another operating division, ZZ Immobilien, which became the group's real estate arm. That subsidiary was later renamed as Plaza Immobilien.

The following year, the company expanded its sporting goods division through the purchase of Toko AG, a producer of ski wax and ski care products founded in 1916 as Tobler & Co. Originally focused on shoeshine and leather care products, Tobler had opened a factory in Altstätten, Switzerland, in 1926; by 1934, the company had changed its name to Toko. In the years following World War II, Toko emerged as an important name in ski waxes, and expanded again with a new factory constructed in the early 1970s. By 1982,

1912: Zuercher Ziegeleien is founded to produce bricks and building tiles.

1980: The company develops a diversification strategy to reduce reliance on cyclical market trends.

1992: Zuercher Ziegeleien restructures as a holding company.

1994: The company enters machinery and systems engineering, which becomes its largest division.

1996: The company begins selling off construction and building materials operations.

1999: The company changes its name to ZZ Holding and then to Conzzeta Holding; the Foam-Partner group is created.

2005: FoamPartner enters China through a joint venture.

the company had come under the control of the Schmidheiny family, before being transferred to Zuercher Ziegeleien.

DIVERSIFIED HOLDING COMPANY FOR THE NEW CENTURY

In recognition of the company's transformation, Zuercher Ziegeleien changed its structure to that of a holding company in 1992. Although the company remained active in building materials production through the decade, it had also begun seeking a new core operation. In 1994, the company acquired the Bystronic Group, establishing a presence in the machinery and systems engineering market. Bystronic added two major components to the group—sheet metal processing system and glass processing systems—and soon became Zuercher Ziegeleien's largest operation.

The acquisition of Bystronic enabled Zuercher Ziegeleien's exit from the building materials market. The company launched that process in 1996, with the sale of its brick and concrete products businesses in western Switzerland. The company's change in direction was motivated by the increasing consolidation of the European building materials market. Unable to keep pace, the company at last decided that it had become too small to compete in a market that had shifted from a local and regional focus to one of true international scope. By 1999, the company had sold off its tile

production, additional brick products operations, and its production of insulating materials and chimneys, to Austria's Koramic/Weinberger Group.

Following that disposal, the company changed its name, initially to ZZ Holding, before settling on Conzzeta Holding; the two Zs in the company's name maintained its link with its past. The newly streamlined holding company was freed to develop its new core operations. These included Hämmerle AG, a producer of industrial machinery, acquired in 1997. The company next boosted its machine systems business with the purchase of Robert Seckler AG, a specialist in the development of handling systems. Founded in 1975, Seckler had started out as an engineering consultant and sales agent in Biel, Switzerland, before moving into production in the early 1980s. The company's first large scale order came in 1983, when it received a contract to supply automated production systems for fuel injection needles for the automotive industry. Seckler developed automation and robotic systems as a specialty, and created the core for Conzzeta's Automation business unit, formed in 2005.

Conzzeta continued streamlining its operations through the first half of the 2000s. The company sold most of its transport operations, Transall AG, to Camion Transport AG in 2000. In 2002, the company sold off more of its building materials operations, disposing of Hard AG and its stake in Marmoran AG. The company focused instead on building up its core divisions, buying up AFM Fabtek and the Beyeler Group in 2002, both engineering companies. In 2003, the company added two more businesses to its machine systems unit, acquiring Armatec Vierhaus, a manufacturer of machinery, and Pullmax Scandinavia AB, a manufacturer of packaging systems.

Conzzeta meanwhile had also been building up its sporting goods division, buying up Climb High, a U.S.-based distributor of European climbing products. That purchase was expected to help raise the sporting goods group Mammut's profile in the United States and Canada, where it was known primarily for its ropes. In the same year, Conzzeta spun off Arova-Mammut's AG industrial activities into a separate company, transforming Mammut AG into a consumer-products company.

Conzzeta added to this category again in 2003 with the purchase of the Raichle footwear brand. That company, founded in 1909, developed its first hiking boot in 1924, and introduced the first plastic ski boot, known as the Fibre Jet, in 1968. Raichle subsequently repositioned itself in the early 2000s as an "outdoor footwear" specialist.

During the late 1990s and into the 2000s, Conzzeta's foam production business had also been growing.

After the 1998 acquisition of Neutrex AG, which brought the company into the production of natural latex products, the company restructured its foam business into five key business units in 1999. These were then placed under a single brand name, FoamPartner, in 2000. By 2003, that operation grew again, with Fritz Nauer's acquisition of Büttikofer AG.

In 2005, Conzzeta created a new business unit, Automation Systems, to group its Seckler subsidiary and its latest acquisition, Cox Automation Systems, which was located in Illinois. The company also entered China in 2005, forming a venture between FoamPartner and Otto Bock Foam Systems to set up a production plant in Tianjin. In that year, also, Bystronics, which had grown into the group's largest single business, extended its sales network through the purchases of Pullmax Ltd. UK and Pullmax Scandinavia AB.

By mid-decade, Conzzeta's diversification strategy appeared well on its way, as the group's sales topped CHF 1 billion. In 2006, the company completed its exit from building materials, selling off its architectural paints operations, as well as its Prebeton subsidiary, which producted prefabricated concrete components. With its new orientation, Conzzeta looked forward to celebrating its 100th anniverary in 2012.

M. L. Cohen

PRINCIPAL SUBSIDIARIES

Bystronic Laser AG; Bystronic Maschinen AG; Cox Automation Systems, Inc. (USA); FoamPartner Fritz Nauer AG; Mammut Sports Group AG; Plazza Immobilien; Schmid Rhyner AG; Seckler AG.

PRINCIPAL DIVISIONS

Machinery and Systems Engineering; Automation Systems; Foam Materials; Sporting Goods; Real Estate.

PRINCIPAL COMPETITORS

Diethelm Keller Holding Ltd; Georg Fischer AG; Bon appetit Group AG; Valora Holding AG; Galenica Ltd; SGS Societe Generale de Surveillance Holding S.A; SaurerGroup; SYNTHES Inc; Alea Europe Ltd;

FURTHER READING

"Akzo Acquires Paints Producer in Switzerland," *Chemical Week*, May 4, 2005, p. 7.

"Bystronic Acquires Sales Companies in Great Britain and Sweden," *Hugin*, January 10, 2005.

"Climb High to Broaden Line after Purchase by Swiss Firm," *Sporting Goods Business*, December 8, 2000, p. 26.

"Conzzeta Holding Acquires US Automation Company Cox Automation Systems, LLC," *Hugin*, September 1, 2005.

"Conzzeta Holding Sells the Business Activities of PREBETON SA to a Subsidiary of Element Integral AG," *Hugin*, January 18, 2006.

"Conzzeta Holding Sells the Business Activities of Siegfried Keller AG to Ampack AG," *Hugin*, February 10, 2006.

"Conzzeta Holding: Bystronic Glass Acquires Canadian Start-up Company Intra and Establishes a Foothold in PVC Window Manufacturing Technology," *Hugin*, November 30, 2005.

Eiselin, Stefan, "Man Verstickt Sich Nicht in Details," *Tages-Anzeiger*, February 15, 2005.

"Switzerland: Camion to Make Acquisition," *Neue Zuercher Zeitung*, March 25, 2000, p. 14.

Correos y Telegrafos S.A.

Via Dublin 7
Madrid,
Spain
Telephone: +34 91 596 30 60
Fax: +34 91 596 37 72
Web site: http://www.correos.es

State-Owned Company
Founded: 1889 as Ceurpo de Correos
Employees: 64,000
Sales: EUR 1.85 billion ($2.5 billion) (2005)
NAIC: 541990 All Other Professional, Scientific and Technical Services

■ ■ ■

Correos y Telegrafos S.A. (known simply as Correos) is Spain's dominant postal service, providing deliveries of more than 5.5 million letters and parcels each year. Correos, a limited liability company wholly owned by the Spanish government, operates a national network of more than 10,000 facilities, including more than 1,900 multi-service branches, nearly 2,000 distribution centers, and more than 8,600 service centers providing postal and delivery service to the country's rural regions. The company also offers online fax, telegram, and digital delivery services. Altogether, Correos employs more than 64,000 people, and posts annual revenues of more than EUR 1.8 billion ($2.5 billion). In addition to regular mail delivery, Correos operates three subsidiaries. Chronoexprés is the group's express delivery wing, operating 57 offices and a fleet of 2,500 vehicles, with total

deliveries of more than 1.2 million per year. Correo Hibrid specializes in providing mass-media communication services to corporations. The company's Correo Telecom provides telecommunications services, including internet access and e-commerce services.

ROOTS IN THE MIDDLE AGES

The modern Correos inherited a role as Spain's central postal service with a history stretching back into the Middle Ages when messenger services were placed under the authority of King Pedro of Aragon. Over time, the position of Royal Postmaster became an important function within the Spanish kingdom.

Spain played a role in the origins of the modern international postal system as well. In the late 15th century, the Tassis family, led by Francisco de Tassis (also known as Franz von Taxis) established a postal service in Italy. Tassis and brothers Ruggiero and Leonardo later extended their postal services to other parts of the Holy Roman Empire, while another brother, Janetto, was appointed Italy's Chief Master of Postal Services. The family then added postal service to Rome and Naples. At the end of the century, the Tassis' horse-based postal service linked Milan and Vienna; and by the beginning of the new century, the Tassis had added Belgium. In 1506, the Tassis were granted royal approval to establish and operate a postal service to Spain as well. Within a decade, the Tassis postal network been extended to Germany and France. By then, the Tassis's postal service had become indispensable to the Habsburg empire, and the family had been granted a monopoly on postal services throughout the Habsburg empire. This

The aim of our company is to provide a universal postal service, by offering the maximum quality and regularity, affordably and efficiently. This legal commitment is supported by its image as the established benchmark in the post office sector. We are focused on a service offer that meets the increasing needs of users and clients, along with trying to professionally train and develop its employees. The main priorities for all areas and for all the people in the Correos are quality, efficiency, and innovation. We are leaders in the post office sector in Spain in all aspects related to the non-urgent delivery of documentation and merchandise.

monopoly was extended to Spain after the split between the Spanish and Austrian Habsburgs in the 1520s. The Tassis family, which had already been granted titles of nobility in the early 16th century, remained in control of the Holy Roman Empire postal monopoly for centuries.

In Spain, the Tassis family sold their postal service to the new Spanish royal court, when the House of Bourbon, led by Phillip V, ascended to the throne. Under the new king, the Tassis postal service in Spain was placed under direct government operation, becoming a public service for the first time. The Spanish government soon began codifying the postal service's operations, enacting the first round of legislation in 1720. This was later reinforced by the Post Office Act of 1743. In 1755, under the leadership of Rodriguez de Campomanes, the Spanish postal service invented home delivery, establishing the new position of postman. De Campomanes became a prominent figure under the court of King Charles III, playing a important role in developing the country's economy. Under de Campomanes, the Spanish postal service established fixed postal rates and introduced such common features as mailboxes and post codes.

Through the 19th century, however, the postal service remained relatively small, in part because postal fees were more commonly paid by the recipient. This changed in 1850, when the postal service issued its first stamp. With fees now paid up front by the sender, the postal service grew rapidly.

Two years later, another major part of the later Correos y Telegrafos was established: the Spanish telegraph office. The first telegraph line, linking Madrid and Irun, was completed in 1854. In 1855, the passage of new legislation authorized the creation of a national telegraph network, with a mandate to extend the network throughout the country, as well as linking to France and Portugal. That same year, the first public telegraph service began operations. Just ten years later, Spain boasted more than 11,000 kilometers of telegraph lines and a network of 215 offices.

MODERNIZING INTO THE 20TH CENTURY

The creation of Spain's first railroads in the 1880s brought a new expansion to postal services, greatly reducing transportation times and costs. Into the later part of the century, the invention of the bicycle and the automobile provided still greater growth to the country's postal service. In 1889, this service was placed under a new government-controlled office, the Cuerpo de Correos, which took over the monopoly on the country's postal deliveries. In 1900, the company completed its transportation network with the takeover of the country's marine mail operations, controlled by the Spanish Transatlantic Company since the late 1880s. This extended Correos's reach to Spain's outlying islands, as well as to its colonial possessions in North Africa. Despite the introduction of the new transportation methods, horseback delivery remained a feature of the Spanish postal system into the 1920s.

A reform of the country's postal and telegraph sectors under new legislation passed in 1909 created a new organization, Servicio de Correos y Telegrafos. The post office then launched a modernization effort, which included the introduction of a number of new products. Among these were the creation of the Post Office Savings Bank and the introduction of postal money orders. In 1919, the service created a dedicated airmail delivery unit, just two years after the first airmail deliveries launched in Italy.

Still, the automobile became the group's primary means for transport during the early decades of the new century. From just 18 vehicles in service in 1906, Correos' fleet swelled to more than 1,600 by the 1931. The post office had also expanded its network of facilities and by the middle of the 1930s already operated from nearly 8,000 smaller branch and sorting offices, as well as nearly 1,400 main offices. The company's employee ranks had also topped 25,000 by then.

Correos became a central fixture in Spain, not only through its postal services, but also through its savings bank operations. By the outbreak of the Spanish Civil War, Correos already accounted for some 40 percent of the country's savings accounts.

KEY DATES

1506: Tassis family granted monopoly to develop and operate postal service in Spain.

1720: Spanish government under King Philip V buys postal service from Tassis family and institutes first postal legislation.

1755: Postal service launches home delivery, hiring the first mail carriers.

1850: Postal service issues first stamp in Spain.

1852: Establishment of telegraph operations in Spain.

1889: Creation of Ceurpo de Correos, which takes over state postal monopoly.

1900: Correos acquires control of marine mail operations, including deliveries to Canary Islands and North Africa.

1919: Airmail delivery service debuts.

1960: Spanish postal sector is liberalized, and Correos faces competition from private sector.

1981: Domestic express mail delivery service, Correos Exprés, is launched.

1983: International express service, Postal Exprés Internacional, is launched.

1992: Correos y Telegrafos is restructured as a commercial operation.

1997: Operations are restructured as state-owned corporation.

2001: Correos is restructured as limited liability company owned by Spanish government; it merges express service with France's La Poste express service in Spain, creating Chrono-Exprés

2006: Correos launches network of 30,000 Telecentros Internet access terminals for rural market.

The war cut sharply into the Correos's operations, precipitating an extended drop in deliveries, which continued through World War II, as well as the closing of a large number of offices. The service's operations remained on a reduced scale through the end of the 1940s, in large part due to the Franco dictatorship's isolationist policies. By the early 1950s, however, Correos's volumes once again returned to prewar levels.

The 1950s were to mark a new period of expansion for the service, as the Franco regime changed tact, adopting a policy of liberalizing the country's economy.

As a result, Correos grew rapidly through the 1950s and into the 1960s, as its volumes more than tripled.

The liberalization of the Spanish economy provided a huge boost for the country during the 1960s and 1970s, further stimulating Correos's own growth. By the beginning of the 1980s, the service had already topped delivery volumes of more than 4.5 billion letters and parcels per year. Correos's growth came in spite of the fact that Spain was one of the first in Europe to liberalize the post delivery sector, allowing private postal carriers to operate since 1960. Nonetheless, Correos remained the country's dominant postal provider.

NEW STRUCTURE FOR THE 21ST CENTURY

The existence of private competitors encouraged Correos to develop new products and services. In 1981, for example, the post office launched its own express mail operation, Correos Exprés, which began operating both national and internationally. For the international market, the company developed a dedicated international rush service, Postal Exprés Internacional.

Into the 1990s, the Spanish government began taking steps to reshape the Spanish postal service in order to prepare it for the coming liberalization of the European market. In 1992, Correos restructured as an Autonomous State Entity, becoming a commercially oriented body for the first time. The service's restructuring continued through the decade, and in 1997, Correos's status was changed again, becoming a state-owned corporation. This led to a further restructuring in 2001, when Correos was transformed into a fully fledged limited liability company. Nonetheless, into the mid-2000s, the Spanish government retained 100 percent control of the post office.

Through the fist half of the new decade, Correos launched an large-scale investment drive in order to increase its delivery capacity while reducing its operating costs. In 2000, for example, the company began a EUR 240 million spending effort in order to upgrade its automated sorting capacity. The following year, the company spent nearly EUR 50 million opening 54 new branches; the company also began renovating a number of its existing offices.

Correos also worked to develop new products and services. In 2001, the company signed an agreement with La Poste of France to combine their Spanish-based express parcel delivery services into a single entity, ChronoExprés. The company boosted that operation the following year, with the takeover of majority control of another express courier service, Servipack. Also that year, Correos turned to the Internet, opening an online office allowing customers to register parcels, print documents, send faxes, among other services. The company deepened its online operations in 2002, with a plan to launch Internet access, as well as fixed and mobile telecom, television, and other services through its national branch network. For this effort, the company formed a partnership with Telecom, owned by the El Corte Ingles group. In 2005, Correos continued to expand its telecommunications operations, contracting with Telefonica to upgrade and manage the company telephone and internet system. This enabled the company to launch a new online service in 2006, a network of 30,000 Telecentros terminals providing Internet access and online services to Spain's rural markets. With a history reaching back more than 300 years, a thoroughly modern Correos turned its attention to its growth into the future.

M. L. Cohen

PRINCIPAL SUBSIDIARIES

Chronoexprés S.A.; Correo Híbrido S.A.; Correos Telecom S.A.

PRINCIPAL COMPETITORS

El Corte Ingles S.A.; LOGISTA S.A.; Solred S.A.; Telefonica Publicidad e Informacion S.A.; Atento Telecomunicaciones España S.A.; Telvent GIT S.A.; Teleinformatica y Comunicaciones S.A.; Grandes Almacenes FNAC España S.A.; Sociedad General de Autores y Editores de España; Conway, The Convenience Company S.A.; Tecnatom S.A.

FURTHER READING

Bahamonde Magro, A., Martínez Lorente, and G. y Otero Carvajal, L.E.: *El Palacio de Comunicaciones. Un siglo de historia de Correos y Telégrafos*, Madrid: E.P.E. Correos y Telégrafos, 2000.

"Correos Deals with the 'Digital Divide,'" *ePostal News*, March 13, 2006, p. 3.

"Correos to Open Online Office," *Expansion*, October 11, 2002.

"Correos y Telegrafos Expansion Project," *Expansion*, May 1, 2001, p. 7.

"Correos y Telegrafos: mas oficinas con servicios para moviles," *Expansion*, October 4, 2002.

"Post Office to Extend its Services," *EuropeMedia*, August 13, 2002.

"Telefonica Wins EUR 74.8 Mln Correos y Telegrafos Contract," *Telecompaper Europe*, December 7, 2005.

"Vista Capital Exits Courier Service," *European Venture Capital Journal*, October 2002, p. 23.

Crocs, Inc.

———— ■ ————

6273 Monarch Park Place
Niwot, Colorado 80503
U.S.A.
Telephone: (303) 468-4260
Fax: (303) 468-4266
Web site: http://www.crocs.com

Public Company
Incorporated: 1999 as Western Brands LLC
Employees: 260
Sales: $108.6 million
Stock Exchanges: NASDAQ
Ticker Symbol: CROX
NAIC: 316219 Other Footwear Manufacturing

■ ■ ■

Crocs, Inc., is a Colorado maker of unique clogs that became extremely popular in the early 2000s with both men and women. The inexpensive shoes rely on a proprietary closed-cell resin material called Croslite to produce a lightweight, slip-resistant, odor-resistant, non-marking sole. The material also softens with body heat, thus molding the shoe to the foot of the wearer and providing a comfortable fit. Originally intended for use on boats and in other outdoor activities like hiking, fishing, and gardening, Crocs has also found a market with working people who spend a lot of time in their feet, such as health care and restaurant workers. Moreover, Crocs, generally considered an ugly shoe, has attracted the attention of celebrities, thereby making them fashionable. The shoe features a removable back

strap available in 20 colors. In some circles, essentially younger girls, these straps are traded among wearers to provide a different look. Because of their broad appeal, Crocs are available through numerous distribution channels: traditional footwear retailers, sporting goods and outdoor retailers, department stores, uniform suppliers, specialty food retailers, gift shops, health and beauty stores, and catalogs. The company also sells the shoes on its Web site and in kiosks located in places with heavy foot traffic. In addition to the United States, Crocs are sold in more than 40 countries. Beyond its signature clogs, Crocs has taken steps to extend its brand to include clothing, hats, sunglasses, gardening kneepads, and other products. The company maintains manufacturing facilities in Canada, Italy, Mexico, and China. Crocs is a public company listed on the NASDAQ.

END-OF-CENTURY ORIGINS

Before assuming its current name, Crocs was originally Western Brands, LLC, formed in Colorado in 1999. The origins of the Crocs clogs, however, date to 2002, and the shared inspiration of the company's three founders: George B. Boedecker, Jr., Lyndon V. Hanson III, and Scott Seamans. All three were Boulder, Colorado, entrepreneurs. Boedecker was involved in the fast food business, a founder of Oregon Food Concepts LLC, a major franchiser of Quizno's in the western United States. Prior to that, he operated more than 100 Domino Pizza franchises. Boedecker was a high school friend of Hanson, and later both attended the University of Colorado, where Hanson received a master's degree in marketing. He also earned a B.S. in Finance from the University of Wyoming. Hanson then spent 17 years

Despite our rapid success, we still stand behind the core values of Crocs Footwear. We are committed to making a lightweight, comfortable, slip-resistant, fashionable and functional shoe that can be produced quickly and at an affordable price to our customers.

involved in sales and management in the computer hardware, software, and financial services fields. Seamans was another friend of Boedecker. For more than 14 years he ran his own company designing and manufacturing professional photography and related medical equipment, and he held a number of patents for his work in materials engineering and process development. He sold his company in 1996, gaining the free time and financial wherewithal to indulge his twin pastimes: skiing and sailing.

Boedecker shared Seaman's passion for sailing. In 2002 they came across a new boating clog produced by a Canadian Company, Foam Creations, Inc. The Quebec company's closed-cell resin allowed the shoe to be lighter than traditional, rubber-soled boat shoes, and because it molded to the shape of a person's foot it was even less likely to slip on a wet boat deck. In addition, the material absorbed a minimum of odors and the clog design insured that it was well ventilated. While on a sailing trio from Islas, Mexico, to Ft. Lauderdale, Florida, in May 2002, the two friends discussed improvements on the Foam Creation's design and decided they wanted to market this ideal boat shoe. When they returned home they brought in Hanson and acquired the rights to Foam Creations' manufacturing process through Western Brands.

Seamans tweaked the design of the shoe while Boedecker took over as chief executive officer and lined up a host of small investors. Hanson set up most of the operation and oversaw the running of it. As a name for the shoe they settled on Crocs, an abbreviation of crocodile, because the attributes of the animal fit the product: comfortable both on the land and in the water, strong, and long-living. Because they also wanted to convey a sense of fun, the founders played on the non-slip properties of the shoe to coin a initial marketing tagline: "Get a Grip." This playful attitude would also lead to the various colors in which the clogs were offered.

EARLY 21ST CENTURY DEBUT

The Crocs clog made its debut in November 2002 at the Ft. Lauderdale International Boat Show with its first model, "The Beach." Attendees snapped up all 1,000 pairs the company had to offer. Even more important to the growth of the brand was the enthusiastic reception the shoes received from the retailers and sales representatives at its first footwear exhibition, the March 2003 Shoe Market of the Americas. Western Brands quickly lined up retail accounts, which within a year approached 300 in number. The shoe sold well with boaters, but according to *CSIndy*, the shoe quickly won "converts among landlubbers, too. People who spent long hours on their feet, such as restaurant workers and hospital employees, like the softness and the loose fit. They were less expensive than, say, traditional surgical clogs, and they cleaned up nicely in the dishwasher, eliminating unsightly food splatters and body fluids." Moreover, the report continued, "Baby boomers with swollen feet and fallen arches liked the way Crocs felt on hardwood floors. Middle school trend-setters tripped on the bright colors. Gardeners dug the fact that you could hose them off." During their first full year on the market, 76,000 pairs of Crocs were sold, generating 1.2 million in sales. Just one year later, Western Brands sold 649,000 pairs, resulting in revenues of $12.3 million.

Manufacturing to this point had been handled by Foam Creations in Canada. Crocs were proving so successful that in 2004 Western Brands acquired Foam Creations, picking up the rights to Croslite as well as the manufacturing facilities. The company prepared to go public, with the first step coming early in 2005 when Boedecker stepped down as CEO in favor of Ronald R. Snyder. Boedecker remained involved in marketing and continued to serve on the board of directors. His 48-year-old successor, another University of Colorado graduate, had been serving as a consultant for the past year. Snyder was a former vice president of a San Jose, California, electronics company, Flextronics International, which had acquired a Colorado electronics company, Dii Group, he had co-founded. Snyder was well familiar with growing companies, in charge of global sales and marketing as well as mergers and acquisitions when Dii increased its worth from $20 million to $17 billion. His international experience would be put to use as Crocs began establishing distribution operations in Europe and throughout the Pacific Rim. He had also experienced the rigors of taking a company public, completing an initial public offering of stock for Dii in 1993. At the same time as Snyder's hiring, Crocs beefed up its management team with the addition of Caryn Ellison as the new chief financial officer. She had previously served as the president of Classic Sport, a Colorado manufacturer of sporting goods.

1999: Western Brands LLC is formed.
2002: The Crocs shoe is first unveiled at a boat show.
2005: Ronald Sndyer is named CEO.
2006: The company is taken public.

In the spring of 2005, Crocs took another step as it laid the foundation for an initial public offering (IPO), unveiling plans for a new line of apparel and accessories. According to *Rocky Mountain News,* "Small companies wanting to go public often need to branch out first to convince investors they can keep growing over the long haul. Such a strategy would help Crocs fend off competition from others who attempt to copy the Crocs shoe concept." Soon the company was hawking T-shirts, hats, and other items bearing its smiling crocodile logo, such as sunglasses and gardening kneepads. At the same time, Crocs continued to bring out new models of its signature clogs. By the end of the year Crocs could be found in nine models and 17 colors.

Crocs also launched its first national marketing campaign in 2005 to increase the brand's visibility with both consumers and potential investors. The Boulder, Colorado-based shop of TDA Advertising & Design was hired to develop the campaign. Heading the effort was TDA's Jonathan Schoenberg, who began wearing Crocs while traveling as a way to generate some inspiration. According to *Denver Business Journal,* people at airports "would come up to him and say, 'Those are so ugly; where can I get a pair?' It was like a scene from a bad sitcom," said Schoenberg. "I was struggling to find an ad campaign and people were walking up and giving it to me." The result was the "Ugly Can Be Beautiful" print ad campaign. It featured lifestyle shots that poked fun at the clogs' hardly glamorous look. The ads appeared in such national magazines as *Vanity Fair, Rolling Stone, GQ, Men's Journal,* and *Real Simple,* as well as regional magazines on the East and West Coasts, such as *Time Out New York.* Sales for Crocs were already on a sharp upward trend, but the advertising played its part in selling more than 6 million pairs of shoes and achieving $108.8 million in sales in 2005. The company also turned its first net profit, $16.7 million, after losing $1.6 million the year before. *Footwear News* named Crocs its brand of the year in 2005.

GOING PUBLIC IN 2006

The company had already dropped the Western Brands name, adopting Crocs, Inc., in January 2005. In preparation for going public it was then reincorporated in Delaware in June 2005. However, Snyder and his team, along with lead underwriters Piper Jaffray & Co. and Thomas Weisel Partners Group Inc. took their time putting Crocs on the market, spending the rest of the year and the early weeks of 2006 in laying the groundwork for the IPO. In its presentation to investors Crocs revealed plans that called for new shoe models, increased distribution both in the United States and globally, and the pursuit of a Crocs store-within-a-store concept with leading retailers. Dick's Sporting Goods chain was already interested in trying out the idea in 15 to 20 of its locations.

As investor interest in Crocs grew, the company was able to increase its asking price as well as the number of shares it was putting on the market. Initially the company planned to sell 9.9 million shares at a price of $13 to $15 per share. Crocs was able to add more than a million shares and bump its asking price to the $19 to $20 range. A lot of that interest came late as many Wall Street firms that liked to invest in consumer-goods companies were distracted by a heavy load of stock offerings and only began to focus on Crocs in the final hours before its IPO. They generally liked what they saw: a company enjoying exceptional growth and a product that had broad demographic appeal.

In the end, Crocs increased its asking price to $21 a share when the offering was conducted in the first week of February 2006. Almost $208 million was raised, of which $97 million went to current shareholders, including the company's three founders. Early backers of the company were also handsomely recompensed for their participation. They were an assorted lot, including a bodybuilder, a retired architect (Hanson's father), and a boat captain—Ron Oliver, a friend of Seamans who ran a distribution center in Miami in the early days and took stock in exchange for his labor. He received nearly $2 million from the offering and still held shares worth another $9.6 million. The company itself netted $87 million. All told, it was the largest IPO ever for a footwear manufacturer, far exceeding Fila Holdings' $135 million and Nine West's $140 million offerings, both IPOs conducted in 1993.

The enthusiasm for Crocs continued after the IPO, as the shares began trading on the NASDAQ and quickly increased in value by 55 percent before settling down. The company did not rest on its laurels, however, quickly launching a new women's shoe model and its first children's style. A few weeks later it announced plans to open its first concept stores in Austria and Sweden. The company also made inroads in the United Kingdom, inking a deal with giant shoe retailer Clarks to carry the clogs. Crocs also benefited from the large number of celebrities spotted wearing the clogs, such as Faith Hill, Tim McGraw, Ben Affleck, and Jennifer Garner. Another sign of success was the appearance of knock-offs. In February and March 2006 Crocs received patents from the U.S. Patent and Trademark office that covered its manufacturing processes and features related to the styling of several Crocs models. Crocs wasted little time in seeking injunction against 11 companies making similar clogs, claiming patent infringement. It was all part of the growing process for a young, successful company in the contemporary business world.

Ed Dinger

PRINCIPAL SUBSIDIARIES

Crocs Retail, Inc.; Foam Creations, Inc.; Crocs Online, Inc.; Western Brands Holding Company, Inc.

PRINCIPAL COMPETITORS

Deckers Outdoor Corporation; NIKE, Inc.; The Timberland Company.

FURTHER READING

Avery, Greg, "Crocs Fights Knockoffs," *Daily Camera (Boulder, Colo.),* April 4, 2006.

Bryer, Amy, "Crocs: Love Us for Our Sole, Not Looks," *Denver Business Journal,* September 12, 2005.

Kelley, Joanne, "Crocs' Amazing Feat Fuels IPO Rumors," *Rocky Mountain News,* May 26, 2005, p. 1B.

———, "In Short Time, Crocs Shows It Has Legs," *Rocky Mountain News,* February 8, 2006, p. 5B.

Newman, Eric, "Crocs IPO Rallies on Wall Street," *Footwear News,* February 13, 2006, p. 2.

Prendergast, Alan, "A Really Big Shoe," *CSIndy,* November 24-30, 2005.

Scardino, Emily, "Croc Attack," *Footwear News,* December 5, 2005, p. 28.

Schneider, Barbara, "Crocs Rock," *Footwear News,* February 9, 2004, p. 122.

THE DIXIE GROUP

The Dixie Group, Inc.

345 Nowlin Lane, Suite B
1100 South Watkins Street
Chattanooga, Tennessee 37421-7805
U.S.A.
Telephone: (706) 876-5800
Toll Free: (866) 274-9776
Fax: (706) 876-5896
Web site: http://www.thedixiegroup.com

Public Company
Founded: 1920 as Dixie Mercerizing Company
Employees: 1,400
Sales: $318.5 million (2005)
Stock Exchanges: NASDAQ
Ticker Symbol: DXYN
NAIC: 314110 Carpet and Rug Mills; 2200 Textile Mill
    Products

■ ■ ■

Once a leading textile company, The Dixie Group, Inc., began manufacturing floorcoverings in the late 1990s when it could no longer compete with the burgeoning foreign textile market. Dixie struggled between 1993 and 2003 to find a niche in floorcoverings. At first Dixie executives were hesitant to compete directly with the two industry leaders: Shaw Industries, Inc. and Mohawk Industries, Inc. Dixie eventually succeeded by manufacturing several lines of high-quality carpets and rugs. Facilities that did not manufacture high-quality carpet or its materials were eventually sold to pay off the company's debt. In 2003 Dixie was excelling with its

three floorcoverings brands: Dixie Home, Fabrica, and Masland Carpets. The Masland brand made up over half of Dixie's sales in 2005.

EARLY YEARS: 1920–1950

In 1920, several Chattanooga hosiery mill owners and other business leaders founded the Dixie Mercerizing Company to specially treat cotton yarn which was then used to make ladies' stockings. Two of the investors were J. T. Lupton and Cartter Lupton who became, respectively, president and treasurer of the company. In its first year Dixie had sales of $1.8 million and a profit of $56,784.

Named for a British calico printer, the mercerizing process used sodium hydroxide to shrink cotton yarn. This gave the yarn a silklike luster, popular for stockings, and also made it better able to hold dye. The company's biggest problem was finding an adequate supply of quality yarn that could stand up under the high tension required for mercerizing.

The owners of the nearby Dixie Spinning Mills, including the Luptons, decided to build a modern spinning plant to meet that need. According to Dixie's 75th anniversary publication, "a 'model town with 72 artistically designed homes' along with playgrounds and a school were part of the plans for what would become known as Lupton City." The venture eventually cost $9 million. In 1925, Dixie Spinning Mills merged with Dixie Mercerizing Company. During the mid-20s, J. Burton Frierson became treasurer of Dixie.

The company remained profitable during the

Depression, and in 1936, added to its production capability with the purchase of the Durham Hosiery Mills in North Carolina. During World War II, Dixie supplied the military and, experimenting with the "miracle fibers" developed during the war, was among the first spinners in the world to make synthetic yarn for military shoe laces.

After the war, J. Burton Frierson was named president and started expanding the company again. The company purchased two plants in North Carolina and in 1950 built a new spinning plant at Lupton to produce synthetic yarn.

DIVERSIFICATION, 1951–1979

In 1951, Dixie began to diversify, moving into the making of carpet yarn with the purchase of Dalton Candlewick, spinners of cotton yarn for the high-volume tufting industry. In 1963, Frierson retired as president, becoming chairman of the board.

The Candlewick business grew quickly in the 1960s and 1970s, taking up to a 10 percent share in the commodity nylon carpet yarn market. The company's core business had steady growth as well, producing yarns and threads for knitting, sewing, lace, braid, and related apparel uses. During this period Dixie commanded about 5 percent of the commodity apparel yarn market. Recognizing that the term mercerizing no longer reflected the scope of its operations, Dixie Mercerizing Company changed its name to Dixie Yarns, Inc., in December 1964.

To meet the demand for its yarns, the company built new plants for both Candlewick and the Apparel Yarn and Thread Division. It also bought Yarn Crafters, in 1968, and Southern Stretch Yarns, in 1969. Acquisitions continued during the 1970s, with the purchase of Sellers Manufacturing Co. & Sellers Dyeing Co. and the Jordan Spinning Co.

During this period, Don Frierson was named president of Candlewick. In 1979 he became Dixie's president and CEO when his father stepped down as chairman of the board. The senior Frierson had run the company for more than 40 years and the Frierson family had controlled the stock for nearly that long.

THE SPECIALTY YARN NICHE

In 1980, Dixie Yarns operated 17 plants in five states and had a workforce of some 5,000 employees. Revenues that year came to $217 million, with nearly 40 percent of sales coming from commodity apparel and carpet yarns. Those two markets were to prove vulnerable for the company. The surge of inexpensive, imported textiles from Taiwan, Hong Kong, and China severely reduced the demand among Dixie's clients for apparel yarn. At the same time, carpet manufacturers in the U.S. found they could save 10 to 15 percent on the cost of carpet yarn by spinning their own.

Rather than try to compete for those markets, Frierson's strategy was to switch to high-margin specialty yarns, essentially returning Dixie to its roots. As Alyssa Lappan explained in a 1988 *Forbes* article, "Cotton apparel yarn with a stretchable Lycra core costs more to manufacture than traditional, undyed commodity cotton yarn, but it also sells for about one-and-a-half times the price."

To carry out his plans, Frierson had to close plants, lay off 30 percent of the workforce, and change a 60-year corporate culture. He implemented profit sharing and quality circles and set a goal for managers of 20 percent pretax return on capital, backing it up with stock options and a cash bonus. Sales, service, and quality were the focus of staff training, augmented by $50 million spent on new equipment and product development labs.

Frierson also spent money on acquisitions. In 1986 he bought China Grove Cotton Mills Co., which gave Dixie entry into more specialty yarn markets with Nomex, a synthetic fiber used in fire-retardant clothing, and Kevlar, for bulletproof vests and uncuttable safety gloves. Late in the year he took Dixie public. The public offering involved complex stock transactions that enabled Frierson and other members of the management team to retain majority control of the stock and "keep Dixie beyond the reach of predators," according to a 1988 *Textile World* article.

Acquisitions and complex stock deals continued with the $78 million purchase in 1987 of Ti-Caro, Inc.

1920: Dixie Mercerizing Company is founded to specially treat cotton yarn.

1925: Dixie Spinning Mills merges with Dixie Mercerizing Company.

1950: New spinning plant opens in Lupton to produce synthetic yarn.

1964: Dixie Mercerizing Company changes its name to Dixie Yarns, Inc.

1979: Don Frierson becomes president and CEO.

1986: Dixie goes public.

1988: Dixie's revenue peaks at $606 million.

1997: Shareholders vote to change the company's name to The Dixie Group, Inc.

1999: The last of Dixie's textile facilities is sold and the company focuses on floorcoverings.

2000: Dixie's sales decline when the factory-built housing market suddenly plummets.

2003: Dixie sells more subsidiaries and focuses on its Dixie Home, Masland, and Fabrica products.

The addition of Ti-Caro involved Dixie in the making of knit fabrics for the first time through its Caro Knit division which produced 100 percent cotton knit fabrics. It also opened more than 15 new specialty yarn markets and made Dixie the country's leader in three major specialty markets: specialty yarns, knit fabrics, and carpet yarns. Dixie also became the largest supplier of industrial sewing thread used in items ranging from tea bags to baseballs. The two acquisitions doubled the size of the company and moved it to number seven among publicly held U.S. textile companies.

The industry recognized Frierson's talents and vision. He served as president of the American Yarn Spinners Association and chaired the American Textile Manufacturers Institute (ATMI) International Trade Committee. During 1988 alone, he was president of ATMI, chairman of the Fiber, Fabric and Apparel Coalition, and vice president of the National Cotton Council. That year, the editors of *Textile World* chose Frierson as the Textile Leader of the Year. In an interview with the magazine, Frierson described his business strategy: "Our basic markets are knit fabrics, threads, carpet yarns, and fine-count and specialty yarns. What we've tried to do is enhance our position in those four areas through increased productivity or plant improvement, through developing new processes or products, or through

acquisitions." Dixie's revenue in 1988 was $606 million, with the company employing almost 10,000 people in 36 plants. Those sale figures proved to be a peak for the company, however, as sales fell for the next four years.

FOCUS ON FLOOR COVERINGS AND CONSUMER PRODUCTS

Frierson continued to consolidate facilities, cut payroll costs, and modernize the company's equipment, spending over $154 million on capital improvements between 1988 and 1993. Frierson's goal was fairly straightforward: to shift the company's emphasis from producing yarn and textiles for manufacturers to making consumer products with its own yarn and textiles itself. The most reasonable area to focus on was carpets since the company's Candlewick Yarns already was one of the country's largest producers of high-quality yarn used to make carpets for homes and businesses, bath and accent rugs, and floorcoverings for cars.

The carpet industry was going through a period of major consolidations during the early part of the decade, and Frierson made his move in 1993. He began with the acquisition of Carriage Industries. That 24-year-old company was based in Georgia and made carpets for modular homes, recreational vehicles, and trade show industries. Major clients included Fleetwood Enterprises and Homes by Oakwood. The purchase included Carriage's subsidiary, Bretlin, Inc., which specialized in making durable indoor/outdoor needlebond carpets and runners, floor mats, and decorative accent rugs. The Bretlin Broadloom products were sold at home centers, mass marketers, and independent retailers including Home Depot, Lowe's, and Payless.

Dixie already owned shares in Masland Carpets, a manufacturer of high-end, designer-oriented carpets and rugs for the residential and commercial markets, and bought the entire company later that year. In 1994, Dixie bought California-based Patrick Carpet Mills and incorporated it into Masland, marketing its product line under the name Patrick Carpet. Masland customers included Nordstroms, Hilton Hotels, and Applebee's International, and the company was a partner in the DuPont Commercial Flooring Systems Network. At the end of 1996 Dixie bought Danube Carpet Mills, Inc., from Shelter Components Corporation for approximately $25 million. Danube made carpets for the same markets as Carriage Industries and its carpet manufacturing operations were consolidated into Carriage's facilities. Its carpet yarn plant became part of Dixie's Candlewick division.

Between 30 to 40 percent of Candlewick's yarns went to the companies in Dixie's floorcovering business.

Other customers included Magee Automotive Products, Bentley Mills, Regal Rugs, and Fieldcrest. Frierson's research and development efforts at Candlewick led to the development of Weave-Tech, a spun yarn with a spandex core, and Naturesse, a heatset cotton yarn designed for bathroom rugs, which combines the aesthetics of cotton with the durability of synthetics. Three years after the purchase of Carriage Industries, the floorcovering business accounted for two-thirds of Dixie's sales.

The other part of the business, yarns and fabric, also underwent changes during the 1990s. Frierson's strategy in this area was to continue building on Dixie's niche of cotton and high performance specialty synthetic yarns while growing its own apparel business. As with floorcoverings, his goal was to manufacture consumer products.

Dixie Yarns continued to be the foundation for the company's textile/apparel business. While it still produced mercerized high-luster cotton, it also manufactured and marketed Supima and Pima cottons, combed and carded ring spun yarns, and Corespun yarns containing Lycra. Its spinning facilities produced DuPont's Thermastat and Coolmax polyester fibers and Courtauld's Tencel, a Lyocell fiber. By the mid-1990s, Dixie Yarns was providing yarn to seven different markets in addition to various specialty markets: high-end upholstery, home furnishings, sportswear, hosiery, sweaters, underwear, and automotive body cloth.

Caro Knit, which was part of the Ti-Caro acquisition in 1987, continued to produce 100 percent cotton knit fabrics for retailers such as J.C. Penney and Brooks Brothers, catalog retailers including Lands' End and L.L. Bean, and sportswear manufacturer Ralph Lauren/Polo. However, as part of Dixie's customer product focus, Caro Knit began operating as a vertical company, using yarn from Dixie Yarns to make its fabric which was then turned into knit sports apparel by C-Knit, the third company in Dixie's textile and apparel business.

C-Knit began operating in 1995, providing cutting operations in South Carolina to prepare components that were shipped to plants controlled by Dixie in Central America where they were sewn into garments. The finished pieces were then shipped back to C-Knit warehouses in the U.S. ready to be sent to customers. Most of the garments were shirts—polo, henley, crew neck, and fleece—for customers including Ashworth, Coca-Cola, and Cumberland Bay by Fruit of the Loom.

In 1996, Dixie sold its Threads USA division to American & Efird, Inc., a subsidiary of Ruddick Corporation, further honing its concentration on floorcovering and textile/apparel. More than half of Dixie's sales for the year were for consumer products, and the company redesigned its administrative and operating procedures and created a new management structure to respond more quickly and flexibly to changes in the markets.

FURTHER RESTRUCTURING: 1997 AND BEYOND

In May 1997, shareholders voted to change the company's name to The Dixie Group, Inc. With increased sales for the first quarter of 1997 in both its business segments, it appeared that the years of restructuring had served their purpose. Frierson did not, however, rule out additional, "strategically appropriate acquisitions" to augment Dixie's growth. By the end of the 1990s Frierson realized that he needed to end the company's 80-year legacy as a textile enterprise and focus entirely on floorcoverings. Originally Frierson thought that if Dixie found a niche within textiles, the company could survive, but Dixie desperately needed help from the federal government to compete against overseas textiles. "We decided we had to become more efficient, but even that doesn't work when your (foreign) competition has subsidized raw material, subsidized loans, subsidized currencies, lower wages and not the same environmental regulations," Frierson said in a December 1, 2002, interview with Bob Gary, Jr., of the *Chattanooga Times.* In 1998 Dixie began aggressively selling off its textile factories and using the cash to pay off debt. The final textile operation was sold in early 1999.

With shareholders waiting to see what Dixie would do after selling the textile facilities, Dixie executives did not think the company would yield results by manufacturing residential carpet. Dixie first targeted niche markets within the floorcoverings industry to avoid a head-to-head competition with the two largest residential carpet manufacturers: Shaw Industries, Inc. and Mohawk Industries, Inc. The strategy backfired after Dixie acquired Bretlin's outdoor carpet products and Home Depot suddenly increased its orders. The sudden demand made it difficult for Dixie to monitor product quality and keep costs low. "We grew extremely rapidly with Home Depot—candidly, more rapidly than we could control, service and execute," Frierson said in the *Chattanooga Times.* "We were out of control in terms of quality and cost."

Besides the problem with outdoor carpet, Dixie struggled with another niche market. Carriage and other brands owned by Dixie established the company as the industry leader for carpet installed in factory-built homes. The niche composed 20 percent of Dixie's annual sales. When the factory-built housing market suddenly plummeted in 2000, Dixie's profits suffered.

To survive, the company sold some of its factories with high operating costs. Other streamlining measures were made. Between 2000 and 2002 Dixie laid off 27 percent of its work force. It consolidated its dye and tufting facilities from several to only one each. It also centralized its distribution centers to only one location. The profit from selling unwanted facilities during the two-year period was later used to pay off more than $110 million of debt.

Dixie then launched Dixie Home, a line of affordable carpet that Frierson believed would complement his company's high-end Masland and Fabrica products. The Dixie Home startup costs and rising prices for raw materials adversely affected profits in 2003, but Frierson believed that the setback was only temporary. The company focused entirely on its three carpet and rug lines after 2003. The outdoor-carpet brand Carriage, which had generated a large percentage of Dixie's sales in the mid-1990s, was sold to Shaw.

Streamlining the company and focusing on high-end carpet and rugs improved Dixie's stock price and sales. Between August 2003 and March 2005 the company's stock jumped from $3 to $19 per share. The company's sales soared as well. From 2003 to 2005 Dixie's reported revenue rose from $234.1 million to $318.5 million.

Ellen D. Wernick
Updated, Kevin Teague

PRINCIPAL SUBSIDIARIES

Carriage Industries, Inc.; Candlewick-Ringgold, Inc.; Candlewick-Lemoore, Inc.; Dixie Experts, Inc.; Dixie Funding, Inc.; Candlewick Ringgold, Inc.; Fabrica International Masland Carpets, Inc.; Patrick Carpet Mills, Inc.; T-C Threads, Inc.; Threads of Puerto Rico, Inc.

PRINCIPAL COMPETITORS

Beaulieu Group, LLC; Interface, Inc.; Shaw Industries, Inc.; Mannington Mills, Inc.; Wilsonart International, Inc.; Armstrong World Industries, Inc.; Couristan Inc.; Tarkett Inc.

FURTHER READING

Christiansen, Larry, and Jan Sheehy, "Dixie's Dan Frierson Accentuates the Positive," *Textile World,* October 1988, p. 47.

"The Dixie Group Announces Management Change," *Business Wire,* October 7, 1999.

"The Dixie Group Sells Yarn Facility in Ranlo, North Carolina," *Business Wire,* May 28, 1999.

"The Dixie Group Reports Third Quarter Earnings Per Share Up 86%," *Business Wire,* October 27, 1999.

"Dixie Yarns Capitalizes on Auto Yarn Quality," *Textile World,* February 1989, p. 48.

Dixie Yarns: Seventy-Five Years of Workin' Together, Chattanooga, Tenn., 1995.

Gary, Bob, Jr., "Chattanooga, Tenn.–based Carpet Maker's Sales Jump 26 Percent," *Chattanooga Times/Free Press* (Tenn.), October 29, 2004.

———, "Dixie Group Posts Higher Quarterly Sales, Net Income," *Chattanooga Times/Free Press* (Tenn.), April 29, 2005.

———, "Dixie Group Sees Higher Carpet Sales, But Flat Profits," *Chattanooga Times/Free Press* (Tenn.), August 2, 2005.

Jaffee, Thomas, "Whistling Dixie," *Forbes,* August 30, 1993, p. 240.

Lappan, Alyssa A., "Number One in Niches," *Forbes,* February 8, 1988, p. 45.

"Shelter Components Corporation Completes the Sale of Its Carpet Operations," *PR Newswire,* January 2, 1997.

Doux S.A.

BP 22, Zone Industrielle de Lospars
Chateaulin,
France
Telephone: (33) 02 98 86 69 00
Fax: (33) 02 98 86 69 69
Web site: http://www.doux.com

Private Company
Incorporated: 1955
Employees: 15,000
Sales: EUR 1.35 billion ($1.7 billion)(2005)
NAIC: 311615 Poultry Processing; 311611 Animal
(Except Poultry) Slaughtering; 311612 Meat
Processed From Carcasses

∎∎∎

Doux S.A. is the world's leading producer of chickens
and other poultry for the export market, and is also
Europe's single largest producer of chicken, chicken
products and other poultry and poultry products. Over
all, the company is the fifth-largest poultry producer in
the world, with a production of more than 1.1 billion
tons per year, and annual sales of more than EUR 1.3
billion ($1.7 billion). The company, based in the small
village of Chateaulin in France's Brittany region, operates a network of nearly 25 slaughtering and cutting
facilities, chiefly in France and Brazil, but also in
Germany, Spain and Switzerland. The company also
operates 4 processing facilities, 14 hatcheries and 12
feed plants. The company exports its products to more
than 130 countries. Doux's products are sold under a

number of brand names, including global brand Doux,
and local brands Père Dodu and La Janzé in France,
Guts-Gold in Germany, Tio Cosme in France, and Le-
Bon and Frangosul in Brazil. Founded in 1955, Doux
remains a family-controlled company, with Charles
Doux, son of the group's founder, as chairman. Guiding
day-to-day operations, however, is managing director
Guy Odri, who joined the company in 2003.

FOUNDING A POULTRY GIANT IN 1955

The Doux family's involvement in France's food industry
began in the 1930s when Pierre Doux, an Armenian
who fled to France, launched a butcher business in
Nantes in 1933. In 1955, Doux traveled north, to the
Finistère region, where he founded his own
slaughterhouse in Port Launay. From the start, Doux
focused on the poultry sector, and especially chickens
and chicken products. Doux invested in freezing
technology, becoming a primary supplier of frozen
chickens to the French supermarket channel, which was
just beginning to become commonplace in France in the
1950s. In the early 1960s, the company's continued
investments enabled it to become one of the first to
introduce automated processing techniques, allowing the
company to step up its production capacity.

Doux's increased capacity situated the company to
begin preparing its frozen chickens for the export market.
This early involvement in the export market allowed it
to position itself as a major player by the 1970s. An
important part of the group's success came through its
early decision to enter the Eastern European market,

COMPANY PERSPECTIVES

An expert in poultry and innovation since its creation in 1955, the Doux Group and its subsidiaries are present in all of the poultry market segments (chicken, turkey, duck, guinea fowl, etc.) to include fresh and frozen products, whole or cut-up poultry and processed products (breaded products, ready-made meals, poultry deli products). A major player in retail sales, the agri-food industry and foodservice, the Doux Group sells its products in more than 130 countries on the five continents, with a driving desire: bringing everything into play to offer responses that are in line with client and consumer needs throughout the world. This quest for innovation, quality and flavour are represented in a portfolio of internationally recognised brands: Doux, Frangosul, Lebon, Père Dodu, Supreme, Le Janzé, Tio Cosme and Guts-Gold.

and especially the Soviet Union. At the same time, Doux became one of the first to target the Middle Eastern market, where the introduction of frozen chicken prepared according to Western methods and hygiene levels made the company a major player in the region.

Much of the group's expansion during this period was attributed to Pierre Doux's son Charles Doux. By the end of the 1980s, the younger Doux had steered the company to the top level of not only the French and European markets, but of the global poultry market as well. By 1990, the company claimed the number two position on the global export market, and the number three position, behind Tyson Foods and Conagra, of the poultry sector overall. The company had also begun to explore its own international development, starting with Spain. In 1989, the company acquired an 85 percent stake in that country's number two poultry group, Porta-Pygasa.

That year marked a new turning point for Doux. In October 1990, the company agreed to acquire majority control of Père Dodu, the poultry division owned by Guyomarc'h, a member of the Paribas group. The remaining share of Père Dodu was held by another Paribas holding, Soprat. The addition of Père Dodu brought Doux one of France's strongest poultry brands, as well as one of the sector's most innovative. Indeed, Père Dodu had helped pioneer the market for prepared and processed poultry parts and products. The company had been one of the first to market successfully a

prepared Cordon Bleu; other innovations introduced by Père Dodu included turkey roasts and parts, and extended-life packaging materials. The addition of Père Dodu also placed Doux firmly at the lead of a buoyant French market that included such other poultry giants as Bourgouin and Lambert-Dodard-Chancereul. By 1992, Doux's sales had topped FRF 7 billion (approximately EUR 1.2 billion)—some 30 percent of which came from outside the European Union.

In the early 1990s, Doux extended its network again, acquiring Pic'Or, the leading poultry slaughterer and processor in France's Nord region. That purchase brought Doux two more facilities, not only boosting the company's broiler chicken capacity, but also its turkey slaughtering and processing sales. The Pic'Or purchase also positioned Doux closer to the Belgian and German borders, as well as to the United Kingdom, strengthening the company's export operations. Soon after, the company added its first foreign plants, buying up the Guts-Gold brand in order to establish its own slaughtering and processing facilities in Germany.

WEATHERING THE POULTRY CRISIS AT THE TURN OF THE CENTURY

By the mid-1990s, Doux's sales had topped FRF 8 billion. The company continued to seek expansion opportunities, targeting fresh growth in the French market. In 1995, Doux found a new target, that of Codivol, the fourth-largest poultry group in France. Codival, which also had a healthy export business with a focus on the northern European market, had been part of cooperative group Transagra, which acquired the business several years earlier. Yet losses in its poultry division in the early 1990s had forced Transagra to exit that business. The addition of Codivol to Doux gave the company seven new abattoirs, including two dedicated to the processing of turkey, as well as a feed production unit with a capacity of nearly 250,000 tons per year.

By then, however, Doux had begun to feel the effects of the GATT agreement, which imposed quotas and threatened to end export subsidies for the European poultry industry. At the same time, a wave of consolidation within the global poultry industry had begun to threaten Doux's dominance in Europe. In order to avoid the loss of income and business that the end of subsidies would bring, while remaining competitive on the world market, Doux made the bold move of expanding into South America. Brazil was by then already the world's fastest growing poultry producer. In 1998, Doux acquired that country's leading poultry processing company, Francosul.

Closer to home, Doux acquired full control of Père

KEY DATES

1933: Pierre Doux establishes a butcher business in Nantes.

1955: Doux moves to Finistere, opens his own slaughtering facility, and begins frozen poultry processing.

1990: Doux acquires majority control of the Père Dodu brand from Guyomarc'h.

1993: The company acquires Pic'Or, the leader in France's northern regions, and also acquires the Guts-Gold brand in Germany.

1995: Doux acquires Codivol, the fourth largest poultry processor in France.

1998: Doux acquires Francosul, the leading poultry slaughterer and processor in Brazil and acquires full control of Père Dodu.

2000: The company launches a $30 million investment drive in Brazil.

2002: Brazil accounts for 50 percent of group production.

2003: Doux shuts down four plants.

2004: Doux launches an extended range of products in its Fraicheur+ packaging.

2006: Amid the bird flu crisis, Doux is forced to cut back production.

Dodu in 1998, when it bought its shareholder partner Soprat. The purchase, in addition to the Père Dodu stake, also gave a boost to Doux's efforts to increase its share of the fast-growing prepared foods market. Doux also acquired the Le Janzé brand, which specialized in the production of "Label Rouge" poultry—that is, poultry certified to meet a number of quality criteria.

The collapse of chief French poultry rival Bourgoin in 2000 helped raise Doux's profile in France and elsewhere. The company also benefited from the series of scandals that rocked the beef and pork industries at the turn of the century. In the meantime, Doux invested heavily in its Brazilian operations, launching a $30 million spending program to increase capacity at its four existing facilities, as well as constructing a fifth plant, for the production of processed foods. The investment program helped shift the balance of Doux's operations, and by 2002, its Brazilian operations accounted for half of the company's total production.

Yet the company's fortunes were set to take a turn for the worse as it approached mid-decade. The global poultry market had entered into a phase of over-production, causing prices to fall sharply. Worse for the industry was the outbreak of bird flu in Asia, and warnings of a pandemic expected to sweep through much of the world over the next several years. The bird flu threat caused consumers to flee the poultry section in supermarkets, and demand went into a freefall.

In response, Doux was forced to tighten the belt of its operation. In 2003, the company launched a restructuring program, which included the closing of four factories by 2004, with other plant closures, particularly those involving non-core operations, anticipated by the middle of the decade. The effort paid off, helping the company return to profits by the end of that year.

Doux's efforts to expand its range of prepared foods also helped the company through the worst of the bird flu crisis. The company launched a successful line of breaded foods, called Mordicus, for the children's market. The company also launched the Fraicheur+ packaging system that was able to extend the shelf life of poultry parts to as much as 12 days. In 2004, the company launched a range of more than 50 Père Dodu products using the new packaging system, with plans to roll out a line of extended-life products for its Le Janzé brand.

Despite these successes, the company remained at the mercy of the continuing bird flu crisis. With new cases being reported around the world—including the first case in France in early 2006—consumer poultry purchases plummeted. The situation only grew worse in March 2006, when the French government ordered that the country's poultry population be quarantined indoors. The drop in sales that followed forced Doux to cut back its production at nearly all of the company's facilities, laying off a significant proportion of its workers.

Doux responded by launching a communication campaign in order to allay consumer fears about poultry products. The poultry sector's spirits were raised somewhat at the end of May 2006, when the government decided to lift the restrictions that had been placed on the market. Nonetheless, with the memory of the beef and pork scandals still fresh in consumer minds, Doux appeared to have its work cut out in order to restore its growth to its former steady pace.

M. L. Cohen

PRINCIPAL SUBSIDIARIES

Doux Geflügel GmbH (Germany); Doux Frangosul (Brazil); Doux Iberica (Spain); Doux Poultry Ltd. (United Kingdom); Avicola de Galicia S.A. (Spain);

MILSA (Spain); Doux Piensons S.A. (Spain); SODEDIS (Switzerland).

PRINCIPAL COMPETITORS

Cargill Inc.; Tyson Foods Inc.; Irvine's Day Old Chicks Private Ltd.; ROMSILVA; ConAgra Foods Inc; Smithfield Foods Inc.; Agricola Super Ltda.; Proagro C.A.; Sadia S.A; Lambert-Dodard-Chancereul.

FURTHER READING

"Doux Buys Soprat Group," *Eurofood*, May 21, 1998, p. 16.

"Doux Gains a Firm Foothold in Brazil," *Eurofood*, August 13, 1998, p. 18.

Dupont, Gaëlle, "Doux prévoit des licenciements," *Le Monde*, May 16, 2003.

Durupt, Vincent, "En trente ans de métier, je n'avais pas vu un tel déluge," *Le Monde*, March 8, 2006.

Francois, Renard, "La réussite du poulet français," *Le Monde*, October 12, 1990.

"French Poultry Giant Downsizes," *Agra Europe*, May 16, 2003.

"French Poultry Giant Expands," *Agra Europe*, May 15, 1998.

"French Poultry Giant Increases Domination," *Agra Europe*, March 10, 1995.

"Répercussion sur l'emploi dans la filière avicole," *Nouvel Observateur*, March 3, 2006.

Todd, Stuart, "Doux Poultry Giant to Shed Further 200 Jobs." Available at *http://www.just-food.com*, July 26, 2004.

Digital
Entertainment

DTS, Inc.

5171 Clareton Drive
Agoura Hills, California 91301
U.S.A.
Telephone: (818) 706-3525
Fax: (818) 706-1868
Web site: http://www.dts.com

Public Company
Incorporated: 1990 as Digital Theater Systems Corporation
Employees: 314
Sales: $75.25 million (2005)
Stock Exchanges: NASDAQ
Ticker Symbol: DTSI
NAIC: 334310 Audio and Video Equipment Manufacturing; 533110 Lessors of Nonfinancial Intangible Assets (Except Copyrighted Works); 512240 Sound Recording Studios; 512199 Other Motion Picture and Video Industries; 512210 Record Production

■ ■ ■

DTS, Inc., formerly known as Digital Theater Systems Inc., is a leader in the field of digital audio, offering a high-quality playback format that enhances the realism of movies and music by splitting sound into multiple front and rear channels. The company licenses its technology to film producers and consumer electronics firms, and also produces equipment like the XD10 Cinema Media Player and related products that add pre-show programming, subtitles, or audio commentary to

films. Other DTS units convert movies to high-definition video and release multi-channel audio discs.

EARLY YEARS

DTS traces its roots to 1990, when entrepreneur/inventor Terry Beard formed a California-based company called Digital Theater Systems Corporation to develop digital sound technology for motion pictures. Beard had earlier run a firm called Nuoptix that made optical sound recording equipment, and in the mid-1980s he and Jim Ketcham of Lorimar Pictures had begun developing digital multi-channel sound for use in theaters. By 1990 they had created a workable system and applied for several patents.

While multi-channel theater sound had been offered as early as 1940, when Walt Disney's *Fantasia* was presented in eight-channel "Fantasound," and some movies had been released with magnetic stereo soundtracks from the early 1950s, the format had typically only been used for prestigious releases and on a limited portion of the total number of film prints made. In 1975 Dolby Laboratories, Inc., began offering a new stereo playback system that could produce four (later five) channels of sound from a film's photographically-printed soundtrack, but digital audio technology that converted sound into computer code offered an even better prospect for high-fidelity reproduction, as it could be copied and played back without the generational loss and background noise associated with analog formats.

Because film prints were subject to wear during projection that could eventually render sensitive digital information unreadable, Beard and Ketcham decided to create a system that used a separate data storage medium. It would be synchronized to the film via a timecode printed at the unused edge of the soundtrack area, which would be durable enough to last for the life of a print. After abandoning digital audio tape (DAT) because reel changes and splices in the film caused the sound to lose synchronization, they settled on CD-ROM discs which were capable of quick re-synchronization and were cheap to produce. DTS-encoded films would have what the company called 5.1 audio tracks, which consisted of left, right, and center front channels; left and right rear "surround" channels; and an additional "subwoofer" channel, which included very low frequency sound to provide a visceral rumble for special effects and battle scenes.

In 1991 the small firm's audio system was demonstrated to director Steven Spielberg, who was highly impressed with the results. Believing it could enhance the impact of his forthcoming dinosaur epic *Jurassic Park*, Universal Studios allowed DTS to secretly test it on release copies of a low-budget horror film called *Dr. Giggles* before approving it for use with *Jurassic Park*.

1993: IMPORTANT NEW INVESTORS

In February 1993 Universal Studios, Spielberg, and a Beard-led group of investors split equity stakes in the firm, which became known as Digital Theater Systems L.P. Beard and his small staff immediately began working long hours to build playback units for hundreds of theaters in preparation for the June 11 opening of *Jurassic Park*. They were able to install 876 systems around the United States for clients like Cineplex Odeon Corporation, which bought 125 units for its chain of theaters. Exhibitors who did not purchase it were still able to show *Jurassic Park* with the analog Dolby Stereo track printed on the film as a backup in case the digital sound failed to work.

Jurassic Park was a huge hit and the sound got rave reviews, and sales of the company's systems quickly grew as major chains like Carmike Cinemas bought hundreds of units. Studios like Paramount, Warner Brothers, New Line, MGM/UA and others soon agreed to use DTS for some or all of their releases, further enhancing the format's viability. Competitor Dolby Laboratories had already unveiled its own digital sound system with the 1992 release *Batman Returns*, but the optically-printed format offered what some considered lower quality due to the four-times greater digital compression required, while the cost of adding it to a theater already set up for multi-channel sound was more than twice DTS's price of under $6,000 per screen.

In 1994 the firm opened an office in Belgium to facilitate European sales, and by year's end over 3,000 systems were in use and more than 60 films had been released with DTS audio. 1995 saw the company introduce a system that helped visually-impaired persons enjoy films via a separate narrated version of the soundtrack broadcast to wireless headsets. The firm, which now employed more than 40, recorded sales of $12.5 million for the year.

By the start of 1996 DTS systems had been installed in more than 5,800 theaters worldwide, including 3,400 in North America. Dolby Digital was in close to 3,300, and newer rival Sony Dynamic Digital Sound (SDDS) was in just over 1,800. The firm's equipment still cost about half as much as its competitors' systems, though the licensing fee it charged studios for major releases was $40,000, as opposed to $10,000 for Dolby and $9,000 for Sony (which had originally been offered for free). Sales were particularly strong in multi-lingual regions like Asia, Europe, and India, where dubbed versions of films could be produced cheaply by making new CD-ROM audio discs, rather than creating expensive new film prints with different soundtracks. Despite such advantages the firm was falling behind in the number of films released with its sound format—67 in 1995, versus 122 for Dolby Digital.

COHERENT ACOUSTICS DEBUTS IN 1996

Following the pattern set by rival Dolby, DTS had also begun seeking home applications for its technology, and after several years of development the Coherent Acoustics format was introduced in 1996. It enabled playback of up to 8 discrete sound channels for video or music discs, though it was only used in limited-production, high-end

KEY DATES

1990: Terry Beard founds Digital Theater Systems to develop digital movie sound.

1993: Universal Studios and Steven Spielberg invest in firm to fund growth; the first product, DTS-6, is introduced and the first DTS-encoded film, *Jurassic Park*, is released.

1994: European office opens in Belgium.

1997: DTS Entertainment is founded to release music mixed for multi-channel sound.

2001: Consumer audio tops cinema sales for the first time.

2003: The company goes public.

2004: DTS audio is selected as a mandatory format for new High-Definition DVDs.

2005: Firm shortens name to DTS, Inc.

equipment as little content was initially available.

In 1997 the company reached an agreement with Image Entertainment for that firm to put DTS sound mixes on laser videodiscs it produced as well as granting it exclusive distribution rights to DTS audio discs. DTS had recently formed a record label called DTS Entertainment to release licensed 5.1 remixes of albums like The Eagles' "Hell Freezes Over," Boyz II Men's "II," and Marvin Gaye's "Greatest Hits."

In October the firm sold a $12 million ownership stake to a group of private equity investors including Eos Partners and Westin Presidio Capital, using the funds to help build infrastructure and increase research and marketing. The year also saw Dan Slusser named CEO and an office opened in Tokyo, Japan.

In early 1998 the company made a renewed push to sell DTS-enabled audio gear to consumers, with companies like Yamaha, Matsushita, and Kenwood licensing its technology for their product lines. By April some 44 compact discs and 48 laserdiscs that incorporated DTS audio tracks were available, and about 50,000 DTS-enabled home audio devices had been sold. After several delays Image Entertainment also began releasing Universal Studios DVDs with DTS soundtracks, the first of which was Kevin Costner's *Dances With Wolves*. The discs could only play on special machines that incorporated DTS circuitry, as the industry's DVD standards required Dolby's format for all equipment but made DTS optional. Because DTS sound required about four times the data storage space of Dolby Digital (and many reviewers believed it

sounded better as a result), DVDs that included it typically came without bonus features like alternate audio tracks or documentaries. For some high-profile titles both standard DVDs and DTS-enhanced versions were released, the latter of which typically cost $5 to $10 more per disc.

Frustrated that its bid to be included as a mandatory audio format on video DVD players had failed, the company fought hard during 1998 to be included in new DVD-Audio disc standards, which would use the much larger storage capacity of DVDs for more finely-rendered sound. When Dolby and Meridian Laboratories formats were chosen DTS threatened legal action, but the firm was unable to reverse the decision of the industry's standards group. Nonetheless, many manufacturers subsequently agreed to license the company's format for their players, typically paying a dollar per unit.

In 1999 DTS began selling encoding equipment that let content providers make their own audio mixes, rather than requiring it be done at DTS-approved facilities. Yielding to market pressure, the company also began allowing encoding with a lower data bit-rate, which would enable DVDs to have both DTS and Dolby sound plus some bonus features. The year 1999 saw 242 films released to theaters with DTS audio, compared to Dolby's 703, while CEO/vice-chairman Dan Slusser took over the president's duties from the departing Bill Neighbors.

In 2001 the firm brought out its first DVD-Audio discs and worked to promote its consumer 5.1 audio recordings via a month-long national bus tour to retailers, which offered DTS sound demonstrations on-site. In September, eight-year company veteran Jon Kirchner was appointed president and CEO, and he subsequently reorganized the company's management, adding several new positions and expanding others. Dan Slusser would continue to serve as board chair.

The year 2001 also saw the introduction of a software developer's kit for video game makers that enabled them to mix their audio for 5.1 channels, while Electronic Arts, Inc., released several games for Sony's Playstation2 using DTS technology. The DTS-CSS Cinema Subtitling System debuted during the year as well, which used a video projector to add captions to films so that expensive subtitled prints need not be made. Revenues for 2001 hit $28.7 million, and a profit of $3.9 million was recorded. Sales of consumer audio products topped those of cinema equipment for the first time.

In 2001 the firm introduced a new higher-quality digital audio format it called 96/24, for the sampling rate of 96 herz and resolution of 24 bits, as compared to compact disc sound with 44.1 herz and 16 bits. The following year the first DVD-video disc was released using this audio format, rock group Queen's "Greatest Video Hits I," while the DVD-Audio release of that group's "A Night At The Opera" became the best-selling disc of its type to date. Also during 2002, the company expanded its Agoura Hills, California, headquarters.

2003: INITIAL PUBLIC OFFERING

In July 2003 DTS went public on the NASDAQ, raising $63.2 million with a sale of 3.84 million shares. The price quickly jumped from the opening level of $17 to more than $24, making it one of the most successful initial public offerings (IPOs) of the year. In the fall, a 1.5 million-share secondary offering was made, with existing shareholders selling twice that amount. Universal Studios' pre-IPO stake would drop from 18 to 7 percent, Spielberg-affiliated Forth Investors LLC from 18 to 6.6 percent, and the firm's largest shareholder, Westin Presidio Partners, reduced its ownership stake from 33.5 to 16 percent.

Another 2003 introduction was that of the new XD10 Cinema Media Player, which was capable of playing up to ten channels of sound in the 96/24 format, using a computer hard drive that could store up to 30 feature film soundtracks. In the fall a new Acura model became the first U.S. automobile to feature DTS sound as standard equipment, and a David Bowie concert was broadcast live from London mixed in DTS 5.1 sound. The year also saw record industry giant EMI begin releasing DTS-encoded DVD-Audio discs, the introduction of products incorporating DTS sound for home computers, and the opening of an office in Guangzhou, China.

By this time DTS equipment was installed at 23,000 cinema screens as compared to Dolby's 40,000, but consumer products incorporating the firm's audio technology or intellectual property had zoomed past 200 million units. Consumer audio accounted for 69 percent of DTS's sales by 2003.

In 2004 the company added software-based security enhancements to its cinema sound systems to help allay concerns about piracy, while introducing a new "lossless" technology that made cinema soundtracks identical to master recordings bit for bit, rather than omitting some information in the compression process. The firm was also battling a host of Chinese electronics companies making equipment with DTS technology without paying royalties, and won a $2.6 million judgment against a firm called Mintek that had used its trademark without authorization.

In September 2004 DTS's 5.1 format was chosen as a mandatory audio technology for both of the next-generation DVD systems Blu-ray Disc and HD-DVD, with the firm's recently introduced DTS-ES extended surround sound allowed as an option. December saw the company pay $11 million to acquire Lowry Digital Images, a four-year old firm that enhanced film and digital video for High-Definition television broadcasts and similar uses. Lowry was subsequently renamed DTS Digital Images. The company had also opened an office in Hong Kong and acquired a Canadian audio/visual research and development firm, QDesign, during the year. Earnings reached a record $61.4 million and profits hit $10 million.

In 2005 the company signed a deal to install XD10 Cinema Media Players in the entire Regal Entertainment theater chain in the United States, and added offices in Paris and Rome. Sound encoding facilities were also opened in China and Argentina, bringing the total to 15 worldwide, and the firm introduced its first product for digital imaging, the JPEG2000 Variable Bit Rate Encoder. The company settled several infringement lawsuits with Chinese firms and shortened its name to DTS, Inc., during the year as well.

In early 2006 the firm upgraded the XD10 Cinema Media Player to automate scheduling, delivery, and screening of pre-show digital advertising and other content via the newly-introduced Cinema Media Network. The movie industry was now gearing up for a shift from film to digital video projection, and DTS was working to define its place in the new paradigm.

More than a dozen years after the release of *Jurassic Park*, the audio format created by DTS, Inc., could be found in cinemas, home theaters, videogames, computers, and automobiles. The firm was busy laying the groundwork for future growth via High-Definition videodiscs and through the movie industry's conversion to digital imaging.

Frank Uhle

PRINCIPAL SUBSIDIARIES

Digital Theater Systems (UK) Ltd. (United Kingdom); DTS (BVI) Ltd. (British Virgin Islands); DTS Canada Holdings, Inc.; dts Japan KK (Japan); International Cinema Services, Inc.; DTS AZ Research, LLC; DTS Digital Images, Inc.

PRINCIPAL COMPETITORS

Dolby Laboratories, Inc.; Sony Corp.; USL, Inc.; Smart Devices, Inc.; Fraunhofer Institut Integrierte Schaltungen; Royal Philips Electronics N.V.; Meridian Audio

Limited; Microsoft Corporation; The Thomson Corporation; SRS Labs, Inc.

FURTHER READING

Arar, Yardena, "Sound Competition – DTS Keeps Pace with Digital Giants," *Los Angeles Daily News*, January 29, 1996, p. B1.

Biddle, RiShawn, "Digital Theater Systems Makes Move to Consumer Electronics," *Los Angeles Business Journal*, January 12, 2004, p. 26.

Brinkley, Joel, "Companies Are On a Quest for Your Ears," *New York Times*, July 21, 1997, p. 9.

"CFA IPO Spotlight: Digital Theater Sys Prospectus Info," *Dow Jones Corporate Filings Alert*, April 30, 2003.

Cole, George, "Sounds Like a Standards Battle," *Financial Post*, June 18, 1997, p. 53.

"DTS Readies Theatrical System for Hearing- and Sight-Impaired," *Warren's Consumer Electronics Daily*, April 19, 2004.

"DTS Sues Chinese DVD Makers," *SinoCast China IT Watch*, November 25, 2004.

Harvey, Steve, "First Look: DTS XD10 Cinema Media Player," *Surround Professional*, June 1, 2003, p. 12.

Johnson, Lawrence B., "Down the Stretch, Dolby's Still in the Lead, But....," *New York Times*, July 7, 1996, p. 14.

La Franco, Robert, "Boom Box," *Forbes*, March 24, 1997, p. 174.

Manafy, Michelle, "Feel the Noise: Dolby Versus DTS for DVD," *EMedia Professional*, July 1, 2000, p. 40.

Parisi, Paula, "3 Sign on For Uni DTS Code," *Hollywood Reporter*, September 2, 1993, p. 1.

Pondel, Evan, "DTS Debuts IPO as Star Sound Firm Makes Best Debut of Year," *Los Angeles Daily News*, July 15, 2003, p. B1.

Rivero, Enrique, "Dolby Still Dominates Sound But DTS Has Some Backers," *Video Store*, May 11, 2003, p. 14.

——, "DTS Moves Theater Sound to Households," *Los Angeles Daily News*, November 18, 1996, p. T1.

Silberg, Jon, "Audiophile Exports," *Hollywood Reporter*, October 8, 2002, p. S-4.

Sporich, Brett, "DTS Is Finding More Studio Support," *Video Store*, April 30, 2000, p. 10.

Turner, Dan, "Digital Firm Changes How We Hear Movies," *Los Angeles Business Journal*, April 8, 1996, p. 1.

Verna, Paul, "DTS Lobbies to Be Included in DVD Audio Spec.," *Billboard*, September 12, 1998, p. 1.

Walsh, Christopher, "DTS' Digital Sound Capabilities Proliferate," *Billboard*, September 20, 2003, p. 62.

Ercros S.A.

—■—

Avda Diagonal 595-5a planta
Barcelona,
Spain
Telephone: (34) 93 439 30 09
Fax: (34) 93 430 80 73
Web site: http://www.ercros.es

Public Company
Incorporated: 1989
Employees: 972
Sales: EUR 432.8 million ($649 million)(2005)
Stock Exchanges: Madrid
Ticker Symbol: ECR
NAIC: 325998 All Other Miscellaneous Chemical Product Manufacturing; 212393 Other Chemical and Fertilizer Mineral Mining; 325131 Inorganic Dye and Pigment Manufacturing; 325181 Alkalies and Chlorine Manufacturing; 325192 Cyclic Crude and Intermediate Manufacturing; 325320 Pesticide and Other Agricultural Chemical Manufacturing; 325412 Pharmaceutical Preparation Manufacturing; 424590 Other Farm Product Raw Material Merchant Wholesalers; 424690 Other Chemical and Allied Products Merchant Wholesalers

■ ■ ■

One of Spain's leading independent chemical producers, Ercros S.A. ranks among the country's top chemical companies overall. Ercros operates through six major divisions. Basic Chemicals produces chlorine, ethyl acetate, caustic soda, sodium hypchlorite, sodium chlor- ate, and caustic potash. Through this division, the company is the largest producer of caustic soda in Spain, with a 37 percent market share; the leading Spanish producer and second-larger European producer of ethyl acetate, holding 32 percent of the domestic market and 17 percent of the European market; and the sole Span- ish producer of caustic potash and potassium carbonate, giving the company 80 percent of the Spanish market for both chemicals. Basic Chemicals, which operates from seven factories in Spain, is Ercros' largest division, accounting for more than half of the group's annual sales. Plastics, the company's second largest division, is Spain's number two producer of PVC, and also produces vinyl chloride monomer in two factories. Much of the company's plastics output is destined for the export market. Pharmaceuticals, which represents 7 percent of company sales, produces erythromycins, phosphomycin, and statins, and other basic and intermediary compounds for the pharmaceuticals industry. The company leads the world in production of phosphomycin, with an 80 percent share of the global market, and is also the second- largest producer of erythromycin base, salts and deriva- tives, with a 10 percent share of the global market.

Ercros's Animal Food division produces phosphates for the feed industry, and also operates two facilities producing plant health products for the agricultural sector. Some 90 percent of the group's animal phosphates are sold in Spain. The company's Emulsion division operates from a factory in Germany and chiefly produces stryrene acrylic, and vinyl and acrylic emulsions for the German market. Ercros's final division is its Water Treatment division, which manufactures water treatment chemicals for swimming pools, as well as for detergents,

COMPANY PERSPECTIVES

Ercros' mission is to consolidate a sound and sustainable industrial project that contributes to the community's wealth and well-being, pays back the trust its shareholders have placed in it and gives those working for it the chance to develop their personal and professional potential to the full. Ercros' operations are designed to increase the company's value and are guided by three basic principles: the highest possible safety standards to protect employees, the local community and facilities; absolute respect for the environment; and complete product quality and satisfaction of customers' needs.

bleaches and cleaning products.

Ercros is listed on the Madrid Stock Exchange, and is led by Chairman and CEO Antonio Zabalza Martí. The company's revenues neared EUR 433 million ($649 million) in 2005. The integration of Derivados Forestal Group, purchased in March 2006, is expected to add more than EUR 200 million to the group's turnover by the end of the year.

MERGING SPANISH CHEMICAL COMPANIES IN 1989

Ercros group was created in 1989 through the merger of two chemical companies, SA Cros and Unión Explosivos Rio Tinto S.A. (ERT). Both companies had been active in one form or another for more than one hundred years. In Cros' case, the company was founded by Francisco Cros, who began producing fertilizers in Barcelona in 1817. The company remained in the Cros family hands, coming under the leadership of Amadeo Cros at the turn of the 20th century.

The younger Cros eyed expansion and diversification into the broader chemicals field, and in 1904 the company was incorporated as SA Cros. In that year, Cros also reached an agreement with Sociedad Electroquímica de Flix to act as the exclusive distributor for Flix's production of chlorine and soda. Flix had been established in 1897 through a consortium of Swiss, German and Spanish investors, who built a production unit on the Ebro River in Tarragona. That factory became one of the first in Europe to use electricity in the production of chlorine.

The relationship between the Flix factory and Cros

remained a lasting one and gradually deepened. Following World War II, Flix incorporated as a limited liability company, and Cros became its majority shareholder. By 1974, Cros had absorbed Flix fully. By then, Flix had developed into one of Spain's leading producers of chlorine and caustic soda, as well as chlorine derivatives, chlorinated solvents and dicalcium phosphate. Into the 1980s, Cros had grown into one of Spain's largest non-government owned chemicals concerns, a position the company solidified with its acquisition of a majority stake in ERT in 1987.

ERT had been founded in 1872 as Sociedad Española de la Pólvora Dinamita in Bilbao. That company was created as part of the network of dynamite production companies established by Alfred Nobel and his family following Nobel's invention of dynamite in 1867. The Polvora company, established in partnership with a group of French and Belgian investors and registered in France, built a factory in Galdácano in order to replace a factory on the other side of the French-Spanish border.

That factory enjoyed a five-year period as the exclusive producer of dynamite in Spain, a monopoly granted by King Amadeo I. The headstart enabled Polvora to weather early competition in the late 1870s, when the exclusivity term expired. Much of this competition came from outside Spain, particularly from Germany and Scotland, including other members of the Nobel network. In 1887, however, the company faced the appearance of a domestic rival, Sociedad Española de la Dinamita, which took over the Galádacano site in 1896. The Polvora company was later renamed as Sociedad Anima Española de la Dinamita y de Productos Quimicos, before being merged into the Sociedad Española de la Dinamita in the late 1960s.

Sociedad Española de la Dinamita branched out into the production of fertilizer in 1927 with the purchase of Sociedad General de Industria y Comercio, based in Cartagena. That company had launched fertilizer manufacturing operations in 1903, building a factory in El Hondón. The purchase of the Cartagena operation also brought mining rights for potassium salt in Cardona. Mining began in 1929 and remained part of the company's operations through the end of the 1980s. The explosives producer continued to grow in the second half of the century, especially through its merger with Compañia Española de Minas de Rio Tinto, a company established in 1954. The newly enlarged company then took on the name Unión Explosivos Rio Tinto S.A. (ERT).

ERT continued growing through the 1970s. In 1974, for example, the company acquired Compañía Española de Penicilina y Antibióticos (Cepa), which had launched production of antibiotics and antibiotic base

KEY DATES

1817: Francisco Cros begins producing chemicals in Spain.

1872: The Sociedad Española de la Pólvora Dinamita in Bilbao is founded to produce dynamite.

1887: The Sociedad Española de la Dinamita is created.

1896: Sociedad Española de la Dinamita acquires Sociedad Española de la Pólvora Dinamita.

1897: The Sociedad Electroquímica de Flix is incorporated to produce chlorine and soda.

1904: Amadeo Cros incorporates his company as SA Cros and acquires exclusive distribution agreement for Flix production.

1927: The Sociedad Española de la Dinamita acquires the fertilizer producer Sociedad General de Industria y Comercio in Cartagena.

1954: The Compañia Española de Minas de Rio Tinto is founded.

1969: The Sociedad Española de la Dinamita merges with Compañia Española de Minas de Rio Tintoto become Unión Explosivos Rio Tinto S.A. (ERT).

1974: Cros acquires full control of the Flix factory; ERT acquires Compañía Española de Penicilina y Antibióticos (Cepa), a leading producer of phosphomycin.

1989: Cros and ERT merge, forming Ercros.

1992: Ercros spins off most of its fertilizer operations into Fertiberia.

1995: The company sells off majority control of Fertiberia and launches a diversification strategy, focusing on basic chemicals, agricultural, veterinary and feed additives, and pharmaceuticals.

2001: Ercros begins construction of a new feed phosphate plant.

2005: Ercros acquires Grupo Aragonesas from Uralita for EUR 180 million.

2006: Ercros acquires the Derivados Forestales Group.

materials in 1949. Cepa became the first Spanish company to produce antibiotics, launching production at a factory in Aranjuez in 1951. In the late 1960s,

Cepa teamed up with Merck to develop a new antibiotic, phosphomycin, launched in 1968. The company remained the world's leading producer of phosphomycin into the 2000s.

In 1973, ERT launched production at a new chemicals facility built at the new petrochemicals industrial zone opened by the Spanish government in Tarragona. ERT's facility produced nitric acid, then added a second facility for the production of ethyl acetate. At the same time, ERT became a founding member of the Industrias Quimicas Asociadas (IQA) joint venture, which built a number of production plants near ERT's Tarragona operations. IQA then established a subsidiary, SA Explosivos Total Aquitaine (SAETA), which launched production of low density polyethylene in the mid-1970s and became the central production plant in the Tarragona zone, with ERT's own operations providing support services. IQA also set up plants producing acetaldehyde and acetic acid in the Tarragona zone. In 1977, ERT bought out its partners, taking full control of SAETA. After IQA went into receivership in the mid-1980s, ERT took over much of IQA's operations.

RESTRUCTURED FOR THE NEW CENTURY

Cros and ERT began transitioning toward their merger in the late 1980s, especially after Cros acquired a majority stake in ERT in 1987. A driving forced behind the merger was the Kuwaiti Investment Office, which, through its subsidiary Grupo Torras, emerged as the newly formed Ercros' majority shareholder, with a 38.6 percent stake.

At its creation, Ercros appeared to be a vibrant new chemicals leader in Spain. Yet the merger quickly turned sour; Ercros' heavy involvement in the production of fertilizer crippled the company into the early 1990s. The Spanish fertilizer market had entered a new phase after the Spanish government liberalized the market in 1986, allowing foreign competitors in for the first time. Spanish fertilizer companies were soon hit by a double blow of oversupply and a flagging economy. In the meantime, extended drought conditions had cut deeply into fertilizer demand. By 1992, Ercros was on the brink of bankruptcy.

The difficulties in the fertilizer sector had already led Ercros to close a number of its fertilizer production sites as early as 1990. In the new decade, the company launched a wider restructuring, selling off a number of operations. Such was the fate of its potash mining subsidiary, Potasas de Llobregat, which was spun off into the merger that formed Comercial de Potasas, also known as Coposa, in 1992. The company also shed its Rio Tinto mining operation.

Yet Ercros's fertilizer division, operating as Fesa-Enfersa, remained a heavy weight on the group's operations, dragging the company toward bankruptcy. Ercros appeared to have found a rescuer, in the form of U.S.-based Freeport-McMorRan Inc., which initially agreed to buy up a 55 percent stake in Ercros. Instead, Ercros worked out a deal with Fesa-Enfersa's main creditor, Morocco-based OCP, which spun off Fesa-Enfersa's assets into a new company, Fertiberia. In exchange, OCP forgave Ercros its debt. Originally, Fertiberia was to be acquired by Freeport McMorRan for a nominal one-peseta purchase price. Instead, Spanish industrialist Juan Villar Mir stepped in with his own bid for 53 percent of Fesa, which had been restructured as the holding company for Fertiberia. Mir won his bid and took control of this part of Ercros' fertilizer operations in 1995. The company remained active in the production of potassium sulfate, however, through subsidiary Potasas y Derivados. This continued involvement enabled the company to take advantage of the upswing in the fertilizer market in the late 1990s.

Through the late 1990s and into the 2000s, Ercros concentrated on the organic expansion of its diversified operations in order to reduce its reliance on its core basic chemicals business and the cyclical nature of this market. The company targeted a number of areas for growth, especially pharmaceuticals, agricultural chemicals, and veterinary and feed additives. The latter category grew strongly and by 2001 accounted for 23 percent of the group's sales. In the early 2000s, Ercros stepped up its feed additives business, building a new feed phosphates plant in the Valle de Escombreras, near Cartagena. This plant came online in 2004.

By then, however, Ercros had decided that organic development was not providing the company with the growth rate it sought. The company instead began targeting acquisitions for its future expansion. By April 2005, Ercros had spotted its first major acquisition target, launching an offer to acquire Grupo Aragonesas from Uralita. By June of that year, Ercros had completed the deal, paying nearly EUR 180 million for Grupo Aragonesas and its subsidiaries. The purchase instantly boosted Ercros's profile, nearly doubling its revenues, which reached EUR 433 million by the end of 2005.

Following the integration of Aragonesas, Ercros restructured again, regrouping its operations into six main divisions. While basic chemicals remained the company's primary revenue source, Ercros had successfully diversified its operations. The company remained on the lookout for new acquisition opportunities. As a result, in March 2006, the company reached an agreement to acquire Derivados Forestales Group. That company was a major producer of formaldehyde and derivatives, among other chemicals in Spain, with four plants in the Barcelona, Tarragona and Valencia regions. The addition of Derivados Forestales was expected to add nearly EUR 200 million to Ercos' sales by the end of 2006.

M.L. Cohen

PRINCIPAL SUBSIDIARIES

Agrocros S.A.; Aiscondel S.A.; Aragonesas Delsa S.A.; Aragonesas Industria y energia S.A.; Ercros Industrial S.A.; Fosfatos de Cartagena SL; Freihoff Chemie GmbH; Ufesys SL.

PRINCIPAL DIVISIONS

Basic Chemicals; Plastics; Pharmaceuticals; Animal Food; Emulsion; Water Treatment.

PRINCIPAL COMPETITORS

Repsol YPF S.A.; Bayer Hispania S.A.; Dow Chemical Iberica S.L.; BASF Espanola S.A.; Arkema Quimica S.A; PPG Iberica S.A; ICI Espana S.A.; Pavasal Empresa Constructora S.A.; IFF-Benicarlo S.A; Acieroid S.A.

FURTHER READING

Beacham, Will, "Ercros Completes Site Sale," *ECN-European Chemical News*, May 24, 2004, p. 8.

"C to Buy Chemicals Firm in Spain," *Chemical Week*, April 20, 2005, p. 5.

Marti, Antonio Zabalza, "Ercros Survives a Fierce Baptism," *Fertilizer International*, May 2002, p. 14.

Robinson, Simon, "Ercros' First Half Profits up Four-fold," *ECN-European Chemical News*, August 8, 2005, p. 10.

——, "New Spanish Buy," *ECN-European Chemical News*, April 18, 2005, p. 8.

"Ercros to Build Phosphates Plant in Spain," *Chemical Week*, February 27, 2002, p. 25.

"State Aid for Newly Reorganised Spanish Chemicals Firm Accepted," *European Report*, July 24, 1999.

Eurazeo

---

3 rue Jacques Bingen
Paris,
France
Telephone: (33) 01 44 15 01 11
Fax: (33) 01 47 66 84 41
Web site: http://www.eurazeo.com

Public Company
Incorporated: 2001
Employees: 92
Sales: EUR 441.0 million ($500 million)(2004)
Stock Exchanges: Euronext Paris
Ticker Symbol: 121121
NAIC: 525910 Open-End Investment Funds

■ ■ ■

Eurazeo is one the world's leading private equity investment groups, with total assets of more than EUR 5 billion. Since 2002, the company has adopted a strategy of focusing its operations on acquiring majority or influential shareholdings in non-listed companies. This strategy helped Eurazeo shift the balance of its portfolio by the mid-2000s, so that more than half of its assets, including real estate holdings, are represented by non-listed entities.

Eurazeo was formed through the mergers of international banking group Lazard LLC's investment vehicles, including Eurafrance and Azeo, and its French real estate holdings Rue Impériale and Société Immobilière Marseillaise, which were merged into Eurazeo in 2004. These mergers served to separate the operations of

Lazard and the holdings of the David-Weill family, as Lazard prepared for its public offering in 2005. Eurazeo remains a major shareholder in Lazard, and that holding accounts for a major part of Eurazeo's total assets (nearly one-third in 2003). Other major Eurazeo holdings include stakes in Rexel, acquired in 2004 in a leveraged buyout together with CDR and Merrill Lynch; Eutelsat (36 percent); Fraikin, the former Fiat-owned truck leasing and rental group; a majority stake in Ateliers de Construction du Nord de la France (ANF), a leading French property management group; and Financière Galaxie, acquired in late 2005, which owns the B&B chain of budget hotels in France and Germany.

In December 2005, Eurazeo entered exclusive negotiations to acquire Groupe Materis, a world-leading producer of specialty chemicals for the construction industry. Eurazeo itself is listed on the Euronext Paris Stock Exchange. Patrick Sayer is company CEO and chairman. While more than 50 percent of Eurazeo is now publicly listed, the David-Weill family, along with other founding families, retains a 21.6 percent stake in the company through the holding vehicle SC Haussmann Percier. Lazard also remains a major shareholder in Eurazeo.

EVOLUTION OF LAZARD FAMILY INVESTMENTS

The creation of Eurazeo in 2000 represented the merging of various investment vehicles developed by Lazard LLC and the David-Weill family since the 1960s, including Lazard's own long-term shareholdings in a number of its major clients, such as stakes in Danone,

Pearson, and Assicurazioni Generali. In 2000, then-Lazard chairman Michel David-Weill completed the consolidation of the various components of the Lazard group into a single entity, Lazard LLC. At the same time, David-Weill began bringing together the several vehicles—including Eurafrance, Azeo, and then Rue Impériale and Société Immobilière Marseillaise—through which the family maintained its control over Lazard. At that time, Lazard was one of the last remaining privately held banking empires.

Lazard stemmed from the fortunes of three brothers from France's Alsace region, Alexandre, Elie, and Simon Lazard, who arrived in the United States in time for the great Gold Rush at the middle of the 19th century. In 1849, the brothers set up a dry goods business in San Francisco, and also began offering banking and currency exchange services. By 1852, the brothers had established a second office, in Paris, called Lazard Frères & Cie, which launched a gold purchasing business. By 1876, Lazard had refocused itself entirely on its banking and financial services operations; the following year, the company established its third office, Lazard Brothers, in London.

Soon after, Lazard cousin Alexandre Weill took over the family business. The Weill family (which later legally adopted the name David-Weill) remained in control of the bank into the 21st century. Throughout most the 20th century as well, the three Lazard offices developed more or less independently. For example, after the British government adopted new rules governing foreign bank ownership, Lazard was forced to sell some 45 percent of Lazard Brothers to SP Pearson in 1919. By 1932, Pearson had acquired 80 percent of Lazard Brothers. In exchange, Lazard gained a significant stake in Pearson as well. This stake, held through investment vehicle Gaz et Eaux, remained at some 10 percent into the late 1990s. In 1999, that vehicle changed its name to Azeo.

OWNERSHIP HISTORY OF GAZ ET EAUX

Gaz et Eaux stemmed from the creation in 1881 of a company dedicated to the distribution of water and gas in France's north and western regions. As with many of France's utilities, Gaz et Eaux also developed significant financial operations, including various investment holdings. In 1945, the company lost its gas concession when the distribution of gas in France was taken over the French government. Gaz et Eaux continued to operate its water distribution business during the post-war years. In 1976, however, Gaz et Eaux abandoned its water distribution operations as well, and in 1977 the company was taken over by the Insitut de Développement Industrier (IDI), and a consortium of banks and insurance groups and others including Mutuelle Générale Française, Paribas, Caisse de Dépots, and Elf Acquitaine.

At that time, Gaz et Eaux became merely an investment holding vehicle with an asset base of FRF 87 million. The company made a number of strategic investments into the first half of the 1980s. For example, in 1980, Gaz et Eaux acquired a stake in Germany's Harpener AG; the sale of that shareholding just six years later provided the group with a profit of approximately FRF 1 billion.

Gaz et Eaux's own shareholder base continued to shift about. In the early 1980s, Escaut & Meuse, a holding company for the Escaut and Meuse families, became a major shareholder, while the IDI transferred its stake to insurance group UAP. When Escaut & Meuse became the target of a takeover attempt in 1985, the family shareholders transferred its shares to a consortium including UAP, certain other shareholders of Gaz et Eaux, and another investment vehicle, Eurafrance. That company, controlled by Lazard and the David-Weill family, had already begun investing in Gaz et Eaux in the early 1980s. Gaz et Eaux then took over Escaut & Meuse, and now boasted total assets of more than FRF 2.2 billion.

By the end of 1985, Eurafrance had become Gaz et Eaux's largest shareholder, after transferring parts of its own investment portfolio. This transfer, including 9.8 percent of Chargeurs and 12 percent of Sovac boosted Gaz et Eaux's total assets to more than FRF 3 billion. Through Eurafrance, Lazard controlled a 45 percent stake in Gaz et Eaux.

EURAFRANCE AS PART OF THE LAZARD INVESTMENT STRATEGY

Eurafrance had been set up in 1969 as Gestion Participations et Placements Parges, and in 1972 acquired control of the insurance group La France, as well as a

KEY DATES

1969: Parges is founded.

1974: Parges becomes Eurafrance and part of Lazard group.

1985: Eurafrance acquires a majority share of Gaz et Eaux (originally founded in 1881).

1999: Gaz et Eaux becomes Azeo.

2000: Eurafrance acquires full control of Azeo and becomes Eurazeo.

2001: Patrick Sayer is named Eurazeo CEO.

2002: Eurazeo adopts a new private equity investment strategy.

2003: The company acquires 36 percent of Eutelsat.

2004: Eurazeo merges with Rue Impériale (Lazard property investment vehicle) and joins the Revel leveraged buyout.

2005: The company acquires Financiére Galaxie, a holding company for the B&B hotel chain.

stake in Eurafrep. Parges came under control of Lazard when that group's real estate vehicle, Rue Impériales de Lyon, which also controlled a majority share of Société Immobilière de Marseillaise, gained a majority stake in 1973. In 1974, Parges took over another majority control of a holding company, CMI Sovac, and changed its name to Eurafrance.

Over the next decade, Eurafrance made a number of important acquisitions, including a stake of nearly 10 percent in conglomerate Chargeurs Reunis in 1974, and a stake in Locatel, among others. In the meantime, the Lazard group acquired other significant shareholdings, including stakes in Chaussures André, Euralux (which owned shares in Generali) and Viniprix through Société Immobilière Marseillaise. Gaz et Eaux, meanwhile, added a number of shareholdings, some of which were transferred from elsewhere in the Lazard group, including stakes in Pearson, Sidel, BSN (later Danone), Sogeit, Société Générale de Belgique, and Eurafrep.

TOWARD TRANSPARENCY IN THE LAZARD GROUP

A first step toward greater transparency—and simplicity—in the Lazard group and the David-Weill family's investment holdings was taken in 1985, when Michel David-Weill, who had by then taken control of the family empire, created Lazard Partners. This group then became the main shareholding vehicle, controlling the U.S. and Paris Lazard companies, as well as the family's stake in the London-based Lazard Brothers. Over the next decade, Lazard Partners continued buying up shares in Lazard Brothers. Into the mid-1990s, David-Weill had gained sufficient control to begin pushing through a consolidation of some of Lazards' operations, including establishing a single company for all of the Lazard group's asset management businesses in 1997. At last in 1998, the family succeeded in acquiring full control, paying Pearson $724 million for its remaining 18 percent in Lazard Brothers. Despite opposition from minority shareholders, David-Weill pushed through the merger of the three Lazard companies, creating a single Lazard LLC, based in New York, by 2000.

The restructuring of the Lazard empire also led to a restructuring of its investment vehicles, including Eurafrance and Gaz et Eaux. These groups provided the David-Weill family and other founding family members with a vehicle for their own long-term investments, and featured the family-owned holding company SC Haussmann Percier (named after the street corner on which the Lazard Paris offices were located) as a major shareholder. At the same time, Eurafrance, Gaz et Eaux, as well as the Lyon and Marseilles property vehicles, each held stakes in Lazard, giving the David-Weill family nearly untouchable control of the bank. In the late 1990s, however, the publicly listed investment companies came under attack: the highly visible French "corporate raider" Vincent Bolloré had gained a 31 percent stake in Rue Impériale, while the banking group UBS Warburg had built up stakes of 10 percent in Eurofrance, 7 percent in Gaz et Eaux (which changed its name to Azeo in 1999, and 5 percent in Immobilière Marseillaise.

These shareholders began to pressure Lazard to simplify its investment holdings, in large part because the complex holding structure was seen as depressing the publicly listed companies' share prices. When UBS Warburg threatened to launch a takeover of Azeo, David-Weill gave in. In 2000, Eurofrance launched a takeover offer for Azeo. After raising its stake to 97 percent, Eurofrance merged with Azeo, forming Eurazeo.

At the time, Eurazeo represented a more or less passive investment group. As *Business Week* described the company at the time, "although Eurazeo was France's largest publicly quoted investment company, it was mostly a sleepy outpost where Lazard parked the stakes it held in traditional clients."

This changed in 2001, when David-Weill brought in a new CEO for Eurafrance, Patrick Sayer, who had been working for Lazard LLC in New York. Sayer agreed to take over the direction of Eurazeo, on the condition that he be granted the right to act independently of Lazard. As Sayer told *Business Week*: "I didn't want to be head of Eurazeo and report to Lazard partners." In the face of continued pressure from Eurafrance's minority shareholders, which demanded that the investment company act separately of Lazard, Weill granted Sayer's request. Eurazeo, in which David-Weill retained the majority of voting rights, also became the family's primary vehicle for its Lazard shareholding (with Rue Impériale and Immobilière Marseillaise also owning shares of Lazard).

EURAZEO AS PRIVATE EQUITY LEADER

In 2002, Sayer led Eurazeo on a redefinition of its strategy. The group now transformed itself into an active capital investment firm with a focus on the private equity and leveraged buyout markets. By then, Eurazeo had already begun to sell off some of its "traditional" holdings, including its stake in Generali. That sale alone raised more than EUR 900 million for the company. The company promptly joined the bidding wars for Royal KPN's yellow pages operation and for Vivendi Universal's selloff of its publishing arm.

Eurazeo struck its first success in February 2003, when the company paid Fiat EUR 764 million to take over majority control of its Fraikin truck and industrial vehicle rental and leasing business. In April of that year, Eurazeo succeeded again, paying EUR 450 million ($486 million) to acquire 23 percent of Eutelsat, the leading satellite operator in Europe. By then, the company had also established a second area of operation, property investment, forming a EUR 100 million real estate investment joint venture with U.S.-based real estate investment specialist Colony Capital.

Lazard had continued to restructure its investment holdings, merging Immobilière Marseillaise into Rue Impériale in 2002. By then, however, David-Weill had given up management control of Lazard to financier Bruce Wasserstein, who was brought in to help revitalize the bank's flagging operations at the end of 2001. Tensions soon grew between Wasserstein and David-Weill, and especially after Wasserstein announced his intention to take Lazard public. In response, David-Weill engineered a merger agreement between Eurazeo and Rue Impériale. In this way, David-Weill strengthened his hold on Eurazeo's shareholding in Lazard, which included veto power over renewing Wasserstein's contract in 2006.

The enlarged Eurazeo now boasted assets of more than EUR 3 billion. The company continued to hone its strategy, adopting an active management approach for its takeover candidates. The company added its next major deal in late 2004 when it joined the leveraged buyout, together with CDR and Merrill Lynch, of leading European electrical equipment distributor Rexel.

Eurazeo, by then already the leading European private equity investment group, struck a new deal in late 2005, when it bought Financiére Galazie, the holding company for the B&B budget hotel chain. By the end of that year, Eurazeo had already launched its next acquisition, gaining the exclusive right to negotiate a takeover offer for Groupe Materis, a leading producer of specialty chemicals for the construction industry. With more than EUR 5 billion in total assets, Eurazeo had clearly established itself a major international private equity group in the new century.

M. L. Cohen

PRINCIPAL SUBSIDIARIES

BlueBirds Participations S.A. (Luxembourg); Catroux; FLM; Fraikin; Fraikin Alquiler (Spain); Fraikin Assets; Fraikin Belgium S.A.; Fraikin Groupe; Fraikin Ltd. (United Kingdom); Fraikin Locamion; Fraikin Locatime; Fraikin Luxembourg; France Asie Participations; Immobilière Fraikin; Locamion; Lotus Asia Investments BV (Netherlands); Lux Tiles (Luxembourg); Malesherbes; RedBirds France; RedBirds Participations S.A. (Luxembourg); SC La Vitrollaise; SCI Cles; SCI Les Boussenots; SCI Les Cars Bleus; Seltra; WhiteBirds France.

PRINCIPAL COMPETITORS

Vanguard Group Inc; Credit Suisse Group ; Landesbank Baden-Wurttemberg AG ; Standard Life Investments Ltd; ING Belgium N.V.; Bermuda Trust Cayman Ltd; TGI Fund I.L.C.; Swisscanto Holding AG.

FURTHER READING

"Colony and Eurazeo Start Eurapean Vehicle," *Estates Gazette*, February 1, 2003. P. 1.

"Duke Street Sells Galaxie to Eurazeo," *European Venture Capital Journal*, September 2005, p. 33.

"Eurazaeo Acquires Fiat Business," *Acquisitions Monthly*, January 2003, p. 56.

"Eurazeo's PE Strategy Evolves," *European Venture Capital Journal*, February 2003, p. 12.

"Eurazeo veut racheter le no. 3 en France de l'hôtellerie bon marché," *L'Expansion.com*, July 8, 2005.

"Lazard regroupe ses holdings," *L'Expansion*, February 25, 2004.

Rossant, John, "Rising Star in the City of Light," *Business Week*, February 24, 2003, p. 48.

Eurocopter S.A.

Aéroport International de Marseille 13725
Marignane,
France
Telephone: (33) 4 42 85 85 85
Fax: (33) 4 42 85 85 00
Web site: http://www.eurocopter.com

*Wholly Owned Subsidiary of European Aeronautic Defence
    and Space Company EADS N.V.*
Incorporated: 1992 as Eurocopter S.A.
Employees: 11,000
Sales: EUR 3.21 billion ($3.8 billion) (2005)
NAIC: 336411 Aircraft Manufacturing; 488190 Other
    Support Activities for Air Transportation; 541710
    Research and Development in the Physical, Eng-
    ineering, and Life Sciences

■ ■ ■

Eurocopter S.A. is Europe's leading manufacturer of
helicopters. Part of the EADS (European Aeronautic
Defence and Space Company) family of companies, its
heritage extends back to the histories of Aérospatiale and
MBB, the French and German companies whose
helicopter businesses were merged in 1992 to form
Eurocopter. Eurocopter manufacturers both military and
civilian helicopters. The company, which boasts the most
extensive product line in the business, typically
dominates the civil/parapublic sector with a 50 percent
market share. A Spanish "pillar" was added in 2005. Eurocopter has forged development, production, and
maintenance partnerships in a few countries outside

Europe, including the United States, China, and Japan.

THE BIRTH OF THE TIGER

Eurocopter S.A., the holding company for the Eurocopter group, was formed in 1992 through the union of the
helicopter operations of Aérospatiale of France and
Germany's   MBB   (Messerschmitt-Boelkow-Blohm).
Aérospatiale held 70 percent of the equity in the new
holding company while MBB had 30 percent. MBB was
part of Deutsche Aerospace (DASA), a unit of Daimler
Benz (later DaimlerChrysler), which later merged with
Aérospatiale to form the EADS group.

France and Germany had been working on a
military helicopter since the 1970s. However the project
did not get official clearance until 1987. It was dubbed
the PAH-2, or Tiger. Eurocopter GmbH, a consortium
of Aérospatiale and MBB, had been set up in 1984 as
prime contractor for the Tiger.

Another consortium, Eurocopter International
G.I.E., was created in May 1991 to manage the commercial helicopter operations of MBB and Aérospatiale.
Eurocopter International was based at the Aerospatiale
Helicopter Division headquarters in La Courneuve, near
Paris. It later became a subsidiary of the Eurocopter S.A.
holding company. The combined helicopter businesses
of MBB and Aérospatiale had revenues of $1.6 billion
in 1990. Aérospatiale's share of the world helicopter
market outside the Soviet Union and U.S. military had
been about 33 percent, about four times that of MBB.

From the beginning, Eurocopter was able to offer

several helicopter types that had been developed by Aérospatiale and MBB. The new company's intent was to sell these aircraft in most of the world's markets, with the exception of North America, where prior sales arrangements were in place, particularly in the case of Aérospatiale, which had a successful line of light planes.

Aérospatiale had sold about 8,700 helicopters before the formation of Eurocopter. Its offerings ranged from the single-engine Ecureuil to the powerful twin-engine Super Puma. MBB's products included the BO105, introduced in the late 1960s by the Bölkow Company as the world's first light twin helicopter. In the 1980s, which MBB had developed the BK117 rescue helicopter, which was based on the BO105, with Japan's Kawasaki Heavy Industries. Both MBB and Aérospatiale were involved in the multi-nation NH90 transport helicopter project, along with Agusta of Italy and Fokker of the Netherlands.

Eurocopter S.A. was originally headquartered near Paris. It had co-chairmen: Heinz Plueckthun from MBB and Jean François Bigay of Aérospatiale's Helicopter Division. Plueckthun soon retired and was replaced by Siegfried Sobotta, former head of Daimler-Benz's busses business.

Eurocopter was soon working with numerous partners all over the world. It tried developing a heavy-lift helicopter with Russia's Mil design bureau, but this project ultimately collapsed. The company had more success with the five-seat, single-engine EC120 Colibri (Eurocopter's smallest helicopter), developed with Singapore Aerospace and China's CATIC. A manufacturing plant was established in Harbin, China. This was designed to replace the Bell 206 and Hughes/McDonnell Douglas MD500 aircraft that had dominated the skies since the 1960s and 1970s. China had begun importing Aérospatiale helicopters in the 1960s, and began manufacturing the Dauphin under license in the 1970s.

CIVIL MARKET CRASHES IN 1993

Eurocopter won orders for its Cougar military transport helicopter from Turkey and the Netherlands in 1993. While it was the best of times for Eurocopter's military business, it was the worst of times for the world's civil turbine engine helicopter market, which, according to *Flight International,* in 1993 saw its lowest sales since 1967. Eurocopter dominated the flat market, however, with a 56 percent market share in terms of value, according to Bigay. Its main rival in the civil sphere was Bell of the United States.

Eurocopter's history in the United States dated back to the 1974 acquisition of Texas-based Vought Helicopter by Aérospatiale. In 1979, MBB also formed a U.S. unit, headquartered in Pennsylvania.

In 1993, Eurocopter posted it first annual loss, amounting to FRF 462 million ($85 million). As a result, the company cut 1,000 jobs in 1993, reducing the work force to about 10,500, followed by a couple more rounds of layoffs in the following years.

Though it remained a worldwide leader, the company could not afford to rest on its laurels. In the mid-1990s, rivals old and new succeeded in whittling away some of the company's market share based on price competition. Eurocopter fought this encroachment through a number of initiatives, reported *Interavia Business & Technology.*

Eurocopter was developing new versions of existing models, such as the Squirrel and the Dauphin, with more fuel efficient engines. At the same time, the company was also offering stripped-down, low-priced versions of military choppers such as the Cougar for sale to developing nations. The product line included more than two dozen aircraft types in all. At the end of 1996, its worldwide fleet numbered 8,000 aircraft in 130 countries. Eurocopter was also paying more attention to after-sales service, making product support a separate business unit. According to *Interavia,* after-sales service typically accounted for a third of revenues.

One important new technology was originally developed in conjunction with client Bristow Helicopters, a specialist in flights to North Sea oil rigs. The Health and Usage Monitoring System (HUMS) used a variety of sensors to monitor tell-tale symptoms of mechanical trouble before they developed into full-blown problems. This lowered maintenance costs while adding a new level of safety.

KEY DATES

1984: Eurocopter GmbH set up to manage Franco-German Tiger helicopter project.
1991: Eurocopter G.I.E. established to market Aérospatiale, MBB helicopters.
1992: Eurocopter S.A. formed through union of Aérospatiale and MBB helicopter businesses.
1996: There are 8,000 Eurocopter helicopters in service throughout the world.
1998: Popular EC120 Colibri light utility helicopter introduced.
1999: France and Germany order 160 Tiger attack helicopters.
2000: Sales exceed EUR 2 billion as European militaries order 243 NC-90 transports.
2005: Eurocopter continues to dominate the civil/parapublic market with a roughly 50 percent market share.

Both the civilian and military markets in Europe had a dramatic upswing in the late 1990s. France and Germany placed a major order for 160 Tiger attack helicopters in 1999.

2000 RESTRUCTURING

A restructuring in 2000 did away with the co-executive structure and put Pierre Bigay in charge of the whole group, which was classified a "société par actions simplifiée" (SAS), or simplified limited liability company. Eurocopter continued to be the largest helicopter manufacturer in the world, controlling a bit less than half of the civil helicopter market and 38 percent of the military market (by unit volume).

Sales exceeded EUR 2 billion in 2000. The company got a big boost when France, Germany, Italy, and the Netherlands ordered 243 NC-90 military transports. Eurocopter logged 531 orders in all, worth EUR 3.5 billion. A highlight of 2001 was the launch of the EC145. Based on the BK117, it was capable of search and rescue missions in thin mountain air.

Eurocopter managed to increase sales to EUR 2.5 billion in 2002 despite the lingering recession and aviation industry turmoil following the September 11, 2001, terrorist attacks on the United States. In fact, the company's market share in civil/parapublic helicopters was up to 60 percent.

Bigay was succeeded as Eurocopter's leader in 2003

by Fabrice Bregier, formerly head of missile manufacturer Matra BAe Dynamics/MBDA. Eurocopter had revenues of about $3.8 billion by 2004. Though exports were up, including those to the United States, the company was laboring under unfavorable exchange rates in relation to the dollar.

BRIGHT OUTLOOK IN 2006

Revenues rose 15 percent in 2005 to EUR 3.2 billion. Eurocopter Spain was added during the year as the company's third "pillar." Highlights of the year included the delivery of the first U.S.-made AS350.

A number of booming markets buoyed Eurocopter's fortunes and prospects for 2006 and beyond. The overall U.S. helicopter market was having a record sales year as high oil prices prompted new investment in offshore oil exploration. There was also a need to replace the aging fleet; an official told *Interavia* that 60 percent of its aircraft in service offshore were more than 20 years old. There were also a great number of 1980s-era rescue choppers coming due for replacement.

Asia and Eastern Europe were a growing source of sales. According to *Interavia,* although China purchased fewer than ten helicopters a year, Eurocopter was expecting the country to become as large a consumer as the United States, which bought ten times as many, by 2015.

Eurocopter was developing an intermediate (six-ton) aircraft, the EC175, to accommodate increasing use of highly automated oilfields popping up further and further from shore. The company was joined in this project by China's Avic II. Deliveries were expected to begin in 2011.

Eurocopter continued its domination of the civil helicopter market, claiming a 52 percent market share by unit sales. It was the leader in several important countries, including the United States and Japan. In 2006 it was preparing to launch a subsidiary in China, where it had been working with local firms for decades. The company also had a long history with in another emerging market, India.

Frederick C. Ingram

PRINCIPAL SUBSIDIARIES

Eurocopter Deutschland GmbH (Germany); Eurocopter España S.A.(Spain).

PRINCIPAL COMPETITORS

AgustaWestland Helicopter Company; Bell Helicopter Textron, Inc.

FURTHER READING

"Eurocopter Ambitions, New Structure," *Les Echos,* September 19, 2000, p. 14.

"France, West Germany Clear New Tiger Helicopter," *Reuters News,* November 30, 1989.

Gamauf, Mike, and Paul Brou, "Operators Give the EC120B Solid Grades," *Business & Commercial Aviation,* February 2005, pp. 30-35.

"Group Formed with MBB to Jointly Sell Helicopters," *Wall Street Journal,* May 7, 1991, p. A15 (W), A18 (E).

Lenorovitz, Jeffrey M., "Aerospatiale, MBB Merge Helicopter Commercial Sectors," *Aviation Week & Space Technology,* May 20, 1991, p. 50.

Macrae, Duncan, "Eurocopter Sitting Pretty," *Interavia Business & Technology,* February 2001, p. 19.

Michaels, Daniel, "Europe Gets Liftoff in Helicopter Sector," *Wall Street Journal* (Europe), January 2, 2004, pp. A1+.

Mordoff, Keith F., "Development Contract Signed for French/German Helicopter," *Aviation Week & Space Technology,* October 10, 1988, p. 31.

Moxon, Julian, "Down, But Not Out: The Market for Civil Helicopters Is Virtually Flat, But Eurocopter President and Chief Executive Jean-François Bigay Is Proud of the Group's Performance," *Flight International,* January 26, 1994, p. 25.

———, "Eurocopter Forced to Cut Back," *Flight International,* June 29, 1994, p. 17.

Musquére, Anne, "High Times for Helo Makers," *Interavia* (683), Spring 2006, pp. 14-18.

Sedbon, Gilbert, "Helicopter Merger Moves Closer," *Flight International,* May 15, 1991, p. 14.

Sparaco, Pierre, "Eurocopter Navigates in Crowded Field," *Aviation Week & Space Technology,* July 4, 1994, pp. 61+.

———, "Eurocopter Seeks Recovery in a Weak Market," *Aviation Week & Space Technology,* September 23, 1996, p. 31.

Sutton, Oliver, "Up-Cyclic in the Crisis: Shrugging Off the General Downturn in the Aerospace Sector, Eurocopter Turned in Another Impressive Set of Figures in 2002," *Interavia Business & Technology,* January/February 2003, pp. 14+.

Taverna, Michael A., and C. Tardif, "Eurocopter Declares War on Costs," *Interavia Business & Technology,* January/February 1997, pp. 28+.

Taverna, Michael A., "East-West Whirlybird," *Aviation Week & Space Technology,* December 12, 2005, pp. 32-34.

———, "The Cutting Edge," *Aviation Week & Space Technology,* June 13, 2005, pp. 167+.

Vechere, Ian, "MBB Consolidates in Eurocopter," *Interavia,* June 1992, p. 22.

Fannie May

Fannie May Confections Brands, Inc.

8550 West Bryn Mawr Avenue, Suite 550
Chicago, Illinois 60631
U.S.A.
Telephone: (312) 453-0010
Toll Free: (800) 243-0245
Web site: http://www.fanniemay.com

Wholly Owned Subsidiary of 1-800-Flowers.com
Incorporated: 1920 as Archibald Candy Corporation
Employees: 900
Sales: $75 million (2006 est.)
NAIC: 311320 Chocolate and Confectionery Manufacturing from Cacao Beans; 311330 Confectionery Manufacturing from Purchased Chocolate

∎ ∎ ∎

Fannie May Confections Brands, Inc. is a regional manufacturer of boxed chocolates. Its brands include Fannie May, Fanny Farmer, and Harry London. The Fannie May brand has long been a favorite in Chicago and surrounding areas, while Fanny Farmer is a venerable East Coast brand. Harry London was based in Canton, Ohio, before combining with Fannie May. Fannie May Confections operates a production facility in Ohio, and corporate headquarters are in Chicago. The company runs roughly 50 retail Fannie May candy shops in the Chicago area. It also sells its candies by mail order, through its web site, and at select grocery chains and other retailers. Fannie May was once the nation's largest boxed chocolate maker, and had hundreds of retail stores throughout the Midwest. The company went bankrupt in 2002 and was later acquired by Utah-based Alpine Confections, Inc. In 2006, Fannie May was bought by the flower and gift basket delivery firm 1-800-Flowers.com.

CHICAGO ORIGINS: 1920

Fannie May Confections Brands, Inc. began as a single candy shop in 1920. H. Teller Archibald and his wife Mildred Archibald opened Fannie May on Chicago's North LaSalle Street, in the heart of the city's central business district, the Loop. Funding for the enterprise evidently came from Mrs. Archibald's family, and the business was very soon a Chicago success. Chicago had a thriving candy industry, which had taken off after the Columbian Exposition in 1893. While most candy makers of that era were small, family-run businesses, new technology introduced in the early 1900s made larger enterprises possible. New equipment enabled manufacturers to mass-produce candies of uniform dimensions and quality. Around the turn of the century, Chicago was home to many large-scale candy companies, such as E. J. Brach & Sons, Wrigley's Gum, Ferrara Pan Candy, and Mars. Cracker Jacks originated in Chicago, as did Frango Mints, the delicacy sold at Marshall Field's department stores. According to Joel Glenn Brenner, author of *The Emperors of Chocolate: Inside the Secret World of Hershey and Mars,* the Archibalds chose Fannie May as the name of their shop to give it a consciously old-fashioned ring. Successful Chicago companies like Wrigley could churn out sweets by the thousands and even export them abroad. Fannie May was meant to hark back to the little shops of the just-vanished last

Fannie May stands for premium chocolate. We developed this by combining a delicious product, stimulating advertising, elegant packaging and selective distribution. Fannie May's standards of excellence include maintaining our product's high quality by requiring special handling during storage and display. Our growing popularity as a premium quality product is due to our innovative approaches in manufacturing, advertising and packaging.

century, with a kindly old lady in the kitchen hand-dipping chocolates. So Fannie May began with a 19th-century aura, even as it rapidly expanded in a quite 20th-century fashion.

By 1930, there were some 35 Fannie May shops across Chicago, and the company was bringing in approximately $300,000 annually. As the enterprise flourished, H. Teller Archibald became almost as well known for his race horses as for his candy company. His horses frequently had "Candy" in their names: Candy Pig, Candy Maid, Candy Queen, and so on, and they were often major contenders in East Coast stakes races. The Archibalds divorced in 1929, and in 1930, the beginning of the Great Depression, Mildred Archibald won $1 million in alimony, plus a house and car, in a delayed settlement. The award attests to both the wealth of the young company and to Mrs. Archibald's part in it. The *New York Times* notice of the alimony award (June 15, 1930) said that Mildred Archibald claimed to have "financed the candy enterprise at its inception and had a great deal to do with the growth and management" of the firm. Nevertheless, H. Teller Archibald continued to run the company after the divorce. He died in 1936, only 56 years old, of a heart attack he suffered at a Boston area racetrack.

After Archibald's death, the company was run by family members, who had married into the family of the cofounder of Montgomery Ward. The Thornes were one of the wealthiest families in Chicago, with a renowned estate on the city's suburban North Shore. The Thornes also were known for their interest in architecture, and Mrs. James Ward Thorne endowed the famous miniature rooms of period furniture at Chicago's Art Institute. Five Thorne brothers had run or been top executives at mail-order pioneer Montgomery Ward from the 1890s until 1920, when they left in a boardroom shakeout. However, members of the Thorne family owned a controlling interest in Fannie May until 1992, when they sold the company to an investment firm.

WORLD WAR II AND AFTER

Fannie May continued to be a Chicago-area institution. During World War II, when chocolate and other raw ingredients were rationed, the company cut its service rather than alter its recipes. In the war years, Fannie May retail shops closed down for the day when their goods were all sold. Immediately after the war, in 1946, the company introduced a new candy—the Pixie, a caramel and pecan confection enrobed in chocolate—that continued as a bestseller for decades. By the 1950s, Fannie May had established itself in grocery stores throughout the Chicago area. It was also one of the first major chocolate manufacturers to sell frozen candies. It retailed through Chicago's ubiquitous Jewel groceries and Osco drugstores, as well as through the Giant food store chain in the Washington, D.C., area.

In 1970, the company came out with another best-selling product, a chocolate and coconut affair called the Trinidad. Under family management, Fannie May seems to have grown slowly and steadily. In the 1980s, the company was headed by Charles Morrow, husband of Martha Thorne. He oversaw the development of a new line of candies, Sweet Persuasions truffles, while Fannie May continued to manufacture its time-tested recipes at its Chicago plant. The company eventually had several hundred retail shops in the Chicago area and beyond, while doing little to update its image or press for expansion. A new chief executive in the 1990s, James Tindall, recalled the company's earlier management style in an interview in *Crain's Chicago Business* (January 21, 1994): "If a retailer was interested in selling Fannie May candies in a freezer case, 'you had to call'," Tindall said. "More than once. It was a test to see how interested (retailers) were." In other words, the company let business come to it, rather than pursuing new opportunities, and even so, Fannie May was not quick to take on new partners. Likewise, in another reminiscence about the firm, *Candy Industry* editor Bernie Pacyniak recalled how a little Fannie May shop had stood for years, basically unchanged, half a block from a west-side Chicago train station. In the January 2004 issue he mused, "I always wondered how the folks at Archibald were able to sustain that site," as apparently it did not seem to do much business. The retailing image was evidently quite staid, though that seemed to suit its customers just fine.

SALE IN 1992

Archibald Candy Corporation had been family owned and operated since 1920. It had grown comfortably,

KEY DATES

1920: Mildred and H. Teller Archibald found Archibald Candy with first the Fannie May shop in Chicago.

1936: H. Teller Archibald dies; the firm passes to the Thorne family.

1946: The company begins selling Pixies.

1970: Fannie May introduces a new candy, the Trinidad.

1992: The Thornes sell the company to investment firm Jordan Co.; Fannie May buys Fanny Farmer.

1999: The company acquires the large Canadian candy maker Laura Secord.

2002: High debt pushes the company into bankruptcy.

2004: The Fannie May and Fanny Farmer brands are acquired by Alpine Confections.

2006: Alpine sells Fannie May Confections Brands to 1-800-Flowers.com.

while doing little to update its image. By the early 1990s, Fannie May was still manufacturing its sweets out of its Chicago plant, and it had 100 retail outlets in the Chicago area. Another 150 or so stores operated in 13 states beyond Illinois. Although the private company did not need to release sales figures, Archibald was said to be profitable. Little seemed to have changed at Archibald over the years, aside from the occasional introduction of new candies and the expansion of its retail shops. Then in 1991, the Thorne family decided to sell the company. The family did not explain the decision, but sold the firm for an undisclosed price to an investment firm called The Jordan Co. The Jordan Co. had been in business only since 1985, and in six years it had acquired 35 private firms. According to the *Chicago Sun-Times* (November 5, 1991), Jordan specialized in making "investments in medium-sized family-run companies" and it let "the people who run them run them." A Jordan executive went on to explain to the *Sun-Times* that the new owners would do little to interfere with Fannie May's way of doing business: "We're very hands off. Usually we have people running our companies who are smarter than we are. We want to grow the company much the way it's grown in the past."

The sale to Jordan was finalized in 1992, but despite the new owner's assurances, the candy company did begin to grow and change rapidly. In August 1992, Fan-

nie May made its first major acquisition, buying Fanny Farmer Candy Shops. Fanny Farmer was a venerable East Coast chain of candy shops that had much in common (though Fannie and Fanny were spelled differently) with its new owner. Fanny Farmer Candy Shops was founded in Rochester, New York, in 1919, making the firm a year older than Fannie May. A businessman named Frank O'Connor started the company, naming it in honor of one of the leading culinary artists of his day, Fannie Merritt Farmer. Miss Farmer had suffered a paralyzing stroke while a teenager. When her disability kept her from finishing school, she turned her attention to cooking. She founded her own cooking school in Boston and taught disabled students at Harvard. O'Connor was not related to Miss Farmer, but rather inspired by her. He changed the spelling of her name when he opened his first shop, perhaps for legal reasons. In any case, Fanny Farmer Candy Shops was in many ways an East Coast parallel to Fannie May: founded in an age of mechanization, it projected an air of hominess; it grew gradually in its region until it encompassed some 330 shops by 1985; and by the 1990s it was afflicted with what *Crain's Chicago Business* (February 21, 1994) called a "dusty image." In the late 1980s, the number of Fanny Farmer retail shops fell to about 200, and the firm was sold to a French company, Midial S.A.

At the time of the acquisition, Fannie May's annual sales were estimated at $85 million, and Fanny Farmer was pegged at approximately $40 million. The combined firm, still called Archibald Candy Corporation, now had some 463 stores, spread across both the Midwest and the East Coast. Production expanded at Archibald's Chicago plant, and the firm became one of the largest chocolate-makers in the United States, along with Russell Stover, See's, and Whitman's. Archibald's big expansion came at a time when the boxed chocolate industry was relatively stagnant. Industrywide sales were some $576 million in the early 1990s, remaining flat or falling. The largest competitors struggled for ways to make their products stand out. Fannie May, for example, began selling truffles, a more elegant candy, in late 1992, apparently in order to compete against European makers and premium chocolateers such as Godiva.

Soon after the Fanny Farmer acquisition, Fannie May got a new chief executive, James Tindall. Tindall introduced non-chocolate products, such as gummy bears, premium coffee, and ice cream, to some Fannie May retail shops. The company also pushed to get its chocolates in many more venues, such as drugstores and supermarkets. However, Tindall resigned to start his own company in 1994, after little more than a year in the job. He was succeeded by Ted A. Shepherd, who came to Fannie May after years of working for candy company M&M Mars. Between 1995 and 1999, Fannie

May greatly increased the number of venues carrying its products, and sales at Fannie May retail shops began to pick up. The company brokered a licensing agreement with card-maker Hallmark in 1998 and began selling Fannie May chocolates in Hallmark's 5,000 retail stores. In addition, Fannie May began buying other candy firms. It bought a California chain of candy stores, Sweet Factory, for $28 million in 1998. Then in 1999, Fannie May acquired Canada's largest chain of chocolate shops, Laura Secord. Laura Secord had 175 stores, selling its own brand of boxed chocolates. The price for the firm was $42 million. These acquisitions boosted Fannie May's revenue to $270 million by the end of the 1990s, and the company had surpassed rivals to become the largest chocolate retailer in North America.

BANKRUPTCY AND NEW OWNERS IN THE EARLY 21ST CENTURY

Fannie May had borrowed heavily to finance its acquisitions in the late 1990s, and by the early 2000s, debt had grown to some $170 million. The company had long been profitable, but only modestly, growing some 2 to 3 percent a year while it was owned by the Thorne family. By 2002, the company could no longer support its debt, and it filed for Chapter 11 bankruptcy. Under Chapter 11, a business can continue operating while it arranges with its creditors for payment of its debt. The company arranged to sell its Canadian subsidiary, Laura Secord, and it was to emerge from bankruptcy in late 2003. But the Laura Secord sale fell through. This sent Fannie May into turmoil. In January 2004, the company announced that the Fannie May and Fannie Farmer brands were being acquired by a Utah-based candy company, Alpine Confections. The deal included the rights to the names and the retail shops, though most of the retail outlets were immediately shut down. Fannie May's Chicago factory also shut down, putting hundreds of people out of work. The sudden loss of Fannie May shops put Chicagoans in a tizzy. When the shutdown was announced, crowds made runs on their favorite Fannie May sweets.

Alpine Confections was founded in 1993 by two Harvard Business School friends, R. Taz Murray and Dave Taiclet. The business was a conglomeration of several candy or sweets businesses, including Maxfield Candy Co., maker of boxed chocolates; Kencraft, known for sugar Easter eggs; the Peppermint Place candy retail stores; licensed products under the Mrs. Fields' Original Cookies name; and several other boxed chocolate manufacturers. The company had sales of $80 million in 2003, and Fannie May's sales that year were $183 million. Alpine paid about $39 million for the distressed Fannie May. Alpine was able to reopen about 50 Chicago-area Fannie May shops about a year after the acquisition, and demand was apparently very strong. Alpine made Fannie May and Fanny Farmer brand candies at its plants in Salt Lake City and in another facility it owned in Canton, Ohio.

Nonetheless, Fannie May's sojourn with Alpine Confections was brief. In 2006, Alpine announced that it had sold three of its brands: Fannie May, Fanny Farmer, and Harry London, as well as its Ohio plant, to the flower and gift delivery company 1-800-Flowers. com. The three units came together as Fannie May Confections Brands, Inc., which became a wholly owned subsidiary of the florist. The purchase price was $85 million. By that time, Fannie May had revenue of about $75 million—far less than in its heyday in the late 1990s. The new owners hoped to be able to grow the candy company again. 1-800-Flowers operated through phone and Internet orders, delivering not only flowers but candy, gourmet foods, stuffed animals, and other gift basket items. It also owned a mail-order subsidiary called Plow & Hearth, which sold mostly home and garden products, the children's toys catalog retailer Hearthsong, a cookie company, a popcorn company, and a gourmet foods subsidiary called GreatFoods.com, so the fit with Fannie May was not hard to see. Fannie May continued to be run out of executive offices in Chicago, with Alpine's Dave Taiclet as chief executive. Although the ownership was new, the company planned to continue to use the same recipes and ingredients on which it had based its fame since 1920.

A. Woodward

PRINCIPAL COMPETITORS

Godiva Chocolatier, Inc.; Russell Stover Candies Inc.; See's Candies, Inc.

FURTHER READING

"Alpine Confections Acquires Fannie May, Fanny Farmer Brands," *Candy Industry,* January 2004, p. 14.

Brenner, Joel Glenn, *The Emperors of Chocolate: Inside the Secret World of Hershey and Mars,* New York: Random House, 1999.

Broekel, Ray, *The Chocolate Chronicles,* Lombard, Ill.: Wallace-Homestead Book Co., 1985.

"Candy Stable Wins Two Miami Races," *New York Times,* January 21, 1927, p. 9.

Chandler, Susan, "Fannie May Bought by Investment Firm," *Chicago Sun-Times,* November 5, 1991, p. 50.

Corman, Linda, "America's Enduring Sweet Tooth," *New York Times,* February 21, 1993, p. A1.

Crown, Judith, "Fannie and Fanny Fight Dusty Image," *Crain's Chicago Business,* February 21, 1994, pp. 4, 49.

"Fannie May Reopens 47 Stores," *Candy Business,* November–December 2004, p. 8.

"Gets $1,000,000 Alimony," *New York Times,* June 15, 1930, p. 22.

"H. Teller Archibald, Manufacturer, Dies," *New York Times,* July 25, 1936, p. 13.

Herman, Eric, "Fannie May 'Would Be a Flagship Brand'," *Chicago Sun-Times,* February 26, 2004, p. 65.

"How Sweet! Alpine to Re-Open 30 Fannie May Stores," *Confectioner,* June 2004, p. 6.

Jackson, Cheryl V., "Sweet Deal: 1-800-Flowers.com Buying Fannie May for $85 Million," *Chicago Sun-Times,* April 6, 2006, p. 53.

Latham, Frank B., *1872–1972 A Century of Serving Customers: The Story of Montgomery Ward,* Chicago: Montgomery Ward, 1972.

"Mrs. Mildred K. Hyde," *New York Times,* February 26, 1937, p. 21.

Obertance, Charles, "Candy Makers Hope Frozen Sweets Will Thaw Summer Sales," *Wall Street Journal,* June 4, 1957, p. 1.

Pacyniak, Bernie, "Too Close to Home," *Candy Industry,* January 2004, p. 8.

Podmolik, Mary Ellen, "Sweet Deal Fannie May Buys Fanny Farmer," *Chicago Sun-Times,* August 5, 1992, p. 59.

Rewick, C. J., "Fannie May: Fatter Sales, Debt," *Crain's Chicago Business,* July 5, 1999, p. 4.

Schultz, Susy, "Charles Morrow, Ex-Fannie May Chief," *Chicago Sun-Times,* March 13, 1998, p. 66.

Floc'h & Marchand

BP 20 111
Kerbethune Moreac
Locmine,
France
Telephone: (33) 02 97 61 66 00
Fax: (33) 02 97 61 66 29
Web site: http://www.jean-floch.com

Private Company
Incorporated: 1989
Employees: 2,300
Sales: EUR 402.76 million ($480 million) (2004)
NAIC: 311611 Animal (Except Poultry) Slaughtering;
    311612 Meat Processed From Carcasses; 311615
    Poultry Processing

■ ■ ■

Floc'h & Marchand is France's leading privately held pork processor, with an output of more than 170,000 tons per year. The company, based in the Brittany region (the heart of the French pork industry) operates in all areas of pork production, from slaughtering to the distribution of fresh meat products to the production of processed and prepared foods, including delicatessen meats, frozen meats, and other products. Floc'h & Marchand, founded by Jean Floc'h and Bernard Marchand in 1969, sells its products under several brand names, including Jean Floc'h, Bernard, and Clermont Salaisons. The company is also a major supplier to the large-scale distribution channel. Floc'h & Marchand

operate ten industrial sites, for the most part located in the Brittany region.

After weathering the swine flu crisis in the French pork industry in the late 1990s and early 2000s, Floc'h & Marchand has been investing in increasing its production in the mid-2000s, including a EUR 6 million expansion of its Clermont delicatessen meats plant in Liffre in 2005. Floc'h & Marchand is a private company and remains under the control of its founding partners. In 2004, the company's sales topped EUR 406 million ($480 million).

EARLY DAYS: PORK PROCESSOR

Jean Floc'h joined in the creation of the pork farmer's cooperative Cooperl in 1966. Based in Lamballe, in the Cote d'Armor region of Brittany, France, Cooperl was formed in order to provide technical assistance and marketing support for its member farmers. The French pork industry was then undergoing a transformation from a largely artisanal, local focus to an increasingly industrialized business. A driving force behind the change in the pork sector was the introduction of self-service supermarkets, and the development of large-scale and nationally operating distribution groups, such as Carrefour, E. LeClerc, Auchan, Casino, and the like. The rising demand for packaged pork products, and the steadily rising purchasing power and pricing pressure exerted by the retail giants, encouraged the growth of farmers' cooperatives such as Cooperl in order to help protect and serve their farmer-members' interests.

Floc'h was one of just 24 founders of Cooperl, but the cooperative grew quickly. By 1970, the group already

KEY DATES

1966: Jean Floc'h is a founding member of Cooperl pig farmer cooperative.
1967: Floc'h's friend, Bernard Marchand, joins Cooperl.
1985: Floc'h and Marchand acquire Clermont Salaisons and begin production of processed meat products.
1989: Company expands slaughtering capacity and adopts name of Floc'h & Marchand.
1990: Company establishes the Jean Floc'h Conserverie and enters the canned meat market.
1995: The Bernard Salaisons subsidiary is launched.
1997: Frozen meat production begins.
1999: A joint venture is begun with Kaufler to provide slaughtering and processing technology to Shandong, China.
2001: Company acquires Charles S.A., a live pig sales agent, and regroups frozen meats business into single factory.

counted 665 members, and production had risen from 8,000 pigs at the beginning to 210,000. By 1975, Cooperl's membership had climbed to 1,300, and the cooperative's total output had doubled to 480,000. While Cooperl's membership was to remain fairly constant over the next thirty years, its production increased dramatically—by the turn of the century, Cooperl represented a total stable of nearly 2.6 million pigs. The vast increase in productivity reflected the huge change that had taken place, not only in France's agricultural sector, but in the retail distribution market, consumer buying patterns. Food technologies and logistics also played a part in the growth of the sector. The development of refrigeration technologies in the 1950s, including refrigerated transport, made it possible to transfer slaughterhouses from France's urban centers to locations close to the country's pork farms. This led to the creation of several specialized slaughterhouses, including the Gilles slaughterhouse, built in Colliney in 1955, which served Cooperl.

Cooperl's operations remained limited to marketing its members' pigs and providing other technical service. Yet the Gilles slaughterhouse's financial crisis in 1977, and its subsequent takeover by the LeClerc supermarket group (which then began supplying its own retail network), led Cooperl to expand its range of functions. In 1978, the cooperative acquired stakes in its first two

slaughterhouses. By 1979, Cooperl had taken over slaughterhouse operations directly.

Floc'h worked for Cooperl into the 1980s, where he was joined by close friend Bernard Marchand. Toward the middle of the 1980s, however, Floc'h and Marchand had begun to hatch plans to leave Cooperl and set up business for themselves. Their plans came to fruition in 1985, when Floc'h and Marchand, together with Floc'h's wife Yvonne and another friend, André Thébault, bought a small, family-owned deli meat producer, Clermont Salaisons. That company had started out as a butcher's shop in the early part of the century, until it was bought by Marcel Clermont in 1957. In 1965, however, Clermont led the business to focus on its production of delicatessen and salted meats (*salaisons*), and Clermont Salaisons quickly established a regional reputation for its fresh, cooked and salted meat products.

Operating Clermont Salaisons whetted the partners' appetite for business. The group soon began exploring other avenues of business and by 1987 had decided to develop upstream operations, buying up a slaughterhouse in Locminé. This business was then named Bernard Locminé. The slaughterhouse facility not only helped supply the Clermont Salaison operation, it also gave the partners direct access to the market for fresh pork cuts. By 1989, the group prepared to expand still further, carrying out a large-scale expansion of the Locminé facility. At the completion of the expansion, the facility grew to a capacity of 35,000 tons per week, becoming one of the largest in the Brittany region. At this time, the founding partners founded a new company for the growing operations, called Floc'h & Marchand.

ACQUIRING SCALE IN THE 1990S

Floc'h & Marchand sought new areas for expansion into the 1990s. The company responded to the fast-rising demand for prepared foods in the early 1990s by founding a new company, Jean Floc'h Conserverie, inaugurating the group's own canning business. The company then added to its range of prepared and salted meat products, forming a new company, Bernard Salaisons, in 1995. A further extension in the category included the creation of Jean Floc'h Salaisons, which specialized in the production of different types of sausage, as well chopped beef products, and fresh pre-seasoned pork meats.

During the 1990s, Floc'h & Marchand rose to prominence as a leading supplier of pork products to the French market. The company also developed a strong export business through the decade, supplying not only other European markets, but markets in North Africa, the Middle East, and Asia. For these markets, the company developed specific products, such as pork-free products for Muslim countries. By the mid-2000s, the export market accounted for some 20 percent of the group's total sales.

Floc'h & Marchand itself made a brief excursion into the international market in the second half of the 1990s. In 1995, the region of Brittany set up an economic cooperation agreement with the Chinese province of Shandong. This led Floc'h & Marchand to join with Kaufler S.A., a supplier of slaughterhouse and meat processing equipment based in Brittany, to form a joint-venture with a local partner in Shandong to develop a business producing delicatessen meats and sausages. Launched in Jining in 1999, that company was later sold to another company and moved to Qingdao.

Closer to home, Floc'h & Marchand had set its sights on further expansion. The company acquired its first site outside of Brittany, at Montigny Le Breton-neux, near Paris, in 1998. That company, set up at the beginning of the 1980s, focused on supplying local butcher shops with cuts of meat. Following its takeover by Floc'h & Marchand, however, the Montigny factory expanded its operations to include the processing and preparation of vacuum-packed meat cuts for the restaurant and catering market. That operation was renamed as Bernard Montigny.

Floc'h & Marchand continued its growth through 1998, acquiring two slaughtering and processing units of fellow Briton Fleury Michon, a producer of packaged delicatessen meats. The first of the two was Loudéac Viandes, originally established in 1965 on a site belonging to the Olida Group, which was subsequently acquired by Fleury Michon in 1992. The second plant, called Ster Goz, was located in South Finistere, established in 1949 as a slaughterhouse. Once under Floc'h & Marchand's control, the Ster Goz site converted its operations to become a major boning facility, preparing meats for canned and salted meat producers, including parent Floc'h & Marchand.

FRENCH PORK LEADER IN THE NEW CENTURY

In the meantime, Floc'h & Marchand had begun developing a new line of business, that of frozen meat products. The company began investing in freezing capacity in 1997, adding flash freezers to several of its sites. The rapid growth of this sector, particularly through the large-scale distribution channel, encouraged Floc'h & Marchand to add a dedicated freezer plant in 2001, regrouping all of the company's frozen foods production.

Floc'h & Marchand faced a setback, however, with the outbreak of a swine flu epidemic at the end of the 1990s. The company saw its sales slip dramatic, amid sensational headlines. The company's international sales were particularly hard hit. A blow to the company came from the banning of pork imports to South Korea, a major export market for Floc'h & Marchand.

Nonetheless, the company continued to invest in its expansion. In 2001, the company acquired Charles S.A., based in Sizun, near Brest. That company had been founded in 1977 and served as a sales agent for live pigs. By 1983, Charles had begun exports to Italy, and especially Sicily. Charles later added exports to Germany and else, as well as becoming a supplier to Floc'h & Marchand's Bernard plant in Kerbéthune.

Into the mid-2000s, Floc'h & Marchand remained a prominent player in the French pork market, and by the middle of the decade had become the country's leading privately owned pork products supplier. Under the continued leadership of founders Jean Floc'h and Bernard Marchand, the company remained committed to its future growth. In 2005, for example, the company spent some EUR 6 million on a major expansion of the its Clermont production facility.

M. L. Cohen

PRINCIPAL SUBSIDIARIES

Bernard Jean Floc'h Locminé; Bernard Locminé; Bernard Montigny; Clermont Salaisons; Jean Floc'h Conserverie; Jean Floc'h Salaisons; Jean Floc'h Surgélation; Ster Goz.

PRINCIPAL COMPETITORS

Danish Crown AmbA; Sovion N.V.; Kerry Group plc; Orkla ASA; Groupe Terrena; Sadia S.A.; SOCOPA S.A.; Glanbia plc; Agrial; Doux S.A.

FURTHER READING

"Crise porcine: l'ensemble de la filière est touché," *Les Echos*, April 30, 1999.

"Fleury Michon se sépare de deux de ses filiales," *Les Echos*, January 15, 1998.

"Floc'h & Marchand crée un joint venture en Chine," *Les Echos*, April 15, 1999.

"Floc'h investit dans le surgelé," *Les Echos*, September 15, 1997.

"Floc'h Marchand revient sur le marché coréen du porc," *Les Echos*, October 29, 2002.

"French Meat Firm Plans Major Investments," *Agra Europe*, August 13, 1999.

"Itinéraires de "self-made patrons": Jean Floc'h, 62 ans," *L'Expansion*, February 3, 2000.

FRANZ INC.

Franz Inc.

———————— ▪ ————————

555 12th Street, Suite 1450
Oakland, California 94607
U.S.A.
Telephone: (510) 452-2000
Toll Free: (888) CLOS-NOW
Fax: (510) 452-0182
Web site: http://www.franz.com

Private Company
Incorporated: 1984
Employees: 43
Sales: $103 million (2004 est.)
NAIC: 511210 Software Publishers

■ ■ ■

Based in Oakland, California, Franz Inc. is a leading vendor of products that software developers use "to build sophisticated, flexible and scalable applications quickly, easily and cost-effectively." The company's products—which are used by the likes of Lucent Technologies, Aluminum Company of America (ALCOA), SRI, and GTE Internetworking—are based on Common Lisp (CL), a general-purpose computer programming language. Franz markets Common Lisp products under the Allegro CL name, which software developers use in a number of different areas, including e-commerce, expert systems, electrical and mechanical computer-aided design (CAD), Internet knowledge-based systems, process control, and scheduling. In addition, the company offers a variety of consulting services, as well as basic, intermediate, and advanced training and certification in Lisp programming.

ORIGINS OF FRANZ: 1974–1983

The List Processing (Lisp) programming language was originally developed in 1958 by artificial intelligence (AI) pioneer John McCarthy, who established the first AI research lab at the Massachusetts Institute of Technology (MIT). Simply stated, AI is the development of machines, or computer systems, that can think and learn. The Lisp language quickly became the standard for developing AI applications.

According to Franz, the company's origins can be traced back to a computer program called Macsyma, which was used to solve complex math problems. Developed at MIT during the early 1970s, Macsyma was first written in a variant of the Lisp language called MACLisp. Along with INTERLisp, MACLisp was one of the most popular Lisp dialects during the 1970s.

As Franz details on its web site, the Macsyma application was so enormous that it required a powerful computer on which to run—a specially configured DEC 10 manufactured by Digital Equipment Corp. The DEC 10 boasted what then was a massive and expensive 2.5 megabytes of memory.

Professor Richard Fateman, who received a Ph.D. in mathematics from Harvard University in 1971 and taught the subject at MIT from 1971 to 1974, was one of the programmers who created Macsyma. Franz explains that after joining the computer science faculty at the University of California, Berkeley, in 1974, Fate-

COMPANY PERSPECTIVES

Franz Inc. has thrived by making it easy for Lisp users to play leading roles in the software industry, and continuously striving to introduce new functionality and features. Further, Franz Inc. understands that it is critical to grow the Lisp market—special academic pricing, educational tools and scholarship programs have all been implemented to ensure that the pool of Lisp users will continue to increase as new people discover this vibrant, dynamic language.

man "continued to access the MIT system over the ARPAnet (the predecessor of today's Internet). In 1978, he learned of a new DEC computer, called the VAX-11/780, which could run Macsyma and many other programs more efficiently and at a much lower cost."

After garnering funds from the National Science Foundation to acquire the university's first VAX computer, Fateman recruited students to "build a version of Lisp that would form the substrate for the version of VAX Macsyma." Among these students were the individuals who would eventually found Franz: John Foderaro, Kevin Layer, and Keith Sklower.

Fateman's students dubbed the new Vax Lisp "Franz Lisp," after Hungarian composer, conductor, and piano virtuoso Franz Liszt (1811–86). The name was meant to convey that the implementation was a quick one, and to mirror the university's "pun-filled" atmosphere.

FORMATIVE YEARS: 1984–1999

According to Franz, Franz Lisp had been distributed for free to thousands of research labs and universities by the mid-1980s. Although the language had been well received by programmers, Fateman and his students were focused on research, not providing technical support. It was this very situation that gave birth to Franz Inc.

As the number of powerful computer workstations began to grow, UC Berkeley graduate student and Scientific Software Support Manager Fritz Kunze foresaw the need for an independent company to "port" and provide support for Franz Lisp. Porting is the process of adapting software for use on different computers or operating systems. The company explains, "Despite a proliferation of free, but unsupported Lisp systems, Kunze believed that important commercial applications would need significant customer support, a high quality product and active development."

With encouragement from Fateman, in 1984 Kunze and students Foderaro, Layer, and Sklower raised $500 and founded Franz Inc., using the seed money to incorporate their enterprise and buy an embosser and blank stock certificates. The firm established its headquarters in a spare bedroom at Kunze's house. Charley Cox and David Margolies were among Franz's first employees.

One major hurdle Franz faced was the $10,000 price tag of a new computer. This was overcome, however, by negotiating a deal with Sun Microsystems. In exchange for porting Franz Lisp to Sun's workstation, the company was able to secure a free workstation.

"Kunze and Foderaro were so nervous that Sun would back out of the deal that they drove down that same day to pick up the computer," the company explains. "Franz continued this practice with every contract negotiated, and soon they had numerous workstations to work with."

Prior to the mid-1980s, the Department of Defense (DoD) had been using different variations of Lisp for research initiatives in the areas of expert systems and artificial intelligence. Almost immediately after Franz was established, the DoD challenged the Lisp community to develop a unified programming language called Common Lisp. A new company called Lucid—which had support from the DoD, Stanford University, and venture capitalists—was formed to develop Common Lisp. Armed with some $25 million in funding, the new firm quickly emerged as an industry leader.

Once developed, Common Lisp differed considerably from the original version of Lisp. In the September 1991 issue of *Communications of the ACM*, Franz cofounder Kevin Layer, along with Franz employee Chris Richardson, described it as "a rich, sophisticated language providing functional, imperative, and object-oriented programming."

The entrance of Lucid was a major crisis for Franz. The company quickly found itself being excluded from much-needed contracts, and it saw support from the Lisp Standardization Committee dwindle. According to Franz, "It was clear that Franz Lisp would need major revisions to become an implementation in Common Lisp." In response, cofounder John Foderaro decided to spend one year working from his home, thereby minimizing distractions, and develop a new version of Common Lisp from the ground up.

As if this situation was not difficult enough, cash was in short supply. Franz weathered the storm by striking its first large deal with a company called Tektronix, which needed a version of Lisp for an artificial intelligence machine it was constructing. Franz beat out Lucid for the contract with competitive pricing and a two-phase deal that involved providing Tektronix with Franz Lisp first, and then Common Lisp when the company's new version was ready.

Franz Inc. launched Extended Common Lisp (ExCL), its version of Common Lisp, in late 1986. As the company explains, this product was eventually renamed Allegro CL in 1988, in keeping with the musical theme that inspired the name Franz several years before. It also was in 1988 that Franz unveiled Allegro CommonLISP 1.0., a Common Lisp implementation for Apple Macintosh programmers. Priced at $600, the new system was developed in tandem with Coral Software.

As the 1980s came to a close, Franz inked another major deal—this time with supercomputer manufacturer Cray Inc. Specifically, Franz ported Allegro CL to the Unicos operating system on the Cray X-MP supercomputer.

Heading into the 1990s, Franz was able to secure a number of smaller customers, but large computer companies like Hewlett-Packard, IBM, and Sun Microsystems continued to repackage Lucid's version of Common Lisp as their own. In addition, Digital Equipment Corp. emerged as a new source of competition with its product, DEC Common Lisp.

Positioned as the industry underdog, Franz competed by demonstrating how its version of Lisp was a better choice than Lucid's. In addition to working on computers with limited amounts of memory, Franz touted that Allegro CL was also faster. Unlike Lucid, Franz made its Common Lisp product hardware independent. On its web site, Franz explained that this strategy enabled the company "to provide direct sales and technical support to its customers, and allowed customers to choose their platform based on best price/performance versus being tied to a particular machine."

In late 1991 Franz worked in partnership with Burlington, Massachusetts–based Symbolics Inc. to develop

Common Lisp Interface Manager (CLIM) 2.0, a next generation set of tools that developers could use to develop graphical user interfaces (GUIs) for applications created with the Lisp programming language. The companies placed CLIM 2.0 specifications in the public domain, and worked with other Lisp vendors to make the tool available for use on other versions of Lisp.

In mid-1992 Franz acquired the rights to Procyon Common Lisp, a Common Lisp product for the Windows operating system. That November, the company introduced the product, renamed Allegro CL£C, at a price of $595. According to *PC Week,* a number of industry analysts were skeptical about Franz's prospects for cracking into the PC object-oriented programming software market, due to competition from other languages and well-funded competitors with established market footholds.

Despite analysts' skepticism, by the fall of 1993 Franz had unveiled Allegro CL£C 2.0 at an object-oriented programming conference, which it expected to sell for $995. By early 1994 Allegro CL£C was being used by the likes of Price Waterhouse. At the company's Price Waterhouse Technology Centre in Menlo Park, California, developers used Franz's development system to create Planet and Venus, two knowledge-based systems for financial auditors. In the March 1994 issue of *AI Expert,* Price Waterhouse Senior Research Scientist Walter Hamscher praised Allegro CL£C for reducing development time.

An important development took place on the competitive front in 1994. That year, Franz arch-rival Lucid declared bankruptcy. According to Franz, Harlequin Inc., one of its principal competitors, acquired Lucid's technology and re-branded it as "Liquid Lisp." By the decade's end a Belgian company had acquired Harlequin, and its Lisp technology was spun off into a new enterprise named Xanalys. These changes to the competitive landscape strengthened Franz's position as an industry leader. In fact, heading into the early 2000s Franz was one of the few remaining Lisp companies.

Another important development that took place in the late 1990s was the 1998 release of Allegro CL 5.0, a new version that was capable of running on either the UNIX or Windows platform. Previously, the company marketed separate versions for each platform.

TAKING LISP ONLINE: 2000 AND BEYOND

The new millennium saw Lisp being applied to Web-based applications in many ways, and Franz's Lisp products were no exception. The company unveiled an open source Web server product called AllegroServe in

June 2000 that developers could use to build complex web sites with dynamically-generated HTML pages.

Lisp quickly became a development tool for both business-to-consumer and business-to-business (B2B) e-commerce. "Critical properties inherent in Lisp make it a great solution for the B2B e-commerce arena," a July 26, 2000 *Business Wire* release explained. "Lisp's internal list-based structure makes catalog-like applications easy to program, enabling the consolidation and standardization of multiple information sources. Furthermore, applications can be modified while they are running, eliminating revenue-losing downtime."

During the early 2000s, e-commerce companies such as Cadabra Inc. and Commerce One Inc. were using Allegro CL as part of their Web development efforts. In addition, ITA Software used Allegro CL to build software that the airline industry used to power the Orbitz travel web site. Franz continued to offer new Web-related technology heading into the mid-2000s, including its NFS Server for Windows in 2004.

Beyond Web applications, Franz saw its Lisp technology used in other exciting ways during the 2000s. For example, Allegro CL was used by NASA contractor Johnson Engineering to develop software for packing equipment into Multi-Purpose Logistics Modules, which the space shuttle used to transport cargo to the International Space Station.

In early 2006 Franz enjoyed a leadership position in the Lisp segment of the computer software industry. From humble roots the company had managed to weather turbulent times and secure a growing customer base. While continuing to serve the AI research community, Franz had played a key role in finding new markets for the Lisp programming language.

According to the company, the future seemed to be a promising one. On its web site, Franz explained: "The increased speed and memory capacity of today's computers, as well as improved software technology, have eliminated many of the concerns that developers had with Lisp in the past as well. Many developers are beginning to view it as the ideal technology for today's software development and delivery needs."

Paul R. Greenland

PRINCIPAL COMPETITORS

Autodesk Inc.; Digitool Inc.; Gold Hill Co.

FURTHER READING

"Allegro CommonLISP: A Complete Microcomputer Implementation of Common LISP," *Byte,* January 1988.

Coffee, Peter, "A Fresh Look at LISP," *eWeek,* February 6, 2006.

———, "'Exotic' Tools Go Mainstream," *eWeek,* February 6, 2006.

———, "GUI Tools Highlight 32-Bit LISP for Windows," *PC Week,* November 7, 1994.

Damore, Kelley, "Object Tools Are Unveiled at OOPSLA; Digitalk, HP, Franz, Show Off Cross-Platform Programming Technology," *InfoWorld,* October 4, 1993.

Enrado, Patty, "Application Watch," *AI Expert,* March 1994.

Foderaro, John K., "LISP," *Communications of the ACM,* September 1991.

"Franz Allegro CL 6.2 Premiers at the National Conference of Artificial Intelligence in Edmonton, Canada," *Business Wire,* August 12, 2002.

"Franz Inc. Releases Web Server; AllegroServe Dynamically Generates HTML, Enabling Developers to Easily Build and Manage Complex, Customized Websites," *Business Wire,* June 1, 2000.

"Franz Inc. Unveils Software Development Suite Allegro CL 6.0: Dynamic Lisp Tools Suited for Internet, Java Connections and More," *Business Wire,* November 17, 2000.

Goggin, Terence, "Get with the Program," *Sm@rt Reseller,* November 29, 1999.

Heller, Martin, "Allegro CL 6.0," *Byte.com,* February 9, 2001.

Howle, Amber, "Franz Ships New Allegro CL Suite," *Computer Reseller News,* July 19, 1999.

"ITA Software Uses Lisp Technology to Help Set Orbitz Apart from Other Travel Sites," *Business Wire,* July 10, 2001.

Layer, Kevin D., and Chris Richardson, "LISP Systems in the 1990s," *Communications of the ACM,* September 1991.

"Lisp Applications Create Solutions to Business-to-Business—B2B—Challenges; Franz Inc. Working with E-Commerce Leaders to Provide More Sophisticated Products and Services," *Business Wire,* July 26, 2000.

"Lisp Emerging as 'The Language of E-Commerce'; Cadabra, Others Built Using Allegro CL," *Business Wire,* June 29, 2000.

"Moving Vans for the International Space Station Get Packed Using Franz Inc.'s Lisp Technology," *Business Wire,* September 5, 2001.

Murphy, Thomas, "Speaking with a LISP," *Computer Language,* March 1993.

Newquist, Harvey P. III, "Lisp for Lunch," *AI Expert,* May 1994.

"Richard J. Fateman," Berkeley, Calif.: University of California at Berkeley, April 10, 2006, Available from http://www.cs.berkeley.edu/~fateman/.

Singh, Jal, "Franz Announces LISP-Based Windows OOP Environment," *PC Week,* October 26, 1992.

Snyders, Jan, "The Reality of the Promise," *Infosystems,* November 1986.

"Stand Up for Their Rights. (Franz Inc. Acquires the Rights to Procyon Common LISP for Windows and Renames It Allegro CL)," *AI Expert,* July 1992.

"Symbolics, Franz to Develop CLIM 2.0," *ISR: Intelligent Systems Report,* December 1991.

The GAME Group plc

Unity House, Telford Road
Basingstoke,
United Kingdom
Telephone: (44) 01256 784000
Fax: (44) 01256 784093
Web site: http://www.gamegroup.plc.uk

Public Company
Incorporated: 1995, as Electronic Boutique Ltd.
Employees: 4,214
Sales: £645.12 million ($1.06 billion) (2006)
Stock Exchanges: London
Ticker Symbol: GMG
NAIC: 443112 Radio, Television, and Other Electronics Stores; 423990 Other Miscellaneous Durable Goods Merchant Wholesalers; 551112 Offices of Other Holding Companies

■ ■ ■

The GAME Group plc is the largest video game retailing specialist in Europe. The company counts over 700 retail sales points—including company owned and franchised stores and in-store concessions—in the United Kingdom, Ireland, France, Sweden, Spain, and Denmark. Based in London, the group's largest business remains in the U.K. and Irish markets, where the company operates more than 400 stores, as well as in-store concessions in department stores, including the Debenhams, House of Fraser, and Fenwick groups. In France, the company operates through the ScoreGames retail chain, that country's leading reseller of video games and software.

The company operates more than 100 stores in France. GAME Group has also expanded into Spain through the acquisition of the CentroMail retail chain, also a market leader with more than 140 stores, as well as a strong online and mail-order business. GAME's Spanish operations have also helped the company expand into Portugal, where it opened a store in 2006. In Scandinavia, the company operates 50 stores, primarily in Sweden, and, since 2004, in Denmark as well. GAME is also present online, operating e-commerce sites under its three primary brands. The GAME Group is listed on the London Stock Exchange and is led by Chairman Peter D. Lewis and CEO Martin Long. In 2006, the company's revenues topped £645 million ($1.1 billion).

PIONEERING THE U.K. VIDEO GAME MARKET IN 1992

The GAME Group stemmed from the earliest attempts to develop a specialized network for video games in the late 1980s and early 1990s. The development of new and more powerful television-based video gaming consoles, accompanied by the arrival of the first graphics-based computer games had created new retail opportunities. In the United Kingdom, a number of retailers, including electronics retailers, department stores, and video games retailers, began offering video games as part of their product mix.

A more limited number of specialized video game resellers also appeared during this time. Among these was Future Zone, established in 1999 by Bev Ripley and Terry Norris. Ripley and Norris had been behind the creation of the Ritz video store chain, through their company City Vision during the 1980s. By the end of

COMPANY PERSPECTIVES

As a specialist it is our continual aim to develop our business, providing our customers with the best shopping experience possible. We aim to constantly review and improve the unique offerings and services that customers see as our unique selling proposition, and therefore maintain our position as the leading specialist retailer in this growing market.

that decade, the pair had built Ritz into England's leading specialist video store retailer, before selling the chain to the United States' Blockbuster Entertainment Corp. for $120 million in early 1992.

Following that sale, Norris and Ripley became interested in the possibilities offered by the growing video game sector. Still in its infancy, and generally looked down upon by the rest of the entertainment sector, the video game sector nonetheless counted a growing number of highly enthusiastic customers. This enthusiasm, further stimulated by the significant strides made in graphics and processor technologies during the first half of the decade, would propel the gaming sector into the lead as the world's fastest-growing and single largest revenue-generating leisure market by the mid-2000s.

Norris and Ripley purchased a shell company called Rhino Group Plc and launched the Future Zone retail format at the end of 1992. Rhino was able to raise some $6 million in initial backing capital, including a reported investment by Blockbuster Entertainment, and by the end of that year, the company had opened the first six of a projected 140 stores.

Ripley and Norris planned to expand the Future Zone primarily through the development of new locations, projecting as many as 50 stores in operation by the end of 1993. The popularity of new generation gaming systems, and especially the Sega Mega Drive and the Super Nintendo, which together shared nearly 55 percent of the total market, helped to drive the group's growth. By the end of that year, Rhino had largely fulfilled its goals, with 46 Future Zone stores already in operation. The company was also close to becoming profitable.

At the end of 1993, however, the company came upon a new opportunity to acquire scale, when Virgin and W. H. Smith announced their intention to sell the 30-store Virgin Games chain, which had been developed

as joint venture. Rhino quickly agreed to buy Virgin Games, paying £12.5 million pounds. According to Ripley, the acquisition came as something of a surprise. As he told *Billboard,* "It's a smashing deal, because I thought we would have to grow organically. We've not taken any of their overhead, and it's a straight bolt-on to our business." With 76 stores in operation, Future Zone claimed a 10 percent share of the U.K. video game market. That market—for both software and hardware—was estimated at nearly £1 billion ($1.5 billion) at the end of 1993. Game software sales alone were estimated at £400 million. Tellingly, sales of CD-ROM based games accounted for just 0.5 percent of the games market.

LINKING WITH ELECTRONIC BOUTIQUE IN 1995

By the early 1990s, another major player on the video game retail front was enjoying its own brisk growth. Founded in the early 1980s as a single kiosk in a shopping mall in Pennsylvania, Electronics Boutique (EB) had developed into one of the United States' leading video game retailers by the end of the 1980s, with more than 75 stores and $30 million in sales. The first video game boom in the early 1990s helped EB build its empire to more than 315 stores by the time Future Zone itself was just starting out.

EB had also launched an international expansion effort in the early 1990s, moving into Puerto Rico, Australia, New Zealand, Korea (the founder's native country), and Europe. For its U.K. growth, however, EB sought out a local partner. EB's opportunity came in early 1995, when it acquired a stake in the Future Zone. By then, Rhino appeared to have run out of steam—while the company struggled for profitability amid the morose British economy of the period, expansion of the group's retail chain had also slowed, reaching just under 120 stores at mid-decade. A downturn in the video game market hit Rhino hard at the beginning of 1995. In a bid for survival, the company agreed to sell 25 percent of its shares to EB.

Following the share purchase, the two companies entered into a service agreement under which Rhino converted its stores to the Electronic Boutique format and signage, gaining purchasing and support services from the U.S. company in exchange for annual licensing fees. Rhino also changed its name, becoming Electronic Boutique Ltd (EBL).

With new backing and a new format, EBL resumed its growth in the second half of the 1990s. The period marked a significant transformation of the video game industry, which within a few short years emerged as one

---

KEY DATES

1992: Bev Ripley and Terry Norris acquire Rhino Group and launch specialist video game retail format, Future Zone.

1993: Rhino acquires 30 Virgin Games stores from Virgin and W. H. Smith.

1995: The Electronic Boutique, Inc. (U.S.) acquires 25 percent of Rhino, which changes its name to Electronic Boutique Limited (EBL) and re-brands its stores.

1997: EBL launches a customer loyalty scheme providing discounts and other preferred customer offers.

1999: EBL acquires GAME, a rival video game specialist with stores in the United Kingdom and Sweden.

2001: EBL acquires CentroMAIL in Spain and Scoregames in France.

2002: The company rebrands as The GAME Group.

2005: The GAME Group acquires AddOn in France and opens its first stores in Denmark.

2006: GAME Group enters the market in Portugal.

---

of the world's most vibrant mainstream leisure categories. Driving the growth was a twofold emergence of technology: a new generation of multimedia-capable personal computers and a new generation of a gaming consoles—including the arrival of the Sony Playstation—featuring 32-bit and then 64-bit graphics capabilities.

The gaming market was divided into two segments based on the device use for playing the games: personal computers and branded game consoles. The console market, which was highly controlled by Sega, Sony, and Nintendo, enjoyed an especially strong degree of repeat business. Loyal customers were eager to be the first to buy new video game titles and console releases, often waiting in line overnight to do so. Recognizing this aspect of the business, EBL introduced a loyalty rewards scheme in 1997 to encourage more consumer activity.

By 1999, EBL had grown to a chain of more than 180 stores, and also boasted a number of in-store boutique concessions housed with other U.K. retailers. Already the leading games retailer in the United Kingdom, EBL cemented its leading position with the purchase of a major rival, GAME, which operated 82 stores in the United Kingdom and in Sweden. The purchase, which cost EBL £97 million, also diluted the

U.S.-based EB's stake in the British chain to 18 percent. EBL decided to retain the GAME retail format alongside its EB store chain during the first years of the new decade. Following the acquisition of GAME, the company also launched the GAME Reward loyalty card. That program attracted some five million customers by the mid-2000s.

In the meantime, EBL developed a number of other outlets, including a wholesaling agreement to supply the the giant Sainsburys retail group. In 2001, EBL acquired failed U.K. online games pioneer Barrysworld, which had gone into liquidation that year. EBL initially operated the site under its original name, then converted it under a new name, www.Game.net.

EBL launched a still more ambitious expansion effort in that year, setting out to build up a European base. The company's first move came in June 2001 in Spain, where it acquired that country's leading specialist video game and computer software retailer, CentroMAIL. The purchase added 70 stores to EBL's holdings.

That acquisition was followed, in October 2001, with a move into France, where EBL bought up that country's ABC Games International and its retail format, ScoreGames. The purchase, worth an initial £7.6 million, gave EBL control of France's second largest video game retailer, with 37 largely Paris-based stores. As Chairman Peter Lewis told *The Birmingham Post*: "The acquisition of Scoregames is another significant step in our European strategy bringing our total number of branded, franchised and gaming outlets in Europe—outside the U.K. and Eire—to 141 compared with four just four months ago."

GAME ON FOR THE NEW CENTURY

EBL broke with Electronic Boutique Inc. in 2002. The U.K. operator changed its name to The GAME Group and carried out a re-branding exercise, renaming all of its stores under the GAME name. GAME Group also attempted to break free of its service contract with EB, which cost the company upwards of $6 million per year. However, EB's right to continue the contract until its 2006 end date was upheld in British court.

Into the mid-2000s, buoyed by the smash successes of such gaming consoles as the Playstation II and the Nintendo Gamecube; the introduction of the Microsoft Xbox, among others; and by the overall success of the video gaming market, the GAME Group's expansion remained strong and steady. In Spain, the company grew rapidly, doubling its number of stores by the end of 2005. At the same time in France, the company's Scoregames unit grew to more than 100 stores, and included a new acquisition, Addon, in 2005. In the United Kingdom, the company, which chiefly operated in the High Street and city center sectors, opened its first out-of-town retail stores, starting in 2003. Not all of the group's expansion efforts were successful, however. The company attempted to launch a new DVD retail format, called Pure Entertainment, opening two stores by this name in Bristol and Reading. These were both closed in early 2005.

At the middle of the decade, GAME became interested in other new markets, such as Denmark, where the first GAME store opened in 2005. Through its Spanish subsidiary, the company also targeted the Portuguese market, opening its first store in that country in March 2006. Given predictions for the future strength of the video game market, with new consoles from Microsoft, Sony, and Nintendo expected in 2006, the GAME Group looked like a winner for the near future.

M. L. Cohen

PRINCIPAL SUBSIDIARIES

ABC Games International S.A. (France); Engine Technology Systems SL (Spain); Game (Stores) Ltd.; Game Digital Ltd; Game Financial Services Ltd.; Game Retail (U.K.) Ltd; Gameplay (GB) Ltd; Game Store Group Ltd; Game Stores Group Sweden AB.

PRINCIPAL COMPETITORS

Stirling Group Ltd.; LG International (U.K.) Ltd.; Prism Leisure Corporation PLC; Yamaha-Kemble Music (U.K.) Ltd.; Windsong Holdings Ltd; Vital Distribution Ltd.; Bell-Fruit Games Ltd.; Namco Europe Ltd.; Pinnacle Entertainment Ltd.

FURTHER READING

Cullen, Drew, "EB Buys Its Way into France," *Register,* October 8, 2001.

Dean, Peter, "A New Future in the Offing for Virgin Games," *Billboard,* December 4, 1993, p. 59.

———, "B'buster Backs UK Vid-game Venture," *Billboard,* November 7, 1992, p. 91.

Dudley, Dominic, "Online Gaming Sector Hits Highs and Lows over Holiday," *New Media Age,* January 8, 2004, p. 4.

"Electronics Boutique and Game Group PLC Severed Their Services Agreement Struck in 1995," *Chain Store Age,* March 2004, p. 14.

Fahey, Rob, "Game to Open Second Out of Town Store," *GI Gamesindustry.biz,* August 22, 2003.

"Game Group plc Christmas Trading Update Conference Call," *Fair Disclosure Wire,* January 10, 2006.

"Game Launches Pay Services on Barrysworld," *New Media Age,* August 29, 2002, p.5.

"Game Seeks Agency for Creative Account," *Campaign,* July 15, 2005, p. 2.

"Game to Score with ArtScience," *Design Week,* September 16, 2004, p. 6.

Pain, Steve, "Electronic Boutique Snaps up Scoregames," *Birmingham Post,* October 9, 2001, p. 28.

Taylor, Paul, "EB in £97m offer for Game," *Financial Times,* April 13, 1999.

Glaverbel Group

Chaussee de La Hulpe 166
Bruxelles,
Belgium
Telephone: (32) 02 674 31 11
Fax: (32) 02 672 44 62
Web site: http://www.glaverbel.com

Wholly Owned Subsidiary of Asahi Glass Company
Incorporated: 1961
Employees: 16,600
Sales: EUR 2 billion ($2.5 billion) (2004)
NAIC: 327211 Flat Glass Manufacturing

■ ■ ■

Glaverbel Group is one of the world's leading producers of raw and processed glass. The company ranks in the world top three and, thanks to early investment in the Czech Republic and Russia, is also the leading producer of glass in Eastern and Central Europe. Based in Belgium, Glaverbel produces glass for the architectural and design markets, as well as for the marine glazing market. The company is also a leading producer of automotive glass, through subsidiary AGC Automotive Europe, formerly known as Splintex. Glaverbel operates production facilities and subsidiaries in Belgium, The Netherlands, France, the United Kingdom, Italy, and Spain in Western Europe, and in the Czech Republic, Poland, and Russia in Central and Eastern Europe. Glaverbel itself has been wholly owned by Japan's Asahi Glass Company since 2002. The company is led by Chairman Arthur Ulens. Glaverbel's sales top EUR 2

billion ($2.5 billion) in the mid-2000s.

BELGIUM GLASSMAKING CONSOLIDATION IN 1961

French-speaking Belgium's involvement in the glassmaking industry stretched back to Roman times. Into the 21st century, the region remained one of the global glass centers, representing some 20 percent of the total world production. The outlines of the modern industry began to appear as early as the 14th century, when glassmaking became the specialty of a small number of families. This led later to the development of industrial glass production in the late 17th century. Already by the mid-1800s, the region boasted the largest number of glass furnaces in Europe. The region's position was further boosted with the invention of the Fourcault mechanical manufacturing process in 1902, which in large part replaced manual glassmaking techniques. By then, more than 85 percent of the glass produced in Belgium was sold internationally.

Yet the increased use of industrialized production techniques and the collapse of the global economy forced a shakeup in the Belgian glassmaking sector at the beginning of the 1930s. The result was a first consolidation of the industry, creating two major companies. The first of these was L'Union des Verreries Mécaniques de Belgique, or Univerbel, created in 1930. The second, S.A. Glace et Verre (Glaver), was founded just one year later.

The companies remained competitors in the postwar period, as the country's glass industry contributed to the country's reconstruction. The massive worldwide demand for glass—particularly strong in devastated Europe—further boosted both Univerbel and Glaver. By the 1950s, Belgium had become the world's largest glass producer. Later in that decade, Univerbel and Glaver joined together in helping to set up a glassmaking factory in Tiel, The Netherlands, which began construction of a glassmaking factory in 1959 under the name of Machinale Glasfabriek De Maas.

Yet the invention of a new glassmaking technique— the "float" method developed by Alistair Pilkington in the United Kingdom—in the late 1950s brought a new crisis in the industry. The new technique, which involved floating molten glass on top of liquid tin, cost less and produced a glass superior to the traditional grinding and polishing methods of producing sheet glass. Float glass quickly became the new industry standard, forcing companies such as Univerbel and Glaver to shut down their existing furnaces and replace them with new float production equipment.

To remain competitive, therefore, Univerbel and Glaver agreed to merge in 1961, creating a new Belgian glassmaking giant, Glaverbel. The new company also included De Maas, which launched production at the Tiel facility in 1964. That subsidiary later became known as Maasglas.

In the meantime, Glaverbel had begun investing in its own float glass technology, and in 1965 opened the first such factory in continental Europe, in Moustier, Belgium. The opening of the new plant helped Glaverbel weather the grueling economic difficulties of the industry through the 1960s. Nonetheless, the company continued to rely heavily on its increasingly outdated sheet glass furnaces. Into the 1970s, the economic crisis battered the company, as well as the rest of the European glassmaking industry.

NEW OWNERS IN 1981

In 1972, Glaverbel was taken over by France's BSN. Later known as Danone, the company was then one of

the two largest glass manufacturers in France, created through the merger of Boussois and Souchon-Neuvesel in 1966. BSN had initially attempted to take over its French rival Saint Gobain, which was also struggling heavily into the 1970s. When that effort failed, the company instead acquired Glaverbel.

The development of still more efficient float glass technology in the early 1970s brought new stress on Glaverbel. Faced with the urgent need to shut down its sheet glass furnaces and convert its production to the new technology, Glaverbel was further hit by the deepening economic recession of the period. As a result, Glaverbel slipped into deep losses by 1975.

The company's losses forced it to undertake a restructuring in 1977. At the same time, Glaverbel adopted a new strategy that called for the company to integrate vertically, adding flat glass processing operations. As part of that effort, the company acquired automotive glass maker Splintex, based in Gilly, in Belgium, founded in 1929. Glaverbel also launched a research and development effort, in part to develop more energy-efficient glass products. The company's success in this area allowed it once again to take its place at the forefront of the industry. Glaverbel also expanded its Splintex division, adding a new tempering plant in Fleurus in 1979.

By the late 1970s, BSN, which also had been developing operations in the processed foods and beverages industry, decided to focus its operations on these markets. The company sold parts of its glassmaking empire to the United Kingdom's Pilkington. Yet Pilkington was not allowed to acquire Glaverbel for antitrust reasons. Instead, BSN found a buyer in Japanese glass major Asahi Glass Company. In 1981, Asahi acquired 80 percent of Glaverbel; by 1983, the Japanese company had taken full control of the Belgian company.

With Asahi's backing Glaverbel continued its expansion through the 1980s. In 1984, for example, the company's De Maas subsidiary opened a new float glass factory in The Netherlands. The Dutch subsidiary then changed its name, to Maasglas.

Asahi took Glaverbel public in 1987, listing the company on the Brussels Stock Exchange. The public offering of 35 percent of Glaverbel set the stage for a new growth period for the company, and particularly its emergence as an international glass production leader. Glaverbel initially targeted the U.S. market. In 1988, the company acquired nearly 20 percent of AFG Industries, formerly part of Saint Gobain, which was then the second largest flat-glass manufacturer in the

KEY DATES

∎

1930: The merger of several Belgian glass producers creates Univerbel.

1931: Glaver is created through the merger of a second group of Belgian glass producers.

1959: Glaver and Univerbel cofound the De Maas glass factory in Tiel, The Netherlands.

1961: Glaver and Univerbel merge and form Glaverbel.

1965: Glaverbel opens its first float glass production facility in continental Europe.

1972: BSN acquires Glaverbel.

1975: Glaverbel acquires Splintex, an automotive glass producer, as part of a diversification strategy.

1981: The Asahi Glass Company of Japan acquires 80 percent of Glaverbel.

1983: Asahi acquires 100 percent of Glaverbel.

1987: Glaverbel is listed on the Brussels Stock Exchange.

1988: Glaverbel acquires a stake in AFG Industries in United States.

1990: The Glaverbel joint venture is established in Canada; a stake is acquired in the glass production operations of Sklo Union in the Czech Republic.

1996: The company sells its stake in AFG to Asahi and refocuses on the European market.

1997: The company acquires 40 percent of Bor Glass in Russia.

1999: Eijkelkamp is acquired in partnership with Akzo Nobel Coatings in The Netherlands.

2002: Asahi acquires full control of Glaverkamp and refocuses the company as its European flat glass operation.

2005: Glaverbel boosts its stake in Bor Glass to 83 percent; a new factory is built in Klin, near Moscow.

United States. By the beginning of the 1990s, Glaverbel and Asahi Glass had together acquired full control of AFG.

In 1990, Glaverbel also entered Canada, joining with two institutional investors to build a float glass manufacturing plant. Glaverbel held 72 percent of that company, Glaverbec. In 1993, Glaverbel bought out its partners in Glaverbec, which was then merged into AFG Industries. The following year, Glaverbel sold part of its share of AFG to Asahi.

GLASS LEADER IN THE NEW CENTURY

Glaverbel's exit from the AFG partnership was inspired by its success elsewhere. In 1990, the company became the first western glass manufacturer to enter the Eastern Bloc region with the acquisition of 40 percent of state-owned Sklo Union's sheet glass division. Glaverbel continued to build up its position in that operation, which was renamed as Glavunion, and later Glaverbel Czech. By 1992, the company controlled 67 percent of the Czech glass group, and by 1994 had increased its stake to 74 percent. By the end of the decade, Glaverbel had acquired full control of the Czech subsidiary. The new operation, located in the Bohemia region, placed Glaverbel close to the German and Austrian borders, providing a strong export market for the Czech operation. The purchase of the Sklo Union also boosted Glaverbel's automotive glass operations; following the acquisition, the Czech auto glass division took on the new name of Thorax.

By 1996, Glaverbel had reoriented its strategy, targeting its growth in Europe, especially in Eastern and Central Europe. As a result, the company sold the rest of its stake in AFG Industries to parent company Asahi Glass.

Soon after, Glaverbel found a new acquisition target, that of Bor Glass Works in Russia. The company initially acquired a 44 percent stake in Bor, for $15 million. The purchase made Glaverbel the first Western group to invest in the predominantly underdeveloped Russian glass market, and as such the company was able to establish a clear leadership position as that market took off in the 2000s.

Glaverbel's next expansion efforts came closer to home, when in 1998 it agreed to acquire the European operations of the United States' PPG Glass Industries. The $240 million purchase gave Glaverbel a new network of factories in Europe, mostly focused on Italy and France. As a result of the PPG Europe purchase, Glaverbel doubled its market share in Europe. The following year, the company joined with Akzo Nobel Coatings to acquire Eijkelkamp, a distributor of float glass and decorative coatings based in The Netherlands. As the company entered the new decade, it shifted its expansion focus to capital investment. In 2000, for example, the company began construction of two float glass facilities in Belgium and in the Czech Republic. Glaverbel also entered Spain, establishing a joint venture with Pilkington to build a float plant in Sagunto.

The difficult economic period, coupled with an oversupply in the Eastern Europe market, slowed Glaverbel's growth, however. At the same time, the consolidation of the global glass market over the previous decade had encouraged Asahi to restructure its own global operations. In order to carry out this restructuring, Asahi moved to reacquire full control of Glaverbel. By 2002, that process was completed, and Glaverbel's listing was removed from the stock exchange.

With Asahi in full control of the company, Glaverbel was refocused as its Japanese parent's European flat glass operation, which was extended to include operations in Poland as well. As part of this restructuring, Glaverbel's automotive glass businesses were regrouped into a single entity, renamed as AGC Automotive Europe in 2004.

Glaverbel continued to build up its position into the middle of the decade. At the beginning of 2005, the company increased its stake in Bor Glass to 83 percent. By then, the Russian company had received some $100 million in investment since its takeover by Glaverbel. In October 2005, the Russian unit was boosted again with the opening of a new glass plant in Klin, near Moscow. That unit, operated by Glaverbel Czech, represented an investment of more than EUR 160 million. The new plant confirmed Glaverbel's position not only as leader in the fast-growing Russian glass sector but as Europe's leading producer of flat glass.

M. L. Cohen

PRINCIPAL SUBSIDIARIES

A.I.V. (France); Agc Automotive Europe (France); Bor Glassworks (Russia); Bradley Glass (U.K.); Daver (France); Eijkelkamp (Netherlands); Energypane; Gedopt; Glacisol (France); Glaverbel Athus; Glaverbel Balticglav (Poland); Glaverbel Barevka (Czech Republic); Glaverbel Batiglav (Czech Republic); Glaverbel Cordoba (Spain); Glaverbel Cuneo (Italy); Glaverbel Glavcentrum (Czech Republic); Glaverbel Glavdas (Czech Republic); Glaverbel Glavetron (Czech Republic); Glaverbel Iberica (Spain); Glaverbel Jumet; Glaverbel Klin (Russia); Glaverbel Kwarcglav (Poland); Glaversun Industries (Italy); Guardiola (Spain); Kempenglas; Miroiterie Hirtz (France); Mirox; Schott Industrial Glass (Jv; U.K.); Schott-Glaverbel Do Brasil (Jv; Brazil).

PRINCIPAL COMPETITORS

Compagnie de Saint-Gobain; CRH plc; Madhvani Group; PPG Industries Inc.; Pilkington plc; Corning Inc.; Guardian Industries Corporation; Nippon Electric Glass Company Ltd.; Nippon Sheet Glass Company Ltd.; Andersen Corporation; KCC Corporation; Central Glass Company Ltd.; Oluwa Glass Company plc.

FURTHER READING

"Arthur Ulens," *Glass Magazine,* February 2006, p. 110.

Bouvy, Catherine, "Le verre en Wallonie...une longue histoire," *Dialogue Wallonie,* September 2003, p. 4.

"Glassmakers Raided in Price Fixing Probe," *Glass Age,* March 16, 2005, p. 4.

"Glaverbel," *Financial Times,* February 19, 2002, p. 20.

"Glaverbel Building New Plant in Belgium," *Glass Magazine,* November 2000, p. 21.

"Glaverbel Consolidates in Russia," *International Glass Review,* Autumn 2004, p. 24.

"Glaverbel Czech Becomes the Largest Flat Glass Producer in Eastern Europe," *Chemical Business NewsBase—Hospodarske Noviny,* November 28, 2002.

"Glaverbel Czech Has Contributed to the Expansion of Its Owner in Russia," *Chemical Business NewsBase—Hospodarske Noviny,* January 25, 2006.

"Glaverbel Czech Still Changing," *Glass,* June 2004, p. 124.

"Glaverbel Free to Take Over PPG's European Float Glass Business," *European Report,* September 2, 1998.

"Glaverbel Licenses Mirror Production," *Glass Age,* February 28, 2003, p. 5.

"Glaverbel Opens in Klin, Russia," *Glass Age,* October 12, 2005, p. 10.

Hijino, Ken, "Asahi Glass to Buy Remaining Glaverbel Stock," *Financial Times,* December 20, 2001, p. 23.

Globo Comunicação e Participações S.A.

Avenida Afrânio de Melo Franco 135
Rio de Janeiro, Rio de Janeiro 22430-060
Brazil
Telephone: (55) (21) 2540-4444
Fax: (55) (21) 540-1037
Web site: http://www.globo.com.br

Private Company
Incorporated: 1982
Employees: 7,841 (TV Globo only)
Sales: BRL 5.56 billion ($2.31 billion) (2005)
NAIC: 511120 Periodical Publishers; 511130 Book Publishers; 512110 Motion Picture and Video Production; 512191 Teleproduction and Other Postproduction Services; 512210 Record Production; 512240 Sound Recording Studios; 515120 Television Broadcasting; 515210 Cable and Other Subscription Programming; 517510 Cable and Other Program Distribution; 518111 Internet Service Providers; 518112 Web Search Portals

■ ■ ■

Globo Comunicação e Participações S.A. is the leading media group in Brazil. It controls Brazil's leading broadcast television network, leading cable-television operator, and leading pay television programmer. Rede Globo de Televisão, or Globo TV Network, the Globo group's main company, has long dominated Brazilian television and is the largest commercial television network outside the United States. Globo also controls Brazil's second largest publisher of books and magazines, produces films, and has several subsidiaries involved in various aspects of the sound-recording and music industries. It also holds a stake in the nation's leading Brazilian satellite direct-to-home television distributor, a controlling interest in the second largest Brazilian printing company, and a half-share in a film-programming service sold to subscription television operators in Brazil.

Most Globo television programs can be found on the Internet through interactive sites provided by Globo.com, Globo's Internet division. Globo is both horizontally and vertically integrated. TV Globo produces, for example, three-quarters of its programs and promotes the recording artists of the music subsidiaries, while Editora Globo S.A., the publishing subsidiary, does the same in its magazines. Similarly, the printing company prints the majority of Editora Globo's magazines. Globo is under the leadership of the three surviving sons of Roberto Marinho, founder of the enterprise, and is indirectly wholly owned by the Marinho family and certain relatives of the Marinho family. It is part of Organizações Globo, an even more diversified media concern that also includes a portfolio of newspapers and a radio network.

Roberto Marinho, Globo's founder, is sometimes called the "Citizen Kane" of Brazil. Unlike William Randolph Hearst, who unsuccessfully ran for mayor and governor of New York and sought the presidency of the United States—or Silvio Berlesconi, who used his media empire to become premier of Italy—Marinho was an uncharismatic figure who operated from behind the scenes. Nevertheless, he exercised at least as much influence over Brazilian politics as two similar Latin American media moguls over their countries: Emilio Azcárraga

As a communication group, our paramount commitment is to the public interest and the truth. Within our core competence—information and entertainment—we are fully aware of our responsibility of generating and satisfying knowledge demands and contributing for the development of a well-informed and politically conscious society.

Milmo in Mexico and Gustavo Cisneros in Venezuela. The family empire that he created includes not only information and entertainment enterprises but also finance companies, shopping centers, cattle ranches, and manufacturers of bicycles, furniture, and microelectronic equipment—in all, about 100 companies.

A MEDIA EMPIRE: 1925–1995

Irineu Marinho, Roberto's father, was a reporter who founded his own daily newspaper but later lost control of it. He launched *O Globo,* a Rio de Janeiro daily, in 1925. Only three weeks later, he died, leaving the paper in the hands of his oldest son, Roberto, a 20-year-old university student. Characteristically, Roberto did not make himself editor-in-chief until 1931, first throughly training himself as a reporter and editor. *O Globo* grew to become, at times, the most-read newspaper in Brazil and still ranks as Rio de Janeiro's leading daily. Marinho launched his first radio station in 1944 and developed it into a national network. He entered the magazine and book publishing business in 1957 under the name Rio Gráfico Editora.

Strongly conservative, pro-business, pro-American, and fearful of communism, Marinho welcomed the overthrow of Brazil's elected president in 1964. He was an enthusiastic supporter of the military governments that ruled the nation until 1985, in spite of their censorship of the media. With funding and technical help from Time-Life Broadcasting Inc., he opened a television station in Rio de Janeiro in 1965. He soon added stations in São Paulo and Belo Horizonte. The modernization of Brazil's telecommunications system and favorable government treatment enabled the fledgling Globo network to expand, by 1972, into Brasilia, the capital, and Recife, a principal city in northern Brazil, giving it truly national reach. Globo became, in terms of audience, the largest network in 1970. By 1980 the network had 36 affiliates, including 6 partly owned by Globo—and by 1985, 46. TV Globo distinguished

itself from the competition by rejecting dependency on U.S. programming and harnessing Brazil's own talents to produce its own programs, hiring many of the nation's best entertainers, actors, writers, and directors. By 1980 the network was winning 60 to 90 percent of the nation's viewers.

TV Globo was transmitting 20 hours a day in 1985, with 80 percent of the material generated internally. Although its fare included sports, variety shows, series, and miniseries, the starring role in its lineup consisted of the telenovelas it showed in prime time: episodes of a story line that continued for months. The telenovela (called, in Brazil, simply a novela) did not originate in Brazil, nor was Globo the first Brazilian network to adopt it. However, Globo, which began producing telenovelas in 1965, swept the field because Marinho hired the best people to mount them and built a state-of-the-art studio to make the product worthy of their efforts. Very little was left to chance. Marinho commissioned pollsters to determine public reaction to different characterizations and situations, enabling, for example, writers and producers to "kill off" certain characters and replace them with actors who had more charisma. By the mid-1980s, Globo was featuring three hour-long telenovelas, six evenings a week. As early as 1970, they were being sold to television stations abroad. They proved a hit in other parts of Latin America, and even in Africa, Asia, and Europe. By 1988 the telenovelas were being exported to 128 countries. (U.S. English-language networks were not interested, however, maintaining that their viewers would not accept dubbing or subtitling.)

TV Globo sandwiched the network's half-hour news program, "National Journal" (introduced in 1969), around the two main telenovelas, enabling Marinho to reach a mass audience with his views on public policy. He briefed his staff in advance on how to treat sensitive topics and followed up with comments, suggestions, and complaints. After military rule ended in 1985, Marinho skillfully cultivated the civilian presidents who followed. The communications minister, an ally, canceled major government contracts with the Brazil unit of Japan's NEC Corp., enabling Marinho to acquire operating control of this financially weakened communications-equipment manufacturing unit. By 1987 Marinho was a billionaire, according to *Forbes,* but Globo suffered embarrassment for its close ties with President Fernando Collor de Mello, who resigned in disgrace in 1992 because of corruption scandals.

Globo continued to expand in this period. In 1985 it acquired Telemontecarlo, a network aimed at French and Italian viewers that won 10 percent of the Italian viewing audience but was sold in 1994. In the early

KEY DATES

■

1925: Roberto Marinho inherits ownership of the Rio de Janeiro newspaper *O Globo*.

1944: Marinho launches his first radio station and later develops it into a national network.

1965: The first Marinho-owned television station begins operations in Rio de Janeiro.

1970: Globo has become Brazil's leading television network, in terms of audience share.

1980: Globo commands 60 to 90 percent of Brazil's television audience.

1988: Globo's wildly popular telenovelas are being shown in 128 countries.

1995: Globo joins a consortium to provide direct-to-home satellite TV in Latin America.

1999: Annual revenues of the Globo organization are estimated at $2.8 billion.

2002: Globo declares a moratorium on payments to service about $1.4 billion in debt.

2005: Creditors agree to refinance $1.23 billion in bonds and bank debt.

1990s it bought 15 percent—the maximum allowed for foreign investors in broadcasting—of the Sociedade Independente de Comunicação (SIC) television network in Portugal, and its programming helped make SIC the nation's leading network. Globosat Programmadora Ltda. was established in 1992 to develop pay television programming in Brazil. Globo Cochrane Gráfica e Editora Ltda. was established as a joint venture with R.R. Donnelley Latin America LLC in 1991.

ENTERING NEW FIELDS: 1995–1999

By the mid-1990s Marinho was nearing 90 and no longer capable of managing his empire; he died in 2003 at the age of 98. Leadership passed to his three surviving sons, and they, in turn, hired a team of professional day-to-day managers in 1998 so that they could concentrate on strategic planning. They were determined to forestall Globo's rivals by entering every field of telecommunications. Globo, in 1995, joined with Rupert Murdoch's News Corp., Mexico's Grupo Televisa S.A., and Tele-Communications Inc., the largest cable TV operator in the United States, to provide direct-to-home satellite television service to all of Latin America. (The latter two were later replaced by Liberty Media International, Inc.) Globo also was investing

heavily in its subscription television units, which included not only Globosat but also Globo Cabo S.A. (later Net Serviços de Comunicação S.A.), which became the leading cable television distributor in Brazil. Globo also founded an Internet portal, Globo.com. It spent $455 million to build state-of-the-art digitalized studios for TV Globo and other entertainment units at Projac, Rio de Janeiro, where the production center covered about 1.5 million square meters.

Since Globo was a private enterprise, it was difficult for outsiders to assess its organizational structure and finances, but the Brazilian business magazine *Exame* made an attempt in 1996, based on copies it had obtained of the enterprise's bank-loan applications. These documents indicated that "Organizações Roberto Marinho," which had no legal existence, was divided into two great branches employing 12,500 people. One branch, controlled by Marinho and his three sons, consisted of television, radio, and newspaper holdings. The other, under a holding company named Globo Comunicações e Participações Ltda. (Globopar), controlled 31 companies engaged in activities such as telecommunications, subscription TV, books and magazines, recordings, real estate, and finance. Each branch represented about half of Globo's estimated $2.4 billion in annual revenue, with TV Globo alone accounting for $1.06 billion, 72-per-cent-owned NEC do Brasil for $640 million, and Editora Globo—the magazine and book unit—for $200 million. The organization's real estate holdings, in additions to the Projac complex, included shopping centers in São Paulo and São José dos Campos; Rio Atlântica Hotel, a five-star hotel in Rio de Janeiro; and apartment and office buildings.

With regard to the communications and entertainment properties, the TV Globo network consisted of its five stations and 86 affiliates, with its signals reaching all but seven of Brazil's 4,491 municipalities. The network accounted for 76 percent of all advertising dollars spent in the television media. *O Globo* was one of the four largest and most influential newspapers in Brazil. Editora Globo, which was turning out 200 books a year and publishing 45 magazines, was 70 percent owned by the Marinho family, through Globopar. Two-thirds of Globo's publications were being printed in Brazil, with the principal Brazilian printer being Globo Cochrane. Globopar's holdings included the recorded music companies Sigla-Sistema Globo de Gravações Audiovisuais Ltda. and RGE. Globosat was the largest supplier of programs for cable TV in Brazil, while Globo Cabo was in charge of their sales and publicity.

Organizações Globo also controlled home video and DVD companies, and movie production company Globo Filmes, which was founded in 1997. In 1999 it established TV Globo International, distributed by satellite and, with a channel in Portuguese, aimed at Brazilians living abroad. That year the enterprise introduced a high-speed broadband service for Globo Cabo's subscribers. A year later, TV Globo introduced its first reality show, produced by Endemol Globo, a company in which it held a half-share. Another holding was Livraria do Globo S.A., a bookstore chain. Organizações Globo's revenues came to $2.8 billion in 1999, and the family's holdings were conservatively valued at $6.4 billion.

GLOBO IN THE 21ST CENTURY

By late 1999, however, Organizações Globo was in financial trouble, after Brazil's economy fell into recession in 1998, forcing it to devalue its currency, the *real*, in January 1999. This, in effect, made it more difficult to service its heavy dollar-denominated debts, and the *real* continued to sink in value against the dollar. Wall Street analysts began looking askance at Globo's finances, forcing the enterprise to abandon some of its cellular phone ventures and to sell nearly 10 percent of Globo Cabo to Microsoft Corp. in 1999 for $126 million. In 2000 it sold 30 percent of Globo.com to Telecom Italia S.p.A. for $810 million.

In late 2002 Globopar declared a moratorium on payments on its debt, which came to about $1.4 billion, mainly incurred by the cable and satellite enterprises. To reinforce the bottom line, Globo now sold some of its peripheral businesses, including a bank, a construction company, and its majority stake in NEC do Brasil. In 2004, it sold a 37 percent stake in cable company Net Serviços to a Brazilian company owned by Telefónos de México, S.A. de C.V. (Telmex) for $370 million. Globopar won approval for its restructuring plan from the holders of all six of its bond issues, who agreed to exchange debt for new securities or cash. This was completed in April 2005, when creditors agreed to refinance $1.23 billion in bonds (80 percent) and bank debts (20 percent).

Shortly after this restructuring, in August 2005, TV Globo and Globopar were merged into an entity named Globo Comunicação e Participações S.A. Broadcast television revenues represented more than 75 percent of the entity's total 2005 revenues on a consolidated pro forma basis. The Globo television network, consisting of the five Globo-owned stations and 118 affiliated ones, held 59 percent of the national viewership in prime time. Globo was producing about 88 percent of the prime time programming and about 74 percent of all the programming it broadcast. Globosat, the most important source of Globo's content and programming revenues, was the leading provider of pay television

programming for cable multiple system operators and satellite television distributors in Brazil. Globo also controlled 51 percent of the voting shares of Net Serviços, the largest multiple system cable operator and pay television distributor in Brazil, which was also a leading provider of broadband Internet access through its Virtua service. It also held a 40 percent stake in Sky Brasil Serviços Ltda., the leading satellite distributor of direct-to-home pay television services in Brazil. Sky Brasil historically obtained all of its programming from Globo's licensing subsidiary, Net Brasil S.A., until a 2004 agreement modified its role to that of providing only Brazilian programming to Sky Brasil. Approval, expected in 2006, of a merger between Sky Brasil and DirecTV Brasil, would reduce Globo's stake in the merged enterprise to 28 percent.

Editora Globo, the publishing arm, was the second largest magazine publisher in Brazil in terms of circulation and advertising revenues. Its titles included *Época,* the second-largest newsweekly, *Quem,* the third-largest celebrity title, and the Brazilian edition of *Marie Claire.* Globo Cochrane, now 81 percent owned by Globo, was printing more than 140 magazines. Globo Filmes, between 1995 and 2005, produced or co-produced 9 of the 10 top-grossing Brazilian movies. Sigla and RGE were producing soundtracks connected to Globo's telenovelas, series, and shows. A third music subsidiary involved the sale of compact discs, DVDs, and other similar items, but most of its assets were sold in 2005. The Marinho newspaper and radio interests remained outside reorganized Globo, which recorded very healthy net income of BRL 1.97 billion ($817.72 million) on net revenues of BRL 5.59 billion ($2.31 billion) in 2005.

Robert Halasz

PRINCIPAL SUBSIDIARIES

Editora Globo S.A. (95%); Globo Cochrane Gráfica e Editora Ltda. (81%); Globosat Programmadora Ltda.; Net Brasil S.A.; Som Livre.

PRINCIPAL COMPETITORS

Abril S.A.; Grupo Bandeirantes de Comunicação; Sistema Brasileiro de Televisão.

FURTHER READING

Chung, Joanna, "Globopar Moves to Refinance Dollars 1.3bn," *Financial Times,* May 10, 2005, p. 47.
Dolan, Kerry A., "Brazil's TV Magnates," *Forbes,* July 3, 2000, pp. 232-34.
Kapp, Michael, "Tuning In," *Latin Trade,* October 2004, pp. 22-23.

Moffett, Matt, "As 'The Other World' Turns, TV in Brazil Gets Downright Odd," *Wall Street Journal,* September 29, 1999, pp. A1, A10.

———, "Brazil's Marinhos Evolve to Keep Clout," *Wall Street Journal,* December 4, 1995, p. A9.

Netz, Clayton, "A Globo Plim-Plim por Plim-Plim," *Exame,* September 25, 1996, pp. 40-42, 44.

Page, Joseph A. *The Brazilians.* New York: Addison-Wesley, 1995.

Riding, Alan, "Brazilian Soap Operas Appeal to Global Tastes," *New York Times,* October 20, 1985, Sec. 2, pp. 25, 32.

———, "One Man's Political Views Color Brazil's TV Eye," *New York Times,* January 12, 1987, p. A4.

———, "On TV, Brazil Is Getting a Clear Picture of Itself," *New York Times,* December 13, 1984, p. A2.

Sinclair, John, "The Globalization of Latin America," *NACLA Report on the Americas,* January 2, 2004, pp. 15+.

Smith, Tony, "Roberto Marinho, 98, Brazilian Media Mogul," *New York Times,* August 8, 2003, p. C11.

Hobby Lobby Stores Inc.

————————————— ■ —————————————

7707 S.W. 44th Street
Oklahoma City, Oklahoma 73179
U.S.A.
Telephone: (405) 745-1100
Fax: (405) 745-1636
Web site: http://www.hobbylobby.com

Private Company
Incorporated: 1972
Employees: 16,000
Sales: $1.5 billion (2005 est.)
NAIC: 451120 Hobby, Toy and Game Stores

■ ■ ■

Hobby Lobby Stores Inc. is a chain of about 370 crafts superstores located in 28 states in the South and Midwest; it is the country's largest privately-owned crafts retailer and third overall behind Michaels and Jo-Ann's stores. The chain specializes in selling products and supplies for arts and crafts, hobbies, picture framing, jewelry making, fashion fabrics, florals, cards and party, baskets, wearable art, home accents, and holiday goods. Always a family-owned operation, Hobby Lobby openly operates strictly on Christian-based principles, and the stores are closed on Sundays to allow employees time for "family and worship." The company's employee turnover rate is considered very low. Hobby Lobby's headquarters is located in a 2.6 million-square-foot Oklahoma City manufacturing, distribution, and administrative complex. Other companies at this complex include Mardel Christian & Educational Supply and Crafts, Etc!, all af-

filiates of Hobby Lobby. Widely successful, Hobby Lobby saw its profits rise in the 1990s more than 1,000 percent. Going into the 21st century Hobby Lobby was opening at least one new store in the United States every month.

BEGINNINGS

Company founder David Green reportedly loved the retail business ever since he was a stock boy at the local five-and-dime in his hometown of Altus, Oklahoma. Green, who chronicled his life and principles in a book titled *More Than a Hobby,* was a preacher's kid, one of six in a household that relied on hand-me-downs and had little disposable income. In 1958, as a high school junior, Green worked some 40-plus hours a week at Mc-Clellan's five-and-dime. Not the best scholar by his own admission, Green found something he was good at and enjoyed: working in retail.

Green would later recall that he learned a lot under the supervision of the store manager, including strong work ethics and the importance of merchandise display. Soon he came to believe that he could manage a store himself. While at McClellan's, Green met a young clerk named Barbara, whom he would marry shortly after high school.

After high school and duty in the Air Force Reserve, Green returned to his job at McClellan's for a short time before taking a position as store manager at another retail outlet called TG&Y. At age 21 Green oversaw a 4,000-square-foot store and a work force of six. Over the next ten years, as his family grew, Green was moved up in the retail ranks while learning the dynamics of retail management through experience.

Green and another TG&Y manager, Larry Pico, had ambitions beyond store management. As Green recalled in *More Than a Hobby,* they "were sitting at the counter one day having coffee when we got to dreaming about what we might start on our own." Green noted that customers were always asking in the craft department for framed canvases they could paint on directly and then hang on the wall. So Pico and Green decided to try manufacturing these picture frames. They secured a bank loan for $600 to purchase supplies and machinery and set up shop in Pico's garage.

They called their new company Greco Products (a combination of the names Green and Pico). Barbara Green and two of the couple's sons helped out by assembling the frames at the kitchen table. The new company received several orders for their product after a salesman Green knew shopped the idea around his territory. Another bank loan helped Greco purchase more materials to fill an increasing number of orders from retailers in Oklahoma and in Texas.

Two years later, on August 3, 1972, Green opened his first store, in Oklahoma City. It was a 300-square-foot arts and crafts center located near the state capitol. Green kept his job at TG&Y for another three years, however, until he was sure that they could make Hobby Lobby succeed.

The shop was a success, and Green soon moved locations to occupy a 1,000-square-foot house. Increasing demand for the frames meant an increased need for assemblers. Barbara Green approached the local Cerebral Palsy Center to contract with the clients there who were seeking gainful employment. Hobby Lobby provided them with training and supervision, and the workers assembled frames and then bagged and labeled them for ten cents apiece.

In 1973, Larry Pico left the business, selling his share of Greco to Green for $5,000. John Seward, a new partner, came aboard the following year to oversee the creative direction of the product lines and the general store operations. Also during this year, Green decided to commit to his Hobby Lobby store full-time. He left TG&Y, and the company opened a second store.

FINANCIAL WOES RESULT FROM RAPID EXPANSION

Sales were good, and in the early 1980s, Hobby Lobby began expanding its reach with new store openings. By 1986, the company had 12 stores in operation. It also began expanding the scope of their merchandise beyond the arts and crafts sector, adding such luxury goods as furniture, fine arts, expensive cookware, and luggage to their offerings. The move was intended to diversify interests and protect the company from fluctuations in different sectors. The move, however, nearly bankrupted the company. Green had seen luxury goods sales increase as the area's oil business boomed; when it went bust, the disposable income of many prosperous Oklahomans and Texans plunged. For fiscal 1985, Hobby Lobby had sales of $25 million but was $1 million in the red. In response, Green shuttered the non-core lines and returned the company's focus to hobby materials, vowing to "grow quality and not quantity," according to *Discount Store News.* The company was able to refinance with another bank, and disaster was avoided. Green regarded the events of the early 1980s as a learning experience provided by God, and he attributed the turnaround to his Christian faith.

Faith informed the opening of Green's Mardel Christian & Educational Supply as well. The enterprise was actually the domain of Green's son, Mart DeLyn Green (and the company name is contraction of his first two names). The concept (Christian books, music, and gifts) was well received in Oklahoma City and eventually became a chain with several locations.

At Hobby Lobby stores, the target market was, according to Green, a woman who wants to improve her home, a woman who appreciates a wide selection of interesting merchandise and enjoys the shopping experience. Moreover, the company sought to carry everything in home decorating and crafting, concluding that people wanted everything they needed to do a project under one roof. A wide selection of merchandise

KEY DATES

1972: David Green opens the first Hobby Lobby store in Oklahoma City.

1997: Hobby Lobby begins featuring full-page Christian message ads during Christmas and Easter seasons.

1998: Hobby Lobby announces that it plans to expand into ten new states by the following year.

2000: United Steelworkers of America fail to unionize Hobby Lobby warehouse.

was therefore important. Hobby Lobby stores had entire departments devoted to crafts, art supplies, baskets, candles, cards and party items, fabrics, florals, frames, garden, hobbies (plastic models, trains, science projects), home accents, jewelry-making supplies, needlework, scrapbooking products, holiday items, small furniture, and wearable art. One of Hobby Lobby's most enduring product lines was its original forte, picture frames.

RETURN TO PROFITABILITY

In the early 1990s, Hobby Lobby consisted of some 30 stores doing over $2 million apiece in volume. Industry analysts began to wonder when the company would go public. Green, however, remained committed to his business being a family operation answering only to himself, his family, and their principles. He had no doubt that a stock offering would net a big profit, but insisted that more money was not as important to him as how he spent the profits the company was already realizing.

Green's Christian beliefs were increasingly reflected in the corporate culture. He averred that Hobby Lobby was not a secular business and that his views were not private. In 1997, the company began taking out full-page ads in local newspapers touting the true meaning of the Easter and Christmas holidays. Although Green admitted that these ads were not traditional for a retailer and were considered by some to be politically incorrect, he claimed that 99 percent of the feedback the store received was positive. Hobby Lobby profits funded a variety of Christian ministry projects, including the publication of Christian literature distributed worldwide.

In 1999 Hobby Lobby opened 30 new stores in ten new states. Each new store typically created about 50 jobs, and each Hobby Lobby Creative Center held between 45,000 and 65,000-square-feet of retail space.

The *Dallas Business Journal* reported in August 1999 that the company's growth projections included operating 1,100 stores by 2003, a figure that figure never materialized.

In 2000, the United Steelworkers of America tried to organize the Hobby Lobby warehouse as a union shop. Their efforts to convince employees to join, however, failed, with 83 percent voting against becoming unionized.

In 2001, Green launched Hemispheres, an upscale home furnishings store concept. The stores did not feature furniture but the furnishing accessories used in decorating, such as lamps, rugs, mirrors, garden fountains. Merchandise was imported from many European and Asian countries, offering customers items not widely available in the United States. Besides the Oklahoma City store, Hemispheres outlets were established in Dallas and St. Louis.

Green continued to serve as CEO, while his son Steve was company president. Green also acted as vice-president of merchandising. While the company retained eight merchandise managers that oversaw 36 buyers, Green remained the home accents merchandise manager and often the actual buyer because he found it the most interesting portion of his work.

By the early part of the 21st century Hobby Lobby was opening a new store almost every two weeks, and the average Hobby Lobby store had about $1.2 million worth of inventory at any given time. Rather than constructing new retail buildings, the company tended to purchase abandoned buildings or to lease existing retail space. By so doing, the company is "able to quickly enter the market, much quicker than had they started from ground zero," Mickey Ashmore, president and CEO of United Commercial Realty, told the *Dallas Business Journal*. The practice could also occasionally take credit for revitalizing a shopping center in dire need of an anchor retail presence. Hobby Lobby affiliate H. L. Construction was responsible for turning a store site into a Hobby Lobby Creative Center, as well as for expanding/remodeling existing centers.

Citing bar code technology as complicated, expensive, and not especially accurate, Hobby Lobby eschewed scanner technology at their checkouts. Instead, store personnel counted goods every week; when less than half of a basic stock was available, more was ordered. An added benefit of this system, according to Green, was that employees became more knowledgeable about their product offerings and better prepared to field customer questions.

Hobby Lobby prided itself on its shopping atmosphere, striving for orderliness, spaciousness, a helpful staff, and a pleasant overall ambience right down to the lighting and background music. Moreover, prices at Hobby Lobby were extremely competitive as much of the stores' product mix was imported from East Asia.

Kim Burton

PRINCIPAL AFFILIATES

H. L. Realty; Bearing Fruit Entertainment; Mardel Christian & Educational Supply; Hemispheres; Crafts, Etc!; Hong Kong Connection; Every Tribe Entertainment; Greco Frame & Supply; Worldwood.

PRINCIPAL COMPETITORS

Michaels Stores Inc.; Jo-Ann Stores Inc.; Wal-Mart Stores, Inc.; Hancock Fabrics, Inc.

FURTHER READING

Green, David, *More Than a Hobby,* Nashville, Tenn.: Thomson Nelson, 2005.

Hemmer, Andy, "Hobby Lobby to Open Seven Stores in Tri-State," *Cincinnati Business Courier,* November 15, 1999.

Howell, Debbie, "Hobby Lobby's Heavenly Ascension," *Discount Store News,* January 24, 2000.

Karman, John R. III, "Hobby Lobby to Open Feb. 1 in Old Home Quarters Site," *Business First of Louisville,* December 1, 2003.

Nannie, Philip, "Idled Hospital Slated for Religious Revival," *Nashville Business Journal,* June 9, 2003.

Sorter, Amy, "Companies Reap Benefits of Leasing Surplus Properties," *Dallas Business Journal,* May 4, 1998.

Tanner, Lisa, "Hobby Lobby, Michaels Plan Metroplex Growth," *Dallas Business Journal,* August 6, 1999, p. 5.

Zganjar, Leslie, "Hobby Lobby Taking Former Wal-Mart Slot," *Birmingham Business Journal,* January 13, 2003.

HOOKER
—— FURNITURE ——
Easy Elegance • Since 1924

Hooker Furniture
Corporation

·

440 East Commonwealth Boulevard
P. O. Box 4708
Martinsville, Virginia 24115
U.S.A.
Telephone: (276) 632-0459
Web site: http://www.hookerfurniture.com

Public Company
Incorporated: 1924 as Hooker-Bassett Furniture
   Company
Employees: 1,400
Sales: $341.78 million (2005)
Stock Exchanges: NASDAQ
Ticker Symbol: HOFT
NAIC: 337121 Upholstered Household Furniture
   Manufacturing; 337122 Nonupholstered Wood
   Household Furniture Manufacturing; 421210
   Furniture Wholesalers

■ ■ ■

Hooker Furniture Corporation is a leading supplier of
furniture in the United States. It was ranked sixth in the
country in 2004. The company specializes in home
entertainment centers and other lifestyle furnishings and
aims to provide quality furniture at mid-market prices.
The 2003 acquisition of Bradington-Young added a
complementary upholstered leather furniture product
line.

The company formed in Henry County, Virginia,
which grew to become a center of the furniture industry
in the 20th century. Since the late 1980s, the company

has been transforming itself from a manufacturer to a
wholesaler of products sourced overseas. Although
imports account for most of the company's revenues,
Hooker does have some manufacturing operations and
distribution centers.

ORIGINS

Hooker Furniture Corporation was formed in 1924 by
J. Clyde Hooker, Sr. At the time, the town of Martinsville, Virginia, was experiencing hard times. Hooker,
then just 29, suggested launching a furniture factory to
provide jobs. Startup capital of about $28,000 was raised
by the community, while a local newspaper publisher
named Rorrer A. James, Jr., contributed 20 acres of
land. Originally called the Bassett-Hooker Furniture
Company, it began operations in the same year as
another well-known Henry County manufacturer, the
Stanley Furniture Co.

The company started by specializing in bedroom
suites. Revenues were about $1 million in the first year,
when the plant employed about 200 people. A line of
dining room furniture was added in 1928.

Clyde Hooker, Sr., had wed Mabel Bassett of the
famous Virginia furniture family in 1920. Their son, J.
Clyde Hooker, Jr., became president of Hooker Furniture
in December 1960 and was named CEO six years later.
Clyde Hooker, Jr., joined the company after attending
Virginia Military Institute and serving in the military in
World War II.

Clyde Hooker, Jr., led the company through decades
of change before stepping down from the CEO position

in December 2000 and resigning as chairman in 2004 due to health issues. He was succeeded by his nephew, Paul Toms, Jr., who told the *Roanoke Times* that Hooker was credited with helping the company survive an influx of low-priced foreign competition by developing niche markets. During the younger Hooker's tenure, sales grew from $4 million in 1961 to $251 million in 2000.

The company spent about $1 million in the mid-1960s to add a warehouse and upgrade equipment. A separate, $2 million expansion was launched in 1969, bringing total production and warehousing space to 500,000 square feet, according to the detailed early history of the company in *Foresight, Founders, and Fortitude: The Growth of Industry in Martinsville and Henry County, Virginia.*

By this time, sales were about $10 million a year. The company had 500 employees. Fifty sales reps covered the country, and Hooker kept showrooms in the furniture center of High Point, North Carolina, as well as in New York City, Chicago, San Francisco, Los Angeles, and Dallas.

In 1970, Hooker acquired a former Burlington Industries and Linwood Co. plant in Kernersville, North Carolina. This site would employ about 300 people.

TRENDS INCLUDE OUTSOURCING AND OUTFITTING HOME OFFICES

Hooker began outsourcing production to the Far East and other low wage areas. This transition began in 1988. By 1999, about one-quarter of the company's products were being imported.

In 1990, the company established the Hooker Furniture Community Improvement Fund. This used proceeds from twice yearly sales of samples and returns to help charities and civic organizations.

Home offices were providing a booming market in spite of a slow economy. Renewed interest in personal computers was fueling the trend, a sales executive explained to *Wood & Wood Products.* The popularity of ever-larger big-screen televisions was giving the company another opportunity to develop new products. A former Thomasville Furniture plant in Pleasant Garden, North Carolina, was acquired in 1993 to provide more capacity for home entertainment center production.

In the mid-1990s, Hooker installed a state-of-the-art logistics system at its warehouses in Virginia and North Carolina. It used wireless bar-code scanners and radio frequency (RF) tags to provide real-time inventory control. The system was credited with raising productivity, increasing shipping accuracy to more than 99 percent, and improving customer service.

Revenues were $145 million in 1995; net income was about $9 million. Hooker averaged double-digit revenue (13 percent) and profit (14 percent) growth through the 1990s.

The company's manufacturing methods were also changing. More automation was used. State-of-the-art sanders and finishing machines were imported from Europe. The company was adopting a low-inventory approach, a plant manager told the *Hickory Record* in 2003. Smaller batch sizes were being run. Responsiveness was one remaining advantage domestic manufactures had, CEO Paul Toms told the *Roanoke Times.*

EMPLOYEE STOCK OWNERSHIP BEGINS

Hooker set up an employee stock ownership plan (ESOP) in 2000. The ESOP acquired a 31 percent holding in the company for $22.5 million. At the time, Hooker had about 2,000 people worked for Hooker, nearly half of them in Martinsville. Management continued to be dominated by family members after the ESOP. Paul B. Toms, Jr., who joined the business in 1983, succeeded his uncle J. Clyde Hooker, Jr., as chairman and CEO in December 2000.

The company was entering joint marketing agreements to expand its customer base. For a few years, Hooker produced trend-spotting guru Faith Popcorn's Cocoon collection aimed at women working from their homes. In 2001, Hooker brought out a line of PGA TOUR® furnishings aimed at people embracing the golfing lifestyle. It also maintained many other brands,

KEY DATES

1924: J. Clyde Hooker, Sr., forms a furniture company; first year revenues are $1 million.
1960: J. Clyde Hooker, Jr., succeeds his father as company president.
1970: The Kernersville, North Carolina, plant is acquired.
1988: Hooker begins importing furniture.
2000: An employee stock ownership plan (ESOP) is established; Paul Toms becomes CEO.
2001: The workforce at the Martinsville plant is reduced.
2002: Stock begins trading on the NASDAQ Small-Cap Market.
2003: Hooker acquires leather seating producer Bradington-Young and closes its first wood furniture plant in Kernersville, North Carolina.
2004: The Maiden, North Carolina, plant closes.
2005: The Pleasant Garden, North Carolina, plant closes.

including Intimate Home, Preston Ridge, Casa del Sol, Waverly Place, Modern Classics, Highgate Manor, Seven Seas, and Kimball Bridge.

Hooker's stock was listed on the NASDAQ Small-Cap Market in June 2002 after being traded over the counter. At the time, the company had about 1,850 employees in Pleasant Garden, Kernersville, and Maiden, North Carolina; Martinsville and Roanoke, Virginia; and other locations.

In 2003 the company made its largest acquisition to date by acquiring the Bradington-Young company of Cherryville, North Carolina, for $24.5 million. Bradington-Young was established in 1978. It made upholstered furniture and leather chairs and recliners and, like Hooker, competed in the higher end of the market. The product lines were seen as highly complementary. The deal added 400 employees to Hooker's workforce and brought its total annual revenues to nearly $300 million.

PLANT CLOSINGS BEGIN

Sales were slipping for domestic furniture, which was more expensive to produce domestically than that outsourced abroad. Hooker significantly cut the workforce at its Martinsville, Virginia, plant in 2001. The company closed a plant for the first time ever in August 2003, when the Kernersville site was shut down. Another, smaller North Carolina, plant, in Maiden, closed in 2004. More than 500 jobs were eliminated in the two closings.

The next year, Hooker shut down its Pleasant Garden, North Carolina plant, which had employed 280 people. A spokesperson explained that it was slated for closure because it was the least flexible of the company's remaining plants. Hooker still had facilities in Martinsville and Roanoke, Virginia.

After several years of top line growth, Hooker's total sales slipped $4 million to $342 million in the fiscal year ended November 30, 2005. Net income was $12.5 million, down nearly a third from the previous year. Bradington-Young contributed $62.5 million of revenues, a record for the unit. Imported furniture accounted for 62 percent of overall revenues; two-thirds of the imports were from China.

Hooker had joined a coalition of U.S. wood bedroom furniture manufacturers seeking higher import duties on furniture from China, which they said was unfairly priced below costs. However, many American retailers were vigorously opposed, and Hooker withdrew from the antidumping coalition after a few months.

Hooker still had a number of manufacturing sites after the plant closings. It was also investing millions in its distribution facilities with the aim of reducing shipment times. Most items were delivered to retailers within a month.

NEW PRODUCTS FOR EVOLVING LIFESTYLES

In the early 2000s, the company continued to respond to changes in technology and domestic home life with products designed for new consumer priorities. One line of innovative new products addressed the proliferation of flat screen televisions in American living rooms. Some of models featured pop-up consoles to conceal the TVs behind a bookshelf or panel while not in use.

Another new niche was the market for juvenile bedroom furniture. Hooker pitched its Youth Furniture for Life line, launched in 2004, as being appropriate for various stages in a growing person's life. It was also suited for guest bedrooms, and was especially appropriate for the the soon-to-be "empty nest" homes of the Baby Boom generation.

Frederick C. Ingram

PRINCIPAL SUBSIDIARIES

Bradington-Young LLC; Triwood, Inc.

PRINCIPAL COMPETITORS

Bassett Furniture Industries, Incorporated; Furniture Brands International, Inc.; La-Z-Boy Inc.

FURTHER READING

"75 Years Later, the Gratitude Goes On," *Roanoke Times,* December 8, 1999, p. B1.

Adams, Duncan, "Adept at Adapting," *Roanoke Times,* Bus. Sec., March 9, 2003, p. 1.

———, "Clyde Hooker Steps Down from Board of Company," *Roanoke Times,* July 2, 2004, p. C8.

———, "Old Chairs Furnish Occasion for Praise; In December, J. Clyde Hooker Jr. Retired from Company His Father Founded," *Roanoke Times,* July 21, 2001, p. A5.

"Better Production: Fluid Workflow Pours Profit Into Hooker Furniture," *Wood & Wood Products,* November 1985, pp. 120–121, 124.

Buchanan, Lee, "Hooker Employees Take Major Stock in Company," *HFN,* September 18, 2000, p. 18.

Cleal, Dorothy and Hiram H. Herbert, "A Community's Faith Is Justified: The Story of Hooker Furniture Corporation," in *Foresight, Founders, and Fortitude: The Growth of Industry in Martinsville and Henry County, Virginia,* Bassett, Virginia: Bassett Printing, 1970, pp. 82–90.

Craver, Richard, "270 Plant Jobs to Go; Hooker to Close Oldest Factory, in Kernersville," *Winston-Salem Journal,* May 29, 2003, p. A1.

———, "Virginia-Based Furniture Company Employees Are Now Majority Shareholders," *High Point Enterprise,* September 15, 2000.

Daniel, Fran, "Planning Ahead; Getting Ready for and Going to Market Is Detailed Process," *Winston-Salem Journal,* October 16, 2002, p. D1.

Garet, Barbara, "Hooker Furniture Sees Growth with Big Screen TVs," *Wood & Wood Products,* April 1997, pp. 22ff.

"Hooker Furniture Moves from Over-the-Counter to Nasdaq Listing," *Business Wire,* June 25, 2002.

"Hooker Furniture Sees the Benefits of Real-Time Information Visibility," *Frontline Solutions,* January 2000, p. 18.

Joyner, Amy, "Va. Furniture Companies Join to Celebrate 75th Anniversary," *Greensboro News & Record,* June 14, 1999, p. B6.

Kaiser, Jo-Ann, "Home Office Market Stays Hot," *Wood & Wood Products,* January 1991, pp. 59ff.

Kitchen, Jane, "Hooker Debuting First Youth Collections," *Home Accents Today,* October 2004, p. SS22.

Kunkel, Karl, "'Hooker U.': A Crash Course for Salespeople," *HFN,* September 3, 2001, p. 22.

Lorimar, Susan, "Hooker Furniture Leaves, Five Other Companies Join Antidumping Coalition," *Wood & Wood Products,* March 2004, p. 13.

Marks, Robert, "Hooker Buys Former Thomasville Plant," *HFD,* February 22, 1993, p. 22.

Nowell, Paul, "Furniture Maker Sees Flexibility as the Key to Surviving Imports," *Hickory Record,* January 5, 2003, pp. B1, B4.

Sexton, Megan, "PGA Tour Furniture Collection Brings Passion for Golf Indoors," *Chronicle-Telegram* (Elyria, Ohio), June 23, 2002, p. H6.

Swensen, Eric, "Hooker Closing Its Last Triad Plant," *News & Record* (Piedmont Triad, North Carolina), July 28, 2005, p. B1.

White, Jack, "Friend: Downtown Will Miss Company," *Winston-Salem Journal,* Metro Sec., June 19, 2003, p. 1.

White, Sharon E., "Hooker Furniture to Acquire Cherryville, N.C.-Based Chair Maker," *Charlotte Observer,* October 9, 2002.

HOP, LLC

---

310 Bristol Street, Suite 150
Cosa Mesa, California 92626
U.S.A.
Telephone: (714) 429-2223
Toll Free: (800) 544-7323
Fax: (714) 429-2294

Wholly Owned Subsidiary of Educate Inc.
Incorporated: 1986 as Gateway Educational Products, Ltd.
Employees: 150 (est.)
Sales: $45 million (2001 est.)
NAIC: 611699 All Other Miscellaneous Services. Not Elsewhere Classified.

■ ■ ■

A subsidiary of Educate Inc., HOP, LLC, produces the "Hooked on Phonics" brand of educational products, including cassettes, CD-ROMS, flash cards, books, and parent guides. Although the Costa Mesa, California–based company is best known for its learn-to-read programs that relies on phonics—associating letters or letter groups with the sounds they represent—it also offers step-by-step learning systems to teach critical reading, math, and study skills. In addition, HOP operates more than 600 reading centers in KinderCare Learning Centers and at other day care providers as an add-on service. HOP's corporate parent also operates the well-known Sylvan Learning Centers, North America's largest network of tutoring services.

"WHOLE-LANGUAGE" APPROACH TO READING EMERGES: EARLY 20TH CENTURY

Teaching children to learn how to read by sounding out letters was hardly a new concept when Hooked on Phonics was created in the 1980s. In fact, it was the predominant way reading was taught at the start of the 20th century. "By the 1930s," according to *Success* magazine, "progressive professors of education from Harvard and Columbia declared that phonics, with its rote memorization of sounds and symbols, was drudgery. They denounced the practice of sounding out words and said children could learn to read as naturally as they learned to talk—if they were allowed to peruse simple words in context. This 'whole-language' philosophy was the basis of the 'Dick and Jane' readers." The approach was controversial and was attacked in the 1950s by the book *Why Johnny Can't Read,* yet it was staunchly defended by mainstream educators who, spearheaded by the International Reading Association (IRA), also spent a great deal of energy over the course of several decades to discredit phonics and implement whole-language reading programs. However, as whole-language gained prominence there was no appreciable gain in literacy. Rather, literacy levels began to steadily slip following World War II, and many children who did learn to read struggled in their efforts, much to the concern of their parents.

One parent frustrated by his son's difficulty in learning to read was John M. Shanahan. He grew up in Boston, educated at a Catholic school where, as a child, he learned to read relying on drills from a tried and true phonetic system. He became a musician, moved to

California, and wrote film scores and commercial jingles. He also became an entrepreneur, starting a business in 1983 called Smart Tapes, producing educational cassettes that among other subjects taught vocabulary and how to prepare for the SAT college entrance exam. He turned his attention to the problem of emerging reading when his son, Sean, became so anxious about learning to read that he begged not to go to school. Shanahan tried to sound out words with his son, the way the nuns had taught him, but Sean had no idea what he was talking about. Deciding to take matters into his own hands, Shanahan took his grade school lesson plans and spiced them up by writing catchy jingles to accompany the drills. He created a study tape for Sean to use and in short order the boy learned to read and caught up with his classmates.

Impressed by Sean's turnaround, Shanahan's neighbors, whose own children were having trouble reading, asked if they could borrow the tapes he made. Shanahan recognized a business opportunity and in late 1986 started Gateway Educational Products Ltd. in Orange, California, to market a learn-how-to-read system he called "Hooked On Phonics." He had a partner, John H. Herlihy, who provided the bulk of the $150,000 in seed money, but Shanahan was the driving force behind the growth of the business, overseeing every aspect of the company. He elected to market the Hooked on Phonics tapes through direct marketing, as he had done with Smart Tapes, but eschewed the services of an ad agency and opted not to outsource the telemarketing and order fulfillment operations. He set up his own telemarketing center, handled the creative work, and bought the media time. It was his idea to use a memorable telephone number for customers to call: 1-800-ABCDEFG. To find out who held that number, he simply dialed it and was connected to a fence company, whose owner had been unaware that his number spelled out the first seven letters of the alphabet. Nevertheless, the man refused to part with the number—until he was persuaded by Shanahan's $10,000 offer.

STRONG GROWTH: 1987–1994

In 1987, its first full year in operation, Gateway generated $100,000 in revenues, but that number would begin to grow exponentially as Shanahan increased his marketing budget, spending heavily on radio and television. According to the Network Radio Marketing Guide, Gateway was the 16th biggest spender on radio by 1990. A year later the company's total radio and television budget topped $41 million, split equally between the two media. In 1992 Shanahan began producing 30-minute infomercials. The media saturation paid off, as sales reached $150 million by 1994. Along the way he made changes to the Hooked on Phonics system and added new products, including Hooked on Math; a Hooked on Phonics Writing Kit; the Hooked on Phonics Classic Achievement Series, which used well-known stories to be read in a family setting; the "We the People" history and civics lesson; and foreign languages programs (German, French, Italian, Japanese, and Spanish) produced with Passport Books. In addition, Shanahan established the Gateway Prison Literacy Project to teach reading to California prison inmates, who experienced a high illiteracy rate. He also made a stab at the retail trade by opening a Hooked on Phonics Store in the heart of Los Angeles' inner city, where he also sold educational toys from Sesame Street, Fisher-Price, and Playskool. Along the way, according to an article published in *Success* magazine, "his success earned Shanahan some powerful enemies in the education establishment."

Writing for *Success,* Duncan Maxwell Anderson and Michael Warshaw reported that "Shanahan faced a powerful adversary [in] the National Education Association (NEA)," which they maintained was a "core constituency of the Democratic Party." The authors suggested that with Democratic President Bill Clinton in the White House, politics was behind the Federal Trade Commission's (FTC) 1992 request for information on Gateway's products and advertising. Wrote Anderson and Warshaw, "Shanahan wasn't alarmed at first; the FTC almost never questioned anyone's right to sell an educational product. But the agency kept coming back for more information. When the FTC requested background information on all the principals in the company, Shanahan retained a lawyer in Washington."

Responsible for regulating advertising, the FTC took on Gateway, claiming that the company did not provide statistical evidence to back their claims that Hooked on Phonics could teach anyone to read. Instead, Gateway relied on testimonials, primarily children who had used the product. In August 1994, Shanahan took the advice of his attorneys and agreed to a consent order from the FTC so that his advertising no longer made claims that could not be backed up by scientific studies. Although Gateway did not admit to any wrongdoing and the company was not fined, agreeing to the consent order was a decision Shanahan would soon regret.

On the eve of the FTC announcement of the agreement in December 1994, the prime-time news show "Dateline NBC" aired a segment that promised "the real story behind Hooked On Phonics." According to *Success,* "It was obvious that the FTC had broken its agreement not to discuss its consent order for Gateway." Moreover, "Dateline" maintained that the FTC had charged Hooked On Phonics with deceptive and misleading advertising, a mischaracterization that was then repeated by other news outlets.

The fallout was immediate and devastating as many Hooked on Phonics customers began to return their products. A number of other customers, on the other hand, supported Gateway during the 60-day period the FTC solicited public comment before issuing a final order. Many people, especially conservative politicians, saw the affair as an attack on home-based education. Although the backlash forced an FTC spokesperson to announce that the agency challenged Gateway's advertising claims, not the product, the admission offered cold comfort for Shanahan, who had already locked in place many media buys before business suddenly dried up.

To make matters worse, the O. J. Simpson murder trial became a television obsession with American viewers and everybody involved in the infomercial trade felt its impact. Shanahan attempted to become less reliant on direct marketing by making the Hooked on Phonics products available through bookstores, educational stores, and other specialty retailers, but an expansion of outlets could not prevent a collapse in sales. In 1995 the company posted sales of just $20 million, an amount that did not come close to covering the bills. Media outlets began demanding payment, and fearful that they might seek liens against Gateway's income, Shanahan filed for Chapter 11 bankruptcy protection in October 1995.

OWNERSHIP CHANGE: 1996

Shanahan sold Gateway to buyout firm Rosewood Capital, LLC in 1996 and turned his attention to other endeavors, in particular a radio network he set up and a half-interest in a media buying agency. He scored another hit by launching the radio talk show of Dr. Laura Schlessinger.

Rosewood was founded in 1986 by Chip Adams as a traditional venture capital firm that began investing in buyouts. A former employee of Bain & Co., a high-powered consulting firm, Adams was familiar with the Hooked On Phonics system because it helped his son, Doug, to learn to read. Adams liked the product but thought it could be improved. The company became Gateway Learning Corporation and the Hooked on Phonics program was redeveloped with the help of educators and others. In the meantime, phonics received a boost when a study sponsored by the National Institute of Child Health & Human Development at the University of Houston contended that not only did phonics work, it was the best way to teaching reading. In June 1996 *Forbes* called the findings "a slap in the face of the education establishment." The magazine reported that in California, where the whole language approach had had a long history in the public schools, parents "were shocked by recent test results that placed their kids last among the nation's students, tied with Louisiana." As a result, California ordered that phonics be taught in every first- and second-grade classroom. Educational publishers and others now began developing their own phonics-based materials.

The new Gateway unveiled its revamped Hooked on Phonics *Learn to read* Program in 1998. It was well received, quickly earning the National Parenting Center Seal of Approval. A year later the company introduced a new Hooked on Math edition, which included games and other activities. Hooked on Phonics was revised further in 2000 when the company brought out the new Hooked on Phonics Classroom Edition. A year later a Deluxe Edition was offered that included an interactive CD-ROM. Also in 2001 Gateway forged an alliance with KinderCare Learning Centers to offer Hooked on Phonics tutoring programs at KinderCare locations across the country. That same year, Gateway expanded beyond basic reading and math, releasing Hooked on School Success to help teach children reading comprehension, study skills, and test-taking strategies.

Gateway had another run-in with the FTC in the early 2000s, accused of selling information about its customers to marketers, renting the information for $95 per 1,000 names, despite promising to keep the data confidential. In July 2004 the company settled the matter by agreeing to pay a fine of $4,600, the amount of money it earned in renting out the data—hardly worth the bad press and legal expenses that resulted.

Rosewood sold Gateway to Baltimore-based Educate Inc. in January 2005 for a reported $13 million. Educate was formed from the tutoring portion of Sylvan Learning Systems, which ran into trouble funding Internet education-related businesses. In 2003 the kindergarten-through-12th-grade tutoring businesses had been sold to insider R. Christopher Hoehn-Saric, who then became Educate's chief executive officer and chairman. What made Gateway attractive in addition to the Hooked on Phonics brand were the company's 600 reading centers in KinderCare and other daycare centers. Gateway was subsequently renamed HOP, LLC, and folded into the Educate operation. The company's new corporate parent decided to expand the retail distribution of Hooked on Phonics products, turning to such outlets as Wal-Mart, Target, and Amazon.com. It also began to add to the Hooked on Phonics product offerings. In December 2005 the company unveiled Hooked on Phonics "Get Ready to Read," a program aimed at the preschool market of three- to five-year-olds.

Ed Dinger

PRINCIPAL COMPETITORS

Laureate Education, Inc.; Multi-Media Tutorial Services, Inc.; Scientific Learning Corporation.

FURTHER READING

Anderson, Duncan Maxwell, and Michael Warshaw, "For Teaching Kids to Read, Entrepreneur John Shanahan Got...Whacked! by the Government, the Media and Educators," *Success,* April 1996, p. 32.

Darlin, Damon, "Back to Basics, Again," *Forbes,* June 17, 1996, p. 46.

Feder, Barnaby J., "Hooked on Ad Claims," *New York Times,* January 5, 1992, p. A42.

Hopkins, Jamie Smith, "Parent of Sylvan Tutoring Centers to Buy Hooked on Phonics Owner," *Baltimore Sun,* January 14, 2005.

Kiley, David, "The Boom In 'Teaching Johnny to Read,'" *Brandweek,* January 28, 1991, p. 20.

Mouchard, Andre, "'Phonics' Maker Files for Bankruptcy," *Orange County Register,* October 13, 1995, p. C1.

Sullivan, J. L., "Hooked on Telemarketing," *Orange County Business Journal,* June 13, 1994, p. 1.

Swartz, Nikki, "Company Fined for Renting Out Customer Data," *Information Management Journal,* September–October 2004, p. 10.

House of Prince A/S

Tobaksvejen 4
Soborg,
Denmark
Telephone: +45 39 55 63 00
Fax: +45 39 55 63 03
Web site: http://www.prince.dk

Wholly Owned Subsidiary of Skandinavisk Tobakskompagni A/S
Incorporated: 1990
Employees: 1,726
Sales: DKK 12.66 billion ($2.15 billion) (2005)
NAIC: 312221 Cigarette Manufacturing

■ ■ ■

House of Prince A/S is Denmark's leading cigarette company, accounting for more than 90 percent of that country's cigarette sales. House of Prince is also the only cigarette manufacturer remaining in Denmark, with a total annual production of more than 12 billion cigarettes per year. The company markets a variety of cigarette brands, including the flagship Prince brand and variations such as Prince Rich, Prince Menthol, Prince Highland, and Prince Golden. Other brands include King's, Looks, and the low-priced brands Corner, North State and LIA, and the 'retro' brand Rockets, introduced in 2006. These brands have also helped House of Prince claim the lead in the Scandinavia, with a 34 percent market share. In addition to the Scandinavian market, House of Prince is also active in Eastern Europe, especially in Poland, but also in Hungary and the Czech Republic, and in the Baltic states, supported by sales subsidiaries in Estonia and Lithuania. Germany and Greece are also important export markets for the company. House of Prince represents the cigarette production and distribution wing of parent company Skandinavisk Tobakskompagni A/S (ST; Scandinavian Tobacco Company), which also includes cigar production units Nobel Cigars and JL Tiedemanns; pipe and rolling tobacco producer Orlik Tobacco Company; and convenience store operator Dagrofa, among others. In 2005, House of Prince posted sales of DKK 12.66 billion ($2.15 billion).

MERGING DANISH TOBACCO INTERESTS IN 1961

House of Prince represented the bringing together of most of the Danish cigarette industry into a single entity. The company dated its origins back to 1750, with the founding of the tobacco importer Christian Augustinus, in Amager. Another important component of the later House of Prince was founded toward the end of that same century, when C. W. Obel opened for business in Aalborg in 1787. The third major part of the later House of Prince was founded nearly 100 years later, with the creation of R. Faerchs Fabrikker, in Holstebro, in 1869. All three companies remained family operated until they merged to form Skandinavisk Tobakskompagni (Scandinavian Tobacco Company) in 1961.

The 19th century saw strong growth in the Danish tobacco industry. Imported tobaccos were increasingly supplemented by tobaccos grown in Denmark. The rising popularity of tobacco use in Denmark, and in Europe

COMPANY PERSPECTIVES

House of Prince (HoP) is ST's international cigarette company with sales in more than 40 countries. To a Dane, a Norwegian or a Swede, HoP is first and foremost associated with the cigarette Prince—so firmly rooted in Scandinavian consciousness that smokers in these three countries regard it as their nationally preferred cigarette brand. But HoP is far more than Prince. Today HoP is strongly positioned as a regional company with international ambitions by virtue of its flexibility and innovation. With the opening of Eastern and Central Europe, HoP has not only created new local brands of high quality but also brands which can succeed across borders.

in general, during that century stimulated the growth of a true tobacco industry in Denmark and elsewhere. By the end of the 19th century, tobacco companies operated throughout the country. A major boost in tobacco consumption had come through the introduction of cigarettes to Europe after the Crimean War in the late 1850s. The Danish market was at first supplied by imported cigarettes, which remained hand-rolled into the second half of the decade. Cigarettes at the time came largely from Russia and Turkey. The first Danish company to begin producing its own cigarettes was Alder & Co, which set up a cigarette rolling workshop in Copenhagen in 1878.

The true boom in cigarette consumption did not occur, however, until the invention of the cigarette rolling machine in 1881. The new machinery dramatically changed the shape of the tobacco industry, shifting its focus from pipes, snuff, chewing tobacco and cigars to cigarettes. These in turn transformed the tobacco industry from a relatively marginal business to one of the world's major industries. The arrival of cigarette machinery in Denmark enabled that country's tobacconists to launch large-scale cigarette production as well. Among them, Christian Augustinus Fabrikker launched its own cigarette production in 1911.

Augustinus emerged as one of the country's leading tobacco companies over the next decades. The introduction of the filtered cigarette in the early 1950s, which followed on the first indications of the harmfulness of smoking, provided a new lift for Augustinus. The first Danish-produced filtered cigarette appeared in the market in 1953. Augustinus followed suit, launching its

own filtered cigarette brands. In 1957, the company launched what was to become its best-selling cigarette brand, Prince. Featuring a so-called "American" blend of tobaccos, Prince enabled Augustinus to outpace its long-running rival, the Danish wing of the American Tobacco Company.

Despite its growing position in Denmark, Augustinus and its counterparts faced a new threat with the creation of the European Union in the late 1950s. In 1961, Augustinus, C. W. Obel and R. Faerchs Fabrikker agreed to merge into a single company, Skandinavisk Tobakskompagni (ST), in order to present a united front against the coming competition from foreign tobacco companies. The Prince brand became the new company's flagship brand as well as its spearhead for ST's international growth. In 1961, the company introduced Prince cigarettes into Sweden, where it quickly became a top-selling cigarette brand. By 1967, the company replicated its success in Norway, and quickly established Prince as the top-selling brand in the Scandinavian region.

RESTRUCTURING THE DANISH TOBACCO MARKET IN 1990

By the early 1970s, ST had beat out the American Tobacco Company, which had changed its name to Nordisk BAT in the interim. In 1972, ST took over its main rival. ST maintained Nordisk BAT's production operations until 1977, when the company merged its cigarette production into a single factory in Saborg. In the meantime, Denmark's entry into the European Common Market opened up new markets for the company, and especially Germany, where the Prince brand was introduced in 1972. By 1986, the Prince brand had established itself throughout West Germany. While the company had more limited success entering other markets in Europe, it nonetheless found success in Greece, which became one of the company's largest export markets.

Through the 1980s and into the 1990s, ST continued to add acquisitions. By the early 1990s, the company had acquired several more Danish tobacco companies, carrying out a de facto consolidation of the Danish tobacco industry. During the period, ST's acquisition included Copenhagen-based AM Hirschsprung & Sonner and P. Wulff, as well as E. Nobel Cigar & Tobaksfabrikker in Nykobing, among others. These acquisitions brought most of Denmark's oldest and most well-known brands into the ST stable.

During this period, ST also continued to develop the Prince brand. In 1979, the company launched its own 'light' brand, Prince Lights. That brand was

KEY DATES

1750: Christian Augustinus Fabrikker is founded in Amager.

1787: C. W. Obel is founded in Aalborg.

1869: R. Faerchs Fabrikker is founded in Holstebro.

1911: Chr. Augustinus Fabrikker launches production of cigarettes.

1957: Chr. Augustinus Fabrikker launches the Prince brand.

1961: Chr. Augustinus Fabrikker, Obel, and Faerchs merge to form Skandinavisk Tobakskompagni (ST); the company begins sales of the Prince brand in Sweden.

1967: The Prince brand is exported to Norway.

1972: ST acquires Nordisk BAT; the company launches cigarette sales in Germany.

1977: The company consolidates all of its cigarette production into a single factory in Soborg.

1990: In a company restructuring, House of Prince becomes an independent cigarette production subsidiary.

2003: House of Prince launches its "luxury" cigarette brand, Christian of Denmark.

2006: The company introduces its "retro" brand, Rockets.

introduced a 100mm version of its ultra light cigarette in 1995, followed by a premium version, Prince Extra Ultra (later renamed as Prince Smooth Taste) in 1999. The latest addition to the Prince brand family came in 2006, with the launch of Prince Highland Taste. The company also headed off increasing competition from low-priced and generic brands, creating its own brands for those segments, including Corner, North State, and LIA.

The creation of House of Prince also enabled the company to focus on expanding its reach into the newly opened Eastern and Central European markets. During the 1990s, the company expanded quickly, setting up new sales subsidiaries in Estonia and Lithuania, as well as Poland, the Czech Republic and Hungary. The company also acquired control of operations in Latvia, bought from the Latvian government, in 2002. Another important growth area for the company was the duty-free market, including sales aboard cruise ships. The company's expansion enabled House of Prince's sales to grow steadily through the 2000s.

Into the mid-2000s, House of Prince remained the strongest cigarette manufacturer in the Scandinavian market, dominating its home market, and holding leading shares in Norway and Sweden. The company continued to seek new means of building its market share. In 2003, for example, the company launched a new "luxury" cigarette brand, Christian of Denmark, The company also targeted the young smoker market, launching the "retro" brand, Rockets, in 2006. Despite pressures on the tobacco industry, House of Prince appeared certain of strong sales for years to come.

M. L. Cohen

subsequently rebranded as Prince Rounded Taste after the European Community banned the use of the word 'light' in cigarette naming in 2003. Other brand extensions launched by ST included Prince 100, introduced in 1985 and featuring the longer 100mm size. That product was followed by a light version in 1987. In 1990, the Prince brand family also added a menthol cigarette, as well as an 'ultra-light' that was subsequently rebranded as Prince Golden Taste.

By the early 1990s, the tobacco industry had come under intense pressure due to increasingly tighter restrictions. At the same time the European Community had begun preparations to eliminate borders among member nations. As a result, while fighting declining sales in its core Scandinavian market, ST also braced itself for a new level of competition for the European tobacco market. In 1990, ST restructured its operations. As part of the restructuring, ST placed all of its cigarette operations into a single, independently operating subsidiary, called House of Prince.

House of Prince continued introducing new variations of its flagship Prince brand. The company

PRINCIPAL SUBSIDIARIES

Scandinavian Tobacco (Estonia); UAB House of Prince Lithuania; Scandinavian Tobacco S.A. (Poland); Scandinavian Tobacco Company Hellas S.A. (Greece); Scandinavian Tobacco S.R.O. (Czech Republic); House of Prince AB (Sweden); Scandinavian Tobacco Hungary Kft.

PRINCIPAL COMPETITORS

Philip Morris International Management S.A; Altria Group Inc; Imperial Tobacco Group PLC; British American Tobacco PLC; Altadis S.A; Reynolds American Inc.; Austria Tabak GmbH and Company KG

FURTHER READING

"Danish Tobacco Company to Conquer Sweden," *Dagens Industri*, January 26, 1999, p. 14.

"House of Prince and Cigars Drive ST Sales," *Tobacco Europe*, January-February 2002, p. 6.

"House of Prince Converts to Christian," *Travel Retailer International*, June-July 2003, p. 46.

"House of Prince Emerges Victorious with Tallink Store," *Duty Free News International*, March 15, 2004, p. 26.

"House of Prince Plans to Begin Production of Wet Snuff in Sweden," *Nordic Business Report*, January 9, 2003.

Lipsith, Gavin, "House of Prince Line Puts Duty Free First," *Duty Free News International*, May 15, 2003, p. 35.

——— "House of Prince Ready to Grasp Opportunity in Custom Concepts," *Duty Free News International*, June 1, 2004, p. 8.

"Norway: High Taxes and a Smoking Ban," *Tobacco Europe*, May-June 2002, p. 12.

"US Launch for Retro Rockets," *Duty-Free News International*, April 1, 2006, p. 23.

HSBC Holdings plc

8 Canada Square
London, E14 5HQ
United Kingdom
Telephone: (44) 020 7991 0588
Fax: (44) 020 7991 4639
Web site: http://www.hsbc.com

Public Company
Incorporated: 1865 as Hongkong and Shanghai Banking
   Company, Ltd.
Employees: 265,285
Total Assets: $1.50 trillion (2005)
Stock Exchanges: London Hong Kong New York Paris
   Bermuda
Ticker Symbols: HSBA; 005; HBC; PHSB
NAIC: 522110 Commercial Banking; 522120 Savings
   Institutions; 522292 Real Estate Credit; 522293
   International Trade Financing; 523110 Investment
   Banking and Securities Dealing; 523920 Portfolio
   Management; 523930 Investment Advice; 523991
   Trust, Fiduciary, and Custody Activities; 524110
   Direct Life, Health, and Medical Insurance Carri-
   ers; 551111 Offices of Bank Holding Companies

∎ ∎ ∎

A leading international banking group, HSBC Holdings
plc (also referred to as the HSBC Group) operates in
about 80 countries and offers comprehensive financial
services encompassing not only commercial and
merchant banking but also capital markets, consumer
finance, securities, investments, and insurance. The
HSBC Group is increasingly international in nature,
despite the group still being centered around the bank
from which it evolved (and from which it gained its ac-
ronymic name)—The Hongkong and Shanghai Banking
Corporation Ltd., the top bank in Hong Kong, known
colloquially as HongkongBank.

HSBC has 9,500 offices spread out across five
continents serving 120 million customers. While a
growing force in many areas of the world, the group is
especially notable for its longstanding presence in China,
where it has been active since 1865. Its foreign
subsidiaries are among the leading banks in Canada,
France, Mexico, and other countries.

FOUNDING OF HONGKONGBANK

The history of HSBC begins with the founding of the
Hongkong and Shanghai Banking Company, Ltd. in
1865. In the early 1860s, Hong Kong's financial needs
were served by European trading houses called "hongs."
This system proved increasingly inadequate as the
colony's bustling trade—primarily in tea, silk, and
opium—burgeoned. By 1864 the first proper banks had
been established, but as these were based in London or
India and controlled from abroad, there was a growing
feeling that a local bank was needed in the colony.

Dissatisfaction led to action when it was discovered
that a group of Bombay financiers intended to set up a
"Bank of China" in Hong Kong, and that this bank,
chartered in London, was to offer only a small proportion of its shares to China coast businesses. Thomas
Sutherland, the Hong Kong Superintendent of the
Peninsular and Orient Steam Navigation Company,

COMPANY PERSPECTIVES

We believe long-term success and good corporate behaviour are linked. Corporate Social Responsibility has been a vital ingredient in HSBC's 140 years of success. We have always maintained that a company's first social responsibility is to be successful. Success allows us to invest in new products and services for our customers. It enables us to pay the dividends which form an important part of the long-term savings and pension plans of our shareholders. It allows us to contribute to public services through the taxes we pay to governments. It creates jobs for our colleagues and suppliers.

proposed the foundation of a new bank modeled on "sound Scottish banking principles." The proposal was promptly taken up by others of the Hong Kong business community; within days a provisional committee had established a banking cooperative capitalized at HKD 5 million. The move effectively preempted the proposed "Bank of China," whose representative, when he arrived later in Hong Kong, could find no market for his shares.

The Hongkong and Shanghai Banking Company Ltd. opened on March 3, 1865, with a second branch inaugurated in Shanghai on April 3. A London office was opened later in the year. Members of the cooperative included American, German, Scandinavian, and Parsee Indian merchant houses, as well as representatives from the Bombay-based David Sassoon & Company and Hong Kong-based Dent & Company. The largest companies in Hong Kong, Jardine Matheson and the American firm Russell & Company, were not represented. The highly favorable response to the bank by foreign interests and compradores (native businessmen who acted as intermediaries with the Chinese community), however, led both to reconsider and join.

An international financial crisis in 1865–66 could have destroyed the bank. Instead, with financial support from its members, the bank took over the operations of failed competitors and hired their staff. Dent, meanwhile, the dominant Hong Kong member of the group, went bankrupt. Instead of hurting the cooperative, however, Dent's failure allowed broader representation by more diverse local interests.

Initially, the bank was established under the local Companies Ordinance as the Hongkong and Shanghai Banking Company Ltd. Under the colonial law of the

time, a bank had to incorporate either under a royal charter in compliance with the Colonial Banking Regulations or else according to British banking legislation. The bank's founders objected to these options, however, as they had particularly designed their enterprise as a local concern. Eventually a deal was struck with the Treasury whereby the bank (renamed The Hongkong and Shanghai Banking Corporation), under a unique ordinance, could retain Hong Kong headquarters while complying with the Colonial Banking Regulations.

EXPANDING RAPIDLY IN THE LATE 19TH CENTURY

HongkongBank expanded rapidly throughout the 19th century. By 1900, it had branches in Japan, Thailand, the Philippines, Singapore, and the countries now known as Malaysia, Myanmar, Sri Lanka, and Vietnam. In some Asian cities, HongkongBank was the first to usher in principles of modern Western banking and was indeed Thailand's very first bank, printing that country's first bank notes. In the United States and Europe, HongkongBank branches opened in San Francisco in 1875, New York in 1880, Lyons in 1881, and Hamburg in 1889. Except in New York, where a Canadian bank already operated, HongkongBank was the first foreign bank in each of these cities.

In Hong Kong, operations experienced a setback in the 1870s when the bank made some unwise investments in local Hong Kong industry—its reserves fell from HKD 1 million to HKD 100,000—but the company soon regained its footing under the leadership of a new chief manager, Thomas Jackson, who brought the bank back to a renewed emphasis on its field of expertise, trade finance. By the end of Jackson's reign, in 1902, HongkongBank's paid-up capital stood at HKD 10 million, and its published reserves at HKD 14.25 million, with additional estimated inner reserves of HKD 10 million.

The bank had, however, developed another lucrative role—that of banker to governments. By the 1880s, HongkongBank was operating in this capacity to the government of Hong Kong and had acquired the Treasury Chest (the British government's military and foreign service) business for China and Japan. In addition, the HongkongBank issued bank notes for Hong Kong and for the Straits Settlements (Singapore and Penang). Since these notes were not, at the time, legal tender, their popularity reflected the public's trust in HongkongBank. Through a powerful compradore in China, the bank established contacts with local officials in Tianjin and Beijing. The bank was later asked to issue

KEY DATES

1865: Hongkong and Shanghai Banking Company, Ltd. is established.

1918: Shareholders' funds are £9.1 million.

1940: The Japanese occupy Hong Kong during World War II.

1950: Mainland industrialists flee the communists to Hong Kong.

1959: HSBC buys London's Mercantile Bank and the British Bank of the Middle East.

1960: The bank forms the Wayfoong consumer financing group.

1972: Merchant bank subsidiary Wardley Ltd. is established.

1980: The California subsidiary is divested; HSBC acquires control of Buffalo, New York's Marine Midland Bank.

1991: Holding company HSBC Holdings plc is formed.

1992: Midland Bank, the United Kingdom's third largest, is acquired for £3.9 billion ($7.2 billion).

1997: The United Kingdom transfers control of Hong Kong to the People's Republic of China.

2000: HSBC acquires venerable Crédit Commercial de France (CCF) for $11 billion.

2002: Mexico's Grupo Financiero Bital is acquired and recapitalized for $2 billion.

2003: A new headquarters is opened; Household International of the United States is acquired.

2004: HSBC acquires Bank of Bermuda and Marks & Spencer's retail financial services unit.

2005: Total assets are $1.5 trillion.

a public loan on behalf of the Chinese government, and directed several more in ensuing years. While some of these loans financed China's war against Japan (1894–95) and the enforcement of peace during internal conflicts such as the Boxer Rebellion in 1900, the bulk was used for infrastructural projects such as railroads, coal mines, and shipping lines.

The bank was able to develop a very favorable rapport with the government and business interests in China mainly because it had a widespread presence in China and was incorporated in Hong Kong. By 1910 it was the favored intermediary of the multinational China Consortium, a result of the demonstrated effectiveness of the Bank's London manager, Sir Charles Addis.

WORLD WARS LEADING TO NUMEROUS DIFFICULTIES

World War I deeply divided the bank, still well represented by both Germans and Britons. The German members of its board, identified in the press as "hostile interests," eventually resigned, marking a more or less permanent end to German participation in the company. Still, the bank's Hamburg office remained open for the duration of the war.

The high price of silver after the war led the bank to make a rights issue to finance an expansion. Chief Manager A.G. Stephen presided over the construction of new facilities in Hankow, Bangkok, Manila, and especially Shanghai, where a new office was opened in 1923. An office opened in Vladivostok in 1918 but was forced to close in 1924, when Russian revolutionary forces completed their consolidation of control over Siberia.

The optimism of the early 1920s crashed after 1929 and continued to deteriorate through the 1930s, as Japanese interests moved into China, this time supported by Japanese guns. At first, the Japanese domination of China was limited to the rich hinterlands of Manchuria and consisted mainly of the commercial exploitation of resources. While the bank was permitted to establish offices in the Manchurian cities of Dairen, Mukden, and Harbin, its operations were limited only to foreign trade. Meanwhile, in the rest of China, the bank experienced new competition from an increasingly sophisticated Chinese banking community.

At the same time, the bank was losing business from the Philippine government and was discriminated against in Indonesia and Vietnam by Dutch and French colonial authorities. Despite generous lending and other support tactics for customers involved in rubber and other volatile commodities trades, bank profits continued to deteriorate. In many cases, competitors complained that the bank's extraordinary care "exceeded the limits of prudent lending." The bank was, however, founded on cooperative precepts, and continued to operate on that basis. Still, it was the shareholders who suffered; shareholders' funds fell from £9.1 million in 1918 to £8.6 million in 1940.

The number of Hong Kong dollars in circulation, 80 percent of which was printed by the Hongkong and Shanghai Bank, increased from HKD 50 million in 1927 to HKD 200 million in 1940. In effect, the bank backed HKD 160 million of the colony's currency—a dangerous exposure to the local economy, despite transferring the currency from a silver to sterling standard. The bank became involved in an even more unmanageable currency-stabilization effort in Shanghai, from which it eventually had to bow out, turning the scheme over to a government board.

The Japanese occupation of China, meanwhile, had become extremely brutal. Terror bombings, invasion, and a Japanese military riot in Nanking stifled commerce in China and isolated Hong Kong from its Chinese hinterland. Sensing imminent danger, the bank's chief manager, Vandeleur Grayburn, authorized the immediate transfer of silver reserves into sterling assets in London. On December 8, 1940, shortly after completing the transfer, Japanese troops stormed through Hong Kong's New Territories, and on December 25 won a surrender.

Bank employees in Manchuria, Japan, and Indochina were repatriated, and those in Burma and Singapore escaped to India. Employees in China, particularly Foochow, managed to reach Chungking, where the bank opened a formal office in 1943. The staff in Hong Kong was much less fortunate; most of them who were of European descent were imprisoned.

Under prearranged orders from Grayburn, the bank's London manager, Arthur Morse, assumed managerial control of the bank. Morse transferred the dollar-denominated assets located in Hong Kong to London, fearing that if the Japanese gained control of them, the assets would be frozen by the U.S. government. In light of the circumstances—the bank's board was interned in Hong Kong—Morse was named both chief manager and chairman. During the occupation, Japanese authorities forced the bank to issue additional currency in order to support the local economy. Grayburn and his designated successor, D.C. Edmonston, meanwhile, died in prison.

The war ended so suddenly in August 1945 that Hong Kong remained occupied when Japan surrendered. With colonial authorities back in control, the bank began the difficult and costly task of rebuilding. The amortization of bank notes issued under the occupation cost HKD 16 million, and new legislation only permitted the bank to collect debts from enemy interests in depreciated occupation currencies.

POSTWAR RECOVERY AND EXPANSION

Despite its weakened condition, the bank played a major role in the reconstruction of Hong Kong, a task Morse began planning well before the war ended. All the company's branches were reopened—with the exception of Hamburg which, again, had remained open during the war—including those in Japan. By 1947, however, new problems arose in China, where the wartime alliance between Chiang Kai-shek's nationalists and Mao Tse-tung's communists had degenerated into a civil war. The immediate effects were severe inflation and increasing public disorder.

By October 1949 the communists had gained control of the mainland and the nationalists had fled to Taiwan. When an initial plea by the communists for reconstruction in cooperation with capitalists was suddenly reversed in 1950, industrialists fled China—especially Shanghai—for Hong Kong. The bank maintained offices in Shanghai, Beijing, Tianjin, and Shantou until 1955, when all but the Shanghai branch were closed. The Chinese, it seemed, preferred to do all their business through Hong Kong.

After the war, the British government practiced a "non-extractive" economic policy in Hong Kong, which, coupled with the entrepreneurial talent of industrialists transplanted from Shanghai and a labor force swelled by thousands of mainland refugees, created a powerful economic base. The bank financed hundreds of new ventures that helped the colony achieve unprecedented export-led growth. The growth of the textile industry in Hong Kong, however, led the bank to fear that it had become overexposed to that one industry.

Under Michael Turner, the HongkongBank adopted a new strategy of expansion using subsidiaries during the mid-1950s. Initially made necessary by American banking legislation, the subsidiary form of organization was first used in 1955 to establish a branch in California—one step toward reducing its dependence on Hong Kong.

Because Britain relinquished much of its empire after the war, British companies were forced to rationalize, by merger, acquisition, or nationalization. Indeed, many went bankrupt. Two such companies, the Mercantile Bank (formerly the Chartered Mercantile Bank of India, London, and China) and the British Bank of the Middle East (known as BBME, formerly the Imperial Bank of Persia), were purchased by the Hongkong and Shanghai Bank in 1959. The addition of the Mercantile Bank, with an extensive branch network in India, and the BBME, strongly represented in the Persian Gulf, made the HongkongBank the largest foreign bank in most of the countries from the Far East to southwest Asia.

Having reduced its exposure to Hong Kong, the bank moved next to diversify operationally. In 1960 it created Wayfoong, a consumer financing group whose name translates loosely as "focus of wealth."

A banking crisis in Hong Kong in 1964 led to a serious run on a competitor, the Hang Seng Bank. As the primary financial institution in Hong Kong and de facto central bank, the HongkongBank, while under no statutory duty to do so, acquired a majority interest in Hang Seng in 1965. Hang Seng subsequently recovered, and was the second largest bank incorporated in Hong Kong into the 1990s.

The HongkongBank's expansion through subsidiaries began in earnest with the creation in 1972 of Wardley Ltd., a merchant bank, and an insurance company called Carlingford. The bank also made numerous other investments—in Cathay Pacific Airways, the World-Wide shipping group, and the South China Morning Post. All these investments proved highly profitable in light of Hong Kong's rapid economic growth. In addition, the BBME benefited greatly from the newly prosperous oil-based economies in the Persian Gulf. In 1978, however, BBME branches in Saudi Arabia were taken over by the Saudi British Bank, a Saudi-controlled bank in which BBME retained management control, but only 40 percent ownership.

Under the leadership of Michael Sandberg, the HongkongBank reexamined its position in America as part of a wider strategy to gain greater representation in the major Western economies. The Hongkong and Shanghai Bank of California was sold and the bank purchased a 51 percent share of Marine Midland Bank, a Buffalo, New York-based bank holding company, in 1980. The HongkongBank bought the outstanding shares of Marine Midland in 1987. This acquisition inspired substantial debate in the U.S. Congress about whether banking laws should be strengthened to prevent foreign companies from gaining control over American banks.

The bank expanded in several ways during 1980. In China, the Shanghai branch was expanded and a representative office was established in Beijing. In addition, the BBME relocated from London to Hong Kong, and the bank gained control of Concord International, a leasing and finance group, and Anthony Gibbs, a British merchant bank. The following year, a Canadian subsidiary, the Hongkong Bank of Canada, was established in Vancouver. In 1986 the Hongkong Bank of Canada acquired the business of the Bank of British Columbia, bringing the number of branches across Canada to 61.

A bidding war over the Royal Bank of Scotland Group between the HongkongBank and Standard & Chartered (issuer of Hong Kong's other currency) was halted in 1981 by the British Monopolies & Mergers Commission, which ruled against both bids. Meanwhile, the bank succeeded in establishing a presence in Africa in 1981 through the acquisition of a controlling interest in Equator Bank by its merchant bank subsidiary Ward-

ley; in Cyprus in 1982, also primarily through Wardley; and in Australia in 1985, when it established HongkongBank of Australia. Back in North America, HongkongBank entered into a strategic alliance with California-based Wells Fargo Bank in 1989. Also that year, HongkongBank was registered under the Hong Kong Companies Ordinance, at which time it adopted the name The Hongkong and Shanghai Banking Corporation Ltd.

HongkongBank's expansionist policies were not always successful. Its acquisition of Marine Midland, said initially to have boosted the bank's assets from HKD 125.3 billion to HKD 243 billion, soon proved a debacle. Ill-advised forays into real estate and Latin American lending led to significant losses, prompting the parent company in 1991 to completely overhaul its subsidiary—at a purported cost of $1.8 billion. Other high-profile failures of the 1980s included the bank's financing of an Australian tycoon, Alan Bond, who went bankrupt.

FORMING HSBC HOLDINGS PLC IN 1991

In 1984 Great Britain and the People's Republic of China signed a historic agreement, slating for July 1, 1997, the return of Hong Kong to Chinese control, and providing added impetus to HongkongBank's overseas expansion. Keen to beef up its presence in Europe, the bank acquired James Capel, a leading U.K. securities firm, in 1986. Of still greater importance was the beginning in December 1987 of an association between HongkongBank and Midland Bank, one of four major British clearing banks. In December 1987 Hongkong-Bank made the friendly acquisition of 14.9 percent of Midland's stock, agreeing not to increase its stake in Midland until the expiration of a three-year agreement in December 1990. Staking its future in Europe to that of Midland, HongkongBank transferred control of its branches on the European continent to Midland and in turn acquired Midland's branches in Canada and South Korea. In 1990 Hongkong Bank of Canada expanded still further through the purchase of Lloyds Bank Canada, becoming the seventh largest bank in Canada by the early 1990s.

HongkongBank and Midland entered into merger talks in 1990, but the talks broke off late in the year because of what were termed "financial difficulties." Nevertheless, HongkongBank held onto its stake in Midland following the expiration of the three-year agreement.

Like many Hong Kong-based companies facing the uncertainties of 1997, HongkongBank made some major organizational changes well before the handover. In 1991 it created a new holding company, HSBC Holdings plc, making HongkongBank a subsidiary of the U.K.-incorporated but Hong Kong-based HSBC Holdings. HSBC stock was set up on both the London and Hong Kong markets, showing the importance Hong Kong Bank placed on Europe (and London) for its future. For HongkongBank, the establishment of a new holding company relieved it of management responsibility for the group's more than 500 subsidiaries in 50 countries. The bank thus could focus primarily on the Asia-Pacific region it knew so well.

HSBC completed the long-anticipated takeover of Midland in 1992, gaining full control of what became its flagship in Europe. HSBC made an initial friendly offer in March for Midland. The following month Lloyds stepped in with a larger, hostile offer. HSBC soon put an end to the takeover battle with a 480p per share offer in June, prompting Lloyds to bow out. HSBC ended up paying £3.9 billion ($7.2 billion) to acquire Midland. As a condition of the acquisition, HSBC was required by the regulatory Bank of England to move its main office to London, which it did in January 1993. The headquarters of HongkongBank remained in Hong Kong.

The acquisition of Midland was a coup, providing HSBC with the significant presence in Europe it had previously lacked. Variously described as a merger and a takeover, the amalgamation virtually doubled HSBC's assets (from £86 billion to £170 billion) and workforce. The venerable Midland, the U.K.'s third largest bank, was not performing to standard at that time, being the least profitable of Britain's "big four" banks. Nevertheless, the financial health and the international experience of the parent company began attracting larger corporate customers to Midland. In addition, many individuals were subsequently won over by the telephone banking service, First Direct, introduced by Midland in 1989 and strongly backed by HSBC. HSBC's lead in technology—used, for example, to automate credit decisions and limit staff expenditure—also played a part in Midland's recovery.

Although under the HSBC umbrella structure individual subsidiaries acted, in large part, autonomously, the company also moved to coordinate some operations. Soon after the takeover of Midland, HSBC integrated its treasury operations in London, New York, and Tokyo and established common technological standards. Also in 1992 HSBC opened a trading room in London for the dealing business of Midland, James Capel, and HSBC Greenwell. This became the largest treasury trading operation in Europe. That year also saw the establishment of the HSBC Investment Banking Group,

which coordinated the merchant banking, securities, and asset management business (HSBC Asset Management) of the entire HSBC Group.

HongkongBank, which had long acted as a quasi-central bank, was relieved of some of these unofficial duties in 1992, when the Hong Kong Monetary Authority was established. The following year HongkongBank divested its holding in Cathay Pacific Airways. In 1994 it became the first foreign bank to incorporate locally in Malaysia through the establishment of Hongkong Bank Malaysia Berhad. In the mid-1990s the bank greatly expanded its personal banking business through the opening or upgrading of personal banking units in Australia, Bangladesh, Brunei, Hong Kong, Indonesia, Mauritius, New Zealand, the Philippines, Saipan, Singapore, Sri Lanka, Taiwan, and Thailand. The bank also expanded its presence in China during this period, maintaining good relations with the Chinese government—which was extremely important as 1997 approached.

HSBC Holdings continued to expand in the mid-1990s under the leadership of Chief Executive John Bond. In 1995 HSBC and Wells Fargo established Wells Fargo HSBC Trade Bank in California, a joint venture (40 percent owned by HSBC) providing trade finance and international banking services in the United States. Marine Midland was bolstered in 1996 with the acquisition of Rochester, New York-based First Federal Savings and Loan Association for $620 million. Latin America was the subject of several 1997 transactions: the purchase of a 10 percent stake in Banco del Sur del Peru; the founding of a new subsidiary in Brazil, Banco HSBC Bamerindus S.A., which took over assets of Banco Bamerindus do Brasil; the increase in investment in Banco Santiago in Chile to 6.99 percent; the acquisition of Roberts S.A. de Inversiones of Argentina (renamed HSBC Roberts S.A. de Inversiones); and the purchase of a 19.9 percent stake in Grupo Financiero Serfin of Mexico.

Although HSBC seemed to suffer no ill effects from the handover of Hong Kong to Chinese control on July 1, 1997, it did feel the effects of the Asian economic crisis of the late 1990s. The group was particularly hard hit in troubled Indonesia, where it had to set aside about $2.5 billion in provisions for bad loans. Nevertheless, its earlier moves into Europe and the Americas paid off handsomely, as higher profits in these regions helped offset weaker results in Asia. Meantime, the Hong Kong Monetary Authority, in an attempt to thwart currency speculators, made a significant intervention in the Hong Kong Stock Market in August 1998, purchasing large stakes in several prominent companies. The government of Hong Kong thereby became HSBC Holdings' single largest shareholder, with an 8.9 percent stake. In October 1998 HSBC announced that it had signed a 999-year lease for a new 1.1 million-square-foot headquarters building at Canary Wharf in London, scheduled for completion by early 2002. The following month HSBC said that it would unify the HSBC Group under the HSBC name and logo, thereby establishing a more global corporate identity. Among the units whose marketing names would change to HSBC were Banco HSBC Bamerindus, the British Bank of the Middle East, Hongkong Bank Malaysia, Hongkong Bank of Australia, Hongkong Bank of Canada, HSBC Banco Roberts, Marine Midland, Midland Bank, HSBC Equator Bank, HSBC Investment Banking, and even the flagship Hongkong-Bank itself. Eventually the legal names of many HSBC Group subsidiaries would also be changed. In a press release, Bond said: "We want the HSBC brand to be known in every country and in every sector in which we operate as synonymous with integrity, trust, and excellent customer service. I am confident that a unified brand and the strong recognition it will bring for HSBC's exceptional strengths is an important step forward as we work to maximise shareholder value." The implementation of this significant change was sure to require much of HSBC's attention at the onset of the 21st century.

HSBC shares began trading on the New York Stock Exchange in 1999. Later in the year, the group bought Republic New York Corporation and Safra Republic Holdings S.A. Acquisitions also were giving HSBC a considerable presence in Europe. The company bought Crédit Commercial de France (renamed CCF S.A. and ultimately HSBC France) for $11 billion in 2000. CCF had been formed in 1894 and operated 650 branch offices. In July 2000, when the deal closed, HSBC shares began trading on the Paris Stock Exchange.

HSBC bought out Australia's NRMA Building Society Ltd., Turkey's Demirbank, and Taiwan's China Securities Investment Trust Corporation in 2001. It also was picking up minority shares in others such as the Bank of Shanghai and Ping An Insurance Company, China's second largest insurance provider. Ping An underwent an initial public offering in 2004, diluting HSBC's stake to about 10 percent, but in August 2005 raised its holding to 19.9 percent at a cost of $1 billion.

"THE WORLD'S LOCAL BANK" IN 2002

The company spent about $2 billion in 2002 to buy and recapitalize Mexico's Grupo Financiero Bital. HSBC gained 5.5 million new customers at 1,400 new branches. During the year, HSBC began billing itself as "The world's local bank." HSBC opened its impressive new headquarters at London's Canary Wharf in April 2003. About 8,000 employees were based there.

Part of HSBC's sensitivity to local cultures included support of environmental causes such as the World Wildlife Fund. In December 2004, the company became the first bank to set the goal of becoming "carbon neutral," a status it achieved within a year.

In 2003, the group made a major acquisition in the United States, taking over Household International Inc., which had more than 1,300 branches and 53 million consumer finance and credit card customers. In Brazil, HSBC also bought a leading consumer finance company, Losango Promotora de Vendas Limitada, as well as Banco Lloyds TSB S.A.-Banco Múltiplo. Among other 2003 deals was the purchase of Keppel Insurance Pte Ltd., which supplied insurance in Singapore.

The mergers and acquisitions activity continued in 2004, adding the Bank of Bermuda Ltd. and Marks and Spencer's Retail Financial Services Holdings Ltd. (d/b/a M&S Money). By this time, most of the group's existing subsidiaries had changed their names to include the HSBC initials. Household International, renamed HSBC Finance Corporation, and others were combined into the HSBC North America unit.

China was the hub of much of the group's investment activity in 2005. While raising its holding in Ping An Insurance, it also bought a 19.9 percent stake in Bank of Communications Ltd. HSBC was also opening new bank branches. In March 2005, its Beijing branch began providing local currency services, a first for a foreign bank. Elsewhere in the world, U.S. credit card issuer Metris Companies Inc. was acquired by HSBC Finance for $1.6 billion in December 2005.

The group's chairman since 1988, Sir John Bond, was retiring in May 2006. He was leaving a much larger company than the one he had joined. HSBC posted pretax profits of $21 billion in 2005, up 11 percent from the previous year. Total assets were $1.5 trillion (£873 billion; HKD 11.65 trillion). The group employed a virtual army of 265,285 employees worldwide, serving nearly 100 million customers.

Robin DuBlanc
Updated, David E. Salamie; Frederick C. Ingram

PRINCIPAL SUBSIDIARIES

The Bank of Bermuda Ltd.; Hang Seng Bank Ltd. (Hong Kong; 62.14%); HFC Bank Ltd.; HSBC Asset Finance (UK) Ltd.; The Hongkong and Shanghai Banking Corporation Ltd. (Hong Kong); HSBC Bank A.S. (Turkey); HSBC Bank Argentina S.A. (99.99%); HSBC

Bank Australia Ltd.; HSBC Bank Brasil S.A. – Banco Múltiplo; HSBC Bank Canada; HSBC Bank Egypt S.A.E. (94.53%); HSBC Bank Malaysia Berhad; HSBC Bank Malta plc (70.03%); HSBC Bank Middle East Ltd. (Jersey); HSBC Bank plc; HSBC Bank USA, N.A.; HSBC La Buenos Aires Seguros S.A. (Argentina; 99.53%); HSBC Finance Corporation (United States); HSBC France (formerly CCF S.A.) (99.99%); HSBC Guyerzeller Bank AG (Switzerland); HSBC Insurance (Asia) Ltd. (Hong Kong); HSBC Insurance Brokers Ltd.; HSBC Investments (Taiwan) Ltd. (formerly HSBC Asset Management (Taiwan) Ltd.); HSBC Investments (UK) Ltd. (formerly HSBC Asset Management (Europe) Ltd.); HSBC Life (International) Ltd. (Bermuda); HSBC Life (UK) Ltd.; HSBC Private Bank (Guernsey) Ltd. (Guernsey); HSBC Mexico S.A. (99.74%); HSBC Private Bank (Suisse) S.A.; HSBC Private Bank (UK) Ltd.; HSBC Securities (USA) Inc.; HSBC Seguros (Brasil) S.A. (97.92%); HSBC Technology & Services (USA) Inc.; HSBC Trinkaus & Burkhardt KGaA (Germany; 77.89%); Maxima S.A. AFJP (Argentina; 59.99%).

PRINCIPAL DIVISIONS

Europe; Hong Kong; Rest of Asia-Pacific, including the Middle East and Africa; North America; South America.

PRINCIPAL OPERATING UNITS

Grupo Financiero HSBC, S.A. de C.V. (99.8%); HSBC Bank plc; HSBC France (Netherlands); HSBC Insurance Holdings Ltd.; HSBC Investment Bank Holdings plc; HSBC Latin America Holdings (UK) Ltd.; HSBC North America Holdings Inc.

PRINCIPAL COMPETITORS

Lloyds TSB Group plc; Barclays plc.

FURTHER READING

Blanden, Michael, "After the Dust of Battle," *Banker,* August 1992, p. 36.

Chambers, Gillian, *Hang Seng: The Evergrowing Bank,* Hong Kong: Hang Seng Bank, 1991.

Collis, Maurice, *Wayfoong: The Hong Kong and Shanghai Banking Corporation,* London: Faber and Faber, 1965.

"An Empire at Risk," *Economist,* September 7, 1996, pp. 71–72.

Engardio, Pete, "Global Banker," *Business Week,* May 24, 1993, pp. 42–46.

Engardio, Pete, and Paula Dwyer, "Hongkong & Shanghai vs. the World," *Business Week,* August 7, 1995, pp. 59–60.

"Far Eastern Promise and the Global Gamble," *Investors' Chronicle,* January 29, 1993.

Graham, George, "HSBC Reaps Fruits of Growth Strategy," *Financial Times,* February 24, 1998, p. 26.

"Greater Than the Sum of His Parts," *Financial Times,* March 1, 1994.

Green, William, "Bland—And Proud of It," *Forbes,* July 7, 1997, pp. 94–96, 98–99.

Holmes, A. R., and Edwin Green, *Midland: 150 Years of Banking Business,* London: Batsford, 1986.

"HongkongBank's Global Gamble," *Economist,* March 21, 1992, pp. 107–08.

"Hong Kong/China Boom Spawns a Global Banking Colossus," *QL Stockmarket Letter,* July 1, 1993.

"HSBC Maps Strategy for US Market," *South China Morning Post,* January 14, 1993.

Irvine, Steve, "The Culture That Powers Hongkong Bank," *Euromoney,* February 1997, pp. 44+.

Jones, Geoffrey, *The History of the British Bank of the Middle East,* 2 vols., Cambridge: Cambridge University Press, 1986–87.

King, Frank H. H., *The History of the Hongkong and Shanghai Banking Corporation,* 4 vols., Cambridge: Cambridge University Press, 1987–91.

———, *The Hongkong Bank in the Period of Development and Nationalism, 1941–1984: From Regional Bank to Multinational Group,* New York: Cambridge University Press, 1991.

King, Frank H. H., ed., *Eastern Banking: Essays in the History of the Hongkong and Shanghai Banking Corporation,* London: Athlone Press, 1983.

King, Frank H. H., Catherine E. King, and David J. S. King, *The Hongkong Bank Between the Wars and the Bank Interned, 1919–1945: Return from Grandeur,* New York: Cambridge University Press, 1988.

———, *The Hongkong Bank in Late Imperial China, 1864–1902: On an Even Keel,* New York: Cambridge University Press, 1987.

King, Frank H. H., David J. S. King, and Catherine E. King, *The Hongkong Bank in the Period of Imperialism and War, 1895–1918: Wayfoong, the Focus of Wealth,* New York: Cambridge University Press, 1988.

Leung, James, "HongkongBank Extends Personal Touch," *Asian Business,* February 1997, p. 22+.

"Loan Masters," *Economist,* August 28, 1993, pp. 65–66.

Lucas, Louise, "Hongkong Bank Chief to Quit in HSBC Rejig," *Financial Times,* October 16, 1998, p. 25.

———, "Profits Growth Limited at HongkongBank," *Financial Times,* August 5, 1997, p. 20.

Meyer, Richard, "Lessons from Buffalo," *Financial World,* July 23, 1991, pp. 37–39.

Morris, Kathleen, "Back to the Future," *Financial World,* June 20, 1995, pp. 42–44.

Muirhead, Stuart, *Crisis Banking in the East: The History of the Chartered Mercantile Bank of India, London and China, 1853–93,* Aldershot, England: Scolar Press, 1996.

Sender, Henny, and John McBeth, "Living Dangerously: Hongkong Bank Is Mired in an Indonesian Nightmare," *Far Eastern Economic Review,* February 29, 1996, pp. 52–53.

Silverman, Gary, "Look British, Think Chinese: Hongkong Bank Stays No. 1," *Far Eastern Economic Review,* December 28, 1995, pp. 64–65.

Tanzer, Andrew, "The Bank," *Forbes,* December 11, 1989, pp. 43–44.

Vander Weyer, Martin, "Hongkong Officer Corps Builds a Global Empire," *Euromoney,* April, 1993, pp. 52–56.

"Waiting for the Griffin to Pull Its Weight," *Financial Times,* March 16, 1993.

"You Organise Your Bank Around Your Customers," *Daily Telegraph,* March 22, 1993.

"Your Future Is Our Future," Hong Kong: The Hongkong and Shanghai Banking Corporation Ltd., 1997.

Janssen Pharmaceutica
N.V.

Turnhoutseweg 30
Beerse,
Belgium
Telephone: (32) 014 60 21 11
Fax: (32) 014 60 28 41
Web site: http://www.janssenpharmaceutica.be

Wholly Owned Subsidiary of Johnson & Johnson
Incorporated: 1953
Employees: 4,000
Sales: EUR 1.93 billion ($2.44 billion) (2005)
NAIC: 325412 Pharmaceutical Preparation Manufacturing; 325320 Pesticide and Other Agricultural Chemical Manufacturing; 325998 All Other Miscellaneous Chemical Product Manufacturing; 541710 Research and Development in the Physical Sciences and Engineering Sciences

■ ■ ■

Belgium-based Janssen Pharmaceutica N.V. is one of the world's most successful specialist drug discovery companies, responsible for the development of more than 80 drugs since its founding in the early 1950s. Among the company's most successful drugs have been the anemia treatment eprex, and risperdal and haloperidol, both for the treatment of schizophrenia. Five Janssen drugs are featured on the World Health Organization's list of essential drugs, including haloperidol, levamisole, miconazole, and ketoconazole. The company has functioned as an autonomous drug development subsidiary of Johnson & Johnson (J&J)

since 1961, and remained J&J's largest single pharmaceutical sector acquisition until its merger with Centacor in 1999.

Janssen operates research and development facilities in Belgium and the United States, chemical production plants in Belgium, Ireland, Switzerland, and the United States, and pharmaceutical production sites in Belgium, France, Italy, Switzerland, Portugal, and Puerto Rico. Janssen also has maintained a production presence in China since 1983, through its joint venture Xian-Janssen Pharmaceutical Co. In addition to its production and research facilities, Janssen operates a global marketing network through its participation in the Janssen-Cilag marketing group, in partnership with sister J&J subsidiary Cilag. Janssen-Cilag operates subsidiaries in 40 countries, with more than 27,000 employees; Janssen itself employs more than 4,000 people. In Asia, the company's products are marketed through local joint ventures including Xian-Janssen (China), Janssen-Kyowa (Japan), and Janssen Korea names, as well as through Janssen-Cilag. Janssen's products are marketed under various names, including Janssen Pharmaceutica and Janssen-Ortho, as well as Ortho Biotech and Ortho-McNeil, also part of the J&J group. Aijit Sherry is company CEO.

ROOTS IN BELGIAN MEDICINE IN 1933

The Janssen family's involvement in the pharmaceutical field began in the early 1930s, when Constant Janssen, a general practitioner in the rural area of Turnhout, in northern Belgium near the Dutch border, began seeking

COMPANY PERSPECTIVES

Based in Belgium, Janssen Pharmaceutica was established in 1953 by a young medical doctor, Dr Paul Janssen. Unlike most pharmaceutical companies, it was created not as a subsidiary of a chemical factory but solely with the aim of conducting pharmacological research. The one objective of the company has always been the continuous development of better drugs to improve the quality of life.

better means of treating his patients. At the time, few drugs existed, meaning Janssen could offer medicinal treatment to very few of his patients. Janssen came into contact with the Richter pharmaceutical company, based in Budapest, and began importing Richter's products to treat his patients. The Richter company's preparations were, in large part, vitamins; nonetheless they represented a step ahead in the treatment of patients at the time. By 1933 Constant Janssen had acquired the exclusive right to import Richter's products into Belgium, The Netherlands, and the Belgian Congo, establishing his own business, in addition to his medical practice. Janssen later began developing his own pharmaceutical preparations, and by the outbreak of World War II had retired from medical practice to devote himself full-time to his pharmaceutical company.

Constant Janssen provided a great deal of inspiration for his son, Paul Janssen, who became determined to enter medicine when his younger sister died when he was only eight. Janssen traveled to Namur to attend school at the Faculté Notre Dame de la Paix, where he studied physics, biology, and especially chemistry. At the end of the war, Janssen left to study medicine at the Catholic University of Leuven. Yet Janssen's earlier studies had convinced him that there was an inherent connection between the chemistry of drugs and their effects as medicines. This led Janssen to travel to the United States in 1948, where he studied chemical research and pharmacology. Returning to Europe, Janssen completed his medical studies at Leuven, then earned his medical degree at the University of Ghent in 1951.

Nonetheless, Janssen had become determined to pursue a career in pharmaceutical research. Called up to complete his military service, Janssen was stationed in Cologne, Germany, where he was able to continue studying chemistry and pharmacology at Cologne University. There, Janssen studied under Nobel Prize winner Corneel Heymans. In 1956, Janssen had

completed his thesis in pharmacology and earned his teaching certification.

By then, however, Janssen had launched his own pharmaceutical company. Returning to Turnhout in 1953, Janssen had set up his own laboratory on the third floor of his father's company. There, Janssen began pursuing his goal of applying modern research techniques toward uncovering the relationship between the chemical structure of a compound and its pharmaceutical effects on patients. Constant Janssen was said to have been skeptical at first, but the younger Janssen quickly proved the firm foundation for his research. Janssen's work consisted of synthesizing molecules, and by 1954, Janssen had synthesized his fifth molecule—R5, better known as ambucetamide. The new compound proved to be a potent antispasmodic, and was especially effective in treating menstrual pain. By 1955, Janssen had released the drug under the brand name Neomeritime. That product remained an important seller for the company into the twenty-first century.

The success of Neomeritime led the Janssen family to reincorporate its business as NV Laboratoria Pharmaceutica Dr. C. Janssen in 1956, and Paul Janssen left Cologne to work full-time in the new pharmaceutical company.

The company's next success was not long in coming. In 1959, Janssen launched a new drug for the treatment of schizophrenia, called haloperidol. The development of that drug highlighted Janssen's novel approach to drug discovery and especially the relationship between chemistry and biology. As reported by *The Lancet*, Janssen had been inspired by the case of a bicyclist who had won a race while under the influence of amphetamines. "Even as he was pulled off his bike and congratulated by a reporter, he tried to continue cycling," Janssen recalled, convincing him that "finding a treatment for amphetamine intoxication would provide a cure for paranoid schizophrenia." Janssen successfully conducted trials of haloperidol on mice, then turned to clinical testing on a young schizophrenic patient in Liege. The test was conclusive—and the patient had gone on to lead a normal lifestyle. Marketed as Haldol, the new drug represented a revolution in the treatment of schizophrenia, allowing patients to be treated at home, instead of being institutionalized.

INTERNATIONAL SUCCESS: MIDDLE TO LATE 20TH CENTURY

Janssen began expanding its facilities, acquiring land in Beerse that later developed into a campus of more than 56 hectares. By the early 1960s, the company had grown

KEY DATES

1933: Constant Janssen acquires distribution rights to Richter (Hungary) pharmaceutical products in Belgium.

1953: Paul Janssen establishes a research laboratory as part of the family business.

1954: The company develops its first successful compound, ambucetamide.

1956: The company changes its name to NV Laboratoria Pharmaceutica Dr. C. Janssen.

1959: Haloperidol, a treatment for schizophrenia, is launched.

1961: Janssen is acquired by Johnson & Johnson.

1964: The company's name is changed to Janssen Pharmaceutica.

1972: A U.S. subsidiary is established in the J&J facility.

1980: The company launches the first technology transfer agreement in China.

1985: The company forms a joint venture in China and builds a factory in China, completed in 1989.

1990: The company merges its global sales and marketing network with those of sister companies Cilag and J&J Biotechnology, creating Janssen-Cilag.

1991: Paul Janssen retires.

1992: The U.S. branch opens a new 270-acre campus in Titusville, New Jersey.

2003: Construction of a new API plant in Ireland is launched.

2004: Paul Janssen dies at age 77.

2006: The company merges its primary care and hospital products operations with those of sister company Ortho-McNeil Pharmaceuticals, creating a new entity, Ortho-McNeil Inc.

1961, Janssen and J&J began negotiations that led to the acquisition of the Belgian company by the U.S. giant. As part of the agreement, however, Janssen was guaranteed that it would remain an independently operating company within the Johnson & Johnson group. This agreement fit in neatly with J&J's own organizational structure. Janssen himself described the merger, as reported by the *British Medical Journal:* "During the negotiations that led to this co-operation, the future and the protection of our company were uppermost in my mind. For me and my employees, the merger was a sort of life insurance."

J&J's backing enabled Janssen to push ahead with its expansion, as the company continued to develop new and innovative pharmaceutical preparations. The company's expansion also included a move into the development of drugs for veterinary applications. Meanwhile, the company had achieved another major breakthrough, that of the development of fentanyl. Released in 1963, that drug became the world's most prescribed anaesthetic.

Other successes followed in the 1970s, including the launch of pimozide, used in controlling Tourette's syndrome, chronic psychosis, schizophrenia, and other mental disorders; mebendazole, a worm treatment known by brand names such as Vermox, in 1972; and loperamide, used to treat gastrointestinal disorders, and popularly known under the Immodium AD brand. Later successes by Janssen included risperidone, an important antipsychotic.

Through this period, Paul Janssen remained directly involved in the company's research and development efforts. Over the course of his career, Janssen was to generate more than 100 patents, as well as publish more than 850 papers. Janssen, however, continued to be backed by the company's steady growth, particularly internationally. In 1973, the company turned toward the United States, setting up a subsidiary at J&J's headquarters. The growth of its U.S. operations soon led Janssen to open its own dedicated facilities nearby. At the same time, Janssen extended its sales and marketing network. The company first targeted expansion in Europe, adding subsidiaries in most of the major markets. In 1980, the company entered the United States, establishing a sales network where previously it had marketed its products through other J&J subsidiaries or under third-party brands.

Through the 1980s, Janssen continued to add new markets, such as South Africa in 1984. By then, the company had marked another significant expansion step. In 1980, Janssen became the first Western company to develop a technology transfer agreement in China. By 1983, the company had assisted in the construction of a

to more than 300 employees. Yet in order to support the company's continued expansion—and especially its rapid growth in the international pharmaceuticals market—Janssen recognized that he needed to find a larger partner. This brought him in contact with Johnson & Johnson, which had been actively seeking to expand its own pharmaceuticals operation. In 1959, for example, Johnson & Johnson had acquired Switzerland's Cilag-Chemie and the United States' McNeil Laboratories. In

factory for the production of mebendazole there. Two years later, Janssen established a joint venture in China with four government-owned businesses. That partnership began construction of a factory in Xian, which launched production in 1989.

DRUG DISCOVERY LEADER IN THE NEW CENTURY

Paul Janssen stepped down from active leadership of the company in 1991; nonetheless, Janssen remained an active researcher until his death at age 77 in 2004. Janssen left one of the most impressive legacies in modern pharmaceutical history: In addition to his record of patents and published papers, Janssen had received a total of 80 medical prizes, and more than 20 honorary doctorate degrees.

Janssen also left behind a company that had taken a firm position among the world's leading drug discovery groups. An important boost for the company's international sales and marketing effort came in the early 1990s, when its marketing network was merged with those of sister companies Cilag and Johnson & Johnson Biotechnology, creating a new J&J subsidiary, Janssen-Cilag. That company became one of the world's largest pharmaceutical sales organizations, with subsidiaries in some 50 countries and more than 27,000 employees.

Janssen continued to develop its research and production wings as well. The company's U.S. branch moved to larger headquarters, a 270-acre campus in Titusville, New Jersey, in 1992. Janssen's group of production facilities also had grown to include chemical production sites in Ireland and Switzerland, and pharmaceutical production plants in France, Italy, Switzerland, Portugal, and Puerto Rico. In 2003, the company expanded its Irish site with the launch of construction of a facility for the production of active pharmaceutical intermediates (APIs).

Into the mid-2000s, Janssen remained an important part of Johnson & Johnson's pharmaceuticals operations. Although Janssen retained its independence with the J&J organization, it nonetheless participated actively in the parent company's overall strategy. An example of this was provided by the merger of Janssen's primary care and hospital products resources unit with that of sister company Ortho-McNeil Pharmaceuticals, creating a new entity, Ortho-McNeil Inc. Janssen Pharmaceutica

looked back on more than 50 years of developing innovative pharmaceutical products.

M. L. Cohen

PRINCIPAL SUBSIDIARIES

Janssen Pharmaceutica Inc. (United States); Janssen Pharmaceutica N.V./Janssen Research Foundation (Belgium); Janssen-Cilag Mexico; Janssen-Cilag N.V. (Belgium); Janssen-Ortho Inc. (Canada); Johnson & Johnson Pharm. Partners (Puerto Rico); Ortho Biotech Inc. (United States); Ortho-McNeil Pharmaceutical Inc. (United States); Xian-Janssen Pharmaceutical Co. Ltd. (China).

PRINCIPAL COMPETITORS

Pfizer Inc.; Astrazeneca S.A.; GlaxoSmithKline; Bayer AG; Sanofi-Aventis; Novartis Inc.; Celesio AG; Roche Holding AG; Abbott Laboratories; Merck and Company Inc.

FURTHER READING

Conn, Joseph, "Paul Janssen: Helped Introduce Haldol," *Modern Physician,* December 1, 2003, p. 23.

"International Pharmaceutical Companies Swarming into the Chinese Market," *China Chemical Reporter,* April 6, 2000, p. 8.

"Janssen Builds API Plant in Ireland," *Chemical Week,* April 2, 2003, p. 45.

"Janssen Pharmaceutica," *Drug Topics,* January 17, 1983, p. 48.

"Johnson & Johnson: (A focus on Janssen, Ortho Biotech, and Ortho-McNeil)," *Formulary,* October 2000, p. S49.

Muller-Wainwright, Carrie, "Drug Discovery Program Discovers American Market," *Drug & Cosmetic Industry,* December 1985, p. 22.

Oransky, Ivan, "Paul Janssen (Obituary)," *The Lancet,* January 17, 2004, p. 251.

"Ortho-McNeil (Ortho-McNeil Pharmaceuticals Inc. and Janssen Pharmaceutica Products LP Merges)," *Chain Drug Review,* January 16, 2006, p. 55.

"Overactive Bladder Alliance Struck with Johnson & Johnson," *Women's Health Weekly,* January 29, 2004, p. 42.

Prizinsky, David, "Major Boost for Biotech Firm," *Crain's Cleveland Business,* October 17, 1994, p. 1.

Rodgers, Katie, "Janssen Launches New Treatment for Schizophrenia," *Drug Topics,* April 11, 1994, p. 30.

Jotun A/S

PO Box 2021
Sandefjord,
Norway
Telephone: (47) 33 45 70 00
Fax: (47) 33 45 72 42
Web site: http://www.jotun.com

Private Company
Founded: 1926 as Jotun Kemiske Fabrik A/S
Incorporated: 1972 as Jotungruppen (The Jotun Group)
Employees: 5,009
Sales: NOK 6.07 billion ($1.04 billion) (2005)
NAIC: 325510 Paint and Coating Manufacturing

■ ■ ■

Jotun A/S is one of the world's top producers of paints and coatings; the company ranks number ten worldwide, and is also the leading supplier of paints and coatings to the Scandinavian market. Jotun is active through four primary divisions: Jotun Coatings, including marine coatings and other protective coatings; Jotun Dekorative, which focuses on the decorative paint market in Scandinavia; Jotun Paints, which oversees the group's worldwide production of decorative paints; and Jotun Powder Coatings, which produces thermosetting coatings.

Based in Norway, Jotun operates through nearly 70 subsidiaries, operating nearly 40 production units, in Europe, Asia, North and South America, Africa, and Australia. In 2005, the company generated turnover of more than NOK 6 billion ($1 billion). Jotun remains a private company controlled by the founding family. Odd Gleditsch d.y. ("the younger"), the founder's grandson, is company chairman. Knut Almestrand serves as managing director overseeing the company's day-to-day operations.

FOUNDING A NORWEGIAN PAINT PRODUCER IN 1926

Odd Gleditsch already had a varied career when he founded Jotun in 1926. As a youth, Gleditsch had served aboard a processor vessel serving whale hunters in Antartica, and later worked on the hunting vessels themselves. In 1916, however, Gleditsch came ashore to begin work for a stockbroker. When that business went under in 1920, Gleditsch set up in business for himself, opening a paint supply shop. Gleditsch's shop also carried supplies for the local whaling industry, including marine paints for whaling vessels. Gleditsch quickly became an important supplier of paints to whalers in Tonsberg, Larvik, and Sandefjord.

By 1926, Gleditsch had decided that the shop would begin manufacturing the paint they sold. The opportunity came when the oil mill in Gimle, near Sandefjord, which supplied Gleditsch's shop with marine paints and other oil-based products, ran into hard times. Gleditsch gathered a group of investors to buy the ailing mill, founding a new company, Jotun Kemiske Fabrik A/S. The company was named after Jotun, a giant from Norse mythology, and the Jotunheimen mountains of Norway. Gleditsch became the group's first general manager.

From the start, Jotun focused on the production of

quality paints. In support of its operations, the company
acquired its own vegetable oil refinery, Vera Fedtrafeneri,
in 1930. The expanded operation allowed the company
to develop new paint types, and Jotun soon became
known for its record of innovation. One of the first of
the company's new products came after it acquired the
patent for oil-based Arcanol in 1931. The product was
highly successful and enabled Jotun to grow despite the
disastrous economic climate of the time.

Gleditsch also displayed a keen commercial sense.
In 1935, for example, the company launched a new
paint line, called Femkronerslakken, or "five-kroner
varnish." The new premium quality floor varnish was
much more expensive than competing varnishes, yet
Gleditsch wagered that its customers would be attracted
to the high-quality of the product, reinforced by including the higher price in its name. The new product
enabled Jotun to expand from its focus on the whaling
industry into the far-larger consumer market.

Jotun beefed up its focus on developing its own innovative products in the postwar period when the
company opened a new factory in Gimle. The facility
also featured the group's own laboratory, staffed with a
team of design engineers. The investment quickly paid
off: by 1953, the company had launched a new thixotropic interior paint, called Fenom, which was a major
technological advancement in the paint industry at the
time. A thixotropic substance exhibited the property of
becoming more liquid when shaken or stirred, then
returned to its original state when allowed to stand,
presenting an obvious advantage for the mixing of paints.
Fenom helped transform Jotun into a leader in the
Norwegian paint market. Fenom featured a flat, matte
finish; in 1954, the group launched Fenolux, a glossy
thixotropic paint. By 1959, the company had added
Fenomix, a semi-gloss variant which outsold its
predecessors.

MERGING FOR SURVIVAL IN 1971

Odd Gleditsch was joined in the family business by son
Odd Gleditsch, Jr. The younger Gleditsch quickly steered
the company toward an expansion on the international

market. The group's first target was Libya, then a poor
kingdom that promised to see a change in its fortune
following the discovery of oil there in 1959. The first
international Jotun production facility, called Libyan
Norwegian Industrial Company, or Linoco (not to be
confused with the Libyan National Oil Corporation),
opened for business in 1962, and remained an important
part of the company's operations into the 1980s. The
North African facility provided a springboard for Jotun's
expansion into the Middle East.

Toward the end of the 1960s, Jotun had begun to
seek out further expansion opportunities. The group
entered the coatings business for the first time in 1968.
This rapidly became one of Jotun's major operations. In
that year the company also entered the Southeast Asia
market, establishing a subsidiary in Thailand. The
company eyed expansion in Europe, and especially the
United Kingdom, where it acquired Henry Clark &
Sons in 1970. This acquisition positioned the company
as a major supplier to the British shipping industry.

Intensifying competition and the growing number
of competitors in Norway's paint industry had begun to
put limits on Jotun's domestic growth into the 1970s.
Gleditsch, Jr., who was by then in charge of the
company, recognized that the cost of a price war among
the country's paint companies would be detrimental to
all. Gleditsch's reasoning was that not only would the
companies themselves suffer, but the resulting financial
difficulties would make them all attractive takeover
targets for foreign paint producers seeking entry into the
Norwegian market. In an effort to head off this possibility, Gleditsch entered talks with the country's three
other major paint producers: Alf Bjercke, Fleichers
Kjemiske Fabrikker, and De-No-Fa Lilleborg Fabrikker.
These talks resulted in the merger of the three companies
with market leader Jotun, creating a new company, A/S
Jotungruppen, in 1972. Gleditsch himself took up the
position of group chairman.

The newly enlarged company then set a course for
further international expansion. Jotun entered the United
States, for example, in 1974, through its acquisition of
marine coatings producer Baltimore Copper Paint Co.
The following year, Jotun extended its reach into the
Middle East, establishing a production subsidiary in
Dubai. The company added a second Dubai plant, for
the production of fiberglass pipelines, in 1977. In the
meantime, Jotun had boosted its Southeast Asian presence with the opening of a production facility in Singapore and the launch of a second Thai factory,
completed in 1978. Back at home, Jotun was hit hard
by a fire that destroyed its main Gimle production facility in 1976. Although the company rebuilt its factory by
April of the following year, its profits were affected by

KEY DATES

1920: Odd Gleditsch opens a retail paint store and begins selling paint to the local shipping industry.

1926: Gleditsch buys an oil mill and establishes the paint production company, Jotun Kemiske Fabrik A/S.

1935: The company markets Arcanol, its first consumer-oriented product.

1951: In-house research and development operations are established.

1962: International expansion begins in Libya.

1968: The company enters Thailand.

1972: The merger of Norway's four largest paint producers creates Jotungruppen.

1983: International expansion efforts continue with new subsidiaries in Egypt, Malaysia, Oman, and Saudi Arabia.

1993: The company enters China through a joint venture with COSCO.

1999: Jotungruppen acquires Valspar's U.S. and Canadian marine operations.

2005: The company enters Indonesia and India.

2006: New factories are opened in China and Yemen.

the tragedy, resulting in several years of losses.

During the 1970s, the company maintained its record of innovation, launching a new wood protection product, Demidekk Dekkbeis in 1973. Some 30 million liters of this product were sold before it was withdrawn from the market amid negative publicity in 1984. Broader success came from the 1975 launch of the group's long-life antifoulings system, Seamaster, which gave the company a strong entry into the international shipping market.

Jotun maintained its growth pace during the 1980s, in large part through targeting its international development. The company entered a number of new markets, including Saudi Arabia, Egypt, Oman, and Malaysia, in 1983 alone. The company left the U.S. market the following year, shifting its focus back to Europe. In 1985, Jotun added a second subsidiary in the U.K., and built a new factory there as well. The company also entered Turkey, acquiring that country's powder coatings producer Toz Boya. Also that year, Jotun added to its presence back home, buying up Oslo-based Scandia Kjemiske.

INTERNATIONAL LEADER FOR THE TURN OF THE CENTURY

Acquisitions remained a strong part of Jotun's growth through the 1990s and into the 2000s. The company extended its presence in the Middle East through the creation of a new coatings subsidiary in Dubai in 1990. Jotun also acquired Spain's Torné and Australia's Denso Dimet that year. One year later, Jotun added its first facility in South Korea, producing marine coatings, and opened a new paint factory in Turkey. The company also entered the Italian market, launching subsidiary Jotun Brignola, before branching out into the eastern European market, setting up a subsidiary in the Czech Republic.

Jotun's strong presence in the Asian region led it to expand into the vast Chinese market as well. In 1993, the company set up a joint venture with state-owned shipping group COSCO. Elsewhere in Asia, the company entered Indonesia in 1996 and Vietnam in 1997. The group's Middle East operations remained a fast-growing part of the group, with new subsidiary acquired or launched in Saudi Arabia. The company also moved into South Africa, establishing its subsidiary there in 1997.

At the end of the decade, Jotun moved to return to the North American market after an absence of some 15 years, buying up Valspar's U.S. and Canada-based marine paints business in 1999. One year later, the company raised its profile in the United States still higher, buying up that country's marine coatings producer PRS Inc. That year also marked the debut of a new tin-free antifouling, SeaQuantum. Also in 2000, Odd Gleditsch, Jr., retired, ceding the chairmanship to son Odd Gleditsch d.y. (d.y. meaning "the younger").

Faced with a difficult market in the early 2000s, Jotun restructured its operations, creating four primary divisions: Jotun Coatings, Jotun Dekorative, Jotun Paints, and Jotun Powder Coatings. Despite difficult market conditions, the company maintained its policy of investment, opening new plants in Dubai and Vietnam in 2004, and in India and Indonesia in 2005. Jotun showed little sign of slowing up at mid-decade: in early 2006, the company opened two new factories in China and Yemen. By then Jotun ranged among the world's top ten producers of paints and coatings.

M. L. Cohen

PRINCIPAL SUBSIDIARIES

Demidekk Optimal Utendørsmaling AS; Drygolin Værbestandig Oljemaling AS; El-Mohandes Jotun S.A.E.

(Egypt); Jotun GmbH. (Germany); Jotun Ltd. (Ireland); Jotun Sdn. Bhd. (Malaysia); Jotun Pte. Ltd.(Singapore); Jotun Ltd. (United Kingdom); Jotun Abu Dhabi Ltd. (L.L.C.); Jotun Australia Pty. Ltd.; Jotun B.V.; Jotun Coatings Co. Ltd. (Zhangjiagang, China); Jotun COSCO Marine Coatings Ltd. (Hong Kong); Jotun Danmark A/S; Jotun Do Brasil Ltda.; Jotun France S.A.S.; Jotun Hellas Ltd. (Greece); Jotun Iberica S.A. (Spain); Jotun Italia S.p.A.; Jotun Paints Ltd. (Hong Kong); Jotun Paints Co. Ltd. (Vietnam); Jotun Paints Co. L.L.C.; Jotun Paints Inc. (United States); Jotun Paints O.O.O. (Russia); Jotun Paints South Africa (Pty.) Ltd.; Jotun Polska Sp.zo.o. (Poland); Jotun Portugal Tintas SA; Jotun Powder Coatings AS; Jotun Sverige AB; Jotun Thailand Ltd.; Lady Interiørmaling AS; P.T. Jotun Indonesia Paints & Chemicals; Scanox AS.

PRINCIPAL COMPETITORS

Akzo Nobel nv; ICI Paints; PPG Industries Inc; The Valspar Corporation; SigmaKalon Group bv; DuPont Performance Coatings; BASF Coatings AG; RPM International Inc; Deutsche Amphibolin-Werke.

FURTHER READING

"Jotun Builds Paints in China," *Chemical Week,* February 15, 2006, p. 9.

"Jotun Introduces New Flexible Top Coat," *Coatings World,* January 2005, p. 26.

"Jotun Opens Plant," *Asia Pacific Coatings Journal,* December 2005, p. 10.

"Jotun Plans Breakthrough in Decorative Paint Market," *Saigon Times Daily,* September 18, 2003.

"Jotun Post Sales of NOK 4260m," *PPCJ Polymers Paint Colour Journal,* December 2004, p. 6.

"Jotun's Sales Growing," *PPCJ Polymers Paint Colour Journal,* July 2005, p. 4.

McColloch, Louis, "Top 50 Paint Companies—the Complete Individual Listings," *PPCJ Polymers Paint Colour Journal,* October 2005, p. S180.

Nambiar, Presenna, "New Products Set to Boost Jotun Growth," *Business Times,* May 20, 2005, p. 24.

Quoc Hung, "Jotun to Market Decorative Paint in Early 2005," *Saigon Times Daily,* March 26, 2004.

Juicy Couture, Inc.

12720 Wentworth Street
Arleta, California 91331
U.S.A.
Telephone: (818) 767-0849
Fax: (818) 767-1587
Web site: http://www.juicycouture.com

Wholly Owned Subsidiary of Liz Claiborne, Inc.
Incorporated: 1997 as Travis Jeans Inc.
Employees: 10
Sales: Sales: $500 million (2005 est.)
NAIC: 448150 Clothing Accessories Stores

■ ■ ■

Juicy Couture, Inc., (Juicy) an upscale American fashion apparel company, became a subsidiary of Liz Claiborne, Inc., in April 2003. The Juicy brand of women's and men's clothing is available in some 30,000 retail establishments worldwide, as well as in freestanding Juicy Couture stores. Under the parentage of Liz Claiborne, Juicy is managed by co-founders Gela Taylor and Pamela Skaist-Levy, who serve as co-presidents of the company. Claiborne, whose image is rather conservative, nevertheless allowed Juicy Couture to operate autonomously and to remain as colorful as its co-founders, Gela Taylor and Pamela Skaist-Levy.

TWO FRIENDS START A FASHION EMPIRE

Juicy Couture was founded by Gela Taylor and Pamela Skaist-Levy. Taylor was a native New Yorker who held a college degree in drama and had appeared in Broadway productions as well as on some weekly television series in the 1980s. Skaist-Levy, on the other hand, was born in California and attended the Fashion Institute of Design & Merchandising, where part of her curriculum was designing a hat that received favorable notice and was eventually carried at upscale retailers Barneys New York and Fred Segal.

Taylor and Skaist-Levy met in 1988, when a mutual friend introduced them at her clothing boutique in Los Angeles. Taylor was pregnant at the time and dismayed at the dearth of chic maternity wear, so the two began their collaborations with a line of maternity jeans, which they fashioned after experimenting with elastic and a pair of Levi's. The jeans were marketed to maternity boutiques under the brand name Travis Jeans, after Taylor's newborn son Travis. Sales of the jeans were bolstered when actress Melanie Griffith was photographed wearing a pair.

From there, the partners went on to design a T-shirt made to be especially flattering for women. In an interview that appeared in a November 2000 issue of *People,* Skaist-Levy said, "We wanted to revolutionize the T-shirt." Form-fitted, with plunging V-necklines, and available in a variety of bright colors, the cotton T-shirts proved wildly popular. During this time the women adopted the business moniker Juicy Couture, which, Skaist-Levy noted in *People,* was chosen because the shirts were so colorful and enticing that "you just want to eat" them. The company remained based in Taylor's Los Angeles apartment before moving to an industrial park in the San Fernando Valley. Manufacturing was all done in the United States, and clothing labels read "Made in the Glamorous USA."

LAUNCH OF THE FAMOUS TRACKSUIT IN 2001

The company's biggest success would come with the introduction of the Juicy Couture tracksuit. Made of soft feminine fabrics, such as velour and terry cloth, the tracksuits were tailored to accent a woman's curves, with low-slung pants and fitted tops, and they became a genuine fashion craze. Taylor and Skaist-Levy actively cultivated celebrity endorsements of their clothing. According to an article in the *Los Angeles Times:* "Much of the brand's success was founded on celebrity relationships. Early in the company's history, the designers hosted a suite at the Cateau Marmont in Hollywood and invited young celebrities to stop by for free clothes. Having Madonna, Jennifer Lopez and Cameron Diaz, as well as countless others, photographed in their track suits proved invaluable."

The tracksuits retailed for about $200 and were also made available in cashmere. Another unique feature of the Juicy brand was that tracksuits and "hoodies" (hooded shirts) could be personalized to suit with words, names, or initials embroidered on the back.

Soon much of Hollywood was purchasing Juicy, and, in turn, most retail outlets, including upscale retailers Nordstroms and Bloomingdale's, were having difficulty keeping Juicy merchandise on the shelves. Women were attracted to the clothing for both its comfort and its sex appeal.

Taylor and Skaist-Levy forged a unique style based on their own tastes and often ignored other fashion trends, including the color palates dictated every season by the major designers. Their own colors were always bright and feminine. Above all, they insisted their clothing be fun, playful, and what they referred to as "girly." They also believed that their T-shirts, jeans, and tracksuits could serve as wardrobe staples, with which women could have, according to Jenny Rubinfield in Harper's Bazaar, "the freedom to incorporate any designer piece they desire." Taylor and Skaist-Levy themselves could be seen wearing Juicy Couture T-shirts, for example, paired

with another designer's formal skirts. The look was referred to by some observers as "casual luxury" and others as "casual chic."

Over the next few years, Juicy Couture grew in size and geographic scope. In mid-2001, Amanda Lewis joined the company as director of European operations in an effort to strengthen overseas sales. Despite a competitive designer label climate in London, Lewis believed that the lack of vivid color selections there would only strengthen the Juicy appeal. Europe and Canada would eventually account for 15 percent of the company's sales, while Japan would represent 10 percent. In 2002, Juicy Couture reported total sales of $47 million.

NEW OWNERSHIP IN 2003

The rapid success of Juicy Couture naturally attracted the notice of the fashion conglomerates. On April 7, 2003, Liz Claiborne added Juicy Couture, Inc., to its holdings, acquiring 100 percent of the company's stock for an undisclosed sum estimated to be around $45 million, with an additional "earn-out payment" (perhaps approaching the amount of the purchase price) to be based on the company's earnings. Under terms of the agreement, Taylor and Skaist-Levy sold their label but retained creative control and roles as co-presidents. In a 2006 article in *WWD,* Skaist-Levy asserted that the Claiborne acquisition had no ill effects on the corporate culture of Juicy Couture: "We still keep it very personal and very real. Claiborne totally let us be. We're completely Juicy."

Skaist-Levy also told readers of *WWD* that they sold Juicy because they "wanted a sugar daddy to help finance what we want to do." Under the parentage of Liz Claiborne, Juicy Couture was definitely able to focus on expansion. In November 2003, the company introduced a line of handbags and accessories, which proved successful. The items were Hollywood hits and included leather handbags as well as a genuine Louisiana alligator-skin bag that wholesaled for about $500. Discussing the line in *WWD,* Ed Bucciarelli, president of Claiborne's accessories division, stated that "We have worked to stay true to the Juicy brand." The article reported that "his team worked closely with Skaist-Levy and Taylor to develop the collections, with company executives flying back and forth to Southern California to show them the handbag and jewelry samples."

Another new area for Juicy was men's clothing. Remaining loyal to their principles of comfort, bright colors, and sex appeal, the company introduced men's polo shirts and jerseys and pants. Again, celebrity

```
┌─────────────────────────────────────────────┐
│                                               │
│              KEY DATES                        │
│                   ■                           │
│  1988:  Gela Taylor and Pamela Skaist-Levy    │
│         meet and start a business designing   │
│         and making maternity jeans.           │
│  1997:  The line expands to include T-shirts  │
│         and the company is incorporated.      │
│  2001:  The Juicy Couture tracksuit debuts,   │
│         and company sales for the year        │
│         surpass $45 million.                  │
│  2003:  Company is acquired by Liz Claiborne, │
│         Inc.                                  │
│  2004:  The first Juicy Couture retail outlet │
│         is opened in Las Vegas.               │
│                                               │
└─────────────────────────────────────────────┘
```

endorsement played a role in the growing popularity of the line; actor Billy Bob Thornton and recording artist Lenny Kravitz each reportedly placed large orders for Juicy's menswear. Juicy for men retailed at such upscale stores as Barneys New York, Fred Segal, Saks Fifth Avenue, and Scoop.

As Juicy Couture grew, so did its leadership ranks. Manufacturing, distribution, and accounting were among the duties the co-presidents would delegate. Michelle Sanders came from Vogue where she worked as the accessories director to serve as vice-president and fashion director at Juicy Couture. She was primarily "another pair of eyes," according to Skaist-Levy cited in *WWD*. Then, Rebecca Blair from the Gucci Group became vice-president and general manager of merchandise and sales in February 2004.

Next in the rapid expansion of the Juicy line was a foray into children's clothing, which was well received. In the traditional women's line, new fabric choices included tweeds, wools, and fur accents, and new products included swimsuits.

Later that year, the company opened its first freestanding store, in Las Vegas, Nevada, at the Caesars Palace Forum Shops. A celebrity-studded grand opening ensued. Two more stores opened in 2005 in Dallas and Atlanta. During this time, the colorful founders of Juicy Couture, having received much press themselves as entrepreneurs and trendsetters, were tapped as models for a new line of Mattel Barbie dolls. The dolls were dressed in Juicy tracksuits and came with pet dogs.

As Juicy Couture looked to the future, plans were being made for Juicy Couture shoes, jewelry, sunglasses, and a signature fragrance, as well as a line of apparel for infants. New store openings also topped the company's priority list, as sites for some 17 new boutiques had been established, including several in Europe and Japan, and two in San Francisco, slated to open in 2007. While some analysts suggested that with wider availability, the brand might lose some of its cache, others saw no signs that Juicy would fade from the fashion scene. As the company continued to prosper, the founders showed no signs of stepping down. In a 2005 article in *Business Week*, Skaist-Levy jokingly asserted that when enough years had passed they would introduce "Juicy Geriatric."

Brenda Kubiac

PRINCIPAL COMPETITORS

Tommy Hilfiger Corporation; Polo Ralph Lauren Corporation; Sean John Clothing Inc.; Calvin Klein Inc.

FURTHER READING

Apodaca, Rose, "On the Right Track," *WWD*, March 27. 2006, p. 38B.

Bowers, Katherine, "Juicy Goal: $10 Million in Europe," *WWD*, June 18, 2001, p. 11.

Cunningham, Thomas, "Juicy Couture Price Could Approach $100 Million," *Daily News Record*, April 14, 2003, p. 23.

DeCarlo, Lauren, "Juicy Couture Makes Good on Its Name," *WWD*, October 27, 2005.

DeCarlo, Lauren, and Emily Holt, "Juicy Grows Up and Outward," *WWD*, March 24, 2005, p. 9.

Edelson, Sharon, "Juicy Couture Aims for $1 Billion in Sales," *WWD*, March 21, 2006, p. 10.

Friday, Kim, "Super Suite," *WWD*, August 6, 2001, p. 10.

"Girls Know What Guys Want," *GQ*, December 2003, p. 68.

Ingrassia, Caitlin, "Juicy Couture: Packed with Vitamin See," *Times Herald-Record*, September 9, 2002.

"Juicy Couture," *Vogue*, April 2003, pp. 376–78.

Kletter, Melanie, "Juicy Squeezes into Jewelry, Handbags," *WWD*, November 3, 2003, p. 20.

Moore, Booth, "Juicy Couture Suits Up for the Big Time," *Los Angeles Times*, December 12, 2004, p. M3.

Nygaard, Sandra, "Ripe for the Picking; Juicy Couture Men's Has Grown Aggressively Despite a Laid-Back Sensibility," *Daily News Record*, June 27, 2005, p. 23.

Palmeri, Christopher, and Nanette Byrnes, "To Live and Thrive in L.A.," *Business Week*, March 28, 2005, p. 73.

Rubinfeld, Jenny, "Inside the Closets of Juicy Couture," *Harper's Bazaar*, September 2004, p. 235.

"Tee for Two," *People*, November 6, 2003, p. 100.

KANSAI PAINT CO.,LTD.

Kansai Paint Company Ltd.

■

4-3-6 Fushimi-machi, Chuo-ku
Osaka,
Japan
Telephone: (81) 06 6203 5531
Fax: (81) 06 6203 5018
Web site: http://www.kansai.co.jp

Public Company
Incorporated: 1918
Employees: 6,388
Sales: ¥196.78 billion ($1.84 billion) (2005)
Stock Exchanges: Tokyo Osaka
Ticker Symbol: 4613
NAIC: 325510 Paint and Coating Manufacturing;
332812 Metal Coating, Engraving, and Allied
Services (Except Jewelry and Silverware) to
Manufacturing

■ ■ ■

Kansai Paint Company Ltd. is one of the world's top
ten producers of paints and coatings for the automotive,
industrial, marine, decoration, and other industries.
Kansai is also an industry leader in the research and
development of new paint and coating technologies,
such as its RETAN PG HYBRID, a one-pack basecoat
for the automotive market, launched in 2005; "Super
Silicone" roof paints and environmentally friendly home
decoration paints; water-based can coatings for the
industrial market; and plant-based paints launched in
2006. Products coated in Kansai paints range from
automobiles to buildings to soft drink cans to cruise lin-

ers to home appliances. Kansai has established a global
production and marketing presence.

The company has targeted the Asia market, and
operates production facilities and subsidiaries in China,
Thailand, Singapore, Malaysia, Taiwan, Hong Kong,
and the Philippines, as well as in India, where it owns
the number two company in that market, Goodlass
Nerolac Paints. Kansai is also present in the United
States and Mexico. In 2005, the company established an
automotive coatings joint venture with PPG that services
the North American and European market. Kansai is
also directly present in Europe, with a subsidiary in the
United Kingdom. Listed on the Osaka and Tokyo Stock
Exchanges, Kansai posted sales of ¥196 billion ($1.84
billion) in 2005. The company is led by President Shoju
Kobayashi.

LAUNCHING A NATIONAL INDUSTRIAL BASE IN 1918

Kansai Paint was founded in Amagasaki, Japan, in 1918
by Katsujiro Iwai. A native of the Kyoto region, Iwai
had moved to Osaka around the start of the 20th
century, where he started his career as a merchant and
trader. Iwai soon became an active proponent of Japan's
early efforts to develop its own industrial base. This
policy sought to reduce the country's reliance on
imported goods, while stimulating the growth of the
national economy. By the beginning of the 1920s, Iwai
had become the driving force behind the creation of six
industrial companies, including Kansai Paint.

Kansai Paint, like Iwai's other businesses, struggled
through the economic instability that marked Japan in

the 1920s and 1930s. Yet by 1926, Iwai had launched its first true product, CELVA, the first lacquer paint to be developed in Japan. The new product established Kansai Paint as a force to be recognized in the Japanese paint market, and by 1933, the company had expanded its operations, opening an office and factory in Tokyo.

The company resumed growth in the postwar period, opening a new headquarters and primary plant in Osaka in 1950. In the next decade, Kansai launched a new expansion of its production capacity, opening a plant in Hiratsuka in 1960. That facility was joined the following year by another plant in Nagoya. In 1965, Kansai boosted its research and development capabilities, opening a new facility in Hiratsuka. The new operation helped Kansai emerge as one of the leading innovators in the paint and coatings industry. During this period, the company linked up with Nissan Motor Company, a relationship that lasted into the beginning of the twenty-first century and that provided an important foundation for Kansai Paint's growth.

By the mid-1960s, Kansai Paint had begun to establish itself as a leading player in the international paint and coatings market as well. The company established its first foreign operation in Singapore in 1965, setting up a joint venture. The company next turned to Thailand, establishing a new joint venture with Thai Huat in 1968. After opening a new plant in Kanuma in 1971, the company returned to its international expansion, entering Hong Kong in 1974. In 1983, Kansai entered a technology cooperation partnership with India's Goodlass Nerolac Paints, part of the Tata group, and Japan's Nihon Tokushu Toryo. In 1986, Kansai acquired a 36 percent stake in Goodlass Nerolac. By the mid-1980s, the company had added a subsidiary in Taiwan, in another joint venture formed in 1985.

Kansai Paint continued its record of innovation as well. The company developed a new water-based, air-drying synthetic in the early 1970s, which was launched commercially as ASCA in 1974. This was followed by Fantac, a marking film, released in 1985. The following year, Kansai Paint gave a new indication of the flexibility of its technology, when it launched a photoresist for printed circuit boards, called Sonne Eduv, developed in partnership with Mitsubishi. By then, the company had begun construction on a new color research laboratory, which opened in 1986 in Hiratsuka. That facility later took the name of Color Designing and Development Laboratory.

ENTERING NEW MARKETS IN THE FINAL DECADES OF THE 20TH CENTURY

Kansai continued its international expansion as well. In 1987, the company entered the North American market, launching its Kansai Paint (America) marketing subsidiary. The following year, the company entered South Korea, forming the KDK Automotive Coatings joint venture. Also that year the company launched a new global brand name, Alesco. Back in the United States, Kansai formed a joint venture with Dupont to develop automotive coatings for that market in 1990. The two companies had been cooperating on the development of automotive coatings since the late 1970s; in 1989, Dupont also acquired the production technology and marketing rights in North America and Europe to Kansai's Sonne Eduv product. Kansai itself entered the European market directly, opening a subsidiary in the United Kingdom in 1990.

In the early 1990s, however, Kansai turned its attention toward developing its presence in the newly opening and rapidly expanding Chinese market. The company established its first production subsidiary there in 1992, in a joint venture facility located in Tianjin. The mainland market not only offered Kansai access to lower production costs, but it also gave the company a presence in what was shortly to become the world's most dynamic market.

Kansai continued to expand its Chinese presence into the mid-1990s, launching a new joint venture in Shenyang in 1994. This was followed by a second production facility in Tianjin, the Tianjin Beacon Kansai Paint & Chemicals Co., founded in 1994. China remained a focus for the company's growth into 1995, with the founding of two more joint ventures that year, Chongqing Kansai Paint Co., and Hunan Kansai Automotive Coatings Co., located in Changsa.

Meanwhile, Kansai had not been neglecting its growth elsewhere. The company opened its new Ono factory in Japan in 1992, then built an automobile

KEY DATES
■

1918: Katsujiro Iwai founds Kansai Paint in Amagasaki, Japan.

1926: The company introduces the first lacquer developed in Japan.

1960: The company opens a plant in Hiratsuku.

1965: A joint venture is launched in Singapore.

1968: The company enters Thailand through a joint venture.

1974: A subsidiary is established in Hong Kong.

1985: The company enters Taiwan.

1986: The company buys a stake in Goodlass Nerolac in India.

1987: A U.S. marketing subsidiary is established.

1990: A European subsidiary is founded in the United Kingdom.

1992: The company enters the mainland Chinese market.

1995: The company enters Malaysia.

1999: The company acquires majority control of Goodlass Nerolac.

2000: The company sets up a joint venture production subsidiary in Indonesia.

2001: The company founds the Ecosystems joint venture with Nippon Paint.

2002: The company enters the Philippines through a joint venture.

2004: An automotive coatings partnership with PPG Industries is founded.

2005: A production joint venture is founded in China with COSCO International Holdings.

2006: The company acquires a stake in the Hunan Xiangjiang Kansai automotive paint joint venture; a water-based automotive plant is built in Guanzhou, China.

TOP TEN PAINTS PRODUCER IN THE NEW CENTURY

By then, Kansai Paint ranked at the top of the Japanese paints and coatings industry, operating six factories in Japan and ten more internationally. Despite the company's international growth, the largest part of the group's revenues remained in Japan, which accounted for some 90 percent of group sales in the late 1990s.

Into the 2000s, however, Kansai Paint targeted the wider Asian market for further growth. A major step forward for the company came in late 1999, when the company bought out the Tata group's stake in Goodlass Nerolac, giving Kansai majority control of that company. By then, Goodlass had gained the position of second place in the Indian paint and coatings market.

Kansai's expansion continued into the middle of the decade. The company entered Indonesia in 2000, establishing subsidiary PT Kansai Paint Indonesia. Formed in partnership with local group Gajah Tunggal Praksa, the venture constructed a 350 ton-per-month automotive paint production facility. The following year, the company established two new Japanese operations, Ecosystems, in partnership with Nippon Paint, and NOF Kansai Marine Coatings Co. In 2002, Kansai Paint entered a new market, with the creation of Kansai Paint Philippines. The company also boosted its operations in Malaysia that year, adding a new subsidiary, Sime Kansai Paint. Also in 2002, Kansai Paint acquired a 70 percent share of its Philippines sales agent, PACM.

In addition to adding new subsidiaries and markets, Kansai Paint began investing in expanding production at existing facilities. At the beginning of 2003, for example, the company earmarked more than $4.2 million in a number of its Chinese facilities, doubling its automotive paint production and significantly increasing its marine paint production. By the middle of that year, the company had announced more than $27 million in new investments, in order to triple production at its Tianjin site and more than double production at its Hunan joint venture. By 2004, the company had boosted production at its plants in Shanghai as well.

After winding up its joint venture with Dupont in the early 2000s, Kansai Paint found a new partner in PPG Industries, which created an automotive coatings alliance between the two companies, targeting the North American and European markets. The new company took the name of PPG Kansai Automotive Finishes, and was expected to expand to include marketing and sales operations in China and other parts of Asia.

Through 2005, Kansai Paint continued to build up its stake in Goodlass Nerolac, boosting its share from 64.5 percent to nearly 80 percent. Kansai Paint then

refinishing center in Hiratsuka in 1994. The company launched a second refinishing center in Amagasaki in 1998. In 1996, the company expanded its operations in Thailand, founding a new subsidiary, Kansai Resin (Thailand) Co. The company also entered Malaysia, through its Singapore subsidiary, setting up KPS Coatings (Malaysia) Sdn. Bhd. in November 1995. That subsidiary began production in July 1996. Back in Japan, Kansai added two more facilities before the end of the century, opening its Technology & Products Development Laboratory in Hiratsuka and its Technical & Business Office in Tokyo in 1999.

joined with Goodlass Nerolac to form a joint venture in order to acquire Malaysia's Sime Coatings in late 2005. By the end of that year, Kansai Paint once again expanded its Chinese presence as well, establishing a joint venture with COSCO International Holdings in December 2005. The new partners then began building a production facility in Zhuhai.

Kansai Paint remained in expansion mode into 2006. The company launched a new investment program of more than ¥13 billion ($108 million) in order to increase production at all of its non-Japanese production facilities in Asia. In March 2006, the company's Chinese presence grew once again, with the purchase of a stake in a new company, Hunan Xiangjiang Kansai Paint, which operated a 2,000 ton-per-month automotive paint plant. Kansai Paint also announced plans to build a new water-based automotive paint facility in Guangzhou, expected to start production in the summer of 2006. Kansai Paint's history of expansion had placed it firmly among the world's leading paint and coatings producers.

M. L. Cohen

PRINCIPAL SUBSIDIARIES

Chongqing Kansai Paint Co., Ltd. (China); Goodlass Nerolac Paints Ltd. (India); Hunan Kansai Automotive Coatings Co., Ltd. (China); Kansai Paint (America), Inc.; Kansai Paint (Asia) Pte. Ltd. (Singapore); Kansai Paint (Singapore) Pte. Ltd.; Kansai Paint Europe Limited (U.K.); Kansai Paint H.K. Ltd.; Kansai Paint Philippines, Inc.; Kansai Resin (Thailand) Co., Ltd.; KDK Automotive Coatings Co., Ltd. (Korea); P.T. Kansai Paint Indonesia; PPG ALESCO Automotive Finishes Mexico, S. de. R.L. de C.V.; PPG Kansai Automotive Finishes Canada, LP; PPG Kansai Automotive Finishes UK, LLP; Shanghai Cosco Kansai Paint & Chemicals Co., Ltd. (China); Shenyang Kansai Paint Co., Ltd. (China); Sime Kansai Paints Sdn. Bhd. (Malaysia); Taiwan Kansai Paint Co., Ltd.; Thai Kansai Paint Co., Ltd.; Tianjin Cosco Kansai Paint & Chemicals Co., Ltd. (China); Tianjin Winfield Kansai Paint & Chemicals Co., Ltd. (China).

PRINCIPAL COMPETITORS

Akzo Nobel Coatings N.V.; PPG Industries Inc.; Sherwin-Williams Co.; DuPont Coatings & Color Technologies Group; ICI Paints; BASF Coatings AG; Valspar Corporation; SigmaKalon Group B.V.; Nippon Paint Co. Ltd.; Kansai Paint Co. Ltd.

FURTHER READING

"COSCO International to Set Up JV with Kansai Paint in Zhuhai," *Alestron*, December 1, 2005.

"Goodlass Nerolac Paints: A Nice Growth Story," *India Business Insight*, December 21, 2003.

"India's Goodlass, Japan's Kansai Paint to Invest in Malaysian Co.," *Asia Pulse*, October 12, 2005.

"Kansai and Nippon Set Sights on Asia," *Asia Pacific Coatings Journal*, December 2000, p. 4.

"Kansai Builds Up Automotive Paint Business in China," *Chemical Business Newsbase*, March 30, 2006.

"Kansai Paint Patents Plastic-Coated Metal Plate," *Coatings World*, February 2006, p. 15.

"Kansai Paint to Build Container Coating Plant in China," *Chemical Business Newsbase*, December 15, 2005.

"Kansai Paint to Up Coatings Output in Asia Over 30,000 tonnes/mo," *Chemical Business Newsbase*, December 15, 2005.

"Kansai Paint Triples Capacity at 2 sites in China," *Chemical Business Newsbase—Chimie Hebdo*, June 30, 2003.

"Plant-Based Paint, Sharp Idea," *Journal of Property Management*, March–April 2006, p. 7.

"Playing the Game," *Asia Pacific Coatings Journal*, August 2002, p. 7.

"PPG, Kansai Paint to Launch Automotive Coatings Venture," *Paint & Coatings Industry*, January 2005, p. 22.

"Splashing Out: A Profile of the Southeast Asian Automotive Coatings Market," *Chemical Business Newsbase*, April 26, 2004.

Kerasotes ShowPlace Theaters LLC

———————————————— ■ ————————————————

224 North Des Plaines, Suite 200
Chicago, Illinois 60661
U.S.A.
Telephone: (312) 756-3360
Fax: (312) 777-0480
Web site: http://www.kerasotes.com

Private Company
Incorporated: 1909
Employees: 2,200
Sales: $155 million (2005)
NAIC: 512131 Motion Picture Theaters (Except
Drive-Ins)

■ ■ ■

Kerasotes ShowPlace Theaters LLC operates one of the ten largest movie theater chains in the United States, with nearly 80 theaters and more than 600 screens in Illinois, Indiana, Iowa, Minnesota, Missouri, and Ohio. Some of its theaters are located in the Chicago metropolitan area, but most are in small and mid-size markets where they have little or no competition. The company is run by third-generation members of the family of founder Gus Kerasotes, and is co-owned by his heirs and Providence Equity Partners, Inc.

ORIGINS

The roots of Kerasotes ShowPlace Theaters date to the earliest years of cinema exhibition in the United States. Company founder Gus Kerasotes was a 17-year-old immigrant from Sparta, Greece, who originally moved to Chicago in 1890 to work making candies and ice cream. After he was stabbed by a disgruntled customer he decided to leave the big city and head south to Springfield, Illinois, where he opened a candy store with a partner.

The turn of the century saw the first motion pictures exhibited at places like vaudeville houses and nickelodeons, primitive storefront theaters where short movies were shown throughout the day, often with live piano accompaniment, since the films were silent. Inspired by the success of a friend in St. Louis, in 1909 Kerasotes decided to convert his shop into a nickelodeon that he named the Royal. It proved so popular that he added a second—the Savoy—three years later.

Movie exhibition was maturing in the 1910s as longer-duration feature films appeared, and soon lavish movie theaters began to replace nickelodeons. In 1921 Kerasotes bought the First National Bank building next to the Savoy and converted it into a 900-seat theater called the Strand, which would feature westerns by the likes of Tom Mix and Buck Jones, as well as live vaudeville acts. Five years later he constructed a three-story building in downtown Springfield to house the firm's headquarters, and in 1929 Kerasotes bought Springfield's Gaity theater, which he renamed the Senate.

Sound movies began to displace the silents beginning with Warner Brothers' 1927 smash *The Jazz Singer*, and despite Gus Kerasotes' belief that they were merely a fad, his oldest son George convinced him to invest in equipment to exhibit "talkies." In 1933 University of Illinois business graduate George Kerasotes became the firm's general manager.

Under his leadership Kerasotes Theaters soon began to expand outside of Springfield into small Illinois towns like Havana, Onarga, and Highland. In 1937 the company partnered with Peoria developer J. Fletcher Lankton to build the 900-seat Beverly Theater in that city, and they later added the Varsity Theater near the campus of Bradley University.

By the mid-1940s the Kerasotes company was operating a total of 11 theaters in mid- and southern Illinois, and Gus's sons George, John, Nicholas, and Louis were all working for the firm (a fifth son, Dr. Anthony Kerasotes, died in World War II). The company continued to expand during the decade, and added theaters in Illinois towns like Chillicothe, LaSalle, Rockford, Decatur, and Champaign-Urbana.

DRIVE-INS SPUR GROWTH

The introduction of television in the late 1940s and early '50s put a damper on ticket sales industry-wide, and movie studios struggled to lure back patrons with 3-Dimensional and widescreen films while many exhibitors turned to drive-ins. The open-air theaters appealed to families with small children, amorous teens, and people who worked late shifts, and despite their seasonal nature (in northern states most were closed during winter months), for a time drive-in movie theaters became the company's most profitable business area. The company's first was added in Decatur, Illinois in the late 1940s; by 1957 6 of its 21 theaters were located outdoors.

In 1958 company head George Kerasotes was elected president of the National Association of Theater Owners, and after Gus Kerasotes' death in 1960 he was officially named the firm's president, though he had effectively been serving as such since 1935. Brother Nicholas was vice-president, Louis was secretary, and John was the company's treasurer.

Expansion continued during the early and mid-1960s, with the 50th Kerasotes theater opening in 1967. By now drive-ins had come to account for about 40 percent of the total business, and the firm had also added its first out-of-state location in Missouri.

During this period theater owners began to discover the economic benefits of showing movies on multiple, adjacent screens with staggered start times, allowing staff to keep busy selling tickets and highly-profitable popcorn and candy, rather than remaining idle for up to two hours while a single film ran. During the early 1970s some Kerasotes theaters were converted into two-, three- and four-screen configurations, while other "multiplexes" were built from scratch, including the four-screen Esquire in Springfield.

Growth was steady during the decade, and by the early 1980s Kerasotes Theaters had grown to become the ninth-largest cinema chain in the United States, with 220 screens in small- and mid-sized markets in Illinois, Indiana, Missouri, Arkansas, and Ohio. In many cases the firm owned most or all of the venues in a particular city.

GEORGE KERASOTES LEAVES IN 1985

In 1985, as several family members later told *Variety*, George Kerasotes made a side deal to buy the 21-screen W.S. Butterfield chain in Michigan by putting up company property as collateral. When his brothers protested the offer of a minority ownership stake, George declared the family partnership over and left to form his own company. After the split his new Springfield-based George Kerasotes Corporation (GKC) would own 75 former Kerasotes Theaters screens in Illinois as well as all 21 of the Michigan ones obtained from Butterfield.

Rocked by this turn of events, his three younger brothers struggled to carry on. With the same overhead as before, but a third fewer theaters, they decided to expand aggressively to catch up and by late 1989 had added 86 screens, including 22 acquired from General Cinema the year before. Following the breakup Louis Kerasotes served as company president until his death in 1988, then brother Nicholas took over until he passed away the next year. Louis' sons Tony and Dean and John's son Denis had by this time taken charge of the firm's day-to-day operations, with John serving as secretary and treasurer of the company and the president and CEO roles left empty.

The mid-1990s saw Kerasotes launch an even more aggressive expansion effort that would boost it from 350 to 500 screens by the end of the decade. In 1996 the firm began constructing two new 16-screen "megaplex" theaters in South Bend, Indiana, and Rockford, Illinois, and a 12-screen version on the site of a drive-in in Pekin, Illinois, that had burned down five years earlier.

KEY DATES

1909: Gus Kerasotes opens his first nickelodeon in Springfield, Illinois.

1921: The Kerasotes-owned Strand theater opens in Springfield.

1933: Gus's son George Kerasotes named general manager of the firm.

1967: The Kerasotes chain opens its 50th theater.

1985: George Kerasotes splits from his three brothers to form GKC Theaters.

2000: The company headquarters are moved to Chicago.

2003: Providence Equity Partners buys a stake in the firm for $75 million.

2005: The company's 600th screen is added.

The new facilities would feature tiered stadium seating with cup holders, huge screens, state-of-the-art sound systems, and large lobbies with multiple concession counters and dynamic architectural styling.

The firm's new megaplexes were often built in markets where it already had smaller theaters, and these now-outdated venues typically began to feature bargain price second-run films before eventually being closed. A few won designation as historic landmarks and were sold to civic organizations with the stipulation that they not show films, while others were demolished to make way for new office buildings or other projects. Drive-ins, which the firm had once operated 72 of, were now all but a memory as the land they were built on provided ideal locations for new megaplexes.

In early 1997 Kerasotes Theaters secured a $115 million line of credit from Bankers Trust to fund its expansion program, which now included 16-screen megaplexes in Ohio and Minnesota. 1998 saw the firm also announce plans for a new $10 million, 16-screen theater in Indianapolis, Indiana, its first in that city, as well as another in Evansville, Indiana. The company was calling many of its new locations ShowPlace Theaters, though the Evansville operation would be known as the Stadium 16, as another theater owner there already operated one called Showplace Cinemas.

By spring of 1999 the company had a total of 468 screens, while offshoot GKC had grown to 320. John Kerasotes had recently retired and Tony Kerasotes was now serving as the firm's president and CEO, with his brother Dean holding down the jobs of executive vice-president and chief operating officer.

In mid-2000 Kerasotes Theaters' headquarters were moved to Chicago, where the company was seeking to expand, though some operations remained at the Kerasotes Building in Springfield. March of 2001 saw former President George Kerasotes die at age 89, after which his daughter Beth auctioned off a number of GKC theaters and undeveloped properties. Kerasotes Theaters then had 82 locations and 525 screens.

In the early 2000s the firm began running commercials for products like Coca-Cola and video games before films, in addition to previews of coming attractions and less-intrusive ads for local businesses on slides. Because up to 90 percent of ticket revenues went to a film's distributor, exhibitors were forced to look for profits in concession sales (whose prices, to the dismay of patrons, were steadily going up) and other areas. With advertisers finding it more and more difficult to get their message through to consumers who could zap past TV commercials or avoid them entirely by watching DVDs, they began courting the completely captive audience in theaters, spending an estimated $300 million nationwide to put ads on the big screen in 2002.

PROVIDENCE EQUITY PARTNERS BUYS STAKE IN 2003

Several of the largest national movie chains had entered bankruptcy protection after a binge of new theater construction in the 1990s was followed by a ticket sales slump in the early 2000s, but Kerasotes avoided such consequences by expanding in a more measured way and in areas where it faced little or no competition. After putting growth on hold for several years, in October of 2002 the firm secured a $170 million loan guarantee from Deutsche Bank and in June 2003, Providence Equity Partners, Inc., bought a stake in the company for $75 million. Its name was later changed to Kerasotes ShowPlace Theaters LLC.

In the fall of 2003 a new 12-screen theater was opened in Springfield on the site of a long-shuttered drive-in, and the year also saw openings of an 11-screen theater in Richmond, Indiana, an 8-plex in Galesburg, Illinois, and a 6-screen site in Quincy, Illinois. The company had scaled back the size of its theaters, as 16-screen and larger multiplexes were now viewed as having more capacity than the movie studios' output warranted.

In 2004 Kerasotes opened a 12-screen theater in Schererville, Indiana near a 16-plex that it already owned, plus a 14-screen site in New Lenox, Illinois, and a 12-screen theater in Indianapolis. The company added screens to its Pekin and Matoon, Illinois, theaters during the year as well.

2004 also saw a number of the firm's locations begin featuring special daytime shows called Matinee Movie

Magic, which were targeted at parents with very young children. Auditorium lights were raised to a higher level so toddlers could safely wander the aisles, and sound was lowered so babies could sleep while their parents tried to enjoy the film. The large number of screens at the firm's megaplexes also allowed it to sometimes feature one or more special-interest "art-house" titles, in addition to the popular mainstream films.

In the fall of 2004 the firm secured an additional $300 million in funding through Deutsche Bank, part of which would be used to pay a $100 million dividend to Providence Equity Partners. Though Kerasotes had historically operated theaters in smaller towns where it had little or no competition, it was now seeking a greater share of the Chicago metropolitan market, where it had become the fourth-largest cinema chain. At this time plans were announced to add 174 new screens by 2007, some 90 of which would be in that area.

In 2005 new 14-screen theaters opened in Michigan City, Indiana, and Machesney Park, Illinois, along with 12-plexes on the east side of Indianapolis and in Muncie, Indiana, which boosted the company's total to 609 screens at 77 locations. Amenities at the new theaters included stadium seating, online ticket sales, free refills on popcorn and drinks, game arcades in lobbies, Dolby Digital sound, and large, curved screens. A typical auditorium was between 200 and 300 seats in size.

In April of 2005 the 30 theaters and 263 screens of splinter company GKC were purchased for $66 million by Carmike Cinemas, Inc., from George Kerasotes' heirs. Carmike, which had emerged from Chapter 11 bankruptcy protection, was one of the top four chains in the United States with 280 theaters and 2,173 screens in 36 states.

SALE/LEASEBACK DEAL COMPLETED IN 2005

In September 2005 Kerasotes ShowPlace sold 17 of the theater properties it owned to Realty Income Corporation for $200 million, which would then lease them back to the firm. The transaction reduced the number of sites the company owned from 65 percent of the total to 40 percent. The funds would be used for ongoing expansion and to pay down debt.

In the fall a handful of Kerasotes' theaters installed Real D digital projection systems for the opening of Disney's *Chicken Little*, which enabled patrons to watch it in 3-D. The industry was slowly beginning to convert to digital projection from the acetate-based film in use since the medium was born. Exhibitors would have to make a substantial investment in new equipment akin to that of the late 1920s when "talkies" arrived, but it

would save distributors huge sums on manufacturing and shipping heavy 35mm film prints and theoretically enable projection of a perfect image every show without the splices, scratches, and dirt that inevitably accumulated on film.

In May 2006 the company opened a new 12-screen ShowPlace theater in Hobart, Indiana, which joined a ten-screen facility there purchased from Loew's Cineplex late the previous year. Plans for another in Chicago's Uptown area were cancelled due to the high expense of construction, but the firm was reportedly also seeking to buy several in the city from AMC Entertainment, which had been forced to sell some locations due to a merger with Loews. Kerasotes had 614 screens at 76 theaters, with new ones under construction in Naperville, Cicero, and Niles, Illinois, and Kokomo, Indiana. Six more were on the drawing board for Chicago and other locations in Illinois, as well.

After almost a century in the movie business, Kerasotes ShowPlace Theaters LLC had established itself as the dominant exhibitor in small and mid-size markets in Illinois and several neighboring states. It was seeking to boost its presence in the competitive Chicago metropolitan area, while continuing to expand in its traditional stronghold. Under the third generation of family management, the company looked poised for many more years of profitable operation.

Frank Uhle

PRINCIPAL COMPETITORS

Carmike Cinemas, Inc.; AMC Entertainment, Inc.; Cinemark, Inc.; Regal Entertainment Group; The Marcus Corp.

FURTHER READING

Boehme, Natalie, "Shaping The Century: Get the Picture? The Kerasotes Family Did," *State Journal-Register (Springfield, Ill.)*, April 28, 1999, p. 5A.

Coppens, Julie York, "Kerasotes Reaching Out to Indie Film Fans," *South Bend Tribune*, September 7, 2001.

Craft, Dan, "George Kerasotes—After 60 Years, He's Still Playing Movies at a Theater Near You," *Pantagraph (Bloomington, Ill.)*, August 30, 1991, p. C1.

———, "Parallel Lives, Parallel Histories," *Pantagraph (Bloomington, Ill.)*, March 29, 2001, p. G3.

Dietrich, Matthew, "Coming Attraction: New 16-Screen Kerasotes Theater," *State Journal-Register (Springfield, Ill.)*, June 29, 1996, p. 1.

———, "George Kerasotes Dies at 89," *State Journal-Register (Springfield, Ill.)*, March 17, 2001, p. 7.

Elejalde-Ruiz, Alexia, "Theater Sold, But Kerasotes Still Running Show," *Chicago Daily Herald*, September 21, 2005, p. 4.

Gallun, Alby, "Multiplex Mogul: Flush with Cash, Kerasotes Theater Chain Looks to Double its Chicago-Area Screens," *Crain's Chicago Business*, January 31, 2005, p. 3.

Ingram, Bruce, "Kerasotes Chain Doesn't Nix Stix," *Variety*, December 6, 1989, p. 102.

Morris, Natalie, "Kerasotes Takes on Partner," *State Journal-Register (Springfield, Ill.)*, July 3, 2003, p. 21.

Prescott, Heidi, "Show Time for Kerasotes," *South Bend Tribune*, May 14, 1998, p. A1.

Rogers, Nick, "Springfield's New Screen Scene," *State Journal-Register (Springfield, Ill.)*, September 25, 2003, p. 11.

Springer, P. Gregory, "Kerasotes at 190, Going to 200," *Variety*, February 13, 1980, pp. 29-30.

———, "Kerasotes Now Split in 2 After 75-Plus Years," *Variety*, December 4, 1985, p. 87.

Wilson, Kelly, "Kerasotes Sells Satisfaction," *Quincy Herald-Whig*, March 10, 1996, p. G23.

Knoll

Knoll, Inc.

———————■———————

1235 Water Street
East Greenville, Pennsylvania 18041
U.S.A.
Telephone: (215) 679-7991
Toll Free: (800) 343-5665
Fax: (215) 679-1755
Web site: http://www.knoll.com

Public Company
Incorporated: 1938 as Knoll Furniture
Employees: 3,775
Sales: $807.96 million (2005)
Stock Exchanges: New York
Ticker Symbol: KNL
NAIC: 337120 Household and Institutional Furniture Manufacturing; 337127 Institutional Furniture Manufacturing; 3372 Office Furniture (Including Fixtures) Manufacturing; 33721 Office Furniture (Including Fixtures) Manufacturing; 337211 Wood Office Furniture Manufacturing; 337214 Office Furniture (Except Wood) Manufacturing; 337215 Showcase, Partition, Shelving, and Locker Manufacturing

■ ■ ■

Knoll, Inc., is a leading U.S. manufacturer of office furniture. Its products include chairs, wood casegoods, files and storage mechanisms, and full office systems. Knoll also produces textiles on contract and markets computer support accessories. The company sells its products through showrooms, sales offices, and dealer-ships in about 500 over 300 U.S. locations. It also sells through independent dealers in Europe, the Pacific Rim, and Latin America.

1938–1946: EARLY YEARS

Knoll was founded in 1938 by Hans Knoll. Knoll, the son of a German furniture maker, was living in New York at the time. Hans, like his father, was a craftsman, but he believed that new woodworking and manufacturing technology being introduced at the time could be integrated with his skills. His primary goal was to produce furniture that was elegant and functional but also affordable. That design philosophy would be hugely successful for Knoll and would guide the company not only through the 1940s but even into the 1990s. Knoll found a willing local market for his furniture designs during the late 1930s and early 1940s.

Knoll's design philosophy was heavily influenced by the famous Bauhaus school of design that was becoming dominant at the time. The Bauhaus was founded in 1919 by architectural renegade Walter Gropius, who merged an art academy and an arts-and-crafts school. He based the school on the canon that no distinction should be made between fine arts and practical crafts, including furniture. Furthermore, the school held that modern art and architecture must be responsive to the aesthetic and engineering needs of the industrial world. The Bauhaus style, or "International Style," adopted by Knoll and other progressive designers was distinguished by minimal ornamentation and an emphasis on simplistic beauty. Famed architect Ludwig Mies van der Rohe was running the school shortly before it was shut down by the Nazis in 1933. By that time, however, its principles were being adopted worldwide. In fact, many of the school's faculty immigrated to the United States where they influenced designers such as Knoll.

1946–1983: EXPANSION

In 1946 Knoll married designer Florence Schust. Schust had been trained as an architect and would ultimately be recognized as one of the most influential women in 20th-century design. The two formed Knoll Associates to help customers realize the value of design in the modern office. Their major breakthrough came shortly after they were married when they were hired to design the Rockefeller family offices in Rockefeller Plaza. The job was heralded as a benchmark for office designs of the day, and it became a springboard for Hans and Florence into other high-profile office design jobs.

During the 1940s and 1950s Florence Knoll worked closely with clients to design their spaces. Importantly, she pioneered the concept of developing a relationship with the client and designing to meet their needs. She began each project with a series of intensive interviews of executives and support staff to discover exactly what they needed. She would then use that information to design spaces and to help Hans design the furniture. Although that type of partnering relationship became

commonplace in the design field during the middle and late 1900s, it was considered revolutionary at the time.

Hans Knoll remained focused on the manufacturing end of the business. In 1945 he moved the company's production facilities from New York to an old mill in East Greenville, Pennsylvania, which is in the Upper Perkiomen Valley. That region provided a skilled and dedicated labor force for Knoll's furniture operations for several years. Indeed, during the 1950s and 1960s Knoll became known for its innovative designs and high-quality office furniture. Besides its good reputation, Knoll benefited from spiraling office furniture markets during the post-World War II economic and population boom.

Throughout the 1950s, 1960s, and much of the 1970s, corporate America built and furnished billions of square feet of office space throughout the country. To exploit that surging demand, Knoll expanded throughout most of the country with sales offices, showrooms, and dealerships that emphasized contract sales. Knoll's furniture designs evolved to keep up with a changing office marketplace during that period, but innovation, thoughtful design, and affordability remained its cornerstone creed. Well-known designers that worked for Knoll included Vico Magistretti, Kazhuhide Takahama, Warren Platner, and Tobia Scarpa. In recognition of Knoll's contribution to modern design, the world-renowned Louvre's Musee des Arts Decoratifs in Paris staged a 1972 exhibit devoted solely to the company's furniture.

Importantly, Knoll introduced its first open-office furniture system in 1973. The Stephens System, designed by Bill Stephens, capitalized on the dominant trend during the 1970s and 1980s toward open offices, as opposed to walled-in spaces. Despite increases in open-office products, the overall office furniture industry stumbled during the commercial construction drought of the late 1970s and early 1980s. Although the market would recover, the downturn marked an end to the booming traditional office furniture markets of the mid-1900s when many corporations spared little expense in furnishing their offices. The office furniture industry bottomed out in the early 1980s. During that time, Knoll, still privately held, was bought out by floor-covering manufacturer General Felt Industries Inc. General Felt took Knoll public in 1983 (as Knoll International) in a stock offering that raised about $56 million. Unfortunately, Knoll languished under General Felt's control.

1983–1996: STAGNATED GROWTH AND OWNERSHIP TURNOVERS

Knoll's problems during the 1980s were partially caused by evolving and volatile office-furniture markets.

KEY DATES

1938: An admirer of the German-based Bauhaus style, Hans Knoll begins making furniture.

1945: Knoll moves from New York to an old mill in East Greenville, Pennsylvania.

1946: Hans Knoll marries designer Florence Schust.

1973: Knoll introduces its first open-office furniture system.

1983: General Felt takes Knoll public in 1983 in a stock offering that raises some $56 million.

1986: General Felt spends an estimated $38 million to take Knoll private.

1990: Westinghouse purchases Knoll for an undisclosed amount of cash.

1996: Westinghouse sells Knoll for $565 million to Warburg, Pincus Ventures.

1997: Knoll goes public for the second time.

1999: Knoll becomes a privately owned company.

2001: An economic slump reduces the entire office industry's orders by 16 percent.

2004: Knoll goes public for a third time.

However, they were also the result of decisions made at General Felt, which was headed by Marshall Cogan and Stephen Swid. Cogan worked at CBS and investment firm Orvis & Co. before taking a job as an auto analyst in 1964 at Carter, Berlind & Weill. Interestingly, that entrepreneurial investment company flourished under the direction of talents like Rober Berlind (the successful Broadway producer) and Arthur Levitt, who became president of the American Stock Exchange. The company became the nucleus of Shearson, Leob Rhoades, which was sold in 1981 to American Express for $900 million. Cogan profited handsomely as an executive at the company, but was pushed out shortly after the American Express buyout.

Cogan teamed up with money manager Stephen Swid in 1982 to purchase the money-losing General Felt, a carpet underlay business. They quickly returned the company to profitability. A few years later they purchased Knoll with the intent of improving it as they had General Felt. Cogan and Swid, through General Felt, also purchased "21," a high-profile New York restaurant. The partners' strategy seemed sound at first, but the hard-charging Cogan gradually got carried away. He tried to take over the Boston Red Sox, the prestigious Sotheby's auction house, and the respected Wall Street investment firm of L.F. Rothschild Unterberg Towbin.

After those defeats, General Felt succeeded in buying steering wheel and dashboard manufacturer Sheller-Globe.

Knoll posted profits during its first few years under General Felt's wing, but the venerable furniture maker eventually got lost in the shuffle. Knoll retained its status as one of the largest contract office furniture manufacturers in the nation, but its profits began to slide in 1986. By that time, General Felt had amassed a mountain of debt and all of its companies were struggling. Knoll had supplied about 80 percent of the cash flow generated by General Felt's three holdings in 1985, but by 1986 Knoll was losing money. Swid wanted to settle down and focus on improving existing operations while Cogan was eager to do more deals. The two had a falling out and Cogan kicked out Swid. To make matters worse, Cogan infuriated investors late in 1986 when he offered to buy back shares of Knoll for $12 each—he had sold them in 1983 for $16. GFI finally did spend about $38 million to take Knoll private in 1986.

Despite Cogan's blunders, Knoll claimed some gains during the mid-1980s. In 1986, for example, the company tapped the cash from the public offering to pay for a $20-million expansion of the East Greenville manufacturing plant. In addition, Knoll introduced its successful KnollStudio collection in 1985. That line, which was designed for executive offices and residences, integrated classic icons of modern furniture by renowned designers like Mies van der Rohe, Marcel Breuer, Harry Bertoia, and Eero Saarinen. New product introductions and increased production capacity allowed Knoll to take advantage of surging office furniture markets during the late 1980s. The industry became increasingly consolidated and competitive during that period, however, and the company was ill-prepared to deal with the inevitable slowdown.

The office furniture market finally did crash beginning in the late 1980s and during the early 1990s. New office construction levels plummeted throughout the nation. At the same time, cost-conscious companies began looking for ways to reduce costs, including those related to furnishings. With sales dropping, General Felt began looking for a buyer for Knoll. In 1990 Westinghouse purchased Knoll International for an undisclosed amount of cash, $112 million worth of stock, and assumption of the company's $111 million of debt. Shortly before buying Knoll, Westinghouse had bought furniture makers Shaw-Walker and Reff Inc. in deals worth a combined total of about $250 million. In 1990, Westinghouse combined Knoll, Shaw-Walker, Reff, and Westinghouse Furniture Systems into a single subsidiary called Knoll Group Inc. The consolidation boosted

Knoll's status from fourth to third largest contract office furniture manufacturer in the United States (behind Steelcase and Herman Miller).

Given the industry downturn, the operations of Knoll Group were bloated. To whip the new company into shape and to combat proliferating competition, Westinghouse initiated a reorganization of all of Knoll's operations. The effort was designed to cut costs, improve efficiency, and conform to evolving market demands for cost-efficient office systems. Knoll Group, under the direction of Chief Executive Maurice C. Sardi, immediately began laying off workers and shifting production. Two Pennsylvania manufacturing facilities were shuttered and about 20 percent of Knoll's work force was eliminated between 1991 and 1993. That brought the total number of employees to about 4,200, roughly 1,200 of whom worked at the East Greenville facility. At the same time, the company invested an average of about $30 million annually to update plants and product lines.

Lagging furniture markets in effect canceled Westinghouse's efforts to streamline its furniture operations. Sales increased to $673 million in 1991, but the company still posted a disappointing net loss in 1991 of more than $1 million. Deep industry discounting and stagnant markets contributed to a much greater loss in 1992 of about $15 million on diminished sales of $576 million. Frustrated and seeking a narrower definition of its own operations, parent company Westinghouse decided early in 1993 to sell off Knoll Group. However, Westinghouse had trouble finding a willing buyer and by late 1993 was still trying to dump the division. Sardi took early retirement late in 1993 and was replaced by 51-year-old Burton B. Staniar.

Under Staniar's leadership, Knoll continued to pursue two goals reflective of the new office furniture environment: developing products aimed at the value segment of the market and intensifying effort to reach the small business and individual consumer. To that end, Knoll revamped its offerings during the early 1990s and converted its contract showrooms into more visible, consumer-oriented sales centers. Knoll introduced a new line of stand-alone furniture for the home-office crowd with desks retailing for less than $1,000. It also introduced several new products geared for ergonomically conscious buyers and for disabled users. It also beefed up offerings in its core office environments furniture lines with, for example, more convenient and comfortable desks and storage units.

Knoll continued to lose money in 1994, although its losses were considerably less than those suffered in 1993. Westinghouse was also on the rebound and had even temporarily decided, early in 1994, not to sell

Knoll Group. Significant new products being marketed in 1994 and 1995 included the Gehry Collection, which was composed of bentwood tables and chairs, and the propeller Table, a line of innovative conference and training tables designed with modern electronic technology in mind. In mid-1995 Knoll Group was employing about 4,000 people worldwide and supporting approximately 500 locations. Knoll's main goal, as it had been since Hans Knoll founded the company in 1938, was to be a leader in the production and sale of innovative, functional, affordable office furnishings.

1996 AND ONWARD

After years of uncertainty under Westinghouse's ownership, Knoll was finally sold in 1996 for $565 million to Warburg, Pincus Ventures LP, a New York-based financial services company. Westinghouse used the sale to pay down some of its $5.4 billion debt incurred from acquiring the television network CBS Inc. in 1995. Westinghouse's reputation as an electrical company was not regarded as the best fit for Knoll. Knoll's disappointing sales for 1994 also prompted the sale.

By the time the sale was completed with Warburg Pincus in early 1996, the furniture industry had improved and Knoll was posting higher earnings. The firm went public again in May 1997 under its new CEO John Lynch. Funds raised by the offering helped Knoll's sales in 1997 leap 26.6 percent above the previous year. Knoll also released a successful line of furniture designed by Maya Lin, the architect of both the Civil Rights Memorial in Montgomery, Alabama, and the Vietnam memorial in Washington, D.C.

When Knoll announced plans to return to private ownership, its shareholders filed a lawsuit that was eventually settled in 1999. Warburg Pincus and a Knoll management group then purchased the remaining shares for nearly $500 million. Knoll was once again a privately owned company. Even though the employment for office jobs was strong in 1999, the office furniture industry had slumped. Industry analysts blamed the plummeting Asian economies, corporate mergers, and even the widespread trepidation concerning the Y2K problem. It was assumed that electronic devices would not be able to handle the dating algorithms for the new millennium. Businesses, fearing that they would soon be replacing all of their electronic equipment, were sheepish about upgrading their office furniture.

In 2000 the office furniture industry finally caught up with America's inflated economy, but soon after the U.S. economy plummeted. The office furniture industry's upswing was short-lived; in 2001 shipments were down 16 percent from the previous year. Knoll began layoffs at several of its manufacturing facilities to cut costs and weather what many were calling a recession. CEO John Lynch was replaced by Knoll's COO Andrew Cogan. In 2002 the new CEO oversaw the spending of millions on manufacturing upgrades. Knoll also introduced its award-winning LIFE chair, a high-end office chair that bolstered overall sales for the company. Knoll posted net profits of $15.3 million during the first half of 2003.

In 2004 Knoll once again went public, hoping to raise as much as $230 million from the IPO. Knoll quadrupled its storage product offering by launching the Knoll Essentials collection, a line of chairs, desks, tables, file cabinets, and other office furniture. In 2005 the collection and an improved economy had helped Knoll post net profits that were 14.4 percent greater than the previous year. There was also a nationwide increase in new commercial construction and decrease in overall business space vacancies. Executives at Knoll began reducing the release of new textiles such as upholstery, panel fabrics, wall coverings, and drapery. They began focusing more on a furniture collection called Knoll-Studio, a throwback to mid-century styling that was partially pioneered by Hans Knoll and Florence Schust. Consumers had a shown a renewed interest in the style and Knoll promptly responded. The company remained a world leader by selling its goods through over 100 showrooms and regional offices, along with a network of over 200 Knoll dealerships.

Dave Mote
Updated, Kevin Teague

PRINCIPAL SUBSIDIARIES

Knoll International Ltd. (United Kingdom); Knoll International S.A. (Belgium); Knoll International GmbH (Germany); Knoll International S.p.A. (Italy); Knoll International S.A. (France).

PRINCIPAL COMPETITORS

Haworth, Inc.; Herman Miller, Inc.; HNI Corporation; Inscape Corporation; Jami Inc.; Steelcase Inc.; Teknion LLC; Trendway Corporation.

FURTHER READING

Blake, Laura, "Knoll Dialing in Consumer Market," *Grand Rapids Business Journal,* May 24, 1993, p. 1.

Brammer, Rhonda, "Staniar Cites Knoll Group's Improvement," *Grand Rapids Business Journal,* November 7, 1994, p. 1.

———, "Will This Scuffed-Up Group Shine Again?," *Barron's,* April 5, 1999, p. 28.

Dearning, Sean, "Knoll Group on the Selling Block," *Wood & Wood Products,* February 1993, p. 44.

Harrison, Kimberly P., "New Player Rolls into Local Office Furniture Market," *Crain's Cleveland Business,* March 13, 1995, p. 4.

Kirkbride, Rob, "140 Knoll Workers Latest Layoff Victims," *Grand Rapids Press,* August 8, 2001, A7.

———, "Office Furniture in for 'Rough Ride,'" *Grand Rapids Press,* August 17, 2001, p. A1.

The Knoll Group: History, East Greenville, Pa.: Knoll Group, Inc., 1995.

"Knoll Group May Soon Be Up for Sale," *Grand Rapids Press,* December 15, 1995, p. C7.

"Knoll, Inc. Reports Continued Double Digit Growth for the Fourth Quarter and Full Year of 2005," *PR Newswire,* February 2, 2006.

"Knoll Reports Record Sales In Quarter," *Grand Rapids Press,* July 24, 1998, p. D6.

Leith, Scott, "The Office Furniture Industry May Finally Be Catching Up With the Booming Economy," *Grand Rapids Press,* June 14, 2000, p. B6.

Luymes, Robin, "Furniture Firms Fight Big Slide," *Grand Rapids Business Journal,* December 30, 1991, p. 2.

Shope, Dan, "Westinghouse Plans to Touch Up Knoll Before Selling the Company," *Allentown Morning Call,* October 24, 1993, Bus. Sec.

Slutsker, Gary, "The Sour Smell of Success," *Forbes,* January 26, 1987, p. 54.

von Hassell, Agostino, "Furniture Maker Picks TPEs for Arm Rests," *Plastics World,* August 1991, p. 15.

"Wolverine Sales, Earnings Decline," *Grand Rapids Press,* April 22, 1999, p. E8.

⊞ KOPIN

Kopin Corporation

200 John Hancock Road
Taunton, Massachusetts 02780
U.S.A.
Telephone: (508) 824-6696
Fax: (508) 824-6958
Web site: http://www.kopin.com

Public Company
Incorporated: 1984
Employees: 379
Sales: $90.3 million (2005)
Stock Exchanges: NASDAQ
Ticker Symbol: KOPN
NAIC: 541710 Research and Development in the Physical, Engineering, and Life Sciences

■ ■ ■

Kopin Corporation is a Taunton, Massachusetts-based developer and manufacturer of high-performance transistor wafers and ultra small active matrix liquid crystal displays (AMLCDS), both of which rely on nanotechnology. The company's heterojunction bipolar transistors (HBT) are called III-V products because the raw materials are drawn from the III and V columns of the periodic table of elements, including Indium Phosphide, Gallium Nitride, and Gallium Arsenide-based substrates. Unlike silicon-based transistors that are laid out horizontally, HBTs are constructed vertically, atomic layer by atomic layer, by means of Metalorganic Chemical Vapor Deposition production growth processes. The resulting transistors are smaller, faster, and need less power than conventional transistors, making them ideal for use in such electronic items as cellular phones and other wireless and high-speed communication applications.

One in three wireless handsets in the world rely on Kopin's HBTs. The company's CyberDisplay AMLCD product relies on nanotechnology to produce what the company calls CyberLites, light emitting diodes grown on sapphire substrates. They can be turned off and on and change colors to produce monochrome and color displays that are less than one-inch in size vertically. The images can be magnified to produce images comparable to what can be found on a 20-inch display. The product offers high resolution, bright images, quick performance, and low power consumption. CyberDisplay is found in camcorders, digital camera viewfinders, wireless devices, virtual reality gaming, simulation, and surgical headgear. Kopin's roster of customers include a large number of major corporations, including JVC, Konica Minolta, Panasonic, Samsung Electronics, Boeing, Kaiser Electronics, and Raytheon. Kopin is a publicly trade company listed on the NASDAQ.

FOUNDER RAISED IN POST-WORLD WAR II HONG KONG

Kopin was founded by its long-time President, Chief Executive Officer, and Chairman Dr. John C. C. Fan and his research colleagues. He was born in Shanghai, China, during World War II, and was raised in Hong Kong. At the age of 18 he came to the United States in the early 1960s to study electrical engineering at the University of California at Berkeley. After receiving his

COMPANY PERSPECTIVES

The company's breakthroughs have produced a host of efficient, compact and powerful products that are transforming the way people see, hear and communicate. The recurring themes throughout our products are small size, low power consumption, high quality, superior performance, enabling the next generation of consumer and industrial mobile products.

undergraduate degree, he relocated to the East Coast, earning master's and doctorate degrees in applied physics at Harvard University. Upon graduation in 1972 Fan was planning to return to California when he elected instead to accept a research post at Lincoln Laboratory, a Massachusetts Institute of Technology outpost in the Boston suburb of Lincoln.

Lincoln Laboratory had been founded in 1951, funded by the military but run by MIT, to apply science and advanced technology to matters of national security, in particular air defense. Over the years, the lab's purview expanded to include such areas as communications, space surveillance, and air traffic control. Lincoln was an applied research lab, as opposed to basic research, meaning that the focus of its scientists was to develop products from their research efforts. It was no surprise, therefore, that Lincoln encouraged the commercial exploitation of products that arose from the defense research. Over the years, scores of start-up companies were spawned at Lincoln.

Fan's research focus at Lincoln was semiconductors, crystalline structures that had both conducting and insulating properties, and could be chemically manipulated to control the flow of electric current in electronic components. Working in the lab's Electronic Materials Group, he researched semiconductor materials, including alloys of dissimilar materials, in hopes of finding the ideal one to produce the best performance for a specific application. As he told the *Providence Journal* in a 2000 profile, it was like genetic engineering, taking "the good things" from each material and leaving the "bad things." Fan had an opportunity to see how genetic engineers approached their research because they could be found splicing genes in a nearby lab. Fan decided to apply comparable splicing techniques to bring together desirable materials. It became known as wafer engineering, and as the technology gained an international reputation, venture capitalists soon took notice. "VCs

were making money from companies like Genentech and Amgen, so people began to see that you could make money from gene slicing," Fan told *Mass High Tech*. He continued, "So they thought, 'Maybe we can make money splicing materials.'" Venrock Associates, the venture capital arm of the Rockefeller family which maintained an office in Cambridge, Massachusetts, began urging Fan and his research colleagues to leave Lincoln and start a company to exploit their findings commercially. In 1984 he was won over and Kopin Corporation was incorporated in Delaware. According to *Providence Journal*, "Kopin is an amalgam of the Chinese words Ko and Pin, which, loosely translated, mean a good product for a fair price."

Fan and his team had not yet set up shop when they were contacted by Massachusetts Governor Michael Dukakis who invited Fan to pay him a visit. "Somehow he had heard of this new technology we were working on, this new way to make integrated circuits," Fan recalled for *Providence Journal*, continuing, "and so I went over to the State House and he told me he wanted me to go down to Taunton to have a look." In Taunton was an industrial park where the governor hoped Kopin would locate. A manufacturing town that had come upon hard times, Taunton was attempting a comeback through the Myles Standish Industrial Park launched by area businessmen. Fan was offered tax breaks to move there, but he was also attracted to the site for other reasons, as he explained to *Providence Journal:* "There was no traffic, housing was much cheaper and there was a plentiful supply of labor from New Bedford, Fall River and Providence. And you could still get back to Boston quite easily."

Kopin established its operations at the Industrial Park. Initial funds of $300,000 came from Venrock and another venture capital firm, Cardinal Partners, based in Princeton, New Jersey. According to *Providence Journal*, "When Kopin moved into the park, Fan said, he had with him a group of about 30 scientists, including 'seven or eight' from MIT. The new company licensed the wafer-engineering Fan and his team had developed at Lincoln and related technology in 1985, and then spent the next half-dozen years on additional research, Fan said, and then, 'in the early '90s,' the focus narrowed to product selection and manufacturing processes."

GOING PUBLIC: 1992

During this incubation stage, Kopin continued to raise the money needed to fund research. In a second round of funding in April 1987, the company received another $8 million. New backers included State Farm Insurance; Boston-based Charles River Ventures; BancBoston Ventures, the venture capital investment arm of Fleet-

KEY DATES

1984: The company is founded.
1992: Kopin makes its initial public offering of stock.
1995: HBT transistor wafers are introduced.
1997: CyberDisplay is introduced.
2000: Kopin acquires Super Epitaxial Products, Inc.
2002: CyberLite is introduced.

Boston Financial; and Eberstadt Fleming Inc. (a VC firm that had recently been created by the merger of New York investment bank F. Eberstadt & Company and Robert Fleming Holdings Ltd., a major British merchant bank). Kopin then went public in April 1992, with an IPO that raised $15 million. Later in the year Kopin sold another $2.6 million of common stock in a private placement with AT&T State Street.

By the early 1990s, Kopin was generating modest revenues from government contracts and the sale of electronic circuits, but major corporations were well aware of the company's work, increasingly impressed by the demonstrations it presented. In addition to using wafer technology to produce advanced integrated circuits, Kopin was also working on flat panel displays by essentially creating transparent integrated circuits. "At engineering school," Fan told *Computer Design* in 1994, "I learned that any material, if made thin enough, will transmit light. LCD's based on thin, single-crystal silicon—the mainstay of most integrated circuits—are transparent." In 1994 Kopin demonstrated what it called a Smart Slide, developed in conjunction with Lincoln, a high resolution, full color imaging device. Although it was not yet a commercially viable technology, Smart Slide was impressive enough to convince the likes of Boeing, Rockwell International, the Defense Advanced Research Projects Agency (DARPA), and the U.S. Department of Commerce to either buy stock or award the company research grants. DARPA, for example, gave Kopin $3 million in research money to pursue its display technology for use in a helmet mounted vision system for the military, and in 1994 the company landed a further $2 million from the Department of Defense to accelerate the development of video-speed AMLCDs. Along the way, starting in 1994, Kopin became an investor itself by buying an interest in Forte Technologies, Inc., a developer of virtual reality head-mounted systems for gaming and other entertainment markets. Kopin eventually gained a majority stake in Forte, but

the investment failed to pan out. Forte filed for Chapter 11 bankruptcy protection in 1997 and its assets were subsequently sold.

On a parallel track, Kopin continued to work on HBT transistor wafers, and in 1995 launched its first commercially successful product on the market. The advanced wafers quickly found a market with manufacturers of cellular phones, other wireless products, and ultra-portable products. Product revenues jumped from $2.8 million in 1994 to $7.2 million in 1995 and $11.7 million in 1997. Another revenue stream began contributing to the balance sheet in April 1997 when Kopin introduced CyberDisplay, the smallest display on the market. It used a lens and backlight to produce larger high resolution images.

Kopin again tapped the public equity market in February 1998, netting close to $17.8 million. Although the company had yet to turn a profit—it would lose nearly $3 million in 1998, even as total revenues increased from $16.4 million in 1997 to $26.9 million—it had plenty of cash on hand to continue to develop its innovative products and carve out an increasing market share. Over the course of 1998, Kopin continued to improve manufacturing yields of Cyber-Display and the production capacity of its transistor wafers.

Kopin prospered further in 1999, as once again it was able to complete a public offering of stock, this time raising $73.2 million. Demand was so strong for its Gallium Arsenide HBT transistors that the company launched a $15 million expansion of the Taunton facility. The year also brought with it the first consumer product to incorporate the CyberDisplay, a viewfinder in a JVC camcorder. Panasonic soon signed up as another Cyber-Display customer in a deal announced in January 2000. In addition to those notable milestones, Kopin enjoyed a record year financially. Revenues totaled $38.7 million and for the first time in company history Kopin recorded a full year profit: $775,269.

STOCK PRICE SURGE: 2000

Kopin began the new century flying high. The price of its stock took off after the Panasonic deal was announced. Worth around $40 per share at the start of 2000, Kopin stock approached the $100 mark by early February. Kopin also bolstered its semiconductor materials business by acquiring Super Epitaxial Products, Inc., a company with expertise in gallium nitride that added complementary technology that could lead to new opto-electronic products. In 2001 Kopin also introduced indium phosphide HBTs, the next-generation in HBTs. The technology was especially suited for increasing the bandwidth of fiber optic networks, and Kopin began collaborating with the likes of Rockwell to produce high-speed components using the new transistors to increase fiber optic network performance. Kopin's CyberDisplay business also continued to grow, as the company added more major customers, including Samsung Electronic Co. and Panasonic. For the year 2000, sales more than doubled to $92.6 million and net income soared to $6.3 million.

Kopin's momentum was stunted in 2001 due to a sluggish economy and other factors that resulted in what some described as a "perfect tech storm." The Cyber-Display business continued to grow, with sales improving from $18.98 million in 2000 to $22.2 million in 2001, but that could not make up for the collapse in HBT sales. For the year Kopin recorded total revenues of $50.3 million and a net loss of $22.7 million. The company did its best to control costs while continuing to invest in research and development, and given that it had no long-term debt and held $104 million in cash and marketable securities, Kopin was in a strong position to wait out poor market conditions.

CyberDisplay sales continue to grow at a robust clip in 2002, increasing 87 percent to $44.1 million, and as a result total revenues rebounded to $76.8 million. But once again the company lost money, although the $31.9 million loss it reported was inflated by the adoption of new accounting standards and investment transactions. More important for the company's long-term success was the introduction of CyberLite, a new high-brightness light-emitting diode. Revenues held steady in 2003, when Kopin lost another $7.7 million, mostly due to the development of CyberLite. While revenues increased to $87.3 million in 2004, Kopin recorded a net loss of $13.8 million, again related to investments in Cyberlite. In 2005 the company returned to profitability, netting $11.7 million on revenues of $90.3 million, with HBTs leading the way for a change. The company introduced a new generation of HBT transistors, the GAIN-HBT, especially suited for the advanced cell phones coming onto the market. Also in 2005 Kopin introduced its Digital iVision products for mobile video applications, a young market expected to grow as video eyewear—essentially small movie screens on glasses—became more commonplace and gained in popularity. Kopin appeared well positioned to enjoy even stronger results in the years to come.

Ed Dinger

PRINCIPAL SUBSIDIARIES

VS Corporation; Kowon Technology Co., Ltd.; Kopin Display Corp.; Kopin Optical, Inc.; Koptron U.S.A.

PRINCIPAL COMPETITORS

EMCORE Corporation; Hitachi, Ltd.; RF Micro Devices, Inc.

FURTHER READING

Caywood, Thomas, "Kopin's Process Fuels Soaring Stock," *Providence Business News,* February 21, 2000, p. 1.

Churbuck, David C., "Crystal Clear," *Forbes,* January 4, 1993, p. 258.

Colt, Tim, "MIT Scientists Found Taunton, Mass., Company, Produce High-Tech Products," *Providence Journal,* July 9, 2000.

Kelly, Matt, "Kopin's Early Success With LEDs Bolsters Bottom Line," *Small Times Correspondent,* October 6, 2003.

"LCDs Posture for Portables," *Computer Design,* March 1994, p. OEM4.

Miller, Jeff, "Kopin's Founder Says Change Is No Problem," *Mass High Tech,* http://directory.masshightech.com/as-fan.asp.

Kwang Yang Motor Company Ltd.

35 Wan Hsing Street
Sanmin District
Kaohsiung,
Taiwan
Telephone: (886) 07 382 2526
Fax: (886) 07 384 0112
Web site: http://www.kymco.com

Private Company
Incorporated: 1963
Employees: 3,650
Sales: $3.7 billion (2002 est.)
NAIC: 336991 Motorcycle, Bicycle, and Parts Manufacturing

■ ■ ■

Kwang Yang Motor Company Ltd. (Kymco) is one of the world's leading manufacturers of powered two-wheel vehicles (PTWs) and other motorized vehicles. The company produces a range of scooters, mobility scooters, all-terrain vehicles (ATVs) and, especially since the 2000s, both light and heavy motorcycles. Kymco markets its vehicles worldwide under the Kymco brand, and also produces PTWs and ATVs as an original equipment manufacturer for third-party brands. The leading manufacturer of PTWs in Taiwan, where nearly one out of every two people own a scooter, Kymco has successfully expanded its exports to some 75 countries worldwide. In support of its international operations, the company has developed a network of manufacturing facilities in Taiwan and in mainland China. The company also operates production joint ventures in mainland China, Vietnam, the Philippines, and Indonesia. Kymco was founded in the 1960s as a producer of components for Honda Motors of Japan, before developing its own fully independent operations in the 1990s. Honda remains a significant shareholder in the privately held company.

FROM BICYCLES TO MOTORBIKES BEGINNING IN 1963

Kwang Yang Motor Company, or Kymco, was established in 1963 as a joint venture with Honda Motor Co. of Japan to produce bicycles, motorcycles, and components. Both bicycles and motorcycles were product categories targeted by the Taiwanese government as part of its effort to transform Taiwan into one of the region's industrial powerhouses. Honda had entered the Taiwanese market in the early 1960s, launching its first production operations there in 1961. Kymco was officially inaugurated in June 1964, and by 1967 had constructed its own headquarters. Construction also began on the company's first manufacturing plant, which was completed in 1970.

By the mid-1970s, Kymco had expanded its production from components to complete vehicles. This led Kymco to begin building its second plant, completed in 1977. The company quickly became Taiwan's leading producer of scooters and light motorcycles. By 1978, the company had been granted status as one of the country's Grade A Motorcycle Manufacturers. By the end of that year, Kymco's total motorbike production had topped 500,000.

COMPANY PERSPECTIVES

It is our goal to bring KYMCO into the international community. We have performed intensive R&D to live up to the needs of our customers. No effort has been spared to reach new highs, developing and manufacturing innovative products, and adding customer satisfaction. We wish to provide the optimal choice of transportation for everyone.

Committed worldwide, we aspire to increase customer satisfaction and contribute to the satisfaction and contribute to the society through constant innovation in the tacking of challenges. It is our hope that our dedication can provide consumers access to the choice of optimal vehicles, so they can share with us the results attained from our endeavors. The making of a respectable global brand The "KYMCO" name represents our firm dedication and responsibility to customers. To ensure KYMCO's perpetuity, we wish to make KYMCO a world-class name brand, setting an exemplary model in the building of brand names in the world.

Taiwan's rising economic strength led more and more people to abandon bicycles for scooters and motorbikes. The growing demand enabled Kymco to step up production, and by 1983, the company's total production had passed the one million mark. In order to meet the steadily building demand, Kymco began a major new expansion program for its second plant in Taiwan, which was completed in 1989. By then, the company had produced its two millionth cycle since launching production in the early 1970s.

An oil crisis in Taiwan in 1987 prompted the Taiwanese government to enact new legislation banning imports of heavy class motorcycles of 150cc and larger. The ban helped boost Kymco's own position in the domestic market, although it limited Kymco's own ability to branch out into the heavy classes of PTWs. The import ban nonetheless encouraged Kymco, which had continued to rely on Honda's technology, to begin developing its own in-house design and engineering capacity. As part of the effort, Kymco began building its own research and development center, with the first phase opened in 1989. By 1991, Kymco also had installed its own integrated motorcycle test field, the first of its kind in Taiwan.

INTERNATIONAL BRAND BY THE END OF THE 20TH CENTURY

In a reflection of Taiwan's own emergence as a global technological and industrial center, Kymco now prepared itself to become a fully independent, and international, player on the international PTW market. While Honda remained a significant shareholder in the company, Kymco launched its own branded line of motorcycles, components, and accessories under the Kymco name. Kymco's production not only targeted the Taiwanese market, where the company claimed as much as one-third of the total PTW market, but also the international market, including Southeast Asia and Latin America, both important markets for scooters and light class motorcycles, and Europe and the North American markets as well.

In support of its effort to develop into an internationally competitive group, Kymco initiated an ambitious manufacturing expansion program through the 1990s. In 1993, the company opened its third Taiwanese production facility, in Lu Chu. In that year as well, Kymco shifted part of its production to the Chinese mainland, taking over control of a production plant in Hunan, which was then named Hunan Kwang Nan Motor Co. Ltd. The company also developed a second joint venture in Hunan that year, Hunan Kinlon Kwang Yang Motor Co., Ltd.

Kymco continued to step up production, topping four million total units in 1994. In that year, the company expanded its production capacity in Taiwan, completing the second phase of construction of the Lu Chu plant. The company also boosted its presence in the fast-developing mainland Chinese market, adding a new joint venture subsidiary, Changzhou Kwang Yang Motor Co. Kymco's entry into the mainland also enabled it to shift production of some of its components from Taiwan to lower-cost China. This strategy became particularly important for the company ahead of Taiwan's entry into the World Trade Organization, and the opening of the Taiwanese market to a whole new level of import competition. Completed in March 1995, the Changzhou unit launched production of scooters and light motorcycles, with a total production capacity of 10,000 per year—compared to the production capacity of Kymco's Taiwan plants of 300,000 per year. By then, Kymco had become technically independent of Honda Motor.

Changzhou was the site of the group's next expansion, with the creation of Changzhou Kwang Hsing Precise Machine Co., Ltd. in 1995. The unit launched production of motorcycle components, including engines, engine components, engine assemblies, and other parts in 1997. In that year as well, the company's

KEY DATES

1963: Kwang Yang Motor Company Ltd. is established to produce bikes and components in a joint venture with Honda motorcycles in Taiwan.

1964: Kymco opens its first production plant.

1977: A second manufacturing plant is opened.

1978: Kymco is designated as a Grade A Motorcycle Manufacturer by the Taiwanese government; the company's 500,000th motorcycle is produced.

1983: Total motorcycle production tops the one million mark.

1987: The Taiwanese government enacts a ban on heavy class (150 cc and higher) motorcycles.

1988: Kymco passes the two million mark for total motorcycle production.

1989: The company completes expansion of its second manufacturing plant and begins production of a research and development center in order to develop an independent manufacturing process.

1992: The company creates the Kymco brand and begins targeting international market.

1993: The company opens its third Taiwan plant in Lu Shu; the Hunan Kwang Nan Motor Co.

Ltd. in mainland China is acquired; joint venture Hunan Kinlon Kwang Yang Motor Co., Ltd. is established.

1995: A joint venture in China, Changzhou Kwang Yang Motor Co., launches production; Kymco becomes technically independent of Honda.

1996: A production joint venture is established in Indonesia.

1999: A second research and development facility is opened in Taiwan.

2000: The company launches its first 250cc models for the export market.

2001: The company adopts a new diversified vehicle strategy, developing ATV and mobility scooters.

2002: The first ATV model for the export market is launched.

2005: The company forms a production joint venture in Vietnam.

2006: The company launches its first 500cc ATV model.

---

second Hunan unit launched its own production of motorcycle components.

GLOBAL POWERSPORTS LEADER IN THE NEW CENTURY

By 1996, Kymco's total production had passed four million units. In that year, Kymco began to broaden its regional interests, where the fast-growing economies in the Southeast Asian region provided a massive demand for scooters and light motorcycles. The company turned to Indonesia in 1996, forming a joint venture with that country's Lippo group. That subsidiary, PT Kymco Lippo Motor Co., began producing a range of Kymco models and components before the end of the decade.

The company added a new production plant in Tibet in 1998, called Tibet Summit Kwang Yang Power Machinery Co. Ltd. In that year as well, the group's total production topped six million units. In the meantime, Kymco had begun construction of a new

research and development unit, completed in 1999. The new unit became part of the group's bid to expand its product range to become a true "powersports" manufacturer, under a new strategy launched in 2001. This effort included the development of new scooter and motorcycle models with larger displacements, as well as a branching out into the four-wheel ATV category.

By 2000, Kymco had developed a new 250cc scooter, the B&W, which it launched on the export market that year. By the end of that year, Kymco had added a second 250cc vehicle, a motorcycle featuring a V-type engine called the Venox, which also joined the group's range of export models. These larger PTWs enabled Kymco to position for a rapid deployment in the domestic market, as the Taiwanese government lifted the ban on heavy bikes in July 2002. In addition to rolling out the Venox in Taiwan, the company added two more 250cc bikes, the Ego and the Grand Dink heavy scooter. The latter had achieved a degree of success in the international market, notably in Europe, and was capable of being scaled up to displacements as high as 700cc.

Kymco added its first ATV model in early 2002, with the launch of the MXer 150. The company also continued to develop its line of heavy bikes, debuting a 500cc scooter, the Xciting, in 2003. In that year, the company added another new product category, mobility scooters, that is, electric vehicles for people of reduced mobility, launching its first electric-powered scooter, called the Energy.

Kymco's ATV offering also was expanded in 2003, with the launch of a new 250cc model. The larger displacement was specifically designed to target the group's entry into the North American market. The 250 cc model also helped drive Kymco's rapidly growing status in Europe. By mid-2004, the company was able to claim the lead in the European ATV market.

Kymco continued seeking out new international expansion opportunities into the mid-2000s. India became an important target market for the company, where the growing economic status of its roughly one billion citizens promised a potentially huge market for Kymco's vehicles. The company began actively seeking out a local partner to aid its entry into the Indian subcontinent.

At the same time, Kymco established a foothold in the Middle East, forming a technical partnership with Iran's Hongkings Co. The company also entered Vietnam, launching a joint venture, Hoalam Kymco Motor Corporation, in Ho Chi Minh City, in 2005. By then, the company had completed construction of a new production plant in Taiwan, specifically for the development and production of the group's mobility scooters and ATV segments. The latter category remained the group's spearhead into the important North American market. By 2006, the company had successfully launched a full range of ATVs in the United States and Canada, ranging from an entry-level 50cc model, to its latest and largest, a 500cc ATV. After 40 years in business, Kymco had established itself among the world's leading "powersports" vehicles producers.

M. L. Cohen

PRINCIPAL SUBSIDIARIES

Changzhou Guangri Precision Machinery Co., Ltd. (China); Changzhou Kwang Hsing Precise Machine Co., Ltd. (China); Changzhou Kwang Yang Motor Co., Ltd. (China); Hoalam Kymco Motor Corporation (Vietnam; 50%); Hunan Kinlon Kwang Yang Motor Co., Ltd. (China; 50%); PT. Kymco Lippo Motor Indonesia (Philippines; 50%).

PRINCIPAL COMPETITORS

Yamaha Motor Company Ltd.; Chunlan (Group) Corporation; Hero Cycles Ltd.; Piaggio and C. S.p.A.; Sanyang Industry Company Ltd.

FURTHER READING

Ebert, Guido, "Kymco Grows Global Presence," *Powersports Business,* February 13, 2006, p. 4.

Freund, Ken, "Taiwanese Cycle Exports Led by Kymco," *Powersports Business,* September 5, 2005, p. 24.

Kelley, Jerrod, "A Big Boost," *ATV Magazine,* May 2006, p. 54.

———, "Kymco Joins ATVEA," *Powersports Business,* April 25, 2005, p. 26.

"Kymco Enters Canada," *Powersports Business,* March 14, 2005, p. 3.

"Kymco No. 1 ATV Brand in Europe in First Half," *Taiwan Economic News,* July 30, 2004.

"Kymco Scooters Find Success in United States," *Powersports Business,* November 15, 2004, p. 20.

"Kymco, SYM Mainland Subsidiaries to Produce Low Price Export PTWs," *Taiwan Economic News,* April 10, 2006.

"Kymco to Tie Up with Vietnamese Partner in Scooter Production," *Taiwan Economic News,* December 27, 2004.

"Kymco's Overseas Investment Projects Hit Snags," *Taiwan Economic News,* September 3, 2004.

Liang, Quincy, "Competitions Between Taiwan's Top Two PTW Makers Extended Overseas," *Taiwan Economic News,* January 7, 2005.

"Taiwan Scooter Makers Slash Prices to Boost Sales," *Taiwan Economic News,* July 25, 2003.

L. M. Berry and Company

3170 Kettering Boulevard
Dayton, Ohio 45439
U.S.A.
Telephone: (937) 296-2121
Toll Free: (800) 366-2379
Fax: (937) 296-2011
Web site: http://www.theberrycompany.com

Wholly Owned Subsidiary of BellSouth Corporation
Incorporated: 1924
Employees: 2,600
Sales: $1 billion (2005 est.)
NAIC: 541870 Advertising Material Distribution
    Services.

■■■

A subsidiary of BellSouth Corporation, L. M. Berry and Company is the largest Yellow Pages advertising sales agency in the United States. Through The Berry Company unit, the Dayton, Ohio-based operation serves more then 100 telephone systems, approximately 1 million advertisers, and more than 100 million telephone customers in over 700 markets, distributing 28 million telephone directories. In addition, Berry Network, Inc., is a business-to-business company that offers Yellow Pages marketing services such as research, media planning, and ad design, plus interactive media services. Berry Sales and Marketing Solutions offers domestic and international clients a wide range of sales and marketing consulting services, including sales strategy, sales force recruitment and readiness, sales manager development, marketing strategies, and product development.

FOUNDER BORN: LATE 19TH CENTURY

The man behind the founding of L. M. Berry and company was Loren M. Berry, born in Wabash, Indiana, in 1888. His father died when he was just four years of age, and he quickly learned the value of hard work as he began to help his mother who struggled to support the family through sewing and work as a maternity nurse. When he was just 8 years old he made and sold horse-radish door to door as well as maintaining *Saturday Evening Post* and laundry routes. He became familiar with newspaper work during his high school years working as a reporter for the *Wabash Plain Dealer* and writing for his school's monthly paper. He also served as the business manager for both the paper and the school annual. In his business function Berry learned the basics of selling advertising space, which he would put to good use after graduation by starting a business, the Ohio Guide Company, to sell advertising in the timetables published by the electric interurban rail lines serving Midwestern cities. In 1909 he traveled to Marion, Indiana, to sell timetable ads and was asked by the manager of The United Telephone Company in Marion (Berry's uncle, according to the *New York Times*) if he could sell advertising for his upcoming telephone directory, a task another man had recently abandoned after putting in little effort and achieving no success.

Telephone directories were hardly new. Neither was the selling of advertising in them. The first directory

COMPANY PERSPECTIVES

At the core of our company is the drive to go beyond your expectation to satisfy every need. It is all about connections: yours with us, ours with your advertisers, the advertisers with their customers. We work to make those connections smart, strong and unbreakable.

been produced in 1878 in Connecticut by the New Haven District Telephone Company just two years after the telephone was invented. It was a crude one-page listing of 47 subscribers and that at the very least separated business from residential customers, although the names were not listed alphabetically, nor were the phone numbers included. Instead, the 11 residential customers were lumped together haphazardly, followed by three physicians, two dentists, 20 "Store, Factories, etc." four meat and fish markets, a pair of hack and boarding stables, and another eight telephones ascribed to "Miscellaneous" customers, including the police and post office. In the early years telephone companies treated directories as a necessary evil—and expense—and thus were published irregularly. According to lore, in 1883 a telephone directory printer ran out of white paper and substituted yellow rather than wait for a shipment. Thus, the term "Yellow Pages" was born.

In the 1880s the commercial printing firm RR Donnelley formed the Chicago Directory Company to print the Chicago telephone directory, and its founder's son, Reuben H. Donnelley, established the first classified telephone directory advertising and laid the foundation for the Yellow Pages industry. Telephone companies across the country followed Donnelley's lead and began to offset printing costs by selling advertising, but generally they devoted little effort to the task, delegating it to telephone company employees with other jobs or to the employees of their printer. It was not surprising that the ads were sold with little enthusiasm and businessmen eyed them with suspicion, regarding directory ads as just another way the local phone company was trying to bilk them. As a result, there were few ads, few telephone customers referred to the directory for sales help, and the unimportance of the telephone directory became a self-fulfilling prophecy.

Loren Berry, however, was not a man to short shrift any job. Already familiar with Marion businessmen after selling timetable ads to many of them, he went to work on the telephone directory and in little more than a

week sold $780 worth of ads, an amount of money that not only covered his commission and the cost of printing a 150-page directory but also earned The United Telephone Company a small profit. It was a successful debut for Berry, who soon traveled to Kokomo and Logansport, Indiana, and used his results at Marion as a calling card with two more telephone companies that were in need of new directories. Again, Berry's efforts paid off for his clients, and he decided to launch a business dedicated to the telephone directory business.

In 1910 22-year-old Berry and his wife moved to Dayton, Ohio, centrally located in the Midwest and a town with a booming economy. They lived in a $12-a-week boarding house while he set up shop at a rented desk in a downtown office building. His first client was the Home Telephone Company, one of two phone companies serving the community. After performing well for the customer, he was then able to sell his services to the parent company, The United States Independent Telephone Company of Columbus, Ohio, which ran 20 telephone companies in the state. Berry was awarded the business of eight directories that had never sold advertising. In order to handle the influx of business, Berry took on a partner, a neighbor in his office building, George Craven, who had been working as a life insurance agent. The expanded operation, called Craven and Berry, was now able to solicit and win business from other Midwestern telephone companies located in larger towns like St. Louis, Indianapolis, and Louisville. New salesmen were employed and given common sense tricks to developing leads, such as read the local newspapers, jot down the names on the side of delivery trucks and wagons, and even visit the silent movie theaters to see what businesses were willing to pay to have their names projected on the screen before the show.

TURNING POINT: 1921

A turning point in Berry's history came in 1921 when the U.S. government finally decided that local telephone competition caused more problems than it was worth, and legislation was passed to allow for natural monopolies and the consolidation of rival phone companies. Although Berry lost some major customers during the shakeout, in the long run the change was good for the company. No longer did advertisers have to decide if they were going to advertise in more than one directory, and they could be assured that they would reach all telephone customers in a community and not just a fraction.

Craven's health began to falter in the early 1920s, forcing the dissolution of Craven and Berry. Thus, in 1924 the firm took the name L. M Berry and Company.

KEY DATES

1910: Loren M. Berry founds company.
1924: After Berry's partner retires, company takes the name L. M. Berry and Company.
1931: The first Bell contract won.
1963: John Berry succeeds father as president.
1980: Loren Berry dies.
1986: BellSouth acquires the company.
2006: Last of the Berry family retires.

It continued to grow, as did the use of the telephone and the importance of the "Yellow Pages" for both advertisers and telephone customers. By the start of the 1930s Berry's annual directory volume had reached one million copies, a considerable improvement over the 8,000 directories of 1910. The company achieved a major coup in 1931, signing its first Bell System contract, covering the Dayton area for the Ohio Bell Telephone Company. In that same year, the company was forced for the second time since the departure of Craven to relocate its Dayton headquarters to larger accommodations. In addition, Berry maintained offices in a number of other cities, as far away as Philadelphia, Pennsylvania, and Tampa, Florida.

A second generation of the Berry family became involved in the company in the 1940s. Loren Berry's son, John William Berry, had learned the business while growing up, working after school, on weekends, and during his summers. When he was 18, in 1941, the younger Berry got his first taste of sales by heading up the directory sales campaign in Franklin, Ohio, and in the process demonstrated a great deal of potential. In just half the time as the previous year's effort, his team doubled the number of Yellow Page advertisers. John Berry did not join the company until 1946, after earning a business administration degree at Dartmouth University in 1944 and serving a stint in the military at the end of World War II. He quickly assumed greater levels of responsibility at Berry Company, becoming general sales manager in 1948.

It was during the postwar years that the telephone became ubiquitous in the homes of average Americans, and as a consequence the Yellow Pages took on a greater importance and the fortunes of the Berry Company rose accordingly. Between the end of the war and 1950, the Bell System installed 14 million telephones, the same number put in service during the company's first half-century. Moreover, the consumer advertising industry came of age and the Yellow Pages became part of a greater

trend impacting consumers and merchants alike. In the generation after the war, Berry expanded across the country. It added Bell customers throughout the south, as well as in New York and Wisconsin, and won the business of nearly 200 non-Bell customers. In addition, Berry became more vertically integrated. Not only did it sell advertising, it would now be able to handle all facets of a sales campaign, plus bill the advertisers, compile the directory, print, and deliver it.

The 1960s brought other changes to berry. John Berry became Managing Director in 1960, then succeeded his 75-year-old father as president in 1963, the same year the business was incorporated. Although Loren Berry would remain involved, serving as chairman of the board, the company was under the guidance of John Berry, who during his tenure would take the business beyond the United States borders. In 1966 he formed a joint venture with International Telephone and Telegraph Corporation (ITT), creating ITT-World Directories to publish directories and sell advertising for telephone companies around the world. By the start of the 1970s the business was publishing in nine languages in 17 countries, some of which never before had a classified telephone directory. Also of note, they were not necessarily the Yellow Pages. In Australia, for example, they became the Pink Pages, and in Europe the Golden Pages.

Stateside, in the meantime, Berry made a number of West Coast acquisitions in the 1960s and as a result opened the first office west of the Rockies. By the early 1970s Berry was responsible for one out of every four telephone directories published in the United States, serving more than 10,000 communities in 42 states. The company also began doing business in Canada, forming L. M. Berry-Canada, Ltd., to produce the Yellow Pages for The New Brunswick Telephone Company.

Loren Berry died in 1980 at the age of 91 and did not witness the major changes that occurred in telecommunications and the Yellow Pages, prompted in large part by the government-mandated breakup of AT&T and the deregulation of the industry. The Yellow Pages had become a significant cash cow for the Bell System, generating about $3.5 billion in advertising revenues in 1982. The profit potential had not been lost on others, of course, and already companies like GTE Corporation and Continental Telecom, Inc., had begun to launch directories to rival the Yellow Pages produced by the local AT&T company. For years other independents had carved out smaller, neighborhood directories that often proved more useful to consumers than the thick, unwieldy AT&T Yellow Pages that covered an entire telephone service area. Of the 6,000 Yellow Pages directories published in the United States in the early

1980s, 1,000 were produced by small independents. Nevertheless, the Bell companies took in 80 percent of all Yellow Pages revenues, retained their status with merchants, and had the added advantage of controlling access to the white pages listings, including new phone numbers, deletions, and changes.

BELLSOUTH ACQUIRES COMPANY: 1986

After the divestiture of AT&T in 1984, the resulting "Baby Bells" began competing with one another, all of them looking to build a lucrative Yellow Pages business. Berry, the second-largest independent advertising sales agent for Yellow Pages directories in the United States, at the time representing 800 directories in 31 states and generating $750 million in annual revenues, was an obvious prize and a natural fit for BellSouth, which in 1986 bought the company from John Berry, who had long since bought out his siblings. He would then use the proceeds to found Berry Investments and also support his philanthropic interests, in particular Dartmouth University.

As a BellSouth subsidiary, The Berry Company lost a number of customers who were in competition with its corporate parent. As a result Berry lost some accounts that it had held for six decades and it took some time to rebuild the customer base. Another factor was increased competition from rival telephone directories in the 1990s. The rise of the Internet, however, also brought a new outlet for the Yellow Pages and new opportunities for Berry. Another industry shift occurred at the end of the century when telecommunications companies began to sell off their directory services, providing Berry with a chance to sell consulting and other services to the restructured operations.

Although BellSouth now owned Berry, the company maintained ties to the Berry family. John Berry, Jr., remained with the company until his retirement in 1994.

His brother, Chuck Berry, was the last of the family to be employed. He had joined the business in 1976 and worked in a number of departments over the years. In the final years of his tenure he took a position in Community Affairs, an area that he described as his true passion, affording him a chance to represent the company his grandfather founded in a number of Dayton-area philanthropic programs. He retired in January 2006. It was the passing of an era for the company, and possibly the start of a new one was on the horizon, as BellSouth reached an agreement to be acquired by AT&T, which Berry also served, for $67 billion. The two companies also jointly owned yellowpages.com. As a result, Berry's looked forward to an uncertain, yet promising, future.

Ed Dinger

PRINCIPAL SUBSIDIARIES

The Berry Company; Berry Network, Inc.; Berry Sales & Marketing Solutions.

PRINCIPAL COMPETITORS

TransWestern Publishing Company LLC; Verizon Information Services; Yellow Book USA.

FURTHER READING

Berry, Loren M., *L. M. Berry and Company, 1910-1971,* New York: Newcomen Society in North America, 1971 24 p.

Johnson, Kenneth O., "The Yellow Pages Walk Into a New Marketing Age," *Telephone Engineer & Management,* June 15, 1987, p. 108.

Nolan, John, "Berry Waits for Merger's Ripple," *Dayton Daily News,* March 7, 2006.

Saxon, Wolfgang, "John William Berry Sr., 75; Made Fortune on Yellow Pages," *New York Times,* May 23, 1998, p. D16.

Sherrid, Pamela, "How Many Fingers Can Walk to the Bank?," *Forbes,* October 10, 1983, p. 108.

Stern, Aimee, "The Battle of the Yellow Pages," *Dun's Business Month,* April 1986, p. 62.

Labeyrie SAS

Saint Geours de Maremne
St-Vincent-de-Tyrosse,
France
Telephone: (33) 05 58 56 73 00
Fax: (33) 05 58 57 30 41
Web site: http://www.labeyrie.fr

Wholly Owned Subsidiary of Alfesca
Incorporated: 1946
Employees: 1,350
Sales: EUR 345 million ($414 million) (2004)
NAIC: 311612 Meat Processed From Carcasses; 311711
   Seafood Canning

■ ■ ■

Labeyrie SAS is Europe's leading producer of luxury grade "festive foods," including foie gras, smoked salmon, seafood spreads, blini (a sort of pancake originally from Russia and typically served with seafood spreads), caviar, and related specialties.

Based in France's Landes region—the heart of the country's foie gras industry—Labeyrie clearly dominants its primary categories in France and elsewhere, maintaining the number one position in France, Belgium, Switzerland, Spain, and Luxembourg, and holds the number two or three in a number of other European markets. In France, the company's market share for foie gras tops 24 percent, while its share of the smoked salmon market stands at 26 percent. Labeyrie's operations also include those of Blini, the leading producer of blinis, as well as seafood spreads and other

spreads, in France; Vendy, the Spanish smoked salmon leader; and Farne of Scotland. Altogether, the company operates six production facilities in France, Scotland, and Spain.

Seafood, and especially smoked salmon, represents nearly 55 percent of Labeyrie's sales, which reached EUR 345 million in 2004. Foie gras products generate 36 percent of the company's sales, while blinis and spreads add 10 percent to the group's revenue. Labeyrie itself was acquired by Iceland's Alfesca (formerly SIF) in late 2004 for EUR 332 million, and has become the spearhead of that company's European expansion strategy. Following the acqustion, Labeyrie has also been integrating the operations of Alfesca's SIF France subsidiary. Xavier Gavare is the company's CEO.

SUPERMARKET CHANNEL TO SUCCESS 1946 TO 2000

Labeyrie was founded by Robert Labeyrie in Saint Geours de Maremne, not far from Biarritz in France's Landes region along the Atlantic coast. Launched in 1946, Labeyrie grew into one of the region's most prominent producers of foie gras, and other so-called "festive foods"—in France, foie gras was traditionally consumed during the Christmas holiday season. The company specialized in the production of foie gras made from duck liver, as per the regional specialty. A major factor in Labeyrie's rise to market leadership was its early entry into the country's supermarket channels. Into the early 1960s, foie gras and related products tended to be sold in markets and in the country's small grocer shops. Yet the introduction of American-style

KEY DATES

1946: Robert Labeyrie begins the production of foie gras.

1963: Labeyrie makes his first sales to the supermarket sector.

1986: Labeyrie's company is acquired by Européenne de Gastronomie, a part of Bank Suez.

1987: Labeyrie's first television advertising campaign is launched.

1989: The company builds new salmon processing and smoking facilities.

1991: Labeyrie Norge is established in Norway; the company enters a supply agreement with Palmitou.

1992: A new foie gras processing plant, including slaughterhouse, is built.

1996: Labeyrie acquires a majority stake in Palmitou.

1997: The company acquires Salmona, a producer of smoked trout.

1999: Labeyrie makes a public stock offering on Paris Stock Exchange and acquires full control of Palmitou.

2000: The company acquires Vendy, the leading brand of smoked salmon in Spain.

2003: Labeyrie acquires Blini, the French market leader in blini and seafood spreads.

self-service supermarkets in the 1950s had also stimulated demand for a wider range of pre-packaged and prepared foods. In 1963, Labeyrie launched its first sales to the supermarket sector.

This early appearance on the France's supermarket shelves quickly made Labeyrie one of the most recognized foie gras brands among French consumers. Over the next decades, Labeyrie expanded to include another important festive foods category, smoked salmon, which, like foie gras, was a staple food for the country's holiday and festive meals.

Labeyrie's emergence as the dominant player in the French festive foods market came in the mid-1980s when the company was purchased by Européenne de Gastronomie, part of SI Finance, a subsidiary of French financial giant Suez Bank. Under Européenne de Gastronomie, Labeyrie was turned more firmly toward the mass retail sector, which by then had already succeeded in dominat-

ing the French grocery market. The new financial backing enabled Labeyrie to invest in modernizing and expanding its production. In 1989, for example, the company built a new state-of-the art salmon smoking facility. This was followed by a full-scale foie gras production facility, including slaughterhouse, in 1992.

At the same time, Labeyrie had launched its first television-based advertising campaign in 1987, becoming the first foie gras producer to do so. The company's slogan—"Labeyrie à tous ceux qui savent vivre" (Labeyrie for all those who know how to live)—proved highly successful and confirmed Labeyrie's position as market leader.

By 1990, Labeyrie had firmly targeted the mass retail sector as its core distribution channel. In order to meet the volumes necessary to supply its large-scale clients, the company took steps to assure its own supply chain. As part of that effort, the group reached a supply agreement with Palmitou, an independent cooperative organization of duck farmers, including both breeders and force-feeders. By 1996, Labeyrie had acquired a majority stake in Palmitou, completing its control by 1999.

Similarly, Labeyrie sought to ensure its supply of salmon, and in 1991, the company established a dedicated purchasing subsidiary, Labeyrie Norge, which worked with salmon breeder-suppliers in Norway. Back in France, the company also entered into an agreement with agricultural cooperative Lur Berri during that decade, in order to supply duck livers for the company's foie gras production.

PUBLIC OFFERING IN 1999

In the late 19990s, Labeyrie began seeking out new markets. In 1997, for example, the company acquired Salmona, which, despite its name, specialized in the production of smoked trout. The acquisition enabled the group to extend its production into the smoked trout category, which, although only one-tenth the size of the salmon market, was not as closely linked with the holiday season. This not only enabled Labeyrie to spread out its sales more evenly throughout the year, but also to make more efficient use of its salmon preparation and smoking facilities. By the end of the decade, the company had largely substituted its own brand for the Salmona brand.

Labeyrie also entered new food categories, including the production of high-end dried hams, such as Parma hams and Bayonne ham varieties. The company launched the new luxury grade Grand Cru free-range ham at the end of the decade. Labeyrie also extended its range of duck-based products into the next decade. In the meantime, Labeyrie's foie gras production benefited from the creation of a new "Indication Geographique Protegee" appellation, establishing criteria for Landes foie gras. This enabled the company to further outdistance its closest competitors, which produced their foie gras outside of the Landes region.

As it turned toward the new century, Labeyrie prepared for still more growth, and accordingly the company went public in 1999, listing on the London stock exchange. In that year, also, Labeyrie launched an e-commerce capable web site, featuring gift packs and other items for year 2000 celebrations.

The company's public offering permitted it to go on a spending spree in the first years of the new century. In 2000, for example, the company moved into Spain, acquiring that country's market leader Vensy in January of that year. In 2001, Labeyrie entered a new category, that of the production of blini and seafood spreads and other spreads, such as tarmaslata and hummous, acquiring the Prince Egor brand. Although number two behind segment leader Blini, the new subsidiary grew strongly under Labeyrie. In particular, Labeyrie was able to increase the Prince Egor brand's penetration of the mass retail sector. As the clear market leader in its foie gras and salmon categories, Labeyrie had successfully established itself as a "must-have" food item for supermarket shelves, placing the company in a position of relative power vis-à-vis the large scale distribution groups.

In 2001, Labeyrie responded to the merger of two its chief rivals—Montfort and Bizac—with the acquisition of supply partner Lur Berri's Pierre Guéraçague brand of foie gras and delicatessen meats, as well as that company's slaughtering and processing facilities. By the end of 2001, Labeyrie's sales had topped EUR 200 million. The company was not only the market leader in France, it also enjoyed strong international sales, which accounted for nearly 20 percent of total revenues.

ALFESCA FLAGSHIP IN 2006

In 2002, Labeyrie found a new financial partner when Européenne de Gastronomie sold its 67 percent stake in the company to Financière de Kiel, a France-based investment subsidiary of Industri Kapital. Under new management, led by Xavier Gavare, Labeyrie returned to its expansion drive. In 2003, the company acquired Blini, the market leader in the blini and seafood spreads market. Established in 1980, Blini had grown to claim more than 35 percent of its market, through sales of its own Blini brand and through its supply to private label brands.

Following the Blini acquisition, Labeyrie turned to boost its share of the European salmon market. In 2004,

the company turned to Scotland, where it bought Farne of Scotland, a leading breeder and producer of salmon products. That company had been founded in 1982, with just six employees; by 1984, Farne had already launched exports, becoming a major name in the European smoked salmon market.

Labeyrie found itself under new ownership by the end of that year, when Industri Kapital sold its stake in the company to Iceland-based SIF. That company had been engaged in a change of strategy, exiting its U.S. holdings (Iceland Seafood Corporation) in order to refocus itself on the European market. The purchase of Labeyrie helped transformed SIF from a largely seafoods-oriented company to a pan-European luxury foods powerhouse. Labeyrie quickly became the flagship for the "new" SIF—which changed its name to Alfesca in 2006.

Through 2005 and into 2006, Labeyrie focused on integrating its parent company's SIF France operations, which included the Delpierre brand of prepared and marinated seafood. As the jewel in the crown of its new parent company, Labeyrie looked forward to further expansion throughout the European luxury foods market and beyond.

M. L. Cohen

PRINCIPAL SUBSIDIARIES

Blini SAS; Farne Salmon and Trout Ltd; Financiére de Kiel SAS; Gueradis SARL; Labeyrie Norge AS; Palmitou SAS; Pierre Guéracague SAS; SIF France SAS; Vensy Espana S.A.; Vensy Portugal LTDA.

PRINCIPAL COMPETITORS

Floc'h et Marchand; Doux S.A.; Cooperative des Eleveurs de la Region de Lamballe; ALH Loudeac; Societe Vitreenne d'Abattage Jean Roze; Fleury Michon S.A.; Compagnie Generale de Conserve; Socopa; Madrange S.A; SODEBO; William Saurin; Compagnie Saupiquet S.A.; SOVIBA S.A.; Arca.

FURTHER READING

"French Foie Gras Producer, Labeyrie, Acquired by Investment Fund," *European Report*, April 6, 2002, p. 600.

"Icelandic Seafood Group Plans to Buy French Salmon and Foie Gras Producer," *Europe Agri*, October 28, 2004, p. 502.

"Labeyrie has New Owners," *Eurofood*, March 28, 2002.

"Labeyrie," *Le Livre des Grandes Marques*, September 21, 2005, p. 2.

"Premier CyberNoël pour Labeyrie," *Le Journal du Net*, November 9, 1999.

"SIF Changes Strategy, in Final Talks to Acquire Labeyrie Group," *Nordic Business Report*, October 26, 2004.

"Suez pourrai se retirer du capital de Labeyrie," *Capital.fr*, March 15, 2002.

EDUCATION SERVICES

Laidlaw International, Inc.

55 Shulman Boulevard, Suite 400
Naperville, Illinois 60563
U.S.A.
Telephone: (630) 848-3000
Fax: (630) 579-6438
Web site: http://www.laidlaw.com

Public Company
Incorporated: 1924
Employees: 87,400
Sales: $3 billion (2005)
Stock Exchanges: New York
Ticker Symbol: LI
NAIC: 485210 Interurban and Rural Bus Transportation

∎ ∎ ∎

Laidlaw International, Inc., is a Naperville, Illinois-based transportation company with three main divisions. Greyhound Services is the United States's only national provider of scheduled inter-city bus transportation services. Laidlaw Education Services operates 39,000 school buses transporting more than two million students, making it North America's largest school bus operator. The third unit, Laidlaw Transit Services, offers both fixed-route municipal bus service and specialized transportation services for riders with disabilities. Laidlaw is a public company listed on the New York Stock Exchange.

TRUCKING ROOTS: EARLY 20TH CENTURY

Laidlaw International was founded by Robert Laidlaw as a trucking company in 1924 in Haggersville, Ontario, Canada. While the company continues to bear his name, in reality the man behind its growth was Michael G. DeGroote, who bought Laidlaw in 1958. Born on a farm in Belgium in 1933, DeGroote emigrated to Canada with his parents in 1948, settling in southwestern Ontario and struggling to make a living on a tobacco farm. He soon dropped out of high school to take a job driving a truck to help support his family. He went into business for himself at the age of 18 and was able to raise enough money to buy a surplus army truck, which he used to transport dairy farm manure to area tobacco farmers. Just a year later he bought four gravel trucks and set himself up as a fleet operator. He took advantage of a uranium boom in northern Ontario to become a millionaire by the age of 21. When the U.S. government cancelled its order, however, DeGroote was overextended, the business collapsed, and in 1958, at the age of 25, he was forced into bankruptcy. It was just a temporary setback for the ambitious young man. Before the year was out he relocated to the city of Hamilton, secured a $75,000 bank loan, and bought Laidlaw's Transportation Ltd. for $75,000 down and another $250,000 to be paid over ten years.

DeGroote took over 21 trucks and inherited but a single customer, Toronto's Canadian Gypsum Co. Ltd., a business that generated about $400,000 a year. De-Groote wasted little time growing Laidlaw through acquisitions, proving adept at recognizing hidden value and negotiating an advantageous price. To achieve his

COMPANY PERSPECTIVES

Laidlaw International, Inc. is a holding company for North America's largest providers of school and inter-city bus transportation and public transit services.

goal of realizing 25 to 30 percent growth each year, he acquired scores of small trucking outfits. After ten years he was operating some 200 trucks and generating annual revenues of $5 million. In 1969 he took Laidlaw public, its shares being listed on the Toronto Stock Exchange.

Also in 1969 DeGroote began to expand beyond trucking by acquiring a solid waste management company. In the 1970s he would increasingly focus on waste management and other areas, shifting away from the boom-or-bust trucking industry, which had a tendency to rise and fall with the economy. Garbage, on the other hand, always had to be dealt with. Moreover, in 1972 he achieved some diversity by acquiring a Canadian intercity and charter bus company. In 1978 DeGroote moved into the United States solid waste industry. Another recession-proof transportation business that caught his eye during this period was school bus transport. In 1979 he acquired his first school bus business in Canada. DeGroote remained committed to the trucking business, acquiring Buffalo's Boss-Linco Lines Inc. in 1979. However, when the economy stalled, Boss-Linco floundered, forcing Laidlaw to take a $5.9 million write-off in 1982. Two years later, Laidlaw dropped out of the trucking business entirely.

In the meantime, in 1983, Laidlaw entered the U.S. school bus transportation market and in that same year began listing its shares in the United States on the NASDAQ. The main thrust of the company at this stage, however, remained solid waste management. By 1983 a Laidlaw subsidiary was the fourth-largest solid waste management firm in the United States. DeGroote, however, launched an aggressive bid in the U.S. school bus market. A major deal in this regard was the acquisition in two separate transactions in 1983 and 1984 of Van Nuys, California-based ARA Transportation Inc, operator of 4,500 school buses covering school districts throughout the United States. Laidlaw acquired another 11 bus transportation companies in 1985. As a result, Laidlaw became the largest school bus operator in North America, operating about 11,000 buses in the United States and Canada. Busing also became the biggest contributor to Laidlaw's balance sheet, accounting for

half of the company's $550 million in revenues in 1985. Waste disposal accounted for 40 percent, while the soon-to-be-divested trucking segment brought in just 8 percent.

While Laidlaw may have been the largest school bus company on the continent, there was plenty of room for further growth, since the company only controlled about 5 percent of the market in the United States, where approximately 70 percent of the business was done by public contractors. School boards, beset with rising costs, were now looking to turn over busing to private operators like Laidlaw. In addition, small- and medium-sized school bus operators were getting squeezed out of the market by rapidly rising insurance costs. In 1986 Laidlaw attempted to achieve a major growth spurt by acquiring Mayflower Group Inc., known for its moving vans but a company that was also heavily involved in school buses, operating 4,500 of them, thus making it Laidlaw next closest rival. The offer was not welcomed by Mayflower, leading to a hostile takeover attempt by DeGroote. Mayflower implemented anti-takeover measures and in the end he backed off.

DEGROOTE SELLS OUT: 1980-1990

In 1988 DeGroote sold his 47 percent controlling stake in Laidlaw to Canadian Pacific for $450 million in cash and stock. He agreed to stay on as CEO and chairman but in June 1990 retired to Bermuda, where the 56-year-old soon grew bored and again turned his attention to the waste management business. He became the head of a new company called Republic Waste Industries, much to the displeasure of many Laidlaw shareholders who questioned how Canadian Pacific could have possibly allowed DeGroote to leave without signing a non-compete agreement. He was later joined by Wayne Huizenga of Blockbuster Video fame, and the company was renamed Republic Industries. The hazardous waste disposal business was spun off, then through a series of acquisitions ventured far afield and evolved into Century Business Services, Inc., a company that offered outsource business services to small and medium-sized businesses, including accounting and tax preparation, employee benefits, payroll, property and casualty insurance, and consulting.

Replacing DeGroote at Laidlaw Inc. (the company having changed its name earlier in 1990) was Donald K. Jackson, a former competitor DeGroote handpicked. It was also in 1990 that Laidlaw gained a listing on the New York Stock Exchange for its Class A and Class B shares. Jackson had founded a Canadian transportation leasing firm, a company like Laidlaw that was involved in both trucking and waste services. He took over Laidlaw when it was ripe for a fall, however. After posting a

KEY DATES

1924: Robert Laidlaw starts a Canadian trucking company.
1958: Michael DeGroote acquires Laidlaw Transportation.
1969: Laidlaw is taken public on Toronto Stock Exchange.
1979: Company becomes involved in Canadian school bus sector.
1983: Laidlaw enters U.S. school bus market; company is listed on NASDAQ.
1990: DeGroote retires.
1993: Laidlaw acquires MedTrans, an American ambulance service company.
1998: Greyhound Lines is acquired.
2001: Laidlaw files for bankruptcy protection.
2003: Laidlaw emerges from bankruptcy.
2005: The company's health care interests are divested.

net profit of $215 million in fiscal 1990, Laidlaw lost $344 million a year later, while the value of its stock dropped 70 percent. According to *The Economist*, tougher environmental laws created a bureaucracy that was expensive to navigate, but this was only part of the company's problems: "Laidlaw has suffered more than many of its rivals. Mr. DeGroote's acquisition spree was haphazard. In some cities, Laidlaw trucks carry rubbish to other companies' landfills. In others, Laidlaw owns the dumps but not the trucks. None of this mattered much when business booming." In addition, Laidlaw was saddled with a pair of DeGroote-engineered deals that caused more trouble than they were worth: a 35-percent stake in Attwoods, a United Kingdom-based waste-management group that was deep in debt, and the Bermuda-based ADT Ltd. security-systems firm, headed by entrepreneur Michael Ashcroft, with whom Jackson clashed because of ADT's mystifying accounting practices.

In 1991 Laidlaw sued ADT for employing "contrived transactions to fabricate a continuing stream of 'profits' and asset growth." The two parties settled the matter with ADT agreeing to four Laidlaw nominees to its board. Jackson also took steps to reorganize Laidlaw's waste-management unit, including the withdrawal from several U.S. cities. He tried to diversify the bus business by adding commuter bus lines in a number of cities, including Denver, Los Angeles, and San Francisco. He

looked overseas, acquiring waste management companies in Italy. In addition, he took Laidlaw into the U.S. ambulance sector with the June 1993 acquisition of MedTrans. Medical transportation was not only highly lucrative but also a very fragmented industry: No company controlled more than 2 percent of the market. Jackson maintained that Laidlaw was on the verge of strong growth, but by now he had fallen out of favor with his board of directors, and in October 1993, following a board meeting, he tendered his resignation.

Jackson's successor was James Bullock, the former CEO of Cadillac Fairview Inc., one of Canada's largest commercial real estate companies. Canadian Pacific gave Bullock a free hand in restructuring the company, and over the next four years he cast off a number of assets and acquired many others. He dumped the company's stock in ADT and sold off Laidlaw's solid-waste interests. He also followed Jackson's lead and committed the company further into the medical transport sector. In 1995 Laidlaw's MedTrans subsidiary acquired, Santa Ana, California-based CareLine Inc., one of a handful of consolidators in the industry and the third largest ambulance company in America. Since its founding in 1992 CareLine had acquired 22 small ambulance companies located in nine states. MedTrans vied with American Medical Response (AMR) to become the largest ambulance company in the country. In 1996 Laidlaw acquired AMR for $2.2 billion. A year later Laidlaw got involved in a related field that it believed was primed for consolidation, paying $400 million in cash for Dallas-based E Holdings Inc., the United States' largest private operator of hospital emergency rooms. Also in 1997 Laidlaw acquired Spectrum Healthcare Services. The idea was to bundle emergency transportation with physician services in prepaid managed care. Another 1997 acquisition was the DAVE Companies, which specialized in para-transit.

Bullock was active on other fronts as well. In 1997 Laidlaw Environmental acquired Safety-Kleen Corporation, an industrial services provider, and assumed its name. Bullock expanded Laidlaw's passenger-transportation business, adding intercity buses by acquiring Greyhound Canada in 1997 for $44.4 million. A year later Laidlaw acquired Greyhound Lines Inc. in the United States for $816 million and the assumption of $416 million in debt. By reuniting Greyhound, Bullock expected to realize savings in such overhead items as insurance, financing, and head-office expense. Laidlaw also continued to build its school bus business, which Bullock initially considered divesting. Bullock told *Canadian Business,* "The more I looked at the business, the better I liked it." In 1995, a decade after DeGroote failed in his bid to take over Mayflower, Laidlaw acquired its school bus and other passenger transportation business for $157 million. A year later Laidlaw acquired Canada's Charterways and National School Bus Service, based in Buffalo.

BANKRUPTCY TO CLOSE CENTURY

Unfortunately for Bullock, he grew Laidlaw too quickly and took on more debt—approximately $3.1 billion —than the company could handle. By 1999 Laidlaw was in trouble and began taking corrective action. Merrill Lynch & Company was hired to advise the company on the sale of assets to reduce its debt load. Laidlaw elected to sell off Safety-Kleen and its health care operations, hoping to raise more than $2 billion. While buyers were lined up, Laidlaw's directors met in December 1999 and voted to remove Bullock from office. He was replaced by Chief Operating Officer John Grainger.

Laidlaw began negotiating with its principal lenders in 2000 and after a year of talks, the two sides came to an agreement, so that in June 2001 Laidlaw was able to file for Chapter 11 bankruptcy protection and put into effect a restructuring of its massive debt. While this was worked out over the next year of so, a new chief executive was installed in September 2002, Kevin E. Benson. He was the former CEO of Canadian Airlines and prior to joining Laidlaw had served as the president and CEO of the Insurance Corporation of British Columbia.

Laidlaw emerged from bankruptcy protection in June 2003, at which point it assumed the name Laidlaw International Inc. While the company had been able to sell off its interest in Safety-Kleen, it retained AMR and EmCare. The holdings, management believed, were too diverse and made it difficult to sell Laidlaw to investors. It was clearly only a matter of time before the health care business were sold off. In February 2005 a deal was struck, with AMR and EmCare fetching $798 million. The money, along with a new credit facility, was then used to retire more expensive and restrictive debt that was hindering Laidlaw's growth. In addition, $85 mil-

lion was spent to retire some 3.8 million shares of common stock. As a result, management hoped the company was now positioned to grow its remaining assets, but only time would tell if school busing, intercity transport, and para-transit would prove to be a workable combination.

Ed Dinger

PRINCIPAL DIVISIONS

Greyhound Services; Laidlaw Education Services; Laidlaw Transit Services.

PRINCIPAL COMPETITORS

Coach USA, Inc.; First Student, Inc.; National Express Corporation.

FURTHER READING

Aguayo, Jose, "The Consolidator," *Forbes*, October 6, 1997, p. 56.

Ferguson, Ted, "Big Wheel at Laidlaw," *Canadian Business*, September 1986, p. 96.

Greenberg, Larry M., and Wade Lambert, "Laidlaw Suit Says Its ADT Affiliate Gave False Data," *Wall Street Journal*, April 2, 1991, p. B10.

Heinzl, Mark, "Laidlaw Hopes to Raise Over $2 Billion in Sale of Ambulance Unit, Other Assets," *Wall Street Journal*, September 14, 1999, p. 1.

———, "Laidlaw's Board Opts to Remove Chief Executive," *Wall Street Journal*, December 21, 1999, p. 1.

Higgins, Will, "Who is Michael DeGroote?," *Indianapolis Business Journal*, June 6, 1986, p. 1.

Holloway, Andy, "Road to Redemption," *Canadian Business*, May 26, 2003, p. 137.

Waal, Peter, "Ambulance Chaser," *Canadian Business*, November 14, 1997, p. 82.

"Well-Timed Exit: Laidlaw," *Economist*, December 7, 1991, p. 86.

Lenovo Group Ltd.

One Manhattanville Road
Purchase, New York 10577-2100
U.S.A.
Telephone: (914) 701-2800
Toll Free: (866) 96-THINK
Web site: http://www.lenovo.com

Public Company
Incorporated: 1988
Employees: 21,000
Sales: HKD 22.56 billion ($2.90 billion) (2004/05)
Stock Exchanges: Hong Kong ADR
Ticker Symbols: 992; LNVGY
NAIC: 334111 Electronic Computer Manufacturing;
334119 Other Computer Peripheral Equipment
Manufacturing; 423430 Computer and Computer
Peripheral Equipment and Software Merchant
Wholesalers; 541511 Custom Computer Programming Services

■ ■ ■

Lenovo Group Ltd. is a leading global manufacturer of
personal computers (PCs). The company was already the
largest PC manufacturer in China when it acquired
IBM's Personal Computing Division in 2005. In addition, the parent Lenovo Group produces PDAs and
mobile phones, and operates consulting and Internet
ventures. It has several manufacturing sites in China in
addition to IBM's former facility in Raleigh, North
Carolina.

HUMBLE ORIGINS

Like many other high-tech start-ups, Lenovo grew from
modest origins. The Zhongguanchun (Zhong Guan Can)
district of Beijing had a reputation as an electronics
black market; the area would eventually be called the
Silicon Valley of China.

Lenovo is a spinoff of the Legend Group, which
was established in 1984 by a group of eleven computer
scientists led by Liu Chuanzhi. Liu managed with a very
authoritarian style, at least in the beginning, according
to later interviews.

Liu was born in Shanghai; his father worked for the
Bank of China. Liu studied radar systems at the Military
Communication Engineering College until 1966, then
went to work for the China Academy of Sciences (CAS)
in Beijing. Some ill-timed criticism of the Cultural
Revolution got him transferred to a rice paddy in the
late 1960s in an effort to rehabilitate his bourgeois
thinking.

In 1970, Liu began working for the CAS's
Computer Technology Institute. In the early 1980s, as
Deng Xiaoping was reforming the economy, Liu successfully lobbied to start a new computer company (there
was already another state-owned computer
manufacturer).

The CAS provided start-up capital of CNY 200,000,
or $24,000. Legend began by importing a wide range of
equipment from abroad, including roller skates, an
employee told *Time International.* Color televisions and
electronic watches were early flops. An important
technical achievement was the creation of a Chinese
character set for computing in 1985.

Legend was the Chinese distributor for Hewlett-Packard Co. (HP) throughout the 1990s. Liu considered HP "our earliest and best teacher." While distributing HP and Toshiba, the company built the country's first nationwide computer distribution network. This would be a key to its dominance of the market for decades to come. The company's state ownership had given it another advantage in the domestic market, which was rooted in the Communist system.

PUBLIC IN 1994

Legend made its first PC under its own brand in 1990. Four years later, the company was celebrating its one millionth PC built. Also in 1994, some shares of Legend Holdings were listed on the Hong Kong Stock Exchange. The offering raised almost $30 million. The Chinese Academy of Science and Technology remained a major shareholder. Legend became first to bring Western-style stock options and other incentives into the People's Republic, offering stock options as a hiring bonus for new talent.

In 1997, Legend surpassed IBM as the leader in the Chinese market for PCs. It was quick to update its offerings, installing new Pentium chips in its machines while starting, and winning, an aggressive price war with its foreign competitors. By 1999 its market share was about 27 percent. Its closest domestic rival, Founder, had about an 8 percent share. Legend had revenues of $2.4 billion in 1999.

The People's Republic was experiencing an ever-growing demand as businesses modernized to keep up with the expanding economy. There was also a large untapped market for home users. According to *The Economist*, only 4 percent of Chinese households had

PCs in 2001, compared with 60 percent in the United States.

A SUCCESS IN THE NEW MILLENNIUM

Legend, of course, benefited from the low production costs that had foreign electronics manufacturers outsourcing their own production to China. It also knew its home market well, Liu told *Time International*. Legend's Tianxi (Millennium Computer) allowed brand new users to connect to the Internet simply by pushing a button.

The burst of the tech bubble slowed demand for personal computers in the rest of the world, but China's market continued to grow. By 2002, according to *Time International*, it was worth $10 billion, making it the world's third largest behind those of the United States and Japan.

Legend's services unit was spun off as a separate company in June 2001. This included the distribution business, which handled foreign-branded equipment such as Hewlett-Packard PCs and printers and Toshiba notebooks. Legend was building up its IT consulting and systems integration businesses through acquisitions.

Legend Holdings Ltd., the parent company of the Legend Computer Systems Ltd. PC manufacturing business, was developing into a conglomerate. In September 2001 it set up a property development unit called Rong Ke Zhi De. It also established a $30 million venture capital fund. Legend Digital China Holdings, formerly Legend Technology, handled Legend Group's fourth line of business: software and e-commerce services. The company was itself a dedicated user of e-commerce. According to *Business Week*, its 2,000 retailers could order from the entire catalog online.

The Internet was a key part of Legend's growth plan. It acquired a number of portals in the late 1990s, and was in Web-related technology partnerships with Microsoft and others. It also had started manufacturing mobile phones and PDAs.

China's entry into the World Trade Organization opened Legend to new competition from abroad as its foreign rivals were permitted to form their own distribution networks. World leader Dell Inc. soon became Legend's top threat, tying IBM for fifth place in the Chinese market, by bringing its famous low-cost, low-inventory techniques to assembly centers in China.

BUYING IBM PCS IN 2005

Legend Computer Co. Ltd. was renamed Lenovo Group Limited in 2003. Lenovo Group's acquisition of IBM's

KEY DATES

1981: IBM forms a Personal Computing Division (PCD).
1984: Legend is founded in China.
1985: Legend creates a Chinese character set for computing.
1990: Legend builds the first PC under its own brand.
1994: Legend builds its one millionth PC; the company goes public in Hong Kong.
2002: Legend starts making mobile phones.
2003: Legend is renamed Lenovo.
2005: Lenovo acquires IBM's Personal Computing Division.

PC business for $1.75 billion (including $500 million in assumed liabilities) was announced in late 2004. Lenovo officially took over the business in May 2005. As part of the deal, IBM obtained an equity stake in the new company, helping it improve its participation in the Chinese market. Three U.S. private equity firms later invested $350 million.

IBM had introduced the world's first serious personal computer in 1981, freeing corporate IT departments from the mainframe and launching a technology boom. Cutthroat competition from new rivals emerged, and IBM left the retail PC market in 2000. Its PC business slipped from annual revenues of more than $10 billion to $5 billion by 2004. The quality reputation of its Thinkpad series remained high, however. Lenovo retained the right to the IBM brand for five years, but quickly worked to publicize its own name in its new sales territories. Part of the campaign was China's first Olympics equipment sponsorship deal.

Almost all of its 10,000 PC-related employees remained at the unit after the acquisition by Lenovo, at least for a year. Its CEO, Stephen Ward, was replaced after a year by Dell's Asia-Pacific chief, William Amelio. Liu's successor, Yang Yuanqing, had become president and CEO a couple of years earlier while still in his 30s. He became chairman after the IBM deal.

A restructuring followed Lenovo's IBM purchase, which created the world's third largest PC manufacturer after Dell and Hewlett-Packard. Lenovo relocated its headquarters from Beijing to Purchase, New York, near IBM's home, while adding IBM's ThinkCenter in Raleigh, North Carolina to several manufacturing sites in China. Plans to relocate the headquarters to Raleigh

were announced in March 2006; the company also was laying off about 5 percent of its more than 21,000 employees.

In April 2006, the company committed to buy genuine Windows software, a deal worth $1 billion a year for Microsoft Corp. In China, most PCs were sold without operating systems installed and cheap pirated versions were rampant. Lenovo was making emerging markets such as India and South America an important part of its growth strategy.

Frederick C. Ingram

PRINCIPAL COMPETITORS

Dell Inc.; Hewlett-Packard Co.

FURTHER READING

Berdon, Caroline, "Paying Catch-Up: Lenovo's $1.25 Billion Purchase of IBM's PC Division Pushed It Up to Third Place in the World Rankings of Largest PC Vendors. And the Chinese Company May Just Have What It Takes to Close the Gap on the Top Two Still Further," *Office Products International,* July 2005, pp. 25f.

Cordon, Matthew, "Liu Chuanzhi 1944–," in *International Directory of Business Biographies* (Vol. 2), ed. Neil Schlager, Detroit: St. James Press, 2005, pp. 495–97.

FlorCruz, Jaime A., and Isabella Ng, "China's Legend in the Making," *Time International,* May 15, 2000, pp. 10f.

Hamm, Steve, Pete Engardio, and Frederik Balfour, "Big Blue's Bold Step into China," *Business Week,* December 20, 2004, p. 35.

Hansen, Fay, "International Business Machine," *Workforce Management,* July 1, 2005, p. 37.

Heim, Kristi, "Chinese PC Giant Takes on Big Role in Piracy Fight; Lenovo Strikes Deals with Microsoft to Pre-Install Genuine Windows; Company Says It Will Help Growth Strategy," *Seattle Times,* April 18, 2006, p. C1.

Hui Yuk-min, "Legend Chases Conglomerate Dreams," *South China Morning Post,* March 9, 2002.

Hung, Faith, "Legend Extends Deeper into China's Telecom Market—Acquires Assets of Network Systems Integrator," *Computer Database,* November 4, 2002, p. 2.

"IBM Completes Sale of PC Business to Lenovo; IBM and Lenovo Made Minor Modifications to the Terms of the Sale to Win U.S. Government Approval," *InformationWeek,* May 2, 2005.

"A Legend for How Long?," *Business Week,* May 15, 2000, p. 30.

"Legend in the Making: Face Value," *The Economist* (U.S.), September 15, 2001.

Powell, Bill, "The Legend of Legend: Once Upon a Time, a Little Chinese Computer Company Lapped Up the Wisdom of Its Foreign Friends. Then It Ate Their Lunch. What's

Next?," *Fortune International* (Asia ed.), September 16, 2002, pp. 34f.

Rifkin, Glenn, and Jenna Smith, "Quickly Erasing 'I' and 'B' and 'M'," *New York Times,* April 12, 2006, p. C9.

Roberts, Dexter, and Louise Lee, "East Meets West, Big-Time; Lenovo's Deal for IBM's PC Unit Led to a Merger of Talent—And a Threat to Dell," *Business Week,* May 9, 2005, p. 74.

Roderick, Daffyd, "For Whom the Dell Tolls: Can Legend Computer Save China from the World's Largest Boxmaker?," *Time International,* March 25, 2002, pp. 44f.

Sima, Katherine, "Lenovo's Design Strategy Drives Success," *Plastics News,* December 19, 2005, p. 13.

"Special Report: The IBM-Lenovo Deal," *VARbusiness,* January 10, 2005, p. 14.

Walsh, Lawrence M., "Growing Pains—Lenovo Switches Leaders," *VARbusiness,* January 9, 2006, p. 16.

Life is good, Inc.

745 Boylstone Street, Suite 400
Boston, Massachusetts 02116
U.S.A.
Telephone: (617) 266-4160
Toll Free: (888) 878-2987
Fax: (617) 266-4260
Web site: http://www.lifeisgood.com

Private Company
Incorporated: 1997
Employees: 167
Sales: $59 million (2005)
NAIC: 315223 Men's and Boys' Cut and Sew Shirt
(Except Work Shirt) Manufacturing; 315232
Women's and Girls' Cut and Sew Blouse and Shirt
Manufacturing; 422320 Men's and Boys' Clothing
and Furnishings Wholesalers; 422330 Women's,
Children's, and Infants' Clothing and Accessories
Wholesalers; 422340 Footwear Wholesalers; 448140
Family Clothing Stores

■ ■ ■

Life is good, Inc. (LIG) designs and markets T-shirts,
other apparel, and accessories. After coming up with
Jake, the grinning stick figure mascot, and the "Life is
good" slogan in 1994, the company quickly became one
of the fastest-growing in the apparel business, a veritable
textbook case in viral marketing. It quickly diversified
beyond T-shirts into a wide variety of casual clothing
and accessories.

Life is good has been described as a lifestyle brand à
la Ralph Lauren or Nike, except that instead of social
status or athleticism, its adherents aspire to appreciate
life's simple pleasures. The corporate culture is reportedly hardworking but casual. The dress code permits not
just T-shirts but flip-flops and shorts. Ideas are brain-
stormed over beer and sandwiches, not power lunches.

Whatever the company's methods, its results have
attracted the attention of the press, and several suitors
interested in buying out the company. Company
president Bert Jacobs has said that he and his brother
have no interest in selling. They see LIG as a force for
good in the American culture, and spend their advertising dollars on festivals to raise money for charity rather
than on slick media campaigns.

HUMBLE BEGINNINGS

The Life is good, Inc. story is a feel-good tale of two
brothers, John and Bert Jacobs. They grew up the
youngest of six siblings in a suburb of Boston. John
studied art and English at the University of
Massachusetts; Bert majored in communications at Vill-
anova University. They both graduated but then took a
step off the conventional career path.

They decided to sell T-shirts and began selling
products of their own design in 1989. They traveled the
Northeast, hawking their wares at college dorms. A Plymouth Voyager was their mobile boutique.

They lived a low-margin existence, but were able to
land odd jobs such as delivering pizza or substitute
teaching during some of the dry spells. The brothers
reportedly launched the next phase of their adventure
with $78—their accrued earnings of five years.

CREATING "JAKE" IN 1994

Their ticket to material abundance lay in a drawing they had pinned to the wall of their Boston apartment. It was a stick figure John Jacobs had penned that they called Jake—a nickname the Jacobs brothers shared as teenagers. Simple enough for a child to draw, the image would be replicated millions of times on LIG's distinctive, garment-dyed T-shirts.

Jake's infectious grin (the smile taking up half his pie-shaped face) was an instant hit; he made his debut at a 1994 fall craft fair in Cambridge, Massachusetts. The Jacobs brothers sold out of their first batch of four dozen Jake shirts before lunch. Soon about 14 local merchants were stocking the shirts. First year revenues were $80,000, according to the Associated Press.

The *Boston Herald* later revealed that the shirts originally had Jake wearing a beret above the word "draw." The brothers soon realized, however, that artists were not the most lucrative market. Instead, a more universal slogan, "Life is good," completed the T-shirt design. "Those three words mean a lot," Bert Jacobs later said in *Worthwhile* magazine. "Appreciate everything around you. Celebrate today, don't wait until tomorrow." The phrase was chosen from a list of candidates in an informal opinion poll among friends.

There was a simple but important philosophy behind Jake. The message was one of humble optimism. It would be reflected in the company name Life is good, Inc. The company was incorporated in Massachusetts on August 18, 1997, but counts 1994, when Jake was created, as its founding date. It had taken the brothers three years to trademark the "Life is good" name, according to the *Daily News Record*.

The brothers gravitated to different roles. John, the art major, focused on the creative end and Bert, as company president, concentrated on growing the business. The pair apparently did not let administrative details get in the way of having a good time. At Life is good, sandals and shorts would be acceptable corporate attire.

COOL AS EVER IN 1998

By 1998, Life is good products were available at more than 500 outlets. Revenues were an estimated $2 million to $3 million, according to the *Daily News Record*. The company had ten employees at its headquarters in Needham, Massachusetts (the Boston suburb where the brothers grew up), and 21 independent sales reps.

New props and scenarios were created for Jake, often at the request of customers. Many harkened back to the simple pleasures of childhood, such as enjoying an ice cream cone or peanut butter and jelly sandwich (the latter was also the food that sustained the founders through the Jacobs brothers' first few years as entrepreneurs). Whatever hobby or pastime Jake took up, he was always having a good time. Sometimes the graphic did not include Jake but a simple emblem such as a guitar or a mountain. A canine companion, Rocket, was created for Jake in 2003. (A female character, Jackie, had been scrapped, however.) By this time, the company also was pitching pet products.

Baseball caps, knit hats, and shorts were early hits outside of the T-shirt genre. In 1998, the company brought out some products for cooler weather, such as long-sleeved T-shirts and sweatshirts. The company also branched out into loungewear, backpacks, and stickers. Specific products were developed for the golf and yoga markets. The range of accessories extended to coffee mugs, Frisbees, and more.

Although brand extensions were a classic tactic for capitalizing on success, LIG was not willing to skimp on quality to improve margins, Bert Jacobs told *American Executive.* In another interview in *SGB,* he said they were focused on quality, rather than growth per se. "We're much more focused on making higher-quality products, having better merchandising at retail, and servicing better. The idea is not necessarily to get bigger."

The headgear was being made in China. T-shirt manufacturing was contracted to plants in North and South Carolina. In January 2001, LIG licensed production to The Shirt Factory in Derry, New Hampshire; it would buy the company four years later. Even then, it continued to outsource some printing due to demand.

Like other young, hip brands, Life is good benefited from a little celebrity exposure, draping the torsos of notables such as Drew Carey, Matthew McConaughey, and Stephen King, noted *Entrepreneur.* Revenues were up to $3.1 million in 2000 and reached $10 million in 2002.

LAUNCH OF THE PUMPKIN FESTIVAL IN 2003

Philanthropy was an integral part of the company's mission. LIG favored children-related charities such as

KEY DATES

1989: Brothers Bert and John Jacobs design their first T-shirt.
1994: The "Jake" stick figure makes his debut at a Cambridge, Massachusetts, street fair.
2000: Revenues exceed $3 million.
2003: An international unit is established.
2004: LIG sells one million T-shirts in its tenth anniversary year.
2005: LIG buys licensee The Shirt Factory in New Hampshire; annual sales approach $60 million.

Project Joy, an expressive therapy program in Boston, and Camp Sunshine, a Casco, Maine, retreat for children with life-threatening illnesses.

In 2003, the company launched a festival in Portland, Maine, to raise money for Camp Sunshine. The main event was a near miss at setting a new world record for number of jack o'lanterns lit at one time. The charity gained $52,000. Soon the company added a second festival in Boston. One 2005 fundraiser brought in $100,000 while fostering competition in "backyard" events such as watermelon seed spitting.

Such festivals helped introduce people to the brand. The company had gotten even this far without doing much marketing beyond a little trade advertising. According to *American Executive*, the company had developed radio spots but at the last minute decided to allocate the funds toward charitable causes. Proceeds from a special flag-themed T-shirt raised money for the United Way after the September 11, 2001, terrorist attacks on the United States.

Life is good International Inc. was set up in 2003. When the product was exported to non-English-speaking areas, the Life is Good slogan remained in English to preserve the brand and to add an air of mystery, said Bert Jacobs in *American Executive*. Foreign partners were required to support the company's charitable activities; LIG aimed ultimately to take the Pumpkin Festivals to world capitals overseas.

TENTH ANNIVERSARY IN 2004

Revenues were $35 million in 2004, the year Life is good celebrated its tenth year in business. By this time, more than 3,000 retailers were carrying LIG's products. The company was selling more than one million T-shirts a year.

LIG bought its licensee The Shirt Factory in Derry, New Hampshire in March 2005. Financing of $16 million was arranged. The operation was relocated to Hudson, New Hampshire, a few months later due to a need for more space to accommodate an expanding product line, including bulky fleece items.

LIG's products were being distributed as far as Japan and Europe by 2005. The company then had revenues of $59 million and employed about 170 people. Most were based in the small town of Hudson, New Hampshire.

The company had established a new design center and headquarters on Newbury Street in Boston. This became the location of its first store in Boston in July 2005 (in addition, company stores were located in Newburyport, Massachusetts, and Portland, Maine).

By this time, the T-shirt business was accounting for less and less of revenues, percentage-wise. Bert Jacobs told *SGB* the company was developing products using high-performance synthetic fabric for the athletic market. Another new product line was jewelry made of natural materials such as stone and leather.

Large sporting goods chains such as REI and Dick's had embraced the brand for years; many had brand boutiques inside their stores. Bert Jacobs told *SGB*, however, that most of the company's business was coming from small specialty retailers. By early 2006, there were more than two dozen "Neighborhood Shoppes" devoted to stocking LIG products. These were operated by independent retailers who had so much success with LIG products that they stopped carrying other brands.

The press pondered the secret of the company's stellar climb. Perhaps positive sentiment was what the country needed after a couple of decades of cynicism, irony, and negativity. Bert Jacobs took a longer view. "The foundation of our brand is optimism, and optimism is timeless," he told *SGB* magazine. It was a brand the whole family could enjoy, he added.

Life is good was looking forward to eventually being able to raise $100 million a year for charitable causes. The founders reportedly had no plans to sell the company or go public.

Frederick C. Ingram

PRINCIPAL COMPETITORS

Columbia Sportswear Company; Nike, Inc.; Patagonia, Inc.

FURTHER READING

Aull, Liz, "Ain't Life Good?," *Impressions*, December 2005, p. 14.

"Forever Young: Even a Reluctant Economy Can't Curb the Drive and Ambition of These Young Millionaires," *Entrepreneur,* November 2001, pp. 64+.

Goodison, Donna, "Square Preps to Get Taste of the Good Life in Jake Store," *Boston Herald,* March 14, 2006.

Hendrick, Bill, "A Word to the Wise Can Be a Gold Mine," *Atlanta Journal-Constitution,* February 9, 2004, p. A1.

Hurt, Melonee McKinney, "Life Is Good," *American Profile,* November 5, 2005.

"Life is good Inks Loan, Buys N.H. Shirt Finisher," *Boston Business Journal,* March 23, 2005.

McCord, Michael, "Life Has Been Good for Life Is Good Duo," *New Hampshire Business Review,* February 7, 2003, p. A18.

McKinney, Melonee, "Everything's 'Jake' at Life is Good," *Daily News Record,* September 4, 1998, p. 6.

Powell, Jennifer Heldt, "Jake-Pot! 'Good' Life Gets Better," *Boston Herald,* June 6, 2005.

Reimer, Susan, "Message Suits to a T," *Buffalo News,* August 31, 2005, p. C3.

Rose, Jill, "The Right Thing," *American Executive,* August 2005.

Ryan, Thomas J., "Lust for Life; Business Is Good for This Lifestyle Apparel Vendor," *SGB,* January 2006, pp. 30–31.

Soong, Jennifer, "The Sunshine Boys," *Worthwhile,* Premiere Issue, 2004, p. 43.

Spiller, Karen, "Life is good Clothiers Shifts Manufacturing Plant to Hudson, N.H.," *Telegraph* (Nashua, N.H.), July 22, 2005.

Live Nation, Inc.

—■—

9348 Civic Center Drive
Beverly Hills, California 90210
U.S.A.
Telephone: (310) 867-7000
Web site: http://www.livenation.com

Public Company
Incorporated: 1997
Employees: 3,000
Sales: $2.94 billion (2005)
Stock Exchanges: New York
Ticker Symbol: LYV
NAIC: 711310 Promoters of Performing Arts, Sports, and Similar Events with Facilities; 711410 Agents and Managers for Artists, Athletes, Entertainers, and Other Public Figures

■ ■ ■

Live Nation, Inc., is one of the largest owners and operators of venues for live entertainment in the world. Since its founding in 1997 the company has acquired many of the largest concert promotion companies in the United States, Canada, and Europe. It promotes or stages about 30,000 events a year attracting around 60 million attendees. Approximately 90 percent of revenues come from this area. Live Nation companies also manage sports celebrities, promote monster truck shows, and put together touring theatrical productions. The business was acquired by Clear Channel Communications in 2000 and spun off as an independent company five years later.

ORIGINS

SFX founder Robert F. X. Sillerman was born in 1948 and grew up in the world of entrepreneurship and entertainment. His father, Michael McKinley Sillerman, founded the Keystone Radio Network, which went bankrupt when Robert was 13. The younger Sillerman took to the world of business from an early age, founding a greeting card company while still in his teens and a marketing consultation firm while an undergraduate at Brandeis University. Following graduation he worked in the field of marketing, founding National Discount Marketers, Inc., in 1974. In 1978 he formed a business partnership with legendary New York radio personality Bruce "Cousin Brucie" Morrow. Sillerman-Morrow Broadcasting Group bought eight radio stations and a TV station before selling out in 1985. Sillerman continued investing in radio and founded SFX Broadcasting, Inc. with Steven Hicks in 1992 to acquire the stations owned by Command Communications and Capstar Communications. The company's name was created by scrambling Sillerman's middle and last initials. In 1993, SFX Broadcasting went public.

Sillerman was ahead of the curve in radio consolidation, buying up stations at a time when they were relatively cheap. In the early 1990s the Federal Communications Commission loosened rules forbidding ownership of multiple stations in the same market, which helped make owning a string of stations more profitable. SFX acquired additional stations over the next several years, and when the 1996 Federal Telecommunications Act further lifted ownership restrictions, the company went on a buying spree. Purchases of Multi-Market Radio, Inc., ABS Communications, Prism Radio

Our strategy is based on providing the artist and fan with memorable and meaningful live experiences that they will remember for the rest of their lives. The company's focus is on creating those special moments where the live entertainment experience will take fans around the world beyond ordinary and into the extraordinary. We will provide fans with a true connection to their favorite artists and to each other. We believe that fans who have connected with their favorite artist at our live events will download, buy, listen and share memories of the show in ways that represent significant growth opportunities for Live Nation.

Partners, Liberty Broadcasting, and Secret Communications soon increased the company's portfolio to more than 70 stations in 20 markets.

In late 1996 SFX made its first foray into the world of concert promotion with the acquisition of Delsener/Slater of New York, one of the top concert promoters in the northeastern United States. The $20 million deal gave SFX a company that staged concerts at a number of different venues and also operated an 11,000-seat amphitheater on Long Island. Within a few months this new line of business was expanded through the $55 million acquisition of Sunshine Promotions, Inc. of Indiana. Sunshine owned two amphitheaters and an indoor theater and held leases on several others. A new division, SFX Concerts, was formed to operate the two companies. SFX's goal was to utilize its chain of radio stations to advertise the events promoted by this division.

In August 1997 SFX announced that it would be acquired by the Capstar unit of Dallas-based Hicks, Muse, Tate & Furst, led by former Sillerman partner Steven Hicks. The deal was put on hold, however, because of scrutiny by the Justice Department's antitrust division. Meanwhile, SFX was expanding its concert promotions division dramatically. In mid-December four major companies were acquired, including top promoters Bill Graham Presents of San Francisco, Contemporary Group of St. Louis, and Concert/Southern Promotions of Atlanta, as well as Network Magazine Group and SJS Entertainment, a radio and concert industry publishing, research, and production firm. The combined cost was more than $230 million. Just two weeks later a $155 million deal to buy PACE Entertainment Corp. and subsidiary Pavilion Partners was announced. The

Houston-based PACE was the largest producer of touring theatrical productions outside New York City and also promoted concerts and motorsport events, while Pavilion owned 11 amphitheaters around the country. To support the buying spree, SFX sold $350 million in bonds and made arrangements for $300 million in credit.

SFX GOES SOLO; ACQUISITIONS COME FAST AND FURIOUS IN 1998

In the spring of 1998 SFX Broadcasting received clearance for its acquisition by Hicks, Muse, Tate & Furst, with newly christened SFX Entertainment, Inc. to be spun off as a separate entity. Shortly thereafter, five more major acquisitions were announced. SFX Entertainment would spend $227 million to purchase concert promoters Avalon Attractions of Los Angeles and Don Law's Blackstone Entertainment of New England, souvenir company Event Merchandising, Inc., the Oakdale Theater of Wallingford, Connecticut, and Falk Associates Management Enterprises (FAME), an agency that represented basketball stars such as Michael Jordan and Patrick Ewing. After this batch of acquisitions, SFX asserted that it had gained control of more than 40 percent of the concert market nationwide.

SFX's national buying binge was causing much consternation within both the investment community and the traditionally fragmented, regionally based concert touring business. Some questioned the premium prices being paid for promotion companies, whose take on a typical event was usually only three to four percent of the gross. Others wondered about Sillerman's agenda, insisting that he was merely repeating his radio game plan of consolidating a fragmented industry so that he could drive up prices and sell out when the market peaked. He denied this charge, insisting that he expected his then six-year-old daughter to take over the company from him when she grew up. Entertainment business insiders predicted a negative impact on up-and-coming acts, who would not have the name recognition to be booked into SFX's nationwide circuit of venues. Some talent agents also feared that performers would book tours directly with SFX, eliminating the need for their services in dealing with multiple promoters across the country. Most observers predicted that SFX would ultimately have to raise ticket prices in order to turn a profit, possibly causing a backlash among audiences in the process. The company denied this, too, stating that the best seats would likely become more expensive, but that others in the rear could be reduced in price and the overall balance would remain the same.

In July 1998 SFX purchased sports marketing firm Marquee Group for $100 million. Sillerman had helped

KEY DATES

1996: SFX Broadcasting buys concert promoter Delsener/Slater.

1997: The SFX Entertainment division is founded; Bill Graham Presents and other properties are acquired.

1998: SFX Entertainment, Inc. is spun off; an exclusive deal with Ticketmaster is signed.

1999: The company completes its first European acquisitions; the SFX Sports Group is formed.

2000: Clear Channel Communications buys SFX Entertainment.

2002: SFX Entertainment is renamed Clear Channel Entertainment.

2005: The company is spun off as Live Nation, Inc. on the New York Stock Exchange.

launch it in 1994 and owned nine percent of its stock. A month later Magicworks Entertainment, Inc. was acquired, also for $100 million. This Miami-based company promoted concerts and managed touring events such as magician David Copperfield and the musicals *Jekyll & Hyde* and *Evita*. It had been a partner of PACE unit PACE Theatricals for some time. Also acquired was production company American Artists, which controlled several theaters in the Boston area.

A big coup for SFX came in August, when it made a deal to buy Cellar Door Companies for $105 million. Cellar Door promoted concerts in the Midwest and South, and had been one of the last major holdouts against the SFX onslaught. Jack Boyle, Cellar Door's head, was placed in charge of SFX's music division. The company also formed a new unit, SFX Live, which was to market entertainment events on a national basis.

CONTROVERSY FOLLOWING SFX'S RAPID GROWTH: 1998–1999

In late summer the U.S. Justice Department launched an informal inquiry into whether the company was attempting to monopolize the concert promotions business. Several major entertainment industry figures also were criticizing SFX in the press, including top Creative Artists Agency agent Tom Ross and USA Networks CEO Barry Diller, whose company owned Ticketmaster. Each of these sparks soon fizzled, however. The Justice probe was dropped by the end of the year, Ross left CAA in part because of his comments about SFX, and the company suddenly signed a deal with

Ticketmaster giving the latter exclusive ticketing rights to all SFX events for seven years. SFX-owned companies Next Ticketing and Capital Ticketing were to be folded into Ticketmaster as part of the arrangement.

In January 1999, SFX spent $18 million for talent agency Integrated Sports International and quickly followed this up with a $100 million deal to acquire interest in seven concert venues. April saw the announcement of a plan to buy TourVen, Inc., a promoter of traveling shows such as "Barney's Big Surprise." In the summer SFX stock moved from the NASDAQ to the New York Stock Exchange, and the company acquired Hendricks Management Co., a baseball player representation firm. SFX also launched an online ticketing site, SFX.com, in conjunction with Ticketmaster.

The summer of 1999 saw court approval granted for the $96 million purchase of the bankrupt Livent, a deal that had been initiated a year earlier. Livent, once one of the premier theatrical production companies, owned such touring shows as Ragtime and Fosse, as well as a number of venues in Canada and the United States. Its bankruptcy had been attributed to widespread accounting fraud.

More acquisitions followed, including the purchase of figure skating promoter Candid Productions and SFX's first European company, Apollo Leisure Group of the United Kingdom. The $254 million Apollo deal gave SFX control over more than 25 theaters in the United Kingdom as well as Tickets Direct, a ticketing agency. To keep the ball rolling, SFX arranged for another $1.1 billion in credit and offered 8.6 million new shares of stock at $41 each. A deal with American Express to become SFX's official card also was signed, one of a string of relationships with corporate sponsors such as Levi's, VH1, and Ford that the company had negotiated. One of SFX's goals was to increase the amount of national advertising at each venue it controlled, with the company now running commercials on giant video screens before some performances.

In the face of SFX's increasingly firm grip on the market, 11 of its competitors formed the Independent Promoters Organization (IPO) to collectively bid for the services of major acts. Members of IPO would include number two U.S. concert promoter Universal Concerts, Metropolitan Entertainment, Belkin Productions, and others. Some performers, including Eric Clapton, Celine Dion, and Shania Twain, had avoided SFX venues at their agents' insistence. The company produced successful tours of its own, however, including those of 'N Sync, Cher, and the Backstreet Boys. Ticket sales in general were up, and SFX claimed $750 million worth had been sold during the year compared with $600 million for 1998.

ENTERING THE 21ST CENTURY: A GROWING PRESENCE IN EUROPE

European expansion was now on SFX's agenda, and in September Midland Concert Promotions Group Ltd. was acquired. The British company produced concerts, wrestling, and motorsport events and had sizable real estate holdings. SFX also had bought Barry Clayman Corp. of the United Kingdom in August, and EMA Telstar Group of Stockholm in September. A month later SFX acquired 80 percent of Mojo Works of the Netherlands, the leading promoter in that country.

The company also was building its sports business. New purchases included SME Power Branding, a sports brand identity firm whose clients included Major League Baseball, and Tellem and Associates, a baseball talent agency. At year's end SFX consolidated the 14 sports companies it owned into SFX Sports Group, which would be headed by FAME CEO David Falk. The company also was concentrating on building its own brand identity, and over the next few months began to add the initials SFX to the names of its subsidiaries.

SFX was adding to its online presence as well, making a minority investment in David Bowie's Ultra-Star Internet Services LLC, which hosted official web sites for entertainers and sports teams. The company also formed a joint venture in Europe with World Online to create a music, sports, and theater Internet portal.

Early March 2000 saw the predictions of some of Sillerman's detractors come true when it was announced that SFX would be sold to radio giant Clear Channel Communications of Texas. The deal would give SFX stockholders $3 billion, with Clear Channel also taking on $1.1 billion in debt. Clear Channel owned 867 radio stations and 19 television stations in the United States, as well as 550,000 outdoor advertising displays. SFX now owned or operated 120 entertainment venues in 31 markets, offered touring Broadway shows in 55, and was the largest promoter of monster truck shows in the country. SFX Sports represented 650 athletes and sports broadcasters.

While the deal was being finalized, SFX continued its buying spree, picking up Electric Factory Concerts of Philadelphia and Jujamcyn Productions of Minneapolis, a touring theatrical production company. SFX already owned half of Jujamcyn, acquired through PACE Entertainment. Sports Management Group also was purchased by the company in May 2000 and was promptly folded into SFX Sports Group. Shortly thereafter, Canada's second largest concert promoter, Core Audience Entertainment, was acquired.

SFX stood unchallenged as the leader of the U.S. live entertainment field. The changes its frenetic buying activity had wrought in the marketplace were still being assessed, however, and SFX was still developing its own identity as a company rather than as merely the sum of many parts. Acquisition by the nation's largest radio conglomerate would create further opportunities for expansion and new marketing synergies, but it would take time before the full impact of this relationship became known.

Clear Channel officially acquired SFX Entertainment Inc. in August 2000; it was renamed Clear Channel Entertainment (CCE) two years later. A number of its subsidiaries continued to retain the well-known SFX prefix in their names.

The expected synergies of a top radio network owning a top concert promoter failed to materialize in the few short years that Clear Channel owned the former SFX Entertainment. The division had 2004 sales of $2.8 billion, or nearly 30 percent of Clear Channel's total revenues, and a meager net income of $16.3 million. Its 3,300 full-time employees (and up to 15,900 summer part-timers) produced 28,500 events during the year.

Overall concert attendance was slipping, though some marquee acts were commanding ticket prices in the three-digit range. Live Nation produced tours for the likes of Sting and Madonna in 2004, while staging productions of successful plays including *Chicago* and *The Producers*.

SPIN OFF IN 2005

In May 2005 Clear Channel suddenly announced the spin-off of its entertainment business. (The outdoor advertising unit was also being made independent.) The tax-free spin-off to shareholders was completed in December 2005, after which the unit, called CCE Spinco, Inc. for a time, was renamed Live Nation, Inc. Its shares were listed on the New York Stock Exchange. The unit's headquarters was relocated to Los Angeles, home to Michael Rapino.

Rapino, a Toronto native, had been named CEO in September 2004 after heading the group's European music operations. One of his first acts was to bring back the brand identities of a dozen different United States promoters that CCE had acquired over the years and then squelched, such as Cellar Door and Electric Factory. These brands were applied to newly organized regional divisions. The company's aim in the United States was to return to a more traditional way of developing bands, Rapino said in *Amusement Business*. It had been the company's practice in Europe to retain well-known names there.

Revenues were more or less flat at $2.9 billion in

2005; the global music business accounted for 79 percent of the total. Live Nation dipped into the red in the fourth quarter with a $134.9 million loss. This resulted in a $130.6 million deficit for the year. In the last half of 2005, the company cut 300 jobs and scaled back its network of regional offices. While valued at more than $1 billion, the company had a total debt of about $367 million, noted *Billboard.*

According to *Billboard,* Live Nation was considering taking over food and beverage sales at its shows as a way to boost revenues. These concessions were then operated by Aramark, whose contract was ending in 2007. CEO Michael Rapino was also reexamining ticket sales, which were mostly handled by Ticketmaster, whose exclusive arrangement was up for renewal in 2008. Rapino suggested developing LiveNation.com into a kind of entertainment portal.

Live Nation was also increasing its stadium management business, inking a deal to run London's Wembley Arena for 15 years. Live Nation owned more than 40 of its own amphitheaters, and rented out more than 100 venues.

Live Nation added a novel new revenue stream with its mid-decade investment in the rock group Korn (a 30 percent stake of which the recording label EMI already owned); in January 2006, the company bought a 6 percent share of the band's future revenues for $3 million.

Frank Uhle
Updated, Frederick C. Ingram

PRINCIPAL SUBSIDIARIES

American Artists Ltd., Inc.; Live Nation (Venues) UK Ltd.; Atlanta Concerts, Inc.; Avalon Acquisition Corporation; Barry Clayman Corporation Ltd. (United Kingdom); Bill Graham Presents, Inc.; Cellar Door Holding Company; Concert Southern Chastain Promotions; Contemporary Group, Inc.; Delsener/Slater Enterprises, Ltd.; DLC Corporation; Electric Factory Concerts, Inc.; EMA Telstar Gruppen AB (Sweden); Event Merchandising Inc.; Irving Plaza Concerts, Inc.; Jujamcyn Productions Company, LLC; Magicworks Concerts, Inc.; Live Nation (Music) UK Limited; Mojo Works b.v. (Netherlands; 80%); NEXT Ticketing, LLC; Oakdale Theater Concerts, Inc.; PACE Entertainment Corporation; Rainbow Concert Productions, Inc.; SFX Broadway, Inc.; SFX Entertainment, Inc.; SFX Family Entertainment, Inc.; SFX Marketing, Inc.; SFX Rights, LLC; SFX Sports Group LLC; SFX Theatrical Group, Inc.; Sunshine Concerts LLC; Westbury Music Fair LLC.

PRINCIPAL DIVISIONS

Global Music; Global Theater.

PRINCIPAL COMPETITORS

Anschutz Entertainment Group; House of Blues Entertainment, Inc.; Nederlander Producing Company of America, Inc.; SMG Entertainment, Inc.

FURTHER READING

Brownlee, Lisa, "Texas Titan's Big Corral—Radio Cowboy's New SFX Deal Jacks Up His Entertainment Clout," *New York Post,* March 5, 2000, p. 62.

Cavazos, Nick, "The New America: SFX Broadcasting, Inc. Riding a Strong Rebound in Radio Industry," *Investor's Business Daily,* January 24, 1995, p. A4.

"Clear Sign of Times: Conglom to Spin Off Live Entertainment Arm," *Daily Variety,* May 2, 2005, p. 5.

Conniff, Tamara, "Q&A: Clear Channel Chairman/CEO Becker Discusses Industry, the Future," *Amusement Business,* November 3, 2003, p. 4.

Furman, Phyllis, "SFX Marks the New Spot: Radio's Sillerman Ready to Go Live from New York," *New York Daily News,* March 9, 1998, p. 20.

Gosselin, Peter G., "SFX Chief Spends $1B to Become Concert King," *Boston Globe,* November 15, 1998, p. A1.

Hamerman, Joshua, "Live Nation Gets Serious About Entertaining M&A," *Mergers and Acquisitions Report,* March 27, 2006.

Harrington, Richard, "A Concert Promoter Out to Steal the Show?" *Washington Post,* August 28, 1998, p. B1.

La Monica, Paul R., "Live Nation: A Hot Ticket?" *CNNMoney.com,* January 4, 2006.

Lorek, L.A., "Clear Channel Spinoff Falls After NYSE Debut," *San Antonio Express-News,* December 23, 2005.

Milner, Brian, "Courts Approve Livent Sale to SFX," *Globe and Mail,* July 9, 1999, p. B3.

Morse, Steve, "SFX Deal Is Part of Industry Trend: Fallout for Concertgoers and Musicians Unclear," *Boston Globe,* May 5, 1998, p. C1.

Newman, Melinda, "Indie Concert Promo Biz Reshaped by SFX's Rise," *Billboard,* September 4, 1999, p. 1.

Petrozzello, Donna, "Robert F.X. Sillerman," *Broadcasting & Cable,* July 11, 1994, p. 69.

Sandler, Adam, "Sea Change—SFX Rewrites Rules of Concert Game," *Daily Variety,* July 30, 1998, p. A1.

Sixel, L.M., "Live Nation Is Going to L.A.," *Houston Chronicle,* Bus. Sec., December 23, 2005, p. 1.

Stieghorst, Tom, "SFX Broadcasting Goes on Buying Spree in Concert-Promotion Business," *Knight-Ridder Tribune Business News,* February 15, 1998.

Sullivan, Jim, "When It Comes to Pop Concerts, He Is the Player," *Boston Globe,* May 16, 1999, p. N1.

Waddell, Ray, "Giant SFX Makes $750M in '99 Grosses," *Billboard,* January 8, 2000, p. 106.

——, "Giant SFX, Ticketmaster Strike Deal," *Amusement Business,* November 23, 1998.

————, "Korn's Live Nation Deal Likely to Be a Winner," *Billboard*, January 28, 2006, p. 26.

————, "Live Nation Adjusting to 'Public' Life: CEO Michael Rapino Keeps Door Open for Change at Venues," *Billboard*, January 28, 2006, p. 16.

————, "Live Nation Eyes Concessions, Ticketing to Drive Revenue," *Billboard*, March 4, 2006, p. 8.

————, "Radio's SFX Buys Delsener/Slater," *Amusement Business*, October 21, 1996, p. 6.

————, "SFX Buys Three Concert Promoters," *Billboard*, December 27, 1997, p. 98.

Wilker, Deborah, "Clear Channel Plays the Classics: Company Is Using Promoter Labels of the Past as Part of New Plan to Conduct Business," *Amusement Business*, January 2005, pp. 6f.

LÖWENBRÄU

Löwenbräu AG

Nymphenburger Strasse 7
Munich, 80335
Germany
Telephone: (49) 89 52 00-0
Fax: (49) 89 52 00 3412
Web site: http://www.loewenbraeu.de

Wholly Owned Subsidiary of Spaten-Löwenbräu-Gruppe
Incorporated: 1872
Employees: 250
Sales: DEM 107 million ($68 million) (2003)
NAIC: 311213 Malt Manufacturing; 312111 Soft Drink Manufacturing; 312112 Bottled Water Manufacturing; 312120 Breweries

■ ■ ■

Löwenbräu AG brews a range of beverages including light beer and soft drinks. It has production joint ventures in dozens of countries, but has resumed direct imports from Munich to the United States and the United Kingdom. The company replaced its partners in those markets after its brand languished from a lack of marketing support.

In the 1970s, Löwenbräu led the development of the U.S. imported beer market. Sales plummeted, however, after Miller Brewing Company took over American distribution and diluted the integrity of the brand by brewing a domestic imitation. In the late 1990s, Löwenbräu replaced its partners in the United States, the United Kingdom, and Canada.

A series of mergers combined Löwenbräu with the venerable Spaten brewery group. This was acquired by Interbrew in 2002. Since Interbrew merged with AmBev to form InBev, the Löwenbräu brand has been supported by the largest brewing group in Germany and the world.

BEGINNING A BRAND IN 1383

Löwenbräu, German for "lion's brew," is considered to be one of the world's oldest brand names. It dates back to a beer made by the proprietor of Munich's Zum Löwen, or Lion's Inn, in 1383. One story, retold in the brand's U.S. television ads of the 1980s, maintains that the lion was chained to the beer barrels to discourage pilferage. The earliest recorded instance of the word "Löwenbräu" is in the 1746 Munich brewers' registry. The Löwenbräu trademark was first registered in the United States in 1897.

No country is more closely associated with beer than Germany, and Bavaria is the source of much of the country's drinking culture. A number of brewing regulations have come from the region since the 12th century, some of them detailing medieval punishments such as beatings, exile, or death for bad brewing. In 1516, Germany's famous "Reinheitsgebot" purity law was decreed by Wilhelm IV, Duke of Bavaria (a similar code had been adopted by Munich brewers some 30 years earlier). The Reinheitsgebot allowed only four ingredients for beer: water, barley malt, yeast, and hops. It remained in practice centuries later—minus the rule limiting the price of a liter to one or two pfennig. (The law did not become mandatory throughout the whole of Germany until 1906.)

COMPANY PERSPECTIVES

When trying to impress a beautiful Fraulein, order her a Löwenbräu. Once it arrives at the table, lean in close and say: Did you know—Löwenbräu is a traditional Munich-style beer that's exclusively imported from the Löwenbräu brewery in Munich. Löwenbräu Original Lager beer is made from the highest quality ingredients giving it a superb natural head, golden color, distinctive, refreshing flavor and a pleasant, enjoyable aftertaste. Brewed according to the Bavarian "Reinheitsgebot" (Purity Law) dating back to 1516.

Löwenbräu beer's production was rooted in the local geography. Water flowed from pristine Alps. Southern Germany was famous for its hops. The locale had its drawbacks; it was far from seaports, which would make exporting expensive.

FIRST OKTOBERFEST IN 1810

Located in Munich, Löwenbräu has remained one of a handful of brewers allowed to participate in Oktoberfest. Its history at the event goes back 200 years. The first of these festivals was held in 1810 to celebrate the marriage of crown prince Ludwig of Bavaria and Therese of Saxon-Hildburghausen.

Georg Brey acquired Löwenbräu in 1818. He and his son Ludwig relocated the brewery to Munich's Nymphenburger Strasse between 1826 and 1851. This would remain its home for more than 150 years. By 1863, Löwenbräu was Munich's leading brewer, according to *Datamonitor*. It became a joint stock company in 1872 after the Breys sold it.

By 1900, according to company literature, the brewery was one of the biggest in Europe. Production was halved during World War I due to rationing. Löwenbräu merged with Unionsbrauerei Schülein & Cie. in 1921, and returned to rapid growth between the wars. The company began making a wheat beer in 1927. Production exceeded one million hectoliters (26 million gallons) in 1928.

Allied bombing devastated the brewery during World War II, however. It was rebuilt after the war and soon expanded its international distribution. It became a leader among the 2,000 breweries in West Germany alone. By the mid-1970s, Löwenbräu, which produced its own malt, was using about 20,000 tons of barley a year.

The United States was then importing only 1 percent of its beer, according to *Beer Blast*. Löwenbräu had become its top German import, more or less tied with Heineken of The Netherlands in market share. A shift to local brewing, however, ended up watering down the brand.

U.S., U.K. PARTNERS IN 1974

After Miller, a subsidiary of Philip Morris, Inc., took over the brand in America in 1974, it made some changes to the formula in addition to setting up its own production and reportedly obscuring its U.S. origin on labeling. Other grains, such as corn grits, were added to the barley in the malt, alleged a Federal Trade Commission complaint by Miller's rival Anheuser-Busch, Inc., and there were shortcuts in the fermentation process.

In 1982, the family of businessman August von Finck, reportedly the wealthiest man in Bavaria, acquired 90 percent holding in Löwenbräu AG (through the holding company Agricola Verwaltungs-Gesellschaft). According to London's *Financial Times,* von Finck acquired the company because of his love of beer. About 10,000 acres of land near Munich was acquired along with the brewery.

In the United States, the brand was being pitched under the tagline, "This world belongs to Lowenbrau," and, indeed, Löwenbräu's influence was being felt globally in the mid-1980s. By one count, the beer was being exported to 140 countries. In 1983, Löwenbräu signed an agreement to have Asahi Breweries, Ltd. brew the drink for Japan, where the German version had been imported for six years. It also was being brewed under license in several other countries.

Later, the slogan was modified to "This night calls for Lowenbrau" (which was coincidentally quite similar to a Michelob campaign, noted *Advertising Age*). The television advertising was elaborate, featuring a troop of professional dancers and techno music. Miller Brewing Co. spent $20 million in 1986 to promote the brand in the United States, according to *Advertising Age*. The TV advertising was later cut, however, to focus on point-of-sale promotion. In spite of the marketing efforts, U.S. sales of Lowenbrau fell 30 percent by 1989. Miller tried producing a light beer version.

Löwenbräu ended the 1980s with a number of new ventures. Siegsdorfer Petrusquelle and Staatlicher Mineralbrunnen were acquired to bolster Löwenbräu's mineral water business. The company was brewing in China, and had bought a former Carlsberg brewery in Greece. In 1989 it acquired a 95 percent stake in Rosenheim, Germany's Schlossbrauerei Hohenaschau, established in 1549.

KEY DATES

1383: The proprietor of Munich's Zum Löwen begins brewing beer.

1516: The Bavarian "Reinheitsgebot" (Purity Law) is decreed.

1746: The "Löwenbräu" name appears in the Munich brewers' registry.

1810: Löwenbräu flows at the very first Oktoberfest.

1818: Georg Brey acquires the brewery.

1872: Löwenbräu becomes a joint stock company.

1851: The brewery relocates to Nymphenburger Strasse in Munich.

1897: The Löwenbräu trademark is registered in the United States.

1928: Annual production exceeds 26 million gallons (one million hectoliters).

1945: The brewery is rebuilt after World War II.

1970: Production is 40 million gallons (1.5 million hectoliters).

1974: Licensing deals are signed in the United States and the United Kingdom.

1982: The Von Finck family acquires a 90 percent stake in Löwenbräu AG.

1992: Löwenbräu posts its first annual loss in decades.

1997: Spaten-Franziskaner-Brau KGaA buys a majority of Löwenbräu AG.

1999: Labatt USA takes over Löwenbräu in the United States.

2002: After a return to Britain, Löwenbräu Original is again exported from Munich to the U.S. market.

2004: InBev acquires Spaten and Löwenbräu.

INTO THE RED IN 1992

The brewery posted its first annual loss in decades, about DEM 8 million, for the 1991–92 fiscal year. Production volume slipped to about four million hectoliters and turnover fell slightly to DEM 342 million. At the time, Löwenbräu AG was changing into a holding company overseeing three operational units: brewing, soft drinks, and real estate. It was suffering from losses at a former Calsberg brewery it took over in Greece.

Lowenbrau established a U.K. subsidiary in 1993. The brew remained a top seller in its category in the United Kingdom through the early 1990s, in spite of minimal marketing support from its distributor there,

according to *Campaign*. The brand had been controlled in Britain by Allied Domecq. It was part of the Carlsberg-Tetley taken over by rival brewer Carlsberg in 1993. Löwenbräu then formed another U.K. unit, and in 1998 handed off this business to Ushers of Trowbridge.

In 1996, Miller was introducing a line of "Lowenbrau Craftbiers" to compete for the "more adventurous" U.S. consumer, reported *Advertising Age*. Miller had been producing Special and Dark varieties under the Lowenbrau brand. By this time, Miller's annual ad support for the brand had dwindled. U.S. sales fell as well, to about 400,000 barrels a year from a mid-1970s peak of more than one million. Domestically, Löwenbräu was having a tough time competing against its neighbors in the alcohol-free segment.

BOUGHT BY SPATEN IN 1997

A well-known Upper Bavaria brewing group, Gabriel Sedlmayr Spaten-Franziskaner-Bräu KGaA, acquired a 96 percent interest in Löwenbräu AG in October 1997. (Von Finck's holding company had been renamed "Custodia Holding AG" a couple of years earlier.) While Löwenbräu would brew separately from the group's other brands (Spaten, Franziskener wheat beer, etc.), there was some opportunity for cost savings by combining marketing, administration, and other functions.

The brewery had been losing money, posting a net deficit of DEM 18 million in 1996–97. The loss was cut in half the next year, though sales fell 13 percent to DEM 250 million. Financial troubles in Asia and Eastern Europe cut sales to those regions, while Austria, Italy, Spain, and Latin America were growth markets. Löwenbräu continued to sign up new joint venture partners. By 1999, Löwenbräu was being brewed in a dozen countries, including India, Israel, and Egypt. Löwenbräu's sales were DEM 121.6 million in 1998, when the company posted a $5.8 million loss.

LABATT TAKING OVER IN THE UNITED STATES IN 1999

Löwenbräu AG replaced Miller as its U.S. partner with Labatt USA in September 1999. Labatt USA, a joint venture between Canada's Labatt Brewing Co. Ltd. and Mexico's FEMSA Cerveza S.A. de C.V., had a mandate to increase ad spending for the brand. Labatt had taken over Löwenbräu's production in Canada two years earlier, replacing Molson Brewery. Labatt Brewing was owned by Belgium's Interbrew S.A. Labatt promptly returned production to the few ingredients specified in the German purity law.

Löwenbräu's total sales slipped to DEM 103 million in 2000; however, the company was able to post a profit of DEM 499,000 after losing DEM 7 million in the previous two years. By this time, its brands included Loewenbraeu Muenchener Hell, Loewenbraeu Premium Pilsener, Loewenbraeu Premium Lager, Loewenbraeu Special, Loewen Weisse, Loewenbraeu Alkoholfrei, and Loewenbraeu Light.

After the closure of its brewing partner Ushers, Löwenbräu was relaunched in Britain in 2001 by Refresh UK PLC, a new drinks marketer. This time, it was imported directly from Munich.

PART OF A LEADING GLOBAL GROUP IN 2004

The Belgian brewery giant InBev bought the brewery operations of the Spaten group for DEM 477 million ($537 million) in 2004. Spaten, which had been brewing for more than 600 years, was shifting to the real estate business. Its brewery business, including Löwenbräu, was officially combined with InBev affiliate Interbrew Deutschland in October 2004. This made Interbrew Deutschland, which also included Beck's, the top brewer in Germany based on total sales.

InBev had been formed by the merger of Interbrew with Companhia de Bebidas das Américas (AmBev). The largest brewing group in the world, InBev was taking the Löwenbräu brand to Romania in 2006. It also took over a licensed operation in Russia from a unit of Heineken N.V.

Frederick C. Ingram

PRINCIPAL COMPETITORS

Diageo PLC; Heineken N.V.; Paulaner Brauerei GmbH & Co. KG; Scottish & Newcastle PLC.

FURTHER READING

Arndorfer, James B., "Labatt to Up Ad Spending Behind Lowenbrau in U.S.: Brewer Demanded More Support After Dropping Miller," *Advertising Age*, August 25, 1997, p. 28.

"Austrian Becomes New Chairman of Loewenbraeu," *Boersen-Zeitung*, September 22, 1992, p. 9.

"Banker with a Bent for Brewing," *Financial Times* (London), Sec. III, Financial Times Survey, West German Banking and Finance, June 9, 1982, p. VII.

"Beermaker May Export Famed Brew," *St. Louis Post-Dispatch*, April 16, 1989, p. 1E.

Behringer, Wolfgang, *Löwenbrau: von den Anfängen des Münchner Brauwesens bis zur Gegenwart*, München: Suddeutscher Verlag, c1991.

"Ein Bier Wie Bayern," *Horizont*, July 31, 1997, p. 71.

"Foreign Beer Prod. Will Start Here," *Japan Economic Journal*, January 25, 1983, p. 17.

Garfield, Bob, "Lowenbrau Light Makes Bow to Germanic Artistic Imagery," *Advertising Age*, November 20, 1989, p. 46.

"Inbev Launches New Brand in Romania, Targets Wider Market Presence," *SeeNews*, April 5, 2006.

"Interbrew Agrees to Buy German Brands," *FT Investor*, September 18, 2003.

"Interbrew Pays £332M for Lowenbrau Maker," *The Independent* (U.K.), September 19, 2003.

Jack, Ian, "Labatt to Brew Lowenbrau," *Financial Post* (Toronto), Sec. 1, August 19, 1997, p. 3.

Khermouch, Gerry, "Miller Hands Off Lowenbrau to Labatt," *Brandweek*, August 18, 1997, p. 1.

Kramer, Larry, "Brewer Sues [*sic*] U.S. Maker of Lowenbrau," *Washington Post*, November 11, 1977, p. F1.

"Lion-Hearted," *Financial Times* (London), Sec. I, August 12, 1983, p. 8.

"Loewenbraeu Acquires Carlsberg Atalanti Brewery," *Frankfurter Allgemeine Zeitung*, August 31, 1989, p. 16.

"Loewenbraeu AG of West Germany Plans to Expand Its Presence on the Mineral Water Market," *Frankfurter Allgemeine Zeitung*, January 26, 1988, p. 17.

"Loewenbraeu Falls into the Red in 1991/92," *Frankfurter Allgemeine Zeitung*, April 1, 1993, p. 20.

"Loewenbraeu—Profits Expected in Two Years," *Frankfurter Allgemeine Zeitung*, May 22, 1998, p. 24.

"Loewenbraeu to Set Up Brewery in Egyptian Venture," *European Report*, January 8, 1997.

"Lowenbrau AG—History," *Datamonitor Company Profiles*, July 17, 2004.

"Lowenbrau Forays into Indian Beer Mart, Floats Local Arm," *India Business Insight*, March 8, 2001.

"Lowenbrau in Comeback," *Off License News*, April 6, 2001, p. 11.

"Lowenbrau on the Right Path (Lowenbrau ist auf gutem wege)," *Suddeutsche Zeitung*, May 14, 1999.

Mahood, Casey, "Labatt Wins Lowenbrau Deal; Brewer Will Take Over Job from Miller, Molson and Supply All of North America," *Globe and Mail* (Canada), August 19, 1997, p. B4.

Pruzan, Todd, "Lowenbrau Expands Its Line; Specialty Craftbiers May Give Needed Lift to Miller," *Advertising Age*, July 22, 1996, p. 8.

Saraikin, Anton, "Lowenbrau uxodit ot Heineken, bavarskoe pivo budet razlivat' InBev," *Vedomosti*, October 10, 2005, p. 189.

"Shareholders at Loewenbraeu Holding AGM Approve Name Change," *Süddeutsche Zeitung*, May 13, 1995, p. 31.

"Shares in Loewenbraeu Subsidiaries in Unexpected High Demand," *Boersen-Zeitung*, August 12, 1994, p. 17.

"Spaten bringt Löwenbräu auf Kurs," *Süddeutsche Zeitung*, April 18, 1998, p. 23.

"Spaten-Franziskaner-Braeu Takes Over Struggling Loewenbraeu," *Frankfurter Allgemeine Zeitung,* September 6, 1997, p. 22.

"SUN Interbrew Limited Announces Changes in Production and Distribution of Lowenbrau in Russia," *SKRIN* (Russia), October 19, 2005.

Teinowitz, Ira, "Lowenbrau Links New Spots to Old Tale of Chained Lion," *Advertising Age,* February 22, 1988, p. 4.

Van Munching, Philip, *Beer Blast: The Inside Story of the Brewing Industry's Bizarre Battles for Your Money,* New York: Times Business/Random House, 1997.

Weiner, Michael A., *The Taster's Guide to Beer: Brews and Breweries of the World,* New York: Macmillan Publishing Co., Inc., 1977.

White, Hooper, "Beers Battle to Take Over the Night," *Advertising Age,* September 22, 1986, p. 73.

Manhattan Group, LLC

———— ■ ————

430 First Avenue North, Suite 500
Minneapolis, Minnesota 55401
U.S.A.
Telephone: (612) 337-9600
Toll Free: (800) 541-1345
Fax: (612) 341-4447
Web site: http://www.manhattantoy.com

Private Company
Incorporated: 1979
Employees: 50
NAIC: 339931 Doll and Stuffed Toy Manufacturing

■ ■ ■

Manhattan Group, LLC, which conducts business as Manhattan Toy, is tiny compared to such toy manufacturing giants as Mattel and Hasbro. However, by creating several high-quality stuffed toys sold only in specialty stores, Manhattan Toy steadily increased its sales throughout the 1980s and 1990s. The company's first toys were partially stuffed to give the toy a floppy quality that stood out from toys that were stuffed to full capacity. Manhattan Toy's brands include Whoozit, Manhattan Toy Baby, and Puppets. The company's most successful line, targeted at girls between the ages of 3 and 12, are Groovy Girls stuffed dolls, referred to as "the opposite of Barbie." The dolls are marketed with a line of modest and tasteful outfits that encourage girls to develop their own individual clothing styles. The company also offers a web site for fans of Groovy Girls

to socialize online. Other Manhattan toys are targeted at infants, toddlers, and preschoolers of both sexes.

THE EARLY YEARS, 1978–1986

Before Francis Goldwyn was known as the founder of Manhattan Toy, he was famous as the grandson of Hollywood studio mogul Samuel Goldwyn. Growing up in the Hollywood environment, Francis Goldwyn spent many of his weekends watching movies at his grandfather's Beverly Hills mansion. After a few years of working in the movie industry, Francis Goldwyn became an accountant and left his family's Hollywood legacy for New York. "I like to say I was run out of California because I wasn't mellow enough," Goldwyn said in a February 1990 interview with *Nation's Business*. He explained, "I was always raised with the attitude that you're a Goldwyn, you've got to do better. I said, as I looked around the country, where is the competition toughest? It was New York. It's very kind of in-your-face competitive here, and I like that." Once he moved to the East Coast, Goldwyn was hired at the accounting firm Coopers & Lybrand (later PricewaterhouseCoopers).

In 1978 Francis Goldwyn ended his Coopers & Lybrand apprenticeship to found the Manhattan Group. Instead of borrowing money from his family, Goldwyn independently approached a New York investor who loaned him the needed seed money. A toy line called Oids was the first of many floppy stuffed toys made by Manhattan Toy. It was also the company's first financial flop. For the first half of the 1980s, Manhattan Toy struggled to stave off bankruptcy. After repeatedly borrowing money from more New York investors, the

COMPANY PERSPECTIVES

Play is discovery and exploration, and joy, and growth, and learning, and so much more. And for us play is serious work. So when we bring play to life, we do it with a commitment to the finest in craftsmanship and creativity. All of our products, from the newest concepts to our time-tested classics, are innovatively designed to inspire imaginative play and delight our consumers large and small. Play is not only fun, it's essential to a child's cognitive, emotional, and social development. Our design process blends science and whimsy to produce toys that offer children a rich array of visual and tactile stimulation and unlimited opportunities for imaginative exploration.

company finally produced a hit in 1984 with its plush dinosaur (plush being a style of soft fabric made from polyester). The dinosaur's availability was limited to top-end retailers such as Neiman Marcus, Bloomingdale's, and F.A.O. Schwarz.

Manhattan Toy's plush dinosaurs eventually bolstered the company's profits after such a grueling beginning. In 1985 Manhattan Toy reportedly generated $200,000 in sales. Goldwyn remained inspired by the budding signs of success and continued making toys. In an interview with *Nation's Business*, Goldwyn recounted the time he shared an elevator with a father accompanied by his young daughter. After noticing the girl's yellow dinosaur, Goldwyn said, "'Hey, that's some dinosaur. What kind of dinosaur is that?' She said, 'That's a triceratops.' I said, 'You like that, huh?' Her father said, 'It's her favorite toy. She won't let it go.' I said, 'That's really neat to hear. I make those.'"

RISING SALES: 1986–1999

Goldwyn's persistence paid off. Thanks to the toymaker's mainstay plush dinosaur, Manhattan Toy sales reportedly climbed to $5 million in 1986 according to the *Wall Street Journal*. Much larger companies began to take notice and generate similar plush products, among them Gerber Products Company. In 1987 Goldwyn filed a claim that a new and less expensive stuffed dinosaur made by Gerber infringed upon Manhattan Toy's copyrights. Goldwyn was quoted in a June 15, 1987, edition of *Wall Street Journal* as saying, "the big companies take the following attitude: 'We have the

money. These little companies don't have the resources to fight us.' Unfortunately, they're right. This time, though, the puppy dog they kicked, bites."

One recent addition under Article III of the U.S. Constitution had hedged Manhattan Toy's litigation. In 1982 the U.S. Court of Appeals for the Federal Circuit had been established. It imposed a uniform appeal process that leveled the playing field for smaller businesses infringed upon by conglomerates like Gerber. Later that year a federal court banned the dinosaur made by Gerber. Manhattan Toy was also paid for Gerber's profits that resulted from Gerber's imitation dinosaurs. Manhattan Toy's attorney, Norman H. Zivin, said that the payout was in the "six figures" according to a June 15, 1987, edition of *Wall Street Journal*. In the same publication one Gerber spokesperson said that his company did not "see this settlement as a win for either side." The spokesperson continued, "We don't agree that it's a win for them. It was never established that there was a true copyright infringement and if there was, we were an innocent bystander because the foreign supplier who furnished us with the product said he had the rights to the design."

In the late 1980s Manhattan Toy's sales of plush dinosaurs began declining. The company released other products like its animal-themed hand and finger puppets. Goldwyn wanted all Manhattan Toy products to appeal to both parents and children. He referred to this approach in *Nation's Business* as making "classic" toys that would outlive other toy fads. The puppets' simple designs allowed children and parents to operate them; typically only the puppets' mouths moved. They were also partially stuffed to give the toys a dangling quality similar to other Manhattan Toy products.

In 1998 Manhattan Toy released a line of stuffed dolls known as Groovy Girls, which would eventually become a huge hit. The dolls were created as wholesome alternatives to such doll brands as Mattel's Barbie and MGA Entertainment's Bratz, both of which more closely resembled supermodels than young girls. Targeting females between 3 and 12 years old, Manhattan Toy sought to encourage girls to discover their unique fashion styles through a variety of outfits, furniture, environments, and vehicles sold as Groovy Girls accessories.

Roger Bildsten, who previously served as a vice-president at Anagram International, Inc., a manufacturer of Mylar balloons and party products, became CEO of Manhattan Toy in 1998. The new executive was a major advocate of Groovy Girls. "America has literally and figuratively embraced the Groovy Girls. Fans of the dolls have actually become the inspiration for additions to the Groovy line," Roger Bildsten proclaimed in a Manhattan Toy press release. "Groovy Girls are a very special brand. You can look forward to some amazing innovation as their world continues to grow," he continued. Under Bildsten's guidance, Manhattan Toy continued creating Groovy Girls dolls with body shapes and ethnicities to reflect the realistic diversity among young American girls.

BRAND EXPANSION, 1999–2004

In 1999 a licensing partnership between Manhattan Toy and Dr. Seuss Enterprises sparked the creation of stuffed Dr. Seuss plush toys and puppets. In anticipation of the 2000 release of the motion picture *The Grinch* starring Jim Carrey, Manhattan Toy released a selection of Grinch dolls and other toys based on characters from the movie. Similar stuffed toys were released in August 2003 for the November release of *The Cat in the Hat* starring Mike Myers. Other Dr. Seuss characters such as Fox in Socks, the "mossy, bossy" man-like creature titled Lorax, and the blue elephant Norton materialized as Manhattan Toy stuffed toys. Norton was released as a 52-inch-long Dr. Seuss Sit Upon toy that small children could, as the name implied, sit upon. Other Dr. Seuss toys, including Hug Arounds and puppets, were created to encourage children to physically interact with Dr. Seuss characters as they read about the characters in Dr. Seuss books.

Product launches after 2000 were in excess of 100 products per introduction and across all brands. Besides new additions to Dr. Seuss and Groovy Girls lines, the company released new products under such other brand names as Whoozit, Manhattan Toy Baby, Manhattan Toy Plush, Manhattan Toy Puppets, and Manhattan Toy Dolls.

In 2004 Manhattan Toy launched its Groovy Girls website at www.GroovyGirls.com, allowing girls to create online accounts and create their own digital doll figures. After their digital dolls had been dressed virtually on the Internet, website members could enter virtual rooms and text-chat with other girls around the world. Cyber parties allowed the girls' dolls to dance and have "Slumberrific Sleepovers." The site also allowed girls to create wish lists, from which parents could purchase items. The online chatting was touted as child-friendly, meaning that only prewritten questions and answer combinations accessed from a user-friendly database could be used to communicate. A typical online chat would begin, "What do you usually do on Saturdays?" To which a girl could reply, "Sometimes I go to the movies on Saturday" or any other prewritten response to the question. The structure kept girls safe from online predators. "It's wholesome girl fun," Amy Susman-Stillman, a developmental psychologist at the University of Minnesota and occasional Manhattan Toy consultant, said in a February 3, 2005, edition of the *Saint Paul Pioneer Press*. She added, "It's not about girls and boys, just girls doing girlfriend things." Manhattan Toy hoped its web site would create an advantage over giants such as Mattel's Barbie and MGA Entertainment's Bratz dolls, whose web sites, Manhattan alleged, offered little in entertainment and served more as online stores.

In 2004 Manhattan entered into a licensing agreement for Groovy Girls with Scholastic Corporation, the children's publisher and media giant. The partnership resulted in a series of Groovy Girls books and magazines that encouraged girls to develop their own personal style and to learn about the power of friendship. The publications were sold through a monthly book club that was launched September 2004. The book club continuity program targeted girls from third to fifth grade. At the time, over 100 different Groovy Girls dolls were available in more than 5,000 specialty retailers worldwide. Manhattan Toy also began licensing the brand to other select companies that could make Groovy Girl doll fashion accessories, sleepwear, jewelry, activity kits, fashion toys, games and puzzles.

In December 2004, Roger Bildsten left Manhattan Toy to become the president of Grand Toys International, Inc. Manhattan Toy filled his position seven months later by hiring Arete Passas, an executive with previous leadership positions at brands such as Oil of Olay, Crayola, Scholastic, Dixie, and Mattel. Passas also served on the Board of the Girl Scout Council of Greater Minneapolis. In early 2005 Manhattan Toy's infant brand, Manhattan Baby, was updated with a series of educational toys including Big Top Sounds, an interactive toy using motion-sensored sounds.

RETAIL EXPANSION: 2004 AND BEYOND

Thanks to a new relationship with the Target Corporation, Manhattan Toy brands were sold by more than 10,000 retailers in 2005, which was double the amount reported by the company in 2004. For the first time in Manhattan Toy's history, a limited selection of its Groovy Girls and Whoozit branded toys appeared inside the large retailer Target Stores, representing a drastic change from its exclusive availability in specialty toy retailers. Some owners of some small retailers reportedly felt betrayed by the new Target relationship. Many had a vested interest in Manhattan Toy after promoting the brand for over two decades. "We worked hard building that brand, and Target's reaping the benefit," Sonya Kalajian, owner of the Toy Shop in Connecticut, said in a September 2005 edition of *TDmonthly*, a trade publication for toys, hobbies, games, and gifts.

Hugh Kennedy, the vice-president of business development for Manhattan Toy, explained that as Target increased the popularity of Manhattan Toy brands, the sales inside specialty stores would also increase. The price of Groovy Girls dolls was the same in both Target and specialty stores. New Groovy Girls dolls were released to specialty stores six months before they were made available at Target.

In 2005, the Groovy Girls products expanded to include Groovy Girls Minis, a 2.5" miniature version of the larger Groovy Girls doll. The new Minis included a range of accessories. Launched in January 2005, they exploded in popularity in both specialty stores and later in mass channels. Following this brand extension was the April 2006 launch of Groovy Girls PetRAGEOUS!, a line of "funky fashion pets" that were as diverse as their doll counterparts. Capitalizing on the fashionable pet trend going on in the celebrity world, the new stuffed animals and their accessories were a successful addition to the Groovy Girls products.

Manhattan Toy consistently gave back to the community with large product donations throughout the year. Toys for Tots, a charity organization, received more than 100,000 toys between 2004 and 2006. Less than a year after becoming Manhattan Toy's president, Passas oversaw the donation of more than 60,000 Groovy Girls dolls to girls who survived Hurricane Katrina. With the help of the Girl Scout Council of Greater Minneapolis, Groovy Girls were first given to displaced hurricane survivors who relocated to Minnesota. The remaining dolls were distributed throughout the Gulf Coast. The relief effort was also overseen by the non-profit Hope for the City organization.

Kevin Teague

PRINCIPAL COMPETITORS

Gund, Inc.; Hasbro, Inc.; Infantino, LLC; Learning Curve International, Inc.; Mattel, Inc.; MGA Entertainment, Inc.; Toy Quest; Ty Inc.

FURTHER READING

"Battle of the Toy Dinosaurs Leaves One Species Extinct," *Wall Street Journal*, July 9, 1987.

"Choking Hazard Spurs Pull-Toy Recall," *Cleveland Plain Dealer*, February 9, 2000, p. 2C.

"CPSC, Firms Announce Recall of Teethers And Oil Burning Candles," *M2 Presswire*, July 21, 2000.

Galante, Steven P., "Small Firms Quicker to Fight Giants Who Copy Their Ideas," *Wall Street Journal*, June 15, 1987.

Ojeda-Zapata, Julio, "Groovy Girls Doll Company Uses Internet to Attract Young Customers," *Saint Paul Pioneer Press*, February 3, 2005.

"Product Recalls," *Providence Journal*, February 13, 2000, p. F4.

"Roger Bildsten as President of Its North," *Market News Publishing*, August 11, 2005.

Salas, Teresa, "Toymakers Forecast A 'Good, Not Great' '89," *Playthings*, January 1, 1989, p. 64.

The Mark Travel Corporation

8907 North Port Washington Road
Milwaukee, Wisconsin 53217
U.S.A.
Telephone: (414) 228-7472
Toll Free: (800) 715-4030
Fax: (414) 934-1589
Web site: http://www.marktravel.com

Private Company
Incorporated: 1983
Employees: 2,300
Sales: $266.4 million (2005 est.)
NAIC: 561520 Tour Operators

■ ■ ■

The Mark Travel Corporation is a Milwaukee-based private company that sells leisure travel packages to more than 200 destinations through 16 travel companies. The flagship brand, and founding company, is Funjet Vacations, specializing in vacations to 60 destinations in the United States, the Caribbean, Mexico, and Europe. Mark Travel also offers vacation packages in partnerships with United Airlines, Midwest Airlines, Southwest Airlines, and the MGM MIRAGE family of Las Vegas and Biloxi, Mississippi resorts. Mark Travel is owned and operated by Chairman William La Macchia and his family, part of La Macchia Enterprises.

EARLY 20TH-CENTURY ROOTS

Bill La Macchia was born into the travel business. His grandfather, Eugenio La Macchia, was an Italian im-migrant who settled in Kenosha, Wisconsin, in the early years of the 1900s, where he opened a grocery store. As a sideline he began to sell steamship tickets to fellow immigrants bringing family members over to the new world as they could afford to do so. His son Edmund, a Marquette University graduate, turned the endeavor into a full-fledged business in 1931, launching La Macchia Travel to serve primarily Italian immigrants, offering steamship tickets and railroad tickets, as well as notary services, translation, accounting, and other help that newly arrived immigrants might need to navigate an unfamiliar government bureaucracy. The agency became involved in airline ticket sales in the early 1940s, a busi-ness under the direction of his wife Emma. Airline tickets would soon supplant the Trans-Atlantic Steamship busi-ness in importance and begin to experience strong growth in the 1950s. Edmund and Emma's eldest son, Eugene, another Marquette graduate, became involved with the family business, which underwent a major change in the 1960s. No longer did the La Macchia family business focus on immigrants, instead taking advantage of the rise of the leisure vacation market to become involved in leisure travel, as well as corporate travel.

Unlike his elder brother, Bill La Macchia did not go to college, preferring to go to work at the American Motors plant in Kenosha, taking a job on the assembly line. In 1963, at the age of 21, he joined the family travel agency, becoming a manager. With his brother in line to take over one day, Bill La Macchia broke away four years later, answering a newspaper ad to find work with Manpower Inc.'s travel services subsidiary, Travelpower. He would become the head of the opera-

The people of The Mark Travel Corporation proudly service 2.6 million vacationers each year. Superb care has been our business for 30 years. That's why 16 leading vacation companies trust their customers to us.

tion and over the years grow increasingly frustrated with the wholesale tour companies with which he dealt. In response, he founded a wholesale division at Travelpower in 1974 called Funway Holidays. In the first year it booked more than 10,000 travelers. The company's methods were hardly high-tech. At the time, La Macchia told *TravelAge West* in a 2004 profile, "Everything was done manually on cards. We had a big grease board that showed available bookings and the phone wasn't very efficient. It was cumbersome and there was lots of room for errors." In 1975 a charter airplane division called Funjet was added to Travelpower's assets. When Parker Pen acquired Manpower in 1976, La Macchia and a Manpower executive named James Scheinfeld, who provided the funding, bought the Manpower travel assets, forming Travway, Inc. By now Funway was booking more than 100,000 vacations, warranting the opening of an office in Las Vegas in 1977. In 1979 Funjet began selling vacations to Mexico.

STRIKING OUT ON HIS OWN: 1980

La Macchia became a solo operator when he and Scheinfeld divided the business in 1980, with La Macchia taking the wholesale operations, Funway Holidays and Funjet. The Mark Travel Corporation was formed in 1983 and Funway Holidays and Funjet were folded into it. The two subsidiaries were merged in 1986, becoming Funway Holidays Funjet.

Funway Holidays continued to prosper packaging Las Vegas tours, and in 1982 was recognized as Tour Wholesaler of the Year by the Las Vegas hotel and motel industry. To this point Milwaukee was the only origin city, and destinations were limited to Las Vegas, Orlando, and Mexico. In 1982 the company began a diversification bid by opening a service office in Denver to establish a second origin market. Moreover, Funjet, which had been booking seats on scheduled air flights now began chartering its own jets. More origin cities and destinations would now be added at a steady clip. "We wanted to control our own destiny," Bill La Macchia explained

to the *Business Journal-Milwaukee*. A Chicago service office was opened in 1985, and Dallas and Houston service offices were added in 1988. Mark Travel closed the decade with another expansion of its business, selected to operate Southwest Airlines Vacations. Also in 1989 Funjets began scheduling regular charters to Mexico.

By the start of the 1990s, Mark Travel had more than 40 origin cities and more than 200 destinations. It added United Airlines as a partner in 1990, taking over the back office operations for the airline's vacation program, handling reservations. In 1994 Mark Travel assumed complete control of the travel business, including product design, promotion, and marketing. United Vacations, established in 1984, offered trips to Hawaii, the Orient, Europe, Mexico, and the Caribbean, as well as a number of U.S. destinations. The airline continued to control seat inventory and pricing, however. In the meantime, Funway Holidays International was established in 1992, a London service office was opened, and Funjet began providing service to Europe. In 1993 Mark Travel began operating another airline wholesale operation, US Airways Vacations, and in that same year opened a San Diego service office. Funway changed its name once again in 1994, 20 years after its founding, becoming Funway Vacations. A year later the company opened a Des Moines service office. By the end of 1995 Mark Travel had annual passenger volumes in the 1.5 million range, and sales volume exceeded $500 million.

The second half of the 1990s was punctuated by the steady acquisition of other travel companies to expand the Mark Travel portfolio. Mountain Vacations, a Denver-based ski operator, was acquired in 1996. Established in 1987, Mountain Vacations packaged ski vacations to U.S., Canadian, and European destinations. In another 1996 development, Mark Travel and MGM MIRAGE forged a joint venture, MGM MIRAGE Vacations, to package tours to MGM MIRAGE's Las Vegas properties: MGM Grand, Mandalay Bay, THEhotel, The Mirage, Treasure Island, Monte Carlo, New York-New York, Luxor, Excalibur, and Circus Circus, as well the Bellagio under construction in Las Vegas and the soon-to-open Beau Rivage in Biloxi, Mississippi. In 1997 Mark Travel added Pleasure Break Vacations, a 25-year-old Rolling Meadow, Illinois tour and charter operator that offered vacations to Mexico, the Caribbean, Belize, Costa Rica, and Europe. The products were sold exclusively through travel agents, catering mostly to residents of Illinois, Indiana, Iowa, Wisconsin, Minnesota, and western Michigan.

SUN COUNTRY AIRLINES ACQUISITION: 1997

Also in 1997 Bill La Macchia and Mark Travel became involved in the airline business, paying $41 million to

```
┌─────────────────────────────────────────┐
│                                         │
│             KEY DATES                   │
│          ─────────────                  │
│                                         │
│  1974:  Bill La Macchia founds Funway   │
│         Holidays as a Travelpower       │
│         division.                       │
│  1976:  La Macchia and partner acquire  │
│         Travelpower assets and form     │
│         Travway, Inc.                   │
│  1980:  La Macchia and partner divide   │
│         the business.                   │
│  1983:  Mark Travel is formed.          │
│  1992:  Funway Holidays International    │
│         is established.                 │
│  1994:  Mark Travel begins operating    │
│         United Vacations.               │
│  1997:  Mark Travel acquires Sun        │
│         Country Airlines.               │
│  2002:  Bankrupt Sun Country is sold.   │
│                                         │
└─────────────────────────────────────────┘
```

acquire a 75 percent controlling interest in Minneapolis-based Sun Country Airlines. The charter outfit had been a profitable venture for the past 16 years, and now transported about three million passengers a year in its 15 jets. Again, the idea was to control Mark Travel's destiny by securing more reliable access to airline seats, but Bill La Macchia proved to be out of his element in the airline business. Almost immediately he had to contend with expected losses, and then he made the mistake of directly taking on Northwest Airlines, which dominated the Minneapolis market but was grounded in 1998 because of a pilots' strike. For a time Sun Country benefited from Northwest's misfortune. Unfortunately for Mark Travel, La Macchia's plan to sell seats to other charter companies did not pan out because major airlines began to poach on this business, and when Sun Country began offering scheduled flights in 1999 to compete with Northwest it was unable to survive an ensuing price war. After losing more than $100 million in three years, Sun Country suspended all scheduled flights in December 2001 and reverted to charter service only, leading to mass layoffs. Sun Country would not, however, charter flights for Mark Travel or anyone for some time. It soon filed for bankruptcy protection and in 2002 was sold to an investment group for about $5 million and began a comeback under new management.

During—and despite—the travails of Sun Country, Mark Travel continued its expansion spree during the late 1990s. In 1998 it bought Hamilton, Miller, Hudson & Fayne Corp., a Detroit-based charter operator, and Albuquerque-based Blue Sky Tours. Founded in 1981, Blue Sky sold scheduled air products to Hawaii. Also in 1998, Mark Travel entered the Canadian market by acquiring a 49 percent minority interest in Conquest Tours Limited, a Toronto vacation charter flight company. Origin cities included Calgary, Edmonton, Toronto, Vancouver, and Victoria. Destinations included Florida, California, Las Vegas, and Hawaii in the United States, and overseas to the United Kingdom, Ireland, Europe, and Australia. Another important development in 1998 was Mark Travel's international subsidiary establishing inbound programs to the United States from more than 30 other countries. In 1999 Funjet celebrated its 25th anniversary by expanding the flights for its Las Vegas vacations to seven days a week and adding a new destination: Punta Cana, Dominican Republic. Mark Travel also supplemented its Las Vegas business by acquiring sightseeing company Showtimes Tours, and its Mexico business by adding AeroMexico Vacations. In addition, Minneapolis charter company TransGlobal Vacations was purchased.

Mark Travel lined up another influential partner in 2000 when it formed a 50-50 joint venture, eLeisure Network, with Carnival Corp. The subsidiary was established to market and distribute the products of both companies over the Internet, targeting travel agents and their clients. Also on the technology side, in 2000 Mark Travel spun off its information technology division, Trisept Technology, which became Trisept Solutions. Trisept had been responsible for developing the booking agent engine, VAX VacationAcess, used by eLeisure and others, as well as software used by Sun Country and the Las Vegas Convention and Visitors Authority, which needed a way to track hotel room bookings. But Trisept's ties to Mark Travel had proven to be a drag on its growth. It was pigeonholed by potential clients as a software company limited to vacation packages rather than a travel industry generalist. There was also a problem with conflict of interests, preventing Trisept from taking assignments from Mark Travel's competitors.

In the early months of 2001 Mark Travel continued to add to its stable of brands, acquiring three businesses from Dallas-based Sammons Enterprises. It acquired Adventure Tours USA, a 30-year-old Dallas-based company that sold vacation packages to Florida, western United States ski destinations, Mexico, Costa Rica, and the Caribbean. Other additions in June 2001 were Town & Country Tours of Phoenix and Buffalo's Santo Tours. Adventure Tours would be allowed to operate as an independent entity in Dallas, but Town & Country was relegated to a Mark Travel brand and Santo Tours was folded into Funjet Vacations.

As was the case with most companies involved in the travel industries, business was severely impacted by the terrorist attacks that took place on September 11, 2001. In the aftermath, Americans were especially reluctant to fly to destination sites. Forced to adjust to this difficult climate, Mark Travel within the month laid off more than 20 percent of staff across the country, including the entire 150-employee reservation center in Bloomington, Minnesota, in early October, and another 350 people, mostly at its headquarters. The drop in travel also sounded the death knell for Sun Country Airlines as it lapsed into bankruptcy before the year was out.

Over the next few years Mark Travel and the travel industry rebounded as separation occurred from the events of September 11. In 2003 Mark Travel was tabbed to operate Midwest Airlines Vacations. By now Bill La Macchia's son and namesake was a seasoned travel executive and serving as Mark Travel's chief operating officer. Bill La Macchia also turned over the presidency of Funjet to Ray Snisky in 2004. The young La Macchia denied that a changing of the guard was taking place in an interview with *Travel Weekly*, maintaining, "This is just an evolution of the vision that my father had when he started this company 30 years ago, to be the kind of tour operator that he wanted to do business with when he was a travel agent—and we accomplished that."

Ed Dinger

PRINCIPAL DIVISIONS

Adventure Tours USA; AeroMexico Vacations; ATA Vacations; Blue Sky Tours; Funjet Vacations; Mark International; MGM MIRAGE Vacations; Midwest Airlines Vacations; Mountain Vacations; Southwest Airlines Vacations; Spirit Vacations; TransGlobal Vacations; United Vacations.

PRINCIPAL COMPETITORS

American Express Company; BCD Travel; Carlson Wagonlit Travel, Inc.

FURTHER READING

Cogswell, David, "In the Hot Seat: Bill La Macchia Jr.," *Travel Weekly*, June 21, 2004, p. 9.

Jennings, Lisa, "Hitting the Mark," *TravelAge West*, March 29, 2004, p. 43.

Kennedy, Tony, "The Money Man," *Star Tribune* (Minneapolis, Minn.), April 25, 1999, p. 1D.

Kueny, Barbara, "Mark Travel Profits As Mid-America Flies Funway," *Business Journal-Milwaukee*, May 28, 1990, p. X26.

Rice, Kate, "A Family Legend," *Leisure Travel News*, September 20, 1999, p. 1.

Martin Franchises, Inc.

422 Wards Corner Road
Loveland, Ohio 45140
U.S.A.
Telephone: (513) 351-6211
Toll Free: 800-827-0207
Fax: (513) 731-0818
Web site: http://www.martinizing.com

Private Company
Incorporated: 1949
Employees: 16
NAIC: 533110 Owners and Lessors of Other Non-Financial Assets; 423850 Service Establishment Equipment and Supplies Merchant Wholesalers; 812320 Drycleaning and Laundry Services (Except Coin-Operated)

■ ■ ■

Martin Franchises, Inc., is the company behind the One-Hour Martinizing chain of dry cleaners. The Martinizing process, named after chemist Henry Martin, was safe enough to allow dry cleaning facilities to be built within city limits. Martinizing became a household name in the 1950s and 1960s as advertising promised garments "As fresh as a flower, in one hour." Martin Franchises, Inc. licenses the well-known Martinizing name to local business operators and provides training and other support. While it focuses on relationships with multiple-store chains, it also supplies a number of individual facilities. There are more than 600 franchised Martinizing loca-

tions worldwide; nearly two-thirds are located in the United States.

SAFER DRY CLEANING PROCESS DISCOVERED IN 1949

A random discovery in 1848 had launched the dry cleaning industry. The owner of a textile dying operation spilled paraffin lamp oil onto fabric, and noticed that it dissolved a greasy stain. Though effective, this procedure naturally carried with it a risk of fire, requiring dry cleaning plants to be located far from city centers.

The story of Martin Franchises, Inc. begins in the late 1940s, when chemist Henry Martin of Buffalo, New York's Martin Equipment Co. discovered a new process for cleaning clothes. The new process used solvents that were less dangerous than previous dry cleaning processes, allowing Martin to locate small cleaning plants within city limits, beginning with one in New York in 1949. Previously, the dry cleaning industry had collected garments for cleaning at "dry stores," while the volatile cleaning chemicals were held at sites in the countryside.

By cleaning clothes on the spot, the chain was able to offer one-hour service when its competitors had a turnaround of as much as ten days. After being dry cleaned at a Martinizing shop, garments were odorless, sanitary, mothproofed, cleaner, and stayed pressed longer, according to company advertising of the day. The stores typically also offered a traditional laundry service, washing and drying shirts in three hours.

Martin's business was soon acquired by the

COMPANY PERSPECTIVES

Martinizing pioneered one hour, on-premise cleaning, providing franchisees with the most efficient cleaning procedures available. Martinizing is the most recognized name in drycleaning. When you own our franchise, you benefit from that name recognition, which helps build your business. Martinizing has been and continues to be the leading dry cleaning franchise in the industry. We've built a track record of helping our franchisees grow their businesses.

American Laundry Machinery Company of Cincinnati, where it was called the Martin Equipment Division or Martin Equipment Sales. The unit's manager was William R. Wallens, who was referred to as the inventor of the Martinizing process by the *New York Times* in a 1963 story on a separate water filtration process he had developed.

In the 1960s, the chain grew to a peak of more than 1,000 sites in Europe and America. "Fresh as a flower in just one hour" was its pitch. Store signage read, "One Hour 'Martinizing': The Most in Dry Cleaning." The chain was advertising for franchisees as well as clients. In 1963 ads for Cincinnati's Perdrix Machinery Sales Co. offered prospective business owners a profitable opportunity "to satisfy the good appearance needs of every family in your community."

The chain was among a number of enterprises, led by the likes of McDonald's and Howard Johnson's, that expanded rapidly through franchising. At the beginning of the 1970s, there were perhaps 3,000 One-Hour Martinizing stores in the United States, according to a *New York Times* story on the strip mall phenomenon. The total number of laundry, cleaning, rental, and valet service establishments was in excess of 110,000, according to the *Monthly Labor Review*.

However, the chain suffered from the introduction of polyester and permanent press fabrics in the 1970s. Many consumers cut back on personal services such as dry cleaning during the economic downturn. The company saw its network scaled back by half, a loss of hundreds of franchises during the decade.

NEW OWNER IN 1978

George Strike acquired the company in 1978. American Laundry had reportedly been preparing to shut down

Martin before Strike offered to buy it. A native of Salt Lake City, Strike had become president of American Laundry in 1962. His Harvard-educated son, Anthony, had worked at a consulting firm and had become an executive at Ohio's Hess and Eisenhardt, a specialized vehicle manufacturer, before joining his father in Martin Franchises. The father and son team would lead Martin Franchises beyond the end of the 20th century.

The Strikes had community ties to both Utah and Ohio. The elder Strike also bought a share in the Cincinnati Reds baseball team in 1981. Other key executives would come from the Beehive State, such as director of franchise development Frank Knowles, who had worked for Utah's Spudnuts doughnut chain before joining Martin Franchises in 2002.

NEW FRANCHISE STRUCTURE IN 1987

Under the Strikes, the company changed from being a licenser to a full-fledged franchiser. Martin instituted a more comprehensive support package for its franchisees in 1987. Afterwards, its franchisees would pay a four percent royalty, plus an initial startup fee. The company developed a three-week initial training program.

The dry cleaning industry was booming in a decade identified with nattily dressed corporate types. Industry-wide sales rose nearly 25 percent to $4 billion in 1987 according to International Fabricare Institute figures cited in *The Business Journal Serving Greater Tampa Bay*. An increasing number of two-paycheck families was one factor, said an IFI spokesperson. Martinizing had no shortage of competition; there were more than 24,000 dry cleaning stores in the United States in the early 1990s.

50TH ANNIVERSARY IN 1999

Martin signed up with local laundry chain New Tanabe to open a series of franchises in Japan beginning in 1991. The company announced ambitious goals of 1,000 stores and annual sales of ¥50 billion there within three years. There were 156,000 cleaning establishments in the country; most of the dry cleaners did not process clothes on site.

The company used the "master franchiser" concept—recruiting a local partner to help attract other franchisees—in other areas as well, such as Latin America. Japanese gas retailer Mobile Sekiyu KK began experimenting with putting Martinizing shops in its convenience stores in the late-1990s.

The company was also pushing into exotic locales as far away as Ecuador, Qatar, and Indonesia. By the

KEY DATES

1949: Chemist Henry Martin discovers a safer, less flammable dry cleaning process. His equipment company, along with the new process, is soon purchased by the American Laundry Machinery Company of Cincinnati.

1970: There are perhaps 3,000 One-Hour Martinizing stores at the height of the franchising boom.

1978: Cincinnati businessman George Strike buys Martin Franchises.

1987: The franchising structure is revamped.

1991: Martinizing is expanding in Japan and other countries.

1999: At the half-century mark, the company has 800 stores in 17 countries.

2003: The company moves to new headquarters in Cincinnati.

time of Martin's 50th anniversary in 1999, there were 800 Martinizing locations in 17 countries around the world. Within the United States, the Denver, Indianapolis, and Louisville markets were booming, an official told the *Greater Cincinnati Business Review* in 1995.

The franchise fee then ranged from $30,000 to start a brand new store to $10,000 for opening a second one. Martin also received a royalty based on sales for newer stores, and a flat fee (adjusted for inflation) from older ones. Total start-up costs were roughly $200,000 to $300,000, plus another $50,000 or so for traditional laundry equipment, noted *Entrepreneur* magazine.

Some of the Martinizing franchises began using less toxic alternatives to the industry-standard perchloroethylene (perc) solvent, which was suspected of health and environmental risks and banned in Canada, Brazil, and Sweden. Downsides to the new eco-friendly processes such as Green Earth's were that they tended not to clean as thoroughly and took longer. Though some of the necessary equipment was more expensive (an expense offset by lower disposal and cleanup fees down the road), the new methods were embraced by operators in environmentally conscious areas such as Malibu, California and Tampa, Florida. (Another process using liquid carbon dioxide was being championed by upcoming rival Hangers Cleaners Inc. of Raleigh, North Carolina.)

NEW HQ, NEW FOCUS FOR FUTURE

In 2003, the company leased 11,000 square feet of nondescript office and warehouse space near Cincinnati for use as its new headquarters, where only about 16 people worked. Martin was restructuring its marketing and real estate departments to prepare for an aggressive new growth program.

In 2004, Martin had 619 locations operated by 214 franchisees; about two-thirds of these stores were in the United States. About 80 percent had signed up before the company's licensing structure was changed in 1987. Throughout its history, Martinizing had been the leading brand in the dry cleaning business. Though there were then 30,000 dry cleaning stores in business in the United States, most were mom and pop shops. Its greatest competition, an official told *Small Business Opportunities,* was strong regional chains, though there were also a couple of emerging national chains, such as Zoots Corporation and DryClean U.S.A. Inc.

The company was looking to double its traditional growth rate by adding up to 40 stores a year, its franchise chief said in *The Enquirer* of Cincinnati. Though the company continued to work with single-unit owners, Martin was principally interested in entrepreneurs who wanted to start chains of five to ten stores within designated territories in booming markets such as central Florida, southern California, Nashville, Phoenix, and Pittsburgh. According to *Small Business Opportunities,* Martin hired the demographic research firm Claritas to help identify target markets. The company also began working with franchise consultants; a spokesperson told *Franchising World* that these were accounting for 55 percent of its new franchises.

Despite the new focus on recruiting multiple unit owners, Martin still preferred to franchise hands-on operators rather than absentee owners. In prior years, typical Martinizing franchisees had come from blue collar backgrounds, said *Small Business Opportunities.* The newer crop of owners included a number of downsized executives with substantial assets. The company was thus poised for continued growth; as a company official noted, its dry cleaning services were as in demand as ever since busy families had less time to clean and press clothes.

Frederick C. Ingram

PRINCIPAL COMPETITORS

Comet Cleaners; Dry Clean U.S.A., Inc.; Hangers Cleaners Inc. (MiCELL Technologies Inc.).

FURTHER READING

Besch, Dawn, "Dueling Cleaners Close Competitors," *The Business Journal (Serving Greater Tampa Bay),* May 29, 1992, pp. 1f.

"Biggest U.S. Dry Cleaning Chain Coming to Japan," *Japan Economic Newswire,* January 22, 1991.

Callison, Jenny, "Ready to Clean Up: Dry-Cleaning Company Plans New Stores Nationwide," *Enquirer* (Cincinnati), July 7, 2004, pp. D1, D2.

"Dry Cleaner Seeks Goal of Environmentally Friendly Stores," *PR Newswire,* May 28, 1992.

Eggleton, Rick, "Matchmaking for the Millennium," *Franchising World,* November/December 1997, pp. 28+.

"Environmentally Friendly Dry Cleaner Open for Business," *Osprey Observer* (Bloomingdale/Fishhawk, Florida), June 2004.

"Expanding an Empire: A Legendary Brand Puts New Great Spin on Plans for Growth," *Small Business Opportunities,* November 2004, pp. 62–64, 138.

"Fifty Years and One Hour," *American Drycleaner,* June 1999, p. 182.

"Franchise Owners See Both Perks, Downsides to Work," *Frederick News-Post* (Maryland), April 3, 2005, p. B11.

Gabler, Ellen, "Dry Cleaning Chain Targets Suburbs, Plans 30+ Stores," *Minneapolis/St. Paul Business Journal,* March 11, 2005.

Gomez, Henry, "Martinizing Franchiser in Market for More Stores," *Crain's Cleveland Business,* August 9, 2004, p. 21.

Griggs, Robyn, "Franchise Follies," *Colorado Business,* March 1996, pp. 32ff.

Groeneveld, Benno, "New Formulas and Machines Are Sprucing Up Dry Cleaning," *Minneapolis/St. Paul Business Journal,* February 4, 2002.

"Hunts Policeman Who Caused Him to Miss Ill-Fated Plane," *Mansfield, Ohio News-Journal,* February 13, 1955, p. 17.

Kincaid, Valerie Bott, "Martin Eyeing International Expansion," *Greater Cincinnati Business Record,* October 30, 1995, p. A18.

Kneeland, Douglas E., "Garish Strips Stir Hostility, Coast to Coast," *New York Times,* November 28, 1971.

"Lapels, Others Named to 'Franchise 500'," *American Drycleaner,* April 2005, pp. 6–8.

"Life, Death and Japan's Small Laundromats; Martin Franchises Aims to Clean Up Lucrative Trade," *Japan Economic Journal,* March 9, 1991, p. A1.

MacGregor, Scott, "Buying Reds Matter of Dollars and Sentiments," *Enquirer.com* (Cincinnati), September 12, 1999.

Maddocks, Todd D., "Clean and Mean," *Entrepreneur Magazine,* June 1, 2000.

"Martinizing Targets Chain Franchises," *American Drycleaner,* June 2004, p. 82.

"Mobile Sekiyu Unveils Dry Cleaning Petrol Station," *Reuters News,* March 17, 1998.

"New Dry Cleaning Shop Ready for Business," *Coshocton, Ohio, Tribune,* March 27, 1955, p. 26.

Peale, Cliff, "Cleaning Up: Low Overhead, Big Name Keep One-Hour Martinizing Looking Good," *Cincinnati Business Courier,* Small Business Monthly Sec., September 5, 1994, p. 10B.

———, "Franchises Offer a Foot in the Door," *Cincinnati Post,* March 19, 1998.

"Re-Martinizing Chicagoland," *Crain's Chicago Business,* August 15, 1988, Street Talk Sec., p. 8.

Vickery, Mary L., "New Technology in Laundry and Cleaning Services," *Monthly Labor Review,* February 1972, pp. 54–59.

"Water Reclaimed by a New Process," *New York Times,* November 4, 1962.

"When School Starts, Harried Mothers Find Relief at Martinizing," *Port Arthur News* (Texas), August 7, 1968, p. 12.

Zate, Maria, "Many Santa Barbara, Calif.-Area Cleaners Use Controversial Solvent," *Santa Barbara News-Press,* September 9, 2003.

Maryland & Virginia
Milk Producers Cooperative Association, Inc.

Maryland & Virginia Milk Producers Cooperative Association, Inc.

■

1985 Isaac Newton Square
Reston, Virginia 20190
U.S.A.
Telephone: (703) 742-6800
Fax: (703) 742-7459
Web site: http://www.mdvamilk.com

Private Company
Founded: 1920
Employees: 550
Sales: $821.9 million (2005)
NAIC: 311511 Fluid Milk Manufacturing; 311512 Creamery Butter Manufacturing; 311514 Dry, Condensed, and Evaporated Dairy Product Manufacturing; 311520 Ice Cream and Frozen Dessert Manufacturing

■ ■ ■

With its headquarters in Reston, Virginia, Maryland & Virginia Milk Producers Cooperative Association, Inc. serves the interests of approximately 1,500 dairy farmers located in 11 mid-Atlantic and Southern states, including Pennsylvania, Maryland, Delaware, Virginia, West Virginia, Kentucky, Tennessee, North Carolina, South Carolina, Georgia, and Alabama. Member farms may be smaller than 100 cows or larger than 2,000. Maryland & Virginia markets members' products at competitive prices and pools their collective buying power to purchase agricultural equipment and supplies for them. The Association also employs a field staff to help members with their milk production, offers equipment loans, and lobbies the government on their behalf. Maryland & Virginia markets more than three billion pounds of milk each year, serving such major urban markets as Baltimore, Richmond, Charlotte, Atlanta, and Washington, D.C.

The raw milk is sent to the co-op's four processing plants. Located in Newport News, Virginia, Marva Maid Dairy produces whole, lowfat, and reduced fat milk as well as buttermilk, flavored milk, eggnog, and orange juice. The Maola Milk and Ice Cream unit, based in New Bern, North Carolina, produces fluid milk, ice cream, ice cream novelties, and juice for consumers in North Carolina, South Carolina, and Virginia. Maryland & Virginia also operates a manufacturing plant in Laurel, Maryland, that uses excess milk to produce butter, condensed milk, and nonfat dry milk to be sold to food companies as ingredients for such products as infant formula and baked goods. Finally, the co-op sends some of its milk to Valley Milk Products LLC, a Strasburg, Virginia-based, majority-owned joint venture with Utz Lake Inc., to produce butter, cream, dried milk powder, and condensed milks, which are then sold as ingredients for bread, baby food, ice cream, and frozen dinners. Maryland & Virginia also maintains an equipment warehouse in Frederick, Maryland, offering 1,500 agricultural items in stock. Although orders are shipped throughout the country, co-op trucks are able to make monthly deliveries to member farms in parts of Delaware, Maryland, Virginia, and Pennsylvania.

The co-op is governed by a 23-member board of directors. Each of the organization's 22 districts elects a director, and a public director serves to provide an outsider's perspective.

COMPANY PERSPECTIVES

From branded fluid milk to commercial ingredients like cream and high heat powder, Maryland & Virginia products represent an important sector of America's food chain.

RISE OF COOPERATIVES LINKED TO INDUSTRIAL REVOLUTION

The cooperative concept arose in Europe in the late 1700s and early 1800s, in response to societal changes brought about by the Industrial Revolution. Rural residents who once produced their own food now went to work in city factories and were very much at the mercy of shopkeepers or company stores where prices were high and products often adulterated to squeeze out further profit. In England consumers fought back, as groups began pooling their money to buy groceries from wholesalers. The first to form a lasting co-op was the Rochdale Equitable Pioneers Society, which opened a store in 1844 to serve the needs of striking textile workers in Rochdale, England.

In colonial America, Benjamin Franklin established one of the earliest co-ops in Philadelphia for mutual fire insurance. For the most part, however, American co-ops were formed by farmers, who used them to purchase equipment and supplies, provide storage or processing services, and in some cases market their products at the best price. Most of them were short-lived, however, the victims of poor organization and management.

Not until the 1890s did the cooperative movement in America truly take shape and begin to have an impact on the country's commerce, as farmers rebelled against the power wielded by the railroads, bankers, and manufacturers. Buying power was one advantage, but farmers also began to form co-ops along commodity lines to gain marketing leverage. In 1893, for example, several local associations were united into one organization, the Southern California Fruit Exchange, which established a formula for all cooperatives that followed. To stimulate sales, the Exchange began advertising its lemons and oranges under the "Sunkist" label.

Because of anti-trust legislation, co-operatives operated in a shadowy area of the law, since in theory they could be considered an unreasonable restraint of trade. But the cooperative movement, which enjoyed its most explosive growth from 1919 to 1922, had political allies, the Farm Bloc Members of Congress from Southern and Midwestern states, and in 1919 the National Coopera-

tive Milk Producers' Federation tried to pass legislation that was favorable to co-ops. It was defeated by commercial groups, but was rewritten and introduced by Senators Arthur Capper and Andrew Volstead a year later. The landmark Capper-Volstead Act finally passed in 1922, allowing farmers and ranchers to join marketing co-ops without fear of antitrust litigation.

SWITCH TO COOPERATIVE STATUS: 1923

Maryland & Virginia was established during this period, adding to the membership of the National Cooperative Milk Producers' Federation. It was organized and incorporated in September 1920 as a nonprofit corporation. Legally an association, it would not become a cooperative until 1923. It immediately hired a manager, who began signing up member dairy farmers. They agreed to pay the new co-op one-fifth of one cent per gallon to market their milk. Unfortunately distributors refused to pay the price the organization wanted and for a time members were no better off than before. In fact, the Association was in debt to the tune of $108,000 by 1924. The passage of Capper-Volstead provided some clout, but more important was a Virginia law, the Milk and Cream Act of 1925, which allowed the state to set the minimum price for milk to save producers from price cutting, which in the long run could endanger supply, and called for the use of an arbitrator to settle differences between producers and dealers. The law was challenged but ultimately upheld by the United States Supreme Court in 1937. The leadership of Maryland & Virginia's second general manager, John McGill, and president Frank Walker also played a key role in the turnaround of the organization, which got out of debt and by the close of the 1920s had built up a surplus of nearly $180,000.

With legal backing, Maryland & Virginia began to enjoy strong growth in the 1920s. It built a pair of processing plants, and also joined forces with a Baltimore association to create a common marketing agency. The foundation established was strong enough to withstand the tribulations of the 1930s, as the stock market crashed in 1929 and America descended into the decade-long Great Depression. It was a difficult period for the Association, which had to go to court in order to sell its products in the Arlington and Alexandria, Virginia area. Maryland & Virginia also had to contend with cheap uninspected, "bootleg" cream that flooded the Washington, D.C., market. The co-op went so far as to hire a private detective agency to keep an eye out for the offenders and offered a $500 reward to anyone with information about the sources of illegal cream. In 1939 the District's Embassy Dairy was caught with 200 cans

KEY DATES

1920: Incorporation of Maryland & Virginia Milk Producers Cooperative Association, Inc. as a nonprofit entity.
1923: The association converts to cooperative status.
1955: The Olney Acres manufacturing plant is acquired.
1962: The Marva Maid milk processing plant is opened.
1971: Colony Farms Dairy is acquired.
1999: The association merges with Carolina Virginia Milk Producers.
2003: The Maola Milk and Ice Cream Co. is acquired.
2006: Giant Food's plant is acquired by the association.

of Indiana cream by local officials. Although the plant was fined a nominal $10, the event spurred a Congressional investigation into the matter.

The United State's entry into World War II in late 1941 provided the stimulus needed to finally bring the Depression to an end. But for Maryland & Virginia and other milk producers the war did not lead to a boon. To put industry on a war footing and make the best use of resources, the government imposed price controls. Milk producers had hoped to see a price increase but government intervention prevented it and they had to wait to enjoy better economic times. Maryland & Virginia did its part during the war by donating milk to the Stage Door Canteen, a Broadway theatre café that catered to soldiers, sailors, and marines. The Association also donated money to the Red Cross. During the first 20 years of its existence, surplus milk had been a perennial problem, but during the war years the Association had difficulty satisfying contracts—and still had to contend with low milk prices that usually resulted from surpluses. Federal subsidies helped, but they were lifted at the close of the war, forcing Maryland & Virginia to contend with the usual forces of supply and demand in the marketplace.

Following a brief recession at the end of hostilities, the U.S. economy soared in the post-war years, and so did Maryland & Virginia, as returning servicemen married and began raising the baby boom generation, which would drink massive amounts of milk. To support members it opened a pair of equipment operations in Frederick, Maryland, by the end of the 1940s. Expan-

sion continued in the 1950s, spurred to some extent by the introduction of new technology in the dairy industry. For example, the first bulk farm tank came into use in the early 1950s. Prior to this, farmers had to store their milk in cans for transportation to processing facilities. Members took advantage of the new bulk tanks and in the summer of 1951 the Association established two truck routes to service 14 farm tanks, the operations of which ranged in capacity from 200 to 600 gallons. In another important industry development, processors were now also allowed to use chemical sterilization methods on their milking equipment rather than rely solely on steam. The Association also expanded during this period. It acquired Embassy Dairy in 1954 and the plant began to process members' surplus milk. Maryland & Virginia's processing capacity was bolstered even further a year later when Olney Acres' manufacturing plant was purchased in Laurel, Maryland. The addition of these two plants solved the long-time problem of what to do with surplus fluid milk: It could now be converted into storable products, thereby taking fluid milk off the market and supporting prices.

MARVA MAID PLANT BUILT IN 1962

In 1962 Maryland & Virginia began the construction of the Marva Maid plant in Newport News, Virginia. When milk processing began a year later, Maryland & Virginia was able to extend its marketing reach to Virginia's Tidewater Region. The 1960s was also a period of consolidation in the dairy industry, as a number of cooperatives merged, such as the Middle Atlantic Diary Council. Maryland & Virginia worked with other associations when a drought led to lower milk production. Unable to provide enough milk to its processing plants, Maryland & Virginia worked with other co-ops to process their excess milk. Furthermore, the Association joined forces in 1968 with Inter-State Milk Producers' Cooperative and Maryland Cooperative Milk Producers, forming the Pennmarva Dairyman's Federation to serve as a common marketing agency.

The 1970s saw significant milk production increases across the country. Maryland & Virginia expanded its operations during this time by acquiring Colony Farms Dairy in 1971. It was then merged with Marva Maid. Another important development came in 1976 when Maryland & Virginia became affiliated with the Land O'Lakes butter operation.

Milk production increases and further expansion continued into the 1980s. The Laurel plant added new receiving facilities, and to relieve the problem of surplus milk the Association joined with others to develop a method for freeze-drying milk solids. In addition, members took advantage of two government programs that kept milk supplies in check: the Dairy Diversion program, through which farmers received payments for lowering production in 1984 and 1985; and Whole Herd Buyout (or the Dairy Termination Program), which paid farmers to slaughter their dairy cows and agree to stay out of dairy farming for at least five years. While Maryland & Virginia lost some members in this way, it also added some when Capitol Milk sold its assets to Southland Corporation, the holding company for the 7-Eleven convenience store chain, and its producers became members of the Association. Another important change in the 1980s came in 1983 with the passage of the Dairy and Tobacco Adjustment Act, which opened the door to national advertising and the promotion of dairy products. In 1986 The Middle Atlantic Milk Marketing Agency was formed to handle the co-op's promotional activities, with member farms charged a 15-cent deduction to support the effort.

At the start of the 1990s, Maryland & Virginia's milk production topped the two-billion-pound mark, which resulted from changes at the Laurel Plant in 1992, as the drying, evaporation, and handling facilities were renovated and enlarged. By now the Association's annual revenues were in the neighborhood of $350 million, but despite growth it faced a challenging future. It was losing members in its core territory as dairy farmers had to contend with the rising cost of feed and other essentials while the price their milk fetched remained flat at best. Moreover, the Washington, D.C. suburbs, where dairy farms were once prevalent, had become more valuable for housing developments, and land speculators convinced many farmers to sell their property and their herds and start a new life. As a result, the city's fresh milk supply crept further south and west. The trend continued over the course of the 1990s and by the end of the decade changes were in order for the Association. Maryland & Virginia merged with Carolina Virginia Milk Producers, adding 400 members and increasing the Association's milk production to three billion pounds a year. Later in 1999 the Association also bought Valley Milk Products LLC to handle some of that extra milk.

In January 2000, the Association took another major step by joining forces with Land O'Lakes East and Southeast Milk, Inc. to form the Advantage Dairy Group as an East Coast milk marketing operation. Several months later, two more co-ops, Lone Star Milk Producers and Arkansas Dairy Cooperative Association joined. A year after that, Land O'Lakes looked to take the idea one step further and merge with Maryland & Virginia, Lone Star, and Arkansas Dairy. Essentially Land O'Lakes would be absorbing the three smaller co-ops. The idea did not sit well with Maryland & Virginia members,

who immediately circulated a petition to force a special session. In a matter of weeks the merger was scrapped. Nevertheless, the milk industry continued to consolidate.

Maryland & Virginia took its own steps to keep growing. In 2003 it acquired North Carolina's Maola Milk and Ice Cream Co. At the same time it had to contend with depressed wholesale prices, which were continuing to drive dairy farmers out of business. One idea launched by the National Milk Producers' Federation, was Cooperatives Working Together, a private program to trim cattle herds to reduce production and increase prices. Maryland & Virginia also made efforts to cope with low dairy prices by making its manufacturing operations more productive, to the benefit of its members. In 2005 the Laurel plant added robotic palletizing to more efficiently package butter, an investment that the Association expected to pay off in less than two years. In 2006 Maryland & Virginia also increased its production capabilities by acquiring Giant Food's dairy processing plant in Landover, Maryland, which processed 700,000 pounds of milk each day, supplying nearly 200 grocery stores. For the past 30 years, Maryland & Virginia had been the plant's only milk supplier, so in effect the Association would be reaping further benefits from the milk its members produced.

Ed Dinger

PRINCIPAL SUBSIDIARIES

Marva Maid Dairy; Maola Milk and Ice Cream; Valley Milk Products LLC.

PRINCIPAL COMPETITORS

Dairy Farmers of America, Inc.; Dean Foods Company; Land O'Lakes, Inc.

FURTHER READING

Chan, Sewel, "Dealing With the Demise of the Dairy," *Washington Post*, August 3, 1997, p. V1.

DuMont, Amber, "October is the Month to Celebrate 85 Years of Maryland & Virginia's Cooperative Heritage," *Pipeline (Maryland & Virginia Milk Producers Cooperative Associations)*, September/October 2005, p. 4.

"Land O'Lakes Merger Nixed," *Dairy Foods*, November 2001, p. 12.

O'Neill, Jeff, "Palletizer Keeps Butter Churning," *Modern Materials Handling*, January 2006, p. 31.

Rath, Molly, "Milk Cooperative Squeezed by Loss of Farms," *Washington Business Journal*, September 10, 1990, p. 23.

Robinson, Ryan, "Dairymen Unite, Fight Falling Milk Prices," *Lancaster New Era*, April 29, 2003.

The MathWorks, Inc.

———————————■———————————

3 Apple Hill Drive
Natick, Massachusetts 01760-2098
U.S.A.
Telephone: (508) 647-7000
Fax: (508) 647-7001
Web site: http://www.mathworks.com

Private Company
Incorporated: 1984
Employees: 1,000
Sales: $350 million (2005 est.)
NAIC: 334515 Instrument Manufacturing for Measuring and Testing Electricity and Electrical Signals; 334516 Analytical Laboratory Instrument Manufacturing; 511210 Software Publishers

■ ■ ■

The MathWorks, Inc., is a leading publisher of technical software. Its flagship product, MatLab, the add-on Simulink, and other products have applications in a number of high-tech industries and are a staple of engineering curricula at more than 3,500 universities around the world. The company is owned by CEO John N. (Jack) Little, chairman and chief scientist Cleve Moler, and Steve Bangert, who together launched the company in 1984 and own most of its equity.

ORIGINS

The MathWorks, Inc. was formed in Palo Alto, California by John N. (Jack) Little, Cleve Moler, and Steve Bangert. It was originally incorporated as a

California company on December 7, 1984. It soon moved to the Boston area and was registered in Massachusetts on June 18, 1986. (A Delaware corporation of the same name was organized in 1997.)

Moler, an accomplished applied mathematician and chair of the computer science department at the University of New Mexico, would become the company's chief scientist and chairman. Jack Little took the titles of president and CEO and was at first the only employee. Little, who had studied electrical engineering at both MIT (where his father was a professor) and Stanford University (where he earned his master's degree), had previously led CAD/CAE package design at a firm called Systems Control Technology. According to the *Boston Globe,* Little's idiosyncratic personality helped keep the company together. He described his management philosophy with a Japanese proverb: "The more power you give up the more power you have."

MathWorks had been formed to commercialize a technical computer programming language and interactive environment Moler had originally created in Fortan for mainframe computers in the late 1970s. Called MatLab, a personal computer (PC) version was translated into C several years later by Little and another engineering consultant, Steve Bangert.

MatLab was designed to compute large arrays of data in matrixes. It was faster than older programming languages such as Fortran at processing large amounts of data. Originally used at research universities, it was soon adopted by industry.

According to the *Boston Globe,* the Massachusetts Institute of Technology bought the first ten copies of

COMPANY PERSPECTIVES

At The MathWorks, we express who we are as an organization through our guiding principle, our mission, and our core values. Developed over time, each represents a philosophy or goal that is intrinsically important to the organization. Our guiding principle is "Do the Right Thing." This means doing what is best for our staff members, customers, business partners, and communities for the long term, and believing that "right" answers exist. It also means measuring our success, not merely in financial terms, but by how consistently we act according to this principle. Our mission and core values express what "doing the right thing" means in our day-to-day work. Our mission articulates our goals as a company and how we go about achieving them. Our core values set out the principles that define who we are and how we work together. We invite you to explore these two different ways of understanding The MathWorks.

MatLab for $500. The disks were likely packaged in Zip-Loc bags, if company lore is to be trusted.

MatLab 2.0 was retailing for $395 in 1987. *PC Magazine* described it as powerful, fast running, and easier to use than other languages such as Pascal. By the time version 4.0 was released in 1991, the software was selling for $2,995. MatLab 4.0 featured color graphics, allowing for display of four dimensions of data on graphs.

Another important and enduring product line was Simulink (originally called SIMULAB). Simulink was an add-on to produce block diagrams. It would be expanded with other graphic tools for studying and modeling dynamic systems. The Simulink C Code Generator retailed for $13,000 when it was introduced in 1992; a bundle of it with MatLab and some other components was priced at $30,000.

The software was expanded to include a variety of system design, modeling, and simulation tools. It was installed in both desktop PCs and supercomputers and counted more than 100,000 users in more than 50 countries by the early 1990s.

BOOMING IN THE NINETIES

In 1991, MathWorks laid out a mission involving four components: technological, business-related, human,

and social. Its 100 or so staffers received eight paid hours a year for volunteer opportunities. "I think employees appreciate that the company is acknowledging their work, and the community we live and work in appreciates us as a fellow community member," a spokesperson told the *Boston Business Journal.* "It's what makes this company different."

In 1994, Cleve Moler developed a software-based correction for the notorious floating-point error discovered in the Pentium chip. For good measure, he posted Intel's correspondence related to the crisis on his own company's web site. "You've got to [be able to] trust a computer's arithmetic," he told the *Washington Post.* "It's a question of confidence."

The work force was growing rapidly, numbering 380 employees by 1997. In many ways The MathWorks was the prototypical software outfit, emphasizing a fun creative environment and a high degree of employee autonomy. Its perks and quirks were intended to foster creativity in a highly competitive business. "Every cent we've spent on the people who work here has paid for itself many times over," Little explained to the *Boston Globe.*

MathWorks did not, however, follow the Silicon Valley crowd of tech firms rushing to go public as the Internet bubble expanded to bursting. "He doesn't want to lose control," cofounder Steve Bangert told the *Boston Globe* of CEO Jack Little. "He doesn't want to deal with a bunch of stockholders."

Cambridge Control, a U.K. software producer and engineering firm, was acquired in October 1997. It had itself been established in 1984 and it became a MathWorks distributor in 1988. Cambridge Control was renamed The MathWorks Ltd. in June 2000, and the consulting arm was dubbed Cambridge Consulting Group. The MathWorks, Inc. also was launching subsidiaries in other European countries.

At the turn of the millennium, MathWorks had about 1,000 employees. It had sales of about $200 million in 2001. Half of this was related to dynamic control-system software, according to information from the Justice Department. The agency filed an antitrust lawsuit against the company over its agreement to take over the MatrixX line of software from Alameda, California's Wind River Systems Inc.

20 IN 2004

Many of the complicated engineering design feats of the previous two decades had been made possible by MatLab and other software produced by MathWorks, which made the calculation of complex algorithms possible. "Without it, these mathematical techniques simply

```
┌─────────────────────────────────────────┐
│                                          │
│             KEY DATES                    │
│         ──────────●──────────            │
│                                          │
│  1984:  The MathWorks, Inc. is formed to │
│         market MatLab technical computer │
│         language.                        │
│  1992:  The company has more than 100    │
│         employees, 100,000 users.        │
│  1995:  The company has more than 220    │
│         employees, distributors in more  │
│         than 160 countries.              │
│  2001:  Sales are reportedly about $200  │
│         million; the company has about   │
│         1,000 employees.                 │
│  2005:  Sales are reportedly about $350  │
│         million.                         │
│                                          │
└─────────────────────────────────────────┘
```

wouldn't be available to the engineers," Moler said in the *Philadelphia Business Journal*. Modeling software was being applied to new areas of science, notably biology and chemistry, and even the financial world. Mathlab and Simulink were much in demand in the electronics industry as product development cycles shortened. After 20 years in business, the company had reportedly never posted a loss.

The company was proud of its record of social responsibility. It also benefited from support in the local community. According to the *Boston Business Journal*, the town of Natick, Massachusetts was arranging tax breaks to allow MathWorks to buy and improve buildings it had been leasing. In November 2004, the company bought its two headquarters buildings for $49.7 million in one of the largest corporate real estate deals the area had seen in years. The three- and four-story buildings together had more than 300,000 square feet.

MatLab products, long dominant in simulations, were extending their usefulness into the evolving electronic design automation (EDA) market. A number of traditional EDA vendors were creating links between their products and MatLab, allowing engineers to use the same language for simulation and implementation.

MatLab Central, MathWorks' Web-based resource for product news and support, was quick to incorporate RSS feeds as a way to push content to users. Launched in January 2004, it was logging 50,000 feed hits a month by June 2005.

Sales for the privately held company were reported as being $350 million in the *Boston Business Journal*. In 2006, the company was heavily involved in the aerospace and defense industry, and was participating in the U.S. Army's multibillion dollar Future Combat System.

Frederick C. Ingram

PRINCIPAL SUBSIDIARIES

The MathWorks, Ltd. (United Kingdom).

PRINCIPAL COMPETITORS

Cadence Design Systems Inc.; Mentor Graphics Corporation; National Instruments Corporation; Visual Numerics, Inc.; Wolfram Research, Inc.

FURTHER READING

Blanton, Kimberly, "At Mathworks, Support + Fun = Success; CEO Jack Little Believes in Power of His Workers—And Their Ideas," *Boston Globe*, April 20, 1997, p. J1.

———, "This Boss Puts His Employees First: Mathworks' Success Owed to Offbeat Style of CEO," *San Francisco Chronicle*, April 25, 1997, p. C3.

Burschka, Martin A., "MatLab," *PC Magazine*, April 14, 1987, p. 168.

Corcoran, Elizabeth, "How to Drive a Chipmaker Buggy; A Math Maven Says the Laws of Flaws Make It Tough for Intel to Avoid Pentium's Woes," *Washington Post*, February 9, 1995, p. D10.

Edwards, Chris, "MatrixX Future in Doubt As Rights Pass to Mathworks," *Electronic Engineering Times*, March 5, 2001, p. 22.

Emigh, Jacqueline, "Mathworks Creates 'Software Fix' for Pentium Error," *Newsbytes*, November 29, 1994.

"The Evolution of MatLab and Simulink," *EDN*, March 3, 2005, p. 28.

Ferranti, Marc, "Color Graphics to Add Luster to MatLab 4.0," *PC Week*, December 16, 1991, pp. 33f.

———, "MathWorks Tools Will Ease Design of Control Systems," *PC Week*, November 30, 1992, p. 63.

Field, Karen Auguston, "RSS Feeds: Not Just for ESPN and CNN Anymore," *Design News*, September 26, 2005, pp. 56, 58.

Goering, Richard, "MatLab Edges Closer to Electronic Design Automation World," *EE Times Online*, October 4, 2004.

———, "Tool Vendors Dispute Report of Downturn in ESL," *EE Times Online*, December 20, 2004.

Goodspeed, Linda, "Corporate Civic-Mindedness Is Factor in Worker Loyalty," *Boston Business Journal*, December 20, 2002.

Hillman, Michelle, "711 Atlantic Fetches $17M," *Boston Business Journal*, August 16, 2004.

McEachern, Christina, "MathWorks Links to Bloomberg, Live Data for Efficient Modeling," *Wall Street & Technology*, April 2000, p. 44.

"Mathworks Purchases Natick HQ for $49.7M," *Boston Business Journal*, November 10, 2004.

Moretti, Gabe, "Design Complexity Requires System-Level Design," *EDN*, March 3, 2005, pp. 26–32.

Qualters, Sheri, "Mass. Equips the High-Tech Army," *Boston Business Journal*, February 20, 2006.

Richards, Gregory, "Tech Help with Doing the Math," *Philadelphia Business Journal,* July 8, 2002.

Schweber, Bill, "The MathWorks' Andy Grace on Simulation,"

EDN, September 1, 2005, p. 26.

Seper, Jerry, "2 Software Firms Accused of Violating Antitrust Law," *Washington Times,* June 22, 2002, p. C11.

Misonix, Inc.

1938 New Highway
Farmingdale, New York 11735
U.S.A.
Telephone: (631) 694-9555
Toll Free: (800) 694-9612
Fax: (631) 6940941
Web site: http://www.misonix.com

Public Company
Incorporated: 1967 as Heat Systems-Ultrasonics, Inc.
Employees: 214
Sales: $45.9 million (2005)
Stock Exchanges: NASDAQ
Ticker Symbol: MSON
NAIC: 339111 Laboratory Apparatus and Furniture
  Manufacturing

∎ ∎ ∎

Misonix, Inc., primarily designs, manufactures, and markets ultrasonic medical devices using High Intensity Focused Ultrasound. Applications include the removal of cancerous tumors, laparoscopic procedures (minimally invasive surgery in the abdominal area), neurosurgery and general surgery, plastic surgery, urology, and wound care. In addition to medical products, Misonix operates a Scientific Products Group that uses ultrasonic technology to produce cleaning systems for medical and dental instruments; a fluxless soldering system; a spraying system with a wide variety of industrial applications, including painting and coating, printing, combustion, and optics; ductless laboratory fume hoods; and the

company's first product, the Sonicator, a liquid processor that transforms AC current into a 20 kHz signal to power a horn/probe used in the laboratory to mix compounds, accelerate reactions, create emulsions and suspensions, and other applications. Misonix is also involved in air pollution control, offering the MYS-TAIRE scrubber, which provides gas, mist, odor, aerosol, and particulate matter removal for such industries as semiconductor, pharmaceutical, mining and metallurgical, food and beverage, hazardous waste treatment, and process and specialty gases. Based in Farmingdale, New York, Misonix is a public company listed on the Nasdaq.

FOUNDER STARTS COMPANY IN 1955

Misonix was founded in Great Neck, New York, in 1955 by Howard Alliger as a sole proprietorship called Heat Systems. Alliger was born in Brooklyn, New York's Flatus section. Although his father was involved in real estate, he developed a love for science, leading him to enroll at the Cornell University School of Engineering following a stint in the Navy where he studied radar in 1946. Alliger spent four years at Cornell but the fifth and final year of his program proved too difficult and he dropped out. He transferred to Allegheny College in Maxville, Pennsylvania, graduating in 1952 with a B.A. degree in economics.

After college Alliger went to work selling environmental test chambers and ovens to laboratories. During the course of his job he met a man named Stan Jacks who told him that he had invented a "funny looking" ultrasonic probe in his basement and he enlisted

Alliger's help in finding a use for it. Alliger took it with him to the laboratories and soon it was discovered that the probe was a good cell disputer, ideal for biochemical laboratories where researchers were interested in determining the inner workings of cells. Alliger now developed the idea of ultrasonic disruption of cells and tissues, eventually leading to his receiving a patent on the Ultrasonic dissector.

Alliger set up shop in 1955 with a secretary in a Great Neck office complex to sell the ultrasonic disintegrator he developed using Jacks's probe, called the Sniffer. Alliger sold the devices, which Jacks manufactured in his basement. The device was sold to laboratories to disintegrate cells, releasing DNA, enzymes, and other cell contents. It was also used to mix liquids, a function the device continues to perform today. Convincing scientists that the device actually did what Alliger claimed it could proved to be painstakingly slow, however. He did not hire his second employee until 1959 and did not move to a new office, in Plainview, New York, until 1963. (The company was incorporated as Heat Systems-Ultrasonics, Inc. in 1967 and moved to Farmingdale, New York, in 1982.) After about a decade, however, every biochemical laboratory in the country was aware of the device and eventually the ultrasonic disintegrator became standard equipment. In the meantime, in 1960 Jacks sold the Sniffer to Branson Instruments, a Connecticut company that was a pioneer in ultrasonic technology for industrial purposes. When Branson began selling to his customers, Alliger started manufacturing the device himself, which in 1962 he called the Sonicator, a product that Misonix continues to sell.

In the 1970s Alliger began looking for further applications of ultrasonic technology. He was interested in developing an ultrasonic device that could be used in the cleaning of dental instruments. This work led him to experiment with chlorine dioxide as a sterilizer as part of the system. Straight chlorine dioxide did not work, but he found a formulation that did and called it Alcide to exploit the chemical. He then discovered that the chemical worked just as well without the ultrasonic

device. He formed another company called Alcide, then took it public in 1983 and sold his share of the business.

FOCUS ON MEDICAL DEVICES: 1987

The MYSTAIRE scrubber was another product that was developed to make use of ultrasonic technology. According to an interview with Alliger, the air pollution product was put on the market in the early 1980s and sold to industrial customers. It wasn't until 1987 that the company launched a concerted effort to apply ultrasonic technology to the development of medical devices that could help remove or disintegrate tumors. The company also tried to develop an ultrasonic system to remove plaque and red blood clots from around the heart. Called the Star System (Sonic Transluminal Atheroma Removal), it relied on the insertion of a titanium wire through the chest and into the heart to perform the procedure, but according to Alliger when the wire began to curve it lost power and the concept did not ultimately pan out.

Heat-Systems-Ultrasonics changed its name to MedSonic, Inc. in August 1991 to reflect the new emphasis on the medical field. In that month the company also brought in a new president and chief executive officer. (Alliger had served as president until 1982 and continued to hold the chairmanship.) The new CEO was Michael Juliano, who had experience in the medical devices field with Wright Laboratories, which he co-founded. Juliano now prepared to take MedSonic public. Underwritten by Josephthal Lyon & Ross Inc., the company completed its initial public offering of stock in January 1992, netting almost $8.7 million. The stock was then listed on the Boston Stock Exchange and the Nasdaq. A month later MedSonic used some of that money, about $550,000, to acquire a 81.4 percent interest in Labcaire Systems, Ltd., a United Kingdom-based company that would manufacture some of MedSonic's industrial products and also help distribute some of the parent company's other products in Europe. The remaining interest in Labcaire was acquired over the course of the next several years. Before this acquisition, MedSonic sold about 16 percent of its products overseas through distributors, but it was not a focused effort. Now with Labcaire in the fold, not only would MedSonic be able to better support European sales, it would also have the ability to launch medical products in Europe, where regulations were less strict, while seeking approval in the United States.

The use of the MedSonic name proved to be short-term. In 1993 Medtronic Inc. objected and filed a lawsuit claiming trademark infringement. Although MedSonic did not believe the charge was valid, it was not interested in spending the money or taking the time to make a

KEY DATES

1955: Company founded by Howard Alliger as Heat Systems.
1967: Company incorporated as Heat Systems-Ultrasonics, Inc.
1982: Headquarters move to Farmingdale, New York.
1992: Company taken public.
1994: Heat Systems is renamed Misonx, Inc.
1996: Alliger retires as chairman.
2005: Company proposes spin off of scientific and laboratory businesses.

defense. Instead it agreed to find a new name, and in January 1994 adopted the Misonix Inc. name.

At this stage, the company was beginning to move from the research and development phase to product development in the medical devices industry. Sales continued to come from laboratories and the environmental segment, but Misonix recorded annual losses for several years as it worked to bring commercial medical devices onto the market. While the STAR System proved to be a disappointment, the company had better luck developing a product to use disruptive ultrasound to fragment body fat. In October 1996 Misonix licensed its ultrasonic cutting technology to United States Surgical Corporation for use in devices performing laparoscopic surgery. Plastic surgeons would also find a use for the technology in liposuction procedures, which previously had relied on a high suction vacuum to literally tear out flesh. The procedure also removed a great deal of blood, so that a large percentage of patients required blood transfusions. Ultrasound offered a far less traumatic option.

Misonix underwent changes in management in the mid-1990s. Joseph Librizzi was named president and chief executive officer in March 1995. With a doctorate in applied mechanics and aerospace engineering from Polytechnic Institute of Brooklyn, Librizzi had been with the company since 1986. Next, Alliger resigned as chairman of the board in March 1996, although he stayed on as a director. Despite his 70 years, Alliger now devoted his time to building yet another business, Frontier Pharmaceutical, Inc., which continued his earlier work on chlorine dioxide to develop oral care, skin care, wound care, and surface treatment products.

RETURN TO PROFITABILITY: 1996

Misonix finally hit its stride in fiscal 1996 (the year ending June 30, 1997), when the price of its stock increased from less than $1 to about $8. The company also posted its first profitable year since going public, netting almost $400,000 on sales that approached $10 million. The following year proved even more successful, spurred in large part by the September 1996 introduction of the company's first ultrasonic medical device, the Lysonix 2000, a soft tissue aspirator used by plastic surgeons to perform liposuction operations. It was sold by licensee Lysonix Inc. With this new revenue stream, Misonix was able in fiscal 1997 to increase sales 77 percent to $17.6 million and record a second straight profitable year with net income of $177,000. Moreover, the company declared a three-for-two stock split in September 1997. Not only did the Lysonix 2000 do well, but the ductless fume enclosure outperformed expectations and the Mystaire product continued to do well too. Unfortunately for Misonix the technology used in the Lysonix system became the subject of a patent infringement lawsuit filed by Mentor Corporation, a cosmetic surgery equipment and supplies company. The matter would wend its way through the court for the next several years, serving as both a distraction and a cloud over Misonix's prospects.

Misonix endured a rough patch in 1998, when a delay in orders sent the company's stock price tumbling from a high of $22.75 to less than $7. But when the fiscal year came to a close, Misonix again realized record results. Revenues improved 52 percent to $26.8 million and net income jumped to more than $5.3 million. The January launch of a second medical device played a important role in the company's continued growth. US Surgical Corporation introduced the Auto Sonix, an ultrasonic cutting and coagulating system used by surgeons.

Despite the overall strong performance of Misonix while he was CEO, Librizzi did not have the confidence of the board of directors, which did not choose to renew his contract when it expired in September 1998. To replace him they brought in one of their own, board member Michael A. McManus, Jr., to take over as chief executive. A former assistant to President Ronald Reagan with a law degree from Georgetown University, McManus was no stranger to the medical field, having worked at Pfizer Inc. as corporate counsel and vice president of strategic planning. He also had experience in law, government, acquisitions, and banking, having served as the CEO of New York Bancorp Inc. and holding positions at Revlon Group and Jamcor Pharmaceuticals.

Misonix's sales slipped to $24.8 million in fiscal 1999 and net income fell below $2 million. In fiscal

2000 the company regained some momentum, improving sales and also making some strategic investments to position the company for continued growth in the ultrasonic field. In November 1999 it paid $1.4 million to acquire a controlling interest in Acoustic Marketing Research, which did business as Sonora Medical Systems. It was a Colorado-based refurbisher of ultrasound systems. Over the next year Misonix acquired the rest of the company. The company also bought a stake in Focus Surgery Inc, an Indiana-based company that was developing medical devices that could destroy difficult-to-reach diseased tissue, in particular prostate cancer. In addition, Misonix invested in Hearing Innovations, Inc., a company developing medical devices that used ultrasound technology to treat deafness and other hearing disorders. (Misonix would acquire Hearing Innovations out of bankruptcy in 2005.)

Revenues rebounded to $29 million in fiscal 2000 and enjoyed modest growth in fiscal 2001 when sales reached $30.8 million. The company launched a new product developed by Sonora, the SONOReal, an ultrasound device that could produce three-dimensional images of babies in the womb. Misonix also continued to expand its capabilities through another acquisition. In February 2001 it acquired Chicago-based Fibra Sonics Inc., a small manufacturer of ultrasonic medical devices, the addition of which gave Misonix entry into three new medical markets: neurosurgery, urology, and ophthalmology.

The September 11, 2001, terrorist attacks on the United States took place during the 2002 fiscal year for Misonix, and the subsequent anthrax attack scares spurred the sales of the company's ductless fume enclosures, which could be used to safely open suspicious letters, and led to a boost in the price of the stock. The year also saw the resolution of the patent infringement lawsuit by Mentor. Misonix agreed to pay $2.7 million to settle the matter. When the year ended, Misonix posted a slight loss in revenues to $29.6 million, but rebounded in fiscal 2003 to record sales of nearly

$35 million, due mostly to a sharp increase in the sale of medical devices. Revenues increased to more than $39 million the next year, again led by strong sales in the medical device segment. The pattern continued in fiscal 2005 when revenues approached $46 million. A month after the fiscal year came to a close, in July 2005, Misonix announced that it had hired San Francisco's ThinkEquity Partners to develop a plan to spin off its Laboratory and Scientific segments in order to focus all of its attention on the development of medical devices. Should that plan come to fruition, it would mark the beginning of a new era for the company.

Ed Dinger

PRINCIPAL SUBSIDIARIES

Acoustic Marketing Research Inc.; Labcaire Systems, Ltd.; Misonic, Ltd.; Fibra-Sonics (NY) Inc.; Hearing Innovations, Inc.

PRINCIPAL COMPETITORS

Met-Pro; Sonics & Materials, Inc.; Valpey-Fisher Corporation.

FURTHER READING

Bernstein, James, "Misonix: Sales Of Fume Device Up," *Newsday,* November 6, 2001, p. A47.

"CEO Interview: Medsonic Inc. (MSON)," *Wall Street Transcript,* March 8, 1993.

Long, Don, "Misonix to Spin Off Lab/Science Division to Focus on Devices," *Medical Device Week,* July 26, 2005.

Martorana, Jamie, "Board Member Picked As New Misonix Chief," *Newsday,* November 3, 1998, p. A36.

Unger, Michael, "Misonix Inc. Hits a Trouble Spot," *Newsday,* January 12, 1998, p. C18.

Moliflor Loisirs

26 rue Bellecordière 69292
Lyon Cedex 02,
France
Telephone: (33) 472 56 22 30
Fax: (33) 472 56 22 59
Web site: http://www.moliflor.com

Private Company
Incorporated: 1956
Employees: 1,505
Sales: EUR 273 million ($320 million) (2005)
NAIC: 721110 Casinos (Except Casino Hotels); 713210
Hotels (Except Casino Hotels) and Motels

■ ■ ■

Moliflor Loisirs is France's third-largest casino operator and one of the fastest-growing as well. Since the start of the 2000s, Moliflor has more than tripled the number of casinos under its operation, for a total of 21 casinos in 2006, generating annual revenues of EUR 273 million ($320 million). Headquartered in Lyon, Moliflor operates casinos throughout France, but especially in the country's southern coastal areas. Altogether the company's casinos feature more than 1,800 slot machines, as well as traditional French and international gaming tables, including le Jeu de la Boule and "English-style" Roulette, Poker, Blackjack and the like. In addition, most of the group's casinos feature a combination of restaurants, hotel accommodations, and entertainment facilities, including theaters and discotheques, as well as other amenities, such as private beach areas and beach facilities. Moliflor was founded in 1948 and controlled by the founding Moliner-Florensa family until its acquisition by PPM Ventures in 1999. The company was subsequently acquired by Bridgepoint Capital in November 2005, which then sold a minority interest to Loto Quebec in 2006. Moliflor Loisirs is led by CEO Marc Leonard.

THE FIRST FIFTY YEARS: 1948 TO 1998

Adrien Moliner had already gained experience in the hotel business when, in 1948, he purchased his first casino location, in Canet-en-Roussillon, on the Mediterranean coast near Perpignan, in the south of France. The actual casino was closed at the time of Moliner's purchase of the site and remained so into the mid-1950s. In 1956, however, Moliner received permission to re-launch casino operations. Joined by nephew Claude Florensa, he incorporated a new company to operate the casino, which later became known as Moliflor.

Initially, the Canet casino's gaming facilities remained somewhat limited, and the property was not considered to be a full-fledged casino. This changed in 1965, when Moliflor was granted the right to add roulette tables. With one casino under its belt, Moliflor began eyeing expansion into other locations. The company at first targeted the regional market, staying close to home with the purchase of the Casino de Boulou, also in the western Pyrénées region.

Moliflor remained a two-casino business into the 1970s. The company added its third casino in 1976, buying a controlling stake in the casino in another coastal

KEY DATES

1948: Hotel owner Adrien Moliner acquires a non-operational casino in Canet.

1956: Moliner's nephew, Claude Florensas, joins the group, which then launches casino operations at the Canet site.

1965: The Canet casino adds roulette tables, becoming a full-scale casino.

1976: The Moliner group acquires its third casino.

1980: Claude Florensas becomes head of the company.

1987: The group incorporates as Moliflor Participations and receives authorization to add slot machines to all of the group's casinos.

1997: The company changes its name to Moliflor.

1998: Moliflor goes public on Paris stock exchange.

1999: PPM Ventures acquires the company, which is reincorporated as Moliflor Loisirs.

2000: An expansion drive begins with the acquisition of casinos in Antibes, Luxeuil-les-Bains, and Montrond-les-Bains.

2005: Bridgepoint Capital becomes a majority shareholder.

2006: Loto Quebec acquires a 38% stake in Moliflor.

site, Saint Cyprien. This operation was complemented by a fourth site in the region, in Argèles, acquired in 1980. The Argèles casino was located directly on the beach, and like the company's other casinos, featured its own restaurant in addition to gaming facilities. Also in 1980, Claude Florensa took over as the head of the company.

Florensa reincorporated in 1987, and renamed the company as Moliflor Participation. The new company then received authorization from the French government to install slot machines in the group's casinos for the first time. The addition of slot machines helped popularize the casino market for French consumers, lowering the threshold for entry into gambling. The company quickly began adding slot machines to its casinos: the Canet facility would eventually add some 160 machines to its floor, while the Boulou casino boasted 80 machines. Both the Argèles and Saint Cyprien sites remained more modest, at 32 machines and 49 machines, respectively.

Slot machines soon accounted for the largest share of the company's revenues, driving its growth into the

1990s and enabling it to continue its expansion through acquisition. The next property added by the company came in 1992, when the company acquired a controlling stake in the casino in Lamalou-les-Bains, a thermal spa resort village situated in the Haut Languedoc National Park and located near Beziers.

By the time the company celebrated its 50th anniversary, it had already acquired its sixth casino, in the ski resort area of Ax-les-Thermes. In that year, the company changed its name again, to Moliflor SA and went public with a listing on the Paris stock exchange in July 1998. With the capital raised from the public offering, Molifor returned to its external expansion, acquiring a seventh casino, in Amélie-les-Bains, a village noted for its thermal spring spas. Like many casinos in France, the new casino was a modest affair, featuring only a small gaming room with no slot machines.

By the late 1990s, however, Moliflor was confronted with the rapidly changing French casino landscape, as a small number of groups, led by chief rival Partouche, had launched a widespread consolidation of the market. A major driving force behind this consolidation was the French government's decision to place tight limits on the addition of new slot machines in the country's casinos. As its competitors began buying up the smaller casino groups in the country, Moliflor became a target as well.

In response, the company decided to take itself off the market, allowing the venture capital group PPM Ventures, part of the British-based Prudential group, to take 92 percent of Moliflor. At the same time, PPM acquired an additional casino in Uriage. This casino was then merged into Moliflor and both companies were regrouped under a new company, Moliflor Loisirs. Taking the lead of the new company was managing director Marc Leonard, who had built his own career within one of France's leading hotel and casino groups, Lucien Barriere.

GAMBLING ON LEADERSHIP IN THE NEW CENTURY

With Leonard in the lead and backed by PPM, Moliflor entered a new growth phase that was to take it to the top ranks of the French casino industry before the middle of the 2000s. Acquisitions formed the core of Moliflor's growth strategy, while the company also invested strongly in expanding and upgrading its portfolio of casinos. As such, the group's Amélie-les-bains casino was expanded in April 2000 with the addition of a new room housing 30 slot machines.

By then, the group had already completed its first new acquisition, taking over the Casino d'Antibes "La

Siesta" located on France's exclusive Côte d'Azur. One of the largest single casinos in France—and one of the last independent casinos before its acquisition by Moliflor—the Antibes casino boasted 180 slot machines, as well as a gaming room, restaurant, private beach, and the region's largest open-air discotheque. The acquisition of the Antibes casino raised the group's revenues past the EUR 100 million mark for the first time. The company quickly added two more casinos in 2000, in Luxeuil-les Bains and in Montrond-les-Bains; the latter was among France's 15th largest casinos while the former represented Molifor's first venture in the French northeastern region.

Moliflor added five more casinos in 2001. The first, located at Gerardmer, in the Haute Vosges region, also featured its own 600-seat cinema. The company continued to move north, adding two Normandy locations, at Saint-Pair-sur-mer and at Saint-Aubin-sur-mer. The company filled in its eastern presence with the purchase of the Santenay casino in April; by July, the company had entered the western Atlantic region as well, in Port Crouesty. That casino, built by Molifor, added a 50-machine slot room the following year.

Moliflor acquired new shareholders in 2002, when PPM sold its stake in the company to an investment partnership between the Royal Bank of Scotland and Legal & General Ventures. Nonetheless, the company remained focused on its expansion drive, buying up the Casino d'Etretat, located near Le Havre in the north of France. The company also invested in upgrading its facilities, completing a renovation of its Montrond casino complex.

By the end of 2002, Moliflor had entered new territory, buying up the Bordeaux-based Groupe Etoile. The purchase added sites along the southwestern Atlantic coast, in Saint Paul-les-Dax and in Saint Jean de Luz, as well as a leisure base in Casteljaloux. The purchase of Groupe Etroile added some EUR 20 million to Moliflor's total revenues, which topped EUR 250 million that year. This placed the group in the number four position in the French casino sector in terms of revenues. With 19 casinos now under its control, the company had also claimed the number two position in terms of locations.

At the beginning of 2003, Moliflor added its 20th casino, returning north to acquire the Tréport casino. Yet that year marked a pause in the group's external expansion as it focused on expanding and upgrading its existing properties. The company unveiled its newly renovated Santenay casino in April 2003; by August, the company had received authorization to add nearly 90 new slot machines among its casinos in Uriage, Antibes, Boulou and Port Crouesty. The company also carried out renovations of the Saint Cyprien casino and its

original Canet casino, with both completed in September of that year. By the end of 2003, the company had received authorization to add nine new slot machines to its St. Aubin casino, as well. This was followed by the addition of 20 new machines in Santenay at the beginning of 2004. Also in 2004, the company won the bid to construct a new casino in Lans en Vercors, which they expected would be opened in 2008.

Marc Leonard was named group CEO in 2005 as Moliflor found new owners, in the form of Bridgepoint Capital, which took over as the group's majority shareholder that year. By the end of that year, Bridgepoint had sold a minority shareholding in the company to Canada's Loto Quebec, which became the group's second-largest stakeholder with a 38 percent share. The new partnership allowed Moliflor to re-launch its expansion drive, which had been largely put on hold during 2005, with the purchase of its 21st casino, the "Les Pins" casino in Sables d'Olonne. That purchase helped complete Moliflor's geographic presence, adding its first site in the middle western seaboard region of France. With new financial backing, Molifor appeared a sure bet to play among the leaders in the French casino market.

M.L. Cohen

PRINCIPAL SUBSIDIARIES

Moliflor Loisirs operates casinos in Amélie-les-Bains, Antibes, Argelès, Ax-les-Thermes, Le Boulou, Canet, Etretat, Gérardmer, Lamalou-les-Bains, Luxeuil-les-Bains, Montrond-les-Bains, Port Crouesty, Les Sables d'Olonne, Saint-Aubin sur Mer, Saint-Cyprien, Saint-Jean de Luz, Saint-Pair sur Mer, Saint-Paul-les-Dax, Santenay, Tréport, and Uriage-les-Bains.

PRINCIPAL COMPETITORS

Groupe Partouche; Groupe Barrière SA; Accor Casinos; Société des Bains de Mer et du Cercle des Étrangers à Monaco; Compagnie Européenne de Casinos; Groupe Tranchant; Groupe Moliflor; Groupe Emeraude SA; Hôtels et Casino de Deauville SA; Société Fermière du Casino Municipal de Cannes.

FURTHER READING

"Double Acquisition for Bridgepoint," *Acquisitions Monthly*, December 2005, p. 39.

"Loto Quebec Acquires a Minority Interest in the French Company Moliflor," *CNW Group*, December 21, 2005.

Malepeyre, Luc, "Casino d'Amélie les bains: Le casino-jeux déficitaire pour la 3e année," *Midilibre.com*, November 25, 2005.

"Moliflor Gambles on South West," *La Tribune*, November 8, 2002.

"PPM Ventures Hits the Jackpot," *European Venture Capital Journal*, April 2002, p. 33.

Smith, Peter, "Bridgepoint to Buy French Casino Group,"

Financial Times, October 1, 2005, p. 17.

Thompson, Andy, "PPM Takes a Gamble in France," *European Venture Capital Journal*, August 1, 1999.

Wootliff, Benjamin, "Royal Bank Takes a Chance on Casino Bid," *Scotland on Sunday*, January 13, 2002, p. 3.

Morgans Hotel Group Company

——— ■ ———

475 10th Avenue
New York, New York 10018
U.S.A.
Telephone: (212) 277-4100
Toll Free: (800) 697-1791
Fax: (212) 277-4260
Web site: http://www.morganshotelgroup.com

Public Company
Founded: 1984
Employees: 2000
Sales: $260.3 million (2005)
Stock Exchanges: NASDAQ
Ticker Symbol: MHGC
NAIC: 721110 Hotels (Except Casino Hotels) and Motels

■ ■ ■

Based in New York City, Morgans Hotel Group Company operates nine luxury boutique hotels, five owned by the company and four under a management agreement. Each property is unique and theatrical in its presentation, taking into account the locale — unlike the endlessly duplicated models of major hotel chains. Each Morgans hotel also boasts trendy bars, nightclubs, and restaurants. Morgans owns three New York properties, including the company's first hotel, Morgans, as well as the Royalton and the Hudson. The company also owns the Mondrian in Los Angeles and the Delano in Miami. Managed hotels include the Clift in San Francisco, the Shore Club in Miami, and London's St.

Martins Lane and the Sanderson (in which Morgans holds a 50-percent interest). Morgans is a public company, having completed an initial public offering (IPO) in 2006, and is listed on the NASDAQ.

FOUNDERS: DISCO-ERA KINGPINS

Morgans was founded by Steve Rubell and Ian Schrager, the infamous owners of New York's Studio 54, a nightclub that defined the disco era of the 1970s. Both were Jewish and Brooklyn born, Rubell the older and more flamboyant of the two. His parents had fled persecution in the Soviet Union to come to America. Once a rabbi, Rubell's father went to work for the post office while his mother taught high school Latin. His father also played tennis, a game that would provide the young Rubell with a partial scholarship to Syracuse University, where he earned bachelor's and master's degrees in finance. It was also at Syracuse that he first met Schrager, four years younger, who joined Rubell's fraternity. Schrager's background was less certain than his future business partner's. According to a 1969 *New York Times* article, his father, Louis Schrager, ran an illegal gambling operation — "numbers," an underground lottery — and was an important member of the notorious Meyer Lansky organized crime syndicate. As a matter of public record, he served time in prison for conspiracy in the 1950s. Schrager would later claim that he did not recall his father's absence, but later admitted to the *New York Times Magazine,* "I always knew my father wasn't a 9-to-5 guy."

Graduating college in the 1960s, Rubell served a

COMPANY PERSPECTIVES

We want the experience of visiting one of our hotels to be more like seeing a great movie, reading a wonderful book, or watching a memorable place — not just as a place to sleep, but a place where you feel an honest, emotional connection — where he feel like you are an integral part of the magical story that is unfolding around you — because you are.

stint in the National Guard in an intelligence unit before attempting to launch a Wall Street career, which he quickly realized did not appeal to him. Instead he borrowed money from his father and friends to become a restaurateur, opening the Steak Loft in Rockville Centre, Long Island, in the early 1970s. Success came rapidly, so that by 1974 he opened a dozen more Steak Lofts in New York, Connecticut, and Florida. He also owned stakes in a pair of Queens' discotheques. It was at this point that he turned to Schrager, who had become a real estate lawyer, to help him run his enterprise and provide the kind of organizational skills he lacked. Together they opened a successful disco, only to have it shut down when disgruntled neighbors sued them. They now turned their attention to Manhattan and looked for a locale where late-noise was more acceptable. They found it in a former CBS television studio on West 54th Street. As they would later do with their hotels, Rubell and Schrager bucked conventional wisdom, hiring sound and lighting engineers who had no disco experience. Their new club, Studio 54, opened on April 26, 1977, and from the beginning it became a magnet for celebrities, lorded over by the likes of Truman Capote, Andy Warhol, and Mick and Bianca Jagger. Others who wanted to join the party had to pass muster at the velvet-roped entrance where often five-foot-five Rubell, flanked by beefy body guards, decided on who was worthy to enter, intent on selecting the right mix of people for the raucous party inside. This casting approach would also be duplicated later when Rubell and Schrager hired hotel staff. Rubell once turned away the King of Cyprus, according to Rubell, because "he looked like somebody from Queens."

Studio 54 became a sensation, known for its celebrities, drugs, and frolics in the dark balcony. It also generated piles of cash, which the partners made a habit of skimming before counting it. On December 14, 1978, 32 months after Studio 54 opened, 30 Internal Revenue Service agents raided the club. Above some ceiling panels

in the basement they found garbage bags containing $600,000 and a second set of account books. There was also the matter of five ounces of cocaine. Rubell and Schrager were arrested and ultimately convicted, fined $20,000, and sentenced to 3.5 years in prison. In addition, they were saddled with back taxes of about $750,000 and lawyer bills in the $1 million range. In February 1980 they were incarcerated and began cooperating with the authorities in their investigation of other city club owners. As a result, their prison terms were reduced to 20 months and they were moved from a New York City facility to a minimum security prison in Alabama for the final six months of their sentence. Here Rubell used his winning personality to become like "the mayor of jail," as Schrager described it. Together they also began to plot their business comeback when released. Instead of nightclubs they decided to direct their attention to hotels, determined to return glamour to a tired industry, to in essence reinvent hotels as theater.

While still in prison, in January 1981, Rubell and Schrager sold the lease to Studio 54 to hotel and restaurateur Mark Fleischman, who took over a club that was past its glory and would close two years later. The building that housed Studio 54 was sold to real estate developer Philip Pilevsky. As a result, the partners were able to pay off their bills and were not destitute when they were released from prison later in the year. They flew back to New York and immediately paid a visit to the hot new hotels in town, the Helmsley Palace and Grand Hyatt. To enter the hotel business they needed funds, and while they turned down offers of help from friends, they were rejected by banks and other investors, who might have backed Rubell and Schrager if they had wanted to open a new club, which would have undoubtedly benefited from tremendous press build up and attracted a celebrity clientele. But they were more than reluctant to invest in their concept of a hotel.

Fleischman was the key to Rubell and Schrager's entry into the hotel business. They still held notes from Fleischman from the sale of the Studio 54 lease and when he mentioned that he was interested in unloading the Executive Hotel he owned at 37th Street and Madison, they struck a deal to buy the property from him, paying $60,000 as a down payment and granted several months time to raise the rest. They continued to have difficulty finding backers. They approached Pilevsky, who saw an opportunity. For half ownership in the hotel, he invested no money but agreed to act as the front man, opening the door to his banking connections. Rubell and Schrager now had the money they needed to turn the fleabag Executive into the exclusive Morgans Hotel.

KEY DATES

1976: Founders Steve Rubell and Ian Schrager open Studio 54.
1984: After serving a prison sentence, Rubell and Schrager open the Morgans hotel.
1989: Rubell dies of AIDS.
1998: Northstar Capital Investment Corporation gains majority stake.
1999: First London property opens.
2005: Schrager resigns as CEO.
2006: Morgans is taken public.

MORGANS HOTEL OPENS: 1985

French designer Andree Putmen was put in charge of the renovation. The lobby was eliminated, the marquee removed, and the bed legs cut off to make the small rooms look larger than they were. Rubell did the hiring — in effect, casting (he even thought about hiring a Hollywood director) — preferring people with glamorous looks and no prior experience in the hotel business. Morgans opened to no announcement on October 1, 1985. With no marquee the new hotel could have easily been mistaken for an apartment building. But among the Morgans' first guests were Bianca Jagger and Cher, the news was fed to the gossip columns, and in short order the 113-room Morgans, which charged $200 a night, had a 91 percent occupancy rate, the highest in the city.

Once again Rubell and Schrager were in the limelight and the darlings of the tony set, having reinvented themselves as cutting-edge hoteliers. They took their hotel-as-theater concept a step further in 1988 when they opened their second property, the 205-room Royalton, located across the street from the famous Algonquin on 44th Street. According to the *Wall Street Journal* in a 1989 article, "The help is gorgeous, the décor stainless-steel surreal. No comfy overstuffed chairs there; everything is very sharp-edged. Visitors to the Royalton's public mens' room encounter no ordinary urinals; there is, however, a waterfall activated by electric eye. To reach their rooms, guests first navigate dark corridors because as the Royalton's designer Philippe Starck puts it, 'before the opera starts, the place is dark.'"

With two successful properties in the stable of their hotel management company, which they called the Morgans Hotel Group — as well as other real estate investments and the creation of the Palladium, the club of the year in Manhattan in 1985 — Rubell and Schrager

next turned their attention to Times Square, a once glamorous neighborhood gone to seed but about to enjoy a rebirth. They bought the massive 610-room Century Paramount hotel, that like the area had seen better days, now reduced to offering rooms in the heart of Manhattan at less than $50 a night on average. The idea for the Paramount was to offer a less expensive hotel experience for a market that had similar tastes as the people who stayed at the Morgans and the Royalton but whose pockets were not as deep. Room rates were capped at $100 per night. Rubell would not see the third property open, however. In July 1989, at the age of 45, Rubell died from septic shock and hepatitis, presumed now to be the results of AIDS, although not acknowledged at the time. His gravestone was inscribed, "The Quintessential New Yorker."

The more reserved Schrager was now left on his own to run Morgans Hotel Group. He was able to open the Paramount in October 1990, and like the Morgans and Royalton it was an immediate hit. But beneath the glittery surface all was not well with the company, which had taken on too much debt in its rise to prominence and was unable to generate sufficient cash flow as a recession adversely impacted the hotel industry. The Morgans hotel filed for bankruptcy in 1991, followed by the Royalton in 1994.

Schrager managed to hold onto his properties, however, and soon returned to expansion mode. For several years he had his eye on the Miami market, and in 1993 Morgans bought the 328-room Delano hotel in Miami Beach, having it redesigned as a contemporary family resort. It opened to considerable acclaim in 1995. In that same year, Schrager brought in some executive help, hiring Steven A. Hicks, a former Marriott hand, to serve as director of operations, and William Sheehan, former Omni chairman, to serve as chief financial officer. Schrager was now free to look for new opportunities. He set his sights on Los Angeles, acquiring the 237-room Mondrian hotel, located on Sunset Boulevard, and reopening it in 1996. Also in 1996 Morgans acquired the venerable 375-room Clift in San Francisco.

NORTHSTAR INVESTS: 1998

To fund his growing portfolio of boutique hotels, Schrager took on new partners in 1998, joining forces with Northstar Capital Investment Corporation, a New York real estate investment trust. The hotels were consolidated under a new company, Ian Schrager Hotels. While Northstar held a 84 percent interest, at a cost of more than $250 million, Schrager was given a free hand to grow the company, and a spate of deals quickly followed as he looked to spread the Morgans' vision to other major U.S. cities and around the world. In April

1998 Schrager acquired the faded St. Moritz on Central Park South in Manhattan, followed a month later by the addition of the Barnizon, a former women's hotel that was well situated in the shopping district of the Upper East Side, and the Empire, located in the Lincoln Center area. Schrager also took over the Miramar in Montecito, California, in March 1998, converting it into a resort, and took his first steps overseas. In 1999 he opened the 204-room St. Martin's Lane in London, followed by the 150-room Sanderson, located in the city's trendy Soho district. Other Schrager deals in the late 1990s included the acquisition of the Henry Hudson, located on West 57th Street in Manhattan. Once renovated it offered more than 800 rooms after it opened as more of an economy hotel in 2000. Another addition was the McAlpin on West 34th Street, another large property, reopened in 2000.

Schrager's ambitions continued to grow in the new century. The company opened the Shore Club in Miami in 2001, holding a modest stake in the oceanside resort for which it served as a manager. Schrager was also especially interested in making Morgan's into a lifestyle brand. There was even talk of launching a retail chain of stores called "Shop" to market a wide variety of goods, many designed by Philippe Starck. The idea was supposed to be launched in the Morgans' hotels in 2001, but other events intervened to derail the plans: the economy soured and, more importantly, the terrorist attacks of September 11, 2001, had a dramatic impact on New York City's hotels and tourist industry. Business began to pick up in 2002, and now Schrager was turning his attention to Las Vegas, putting down a deposit on the Maxim casino-hotel.

Once again a period of expansion resulted in overbearing debt for Schrager, who in 2003 breached bank covenants of $355 million and the Clift was forced to file for bankruptcy protection. Aside from a drop in travel that hurt occupancy rates across the board in the hotel industry, he also had to contend with imitators, like the W hotels that opened in 1998 and drew on elements developed by the Morgans' hotels, such as (according to the *New York Times Magazine)* "arty black-and-white photographs, large mirrors leaning against walls, [and] a staff of fashionistas." The stable of hotel properties was trimmed to nine: the original Morgans, Royalton, Hudson, Delano, Mondrian, Clift, St. Martin's Lane, Sanderson, and the Shore Club.

In July 2005 the 58-year-old Schrager stepped down as CEO of Morgans Hotel Group, which had lost money since the start of the 2000s. He retained an ownership stake and consulting contract, but now devoted his attention to the development of apartments and condominiums. Replacing him was W. Edward Scheetz,

North Star's co-chief executive officer, who looked to grow Morgans. In February 2006 he took the company public, netting approximately $275 million. The stock did not fare well once it debuted on the Nasdaq, however, quickly dropping below its IPO price. Apparently, investors were not sufficiently impressed with the projects in Morgans' pipeline, which included the development of a new Miami property located across the street from the Delano, the acquisition of the James Hotel in Scottsdale, Arizona, the development of a pair of hotels in Las Vegas. In May 2006 investors bid down the price of Morgans' stock even further, to a new low around $16, a response to the company's announcement that it had agreed to pay $770 million in cash for the Hard Rock Hotel & Casino in Las Vegas. In the opinion of Wall Street analysts Morgans had overpaid and already had too much debt to contend with. In some ways, the Hard Rock property was in keeping with Morgans' desire to be perceived as a hip venue. It could be certainly argued, however, that it was not boutique in spirit and nothing like the original vision of Rubell and Schrager that had caused people to seek out a hotel with no name out front, one that even New York cab drivers did not know existed. Whether that experience, like that of Studio 54, could ever be duplicated was another question.

Ed Dinger

PRINCIPAL COMPETITORS

The Ritz-Carlton Hotel Company,LLC; Starwood Hotels & Resorts Worldwide, Inc.; WHM, LLC.

FURTHER READING

Bagli, Charles V., "A Hotelier for Jaded Boomers," *New York Times,* July 19, 1998, p. 3.

———, "Schrager Quits Hotel Company For Apartments," *New York Times,* July 12, 2005, p. B5.

Chandler, Peter, "That's Entertainment; Steve Rubell," *Times (London),* July 29, 1989.

Freedman, Alix M., "White Collar Chic: Studio 54 Partners Are Even More Successful As New York Hoteliers," *Wall Street Journal,* January 19, 1989, p. 1.

Gabriel, Frederick, "Schrager's Allure," *Crain's New York Business,* May 26, 1997, p. 1.

Gordon, Meryl, "The Cool War," *New York Times Magazine,* May 27, 2001, p. 34.

Rowe, Megan, "Schrager Spreads His Wings," *Lodging Hospitality,* August 1995, p. 20.

Weiss, Lois, "Nightclub King Takes On New Hotel Projects," *Real Estate Weekly,* October 12, 1994, p. 13.

Morton International, Inc.

100 North Riverside Plaza
Chicago, Illinois 60606
U.S.A.
Telephone: (312) 807-2000
Toll Free: (800) 789-7258
Fax: (312) 807-2949
Web site: http://www.mortonsalt.com

Wholly Owned Subsidiary of Rohm and Haas Company
Incorporated: 1910 as the Morton Salt Company
Sales: $706 million (2004 est.)
NAIC: 311940 Seasoning and Dressing Manufacturing; 325188 All Other Basic Inorganic Chemical Manufacturing

■ ■ ■

Morton International, Inc.—probably best known for its popular blue canister of table salt, featuring a raincoat-clad girl with an umbrella and the tagline, "when it rains, it pours"—is a diversified wholly owned subsidiary of the chemical maker Rohm and Haas Company. Morton's focus is on two industry segments: the manufacture and sale of salt for consumer and industrial use, and the manufacture and sale of specialty chemicals. In 1986 the company, then called Morton Thiokol, gained notoriety for its part in the explosion of the NASA space shuttle Challenger. The accident precipitated a crisis that led Morton to spin-off the Thiokol rocket business in 1989. Both companies now operate as completely independent enterprises. The late-1990s acquisition of Morton was

attractive to Rohm and Haas because salt was used to manufacture many of its products. After purchasing Morton in 1999, Rohm and Haas sold several of Morton's overseas facilities to pay off debt and closed some other underperforming facilities as well. Rohm and Haas endured a rash of environmental and safety-related issues that were connected to chemical plants previously under Morton's control, but after three years the majority of issues related to Morton were resolved. In 2003 Morton was honored as an industry leader by the National Safety Council.

EARLY YEARS: 1879–1967

Morton began as a small agency distributing salt in the American Midwest, from shipments routed from the eastern seaboard on the Erie Canal. After the Civil War, the demand for salt kept pace with the expansion of the meat-packing industry, particularly in Chicago, where both the meat-packing and salt industries became well established. In 1879 a 24-year-old clerk named Joy Morton joined the agency, and by the age of 30 he owned it.

Morton soon came to dominate at least a third of the salt market, becoming the product's only nationwide distributor. Morton experienced moderate success, maintaining a large share of a stable and profitable market with few competitors. However, by the mid-twentieth century, the salt industry had fully matured. In the 1950s, Morton diversified into specialty chemicals, including bromides, adhesives, dye stuffs, and polymers. In 1965 Morton Industries went public and decided to diversify further.

KEY DATES

1879: Joy Morton is employed by small Midwest company that sells salt.

1886: Morton buys the company and names it Joy Morton & Co.

1902: Joy Morton forms the International Salt Co. of Illinois.

1910: Company is incorporated as the Morton Salt Co.

1965: The enterprise is renamed Morton Industries, goes public, and begins to diversify.

1969: Morton merges with Norwich Pharmaceuticals.

1982: The rocket fuel company Thiokol merges with Morton.

1986: Morton Thiokol engineers are blamed for NASA Challenger disaster.

1989: Morton spins off Thiokol but retains the profitable airbag division.

1997: Morton spins off its airbag division.

1999: Rohm and Haas acquires Morton.

2001: Rohm and Haas pays $38 million for Mississippi environmental damages.

2003: Morton receives award for safest company in its industry from National Safety Council.

DIVERSIFICATION: 1969–1982

Morton's first major acquisition was Simonize, a maker of auto wax and household cleaners, in 1965. Four years later, Morton merged with Norwich Pharmaceuticals, which manufactured prescription drugs as well as such over-the-counter products as Unguentine, Chloraseptic, and Pepto-Bismol.

However, the Morton-Norwich merger was problematic in that Morton did not possess the financial resources to revitalize Norwich. Despite its established product line, Norwich was slowed in its growth by an inadequate research and development budget; at the time, the marketing of a new drug could incur costs of $50 million, a figure far exceeding Morton-Norwich's entire research budget. As a result, from 1969 to 1971, Morton-Norwich's dividends remained negligible, and its stock shares sold for only eight times dividends, which was low for pharmaceutical companies. To remedy the situation Morton-Norwich went into partnership with Rhone-Poulenc, a French drug manufacturer. In exchange for 20 percent of its stock, Morton-Norwich received right of first refusal on any of Rhone-Poulenc's new products. Moreover, Rhone-Poulenc had ample research facilities.

However, the partnership with Rhone-Poulenc was beset with difficulties. "We couldn't run our business with those people," said Charles Locke, then president of Morton. Moreover, Rhone-Poulenc was eventually nationalized by French President Mitterand, and the company decided to sell its stock in Morton-Norwich. The French company did not abide by an earlier agreement to refrain from selling its share of Morton-Norwich to a single buyer, so Morton-Norwich found itself a potential takeover candidate.

THIOKOL MERGER: 1982–1989

In 1982 Morton sold Norwich and used part of the proceeds to buy back its stock from Rhone-Poulenc. However, Morton remained a potential candidate for takeover due to the steady income from its salt operation. Its stock was selling for $30 a share, but with only $20 a share cash reserves, the management at Morton decided to take action. As a result, management began to look for an eligible specialty chemicals company to purchase or merge with.

Thiokol, with its 20 percent annual growth rate, was Morton's prime candidate for a merger. Thiokol controlled 40 percent of the solid rocket fuels market, and its Texize division manufactured a popular and profitable line of household cleaners that included the brand Glass Plus. Morton decided that the household products divisions in both companies would complement one another, and in 1982 the two companies completed the finalization of their merger.

One year later, however, a severe disagreement arose between the upper management leaders of the two companies. As a result, the top management at Thiokol walked out. Among the defectors was Robert Davies, president of Thiokol, considered one of the brightest executives in the aerospace and chemical industries. Four other high level executives with experience in aerospace either retired or quit when Davies left. Consequently, Morton's Charles Locke was given complete control of both companies.

Despite these defections, few industry analysts questioned the wisdom of the Thiokol-Morton merger. In the first year after the merger the company posted record earnings. Two years later earnings per share increased 26 percent. Morton's and Thiokol's specialty chemicals divisions were working well together, and the new company offered chemical purification products, metal recovery chemicals, coatings, polymers, and chemicals for the electronics industry. The household products division saw many of its brands, including

Glass Plus, Yes Detergent, and Spray & Wash, achieve 10 to 20 percent market growth in a crowded and highly competitive field. To further strengthen its position in the household products market during this time, Morton Thiokol began to manufacture its own packaging materials, becoming one of the first manufacturers in the industry to do so. In 1985 the household products division was sold to Dow Chemical Company in order to prevent an attempted takeover by that chemical firm.

In the mid-1980s, Morton Thiokol's staff of engineers was gaining acclaim for its work on materials for the aerospace industry, and the company won a contract to produce rocket boosters for NASA's space shuttle Challenger. On January 26, 1986, Morton Thiokol engineers are alleged to have approved the launch of the Challenger space shuttle, despite the below freezing weather conditions. Seventy-three seconds after lift-off an explosion occurred that destroyed the rocket and killed its crew. The explosion was attributed to the failure of rubber O-rings on Morton Thiokol's rocket boosters.

Morton Thiokol chair Charles Locke shocked the public when, shortly after the accident, he told reporters that "the shuttle thing will cost us ten cents a share." Although he was quoted out of context, the remark nonetheless ensured Locke a reputation as being tactless and insensitive. In 1989, despite performing $400 million worth of redesign work at cost and the resumption of shuttle flights, Morton Thiokol lost a bid for a new booster design to Lockheed. At this point, Locke decided to spin off the Thiokol division.

FURTHER EXPANSION: 1989–1999

Before dividing the companies, Locke transferred Thiokol's chemical businesses to the Morton side of the company. Morton also retained Thiokol's promising automotive airbag business. The companies were officially split on July 1, 1989. Morton International, with $1.4 billion in sales and 8,000 employees, remained concentrated mostly in chemicals and salt. But the company also invested nearly $100 million in its airbag business.

Airbags, designed to inflate upon the impact of a car crash, protected drivers from colliding with an automobile's dashboard and windshield. After Mercedes-Benz ordered the first airbag, other auto manufacturers found it to be a competitive advantage. Chrysler incorporated airbags into its designs in 1987, and others followed. The most important development in the airbag market occurred in 1991, when congress passed legislation making airbags mandatory on all new cars. At the time, Morton dominated the market with 55 percent

of the market, while its closest competitor, TRW, held 35 percent.

Morton also actively expanded its chemical operations after its divestiture of Thiokol, taking over the Whittaker Corporation's coatings and adhesives business for $225 million. In taking over this business, Morton integrated vertically into the polyester market. Subsequent acquisitions included the K.J. Quinn and German Iromer Chemie and Sandoz-Quinn Produckte companies, which were added to Morton's Dynachem and Bee Chemical divisions. The company's specialty chemicals business grew to include adhesives, coatings, sealants, electrical chemicals, dyes, sodium borohydride, biocides, tin stabilizers, and laser and semiconductor materials. In late 1991 Morton sold its food and cosmetic colors business to Milwaukee-based Universal Foods in order to concentrate on its industrial dyes operations.

After the spinoff, Morton managed consistently higher earnings than Thiokol, possibly a result of Morton retaining Thiokol's most promising businesses before the two companies split up. As it approached the 21st century, Morton concentrated its investments on high-growth niche markets. In the mid-1990s Morton completed a flurry of mergers and alliances. It also invested heavily in a France-based salt enterprise, purchased the European powder coating company Pulverac, and released new products. In 1997 Morton sold its automotive safety company to Autoliv AB, thus forming the world's largest airbag company with 15,000 employees and over $3 billion in sales. The same year Morton merged with Nippon Synthetic Chemical Industry to produce photoresist film, a compound used in semiconductors. Also in 1997 Morton agreed to supply and distribute coil coatings made by two subsidiaries belonging to the German-based Grebe Group. Grebe Group was one of Europe's leading producers of non-stick sealants and decorative coatings.

On April 13, 1998 an explosion rocked one of Morton's New Jersey factories. The Patterson-based factory made dyes for petroleum products. An out-of-control chemical reaction detonated in a vat of dye that injured nine employees. Homes as far as 15 blocks away felt the blast, and a cloud of yellow dust settled on the surrounding neighborhood. OSHA fined Morton $7,000. The plant was lambasted in a report filed by the U.S. Chemical Safety and Hazard Investigation Board. According to the *Knight Ridder Tribune Business News Service*, Morton was accused of not informing its workers about the dyes' well-known explosive properties. Despite the bad press, Morton continued to prosper and posted $2.5 billion in sales for 1998.

Hoping to reduce costs and focus on mainstay products such as salt, Morton sold its highway markings and paints business in early 1999. The factories were located in Los Angeles and Salem, Oregon. The Morton's Salt brand made up 12 percent of the company's total revenue in 1999.

ROHM AND HAAS: 1999–2006

Morton was acquired by Rohm and Haas in 1999 for $4.9 billion. Rohm and Haas was a Philadelphia-based company that used Morton's salt to produce its own line of industrial chemicals. The global conglomerate was separated into six divisions, the largest being the coatings group, which made chemicals that were sold to paint makers. To reduce costs by $200 million, the new owners cut 1,150 jobs soon after the Morton acquisition.

Unfortunately for Rohm and Haas, it acquired Morton's safety, health, and environmental troubles as well. The worst surfaced in 2000 at a Moss Point, Mississippi, facility. The U.S. Environmental Protection Agency, the Department of Justice, and the State of Mississippi filed charges against Rohm and Haas after it was discovered that Morton's chemical byproducts were dumped into an underground well. The factory's troubles dated back to 1996 when a Morton environmental manager was caught falsifying reports about waste water discharge and groundwater monitoring. The false reports were discovered and disclosed publicly by Morton in 1996. The manager was fired soon after.

Rohm and Haas paid a total of $38 million to resolve the Moss Point fiasco, including fines for civil penalties that reached $20 million. At least $2 million of criminal penalties were imposed on Rohm and Haas. The company was also required to spend millions on a plant waste minimization project to upgrade the city's waste water facility and to donate $2 million to pollution prevention research at the University of Southern Mississippi's School of Polymer Science. To pay off debt, Rohm and Haas sold Morton's European salt operations and Morton's thermoplastic-polyurethane business for $390 million in 2000. The businesses' sales were collectively $295 million the year before.

After a few years of litigation and factory renovations, Rohm and Haas curbed the amount of incoming lawsuits, some of which involved asbestos overlooked in old Morton factories. In 2003 the National Safety Council proclaimed Morton International was the safest business in its industry, determined by the Standard Industrial Classification code system, and sales for Rohm and Haas continued to soar. Overall revenues from 2003 to 2005 rose from $6.42 billion to $7.99 billion.

John Simley
Updated, Kevin Teague

PRINCIPAL SUBSIDIARIES

Bee Chemical Company; CVD, Inc.; The Canadian Salt Co., Ltd. (Canada); Inagua Transports, Inc. (Liberia); Morton Bahamas, Ltd. (Bahamas); Morton Coatings, Inc.; Morton International, B.V. (Netherlands); Morton International GmbH. (Germany); Morton International, Ltd. (Canada); Morton International, Ltd. (Japan); Morton International S.A. (France); Morton International S.p.A. (Italy); Morton Japan Ltd. (Japan); Morton Overseas, Ltd.; Morton International S.A. de C.V. (Mexico); Morton Yokohama, Inc.; N.V. Morton International S.A. (Belgium); Nippon-Bee Chemical Company, Ltd. (Japan); Toray Thiokol Company, Ltd. (Japan); Toyo-Morton, Ltd. (Japan).

PRINCIPAL COMPETITORS

The Dow Chemical Company; E. I. du Pont de Nemours and Company (DuPont); Cargill, Incorporated; Compass Minerals International, Inc.; IMC Global Inc.; Rockwood Holdings, Inc.; Eastman Chemical Company; Nippon Fine Chemical Co. Ltd.; Sovereign Specialty Chemicals, Inc.

FURTHER READING

"A High-Stakes Bet that Paid Off," *Fortune*, June 15, 1992, pp. 121-22.

"After an Aerospace Spin-off, Morton is Ready for an Upswing," *Chemical Week*, May 23, 1990, pp. 14-19.

Carberry, Sonja, "Distributor Joy Morton Poured It On When It Rained," *Investor's Business Daily*, March 7, 2006, p. A4.

Casey, Michael, "Rohm and Haas to Close Chemical Plant in Paterson, N.J.," *Knight Ridder Tribune Business News*, May 16, 2001.

Davis, Ann, "Treating On-the-Job Injuries as True Crimes," *Wall Street Journal*, February 26, 1997, p. B1.

Grant, Alison, "Morton Salt Retirees Granted A Day in Court," *Plain Dealer*, April 28, 2006, p. C6.

"Life Beyond Challenger," *Forbes*, September 21, 1987, p. 44.

"Morton Sells Colors Business," *Chemical Week*, August 7, 1991, p. 5.

"Morton Thiokol Completes Spinoff," *Journal of Commerce*, July 6, 1989.

"Morton Thiokol is to Spin Off Chemical Line," *Wall Street Journal*, February 28, 1988, p. A3.

"Morton Thiokol: Reflections on the Shuttle Disaster," *Business Week*, March 14, 1988, pp. 82-91.

"Redemption," Forbes, January 7, 1991, p. 307.

"Rohm and Haas Says It Agreed to Sell Units In $390 Million Deals," *Wall Street Journal*, July 21, 2000, B2.

"Rohm and Haas Says It Could Face Fines Over Falsified Records," *Wall Street Journal*, November 18, 1999, C22.

"Rohm and Haas Settles Environmental Violations In
    Mississippi," *PR Newswire*, October 26, 2000.

MWI Veterinary Supply, Inc.

---

651 South Stratford Drive
Suite 100
Meridian, Idaho 83642
U.S.A.
Telephone: (208) 955-8930
Toll Free: (800) 824-3703
Fax: (208) 955-8902
Web site: http://www.mwivet.com

Public Company
Incorporated: 1980 as MWI Drug Supply, Inc.
Employees: 596
Sales: $496.7 million (2005)
Stock Exchanges: NASDAQ
Ticker Symbol: MWIV
NAIC: 446199 All Other Health and Personal Care
   Stores

∎ ∎ ∎

MWI Veterinary Supply, Inc., distributes animal health products to approximately 14,000 veterinary practitioners, clinics, and veterinary hospitals across the United States as well as to livestock producers. The Meridian, Idaho-based company offers a wide range of supplies, some 11,000 in total from more than 400 vendors, meeting the needs of animals of all sizes, from mice to cows. Products include pet food and nutritional products, pharmaceuticals, vaccines, parasiticides, dental, diagnostics equipment, grooming, apparel (including gowns, scrubs, masks, gloves, and eyewear), identification products, surgical equipment, X-ray machines, and even office fixtures, lighting, and flooring.

In addition, MWI provides such services as online ordering, pharmacy fulfillment, equipment procurement help, and inventory management. The company maintains pharmacies in Texas, Pennsylvania, and Idaho. Warehouses are located in nine states: Arizona, California, Colorado, Georgia, Idaho, Michigan, Pennsylvania, Washington, and Texas, which has facilities in San Antonio and Grand Prairie. About two-thirds of sales come from veterinary practices and the rest from the sale of supplies needed for the production of livestock. The $4.7 billion veterinary supply market is highly fragmented, and after going public in 2005, MWI positioned itself to be one of the major consolidators in the industry, as it seeks to not only expand the products and services it can offer to customers through internal growth but to also grow its business through acquisitions. Although MWI stock trades on the Nasdaq, the company is majority-owned by New York-based venture capital firm Bruckmann, Rosser, Sherrill & Co.

1970S ORIGINS

The man behind the MWI initials was Millard Wallace Ickes. Ickes was a practicing veterinarian in the early 1970s, working with partners at Caldwell, Idaho's family-run Kindness Animal Hospital. Like other clinics in the Northwest, Kindness had to contend with escalating drug prices. Moreover, being a small operation and located far away from the major distributors, it was not able to place the kind of large orders that would receive a discount, or decent customer service. According to *Investor's Business Daily,* Ickes "wisely started cutting

Our family of over 600 employees responds quickly to customer needs. This "What Ever It Takes" attitude is proudly felt by all departments within the company.

costs by ordering his pharmaceutical supplies in bulk. What his customers didn't use, he sold to neighboring veterinarians and suppliers." MWI's chief executive officer, James Cleary, added, "After a while, he had more medicine in his cages than dogs and cats. So he turned it into a distribution business."

Founded in 1976 the enterprise was called Ickes Drug Co. At first it was very much a shoestring affair operating out of the hospital. According to company information, "A calculator and a few notepads were purchased, and they converted some of the kennels into storage rooms. News of the distributorship began to grow."

The business was received so well that it soon outgrew the hospital. Ickes was now faced with a decision: continue to practice veterinary medicine or take a chance on the distributorship. He opted for the latter and left the hospital he had served for more than 25 years. Ickes hired some salesmen, rented a small warehouse, and began to expand his product lines beyond the original drugs he carried. He also extended the company's reach so that soon the company was delivering to veterinaries and clinics throughout Idaho and made inroads into the neighboring states of Oregon, Utah, and Nevada. He found ready customers in veterinarians like himself, providing the kind of service he had always wanted. The company took pains to provide superior customer care, and it did not require customers to place large volume orders to receive competitive prices.

In 1980 Ickes incorporated the business in Idaho as MWI Drug Supply, Inc. A year later he sold control of the company to Agri Beef Company, which would take MWI to the next level and begin to grow the distributorship beyond the Northwest. Based in Boise, Idaho, Agri Beef primarily raised cattle but it had deep enough pockets to grow MWI. Over the next few years MWI was able to develop a robust data processing system to help the company efficiently buy and move greater volumes of merchandise, which continued to expand in

breadth. Customer service also improved, as MWI purchased vans to accommodate an increasing level of next-day delivery service.

DENVER ACQUISITION: 1990

MWI steadily entered new markets in the 1980s. The company's expansion was accelerated in 1990 with the acquisition of Jones Veterinary Supply, a Denver based distributor. As a result, MWI's sales territory now covered 18 states. Because the company had expanded well beyond the basic drugs Ickes had once stockpiled in cages to include foods, supplies, equipment, and instruments, the name was changed to reflect this broader business mix. In September 1994 the business was incorporated as MWI Veterinary Supply Company, and it became a full-fledged subsidiary of Agri Beef.

Agri Beef continued to oversee MWI until the early 2000s, at which point it opted to sell the company, which was by now generating about $250 million in annual sales. Los Angeles investment banking boutique Grief & Co. was hired to broker the deal. Launched in the early 1990s by Lloyd Grief, a veteran of old-line San Francisco stock brokerage Sutro & Co., the firm specialized in helping middle-market companies in pursuing strategic acquisitions or putting themselves or subsidiaries up for sale. A suitable buyer for MWI was found in 2002 in New York City-based Bruckmann, Rosser & Sherrill Co. II L.P., a private equity investment firm. Bruckmann Rosser had been founded in 1995 by former investment officers of Citicorp Venture Capital, Ltd. It focused on middle market companies that exhibited strong growth potential and were leaders in their fields. MWI clearly fit the bill. The veterinary supply industry was large and growing and heavily populated with mom-and-pop operations. Along with Webster Veterinary Supply and a handful of other distributors, MWI was a dominant player in a field where consolidation was just beginning to take shape. Hence, it was no surprise that Bruckmann Rosser would find MWI a worthy acquisition.

In June 2002 Bruckmann Rosser formed MWI Holdings, Inc., to acquire 71.5 percent of the MWI stock from Agri Beef at a cost of $19.6 million. Agri Beef retained nearly 18 percent of the business. When the transaction was completed James F. Cleary, Jr., was appointed chief executive officer. A 1990 Harvard Business School graduate, Cleary had spent six years with Morrison Knudsen Corporation, a construction and engineering firm, before joining Agri Beef in 1996. He became vice-president of demand generation before moving over to MWI in 1998 to become director of

KEY DATES

1976: Howard W. Ickes founds a pet drug distributorship.

1981: Agri Beef Company acquires Ickes's business.

1994: MWI Veterinary Supply becomes a separate Agri Beef subsidiary.

2002: Venture capitalist firm Bruckmann, Rosser, Sherrill & Co. acquires company.

2005: MWI is taken public.

national accounts. He was then named MWI's president in 2000. In addition to serving as CEO, Cleary sat on the board of directors along with Bruckmann Rosser managing directors Bruce C. Bruckmann and Stephen C. Sherrill, and principal Brett A. Pertuz.

Under new ownership MWI over the next two years accelerated its already steady growth, driven in large part by the addition of new products and customers. In September 2000 the company had 8,000 products to offer. That number increased to 10,000 by September 2004. An important new source of revenue came from the 2002 introduction of a new line of diagnostic equipment and supplies. To land more customers, the company continued to beef up its sales force. Shortly after Bruckmann Rosser acquired control, MWI employed 82 field sales representatives. A dozen new reps would be hired over the next year and another 18 in fiscal 2004. The additional personnel helped the company to reach out to new markets, especially in the northeastern and southeastern parts of the United States. The positive impact of all these factors became evident on MWI's balance sheet. Sales increased from $281.2 million in fiscal 2002 (ending September 30, 2002), to $341.7 million in 2003, and $394.3 million in 2004.

MWI made its first move in pursuing external growth in November 2004 when it completed the $400,000 acquisition of a pet crematorium from Memorial Pet Care, Inc. Located in Meridian, Idaho, the crematorium would serve veterinary practices in the southwest portion of the state as well as eastern Oregon. Then, in January 2005, MWI spent approximately $5 million to acquire Vetpro Distributors, Inc. Based in Holland, Michigan, Vetpro was a regional animal health products distributor. Its addition allowed MWI to significantly expand its presence in the Midwest and improve its ability to distribute products in such states as Illinois, Indiana, Michigan, Ohio, and Wisconsin.

GOING PUBLIC IN 2005

With a strong track record of growth to promote, MWI was ready in 2005 to make an initial public offering (IPO) of stock. The IPO was underwritten by Banc America Securities LLC, Williams Blair & Company, LLC, and Piper Jaffray & Co. and took place on August 8, 2005. Demand among investors proved strong, and instead of pricing the stock in the announced range of $14 to $16 per share, MWI was able to command $17. With the sale of five million shares, MWI netted $76.8 million, money that was used to retire debt and redeem outstanding shares of preferred stock held by Bruckmann Rosser and Agri Beef. MWI stock was listed on the Nasdaq, and on the first day of trading soared past the $20 level. In keeping with Nasdaq listing standards that required a majority of independent directors, MWI's board of directors underwent some changes by the end of 2005. Sherrill and Pertuz resigned, and the first chairman of the board was also named (albeit a non-executive position). Director John F. McNamara was named chairman. He was the former CEO and chairman of AmeriSource Corporation and a 20-year veteran at McKesson Corporation, and was also well connected, having served as chairman of the International Federation of Pharmaceutical Wholesalers and Chairman of the National Wholesale Drug Association.

Fiscal 2005 proved to be a banner year for MWI, and when the results were announced they reflected why investors had been so enthusiastic about the stock offering. Revenues grew 26 percent to $496.7 million and net income increased 80.5 percent to $4.6 million. Memorial Pet Care and Vetpo made important contributions, especially the field reps that came over from Vetpro, who were responsible for $13.7 million in new sales in fiscal 2005. Also helping out — and poised to provide greater benefits — was a new, larger, and more efficient distribution center that opened in Nampa, Idaho, in April 2005 and which would help serve northwestern customers. Other improvements to the distribution network was also in the works for fiscal 2006. In December 2005 a new 58,000 square-foot distribution center in Denver opened to better serve Rocky Mountain area customers. A new 30,000 square-foot distribution center in Orlando, Florida, would also open later in the year to help MWI expand its reach into the southeast. Furthermore, the company looked to build revenues through the addition of value-added services, such as the pharmacy fulfillment program, MWI's e-commerce platform, and its Sweep Inventory management system. Furthermore, the company was eyeing possible acquisitions. In May 2006 MWI found a purchase to its liking, paying $4 million in cash and stock to land Northland Veterinary Supply, Ltd. Northland was a Clear Lake, Wisconsin-based distributor of animal health products to 500 Midwestern veterinary practices. The addition of Northland was likely one of the opening moves in the next phase of MWI's growth, as it sought to fill out a national distribution network.

Ed Dinger

PRINCIPAL SUBSIDIARIES

MWI Veterinary Supply Company.

PRINCIPAL COMPETITORS

Burns Veterinary Supply; Patterson Companies Inc.; Professional Veterinary Products, Ltd.

FURTHER READING

Anderson, Steven, "Meridian Veterinary Firm MWI Goes Public with Nasdaq Listing," *Idaho Business Review,* August 22, 2005.

Carlson, Brad, "MWI Veterinary Supply Leases part of Ex-Micronpc Call Center," *Idaho Business Review,* August 18, 2003.

Elliott, Alan R., "Distributor of Animal Products Eyes Wider Market Reach," *Investor's Business Daily,* April 21, 2006, p. A05.

Phillips, Kyra, and Matthew Chance, "MWI Veterinary Supply, Unice Corp. IPOs Price," *America's Intelligence Wire,* August 3, 2005.

Srinivasan, Kirsten, "Howling Success," *U.S. Business Review,* March 2006, p. 111.

Nordisk Film A/S

—■—

Mosedalvej 14
Valby, 2500
Denmark
Telephone: (45) 36 18 82 00
Fax: (45) 36 18 93 00
Web site: http://www.nordiskfilm.com

Wholly Owned Subsidiary of Egmont Group
Incorporated: 1906 as Nordisk Films Kompagni
Employees: 1,200
Sales: $426 million (2005)
NAIC: 512110 Motion Picture and Video Production;
515120 Television Broadcasting; 515210 Cable and
Other Subscription Programming; 512191 Telepro-
duction and Other Postproduction Services; 512131
Motion Picture Theaters (Except Drive-Ins)

■ ■ ■

Nordisk Film A/S is the largest film and television
company in Scandinavia, and one of the oldest continuously operating ones in the world. The Danish firm
makes television programs, theatrical films, commercials,
cartoons, and music videos; distributes its own films and
those of other companies to theaters in Scandinavia;
operates a chain of Danish and Norwegian movie
theaters; and distributes videos, videogames, and Sony
PlayStation equipment in Scandinavia. Nordisk also has
several joint ventures with other studios, co-owns a music
firm, and operates on-demand broadband and cable
television service TV2 Sputnik with Danish broadcaster
TV2. The firm is a unit of Egmont, a Danish media

group with operations in 21 countries.

BEGINNINGS

The company now known as Nordisk Film traces its
origins to 1906, when Ole Olsen started producing motion pictures in Denmark. The first title completed by
Olsen, who a few months earlier had opened a film
theater in Copenhagen, was a two-minute silent film
called *Duer og Maager* (*Pigeons and Sea Gulls*), and others soon followed. On November 6, 1906, he officially
founded Nordisk Films Kompagni and by year's end offices had been established at Vimmelskaftet, along with
outdoor studios at Valby and a film laboratory at
Frihavnen. The firm was now operating in Germany and
Sweden, and had adopted a logo of a polar bear standing atop a globe.

Over the next several years the firm continued to
grow, gaining affiliates in Austria, Britain, and the United
States. In 1908 an indoor studio was opened at Valby,
and a second followed in 1910. In 1911 Nordisk began
producing feature films of approximately 45 minutes in
length, the same year that its stock began trading
publicly. Over the next four years three additional Valby
studios were opened, and during 1914 the company
produced a record 143 fiction and 46 nonfiction films,
of which more than 7,000 copies were sold to
distributors.

Screen stars of this era included Olaf Fonss, Clara
Wieth Pontoppidan, and Valdemar Psilander. The latter
was hugely popular and completed more than 80 films
between 1911 and 1916, but his salary demand of DKK
250,000 and the impact of World War I on film

distribution caused the company to begin running deeply in the red. Nordisk's New York affiliate closed in 1916 and in 1917 Olsen gave up his German operations, which had grown to include 60 movie theaters and a production company.

In the 1920s Nordisk strove to regain its momentum, with director A.W. Sandberg contributing a number of popular releases, including several Dickens adaptations. In 1922 Ole Olsen stepped down as the firm's managing director, and by 1928 production had fallen to a single fiction film, *Jokeren* (*The Joker*), which was directed by a German and starred non-Danish actors.

1929: REORGANIZATION UNDER CARL BAUDER

In 1929 majority shareholder Carl Bauder took control of the firm, and Nordisk's first sound feature, *Praesten I Vejlby* (*The Vicar of Vejlby*), was released two years later. Bauder also owned a theater called Palads Teatret and held control of several sound patents, and in 1934 won a lawsuit that forced American studios like Paramount, Fox, and MGM to pay Nordisk a licensing fee to use so-called "noiseless" sound reproduction technology in the Scandinavian countries.

In 1936 Holger Brondum was appointed managing director of the company, a post he would hold for nearly three decades. During World War II the German occupation of Denmark caused the firm to suffer several major losses, with the Valby Studios and its Kino-Palaeet movie theater both destroyed in 1944. After the war Valby's Studio 4 was rebuilt and it resumed operations in 1946.

In 1951 the company founded Nordisk Film Junior to make children's films, documentaries, commercials, and Danish remakes of foreign titles, and five years later

the firm's first color movie, *Kispus,* was released. Nordisk was now beginning to produce movies in Greenland, with *Kispus* director Eric Balling producing a feature there called *Qivitoq* during the year. The latter film was nominated for an Oscar in 1957, the same year that Balling was named a managing director of Nordisk Film. Balling's successes as a movie director continued throughout the 1960s, and included the 1963 *Sommer I Tyrol* and several James Bond-inspired secret agent comedies in 1965 and 1966.

TELEVISION PRODUCTION BEGINNING IN 1970

Balling continued to be a creative leader for Nordisk, bringing it to the small screen in 1970 with the long-running series *Huset Pa Christianshawn* (*Friends and Neighbors*). Because of the show's success, as well as a popular series of "Olsen Gang" comedy films, the company was able to continue operating at a time when several other Danish studios were closing, as well as rebuilding Valby's Studio 3. Another successful Balling-directed TV program, *Matador* (*Monopoly*), was begun in 1978 and became Denmark's most popular series over a four-year run.

In 1982 the firm named Jens Jordan its managing director, and during his tenure the renovation and expansion of Carl Bauder's Palads Teatret was completed. The early 1980s was a fertile period for Nordisk, with successful films by directors like Kaspar Rostrup, Nils Malmros, Bille August, Ole Roos, Lars von Trier, and Balling winning numerous Danish and international film awards.

In 1984 Hans Morten Rubin was named to head the firm's Valby operations, and with investors, including publishing firm Gutenberghus, he quickly established Denmark's first privately owned local television station, Weekend-TV. Although it broadcast several popular shows, the station was not allowed to show advertisements, and with losses skyrocketing it was shut down two years later.

The firm had long been owned by a joint partnership of the Ema and Carl Bauders Foundation and Carl Bauder A/S, but during 1985 company head Jens Jordan was allowed to acquire a stake in its film production unit. In addition to subsidiaries devoted to technology, video, and distribution, Nordisk now controlled 40 percent of the movie theaters in Denmark. The year 1985 also saw Nordisk join with Gutenberghus to found a film production company called Dansk Reklame Film A/S.

In 1987 the company formed a group to plan strategy for television broadcasting, which led to the

KEY DATES

1906: Theater owner Ole Olsen begins making short films in Denmark.

1929: Carl Bauder takes control of the insolvent firm and reorganizes operations.

1944: The studios and movie theater are destroyed during World War II.

1970: Eric Balling's *Friends and Neighbors* is produced for television.

1984: Weekend-TV joint broadcast venture is formed, but lasts only two years.

1988: Nordisk-produced *Babette's Feast* wins the first Danish best foreign film Oscar.

1989: Pathe buys 50 percent of the firm's exhibition/distribution operations.

1992: Nordisk is acquired by Egmont.

1996: The firm is split into two units, with Egmont Entertainment handling distribution.

2002: Egmont Entertainment is merged back into Nordisk.

2004: TV2 Sputnik broadband video service is launched with Danish TV2.

2006: Michael Ritto is named to head the firm; Nordisk takes a stake in his record company.

creation of a unit called Nordisk Film Broadcast and the acquisition of a 30 percent stake in Kanal 2, a private television station in Copenhagen. In 1988 the firm began to produce shows for the new Danish national network TV2, which included a Danish version of the hit game show *Wheel of Fortune*.

The year 1988 also saw Gabriel Axel's Nordisk production *Babettes Gaestebud* (*Babette's Feast*) win Denmark's first-ever Academy Award for Best Foreign Film, and another of the studio's productions, Bille August's *Pelle Erobreren* (*Pelle the Conqueror*) won a year later. In 1989 the French company Pathe bought a 50 percent stake in the firm's distribution and exhibition division for DKK 185.4 million, after which it became known as Pathe-Nordisk A/S. A year later the unit formed a joint partnership with Svensk Filmindustri called Scandinavia Media Alliance to buy distribution, broadcast, and video rights to films from CBS/FOX, Orion, and RCA/Columbia, which would control close to 30 percent of the Scandinavian film market.

In late 1991 Union Bank of Finland formed a joint venture with Nordisk to create a holding company that would operate the firm's theater chain as well as 86

Finnkino theaters in Finland. Each company controlled approximately two-thirds of the screens in their home countries. The partnership hit rocky ground in late spring, however, and after months of negotiations Nordisk dropped out and sold a minority stake it had acquired.

MERGER WITH EGMONT IN 1992

In the summer of 1992 Nordisk merged with Danish media and publishing conglomerate Egmont Group, which had previously been known as Gutenberghus. Egmont owned a 20 percent stake in Norway's TV2, which was about to begin running advertisements, as well as other film/video production and distribution units in Scandinavia and Germany. Nordisk's new parent company had sales of approximately $1 billion, of which its newly conglomerated film/video units were expected to contribute a fifth. The Scandinavian Media Alliance joint venture subsequently began acting as Egmont's purchasing unit, while Nordisk took over the distribution company formerly split jointly with Pathe, and the still co-owned chain of theaters became Nordisk-MGM Biografer, adopting Pathe's parent company's name.

In the fall of 1993 the firm was restructured into six divisions, as follows: television production facilities; feature film and TV fiction production; theatrical distribution/exhibition/radio; video distribution; Scandinavian TV services/foreign film and TV sales; and business development/joint venture projects. The firm's Andrsteierne film laboratory and IFT subtitling units would remain standalone operations.

The year 1993 also saw Nordisk buy a 50 percent stake in a unit of Scanbox Denmark A/S called Dansk Video Service (DVS), which distributed videotapes to gas stations and convenience shops; form a joint venture with John De Mol Productions to make game show and reality TV programs; win the right to rent out Nintendo videogames in Norway and Denmark; and take over Danish film distribution for 20th Century Fox.

In 1994 the Scandinavian Media Alliance was dissolved, ending what some had criticized as a virtual monopoly of the market. The firm would continue to work with Svensk Filmindustri on select projects afterward, however.

MANAGEMENT SHAKEUP/ RESTRUCTURING IN 1995

In August of 1995 Nordisk entered a period of crisis when managing director Jens Jordan was fired by the firm's board, reportedly because he had backed six executives who wrote a letter seeking greater independence from Egmont. The firm's newly appointed chief operating officer, Henrik Slipsager, also was let go and more than a dozen other executives subsequently quit. Jensen later filed suit and Egmont parent the Egmont Foundation stopped holding board meetings because Jordan was a member and could not be dismissed due to a provision in his contract. In December the Danish Ministry of Justice found in favor of Jordan, and he was invited to rejoin the board and several lawsuits were dropped. That same month saw the firm appoint three new executives to head Nordisk's major units of distribution, production, and finance. Each would report directly to Egmont CEO Jan Froeshaug, with Nordisk's CEO job eliminated.

The year 1995 also saw Nordisk form a classic film unit to market special interest and art film titles, and found Nordisk Film Format Distribution to scout foreign markets for new program ideas while selling Scandinavian ones abroad. The firm now had 600 employees and annual revenues of more than DKK 1.5 billion, equal to $246 million.

In 1996 Nordisk Film split into two units, Nordisk Film & TV Production and Egmont Entertainment, the latter of which would handle distribution chores. The company also completed *Bryggeren* (*The Brewer*), a TV miniseries about the founder and history of the Carlsberg brewery. It was the longest and most expensive program of its type filmed to date in Scandinavia, costing about DKK 90 million. The firm also sold radio unit Nordisk Film Radio to Uptown Radio, bought a 41 percent stake in troubled broadcaster TV Linkoping, and acquired TV production firm VipVision of Finland during the year.

In early 1997 the company launched network gaming services via Egmont Online, a Nordisk subsidiary that offered educational and shopping options. In 1998 Nordisk bought a production company called Victoria Film, which was merged with the firm's Per Holst Film unit, and 1999 saw formation of children's film unit Egmont Bornefilm, as well as the acquisition of film laboratories in Copenhagen and Stockholm that had formerly been operated as a joint venture, giving Nordisk leadership in this category in Scandinavia. The firm also purchased advertisement producer Tinmen Filmproduksjon A/S and underwent another restructuring during the year, with filmmaker Per Holst appointed creative director.

During 2000 Nordisk added new post-production facilities in Valby and created a new feature film production unit. Revenues totaled $92.3 million for the year, with a loss of $2.5 million recorded. In early 2001 the company laid off 30 employees after the long-running *Wheel of Fortune* was canceled by TV2.

MERGER OF NORDISK FILM AND EGMONT ENTERTAINMENT IN 2002

In 2002 Nordisk Film and Egmont Entertainment were merged back together as the two companies' parent sought to create the "largest Nordic producer and distributor of electronic entertainment," according to a press release. The firm's employment ranks would grow to 1,350 and its revenues to more than $474 million under the leadership of Egmont Entertainment director Kenneth Plummer.

In 2003 a miniseries called *The Royal Family* was a major success and it was sold to numerous TV networks abroad. Nordisk was experiencing growth in other areas, as well, racking up the one millionth sale of Sony PlayStation 2 videogame consoles in Scandinavia and acquiring Pinkfloor A/S, maker of a videogame for teenage girls called "PowerBabe." During the year the firm also opened a U.S. office, shut down its advertising film production unit, and boosted the production of feature films for the Scandinavian market.

In 2004 the company joined with Danish TV2 to launch TV2 Sputnik, an on-demand television channel that would give subscribers access to TV2 programs and several hundred Nordisk film titles. It was initially available only through broadband Internet connections, but a cable television option was later added via TDC Kabel TV. The firm subsequently added an online video rental store called Sputnik Film, as well. Videogame subsidiary Nordisk Films Interactive sold one million software units during the year, and the firm also had success with "reality" TV titles like *FC Zulu* and *Jakten pa Kjaerligheten,* the latter of which became the most popular TV series in the history of Norwegian television.

During 2004 the company continued to find success distributing imported films in Scandinavia like American hits *Kill Bill* and *Spiderman 2,* while opening a new movie theater, BioCity Aalborg, and installing new all-digital projection equipment on three screens. Nordisk sold a 40 percent stake it owned in videogame maker IO Interactive to Eidos of the United Kingdom, as well.

In 2005 the company bought a 20 percent stake in Matila Rohr Productions of Finland, that country's largest production company, and expanded its movie theater chain to 16 units with a new location in Frederiksberg, near Copenhagen. In the videogame sector the firm launched the Sony handheld PlayStationPortable, selling 125,000 units, and had success with so-called "social games" like "Buzz," "Sing Star," and "Eye Toy." The year 2005 also saw a joint venture launched with Sonofon to provide film information and previews and other content to mobile telephones, while Nordisk Film Interactive began working to develop games for mobile phones.

During 2005 the company signed deals with production firms including Fluid Films, Affinity Films, and Cristaldi Pictures, which gave Nordisk distribution rights and an equity stake in exchange for investing 10 to 15 percent of the films' budgets. The year saw Nordisk acquire 104 international films for distribution while also handling 55 Scandinavian-produced titles.

In early 2006 Michael Ritto was appointed to the post of managing director, taking the place of the recently departed Kenneth Plummer. Nordisk would simultaneously acquire an ownership stake in Ritto's record company Music Business Organization A/S, as it sought to broaden its activities in this area. The year 2006 also saw the sale of DVS Entertainment to Scanbox and the acquisition of several Danish movie theaters from Sandrew Metronome.

Starting its second century in business, Nordisk Film A/S had broadened its scope beyond film and television to include music, videogames, and digital interactive content. The industry leader in its home country of Denmark, Nordisk was a powerful presence throughout Scandinavia, as well.

Frank Uhle

PRINCIPAL SUBSIDIARIES

Nordisk Film Biografer A/S; Nordisk Film A/S; Nordisk Film Post Production A/S; Per Holst Film A/S; Nordisk Film Interactive.

PRINCIPAL COMPETITORS

Svensk Filmindustri; Sandrew Metronome AB; Zentropa Entertainments; Nimbus Film Produktion ApS; Scanbox Entertainment A/S; Thura Film A/S; Koncern TV & Filmproduktion A/S.

FURTHER READING

"Danish Egmont to Invest in Pinkfloor," *Danish News Digest,* January 21, 2004.

"Danish Sonofon Provides Service in Co-operation with Nordisk Film," *Danish News Digest,* January 6, 2005.

Edmunds, Marlene, "Duo Launch Sputnik Broadband Unit," *Daily Variety,* November 18, 2004.

———, "Egmont Exec to Exit," *Daily Variety,* March 13, 2005.

———, "Nordisk to Back Pack of English Pix," *Daily Variety,* May 11, 2005.

———, "Scandi Film Giants Butt Heads Over Local Pix," *Daily Variety,* May 12, 2005.

"Egmont Media Merges Two Branches and Joins Bidding for Danish TV2," *TV Meets the Web,* August 20, 2002.

Ferro, Charles, "Danish Vet Ritto Steps into Film Biz," *Billboard.biz,* February 6, 2006.

Keller, Keith, "Egmont, Nordisk Pact May Ignite Competition," *Hollywood Reporter,* September 1, 1992, p. 1.

———, "Jordan Affair Shakes Egmont at Foundation," *Hollywood Reporter,* November 21, 1995, p. 11.

———, "Nordisk, Egmont Wrap Merger," *Hollywood Reporter,* June 22, 1992, p. 1.

———, "Nordisk Gets New MGM Deal," *Hollywood Reporter,* February 1, 1993, p. 6.

———, "SF, Nordisk End Media Alliance," *Hollywood Reporter,* July 6, 1994, p. 7.

Lundborg, Pia, "Films, Games Push Up Egmont Earnings," *Daily Variety,* March 14, 2006.

———, "Finnish Shingle, Scandi Nordisk Link," *Daily Variety,* October 12, 2005.

"Nordisk Eyes International Market," *Television Business International,* April 1, 1996, p. 132.

"Nordisk Film & TV Strengthens Creativity," *DocTV,* June 23, 1999.

"Nordisk Film to Attract Nordic Audience," *Danish News Digest,* April 29, 2003.

"Nordisk Unveils Restructure," *Hollywood Reporter,* September 17, 1993, p. 16.

"One Mln PlayStation 2 Consoles Sold in Nordic Countries," *Danish News Digest,* November 3, 2003.

Olga's Kitchen, Inc.

1940 Northwood Drive
Troy, Michigan 48084
U.S.A.
Telephone: (248) 362-0001
Fax: (248) 362-2013
Web site: http://www.olgaskitchen.com

Private Company
Incorporated: 1976
Employees: 1,240
Sales: $47 million (2005 est.)
NAIC: 722110 Full-Service Restaurants

■ ■ ■

Olga's Kitchen, Inc., is a chain of casual dining restaurants best known for a wide variety of sandwiches available on its trademarked pita-like Olgabread. The best-selling Original Olga features seasoned beef and lamb, onions, tomatoes, and a yogurt-based Olgasauce, while the Olga menu also offers spinach pie and Greek salads as side dishes. While the majority of Olga's restaurants in the chain are scattered throughout the Metropolitan Detroit area, some are found in Illinois and Ohio, and all are located in enclosed shopping malls or strip malls. One of the original investors in Olga's, Michael A. Jordan, heads up the company.

1970: ORIGINS

Olga's Kitchen was founded by Olga Loizon, who opened her first restaurant, Olga's Souvlaki, in 1970. During a family vacation to Greece a few years prior,

Loizon had conceived the idea of transforming the Greek souvlaki sandwich that she enjoyed into her own Greek-inspired pita wrap. While in Greece, Loizon spent $300 on the vertical broiler necessary to cook the spiced beef and lamb, and then back home in Michigan she spent another couple of years perfecting her famous pita bread recipe. Discussing the unique sandwich, Elizabeth Rhein of Restaurant Business noted that "Only people who had eaten souvlaki in the street stalls of Athens had ever seen a sandwich like this before." Loizon's first sandwich shop, in upscale Birmingham, Michigan, offered one sandwich: The Olga Sandwich, comprised of thinly sliced strips of beef and lamb topped with onions and tomatoes and served on bread made from Olga's secret recipe. Loizon's son William helped with the fledgling enterprise, which provided the community a welcome alternative to the traditional burger and fries.

The Loizons' first day of business was March 14, 1970, and their total sales for the day were $15. Gradually the restaurant gained more customers; what reportedly kept original customers coming back was the Olgabread. The bread was sweeter than pita, and the Olga sandwich was not as spicy or garlicky as a traditional gyro. Also unique and popular at the Loizons' restaurant was the side of homemade yogurt sauce that came with the sandwich. Eventually, a hotdog wrapped in Olga's bread became part of the menu, along with a salad—when Loizon had the time and inclination to make it.

Olga and William Loizon brought the locals into their 600-square-foot store regularly, where there wasn't even enough room for Loizon to bake bread; she reportedly made the bread at her home and then brought it in to the restaurant. The Loizons next expanded their business to include catering of private parties. Following one such party, Loizon was approached by some of the guests, a group of businessmen, who were so impressed with the Olga sandwich that they offered to invest in the concept and promote it. In 1975, this group of investors purchased Olga's Souvlaki and hired local restaurateur Michael Jordan to run the company. The following year, the restaurant's name was changed to Olga's Kitchen, and the parent company was incorporated.

Jordan had begun in the restaurant business with Greenfield Mills Restaurants in the early 1960s, which were scattered throughout the metropolitan Detroit, Michigan, area. Jordan had worked his way up from the kitchen to management and had remained there until he joined a food service consulting company in 1971. As president of Olga's Kitchens in the 1980s, Jordan would oversee a period of expansion.

While Olga Loizon held neither a position in the company nor any stock in it, she remained a presence in Olga's Kitchens, serving as "chief critic, chief customer and chief creator," according to vice-president of marketing, Ron Crews, as cited in *Restaurant Business.* By the early 1980s, every year Loizon made an effort to visit her Detroit-based restaurants to mingle with her customers, and while there she never merely sat on the sidelines but helped out.

EXPANSION

In an October 1987 issue of *Restaurant Business* Jordan reflected on his decision to expand the Olga's chain: "We were doing so much business and there was so much demand for the product that we decided to find out how good this could really be." In the late 1970s and early 1980s, the company established some 30 restaurants scattered throughout Michigan, Ohio, California, Texas, Missouri, Wisconsin, Illinois, Florida, and Pennsylvania.

In an effort to offset the cost of expansion, the company considered an initial public offering of stock but instead eventually settled on franchising the chain.

To oversee those operations, it formed Olga's Kitchens Licensing subsidiary. In 1985, Olga's Kitchens began franchising, and outlets were opened in Oklahoma City, Oklahoma; Austin, Texas; Rochester, New York; and Gaithersburg, Maryland. Although the restaurants were well established and successful in Detroit, however, the company experienced its share of growing pains out of state, and some five underperforming Olga's Kitchens were shuttered.

Franchisees paid anywhere from $200,000 to $400,000 for the Olga's concept and six weeks of training at the Bloomfield Township, Michigan, restaurant. Then, Olga's management staff took an additional four weeks assisting the new franchisees with the hiring and training of approximately 45 employees. Jordan's long-term goal was for franchises to represent two-thirds of all Olga's Kitchens, a goal that was never reached due to operational issues.

On average, according to Jordan, Olga's Kitchens were generating $800,000 annually with some reaching an impressive million-dollar mark by 1985. The majority of restaurants during this time were located in shopping malls or their food courts, with only four freestanding locales. By 1987, there were 30 company-owned and another seven franchised Olga restaurants in operation, and the company's annual sales had reached $30 million. The menu now included a variety of salads, but the Olga bread was still credited for much of the chain's success. From a facility near corporate headquarters, the dough was prepared, rolled into balls, frozen, and distributed to each Olga's Kitchen unit, and the recipe remained a guarded secret.

In addition to the Original Olga, new fillings were introduced in the late 1980s and early 1990s. The Vegetarian Olga became popular, as did the chicken and steak fajita fillings for Olga sandwiches. The company even introduced a peanut butter and jelly Olga for kids. Soups proved a popular addition as did curly french fries. Fresh ingredients remained a priority at the restaurants. Advertising efforts, however, remained modest and consisted of coupons available in local newspapers and in-store promotions.

1997 BEGINS A PERIOD OF CONSOLIDATION

By the mid-1990s, there were 52 Olga's Kitchens in operation. Company profits, however, were suffering as same-store sales declined. By 1997, Jordan had instituted a consolidation plan that included shuttering some restaurants and renovating the most successful of its units. The number of Olga's Kitchens was slashed from 52 to 26. In 1998, Olga's was listed as 186 on *Crain's*

KEY DATES

■

1970: Olga Loizon opens her first sandwich shop located in Birmingham, Michigan.
1976: Olga's Kitchen, Inc., is incorporated with four additional restaurants in Metro Detroit.
1983: Olga's Kitchens Licensing Inc. is formed.
1998: Olga's Kitchen tops *Crain's Detroit* list of the top 200 privately held companies by revenue.
2004: Olga's enters into an agreement with Team Schostak Family Restaurants to open 15 restaurants over a five-year period.

Detroit list of the leading private 200 companies based on revenues.

By this time, the Olga's menu had expanded considerably. Variety set Olga's apart from its competitors, and there were some 20 different types of Olga sandwiches from which to choose, including the California-Style Olga; Bacon, Lettuce and Tomato Olga; Olga Burger; Smoked Sausage Olga; Stir-Fry Oriental Vegetable Olga; Three Cheese Olga; Turkey Club Olga; and the Chicken Oriental Olga. The restaurant also offered Olga's Salad, spinach and apple pie, frozen "Olgurt" and the trademark Orange Cream Cooler. The company introduced Kids' Surprize Meals, as well as an a la carte menu for children ten and under.

2000 AND BEYOND

In April 2004, Olga's entered into an agreement with Schostak Brothers & Company's restaurant division, Team Schostak Family Restaurants located in Southfield, Michigan, to put in place 15 restaurants over a five-year period. Schostak, already a large Burger King franchisee in the area, took part in locating and developing the new Olga's, while gaining the title of part owner of the properties. At that time, sales at each Olga's location were averaging about $1.8 million (on average customer tabs of $9), with each new restaurant costing some $750,000 to develop. The company began to focus on freestanding locales versus its typical mall-based outlets. The majority of these freestanding sites were located in Michigan and in Toledo, Ohio.

Responding to gourmet trends in the food industry, Olga's Kitchens introduced Suncoast Smoothies beverages and Olga wrap sandwiches. New fillings included such varieties as Thai Chicken, Roasted Veggie Pesto, and the Bleu Cheese Burger. Coupons for new fare and nutritional information were made available on the company's new web site. Another new trend, the low-

carb diet, prompted Olga's Kitchens to introduce a new bread that was low in carbohydrates as well as another fat-free version. While these proved less popular than hoped, the company continued to offer them as an option on its menu.

In 2005, there were 23 Olga's in Michigan, two in Illinois, one in Ohio, and one in California. Despite a sluggish economy, some casual restaurants, including Olga's, seemed to be faring well in the Detroit Metropolitan area, and plans were underway for modest expansion including new sites in Allen Park, Bloomfield Hills, and St. Clair Shores, all in Michigan. In 2005, at a reopening of the Toledo restaurant originally established in 1982, Olga Loizon made a guest appearance. In her seventies, she resided in the Detroit area and continued to drop in at the restaurants to meet customers and ensure that everything was operating up to her standards.

Brenda Kubiac

PRINCIPAL COMPETITORS

Panera Bread Company; Arby's Inc.; Great Harvest Bread Company.

FURTHER READING

Bodwin, Amy, "Olga's Name, Secret Recipe Keys to Company Expansion," *Crain's Detroit Business*, February 18, 1985, p. 27.

"Crain's List," *Crain's Detroit Business*, May 31, 1999, p. 26.

"Crain's List," *Crain's Detroit Business*, May 1, 2000, p. 28.

Crumm, David, "Olga Turns a Little Dough Into...Big Bucks From One Chain of 35," *Detroit Free Press*, January 5, 1984, p. 7A.

Deck, Cecilia, "Keeping on Top of Trends is the Meal Ticket for Olga's," *Detroit Free Press*, April 16, 1990, p. 1F.

Rhein, Elizabeth, "Olga's Finds a Niche," *Restaurant Business*, October 10, 1987, pp. 154–158.

Rogers, Monica, "Building on Tradition: Doug Hetherington Puts a Contemporary Spin on Olga's Kitchen's Culinary Heritage," *Chain Leader*, May 2006.

Snavely, Brent, "Eateries Take Second (and Third) Helpings," *Crain's Detroit Business*, July 4–10, 2005, p. 3.

———, "Let Them Eat Bread," *Crain's Detroit Business*, February 14–20, 2005, p. 1.

———, "Olga's Kitchen, Schostak Ink Deal for 15 Restaurants," *Crain's Detroit Business*, May 3–9, 2004, pp. 1–2.

———, "Restaurant Operators Defy Slow Economy," *Crain's Detroit Business*, May 29, 2006, p. 14.

Strickland, Daryl, "Olga's Going to be a Part of it, New York," *Detroit Free Press*, July 21, 1986, p. 1D.

Walkup, Carolyn, "Olga's Poised to Resume Growth After Consolidating," *Nation's Restaurant News*, November 10, 1997, p. 98.

Palmer Candy Company

311 Bluff Street
Box 326
Sioux City, Iowa 51103
U.S.A.
Telephone: (712) 258-5543
Toll Free: (800) 831-0828
Fax: (712) 258-3224
Web site: http://www.palmercandy.com

Private Company
Incorporated: 1914
Employees: 130
Sales: $31 million (2004 est.)
NAIC: 311330 Confectionery Manufacturing from Purchased Chocolate; 311911 Roasted Nuts and Peanut Butter Manufacturing

■ ■ ■

Most Iowans know niche-market chocolatier Palmer Candy Company as the maker of Twin Bing, a candy bar made with cherry-flavored nougat and fondant fillings coated with crushed peanuts and milk chocolate. The bumpy Twin Bing has been a top seller in Iowa and a few surrounding states since the 1920s while remaining relatively unknown across the greater United States. Palmer Candy is a small player compared to the three candy-making giants—Mars, Inc., The Hershey Company, and Nestlé S.A.—that control 90 percent of America's candy industry. Nonetheless, Marty Palmer, the fifth generation of Palmers serving as president for Palmer Candy, is content with his company's standing.

The Twin Bing fit into a cherry-flavored niche that the larger companies avoid. Twin Bings are one of the last candy bars still assembled by hand, and Palmer Candy claims the longest family ownership in the United States for a candy maker of its size. Despite the down-home reputation, Palmer Candy generates most of its money by mechanically rebagging other company's candies and producing its own bulk candies ranging from chocolate-covered peanuts and malted milk balls to caramel corn and hot tamales. In the early 2000s, Palmer Candy was the nation's second-largest producer of coated pretzel products after Nestlé. Its bulk candies are sold to such supermarket chains as Iowa-based Hy-Vee Food Stores and St. Louis-based Schnuck's Markets.

EARLY YEARS: 1871–1923

Before people were eating chocolate, they were drinking chocolate. The first European to discover the cacao-sweetened nectar was the Spanish conquistador Hernando Cortez, who took the drink's recipe from the Aztec Indians and brought it back to Spain in 1529. From Spain the chocolate drink's popularity spread throughout Europe. Chocolate would not be available in a non-liquid form until the 1800s.

Edward Palmer's first product was not chocolate, it was fruit. In 1871 a fire in St. Joseph, Michigan, destroyed the businessman's home and fruit store. Instead of rebuilding in Michigan, he transplanted to the burgeoning frontier town of Sioux City and purchased a wholesale grocery operation. In 1878 Edward Palmer expanded his business with a candy and fresh fruit section and renamed his company Palmer and Company. He sold bulk candy in the back of his store from wooden containers. In 1892 Edward Palmer's oldest son, William, opened a second wholesale fruit company. Soon after, Edward, his son William, and a younger son named Charles united their businesses. Candy remained a sideline product for the family-owned operation with the mainstay being fresh fruit.

In 1900 the three Palmers moved their Sioux City business into a four-story, red brick factory on Douglas Street. The new facility came equipped with cold storage lockers, an electric generator, and candy-making equipment that included steam boilers. In the new facility Palmer and Company began hand-dipping chocolate and making gumdrops, marshmallows, and low-cost candies to be sold in bulk. A fifth floor was added to the factory in 1908. Products made by Palmer and Company were delivered daily by the company's fleet of horse-drawn wagons. Each wagon would ride as far as it could in one day to deliver products to towns outside of Sioux City. Wanting to diversify its business in 1914, Palmer and Company incorporated the candy business as Palmer Candy Company and the fruit business as Palmer Fruit Company. Candy was produced in the Douglas Street factory, but the fruit enterprise was moved to a warehouse on Pearl Street.

CHOCOLATE BAR BOOM:
1923–1973

Milton S. Hershey, a Pennsylvanian businessman who made his fortune selling caramels, began mass-producing chocolate bars in 1884. Candy bars from other confectionaries soon followed, but the candy bar industry was not catalyzed until World War I. Several American candy makers were commissioned by the U.S. Army Quartermaster Corps to make chocolate for American soldiers fighting in Europe. At first blocks of chocolate were shipped overseas. Once in Europe, the 20- to 40-pound blocks were broken into smaller pieces for each soldier. By the war's conclusion, factories were shipping chocolate in single-serving sizes. After the ceasefire on the Western Front, American soldiers returned home with a newfound craving for chocolate. Throughout the 1920s an estimated 40,000 American candy bar brands were created. Many were spawned by regional confectionaries, with each candy bar reflecting the personality of its town. Consumers began buying candy in single servings from drug stores and grocery stores instead of from bulk containers. When the demand for candy bars reached Sioux City, Palmer Candy responded with the Bing Bar.

Bing Bars originally came in four different flavors: cherry, pineapple, maple, and vanilla. The distinguishing flavors were inserted in the middle of the candy bar as a nougat and fondant mixture. Nougat was a sugary paste with nuts. Fondant was a mixture of water, sugar, and corn syrup. The nougat and fondant were mixed into a cream, scooped into balls, and coated with a thin layer of chocolate to keep the cream from hardening. A layer of crushed peanuts and chocolate referred to as hash was added last. It was the hash's unruly texture that made Bing Bars difficult to make by machine. The hash could not be extruded or processed with an enrober, the two methods of mass-producing food products. The first Bing Bar was sold in 1923, the same year that Milky Way, Butterfinger, and Reese's Peanut Butter Cups were introduced. The same style of printed wrapper that was used on the first Bing Bar would be used on future Bing products.

In 1941 Palmer Candy purchased Sioux City's Soo Candy Company and its peanut-roasting facility. This marked the company's first venture into nutmeats, which would continue for more than sixty years. In 1956 the expanded Palmer Candy was able to purchase the candy division of the Johnson Biscuit Company, which included the La Fama chocolate bar brand. Acquiring other candy companies helped Palmer Candy drift into the rebagging business. First it purchased candy in bulk from other companies, then Palmer Candy used its machinery to bag the candy for in-store rack displays.

AGE OF THE TWIN BING:
1973–1998

As Palmer Candy gradually outperformed the family's Palmer Fruit Company, the latter was closed in 1969. Palmer Candy had also discontinued its three less popular

KEY DATES

1871: Fire destroys E. C. Palmer's original store in Michigan so he moves to Sioux City, Iowa, and purchases wholesale grocery operation.

1878: Palmer adds a candy and fruit section to his grocery store called Palmer & Company.

1900: Palmer & Company moves its candy and fruit business into a four-story factory building.

1914: Palmer & Company splits the candy business from fruit wholesaling and incorporates as the Palmer Candy Company.

1923: Bing candy bars, including the Cherry Bing, are introduced.

1940: Palmer Candy purchases Soo Candy Company and its peanut-roasting department.

1956: Palmer Candy purchases the Johnson Biscuit Candy division, claiming the rights to the La Fama candy brand.

1969: With the end of its fruit business, Palmer Candy concentrates on its candy business.

1973: Palmer Candy releases the Twin Bing to justify a price increase.

1979: Palmer family moves to a new headquarters and enjoys success with improved production, warehousing, peanut roasting, rebagging and shipping systems.

1986: Palmer offers a triple bump Bing, The King Bing.

flavors of Bing Bars to focus on its best-selling cherry flavor. In 1973, after the rising costs for sugar and coca forced the Bing Bar to increase from ten to 15 cents a bar, Palmer Candy introduced the Twin Bing, a double hump version of the original. Palmer Candy hoped that the larger bar justified the price increase. Palmer Candy's business was doing so well that in 1979 it moved to a larger factory on Bluff Street. The new building was designed solely for candy making and facilitated the business's peanut roasting, rebagging department, candy making, business offices, and candy storage. The bottom floor of the company's original building was converted to Palmer's Old Time Candy Shoppe, which sold Palmer Candy products and displayed Palmer Candy memorabilia. The shop was scheduled to operate seasonally; but after being more profitable than originally expected, it stayed open year round.

In the 1980s Marty Palmer led Palmer Candy as the company's fifth-generation Palmer president. According to an interview he gave in Steve Almond's award-winning book *Candyfreak: A Journey through the Chocolate Underbelly of America*, Marty Palmer did not plan on joining the family business after he graduated from the University of Colorado. He considered Palmer Candy an "overgrown candy shop." When relatives asked him to return home and help them sell the company or preside over it, Marty became president and expanded its products. "I realized there was huge growth possible and there was going to be risk to it, but it could work, if we were willing to work hard," Palmer said. As other candy bar manufacturers introduced their king-size candy bars in the 1980s, Palmer Candy responded with a triple hump bar called a King Bing. Larger companies tried purchasing Palmer Candy, but Marty Palmer always responded with a sales price that was what he thought the business would be worth in ten years. The tactic thwarted acquisitions. By the late 1990s Palmer Candy was manufacturing an average of 50,000 Twin Bings every day. Pumps were installed in the factory's basement to move the melted chocolate from a 60,000 pound container in the basement to the upstairs production line. Before the pump was installed, the chocolate was hand broken, melted down, and transported via buckets to the upper floors.

PRODUCT LINE EXPANSION: 1998–2003

In 1998 Palmer Candy celebrated 75 years of making its Bing candy bars with a public celebration in Sioux City. "We've had a lot of successful products in and out, but for 75 years the Bing has done the job," Marty Palmer was quoted by the *Associated Press Newswires*. "It's made the difference in us surviving." A special 150-pound Twin Bing was put on display at Palmer's Olde Time Candy Shoppe. Employees made the colossal candy bar's outer coating with a three-foot-deep bowl. The two cherry cream centers were molded with a basketball-sized stainless steel mold. The huge treat was later divided amongst three local charitable organizations: Boys and Girls Family Services, Girls Inc., and the Boys Club.

According to Marty Palmer, the celebration sparked new product ideas among the company's upper management. Marty Palmer told the *Omaha World-Herald* that when the original Bing Bar was created in 1923, peanut butter wasn't as popular as it had become in the late 1990s. The observation resulted in the Peanut Butter Bing. A broad selection of employees taste-tested the new candy bar through its development. "We struggled for about a year to perfect this," Marty Palmer was quoted by the *Associated Press Newswires* in 1999. "We ended up with a formulation that is not just a hunk of peanut butter. It's actually a peanut butter creme. It includes a lot of peanut butter. It also has peanut flour, and even a little flavoring."

Sales for the Peanut Butter Bing pushed Palmer Candy to full production capacity after its May 1999 launch. Even with increased weekend shifts, Palmer Candy couldn't keep up with new orders. Marty Palmer hoped that the early success was a signifier that the Peanut Butter Bing would be distributed nationally. "[Distributors] know peanut butter, chopped peanuts and chocolate are going to be a winner," he was quoted, when the Peanut Butter Bing debuted, by *Associated Press Newswires*. "They are really excited about it. We're really hoping this might be what takes the Twin Bing to a much larger area." In 2001 executives at Palmer Candy agreed that the Peanut Butter Bing had too much peanut flavor; so the company released an altered version of the Peanut Butter Bing. The new candy bar, shipped in a new gold wrapper, featured crisped rice instead of chopped nuts. The caramel added to the center scored higher with the Palmer Candy taste testers than the peanut center of the Peanut Butter Bing.

In 2003 the various Bing bars still hadn't expanded far outside of Palmer Candy's original distribution footprint. "Despite our best efforts, we have been unable to make that go nationally," Palmer told the *Sioux City Journal*. "It just takes so many advertising dollars." While the improved Peanut Butter Bing, which was later renamed the Crispy Peanut Butter Caramel Bing, sold well, it never outsold its cherry-flavored predecessor.

EXPANDING BEYOND CANDY BARS

Undaunted, Marty Palmer beefed up his company's resources and in 2003 consolidated the company into a colossal 220,000-square-foot warehouse. Besides adding more space, the warehouse solved a logistical problem of having the company's supplies stored in five smaller warehouses throughout Sioux City. The new warehouse became the new center for Palmer Candy storage and production. The space allowed Palmer Candy to increase its rebagging and bulk candy production for super markets, food clubs, and other retailers. The bags of candy would then be sold on racks typically for 50 cents or $1 each. Palmer Candy was also making niche candies like holiday divinity and fudge peanut brittle. The company was flexible enough to make candy exactly to a customer's specifications, unlike larger candy makers.

In 2003 a Minnesota-based competitor, Shair Candy, which was also a family-run business, closed. Palmer Candy was able to collect some of Shair Candy's rebagging customers. Shair Candy's fate reflected a growing trend in the candy industry. In the 1980s there were about 300 family-run candy makers in America. In 2004 only about 30 remained.

Early in the new millennium Palmer Candy was still growing and employed about 100 full-time people. The seasonal candy business increased so much during the fall, with Halloween being the largest candy-consuming holiday, Palmer Candy hired an extra 100 part-time employees and operated its candy factory for 24 hours a day. "Everybody digs in and just gives it their all," Marty Palmer said in the *Sioux City Journal*, adding "Then Christmas comes and we just breathe a sigh of relief and have a little time with our families."

After 125 years of successful candy making, Palmer Candy and its fifth-generation president were content with their candy-making role in America. In 2004 the company operated four successful ventures: the bulk sales of candies to grocery and specialty stores, custom candy manufacturing, rebagging other company's candies, and the production of Bing candy bars. The latter didn't have a national presence, but the factory provided jobs for hundreds of Sioux City residents. Amongst self-proclaimed candy fanatics, the Twin Bing had accumulated somewhat of a cult following. In his book *Candyfreak*, Steve Almond devoted an entire chapter to the Twin Bing. Almond believed that the Twin Bing was one of the last great regional candy bars and something to be cherished.

"There are people who make more candy in a day than we make in a year," Marty Palmer said in a 2004 interview with the *Sioux City Journal*. "We don't try to compete with Mars and Hershey. We don't try to go head to head against the same products that might be produced by someone who is huge," Palmer continued. "We make some very interesting candy, and we do it really, really well. We provide a selection and variety and level of service that nobody else can match. So, we're growing a lot every year."

Kevin Teague

PRINCIPAL COMPETITORS

Alpine Confections, Inc.; Brach's Confection, Inc.; Spangler Candy Company; Tootsie Roll Industries, Inc.; World's Finest Chocolate, Inc.

FURTHER READING

Almond, Steve, *Candyfreak: A Journey Through the Chocolate Underbelly of America*, North Carolina: Algonquin Books of Chapel Hill, 2004, 158-172 pp.

Andres-Frantz, Alyce, "Open Trade's Benefits Outweigh Disadvantages." *Market News International*, May 1, 2002.

Dreeszen, Dave, "Palmer Candy's Newest Candy Goes Peanut Buttery," *Associated Press Newswires*, June 28, 1999.

Feran, Tom, "Candy Fan Unwraps Truth Of Lost Treats," *Plain Dealer*, June 4, 2004, p. E1.

Magee, Patricia L., "Palmer Finds Its Niche in Specialized Marketing," *Candy Industry*, May 1985, p. 30.

Mogul, Fred, "Celebrating With a Big Bing," *Omaha World-Herald*, July 25, 1998, p. 19SF.

"Palmer Candy Celebrates Candy Bar's 75th Year With Giant Production," *Associated Press Newswires*, July 22, 1998.

Puig, Claudia, "'Big' In-Their-Face Documentarian's 'Random Thoughts'," *USA Today*, April 16, 1998, p. 4D.

Turnquist, Kristi, "We Want Candy," *Oregonian*, October 31, 2005, p. D1.

"Twin Bing Candy Maker Says Peanut Butter to Key Growth," *Omaha World-Herald*, June 29, 1999, p. 17.

PHI, Inc.

Post Office Box 90808
Lafayette, Louisiana 70509
U.S.A.
Telephone: (337) 235-2452
Fax: (337) 232-6537
Web site: http://www.phihelico.com

Public Company
Incorporated: 1949 as Petroleum Bell Helicopters, Inc.
Employees: 2,175
Sales: $363.61 million (2005)
Stock Exchanges: NASDAQ
Ticker Symbol: PHIIK PHII
NAIC: 481211 Nonscheduled Chartered Passenger Air Transportation; 481212 Nonscheduled Chartered Freight Air Transportation; 488190 Other Support Activities for Air Transportation; 621910 Ambulance Services

■ ■ ■

Petroleum Helicopters, Inc. (PHI), based in Louisiana, operates one of the largest fleets of commercial helicopters in the world. It provides a wide and diverse range of transportation services to the petroleum industry, principally in the Gulf of Mexico. It has contract operations at other places throughout the world, including South America, Asia, and Africa. The company also provides medical and emergency evacuation services, including a growing air ambulance operation. In addition, PHI conducts its own extensive pilot and crew training and helicopter-repair services, which in no small measure accounts for its excellent safety record. Chairman Al Gonsoulin became the company's largest shareholder in 2001, after buying out the founding Suggs family's holdings.

1949–1959: STARTING OUT TO FILL OIL INDUSTRY NEEDS IN LOUISIANA

With the close of World War II, a marshland and offshore oil and gas industry began emerging in states bordering the Gulf of Mexico, notably Texas and Louisiana. The placement of drilling rigs in remote or difficult to access places posed significant problems. In Louisiana, seismograph crews often had to traverse rugged terrain in four-wheel drive jeeps and trucks, and marshes and swamps in swamp buggies, sometimes getting bogged down. It was a slow and fairly dangerous way to get to potential drilling sites.

Jack Lee, who was then president of a seismographic company, was appalled by the situation and anxious to find a viable alternative. Thinking that helicopters could provide both a more efficient and safer mode of transport for his crews, Lee approached Robert L. Suggs and Maurice M. Bayon with his idea. Suggs and Bayon had been operating a radio navigation company called Offshore Navigations Inc. from a houseboat, according to Bayon's 2001 obituary in the *Times-Picayune*.

Under the leadership of Suggs, the new company, named Petroleum Bell Helicopters, Inc., officially went into business on February 21, 1949, with an initial investment of $100,000, three Bell 47 D model helicopters, and a small workforce of eight employees.

COMPANY PERSPECTIVES

PHI is the Total Helicopter Company. As the offshore oil and gas industry moves further out into the Gulf of Mexico, the air medical industry gets more advanced and, as international arenas open, PHI plans to be able to meet the needs of all customers in all locations. PHI provides customers with the safest, most reliable helicopter transportation in the world and they are prepared to move anywhere their services are needed. As one of the largest helicopter companies in the world, PHI has the ability to expand and grow which allows for greater flexibility and improved service. Thus, as the industry progresses into the 21st century, PHI is primed for any challenge.

Potential use of PHI's services quickly increased when, in the 1950s, offshore drilling in the Gulf of Mexico started its rapid expansion. The company was already positioned to provide timely transport services to and from drilling rigs and platforms, not just for seismic crews but for other industry offshore workers and equipment. By 1952, it also began expanding its services on an international scale, starting up operations in oil field locations throughout the contiguous 48 states of the United States. By the end of the decade, it had operations in Alaska, Canada, Bolivia, Colombia, Puerto Rico, and Greenland, as well.

As the nature of its services changed, the company required larger aircraft, and in 1955, PHI began using Sirkorsky S-55s. In the same year, the company designed and built offshore refueling facilities in the Gulf of Mexico for its growing fleet of rotary-blade aircraft. By 1959, it had added Sirkorsky S-58s to its fleet and, among other things, used them to transport power poles over mountainous terrain in Puerto Rico. Such special use of its helicopters demonstrated PHI's willingness to adapt to the needs of its customers.

It was also in the 1950s that PHI began taking significant steps towards achieving the industry's premier safety record. At that time there was a paucity of helpful guidelines for helicopter maintenance and operation, and few reliable ground rules for ensuring the safe and efficient use of the aircraft. In 1956, the company established its own in-house training program, something that thereafter played a major part in its enviable reputation for safety and high quality of service.

1960–1969: CONTINUED EXPANSION AND UNIQUE MISSIONS

In the 1960s PHI continued to expand its operations both at home and abroad. Demand for its services was quickly growing. Between 1961 and 1963, its number of flight hours increased from 200,000 to 300,000 hours. Eventually, customer needs would take the company to 42 countries, where it established associations that in some cases lasted to the end of the century. An important step occurred in 1967, when PHI began operating in Africa, in Angola, or what was then Portuguese West Africa. The long range development of Angola's Cabinda Gulf Oil Company kept a fairly sizable number of PHI aircraft and personnel working there for decades.

Starting even earlier, in the 1950s, PHI also established a reputation for public service, conducting the extremely dangerous work of saving lives during disasters, notably the great hurricanes that ravaged the Gulf of Mexico and the Caribbean. For instance, in 1961, when Hurricane Carla slammed into the Texas coast with winds of 145 mph, PHI pilots rescued 500 people. During the decade, such heroic efforts won several PHI pilots Winged S Awards for rescue work under hazardous conditions. It was in the mid-1960s that PHI also engaged in the first of many unique missions for the U.S. government when one of its pilots undertook the mid-air retrieval of a rocket-launched space module upon its return to earth. Thereafter, PHI often worked for NASA, retrieving objects released from spacecraft. The company was also undertaking some unique assignments for other agencies and businesses, developing a diverse range of uses for its craft and crews outside petroleum industry needs.

By the end of the 1960s, PHI's fleet of aircraft numbered 87. The rapid growth of the offshore oil industry in the Gulf of Mexico fueled PHI's own expansion. As a result, in 1969 PHI built a new facility, the Lake Palourde Heliport at Morgan City, Louisiana, which was then the largest heliport in the world. The growth also required a tracking system that would allow reliable communications between pilots and flight-following facilities throughout their missions. PHI began developing such a system, one that would ultimately become a computerized network allowing effective and dependable communications with airborne pilots from Texas to Florida.

1970–1979: OIL BOOM LEADS TO PHI'S ACCELERATED EXPANSION

No decade in the 20th century matched that of the 1970s for the petroleum and related industries in the United States. It was boom time, pure and simple. By

KEY DATES

1949: The company is founded by Robert L. Suggs and Maurice M. Bayon.

1952: PHI begins its international expansion.

1956: PHI begins an in-house training program.

1966: The company's aerospace role begins with work for NASA.

1970: PHI reaches over one million flight hours.

1981: PHI starts up its Aeromedical Services Division.

1982: The oil bust hits the industry hard, but diversification helps PHI.

1989: Robert Suggs, PHI's founder, dies.

1990: Carroll Suggs becomes chairman, president, and CEO.

1991: PHI reaches seven million flight hours.

1997: The company acquires Air Evac Services.

1999: PHI opens a new heliport facility in Boothville/Venice, Louisiana, and begins construction of new operations and maintenance facility in Lafayette, Louisiana.

2001: Al Gonsoulin acquires a 52 percent stake in the company from the Suggs family.

2006: The company is officially renamed PHI, Inc.

the time that it began, PHI already had in place techniques and procedures for ensuring safety and quality service, setting industry standards.

By the decade's first year, PHI had logged over 1 million flight hours, the first commercial helicopter company in the world to achieve that milestone. Two years later, in 1972, PHI placed a major order for new helicopters costing about $5 million. The purchase increased the company's fleet to 233 aircraft by 1974, when PHI was employing almost 1,000 people. The company continued to find diverse uses for its fleet of rotary-winged aircraft. In 1971, in Costa Rica, its pilots fashioned a sling load technique for transporting goods to offshore rigs, including pallets of bananas weighing two tons.

PHI growth was steady and very strong through the entire decade. At the time of its 25th anniversary in 1974, it was maintaining operations at 13 Gulf Coast and five foreign bases. By the end of the decade, the company's fleet reached 308 aircraft, the largest non-military fleet of helicopters in the world. Only the fleets of the U.S. and Soviet Union militaries were larger.

1980–1989: PHI WEATHERS THE OIL INDUSTRY'S COLLAPSE

Unfortunately for U.S. oil and related industries, the boom did not last, and with the resulting collapse in the early 1980s, PHI faced the prospect of a major decline in the oil field's need for its services. Robert Suggs and his staff knew that the company's continued growth would depend on increasing diversification. An important step was taken in 1981 when, in support of Acadian Ambulance's newly created Air Med Program, PHI put its Aeromedical Services Division into operation. The company quickly became one of the major providers of air medical services, expanding beyond its Louisiana base by mid-decade.

In 1984, it reached another milestone when it logged its five-millionth flight hour. At that time, it was operating a fleet of 417 aircraft. Nationally, it also greatly enhanced its profile through support of the Los Angeles Olympics and participation in the Louisiana World's Fair Exposition, where it prominently displayed one of its Sirkorsky S-76 helicopters on the deck of an oil rig erected for the event. It was the same model helicopter that in 1986 PHI put into use for its medical helicopter support of the Cleveland MetroHealth Medical Center's services. It was also in 1986 that PHI introduced innovations in training services with in-house courses focusing on the impact of human factors on pilots and their decision making. Another innovation came in 1988, when the company established PHI Technical Services, a new business providing maintenance services to third-party customers.

When founder Robert Suggs suffered a fatal heart attack in 1989, there was some apprehension about PHI's future, including a possible corporate raid, but Carroll Suggs, his widow, quickly allayed concerns when, in 1990, she took over the company's reins as chairman, president, and CEO. In an industry dominated by males, she demonstrated that she could get the job done, garnering several awards in the process.

1990–2000: PHI TIGHTENS CORPORATE BELT BUT CONTINUES TO GROW AND DIVERSIFY

In 1990, PHI had a fleet of 291 copters or one out of every 69 non-military whirlybirds in the world. In its primary use market, that of transporting crews and equipment to and from offshore oil platforms in the Gulf of Mexico, PHI held about a 60 percent share, thrice that of Offshore Logistics, its closest competitor. The company had started a strong turnaround from the dark days of the 1980s, when inexpensive foreign oil wreaked havoc with the American oil industry. For the fiscal year ending in April, 1990, the company had netted almost $10 million from revenues of $188 million, or $1.63 per share, its best performance since just before the oil bust hit in 1982. Still, the profits came in part from some downsizing measures, including the sell-off of some of its assets. Among these were some of its older aircraft. In fact, even with a mild resurgence of the oil industry in the mid-1990s, PHI was forced to continue to make belt-tightening efforts such as reducing its work force, selling equipment, and using other cost-cutting measures. The Gulf of Mexico, although remaining PHI's principal source of business, lagged way behind in its pre-bust rig count throughout the decade. Also, technological advances in the industry reduced the number of workers needed on rigs, thereby cutting back on transportation needs. As a partial solution to the Gulf oil drilling doldrums, PHI looked for new international markets to tap for potential growth in South America and Asia.

Despite the U.S. oil industry's stagnation, PHI continued to grow. By 1991, it had logged its seven millionth flight hour. It was also reaching some other important milestones. Under Carroll Suggs' leadership, the company attained a new level as a service-orientated and customer-driven organization, one able to customize operations to fit the specific needs of its clients. Suggs also stressed PHI's continued commitment to both safety and diversification. In order to improve its already enviable safety record, the company dedicated a million dollars annually to a safety incentive program. The result was that PHI's accident rate fell to one-seventh of the national average. Its excellent safety record earned the company international recognition and several awards, including, in 1996, the Federal Aviation Administration's High Flyer Award.

Among other new challenges, in 1994, during the Haiti embargo, PHI put some of its craft to use patrolling the Haiti-Dominican Republic border, making it the first civilian company chosen for such a service. In 1997, it was also selected as the first civilian operator to support the National Science Foundation's Antarctica Program. It was a landmark year in other ways. Among other important measures, PHI established Acadian Composites, Inc. to repair and overhaul structural composite panels on helicopters. It also acquired the Arizona-based Air Evac Services, Inc., the country's largest air medical transport service.

Through the decade, PHI continued to play a major role during disasters. For instance, in 1997 it began fighting fires for the U.S. Forestry Service, and in the following year helped transport food and medical supplies to Nicaragua, which had been ravaged by flooding caused by Hurricane Mitch.

A new downturn in oil prices in the late 1990s led to a further reduction in drilling activity in the Gulf of Mexico with disappointing results for PHI. The worst year was 1999, when the Gulf drilling rig count dropped to its lowest point on record and, in real dollar terms, the price of crude oil plummeted to lows not posted since the Great Depression. Although the company realized record revenues, its flight hours in the area and income from its transport services declined from the previous year and resulted in some further belt-tightening measures, including the sale of underused assets and a reduction in labor costs. However, a solid increase in revenues from its Aeromedical and Technical Services operations helped offset the impact of the decline in production rigs. Between them, the operations produced an increase in revenue of $14.3 million, a growth, respectively, of 30 and 25 percent over the previous year.

At the close of the 20th century, despite the volatility of the oil market, PHI remained very upbeat. It looked for new ways to use its air fleet and planned for additional growth. In August 1999, it ended construction and put into operation a new, state-of-the-art heliport in Boothville/Venice, Louisiana, named the Robert L. Suggs Heliport, in memory of PHI's founder. It was also completing its new operations and maintenance facility in Lafayette, Louisiana.

PHI scaled back its air-ambulance operations in Arizona in late 1999. Entering 2000, PHI had 1,875 employees, 275 helicopters, and ten fixed-wing airplanes. Lance F. Bospflug was appointed president in September 2001 and replaced Carroll Suggs as chief executive about a year later. Suggs remained chairman of the board.

Though new to the aviation industry, Bospflug had been credited with helping turn around T.L. James & Company, Inc., a Gulf Coast dredging, construction, and timber business, and it was hoped he could return PHI to profitability. Bospflug led a restructuring effort that resulted in some one-time charges and a loss of $12.3 million for 2000 on revenues of $235.3 million. The company had lost $5 million in 1999.

Another round of job cuts in early 2001 reduced employment by 220 workers (none of them pilots). Most of these were in administration or maintenance. PHI was trying to boost profits and a lagging stock price, a spokesperson told the *Times-Picayune*.

2001: NEW LEADERSHIP

Company co-founder Maurice M. Bayon passed away in March 2001 at the age of 92. He had retired from PHI in 1990. In August 2001, the Suggs family sold its 52 percent stake to Houston oilman Al A. Gonsoulin for $30.4 million. Gonsoulin had formed the Sea Mar supply boat company in 1977; it was eventually acquired by drilling firm Nabors Industries.

Gonsoulin subsequently succeeded Carroll Suggs as board chairman. At the same time, the company was preparing to relocate its corporate offices in Metairie into the operations center in Lafayette.

By this time, evidence of a recovery was in hand, according to *Helicopter News.* Several months of contentious negotiations with its new pilots' union (the Office and Professional Employees Union) had resulted in a new three-year contract. Sources told the *Times-Picayune* that the exhausting talks, the culmination of several years of fighting against unionization, helped hasten Carroll Suggs' retirement.

There were more executive transitions in store. Lance Bospflug stepped down as CEO and president in May 2004 citing personal reasons. His duties were taken up by chairman Al Gonsoulin.

Although revenues dipped to $270 million in 2003 after holding flat at about $283 million for two years, the company continued to increase its business. By 2005, operating revenues were up to $364 million; net earnings were $14 million, versus $4 million in 2004 and $1 million in 2003. PHI's helicopter fleet numbered 223 aircraft. The company also owned several fixed-wing planes, and operated a dozen rotorcraft on behalf of clients.

PHI was affected by the storms that hammered the Gulf in 2005. Hurricane Katrina flooded its Boothville, Louisiana, base in late August, putting it out of service for a year. A month later, Hurricane Rita wiped out PHI's base in Cameron, Louisiana. Other facilities were damaged. The company experienced no loss of life or aircraft in either case.

The company began 2006 with a new name, PHI, Inc. The move was made to unite its broad range of operations under a single brand. Its old NASDAQ ticker symbols (PHEL, PHELK) were replaced by new ones (PHII, PHIIK), as well.

John W. Fiero
Updated, Frederick C. Ingram

PRINCIPAL SUBSIDIARIES

International Helicopter Transport, Inc.; Evangeline Airmotive, Inc.; Air Evac Services, Inc.; PHI Air Medical Services, Inc.; Petroleum Helicopters International, Inc.; Helicopter Management, LLC; Helicopter Leasing, LLC; HELEX, LLC; Sky Leasing; PHI Angola (Angola); Petroleum Helicopters Angola Limitada (Angola; 49%); PHI International, LTD (Cayman); Energy Risk LTD (Bermuda).

PRINCIPAL DIVISIONS

Domestic Oil and Gas; Air Medical; International; Technical Services.

PRINCIPAL COMPETITORS

Bristow Group, Inc. (Air Logistics); Rowan Companies, Inc. (Era Aviation Inc.).

FURTHER READING

Antosh, Nelson, "Petroleum Helicopters Flies Into Local Hands," *Houston Chronicle,* September 7, 2001, p. 2.

Barrett, William P., "Do I Look like a Haggard Cat?," *Forbes,* October 29, 1990, p. 44.

Biers, John M., "Chairman of Gulf's Largest Copter Firm to Step Down; Carroll Suggs Sells Majority Stake in Firm After Losing Union Battle," *Times-Picayune* (New Orleans), September 8, 2001, Money Sec., p. 1.

———, "Copter Strike Averted; PHI, Pilots Union Get Over Hump," *Times-Picayune* (New Orleans), April 28, 2001, Money Sec., p. 1.

———, "Helicopter Firm to Get New Home," *Times-Picayune* (New Orleans), January 5, 1999, p. C1.

Gonzales, Angela, "Air Evac Parent Lays Off 70 Workers, Unloads Assets," *Business Journal of Phoenix,* November 19, 1999.

Griggs, Ted, "Exec Tells Challenges of Business," *Advocate* (Baton Rouge), November 6, 1999, p. 1C.

Guardiano, John, "PHI Appoints New President," *Helicopter News,* October 6, 2000.

———, "PHI President Promoted to CEO," *Helicopter News,* September 6, 2001.

"Helicopter Firm Cuts 220 Jobs; Lafayette Company Tries to Boost Stock After 2-Year Profit Spiral," *Times-Picayune* (New Orleans), Money Sec., February 8, 2001, p. 1.

Lear, Calvin, "Larger Facility Planned to Keep PHI in Lafayette," *Advocate* (Baton Rouge), October 23, 1996, p. 3B.

"Maurice M. Bayon, 92, Founder of PHI," *Times-Picayune* (New Orleans), March 29, 2001, Metro Sec., p. 3.

"PHI 50th Anniversary," special issue of *Daily Advertiser* (Lafayette, La.), February 19, 1999, pp. 1-56.

Plexus Corporation

———— ■ ————

P.O. Box 156
55 Jewelers Park Drive
Neenah, Wisconsin 54957-0677
U.S.A.
Telephone: (920) 722-3451
Fax: (920) 751-5395
Web site: http://www.plexus.com

Public Company
Incorporated: 1979
Employees: 6,800
Sales: $1.23 billion (2005)
Stock Exchanges: NASDAQ
Ticker Symbol: PLXS
NAIC: 334412 Bare Printed Circuit Board Manufacturing; 334418 Printed Circuit Assembly (Electronic Assembly) Manufacturing; 541330 Engineering Services; 541710 Research and Development in the Physical, Engineering, and Life Sciences

■ ■ ■

Plexus Corporation refers to itself as a "product realization service," that is, it helps corporations design, develop, and manufacture electronic components and other products. The company offers a full range of product realization services, including hardware and software design; printed circuit board design; prototyping services; new product introduction; material procurement and management; printed circuit board and higher level assembly; functional and in-circuit testing; final system box build distribution; and after-market services.

Since 2000, the company has worked to develop a global manufacturing network to meet the needs of its clients. The company's major markets include wireline/networking (38 percent of 2005 net sales), medical (30 percent), industrial (22 percent), wireless infrastructure (10 percent), industrial/commercial (17 percent) and defense/security/aerospace (5 percent). In 2005 Juniper Networks, Inc. accounted for 19 percent of Plexus's sales, and General Electric Corp. for 12 percent.

BEGINNING OPERATIONS IN 1980

Plexus was incorporated in Wisconsin in 1979 and began operations in 1980. The company was founded by Peter Strandwitz, John Nussbaum, and a group of other entrepreneurs interested in a venture to design and build computer circuit boards by contract. Located in the eastern Wisconsin city of Neenah, on Lake Winnebago, the new company found the bulk of their early work through contracts with IBM.

The business grew, and by 1987, Plexus reported revenues of $24.5 million. The company also reported a net loss of $1.3 million, however. Turnaround was quick, and the next year the company saw revenues of $53.2 million and net income of $393,000, a dramatic increase in sales of 117 percent. To effect this change, management had cut operating expenses as a percentage of sales by 50 percent. The company's stock, then traded over-the-counter, responded in 1989 by nearly doubling in the first six months. Sales in 1989 again rose substantially to $78.1 million.

By the end of the 1980s Plexus had organized its business among three subsidiaries. One, Technology Group Inc., was headquartered in Neenah, Wisconsin, and focused on electronic product development and testing. The other two subsidiaries were the company's dual contract production units, Electronic Assembly Corp. and Electronic Assembly Inc., with facilities in Neenah as well as in Richmond, Kentucky.

QUALITY CONTROL LEADING TO STRONG SALES: 1990–1994

Strong sales growth continued in the 1990s as Plexus developed a reputation for quality control in producing its electronic circuit boards. With the quality of boards produced in the Far East and the Pacific Rim slipping, more companies were buying boards made in the United States. Sales in fiscal 1991 reached $120.4 million, representing a five-year growth rate of 26 percent.

By 1991 the two contract production units had been merged into one, Electronic Assembly Corporation. The other subsidiary, Technology Group Inc., focused on product design and development. The company's customers ranged in size from giant IBM to a small Wisconsin-based maker of telecommunications devices for the deaf. The company's CEO and founder Peter Strandwitz told the *Business Journal-Milwaukee:* "Three key factors in Plexus' success are state-of-the-art technology, a high-quality, motivated labor force, and the quality demands of its customer base." Analysts agreed that the quality of Plexus' technology was among the industry's best. Due to its board testing equipment, Plexus could test board designs even more thoroughly than some of its customers, noted one analyst.

For 1992 sales rose 32 percent to $157.4 million, while net income jumped 39 percent to a record $5.1 million. In 1993, however, sales were flat at $159.6 million, and net income plunged about 50 percent to $2.6 million. Sales improved to $242.5 million in 1994; net income was about $3.1 million.

The company had completed work on its new 175,000-square-foot Advanced Manufacturing Center in Neenah. Costs associated with bringing the facility on-line had affected profits in 1993. The new facility added capacity in anticipation of future business from outsourcing by major electronic manufacturers. Major customers included IBM and GE Medical Systems.

EXPANSION AND ALLIANCES: 1995–2000

In 1995 Plexus expanded by hiring 500 people in the fourth quarter. Some of the new employees were hired through Wisconsin's Department of Vocational Rehabilitation, leading the company to hire workers with physical disabilities primarily for basic assembly jobs. Plexus also developed new training methods and established its Mentor Training Program, wherein volunteer mentors helped new employees through their first days and weeks at the company. Workforce diversity and training objectives became part of the company's strategic plan in 1996, and in 1998 Plexus was given the Governor's Exemplary Employer Award.

In 1997 Plexus gained marketing clout through a design and marketing agreement with Cadence Design Systems Inc., the world's largest software design company. Under the agreement, Cadence's 450-person sales force would market Plexus products and services to its customers. Plexus, with its large staff of engineers, provided the electronics industry with design, manufacturing, and testing services, but had a minimal sales force.

In April 1997 a new assembly plant in Green Bay, Wisconsin, began operations. The $22 million, 110,000-square-foot facility was built by Plexus on an Oneida reservation. Plexus and the Oneida tribe collaborated on the building and equipment for the facility, which was financed and owned by the Oneidas but operated by Plexus. It was Plexus's third electronic manufacturing services plant in addition to plants in Neenah and Richmond, Kentucky. The Green Bay facility featured five cells; the first became operational in April 1997, and others could be brought on line as business increased. Plexus also opened a design center in Raleigh, North Carolina, in 1997.

To help it land corporate research and design contracts, Plexus formed alliances with other research and design companies. In addition to its alliance with Cadence Design Systems, Plexus formed an alliance with Adaptive Microwave, a digital compression company based in Fort Wayne, Indiana, with expertise in video compression. Another alliance was established with IDEO of Palo Alto, California, the world's largest private firm in industrial design and engineering. Plexus's acquired printed circuit board assembly production facilities in the Chicago area from Shure Inc. for the RF/wireless technology market.

In addition to expanding its research, development, and production capabilities, Plexus continued to develop new technologies. Late in 1999 the company announced that it had designed an inexpensive radio module that allowed computers to communicate by radio wave from ten miles apart, compared with ten feet permitted by current technology. In addition, the high frequency wireless band used in this new technology could send ten to 20 times the amount of data that existing systems could handle. The technology also allowed computers within the confines of a building to communicate several hundred feet apart. Using this technology computers would be able to communicate directly with one another in real time while bypassing all wired infrastructures.

Plexus focused on the high-end, low-volume aspect of the electronics business, which resulted in smaller sales growth than companies focused on high-volume commodity electronics have realized. As a result Plexus's stock was not given a high valuation by Wall Street and was considered undervalued by investors during 1999. By March 2000, however, the company's stock price had jumped from $34 a year before to about $56, and Plexus's market capitalization exceeded $1 billion for the first time.

BUILDING A GLOBAL SUPPLY CHAIN IN 2000 AND BEYOND

Plexus's high degree of engineering skill made it a leader in supplying contract engineering and manufacturing as well as design and testing services to the electronics industry. As the company sought to expand its capabilities, it hoped to establish an overseas presence; at the end of 1999 all of its facilities were located in the United States.

Through acquisitions and internal expansion, the company was increasing its engineering staff and opening facilities in Mexico and Europe. In May 2000 it completed the acquisition of the electronic contract manufacturing operations of Elamex, S.A. de C.V. in Juarez, Mexico, for approximately $54 million. It was the company's first expansion outside the United States. Plexus would operate two facilities in Juarez, a newly constructed 210,000-square-foot electronic manufacturing plant and a 40,000-square-foot service center.

Revenues were $752 million in 2000. In May of that year, Plexus closed the acquisition of Boston-based Agility Inc. A couple of months later, it bought Keltek Holdings Ltd. of Kelso, Scotland, another privately owned EMS provider. The company aimed to use Keltek

---

KEY DATES

1979: Plexus is incorporated as a Wisconsin corporation.

1988: Sales increase 117 percent, and the company turns a profit.

1994: A new 175,000-square-foot Advanced Manufacturing Center in Neenah is completed.

1999: The company acquires SeaMED, an electronic design and manufacturing services provider for the medical market.

2000: The company acquires a manufacturing facility in Mexico, the company's first expansion outside the United States.

2001: Plexus cuts its workforce 10 percent while buying e2E, Qtron; sales exceed $1 billion.

2002: The MCMS acquisition adds manufacturing capacity in Asia.

2004: A second Malaysia plant is acquired to meet demand for low-cost manufacturing.

---

longest-standing alliance was with Battelle Institute of Columbus, Ohio, a private research and development company with $1 billion in sales. For fiscal 1998 net sales were $396.8 million, with net income of $19.2 million. The company had about 2,400 employees.

In early 1999 Plexus expanded its Raleigh, North Carolina, design center, which was originally opened in September 1997. It also opened its third regional design center in Louisville, Colorado, near Boulder. The 14,000-square-foot facility was designed to house up to 60 engineers. Plexus began by transferring a core team of eight to ten engineers from Neenah, then hired more engineers in Colorado. Overall, Plexus planned to double its engineering staff to 500 nationally over the next three years. The company's geographic expansion was guided in part by a desire to locate in high quality-of-life areas that would attract highly qualified technical candidates. Future expansion plans included the West Coast, Boston, Texas, and Europe. Expansion was seen as necessary to win contracts from global corporations.

In mid-1999 Plexus acquired SeaMED, a medically focused electronic design and manufacturing services provider in the Seattle, Washington area. The acquisition added 135 engineers and support personnel to the company's Design Center staff. SeaMED's customers included Boston Scientific, Johnson & Johnson, Medtronic, and Novoste. Later in the year Plexus

as a base for opening regional design centers throughout Europe, an executive told EBN.

Unfortunately, as a supplier to original equipment manufacturers (OEMs) in the electronics industry, Plexus was affected by the enduring slowdown following the collapse of the tech bubble. By the end of 2001, the company had reduced its workforce by about 10 percent as a result.

At the same time, Plexus made a couple of strategic acquisitions. The purchase of Hillsboro, Oregon-based e2E Corp. for about $25 million in stock and assumed debt bolstered its PCB engineering capabilities. E2E had 100 engineers based in a handful of cities in the United States and abroad. Adding hard-to-find design talent was a priority for Plexus. The acquisition of San Diego-based Qtron Inc., a $75 million EMS provider, brought advanced wireless infrastructure technology as well as two Southern California manufacturing plants.

Plexus added manufacturing capacity in Malaysia, China, and Nampa, Idaho via the January 2001 acquisition of five plants of bankrupt MCMS Inc. of San Jose, California from MPC Computer (formerly Micron Electronics Inc.). Plexus continued to cut its workforce by about 10 percent a year. It was, however, hiring more engineers at its Research Triangle, North Carolina facility.

The company's plants were running at half capacity in the post-bubble economic slump. Plexus lost $4 million in 2002 on sales of $884 million. In the next two years, the company closed manufacturing facilities in Bothell, Washington; San Diego, California; Richmond, Kentucky; and its oldest facility in Neenah, Wisconsin. Operations in Nashua, New Hampshire and Tel Aviv, Israel were sold to former employees. A second plant was acquired in Penang, Malaysia in fiscal 2004.

Thomas B. Sabol, the company's chief financial officer, told the *Wall Street Transcript* that what set the company apart from its competitors was its "passion for customer service." Plexus continued to avoid the high-volume commodity and consumer markets in order to focus on its niches: medical, optical, wireless, networking, data communications, and industrial. Another distinguishing factor, an analyst told *EBN,* was Plexus's strength in new product introduction (NPI) capacity. After buying Agilent, Plexus had doubled the size of its facility for use as an NPI Plus center.

Plexus landed a contract for broadband equipment from Next Level Communications in 2003. This work was allocated to the newly acquired Nampa, Idaho plant. By this time, Plexus was running 14 manufacturing plants around the world.

Net sales rose nearly 20 percent in 2004 to exceed $1 billion. This was not enough to stem the flow of red ink, though the company did manage to reduce its previous year loss of $68 million by more than half. After losing $31.6 million in 2004, Plexus posted a $12.4 million deficit in 2005, when sales were $1.3 billion. The company had added the defense/security/aerospace market to its list of chosen niches.

David P. Bianco
Updated, Frederick C. Ingram

PRINCIPAL SUBSIDIARIES

Plexus Services Corporation; Plexus International Services, Inc.; PTL Information Technology Services Corporation; Plexus Management Services Corporation.

PRINCIPAL OPERATING UNITS

United States; Asia; Mexico; Europe.

PRINCIPAL COMPETITORS

Solectron Corporation; Flextronics International Ltd.; Sanmina Corporation.

FURTHER READING

Bach, Pete, "Recovery a Priority at Neenah, Wis.-Based Electronics Manufacturer Plexus," *Post-Crescent* (Appleton, Wis.), February 13, 2003.

Boardman, Arlen, "Acquisition of Hillsboro, Ore., Circuit Board Firm Brings Plexus 100 Engineers," *Post-Crescent* (Appleton, Wis.), October 3, 2000.

———, "Neenah, Wis.-Based Plexus Corp. Develops Computer Radio Module," *Knight-Ridder/Tribune Business News,* November 18, 1999.

———, "Neenah, Wis.-Based Plexus Shifts Its Recruiting Philosophy," *Post-Crescent* (Appleton, Wis.), February 13, 2001.

———, "The Post-Crescent, Appleton, Wis., Arlen Boardman Column," *Knight-Ridder/Tribune Business News,* March 9, 2000.

———, "Wisconsin-Based High-Tech Firm Needs Mexican Labor for Expansion," *Knight-Ridder/Tribune Business News,* March 5, 2000.

———, "Wisconsin's Plexus Signs Deal with Software Design Giant," *Knight-Ridder/Tribune Business News,* February 13, 1997.

Carlson, Brad, "Plexus Corp. Lands Next Level Communications Contract," *Idaho Business Review* (Boise), February 24, 2003.

"Company Interview: Thomas B. Sabol, Plexus Corp.," *Wall Street Transcript,* Bear, Stearns & Co. 13th Annual Technology Special, June 2002.

"Company Interview: Thomas B. Sabol, Plexus Corp.," *Wall Street Transcript,* Needham & Company Growth Special, January 2002.

Dries, Michael, "Plexus Corp.," *Business Journal-Milwaukee,* January 29, 1994, p. 9.

Gallagher, Kathleen, "Plexus Keeps on Soaring, with Stock Splitting 2-for-1," *Milwaukee Journal Sentinel,* Bus. Sec., September 2, 2000, p. 1.

Gertzen, Jason, "Plexus Acquiring San Diego Firm," *Milwaukee Journal Sentinel,* Bus. Sec., May 3, 2001, p. 1.

Haber, Carol, "Oneida Tribe, Plexus Team on Plant," *Electronic News,* March 24, 1997, p. 46.

Hawkins, Lee, Jr., "Plexus to Buy Five Plants from Bankrupt Company," *Milwaukee Journal Sentinel,* Bus. Sec., November 29, 2001, p. 3.

Hudson, Kris, "Firm to Open Electronics Design Center in Louisville, Colo., Business Park," *Knight-Ridder/Tribune Business News,* February 16, 1999.

"In Neenah, Wis., Plexus Tells Shareholders to Expect Bigger Projects," *Knight-Ridder/Tribune Business News,* February 13, 1998.

Kueny, Barbara, "Plexus Corp.," *Business Journal-Milwaukee,* July 25, 1992, p. 6B.

McKeefry, Hailey Lynne, "Plexus Looks to Strengthen Global Presence—Acquisitions, New Infrastructure Play Key Roles,"
EBN, January 15, 2001, p. 72.

Matzek, MaryBeth, "Plexus Charts Future Growth," *Post-Crescent* (Appleton, Wis.), March 9, 2005.

"Neenah, Wis.-Based Product Design Firm to Form Division in Colorado," *Knight-Ridder/Tribune Business News,* April 11, 1999.

"Plexus Corp.," *Business Journal-Milwaukee,* December 10, 1990, p. 19.

"Plexus Corp.," *Business Journal-Milwaukee,* July 31, 1989, p. S14.

"Plexus Corp.," *Business Journal-Milwaukee,* February 27, 1989, p. 24.

Schaff, William, "Give Plexus Its Due," *InformationWeek,* September 13, 1999, p. 192.

Serant, Claire, "Consolidation Adds Muscle to Midtier—Plexus, EFTC Lead the Way in Acquiring Smaller, Private EMS Companies," *EBN,* May 14, 2001, p. 64.

———, "Contractor Hones Supply Chain Management Skills," *EBN,* August 27, 2001, p. 34.

———, "Plexus Continues Global Expansion, Eyes Asia," *Electronic Buyers' News,* August 7, 2000, p. 72.

Squires, Susan, "Plexus Wins Wis. Governor's Exemplary Employer Award," *Knight-Ridder/Tribune Business News,* June 4, 1998.

Provimi S.A.

9-11 Avenue Arago
Trappes,
France
Telephone: (33) 01 34 82 79 01
Fax: (33) 01 34 82 79 10
Web site: http://www.provimi.com

Public Company
Founded: 1927
Employees: 8,905
Sales: EUR 1.59 billion ($1.95 billion) (2005)
Stock Exchanges: Euronext Paris
Ticker Symbol: VIM
NAIC: 311119 Other Animal Food Manufacturing

■ ■ ■

Provimi S.A. is one of the world's leading producers of animal feed, pet foods and animal nutrition products and is also the world's largest pure-play feed producer. Provimi, formed in 2001 through the breakup of Eridania Beghin Say, has its roots in the Netherlands, which remains the site of the holding company, but operates from its corporate headquarters in Trappes, France. The company is present in more than 30 countries, with over 100 manufacturing facilities.

Provimi produces a complete line of feed, including proteins, vitamins and minerals, for all livestock categories, and is also a major producer of fish feed, including specialized feed for eel, marine fish, turbot, halibut, cod and tilapia, as well as for trout and salmon. Since its relaunch as an independent, public company,

Provimi has also stepped up its production of domestic pet food products, and especially for dogs and cats. Europe remains Provimi's core market, accounting for 75 percent of the group's total sales, which topped EUR 1.5 billion ($1.9 billion) in 2005. The company is present in the North American market largely through subsidiary North American Nutrition Companies (NANCO). The group's North American sales accounted for 11 percent of total group revenues in 2005. The company is also building a growing presence in the Asian region, notably through its control of Peter Hand in China. Provimi is listed on the Euronext Paris stock exchange. Wim Troost is group chairman.

SALT PRODUCER IN 1927

Provimi stemmed from a business set up in the Netherlands by the Bonda family in 1927. Bonda originally sold salt to feed producers but quickly recognized an opportunity to expand into the production of nutritional feed supplements, developing a concentrated mix of proteins, vitamins and minerals to improve feed quality. By the 1930s, the company had begun marketing its concentrate as Provimi (from PROteins, VItamins, MInerals), based on the main ingredients in its feed concentrate. The product helped establish the Bonda family at the forefront of animal nutrition in the Netherlands, and later throughout Europe, under the name Industriele B Bonda-Rotterdam N.V (Bonda International Corporation).

Over the next decades, Bonda diversified into the production of feed as well as feed supplements and expanded its sales and production network to include

Our Vision is to play a major role in feeding a growing and increasingly affluent global population with high quality, safe nutrition products, using our international resources of research and development that have been built up over decades of industry experience. In addition, we will extend our technical expertise in animal nutrition to provide safe and tasty pet food to companion animals all over the world.

most of Western Europe. Through the end of the 1960s, the company, which remained under family ownership, also diversified beyond its core feed operations, adopting something of a conglomerate status. By the early 1970s, Bonda's sales topped $100 million, backed by an extensive sales network spanning more than 25 countries, with feed plants operating in seven countries in Europe, as well as in Canada.

Bonda's strong European position brought it to the attention of Central Soya Company, based in the United States. Like Bonda, Central Soya had started out as a producer of feed supplements, then grew into one of the United States' leading feed producers, before diversifying to become a major agro-industrial foods group. By the early 1970s, Central Soya had launched an effort to expand into the international market, which led it to acquire Bonda in 1971. Central Soya then began marketing its products in Europe under the Provimi name, at first in Europe, then on an international level. Under Central Soya, also, Provimi—as the unit came to be called—streamlined its own operations to focus exclusively on its feed and feed supplements business.

The later Provimi operation grew during the 1980s, as Central Soya moved to boost both its domestic and international feed production operations through a series of acquisitions. In 1980, for example. Central Soya added new feed operations in Portugal, which were followed by two factories in Belgium operated by Aliments Protector.

Into the late 1980s, however, Provimi found itself under new ownership. In 1985, full control of Central Soya was acquired by Shamrock Capital, a holding company owned by the Roy Disney family, which had already held a majority stake in Central Soya. Under Shamrock, Central Soya underwent a significant streamlining, becoming refocused around a narrower field of activities. At the end of that restructuring in 1987, Shamrock sold Central Soya to Ferruzzi Agricola Finanziario, part of Italy's fast-growing Ferruzzi agro-

industrial group, which also controlled the leading Italian sugar producer, Eridania, as well as the leading French sugar group Béghin Say. The Ferruzzi group had begun transforming the merged Eridania Béghin Say into a diversified agro-industrial group in its own right. Ferruzi in turn was controlled by the Italian conglomerate Montedison.

Placed under Eridania-Béghin-Say (the merger entity was formalized in 1992), Central Soya's feed production operation began to target new expansion. The newly opening Eastern Europe markets provided a strong opportunity for growth. The company acquired its first subsidiary in Poland in 1989, followed by an entry into Hungary in 1990, through a feed production joint venture with Central Soya called Agrokomplex. The company then extended into a number of other Eastern European markets, including Bulgaria and Russia.

The first half of the 1990s represented a period of extended growth for Provimi as it expanded throughout much of central and Eastern Europe, while also strengthening its western European base. By the middle of the decade, the company had completed a series of acquisitions, adding operations in Italy, France, Ireland, the United Kingdom, Spain, Greece, and Switzerland, as well as in Poland. In this way, Provimi emerged as the European leader in the feed market.

INTERNATIONAL PURE-PLAY LEADER IN THE 21ST CENTURY

Acquisitions formed a major part of Provimi's growth through the second half of the 1990s and into the 2000s. The company's purchases were carried out in large part in support of a two-pronged strategy of, on the one hand, diversifying into other feed areas, including fish feed and pet foods, and on the other hand, of developing a truly international operation beyond Europe.

The company's geographic expansion led it to acquire positions in new markets including Argentina, Brazil, the United States, India and South Africa through the end of the 1990s. At the same time, the company completed a series of smaller bolt-on acquisitions, reinforcing its leading position in Europe.

Meanwhile, Provimi launched a string of acquisitions in such markets as Denmark, Chile, Spain, the Netherlands, the United Kingdom, and the Czech Republic in an effort to gain a rapid and major position in the international fish feed market.

As it turned toward the new century, Provimi intensified its acquisition drive. Between 1999 and 2005, the company carried out well over 30 acquisitions. These included 51 percent of Chilean fish feed group Alitec

KEY DATES

1927: The Bonda family begins supplying salt to feed producers.

1971: Industriele B Bonda-Rotterdam N.V (Bonda International Corporation) is acquired by Central Soya Company of the United States and refocuses around core of feed products, becoming the parent company's European branch.

1980: Two feed production units from Aliments Protector of Belgium are acquired.

1985: Central Soya is acquired by Shamrock Capital, which begins streamlining.

1987: Central Soya is acquired by Eridania-Béghin Say which launches an expansion of feed business.

1989: Provimi enters Poland.

1990: A joint-venture in Hungary with Central Soya is established as part of expansion throughout Central and Eastern European region.

1997: Company launches new strategy to add operations in fish feed and pet food, as well as develop expanded international operations.

2001: Eridania-Béghin-Say is split up into four companies, including Provimi, which is listed on Euronext Paris exchange.

2002: Majority stake in Provimi acquired by CVC Capital Partners and PAI Partners through Provimlux Investments.

ing the 1990s. The agro-industrial operation in particular was hard hit by a series of crises, in Southeast Asia, as well as in Russia and Brazil, which had left it hemorrhaging badly. In 2001, Montedison's shareholders agreed to break up Eridania-Béghin-Say into its four primary operating areas. As part of that breakup, Provimi took over the group's feed business, becoming the world's leading pure-play feed and animal nutrition group. Provimi, operated under a Netherlands-based holding company, was registered in France, with its headquarters in Trappes, and a listing on the Euronext Paris stock exchange. In 2002, Montedison, which by then had begun to refocus itself around its core energy business, agreed to sell its 53.7 percent of Provimi to an investment partnership between CVC Capital Partners and PAI Management.

Throughout the change in corporate status, Provimi maintained its fast-paced growth. By 2002, the company had launched a new round of acquisitions, starting with Hercules in Russia, Sanogold in Germany, Danafeed in Denmark, Comptoir de Gives in Belgium, and Sunglo Feeds in the United States. In that year, also, the company acquired the remaining share of Alitec in Chile. The company also boosted its pet foods operations into the mid-2000s. For this market, the company targeted especially the fast-growing private label segment, avoiding head-to-head competition with the major branded products leader. As part of its pet foods extension, Provimi purchased the Netherlands' Rocofa in 2003, as well as Viand, based in Bulgaria, and Agvet, an animal health specialist in India. By the end of 2005, Provimi had added pet foods operations in Hungary, Poland, and Slovakia as well. As it turned to the second half of the decade, Provimi had become the world's leading pure-play animal nutrition group, with significant global positions in the three major feed categories.

M. L. Cohen

and Spanish pet food producer Nutral in 1999. The following year, the company added fish feed united in Spain and Denmark, as well as a premix and specialty feed producer in Spain, and a full-range feed unit in Poland. Into 2001, the company acquired Australian premix producer Agribusiness, as well as Poland's Rolimpex, France's Sofrada, Brazil's Nutron and the United Kingdom's Nutrec. That year also marked the company's entry into the Asian market, with the purchase of a 51 percent stake in China's Guangxi Peter Hand, which also operated two production units in Vietnam.

While continuing its buying spree, Provimi found itself once again under a change of ownership. The Montedison group, and especially its Eridania-Béghin-Say unit, had fallen into deep financial difficulties dur-

PRINCIPAL SUBSIDIARIES

Agrokomplex (Hungary); North American Nutrition Companies Inc. (NANCO) (United States); Alimental (Argentina); Alitec (Chile); Bonimex (Netherlands); Bonimex South America (Chile); Celtic (France); Centralys (France); Comptoir de Gives S.A. (Belgium); Dana Feed (Denmark); Dana Feed (Poland); Joosten Products (Netherlands); Mervo products (Netherlands); Mixrite (Ireland); Neolait (France); NuTec (France); NuTec (Ireland); NuTec (Provimi Ltd) (United Kingdom); NuTec South Africa; Nutral (Spain); Nutron (Brazil); Pet Hungaria; Peter Hand Chong Qing (China); Peter Hand Vietnam; ProAqua (Brazil); ProAqua (Spain); Protector (Switzerland); Provimi Australia; Provimi Azov

(Russia); Provimi B.V. (Netherlands); Provimi Bejing; Provimi Belgium; Provimi Bulgaria; Provimi Canada; Provimi Gan Yu (China); Provimi Hellas (Greece); Provimi Italia; Provimi Jordan; Provimi Moscow Ltd (Russia); Provimi Pet Food CZ s.r.o. (Czech Republic); Provimi Portuguesa; Provimi Samara (Russia); Provimi Zootrofiki (Greece); Provimi-Rolimpex S.A. (Poland); RoCoFa B.V. (Netherlands); SanoGold (Germany); SCA Iberica (Spain); Sodial (France); Sofrada (France); Vetcare (India); Viand AD (Bulgaria); Vipromin 2000 (Romania); Zootech (France).

PRINCIPAL COMPETITORS

Cargill Inc.; Archer Daniels Midland Co.; Eli Lilly and Co.; ConAgra Foods Inc.; Uganda Grain Milling Company Ltd; Namib Mills Proprietary Ltd; Land O'Lakes Inc; Proagro C.A.; Edison S.p.A; CJ Corporation; Maple Leaf Foods Inc; Kerry Group plc; Nutreco Holding N.V.

FURTHER READING

Howie, Michael, "Eridania Shareholders Vote in Favor of Demerger," *Feedstuffs*, July 9, 2001, p. 7.

——, "Provimi Cites US Operations Improvement," *Feedstuffs*, June 24, 2002, p. 6.

——, "Sale of Provimi Finalized by Provimlux Investments," *Feedstuffs*, December 9, 2002, p. 7.

Mallet, Victor, "Edison Agrees to Sell Provimi Unit," *Financial Times*, August 12, 2002, p. 15.

"Provimi Acquires Belgian Comptoir de Gives Group," *Europe Agri*, January 25, 2002.

"Provimi Buys Nama in Slovakia," *Feedstuffs*, October 25, 2004, p. 27.

"Provimi Buys Two Animal Feed Producers in Russia," *Europe Agri*, September 27, 2002, p. 501.

"Provimi Cites Product Mix," *Feedstuffs*, January 9, 2006, p. 6.

"Provimi Expands in Asia, Europe," *Feedstuffs*, June 14, 2004, p. 7.

"Provimi Expands in Pet Food Industry," *Feedstuffs*, June 9, 2003, p. 7.

"Provimi Opens New Premix Plant in Brazil," *Feedstuffs*, March 28, 2005, p. 17.

"Provimi Strengthens Presence in Asia," *Feedstuffs*, December 10, 2001, p. 7.

"Russian Acquisition," *Feedstuffs*, November 21, 2005, p. 17.

Pulaski Furniture
Corporation

---

301 Madison Avenue South
Pulaski, Virginia 24301
U.S.A.
Telephone: (540) 980-7330
Fax: (540) 994-5756
Web site: http://www.pulaskifurniture.com

Private Company
Incorporated: 1955
Employees: 830
Sales: $242 million (2005 est.)
NAIC: 337120 Household and Institutional Furniture Manufacturing; 337129 Wood Television, Radio, and Sewing Machine Cabinet Manufacturing; 337211 Wood Office Furniture Manufacturing; 423210 Furniture Merchant Wholesalers

■ ■ ■

Pulaski Furniture Corporation makes mid-priced wooden bedroom, dining room, and occasional furniture for the home, such as credenzas and chests, home entertainment centers, and curio cabinets, and desks, bookcases, and consoles for the home office. In addition, the company imports accent pieces and parts, which it includes in its furniture. Pulaski Furniture is distributed through independent retailers, regional chains, national chains, department stores, and catalog houses. The company operates factories in Virginia and Missouri and a distribution center in North Carolina. It is credited with introducing eclectica to an industry that once primarily sold suites.

1955–1972: CREATING A NICHE IN THE OCCASIONAL FURNITURE MARKET

In 1955, Thomas J. McCarthy, Sr., Fred A. Stanley, Sr., and Colin Richardson founded and incorporated the Pulaski Veneer and Furniture Corporation, taking the name for their new venture from the Virginia town in which it was located. The company's original home was an old RCA Victor cabinet shop in downtown Pulaski that had been closed since 1948 as a result of the region's depressed economy.

The company began by making a couple of inexpensive bedroom and dining room suites. Designs were simple to provide for low pricing and ease of manufacture as the factory personnel's skill developed. Business was generally good for the new company, although, in the early years, employees sometimes received goods, such as hams and flour, from the Richardson family's farm in lieu of cash paychecks.

Pulaski Corporation acquired its first permanent showroom space in Chicago, Illinois, at the American Furniture Market in October 1957. In 1960, it acquired Morris Novelty Corporation of Martinsville, Virginia, producers of small occasional tables and other novelty furniture items. From this point forward, Pulaski began to expand into the production of curio cabinets, designed for the express purpose of displaying collectibles. Thanks mostly to the "Pulaski look," a highly stylized line that was a bit more difficult to manufacture and looked more expensive than it actually was, business was brisk.

The company changed its name from Pulaski Veneer and Furniture Corporation to Pulaski Furniture

The Pulaski success is directly attributable to defining our niche in various core competencies and servicing it well with proper products, prices, and quality to make our products highly desirable in a specific marketplace. 2005 marks Pulaski Furniture's 50th Anniversary. We celebrate our rich history and look forward to the next 50 years.

Corporation in 1962. By the mid-1960s, sales had reached about $7 million, and in 1967, Bernard "Bunny" C. Wampler became the company's chief executive officer, a role he occupied for the next 30 years. Under Bunny Wampler, Pulaski continued to expand and diversify, adding accent pieces, occasional tables, and hand painted armoires.

1973–1987: A SIGNIFICANT GROWTH PHASE

The company positioned itself for future growth by building a new case goods plant in Dublin, Virginia, in 1973. Twice the size of the original Pulaski case goods factory, this plant was the most modern of its time and huge for its day at 550,000 square feet.

In spring of 1976, with the nation's Bicentennial celebration under way, Pulaski introduced a line of golden oak furniture called Keepsakes, a 45-piece, "turn of the century" Victorian bedroom, dining room, and accent furniture collection that looked a lot like furniture that for many years had been considered old-fashioned. Extremely popular, this collection eventually grew to 90 pieces, and in December 1980, Pulaski cut its one millionth piece of Keepsakes.

The introduction of Keepsakes initiated what was to become a significant growth phase for Pulaski. Shortly thereafter, at an auction in 1983, Pulaski bought Coleman Furniture, a case goods manufacturer, whose primary business was manufacturing contract furniture for hotels and the government. Coleman was a very large bedroom manufacturer with more than 1,000,000 square feet of production and warehouse space. This purchase helped to consolidate Pulaski's shift from an older to a modern manufacturing facility, and contributed to its impressive growth in revenues. Pulaski joined forces that year with three other companies to form Triwood, a joint venture focused on the manufacture of plywood; this venture ended in 1995.

Annual sales increased from $48 million in 1981 to $74 million in 1985.

During the latter half of the 1980s, domestic furniture sales benefitted from low interest rates in the United States. These rates made home ownership more affordable, and created new homeowners in need of furniture. Pulaski's growth accelerated in 1985 with the $9.4 million acquisition of Gravely Furniture Company, which operated as Ridgeway Clock Company, a world-renowned manufacturer of grandfather, wall, and mantel clocks. Combined, the two firms had annual revenues of about $90 million from four plants and employed around 1,850 people.

The Ridgeway plant was a good fit for Pulaski because the clock business, like the curio business, provided accent pieces for decorating. The timing for this purchase was also ideal as, in the mid-1980s, consumers turned away from avant garde designs and toward nostalgic recreations of old American furniture styles. With the total number of sales for the Keepsakes collection at 1,300,000 pieces, the company added the 30-piece Sagamore Hill collection, which tapped into the same spirit of nostalgia in consumers.

In 1987, Pulaski held its initial public offering (IPO) of stock, and one year later, in 1988, the company purchased Craftique, a high-end manufacturer of solid mahogany reproductions of 18th-century furniture pieces. In 1989, it launched its Accentrics line, which departed from the company's traditional focus on nostalgia to incorporate high-end, mixed-media designs at medium price points. In 1990, the company also started a seated upholstery plant in Christiansburg, Virginia.

1987–2005: A DOWNTURN IN THE FURNITURE INDUSTRY

Unfortunately, the stock market crash of October 1987 had inaugurated a downturn for the entire furniture business. Although the industry recovered briefly in 1988, consumer confidence faded during the mini-crash of 1989, by which time the nation's seven-year economic expansion was ending, and a national recession was underway. Waves of layoffs across the nation cut into consumers' willingness to spend. Although sales for Pulaski reached $100 million in 1987 and continued to grow through the remainder of the 1980s, the company also began to look for ways to reduce its production costs.

During this time, Pulaski began to establish its Asian connections, bringing in both ready-to-finish and completely assembled goods from overseas at least partly as a means of economizing on production. (By 2005,

KEY DATES

1955: The company is founded by Thomas J. Mc-Carthy, Sr., Fred A. Stanley, Sr., and Colin Richardson.

1960: Pulaski acquires the Morris Novelty Corporation of Martinsville, Virginia.

1962: The company changes its name from Pulaski Veneer and Furniture Corporation to Pulaski Furniture Corporation.

1967: Bernard Wampler becomes the chief executive officer.

1973: The company acquires a case goods plant in Dublin, Virginia.

1976: The company introduces its Keepsakes collection.

1983: Pulaski acquires Coleman Furniture; the company takes part in a joint venture to form Triwood.

1985: Pulaski purchases Ridgeway Clock.

1987: The company holds its initial public offering.

1988: Pulaski upgrades its original plant and acquires Craftique.

1990: Pulaski enters the seated upholstery business.

1995: Pulaski sells Triwood.

1998: The company sells Craftique and its seated upholstery business.

1999: The company purchases Dawson Furniture.

2000: Management leads a buyout with support from Quad-C Management; Pulaski closes its Martinsville, Virginia, plant and sells its Dublin, Virginia, plant.

product niche was organized into a "strategic business unit," and the company designed its products to be easy to coordinate and, thus, easy to sell. Having worked for the family business from the age of 15, John Wampler, who would became chief executive officer in 1997, oversaw big changes in the 2,250-employee, ten-factory company. The company upgraded machine and information centers, to "make more furniture with the same number of people, and to make it faster," according to Wampler, as quoted in an October 1996 *High Points* article.

Wampler also led the move to restructure the company along product lines and refocus on its core competencies. This led to selling the Craftique division and closing the upholstery division in 1997, while reorganizing production to assign products to the plant most efficient for their manufacture. To further extend its product lines, Pulaski began manufacturing furniture for hotels and motels in 1998, and purchased Dawson Furniture of Missouri, a manufacturer of both promotional and unfinished furniture in 1999.

Pulaski also increasingly focused its attention on its curio cabinets. With adult collectors numbering more than 36 million in the United States in the late 1990s, and curio cabinets representing a domestic market with sales of about $500 million, the company began to introduce themed curio cabinets and lines of furniture. In 1996, it joined forces with Heilig-Meyers stores to unveil its 15-item Nascar-themed collection, featuring black-and-white checkered armchairs, toolbox end tables, and a curio for die-cast Nascar racers with carved car pediment and a mirrored racetrack background.

In 1998, Pulaski became a licensee for Precious Moments collectibles and began to make cabinets specifically to hold figurines. Another curio for golfers had tees set into glass shelves. And a cabinet for dolls, which accounted for 57 percent of the collectibles market, employed standard light bulbs because halogen bulbs, usual for most other curio cabinets, changed the color of a doll's hair. By 1999, Pulaski had sales exceeding $200 million, and curios represented half of its business.

In 2000, John Wampler and other senior executives, with the support of an affiliate of Quad-C Management, bought out the company for $125 million. That year's sales peaked at somewhere around $240 million. However, business dropped during the 2001 recession, leading to layoffs, and continued to shrink during the next three years in the face of increased import competition. By 2003, total sales had dropped to $160 million, moving Pulaski from its position as the 18th largest domestic furniture manufacturer and importer in 2001 to just outside the top 25 manufacturers.

more than half of the company's business came from Asian imports.) In the wake of poor results for its Craftique division in 1993, the company introduced a new line of promotionally priced items, curios, hall trees, consoles, and gun cabinets in 1994. It also built a highly mechanized $10 million curio manufacturing facility to maintain its presence in the mid- to lower-end furniture market. The 75,000-square foot small plant, Pulaski's "miniplant," was a complete manufacturing facility with rough milling, finishing, and packaging capacity in which a curio cabinet could go from cut lumber to being boxed for shipping in three to five days.

With leadership from John Wampler, Bunny Wampler's son, starting in 1993, the corporation became increasingly market-driven, focusing on what the company's customers and their consumers wanted. Every

Despite its contracting sales, Pulaski entered into a new licensing agreement with PBS in 2003 to produce its "Antiques Roadshow" Collection, 60 modern adaptations of American designs of the 1800s, including two bedroom and two dining room collections and accent pieces such as Bombay chests, curio cabinets, painted trunks, and grandfather clocks. "The collection is special," offered Wampler in a 2003 *San Francisco Chronicle* article. "It's authentic furniture based on real antiques, real people, and real stories about home furnishings." Each piece came with a logo and a hangtag complete with photo and history of the antique that inspired it.

Rather than close plants as domestic capacity decreased in the early 2000s, Pulaski sold facilities, first its Dublin and Martinsville, Virginia plant, and then, in late 2004, its Ridgeway Clock division to Howard Miller. These sales were part of a refining of focus led by Lawrence E. Webb, Jr., who became chief executive of Pulaski in 2003, to concentrate on bedroom, dining room, case goods, and occasional furniture. Under Webb, the company's different product lines were assigned to a specific plant of manufacture to create facilities better equipped to compete in a specific niche.

Furniture manufacturers as a group experienced an upswing in sales by 2004, in the long-term wake of 9/11 and Internet growth, as Americans spent more time at home. Pulaski's 2004 sales improved nearly five percent to an estimated $178 million and it added another line of furniture, the Casa Cristina collection, which targeted the growing population of Hispanic home owners.

In 2005, with revenues close to $200 million, Pulaski introduced a new lighting system in its curios in response to customer demand and reintroduced its line of Keepsakes curios and its Accentrics line of stand alone occasional items. The company was looking optimistically to the future. "When we asked customers about their...Pulaski curios and accent furniture, 96 percent of respondents said they were satisfied," Webb reported of a customer survey in a 2005 *Furniture Today* article. "Forty-two percent said they had plans to purchase another piece."

Carrie Rothburd

PRINCIPAL COMPETITORS

Ethan Allen; Furniture Brands International; Hooker Furniture; Thomasville; Lexington; Ashley Furniture; Bassett Furniture; Chromcraft Revington; Stanley Furniture

FURTHER READING

Evans, Lynette, "Everything Old Is New Again," *San Francisco Chronicle,* May 17, 2003, p. 1WB.

"Fast Forward," *High Points,* October 1996, p. 26.

Hamilton, William, L., "The Real You, Now on View," *New York Times,* November 18, 1999, p. F14.

Hinden, Stan, "Solid Profit Picture Builds Up Pulaski Furniture's Stock," *Washington Post,* May 19, 1986, p. 39.

Koncius, Jura, "Learning Latin; Furniture Plays to Hispanic Shoppers With a Spanish Talk-Show Star," *Washington Post,* December 2, 2004, p. H1.

Linville, Jeff, "Pulaski Eyes Growth," *Furniture Today,* June 6, 2005, p. 1.

Quidel Corporation

—◼—

10165 McKellar Court
San Diego, California 92121
U.S.A.
Telephone: (858) 552-1100
Toll Free: (800) 874-1517
Fax: (858) 546-8955
Web site: http://www.quidel.com

Public Company
Incorporated: 1979 as Monoclonal Antibodies, Inc.
Employees: 255
Sales: $92.3 million (2005)
Stock Exchanges: NASDAQ
Ticker Symbol: QDEL
NAIC: 325413 In-Vitro Diagnostic Substance Manufacturing

◼ ◼ ◼

San Diego-based Quidel Corporation develops, manufactures, and markets rapid point-of-care (POC) diagnostic tests. They are used to detect certain illnesses and medical conditions, especially those affecting women's health. Sold under the QuickVue label, the tests serve women by verifying pregnancy, the presence of bacterial vaginosis, or osteoporosis. Quidel also provides diagnostic tests for infectious diseases, including influenza, Strep A, infectious mononucleosis, *H. pylori* infection (the cause of stomach ulcers), and Chlamydia (a bacteria similar to gonorrhea, mostly affecting teens and young adults). The products are used in hospitals, clinical laboratories, doctor's offices, and wellness screen centers, and sold through a direct sales force as well as major distributors, including Cardinal Healthcare Corporation, Physician Sales and Services Corporation, and National Distribution Corporation. In addition, Quidel offers the over-the-counter RapidVue line of pregnancy tests. Quidel is a public company listed on the NASDAQ.

FOUNDING OF THE ORIGINAL QUIDEL CORPORATION IN 1982

What constitutes today's Quidel Corporation is the result of a 1991 merger between Monoclonal Antibodies, Inc. and the original Quidel Corporation. Monoclonal Antibodies was the surviving corporate entity, but it subsequently assumed the Quidel name. The old Quidel was founded by Dr. David H. Katz in San Diego. He dedicated his life to the medical field in large part because of his mother's poor health while he was a child. "I had to spend a lot of time in hospitals," he explained to the *San Diego Business Journal.* "I wanted to emulate the people who took care of her for so long." Katz earned an undergraduate degree at the University of Virginia, and then received his medical doctor's degree from Duke University in 1968. During his time at Duke, Katz spent time at The Scripps Research Institute, working under one of the leaders in the immunology field, Dr. Frank J. Dixon. It was this experience that led Katz to become a researcher rather than a practicing physician. To fulfill his military commitment at the height of the Vietnam War, he spent four years at the National Institutes of Health (NIH) involved in immunological research. "That's where I really learned immunology for the first time," he told the *San Diego Business Journal.* "The field

COMPANY PERSPECTIVES

Our ultimate and all-consuming mission is to enhance the health and well-being of people around the globe.

was moving in a new direction in the late '60s." For the first time the importance of the immune system regarding cancer research, organ transplants, and disease was to be fully investigated.

After NIH, Katz taught at Harvard's pathology department and while there stumbled upon a biotechnology he called Suppressive Factor of Allergy, or SFA, for which he would ultimately receive a patent. In 1976 his old mentor, Dr. Dixon, brought Katz back to Scripps, where in the course of the next five years Katz rose to the chairmanship of the cellular and immunology department, which was only a three-person affair when he began but would grow to significantly more than 100 by 1981. At this point he resigned to launch a biotech start-up company primarily to exploit SFA, a technology that he believed had the potential to create a drug that could eradicate all known allergies.

With $1.5 million in seed money from the venture capital firm Brentwood Associates, Katz established Quidel Corporation in 1982 in Torrey Pines Mesa, near San Diego. For the company name, he eschewed the use of common prefixes such as "bio," "tech," or "immuno." His initial idea was to call it Lidan, drawing on the names of his daughters, Lisa and Danica, but it had already been trademarked by a Los Angeles investment firm that had no interest in changing their name to accommodate him. Over wine with some friends, Katz coined Quidel, a variation of the Chinese word Quided, which meant "to advance very rapidly." In addition to for-profit Quidel, Katz also established a nonprofit sister company, Medical Biology Institute (MBI), which conducted basic research on a number of diseases, relying mostly on government grants. Although MBI did not serve as the research arm of Quidel, there was interaction between researchers, who shared much of the same facilities and even teamed up to form a coed softball team, Quimbi.

While Quidel worked to develop an SFA drug, it developed some interim products to bring in money. One of them was a self-test pregnancy test kit, introduced in 1985 and marketed under the QTest name by Becton, Dickinson & Co. Other test products followed, including a home ovulation test, a "dipstick" strep throat test for physicians, and a dairy cow fertility

test that grew out of the company's human fertility work. Quidel filed to make an initial public offering of stock in 1986, but had to back off when market conditions deteriorated. The company, strapped for cash, raised $9 million in a private placement of stock with a number of venture capitalists, but troubles continued and in 1988 Katz fell out with the directors and resigned.

FINDING A MERGER PARTNER IN 1990

Katz was replaced as CEO by Scott Glenn, who had been with Quidel since the beginning. In 1989 he engineered a restructuring of the business, spinning off the therapeutics division as La Jolla Pharmaceuticals to develop and market drugs for antibody-mediated autoimmune diseases, such as lupus and antibody-mediated thrombosis. What remained of Quidel was the diagnostic products, but it was a small company attempting to survive in a competitive field. To become a larger player, Quidel, in 1990 found a suitable, and willing, merger partner in Monoclonal Antibodies, Inc.

Monoclonal Antibodies was founded in Mountain View, California, in 1979 by Thomas A. Glaze, a graduate of Stanford's MBA program. Backed by legendary Silicon Valley venture capitalist Arthur Rock, it was one of a number of companies looking to exploit the hot new field of monoclonal antibodies, which sought to use pure antibodies to target specific parts of the body as a way to combat cancer and other serious diseases. Dr. Cesar Milstein and Dr. Georges Kohler developed the technique to produce these antibodies in mice at their laboratory in Cambridge, England in 1975, and nine years later would win the Nobel Prize in Medicine for their work. According to the *Wall Street Journal*, "Monoclonal antibodies are the products of hybridomas, the fusion of fast-growing cancer with an antibody-producing cell. The antibody produced is free of impurities that could confuse its natural radar system. At least in theory, it can be armed with therapeutic agents and aimed." Unfortunately, monoclonal antibodies was yet one more magic bullet that failed to work, as the complexities of the human body as well as cancer proved too great. The drugs that were developed—using mouse proteins that were treated as invaders by the body—were unable to penetrate "tumors to reach their target proteins." But, as the *Wall Street Journal* further reported, "The specificity of the antibodies in seeking out a single protein made them immediately useful in diagnostics." Early on Monoclonal steered away from cancer therapy and focused on the potentially lucrative diagnostics market.

Monoclonal went public in 1981 and began marketing diagnostic test kits using genetically

```
┌─────────────────────────────────────────────┐
│                                               │
│              KEY DATES                        │
│                    ■                          │
│  ──────────────────────────────────────       │
│                                               │
│  1979: Monoclonal Antibodies, Inc. is founded.│
│  1981: Monoclonal is taken public.            │
│  1982: Quidel Corporation is founded.         │
│  1986: Monoclonal loses a patent dispute.     │
│  1991: Monoclonal and Quidel merge.           │
│  1996: An alliance with Glaxo Wellcome is formed.│
│  2000: Litmus Concepts, Inc. is acquired.     │
│  2004: Caren L. Mason is named CEO.           │
│                                               │
└─────────────────────────────────────────────┘
```

engineered antibodies. Growth was sidetracked in 1984 when Hybritech Inc., another diagnostics test provider, sued Monoclonal, alleging infringement on a patent it received a year earlier. According to the *San Francisco Chronicle,* "The patent in question pertains to the use of monoclonal antibodies in a technique known as sandwich immunoassays. ... Thomas Glaze, president of Monoclonal, said sandwich immunoassays were developed and not patented in the late 1960s using conventional antibodies to measure biological compounds. His company used the technique with monoclonal antibodies to develop products such as a home pregnancy test. Glaze said six of his company's seven current products use the sandwich technique that Hybritech claims to have patented."

In August 1985 Monoclonal achieved what it considered a major court victory when a federal judge dismissed the case, noteworthy because it was the first genetic engineering patent dispute to be settled in court. A month later the company signed a major agreement with a Johnson & Johnson unit to develop and supply home diagnostic tests, and it appeared Monoclonal was on the cusp of prosperity. In 1986 it achieved profitability on revenues of $7.7 million. But even as it was posting record results the company met with serious problems. In August 1986 Johnson & Johnson pulled out of its deal to sell an ovulation test because of shelf-life problems. A month later a federal appeals court reversed the prior lower court decision and upheld the validity of the Hybritech patent, and then in March 1987 Monoclonal was ordered by the court to cease selling products that infringed on the patent, eliminating 80 percent of its revenues. On the verge of bankruptcy, the company slashed its workforce by a third to cut costs while it negotiated a settlement with Hybritech. In July 1987 Monoclonal agreed to pay Hybritech $2.25 million to settle past claims and acquired a one-year license with a 15 percent royalty to sell its products until they were reformulated.

Monoclonal began to rebuild sales in the final years of the 1980s, but the company was eager to merge with Quidel in 1990. The agreement was contingent upon the infusion of $7 million from private investor David Blech. When he backed out, the merger stalled until J.P. Morgan & Co. and other institutional investors stepped in to provide $11 million in financing, of which $7 million came from the purchase of stock. When the merger was completed in January 1991, the result was a company employing nearly 300 people with combined sales of $30 million. Although Monoclonal contributed just a third of that amount, as a public company it became the surviving entity. But it immediately assumed the Quidel name and set up its headquarters in San Diego, and steps were taken to shut down Monoclonal's Sunnyvale facilities. Glaze, who took over as chairman, did not lament the name change, telling the *Business Journal of San Jose,* "We felt for a long time that the name (Monoclonal) was just too long." Glaze held the chairmanship until 1995, then stayed on as a director.

By combining operations the new Quidel was able to save about $2.3 million over what the two companies would have paid if on their own. As a result, in the fiscal year ending March 31, 1992, the company reached profitability, netting nearly $900,000. In the fall of 1992 the company received more good news when the 1,800-unit Walgreen drugstore chain agreed to carry Quidel's ovulation detection kit, Conceive, priced at $9.99, packaged in a box with a smiling baby on the front. Quidel also marketed a plain wrapper pregnancy test called RapidVue at a price point of $6.99. But they were actually the same product packaged differently. According to *Forbes,* "What's different is the market. 'The market definitely divides between the women who want babies and those who don't,' explains Quidel Chief Executive Steven Frankel. He explains why the smiling baby sells for more than the plain-wrapper product: 'It's like what Charles Revson said about cosmetics: People buy hope. In our case, they pay more for hope than for possible relief.'"

Business tailed off in fiscal 1994 and fiscal 1995, when Quidel lost nearly $6 million. But the company was in the process of switching its business model from one dependent on selling kits under others' brand names to one dependent on branded sales. Quidel returned to profitability in 1996, netting $579,000 on sales of $33.5 million. The company also forged an important alliance with Glaxo Wellcome in 1996, as the two collaborated to develop the Quick Vue Influenza Test, which received FDA approval three years later. They signed another collaborative agreement in 1997 to develop diagnostic tests to detect genital herpes. In addition, Quidel established an alliance with Procter and Gamble in fiscal 1997 to co-market a *H. pylori* test, which a year later would result in a 45 percent increase in sales in the *H. pylori* category. In April 1999 Quidel's women's health business received a major boost when the company signed an exclusive agreement with Perrigo Company, a global leader in store brand healthcare products. In addition, in March 1999, Quidel struck an agreement with Merck-Medco Managed Care, L.L.C. to provide the Quick Vue H. Pylori tests in Merck-Medco's pharmacy disease management program. By the end of the 1990s, Quidel eliminated less profitable products, shut down three unprofitable international subsidiaries, and narrowed its focus to women's health and infectious diseases. In the year 1999 (Quidel's fiscal year now ended on December 31), the company recorded sales of $52.2 million and net income of $5.9 million.

MAJOR ACQUISITIONS: 2000

In 2000 Quidel acquired Litmus Concepts, Inc., a diagnostic company that made women's health products. As a result, Quidel picked up multilayered thin film technology, used in the mass production of disposable tests, as well as 21 associated patents. Also in 2000, Quidel began selling a urinalysis product line, Quick Vue UrinChek, an improved *H. pylori* test for peptic ulcer disease in the U.S. market, began selling an over-the-counter influenza test in Europe, and received permission to market its influenza test in Canada as well. For the year global sales increased 31 percent to $68,351.

In 2002 Quidel began to offer products using the layered thin film technology acquired from Litmus Concepts. Sales continued to grow, reaching $92.5 million in 2003, while net income approached $20 million. The year 2004 brought a change in management as Caren L. Mason was named president, CEO, and a member of the board of directors after the company reported disappointing quarterly results and CEO S. Wayne Kay was asked to leave. She brought to the job more than 25 years of healthcare experience, involved with the running of a number of fast-growth, high-tech healthcare companies. She took over as Quidel was contending with a drop-off in business caused by an unusual flu season that peaked much sooner than normal. Hence, sales dipped to $78.7 million and net income fell to $1.6 million. Revenues rebounded to $92.3 million in 2005, and the year ended on a good note when the FDA agreed to allow Quidel to promote its flu-test kit as being useful in detecting avian flu, as well as highly effective in diagnosing the common influenza A strain. The effects of the decision were felt immediately, as Quidel achieved record results in the first quarter of 2006, led by sales of its influenza tests.

Ed Dinger

PRINCIPAL SUBSIDIARIES

Pacific Biotech, Inc.; Metra Biosystems, Inc.; Osteo Sciences Corporation; Litmus Concepts, Inc.

PRINCIPAL COMPETITORS

Abbott Laboratories; Beckman Coulter Inc.; Hemagen Diagnostics, Inc.

FURTHER READING

Chase, Marilyn, "Monoclonal Says Judge to Order a Halt on Sales of Firm's Biggest-Selling Items," *Wall Street Journal,* March 25, 1987, p. 1.

Dower, Rick, "Katz Seeks Separate Successes at Quidel and MBI," *San Diego Business Journal,* September 14, 1987, p. 24.

Goldman, James S., and Michael Krey, "Companies Merge (Monoclonal Antibodies; QUIDEL)," *Business Journal of San Jose,* November 12, 1990, p. 16.

Kinsman, Michael, "San Diego-Based Medical Products Maker to Fire CEO After Earnings Warning," *San Diego Union-Tribune,* July 14, 2004.

Koselka, Rita, "Hope and Fear As Marketing Tools," *Forbes,* August 29, 1994, p. 78.

Lancaster, Hal, "Efforts to Develop Monoclonal Antibodies Are Moving More Slowly Than Expected," *Wall Street Journal,* May 1, 1984, p. 1.

Pollack, Andrew, "The Birth, Death and Rebirth of a Novel Disease-Fighting Tool," *New York Times,* October 3, 2000, p. F1.

Rose, Craig D., "FDA Lets Quidel Boost Claims for Its Flu Test," *San Diego Union-Tribune,* December 30, 2005.

Russell, Sabin, "Monoclonal Rebounding," *San Francisco Chronicle,* September 8, 1988, p. C1.

Reddyice

Reddy Ice Holdings, Inc.

———— ■ ————

8750 North Central Expressway
Suite 1800
Dallas, Texas 75231
U.S.A.
Telephone: (214) 526-6740
Fax: (214) 443-5357
Web site: http://www.reddyice.com

Public Company
Incorporated: 1927 as Southland Ice Company
Employees: 2,100
Sales: $319.8 million
Stock Exchanges: New York
Ticker Symbol: FRZ
NAIC: 312113 Ice Manufacturing

■ ■ ■

Listed on the New York Stock Exchange under the appropriate ticker symbol FRZ, Reddy Ice Holdings, Inc., is the United States' largest maker of ice and packaged ice, about three times larger than its nearest competitor. The Dallas-based company divides its activities between two business segments: ice products and non-ice products and operation. The former includes the manufacture and delivery of ice (some of which are blocks as large as 300 pounds for commercial use) as well as the installation and operation of The Ice Factory, a self-contained, on-site proprietary system that makes and packages bags of ice for customers of convenience stores, supermarkets, and other retail outlets. Reddy Ice focuses on Sunbelt states where the demand for ice is more consistent, and

overall it services some 82,000 customer locations in 31 states and Washington, D.C. The company also maintains 58 manufacturing facilities and 52 distribution centers. The non-ice business includes the operation of five cold storage warehouses, and a bottled water plant.

HERITAGE DATES TO 1927

Reddy Ice shares its origins with the 7-Eleven convenience store chain, a business that actually grew out of the activities of Southland Ice Company. Southland was founded in 1927 by Joseph C. Thompson and a group of investors. The operation included eight ice plants and 21 retail ice docks. The idea behind the company was to sell block ice to customers who owned automobiles. But not only did these customers like the convenience of pulling up to the neighborhood icehouse to buy block ice (needed to keep food cool in the ice boxes in use at the time), they began to ask for bread and milk as well. A manager of one of the ice docks, John Jefferson Green, convinced Thompson to allow him to sell other staples in addition to ice. The icehouse now began to offer a dozen items, including milk, bread, canned goods, and cigarettes. The result was the world's first convenience store. In 1928 another Southland manager, after making a visit to Alaska, planted a souvenir totem pole in from of his store. It proved to be an attraction, and soon the other Southland ice docks added them, and the stores now became known as "Tote'm Stores," a name appropriate on two levels: the stores were known for the totem poles out front and customers toted away their purchases, instead of having them delivered.

In the early 1930s Southland's horse-drawn ice

COMPANY PERSPECTIVES

Reddy Ice will remain the recognized leader in the packaged ice industry by producing the highest quality of pure, clean and odorless ice products, by maintaining the highest level of customer service and satisfaction, through the relentless pursuit of excellence in technology and merchandising equipment, and by maintaining and growing the broadest geographic distribution network in the ice industry.

delivery wagons were replaced by trucks. The company struggled at the beginning of the Great Depression that was brought on by the stock market crash of 1929 and was forced into receivership. It soon emerged reorganized, with Thompson serving as president, and the chain of Tote'm Stores resumed its strong growth, especially benefiting from the repeal of Prohibition, which allowed the stores to now sell beer, one of the three staples of the convenience store business along with soda and cigarettes. (A fourth, it might be argued, was gasoline, and in the 1920s Southland first dabbled in the business, building and leasing gas stations at ten of its stores.) It was also not surprising that the sale of ice showed dramatic improvement with the repeal of Prohibition.

By the end of the 1930s Southland owned 60 Tote'm Stores in the Dallas-Fort Worth area. These accounted for most of Southland's revenues. Southland also began to become vertically integrated in the 1930s. It added Oak Farms Dairies to meet the milk needs of the Tote'm Stores. Nevertheless, the ice business remained very important. Demand for ice again surged after America's entry into World War II in late 1941. For example, Southland supplied most of the ice needed for the construction and operation of the U.S. Army's chief training facility, Camp Hood. During this period Southland expanded its ice operations by acquiring City Ice Delivery, Ltd., picking up a pair of modern ice-making plants and 20 retail outlets. Southland was now the largest ice company in Dallas.

POSTWAR INCREASES ICE DEMAND

In the post-World War II years, Tote'm Stores were renamed "7-Eleven," A reference to the stores' hours: 7:00 in the morning until 11:00 at night, seven days a week. While the popularity of the convenience stores continued to grow, demand for Southland ice also increased. Home refrigerators were not yet commonplace and for some time to come ice boxes would still need to be regularly supplied with block ice.

Southland's 7-Eleven stores were introduced outside of the Dallas area in the early 1950s when units opened in Austin, followed by new outlets in Houston. The chain expanded beyond Texas in 1954 with stores in Miami and Jacksonville, Florida. In 1958, the first "northern" 7-Eleven stores were opened in Maryland, Virginia, and Pennsylvania. After Southland was incorporated in 1961, 7-Eleven expanded even more rapidly, as the chain spread to all parts of the country, its growth accomplished in some measure by the acquisition of smaller convenience store chains. By the mid-1960s there were more than 1,500 7-Eleven stores, and by the end of the decade there would be more than 3,500 units in the United States and Canada. The 5,000 mark was reached in 1974, when 7-Eleven began to spread around the world. Southland also became a public company and gained a listing on the New York Stock Exchange in 1972.

By this point Southland's ice business, now called the Reddy Ice Division, was the largest ice operation in the world, but it was just a small part of a large, vertically integrated retail enterprise. The sale of gasoline was a far more important revenue generator than packaged ice, and in 1983 Southland acquired Citgo Petroleum Corp. for $780 million, to ensure a steady supply of gas for 7-Eleven, which had become the largest independent retailer of gasoline in the United States. It was an ill-fated decision, however, that had an impact on Reddy Ice and other Southland units. Just as excess refining capacity came on line, the demand for gas dropped, resulting in a $50 million pre-tax loss for Southland in 1984. To make matters worse, Southland had to contend with a hostile takeover bid in 1987. Joseph Thompson's three sons decided to ward off the attack by Canadian corporate raider Samuel Belzburg by forming a holding company to take Southland private. But in order to finance the $3.7 billion plan, they had to sell off some assets. One of these was Reddy Ice; it was put on the block in July 1987.

In March 1988 Southland sold Reddy Ice to Kaminski/Engles Capital Corporation for $26 million, with the bulk of the financing provided by Citicorp. This was the first non-real estate transaction for the Dallas investment firm headed by former real estate executive Robert Kaminski and lawyer Gregg L. Engles. They took over a company that generated $17 million a year in revenues by producing 156,000 tons of ice each year, operating five plants in Texas as well as facilities in Davie, Florida, and Las Vegas, Nevada. Engles would become

KEY DATES

1927: Southland Ice Company is formed to sell ice directly to customers with cars, during an era when ice is typically still delivered to homes. The convenience store concept is born when ice dock managers begin selling staples such as bread and milk, in response to customer request.

1946: Southland stores, which had become known as "Tote'm Stores" are renamed "7-Eleven."

1988: Southland sells Reddy Ice to the Kaminski/Engles Capital Corporation.

1983: Kaminski/Engles enters the dairy business with the acquisition of Suiza.

1998: Suiza Foods sells Reddy Ice to Packaged Ice.

2003: Trimaran Capital Partners acquires Packaged Ice, renamed Reddy Ice.

2005: Reddy Ice is taken public.

the driving force behind Reddy Ice's growth over the next decade. A Yale law school graduate, he had quickly lost interest in a legal career and in the 1980s became involved in Texas real estate with dismal results. He had better success with Reddy Ice, but was not content to just pursue the limited ice business. According to *Forbes,* Engles soon realized that the ice and dairy businesses were quite similar: "Both were produced in aging, undercapitalized plants; perishability dictated that each had to be shipped directly to stores; both were highly fragmented businesses. In 1993 Engles did a $100 million LBO of a down-and-out Puerto Rican dairy called Suiza (Spanish for Swiss)." With this as a base, Engles began acquiring other dairies in the United States, along the way picking up such venerable brands as Borden and PET. With both his growing dairy and ice assets, Engles strengthened his business interests by reducing redundancy in capacity and distribution routes, and upgraded infrastructure and equipment. In 1996 he made an initial public offering of Suiza Foods Company, which included Reddy Ice. A year later Suiza reached the $1 billion mark in annual sales. That number grew to $2.5 billion in 1997, of which Reddy Ice contributed 4 percent or $66.3 million.

SOLD TO PACKAGED ICE: 1998

Reddy Ice was hardly a major component of Suiza, and so in 1998 Engles recouped his investment in the company by selling it to Houston-based Packaged Ice

Inc. for around $180.8 million in cash. In this way Suiza could focus on its diary business and allow Reddy Ice to fulfill its potential as well. Packaged Ice was an up-and-coming company in an industry that was rapidly consolidating. While it recorded sales of just $29 million in 1997, it had completed a number of acquisitions before adding Reddy Ice which would have increased sales to the neighborhood of $90 million.

Packaged Ice was founded in 1990, with backing from a pair of venture capital funds, by James Stuart, a former accountant for the Houston office of Big Five accounting firms. According to *Houston Business Journal,* "Stuart embarked on his second career after looking around for something new to invest in and coming across a technology that allowed for ice to be manufactured, bagged and sold in the store." Stuart's idea was to modernize the traditional model of ice production by transferring the manufacturing and distribution process from a faraway plant to the point of sale using this new technology. Stuart bought the prototype of what would become The Ice Factory in 1986. After devoting the next five years to refining it for retail operation, he began pitching the idea to supermarket chains, including Randalls Foods Stores and Kroger Stores. Packaged Ice owned the machines and companies paid a usage fee to install one or more of The Ice Factory units onsite.

Soon after The Ice Factory machines began finding their way into the marketplace, Stuart began to buy ice companies from owners who could not compete with his innovative technology. While he was banking on The Ice Factory to become the major source of revenue, and ideally 100 percent of the business, Stuart took advantage of the opportunities presented to him and began acquiring traditional ice manufacturers. These soon accounted for the bulk of Packaged Ice revenues.

Meanwhile, Packaged Ice was not the only company buying up small to mid-sized ice companies in the 1990s. Reddy Ice had been completing its share of acquisitions, as had Artic Group of Canada, the only public company in the industry until 1999. After its successful 1998 acquisition of Reddy Ice, Packaged Ice took its company public with an initial public offering of stock that netted $91 million. With Reddy Ice in the fold, Packaged Ice was now the undisputed leader, generating sales of $231.7 million in 1999 and $244 million in 2000. The company was not highly valued by Wall Street, however, so in 2001 Packaged Ice began to focus on refining its corporate structure. Since the Reddy Ice acquisition, the company had maintain dual headquarters in Houston and Dallas. In 2001 it initiated plans to shut down the Houston operations and realize some cost savings by bringing everything to Dallas. Moreover, Stuart stepped down as chief executive officer, replaced by William Brick, who had run Reddy Ice for Suiza and had come with the acquisition.

The price of Packaged Ice stock continued to languish, and in 2003 the ownership of the company changed hands when Trimaran Capital Partners, a Bear Stearns & Company private equity unit, agreed to pay $450 million for the outstanding stock to take the business private. In May 2003 Reddy Ice Holdings Inc. was formed to house the assets of Packaged Ice, which was also renamed Reddy Ice Group, Inc. Clearly, the new owners believed the Reddy Ice brand still carried considerable clout in the marketplace. Under Trimaran, Reddy Ice continued to grow through acquisitions, adding a pair of companies in 2003, and another 11 in 2004. As a result sales increased to $285.7 million.

Trimaran was now ready to take Reddy Ice public once again. In August 2005 the company completed an IPO that raised close to $190 million. The offering was well received by investors who paid $18.50 a share, above the $16 to $18 range that had been projected. The stock then climbed in value as it began trading on the New York Stock Exchange. Reddy Ice's proceeds from the offering, $127.9 million, were earmarked, according to the prospectus, for the paying down of debt. However, according to the *Dallas Morning News,* "The company will probably use its increased capital to expand further in the South and Southeast and push deeper into California, a lucrative area, said Jane McEwen, executive director of the International Packaged Ice Association. 'Expansion is one of the foremost reasons for this IPO,' she said. 'They're positioning themselves to service some very desirable parts of the country—and service them widely."

Ed Dinger

PRINCIPAL SUBSIDIARIES

Reddy Ice Group, Inc.

PRINCIPAL COMPETITORS

Home City Ice Company, Inc; The Manitowoc Company, Inc.

FURTHER READING

Apte, Angela, "Hot Ideas For A Cool Business," *Houston Business Journal,* April 30, 1999, p. 27.

Colley, Jenna, "Packaged Ice Hopes For Hotter Profits in Dallas," *Houston Business Journal,* May 4, 2001, p. 2.

Cook, Lynn J., "Got Growth?" *Forbes,* May 12, 2003, p. 102.

Halkias, Maria, "Suiza Selling Reddy Ice," *Dallas Morning News,* March 31, 1998, p. 5D.

Robertson, Jordan, "For Reddy Ice, First Day of Trading Is Warm One," *Dallas Morning News,* August 11, 2005.

Simnacher, Joe, "Southland To Sell Off Reddy Ice," *Dallas Morning News,* July 7, 1987, p. 1D.

Weiss, Michael, "Investment Firm To Buy Reddy Ice," *Dallas Morning News,* March 4, 1988, p. 1D.

Rémy Cointreau Group

21, Boulevard Haussmann
Paris, 75009
France
Telephone: (+33) 01 44 13 44 13
Fax: (+33) 01 45 62 82 52
Web site: http://www.remy-cointreau.com

Public Company
Incorporated: 1724 (Rémy Martin), 1849 (Cointreau)
Employees: 1,945
Sales: EUR 905.3 million ($1.08 billion) (2005)
Stock Exchanges: Euronext Paris
Ticker Symbol: RCO
NAIC: 312130 Wineries; 312140 Distilleries

∎ ∎ ∎

Acclaimed the world over for its Rémy Martin cognacs, the group Rémy Cointreau Group is also a leading producer and distributor of liqueurs, spirits, wine, and champagne. The company's VSOP, XO Excellence, top-of-the-line Louis XIII, and other cognacs are enjoyed throughout the world. Rémy Cointreau produces and distributes fine champagnes under the Piper-Heidsieck and Charles Heidsieck labels. Rémy Cointreau's family of liqueurs and spirits include the famed Cointreau, a white liqueur based on orange peels, as well as the passion fruit-based Passoä, and rums under the Mount Gay, Metaxa, and St. Rémy brands. Rémy Cointreau also built up an impressive worldwide distribution network.

ORIGINS

Founded in 1724, Rémy Martin would hold a prominent place in the growth and definition of the cognac category. Established near the town of Cognac, in the Charentes region north of Bordeaux, Rémy Martin developed a reputation for the singularity of its brandy. This singularity would soon be recognized by law. In 1850, a direct correlation was made between the Cognac region's soil and the quality of the area's "eaux de vie." This correlation would lead to the official delimitation of the Cognac region, into six zones surrounding the city of Cognac itself, in 1909. From there, the law fixed the various cognac appellations, beginning in 1936. Rémy Martin, purchasing from some 2,000 vineyards in the region, concentrated on the highest appellation of "fine champagne Cognac," which required that at least 50 percent of the cognac's contents came from the Grande Champagne zones immediately bordering Cognac.

Rémy Martin remained focused on its line of cognacs until well into the 1960s; the company had remained relatively small, however, ranking only 25th among the region's cognac houses. The death of André Renaud, inheritor of the Rémy Martin tradition, in 1965 would lead the company to the next phase in its growth, that of developing a worldwide distribution network. Renaud's will bequeathed the company to his daughters, with 51 percent going to oldest daughter Anne-Marie Hériard Dubreuil, and 49 percent going to her younger sister Geneviève Cointreau. This development would also represent a first step in the later merger between the Rémy Martin and Cointreau families—and set the stage for a long-running family feud: Geneviève Cointreau was married to Max Cointreau, one of the

COMPANY PERSPECTIVES

Rémy Cointreau offers the connoisseur a unique and rare range of premium wine and spirit brands, known and recognised throughout the world. Rémy Cointreau is committed to constant improvement and innovation. The Group continues to add value to its brands, while remaining true to its long term in goals. Rémy Cointreau stands out as a "quality benchmark" in the wines and spirits market and anticipates and interprets the demands of contemporary consumers. The success of the Group's brands is due to a unique mix of prestige and pleasurable discovery, the demand for perfection and contemporary aspirations, and their excellence.

heirs of the popular French liqueur. André Hériard Dubreuil, husband of Anne-Marie and majority shareholder, was named president of the company, taking active control of operations, while Max Cointreau was named director-general.

The Cointreau company had been founded by Edouard Cointreau and his brother Adolphe near the town of Angers in 1849 to produce a white liqueur, flavored with orange peel, that would grow to become one of France's most popular specialty drinks, particularly with its ready status as a mixer in cocktails. Cointreau, too, would remain entirely a family-run operation. In 1948, a new generation of Cointreaus took over the company's leadership—brothers Robert and Max, and their cousin Pierre—dividing the running of the company among them, with Pierre overseeing the Angers factory, Robert in charge of developing international development, and Max in charge of the distribution network.

Max Cointreau's marriage to Rémy Martin heir Geneviève in 1946 would lead the two companies to a combining of forces in the late 1960s. Both companies were seeking to expand their operations, if only to maintain their independence in an industry that was beginning to show signs of consolidation. In 1969, Cointreau and Rémy Martin joined together to form a distribution network to develop both companies' brands worldwide. In the 1970s, both Cointreau and Rémy Martin would begin expanding their product offerings, acquiring brands and production and distribution agreements to offer a more extensive line of alcoholic beverages.

In 1973, Cointreau acquired Picon, an orange-peel

and quinine-based aperitif invented in 1837, as well as the rums of Saint James de Martinique. In the early 1980s, Cointreau would also add the Scotch whiskey Glenturret and the Izarra and Clé des Ducs lines of liqueurs; the company was also preparing new products, including a peach-flavored liqueur Péché Mignon, introduced in 1983, and the passion fruit-flavored liqueur Passoä, launched in 1987. For its part, Rémy Martin focused on expanding its cognac distribution, while acquiring the first of its champagne labels, Krug, in 1977, and diversifying into Bordeaux wines, acquiring the De Luze wine purchasing and exportation firm in 1980. In the mid-1980s, Rémy Martin added two new champagne labels, Charles Heidsieck and Piper Heidsieck, and toward the end of the decade added the Italian liqueur Galliano and the Barbados-based Mount Gay brand of rum. By the late 1980s, Rémy Martin, under André Hériard Debreuil's leadership, had raised itself to the position of the third largest cognac house. By then, Rémy Martin's sales had topped FRF 4 billion.

LEADERSHIP CHALLENGES BEGIN IN 1978

Trouble was brewing in the Cointreau family, however. In 1973, Max Cointreau installed son André as head of the newly acquired Picon label. Yet André Cointreau's leadership was called into question by other members of the Cointreau family, in particular by Robert Cointreau. With 40 percent of the company's stock against the 20 percent each held by Max and Pierre, Robert Cointreau called for an audit of the company's operation in 1978, and restructured the company under a holding company—ending the three-member governance of the company—in which he took majority control. At the same time, Robert instituted an amendment in the company's charter restricting sales of the family-held shares to a third party. While Pierre was named president of the new holding company, Max Cointreau was named president of Cointreau S.A., which continued to represent some 70 percent of the company's sales of FRF 1.6 billion.

Max Cointreau would not remain long as president of Cointreau—in 1982, Robert and Pierre joined together to relieve their relative of his position. Max Cointreau, in turn, threatened to sell off his 20 percent of the company to a third party, leading Robert and Pierre and the other family shareholders to harden the restrictions on stock sales to third parties. Max Cointreau was effectively forced out of all control of the company. The feuding within the family ranks was dampening the position of the otherwise healthy company. As the battle for control raged on, the company's distribution activities fell into disarray. In

KEY DATES

1724: Establishment of the Rémy Martin House of Cognac.

1849: Establishment of Cointreau & Cie by Adolf and Edouard-Jean Cointreau in Angers.

1924: Acquisition of E. Rémy Martin & Cie by André Renaud.

1965: André Hériard Dubreuil succeeds his father-in-law André Renaud.

1970: Beginning of worldwide distribution under the network Rémy Associés.

1980: Rémy Martin acquires the merchant house De Luze in Bordeaux.

1985: Rémy Martin acquires the Charles Heidsieck Champagne house.

1988: Rémy Martin acquires the champagnes Piper-Heidsieck Champagne houses.

1989: Rémy Martin acquires the brands Galliano and Mount Gay Rum.

1990: Merger of Rémy Martin & Cie and Cointreau SA.

1991: Creation of the Rémy Cointreau Group.

1998: Dominique Hériard Dubreuil becomes chairman and CEO.

2000: Acquisition of the vodka and spirits group called Bols NV.

2004: Dominique Hériard Dubreuil steps down as CEO and remains as chairman.

2006: Rémy Cointreau sells Bols to focus on its key brands.

1985, however, the company moved to improve its distribution position, forming a partnership with IDV and Cinzano.

Max Cointreau, meanwhile, was faring no better on the Rémy Martin side. Tensions between the two sisters—and their husbands—flared by the early 1970s. In the late 1960s, Max Cointreau was already suggesting a combination of the Cointreau and Rémy Martin operations—envisaging himself at the lead of the combined groups, a vision that undoubtedly ran counter to those of Robert and Pierre Cointreau on one side, and André Hériard Debreuil on the other. By 1973, Max Cointreau, running for local office, reportedly suspected his brother-in-law André Hériard Debreuil of backing an opposing candidate. Cointreau won the election, but the tension among the family was mounting. The death of Anne-Marie and Geneviève's mother added

to the simmering battle for succession of the family operation, with Max and Geneviève chafing under their minority position. The tension finally erupted into an all-out feud in the early 1980s, when the Hériard Debreuils sought to increase the company's capitalization, a move opposed by the Cointreaus. A flurry of court battles—some 22 or more—ensued, lasting until the end of the decade.

A 1989 MERGER

The parallel feuds with Max Cointreau had, perhaps, another effect: forging closer relations between Cointreau, led by Robert and Pierre, and Rémy Martin, led by André Hériard Debreuil. Faced with the growing consolidation of the beverage distribution industry, and competition against such industry giants such as Guinness, Seagrams, and Grand Metropolitan, Cointreau and Rémy Martin reinforced their joint distribution activities, forming partnerships especially focused on the Far East and the U.S. markets. The agreement would provide a boost to Cointreau, which had had only limited success in these markets. For Rémy Martin, which had based much of its growth on conquering these markets—carrying the company to the number three position in cognac sales—the addition of the Cointreau labels enabled it to present a full line of beverages. In 1988, the two companies further strengthened their links when Robert and Pierre Cointreau purchased 10 percent of Rémy Martin's stock.

That link proved to be a bridge in November 1989 when Rémy Martin and Cointreau announced their agreement—kept secret from Max Cointreau and sons—to merge the two companies. Effected in 1990, the merged operations soon adopted the new name of Rémy Cointreau. Soon after the merger, Max Cointreau and his family sold off their shares—19 percent of Cointreau and 49 percent of Rémy Martin—to competitor Grand Metropolitan.

The merger created a company with more than FRF 6 billion in annual sales, and an extensive worldwide distribution network boasting many of the industry's most respected brands. The first half of the 1990s proved difficult years for the company: the recession of the early years of the decade, and its lingering effects on Europe, helped dampen sales of the company's luxury-oriented products. The slipping Japanese economy—an important market for Rémy Cointreau's cognacs—also hurt sales of the company's core revenue generator. Nevertheless, the company's overall revenues would post steady growth toward the middle of the decade, rising from FRF 6.4 billion in 1994 to FRF 6.8 billion in 1996. Rémy Cointreau's sales dropped FRF 622 million in 1998 as Asia's "tiger" economies continued to suffer. Industry analysts were suggesting that if something was not done soon to stop the company's rising costs and spiraling revenues, it would not survive.

1998 AND BEYOND

Salvation came in the form of Dominique Hériard Dubreuil, the daughter of André Hériard Dubreuil who took the helm as Rémy Cointreau's chairman and CEO in January 1998. Famous for her tough management and unwavering vision, along with her ability to transcend above family politics, Hériard Dubreuil began selling her company's less profitable subsidiaries to reduce debt. She also bolstered advertising for Rémy Cointreau's already successful key brands. In 1999 Hériard Dubreuil sold Krug Champagne for about $176 million, Bordeaux negociant Grands Vins de Gironde for $156 million, and the company's 40 percent stake in the barrel maker Seguin Moreau. To expand distribution she aligned Rémy Cointreau with Highland Distillers and Fortune Brands' Jim Beam to create a distribution joint venture called Maxxium Worldwide BV. Maxxium would grow to include Sweden's V&S Vin & Spirit AB, the makers of Absolut vodka, and distribute spirits globally to 35 countries excluding the U.S. and the Caribbean.

In 2000 Rémy Cointreau ventured into the vodka market when it acquired the Netherlands-based Bols NV, a distillery that made mostly vodkas but also gin and other drinks, including the popular Blue Curaçao liqueur. After the acquisition of Bols, Rémy Cointreau stopped acquiring and began consolidating. This strategy differed from the industry trend but helped narrow Rémy Cointreau's champagne and wine portfolio and tripled the operating profits of its four key brands in just two years. Although Rémy Cointreau was becoming more efficient, an industry analyst by the name of Canadean noted in a November 8, 2005, publication of the beverage industry news source *Just-Drinks* that by reducing its size, Rémy Cointreau had opened itself up to be acquired by a larger group.

In 2004 Hériard Dubreuil restructured the company's upper management. Jean-Marie Laborde became CEO. Hériard Dubreuil continued her tenure as executive chairman but no longer handled the day-to-day operations. She also continued supporting Rémy Cointreau's investor relations and ongoing business strategy. Even though sales had dropped at the start of the year, they had rebounded by July. Analysts were giving Hériard Dubreuil credit for reviving a company of which she also held a considerable stake. In March 2004 the Hériard Dubreuil family owned the company Andromède, which possessed 88.7 percent of Orpar SA, a company that owned 44.29 percent of Rémy Cointreau's capital. Other Rémy Cointreau shareholders included

the General Public (30.69 percent), Arnhold and Bleichroeder (9.99 percent), and France's treasury (1.41 percent.)

Streamlining the company even more, in June 2005 Rémy Cointreau sold the rights to distribute and produce Bols vodka in Russia and Poland. Six months later it put the entire Bols brand up for sale. Hidde van der Pol, the international brand director for Bols, said in *Just-Drinks,* "Rémy Cointreau has stated that its main strategy is to focus on its very premium brands and that's where they're focusing right now." In March 2006 Rémy Cointreau announced that it had completed the sale of not just Bols but also its other Dutch brands, including Bokma, Coebergh, Corenwyn, and Pisang Ambon. It had also sold off its two Italian liqueurs, Galliano and Vaccari. Rémy Cointreau's key brands—Heidsieck Champagne, Piper Heidsieck, Cointreau liqueur, and Rémy Martin cognac—continued to grow. In April 2006 the company reported that its consolidated sales jumped 6.4 percent for the fiscal year in 2006 over the previous fiscal year. By focusing on its top-shelf cognacs, champagnes, and wines that had made Rémy Cointreau famous, the enterprise had become one of the largest drink groups in Europe.

M. L. Cohen
Updated, Kevin Teague

PRINCIPAL DIVISIONS

Spirits; Liqueurs; Champagne; Partner Brands.

PRINCIPAL COMPETITORS

Allied Domecq plc; Diageo plc; Constellation Brands, Inc.; LVMH Moët Hennessy Louis Vuitton S.A.; Pernod Ricard S.A.; Bacardi & Company Ltd.; Beam Global Spirits & Wine, Inc.

FURTHER READING

"ABN Amro Unit Buys Liqueur Brands From Remy Cointreau," *Dow Jones International News,* March 9, 2006.

Barjonet, Claude, "Cointreau Contre Cointreau," *L'Expansion,* December 19, 1986, p. 71.

"First-Half Profits Soar At Rémy Cointreau." *Just-Drinks,* December 8, 2005.

Gallois, Dominique, "Une Querelle 'Quinze Ans d'Age,'" *Le Monde,* November 11, 1989, p. 44.

Iskandar, Samer, "Remy Cointreau Sees Return to Black." *Financial Times,* December 16, 1998, p. 26.

"Keep It In the Family—Part Four." *Just-Drinks,* November 8, 2005.

"Rémy Cointreau Nine-Month Sales Up—Just." *Just-Drinks,* January 18, 2006.

"Remy Sales Up But Core Brands Flat." *Just-Drinks,* October 20, 2005.

Rogers Corporation

1 Technology Drive
Rogers, Connecticut 06263-0188
U.S.A.
Telephone: (860) 774-9605
Fax: (860) 779-5509
Web site: http://www.rogerscorporation.com

Public Company
Founded: 1832 as Rogers Paper Manufacturing Company
Employees: 1,975
Sales: $356.1 million (2005)
Stock Exchanges: New York
Ticker Symbol: ROG
NAIC: 524211 Plastics Material and Design Manufacturing

■ ■ ■

Rogers Corporation is a global specialty materials company that maintains its headquarters in the small town of Rogers, Connecticut, which assumed the name in the 1950s after the company agreed to pay the electric bill for the street lights.

Rogers focuses on the portable communications, communication infrastructure, consumer products, computer and office equipment, ground transportation, and aerospace and defense markets, manufacturing and selling high-performance specialty materials in four business segments. The Printed Circuit Materials segment produces flexible materials such as circuit ribbons used to link components in laptops and cell phones, and high-frequency circuit laminates used in antennas for cellular base stations, low noise block down-converters (LNBs) for direct broadcast satellite television receivers, radar systems, and high-performance wireless components. The High Performance Foams segment produces urethane, silicone, and nonwoven materials used in a wide variety of applications in the communications, computer, transportation, printing, and consumer markets. The materials are used to make gaskets in appliances, and a variety of gaskets and seals in automobiles, aircraft, and trains; serve as cushions and seals in cell phones and other handheld devices; act as padding for medical and prosthetic skin contact devices and protective garments; and provide shock absorption and cushioning in footwear and sporting equipment. The Custom Electrical Components segment is composed of the electroluminescent (EL) lamps and inverters used as backlighting for displays, dials, and keypads. Applications include portable devices and automobiles. Also in this segment, busbars are used in locomotive trains to distribute the power generated by the diesel engine to the electric motors that move the train. Rogers's Other Polymer Products segment makes products such as floats used in automobile fuel tanks; rollers used in printers, copiers, and mail processing systems; foam padding used in printing applications; and laminates for shielding of cables and for various automotive and industrial applications.

In the United States Rogers maintains manufacturing plants in Connecticut, Arizona, and Illinois. Foreign manufacturing operations are located in Belgium, China, and Korea. Sales offices are located in Japan, Hong Kong, China, Taiwan, Korea, and Singapore. Rogers has joint

COMPANY PERSPECTIVES

Rogers Corporation is a manufacturer of specialty materials for applications in portable communications, communication infrastructure, consumer products, computer and office equipment, ground transportation, and aerospace and defense.

ventures in Japan and China with Inoac Corporation, in Taiwan with Chang Chun Plastics, and in the United States with Mitsui Chemicals. Rogers Corporation is a public company listed on the New York Stock Exchange.

19TH-CENTURY ORIGINS

The founding of Rogers Corporation dates back to 1832 when a Dutch immigrant named Peter Rogers opened a paper mill in Manchester, Connecticut. Named Rogers Paper Manufacturing Company, this company produced paperboard used in the thriving textile industry of New England. When Peter died in 1841, his son, Henry Rogers, took over the business. It was Henry who established a culture of innovation, and was instrumental in the development of a number of advances in papermaking, including the bleaching of colored paper and the recycling of waste paper, the latter an extremely important contribution to the industry. In 1890 Henry Rogers retired and his son, Knight, and daughter, Gertrude, ran the business. Under their stewardship, Rogers Paper became a supplier of transformer insulation board for the emerging electrical power transformer industry at the dawn of the 20th century. This business spurred growth in sales approaching $1 million.

In 1901 the company incorporated in Connecticut, with all stock owned by the Rogers family. In 1927 Rogers Paper was reincorporated in Massachusetts and taken public, the first step in removing direct involvement of the Rogers family after almost a century of control. In 1920, seven years after Knight Rogers died, his sister installed the first nonfamily member to run the business: Charles Ray, a seasoned executive who came from the Troy, New York–based Manning Paper Company. In 1927 Ray bought all of Gertrude's company stock. A year later he took steps to diversify the company, bringing in a technical director, Saul M. Silverstein, who held a chemical engineering degree from the Massachusetts Institute of Technology. Silverstein, in turn, recruited M.I.T. classmate Raymond A. St. Laurent to take over sales and develop new markets for the company's paperboard products.

The diversification effort was well timed. It began to bear fruit as the United States suffered the stock crash of 1929, which ushered in the decade-long Great Depression. New products included tympana printing board, rail joints, artificial leather, and motor insulation materials. Not only did Rogers survive the economic downturn of the 1930s, it was able to invest in the research and development of new phenolic resin plastics. It was the addition of these products that brought the company to Goodyear, Connecticut, the village that would one day bear the Rogers name. Originally known as Williamsville, it became Goodyear around the start of the 20th century because Goodyear was its largest employer. In 1936 the company sold its plant for $250,000 to Rogers, which continued to maintain three small manufacturing units in Manchester. The village retained the Goodyear name until 1953 when Rogers's president, Saul Silverstein, was so miffed at seeing Goodyear—a competitor in molded rubber products—on his company's letterhead that he struck a deal with the village to pay for the 22 streetlights in the center of town if the village name was changed to Rogers. On the basis of a handshake, the change was agreed to and went into effect in 1954.

DEPRESSION-ERA DEVELOPMENTS

In the final years of the 1930s, Rogers transferred production to the former Goodyear plant and consolidated the Manchester operations. Diversification continued in the 1940s, as Rogers now became involved in footwear. Rogers Paper Manufacturing Company no longer seemed an appropriate name, and in 1945 the company became the Rogers Corporation. The company's focus continued to move further away from paper products in the postwar years. In 1949 Rogers added new fiber-reinforced polymer materials for use in electrical insulation and gaskets. Four years later glass and ceramic fiber were incorporated to make chemical-resistant gaskets. Company researchers would continue to combine polymers and chemicals with natural and synthetic, organic and inorganic fibers to create a host of new products. During this period Rogers also added product lines by acquiring Cellular Rubbers Products, Inc., a Willimantic, Connecticut–based elastomer fabrication company, maker of molder circuits in switches and timers for cars, appliances, and industrial uses.

The 1950s also saw Rogers make its first international move, licensing its phenolic molding materials to Vynckier N.V. in Ghent, Belgium, in 1958. The decade was a watershed period for Rogers in another way as well. The company began to implement long-

KEY DATES

1832: The company is founded by Peter Rogers as Rogers Paper Manufacturing Company.
1841: Peter Rogers dies.
1901: The company is incorporated, with all stock owned by the Rogers family.
1927: The company is taken public; the Rogers family ends its connection to the company.
1936: The Goodyear plant in Goodyear, Connecticut is acquired.
1945: The company name is changed to Rogers Corporation.
1954: Goodyear, Connecticut, changes its name to Rogers.
1960: Rogers is listed on the American Stock Exchange.
1968: Rogers acquires a plant in Woodstock, Connecticut to house production of PORON® urethanes.
1969: The first European plant opens.
1970: Rogers opens the Lurie Research and Development Center at its headquarters in Rogers, Connecticut.
1984: Rogers Inoac Corporation is formed as a 50/50 joint venture with Inoac Corporation.
1992: Strategic restructuring is initiated.
1996: Rogers acquires Bisco Products from the Dow Corning Corporation.
2000: Rogers stock begins trading on the New York Stock Exchange.
2002: Rogers opens a manufacturing facility in China with expansions in operations in the ensuing years.
2003: The High Performance Foams Division of Rogers opens a new facility in Carol Stream, Illinois.
2004: A total of 65 percent of Rogers's sales are outside the United States.
2005: More than 6 percent of Rogers's sales are outside the United States.

range planning, identifying new markets—in particular the fast-growing electronics industry. For example, in 1959 Rogers became involved in the mainframe computer market by developing a busbar, a laminated circuit that distributed power in IBM's new transistorized computer. Within a few years Rogers was supplying busbars to almost all mainframe computer manufactures. As part of its planning effort, Rogers established a goal of doubling revenues and profits every five years. Thus sales that totaled $5 million in 1958 doubled to $10 million by 1963. Also of importance, the company had in 1960 gained a listing on the American Stock Exchange, providing a higher profile with investors.

Although Rogers continued to produce transformer insulation board, the company's growth was now linked to new products used in electronics and consumer goods. In the early 1960s Rogers introduced materials used to make breathable footwear, chemical-resistant floats, and high-temperature, synthetic fiber-based materials. In 1966 Rogers acquired technology from Westinghouse Electric Corporation that would not have an immediate commercial impact but would one day be used in the development of flexible circuits that would be needed in increasing numbers in computers, cell phones, and other electronic devices. With so much of the electronics industry operating in the western United States, Rogers opened a 40,000-square-foot plant in Chandler, Arizona, in 1967 to house the new Circuit Systems Division. A year later Rogers bought Woodstock, Connecticut–based Litho Chemical & Supply Co., Inc. to establish a new PORON Division to produce the high-density, flexible foam used in footwear as well for medical and other applications. Rogers closed the 1960s by forming its first international company, Mektron N.V., established in May 1969 in Ghent, Belgium, to produce busbars and interconnection products for the European market. Rogers also cast its attention elsewhere in the world, licensing Mektron interconnection products to Nippon Oil Seal Industry Co., Ltd. and establishing Rogers Mexicana in Agua Prieta, Mexico.

Rogers's annual sales by the start of the 1970s approached $30 million, about 28 percent of which came from the electronics markets, in particular data processing. Electronics would become even more important over the next dozen years, so that by 1982 it accounted for 72 percent of Rogers's revenues. Growth was so steady that Rogers continually expanded its production capacity. By 1973 the company was operating 14 plants in seven states and three countries. Another plant was bought in Lithonia, Georgia, in 1976, and in 1979 the Manchester facility was expanded as was the Mexico operation. Another plant was acquired in Mesa, Arizona, in 1980, and a new production facility was added in France. In 1982 the Chandler operation was supplemented by a second plant.

A key to Rogers's growth was its ongoing commitment to research and development. In the early 1970s the company opened the Lurie Research and Development Center in Rogers, Connecticut, the facility named after a former technical director. Throughout the 1970s and early 1980s, Rogers developed a host of new products, including materials for microwave stripline circuitry, micromotion membrane keyboards, and asbestos-free gasketing materials. The company also expanded through acquisition and joint ventures. In 1980 Rogers acquired Soladyne, Inc., a San Diego maker of microwave stripline circuits. Rogers formed a joint venture with Inoac Corporation in Nagoya, Japan, in 1984 to produce high-performance elastomers for the Asian market. Then, in 1988, Rogers and 3M created Durel Corporation, a joint venture that manufactured electroluminescent backlighting systems.

Rogers experienced a drop in earnings in the late 1980s, prompting the company to search for ways to cut costs. One of the areas it looked at was the $500,000 electric bill for the year. One item stood out: $2,600 to pay for the streetlights in Rogers, Connecticut. No one in management knew of the 1950s' agreement with the village and it was decided to let the taxpayers foot the bill. Neither the village nor the local fire district that included Rogers stepped in to pick up the tab, and so in October 1989, the lights went out. Soon, one arson and at least two burglaries took place, prompting residents to meet in a local church to vent their anger at the company and begin taking steps to change the name of the village back to Williamsville. The effort was spearheaded by Charles A. Spaulding, who had lived in the town for 44 years and worked for the company for 34, and one of the few people still alive who remembered Saul Silverstein's handshake agreement. The cost of changing letterhead and signage, as well as bad community relations, were not worth the $2,600 in savings, and Rogers Corporation quickly agreed to pay for the streetlights for at least another 14 years. Peace was restored, and maps of Connecticut did not have to be redone.

END-OF-CENTURY CHANGES

In 1992 a new chief executive officer, Harry Birkenruth, initiated a strategic restructuring of Rogers to focus attention on the company's specialty polymer composite materials businesses, which in the past 30 years had emerged as the primary engines of growth. Over the next few years Rogers shed a number of divisions and products. In March 1992 the Circuit Components Division plant in Tempe, Arizona, was sold. A year later Rogers Flexible Interconnections Division and a half-interest in a related joint venture, Smartflex Systems, were sold to Ampersand Ventures. The Power Distribution Division was sold to Method Electronics in 1994. The Soladyne Division was sold at the end of 1995. Rogers also built on its core product lines by acquiring Bisco Products from the Dow Corning Corporation in a

deal that closed at the beginning of 1997. The Elk Grove Village, Illinois–based business sold high-performance cellular silicone foam products, which Rogers continued to market under the BISCO brand name. In addition, Rogers gained a presence in the European commercial aerospace market. In that same year, Rogers acquired another Ghent, Belgium company, UCB Induflex N.V., maker of multilayer laminates for shielding of electromagnetic and radio frequency interference. Also in 1997, Birkenruth retired, turning over the reins to Walter E. Boomer, who took over at the end of March. He inherited a company that for the year generated sales of $216.6 million and net income of $16.5 million.

In the final years of the 1990s, Rogers opened a sales office in Taiwan; began construction on a new microwave materials manufacturing facility on an unused piece of property the company owned in Chandler, Arizona; acquired the engineering molding compounds business of Cytec Industries, Inc.; and formed a joint venture with Mitsui Chemicals, Inc. to produce specialty flexible laminates for Hutchinson Technology, Inc., the world's largest maker of hard disk drive suspension assemblies. Rogers closed the 1990s posting sales of $247.8 million and profits of $18.6 million.

Rogers had to contend with a rocky period for the technology sector starting in 2000 and lasting well into 2002 after a downturn in the national economy. After sales reached a record $316.8 million and net income totaled a record $26.7 million in 2000, business began to fall off significantly. Sales dipped to $216 million and net income to $18.6 million in 2001. The company enjoyed marginal improvement in 2002 before experiencing a significant rebound in 2003. Along the way, Rogers divested the Manchester Moldable Composites Division; bought out 3M to take a 100 percent interest in Durel Corporation and make it a division of Rogers; and began to relocate the Elastomer Components Divisions to China to be closer to customers. Of more importance, at the close of 2001 Rogers acquired some product lines from Cellect L.L.C., manufacturer of plastomeric and elastomeric high-performance polyolefin foams. As a result, Rogers became the only company to produce all three specialty foams—polyolefin, polyurethane, and silicone—thereby enhancing the company's long-term growth potential.

In the early 2000s Rogers enjoyed especially strong sales of LNBs to the robust satellite TV industry and flexible circuit materials used in cell phones, which as they moved to color displays required eight times as much flexible materials as earlier generation cell phones. In fact, the more tech product sold, the better Rogers performed. Moreover, it had few competitors in the niche markets it pursued and were costly for rivals to enter. Sales soared to $365 million in 2004 before taking a step back to $356.1 million in 2005 when Rogers also recorded net income of $16.4 million. Rogers's continued growth, as it pushed to become a $1 billion company, was likely to be driven by the demand for satellite dishes, cellphones and other handsets, broadband wireless and networking, as well as new high-tech automobile sensors such as tire-pressure sensors and collision-avoidance radar systems.

Ed Dinger

PRINCIPAL SUBSIDIARIES

Rogers Japan Inc.; Rogers China, Inc.; Rogers Specialties Materials Corporation; Rogers Circuit Materials, Inc.; Rogers N.V.

PRINCIPAL COMPETITORS

Cookson Group plc; Kingboard Chemical Holdings Ltd.; Rohn and Haas Electronic Materials.

FURTHER READING

Benesh, Peter, "If Your Clients Can't Come To You, Well ...," *Investor's Business Daily,* June 18, 2004, p. A05.

Hamilton, Robert, "By Letting There Be Light, a Company Remains a Namesake," *New York Times,* January 14, 1990, p. A2.

Lubanko, Matthew, "Killingly, Conn.–Based Manufacturer Sees Bright Future in Small Parts," *Hartford Courant,* January 25, 2004.

Miller, William H., "Textbook Turnaround," *Industry Week,* April 20, 1992, p. 11.

Ronco Corporation

21344 Superior Street
Chatsworth, California 91311
U.S.A.
Telephone: (818) 775-4602
Toll Free: (800) 486-1806
Fax: (818) 775-4664
Web site: http://www.ronco.com

Public Company
Incorporated: 1964 as Ronco Teleproducts, Inc.
Employees: 17,800
Sales: $63 million (2005 est.)
Stock Exchanges: Over the Counter
Ticker Symbol: RNCP.OB
NAIC: 454110 Electronic Shopping and Mail-Order Houses, 454113 Mail-Order Houses

■ ■ ■

Best-known for its fast-paced, late-night commercials and pioneering infomercials, Ronco Corporation has manufactured, sold, and distributed an astonishing array of well-known gadgets and goodies since its inception in the early 1960s. From the Veg-O-Matic and the Pocket Fisherman of the early days to GLH Formula #9 and the Electric Food Dehydrator of the 1990s, Ronco has chalked-up a series of well-promoted hits. In the process, company founder Ron Popeil has garnered quite a bit of media attention. In 1993 friend and fellow Mirage Hotel board member Steve Wynn told *People* magazine, "Ron has a knack for convincing you that you need something." A July 1981 article in *People* magazine

dubbed him "the Horatio Alger of the TV age." The *CBS Evening News* called Popeil "a master, a pioneer, the king of the infomercial, a gadget savant," while television newsmagazine *20/20* dubbed him a "television visionary, the man who turned the hard sell into a blunt instrument, [and] the granddaddy of TV hucksters."

Many successes and a popular leader notwithstanding, Ronco's history has included some challenges as well. After its foundation near Chicago in 1964, the firm went public in 1969. Sales and profits increased erratically throughout the 1970s, but the early 1980s brought intense competition and eventual bankruptcy. Ron Popeil revived his firm in the late 1980s with such products as GLH "Great Looking Hair" Formula #9 (a "spray-on toupee"), the Popeil Automatic Pasta Maker, and the Ronco Electric Dehydrator. Headquartered in southern California, the reincarnated Ronco remained privately and closely held into the mid-1990s until an acquisition brought the company public again in 2005. Although company representatives declined to release annual sales estimates, Popeil's 1995 autobiography titled *Salesman of the Century* boasted that his firm had generated more than $1 billion in retail sales over the course of its more than 30 years in business.

1935–1964: THE BOUNDLESS HUCKSTER

The Ronco saga is as much the story of Ron Popeil as it is a company history. The hyperbolic pitchman was born to Sam and Julia Popeil in 1935 in the Bronx. Sam Popeil was trained by his uncles to demonstrate and sell

Their long, hard days of live demonstrations came to an end in 1964, when Popeil and Korey launched a joint partnership called Ronco Inc. in Elk Grove Village, Illinois. Their first product—and the demonstrative television commercial that promoted it—set the standard for the dozens of Ronco offerings that would follow. The Ronco Spray Gun was manufactured on contract by another company; Ronco acted essentially as a promoter and distributor. The product, a hose nozzle, was a fairly basic, inexpensive household item with a twist: the high-pressure sprayer featured water-soluble tablets of soap, wax, insecticide, or herbicide, and so the nozzle could be used to wash and wax the car, fertilize the lawn, kill weeds or insects, and wash windows. The tablets were a key consideration: they would continue to generate high-profit-margin sales long after the initial purchase of the spray nozzle.

Popeil wrote a script, traveled to a Florida television station to tape the advertisement, and starred in the spot using the motor-mouthed style that had brought him success on the fair circuit. The production cost a total of $550. Korey spent another $400 to place the ad in cheap, late-night timeslots on television stations in Illinois and Wisconsin. They sold the goods on a "guaranteed-sale" basis through local retailers. Popeil defined guaranteed-sale as the direct sale of product to the retailer with the provision that any unsold merchandise would be repurchased by Ronco. Korey eventually placed the Ronco Spray Gun in 100 cities. The campaign featured "trade support marketing"—a mention of the retail outlets that carried the product—a technique pioneered by Popeil Brothers. The spray gun was an undeniable success. Within four years, Ronco had sold almost one million units.

Several elements of Ronco's strategy emerged over the course of the next two decades, some of which were reflected in that initial offering. First, the vast majority of Ronco's products were inexpensive. Until the late 1970s, the company did not float a single item over $20 and most were priced under $10. Also, Ronco avoided manufacturing in the early days, thereby sidestepping the hefty capital outlays and risks involved in mass production. Contrary to popular belief, only a few of the company's products were invented by Ron Popeil. While he often had a hand in "refining" the gadgets, most of the products were purchased from the manufacturer or developer and sold on an exclusive contract. Therefore, Ronco vacillated between retail and mail order distribution.

Finally, one of the most important factors in the long-term Ronco scheme was the continuous introduc-

Other people in our business take the spaghetti approach. They throw a lot of stuff against the wall and hope something sticks. The failure rate is dependent solely on what you're throwing up against the wall. I don't operate that way. If I believe in a product idea, I'll put my time, money, and marketing skills behind it. It might take two-and-a-half years of my life to create and sell a product. But, I enjoy every minute of it!—Founder, Ron Popeil

kitchen gadgets, and he and his sibling Raymond launched Popeil Brothers, Inc. in Chicago in 1947. A 1989 article about the Popeil family businesses noted that their postwar television commercials were among the first to bring live demonstration to the new media, foreshadowing the infomercials and home shopping channels that would emerge decades later. Although Ron Popeil would later downplay his father's influence, a writer for the Journal of Popular Film and Television asserted that Ron "rode to success on the coattails of Popeil Brothers." Ron Popeil's career brought two generations of selling to its ultimate fruition.

He got an early education in the housewares market working weekends in his father's Chicago factory making kitchen products. At 16, Ron began selling Popeil Brothers' "Spiral Slicers" and "Slice-A-Way" gadgets in street markets. Within a year, the teenager had moved out on his own, hawking Popeil Brothers' products on a flat commission basis at the Woolworth's store in downtown Chicago.

There's little doubt that Popeil was a natural salesman. He claims to have made $1,000 each week in the early 1950s—four times an average monthly salary. He earned enough to pay for a year of classes at the University of Illinois, where he met future business partner Mel Korey. But it was hard for Popeil to justify paying for college classes when he was making money hand over fist without an advanced education. So while Korey earned his undergraduate degree, Popeil continued to sell at Woolworth's during the winter and hit the Midwest "fair circuit" in the summer. The fair circuit included county and state fairs, as well as auto, home, and garden shows. Korey joined Popeil upon graduation, selling knives, kitchen gadgets, spray shoe polish, and hobbycraft kits throughout the Midwest.

KEY DATES

1935: Ron Popeil is born in the Bronx.

1945: Ron's father and uncle launch Popeil Brothers, Inc., in Chicago.

1964: Mel Korey and Ron Popeil launch a joint partnership called Ronco Inc.

1969: Ronco makes its first public offering.

1974: Popeil releases his first invention, the "Smokeless Ashtray."

1983: Ronco overstocks the CleanAire Machine for the holiday season.

1984: Ronco files for Chapter 7 bankruptcy and is temporarily out of business; Popeil forms a new partnership with former Ronco salesman Malcolm Sherman.

1987: Trying to rebuild Ronco, Popeil tours the fair circuit and begins selling his food dehydrator.

1989: Popeil begins selling via infomercials.

1991: Ronco releases its first half-hour infomercial starring Popeil.

1993: Launch of the Popeil Automatic Pasta Maker.

1997: Release of the New and Improved Popeil Automatic Pasta and Sausage Maker.

1998: Release of the Ron Popeil Showtime Rotisserie and Barbecue.

2005: Popeil sells Ronco for $55 million.

tion of new products to replace those that had lost their novelty. Toward that end, the company considered a reported 400-plus potential products every year. In order to whittle that daunting list down to the dozen or so annual offerings, the company evaluated each one's potential for demonstration on television, whether it could be positioned as a problem-solving device, its novelty, mass appeal, and profit margin.

However, as Popeil reiterated throughout his book, television marketing was the engine that drove demand. In a rare moment of modesty in his 1995 autobiography, Popeil admitted that "In those [early] days you could advertise empty boxes on TV and sell them. It was hard not to be successful." The salesman's on-screen technique mixed old-fashioned demonstration with breathless hyperbole to convince millions of viewers that his gadgets solved everyday "problems" they did not even know they suffered until that very moment. Such Popeilesque phrases as "as seen on TV," "the perfect Christmas gift," "miracle (add product name here)," and "and that's not all!" would trigger millions of people to reach for wallets

and pocketbooks in the coming decades.

Ronco refined its marketing and distribution techniques with its second televised product, the "Chop-O-Matic." Produced by Popeil Brothers, this "food chopper with rotating blades" had been peddled by Ron Popeil on the fair circuit since the late 1950s. Not only was the commercial for this device longer, at five minutes, but Ronco also made this its first mail-order product. Delighted with the Chop-O-Matic's success, Sam Popeil invented and manufactured the Dial-O-Matic and what would become Ronco's first blockbuster, the Veg-O-Matic. Ron Popeil's television ad fueled the sale of over nine million units for $50 million worth of these rather primitive food processors.

While the Veg-O-Matic was Ronco's best-known product of the era, it was pantyhose that generated over half of the company's annual sales in the late 1960s. Ronco's ads for London Aire Hosiery, the pantyhose "guaranteed in writing not to run," featured Ron Popeil abusing the double-locked-stitch nylons with such outrageous tools as a scissors, a nail file, a scouring pad, and a lit cigarette, all to show that the fabric would not run.

Ronco's sales increased from about $89,000 in 1964 to over $14 million in 1969. Net income multiplied from $4,400 to over $1.25 million during the same period. The company went public as Ronco Teleproducts, Inc. in 1969, selling a $5 million, 22 percent stake.

1970–84: PRODUCT EXPANSION

The 1970s were Ronco Teleproduct's heyday. Over the course of the decade, the company broadened its product line from its base in housewares to personal care products, record albums, and hobbycrafts, while expanding its geographic reach internationally to include Canada, Great Britain, and Australia. In the early 1970s, Ronco ranked among America's top 25 television advertisers. The new offerings formed a panoply of gadgets. Housewares included the Miracle Broom, the Roller Measure, the Salad Spinner, the Glass Froster, the Cookie Machine, and the Miracle Brush. In 1974, Ron Popeil brought out his first invention, the "Smokeless Ashtray." This device filtered cigarette smoke from the air at its source and was offered in both home and car models. Ronco's Egg Scrambler featured a battery-powered needle that whisked yolk and white together while still in the shell.

Craft and hobby products included the Mr. Microphone, the Ronco Bottle and Jar Cutter, the Ronco Rhinestone and Stud Setter, a Candle-Making Kit, a Pottery Wheel, and a Flower Loom. The Pocket Fisherman, developed by Sam Popeil, featured a telescoping rod which was so compact that it could fit into a car's glove compartment. The gadget was one of the company's best-selling (at 35 million units) and best-remembered products. Ronco also started offering record album compilations of popular music during this period, promoting four to six discs each year.

Ronco's line of personal care products included the Trim-Comb hair groomer, the Tidie Drier hair/clothes dryer, the Steam Away clothing steamer, and the Mr. Dentist. The Buttoneer had originally been something of a flop for manufacturer Dennison Manufacturing, but Popeil reduced the price by more than 25 percent and produced one of his typical problem-solving television spots. Buttoneer sales multiplied ten times within just one year.

This rapid series of product launches helped fuel steady sales growth throughout the 1970s, from $16 million in 1970 to $22.2 million in 1975 and $36.9 million by 1980. Ronco's profitability vacillated erratically, however, throughout this period, from a net loss of $796,000 in 1973 to a net income of $1.4 million in 1978.

In an effort to raise its profit margins, Ronco Teleproducts introduced its best-quality, highest-priced product, the CleanAire Machine, in the late 1970s. Essentially a larger version of the "Smokeless Ashtray," the CleanAire Machine featured a charcoal filter that could clean a whole room's worth of air. But the CleanAire machine would also help contribute to Ronco's early 1980s demise. Ronco overbought the device for the 1983 Christmas season and was not up to competition from the likes of Norelco, Remington, and other leading housewares manufacturers, who initiated a price war in the category. Ronco also got burned on its guaranteed sales policy; retailers returned well over two-thirds of the CleanAire machines that year. The reduced cash flow lowered Ronco's all-important advertising budget at a time when TV advertising costs were rising quickly. Without his hallmark television ads to keep products in front of the consumer, revenues dropped by one-third from 1982 to 1983. To make matters worse, Ronco's bank called in the company's $15 million revolving line of credit.

1984–2003: RECOVERING FROM BANKRUPTCY

The company tried to reorganize under Chapter 11 of the federal bankruptcy code but was soon forced into Chapter 7 in 1984 and out of business. Popeil, who did not declare personal bankruptcy, was able to purchase much of Ronco's inventory at auction. He entered into a new partnership with former Ronco salesman Malcolm Sherman shortly thereafter. (Mel Korey had resigned from Ronco's executive team early in 1983.) From 1984 to 1987, Popeil and Sherman concentrated on selling the CleanAire Machine and the Ronco Electric Food Dehydrator. But as the end of the 1980s loomed, Popeil and Sherman parted ways. Sherman got the rights to the CleanAir Machine, while Popeil assumed sole control of the food dehydrator and the partnership.

Popeil went into a period of what he called "semi-retirement" following the demise of his namesake company. He returned to his old hunting grounds on the fair circuit from 1987 to 1990 and emerged from his self-imposed exile from television in 1989. That was when a friend suggested that Popeil team up with mail-order powerhouse Fingerhut, which was testing a home shopping television channel. Although Fingerhut closed down its home shopping operation not long thereafter, Popeil was reinfected with the television bug. In 1991, he produced his first half-hour infomercial.

Titled Incredible Inventions, the long-form ad essentially reproduced Popeil's fair demonstration and offered direct sales via a toll-free phone bank. Production and airing of the ad cost $33,000—a far cry from the $550 that Popeil had spent on his first one-minute spot. But the dehydrator sold for around $60, whereas the Chop-O-Matic had sold for $3.98. The infomercial generated a total of $80 million in food dehydrator sales by 1993.

Popeil followed up the dehydrator success with GLH Formula #9 and the Popeil Automatic Pasta Maker. He bought the first product, a spray-on "toupee" called Great Looking Hair, from its Australian inventors. The fibrous aerosol came in nine colors and cost $39.92 per can. Ronco sold 900,000 cans of the formula within just one year.

In 1993, he launched the Popeil Automatic Pasta Maker, a device that one observer called "the most substantial product Popeil's bizarrely successful company...has ever produced." While promotions via infomercials and the QVC (Quality Value Convenience) home shopping network generated unit sales of over 500,000, the introduction was not without its stumbling blocks. In 1994, Creative Technologies Corporation sued Popeil and the retailers affiliated with his pasta maker for patent infringement, false advertising, and unfair competition. State and federal courts, however, found Popeil and his company not guilty on all counts. While both parties continued to file suits and countersuits through 1995, Popeil was able to continue promotion of his device. In 1994, he forged a contract giving Salton-Maxim the right to distribute the pasta machine in retail outlets. Popeil also hoped to derive additional sales with the introduction of branded pasta mixes.

The 60-year-old Popeil showed no signs of slowing down in 1995. Fresh from the release of his autobiography, he toured the United States promoting the book, himself, and his products old and new. *Salesman of the Century* hinted that future Ronco offerings could include a revival of the Pocket Fisherman and a newfangled spatula called the Popeil Gripper. And no matter what the company introduces, it's liable to be pitched as "amazing."

In 1997 Popeil was back on QVC promoting his latest invention, the New and Improved Popeil Automatic Pasta and Sausage Maker. The updated product was an improvement from the original because it not only made pastas, but also sausages. QVC infomercials featured Popeil adding meats, vegetables, and spices to the Pasta and Sausage Maker while sausage emerged from an opening on the front of the machine. Also in 1997, Popeil publicly expressed interest in selling Ronco. He wanted to continue inventing products and acting as the business's spokesperson but had grown tired of running its day-to-day operations. The most noteworthy company to show interest, LA Group Inc., started negotiations for a possible acquisition, but a sale was never finalized, and Ronco remained in Popeil's control. The LA Group, which operated the Seen on TV website that sold items pitched by infomercials, eventually launched www.Ronco.com. Under a three-year agreement the LA Group received a commission for every Ronco product sold on the website.

In 1998 Popeil released one of his most successful inventions, the Ron Popeil Showtime Rotisserie and Barbecue. Infomercials featured Popeil demonstrating the device by cooking a chicken in three hours. Owners of the product were encouraged to marinate the chicken, place it inside the Rotisserie and Barbecue, and then set the device's timer for three hours. During the advertisement Popeil repeated the phrase "set it and forget it," which became Popeil's latest infomercial catchphrase. According to *HFN—Home Furnishings News* magazine, Ronco generated an estimated $250 million in annual sales for 1999. Popeil explained that the high sales were proportionate to Ronco's media spending. The company spent an estimated $50 million on media in 1999 to advertise the Rotisserie and Barbecue.

2003 AND BEYOND: NEW AND IMPROVED

Richard Allen, a former marketing, brand management, and manufacturing executive, was asked by private investors to acquire a successful importing company. In 2003 Allen approached Popeil, who later agreed to sell Ronco for $55 million. In 2005 Allen raised the needed money with the help of Sanders Morris Harris Group Inc., a Texas-based investment bank. The acquisition process involved Popeil's marketing company Ronco Marketing Corp. acquiring the other companies within Ronco's fold. The new conglomerate then changed its name to Ronco Corporation and finally merged with a holding company called Fi-Tek VII, Inc., which later changed its name to Ronco Corporation. When the acquisition was completed, Ronco was traded over the counter under the symbol RNCP.

Richard Allen became the company's CEO. Popeil remained a product consultant with a $500,000 annual salary. He received an additional $10,000 for every guest appearance he made on television. Popeil was also awarded $50,000 for every new infomercial produced and was given the same amount for every appearance on the television network Home & Garden Television (HGTV), according to the *Los Angeles Business Journal.* "I ran the business like an entrepreneur, not like a businessman," Popeil said in the *Los Angeles Business Journal.* "I had about 170 employees, but I never really got involved. I hate the day-to-day stuff."

The new owners announced plans to expand Ronco beyond its infomercial roots. Because millions had been spent advertising Ronco products for direct sales, Allen believed Ronco products would successfully cross over into retailers such as Wal-Mart.

April Dougal Gasbarre
Updated, Kevin Teague

PRINCIPAL SUBSIDIARIES

Ronco Marketing Corporation (RMC).

PRINCIPAL COMPETITORS

Applica Inc.; The Holmes Group, Inc.; NACCO Industries, Inc.; QVC, Inc.; Thane International, Inc.; Salton, Inc.; ValueVision Media, Inc.

FURTHER READING

Abdeddaim, Michelle N., "CTC, Popeil Swap Tacks for Marketing Pasta Makers," *HFN—The Weekly Newspaper for the Home Furnishing Network,* April 10, 1995, p. 107.

Bailey, Doug, "Still Selling After All These Years," *Boston Globe,* November 7, 1993, p. 77.

Colker, David, "He Sliced and He Diced, and Now He's Really Selling," *Los Angeles Times,* September 1, 2005, p. 3.

Darlin, Damon, "Words to Live By in Infomercial World," *New York Times,* April 8, 2006, p. 1.

Della Cava, Marco R., "From Veg-O-Matics to Spray-On Hair, Infomercials Marking 20 Years," *Tulsa World,* October 26, 2004, p. D4.

Gliatto, Tom, "He Yells! He Sells! Amazing! Pitchman Ron Popeil Strikes Gold with His Spray-on Toupee," *People,* May 3, 1993, p. 154.

"It Slices! It Dices! It Goes Belly Up!" *Newsweek,* February 13, 1984, p. 74.

Koris, Sally, "In the Wee Small Hours, Pitchman Ron Popeil is Never at a Loss for a Miracle," *People,* July 13, 1981.

Myerhoff, Matt, "Infomercial King Sells Company, Ronco Goes Public for Expansion," *Los Angeles Business Journal,* August 29, 2005.

Popeil, Ron, *The Salesman of the Century: Inventing, Marketing, and Selling on TV: How I Did It and How You Can Too!,* New York: Delacorte Press, 1995.

"Popeil Wins an Appeal, and Countersues CTC," *HFN,* June 12, 1995, p. 82.

Rivenburg, Roy, "Still Slicing & Dicing," *Los Angeles Times,* December 15, 1995, p. 1E.

Serwer, Andrew E., "Ron Popeil: The King of Thingamabobs," *Fortune,* June 12, 1995, p. 124.

Stern, Andrew, "Veg-O-Matic Part of Culinary History," *Toronto Star,* July 10, 2004, p. M06.

Thomas, Clarence W., "It Chops, It Slices, It Dices: Television Marketing and the Rise and Fall of the Popeil Family Businesses," *Journal of Popular Film and Television,* Summer 1989, pp. 67–73.

Wilcox, Gregory J., "Simi Reels In Ronco Infomercial Giant to Move In April," *Los Angeles Daily News,* January 12, 2006, p. B1.

Saffery Champness

Lion House
Red Lion Street
London,
United Kingdom
Telephone: (44) 020 7841 4000
Fax: (44) 020 7841 4100
Web site: http://www.saffery.com

Private Company
Incorporated: 1855
Employees: 425
Sales: £1.5 billion ($2.5 billion) (2002 est.)
NAIC: 541211 Offices of Certified Public Accountants

■ ■ ■

Saffery Champness celebrated its 150th anniversary in 2005 as one of the United Kingdom's leading independent accountancy partnerships. The London-based business has developed an extensive presence in the United Kingdom, with offices in Bournemouth, Bristol, Edinburgh, Harrogate, High Wycombe, Inverness, London, Manchester, and Peterborough, as well as an office on the island of Guernsey, providing offshore services through subsidiary Saffery Champness Management International Limited. Saffery Champness provides a full range of accountancy and related financial services, including auditing, tax planning, corporate finance; human resources (HR) consultancy; investment and financial advice; information technology (IT) consultancy; litigation and forensic accounting; offshore structures; payroll; private office; share valuation; tax;

trusts; and value-added tax (VAT).

The company targets a broad client base, with customers including publicly listed companies; barristers; charities; media and entertainment groups; landed estates and agriculture; foreign owned corporations; owner managed businesses; private clients; professional services firms; property; public sector; and regulated businesses. Saffery Champness also provides specialized services through a number of dedicated groups, such as its Professional and Consultancy Services Group, established in January 2006 and focused on the HR and recruitment sectors. Saffery Champness employs nearly 55 partners, supported by a staff of 370. The firm's annual revenues are estimated to top £1.5 billion ($2.5 billion) in the mid-2000s, placing it in the United Kingdom's top 20 accounting firms. Saffery Champness is also a founding member of SC International, a globally operating accountancy association grouping more than 100 independent accountancy firms in more than 50 countries worldwide. Saffery Champness has been led by Chairman Nick Gaskell since July 2005.

PIONEERING U.K. ACCOUNTING IN THE 19TH CENTURY

While accounting had been practiced for centuries, its emergence as a modern profession was still quite recent. The first full-fledged accounting firm was established in the United Kingdom only in the late 18th century. It was not until the passage of the Bankruptcy Act of 1831 that the profession received its first official recognition, when accountants were granted the same status as merchants and bankers for conducting audits. A major

COMPANY PERSPECTIVES

We believe firmly in giving clients added value by: Providing a proactive, friendly and highly personal service which is flexible and responsive to clients' needs; Offering a wide range of skills and specialist services to meet clients' practical requirements; Communicating clearly and openly with clients; Basing all advice on the personal relationship between the clients and a lead director backed up by further specialist resources in Guernsey and throughout the firm; Focusing the firm's resources on developing a team of quality staff, on whose services our clients depend; Working as a team with the clients' existing professional advisers; Providing access to a network of other professional contacts offering complementary services who share our high standards of client service and in-depth technical expertise; Offering a cost-effective service, with fees agreed at the outset wherever possible; Building long-term relationships with clients.

move toward the creation of the modern accounting industry in the United Kingdom came in 1853, with the establishment of the country's first accountants association, the Institute of Accountants in Edinburgh.

Saffery Champness's roots were planted during this early period of the U.K. accounting industry, when Joseph John Saffery established an accountant's office in London in 1855. The original site of the firm's offices was in London's Guildhall Chambers. Soon after founding his firm, however, Saffery formed a partnership with William Palmer, taking up new premises on Basinghall Street.

The accounting industry received a new boost in 1862, with the passage of the Companies Act. Also known as the "accountant's friend," the new legislation created an Official Liquidator, that is, a single person charged with overseeing a company's liquidation. The creation of this function proved an important source of new revenues for the country's accountants. The new opportunities led Saffery to expand his partnership in 1865, linking H. Croysdill to form Croysdill & Saffery.

The British government continued strengthening the legislation governing the nation's corporate sectors through the end of the century. In 1867, for example, a new Companies Act was passed, followed soon after by a new Bankruptcy Act in 1869. Through this legislation and others, accountants became more and more

implicated in the financial lives of the country's companies, both private and public, as well as in the public sector. The rising importance of the accounting industry led to the creation of a number of new locally and regionally focused accountants associations, such as the Institute of Accountants in London. This body, which included Joseph Saffery among its founding members, later grew into the central accountants body, the Institute of Chartered Accountants in England and Wales, or ICAEW.

Another important piece of legislation in the U.K. accounting industry was added in 1879, when a new Companies Act established requirements that all of the country's banks maintain audited accounts. This legislation provided a new revenue stream for accountants. Not all of the legislation governing the corporate sector proved favorable to accountants' interests, however. A large number of accountants overseeing insolvency proceedings had been withholding the money generated during liquidation proceedings; in response, the Bankruptcy Act passed in 1883 established the new office of Official Receiver, which then took over the management of insolvency proceedings. The new legislation represented a major loss of earnings for the accounting industry.

Saffery was joined in business by son Francis Joseph Saffery in 1885. At that time, the firm's name was changed to Saffery Son and Company. The elder Saffery's prominence in the London accounting market was underscored in 1889 when he was elected as president of the ICAEW, a position he held for two years. By then, another Saffery son, Harold Edgar Saffery, joined the firm, which became known as Saffery Sons and Co. in 1889.

EVOLVING THROUGH A SERIES OF MERGERS IN THE 20TH CENTURY

British legislation continued to influence the development of the modern accounting industry. In 1903, for example, the passage of a Revenue Act presented a first definition of an accountant as a member of an incorporated body of accountants, such as the ICAEW. The new legislation, subsequently reinforced following World War I, gave new weight to the accountants bodies, as well as further legitimacy to the accounting profession. In the meantime, the British government extended its requirement for audited accounts from the financial sector to the corporate sector, passing the Companies (Consolidation) Act of 1909. By then, Saffery & Sons had grown as well, adding a new partner, John Skinner. The firm then changed its name to Saffery, Sons and Skinner. After Skinner retired in 1914, and Cecil Francis Saffery joined the firm, the partner-

KEY DATES

1855: Joseph John Saffery opens an accounting office in London.

1868: The Champness and Maclerie accounting partnership is created in London.

1869: The Armitage & Norton accounting firm is founded.

1921: Saffery opens an office in Margate.

1972: Saffery merges with Newman Ogle Bevan & Co.

1973: The name is changed to Safferys.

1974: The firm merges with C. McDonald & Co.; Champness merges with Somerset Cowper & Co.

1977: Safferys opens a Guernsey office.

1980: Safferys opens an Iverness office.

1982: Safferys and Champness merge and become Saffery Champness.

1985: Offices are opened in Edinburgh and Bournemouth.

1986: The firm becomes a founding member of the SC International accounting network.

1987: Saffery and Champness merges with Armitage & Norton; an office is opened in March.

1992: An office is opened in Harrogate.

1994: An office is opened in the northwest region of England.

1995: The March office is transferred to Petersborough.

1998: An office is opened in Bristol.

1999: SC International merges with S&W International.

2005: Saffery and Champness celebrates its 150th anniversary.

2006: The firm creates a Professional and Consultancy Services group focused on the HR and recruitment sectors.

ship readopted the name of Saffery Sons & Co. The firm was to maintain that name into the 1970s.

Saffery grew during the 1920s, adding an additional office in Margate in 1921. Later that decade, the firm added a new partner, Thomas Holdme Nicholson, who joined in 1928. Members of the Nicholson family were to become prominent members of the Saffery partnership, as Nicholson's son Dennis, and then grandson Clive, joined the firm.

Yet Saffery Sons & Co.'s emergence as one of the United Kingdom's top 20 accounting firms really occurred in the 1970s. An important step toward this transition came in 1972, when Saffery Sons & Co. merged with Newman Ogle Bevan & Co. Following this merger, Saffery Sons changed its name to Safferys in 1973. The following year, Safferys grew again, this time merging with C. McDonald and Co. Safferys also added a new office during the 1970s, extending into the offshore market with the opening of its Guernsey branch in 1977. Starting with just one resident partner, the Guernsey office grew into one of the group's largest offices over the next decades. The successful opening in Guernsey led Safferys to seek other areas of expansion, and in 1980 the firm opened an office in Iverness as well.

At the same time, Safferys continued to seek out merger partners in order to maintain its position in the fast-consolidating U.K. accounting industry. This led the firm to its biggest merger to date, when it joined with Champness Cowper & Co. in 1982. That firm was nearly as old as Safferys itself, having been founded in 1868 by J.H. Champness and partner Maclerie. That firm also took up offices on London's Basinghall Street. Champness later formed a new partnership with J. Corderoy in 1886, at which time the firm's name became J.H. Champness Corderoy & Co. Champness grew again in 1945, becoming J.H. Champness Corderoy Beesly & Co. In 1974, the firm merged with Somerset Cowper & Co., a firm originally founded in 1915, becoming Champness Cowper & Co. Following its merger with Safferys, the enlarged firm adopted the new name of Saffery Champness.

Saffery achieved its more or less final form in 1987, when it merged with significant rival Armitage & Norton. Like both Saffery and Champness, Armitage & Norton, originally founded in 1868, had evolved through a series of mergers, especially during the 1970s. The addition of Armitage & Norton not only boosted Saffery Champness's London operations, but also added offices in Edinburgh and High Wycombe. These joined Saffery Champness's own Edinburgh office, opened in 1985, and another new office, established in Bournemouth that same year. Following the merger with Armitage & Norton, Saffery Champness extended its network again, adding an office in March.

U.K. LEADER WITH INTERNATIONAL REACH IN THE NEW CENTURY

The growing international nature of the corporate market, with the emergence of a large number of multi-nationally operating companies, also stimulated the consolidation of the worldwide accounting industry. This in turn stimulated the growth not only of the world's Big Four accounting firms, but also the appearance of a number of international accounting partnerships. In 1986, Saffery Champness moved to safeguard its own competitiveness, becoming the founding member of the SC International accounting network. That body, later chaired by Saffery Champness's Clive Nicholson, grew to include more than 100 partner firms in some 50 countries across the world. In this way, Saffery Champness gained access to a global network with a local character.

The growth of SC International allowed Saffery Champness to focus its own operations on the United Kingdom. The firm grew again in 1992, adding a new office in Harrowgate. Two years later, the company added its first office in the northwest region of England. That office was subsequently moved to Manchester in 1999. Similarly, the firm transferred its March office to Peterborough in 1995. The final addition to the group's local network came in 1998, when Saffery Champness added an office in Bristol. In the meantime, SC International itself grew significantly, after its merger with S&W International in 1999. By the mid-2000s, SC International's billings had grown significantly, representing more than $450 million. Saffery Champness's own revenues were estimated to top £1.5 billion ($2.5 billion).

Part of Saffery Champness's success came in its ability to embrace new accounting trends and markets. As such, the firm became the first to provide audits for the United Kingdom's rapidly growing professional rugby league. In 2006, the firm responded to the specific demands of the fast-growing human resources and recruitment services sector by creating a dedicated Professional and Consultancy Services group for that market. After more than 150 years, Saffery Champness remained at the top of the U.K. accounting industry.

M. L. Cohen

PRINCIPAL SUBSIDIARIES

Saffery Champness Management International Limited (Guernsey).

PRINCIPAL COMPETITORS

Ernst and Young LLP; Grant Thornton Ltd.; BDO Stoy Hayward; PKF; Horwath Clark Whitehill; Deloitte and Touche LLP; BKR Haines Watts; Moore Stephens; Dynamic Commercial Finance plc; ADP Network Services Ltd.; RSM Robson Rhodes LLP.

FURTHER READING

"Accountancy Firm Counts on Flex," *Employee Benefits*, May 2002, p. 11.

"Happy 150th Birthday," *Bristol Evening Post*, January 4, 2005.

"Hill Climbs Up the Ranks at Saffery Champness," *Accountancy Age*, September 15, 2005, p. 18.

"Saffery Champness, Sponsors of the Lifetime Achievement Award," *Harrogate Advertiser*, March 24, 2006.

Sullivan, Ruth, "Moving Places: SC International," *Financial Times*, February 27, 2003, p. 13.

"Tax Opportunities in Asia Pacific," *International Accounting Bulletin*, January 28, 2006, p. 2.

"We're One of the Best to Work For," *Bristol Evening Post*, September 8, 2003.

Sam Levin Inc.

301 Fitz Henry Road
Smithton, Pennsylvania 15479-8715
U.S.A.
Telephone: (724) 872-2055
Fax: (724) 872-2060
Web site: http://www.levinfurniture.com

Private Company
Incorporated: 1920
Employees: 400
Sales: $160 million (2006 est.)
NAIC: 442110 Furniture Stores

■ ■ ■

Sam Levin Inc. is the Smithton, Pennsylvania-based corporate parent of Levin Furniture, operator of a dozen furniture superstores. Half of them are located in the Pittsburgh area, while the others are in the Cleveland and Akron, Ohio markets. Despite operating in flat markets and the far-from-robust furniture retail environment, Levin has been able to grow its business by opening large family-friendly showrooms and offering attractive deferred payment and in-store credit options, which customers can arrange before starting the buying process through easy-to-use self-service kiosks. The company is owned and operated by the third generation of the Levin family.

EARLY 20TH CENTURY ORIGINS

According to Levin family lore, Levin furniture was founded in Mount Pleasant, Pennsylvania, by peddler

Sam Levin in 1920 because his wife Jessie was concerned about marrying off their six daughters, being afraid that the families of would-be suitors might look askance at associating themselves with a child of such dubious parentage. So Levin opened a store in town, one that offered hardware as well as furniture, a common combination of the day. He even offered coal-burning stoves and replacement parts produced by the local foundry. Over time furniture crowded out the hardware inventory and became the focus of Levin and his wife. They managed to survive the difficult 1930s, building a lasting relationship with their customers, who relied on installment buying plans to furnish their homes during the Great Depression that did not abate until the national economy roared back to life in the 1940s and the United States entered World War II. Levin, the former peddler, was more than willing to barter to keep a customer during these lean times, known to accept chickens and eggs and other items in lieu of cash. Thus, working with customers with a tight budget became a hallmark of Levin Furniture from an early date.

In addition to their six daughters, the Levins also gave birth to a son named Leonard, who in 1943 joined his father in running the furniture store. It was Leonard and his wife Sally who took Levin Furniture to the next level. She played key roles in buying, as well as in merchandising and advertising. Sally was also responsible for incorporating professional decorating services into the operation. The second generation of the family bought a townhouse attached to the store and transformed it into "Colonial House," an in-store boutique decorated with Early American furniture and accessories for sale. The attention to period detail was so

COMPANY PERSPECTIVES

Whether your style is clean and simple; traditional; opulent and elegant; or a combination of many styles, you'll find more ways to express yourself at Levin Furniture.

exact that Colonial House became a minor tourist destination, attracting busloads of visitors who viewed the different rooms and learned the history of period pieces.

A third generation of the Levin family, Howard Levin, Leonard and Sally Levin's eldest son, joined the family business in 1978. He spearheaded Levin Furniture's expansion beyond the lone Mount Pleasant store, and entered the much larger market of nearby Pittsburgh, Pennsylvania. In a matter of seven years, Levin Furniture opened five new, full-service furniture stores in the area. At a time when other furniture stores were beginning to struggle, the newcomer emerged as Western Pennsylvania's largest furniture retailer.

After his father died in 1989, Howard Levin began to plan his next major move: entering the Cleveland, Ohio, market. The residents of Cleveland and Pittsburgh, although hated rivals when it came to professional football, were more alike than different, populated by very much the same blue collar demographic. The more Howard Levin researched the market and visited Cleveland, the more convinced he became that it was ideal territory for the Levin Furniture concept.

OHIO MARKET PENETRATED:
1990–2000

The first Ohio Levin Furniture Store opened west of Cleveland in Bedford, Ohio, in 1992. A second area store opened just months later in Mentor, Ohio, followed later in the year by a store in Middleburg Heights. It was a promising start to the fulfillment of Howard Levin's vision, but only two weeks after the third Cleveland-area opening the 40 year old suddenly died of a heart attack. His younger brother, Robert Levin, who was hardly prepared for a career in retailing, took over. After graduating from the Pennsylvania State University with a Bachelor of arts degree in philosophy, he then earned a master's degree in gerontology at the University of Southern California and moved to the Washington, D.C., to work in the health policy field. He now quit his job, returned home, and took over a chain of nine

furniture stores. According to a *Smart Business Pittsburgh* profile, "those first few months after his brother's passing are fuzzy, clouded by the shock of Howard's death and the steep learning curve Robert faced as he tried to acclimate himself to running a business that he previously had little involvement in." Describing the shock he felt at the time, Levin said, "I remember feeling in that first year that I was just hanging onto the tail of the tiger and just trying to keep it together."

Fortunately for Robert Levin, his brother had developed an excellent strategy for the company. He also followed Howard's lead by assuming the marketing and advertising responsibilities. *Smart Business Pittsburgh* explained that as he found his stride, Robert Levin "continued to lead the company with an aggressive marketing and advertising program, leveraging technology to support it." Under his leadership, Levin Furniture twice expanded its distribution operation. He also broadened the chain's product mix.

Levin Furniture enjoyed strong and steady growth in the 1990s and into the new century, despite operating in markets with an aging population and a decreasing number of new homebuyers looking to furnish their empty houses. Levin Furniture was able to find a way to prosper in the replacement business, enticing people to replace that old couch or dining room table. A key to the chain's success was its aggressive marketing, which included a good deal of television and direct mail advertising. In addition, Levin Furniture, because of it growth, gained an increasing amount of cooperative advertising dollars from manufacturers. "It's a cliché," Howard Levin explained to *Smart Business Pittsburgh*, adding, "but the larger you are, the more valuable you are to the wholesaler, who has a limited number of outlets to sell to. The partnership becomes more valuable to them, therefore advertising support becomes more significant. That's one way you can build your business by increasing your advertising, but having the net cost of advertising actually drops. That's been very important in growing the top line." That top line improved at a steady clip under Robert Levin's leadership. Sales reached $57 million in 1997, an amount that would total $140 million by 2004, and increase to around $160 million in 2006.

Another important part of Levin Furniture's program was its attractive deferred payment options, which generated strong sales volumes. Given that for most people furniture was the third largest investment they were likely to make, trailing only a house or car, offering accommodating terms was a key factor in making a sale. Levin offer a "12-month, same as cash" option, in which the customer made monthly payments but interest charges were eliminated or at the very least delayed for one year. A second option, "deferred same as cash," delayed both payments and interest for a full year. At that point, the customer could pay off the balance without interest charges or begin accruing interest as the purchase was paid off in installments. Because Levin Furniture did not have cash on hand to finance loans, devoting its cash flow to inventory, the accounts were sold at a discount to a bank, which also received between 5 and 10 percent of the sale price. The bank then accepted customer payments and handled all the other financial details. There was little money to be made, but banks took on the accounts to gain access to customer information, such as credit rating, as a way to uncover potential new customers. Moreover, the loans represented only a modest risk because the purchased furniture served as collateral.

NEW CENTURY BRINGS TECHNOLOGICAL INNOVATION

Levin Furniture merged technology with its financing plans in the early 2000s, introducing in-store, self-service, credit application kiosks, which essentially eliminated paper credit applications and provided a number of other benefits. Initially, the company created an in-house kiosk system to automate the credit process, but after a brief trial it proved too unreliable. Levin Furniture now turned to a commercial kiosk provider, Apunix Computer Services, which helped the company develop a truly viable self-service credit processing kiosk system tied in with any promotions the stores might be offering. *Self Service Magazine* offered a glimpse into how the system actually worked: "The customer walks in the store and the retail associate is trained to tell people about the incentive and then the sales associate introduces them to the kiosk as a private, secure, and fast way to get the application process done." Each store contained at least two touch-screen kiosks, at which the customer followed prompts to enter the information necessary to perform a credit check. "The customer then gets a slip out of the kiosk that tells them they are approved, account number, and the credit limit with the store. Then the customer can immediately begin shopping." Should a customer be rejected, the kiosk "doesn't tell a customer they are rejected, Rather, it tells a customer to see the front office. A manager will then look at the application and search for an alternative financing method for the customer. In almost every case they are able to find a way to provide the customer a financing option."

The kiosk system provided a number of benefits to Levin Furniture. Because customers preferred the privacy of the system, it significantly reduced man-hours at each store, freeing up sales associates to spend more time with customers instead of processing paperwork. With the credit application now taking place at the beginning of their shopping trip, customers were also more likely to make a purchase and spend closer to their credit maximum, on average about 85 percent to 90 percent of their available credit. Foot traffic was also converted to sales at a much higher rate, and sales associates, knowing the customer's price range could do a more focused and effective job in selling them furniture. Even if customers applied for credit and did not make a purchase, Levin Furniture benefited from the process. As Nick Rossi, the company's Information Technology director, explained to *Self Service Magazine* these non-activated accounts could be marketed it, "so we can find out why they didn't buy. … Knowing why your customer didn't buy is much more important than knowing why they do." Another advantage of the system was that it generated a unique customer number, which was then used to weed out duplicates in the mailing lists, thereby reducing mailing costs.

At the end of the 1990s Levin Furniture maintained its strong growth by turning to a new large showroom format that would replace older stores. The first opened in North Fayette, Pennsylvania, in the summer of 1999. At 70,000 square feet it was the largest furniture showroom in the state and in effect served as a furniture theme park, a destination as much as a store. It featured 100 living room settings on display, one of the largest in-store sleep shops in the United States, and a 10,000-square-foot clearance center. In addition, the store included a children's area where offspring could play on a wooden boat outfitted with slides and climbing apparatuses or watch videos on a big-screen television in kid-size recliners while their parents shopped. A hospitality center, named Sally's Café after Sally Levin, not only offered drinks and snacks, it was tied into the company's support for a local charity, the Free Care Fund of Children's Hospital. Items were ostensibly free but customers were encouraged to make a donation to the fund.

Levin Furniture opened another new showroom in the Pittsburgh area in 2001, this one 74,000 square feet in size. It offered the same features as the North Fayette store and a number of new collections as well: Jessica McClintock for American Drew and Alexander Julian's case goods. A year later, Levin Furniture opened an even larger showroom, 88,000 square feet in size, located in West Mifflin, Pennsylvania, in a renovated former location for big box retailer Builders Square. With the extra space, the store was able to take advantage of its close proximity to the Levin Furniture warehouse to devote 26,000 square feet to a clearance center.

Levin Furniture continued in the 2000s to replace older stores with the new larger prototype. In 2006 the company opened its 12th store, located in Akron, Ohio, and in the works were plans to improve four other stores and add another location in North Hills, Pennsylvania. To keep pace with growing sales, Levin Furniture also

invested $5 million to add 110,000-square-feet of space to its Smithton distribution facility.

Ed Dinger

PRINCIPAL COMPETITORS

Haverty Furniture Companies, Inc.; J.C. Penney Corporation, Inc.; Rooms To Go, Inc.

FURTHER READING

"The Credit Worth Giving a Kiosk To," *Self Service Magazine*, January-February 2004.

Ray, Marano, "Designs on the Market: Levin Furniture Co.," *Smart Business Pittsburgh*, February 1, 2006, p. 24.

Seiling, Donna, "Fancy Financing," *Pittsburgh Business Times*, June 29, 1998.

Sheridan, Patricia, "Fore Levin, At New West Mifflin Store, More is More," *Pittsburgh Post-Gazette*, April 13, 2002.

———, "Levin Creates A New Furniture Theme Park," *Pittsburgh Post-Gazette*, July 21, 2001, p. B2.

———, "Levin to Open State's Biggest Furniture Store," *Pittsburgh Post-Gazette*, July 17, 1999, p. D6.

Saturn Corporation

———————— ▪ ————————

100 Saturn Parkway
Spring Hill, Tennessee 37174
U.S.A.
Telephone: (931) 486-5000
Toll Free: (800) 553-6000
Web site: http://www.saturn.com

Wholly Owned Subsidiary of General Motors Corporation
Incorporated: 1983
Employees: 9,600
Sales: $3.9 billion (est.)
NAIC: 336110 Automobile and Light Duty Motor
Vehicle Manufacturing

■ ■ ■

U.S. automaker Saturn Corporation grew out of a project that General Motors Corporation (GM) began in 1982. The aim of the project was to explore the potential for building a small car of superior quality and value as efficiently as possible, combining the most advanced technology with the newest approaches to management. Saturn realized its goal by producing a car ranked only behind the Lexus and the Infiniti (imported luxury cars produced by Toyota and Nissan) in the 1992 J. D. Power & Associates customer satisfaction survey. Saturn was regarded as more than simply a successful product, however; the company was seen as nothing less than the embodiment of GM's vision of modern corporate ideals. Saturn was the product of an extraordinary effort within GM to create a company from scratch without any preconceived notions and combining the most advanced

techniques and ideas in all areas. From community and employee involvement in decision-making, to environmentally responsible plant design, to dealers trained to avoid the high-pressure sales techniques typical of traditional car salesmen, Saturn sought to embody a 1990s model of corporate enlightenment. Recognized for its innovations in product design and production methodologies, the company received a great deal of positive publicity. At the same time, however, critics noted that its accomplishments were achieved slowly and at great expense.

INDUSTRY CLIMATE: 1950–1983

Saturn grew out of a particular climate within the car industry. Traditionally, the "Big Three" automakers (General Motors, Ford, and Chrysler) had built large cars, emphasizing features and comfort. The industry began to change in the 1950s when foreign car makers (notably Renault and Volkswagen) offered American consumers smaller cars at lower prices. Imports had claimed a 10.1 percent market share by 1959, but they were pushed back to a 4.8 percent share in 1962 after the introduction of the Corvair (GM), the Valiant (Chrysler), and the Falcon (Ford) in 1960.

By the late 1960s, the Big Three began to be challenged by Japanese car manufacturers. The Vega was GM's answer to the challenge. In 1968 GM announced that it would build the Vega from scratch rather than redesign another GM car. The finished product, introduced in 1970, proved disappointing. Vegas were prone to rust, and their aluminum engines warped. The

Chevette, GM's more successful small car introduced in 1975, was nearing the end of its 10-year product cycle when GM began to work on a replacement, code-named the S car. In 1981 GM determined that the S car could be built much less expensively by Isuzu (GM had bought 34.2 percent of Isuzu in 1971). Its next small car (the Chevrolet Spectrum) was built in Japan. This series of events confirmed in some people's minds the suspicion that U.S. automakers couldn't produce small cars competitively. As smaller cars were widely believed to represent the future direction of the industry, the episode called into question the likelihood of the long-term survival of the Big Three. To address this concern, Ford initiated the "Alpha project" and Chrysler began work on "Concept 90."

At GM an internal project to build an affordable, high-quality, small car to compete with the imports was approved in May 1982 by GM Vice-Chairman Howard Kehrl in conjunction with Alex Mair and Robert Eaton, vice-presidents in charge of design and engineering. On June 15 Alex Mair sat down with engineers Joe Joseph and Tom Ankeny to sketch out the plan. By July the project had been dubbed "Saturn," a reference to the Saturn rocket that propelled the American astronauts to the moon during the space race with the Soviet Union.

The project enjoyed strong sponsorship from the highest ranks of the company. In keeping with the emphasis on consensus throughout Saturn, no one in particular is considered the project's founding father. In the words of then-GM Chief Roger Smith, "I don't know who is the father of Saturn around here. I think all of us are promoting it and pushing it. I've been hot for it but I'm not going to tell you that I started it, because that wouldn't be true."

Although the project was to be kept confidential, press leaks began in early 1983. As cooperation with the United Auto Workers union (UAW) was vital to the success of the project, GM had begun behind-the-scenes discussions with Donald Ephlin, the UAW manager for GM. By October, a joint GM-UAW Study Center was agreed upon.

Motivated in part by claims that the company was turning its back on the United States by building cars in Japan, on November 3, 1983, GM announced a new operating unit, the wholly owned Saturn Corporation, with an initial capitalization of $150 million. It would be the first nameplate added to the General Motors ranks since Chevrolet in 1918. Saturn would incorporate the latest technology available. The operations were to be completely computerized, with robots utilized to reduce direct labor costs, and flexible manufacturing techniques and just-in-time inventory systems introduced.

The importance of the project is evident in the wording of its announcement. Chairman Roger Smith announced Saturn as "the key to GM's long-term competitiveness, survival, and success as a domestic producer. ... We expect it to be a learning laboratory," he said. "We also expect that what we learn with Saturn will spread throughout GM." He described Saturn as the key to improving every GM plant and product.

Key staff members recognized for bringing the project to this point included Alex Mair of the Technical Staffs Group, Bob Eaton of Advanced Product & Manufacturing Engineering, Irv Rybicki of the Design Staff, and UAW leaders Don Ephlin and Joe Molotke. Executives appointed to take the company forward included the former head of the Oldsmobile Division, Joseph Sanchez, as president; the former executive director of the Saturn project, Reid Rundell, as executive vice-president for strategic planning; John Middlebrook as vice-president for sales, service, and marketing; Tom Manoff as vice-president for finance; Jay Wetzel as vice-president for engineering; and Guy Briggs as vice-president for manufacturing operations. When Sanchez died suddenly on January 26th, William E. Hoglund was appointed president. Hoglund served until Richard G. "Skip" LeFauve succeeded him on February 3, 1986.

SATURN IS BORN

The company was launched. On December 19, 1983, a joint GM-UAW Study Center was announced. The following February, 99 people ("the Group of 99") were designated to identify key founding principles for Saturn and to search the world for the best ideas in all areas. The group consisted of a functional cross-section of people, including plant managers, superintendents,

```
┌─────────────────────────────────────────────┐
│                                             │
│              KEY DATES                      │
│                    ▄                        │
│  ─────────────────────────────────────────  │
│                                             │
│  1983:  GM launches a small car division    │
│         called Saturn to compete against    │
│         small, high-quality imports.        │
│  1985:  GM decides to build Saturn's plant  │
│         in Spring Hill, Tennessee.          │
│  1985:  The United Auto Workers union (UAW) │
│         agrees to help Saturn design its    │
│         company.                            │
│  1990:  GM chairman Roger Smith drives the  │
│         first Saturn off the production     │
│         line on July 30; the first Saturns  │
│         are delivered to a dealership on    │
│         October 11.                         │
│  1994:  Saturn's best-selling year; 286,003 │
│         units of the S-series are sold.     │
│  1998:  UAW authorizes a strike at the      │
│         Spring Hill plant.                  │
│  1999:  Saturn releases its second model    │
│         called the L-series.                │
│  2000:  Saturn Ion replaces the S-series.   │
│  2002:  Saturn releases its first SUV       │
│         called the Vue.                     │
│  2004:  GM assumes more control of Saturn   │
│         and restructures the entire         │
│         division.                           │
│  2006:  A new Saturn midsize sedan and      │
│         two-seat roadster are introduced.   │
│                                             │
└─────────────────────────────────────────────┘
```

union committee members, production workers, and skilled tradesmen, as well as UAW and GM staff from 41 UAW locals and 55 GM plants.

The group split into seven functional teams to explore stamping; metal fabrication and body work; paint and corrosion; trim and hardware; heating, ventilation, and air conditioning; and powertrain and chassis. In all, the Group of 99 visited 49 GM plants and 60 other companies around the world. They made 170 contacts, traveled two million miles, and put in 50,000 hours of effort.

The group's findings were presented in April 1984. The keys to success identified included ownership by all employees, the assumption of responsibility by all, equality and trust among employees, the elimination of barriers to doing a good job, giving staff the authority to do their jobs, and the existence of common goals. Specific recommendations included the use of a conflict resolution process that had been developed by the group and the formation of consensus-driven partnerships within work teams as well as between the union and company management.

The search for a plant location began immediately after the company was announced. Two days later, Illinois Governor James Thompson became the first to visit GM, advocating a site in his state. By the end of the search process, 24 governors had paid visits to GM and 38 states had expressed interest. Donald Avenson, the Speaker of Iowa's House of Representatives, offered to pay half of the first year's wages for workers ($140 million) if Saturn settled in Iowa. Spring Hill, Tennessee, was confirmed as the plant site on July 30, 1985, and construction began in May 1986.

The plant was a mile long and a half mile wide, totalling four million square feet and consisting of four functional buildings: powertrain (engine and transmission systems), body systems (frames, exterior panels), vehicle interior systems (interior trim), and vehicle systems (final assembly). The facilities' core team, which designed the layout, included employees at all levels. The team considered unique lighting requirements in different areas; placed restrooms and cafeterias conveniently; and designed a sophisticated roadway that separated truck traffic from pedestrians, decentralized loading docks so materials arrived where they were needed, and ensured that no one walked more than five minutes from parking lot to work.

As controlling labor costs was crucial to competing with the imports on a cost basis, cooperation with the UAW was an important factor. During the 1980s GM had suffered losses and had laid off 170,000 UAW workers. The competitive environment spurred both sides to work together on improving the prospects for American car manufacturing. Al Warren, vice-president of GM's Industrial Relations staff, and Donald Ephlin, UAW vice-president and director for the General Motors Department, were instrumental in creating a strong bond between Saturn and the UAW.

On July 26, 1985, the UAW executive board approved a unique labor agreement for Saturn. It reduced the number of job classifications, allowed unprecedented flexibility in job content, eliminated work rules, and set pay rates at 80 percent of the base rate at other GM plants with the difference made up in performance incentives. All Saturn workers were salaried and participated in a "risk-reward" system in which they lost 20 percent of their pay if the company did not reach common goals (e.g., sales goals), but earned proportional bonuses if goals were exceeded. Each team managed its own budget, inventory, and hiring.

Training was an important part of Saturn's human resource strategy. Workers spent between 250 and 750 hours in training to become "job-ready." On the job, they spent a minimum of 5 percent of each year in training. Workers were acclimated to Saturn's philosophy through core courses on conflict management, consensus decision making, and team dynamics. They also received specialized technical training on machinery, parts quality, and working with vendors. The training program sought to promote teamwork, self-direction, initiative, and responsibility. In 1992, Saturn's success in managing human resources could be measured by the lowest absentee rate in the industry: absenteeism at Saturn was 2.5 percent, a far cry from the 14 percent at other GM plants.

As other elements of the company were being developed, product development staff were working on the cars. The first demonstration vehicle was completed on September 15, 1984. Although Saturn was a "no year" project (it had no set launch date), GM chairman Roger Smith was determined to begin production before he retired. He drove the first car off the production line on July 30, 1990, one day before he retired and turned the reins over to Robert Stempel.

The first truckload of Saturns was sent to dealers in California on October 11, 1990. By November the company garnered several awards, including the *Popular Science* "1990 Best of What's New in Automobiles" and an award from the Society of Plastics Engineers for its thermoplastic door panel. In June 1992 the first exports went to Taiwan. Annual production quickly reached 240,000 units, and buyers were lined up on waiting lists, but the company was still losing money. By 1993 Saturn expected to raise production to 320,000, allowing the company to turn its first profit; the product line included seven models of sedans, coupes, and wagons.

In developing parts and manufacturing processes, Saturn employed Product Development Teams (PDTs) consisting of manufacturing engineers, finance staff, materials managers, quality engineers, and UAW technicians. The teams decided what materials to stock and evaluated prospective suppliers for quality, price, and efficient organization.

In keeping with the "complete job-focus" philosophy, a part was manufactured from start to finish in one place. Ergonomics was another important consideration. Equipment, which was "low-tech and people-oriented," was chosen by its users and frequently adjusted to individuals. Whereas workers must crawl inside the vehicle to work on the cockpit of most cars, Saturn cockpits were assembled in a fixture that can be rotated for the comfort of the individual worker. A skillet system allowed workers to ride on a moving platform with the car as it moved down the assembly line. While the basic system was copied from GM's Opel facility in Germany, Saturn widened the platform and turned the cars sideways, saving 40 percent in floor space.

In the engine and transmission area, lost-foam casting was used on a large scale for the first time, providing casting precision, flexibility, material savings, minimal tool wear, and reduced machining. In making trim, plastic colors were mixed at the injection molding machine, reducing change-over time and costs. Other innovative production methods included an environmentally sound waterborne paint process and a method of testing transmissions with air rather than oil.

SERVICE AND MARKETING

Marketing was another central issue at Saturn. The first marketing customer clinic was held in San Francisco in March 1985, five years before production began. The car itself was designed to be adaptable to changing consumer preferences. Whereas older cars depend on exterior panels for structural strength, Saturns are structurally based on a strong "space frame" to which the exterior "skin" is attached, allowing for quick style changes. Saturn's marketing philosophy was concerned with bringing in "plus business" (non-GM buyers). Based upon the profile of imported car buyers, the targeted Saturn consumer would be an average of 38 years old, earning an average of $51,000 annually. A large percentage would live on the West Coast and 50 percent would be college graduates.

The Saturn Marketing Planning Team incorporated the ideas of 16 dealers representing 25 manufacturers. Led by Donald Hudler, the team studied distribution methods of 30 major U.S. corporations and came up with Saturn's Market Area Approach (MAA), which was announced on May 26, 1987. MAA set up 300 "territories" to be handled by individual franchised dealers.

Saturn sought the consistency of service lacking in the GM dealer network. In early 1989 dealers were invited to apply for franchises. Saturn dealers were trained in low-pressure sales and were encouraged to pay salaries rather than commissions. The strong demand for the car, coupled with significant dealership control over territory, enabled Saturn dealers to average twice the unit sales volume of other car dealerships. In addition, the August 3, 1992, *Business Week* noted that a 17 percent gross margin was built into the "no-haggle" sticker price (while other cars averaged 12 percent).

An important step in defining Saturn's marketing strategy was the selection of an advertising agency. Fifty agencies had applied for consideration by a review panel composed of two Saturn executives, two retailers, and a UAW representative, but the agency chosen was not among them. Thomas Shafer, Director of Marketing Services, felt that it was important to consider West Coast agencies since the small car market was most competitive there. As a result, the Hal Riney & Partners agency was named as Saturn's "communications partner" on May 24, 1988. Riney set about creating a "charismatic brand." He felt strongly that model names would detract from the Saturn name and insisted that the cars simply be called "Saturns," with numbers distinguishing various models. Dealerships would be called "Saturn of x" and colors would be "red" rather than the more pretentious "raspberry red." Saturn advertising was designed to be emotionally driven, with a focus on the human element rather than the product. In February 1989 the first print ad appeared, even though cars would not be available for more than a year.

In addition to external marketing work, Riney assisted the new company with internal communications. In April 1989 Riney produced "Spring, in Spring Hill," a documentary explaining the company to employees, suppliers, and the press. It was later aired as an infomercial. In the film, team members explained what the project meant to them. In the words of a Riney executive, "We wanted to get people rooting for Saturn, the company."

Saturn lost $800,000 in 1990 with calendar year sales of 1,881 units. 1991 calendar year sales were 74,493 units, and 1992 sales reached 196,126 units by December 31, with a substantial number of additional units back-ordered. In the 1992 model year Saturn earned a 2.8 percent market share. It was estimated that the company needed to sell 300,000 cars per year to make a profit. Increasing capacity significantly would require further investment in new facilities or the retooling of an existing plant. Building new capacity was problematic as GM continued to close old plants; retooling, however, also presented problems, as duplication of the innovations in the Spring Hill plant was a formidable task. In addition, there were few existing facilities large enough to accommodate the manufacturing of all necessary components at one site, as Saturn did in Spring Hill.

By mid-1992 Saturn cars had 95 percent domestic content and were ranked as the highest-quality American cars, with defect ratings rivaling those of top Honda and Nissan vehicles and customer satisfaction ratings outpaced only by Lexus and Infiniti. On the negative side, the company was far from recouping the undisclosed billions that GM had invested in it and was not operating at full capacity. In addition, an average of 35 hours of labor were required per car, compared to the stated company goal of 20 hours.

In an effort to transfer experience gained at Saturn throughout GM, the company moved several Saturn executives to other divisions. GM President and CEO Jack Smith, who succeeded Robert Stempel in 1992 after the latter's controversial ouster, talked about "Saturnizing" all of GM. Yet, as Donald Ephlin noted, "One of the things GM does very poorly is spread improvements across the system."

In 1993 Saturn was set to sell 200,000 cars, garnering 1.4 percent of the market. Commentators noted that while the cars themselves were not exceptional, the company was truly excelling at advertising and customer satisfaction, giving the Saturn mystique considerable weight. In June 1994, for example 44,000 Saturn owners and their families drove their Saturns to Spring Hill for a three-day "homecoming," a feel-good event in which the relationships between dealer and customers were further cemented. Saturn's sales had fallen, however, from a peak of 25,000 per month the year before to 15,000 per month in 1994. The drop was attributed to several factors. Despite building a reputation for having happy customers, Saturn was presented with several challenges in 1994. GM, which was short of cash, cut back on Saturn's advertising budget, which was halved; plans to expand the dealer network were put on hold, with 285 dealers serving only about 60 percent of the U.S. market; product enhancements, including a facelift and passenger airbags, were delayed from the 1994 to the 1995 model year; and modifications that would decrease engine noise were delayed until 1996. The car was also facing more formidable competition from domestic rivals, including the Dodge and Plymouth Neon. Michael Bennett, president of UAW Local 1853 in Spring Hill, stated that if Saturn didn't build a second assembly plant soon, the company was doomed to extinction much like the American Motors Corp., which was too small to survive. While the Spring Hill plant was capable of producing 325,000 cars a year, Bennett maintained that Saturn needed 500,000 to make a profit. Profitability was impossible for outsiders to assess, as GM refused to release financial data on the company.

In 1995 Saturn reached two important milestones, as its millionth vehicle rolled off the line after ten years of production. Reports indicated that the company planned to add a larger sedan to its offerings, to be built at a plant in Wilmington, Delaware, that was otherwise scheduled for closing. While this was good news for the line, other GM divisions were concerned that expansion by Saturn would cannibalize their own sales. By May, sales of the original line were up 17.5 percent for the year, in a segment that was down 14.4 percent overall. However, officials were concerned about the effects of Saturn's limited product line as the company's target market, the baby boom generation, grew older and became interested in trading up. For their part, critics continued to complain about the Saturn's dull styling and engine noise.

Nevertheless, the experiment continued, as Saturn took the battle for small-car dominance to its most formidable competitors' home turf, appointing six distributors in Japan in 1996. Keith Wicks, general director of Saturn Japan, stated, "We are convinced the high quality of Saturn cars, combined with friendly customer treatment and service at our Saturn retailer, will make a difference even for very discerning Japanese consumers." The right-hand drive vehicles were to be available in ten to 15 showrooms when sales began in 1997. Sales remained strong at home: president Don Hudler stated at mid-year that if the company could produce them, Saturn could sell about 50,000 more cars a year, a number that would generate about $600 million in revenue. In August General Motors confirmed that it would build a midsize Saturn in Wilmington. The car would be based on the same platform as the Vectra, a European offering from GM.

Noting that the car would be built at an existing GM facility, some observers took the decision as a sign that GM was serious not only about investing in Saturn's success, but also about spreading Saturn's accomplishments beyond Spring Hill, to the rest of the company. Drew Winter of *Ward's Auto World* wrote: "From a business standpoint, or even according to Saturn's own mission statement, it probably is too soon to call Saturn an unqualified success. But as sales remain strong, details of a global strategy continue to leak out, and GM's overall customer satisfaction shows marked improvement, it sure doesn't look like a loser."

In July 1998 the UAW squelched its sanguine relationship with Saturn when the union authorized a strike at Saturn's Spring Hill plant. Workers were unhappy about a proposal to outsource the assembly of future Saturns. They were also dissatisfied by the low-yielding goal-based bonus plan and skeptical about GM's long-term commitment to the Saturn brand. Much of GM's marketing budget was being used to stoke the popularity of GM's sports utility vehicles. The UAW only authorized the strike; it was never executed. Both parties resolved their differences by early September. At the year's end, Saturn's president Hudler was transferred to a new Saturn retailing unit. Hudler's vacancy was filled by Cynthia Trudell, who had served as president over GM's IBC Vehicles facility in the United Kingdom.

EXPANDING THE PRODUCT LINE: 1999 AND BEYOND

When Saturn finally did release a new vehicle in 1999 it was the ill-fated L-series, a midsize sedan designed to compete with the Toyota Camry and Honda Accord. The car was built at GM's Wilmington, Delaware, plant. After it was redesigned the L-series was renamed the L-300, and Saturn projected that it would sell 200,000 units a year. In reality, sales peaked at 98,000 units in 2001. In 2002 the L-300 was only ranked 19th out of 25 in a quality survey of midsize sedans conducted by J. D. Power & Associates Inc.

More new models followed. The Saturn Ion was released in 2000 to replace the S-series. Sales for the Ion were less than originally projected. Branching out from the small and midsize automobile market, Saturn released a gas-conscious SUV titled the Vue in March 2002. The Vue's 24 mpg gas mileage was achieved by using a system of pulleys instead of gears, keeping the SUV true to Saturn's alternative-car image. The Vue was criticized by automotive analysts for lacking style and entering the SUV market too late, but demand for the Vue steadily increased. Sales were up 6 percent in 2004 over 2003. Unimpressed, industry analysts predicted that the Saturn brand, which had cost GM billions, was nearing an end. Saturn's best year was 1994 when it sold 286,003 units of the S-series.

In 2004 GM executives decided that if Saturn was going to be profitable, they needed to shake up Saturn's infrastructure. To reduce manufacturing costs, future Saturn models would be designed to use parts shared by other GM divisions. Saturn's rewards program was also discontinued. Workers received a $3,000 bonus in 2004, and instead of rewarding employees when the company accomplished certain goals, the employees were told what their exact pay would be for the following two years. GM then assumed more control over Saturn's upper management.

In late 2004 the production of the unsuccessful L-300 ended. GM then promised to spend $3 billion producing new Saturn models. "You can say that we let the [Saturn] product get too long in the tooth, but I'm optimistic, confident, the new Saturn products will be very well received," Gary Cowger, GM's president of North American operations, said that year in *The Globe and Mail*. In late 2004 Saturn released its first minivan, called the Relay. Saturn then unveiled a convertible roadster, the Saturn Sky, at the 2005 Detroit Auto Show. Designed at GM's Advanced Design Studio in the United Kingdom, the wide-based Sky was one of the first Saturns widely praised for its styling. The Saturn Aura, a midsize sedan that was designed to replace the L-300, was also unveiled at the auto show. Neither the Sky nor the Aura were distributed until 2006. Favorable reviews about Saturn's new additions fanned excitement about the brand's resurrection throughout GM. In 2005 Saturn sold 214,000 vehicles, an improvement over previous years. Also in 2006, Saturn revealed hybrid versions of the Vue and a larger SUV called the Outlook to be available in 2007. Although Saturn still was not performing up to past expectations, and the auto industry in general was faced with enormous economic challenges, GM believed Saturn definitely had a future.

Mary-Sophia Smith
Updated, Paula Kepos; Kevin Teague

PRINCIPAL COMPETITORS

Ford Motor Company; Toyota Motor Corporation; DaimlerChrysler AG; Honda Motor Co., Ltd.; Kia Motors Corporation; Mazda Motor Corporation; Nissan Motor Co., Ltd.; Volkswagen AG.

FURTHER READING

Aaker, David A., "Building a Brand: The Saturn Story," *California Management Review,* Winter 1994.

Booth, David, "Saturn Soars to a Higher Orbit," *National Post,* April 28, 2006, p. DT2.

Butler, Lacrisha, "Sasser Praises Saturn Work," *Tennessean,* Nashville, October 7, 1992.

DeMott, John S., "Saturn Makes Its Debut at GM," *Time,* January 21, 1985.

"First Month Brings 100 Saturn Sales in Japan," *New York Times,* May 8, 1997.

Gilbert, Stuart C., "Observations on the Saturn Project: Site Selection, Financia," *Economic Development Review,* Fall 1994.

Gruley, Bryan, and Ann M. Job, "Saturn Sets Off 'Civil War'," *Detroit News,* January 27, 1985.

Haig, Simonian, "GM Pins Hopes on the Saturn Concept: The U.S. Car Maker Plans to Widen the Scope of Its Innovative Subsidiary," *Financial Times,* August 17, 1996.

——, "Saturn Takes on Japan's Market for Small Cars," *Financial Times,* July 9, 1996.

Higgins, James V., "Saturn's Revolution: How GM Set the Course to Next Century," *Detroit News,* January 13, 1985.

Klayman, Ben, "GM Hourly Workers Authorize Saturn Strike." *Reuters News,* July 19, 1998.

Lippert, John, and Greg Gardner, "Saturn Needs to Expand to Survive, Says United Auto Workers Union," *Knight-Ridder/Tribune Business News,* January 10, 1994.

McGrory, Mary, "Saturn Gives U.S. Autos Some Get-Up-And-Go," *Tennessean,* December 1, 1992.

"Saturn Beats Benz, Acura in Survey," *Flint Journal,* June 30, 1992.

"Saturn: GM's Final Frontier," *Automobile Quarterly,* Fall 1992.

"Saturn Names President From GM British Subsidiary," *Cleveland Plain Dealer,* December 15, 1998, p. 1C.

Serafin, Raymond, "The Saturn Story: How Saturn Became One of the Most Successful Brands in Marketing History," *Advertising Age,* November 16, 1992.

Taylor, Alex, "Blah Car, Bad Book—In the Rings of Saturn by Joe Sherman," *Fortune,* November 29, 1993.

Vaughan, Michael, "We're On The Comeback Trail," *Globe and Mail,* April 13, 2006, p. G2.

Welch, David, "Can Saturn Get Off The Ground Again?" *Business Week,* October 14, 2002, p. 79.

White, John R., "General Motors Should Build Everything As Well As It Builds Its Saturns," *Boston Globe,* November 15, 1992.

White, Joseph B., and Melinda Grenier Guiles, "Rough Launch: GM's Plan for Saturn, to Beat Small Imports, Trails Original Goals," *Wall Street Journal,* July 7, 1990.

Whiteside, David, "How GM's Saturn Could Run Rings Around Old Style Carmakers," *Business Week,* January 28, 1985.

Winter, Drew, "Saturn Turns 10," *Ward's Auto World,* July 1995.

Woodruff, David, "Saturn: GM Finally Has a Real Winner, but Success Is Bringing a Fresh Batch of Problems," *Business Week,* August 17, 1992.

——, "Saturn: May We Help You Kick the Tires?" *Business Week,* August 3, 1992.

Scott Fetzer Company

28800 Clemens Road
Westlake, Ohio 44145
U.S.A.
Telephone: (440) 892-3000
Fax: (440) 892-3060
Web site: http://www.berkshirehathaway.com/subs/
scotfetz.html

Wholly Owned Subsidiary of Berkshire Hathaway Inc.
Incorporated: 1914 as The Scott & Fetzer Machine
    Company
Employees: 4,889
Sales: $1 billion (2004 est.)
NAIC: 551112 Offices of Other Holding Companies

■ ■ ■

Scott Fetzer Company is a holding company for a variety
of companies engaged in providing industrial and commercial products, perhaps the best known of which are
World Book encyclopedias and Kirby vacuum cleaners.
Its Campbell Hausfeld subsidiary makes air compressors
and other power tools. Vacuum cleaners were the
company's sole mainstay until it went on an acquisition
spree in the 1960s and emerged with 31 businesses. A
new CEO later trimmed Scott Fetzer back to concentrate
on some core products. Conglomerate Berkshire Hathaway acquired the company in 1986, and its earnings
have been steady since then.

ORIGINS

Scott Fetzer was founded in a barn in 1914 as The Scott
& Fetzer Machine Company, a joint effort of George H.
Scott and Carl S. Fetzer, who would go on to produce
automotive parts. Together, the men built a machinist
shop producing tools and dies that became known for
their precision. During World War I, the Cleveland-
based Scott & Fetzer manufactured flare pistols.
Overseeing that production was a young entrepreneur
named Jim Kirby, who showed Scott and Fetzer his
designs for a vacuum system. They agreed to manufacture
the Kirby Vacuette, a non-electric sweeper. Moreover,
their company, then known simply as Scott & Fetzer,
became involved in the marketing of the product,
pioneering the concept of the door-to-door sales force
that provided in-home demonstrations. In 1925, Scott
& Fetzer produced for Kirby the Vacuette Electric, which
had a removable handle and nozzle attachment. Ten
years later, Scott & Fetzer were still working with Kirby
and introduced the Kirby Model C vacuum.

The vacuum cleaner was the company's staple for
the next 40 years. In the 1960s, Scott & Fetzer began
diversifying its interests to include a variety of businesses, including chain saw and trailer hitch
manufacturers. In 1967, the company purchased
manufacturer FRANCE, which produced neon
transformers for lighted signs. In 1969, the company
acquired Meriam Instruments which made gauges and
other instruments to measure pressure, calibration, and
flow.

Ralph E. Schey, a Harvard business school graduate,
became president of the company in 1974. Schey was a

KEY DATES

1914: The Scott & Fetzer Machine Company, a manufacturer of parts and tools, incorporates.
1925: Scott Fetzer releases the Kirby Scott & Fetzer Sanitation System.
1964: An acquisition spree begins.
1974: Ralph E. Schey becomes president and begins scaling back on Scott Fetzer's holdings.
1978: Scott Fetzer purchases World Book from Field Enterprises.
1984: World Book sales staff is increased 50 percent.
1986: Berkshire Hathaway purchases Scott Fetzer for an estimated $320 million.
1990: Scott Fetzer releases the first World Book available on CD-ROM.
1998: World Book launches its World Book Online Reference Center.
2000: CEO Schey retires and is replaced by Kenneth J. Semelsberger.

noted venture capitalist who quickly applied himself to trimming and restructuring the company. The company did make one acquisition during this time. Carefree of Colorado, a maker of awnings, joined Scott Fetzer in 1974. By 1976, Schey also held the posts of chairman and chief executive officer at Scott Fetzer. Within four years, Schey reduced Scott Fetzer from 31 to 20 divisions. He concentrated the remaining divisions in brand name goods for consumer markets, based upon his belief that such goods were more recession-proof. In addition, the company's senior managers at that time were primarily marketers rather than manufacturers, and this goal suited their strengths.

Scott Fetzer's new direction was the home improvement market. Schey's first large acquisition was Wayne Home Equipment, a maker of oil and gas burners and pumps, which it purchased in 1978. As a subsidiary of Scott Fetzer, Wayne went from supplying manufacturers to becoming a retail competitor, issuing branded products into mass merchandise stores. By the mid-1980s, Wayne was forming a new operating group—known as Environmental Products & Services—to sell a broad line of air- and water-treatment products, as well as heating, cooling, and home-security products.

While these changes were taking place, Schey was also working on expanding the direct sales arm of Scott Fetzer. The retail arena was experiencing fluctuations at

the time due to rising overhead costs, which led to clerk cutbacks, and an increase in double-income households, which gave consumers less time to shop. Direct selling, also known as door-to-door, avoided both of these obstacles. For $50 million, Schey purchased World Book from Field Enterprises in 1978. At the time, World Book was the market leader in direct sales. The company came with a profitable mail-order business in books and various consumer goods. Encyclopedia buyers proved to be ideal mail-order customers: they had already been found credit worthy—as most encyclopedias were purchased on credit—and were willing to receive products through the mail. World Book's only ostensible competitor was Encyclopaedia Britannica.

After the purchase, Schey spent two years revising World Book by selling off the Japanese division and trimming domestic operations in much the same way as he had Scott Fetzer. Preschool and elementary school lines were expanded so that customers could start buying sooner and then trade up into other sets of encyclopedias as their children grew older. By 1984, World Book had more than 30,000 sales representatives. Scott Fetzer's other prime product, Kirby vacuum cleaners, was also sold door-to-door by dealers who bought the machines for cash. As these sales representatives worked strictly on commission, Scott Fetzer's profit margins grew plump enough to attract attention.

As the sales force of World Book was reorganized in 1981, Scott Fetzer also revised its traditional selling strategies. Instead of attaching salaries only to sales, sales managers were given greater responsibility for expenses and profits. Recruiting, training, motivational, and compensation strategies were all updated, and the sales force was increased by 50 percent in 1984. Around the same time, other direct-selling giants, such as Avon and Mary Kay Cosmetics, were unable to get the number of sales representatives they needed. Direct selling was developed into a science by Scott Fetzer during the early 1980s. Sales people no longer wandered through neighborhoods, knocking on doors and applying charm to random homemakers. Sales representatives now contacted potential buyers first by phone, at fairs, or in shopping malls, and set up appointments. From there, the sales challenges were the same, but Kirby sales representatives in the 1980s boasted one sale out of every three pitches—a good record for a purchase that then ran up to $900, with accessories.

Just as World Book had undergone reconstruction, Kirby too was overhauled between 1977 and 1981. A dramatic change came in 1980, when Kirby eliminated half of its distributors. For the most part, these distributors were independent contractors who recruited their own sales staffs. At the time, a practice called bojacking was in vogue. Bojacking by distributors referred to the practice of buying vacuums from Kirby and jacking up the price, then reselling them with a price tag that undercut Kirby salesmen. This prompted Scott Fetzer to write a new dealer agreement that mandated that Kirby vacuum cleaners be sold in the home. The roughly 700 distributors who disagreed with this new policy were eventually dismissed. Between 1971 and 1981, unit sales plunged by one-third. The company, instead of panicking, concentrated on training its key salespeople to run their own dealerships. This strategy inspired other direct sellers to turn their attention to training as a way to increase productivity.

It also culled compliments from competitors. And it worked. Direct sales traditionally pepped up when the economy dragged, with revenues reflecting the number of available representatives rather than market size. A slowed economy meant cutbacks, which translated to more people looking for work such as direct selling. The sales force thinned as the company recovered. This was not the case, though, during the down-cycle of the late 1970s and early 1980s. Those who usually entered direct sales to help meet family bills went looking for part-time company work instead. The sales force dipped during this time, and when the recovery arrived, there were even fewer candidates. Avon and Mary Kay Cosmetics were especially bruised by this trend; in fact, Avon had to give up on its goal for an increased sales force. Scott Fetzer had already streamlined its sales force and unleashed the highly trained group on consumers. It was so successful that by the mid-1980s, World Book and Kirby vacuum cleaners accounted for more than half the company's sales and operating profits, while direct sales titans like Avon and Mary Kay were wobbling.

CHANGE OF OWNERSHIP IN 1986

Up to this point, Scott Fetzer was prospering rather quietly. In the four quarters leading up to December 1984, sales had risen 17 percent and earnings were up 45 percent. In the takeover craze of the 1980s, however, Scott Fetzer could not go unnoticed. Financier Ivan Boesky began accumulating shares of the company before the spring of 1984, when Schey announced a plan by a group he led to take the company private in a leveraged buyout. Kelso & Company, a New York investment firm, entered the fray with a $61-a-share bid. Kelso's specialty was corporate buyouts through employee stock ownership plans (ESOP). An ESOP would have taken over up to 60 percent of the company within five years, had Kelso's deal gone through. The bid was raised to $62 a share in January 1985, but ultimately the sale was made to Berkshire Hathaway for roughly $320 million in early 1986.

Berkshire was an Omaha-based holding company managed by CEO and part-owner Warren E. Buffett. Buffett became something of a hero in investor circles, with a good record of finding companies whose stock prices did not reflect their intrinsic worth. Using this for a guide, Berkshire acquired interests as diverse as insurance, publishing, candy, and furniture. At the time of the sale, Scott Fetzer was considered well-managed and a good earner, two of Buffett's favorite green lights for a purchase. Berkshire Hathaway specifically sought companies with consistent earnings that it would not have to micromanage, in industries that were not so technical that board members could not comprehend the business.

Scott Fetzer, with 17 businesses at the time, had sales of about $700 million. In addition to World Book, which then accounted for about 40 percent of Scott Fetzer's sales, other businesses included Kirby, Campbell Hausfeld air compressors, and Wayne burners and water pumps. World Book was then selling more sets of encyclopedias in the United States than its four largest competitors combined. After the ESOP plan was scuttled, Buffett wrote to Ralph Schey saying he admired the company's record. Just a week after their first dinner together, the acquisition contract had been signed.

In 1986, World Book's unit volume increased for the fourth consecutive year. Encyclopedia sales were up 45 percent over 1982. The Childcraft unit sales were also growing significantly. Success was in part attributed to good prices and editing and a sales force that was strongly identified as educators. More than half of the active sales force in the mid-1980s were teachers and another 5 percent were librarians. Kirby sales were also strong, with unit sales worldwide growing 33 percent between 1982 and 1986. In Kirby's case, the product was more expensive than most competing cleaners, but it was also known for its longevity. Some homes boasted 35-year-old Kirbys still on duty. Campbell Hausfeld, Scott Fetzer's largest unit, was the nation's leading producer of small and medium-sized air compressors. Its earnings more than doubled in 1986.

Pre-tax earnings for Scott Fetzer rose 10 percent in 1987. At the close of that year, World Book introduced its most extensively revised edition since 1962. The number of color photos had nearly doubled, more than 6,000 articles were revised, and these changes helped unit sales to increase for the fifth year in a row. The company's export business was particularly strong in 1988, when World Book became available in the Soviet Union. World Book had begun a costly decentralization into four locations in anticipation of having to leave its Chicago Merchandise Mart location. At the same time, Kirby's overseas sales more than doubled in two years.

DIGITAL AGE

If Scott Fetzer had been an independent company, it would have ranked close to the top of the *Fortune* 500 in 1990 in terms of return on equity. Despite costs of moving and a small decrease in unit volume, World Book earnings improved. A new Kirby vacuum cleaner was introduced and did very well. However, earnings overall for Kirby did not grow as quickly as sales because of start-up and learning curve costs for the new product. Northland, a division of Scott Fetzer based in Watertown, New York, also kept the company tradition of quiet excellence. It won a design award in 1990 for a redesigned bypass cover that cut production costs by up to $8,000 annually, while producing a more consistent product. International business remained strong, with another 20 percent sales gain in 1990. Campbell Hausfeld had record sales of $109 million that same year, most of which came from products introduced within the past five years.

In 1991, pre-tax earnings declined for World Book and the rest of Scott Fetzer, except Kirby. The following year, Kirby remained steady while World Book and the rest of Scott Fetzer's units increased again. All units again increased earnings in 1993. From the time of its purchase by Berkshire Hathaway in 1986, Scott Fetzer had consistently increased its earnings while reducing its investment in both inventory and fixed assets—using minor amounts of borrowed money outside of its finance subsidiary. It seemed healthy indeed, and Berkshire's continued parenting was proof.

In 1990 Scott Fetzer released the first version of its 22-volume World Book on CD-ROM. In 1992 executives from World Book also began a worldwide tour to promote World Book's new international edition. An estimated $5 million was used to convert the World Book's spelling into British English and expand the book's subject matter, making sure to include more articles about countries where English was not the primary language. The new World Book was marketed to non-Western countries such India, Singapore, the Philippines, and Egypt.

As the technology industry blossomed in the late 1990s, sales for the printed World Book began declining. "I suppose the biggest challenge was arranging for the survival of the company in the mid-'90s," Dom Miccolis, vice-president of World Book, said in the *Chicago Daily Herald*. He noted, "It became a different business." As the information medium transitioned from printed paper to electronic media, the cumbersome 22-volume *World Book* became an increasingly difficult sale for World Book representatives. Sound, video, and images were being added to the CD-ROM versions of *World Book*. For instance, a CD-ROM article about Wolfgang Amadeus Mozart also included sound bites from several of the composer's symphonies.

In 1998 World Book launched its World Book On-line Reference Center, a web site that allowed subscribers to access every *World Book* published since 1922, along with extra articles that had never been published. Moving further into the electronic realm, in 1999 World Book entered into an agreement with the American Education Corporation, the creators of the A+dvanced Learning System. The agreement integrated the A+dvanced Learning System software with World Book's electronic content. Teachers could use the tool to monitor and control their students' learning processes. The final product was sold to U.S. and Puerto Rican schools.

NEW MILLENNIUM

On December 31, 2000, Scott Fetzer's CEO and chairman, 76-year-old Ralph E. Schey, retired. Schey was succeeded by Kenneth J. Semelsberger, who had worked closely with Schey as the chief financial officer, group vice-president, and division president for Scott Fetzer.

As the U.S. economy slumped after the September 11, 2001, terrorist attacks on the United States, Kirby distributors were able to be more selective about whom they hired as their door-to-door sales representatives. Despite a rash of charges that the sales reps hired by Kirby's distributors were targeting the poor, Kirby continued selling only to its select distributors. Direct selling remained a lucrative strategy in the new millennium. According to the Direct Selling Association, in 2002 the sales for the direct sales industry were posted at $28.7 billion, a significant increase over the $15 billion posted in 1993.

One of Scott Fetzer's smaller companies, Northland, laid off several of its workers in 2002. The New York-based company designed AC and DC electric motors, which were then manufactured in Juarez, Mexico. "The business level wouldn't support the employment we had at that time," Scott Wakeman, the company's general manager, told the *Watertown Daily Times*. "We don't see this as a permanent situation," he said. Northland management told the newspaper that they hoped to rehire the employees after the company's profits improved.

In the new millennium, World Book shifted its focus further away from selling printed 22-volume sets. Instead it sold electronic versions of *World Book* to schools and libraries. World Book formed a partnership with America Online Inc. (AOL) to make *World Book* a reference source for AOL's English and Latino web sites. *World Book's* printed set was still the best-selling printed encyclopedia in 2004, but it was World Book's transition to CD-ROM and the Internet that helped the company survive. In 2004 World Book posted the highest profit rate that the company had reported since 1989, according to *Chicago Daily Herald*. Scott Fetzer's performance validated Warren Buffet's reasons for buying the company. In the first 13 years Berkshire Hathaway owned Scott Fetzer, it netted more than $1 billion for the new owners.

Carol I. Keeley
Updated, Kevin Teague

PRINCIPAL SUBSIDIARIES

The Kirby Company; World Book Inc.; Campbell Hausfeld; Carefree of Colorado; Cleveland Wood Products; Douglas Products; ECM; France; Halex; Kingston; Meriam Instrument; Northland; Powerwinch; Quikut; ScottCare; Scot Laboratories; Stahl; United Consumer Financial Services; Wayne Home Combustion Systems; Wayne Water Systems; Western Enterprises; Western Plastics.

PRINCIPAL COMPETITORS

Electrolux AB; Danaher Corporation; Whirlpool Corporation; Black and Decker Corporation.

FURTHER READING

Bianco, Anthony, "The Warren Buffet You Don't Know," *Business Week*, July 5, 1999, p. 54.

Cahill, Joseph B., "Here's The Pitch," *Wall Street Journal*, October 4, 1999, p. A1.

Dorr, Robert, "Critics Charge Omaha, Neb., Firm's Vacuum Seller with Pressure Tactics," *KRTBN Knight-Ridder Tribune Business News*, October 12, 1999.

Gordon, Evelyn, "Encyclopedia Salesmen Knock At Nation's Door During Int'l Tour," *Jerusalem Post*, February 25, 1992, p. 10.

Hight, Bruce, "Kirby Found Liable For Independent Contractor," *Austin American-Statesman*, January 1, 1999, p. D1.

Rasmussen, Jim, "Taking the Long View," *Omaha World-Herald*, July 31, 1999, p. 51.

"Mastering the Process," *Chief Executive*, May 1991, p. 46.

"Personality Clashes," *Development Journal*, September 1989, p. 17.

"A Sale for Scott Fetzer," *Fortune*, January 7, 1985, p. 11.

Saporito, Bill, "A Door-to-Door Bell Ringer," *Fortune*, December 10, 1984, pp. 83-88.

"Scott Fetzer Inc.," *Insiders' Chronicle*, September 30, 1985, p. 2.

"Vacuum-Cleaner Motor Now 84 Percent Quieter," *Appliance Manufacturer*, December 1990, p. 35.

Skipton Building Society

The Bailey
Skipton, North Yorkshire BD23 1DN
United Kingdom
Telephone: (44) 01756 705000
Fax: (44) 01756 705743
Web site: http://www.skipton.co.uk

Private Company
Incorporated: 1853
Employees: 5,000
Total Assets: £9.2 billion ($13.14 billion) (2005)
NAIC: 522292 Real Estate Credit; 522120 Savings
  Institutions; 551112 Offices of Other Holding
  Companies

■ ■ ■

Skipton Building Society is the United Kingdom's seventh-largest building society, the British equivalent of a U.S. savings and loan association. The group operates nearly 80 branches across the country and boasts a membership of some 600,000. In 2005, the mutual posted total assets of £9.2 billion ($13 billion).

Skipton has avoided pressure to de-mutualize, while also maintaining its competitiveness in the British home mortgage and savings markets, by adopting a strategy based on diversifying its range of financial services. As such, the building society has created or acquired a group of more than 13 subsidiaries, adding specialist mortgages, personal loans, wealth management and related services for its customers. The company's consumer-oriented subsidiaries include the Connells estate agency group,

which operates through 150 branches throughout much of England, independent financial adviser Pearson Jones, and Direct Life & Pension Services, a low-cost life insurance provider. Yet a major part of Skipton's diversification program has been to develop a range of services for other building societies.

Group companies include Amber Home Loans, which provides specialist mortgage products to lenders; Pink Homes Loans, providing mortgage products to the intermediary market; Bailey Computer Services Ltd., a provider of computer system services to building societies; Baseline Capital, providing mortgage analysis and credit risk assessment services; the Skipton Information Group, including EuroDirect, GMAP and Callcredit, providing direct marketing, database marketing, market analysis, retail planning, territory planning, credit risk management, fraud prevention, credit referencing and scoring, and related services. Other subsidiaries include majority control of Mutual One Ltd., providing internal audit and other services to building societies; and software provider Jade Software Corporation. Home-grown businesses include Skipton Financial Services, Skipton Business Finance Limited, and the group's offshore deposit taking unit, Skipton Guernsey Ltd. Much of Skipton's diversification drive has been led by managing director John Goodfellow.

SKIPTON'S BUILDING SOCIETY IN THE MID-19TH CENTURY

The building society movement in the United Kingdom developed as a direct offshoot of the country's growing industrialization in the late 18th and early 19th centuries.

COMPANY PERSPECTIVES

At Skipton, we consider ourselves to be a strong and innovative provider in the mortgage and investment markets. But at a time of great competition, the Society has grown by acquiring subsidiary companies which has set us apart from our contemporaries. This group structure enables us to strengthen our position and build for the future—a prime goal in delivering real value to our members. Alongside the Society's core products of savings, mortgages (both residential and commercial) and general insurance, customers have access to other Skipton Group services, including specialist mortgage, personal loans, IHT advice and wealth management. The Skipton group is made up of a number of highly innovative and successful organisations which operate in the Financial Services sector or in support of that sector.

Building societies were originally created to provide direct funding for members building their own homes. By the mid-1800s, however, a new building society model had developed which provided funding to its members in the form of loans. These were then repaid, with interest, back into the pool.

The generation of interest on home loans in turn attracted the interest of investors seeking to place their savings. By the 1840s, building societies had begun accepting members who were not necessarily interested in building a home. This led to the creation of the first "permanent benefit" building societies, based on an idea proposed by James Henry James in 1845. The first permanent building society was established that year. Permanent building societies rapidly overtook the terminating societies as the focus of the movement; nonetheless, a number of terminating societies remained in existence in the late 20th century. The last terminating society was wound up only in 1980.

A major milestone for the permanent building society movement came in 1847, when Arthur Scratchley released his Treatise on Benefit Building Societies. This work not only provided the first written framework for permanent societies, but also provided tables for interest calculation and repayment schedules. The permanent societies quickly began developing new savings accounts and customer services, taking on aspects of the traditional banking industry. The popularity of the new model was such that by 1860, the United Kingdom counted more than 2,700 building societies, the vast majority of which were based on the permanent benefit model.

Among these new societies was the Skipton and District Permanent Benefit Building Society. Founded by George Kendall in 1853, the Skipton society distinguished itself from the outset. As reported by the *Craven Herald*, a Skipton-based newspaper founded during the same period, Skipton "differs from the old building societies, in this, that it is not established for the express purpose of building a certain street or row of houses, but what is much superior, it enables a man to build what he likes, where he likes, and as he likes; or, if a member prefers to buy a house, he can do so, and the Society, if they think the purchase a good one, will advance the money; and if he wishes neither to build, nor buy any buildings, he will receive four and a half per cent compound interest, calculated monthly, and can withdraw at any time on giving a month's notice; thus constituting an investment good in itself, and especially suitable for the weekly savings of the working classes."

Kendall's society quickly attracted members, boasting nearly 200 members and total deposits of more than £2,300 pounds after just one year. The Skipton society grew into one of the region's most prominent through the end of the century, and by the beginning of World War I, the society's total assets had topped £100,000. The mutual's growth had been aided by new legislation, and especially the Building Societies Acts of 1874 and 1894. The new legislation had reformed a number of dubious practices, such as balloting, that had exposed some societies to exploitation by gamblers, while also restricting societies to operating only within the mortgage and savings markets. As a result of the new legislation, the number of building societies shrunk dramatically, with just 1,700 left in operation at the start of World War I.

The number of building societies continued to decline through the 20th century; by the beginning of the next century, only slightly more than 60 societies remained in operation. These, however, had grown significantly in financial status. If, at the start of World War I, the total assets of the 1,700 building societies then in existence amounted to a small but respectable £76 million, by the turn of the next century, the 63 remaining building societies held total assets of more than £170 billion.

SURVIVING THE CONSOLIDATION DRIVE IN THE SIXTIES

Skipton became one of these survivors by maintaining its growth through the early decades of the 20th century.

KEY DATES

1853: The Skipton and District Permanent Benefit Building Society is founded by George Kendall.

1928: The name is shortened to Skipton Building Society.

1942: The organization merges with the Barnoldswick Building Society.

1947: Skipton opens its first branch office, in Harrogate.

1987: Total assets top £1 billion; Skipton launches a diversification strategy, establishing new financial services subsidiaries.

1990: Skipton acquires Mortgage Systems, the leading specialist processor of third-party mortgages in the United Kingdom.

1998: Skipton becomes a founding member and majority shareholder of the Mutual One outsourcing services group for the building society sector.

2001: Skipton acquires majority control of Direct Life and Pensions Services.

2005: The insurance and mortgage operations of Pink Home Loans and Direct Life and Pensions are combined into a new unit, Pink Home Loans Network.

In 1928, the society moved to new headquarters, on Skipton High Street. At the time of the move, the society changed its name, becoming simply Skipton Building Society. Skipton had also launched its expansion beyond the Skipton region. At the end of the 1920s, the society had begun providing services in London through an agency network. By the early 1930s, the society's total assets had topped £2 million.

The transformation of the building society into a smaller pool of far larger societies was given new impetus with the passage of the new Building Society Act of 1939. The new legislation set new mortgage guarantee standards and limited the range of services societies were allowed to provide. The next blow to the society movement came in the years following World War II. In the aftermath of the war and the necessity of reconstruction, the societies faced new competition from the nation's large, wealthy banks, which began competing heavily for the new mortgage market. Rising interest rates demanded by the British government in the early 1950s also cut into the building societies' margin of movement.

Skipton had by then already anticipated the growing drive toward consolidation of the building society movement. In 1942 the society merged with the Barnoldswick Building Society. By the end of the 1940s, Skipton also began to build its branch network, opening its first branch in Harrogate in 1947. By the time of its 100th anniversary, Skipton's total assets had topped £10 million.

Through the 1960s, Skipton continued to expand its branch network. Acquisitions and mergers formed a major part of the group's growth during this period, including mergers with building societies in Ribblesdale, Otley and Bury. In this way, Skipton emerged from the major consolidation of the building society as one of the largest remaining societies, with assets of more than £1 billion in the late 1980s.

DIVERSIFYING FOR THE NEW CENTURY

Skipton was faced with a choice in the late 1980s. In 1986, the British government transformed its financial sector by passing new legislation. As part of the deregulation of the industry, banks and other financial institutes were given new access to the home mortgage market, which had remained the traditional territory of the nation's building societies. The building societies, however, were given the right to "de-mutualize" by abandoning their mutual status through a public offering or by acquisition by another financial group. Over the next decade, many of the country's leading building societies, including Abbey National, completed the conversion process.

As a result of these changes, Skipton found itself under pressure from two fronts. On the one hand, the society faced increasing competition from a wider pool of rivals. On the other hand, the society's members, eager to take advantage of the "windfalls" being paid out to members of converting mutuals, began pressuring the society to de-mutualize as well.

Skipton resisted calls to convert the society's status. Instead, the building society adopted a new and rather novel strategy that called for the diversification of its activities into a variety of financial areas. A central part of the group's diversification drive targeted its emergence as a major provider of financial services to other members of the building society market. In support of this, Skipton set up two new subsidiaries in the late 1980s, Homeloan Management Ltd., which became the United Kingdom's second-largest provider of outsourced mortgage administration services, and Skipton Financial Services Ltd., which became one of the country's top 25 Independent Financial Advisers (IFA). In 1990, the society made its first acquisition, of Mortgage Systems, the leading specialist processor of third-party mortgages in the United Kingdom.

Acquisitions remained a key component in Skipton's diversification drive. In 1996, for example, Skipton acquired Connells Ltd., a leading estate agency operator with nearly 140 estate agencies across the country. The Connells acquisition also added a strong financial services component. In that year also, the society bought Dealwise, a brokerage business, for £3.6 million. Dealwise proved a wise investment for Skipton, and also provided a means of relieving the pressure from members seeking the society's conversion. In 1999, Skipton sold off Dealwise for more than £82, and quickly transferred much of the profit of that transaction in the form of a windfall payment to its members.

Skipton continued building its network into the 2000s. The bank took the lead in creating Mutual One, providing outsourcing services geared to the building society sector, in 1998. In 2000, the group acquired control of Pink Home Loans, one of the few British mortgage "packaging" specialists. The following year, Skipton bought up majority control of Direct Life and Pensions Services, boosting its IFA services operations. In 2005, Skipton combined the insurance and mortgage operations of Pink Home Loans and Direct Life and Pensions into a new unit, Pink Home Loans Network.

By the mid-2000s, Skipton had grown into the United Kingdom's seventh largest building society, with total assets of more than £9 billion. The society operated through a national network of 80 offices, and a diversified financial network of 16 subsidiaries. As it turned toward the second half of the decade, Skipton reaffirmed its commitment to maintaining its mutual status—a commitment strengthened by the continued success of the society's diversification strategy.

M. L. Cohen

PRINCIPAL SUBSIDIARIES

Amber Homeloans Ltd.; Amber Select Ltd.; Baseline Capital Ltd.; Callcredit plc; Connells Ltd.; Connells Relocation Services Ltd.; Connells Survey & Valuation Ltd.; Connell Financial Services Ltd.; Conveyancing Direct Ltd.; EuroDirect Database Marketing Ltd.; GMAP Ltd.; Homeloan Management Ltd.; Jade Software Corporation Ltd.; Mutual One Ltd.; Savings Management Ltd.; Sequence (U.K.) Ltd.; Sharman Quinney Holdings Ltd.; Skipton Business Finance Ltd.; Skipton Financial Services Ltd.; Skipton Group Holdings Ltd.; Skipton Guernsey Ltd.; Skipton Information Group plc; Skipton Investments Ltd.; Skipton Premises Ltd.; The Private Health Partnership Ltd.

PRINCIPAL COMPETITORS

Abbey National plc; Nationwide Building Society; Cheltenham and Gloucester plc; Alliance and Leicester plc; Northern Rock plc; Bradford and Bingley plc; Aviva plc; Britannia Building Society; Bristol and West plc; Portman Building Society; Yorkshire Building Society; Kent Reliance Building Society; Coventry Building Society; Chelsea Building Society; Leeds Building Society; West Bromwich Building Society; Derbyshire Building Society; Cheshire Building Society.

FURTHER READING

Annesely, Christian, "Outsourcing Building Society Shifts IT Systems to Fellow Mutual," *Computer Weekly*, December 13, 2005, p. 8.

Bone, Alison, "John Goodfellow," *Money Marketing*, November 20, 2003, p. 4.

Brown-Humes, Christopher, "Skipton Boosted by Subsidiaries," *Financial Times*, February 23, 1999, p. 24.

Croft, Jane, "Investec Acquires Pounds 100m Mortgage Book from Skipton," *Financial Times*, March 20, 2006, p. 18.

Harris, Clay, "Skipton Always Stays Close to the Ground," *Financial Times*, August 11, 2004, p. 22.

Kay, William, "Credit Where It Is Due," *Independent*, January 26, 2002, p. 3.

Macintosh, James, "UK Skipton Hands Pounds 50m Back to Members," *Financial Times*, July 21, 2000, p. 26.

"Skipton Buys into Protection Specialist," *Money Marketing*, August 23, 2001, p. 7.

"Skipton Looks to FTSE 100," *Financial Adviser*, January 26, 2006.

"Skipton on Trail of IFA Acquisition," *Financial Adviser*, January 29, 2004.

"Skipton Ponders Return to Share Dealing," *Money Marketing*, May 5, 2005, p. 8.

"Skipton to Enter the CTF Market with Homeowners," *Financial Adviser*, January 6, 2005.

"Skipton Uniting Pink and Direct Life," *Financial Adviser*, December 8, 2005.

"Skipton Unveils a Top Flight Reshuffle," *Financial Adviser*, January 12, 2006.

"Step Up Bond from Skipton Guernsey," *International Money Marketing*, June 2004, p. 10.

"The Skipton Keeps the Punters Guessing," *Independent on Sunday*, August 24, 1997, p. 13.

Wright, Greg, "Boom Sees Skipton Soar to Record," *Yorkshire Post*, February 2, 2005.

Sobeys Inc.

115 King Street
Stellarton, Nova Scotia B0K 1S0
Canada
Telephone: (902) 752-8371
Fax: (902) 928-1671
Web site: http://www.sobeys.com

Public Company
Incorporated: 1946 as Sobeys Stores, Ltd.
Employees: 75,000
Sales: CAD 12.19 billion ($9.68 billion) (2005)
Stock Exchanges: Toronto
Ticker Symbol: SBY
NAIC: 422410 General Line Grocery Wholesalers; 445110 Supermarkets and Other Grocery (Except Convenience) Stores

■ ■ ■

Sobeys Inc. is one of Canada's top grocers. The company operates more than 1,300 stores under the IGA, Sobeys, IGA Express, and Price Chopper banners in all ten provinces. Sobeys also has an extensive wholesale distribution business in addition to its retail supermarkets. The acquisition of the Oshawa Group in 1998 tripled the company's size. Sobeys has become Canada's second largest food distribution business. Empire Company Limited, controlled by the Sobey family, owns 68 percent of Sobeys Inc.

ORIGINS

Sobeys Inc.'s story begins in 1907, when John William Sobey acquired a meat delivery business in the coal mining and railway town of Stellarton, Nova Scotia. In 1912, his brother Charles joined him and the two set up their first store, a two-story structure built from logs hewn at the family farm; the second floor served as a residence. The sales area measured 800 square feet. Charles left after a year to become a lumberjack in the Yukon. However, the business would continue to be family-driven throughout the rest of the century.

J.W. Sobey's son, Frank, is credited with expanding the butcher shop into a full-fledged grocery store in 1924; the younger Sobey was taken on as a partner within a couple of years. Frank Sobey was also mayor of Stellarton, and for a brief time owned an interest in a theater. By 1939, the Sobeys had a chain of six stores.

POST-WAR EXPANSION

The firm was incorporated as Sobeys Stores, Ltd. on April 18, 1946. The eight shops, one warehouse, and one bakery of neighboring rival Barkers Stores, Ltd. was acquired soon after for about CAD 159,000.

Around this time, Frank Sobey also acquired Empire Company Ltd., which had some land he had been interested in for his stores. Empire, named after a theater it had owned, would become the family's investment company.

In August 1947, Frank Sobey opened the first modern supermarket in Pictou County, Nova Scotia, which was originally called "Sobey's Wholesale

COMPANY PERSPECTIVES

At Sobeys Inc., our focus is clear and steadfast—we are focused on food, driven by our fresh expertise, supported by superior customer service—in the right-sized, right format stores for each individual market we serve. Our passion for food—supported and enabled by processes and tools that engage our people to get the job done well—sets us apart in a highly competitive marketplace. Our customers see and feel the difference, and their growing patronage is driving our sales and earnings growth.

Groceteria." The format, developed in the United States in the 1930s, had spread to Canada through the Dominion and other chains. Unlike their predecessors, the stores were self-service and did not offer credit or delivery. What they did have was low prices.

According to his biography by Harry Bruce, Frank Sobey picked up the idea while touring America with his wife in 1940; his plans were delayed for the duration of the war. Sobey's competitors and even his father scoffed at the idea. However, it was an instant commercial success, drawing throngs of housewives to its opening in a pattern that would be repeated elsewhere. Sobey's original supermarket, Store Number 25, measured 6,150 square feet.

Sobeys expanded throughout eastern Canada in the 1950s and 1960s. The company had sales of CAD 8 million at 17 stores by 1956. In 1960, the giant Weston-Loblaw group bought a 40 percent share in the company for almost CAD 1 million, according to Harry Bruce's biography of Frank Sobey.

LAWTON'S ACQUIRED IN 1966

Sobeys parent Empire Co. acquired Lawton's Drug Stores Ltd. in 1966. Lawton's had been started as a single pharmacy in Halifax. In late 1996, Sobeys merged its management with Lawton's, which then had a few dozen branches in Atlantic Canada.

Sobeys' sales were nearly CAD 93 million in 1971. By this time, Frank Sobey's three sons, Bill, David, and Donald, had become involved in running the business or the Empire Inc. investment company.

Sobeys Stores Ltd. had sales of CAD 237 million in 1977. During the year, the family's Empire Company Ltd. launched a takeover attempt of M. Loeb, Ltd., a

diversified Ottawa food wholesaler four times the size of Sobeys. This started a bidding war which ended with control of Loeb going to the fast-rising Provigo Inc. of Quebec. Empire, the family's investment company, however, soon amassed a 25 percent holding in Provigo. In 1980, it bought back Weston-Loblaw's holding in Sobeys; a couple of years later, some of the Provigo shares were sold to Caisse de Dépôt et Placement du Québec, for a handsome profit.

Frank Sobey died in 1986, leaving Sobeys Inc. and Empire Co. in the hands of his three sons. By the late 1980s, Empire owned 100 grocery stores in Atlantic Canada (including its first Sobeys store in Ontario), as well as 56 Lawton's Drug stores, 26 shopping centers, 22 theaters, and other holdings, noted Toronto's *Financial Post*. Donald Sobey, the eldest son, liked to tell interviewers that the quality of management was a key to the group's investment choices. Empire was still operating from the same building where J.W. Sobey had set out as a butcher. Sales had passed CAD 500 million in 1983 and were more than CAD 1 billion in 1987.

OSHAWA ACQUIRED IN 1998

Sobeys executed an audacious takeover in 1998 that gave it national reach for the first time. It acquired The Oshawa Group Ltd., a grocery distributor based in Toronto, in a CAD 1.5 billion leveraged buyout. Oshawa was twice Sobey's size. It operated most of the IGA supermarkets in Canada. The purchase added more than 800 stores, making Sobeys Canada's second largest grocery chain after Lowlaw Cos. Ltd. Sobeys annual revenues lept to nearly CAD 10 billion. A new public entity, Sobeys Canada Inc., was created in the Oshawa purchase; this was soon renamed Sobeys Inc.

Oshawa had started 100 years earlier delivering fruit from a horse-drawn wagon. In 1949, Ray Wolfe acquired what was then known as Oshawa Wholesale. A couple of years later he brought Chicago's IGA grocery chain into Ottawa. Oshawa went public in 1957 and entered the retail trade in 1971. It had assets of about CAD 800 million and more than 100 food stores under the banners IGA Dutch Boy, and Food City by the time of Wolfe's death in 1990. After an aggressive expansion program in the mid-1990s, Oshawa underwent an extensive restructuring that did away with many non-food assets, such as drugs stores and a laundry business, right before its acquisition by Sobeys.

NEW LEADERSHIP IN 2000

William G. (Bill) McEwan, formerly with Great Atlantic and Pacific Tea Co. Inc. (A&P), was hired as Sobeys president and CEO in late 2000. When David Sobey,

---

KEY DATES

1907: J.W. Sobey forms a meat delivery service in Stellarton, Nova Scotia.
1946: The company is incorporated as Sobeys Stores, Ltd.
1947: Sobeys opens its first modern supermarket.
1966: Lawton's Drug Stores are acquired by Sobeys parent, Empire Co.
1983: Sobeys sales are more than CAD 500 million.
1987: Sales exceed CAD 1 billion.
1988: Sobeys enters the Ontario market.
1998: The acquisition of the Oshawa Group makes Sobeys the second largest food distributor in Canada.
2002: SERCA Foodservice sold to SYSCO Corporation.
2005: Sobeys begins to streamline store formats and private label brands.

---

outbid by Quebec's Metro Inc. The company shifted its expansion efforts into building new stores and upgrading existing ones.

Sales exceeded CAD 12 billion ($9.7 billion) in the 2005 fiscal year, rising 10 percent. The company had 75,000 employees at 1,314 stores scattered across Canada's ten provinces. These were supplied by 23 distribution centers. Eight million Canadian households in more than 800 communities shopped Sobeys' various stores during the year. In 2005 the company streamlined its private label offerings under the Compliments brand and turned around its Western Canada business.

In 2006 Sobeys was converting stores into one of its five new formats. Its "smart retailing" strategy applied the *kanban*—or continuous replenishment concept of Japanese-style manufacturing—to its produce and bakery departments. Like other supermarket chains, it was preparing for Walmart to finally bring its Supercenters into the Canadian market, though officials did not appear overly worried.

Frederick C. Ingram

grandson of the company founder, retired as chairman in 2001, he was replaced by Sir Graham Day, who had previously led such eminent UK firms as British Aerospace, Rover Group, and Cadbury Schweppes.

In early 2002, Sobeys sold off its SERCA Foodservice business, which it had gained in the Oshawa purchase, to Houston's giant SYSCO Corporation. This allowed Sobeys to concentrate on its grocery business while paying down some of the CAD 1 billion debt from the Oshawa acquisition. The company was also maintaining readiness for other potential acquisitions.

Sobeys was whittling its more than 20 banners down to a handful of key shopping concepts: the full-service stores of Sobeys (and IGA Extra in Quebec); Sobeys Express convenience stores; smaller IGA stores; low-price Price Chopper outlets; and customized markets for rural areas. Sobeys avoided the trend towards ever-larger superstores, but was allowing the Bank of Montreal to set up branches in some of its supermarkets.

In 2004, the company paid CAD 65 million to buy Commisso's Food Markets Ltd., a small southern Ontario grocery chain, as well as Commisso's Grocery Distributors Ltd. (Another unit of Empire Co. was acquiring related properties holdings for CAD 42 million.) This added 15 stores, helping to bulk up Sobeys' involvement in Ontario, though it still had relatively few stores in metropolitan Toronto.

In 2005, Sobeys attempted to buy A&P Canada, which operated Dominion stores in Ontario, but was

PRINCIPAL DIVISIONS

Sobeys Atlantic; Sobeys Ontario; Sobeys Québec; Sobeys West.

PRINCIPAL COMPETITORS

Loblaw Cos. Ltd.; Metro Inc.

FURTHER READING

Anderson, Mark, "Subject: Sobeys Inc.," *National Post Business,* September 2003, pp. 30–32.

Beres, Glen A., "Oshawa's Expanding Agenda: Despite a Host of Challenges, Canada's No. 3 Food Distributor Is Honing a Strategy for Growth," *Supermarket News,* June 19, 1995, pp. 1ff.

Bruce, Harry, *Frank Sobey: the Man and the Empire,* Toronto, Ontario: MacMillan, 1985.

———, "The Grocery Kings from Stellarton," *Reader's Digest (Canadian),* January 1987, pp. 55ff.

———, "The Sobey Boys Meet the Man from Provigo," *Canadian Business,* November 1985, pp. 87ff.

"CEO/Company Interview: Douglas B. Stewart, Allan Rowe; Sobeys, Inc.," *Wall Street Transcript,* November 29, 1999.

"Corporate Parent in Midst of Transforming Business Model," *Chain Drug Review,* May 1, 2006, pp. 204f.

Gattuso, Greg, "Oshawa Group Returning to Its Food Roots," *Supermarket News,* June 1, 1998, p. 12.

Gibbens, Robert, "Sobeys Aim Well Beyond the Wildest Dreams; Royal Family: Takeover of Oshawa Would Put Them Second to Loblaw," *National Post* (Toronto), October 29, 1998, p. C8.

Henderson, Jennifer, "'People' Key to Sobeys' Empire," *Financial Post* (Toronto), Sec. 1, February 29, 1988, p. 7.

Kimber, Stephen, "Bag-Boy Calls," *Report on Business Magazine,* October 2003, pp. 67ff.

"Lawtons' Flourishes Under Sobeys' Wing," *Chain Drug Review,* April 26, 1999, p. 248.

McFarland, Janet, "Sobeys Quietly Empire-Building: Grocery Unit Makes Inroads in Ontario," *Financial Post* (Toronto), Sec. 1, December 4, 1993, p .8.

"Oshawa Chairman Ray Wolfe Dies at 72," *Supermarket News,* January 22, 1990, p. 4.

"Parent Company Fortifies Position in Canada," *Chain Drug Review,* April 28, 2003, p. 230.

Shaw, Hollie, "Sobeys Doesn't Need A&P, CEO Says: Reassures Investors in Wake of Loss to Metro in Bid War," *National Post's Financial Post & FP Investing* (Canada), September 21, 2005, p. FP7.

"Sobeys Connection a Boon for Lawtons," *Chain Drug Review,* October 14, 2002, pp. 66f.

Suhanic, Gigi, "Sobeys Pays $65M for Commisso Grocery Stores: They're Acquiring More Volume in the Ontario Market," *National Post's Financial Post & FP Investing* (Canada), December 4, 2003, p. FP3.

Zwiebach, Elliot, "Sobeys Goes National," *Supermarket News,* February 4, 2002, p. 12.

Spansion Inc.

—————•—————

915 DeGuigne Drive
Sunnyvale, California 94088
U.S.A.
Telephone: (408) 962-2500
Toll Free: (866) 772-6746
Web site: http://www.spansion.com

Public Company
Founded: 1993 as Fujitsu AMD Semiconductor Ltd.
Employees: 7,500
Sales: $2 billion (2005)
Stock Exchanges: NASDAQ
Ticker Symbol: SPSN
NAIC: 334413 Semiconductor and Related Device
   Manufacturing

■ ■ ■

Spansion Inc. is a Sunnyvale, California, manufacturer of Flash memory, which is used to store data in a number of electronic products, including wireless phones, personal digital assistants, automotive subsystems, and networking equipment. One of the fastest growing segments of the semiconductor industry, Flash memory is similar to DRAM found in personal computers. It is able to write and rewrite data, but Flash memory, which is more expensive than DRAM, has the added ability to store and retain information when the power supply for an electronic device is turned off. As the largest Flash memory company, Spansion concentrates on the integrated electronics market; its customers are the leading original manufacturers of automotive electronics,

consumer electronics, and handsets. Spansion is a public company listed on the NASDAQ.

FLASH TECHNOLOGY: LATE
CENTURY DEVELOPMENT

In 1992 "Negative Gate Erase" technology was introduced. This was the first way to maintain erase performance in an electronic device without the need for external power, thus setting the stage for Flash memory. A year later, two of the giants in the semiconductor industry, Advanced Micro Devices Inc. (better known as AMD) and Fujitsu Ltd., joined forces to create a joint manufacturing venture called Fujitsu AMD Seminconductor Limited (FASL), marrying AMD's Flash memory technology with Fujitsu's process technology and high-capacity manufacturing operations. FASL quickly became a leader in the field, responsible for a number of innovations. In 1996 the company introduced the industry's first 2.7-volt flash device, offering the lowest voltage to that point in the Flash market. A year later FASL took the technology a step further, bringing out the industry's first 1.8-volt Flash device. That same year, FASL was responsible for a breakthrough in the automotive electronics field when it unveiled the first Known Good Die (KGD) Flash memory. It was capable of operating under extreme conditions and temperatures as high as 145 degrees Celsius, an important factor when a device is incorporated into an engine or other automotive components where high temperatures are achieved. Another FASL technical achievement of 1997 was the introduction of the simultaneous read/write feature, which for the first time allowed for the reading of data

COMPANY PERSPECTIVES

Dedicated to enabling, storing and protecting digital content, Spansion is the largest company exclusively focused on Flash memory solutions and has one of the most diverse and comprehensive Flash product lines on the market.

while a Flash device was conducting program or erase operations. Simultaneous read/write became a standard for NOR Flash chips, earning *EDN Magazine's* "EDN Innovation of the Year." (NOR stood for the programming expression "not or." NOR chips could read data at high speed, yet were extremely accurate. They were ideal for running the software used in mobile phones and other devices. A second type of Flash memory, NAND—standing for "not and"—was better suited for digital cameras, MP3 players, and other electronic devices. In simple terms, NOR and NAND were two different ways computers searched data and connected the Flash memory cells. NOR chips offered better quality and faster speeds but were more expensive than NAND chips, which weren't as reliable but could store a lot of information at less expense. In a basic cell phone, for example, NOR chips contained key programming code while NAND chips were used for mass storage of less critical information, such as a user's favorite ring tone.

FASL continued to break new ground in the Flash memory industry in the final years of the 1990s. In 1998 the company unveiled the first page-mode flash device, which permitted the fast read speeds required in high-performance applications. A year later FASL took the technology a step further by creating the first burst-mode Flash device, offering even faster read speeds.

NEW CENTURY INNOVATIONS

FASL's breakthroughs continued with the start of the new century. In 2000 the company offered the first product to combine Flash and SRAM in a single chip. The Multi-Chip Product (MCP) was another key advance for the mobile handset market, allowing for smaller devices by delivering a complete memory subsystem in a single small chip. Then in 2001 FASL introduced MirrorBit technology, which led to the first fundamental change in non-volatile storage technology in the semiconductor industry in more than 20 years. It allowed for the storage of two bits per cell while maintaining the same level of performance. Another

FASL breakthrough in 2001 was the development of the first Flash memory device with a 32-bit data bus, resulting in extremely quick system throughput, which was especially useful in automotive applications and printers. The year was also noteworthy because of sagging Flash memory prices, which forced FASL to cut back production at some of its facilities. In 2002 FASL brought out advanced sector protection, providing an even greater level of protection against loss of data.

AMD and Fujitsu deepened their relationship and their commitment to the Flash memory market in March 2003 by establishing FASL LCC, a company that brought together the Flash memory operations of both parent corporations. AMD held a 60 percent controlling interest in the joint venture. AMD also contributed a recent acquisition, Coatue Corp., a startup company that had developed a way to use polymer technology to build arrays of nonvolatile memory cells. As a result, the technology was able to produce a memory chip that combined Flash memory's non-volatility and low power consumption with the speed of DRAM. This new class of polymer-based technologies, Coatue claimed, would be able to create memory chips that handle applications conventional memory chips could not accommodate, including solid-state video storage, instant-boot computers, and single-chip personal computers.

The new FASL would also begin to market its products under a new brand name: "Spansion." according to *ExtremeTech.com* in an article written at the time of the announcement, "By further separating itself from Fujitsu and AMD, the new company will be able to form industry alliances and take the necessary steps to compete in the cutthroat market for flash memory. ... At its inception, FASL LLC will represent the world's second-largest flash memory provider, behind Intel Corp. Although market researcher Semico Research expects flash dollar sales to overtake DRAM in 2004, driven by cell phones, PDAs, and the like, flash pricing has continued to decline, with a 30 percent drop in price per megabyte last year." Out of the gate, the new company, based in Sunnyvale, California (with another headquarters located in Tokyo), would be worth an estimated $2.5 billion. It enjoyed only limited independence, however. Although it maintained its own sales operation, FASL's parent companies would be its only distributors, with AMD given priority status in the Americas and Fujitsu in Europe. The parent companies split the Asian market.

FASL LLC was headed by Dr. Bertrand Cambou, who served as both president and chief executive officer. French-born, he held an engineering degree from Supelec, Paris, and a doctorate in electronics from Paris XI University. He was involved in the development of terminals for secure e-transactions while working at Ingenico, and then went on to Gemplus International SA, a Smart Card maker, where he became chief operating officer and co-president. Before taking charge of FASL, he joined AMD in 2002 to become group vice president of the Memory Division. He also had 15 U.S. patents to his credit.

The new FASL did not let up on product development. In 2003 it used second generation Mirror-Bit flash technology to introduce the industry's first 512-Megabit NOR Flash memory chip, the highest density NOR Flash device available in the market. A year later, in June 2004, FASL took the name Spansion LLC, and in the fall of that year announced a new kind of Flash memory chip that combined NOR and NAND architecture. The new ORNAND chips could serve both the NOR market for flash chips, lead by Intel and Spansion, and the fast-growing NAND market, dominated by Samsung and Toshiba. According to the *San Jose Mercury News,* "Spansion's new trick is to modify its NOR flash chips so that they can mimic the features and lower price of NAND flash. In doing so, the company's ORNAND flash chips could be used in either the NOR or the NAND markets." The hope was that Spansion chips would find their way into a greater number of cell phones, which as they grew more sophisticated, adding cameras and music capabilities, required greater data storage. Spansion offered developments on other fronts as well in 2004. It unveiled the 1.8-volt, 80 megahertz burst-mode Flash memory chip. Combining the lowest voltage of any 256-megabit Flash device on the market with two-bit-per-cell technology, it was ideally suited for wireless applications.

The final quarter of 2004 proved difficult for Spansion, which had to contend with price-cutting competition and as a result reported an operating loss of $39 million, much to the displeasure of AMD's CEO, Hector Ruiz. He told analysts the performance "makes me want to puke." He also made it clear that he was open to anything that would increase value to shareholders, a comment that most observers interpreted as a signal that

Spansion would either be sold or spun off. If so, Spansion would no longer be a drag on AMD's earnings, which reported a net loss of $17.4 million in the fourth quarter, and AMD would be in a better position to challenge its bitter rival, Intel, in the computer processor field. *Barron's* explained why Spansion was becoming such a nettlesome problem for AMD: "Spansion eats up lots of capital, and its main rival is Intel, which puts AMD in a strategically vulnerable spot. Since flash contributes a modest 7% of Intel's revenues, compared with 40% for AMD, should the urge strike, Intel can brutally slash prices. In that event, Intel may bleed a little, but AMD will hemorrhage massively. And when the money-losing Spansion needs more dough, AMD, as one of the joint-venture owners, has to pony up." *Barron's* also contended that if AMD separated itself from Spansion, "Intel may not feel the urge to compete as aggressively. In short, Spansion may be a more valuable business if AMD isn't a majority owner."

2005 IPO

Spansion reported a weak first quarter in 2005, as the Flash memory market continued to experience an oversupply of product and eroding prices, and sales were down 29 percent over the same period the previous year. Essentially, the die was cast for Spansion's future. AMD announced in April 2005 that it would spin off the unit in a public offering of stock. All through the summer and autumn of 2005, Spansion and its lead underwriters, Citigroup Inc. and Credit Suisse First Boston, prepared for the stock offering. In November the company was reorganized as Spansion Inc., and in the meantime company representatives met with potential investors at road show presentations. It proved to be a difficult sale, however. The company was hoping to price the stock between $16 to $18 per share, but as Spansion continued to post quarterly losses, investors grew increasingly wary. The company lowered its asking price to the $13 to $14 range, but on the eve of the December offering, the price to institutional investors fell to $12. In all the sale raised $506.4 million, a far cry from the $750 million figure once bandied about, but still the largest technology stock offering of the year. Given Spansion's string of quarterly losses, however, merely completing the offer was considered a success.

As Spansion entered 2006 as an independent company, its prospects began to improve. Flash chips remained a fast-growing market, and Intel had to reallocate some factory space in order to produce more chipsets because of a shortage. As a result, it produced fewer flash chips, presenting an opportunity for Spansion. Being in control of its own fate was also a major plus. "We're a much better capitalized company than before," Spansion executive Tom Eby told *Investor's Business Daily.* "And we eat, sleep and breathe flash."

Ed Dinger

PRINCIPAL COMPETITORS

Intel Corporation; Samsung Electronics Co., Ltd.; Toshiba Corporation.

FURTHER READING

"AMD Distances Itself From Flash Market," *ExtremeTech.com,* March 31, 2003.

Brammer, Rhonda, "On AMD's Menu: Eating Intel's Lunch," *Barron's,* September 26, 2005, p. 21.

Clark, Don, "Memory Race Turns in a Flash," *Wall Street Journal,* March 7, 2005, p. B3.

Detar, James, "AMD's Shareholders Chipped In to Buck Up Spinoff Spansion's IPO," *Investor's Business Daily,* January 9, 2006, p. A05.

Kharif, Olga and Cliff Edwards, "For AMD, a Thorny Dilemma," *Business Week Online,* June 23, 2005.

Ladendorf, Kirk, "AMD Considers a Future Without Flash," *Austin American-Statesman,* February 13, 2005, p. J1.

Takahashi, Dean, "Sunnyvale, Calif., Firm's Chip Could Shake Up Flash-Memory Market," *San Jose Mercury News,* November 9, 2004.

Specialist Computer Holdings Ltd.

James House
Warwick Road
Birmingham,
United Kingdom
Telephone: (44) 0121 766 7000
Fax: (44) 0121 773 3986
Web site: http://www.specialistcomputerholdings.com

Private Company
Incorporated: 1975 as Specialist Computer Recruitment
Employees: 6,000
Sales: £1.8 billion ($2.9 billion) (2004)
NAIC: 541512 Computer Systems Design Services;
423430 Computer and Computer Peripheral Equipment and Software Merchant Wholesalers

■ ■ ■

Specialty Computer Holdings Ltd. (SCH) claims the title of the world's fastest-growing, privately held IT services group. The Birmingham, England-based company is also one of the European markets top IT services providers, posting sales of nearly £2 billion ($3 billion) in the mid-2000s. The company has targeted a position among the global top 20 IT services companies by 2008. In support of this effort, SCH has established a presence in more than 65 countries worldwide. The company's operates through four primary divisions. SCC Enterprise Solutions provides IT infrastructure design and delivery services to large scale corporations, as well as government and public sector organizations. Global Services provides international IT integration services for internationally operating companies and organizations. Lifecycle develops and delivers network integration software and services. SCC Exchange was created at the end of 2004 in order to focus specifically on the needs of the mid-scale enterprise market. SCH has built up an impressive client list, including British Airways, IKK, Arkopharma, La Poste, Sodexho, RWE, Dusseldorf Airport, La Caixa, Thetis, Vodaphone, and the Dutch Foreign Office, among others. SCH remains 100 percent controlled by founder Peter Rigby, joined by his sons, James and Steven.

COMPUTER SERVICES STARTUP IN THE 1970S

The growing adoption of computer systems by Britain's corporations in the 1970s created a demand for qualified personnel. Peter Rigby recognized the opportunity to get in at the ground floor of what promised to become a major new services market, and in 1975 he founded his own company, Specialist Computer Recruitment (SCR). Rigby's company started out with just £3,000 of Rigby's own savings. Over the next decades, SCR expanded its range of recruitment expertise, providing personnel for a range of positions, including management, administrative, logistics, sales and training, as well as call center and telecom operations.

By the end of the decade, however, Rigby spotted a new opportunity, that of directly providing services to businesses seeking to outsource their computer-related functions. In 1980, Rigby established a new company, Specialist Computer Services, which launched payroll support services, as well as other mainframe-based administrative services.

COMPANY PERSPECTIVES

Our business is about people, about high service content, about a quality approach and, above all, about honest and professional engagement. Our people share the benefits and values of a single, unified, European family. We understand the needs of our customers, adapt quickly to change, and deliver the services and support they need, across Europe and beyond.

Rigby's next extension came just two years later, when he set up the first Specialists Computer Centres dealership. Opened in Birmingham, SCC offered integrated hardware and software packages, as well as systems support services. SCC's first major step forward came in 1983, when the company became an IBM PC dealer, which by then had begun to impose itself as a standard for the personal computer market.

By 1984, SCC had already imposed itself as a major contender in the U.K. IT services market. In that year, the company received a major contract from the Government Communications Headquarters worth £4 million. The contract allowed the company to begin its first geographic expansion, with new offices opened in London and in Liverpool that year. By the end of 1986, the company's network had grown to include offices in Nottingham, Manchester, Southampton, and Glasgow. The company had already completed its first acquisition, of the Byte Shop Group.

One year later, the group's sales had already doubled, from £18 million to £37 million. Rigby formed a holding company for his expanding operations, called Specialist Computer Holdings (SCH) and moved into a new 30,000-square-foots headquarters and logistics facility in Birmingham. The company had also launched a new subsidiary, ETC, which acted as a wholesaler for IBM PC systems. SCC's partnership with IBM helped SCH boost its revenues past £70 million by the end of 1989.

BRITISH TOP FIVE IN THE 1990S

SCC added news offices in London, Edinburgh, and Bristol into the next decade. In 1991, the company made two new acquisitions, of Asystel, boosting its IT services operations, and of Applied Micros' PC and training units. The latter acquisition enabled the company to launch its own software and applications training business, Specialist Computer Education (SCE)

in 1991. Meanwhile, the hugely successful launch of a new generation of the Microsoft Windows operations system in the early 1990s transformed the PC sector. SCH profited strongly from the upsurge in PC purchases, emerging as one of the country's five largest dealers. The company backed up its dealership operation with a launch of a consumer and small business mail order business, Byte Direct Mail Order. The Byte name remained a motor for SCH's growth into the mid-1990s, especially with the successful launch of a new retail format, Byte Computer Superstore, in 1993.

By 1995, the company had already opened 16 Byte stores. Just one year later, Byte became a national brand when SCH reached a deal with Office World to place Byte concessions in its 46 stores in England. At the same time, SCH boosted its range of retailing and wholesaling operations when it acquired Scotbyte Computers and Scotbyte Supplies.

SCH invested some £9 million in expanding its own infrastructure, including the expansion of its logistics facilities, as well as the opening of a new National Response Centre in Oldbury, through 1997. The company then returned to its external expansion that year, acquiring Network SI's maintenance services operation. This permitted the company to launch a new business, Specialist Direct, targeting the small- and medium-sized business market. Next, SCH bought up Qudis, a distributor of Hewlett Packard products, which was then merged with its ETC subsidiary in 1998.

In the meantime, however, SCH's focus on its move into the retail sector had allowed its corporate IT services operations to lag behind its competitors. The company countered this in 1999 with the purchase of Lantec, formerly part of Elcom International. The acquisition helped raise SCH's total revenues past £700, and also placed the company once again among the leaders in the U.K. corporate market.

GLOBAL LEADER FOR THE 2000S

Rigby, who by then had been joined by sons James and Steven, next became determined to expand the company's operations onto a European—and then global—scale. In 2000, the company took its first step onto the European continent, acquiring Info'Products/ Allium from the Netherlands' Buhrmann for £115 million. That acquisition transformed SCH into the leading systems integration and desktop services player in the European market. The company also responded to the growing demand for global service offerings with the creation of a new subsidiary, Specialist Global Services (SGS).

SCH solidified its leader status the following year when it acquired the United Kingdom's number three

```
┌─────────────────────────────────────────────┐
│                                             │
│              KEY DATES                      │
│                   ■                         │
│  ─────────────────────────────────────────  │
│                                             │
│  1975:  Peter Rigby launches Specialist     │
│         Computer Recruitment with a £3,000  │
│         investment.                         │
│  1980:  Company enters the IT services      │
│         market with launch of SCS           │
│         (Specialist Computer Services).     │
│  1982:  The first SCC (Specialist Computer  │
│         Centre) dealership is opened.       │
│  1992:  A mail order business, Byte Direct  │
│         Mail Order, is launched.            │
│  1997:  Company launches Specialist Direct, │
│         providing IT maintenance services   │
│         to small businesses.                │
│  2000:  Company becomes the European market │
│         leader with purchase of             │
│         Info'Products/Allium and launches   │
│         Specialist Global Services (SGS).   │
│                                             │
└─────────────────────────────────────────────┘
```

player, Compelsource. This purchase was followed in 2002 by the purchase of two French distribution businesses, Metrologie France and Metrologie Systems. The company added a third French acquisition that year, buying up system integration specialist EBC Informatique. Then in 2003, the company acquired Hays Payroll UK, before turning to Spain, where it bought up GE Capital IT Solutions Spain. These purchases helped boost the company's total revenues past £2 billion.

In 2003, SCH moved to adopt a single brand for its expanded operations, placing the former Allium, SGS and Info'Products operations under the SCC umbrella. By then, the company had successfully transformed itself into a truly European company, with more than half of its sales coming from the continent.

SCH's expansion continued into 2004, with the creation of a new business unit, SCC Exchange. The new subsidiary allowed the company to provide dedicated services for the mid-sized market. At the same time, SCH continued its acquisition drive, buying up the Unix infrastructure operations of Acuma. That purchase, which placed SCH as the number three largest reseller of Unix-based systems in the United Kingdom, was part of the company's ambition to build this operation into a European leader.

SCH next turned to Germany, where it acquired Triaton GmbH, part of Hewlett Packard, which focused on product supply. The purchase helped the company solidify its position in the manufacturing and health insurance markets, in particular. In Italy, that year, SCC acquired the IT services division of the ATR Group,

placing the company as that market's leader. Meanwhile, the company had completed the integration of a new Dutch unit, Pluz, a hardware distribution joint venture formerly owned by Getronics and Hagermeyer.

SCH showed no signs of slowing down into the mid-2000s. By the end of 2005, the company had completed a new acquisition, buying TBI-Proxis Services. Based in France, that company focused on providing managed services to the small and mid-sized enterprise market. By the beginning of 2006, SCH's sales approached £2.5 billion ($4 billion), and the company had succeeded in capturing the leading position in some eight European markets. SCH hoped to continue building on its success, announcing its plans to break into the ranks of the global top 20 IT services companies before the end of 2007.

M. L. Cohen

PRINCIPAL DIVISIONS

SCC Enterprise Solutions; SCC Exchange; Lifecycle; Global Services.

PRINCIPAL COMPETITORS

Groupe Open; Volvo Information Technology AB; T-Systems GEI GmbH; gedas AG; Transiciel S.A.; Terra Networks S.A.; Sopra Conseil et Assistance en Informatique; GFI Informatique; Oberthur Card Systems; Computacenter France.

FURTHER READING

Driscoll, Sara, "SCC Expects Profitable Exchange," *Computer Reseller News*, August 15, 2005, p. 1.

Hall, Dominic, "SCH Strengthens European Assault with Spanish Purchase," *MicroScope*, February 11, 2003, p. 3.

"Hobby-Cum-Business Swells Rigby Coffers," *Birmingham Post Midlands Rich List*, 2006.

Quicke, Simon, "SCH CEO Gives Thumbs Up to Consolidation Trend," *MicroScope*, October 13, 2003, p. 1.

——, "SCH Turnover Boon Highlights the Benefits of Continental Expansion," *MicroScope*, October 13, 2003, p. 12.

"SCC Exchange Division to Focus on Mid-Market," *MicroScope*, December 13, 2004, p. 5.

"SCC Expands with Acuma Unix Buy," *MicroScope*, July 9, 2002, p. 3.

"SCC move on French front," *Europe Intelligence Wire*, June 6, 2005.

"SCH Happy with Benefits Gained by Staying Private," *MicroScope*, March 15, 2004, p. 4.

"SCH's Organic Plans for 2005," *Newswire*, November 22, 2004.

Stewart's Shops
Corporation

2907 Route 9
Ballston Spa, New York 12020
U.S.A.
Telephone: (518) 581-1200
Fax: (518) 581-1209
Web site: http://www.stewartsicecream.com

Private Company
Founded: 1921
Sales: $500 million (2005 est.)
NAIC: 445120 Convenience Stores

■ ■ ■

Stewart's Shops Corporation is a Ballston, New York–based operator of more than 300 convenience stores spread throughout upstate New York and Vermont, all within a 150 mile radius of Saratoga Springs, New York, where the company got its start. The stores are supplied with milk and ice cream from the company's own dairy as well as with chili, macaroni and cheese, and soups prepared in its own kitchens. The company's 260,000-square-foot processing facility produces approximately 10 million gallons of milk and 3 million gallons of ice cream each year. About three quarters of the products sold in the stores are either produced or distributed by the company. In addition to ready-to-go food and basic groceries, Stewart's Shops sell gasoline, and offer free air, ATMs, and public rest rooms in most units. The company is two-thirds owned by the Dake family, with the rest owned by the employees through a profit sharing program that contributes about 25 percent of each employee's annual pay to their individual accounts. In addition, Stewart's is known for giving back to the communities it serves, donating 5 percent of annual profits to charity. As a result, Stewart's has enjoyed double-digit growth for many years, outperforming larger chains operating in their markets.

EARLY 20TH CENTURY ROOTS IN
ICE CREAM

Stewart's traces its heritage to brothers Percy W. and Charles V. Dake, who in 1921 began producing ice cream in Greenfield, New York, under the Dake's Delicious Ice Cream label. By the end of the decade they were making 100,000 gallons of ice cream a year, attracting the attention of Sealtest, which acquired the business in 1929. As part of the deal, the Dake brothers agreed to a non-compete clause, but while ice cream was off limits to them, milk was not. In 1935 New York passed a law that would require all milk to be pasteurized and the Dakes recognized a business opportunity. They opened a modern dairy plant in 1935 in a former municipal water works building in Saratoga Springs. Area dairy farmers, who had faced the risk of being put out of business, could now sell their raw milk to the Dakes' Saratoga Dairy. They expanded their operation two years later by acquiring a facility in Greenfield, New York, to produce cheese, powdered whey, and casein. Raw milk that supplied this plant came from all over New England and the Eastern United States.

The non-competition agreement with Sealtest expired in 1945 and the Dakes lost little time in making their return to the ice cream business. They bought the

COMPANY PERSPECTIVES

From Plattsburgh to Newburgh, Watertown to Rutland, the company maintains its small-town feel and motto, "We are closer to you."

Stewart Ice Cream Company, owned by Donald Stewart of Ballston Spa, New York, picking up his dairy, ice cream freezer, hardening room, and a retail shop located on heavily traveled Route 50 in Ballston Spa. In addition, the Dakes kept the Stewart's name. The year 1945 also saw the arrival of a second generation of the Dake family in the business, as Charles S. Dake, the son of Charles V. Dake, joined the company. The young man had served in the Army during World War II; now discharged, he was eager to make a go of the newly acquired ice cream business, which was set to thrive as servicemen like himself began returning home and raising families. In short order, shops were opened in Saratoga Springs and South Glen Falls, where customers would line up to buy seven-cent single-scoop cones and ten-cent double cones.

Stewart's grew steadily over the next decade. It made a notable contribution to the ice cream trade in 1948, becoming the first to use folding half-gallon takeout ice cream cartons, developed in conjunction with the Sutherland Paper Company. That same year, Charles' wife, Phyllis, conceived of a bar where people could choose from bowls of toppings to customize their sundaes. The "Make Your Own Sundae" feature was then advertised on the first television station in the area, WRGB, and grew extremely popular. In 1950 both Saratoga Dairy and Stewart's Ice Cream Co. were incorporated and ice cream manufacturing was transferred to the Greenfield facility. By the end of 1955 Stewart's was operating more than 50 ice cream shops.

STORES ADD MILK SALES: 1957

The transition from ice cream shop to convenience store began in 1957 when Stewart's petitioned the Department of Agriculture for approval to sell milk produced by its dairy in its ice cream shops. Permission was granted and Stewart's enjoyed immediate success in the retail milk business. Since the company was able to produce its own milk, it could cut retail prices by 25 percent, thereby attracting a good deal of business. It was only a matter of time before the ice cream shops began offering other dairy products—and non-dairy products as well, including what would be considered the three staples of

convenience stores: beer, soda, and cigarettes.

In 1959 Charles S. Dake also took over the running of Saratoga Dairy, succeeding his uncle. A year later he convinced his brother, William P. Dake, to join him in turning around the dairy, which at this point was losing money. More than just a trusted sibling, Bill Dake was a Cornell University-trained engineer. He used his expertise to restore the dairy operation to profitability. The business of Saratoga Dairy and Stewart's Ice Cream Co. reinforced one another, so that together they grew into one of the most successful private dairy companies in the Eastern United States.

For a time during the late 1960s and early 1970s, Stewart's ran several Farmer in the Dell Shops, but the growth of the company was tied to the success of its expanding chain of Stewart's Shops and the popularity of its ice cream. Another important factor was the retention of employees. In 1974 Employee Stock Ownership Plans (ESOP) became viable with the passage of the Employee Retirement Income Security Act. Stewart's established its own ESOP, in effect selling part of the company to the employees, a stake that over time would become one-third of the company. With an interest in the business, Stewart's employees stayed longer and proved more industrious, in the end making the two-thirds stake in the business more valuable, in the opinion of the Dake family, than if the family had retained full ownership. To further aid in the retention of employees, Stewart's also offered benefits, such as health care, that were quite liberal compared to what other convenience store chains offered.

Another major step in the evolution of Stewart's shops was the addition of self-service gasoline pumps. The decade also brought sadness to the Dake family, as Charles Dake struggled with cancer, eventually succumbing to it in 1978 at the age of 53. His brother William now assumed the presidency of the company and continued to grow the Stewart's chain. In 1981 the 100th shop opened, located in Schenectady. William's son, Gary C. Dake, joined him in 1984 to relieve some of the burden.

Stewart's grew at a steady pace in the 1980s, as did the convenience store industry in general, but after nearly 20 years of impressive growth the sector reached a saturation point by the end of the decade as the number of convenience stores in the United States stalled at around 85,000. In addition, industry-wide profits in 1989 fell off 75 percent from the prior year's total. A subsequent recession made matters even worse, and two of the largest national operators, 7-Eleven and Circle K, which had grown too quickly and taken on too much debt, landed in bankruptcy court. Stewart's, on the other hand, continued to prosper and expand. In a 1991

KEY DATES

1921: Percy W. and Charles V. Dake start Dake's Delicious Ice Cream.
1929: The business is sold to Sealtest.
1935: The Dake brothers launch Saratoga Dairy.
1945: The brothers acquire Stewart's Ice Cream Company and reenter the ice cream business.
1959: Charles S. Dakes, of the second generation, takes charge.
1974: An Employee Stock Ownership Plan is initiated.
1978: Charles Dake dies and is replaced by his brother William.
1993: The 200th Stewart's shop opens.
2003: William Dake's son Gary assumes the company presidency.

interview with *Capital District Business Review,* Bill Dake admitted that the recession adversely affected Stewart's, "but nowhere near as much as most companies." Explaining his company's "contrarian" approach that defied the conventional wisdom of the previous two decades, he said, "We never went public when everyone went public; we never got into debt; we went into [refillable bottles] when everyone was getting out of refillables." Stewart's also benefitted from the retention of employees, but the impact of Bill Dake's management could not be underestimated. He kept his management structure lean, relying on just five district managers to supervise 150 shops. He was also known to be demanding and to surround himself with hard-working, aggressive executives. Thin-skinned, underachievers were not tolerated. A little more puzzling was Stewart's reluctance to embrace technology in the early 1990s, holding out as long as possible on adding electronic checkout scanners. But while Stewart's lacked the ability to track product performance and adjust product mix, the stores retained a personal touch that tied it closer to customers. To better serve those customers, Stewart's introduced ATMs in urban locations, and more remote stores were served by "Scrip" cash machines, a machine to performed all bank functions, including cash withdrawal and transfers, with the exception of deposits. To receive cash a customer received a slip of paper, known as "scrip," which could be handed to the store's cashier in exchange for cash out of the register.

In 1993 Stewart's opened its 200th store and a year later added another 40 units in one stroke by acquiring the Bonfare chain, the integration of which proved difficult. To keep up with the company's growth, a new $4 million, 35,000-square-foot dairy was built. In the second half of the 1990s, Stewart's began an aggressive bid to expand beyond the Saratoga vicinity and into New York's mid-Hudson Valley for the first time. In 2000 the 300th Stewart's store opened in West Sand Lake, New York. Annual revenues at this stage topped the $500 million mark. William Dake's success in growing the chain was also recognized in 2000, honored by the New York Capitol chapter of the American Marketing Association as the year's Marketer of Excellence.

NEW CENTURY REAL ESTATE VENTURES

Stewart's had been involved in the real estate business for a long time, essentially securing land for new stores, but along the way it developed an expertise in the municipal approval process and in 2000 began to dabble in residential and other real estate development activities. It opened a small shopping strip near Saratoga Lake featuring a new Stewart's shop and several rental storefronts. The company also bought a 12,000-square-foot building in central Albany. The former warehouse and mail-order distribution center was converted to include a new Stewart's convenience store, retail rental units, as well as apartments. In Waterford, New York, Stewart's began converting a 14,750-square-foot Grand Union supermarket into a Stewart's Shop plus retail rental units. At 3,600 square feet the convenience store would be larger than the usual Stewart's Shop, which was 2,400 square feet, in order to carry more grocery items and serve area residents—in particular the poor and elderly who would now be without a local grocery store and did not have the means to travel to a distant supermarket. About a dozen other Grand Union supermarkets would also be shut down in surrounding small towns over the ensuing months, due to the sale of Grand Union to another company. The closures may have prompted Stewart's to expand its grocery offering at more than 20 of its stores affected by the closings but in reality it was a move already in the works. "Grand Union is the trigger, but the underlying theme is the big-box player," Bill Dake told Albany's *Times Union.* "As these stores get bigger and the lines get longer, it gets harder to go to them all the time. Instead of going to Stewart's twice a week and going to the grocery stores once a week, people will come to Stewart's three times a week and go to the grocery stores every two weeks." Stewart's Shop not only acted as a supplement to the grocery store, over the years it took on a new function serving as a local hangout, like the coffee shops and diners of another era where neighbors could swap gossip and exchange views about the weather. In order to accommodate customers, the standard Stewart's store design now included three or more dining booths.

William Dake turned over the presidency to his son Gary in 2003 although he stayed on as chairman of the board. Under the younger Dake's leadership, Stewart's anticipated adding 6 to 12 new stores each year. While Saratoga County was saturated with Stewart's Shops, there were plenty of growth opportunities elsewhere in upstate New York. In order to keep pace, the company opened a 56,000-square-foot warehouse in 2004, and a year later began a phased expansion program to increase ice cream production.

Ed Dinger

PRINCIPAL COMPETITORS

7-Eleven, Inc.; Ben & Jerry's Homemade Inc.; Cumberland Farms, Inc.

FURTHER READING

DerGurahian, Jean, "Convenience Store Chains Find Success as Neighborhood Centers," *Albany Times Union,* February 11, 2002.

Furfaro, Danielle T., *Albany Times Union,* March 11, 2001.

Leon, Matt, "Ice Cream Giant Taking Statewide Growth in Stride," *Post-Star* (Glen Falls, N.Y.), March 24, 2005.

Maisto, Michelle, "The Sweet Like," *Mobile Enterprise,* September 2004.

Poe, Amy, "Stewart's Holds Market With Low Price, High Value," *Capital District Business Review,* July 8, 1991, p. 13.

"Stewart's Planning Expansion," *Ice Cream Reporter,* September 20, 2005, p. 1.

Superior Essex Inc.

150 Interstate North Parkway
Atlanta, Georgia 30339
U.S.A.
Telephone: (770) 657-6000
Toll Free: (800) 685-4887
Fax: (770) 303-8807
Web site: http://www.superioressex.com

Public Company
Incorporated: 1930
Employees: 4,100
Sales: $1.8 billion (2005)
Stock Exchanges: NASDAQ
Ticker Symbol: SPSX
NAIC: 331528 Other Nonferrous Foundries

∎ ∎ ∎

Headquartered in Atlanta, Georgia, Superior Essex Inc. is a leading manufacturer of cable and wire. The company is among the largest industry players in North America, and also has a significant global presence. Superior Essex operates 23 production facilities in the United States, Mexico, and Europe and has an established global distribution network. The company's customer base includes cable television and telephone companies, as well as distributors and manufacturers in a variety of industries. Superior Essex offers more than 500 magnet wire and winding wire products. In North America and China, these products are marketed through the Essex Group Inc. The company serves the European market through its EssexNexans joint venture. Accord-

ing to Superior Essex, its magnet wire products are critical components in millions of items, including automobiles, home appliances, generators, motors, transformers, and commercial machinery.

Superior Essex has several other business units that are devoted to specific end markets. As the world's largest producer of outside plant copper communications cables, Superior Essex Communications LP makes a range of different copper and fiber optic communications cables for multiple voice and data applications. Finally, Superior Essex serves original equipment manufacturers and the motor repair market via its Essex Brownell, Essex Express, and Active Industries units, which offer various electrical insulation products. The history of Superior Essex is really a tale of two companies: Essex Group Inc. and Superior TeleCom, which combined to form Superior Essex in 1998.

ESSEX GROUP INC.: 1930–1998

Superior Essex's deepest roots stretch back to Detroit, Michigan, where businessman Addison E. Holton established Essex Wire Corp. in 1930. Holton was a World War I veteran who served in the Navy and attended the University of Michigan. During its formative years, the company's work force produced battery cables, wiring harnesses, and other wire items for the Ford Model A, working from 125,000 square feet of leased space in Ford Motor Company's Highland Park plant.

Expansion happened rapidly at Essex during the 1930s. Shortly after it was founded the company acquired Logansport, Indiana-based RBM Manufacturing Company, a producer of electrical switches and automotive components. In 1932 Essex proceeded to buy a rubber insulation plant in Jonesboro, Indiana. According to the company, the facility was known for producing a brand of building wire called Paranite. Finally, in 1936 Essex acquired a vacant industrial facility in Fort Wayne, Indiana. The site had formerly housed the Dudlo Manufacturing Company, which was founded in 1912 and pioneered the process for enameling magnetic wire.

According to company literature, during the 1940s "Essex was producing enough magnet wire to build the millions of transformers used by America and its allies during World War II. Essex plants also produced thousands of miles of field telephone wire for the Army Signal Corps, as well as wiring harnesses for B-24 bombers. Later, Essex was awarded the highly prestigious 'E' Award by the Secretary of War."

Essex relocated its headquarters to Fort Wayne in 1954. Four years later, Walter F. Probst succeeded Addison Holton as the company's president. Holton retired altogether in 1962, at which time Probst assumed the additional role of board chairman.

By 1965 Essex's sales totaled $355 million. The company had seven divisions, 41 plants throughout North America, and 26 warehouses. It was that year that the company was first listed on the New York Stock Exchange, with 5 million shares. It also was in 1965 that Essex unveiled an $8 million expansion initiative, which included $3.2 million for its Essex Wire and Cable division, $2.5 million for its Essex Automotive division, and $2.3 million for the acquisition, expansion, and improvement of other facilities.

In early 1966 Paul W. O'Malley, who had been with Essex since 1952, was named company president. Probst continued to serve as chairman and CEO. O'Malley was a World War II veteran who earned a metallurgical engineering degree from Pennsylvania State University and a law degree from the University of Michigan Law School.

By 1968 Essex was in the process of building a new 30,000-square-foot facility in Fort Wayne for its Metal

Products division. In all, the company had 67 plants in 30 states and Canada. That year, Essex also acquired Transport Motor Express Inc., one of the nation's largest trucking companies, in a stock deal valued at $12 million. Growth and expansion continued at a rapid pace in 1969, when Essex acquired 14 other companies.

Essex Wire Corporation was operating under the name Essex International Inc. by 1970, and the company's employee base numbered 25,700. While most of its workforce was in the midwestern United States and Canada, Essex also operated a facility in Northern Ireland. At the end of the decade, the company's divisions included: Magnet Wire; IWI; Wire and Cable; Controls; Metal Products and Plastics; Power Conductors; Communications and CATV; Industrial Laboratory Products; Wire Assembly; and Electro-Mechanical.

Sales reached approximately $845 million in 1973, at which time Essex operated about 100 plants. In 1974 the company merged with East Hartford, Connecticut-based United Aircraft Corporation (United Technologies Corporation). The merger of Essex and United created the nation's 30th largest company, with combined 1973 sales of $3.13 billion.

When Walter Probst retired as chairman and CEO in 1974, he was succeeded by Essex President Paul O'Malley. Following the United Technologies merger, O'Malley was elected as Essex group vice president and director. He held this post until 1981, at which time he retired and was succeeded by James A. O'Connor, a 31-year Essex veteran.

During the late 1970s Essex faced criticism from labor leaders for being one of the most anti-labor companies in the industrial north. The AFL-CIO criticized the company for encouraging the presence of multiple unions in order to keep labor decentralized and weak, scattering production to diffuse strikes, paying low wages, and providing no or poor benefits packages to workers. Another black mark on the company came in September of 1978 when the U.S. Justice Department charged Essex and five other wire manufacturers with price fixing. According to the September 27, 1978, issue of the *Fort Wayne Journal Gazette*, while the company denied any wrongdoing, the agency charged that Essex and its counterparts "exchanged information about prices and conspired to restrain trade."

Although a new decade began in 1980, this year also signified the end of an era when Essex founder Addison Holton died at the age of 83. In 1982 Essex Group announced plans to invest $3 million in its Fort Wayne facility, which would become the company's world headquarters. The improvements were scheduled for completion in 1984. By 1983 Essex employed 8,982 workers worldwide, with an annual payroll of $26.8 million.

Essex became a privately owned firm in 1988 when MS/Essex Holdings, an investment group that included members of Essex's management team and the New York securities firm Morgan Stanley Leveraged Equity Fund II LP, bought the company from United Technologies. At this time, John M. Bruce was president and CEO of Essex Group. The buyout came at a time when U.S. wire companies faced growing competition from foreign imports. Essex changed hands again in 1992 when it was purchased by Bessemer Holdings, but remained privately owned. However, in 1997 Essex became a publicly traded firm once again.

During the 1990s, Essex acquired a number of other firms, including magnet wire and electrical motor distributor Brownell in 1995. After being merged into Essex's distribution arm, the new business was named Essex Brownell. The acquisition of Active Industries, a converter/fabricator of electrical insulation products, followed in 1998.

In September 1998 Essex announced that it was being acquired by Superior Telecom Inc. in a deal valued at $1.4 billion in cash, stock, and debt. Finalized in 1999, the acquisition made Essex a subsidiary of Superior and created what then was North America's largest cable and wire manufacturer. Essex Chairman, President, and CEO Steven Abbott became Superior's president and chief operating officer following the deal.

SUPERIOR TELECOM: 1954–1998

Superior Telecom got its start in 1954—the same year that Essex relocated from Detroit to Fort Wayne, Indiana. Established in Hickory, North Carolina, as the Superior Cable Corporation, the firm produced plastic insulated, twisted pair cable and wire. Production took place in a new 32,000-square-foot plant, the construc-

tion of which was authorized by the Hickory Development Corp. at a cost of $160,000. Manufacturing equipment was installed in May, and the company produced its first reel of cable in August, delivering it to the Hickory Telephone Company.

Attorney Walker Geitner was Superior's first president. While most of Superior's cable was used for the telephone industry, Geitner explained that it had broader applications. In the July 26, 1956, issue of the *Hickory Daily Record*, he explained: "The cables which our company manufactures differ from other cables in that all of our cables are concerned with a transfer of intelligence from one point to another point. This intelligence may be in the form of a telephone conversation. It may be an electrical pulse from a fire alarm system, or a traffic control system, or it may be a pulse on a pipe line control system which opens or closes a valve."

In 1959 Geitner was named Superior's chairman. Succeeding him as president was James L. Robb, who had been with the firm since its inception. The following year Superior established a second manufacturing plant in Rocky Mount, North Carolina. By 1962 the company had expanded its headquarters plant three times, reaching a size of 150,000 square feet. Production had expanded to include coaxial cables, as well as wire for use in missile, aircraft, and industrial applications.

In 1963 Superior played a pioneering role in the telephone sector with the roll-out of the industry's first all-plastic drop wire. In order to more effectively serve the southwestern United States, a new cable plant was erected in Brownwood, Texas, in 1964.

By 1965 additional growth had increased the size of Superior's home plant even further, giving the firm 125,000 square feet of manufacturing space, about 35,000 square feet of office space, and a 35,000-square-foot building for warehousing and shipping. The company's annual sales reached nearly $20 million that year. Looking to the future, Superior had plans to construct a separate facility devoted to research and development.

Superior was acquired by Continental Telephone in 1967. As a Continental subsidiary, the firm was renamed Superior Continental Corp. Growth continued under its new owner, with annual sales reaching $90 million in 1969 and approximately $125 million in 1971.

In 1971 Superior Continental announced plans to build an eight-story corporate office facility in Hickory for $3 million. By this time J. L. Robb had become president of manufacturing for Continental Telephone, and Warner T. Smith served as Superior Continental's president. The company's manufacturing plant in Hickory had continued to grow exponentially, reaching 600,000 square feet.

Continental Telephone divested Superior in 1976. In a cash and stock deal, Robert C. Pittman and A. L. Viles purchased the company for $17.1 million. Superior Cable Corporation was reincorporated and became the parent company of the Superior Cable facilities located in Hickory and Rocky Mount, North Carolina, as well as the Brownwood, Texas, plant. Also included in the deal were Hickory Brand Telephone Cords; Keller, Texas-based Communication Apparatus Company; and a non-operating plant in Angier, North Carolina.

Superior was acquired by optical fiber and cable manufacturer Siecor Corporation in 1980. In 1981 Siecor relocated from Horseheads, New York to Hickory. Five years later, Superior changed hands once again when it was divested by Siecor. As an independent firm, Superior went on to market its own line of fiber optic cable. In 1987 Siecor played a pioneering role on the international trade front when, after five years of negotiating, it convinced Japan to purchase some of its fiber optical cable.

The Alpine Group Inc. acquired Superior in 1993. Following this development, the company added premises data cables to its product lineup and proceeded to acquire other firms. A public offering soon followed, and Superior TeleCom Inc. went public in 1996 with a listing on the New York Stock Exchange. Superior's annual sales reached $500 million in 1997. Following the acquisition of Essex International in 1999, Superior changed its name to Superior Essex.

SUPERIOR ESSEX: 1999 AND BEYOND

Superior Essex held about 30 percent of the market for copper building wire by August 1999. At that time, the company announced that it would close three wire manufacturing plants and lay off 469 employees in order to optimize its financial returns in a highly competitive market that was suffering from oversupply. The company closed plants in Glendale, Arizona; Pauline, Kansas; and Tiffin, Ohio. It continued to produce wire at sites in Sikeston, Missouri; Florence, Alabama; Anaheim, California; Lafayette, Indiana; and Columbia City, Indiana.

In 2000 Superior Essex was awarded a three-year contract to supply cable and wire to Alltel Communications Products Inc., which served 8.5 million customers in 25 states with both wireless and wired communication services. The deal was significant because it involved Superior Essex supplying Alltel with all of its cable and wire.

In late 2000 Superior Essex launched an e-commerce Web site in an effort to boost sales in a market that continued to suffer from high competition and oversupply. In addition to order entry, the site allowed the company's customers to track shipments, estimate shipment arrival times, and read industry news feeds. By December 2001 Superior Essex occupied a 228,000-square-foot warehousing and distribution facility in northeast Indiana previously occupied by defense giant Raytheon.

During the early 2000s industry observers took notice of Superior Essex's performance in the human resources realm. The company, which maintained a workforce of 5,000 in 2003, was able to give employees better benefits without increasing their out-of-pocket contributions—despite the national trend of skyrocketing healthcare costs. It accomplished this by streamlining its benefit packages and renegotiating contracts with healthcare providers.

As of early 2004 Stephen M. Carter was CEO of Superior Essex. An important development occurred in April of that year when the company announced its plans to acquire the North American outside plant communications cable and wire operations of Belden Inc. The purchase price of approximately $95 million freed Belden from a market where it had not been able to turn a profit for several years.

Commenting on the deal in the April 2004 issue of *Electrical Wholesaling*, Carter said: "This acquisition will more appropriately align capacity in the outside plant copper communications cable industry with demand, which has declined 50 percent in North America since 2000. We have responded to this decline by consolidating our manufacturing facilities and reducing capacity, but the need to serve our customers with the most efficient production now requires us to look beyond internal solutions. We are confident that we will be able to smoothly transition Belden's customer base, which last year generated approximately $200 million in revenues, and meet their ongoing needs without disruption."

In February 2006, Superior Essex announced that its revenues reached $1.8 billion in 2005, up from $1.4 billion the previous year. Commenting on the company's performance in a news release, Carter said the company was "successful in generating organic growth" in its main North American markets. Carter attributed the firm's increased revenues to consolidating acquisitions. In addition, he pointed to increased earnings despite the burden of skyrocketing energy costs. As the company moved into the second half of the 2000s, it did so from a fortunate position of market leadership.

Paul R. Greenland

PRINCIPAL SUBSIDIARIES

Superior Essex Communications LP; Essex Group, Inc.

PRINCIPAL COMPETITORS

Alcatel; APA Cables and Networks Inc.; General Cable Corporation.

FURTHER READING

"$8 Million Expansion Plan Announced by Essex Wire," *Fort Wayne Journal Gazette*, July 14, 1965.

"Alltel Awards Superior Essex Supply Pact," *American Metal Market*, March 14, 2000.

Baer, Justin, "Essex Sold to N.Y. Firm," *Fort Wayne Journal Gazette*, September 23, 1998.

"Cable Company Process Topic at Rotary Club," *Hickory Daily Record*, July 26, 1956.

"Cable Firm Grows Phenomenally," *Hickory Daily Record*, September 11, 1965.

"Cable Plant Contracts Authorized at $160,000," *Hickory Daily Record*, February 14, 1953.

Chewning, Cherin, "Pair Confident about Firm Buy," *Hickory Daily Record*, November 3, 1976.

"Essex Wire to Acquire Truck Line," *Fort Wayne Journal Gazette*, November 2, 1968.

"Founder of Essex Wire Is Dead at 83," *Fort Wayne Journal Gazette*, September 3, 1980.

Leininger, Kevin, and Karl Kates, "Essex's Influence Extends to Worldwide Market," *Fort Wayne News Sentinel*, May 16, 1983.

Leininger, Kevin, "Investment Group Purchases Fort Wayne Essex," *Fort Wayne News Sentinel*, January 27, 1988.

———, "$3 Million Shot in Arm to Come from Essex Plan," *Fort Wayne News Sentinel*, August 21, 1982.

Murphy, Joan L., "Siecor Plans to Sell Some Assets," *Hickory Daily Record*, June 7, 1985.

Nucifora, Alf, "Customers Don't Give Loyalty—You Earn It," *NJBIZ*, February 3, 2003.

"O'Malley Succeeds Probst as Essex Wire President," *Fort Wayne Journal Gazette*, February 10, 1966.

Pegram, Charles B., "Firm Explains Site Choice," *Hickory Daily Record*, November 27, 1971.

"Production Underway at New Essex Plant," *Fort Wayne Journal Gazette*, August 17, 1968.

Risen, Jim, "Essex, Five Other Wire Firms Charged with Price Fixing," *Fort Wayne Journal Gazette*, September 27, 1978.

———, "Unions Chip Away at Essex's Anti-Labor Reputation," *Fort Wayne Journal Gazette*, June 17, 1979.

"Stockholders Okay Essex-United Tie," *Fort Wayne Journal Gazette*, February 1, 1974.

Yafie, Roberta C., "Superior Essex Launches e-Com Site for Electrical Products Line," *American Metal Market*, September 4, 2000.

———, "Superior to Close Three Wire Plants, Lay Off 469," *American Metal Market*, August 13, 1999.

Tele Norte Leste
Participações S.A.

Rua Humberto de Campos, 425
Rio de Janeiro, 22430-190
Brazil
Telephone: (55) (21) 3131-1314
Toll Free: 0800-31-0800
Fax: (55) (21) 3131-1155
Web site: http://www.telemar.com.br

Public Company
Incorporated: 1998
Employees: 47,107
Sales: BRL 16.75 billion ($6.86 billion) (2005)
Stock Exchanges: São Paulo
Ticker Symbol: TNLP3, TNLP4; TNE
NAIC: 517110 Wired Telecommunications Carrier;
517212 Cellular and Other Wireless Telecommunications; 518111 Internet Service Providers; 518112
Web Search Portals; 551112 Offices of Other Holding Companies

■ ■ ■

Tele Norte Leste Participações S.A. (TNL) is the holding company for Telemar Norte Leste S.A. (Telemar), the largest provider of fixed-line telecommunication services in South America, based on the total number of lines in service. These services are marketed under the Telemar brand name. Telemar has the concession to provide fixed-line telecommunications in 16 states of northern and northeastern Brazil. These 16 of the nation's 27 states, which include Rio de Janeiro—headquarters for Telemar—cover 64 percent of the national territory and take in more than half the population. Besides fixed-line local and long-distance telephone service, TNL also provides wireless services in Brazil through Oi, broadband Internet access through Velox, data transmission through Pegasus, and a variety of value-added services for businesses, including voice data and videoconferencing.

BRAZILIAN TELEPHONY BEFORE 1998

Brazil's experience with the telephone dates from 1876, when Emperor Pedro II visited the Centennial Exhibition in Philadelphia and tried out Alexander Graham Bell's invention. The emperor had a telephone line installed in his palace later that year. By 1940 there were more than 800 telephone companies in Brazil, but rural areas were poorly served. The number of companies grew to over 1,000 by the 1960s, although Canada-based Companhia Telefônica Brasileira was dominant. In 1962 the government created the Brazilian Telecommunications Enterprise (Embratel), which took over the main line and ultimately became responsible for long-distance and international telephone transmission. In 1968 the ministry of communications assumed control of Companhia Telefônica Brasileira, and a constitutional change reserved telecommunications service to the state. Embratel was taken over in 1972 by Telecommunicações Brasileiras S.A. (Telebrás), 80-percent-owned by the Brazilian government.

Telebrás was financed by an unusual system that required potential subscribers to buy shares of stock in exchange for a phone line. By 1992, this entailed an

COMPANY PERSPECTIVES

The major objective of the company is to offer whatever is most modern in telecommunications, surpassing the levels of demand of customers and the market. That is why Telemar invests strongly in the development of new technology and the training of its functionaries, with the aim of providing the best service to its clients.

investment of $4,000. The scheme eventually reduced the government's stake in Telebrás to 52 percent. It also made a private line unaffordable for poor people while acting as a cash cow for the government, which dipped into the funds for other purposes and left Telebrás short of money needed to finance new technology and infrastructure. Nevertheless, Brazil successfully launched communications satellites in 1985-86, enabling telecommunications service to reach all of the enormous nation, including the Amazon basin. Cellular service was available by the mid-1990s. Yet 15 million people were on waiting lists for fixed-line service and another 5 million for cellular phones. Half of Brazil's businesses had no telephone service at all.

TELEMAR'S INCEPTION AND PROGRESS: 1998–2004

Privatization took place in 1998, when Telebrás established 12 new holding companies: eight for mobile telephone operations, a ninth for Embratel, and the other three as fixed-line operators. One of the latter was Tele Norte Leste (TLN), which was privatized and purchased by Consortium Telemar, a six-company union of Brazilian investors headed by the construction group Construtora Andrade Gutierrez S.A. The consortium, which successfully bid BRL 3.43 billion ($2.94 billion) for its concession, was seen as the weakest of the three fixed-line operators because, unlike the others, it did not have a foreign partner to help provide the cash needed to upgrade its system. *The Economist* (November 28, 1998) described it as "a ramshackle group of local investors." All voting shares held by the consortium were acquired in 1999 by Telemar Participações S.A., the parent of TLN. BNDESPar, the investment arm of Brazil's national development bank, held a 25-percent stake.

Telemar's perceived weakness did not keep it from outbidding Telecom Italia S.p.A., which was part of the

controlling group of rival Brasil Telecom Participações S.A., in 2001, for a D-band-frequency license to provide wireless service in the same area where it was providing fixed lines. Telemar paid the Brazilian government $656 million for the right to use this frequency, which was expected to provide improved roaming and faster Internet connections than existing services. Telemar had also purchased the Internet-access arm of the online media company IG and controlled more fixed-line phones than any other Brazilian telecommunications company.

A major reorganization of Telemar also took place in 2001. Fifteen fixed-line subsidiaries, one each in 15 states, were merged into the 16th, whose corporate name was changed to Telemar Norte Leste S.A. TLN retained 82 percent of Telemar's combined shares.

TNL's mobile-phone service, named Oi, began operating in June 2002 and by May 2003 had 2 million subscribers. In order to finance the operation, however, Oi incurred debts of BRL 5.32 billion ($1.85 billion). TNL provided Oi with BRL 562 million ($195 million) to reduce the debt, then sold Oi to Telemar for BRL 1 (35 cents), the equity value assigned to Oi by TNL's advisers, Ernst & Young, and transferred Oi's debt to Telemar. This did not please Telemar's minority shareholders, who argued that Telemar had in effect overpaid by assuming so much debt for an operation that was still losing money.

By mid-2003, Telemar had climbed from third to second place among Brazil's nongovernment and nonfinancial enterprises, advancing on a broad front by offering fixed, mobile, and national and international long-distance telephone services, plus data transmission. The number of its installed fixed-line telephones had grown from 8 million to 17.5 million (31 percent in Rio de Janeiro). The number of Oi's cellular phones had reached 2.2 million. While Telemars local and intraregional services were confined to 16 states, the company also was offering data transmission throughout Brazil and long-distance phone service both interregionally and internationally. Starting in 2003, Oi began to have a significant market share in long-distance calls originated on wireless telephones.

Telemar had acquired, in late 2002, a controlling interest in Pegasus Telecom S.A. in order to offer data-communications solutions in the part of Brazil not within its concessions. It completed the acquisition in 2003. This enabled Telemar to expand its market share in the corporate data segment by offering nationwide bundled services, including third-party network management (outsourcing). In addition, TNL Contax S.A. had been established for call centers and other business

KEY DATES

1998: A consortium wins the concession for fixed-line telecommunications in 16 Brazilian states.

2001: Telemar wins a license to offer wireless service in the same area as its fixed-line concession.

2002: TNL's mobile-phone arm, Oi, begins providing wireless telecommunications service.

2002: Telemar acquires control of Pegasus, a broadband data-transmission provider.

2003: TNL merges Oi into Telemar.

2005: Oi Internet is established as an Internet service provider.

services. (It was spun off to TNL shareholders in 2005 as Contax Participações S.A.)

But it was Oi that Telemar was relying on for rapid growth. "Brazil is the biggest growth market in Latin America," a securities analyst told Michael Kepp of *Latin Trade*. "This is not just because of the country's population and room-for-growth penetration rate, but because the fixed-line sector is a no-growth market, leaving the mobile market to grow and steal market share away from the fixed-line market." Because Oi's license area was the same as Telemar's fixed-line area, it was able to reduce the cost of connecting wireless calls to the fixed-phone system, and lower costs meant it could reduce cellular-phone prices and attract more customers. By the end of 2003 Oi had 7.3 million subscribers. Lower prices were not the only attraction. Oi successfully enrolled youths from every income group as having a cellular phone became an "in" thing to do. Prepaid mobile phones were among the hottest Christmas gifts bought by lower-income parents for their children. Hence, Oi's marketing director told Kepp that the unit's growth plan involved "targeting young and youthful-spirited people who like technology, daring new services and innovative technology."

TELEMAR IN 2005

The Telemar group customer base totaled 26 million by the end of 2005. Telemar had more than 17 million lines, of which nearly 14.9 million were in service, including public telephones as well as residential and commercial ones. Ninety-seven percent of the lines had been digitalized. There was, however, a slight decrease in lines in service, mainly from customer migration to mobile and broadband services. Broadband Internet ac-

cess rose by 80 percent during the year, to 805,000 subscribers. Oi ended the year with more than 10 million customers and 12 percent of the cellular market. Oi Internet was created in 2005 as an Internet-access provider. Other company units included HiCorp, which was providing Internet access to Internet service providers; Pegasus, offering data-transmission services; and Contax, which was offering call-center services to Telemar, Oi, and third-party customers, including major financial institutions. TNL was, in terms of revenue, the second-largest nongovernment company in Brazil in 2005.

Telemar's local services in Region I (the 16 states in which it had obtained a concession) included installation, monthly subscription, measured service, collect calls, and supplemental local services. Telemar was also providing long-distance services between the states in this region and, since 2002, providing interregional long-distance services between its region and the other two in Brazil. Also in 2002, it began providing international long-distance services originating from Region I, using the wireless telecommunications services license granted to Oi. In 2003 it began to offer fixed-line interregional and international long-distance services originating in the two other regions, using the same license granted to Oi. Telemar's fixed-line services also included calls originated from its fixed-line customers to customers of wireless service providers, including Oi. It also owned and operated public telephones throughout Region I, all of them activated by a prepaid card.

Oi's revenues from wireless telecommunications services came from usage fees for outgoing calls made and value-added services such as access to the Internet, data transmission, short messages, forwarding, call waiting, and call blocking; monthly subscriptions; roaming; interconnection fees received from other operators on incoming calls; and sales of handsets. Some 86 percent of its customer base was buying prepaid cards; the postpaid customers paid a monthly subscription fee and were billed on a monthly basis for services provided during the previous month, such as mailbox, caller ID, and conference calls. GPRS service, available in the main cities of Region I, allowed—depending on the handset model—wireless access to the Internet through mobile telephones, laptops, or personal digital assistants (such as Palm Pilots). It also enabled customers to use voice and data services simultaneously. The WAP portal was a service-and-contents channel available to wireless customers.

Telemar's variety of customized, high-speed data-transmission services, through Pegasus, included video-conferencing, video/image transmission, multimedia applications, and interconnectivity between local area networks at data-transmission speeds. Its Velox service was offering high-speed Internet service and other data-transmission services using ADSL technology to residential customers as well as small and medium-sized business customers. The company also was leasing dedicated lines to other telecommunications service providers, Internet service providers, and corporate customers.

TLN was 58-percent-owned by Telemar Participações S.A. in 2005. This company consisted of nine common-stock shareholders, with the largest being BNDES Participações S.A., representing the government development bank and holding one-quarter of the shares. Until late 2004 TNL still owned 81 percent of the combined share capital of Telemar. Then TNL's board of directors approved a proposal to capitalize its new wholly-owned subsidiary, Telemar Telecomunicações Ltda., by transferring to it all the Telemar preferred shares held by TNL. After this change, TNL became a direct holder of 43 percent of Telemar's share capital, indirectly maintaining a holding of 97 percent of the voting capital and 81 percent of the total share capital of Telemar through Telemar Telecomunicações. In May 2006 TNL proposed that its shareholders approve a plan that would make TNL a wholly owned subsidiary of Telemar Participações S.A., exchanging their TNL shares for shares in the parent company.

Robert Halasz

PRINCIPAL SUBSIDIARIES

HiCorp Comunicações Corporativas S.A.; Telemar Norte Leste S.A.–Telemar; Telemar Telecommunicações Ltda.

PRINCIPAL COMPETITORS

BCP S.A.; Brasil Telecom S.A.; Cellular CRT Participações S.A.; Empresa Brasileira de Telecomunicações S.A.; Telefónica Empresas S.A.; TIM Celular S.A.

FURTHER READING

"Brazilian Phone Company Buys Internet Access Concern," *New York Times,* December 25, 2000, p. C2.

Kepp, Michael, "Built for Speed," *Latin Trade,* March 2004, pp. 30-31.

"The Questionable Case of Telemar," *LatinFinance,* December 2000, p. 77.

Rich, Jennifer, "In Quick Recovery, Brazil Sells Three Wireless Licenses," *New York Times,* February 14, 2001, p. W1.

Wheatley, Jonathan, "Brazil Deal Opens Debate on Governance," *Financial Times,* June 9, 2003, p. 28.

Tilcon-Connecticut Inc.

152 Black Rock Avenue
New Britain, Connecticut 06052-0000
U.S.A.
Telephone: (860) 223-3651
Fax: (860) 229-2029
Web site: http://www.tilconct.com

Wholly Owned Subsidiary of CRH plc
Incorporated: 1923
Employees: 300 (2005)
Sales: $37.7 million (2005 est.)
NAIC: 324121 Asphalt Paving Mixture and Block Manufacturing

■ ■ ■

Headquartered in New Britain, Connecticut, Tilcon Connecticut Inc. is a supplier of crushed stone, hot mix asphalt, and ready mix concrete. From the Massachusetts border to the Connecticut shoreline, the company serves customers throughout its home state from 25 different locations. Each year, Tilcon supplies millions of tons of aggregate from five quarries and two sand and gravel pits. The company produces asphalt products at 22 asphalt plants, where computers control the mixing process and certified technicians test mixes for uniformity and quality. At nine ready-mix concrete plants throughout Connecticut, the company uses computer systems to maximize efficiency in the areas of batching control, dispatching, job tracking, and delivery. In addition, skilled professionals are responsible for testing and quality control. As one of Connecticut's largest paving

companies, Tilcon paves and repairs many miles of new roads, bridges, and highways each year. The company has won numerous awards for its work in this area. In addition to using technologically advanced equipment, Tilcon employs experienced road crews, estimators, inspectors, lab technicians, paving superintendents, and quality control engineers. Through its Heavy & Highway Construction division, Tilcon has created paved surfaces and roadways at a variety of sites, ranging from office buildings and manufacturing plants to schools and shopping malls. Finally, Tilcon's Buchanan Marine division is engaged in barge transportation, annually moving some 6 million tons of crushed stone from quarries in northeast Connecticut to New York City and Long Island. This is accomplished via a fleet of 250 aggregate barges and 11 tugboats. In addition to its own shipyard, the company works from various docks throughout Connecticut, Delaware, New Jersey, New York, and Virginia.

HUMBLE BEGINNINGS: 1923–1956

Before Tilcon Connecticut began paving the way for travelers, an Italian immigrant named Angelo Tomasso, Sr., traveled to the United States in search of new opportunities. Born in 1892, Tomasso arrived in America in 1910. Working as a day laborer, he eventually joined a New York contractor who promoted him to the position of foreman. After serving his new country during World War I, Tomasso established a construction company called Angelo Tomasso Inc. in 1923.

Using a lone Bucyrus Erie steam shovel, Tomasso went to work building roads and working on sewer projects. He was among the very first contractors to work on New York's Taconic Parkway, working on construction in the Poughkeepsie area. Tomasso and his wife, Nazzarena, eventually produced four sons (Angelo Jr., Victor A., George A., and William J.). Angelo marked the birth of each son by purchasing a new steam shovel for his fledgling enterprise.

According to the August 5, 1952 issue of the *New Britain Herald,* Tomasso was active outside of the construction business. In addition to founding a number of ethnic organizations, he was considered a leader in the Democratic Party and became friends with Franklin D. Roosevelt while the latter was governor of New York.

During the 1930s and 1940s, Angelo Tomasso Inc. paved the majority of the roads throughout the city of New Britain. The company's first hot mix asphalt plant was erected in 1939. The following year, a quarry in Plainville, Connecticut, was acquired.

On November 19, 1949, Tomasso was hurt on the job while working at his quarry in Plainville, Connecticut. The accident caused a large stone to strike him in the head. Tomasso recovered from the ordeal and, with the help of his wife and sons, continued building his firm.

Angelo Tomasso, Sr., died in his home following a brief illness on August 4, 1952. In the August 5, 1952, issue of the *New Britain Herald,* New Britain Mayor John L. Sullivan remembered Tomasso as "an outstanding citizen" and credited him for improving the city's roadways. Following his father's death, Angelo Tomasso, Jr., became president and CEO of the company.

After graduating from New Britain High School in 1943, Angelo Tomasso, Jr., joined the Navy. He served as a petty officer in the Amphibious Corps during World War II and received a Purple Heart. Tomasso furthered his education after the war by enrolling in Naval Officers Training School at Alabama's Auburn University. Upon earning an undergraduate civil engineering degree, Tomasso returned to New Britain. Securing a position as general superintendent of Angelo Tomasso Inc., Angelo Jr. and his brothers gained a reputation for managing the construction of major highway projects, including Routes 2 and 9, and Interstate Highways 91 and 94.

INITIAL GROWTH & EXPANSION: 1957–1978

Starting in the late 1950s Angelo Tomasso, Jr., led his family's company through a period of growth and expansion. A string of acquisitions allowed the company to gain a number of asphalt plants, concrete plants, and quarries in Connecticut.

Tomasso of North Haven Inc. was established in 1957, following the acquisition of the North Haven Asphalt Co. The purchase of New Britain–based Sherman Sand and Stone Co. in 1961 led to the formation of Sherman-Tomasso Concrete Inc. Arborio-Tomasso Inc. was formed in 1964, after the acquisition of Arborio & Sons in Farmington. A new concrete plant in Middletown was erected the following year.

Angelo Tomasso Inc. reached a productivity milestone in 1968 while working on Interstate 84 in the towns of Farmington, New Britain, and Plainville. On a 9-mile stretch of highway, the company laid 1 mile of concrete per day. Another development took place that year when Angelo Jr.'s four sons formed Tomasso Brothers Inc., a construction and development company, followed by a property management firm called Tunxis Management. The company ended the 1960s by acquiring Bristol-based Helming Brothers in 1969.

Growth and expansion continued in the early 1970s. Angelo Tomasso Inc. began the decade by building its Portland Asphalt Plant in 1970. The following year the company set a world record with cooperation from some of its competitors when, as part of a massive repaving project at Connecticut's Bradley Airport, 18,300 tons of bituminous concrete was laid in only 18 hours time.

In January 1972, Ashland, Kentucky–based Ashland Resources Co.—a division of Ashland Oil Inc.—purchased Angelo Tomasso Inc. Following the acquisition, Angelo Tomasso, Jr., was named a vice-president at Ashland. However, management of Angelo Tomasso Inc. continued under the family, with Angelo Tomasso, Jr., as president; Victor F. Tomasso as first vice-president; William J. Tomasso as second vice-president and assistant secretary; Nazzarena Tomasso as secretary and treasurer; and George A. Tomasso as assistant treasurer.

KEY DATES

1923: Angelo Tomasso Inc. is established.
1972: Ashland Resources Co. acquires Angelo Tomasso Inc.
1979: Thomas Tilling Ltd. acquires Ashland Oil's northeast regional construction group and Angelo Tomasso Inc. becomes Tilcon Tomasso.
1984: The company is acquired by British Tire and Rubber Co.
1990: Tilcon Tomasso changes its name to Tilcon-Connecticut.
1996: The company becomes a subsidiary of CRH Group plc.

At the time of the acquisition, which was rumored to be valued somewhere between $50 million and $83 million, Ashland already owned the New Haven Trap Rock Co., which was then Connecticut's largest supplier of crushed stone. According to Tilcon, "Trap Rock's North Branford quarry was considered the world's largest single-face trap rock quarry with a frontage of 1-¼ miles."

Around this time, Angelo Tomasso Inc. employed approximately 700 workers during the height of construction season. These employees used some 400 pieces of equipment to carry out their work. A January 15, 1972, article in the *New Britain Herald* called the company's plant "a model of automation for a concern dealing in trap rock, concrete and other material," explaining: "A sophisticated arrangement of equipment and control devices allow quick and accurate truck loading with little related confusion, spillage and the like. It has been the subject of several feature stories in the road building and concrete field. A hallmark of the company has been excellent maintenance and care of its vehicles."

UNDER INTERNATIONAL OWNERSHIP FROM 1979 INTO THE 21ST CENTURY

When the United Kingdom's Thomas Tilling Ltd. acquired Ashland Oil's northeast regional construction group in 1979, Angelo Tomasso Inc. fell under international ownership for the first time, becoming a division of Tilling subsidiary Tilcon Inc. Following the ownership change, Angelo Tomasso Inc. was renamed Tilcon Tomasso, and Angelo Tomasso, Jr., provided leadership to both concerns as president and CEO of Tilcon Inc.

Another ownership change came in 1984, when the company was acquired by British Tire and Rubber Co. One possible benefit of this acquisition may have been the ability to secure tires for Tilcon equipment at a reduced cost. This would have been of great help, as tires for some of its large quarry vehicles—standing as high as 10 feet—cost $8,000 apiece. The company's maintenance staff included workers who focused exclusively on the care of tires, performing regular inspections and maintaining detailed records. There was plenty of work to keep them busy; Tilcon changed as many as 5,000 tires each year.

During the mid-1980s, Tilcon moved crushed stone via a massive fleet of 400 to 500 trucks that received fuel from a 100,000-gallon diesel tank, as well as a 10,000-gallon gasoline tank. Oil was delivered to the company in shipments of 6,000 gallons. All of this fuel was drawn using a computerized access control system that monitored fuel usage. In addition to its vehicle fleet, Tilcon also owned its own railroad operation. The firm's fleet included 34 cars, each capable of moving 80 tons of stone.

To repair all of its equipment, Tilcon employed a staff of skilled mechanics. In addition to regular maintenance equipment, cranes were located in the garage for lifting heavy equipment, along with a massive lift for raising earth movers in need of repair. The company also relied on nine staff welders who worked two shifts. In addition to a welding shop, these employees also worked from portable welding vehicles when emergency repairs were needed out in the field.

In 1990 Tilcon Tomasso's name changed to Tilcon-Connecticut, and Angelo Tomasso, Jr., was appointed chairman of Tilcon Inc. That year, Tomasso received an honorary Doctorate of Humane Letters degree from Central Connecticut State University for his many contributions in the realm of community and public service. In the May 12, 1990, issue of the *New Britain Herald,* the university's president, John W. Shumaker, said: "Angelo Tomasso Jr. takes the same dedication and hard work that made him a success in business and applies those talents to improving the quality of life in the communities where he and his employees live and work. When his country, his state and his community have needed balanced, judicious and even gallant service, Angelo Tomasso has unfailingly responded with dedication, vision and generosity."

In a deal that *The London Evening Standard* valued at $279 million, CRH Group plc.—a construction conglomerate based in Dublin, Ireland, with 1995 profits of approximately $77 million—purchased Tilcon in

1996. Prior to the sale, CRH subsidiary Oldcastle Northeast Inc. was required to sell a quarry and two asphalt plants in order to avoid antitrust violations in the Hartford, Connecticut, area.

In 1998 Tilcon received the National Asphalt Pavement Association's National Ecological Award for environmentally friendly operations at its hot mix asphalt plant in Old Saybrook, Connecticut. The facility, located on the Long Island Sound shoreline, was bordered by residential neighborhoods and a fragile wetland. Tilcon implemented a number of measures to keep operations clean and quiet, and to make the site as visually appealing as possible.

According to the December 31, 2000, issue of the *New Britain Herald*, Angelo Tomasso, Jr., retired as Tilcon Inc.'s chairman on January 1, 2001. Following his retirement, the company continued under the leadership of President and CEO Joseph Abate, and his nephew, Carmine Abate, became president and CEO of Tilcon-Connecticut.

During the mid-2000s, Tilcon continued to be recognized by the industry with a variety of awards. In 2004 these included a Quality in Construction Award from the National Asphalt Pavement Association (NAPA); NAPA's Diamond Achievement Commendation for exemplary operations at Tilcon's New Britain asphalt plant; a Commitment to Environmental Excellence Award (honorable mention) from the National Ready Mixed Concrete Association; and a Showplace Award from the National Stone, Sand & Gravel Association for enhancing the appearance of the Tilcon Newington plant.

By 2005 Carmine Abate had been named president of Tilcon Connecticut, and the company remained a part of CRH. That year, the company was named as Habitat for Humanity's Corporate Partner of the Year in the Hartford, Connecticut, area. In addition, Tilcon continued to receive recognition for its work. Honors included an Excellence in Asphalt Pavement Construction Award for the company's work on Interstate 91 in the Connecticut towns of North Haven and Wallingford. The project was carried out under difficult conditions, including a quick turnaround and the requirement that

work could only be performed at night due to high traffic levels. Finally, Tilcon's hot-mix asphalt plants in Waterbury, Newington, North Branford, New Britain, and Manchester received NAPA's Diamond Achievement Commendation for operational excellence.

As of 2006, Tilcon enjoyed a position of market leadership in the northeastern United States. Moving forward into the late 2000s, it appeared that the company Angelo Tomasso, Sr., started with only one steam shovel would continue to grow and prosper.

Paul R. Greenland

PRINCIPAL DIVISIONS

Concrete & Asphalt; Heavy & Highway Construction; Buchanan Marine Transportation.

PRINCIPAL COMPETITORS

O and G Industries Inc.; Lane Construction Corporation.

FURTHER READING

"Angelo Tomasso Jr. to Receive Honorary Degree from CCSU," *New Britain Herald,* May 12, 1990.

"Contractor Dies at Residence Here," *New Britain Herald,* August 5, 1952.

Hathaway, William, "Irish Firm to Purchase Tilcon, Reports Say," *Hartford Courant,* September 4, 1996.

"Hundreds Attend Tomasso Funeral," *New Britain Herald,* August 7, 1952.

"Lean and Green," *Roads & Bridges,* September 1999.

"Quarrying Stone Is a Big Business for Tilcon Tomasso," *Herald Business & Industry Review,* 1984.

"Tilcon Celebrates Over 80 Years of Providing Building Materials for Central Connecticut," *New Britain Herald,* March 30, 1999.

"Tomasso Firm Sold to Kentucky Concern," *New Britain Herald,* January 15, 1972.

Whipple, Scott, "Construction Icon Leaving World of Concrete," *Herald Press,* December 31, 2000.

Tumbleweed, Inc.

2301 River Road
Suite 200
Louisville, Kentucky 40206
U.S.A.
Telephone: (502) 893-0323
Fax: (502) 893-6676
Web site: http://www.tumbleweedrestaurants.com

Private Company
Incorporated: 1995 as Tumbleweed LLC
Employees: 1,800
Sales: $100.9 million (2004 est.)
NAIC: 72211 Full-Service Restaurants; 72241 Drinking
     Places (Alcoholic Beverages)

■ ■ ■

Tumbleweed, Inc., owns, franchises, or licenses more than 50 Tumbleweed Southwest Mesquite Grill & Bar casual-dining restaurants in the United States (primarily in Kentucky and neighboring states) and abroad. Tumbleweed's menu consists of two distinct cuisines: spicy Tex-Mex dishes, such as burritos, enchiladas, and tacos; and mesquite-grilled Southwestern items, such as ribs, steaks, chicken, and seafood. Fresh ingredients are emphasized throughout. The price range of the menu items is fairly broad, in order to appeal to traditional casual dining customers as well as more cost-conscious patrons. The average check price in 2004 was about $8 for lunch and $15.50 for dinner.

1975–1995: FOUNDING AND EARLY GROWTH

Despite its distinctly western-sounding name, Tumbleweed was actually founded east of the Mississippi—in New Albany, Indiana. It was the brainchild of George and Linda Keller, a young married couple who had grown up in the New Albany area, just across the river from Louisville.

In 1975, the Kellers decided to open a Mexican restaurant, convinced by friends in Arizona that the popularity of Mexican cuisine was on the rise. Since Mexican food was in decidedly short supply in Indiana in the mid-1970s, however, the couple had little precedent in the way of recipes and menus. Amassing a collection of cookbooks, they began testing different recipes, using a trial-and-error approach to refine their concoctions. Eventually, they developed a complete menu for the new eatery, which opened in 1976 as Tumbleweed.

Tumbleweed was a big hit right away, with patrons lining up on the sidewalk to wait for one of the restaurant's 28 tables. The venture turned a profit its very first year and continued to do so consistently. Soon, the Kellers came to believe they could turn their single restaurant into a chain; by 1989, they had opened four more Tumbleweeds, all in the Louisville area. In addition, they had sold franchises for five other Tumbleweed locations: two in New Albany, one in Salem, Indiana, one in Lexington, Kentucky, and one in Fort Wright, Kentucky.

By the mid-1990s, the Kellers had expanded their chain to include seven company-owned and seven

COMPANY PERSPECTIVES

Imagine a return to the days of the Great Southwest, filled with the aroma of fresh cut steaks grillin' over a real Mesquite campfire. Where honest flavors and large portions satisfied even the heartiest of appetites. Tumbleweed Southwest Grill combines the hearty flavors of Mesquite grilling with south-of-the-border Mexican-style favorites to create a unique concept — Southwestern Cowboy — that provides a special franchise opportunity.

franchised restaurants in Kentucky, Indiana, and Wisconsin, as well as two joint-venture food-court outlets. The menu had evolved into a combination of mesquite-grilled foods and flavorful, spicy Mexican meals. This dual menu, which created a sort of hybrid between a steak house and a Mexican restaurant, was designed to appeal to a broader range of patrons than either type of restaurant alone could.

The Kellers believed there were tremendous growth opportunities for Tumbleweed. They knew, however, that to take advantage of those opportunities, the business needed an infusion of capital. "Tumbleweed is nowhere near its potential," George Keller said in an address to his employees in December 1994, as reported by the *Louisville Courier-Journal*. Keller said that reaching that potential required "financial resources greater than the current ownership is able to provide." In order to secure the capital necessary for further expansion, Keller worked with one of Tumbleweed's executives to structure a buyout.

The buyout was led by John A. (Jack) Butorac, Jr., a long-time veteran of the restaurant business. In his 27 years as a restaurateur, Butorac had served as owner, operator, consultant, and senior operations executive for a number of chains—including Chi-Chi's, Fuddrucker, Two Pesos Mexican Cafes, and Kentucky Fried Chicken. He had joined Tumbleweed in 1991 as a consultant and had since then played a key role in the chain's growth and development.

Joining Butorac were James Mulrooney, David Roth, and David Cooper. Mulrooney was an accountant with a background in real estate development and restaurant operations. Like Butorac, he had spent several years in management positions with Chi-Chi's. Roth and Cooper were partners in a local law firm. The principles formed Tumbleweed LLC—a limited liability company

established for the express purpose of purchasing the Tumbleweed chain—and set about finding more investors to put up cash for the deal. When the buyout was completed in January 1995, the investor group consisted of more than 60 individuals who, together, put up approximately $15 million. George and Linda Keller received $9.8 million for the company's assets, and an additional $1 million in exchange for signing a non-compete agreement.

Butorac took over as the company's new president and CEO, and Mulrooney served as executive vice-president and CFO. George Keller, who had retained a minority stake in the chain, held a position on its board of directors.

1995–1997: GROWTH THROUGH FRANCHISING

Tumbleweed's new management group had ambitious plans for the chain's growth. Their goal was to have 114 restaurants open by the end of 1998, which would mean adding roughly 24 new restaurants each year. They planned to make no substantial alterations to the restaurants' concept, menu, staffing, or management style—merely to accelerate the pace.

By early 1996, however, Tumbleweed had managed to add only five restaurants, bringing the chain total to 19. Butorac and his team had revised the company's expansion strategy to allow for more modest goals: 40 restaurants open by the end of 1997, and up to 65 by the end of 1998. In a December 1996 interview with *Business First of Louisville*, Butorac attributed the slower-than-projected growth to the company's inability to quickly enlist qualified franchisees.

In order to attract more franchisees, the owners began to review and modify the existing franchise program. One of the first changes they made was designed to offer more flexibility in restaurant size. Up to that point, the average Tumbleweed consisted of approximately 7,000 square feet, with seating for around 275 people. Because of their size, these restaurants were economically viable only in fairly large markets, which limited the pool of potential franchise sites. Butorac realized, however, that there were many smaller markets where a scaled-down version of the restaurant could be profitable.

Soon, Tumbleweed franchisees had three restaurant sizes to choose from: the traditional "maxi," or one of two new, smaller options: the "midi" or the "mini." The midi comprised approximately 5,400 square feet and seated 225, while the 3,500-square foot mini had room for 130. The company's new franchise literature claimed that the flexible Tumbleweed concept was "adaptable for virtually any size market."

Germany, in February 1998. Restaurants in Jedda, Saudi Arabia, and Brussels soon followed. At the same time, Tumbleweed International began construction on three new locations: one in Amman, Jordan, and one in Cairo.

Because Smith's company was a licensee, rather than a franchisee, it had the ability to grant franchises of its own. Within just a few months of signing the licensing deal, Tumbleweed International had sold franchise rights to investors in Lebanon and Turkey. As of May 1998, Tumbleweed International's plans were to have 40 units operational by late 1999.

1998–1999: DIRECT PUBLIC OFFERING

By the end of 1998, the Tumbleweed chain had grown to approximately 40 restaurants in six states and three foreign countries. More than half of the restaurants were corporate-owned. The company had total revenues of $42.8 million, and net income of $1.3 million. In September of that year, Butorac received permission from the Securities and Exchange Commission to take Tumbleweed public. The company hoped to raise $12 million by selling 1.2 million shares priced at $10 each. Because $12 million was a small offering, however, the company leaders knew they would have a hard time finding an underwriter to handle it. Thus the company decided to offer its shares in a direct public offering (DPO), a method that eliminated the underwriter typically used in initial public offerings.

Taking the DPO route meant that the company's executives had to market shares directly to investors. After distributing about 10,000 prospectuses, they managed to attract 1,186 investors, who between them purchased 776,543 shares. Most of the investors were customers or company employees, and 80 percent of them were located in the five-county area around Louisville. Although the offering fell short of its intended goal, it did generate almost $7.8 million, a very good showing, considering the difficulties of going public without an underwriter. In conjunction with the offering, Tumbleweed was reorganized from a limited liability company into a corporation: Tumbleweed, Inc.

While most of the proceeds from Tumbleweed's DPO went to pay down debt, part also went to fuel further expansion and to boost advertising efforts. By the spring of 1999, the company had opened two new franchised stores, and four more sites were contracted for. Management's goal was to open a total of 15 new restaurants by the end of the year. The company also dropped $1 million into a new advertising campaign designed to increase awareness in markets outside Louisville. The campaign—with a "Fun, Food and

Another feature designed to make Tumbleweed attractive to potential franchisees was the company's use of a central commissary for the majority of the individual restaurants' food needs. Whenever possible, cooked food ingredients and sauces were prepared in advance at the commissary and shipped to the restaurants, leaving only the final preparation for the restaurant workers. Because the restaurant itself was not responsible for extensive cooking, it required less kitchen space than it otherwise would have. This allowed for more seating space, and hence the potential for greater income. It also greatly simplified day-to-day operations for the restaurant owners and managers, and ensured consistency in the menu items. The commissary did not operate to make a profit; franchisees were charged only slightly more than the actual cost of the food.

By late 1997, there were 29 Tumbleweed restaurants up and running. Of the 29, 17 were company-owned and 12 were franchised. Although most of its growth to that point had been geographically focused in Kentucky, Indiana, and Ohio, the company was preparing to jump into international markets. In November 1997, Tumbleweed teamed up with Terrance A. (Terry) Smith—a restaurateur in Brussels, Belgium—to put together a licensing deal.

Smith was a Chi-Chi's franchisee with 17 restaurants in ten European, Middle Eastern, and Far Eastern countries. Under the terms of the licensing deal, Smith's newly formed company—Tumbleweed International LLC—was given exclusive rights to develop Tumbleweed restaurants outside North and South America. Smith immediately began converting his 17 Chi-Chi's locations to Tumbleweeds, reopening the first in Ehrlangen,

Friends" theme—emphasized Tumbleweed's South-western-style cuisine, rather than its Mexican dishes.

When Tumbleweed went public, it did not immediately meet the minimum criteria for listing on the NASDAQ exchange. Its shares were instead traded on the less-widely followed OTC Bulletin Board. In April 1999, however, NASDAQ approved the company for listing on its National Market exchange. The NASDAQ listing was important because it gave Tumbleweed stock a far greater exposure. In an April 29, 1999, press release, Butorac called the listing a "corporate milestone" in the company's continuing progress. "This listing will enhance the visibility of Tumbleweed to individual and institutional investors," he said, adding "This should improve the liquidity of the holdings of our current shareholders and help us in our efforts to expand the coverage and sponsorship of the company's shares."

During the first half of 1999, Tumbleweed's expansion rate accelerated. By August, eight new restaurants had been added, bringing the total number to 48. Of the 48 locations, 28 were corporate-owned, five were licensed to Tumbleweed International, and the remainder were franchised. Tumbleweed was also laying the groundwork for further expansion in the near future. In August, the company signed a development agreement with one of its existing franchisees to open at least 11 units in the coming five years. Moreover, in September, a new franchisee in Virginia contracted to open at least 13 new restaurants over a six year period, giving Tumbleweed entry into a new state.

At the end of 1999, five years after Butorac's investor group acquired Tumbleweed, the company remained committed to expansion. Although it had failed to achieve the kind of explosive growth the owners originally aimed for, it had nonetheless made significant strides toward reaching its potential. In the five years since the buyout, the chain had more than tripled in size, expanding into two new states and four foreign markets, all the while remaining consistently profitable.

As Tumbleweed rolled into the new century, its management planned to continue growing the chain through the addition of both franchised and corporate-owned restaurants. The company would likely continue to seek entry into new geographic territories, while at the same focusing on increasing its presence in many of its existing markets.

Tumbleweed Inc.'s total revenues rose 20 percent to $51.4 million in 1999 as the company opened a dozen new mesquite grills. Though pretax profit increased 73 percent to $3.4 million, net income fell by a third to $1.2 million. Unfortunately, the company slipped into the red in 2001, posting a $3.4 million net loss on total revenues of $59.5 million. In 2002, the company's last

full year before being taken private again, the loss was reduced to $964,663 on revenues of $57.6 million.

The 19 international restaurants of licensee Tumbleweed International had total sales of $38 million in 1999, according to *Chain Leader*. Only five of these were Tumbleweed restaurants, all recently opened; the rest were Chi-Chi's.

Tumbleweed, Inc. bought Tumbleweed International, LLC in 2002 for $1.5 million. The licensee had been 40 percent owned by Chi-Chi's International Operations, Inc. In August 2000, Tumbleweed International chief Terry Smith had succeeded Jack Butorac as Tumbleweed, Inc.'s CEO, chairman, and president. The two had worked together years before at Chi-Chi's.

Tumbleweed was refining its casual dining concept, reported *Nation's Restaurant News*. The "blue jeans Texas" atmosphere was being replaced by a "contemporary Southwest" theme, reflected in brighter interior and exterior colors, upgraded décor, and plateware. The menus were also reworked. Steaks and grilled items were becoming more important; the company stopped using frozen steaks and added other fresh ingredients. In addition, Smith told *The Wall Street Transcript*, the chain was rolling out four seasonal menus a year while cutting items that weren't selling enough. He added that an expanded range of side items proved to be a surprisingly significant factor in winning customers.

Relations with franchisees were another area of improvement. According to Smith, Tumbleweed adopted a more inclusive approach to implementing change. This helped get Tumbleweed ranked among the top ten of U.S. franchising companies in *Success Magazine*. The culture within the company was also becoming less hierarchical, added Smith in *The Wall Street Transcript*.

Four underperforming stores were closed in the slow economy of 2002. At year-end, Tumbleweed announced a new $18 million financing package from GE Capital Franchise Finance Corporation. The company then owned 31 Tumbleweed restaurants while its six franchisees operated 19.

An investment group including CEO Terrance Smith, director David Roth, and shareholder Gerald Mansbach owned 46.2 percent of shares. (Mansbach alone had a 40.5 percent holding.) In June 2002 they proposed buying out the rest of the company at a 47 percent premium; the stock was then trading about $1.75 a share. This bid was dropped in November 2002 due to a slowing economy and difficulty obtaining financing.

PRIVATE IN 2003

The company was taken private around Thanksgiving 2003 by buying out small shareholders, reducing the total number of investors from 1,000 to about 120. Smith explained that it was too small to deal with the hassles of trading publicly, particularly after the Sarbanes-Oxley Act of 2002 began requiring more stringent accounting practices and reporting. He told *Nation's Restaurant News* the company had been spending $350,000 a year on the costs of filing the required reports. The market itself had been a roller coaster for the company; its share price had ranged from a penny to more than a dollar in one year.

Domestic systemwide sales rose from $94.1 million in 2003 to $100.9 million in 2004, according to *Nation's Restaurant News*. Tumbleweed marked its 30th anniversary year with a new 340-seat flagship location on the downtown Louisville riverfront. At the end of 2005, Tumbleweed was operating 26 company-owned restaurants and franchising or licensing another 27.

Shawna Brynildssen
Updated, Frederick C. Ingram

PRINCIPAL COMPETITORS

Applebee's International, Inc.; O'Charley's Inc.; Texas Roadhouse, Inc.; Outback Steakhouse, Inc.

FURTHER READING

Boyd, Terry, "Louisvillians to Take Tumbleweed Around the World," *Business First of Louisville*, May 11, 1998.

———, "Tumbleweed Gets Approval for Direct Public Offering," *Business First of Louisville*, September 28, 1998.

"CEO/Company Interview: Terrance A. Smith, Tumbleweed, Inc.," *Wall Street Transcript*, August 20, 2001.

Cooper, Ron, "Tumbleweed Growth to be Spurred by Franchisees," *Business First of Louisville*, December 2, 1996.

Duecy, Erica, "Tumbleweed Goes Private, Blows Off Public Market," *Nation's Restaurant News*, October 20, 2003, p. 8.

Egerton, Judith, "Tumbleweed Restaurant Chain to be Sold: Deal to Help Firm Expand," *Louisville Courier-Journal*, December 29, 1994, p. C1.

Farkas, David, "Mexican Emigration: An American Expatriate in Europe Rebuilds His Business After Chi-Chi's Headed South," *Chain Leader*, February 2000, p. 44.

Grant, Robert L., "CEO's Group Offers to Buy Tumbleweed Inc for $1.75/Share," *Dow Jones Corporate Filings Alert*, June 3, 2002.

"Mansbach Group Drops Bid to Buy Tumbleweed," *Nation's Restaurant News*, November 4, 2002, p. 78.

Mehegan, Sean, "Sell the Sound: Tumbleweed Extends Its Brand Through CD Sales," *Restaurant Business*, February 2006, p. 18.

Papiernik, Richard, "Tumbleweed's Earnings Roll Into 73% Gain in Fiscal 1999," *Nation's Restaurant News*, April 17, 2000, p. 12.

Redding, Rick, "Tumbleweed Sets Expansion Plans after Stock Sale," *Business First of Louisville*, April 5, 1999.

"Tumbleweed Directors Approve Plan to Buy Out Small Investors," *Lane Report*, July 1, 2003, p. 11.

"Tumbleweed Investors Offer to Acquire Company," *Reuters News*, June 3, 2002.

Walkup, Carolyn, "Tumbleweed Dusts Off Growth Plan After Chain Overhaul," *Nation's Restaurant News*, March 21, 2005.

Williams, Shirley, "Taste for Success Spurs Couple to New Ventures," *Louisville Courier-Journal*, November 1, 1989, p. N1.

UFA TV & Film Produktion GmbH

Dianastraße 21
Potsdam, 14482
Germany
Telephone: (49) (331) 7060-0
Fax: (49) (331) 7060-149
Web site: http://www.ufa.de

Private Company
Founded: 1917
Sales: EUR 320 million ($402 million) (2003)
NAIC: 512110 Motion Picture and Video Production;
512120 Motion Picture and Video Distribution;
512190 Postproduction Services and Other Motion
Picture and Video Industries; 512191 Teleproduc-
tion and Other Postproduction Services; 512199
Other Motion Picture and Video Industries

■ ■ ■

From its roots in the 1920s Golden Age of German
film, UFA TV & Film Produktion GmbH has developed
into one of Germany's most successful film production
companies. It produces programming for the country's
leading broadcasters, including ZDF, ARD, RTL, and
SAT 1; its shows are regularly among the most highly
rated on German television. UFA is part of Fremantle-
Media and includes all of Fremantle's production
activities. UFA in turn is divided into six independent
subsidiaries each of which is responsible for a different
production area: UFA Fernsehproduktion, teamWorx,
and Phoenix-Film produce television drama, including

mini-series, made-for-TV movies, and various specials.
UFA Entertainment specializes in documentaries, reality
TV, and other nonfiction genres. Grundy UFA produces
soap operas and prime-time drama series. GRUNDY
Light Entertainment produces a broad spectrum of TV
comedies, quiz shows, music and variety shows, and
panel shows. Altogether in 2004, UFA's various production arms produced 25 daily and weekly TV shows,
more than any other company in the German TV
market.

PROPAGANDA MOVIES AT THE END OF WORLD WAR I

UFA was founded, not by one of Wilhelmine Germany's
pioneer filmmakers, but by an officer in the German
military. In 1917, the tide of World War I was turning
decisively against Germany, and Erich Ludendorff, the
head of the German military and the nation's de facto
dictator, was looking for a way to reverse German public
opinion which had turned against the Kaiser's
government. His solution was to use the new medium
of movies for propaganda. Within months, the German
government, with funding from Deutsche Bank, secretly
purchased Nordisk Films Kompagni, Denmark's leading
film company. The Reichmark (RM) 10 million purchase
price included Nordisk's studios, its distribution
company, and its chain of movie theaters in Denmark,
Germany, and elsewhere in Europe. As a result, when it
was founded on December 17, 1917, Universum-Film
AG was a full-blown film company. It was owned jointly
by the German government and Deutsche Bank; execu-

COMPANY PERSPECTIVES

UFA is one of Germany's oldest and most distinguished entertainment brands, with an artistic heritage of films like *Metropolis, The Blue Angel,* and the German Expressionist films. Today, UFA is a highly competent group of production companies which over the past few years has continuously extended its market leadership among Germany's film and television producers. UFA's programs thrill and inspire millions of viewers every day. UFA evolved from a program designer and TV producer into a content specialist which offers a range of solutions for multimedia technologies—and for an extremely varied set of partners.

tives from Germany's leading firms, including AEG, Dresdner Bank, and the Norddeutscher Lloyd shipping line, sat on its board.

Ludendorff's original idea was to use the film company as a direct—and secret—arm of the German government carrying out its propaganda aims. The involvement of private commercial interests, however, guaranteed that a tug-of-war would eventually develop over control of UFA's artistic direction. What was attractive to all parties was the German public's nearly insatiable appetite for motion pictures during the war. They had been completely cut off from films by the world's largest producers, France and Britain since 1914, and the U.S. since 1916. A German national company—in an industry whose growth had lagged far behind the movie industries of other nations—could operate with a virtual monopoly. UFA set out immediately acquiring other movie companies, especially in Germany. Before the war had ended, it purchased Meester, a producer of films as well as movie equipment; Union-Konzern, a chain of 56 German movie houses; and the foreign arm of Deutscher Lichtbild-Gesellschaft, the latter as part of a never-realized plan to colonize film industries throughout Europe after a German victory. As defeat approached, government control of UFA became more and more tenuous. In 1918 more and more UFA productions were pure entertainment, to distract public opinion and attention, rather than propaganda intended to influence it. When Germany erupted in a revolution that overthrew the Kaiser at the end of the year, government control of the company ended, too.

THE RISE AND FALL OF THE GOLDEN AGE OF FILM DURING THE WEIMAR REPUBLIC

With its other business acquisitions, UFA was also acquiring the most talented members of the German moving picture industry, whose work would usher in the so-called golden age of German film in the 1920s. The most important of these artists early on was director Ernst Lubitsch, whose films brought UFA its first artistic and commercial successes. *Madame DuBarry,* for example, was licensed to American investors for $40,000. They made $500,000 from it in its first two weeks of exhibition. The American rights to Lubitsch's next film, *Anna Boleyn,* were sold for $200,000, about RM 14 million—almost twice as much as it had cost to make the film. Small wonder that Lubitsch became, in 1922, the first important figure to leave Germany for Hollywood.

Once in power, the Social Democrats ended the government's involvement in film almost immediately. In 1920 the government made public its UFA holdings; in 1923 it sold all of its UFA shares to the Deutsche Bank. One reason for the government's exit was a projected loss from film making that could be prevented only by massive infusions of between RM 20 million and RM 100 million. As the new majority shareholder, Deutsche Bank named its director, Emil Georg von Stauss, as UFA chairman. A political nationalist, von Stauss was as deeply committed to the formation of a German film industry as he was to the other new German companies he supported, Daimler Benz and Lufthansa.

In 1921 UFA merged with Decla-Bioscop AG, Germany's second largest film company. Decla was the company that inaugurated the era of "expressionist" film in 1919 with *The Cabinet of Doctor Caligari*; it had also given director Fritz Lang his start. The merger was arguably the most important in UFA's history—it combined two powerful studios, distribution systems, and rosters of stars and technicians. Most significantly, UFA a year later took over the Decla-Bioscop studios in the town of Neubabelsberg, just outside Berlin. By the mid-1920s, "Babelsberg" had become the world's most important studio complex outside of Hollywood and UFA Germany's film studio, featuring stars such as Paul Wegener, Emil Jannings, and Pola Negri, and directors like Lang, F.W. Murnau, and Joe May.

UFA's aggressive business strategies—and the foreign currency its foreign successes brought in—enabled it to survive the catastrophic inflation of 1923 that threatened to bring down Germany's economy and government. The company was a complex business and artistic entity.

KEY DATES

1917: Universum-Film AG is founded.
1921: The German government sells its UFA holdings to the Deutsche Bank; UFA merges with Decla-Bioscop.
1922: UFA takes over the Decla-Bioscop studios in Neubabelsberg.
1925: UFA founds the film duplication company, Aktiengesellschaft fuer Filmfabrikation (Afifa); UFA-Wochenschau, its newsreel series, first goes into production.
1927: Fritz Lang's *Metropolis* is released; Alfred Hugenberg's Scherl-Gruppe acquires UFA.
1930: *The Blue Angel*, featuring Marlene Dietrich, is released.
1937: UFA and other German film studios are sold to the German government and administered by the holding company, Cautio GmbH.
1942: UFA-Film GmbH (Ufi) is founded.
1945: The Russian army occupies the Neubabelsberg studios.
1946: Russians nationalize East German UFA facilities and found Deutscher Filmaktiengesellschaft (DEFA).
1949: American and British occupation authorities launch their first attempts to break up the Ufi conglomerate.
1956: Remaining West German UFA holdings are sold by German government to Deutsche Bank.
1964: Deutsche Bank sells its UFA holdings to Verlagsgruppe Bertelsmann.
1972: Bertelsmann sells UFA-Theater AG to Riech Group.
1984: Bertelsmann and Gruner & Jahr form UFA Film- und Fernseh GmbH.
1992: UFA celebrates its 75th anniversary.
1997: UFA Film- und Fernseh GmbH merges with CLT of Luxembourg to form CLT-UFA.
2000: CLT-UFA merges with Pearson TV to form the RTL Group.

Its structure included production, distribution, and exhibition subsidiaries that operated with complete independence. In 1925 it added another arm, the Aktiengesellschaft fuer Filmfabrikation (Afifa), a film duplication business. Its chain of magnificent first run theaters was famous throughout Europe. Under Erich Pommer, its *wunderkind* production head, UFA released a string of films in the middle 1920s that would one day be considered classics of the Golden Age of Film, movies like *Dr. Mabuse, der Spieler, The Last Laugh, Die Nibelungen, Asphalt,* and *Metropolis.* Yet despite its artistic successes, UFA was approaching the brink of financial ruin.

During the period of inflation, foreign filmmakers ignored Germany. After the 1923 currency reform, however, American films flooded the market, while UFA films found it difficult to get shown in foreign theaters. Receipts fell. Fritz Lang's *Metropolis,* the most expensive film of its time, flopped in the U.S., leaving UFA RM 50 million in debt. To add insult to injury, German film artists, such as F.W. Murnau, Emil Jannings, even production head Pommer, began abandoning Germany to work in Hollywood. Seeking a way out of the desperate situation, UFA turned to its American competitors. Metro-Goldwyn and Paramount provided a sizable loan, for which UFA agreed to distribute twenty of each studio's films in Germany. The Americans were required to distribute only ten UFA productions, and then only if they found the movies to be consistent with American tastes. Another $270,000 loan from Universal required UFA to distribute fifty more American movies in Germany.

Facing insurmountable difficulties, Deutsche Bank decided to get out of the movie business. It sold its complete UFA holdings to Alfred Hugenberg, a media magnate with close ties to a number of right-wing politicians, including Adolf Hitler. Hugenberg acquired UFA at a bargain basement price, only RM 13.5 million, far below the RM 75 million at which the company had been valued. For that bargain price he received UFA's 140 subsidiaries in Germany, Europe, and North America, approximately 3.5 million square feet of studio area in Berlin and Neubabelsberg, and some 100 movie theaters. Hugenberg was willing to take a chance with UFA anyway—he wanted the company more to propagate his nationalist ideological message than to make money.

Despite the trend underway in the United States, UFA hesitated to introduce sound to their motion pictures. An early UFA experiment with sound was met with complete public indifference in 1925. When UFA's business manager visited New York three years later, however, talkies were being shown in virtually every movie theater on Broadway. As soon as he returned to Germany, UFA launched an aggressive move into sound. By 1929 it had built a state-of-the-art sound studio in Neubabelsberg; by the time the Great Depression reached its height in 1932, most of UFA's theaters had been equipped to exhibit talkies. Both moves gave the studio a vast lead over its German competition. Among its first influential sound pictures were *The Blue Angel,* the film that launched Marlene Dietrich's career, and *Die Drei von der Tankstelle,* which ignited a craze for light musicals in Germany that would last until the end of World War II. Sound created new enthusiasm for film in Germany, but it also brought commercial disadvantages. Sound films could not so easily be exported, especially to lucrative markets like the U.S. and Britain, and the initial technical expense required in those economically hard times led to a drop in the number of films produced. Nonetheless, Hugenberg's Spartan cost-cutting measures put the firm back in the black. By the time Hitler came to power in January 1933, Hugenberg had bought out the shares of all foreign investors, making the firm "pure German" and setting the stage for its complete Nazification.

PROPAGANDA FILMS DURING THE THIRD REICH

Before 1933, UFA had produced some films with nationalist themes that were in line with Hugenberg's ideological leanings. The bulk of its releases were innocent comedies, melodramas, musicals, and serious drama. Almost immediately after Hitler's rise, however, UFA fell in line with the new regime. Just eight months after Hitler's appointment as Chancellor, the company released *Hitlerjunge Quex*—Hitler Youth Quex—the story of an idealistic young Nazi allegedly murdered by Communists. UFA film projects that were already underway but which were seen as not conforming sufficiently to the Nazi line were cancelled. Jewish actors, directors and technicians were forced to leave UFA beginning in spring 1933. Other UFA artists, like Fritz Lang and Marlene Dietrich, left Germany to try their luck in the United States. Nazi Propaganda Minister Joseph Goebbels, who believed passionately in the power of film, took steps almost immediately to bring UFA directly under his control.

An important move in securing that control was the incorporation of the Filmkreditbank GmbH, a government-run credit institution that financed the lion's share of film production costs, but required producers to submit to government censorship. Meanwhile the Nazi government began a systematic takeover of all German media, and in March 1937 Alfred Hugenberg had to sell all of his UFA shares to the German government. UFA and other studios were placed in a state-run holding company, Cautio GmbH. The circle had closed. In twenty years time, UFA had gone from a government propaganda agency, to one of the world's most highly respected private film studios, and back again. By 1942 the entire German film industry had been consolidated into two UFA companies: UFA-Film GmbH, which was responsible for production, and UFA GmbH, which handled newsreel production, distribution, and other aspects of film work.

Despite control by Goebbels' Propaganda Ministry, comedies, musicals, and melodramas continued to account for the majority of theatrical movies produced in Germany, although a few military dramas that idealized war, soldiers, and German expansionism, like *Urlaub auf Ehrenwort* and *Pour le Merite,* were important propaganda vehicles. Most propaganda during the Third Reich was presented in UFA newsreels. Footage of German victories was used to boost German morale at home and to demoralize morale elsewhere in Europe. Newsreels of the German invasion of Poland were shown to diplomats from Holland, Belgium, Norway, and Romania, for example, shortly before German armies crossed their borders. UFA celebrated its 25th anniversary during the battle of Stalingrad when the tide turned once and for all against Germany. UFA newsreels continued to urge Germans on to victory. What the public wanted, however, was escape, through productions like the comic fantasy of *Munchhausen,* made in 1943 as millions of German soldiers were being killed or taken into Soviet captivity. Being a movie actor or technician continued to have perks in the last months of the war, as film teams shot their melodramas increasingly in idyllic countrysides far from nightly bombing raids in the cities.

UFA IN THE COLD WAR

On April 24, 1945, Russians occupied the Neubabelsberg UFA studios, and when peace was finally declared they controlled about 70 percent of all Ufi production facilities. The Russians rapidly reorganized those properties into the East German studio Deutscher Filmaktiengesellschaft (German Film Share Corporation), better known as DEFA. In spring 1946 DEFA began production on the first postwar German film, *Die Moerder sind unter uns,* (The Murderers Are Among Us), a powerful drama in the best 1920s UFA tradition that confronted the all-too-recent Nazi past head on.

The western allies banned all German film making. In September 1949 the American military, which had put former UFA head Erich Pommer in charge of their Motion Picture Division, seized the remaining Ufi properties. They announced a plan to break up the old Ufi conglomerate and sell off the parts. At the same time, the names "Ufi" and "UFA" were banned. It was difficult to make UFA disappear however. The 28 movies made in Germany between 1946 and 1948 *all* used former UFA directors, actors, and technicians exclusively.

The proposed break-up also met with the resistance of the West German government, which hoped to reestablish a national German film industry and—secretly—recreate its own government propaganda studio.

By 1953 Cautio GmbH had been dissolved, but Ufi continued to exist. In 1956 UFA history repeated itself once again, when the German government sold the remaining Ufi subsidiaries to the Deutsche Bank for approximately a third of their real value. UFA seemed to have a new lease on life, but as the 1960s began the "reborn" UFA was beset with problems. Unlike DEFA, its East German counterpart, which released popular movies regularly, UFA films couldn't seem to find the West German pulse. Furthermore film popularity in West Germany was waning, and as ticket sales fell, Deutsche Bank got cold feet. It replaced its controversial UFA CEO Arno Hauke, but his replacement spent large sums on a range of films that was too broad for the relatively small German market. By January 1962, the situation was so bad that the UFA board voted to cease theatrical film production and distribution altogether, reducing the once proud firm to a chain of movie houses. At the end of 1963, Deutsche Bank sold UFA's West Berlin studios and its duplication facilities to Becker & Kries. In 1964 the remainder of its UFA holdings—including the UFA music publishing company, UFA's advertising film company, the theater chain UFA-Theater AG, and the rights to all UFA films—were acquired by the publishing giant Bertelsmann AG.

UFA UNDER BERTELSMANN

The acquisition was important for Bertelsmann. It enabled the company to expand into film and TV and helped make it one of Europe's leading media companies. Afterwards Bertelsmann sold the old newsreel company UFA-Wochenschau to the government; its Berlin studios were sold to ZDF, one of two German public broadcasters. Bertelsmann retained the UFA advertising film company, UFA-Werbefilm, and the TV production firm, UFA-Ferhsehenproduktion. In 1972 Bertelsmann sold the UFA-Theater AG to the Riech Group, retaining only its large premier cinemas. Bertelsmann also retained the rights to the UFA name and logo, and licensed their use to Riech. The rights to the old UFA movies were transferred to a nonprofit group, the F.W. Murnau Foundation, on the instigation of the German government, to prevent their being auctioned off individually to private bidders.

Under Bertelsmann, UFA concentrated on producing programming for television. In 1984, when private broadcasting was introduced in West Germany, Bertelsmann and media firm Gruner & Jahr merged their film

and TV production activities into a holding company, the Hamburg-based UFA Film- und Fernseh GmbH. In 1987 UFA Film- und Fernseh purchased the Deutscher Fussballbund—an organization comparable in scope to major and minor league baseball—together with all broadcast rights. In 1991, on the occasion of the company's 75th anniversary, a new UFA logo, based on the famous UFA rhombus of the 1920s, was introduced. The opening of the Berlin Wall in 1989 also paved the way for UFA's return to the Neubabelsberg studios. By the mid-1990s UFA was once again the largest German entertainment company, producing approximately 2000 television programs annually, including made-for-TV movies, mini-series, soap operas, prime time series, sitcoms, and documentary and current events programming. The holding company merged in 1997 with Luxembourg's CLT group to form CLT-UFA. This in turn merged with Pearson TV in 2001 to form the RTL Group. Since then UFA has functioned as the umbrella for FremantleMedia, a firm that encompasses all of the RTL Group's global production activities. The UFA-sponsored Client Satisfaction Study in 2003 confirmed UFA's reputation for professionalism, financial strength, competence, and dependability. The strong ratings for shows such as *Deutschland sucht den Superstar, Gute Zeiten, Schlechte Zeiten, SOKO Leipzig, Hinter Gittern—der Frauenknast,* and *Held der Gladiatoren* indicate that UFA will continue as a producer of German entertainment into the second decade of the 2000s.

Gerald Brennan

PRINCIPAL SUBSIDIARIES

UFA Entertainment GmbH; Grundy UFA TV Produktions GmbH; GRUNDY Light Entertainment GmbH; Objektiv Film; teamWorx Television & Film GmbH; Phoenix-Film GmbH.

PRINCIPAL COMPETITORS

VIVA Medien AG; Bavaria Film GmbH; Senator Entertainment AG; EM.TV & Merchandising AG; Euro-Arts Medien GmbH.

FURTHER READING

Bergfelder, Tim, Erica Carter and Deniz Gokturk (eds.), *The German Cinema Book,* London: British Film Institute, 2002.

Beyer, Friedemann, *Die UFA-Stars im dritten Reich,* Munich, 1991.

Elsaesser, Thomas (ed.), *A Second Life: German Cinema's First Decades,* Amsterdam: Amsterdam University Press, 1996.

Giesen, Rolf, *Nazi Propaganda Films: A History and Filmography,* Jefferson, N.C.: McFarland, 2003.

Kracauer, Siegfried, *From Caligari to Hitler: a Psychological History of the German Film*, Princeton, N.J.: Princeton University Press, 1947, 2004.

Kreimeier, Klaus, *Die UFA-Story: Geschichte eines Filmkonzerns*, Fischer Taschenbuchverlag, 1992.

Lipschuetz, Rita, *Der UFA-Konzern*, Berlin, 1932.

Rotha, Paul, *The Film Till Now* (revised ed.), London: Spring Books, 1967.

Schebera, Juergen, *Damals in Neubabelsberg—Studios, Stars, und Kinopaläste im Berlin der zwanziger Jahre*, Berlin: Edition Leipzig, 1990.

Wollenberg, Hans H., *Fifty Years of German Film*, London: Falcon Press, 1948.

ULVAC, Inc.

2500 Hagisono
Chigasaki, Kanagawa, 253-8543
Japan
Telephone: (81) 467 89 2033
Fax: (81) 467 82 9114
Web site: http://www.ulvac.co.jp

Public Company
Incorporated: 1952 as Japan Vacuum Engineering
    Company
Employees: 3,712
Sales: $1.45 billion (2004)
Stock Exchanges: Tokyo
Ticker Symbol: 6728
NAIC: 333912 Air and Gas Compressor Manufacturing

■ ■ ■

ULVAC, Inc., is a Japanese company, affiliated with Matsushita Electric Industrial Company, that through its three dozen subsidiaries develops, manufactures, sells, and services production systems and products that rely on vacuum-based processing chambers. These products include leak detectors, vacuum evaporation systems, vacuum gauges, Reactive Ion Etching systems, flat panel display systems, and booster, rotary, dry, diaphragm, and diffusion pumps. The products are used in such applications as semi-conductor manufacturing; metallurgy, including precision casting, induction melting, and the production of heat treating equipment; the manufacture of vacuum pumps, vacuum gauges, HELIOT leak detectors, and other vacuum equipment; Industrial equip-

ment such as vacuum freeze drying equipment, automatic leak detectors, vacuum roll coating equipment, and vacuum distillation equipment; and electronic systems, including in-line flat panel display systems, in-line hard disk systems, and the production of optical disks and film magnetic heads. ULVAC maintains operations in China, Germany, India, Japan, Malaysia, Singapore, South Korea, Taiwan, and the United States, where its headquarters is located in Methuen, Massachusetts. ULVAC is a public company listed on the Tokyo Stock Exchange.

VACUUM TECHNOLOGY COMMERCIALLY VIABLE IN 20TH CENTURY

The origins of vacuum technology, creating an advantageous condition of below-normal atmospheric pressure, had its origins in the 1600s when German aristocrat Otto von Guericke took up the question posed by Aristotle about the possibility of a vacuum in nature and the contention of René Descartes that if the air was removed from a container it would simply collapse. Guericke was credited with the invention of the air pump, which he used to create a vacuum within a pair of sealed copper hemispheres. He then made a dramatic public demonstration in which eight workhorses pulling from either hemisphere were unable to pull apart the copped orb. Yet, when air was introduced they came apart easily.

While the principles of the vacuum were then laid out, it was not until the 1900s that vacuum technology found its first major use: electric light bulbs. Electronics then began making use of vacuum technology in the production of electron tubes, and manufacturers discovered the advantages of carrying out certain processes within a vacuum. Lensmakers, for example began to treat lens surfaces under vacuum conditions to increase light transmission and eliminate reflections, as did blood banks in the preparation of plasma, and metallurgists in the production of reactive metals like titanium. The rise of nuclear energy in the 1950s created an even greater need for vacuum equipment, the demand for which grew even greater with the rise of microelectronics.

ULVAC LAUNCHED IN 1952

ULVAC was founded in August 1952 in the Kansai (or "western") Region of Japan by Dr. Jin Imachi, a researcher at Tokyo Shibaura Electric Company, the forerunner to Toshiba Corporation. ULVAC was established to commercialize vacuuming technologies that resulted from university research. Imachi raised ¥1 million in seed money from each of five prominent Kansai businessmen: Konosuke Matsushita, president of Matsushita Electric Industrial Co., Ltd.; Yoshio Osawa of Osawa & Co.; Aiichiro Fujiyama, president of Dainippon Sugar Production Co.; Tamesaburo Yamamoto, president of Asahi Breweries, Ltd., and Gen Hirose, president of Nippon Life Insurance Co. Chosen to serve as ULVAC's first president was Yoshijiro Ishikawa, the former president of Keifuku Electric Railway Company.

The company set up shop as the Japan Vacuum Engineering Company with just a handful of employees and for the first two years served as an importer of vacuum equipment manufactured by a U.S. firm, National Research Corporation. The company also launched its own research and development programs, and in 1954 it ceased to be an importer and now began to produce its own vacuum equipment for the Japanese market.

A key figure in the company's research efforts was Chikara Hayashi, who would one day serve as ULVAC's president and chairman. Hayashi provided a glimpse at the early years of vacuum technology in Japan and the

birth of ULVAC in an oral history recorded by William Sproul of the Society of Vacuum Coaters. Born in 1922, Hayashi attended the University of Tokyo during World War II, graduated in 1944, and was drafted by the Japanese Navy, where he was involved in the production of optical lenses and prisms used in binoculars and periscopes. The anti-reflection coating on these items were produced using vacuum technology. After the war, Hayashi returned to the University of Tokyo to work in the Nuclear Physics Department. Once again he was involved in vacuum technology, used to make components for particle accelerators. Conditions were difficult, however. "Japan was devastated," Hayashi told Sproul, "so there was no budget to get sufficient materials except for paper and pen. Actually, I got some raw material from occupied Army Arsenal and used them by myself to make vacuum systems." He quickly realized that he could not make equipment and pursue physics simultaneously. "I decided to go into the industry to help develop and [aid] in the recovery of the Japanese economy," he said. "The first thing was how to get money. That's why I joined Ulvac." He was recruited by Ishikawa, who Hayashi recalled telling him, "Why don't you join Ulvac because I promise to make a research institute for vacuum technology for you."

Hayashi was one of the six original employees: "One or two were mostly money management and the rest were technical. ... I started as an R&D manager in title and worker in the floor and the street." The institute for vacuum technology did not materialize, but Hayashi was not overly disappointed. "Our purpose was to help recover the Japanese economy," he explained. "So I had no way to object." Within a few years Ishikawa would make him president, a post Hayashi held until 1971, after which he became chairman of the board until his retirement at the age of 70 in the early 1990s. It was Hayashi who was largely responsible for the growth of the company and the one who spearheaded a change in name from Japan Vacuum Engineering Company to Ulvac. "When I took the presidency," Hayashi told Sproul, "I thought, 'technology, technology.' I'm not limited to Japan, so I wanted to change the name. I asked people who wished to vote for the name, and we came up with 'The Ultimate in Vacuum.'" The phrase was then truncated to coin "ULVAC."

For the first 20 years of its existence, ULVAC was a small company. Even while running ULVAC, Hayashi was able to remain very much involved in the technical side. Over the years the company added capabilities which spawned new subsidiaries. In 1964 ULVAC created Reliance Electric Ltd., a manufacturer of drive equipment for industrial machinery, by spinning off a unit and teaming up with a U.S. concern, Reliance Electric and Engineering Company. Also in 1964 Ulvac

```
┌─────────────────────────────────────────────┐
│                                             │
│             KEY DATES                       │
│             ───────■───────                  │
│                                             │
│   1952:  Company founded.                   │
│   1966:  ULVAC Materials, Inc., formed.     │
│   1975:  ULVAC North America Corporation is │
│          formed.                            │
│   1987:  ULVAC Corporation is created.      │
│   1992:  ULVAC Technologies consolidates its U.S. │
│          units.                             │
│   2003:  First Chinese subsidiary is formed. │
│   2004:  Company is taken public.           │
│                                             │
└─────────────────────────────────────────────┘
```

formed Shinku Riko, later renamed ULVAC-Riko, Inc., to specialize in the manufacture of thermal analysers. Furthermore, during the 1960s Hayashi attended a metallurgical conference in New York where he learned about ion plating on nuclear fuel capsules. Hayashi considered it a "nice technology," and ULVAC became involved in ion plating and formed a vacuum metallurgical department. In 1966, the company spun off the unit to create Vacuum Metallurgical Co., Ltd., which ultimately took the name ULVAC Materials, Inc.

In the 1970s Ulvac expanded into other areas as well. In 1971, ULVAC Kiko, Inc., then known as Sinku Kiko, was formed to serve as a specialty manufacturer of compact vacuum pumps, vacuum devices, and peripheral devices. A year later it established the Institute for Super Materials in Chiba, Japan. As Hayashi recalled, "A professor at the NIHON University asked me to help (to support him develop super-conducting materials). But my company was not so strong and very small (in 1970), still learning. So I went to the government, the Science and Technology Agency, and asked those officers if they could help." He was told that the agency could not directly support a professor, but it was willing to provide funding to the company and it in turn could work with the professor. As a result the institute was established. The company launched ULVAC North America Corporation, located in Dover, Delaware, to serve as an importer of ULVAC products to the United States.

Other developments in the 1970s included the 1978 alliance with Showa Shinku Co. Ltd., maker of LC oscillators (used in everyday circuits) and optical thin-film manufacturing equipment. In 1979 ULVAC Service, which serviced both ULVAC and non-ULVAC equipment, was created by spinning off the ULVAC Service Department. It would later take the name ULVAC Techno, Ltd. Also in 1979 ULVAC Coating Corpora-

tion was established by spinning off the ULVAC SI Division. It manufactured hard mask blanks and thin films for semiconductors and flat panel displays.

SUBSIDIARIES AND WORLD GROWTH 1980 ON

ULVAC added a host of subsidiaries during the 1980s. A pair of units were established in 1981: ULVAC Kyushu Co., Ltd., to expand sales activities in Japan's Kyushu region, and ULVAC Cryogenics, Inc., a joint venture with Helix Technology Corporation of the United States to manufacture and sell cryopumps. A year later another joint venture, ULVAC-Phi, Inc., was established with a U.S. company, Perkin Elmer Corporation, to manufacture and sell surface analysis equipment. ULVAC Seiki Co., Ltd., was formed in 1985 as a Kansai business unit plant, and two years later ULVAC Tohoku, Inc., was established in Hachinohe to supplement UL-VAC's large equipment production capacity. The most important development in the decade was the creation of ULVAC Corporation in May 1987. This unit served as the marketing department for all of the ULVAC subsidiaries, as well as providing a way for the various businesses to share information with one another. UL-VAC Corporation also conducted ultra fine powder research in conjunction with Vacuum Metallurgical Co., Ltd. Also of note, during the 1980s, ULVAC was one of several Japanese high-technology companies accused by U.S. lawmakers of withholding certain manufacturing equipment from U.S. microchip makers to prevent them from threatening the dominant market position enjoyed by Japanese chip companies.

ULVAC continued to add to its stable of subsidiaries and fine tune its operation in the 1990s. The company opened a super clean plant at Fuji Susono in 1990 in order to meet the growing demand for better performing manufacturing equipment used by semiconductor makers. In 1992 ULVAC Technologies, Inc. was formed in the United States to bring together ULVAC North America Corporation and other group companies in the United States in order to better serve semiconductor manufacturers in North America and Europe with consolidated sales and service operations. To provide better support for user production technology, ULVAC opened the ULVAC Technical Support Center in January 1994, and to improve the company's industrial technology capabilities, the Industrial Engineering Center was established in 1997. A year later the Purchasing Center was opened to improve the company's purchasing operations and allocation of physical resources. To provide customers with the full range of what Ulvac subsidiaries had to offer, ULVAC Solution was launched in 1998 to essentially serve as a liaison. To close out the 1990s, ULVAC began dealing in used equipment for the first time and it also formed yet another joint venture. ULVAC Taiwan teamed up with Phi of the United States to create Phi-ULVAC Taiwan to provide surface analysis services. Moreover, Ulvac also established in 1999 a major alliance with Ramtron, another U.S. company, to pursue the development of next-generation ferroelectric memory.

At the start of the new century, Ulvac forged a technical alliance with Kodak and Sanyo Electric Co. Ltd. to develop organic light emitting diode (OLED) flat panel manufacturing equipment technology, pioneered by Kodak in the late 1980s. While the United States remained a major market for ULVAC, it was being replaced by China. The market held such great promise that Ulvac had to establish a presence there. In July 2003 ULVAC (Suzhou) Co., Ltd was established in China. A year later ULVAC-TTI Technology (Shanghai) Corporation was established to manufacture and sell control systems in China, and ULVAC Vacuum Furnace (Shenyang) Co., Ltd., was formed to manufacture and sell industrial vacuum furnaces in China.

ULVAC also prepared to go public in 2004. In April of that year, an initial public offering of stock was completed, and the company's shares began trading on the Tokyo Stock Exchange.

Ed Dinger

PRINCIPAL SUBSIDIARIES

ULVAC Corporation; ULVAC Techno, Ltd. ; ULVAC Kyushu Corporation; ULVAC Tohoku, Inc.; ULVAC Seiki Co., Ltd.; ULVAC Equipment Sales, Inc.; Sanko ULVAC Co., Ltd; ULVAC Materials, Inc.; ULVAC Coating Corporation; ULVAC Cryogenics Inc.; Reliance Electric Ltd.; ULVAC Suzhou Co., Ltd.; ULVAC Vacuum Furnace (Shenyang) Co., Ltd.; ULVAC Taiwan, Inc.; ULVAC (Shanghai) Co., Ltd.; ULVAC Inc. (China); ULVAC Technologies Inc. (United States); ULVAC Korea Ltd.; ULVAC GmbH (Germany);

PRINCIPAL COMPETITORS

Axcelis Technologies, Inc.; Intevac, Inc.; Varian Semiconductor Equipment Associates, Inc.

FURTHER READING

"IPO Profile: Ulvac Inc.," *Asia Africa Intelligence Wire*, April 9, 2004.

"Japan Firms Accused of Withholding Gear Used in Making Chips," *Wall Street Journal*, May 7, 1991, p. A16.

Sproul, William, "Oral History Interview with Chikara Hayashi," *Society of Vacuum Coaters*, http://www.svc.org.

"ULVAC Technologies, Inc.," *Solid State Technology*, December 1, 1994, p. S21.

"Vacuum-Industry Supplier Consolidates US Business Units," *Paper, File & Foil Converter*, November 1992, p. 14.

United Talent Agency, Inc.

———————■———————

9560 Wilshire Boulevard, Suite 500
Beverly Hills, California 90212
U.S.A.
Telephone: (310) 273-6700
Fax: (310) 247-1111
Web site: http://www.unitedtalent.com

Private Company
Incorporated: 1991
Employees: 300
Sales: $13 million (2006 est.)
NAIC: 711410 Agents and Managers for Artists, Athletes, Entertainers, and Other Public Figures

■ ■ ■

United Talent Agency, Inc., is one of the top American talent agencies, representing film and television actors, directors, writers, and producers; authors; musicians; video game creators; and corporations seeking media-based marketing opportunities. The firm also packages film, television, and video game projects by bringing artists and financial backers together. Some of UTA's best-known clients include actors Johnny Depp, Harrison Ford, and Charlize Theron; *Sopranos* creator David Chase; *Law & Order* creator Dick Wolf; and writer/directors M. Night Shyamalan, Wes Anderson, and Joel and Ethan Coen. Ownership of the firm is vested in more than 20 of its top agents.

BEGINNINGS

United Talent Agency was founded in January of 1991 by the merger of two California-based agencies, Bauer Benedek and Leading Artists. The former was run by one-time William Morris Agency representative Marty Bauer and entertainment lawyer Peter Benedek, while Leading Artists' senior partners included Jim Berkus and Gary Cosay. Each firm was respected within the industry, but both found themselves overshadowed by giants like Creative Artists Agency (CAA), International Creative Management (ICM), and William Morris, and the two organizations decided to combine forces to boost their stature.

Founded in 1986, Bauer Benedek had become known for representing movie actors and directors, while the ten-year-old Leading Artists had a stronger presence in television. The latter area appeared to offer much potential for growth, and the newly-christened United Talent Agency (UTA) soon began broadening its roster of TV comedy writers, with early clients including contributors to hits like *The Simpsons, Married...With Children,* and *The Wonder Years.* Others represented by the agency included movie writer/directors Lawrence Kasdan, Brian De Palma, Steven Soderbergh, and brothers Joel and Ethan Coen; *Seinfeld* creator/writer Larry David; and actors Mike Myers, Bridget Fonda, Alan Alda, and Charles Grodin. As its business grew, the firm soon began to add agents to the 26 it had started with.

Although the media stereotype of a Hollywood talent agent is a hyper-aggressive individual wearing an Armani suit and clutching a constantly-ringing cellphone (and some do resemble this model), the field is in fact regulated by the State of California and agencies work under contracts with entertainment industry unions. By law agents receive 10 percent of a client's earnings, and those who handle as many as several dozen at once and work long hours are able to earn more than $1 million per year. Top producers at UTA could also be elevated to the status of partner, after which they would share in the earnings of the agency as a whole.

Key to an agent's success is obtaining advance knowledge of upcoming projects that a client's name could be attached to, and each cultivates a network of studio assistants and other low-level industry employees to provide this information. Another popular way for agencies to find clients work is to pre-package a project by attaching several prominent names to a script and then offering it to studios, networks, or other financial backers.

In the fall of 1992 UTA lured six key agents away from rival InterTalent Agency. The experienced agents brought to the firm clients like Laura Dern, Sting, Mia Farrow, and Jason Patric. Three of the six agents, David Schiff, J.J. Harris, and Judy Hofflund, were made partners, joining the ranks of Marty Bauer, Peter Benedek, Jim Berkus, Gary Cosay, Jeremy Zimmer, Robert Stein, and Gavin Polone.

UTA continued to expand its roster of television writers during the early 1990s, and by 1994 the firm's clients included three-fourths of the staff of the hit comedy *Roseanne*. The agency sought those who worked on dramas, adding top names like *Law & Order* creator/writer Dick Wolf and *Homicide: Life on the Street* writer/director Tom Fontana as it expanded in this category as well.

In 1995 pop icon Michael Jackson left industry powerhouse CAA and selected UTA to find him acting work. He would be represented by partner Nick Stevens, who had helped Jim Carrey win roles that made him a star. The firm also formed a TV talent division that would be headed by Stevens and Martin Lesak during

the year, while partner Judy Hofflund left to become a personal manager. Well-known performers on UTA's roster now included comic Martin Lawrence and Barry Humphries, better known as "Dame Edna," and the company was also seeking projects for production companies like Colossal Pictures, which had created animation for MTV's *Liquid Television*.

INDEPENDENT FILM UNIT FORMED IN 1996

In 1996 UTA formed a new division to help independent filmmakers package projects and secure financing, while at the same time providing its other talent with more work. It would be headed by former Turner Network Television executive Howard M. Cohen. Rival agencies like CAA, ICM, and William Morris had also recently formed similar units to capitalize on the growing market for independent films.

In the spring of 1996 UTA dismissed partner and television department head Gavin Polone, after an agent accused him of sexual harassment and threatened to go public if she was not released from her contract. Polone immediately threatened legal action, and UTA soon issued a public apology and agreed to buy out his contract. He was one of the firm's most powerful agents, and his departure cost UTA *Seinfeld's* Larry David, among others. A year later the agency sued Polone, alleging that he was guilty of defrauding clients, sexual misconduct, and other unethical behavior. His subsequent cross-complaint included allegations of improprieties by others in the agency and also revealed that UTA had agreed to pay him $6 million over two years to settle the broken contract as well as for libel and defamation. The suits were resolved several years later with Polone (who had by now begun working with former partner Judy Hofflund) receiving an undisclosed settlement.

The fracas with Polone was one of several during 1996, which had also seen UTA sue agent Jay Sures after he, too, threatened to reveal improprieties if he was not let out of his contract. That case was resolved more amicably, however; Sures stayed with the firm and was later named co-head of its television unit and made a partner. The turmoil of the Polone and Sures situations and partner Robert Stein's move to William Morris, along with other departures, reportedly led the agency to hire an in-house therapist to soothe its staff's frayed nerves.

In June of 1996 UTA's partners voted to name Marty Bauer and Jim Berkus co-chairmen, with Bauer also named president. The firm had always been run by the consensus of its partners, though Bauer had earlier

```
┌─────────────────────────────────────────┐
│                                         │
│            KEY DATES                    │
│              ──■──                      │
│                                         │
│  1991:  The Bauer Benedek and Leading Artists agen-│
│         cies merge to form United Talent.│
│  1992:  Six former InterTalent agents join the firm.│
│  1996:  The independent film division is created.│
│  2001:  The music department is expanded and a TV│
│         reality show unit is formed.    │
│  2005:  A videogame agency is opened in San│
│         Francisco; seven new partners boost the firm's│
│         total to 20.                    │
│                                         │
└─────────────────────────────────────────┘
```

given up the title of president because he reportedly felt his duties were unclear. In 1997 he again stepped down and the following year left the firm to found a management company, leaving UTA to be run by a board of six senior partners led by chairman Jim Berkus.

In 1998 the firm boosted five more agents to partner status, bringing the total number to 12 (out of 60 agents), and wooed Tracey Jacobs away from ICM, who brought with her such clients as Johnny Depp and Jennifer Jason Leigh. A triumph of the late 1990s was the agency's packaging of the HBO series *The Sopranos,* created by client David Chase. It was initially presented to Fox and several other broadcast networks without success before a deal with the pay-cable firm was landed. After its debut in early 1999 the show quickly became a signature franchise of the network, and went on to win numerous Emmy awards.

In the summer of 1999 UTA was named one of the top two broadcast television talent agencies by *Hollywood Reporter,* just behind the William Morris Agency. Series the firm's clients worked on included *God, the Devil and Bob* and *Get Real.* The agency also began representing director Barry Levinson during the year and made 29-year-old Sue Naegle its youngest partner to date. She had started out in UTA's mailroom seven years earlier.

Early 2000 saw the firm take on two major CAA defectors, actress Heather Locklear and pop star Madonna, the latter of whom would use the agency to seek acting work. Others signed during the year included Jonathan Pryce and Hope Davis. The agency's roster also now included actors Kelsey Grammer and Matt LeBlanc, as well as writer/producers Bruce Helford (*The Drew Carey Show*), Gary David Goldberg (*Spin City*), Steve Levitan (*Just Shoot Me*), and Joss Whedon (*Buffy, the Vampire Slayer*).

2001: MUSIC DEPARTMENT EXPANDED; REALITY UNIT FORMED

In 2001 UTA hired well-known agent Rob Prinz to oversee and expand its music department and launch a new booking and touring division. Onetime CAA representative Prinz, who had recently left Artist Group International, brought with him clients like Ricky Martin and Celine Dion. 2001 also saw the firm add names like Sharon Stone and Tori Spelling to its acting roster, while losing Garry Shandling to Endeavor. Several agents were lost to rival firms, as well, while literary agent Barbara Dreyfus joined from ICM.

The success of "reality" television shows like CBS' *Survivor* wrought huge changes in the television industry, and in 2001 UTA formed a new alternative programming department to work in this area. It was headed by Chris Coelen, whose clients included *Who Wants to Be a Millionaire* executive producer Michael Davies, *American High* creator/executive producer R.J. Cutler, and *Monster Garage* creator Thom Beers. The unit would help package programs like the Carmen Elektra vehicle *Livin' Large* and the reality courtroom series *Law & Order: Crime and Punishment* for NBC, which was co-created by Dick Wolf. The unit also worked with international clients like Britain's Wall to Wall and RDF Media, the latter of which produced the British and U.S. hits *Wife Swap* and *Supernanny.*

The year 2002 saw partner and co-head of the firm's television unit Chris Harbert leave to join CAA, while UTA won agent Darren Statt away from Endeavor, along with some of his clients including *Mummy* star The Rock. The following year partner J.J. Harris left to start a management company, though her clients, including Charlize Theron, would continue to be represented by UTA. 2003 also saw the head of the firm's independent film unit, Howard Cohen, leave to found a film distribution company called Roadside Attractions. While at UTA he had helped package and sell more than 50 titles including *Igby Goes Down* and *Girl With A Pearl Earring.* The unit would continue to operate through UTA's motion picture literary department, run by Jeremy Zimmer and Dan Aloni. Also during the year, the agency started a joint venture called UTA Urban Music with Team Lunatics to represent rap and hip-hop performers for tours, film, and TV appearances.

Seeking to spread ownership of the firm to more of its top agents, in 2004 UTA elevated seven to the status of partner, raising the total to 20. They included the heads of its television talent, production, and book departments. 2004 also saw four younger agents let go, and a $10 million lawsuit filed against the firm by Handprint Entertainment after one of that company's staffers was hired by UTA. The suit alleged that he had taken confidential materials with him, and UTA later sued its lawyers, claiming the company had been given bad advice at the time of his hiring. Year's end saw the loss of agent Adam Isaacs to Endeavor, along with his A-list clients that included Keira Knightley, Matt LeBlanc, Juliette Binoche, and Helena Bonham Carter.

VIDEOGAME OFFICE OPENED IN SAN FRANCISCO IN 2005

In January of 2005 UTA opened an office in gaming industry hotspot San Francisco to seek work for its clients in the lucrative videogame market. Industry news Web site founder Jonathan Epstein was hired to head the operation, which would work with both game makers and retailers to seek deals like in-game advertising and marketing partnerships, plus jobs for the agency's talent. Clients would include the likes of Amazon.com and *Destroy All Humans* game maker THQ, Inc., for which UTA would seek product placements and other marketing opportunities in movie and television projects.

By now the firm had nearly 100 agents, and during the year three more were made partners. They included alternative TV unit head Chris Coelen, who had helped package and launch 31 reality series in the previous 12 months; Lisa Hallerman, whose clients included Mary-Kate and Ashley Olsen; and Sharon Sheinwold, who represented Jack Black, among others. Recent hit movies packaged by the firm included *Dodgeball* and *Wedding Crashers,* which featured agency clients including Ben Stiller, Vince Vaughn, and Owen Wilson.

2005 also saw partners Martin Lesak, Jason Heyman, and motion picture literary department head Dan Aloni defect to CAA, taking with them clients like Will Ferrell and directors Tom Shadyac (*Bruce Almighty*) and Christopher Nolan (*Batman Begins*), while partner David Schiff left to start a management firm. Clients added during the year included *Buffy the Vampire Slayer* star Sarah Michelle Gellar and actress Liv Tyler, with losses including Jason Alexander and Paris Hilton. For the 2005–06 television season, according to a survey by TVTracker.com, UTA once again had the second-highest number of clients working on scripted broadcast network shows. Its total of 226 was only slightly behind leader CAA's 231.

The company's efforts to curry favor with assistants and other underlings at sources of gossip like studios, production companies, and law firms continued with a holiday present of a license plate-sized piece of chocolate that featured the UTA logo, which was sent out to 1,400 people. Some also contained vouchers good for cash prizes of between $100 and $5,000.

In early 2006 partner Marty Bowen left to co-found a production firm, while partner and reality unit head Chris Coelen left the agency to run the U.S. subsidiary of RDF Media, after which UTA sued him for breach of contract and theft of confidential information. In the spring the industry press began reporting rumors that UTA was planning to merge with rival agency Endeavor, though both refused comment.

Fifteen years after its founding, United Talent Agency, Inc. had risen to become one of the top talent agencies in Hollywood, representing a wide range of actors, writers, directors, and others. Its roster included many influential names, and despite the sometimes-volatile nature of the industry it appeared well-positioned for continued success.

Frank Uhle

PRINCIPAL DIVISIONS

Motion Pictures; Television; Alternative Television; Digital Media; Books; Music; Marketing; Production.

PRINCIPAL COMPETITORS

Creative Artists Agency, Inc.; International Creative Management, Inc.; William Morris Agency, Inc.; Brillstein-Grey Entertainment; The Endeavor Agency; Paradigm Talent and Literary Agency; The Gersh Agency.

FURTHER READING

Adalian, Josef and Harris, Dana, "Howdy, Partner: UTA Boosts Seven," *Daily Variety,* March 22, 2004.

Chetwynd, Josh, and Stephen Galloway, "Polone Answers UTA's Suit with One of His Own," *Hollywood Reporter,* October 3, 1997, p. 1.

Fleming, Michael, "Agencies No Longer Endeavoring to Wed," *Daily Variety,* March 21, 2006.

Fritz, Ben, "UTA Game For Player." *Daily Variety,* January 11, 2005.

Frutkin, Alan James, "The Art of the Deal Here," *Mediaweek,* July 31, 2000.

Galloway, Stephen, "Bauer, Berkus: UTA Co-Chairmen," *Hollywood Reporter,* June 11, 1996, p. 3.

———, "Vet Music Rep Prinz on UTA Stage," *Hollywood Reporter,* September 26, 2001, p. 3.

Hiestand, Jesse, "UTA Sues Firm Over Guillod Hire," *Hollywood Reporter,* March 19, 2004, p. 4.

Hoffman, Claire, "Talent Firms May Merge to Keep Pace," *Los Angeles Times,* March 13, 2006, p. 1A.

"Jacobs Partnering with UTA," *Hollywood Reporter,* November 3, 1998, p. 3.

Johnson, Ross, "TNT's Cohen to Head UTA Indies," *Hollywood Reporter,* March 23, 1996, p. 3.

———, "UTA Sues to Enforce Agent Pact," *Hollywood Reporter,* May 10, 1996, p. 3.

Katz, Jesse, "How a Pathologically Blunt Producer Makes It in Suck-Up City," *The New York Times,* February 9, 2003, p. 48F.

Kit, Zorianna, "Super Producers Power Reps." *Television Week,* August 8, 2005, p. 1.

———, "UTA Agent Harris Joins Reynolds in Management Firm," *Hollywood Reporter,* January 22, 2003, p. 4.

Moskal, Jerry, "UTA's Defamation Payment to Polone Ruled Not Taxable," *Los Angeles Business Journal,* January 5, 2004, p. 7.

Parker, Donna, "6 ITA Agents Cross to UTA as Block Talks with ICM," *Hollywood Reporter,* October 14, 1992, p. 1.

Petrikin, Chris, "UTA Ups 5 Agents," *Daily Variety,* April 23, 1998.

Rice, Lynette, "One Week in Hollywood: Agent of Change," *Entertainment Weekly,* August 1, 2003, p. 44.

———, "Talent Show: WMA, UTA Tops in Piloting TV Actors," *Hollywood Reporter,* July 2, 1999, p. 1.

Schreiber, Dominic, "Not So Secret Agent," *Television Business International,* September 1, 2003, p. 24.

URS Corporation

600 Montgomery Street, 26th Floor
San Francisco, California 94111-2728
U.S.A.
Telephone: (415) 774-2700
Fax: (415) 398-1905
Web site: http://www.urscorp.com

Public Company
Incorporated: 1957 as Broadview Research Corporation
Employees: 27,500
Sales: $3.92 billion (2005)
Stock Exchanges: New York Pacific
Ticker Symbol: URS
NAIC: 541330 Engineering Services

■ ■ ■

URS Corporation is one of the world's largest engineering design firms. Listed on the New York Stock Exchange, San Francisco-based URS operates in 20 countries, although 90 percent of its sales come from North America. Business is divided among two divisions. The URS division offers planning, design, and program and construction management services to both public and private clients, involved in such projects as mass transit systems, highways, bridges, airports, water supply and treatment systems, manufacturing plants, healthcare facilities, college facilities, grade school and high schools, military housing, courthouses, and the construction of other government buildings. The EG&G division provides planning, systems engineering and technical assistance, and operations and maintenance services to the United States government, primarily the Department of Homeland Security and the military.

COMPANY ORIGINS: 1951

URS was started in 1951 under the name Broadview Research. It was a small private company that was dependent on a modest Army operations contract, employing physical and engineering sciences. The business was incorporated in 1957 as Broadview Research Corporation, and in 1962 changed its name to United Research Services, Inc. Two years later it took the name URS Corporation, the company's current name, though more permutations were to follow over the years. In 1967 the company launched a strategy to become a multidisciplinary services firm. A year later it made an initial public offering of stock, gaining a listing on the American Stock Exchange, and once again changed its name, this time becoming URS Systems Corporation. It also looked to grow externally through acquisitions, making half-a-dozen purchases over the next two years. URS still relied on its military contract, however, and when that expired in fiscal 1970, the company lost money, prompting a change in management and direction.

In March 1970 Arthur H. Stromberg joined URS and became chief executive officer in 1971. (He added the chairmanship in 1976.) Under his direction the company bounced back, recording record earnings for two consecutive years before business fell off during a recession, resulting in three straight years of declining profits. The company at this stage provided architectural and engineering services, mostly to local, state, and

COMPANY PERSPECTIVES

URS is one of the largest engineering design firms worldwide and a leading U.S. federal government contractor. Our business focuses primarily on providing professional and technical services in the engineering, construction services and defense markets. We execute large and complex engineering projects and provide a comprehensive range of professional planning and design, systems engineering and technical assistance, program and construction management, and operations and maintenance services.

federal agencies. Earlier Stromberg diversified somewhat by acquiring Pollution Control Engineering, Inc. in 1973, and URS would continue to add environmental practices, but in 1976 he went far a field by purchasing Advanced Systems, Inc., which produced video-assisted training programs. A year later he added the well-known speed-reading company, Evelyn Wood Reading Dynamics, Inc., for $7 million. It was an unlikely combination, but it at least improved the company's non-government business. The new assets also played their part in URS posting a record $3.8 million in profits in 1977 on sales of about $37 million.

URS enjoyed steady growth for several years, as the number of offices increased from nine to 32 and sales approach $100 million by fiscal 1985. Investors were having a difficult time, however, comprehending a company that on one hand cleaned up toxic waste sites and on the other taught speed reading. To simplify the company, Evelyn Wood was divested and Advanced Systems was spun off, the shares distributed to URS stock holders. The company now became listed on the New York Stock Exchange and enjoyed a nice run, as did the stock of the now independent Advanced Systems.

In 1986 URS had a healthy backlog of contracts and appeared to be well positioned in high growth areas like hazardous waste and pollution control. The company wanted to commit further to this sector and in 1987 began a reorganization, spinning off its consulting business into two companies: URS Consultants Inc. and URS International Inc. The remaining assets now took the name Thortec International, Inc. in November 1987. The plan was to make public offerings of the spin-offs, with Thortec retaining majority stock ownership of both companies. The money raised would then be used to expand Thortec's hazardous- and toxic-waste remediation business into a full-service operation. In addition,

Thortec hoped to build its forensic engineering, project and program management software systems, and other management services. The strategy did not work out as planned, however.

FISCAL 1986 RESULTS DRAW SEC SCRUTINY

Thortec lost money in fiscal 1987 and the situation grew worse in 1988, as it lost $17.3 million on revenues of $113.7 million. Moreover, the company had to admit in its public filings that it had become the subject of a Securities and Exchange Commission investigation of its reported results for fiscal 1986. The SEC contended that the company added $8.4 million to the reported $115.7 in revenues and $8.7 million in revenues, and inflated fiscal 1987 results by another $5 million. Shareholders then filed a class-action suit alleging the company misrepresented its financial situation, and this matter was eventually settled out of court. In the meantime, Thortec's chief financial officer, its chief accounting officer, and its chief operating officer resigned in 1988. Stromberg held out until the spring of 1989, when he relinquished the CEO post and the chairmanship (although he stayed on as a director for several more months). The four executives reached an agreement with the SEC in 1990, agreeing to a permanent injunction that barred them from future securities laws violations, although they neither admitted or denied the charges.

While the SEC matter was being resolved, a group of shareholders, lead by Richard C. Blum — husband of former San Francisco mayor and future U.S. Senator, Dianne Feinstein — took control and launched a reorganization. Blum would also end up with a controlling interest of more than 60 percent after providing $12.5 million in much needed cash in October 1989, adding to a small stake he previously owned. A new CEO had already been brought in several months earlier, Martin M. Koffel, a friend recruited by new director, Bill Walsh, the chairman of buyout firm Sequoia Associates. (Koffel was subsequently named chairman as well.) Walsh told the *Wall Street Journal,* "I knew he was very expert at turnarounds, and we needed help badly." An Australian, Koffel had proven his abilities by turning around, among other companies, Oral-B Laboratories Inc. and selling it to Gillette Co. According to the *Wall Street Journal,* "Koffel spent his first three years at URS shutting down all businesses that had no relation to the company's basic expertise in providing engineering services for large-scale projects such as airport and road construction. 'We had a great reputation for engineering, so I wanted to get back to that,' Mr. Koffel says." In keeping with that plan, the company reverted to the URS name in February 1990. To shore up the company's

KEY DATES

1951: Company is founded as Broadview Research Corporation.
1964: Company first assumes the URS Corporation name.
1971: Arthur H. Stromberg is named CEO.
1989: Martin M. Koffel replaces Stromberg amid an SEC investigation.
1996: Greiner Engineering, Inc., is acquired.
1999: Dames & Moore Group is acquired.
2002: EG&G Federal Services Inc. is acquired.

stock price, which had fallen to the $1 range, he engineered a one-for-ten reverse stock, thus increasing the price ten-fold and making it more visible with investors. Koffel's changes began to have an immediate positive effect, as URS returned to profitability in 1991 on sales of $122 million. The company was strong enough that in June 1991 it was able to return to the public market to raised nearly $20 million in an offering of new shares of stock. Most of the proceeds were used to pay down debt.

By 1995 URS had increased its revenues to $180 million and net income reached $5.1 million. "As it grew," reported industry publication *ENR*, "URS Engineers needed to win the megaprojects that will keep its staff busy and challenged. But the company wasn't getting the respect afforded to companies the size of Sverdrup Corporation and CH2M Hill Cos. Ltd." Koffel now became a consolidator in the engineering field, which was undergoing a industry shakeout that would result in a handful of large international companies and many small specialty firms. His first major step came in 1995 with the $73 million cash and stock acquisition of Greiner Engineering Inc., an Irving, Texas-based firm that for the past three years had been of interest to Koffel. Although it was struggling financially, primarily due to an investment in a California toll road project, Greiner had a solid reputation in airports as well as expertise in surface transportation and bridges, thus providing a better business mix for URS, which was too dependent on environmental projects, as well as federal contracts. Moreover, Greiner added some international assets, operating in Asia.

With Greiner in the fold, URS saw revenues increase to $305.5 million in fiscal 1996 and net income improve to $7.4 million. The next major acquisition occurred in November 1997, when URS added Woodward-Clyde Group, Inc, in a $132.4 million transaction that included

$39.2 million in cash, stock worth $61.9 million, and the assumption of $31.1 million in debt. Denver-based Woodward-Clyde, a major geotechnical engineering and environmental consulting firm, doubled the size of URS, making it the United States' fifth largest engineering firm. The deal lessened URS's dependence on government contracts and expanded the firm's market coverage, which now included offices in Canada, Europe and Latin America.

DAMES & MOORE ACQUISITION: 1999

Revenues increased to $406.5 million in fiscal 1997 and net income improved to $11.5 million, but once Woodward-Clyde was digested and contributing to the balance sheet for the full year, the results would become even more dramatic. Revenues nearly doubled to $806 million, as did net income, which totaled $22.7 million in fiscal 1998. With Greiner and Woodward-Clyde fully assimilated, URS was ready once again on the acquisition trail. In February 1999 the company completed a relatively small purchase, paying $13.6 million and assuming debt to pick up Thorbun Colquhoun Holdings plc, a mid-size United Kingdom based engineering firm that specialized in transportation projects and structural engineering services for manufacturing facilities and stadiums. Thorbun's addition beefed up URS's operations in Europe. A far more significant transaction took place in June 1999 when URS acquired Dames & Moore Group in a $357.4 million deal. Based in Los Angeles, Dames & Moore had fancied itself an industry consolidator, so that its willingness to be acquired by URS came as a surprise to knowledgeable observers. Dames & Moore, in fact, had also attempted to buy Woodward-Clyde. Combined with URS, the result, according to *ENR*, was a "supercompany," one that set a new size standard for design firms. Dames & Moore maintained offices in more than 30 countries, thereby adding to URS's presence in the United States, Europe, and Asia. URS also broadened its areas of expertise by adding nearly 8,000 engineers, planners, and construction managers. With Dames & Moore's partial contribution, URS recorded revenues of more than $1.4 billion and net income of $33.2 million in fiscal 1999. Those totals grew to more than $2.2 billion in revenue and net income of nearly $50 million in fiscal 2000 when Dames & Moore was more fully integrated. During the course of the year, URS also completed a corporate branding program, applying the URS name to all aspects of the now massive firm.

According to *ENR*, URS emerged in 2001 as number one on the publication's annual list of the Top 500 Design Firms. In fiscal 2001, URS increased revenues to $2.32 billion and net income to $57.9 million. The company was not content, however, to stand pat. In August 2002 it completed yet another significant acquisition: the $500 million purchase of EG&G Federal Services Inc. from The Carlyle Group. The Gaithersburg, Maryland-based firm positioned URS to become a major player in the growing markets for homeland security, in the wake of the September 11th terrorist attacks, and government outsourcing. Moreover, EG&G brought other aspects to the table. "EG&G has all sorts of whizbang things but was not allowed to flex its technology wings under Carlyle," an engineering executive told *ENR*. "Now we have a company with a bigger toolbox and we will see them in the market quite quickly and competitively."

URS assimilated EG&G and reorganized the business into two units: URS Division and EG&G. Revenues totaled $3.2 billion in fiscal 2003, when net income reached 58.1 million. In fiscal 2005 revenues approached the $4 billion threshold and the company reported net income of $61.7 million. In a matter of 15 years, URS had gone from the brink of bankruptcy to becoming a dominant international firm, and there was every reason to expect the upward trend to continue for some time to come.

Ed Dinger

PRINCIPAL DIVISIONS

URS Division; EG&G Division

PRINCIPAL COMPETITORS

AECOM Technology Corporation; Bechtel Group, Inc.; Jacobs Engineering Group Inc..

FURTHER READING

Abate, Tom, "URS Growth Strategy Tied to Defense Work," *San Francisco Chronicle,* May 11, 2003, p. I1.

Beckett, Jamie, "Ailing Thortec Shuffles Many of Its Executives," *San Francisco Chronicle,* January 5, 1989, p. C1.

Brown, Paul B., "Divide and Conquer," *Forbes,* August 1, 1983, p. 72.

Carlsen, Clifford, "URS Corp. Ready to Grab Hazardous Waste Market," *San Francisco Business Times,* September 21, 1987, p. 1.

Carlton, Jim, "URS, Once Near Bankruptcy, Is at Pinnacle of Industry," *Wall Street Journal,* December 16, 1999, p. B4.

Gordon, Mitchell, "Engineering Services to Speed Reading: Unlikely Mix Pays Off for URS Corp.," *Barron's National Business and Financial Weekly,* December 11, 1978, p. 36.

Korman, Richard, "Behind The Dames & Moore Deal," *ENR,* May 17, 1999, p. 10.

———, "URS-Greiner Deal: Will Mid-Sized Models Be Obsolete?" *ENR,* June 3, 1996, p. 10.

Pender, Kathleen, "Troubled Thortec Says CEO to Resign," *San Francisco Chronicle,* February 22, 1989, p. C1.

Rubin, Debra K., and Mary Buckner Powers, with Richard Korman, "URS Aims To Boost Stock Price And Market Share With EG&G Buy," *ENR,* July 29, 2002, p. 13.

Vishay Intertechnology, Inc.

63 Lincoln Highway
Malvern, Pennsylvania 19355-2143
U.S.A.
Telephone: (610) 644-1300
Fax: (610) 296-0657
Web site: http://www.vishay.com

Public Company
Founded: 1962
Employees: 26,100
Sales: $2.29 billion (2005)
Stock Exchanges: New York
Ticker Symbol: VSH
NAIC: 335310 Electrical Equipment Manufacturing; 334410 Semiconductor and Other Electronic Component Manufacturing; 335999 All Other Miscellaneous Electrical Equipment and Component Manufacturing

■ ■ ■

Vishay Intertechnology, Inc., is a leading manufacturer of discrete semiconductors (diodes, rectifiers, transistors, and optoelectronics) and the third-largest leading producer of passive electronic components such as resistors, capacitors, and inductors, in the United States and Europe. A Fortune 1000 company, Vishay makes products essential to the operation of anything using an electric circuit; they can be found in computers, automobiles, satellites, telephones, household appliances, and televisions, as well as in medical, military, and aerospace equipment. In the early 21st century Vishay

had operations in 17 countries and employed more than 25,000 people over 50 plants around the world. Felix Zandman, the chairman and previous CEO of Vishay, and his cofounder's widow, Luella Slaner, controlled a majority of the company's voting stock.

1920–1962: FOUNDING FAMILY BACKGROUND

Felix Zandman was born in Poland in the late 1920s, into a family that originally came from the village of Vishay in Lithuania. He survived the Holocaust and, in 1946, went to France. While he knew no French, he dutifully memorized 30 words a day while earning degrees in mathematics and engineering and his doctorate in physics. While a student he developed a new technology that significantly changed how structures were tested for stress.

Up until then, scientists had used a plastic model of a bridge or building or engine part or airplane wing to figure out mathematically how the metal would act under stress. Zandman, however, developed a transparent plastic coating he could apply directly to a structure along with instruments that could measure the results of the stress optically. When viewed through a polariscope, the coating produced patterns that showed a picture of the actual distribution of stress and could help improve the structure's safety.

The response of the French engineering community was very positive, and Zandman decided he might parlay his new process, eventually known as Photostress, into a new business. However, the airplane manufacturer he worked for, although excited about the process, was not supportive of his entrepreneurial dreams.

In 1956, Zandman came to the United States and went to work at the Budd Company, a major Philadelphia manufacturer. Budd had just added strain gauges (electronic measuring devices) to its existing line of railroad cars and automobile chassis, and it soon bought the Photostress process. Although he did not speak English when he arrived, Zandman again memorized 30 words a day in order to learn the language.

While at Budd, Zandman developed a new kind of resistor, the part of an electrical circuit that adjusts and regulates voltage and current, that was not effected by temperature. For resistors used in high precision instruments, such as aircraft guidance systems, temperature change could be disastrous. Again, Zandman saw the potential for a new business if he could translate his concept into reality. But Budd was not interested in funding the project, the marketing people believing there was not a sufficient market for the technology.

1962–1980: COMPANY FORMATION AND INNOVATIONS

In 1962, Zandman turned to his cousin, Alfred P. Slaner, who loaned him $200,000. Zandman put in $4,000 of his own savings, and the new company was born, with the partners each owning 50 percent. They chose the name Vishay, where their great-grandparents had lived, in memory of their family and of those who had died in the Holocaust. In his autobiography, *Never the Last Journey*, Zandman recalled Vishay's first days: "We signed the lease [in Malvern] on February 22, 1962, and the next day we started work. . . . We built our laboratory at night, nailing wallboard and painting and doing everything on a shoestring. I bought furniture and equipment, and a month later we were ready to go."

The company introduced Micro-Measurements strain gauges, developed by James E. Starr and produced

in Romulus, Michigan, which it marketed primarily to the automotive industry. Thinner than a postage stamp, Vishay's gauges could be bonded to any structure easily to change the resistance value when the structure was subjected to stress. And like its resistor, the strain gauge was impervious to temperature. In addition to the millions used to improve structural integrity, the gauges were also used as weight sensors in electronic scales. Zandman had also acquired the rights to his Photostress process and the company included the plastic coatings and instruments among its products.

However, Vishay's early prominence was based on its Bulk Metal resistor, which the company created in about six months. Analysts would later remark that introducing a flat, 0.33 watt resistor into a market of round ceramic resistors rated at one-eighth, one-fourth, or one-half watt was a marketing coup. Actually, according to Zandman's book, it was an accident: "Since we were not working with wires but with foils, we didn't have to wind anything. Ours would be flat. The cheapest material we could use to bond our foil to was not ceramic, but glass. So we used glass as our substrate. Then we needed a case to put the resistor in. I found on the market a small, inexpensive flat case that was made for capacitors. We cut the piece of glass to the size of the case; then we attached the leads. When I measured the power of our now cut-down and encased resistor, I found it was 0.33 watt."

Orders poured in, particularly from the defense industry. Using the Vishay resistor, jet fighter pilots did not have to wait long for their navigational electronics to warm up. The accuracy of weapon guidance systems was no longer limited to plus or minus six-tenths of a mile. And not only U.S. companies wanted the resistor. Orders came in from France, Japan, Germany, and the United Kingdom.

To meet the demand, Vishay began licensing its resistor, beginning with manufacturer Sfernice, the largest resistor manufacturer in France. In 1969, Vishay opened its own manufacturing plant in Israel, and in 1972 Zandman took the company public. However, the company issued only 20 percent of the outstanding shares, leaving the rest in the hands of Zandman and Slaner.

1981–1990: GROWTH THROUGH ACQUISITION

By the early 1980s, Vishay was a world leader in the development of resistors and strain gauges, with 65 percent of its sales in its first 20 years made to defense and aerospace contractors. The company had sales of over $45 million a year, with a cash balance of $35

During 1984 Dale Electronics came on the market, and Vishay began its first major acquisition spree, growing its core resistor business. Dale, a subsidiary of the Lionel Company, was the largest wire-wound resistor maker in the world outside Japan. Lionel had bought Dale years ago to produce the transformers it needed for its model trains, and had left Dale alone to grow into a giant. With annual sales of around $120 million, Dale was more than twice the size of Vishay. Although companies such as Du Pont, Emerson, and Dynamics Corporation of America were interested, Vishay bought 50 percent of the company in 1985, acquiring the rest of the shares in 1988. In making the purchase, Vishay formed a subsidiary, Dale Holdings, Inc., which owned all the common stock of Dale Electronics.

Electronic companies all over the world were up for sale. Leveraged buyouts and takeovers were rampant. But Vishay was not interested in buying a company just to strip it and sell it. In selecting companies to buy, Zandman followed a five-point strategy, according to *Electronic Business*: 1) concentrate only on businesses in which Vishay had demonstrated expertise; 2) focus on profitability while attending to long-term goals; 3) produce and sell in all key markets; 4) provide quality products; and 5) grow through research and development, market penetration, and acquisition.

In 1987 Vishay bought Draloric Electronic, the largest manufacturer of fixed resistors in Germany. Vishay reduced the numbers of managers in both Dale and Draloric and moved some production to Israel, where it opened a second facility. It also purchased the resistor and power capacitor business of Corning Glass. Vishay maintained the brand names of most of its new purchases since they were already so well known and respected.

In 1988 it bought Sfernice, the major French resistor manufacturer with which Vishay had initiated a licensing agreement, with sales of $100 million. As with its other acquisitions, Vishay transferred the Sfernice foil resistor business to Israel and restructured the company. In his book, Zandman pointed out that despite moving certain production lines to Israel, employment at Dale's operations in Nebraska and South Dakota still rose. He explained that the jobs first lost in the United States were those responsible for making older, uncompetitive products. By moving these jobs overseas, these product lines became competitive moneymakers that enabled the company to squeeze out the competition, increase resources, and, in turn, open new product lines in the United States.

During this period, Vishay created a special Class B type of stock in addition to its common stock. Class B could not be traded but carried with it ten votes per share. All current stockholders could convert their stock

KEY DATES

1946: Felix Zandman moves to France after surviving the Holocaust.
1956: Zandman emigrates to the United States and works for the Budd Company.
1962: Zandman and his cousin Alfred P. Slaner cofound Vishay, naming the company after their ancestral village in Lithuania.
1969: Vishay opens its own manufacturing plant in Israel.
1972: Vishay makes its first public offering.
1983: Vishay buys Mann Components, an English resistor manufacturer.
1987: Vishay acquires Draloric Electronic, the largest German manufacturer of fixed resistors.
1990: Vishay moves into the inductor market with the purchase of Nytronic Inductors.
1992: Vishay makes its first capacitor acquisition when it purchases Sprague Technologies.
1996: One-third of the company's work force is located in Israel, Mexico, and the Czech Republic.
1998: Vishay gains complete ownership of the Semiconductor Business Group of TEMIC.
2002: Vishay acquires General Semiconductor for $540 million.
2005: Zandman is succeeded as CEO by the company's president and COO Gerald Paul.

million. But Vishay stock, which sold originally at $8 a share was selling at less than $3. Zandman began considering alternatives to his strategy of internal growth in order to produce a better rate of return. He decided on a course of acquisitions, determining that there was no reason the company could not produce "garden-variety" resistors as well as its ultraprecise components. His timing was right as consolidations were beginning to occur within the passive electronic components industry.

Early in 1983, Vishay bought Mann Components, an English resistor manufacturer with sales of about $2 million. The next year the company acquired Geka, a French competitor, and two small American companies, Angstrohm Precision and Elliot Industries. Sales for 1984 were a record $48.5 million, helped by an expansion in research and development, cost-cutting, and product improvement. Even with the acquisitions, debt was still zero and the cash surplus had not dropped.

to Class B, but to sell it would have to convert it back. Once Zandman and Slaner had converted their shares to Class B, it was unlikely that they could lose control of the company. By the end of 1989, Vishay had sales of $416 million.

1990–1995: THE INDUCTOR AND CAPACITOR MARKETS

In 1990 Vishay began moving into the inductor market with the purchase of Nytronic Inductors, a U.S. company with sales of $10 million. The company continued efforts in that field the following year, acquiring several small inductor manufacturers in Mexico (West-Cap Arizona and Jeffers Electronics) and France (Aztronic Measurements Group).

By the early 1990s Vishay was no longer so dependent on sales to aerospace and defense contractors, which were down to 16 percent. Meanwhile, sales to the computer industry represented 28 percent, telecommunications 12 percent, with the rest to the automotive, instrumentation, and industrial markets.

With the acquisitions of Draloric, Dale, and Sfernice, the company held about one-third of the American resistor market and 40 percent of the European market. Zandman decided the company needed to move into fields other than resistors and inductors if it was to continue its rapid growth. The market he selected was capacitors, components that stored and released electrical energy. The first capacitor acquisition, in 1992, was Sprague Technologies, a part of American Annuity Group.

Sprague had been one of the largest capacitor manufacturers in the United States. The founder of the company, R. C. Sprague, invented the ceramic capacitor in 1926 then went on to invent almost everything that had to do with capacitor technology. Capacitors made radio tuners, telephone receivers, and television receivers possible by allowing the filtering of wave frequencies. In addition to capacitors, Sprague began producing resistors, then transistors. But in the mid-1960s, after the founder retired and his son took over, the company invested heavily in semiconductors. The competition from other companies, both American and Japanese, was too much, and the company lost hundreds of millions of dollars. Sprague was sold to General Cable, which was then bought by Penn Central Railroad, which made Sprague a separate entity controlled by a major shareholder. During these transitions, the company dropped its production of every passive component except capacitors.

While Vishay was negotiating for Sprague, it also began looking for a purchase in Germany to strengthen Draloric's position in the European market. The company settled on Roederstein GmbH, Europe's largest component manufacturer. A huge operation, with sales of over $300 million and plants in Portugal and the United States as well as Germany, Roederstein was rumored to be close to bankrupt.

Initially Vishay planned to acquire Resista, the Roederstein division that made metal film resistors in competition with Draloric and commercial thick film chip resistors to compete with the Japanese. In the end, however, Vishay bought the entire company. They eliminated entire layers of Roederstein's management, closed an obsolete plant, moved some production to Israel, and restructured the company with Draloric. Within nine months Roederstein was profitable again.

In 1993, the market for small specialty tantalum capacitors started growing, and Vishay bought the tantalum capacitor division of North American Philips Corporation. In 1994, Vishay purchased Vitramon, which made multilayer ceramic chip capacitors, from Thomas & Betts for $184 million.

As Vishay continued to acquire companies, its sales continued to increase, as did its earnings. By eliminating or restructuring duplicative sales, distribution, and administrative expenses, it took advantage of economies of scale and kept costs down even as it expanded. This occurred despite a period (1991-93) of general recession in the industrialized countries and a worldwide slowdown in the electronic components industry.

Wanting to increase its internal sales, the company targeted its 30 biggest customers for special attention. Vishay promised 100 percent on-time delivery worldwide and maintained manufacturing capacity for these clients, including AT&T, Hewlett Packard, Bosch, and Siemens.

1995–2004: FURTHER ACQUISITIONS

The passive components industry experienced a growth spurt in 1994 and 1995. To meet the anticipated demand, the company expanded its offshore capacity, spending over $165 million in 1995 on plant and equipment, including new facilities in Israel and the Czech Republic. At the same time, it had to maintain high production levels in the United States, Germany, and France—high-cost countries.

During this time, the company made a move into Asia, buying 49 percent of Nikkohm, a Japanese passive components maker. That year Vishay introduced a resistor chip that helped extend the life of lithium batteries used in laptop computers and other portable electronics.

The worldwide demand for passive components

dropped significantly in 1996 as companies, particularly in the telecommunications and computer industries, found themselves with an oversupply of components, especially capacitors. An economic slowdown in Germany and France combined with a strong U.S. dollar also contributed to Vishay's first decline in annual sales, to $1.1 billion. The company announced a major restructuring, consolidating Vishay Electronic Components operations in the United States, Europe, and Asia into one entity and bringing its sales and marketing activities into a single, worldwide organization. This resulted in laying off about 11 percent of the work force, half in the United States and half in Europe. Vishay was moving towards its goal of having 50 percent of its work force in low-cost countries. At the end of 1996, one-third of the company's work force was located in Israel, Mexico, and the Czech Republic, compared to one-quarter at the beginning of the year. Vishay also announced the appointment of Dr. Gerald Paul, the president of Vishay Electronic Components, Europe, as chief operating officer and executive vice-president.

In May 1996, in a joint venture with the Eisenberg Group of companies, Vishay signed an agreement with the China National Non-Ferrous Metals Industry Corporation, a Chinese government agency, to mine and refine tantalum ore and eventually produce tantalum capacitors for the Chinese market. Analysts expected this to provide Vishay with significant cost savings in the purchase of tantalum powder and wire in the long term.

In 1997, after months of exploring a purchase in the $14 billion discrete semiconductor (integrated circuits) market, Vishay acquired 65 percent of the Taiwan-based Lite-On Power Semiconductor Corporation (LPSC) for $130 million. LPSC produced diodes, discrete semiconductor components used to convert electrical currents from AC to DC, and had plants in Taipei, Shanghai, and Lee's Summit, Missouri. LPSC also owned 40 percent of Diodes Inc., a California-based supplier of discrete semiconductor devices. The acquisition followed Zandman's traditional pattern of acquiring a business with similar technologies to expand the company's geographic reach and product scope. In July of that year, the company entered into an technical collaboration with Electro Scientific Industries, Inc. (ESI), an Oregon-based manufacturer of laser systems, semiconductor equipment, and vision products. The initial collaboration was expected to be on automated machine visual inspection for multilayer ceramic capacitors.

During this time, the passive components market began to recover. That, along with the restructuring, the movement of more production to low-cost countries,

and the LPSC acquisition led various investment firms to encourage the purchase of shares in Vishay.

As companies produced smaller and more compact products, such as notebook computers and pagers, they needed more, and smaller, components to complete the electronic circuitry. A digital cellular telephone, for example, could have as many as 437 resistors, capacitors, and inductors on its circuit board. An average Pentium microprocessor board had 252 total passive components, compared to 124 on the board of an average 486-based machine. The average automobile had more than 2,000 tantalum capacitors and multilayer ceramic chip capacitors. One of the answers to where to put all these components was to mount them on both sides of a circuit board. Vishay was a leader in the development and production of these surface mounted devices (SMDs), which, in 1996, accounted for about half the fixed resistor market. The need for Vishay's products was not about to diminish.

Vishay continued acquiring companies and vesting more capital into the semiconductor market. In 1998 Vishay gained complete ownership of Telefunken and 80.4 percent ownership of Siliconix, both divisions of the Semiconductor Business Group of TEMIC. Telefunken and Siliconix produced semiconductors along with other products that fit within Vishay's five-point strategy. A few years later Vishay would make several attempts to purchase the remainder of Siliconix. When the initial acquisition of Siliconix and Telefunken proved to be a lucrative buyout, Vishay sold Lite-On to focus on the two businesses.

More acquisitions continued from 2000 to 2001 as Vishay collected more passive-component companies such as Electro-Films, Spectrol, North American Capacitor Company (Mallory), and Cera-Mite. During the same period it acquired Infineon Technologies, which made components needed for infrared technologies. In 2002 Vishay offered $463 million to acquire General Semiconductor, a producer of diodes and rectifiers. Rectifiers were a semiconductor that converted alternating current (AC) into direct current (DC). General Semiconductor rejected two of Vishay's acquisition offers. Siliconix, of which Vishay owned 80.4 percent, subsequently sued General Semiconductor for patent infringement. Some analysts suggested that the extra litigation put pressure on General Semiconductor to finally sell for $540 million to Vishay. As a result of the acquisition, Vishay acquired an additional $229 million of General Semiconductor's debt.

In an interview with CNBC correspondent Mark Haines, Felix Zandman explained on the television program *Squawk Box* that "Vishay has been always making acquisitions. We have grown quite strongly through acquisitions, but we never slipped. All the acquisitions have been very, very good for us." One of the company's largest acquisitions during 2002 was that of Netherlands-based BCcomponents, a leading producer of passive components. The new addition reinforced Vishay as the third largest producer of passive electronic components behind Murata Manufacturing Co., Ltd. and EPCOS AG.

With so many companies entering the fold, Vishay could vertically integrate its products. In 2002 Vishay focused on strain gage products, which were used inside electronic scales to convert weight into a voltage output signal. Vishay acquired five strain gage businesses: Sensortronics, Tedea-Huntleigh, BLH, Nobel, and Celtron. The scope of the five companies allowed Vishay to offer a wide range of strain gage products, from the tiny resistance strain gages all the way up to the large testing systems that monitor the output of strain-gage transducers.

2004 ONWARD

In May 2004 the 75-year-old Felix Zandman announced that he would be succeeded as CEO by Gerald Paul, who had served as Vishay's president and chief operating officer. The succession took place on January 1 the following year. Zandman was far from being retired. He remained the chairman of Vishay's board and assumed dual roles as Vishay's new chief technology officer and as the chief business development officer—both newly created positions.

In early 2005 Vishay made several tender offers for the remaining shares of Siliconix. In March Vishay offered to exchange 2.64 shares of its common stock for each Siliconix share. Siliconix, however, advised their shareholders not to sell. Vishay came back in April with a tender offer to exchange 2.9 shares of Vishay and then again with 3.075 shares of Vishay for every Siliconix share. Vishay's shareholders who opposed the pending bid filed class action litigation against Vishay. Finally, however, in May of that year, Siliconix was merged and became a wholly owned subsidiary of Vishay.

Ellen D. Wernick
Updated, Kevin Teague

PRINCIPAL SUBSIDIARIES

SI Technologies, Inc.; Siliconix Inc.

PRINCIPAL COMPETITORS

Maxim Integrated Products, Inc.; Motorola, Inc.; Murata Manufacturing Co., Ltd.; Fairchild Semiconductor International, Inc.; AVX Corporation; General Semiconductor, Inc.; International Rectifier Corporation.

FURTHER READING

Jorgensen, Barbara, "The Minnow That Swallowed the Whale," *Electronic Business*, January 7, 1991, p. 39.

———, "Vishay Gets Bigger, Concentrates on Big Customers," *Electronic Business Buyer*, September 1993, p. 106.

"Dr. Felix Zandman, Chmn Of The Bd And CEO Of Vishay Intertechnology, Inc., Will Transfer His CEO Position To Dr. Gerald Paul, Pres And COO," *Dow Jones News Service*, November 22, 2004.

Levine, Bernard, "Vishay to Enter Ceramic Cap Market Via Vitramon," *Electronic News*, July 18, 1994, p. 2.

Talley, Karen, "Qwest International Plunges 20%; Vishay Drops 16%," *Wall Street Journal*, August 4, 2004, p. C3.

Tanaka, Wendy, "Top Executive to Leave Malvern, Pa, Electronics Parts Maker," *Philadelphia Inquirer*, November 4, 2003.

Tanaka, Wendy, "Vishay Intertechnology Names Its Next President," *Philadelphia Inquirer*, May 13, 2004.

Troxell, Thomas N., Jr., "Profits from Stress: Vishay's Instruments Find and Measure It on Aircraft, Other Equipment," *Barron's*, July 8, 1985, p. 39.

"Vishay Inks Tantalum Pact With PRC," *Electronic News*, May 13, 1996, p. 8.

"Vishay to Revamp Manufacturing, Take Charge," *Electronic News*, June 24, 1996, p. 12.

"Vishay to Settle Siliconix Litigation," *Associated Press Newswires*, April 29, 2005.

Zandman, Felix, and David Chanoff, *Never The Last Journey*, New York: Schocken Books Inc., 1995.

Zipser, Andy, "High-Voltage Performer: Acquisitions Spark Vishay Intertechnology," *Barron's*, August 26, 1991, p. 18.

W. H. Braum, Inc.

3000 N.E. 63rd Street
Oklahoma City, Oklahoma 73121
U.S.A.
Telephone: (405) 478-1656
Fax: (405) 475-2460
Web site: http://www.braums.com

Private Company
Incorporated: 1968
Employees: 100
Sales: $328.1 million (2004)
NAIC: 311511 Fluid Milk Manufacturing; 311520 Ice
    Cream and Frozen Dessert Manufacturing

■ ■ ■

W. H. Braum, Inc., is a family-owned company based in
Oklahoma City, which operates a chain of more than
280 Braum's Ice Cream and Dairy Store outlets located
in Oklahoma, Arkansas, Kansas, Missouri, and Texas.
The stores are all within 300 miles of the company's
farms to ensure freshness. The company is vertically
integrated, controlling all phases of dairy production,
store construction, and distribution of products. Braum
grows its own corn and alfalfa, mixed with grain, to feed
a herd of more than 10,000 dairy cows on seven farms
comprised of some 40,000 acres. The Holstein cows are
milked three times a day at a sprawling 35-acre complex,
and the milk is processed at a nearby, massive state-of-
the art processing plant into finished products: four
kinds of milk, ice cream, sherbet, frozen snacks, sour
cream, cottage cheese, and dips. The company produces

90 flavors of ice cream, and each store offers 27 regular
flavors and a rotating mix of another 50 flavors. Braum
refuses to inject the dairy herd with hormones or feed it
antibiotics to increase milk production, preferring instead
to control the feed mixture and other variables. Manure
and other waste products from the herd are treated and
used to naturally fertilize the crops, reducing the need
for chemicals. A second farm houses a support herd
where all the calves are born and housed in 3,000
individual hutches, and raised to maturity. They then
join the milking herd and return to the support herd
when they are ready to calve.

Braum also makes its own plastic containers for
milk and cartons for ice cream; operates its own
construction unit, which has built private roads and
even a bridge; a cabinet shop to make furniture for the
stores; and an in-house design unit, which produced the
company's award-winning logo. In addition, Braum
operates its own bakery, producing bread, buns, cookies,
muffins, and other baked goods as well as ice cream
cones and roasted almonds and pecans for sundae
toppings. The company operates its own fleet of trucks,
meeting all store needs with trailers that feature three
temperature controlled zones—frozen, chilled, and
dry—suitable for milk, frozen products, and fresh
produce, meat, and baked goods. The retail units are
part convenience store, part ice cream shop, part fast
food restaurant. The fountain serves ice cream cones,
sundaes, milk shakes, frozen yogurt, and other treats,
while the grill offers breakfast items, hamburgers and
other sandwiches, and salads. The stores' Fresh Market
section offers milk and bakery products, as well as fresh
produce and meat—a more recent addition. In the mid-

COMPANY PERSPECTIVES

Braum's is unique in the dairy industry because it is vertically integrated. Braum's "cuts out the middleman" by owning its dairy herd, farms and ranches, processing plant, bakery, retail stores, and delivery trucks. Braum's can offer its customers the highest quality products at the lowest possible prices.

2000s the company began building a beef herd to produce its own high-quality beef products.

1933 ORIGINS

The W. H. Braum company traces its heritage to Henry H. Braum, who in 1933 traded his farm for a small butter and milk processing plant in Emporia, Kansas. He soon began bottling his own milk and in 1940 added ice cream-making equipment. In 1949 he was joined by his son, William H. Braum, whose name the company would one day take. The younger Braum was well familiar with the operation by this time. "I started working for my father when I was 12 years old, helping with curb service," he told *Dairy Field*, in a 2001 profile. He continued to work for his father during high school in the early 1940s. Bill Braum then left home to attend the University of Kansas. He graduated in 1949 with a degree in Business Administration, prepared to play a more significant role in the running of the family business.

Henry Braum sold his wholesale dairy operation in 1952, deciding to focus on the retail ice cream business, which showed promise. A large number of local ice cream parlors and small chains sprouted up in the post-World War II years, as the parents of the baby boom generation looked for wholesome family activities. Braum launched a chain of Kansas ice cream shops under the Peter Pan name. His son Bill would take the company to the next level.

In 1957 Bill Braum bought out his father and took complete charge of the Peter Pan chain and the Emporia processing plant. Over the next ten years he expanded the chain to 61 stores and began the process of vertical integration by establishing a 1,000-cow dairy farm. He also built a new processing plant. The Peter Pan part of the business was so prosperous that it attracted the attention of a large wholesaler, who bought the retail operation in 1967.

TUTTLE MILKING FACILITY READY IN 1975

As part of the sale agreement, Braum was not allowed to sell ice cream in Kansas for the next ten years. He was not prevented, however, from operating in neighboring Oklahoma. Moreover, Braum kept his dairy herd and processing plant. Shortly after the Peter Pan sale, in 1968 Braum launched a chain of Braum's Ice Cream and Dairy Stores in Oklahoma. He wasted little time in establishing a strong base of operations, opening 24 stores in the first year alone. The stores were supplied with dairy products, ice cream, and other supplies from the Emporia facilities. It was not the most efficient way to do business, and after three years Braum opened a new processing plant in Oklahoma City in 1971. The dairy herd remained in Kansas for another four years, however. Then in 1975 a new milking facility was ready in Tuttle, Oklahoma, and the cows were relocated. Further vertical integration took place in 1978 when Braum opened a high-volume bakery in Oklahoma City. It would not only supply the retail stores with cones for ice cream, but other baked goods as well, including hamburger and hot dog buns for use in the grill and resale, and bread, cookies, cinnamon rolls, and muffins.

Braum continued to grow into the 1980s and expand its operation. Over the years it bought additional land near the Tuttle farm, on both sides of the South Canadian River, until the company owned property that was 15 square miles in size. Much of it was waste land and not fully developed when Braum acquired it. The Braum construction unit, when it wasn't building the milk barns and free stall barns, water treatment and waste treatment plants, and other farm facilities, made numerous improvements to the land, such as jetties on the river banks to stabilize the sandy banks during seasonal flooding. The unit also helped to construct a 200-yard private bridge across the South Canadian River, providing the company with access to fields and operations separated by the water. Moreover, the bridge relieved the public roads of Braum's large farm machinery and other vehicles.

In 1987 to accommodate increasing demand for Braum's dairy products, the construction crews built a new state-of-the-art processing center, 260,000 square feet in size. Here the company was able to control all facets of milk processing and dairy product making. Milk was shipped in tankers from the milking barns, where cows were milked around the clock, seven days a week, 400 at a time. The milk was processed and bottled, the half-gallon and gallon containers made on the premises, then made ready for shipment. All told, milk went from the udder to store coolers in about 36 hours. In the 1990s skim milk became Braum's specialty,

KEY DATES

1933: Henry Braum trades his Kansas farm for a milk processing facility.

1940: Braum begins making ice cream to sell to milk customers.

1952: Braum opens a chain of Peter Pan Ice Cream Stores.

1957: Son William Braum buys out his father.

1967: The Peter Pan chain is sold.

1968: The first Braum's Ice Cream and Dairy Store opens in Oklahoma.

1975: The Braum dairy herd moves from Kansas to Tuttle, Oklahoma.

1987: A new Braum milk processing plant opens.

1993: The company builds a new milking complex with capacity for growth.

2005: Braum stores begin carrying fresh meat and produce.

processed through a mechanical vapor recompression system that removed water to increase solids. As a result the milk had more body and flavor and contained more calcium and other nutrients than most skim milk. The plant also produced ice cream and the containers in which it was sold to consumers as well as the 3.5 gallon boxes that held the ice cream served at the stores' soda fountain. In addition, an on-site bacteriological lab handled all product testing. The company's desire to control as many aspects of quality was also demonstrated by the incorporation of a banana ripening room: The bananas were brought in once a week and ripening was controlled with ethylene gas.

The new plant also took measures to maintain sanitary conditions. Because overhead pipes and conduit collect dust, in the new facility the lines for utilities, steam, water, ammonia, and compressed air were all placed under the plant floors. Moreover, an air filtration system was installed as a further way to keep the air fresh and prevent contamination of ice cream and other products exposed to the air. The processing rooms were sloped from the middle to allow water to drain better when equipment was cleaned. It was then recycled to irrigate the fields, just as the manure from the cow barns was processed for use on the fields. Making sure that nothing went to waste was a hallmark of Braum. Controlling quality at every level, from cow to consumer, was another. As company spokesperson Andie Schwab

encapsulated it for *Dairy Field,* "We milk the cows to make the milk to put in the ice cream we place on the cones we make in our bakery to put in our trucks to ship to our stores."

In 1989 the processing plant was expanded, adding 60,000 more square feet of warehouse space, and the processing area was expanded further in 1991. The facility was capable of accommodating 500 stores, meaning that Braum had built in extra capacity to accommodate future expansion of the retail chain. All of these additions to the operation were privately funded, the Braum family priding itself on not accepting government financing, including farm subsidies.

In 1993 the Braum construction unit added a new 35-acre milking complex; according to the company, this was the largest of its kind in the world. It included 17 free-stall barns, in which each animal of the 10,000-cow herd was provided with a four-foot by eight-foot cubicle and a bedding of straw on which it could lie down. The stalls were elevated so that flush water could keep the facility clean, and the barns were built on a three-percent grade to assist in regular flushing and cleaning. The manure was then flushed to on-site waste treatment plants and eventually made it to the fields where the cattle feed was raised. Again allowing for future growth of the company, the complex was built to be capable of milking 15,000 cows if necessary.

As Bill Braum passed retirement age in the 1990s, a third generation of the Braum family, son Drew along with his sisters, became involved in the running of the business. Drew rose to the presidency, although his father continued to serve as chief executive officer well into his 70s. The younger Braum, like his father, grew up in the business, learning it from the lowest ranks. In an interview with the *Daily Oklahoman,* he recalled, "I guess my first job was painting (cattle) feeders and fence in sixth grade, as a summer job. Forty dollars was what I made that summer. My first regular job was in eighth grade here in Oklahoma City, working at the store on Britton Road. I worked behind the counter dipping ice cream. You'd make $1 an hour dipping ice cream. Then I got to go to the loading dock, where you'd make $1. 60, so that was a pretty good pay increase."

NEW CENTURY, SAME PLAN

As Braum entered the new century it continued to grow at its own pace, refusing to locate stores more than 300 miles from its farms to maintain high quality. All revenues came from the stores. Over the years, wholesalers and supermarkets approached the company about carrying their products, but the Braum family was not interested in selling outside of their retail operations.

Moreover, people occasionally asked if they could buy stock in the company, but going public was not in the family plan. "I'd hate to go to stockholders and say I spent this much money and here's my return on investment," Drew Braum joked to a group of Oklahoma City Rotary Club members in a 2005 presentation. "I would be unemployed." He did admit, however, that there was some talk of franchising. Nevertheless there were no franchising plans in the works. Instead, the company was looking to expand its store offerings. In 2005 Braum introduced its "Fresh Market" concept, adding fresh meats, fruits, and vegetables to its store. It was a natural progression for the company, and as in the past, Braum moved to gradually assume control of production as much as possible. To that end, the company began to build up a beef herd to supply the stores with its own beef.

Ed Dinger

PRINCIPAL COMPETITORS

Blue Bell Creameries L.P.; Dreyer's Grand Ice Cream Holdings, Inc.; International Dairy Queen, Inc.

FURTHER READING

Accetta, Pamela, "Storing Success," *Dairy Field,* May 2001, p. 1.

Demetrakakes, Pan, "Do-It-All Dairy," *Food Processing,* June 1998, p. 79.

Mans, Jack, "A Different Kind of Dairy Company," *Dairy Foods,* January 1997, p. 49.

Reiter, Jeff, "Doing Fine in Oklahoma," *Dairy Foods,* December 1994, p. 16.

Robinson, Rick, "Family, Quality Drive Braum's Success," *Daily Oklahoman,* June 2, 2002.

Stafford, Jim, "Braum's May Franchise But Won't Sell Stock, President Says," *Daily Oklahoman,* August 3, 2005.

Wenner Bread Products Inc.

———— ■ ————

33 Rajon Road
Bayport, New York 11705-1101
U.S.A.
Telephone: (631) 563-6262
Toll Free: (800) 869-6262
Fax: (631) 563-6546
Web site: http://www.wenner-bread.com

Private Company
Incorporated: 1975 as Wenner Bread Products Inc
Employees: 489
Sales: $74 million (2005)
NAIC: 311812 Commercial Bakeries; 311822 Flour
Mixes and Dough Manufacturing from Purchased
Flour

■ ■ ■

The commercial bakery Wenner Bread Products Inc.
ranked as the tenth most-used commercial bakery by
retail bakeries, according to a 2002 report published by
Milling & Baking News. The company sold dough that
was shipped frozen and later cooked at retail bakeries. It
also made partially baked (par-baked) and baked bread
that was shaped, frozen, and shipped. What began as a
small New York bakery had skyrocketed into a nearly
500,000 square-foot network of manufacturing and
warehousing facilities by 2006. Wenner Bread capitalized on a trend during the 1990s that saw many retail
bakeries, especially in-store supermarket bakeries, search
for cost-effective ways to supplement a nationwide
shortage of trained bakers. One solution was to order

frozen dough or par-baked breads from commercial
bakeries like Wenner Bread. The exchange allowed
bakeries to sell the same fresh-baked products without
needing onsite bakers. The five sons of the company's
founders would later oversee Wenner Bread, which
provided nearly 500 jobs for Long Island residents.
Wenner Bread prided themselves as a high-quality commercial bakery and as the largest independent frozen-
dough company in Long Island. Wenner Bread won
several awards for safety. It also contracted the California-
based technology business Graviton, Inc., to develop a
wireless sensory network that provided Wenner Bread
with a state-of-the-art self-monitoring production line.
In 2005 Wenner Bread produced more than 500 varieties of breads and rolls for an estimated 20,000 retail
bakeries, in-store supermarket bakeries, and food services.

1956–1980: RISE OF WENNER BREAD

In 1956 William, Sr., and his wife Mary Jane Wenner
opened what would be the first of many Wenner-
operated Long Island bakeries. Located in the town of
Roosevelt, the shop called Wesley's was started with
$2,000; it retailed breads, rolls, and pastries. The store's
fast-growing sales prompted William Wenner, Sr., and
his wife to open a second bakery in West Islip. On the
Wenner Bread website, Wenner, Sr., attributed his
business's success to producing "the freshest, highest
quality breads and rolls that we could, day after day."
Third and fourth retail bakeries soon followed.

The Wenner family began looking for ways to
expand into the commercial bakery business. If dough
was mixed and frozen at one location, it could still be

COMPANY PERSPECTIVES

Your complete satisfaction is our ultimate goal. We are committed to excellence in every facet of delivering superior bread products and support services. As the target for perfection continually moves, we respond by constantly improving our methods and processes. We are continually developing new products, based on consumer demand, your requirements or Wenner innovations. Wenner proudly provides much more than quality bread products, we offer a full range of support services, including planning, training, marketing and more. Wenner's expert staff assists in establishing in-store bakeries, including space planning and display design. Our experienced technicians will teach your employees the skills they need to become bakers in very little time. For our hospitality customers, Wenner helps plan menus, making our best product recommendations based on existing equipment and facilities. We also provide full marketing support, from packaging design to supplying reader friendly product brochures for your customers.

thawed, formed, baked, and sold as fresh bread at another. Wenner Bread opened its first commercial bakery at a 2,500 square-foot warehouse in Deer Park. Before supermarkets were built with in-store bakeries, Wenner Bread sold to food service and retail bakeries that were hoping to reduce labor costs and the amount of space and time needed to prepare dough from scratch. Mary Jane and William Wenner, Sr., were joined by their five sons and the family ended its tenure as a retail bakery. Wenner Bread incorporated in 1975. Two years later Wenner Bread released a successful line of egg twist rolls and frozen challah dough. The latter was ceremonial bread served at Jewish holidays excluding Passover.

1980S: HEALTHY BREADS

Packaged bread that was sold in supermarkets had been a relatively predictable food item until the 1980s. Supermarkets were noticing that the sales growth of healthier breads, such as whole-grain bread and oat bran bread, was outpacing their less-healthy breads such as rye bread and white bread. In the 1980s pricing also became more competitive between the companies supplying commercial bread racks.

One common misconception about bread was that it was fattening. In the 1980s more consumers were realizing that the fat actually came from the spreads used on bread. Bread was increasingly recognized as an excellent source of complex carbohydrates, vitamins, minerals, and fiber. Supermarkets noticed that their customers were reading more nutritional labels on the packaging. Even though in-store bakeries had not yet been popularized inside supermarkets, consumers were seeking higher quality breads. The trend would affect Wenner Bread in the following decade. Between 1984 and 1989 the consumption of whole-grain breads doubled. "The category has increased 25 percent over three years. Consumers are more educated in diet and nutrition than they were before," Gregg Dorner, the director of merchandising at Heinemann's Bakeries, said in a February 6, 1989 issue of the trade publication *Supermarket News*. "The growth of the whole-grain bread category really depends on the area. In the more affluent neighborhoods, the whole-grain breads [are growing even faster,]" Dorner said.

1990–1999: IN-STORE BAKERY BOOM

In the 1990s new supermarkets were being built with in-store bakeries, but the supply of skilled bakers had dwindled. Food service providers and other retailers began relying on the convenience and consistency of commercial bakeries like Wenner Bread. Using commercial bakeries was not just easier, it was sometimes less expensive. In 1993 Ralphs Grocery Co. closed a bakery that was providing bread for its Southern California supermarkets. The Ralphs Glendale-based bakery had become too expensive to operate. Executives tried reducing costs with the layoff of more than 100 employees at the start of 1993, but eventually the company's executives found a more affordable supply of fresh bread. "We tried to make this thing work, but consumers are demanding in-store manufacturing," Gene Brown, senior vice president for Ralphs human resources, said in a May 7, 1993 edition of the *Los Angeles Daily News*. "In addition, commercial bakeries can produce the products like bread and buns for less money," Brown concluded.

In the mid-1990s supermarkets were also improving the marketing for in-store bakeries. Full-page newspaper ads were dedicated to the fresh-baked bread being made inside supermarkets. In-store bakeries slowly understood that consumers would pay higher prices as long as the bread was fresh and made from high-quality ingredients. It was estimated that retail bakeries increased their reliance on commercial bakeries from 62 percent in 1994 to 65 percent in 1995. Bread supplied by Wenner Bread

KEY DATES

1956: William and Mary Jane Wenner open Wesley's pastry store in Long Island with $2,000.

1975: The company incorporates as Wenner Bread Products Inc.

1978: The company introduces the first frozen dough challahs and egg twist rolls.

1999: Sales reach $59 million.

2003: Graviton technology is installed in Wenner Breads production line.

2004: Sales reach $71.5 million.

and other commercial bakeries was typically branded by the supermarket. "We want the store to have the brand. We think it's vital for in-store bakeries to maintain their own identity and not be someone else's bakery," Richard Wenner, the president and chief executive officer of Wenner Bread, said in *Milling & Baking News*. "When you take a brand into your own bakery, you lose control over your own profitability," William Wenner's son continued; "You're becoming an extension of the commercial aisle by using off-premise labels, and you're eliminating your image of freshness."

The freshest method of supplying retail bakeries was to ship frozen dough that could later be baked. Shipping par-baked bread was the second-freshest way to transfer bread from commercial bakeries to retail bakeries. Some retailers purchased already-baked frozen bread which they would then defrost and sell. Bob Wallace, president and chief executive officer of BakeMark Ingredients [East], Inc., said in *Milling & Baking News*, "There's a continuum where [retail bakeries] move from scratch, to mix, to frozen dough to thaw-and-sell, and different chains and different customer segments are always at different points on that continuum," he said. "The continuum generally moves toward more convenience, meaning less labor required."

According to Gale Group Inc., the sale of bread products for Wenner Bread reached $59 million in 1999. The commercial bakery industry was expanding from a niche to a mainstream market. Retail bakeries were ordering frozen dough or par-baked breads and then finishing the product with their signature ingredients or shape just before baking.

2000–2002: ARTISAN BREADS

Artisan-style breads enjoyed a rise in popularity at the start of the new millennium. These breads were made with thick crusts that usually surrounded dense interiors of bread, fruits, nutmeats, and honey. The style originated in Europe where artisan bread had been handmade for centuries. It typically featured a high price tag and was initially considered a luxury item. Wenner Bread offered more than 25 varieties of artisan dough in 2002. Even though the U.S. economy dipped after 2000, Americans' desire for high-end bread was increasing. In 2002 consumers purchased $75 million to $150 million of artisan bread in the United States. Sales were growing 20 percent annually. It was estimated that in the mid-1990s only 10 percent of supermarkets carried artisan breads, but by 2002 the percentage had climbed to 40 percent. "People now talk about a loaf of bread like a bottle of wine," said Frank French, director of technical services for ADM Milling Co., in *Milling & Baking News*. He continued: "People are tearing bread apart. I'm amazed at how many people love to do that."

Industry analysts feared that commercial bakeries would warp the traditional handmade process of artisan bread. Wenner Bread and its competition were aware, however, that consumers would only pay a premium price for the product if it was made with fresh and premium products. Many commercial bakeries still made the dough by hand. "Artisan bread is meant to be baked and sold. It's not meant to be baked, frozen, sold, and distributed across the country and baked again," Wenner said in *Milling & Baking News*.

2002–2003: FACILITY IMPROVEMENTS

While most commercial bakers believed that the flourishing economy and lack of skilled bakers had increased their business, Tim Busta, the product manager at Dawn Food Products, Inc., offered a different theory. In *Milling & Baking News*, Mr. Busta explained in 2002, "The reason the frozen dough market is growing so well is the fact that the quality level has risen from 10 to 20 years ago," he said. "Better technology, ingredients and machinery available today drive down the cost so bakers can have frozen dough without paying a ton to have someone pre-form something for them, and improved ingredient technology has made frozen dough products better."

Wenner Bread's high-tech facility exemplified Mr. Busta's statement. In 2003 Wenner Bread signed a contract with Graviton, Inc., a California-based developer of wireless networks. Graviton installed a state-of-the-art sensory system across Wenner Bread's production line. Monitors were placed throughout warehouses to insure optimal temperature and dough quality. Temperature monitors were also installed inside freezers, refrigerators, and delivery trucks. All of the information was sent wirelessly to a control center, which also alerted factory workers about routine maintenance needed on equipment. To reduce wasted electricity, Graviton installed wireless power meters throughout the production line. "Wenner Bread Products has a proud history of innovation, safety and relentless dedication to quality," Richard Wenner was quoted by *PR Newswire*. "Consistent with that tradition, we are pleased to be working with Graviton to implement this breakthrough technology in our state-of-the-art manufacturing operations."

Wenner Bread's product quality and workplace environment scored well with industry groups. The company earned a superior rating from the American Institute of Baking. The Occupational Health and Safety Administration (OSHA) awarded Wenner Bread with Star Status and titled the company "America's Safest Bakery." Wenner Bread's Long Island facilities allowed the company to produce some 1,200 bread varieties by 2003. In restaurants, where fresh baked bread was not as important as other items on the menu, Wenner Bread provided frozen hamburger buns, breadbasket rolls, Kaiser rolls, and other bread products.

The competition was also improving their manufacturing process. In 2004 a system that provided real-time feedback on the quality of bread products was installed at a Flowers Bakery plant. Flowers Bakery, owned by Flowers Foods, Inc., was one of the nation's largest commercial food companies serving retail bakeries and fast food chains. The system was co-created by Georgia Tech Research Institute, the conveyor systems manufacturer Baking Technology Systems, Inc. (Bake-Tech), the software company Thinkage Ltd., and the manufacturing technology firm Rockwell Automation, Inc. Cameras mounted in the production facilities fed video to computers that inspected the bread for impurities, seed consistency, and proper form. The supervisory system was designed to inspect between 600 and 1,000 buns per minute.

Safety was also a top priority for Wenner Bread. OSHA had reported a reduction in workplace fatalities across America's general population in 2003, but the fatalities for Latino day laborers had increased. OSHA representatives explained that because many Latino day laborers spoke little or no English, they could not fully understand onsite safety instructions. In 2003 OSHA teamed up with Wenner Bread for the OSHA Voluntary Protection Program. The majority of Wenner Bread's employees were non-English speaking. The program required Wenner Bread to provide safety and health information in their employees' native tongues. Wenner Bread was the first business in the New York area to participate in such a program. One 10-hour Spanish

safety course covered proper use of equipment, health hazards in the Wenner Breads factory, and fall protection. Wenner Bread also provided the employees with protective equipment and food throughout the course.

2003 ONWARD

In 2003 Wenner Bread was operating in 150,000 square feet of several different office, production, and warehouse locations. In June the company leased 72,000 more square feet of warehouse and office space in Ronkonkoma, Long Island. The expansion secured Wenner Bread's position as the largest commercial baker on Long Island. Wenner Bread also employed between 400 and 500 employees and sold bread to 20,000 retail locations. "Long Island has a bigger food industry than most people realize," Jeremiah Schnee, a managing partner at the business advisory firm Biscotti, Toback/RFR & Co., was quoted by *Long Island Business News*. He continued, "Food may not be sexy the way high-tech is, but it's a stable industry. Everybody has to eat. It's much more stable and consistent (than tech), while being unsung."

Wenner Bread's sales were estimated by the Gale Group to be $71.4 million in 2004, a substantial increase from the $59 million posted in 1999. In 2005 the U.S. bakery industry had an estimated 2,600 commercial bakeries that were collectively generating $25 billion in sales. The next year Wenner Bread employed 600 workers and was hoping to consolidate its operations, which was spread across 500,000 square feet of production and warehousing facilities. The company was also hoping to reduce transportation costs by adding production facilities closer to their suppliers in the Midwest.

Kevin Teague

PRINCIPAL COMPETITORS

Bakemark USA LLC; Dawn Food Products, Inc.; Flowers Foods, Inc.; General Mills, Inc.; Interstate Bakeries Corporation; Kraft Foods Inc.; Sara Lee Food & Beverage; Unilever.

FURTHER READING

"Breadmaker Sales Rising," *Dayton Daily News*, January 22, 1994, p. 4B.

Denny, Sharon, "Bread: Enough Dough For Everyone," *Current Health 2*, December 1, 1994, p. 25.

"Graviton to Implement Wireless Sensor Network and Control Platform at Wenner Bread Products," *PR Newswire*, February 1, 2002.

Harper, Roseanne, "EDDA Presents Tiffany Crystal Awards," *Supermarket News*, January 15, 1996, p. 41.

Higgins, Kevin T., "Buns Of Fire," *Food Engineering*, April 1, 2004, p. 135.

Krumrei, Doug, "Let The Good Times Roll," *Bakery Production and Marketing*, June 24, 1995, p. 62.

"Large Commercial Bakeries' Sales per Employee in the U.S. Average $150,000," *Business Wire*, April 5, 2006.

"Long Island Commercial Market Getting Stronger, Study Says," *Real Estate Weekly*, August 6, 2003, p. 13.

O'Brien, Dennis, "Shipyard Worker Earns Workplace Safety Award," *Newport News,* November 14, 1998.

Postema, Susan B., "Ralphs To Close Bakery, Lay Off 300," *Los Angeles Daily News*, May 7, 1993, p. N3.

Springer, Judith, "Whole Grains Bring In The Bread," *Supermarket News*, February 6, 1989, p. 23.

Wilkinson Hardware
Stores Ltd.

P.O. Box 20
Roebuck Way
Manton Wood, Worksop
United Kingdom
Telephone: (44) 01909 505505
Fax: (44) 01909 505777
Web site: http://www.wilko.co.uk

Private Company
Incorporated: 1930
Employees: 21,000
Sales: £1.12 billion ($1.9 billion) (2005)
NAIC: 444130 Hardware Stores

■ ■ ■

Wilkinson Hardware Stores Ltd. is one of the United Kingdom's leading retailers catering to the hardware and do-it-yourself (DIY) sector. The company, headquartered in Manton Wood, Worksop, operates more than 265 stores throughout the United Kingdom, and boasts more than 21,000 employees. The company operates several store formats, varying in size, with an emphasis on large-scale 'superstores'. Unlike many of its competitors, Wilkinson stores are typically located in the country's downtown 'High Street' areas. Because of this proximity to its customers, Wilkinson stores tend to feature a broader product assortment than typical hardware stores.

The company's product assortment goes beyond DIY, hardware and decorating and garden items, to include toiletries, household cleaners, kitchen goods, "home living" including bedding and other textiles, pet foods and other pet care items, stationery, and even confectionery. Other items include perfume and fragrances and computer supplies. In this way, Wilkinson Hardware operates as much as an old fashioned variety store as a hardware store. These product categories nonetheless all maintain a common theme—Wilkinson's dedication to remaining a low-priced, discount-oriented retailer. As part of this effort, the company also sells its own branded goods, which account for a significant proportion of the company's sales.

Owned by the founding Wilkinson family, Wilkinson Hardware has been growing steadily into the mid-2000s, averaging 20 new stores per year for more than a decade. The company has targeted an expansion of its retail network to 370 stores by 2010. Tony Wilkinson, son of the company founder and chairman since 1972, retired in 2005, making way for the latest generation under daughter Lisa Wilkinson and niece Karin Swann. In 2005, Wilkinson Hardware posted total sales of nearly £1.12 billion ($1.9 billion).

SINGLE STORE BEGINNINGS IN 1930

Wilkinson Hardware Store was founded by J.K. Wilkinson, who opened a small shop selling hardware items and other variety goods on Charwood Street, in Leicester, in 1930. Wilkinson, described as a canny businessman, founded his business on a simple, yet effective philosophy which was to sell quality goods at discount prices. That strategy quickly paid off, establishing the Wilkinson store as a local favorite. Within a year, Wilkinson had already opened his second store. Yet, as

COMPANY PERSPECTIVES

■

At the heart of Wilkinson is a desire to provide the ultimate shopping experience for our customers and a rewarding place to work for our team members. Our Vision for the business is simple: We are committed to providing our customers on the high street with quality products at everyday low prices and friendly service that exceeds expectations. We invest in team members, logistic and information technology to make this family business a great place to work and shop.

granddaughter and future company director Karin Swann told *Worksop Today*: "I don't think he every dreamed it would grow as big as it is. He simply started off wanting to give people great quality goods for a good price. That way of thinking has remained ever since and it has brought us to where we are now."

By the end of the 1930s, J.K. Wilkinson already operated seven stores. Following World War II, Wilkinson continued to expand the business, opening a number of new stores. In 1960, Wilkinson was joined by son Tony Wilkinson, who had started his working life at the F.W. Woolworth retail group. The younger Wilkinson worked at a number of positions in the Wilkinson organization, and named to the company's board of directors in 1963. By the late 1960s, the younger Wilkinson had emerged as the driving force of the group, and in 1972 he replaced his father as company chairman. A number of other members of the Wilkinson family were also active in the company, including Wilkinson's younger sister, Barbara.

By then, Wilkinson had grown to a network of 20 stores. The company's growth required it to expand not only its headquarters, but its distribution facilities as well. In the late 1960s, the company moved to Worksop, in Bassetlaw, constructing a new head office and distribution center. That site also became the home of the group's test store—a full-scale mockup of a typical Wilkinson store, which enabled the company to test new floor plans, formats, and products.

Wilkinson continued to spread strongly throughout the Midlands and northern regions of England during the 1970s and 1980s. The company's commitment to low prices during a difficult economic climate helped it attract a growing number of customers. As part of its continued efforts to remain a price leader, the company began developing its own branded product range, offer-

ing customers a choice of quality, yet discounted products, as well as the major name brands. Wilkinson's own branded line became an important source of revenues for the company, accounting for as much as 35 percent of its sales.

Into the 1990s, Wilkinson remained committed to its center-of-town locations, despite the growing success of out-of-town commercial zones and the rising number of competitors turning to ever-larger superstore-formats. Indeed, the trend offered a number of opportunities for the company to acquire new sites in the country's town centers. In 1991, for example, the company purchased the freehold to the former Marks & Spencer department store site in Dudley. The strong demand at the store led the company to invest in its expansion, carrying out a £250,000 extension in 1994.

NATIONAL RETAIL HARDWARE LEADER IN THE NEW CENTURY

By then, Wilkinson had already entered into a new growth phase, becoming one of the United Kingdom's fastest growing retailers. Throughout the 1990s and into the new decade, Wilkinson achieved an impressive growth record of an average of 20 percent per year. Part of the secret to the company's success was its willingness to expand its product offering beyond the traditional hardware and DIY market. As such the company's store shelves featured a wide range of household-related items, including cleaning and kitchen products, textiles and clothing, pet care products, and personal hygiene and personal care items—such as perfume. Wilkinson also added a book section, with titles ranging from DIY guides to children's books and fiction. The wider assortment, of more than 25,000 items, helped stimulate traffic in the company's stores. As such, the company's customers typically visited the store an average of two to three times per week.

By mid-1999, Wilkinson operated nearly 160 stores, backed by its one million-square-foot Worksop distribution center and a trucking fleet of more than 500 vehicles. Most of the company's business, however, remained concentrated in the United Kingdom's Midlands and northern regions. As it approached the new century, the company now targeted expansion onto a truly national level, with plans to open new stores in the southeast and Wales.

In the summer of 1999, the company announced its decision to build a new distribution center in Wales, replicating the Worksop site and offering more than 850,000 square feet of warehousing space. This site, like the Worksop center, offered support for as many as 300 stores. Construction began on the site in Magor in 2000,

KEY DATES

1930: J.K. Wilkinson opens his first hardware store in Leicester; within a year, he opens a second store and by the end of the decade operates seven stores.

1960: Son Tony Wilkinson joins company.

1963: Tony Wilkinson becomes a company director.

1969: Wilkinson moves to new site in Worksop and builds a one million square-foot distribution center.

1972: Tony Wilkinson becomes company chairman; Wilkinsons now operates 20 stores.

1999: With nearly 160 stores in operation, Wilkinson targets expansion into Wales and southeast England.

2000: Company opens second distribution center in Magor, Wales.

built one of the country's largest city center-based shopping areas, Eastgate. And extension to this site, Westgate, fitted in with Wilkinson's own expansion plans, and the company opened a store on that site in 2000.

Wilkinson continued adding new locations into the middle of the decade. It added stores in Stroud, Knowle, Armley, West Ealing, Barry, Corby, Brentwood, and Derby in 2005. Most of these were small or medium format, although the Corby store followed the company's extra large format. Into mid-2006, Wilkinson's new store program added locations in Chelmsley Wood, Longton, and Clowne. By then, Wilkinson had come under new family leadership, after Tony Wilkinson retired as chairman. Taking his place was niece Karin Swann, who had joined the company in 1994, and daughter Julie Wilkinson, who became a company director. With sales of more than £1.1 billion and an ambitious growth strategy, Wilkinson planned to remain one of the United Kingdom's leading family-owned retailers into the new decade.

M. L. Cohen

with operations launched in September of that year. At the same time, Wilkinson opened its first stores in its new territories, with a target to reach a total of 250 stores by 2003.

Through the mid-2000s, Wilkinson's expansion effort called for the addition of some 20 stores per year. The success of its new store openings encouraged the company to raise the bar of its growth targets. In 2003, for example, the company set a new goal of 300 stores by 2006, and at the mid-decade the company hoped to operate as many as 370 stores by 2010.

In addition to new store openings, the company also continued to fine-tune its portfolio, transferring existing stores to larger sites—such as its Lincoln store, which took over a site formerly occupied by C&A in 2001. The company remained committed to its city-center market—particularly as this market had been undergoing a transformation of sorts at the turn of the century. With the growing number of out-of-town shopping centers draining people from the country's city centers, a number of city councils had begun to fight back, promoting the development of new large-scale shopping centers within the city center. An example of this could be found in Basildon, in the southeast, which

PRINCIPAL SUBSIDIARIES

Wilkinson Hardware Stores Ltd.

PRINCIPAL COMPETITORS

Kingfisher plc; BandQ plc; Saint-Gobain plc; Focus Ltd; Homebase Ltd; Facey Commodity Company Ltd; Heiton Group plc.

FURTHER READING

"Wilkinson looks at Two Possible Sites for Second Distribution Centre," *DIY Week*, June 25, 1999, p.2.

"Hardware Giants Wilko Marks 75th Birthday," *Worksop Today.co.uk*, May 20, 2005.

"Hardware Giant Wilkinson Celebrates 75th Birthday," *Worksop Today.co.uk*, May 13, 2005.

Meyer, Scot, "Culling Best Practices," *MMR*, June 25, 2001, p. 57.

"Wilko's Magic Numbers," *The Hub*, September 2003.

"Wilkinson Links with Dulux and Polycell," *Marketing*, June 16, 2004, p. 14.

"Wilkinson to Increase Books Offer," *Bookseller*, January 25, 2002, p. 7.

Wright Express
Corporation

———■———

97 Darling Avenue
South Portland, Maine 04106
U.S.A.
Telephone: (207) 773-8171
Fax: (207) 828-5181
Web site: http://www.wrightexpress.com

Public Company
Incorporated: 1983
Employees: 650
Sales: $241.3 million (2005)
Stock Exchanges: New York
Ticker Symbol: WXS
NAIC: 523910 Miscellaneous Intermediation

■ ■ ■

With its headquarters in South Portland, Maine, Wright Express Corporation is a leader in the field of payment processing and information management services for commercial and government vehicle fleets in the United States, Canada, and Puerto Rico. Utah-based subsidiary Wright Express Financial Services Corporation provides fleet and corporate credit cards. When the cards are used, the company is able to collect point-of-sale information, including the identification of the driver and the vehicle, the vehicle's odometer reading, and the amount of the expenditure for fuel or maintenance and its provider. In this way, fleet operators are able to eliminate fraud, such as old-time collusion between a driver and service station attendant to pad a bill. Wright also provides analysis tools to allow customers to use the

data collected to better manage their fleets. Operators, for example, can determine if a vehicle is costing too much to fuel or service and decide if it should be retired. More than 180,000 fuel and vehicle maintenance locations, covering over 90 percent of the America's retail fuel locations, are compatible with the Wright system. Wright is a public company listed on the New York Stock Exchange.

19TH CENTURY ROOTS

Wright Express started out as a sideline for A.R. Wright Company, a family business founded in the 1890s by Augustus R. Wright, which sold coal and ice to Portland, Maine. Later it began selling gasoline and focused on the home heating fuel business. In 1983, according to *New England Business,* Parker Poole III, the grandson of Augustus Wright and an executive in the company, "had a brainstorm: a way to raise capital and expand the oil delivery-based enterprise. The little company had thought a POS credit card system, sort of like an ATM (Automated Teller Machine) network, was the wave of the future and that Wright could be a forerunner in software production and sales." Along with his uncle (and A.R. Wright's president), William Richardson, Poole formed Wright Express Corporation in 1983. The new company with its handful of employees set up shop in the A.R. Wright offices. The business almost proved to be too visionary, however. At the time, less than 3 percent of all gas stations in the United States had the electronic equipment necessary to process MasterCard and Visa transactions, let alone accommodate Wright's plan to collect data and provide fleet operators with useful information.

COMPANY PERSPECTIVES

In the simplest terms, Wright Express, along with its wholly owned subsidiary Wright Express Financial Services Corporation, is a leading provider of fleet and corporate charge cards. Flexible, pre-set cardholder limits and robust data capture from each card transaction provide users with valuable information to better manage corporate expenses. And the powerful back-end processing of those transactions helps streamline your entire process of tracking and paying for employee business expenses, be they for fuel, supply purchases or travel and entertainment.

Wright's modified concept was to offer a WEX fuel credit card that could be used by trucks at three unattended stations in Portland. Fortunately Oakhurst Dairy signed on as a customer. "Simultaneously," wrote *New England Business,* "Shell and Mobil announced plans to launch their own credit business, one very similar to what A.R. Wright had in mind. The proliferation of ATMs in everyday life, the initiation of PIN numbers and itemized billings by banks and major credit card companies gave A.R. Wright the credibility it needed."

With national aspirations, the young company was no longer a good fit for the local home-heating fuel company and required more capital than its parent could provide. Hence in 1985 it was reincorporated in Delaware and Richardson cast about for venture capital, securing some locally and in Boston, and far away as Texas. Now under the control of the venture capitalists, Wright sought out relationships with the major oil companies, hoping to take advantage of their automation programs to make the WEX card accessible at their electronic networks. Moreover, according to *Forbes,* "Wright didn't have the money to send salesmen across the country begging gas station owners to accept a card they had never heard of. Instead, it won over thousands of stations at a clip by selling to large oil companies like Getty, Texaco and Exxon. The oil companies would then tell their stations to take the card as a way to win fleet business."

GETTY ON BOARD: 1987

A major turning point occurred in 1987 when Wright signed its first agreement with a major oil company, Getty Petroleum, which was interested in having a fleet card but not the burden of carrying the credit. In addition, it wanted to deal with just one company and one bank. Wright made the decision to carry the credit and sought out a financial backer. It found one in GE Capital, which was willing to sign on if Getty was. Getty was equally cautious and it took some time before both parties signed on to the deal. "Then relationships with banks evolved," according to *National Petroleum News,* which added, "Wright Express began working with Getty's financial network, Philadelphia National Bank. Wright Express got PNB to accept their card through the PNB network, and the mechanics were in place."

With Getty and GE Capital on board, Wright began adding other oil companies, including 11 majors and semi-major oil companies, over the next seven years. For many the Wright offered a private label card, one under the oil company's name as a way to build brand loyalty with fleet customers. The addition of so many oil company customers also served to, in effect, multiply Wright's sales force. It was not surprising, therefore, that the company signed up fleet customers at a rapid clip, and annual revenues doubled for each of the next several years. Furthermore, as had been the case with Getty, Wright was able to get its cards accepted by the networks used by their other oil company clients. In this way, Wright avoided the expense of creating its own proprietary network. "Fina was on the Buypass systems, so Wright Express got on the system," reported *National Petroleum News.* "Crown and Total were on the JCPenney network, so they got on there. Clark was on Sears and on and on." In 1989 Wright also began to sign up tire, service, and quick-lube companies, which began accepting the WEX card, thus making Wright into a full-service automotive services provider.

By the end of 1990, 50,000 sites accepted the WEX card. Two years later Wright recorded its first profitable year. Not only did the information collected at the post of sale help fleet customers to uncover fraud and better manage their costs, it provided Wright with information that helped its CEO, John R. Birk, who joined the company in August 1992, to anticipate changes in the economy and make preparations. According to a 1995 *Inc.* article: "Ninety to 120 days before the economy comes out of a recession, the number of monthly transactions and the average size of those transactions start to climb. In 1993 Birk's model told him that the economy was in danger of overheating. Consequently, he figured the United States was due for some inflation and a rise in interest rates." Even though Wright was growing quickly and hiring more people, Birk implemented an aggressive cost-control program and restructured his debt before interest rates rose.

To help him pursue the next phase of Wright's growth, Birk also added seasoned executives to the

KEY DATES

1983: Company is founded.
1987: Getty Petroleum is signed as a customer.
1994: Company is acquired by Safecard Services Inc.
1997: Wright Express Financial Services Corporation is formed.
2001: Company becomes a Cendant Corporation subsidiary.
2005: Wright is spun off as public company.

management team in early 1994. Taking over as senior vice-president of product management was Paul J. Novak, formerly with MasterCard International. Coming over from L.L. Bean Inc., where he served as credit manager, was Roland L. Tufts, who now became Wright's vice-president of credit and collections. They joined a company that generated just $11.2 million in revenues in 1993, but Wright clearly held great promise, enough to attract the attention of Cheyenne, Wyoming-based SafeCard Services Inc., a credit card-registration company whose business was to quickly notify credit card issuers when a subscriber's card was lost or stolen. About ten times larger, SafeCard agreed in July 1994 to pay $35.5 million in cash for Wright. SafeCard was headed by Paul G. Kahn, former president of AT&T Universal Card, the telecom's credit card division. After leaving AT&T in 1993 he became SafeCard's CEO and chairman as well as a member of Wright's board of directors. Once he learned more about Wright's business, he became excited about adding it to the SafeCard operation, which would gain product diversification. In turn, Wright would be able to take advantage of SafeCard's platform to expand its geographic reach.

Wright also hoped to tap into SafeCard's cash reserves to further grow the business, but the new ownership soon encountered problems. SafeCard was renamed Ideon Group Inc. and under Kahn ran off the racks. "During his watch," reported *South Florida Business Journal,* "Ideon started and scrapped two expensive and money-losing businesses, ran up overhead, and spent lavishly on parties, a corporate jet and other items. Kahn hired friends, relatives, several personal assistants and a corporate historian. He also paid millions to consultants, including Martin A. Siegel, the ex-Kidder Peabody investment banker/convicted felon." When Kahn's ventures failed to pan out and the price of Ideon stock

plummeted, hundreds of employees were fired to cut costs in 1995. In February 1996, Kahn joined their ranks.

In 1996 Wright reached a milestone when it issued its one-millionth commercial charge card. It also received a new corporate parent that year, when CUC International, Inc. agreed to acquire Ideon in a $375 million deal. Later in the year CUC merged with HFS Incorporated to form Cendent Corporation. This ownership arrangement would last three years. (Before then, Wright would establish, in 1997, a wholly owned banking subsidiary, Wright Express Financial Services Corporation in Utah.) In May 1999 Avis Rent-A-Car agreed to pay $1.8 billion to acquire Cendant's fleet management business, which included Wright as well as the PHH Vehicle Management Services unit. There was no significant impact on Wright, however. It continued to chart its own course with its management team left in place, now headed by CEO Michael E. Dubyak, who had been with Wright for a dozen years before ascending to the top post in 1998. Moreover, Cendant, which held Avis stock, would buy the remaining shares of Avis common stock to gain control of Avis in 2001 and once again become Wright's corporate parent.

INDEPENDENCE: 2005

Wright ended the 1990s with more than 500 employees, a significant increase over the 80 that it employed just eight years earlier. Expansion continued in the new century. The company posted revenues of $126.6 million and net income of $24.4 million in 2002. A year later those totals improved to $156.9 million and $34.6 million. Cendant now felt the time was right to spin off Wright in an initial public offering of stock and announced its intention in November 2004. With Credit Suisse First Boston and Merrill Lynch acting as underwriters, the offering was completed in February 2005, netting $1 billion for Cendant. While Wright did not receive any of the proceeds, it at least gained the use of its stock as currency should it opt to make acquisitions. The spin-off agreement also contained several anti-takeover provisions, perhaps a reflection of management's weariness of having constantly changed hands in the 1990s. The election of the board of directors was staggered so that only one-third could be changed each year. As a result, three years would be required to complete a buy out of the company. The provisions also hindered a party in calling a shareholder election, and once an outside shareholder gained a 15 percent stake in the business, investors received additional rights. While it might have become more difficult to remove poor management, the agreement offered no severance package to Dubyak and other senior members of management. In this way, they did not have an incentive to find a buyer for the company in order to cash in their severance packages.

Investors were not especially excited about the Wright offering, however. The company's stock immediately dipped below its initial $18 price. Nevertheless, the company continued to grow its balance sheet, posting revenues of $241.3 million and earnings of $18.7 million in 2005. Wright also introduced a new business card that it hoped would spur further sales growth. In addition to being accepted at more than 180,000 fuel and service locations and providing information to help a fleet operator manage costs, the new card offered a roadside assistance program; a online employment application screening service to help fleets comply with the U.S. Department of Transportation's mandatory screening requirements; and WrightRewards, a rewards programs that allowed fleet operators to accumulate points on every transaction, redeemable for travel, entertainment, and other retail premiums.

Ed Dinger

PRINCIPAL SUBSIDIARIES

Wright Express Financial Services Corporation.

PRINCIPAL COMPETITORS

Comdata Corporation; Fleetcor Technologies, Inc.; U.S. Bank Voyager Fleet Systems, Inc.

FURTHER READING

Churbuck, David C., "Don't Leave Headquarters Without It," *Forbes,* December 20, 1993, p. 242.

Moore, Bonnie, "Wright's Tough: And Don't Leave Home Without It," *New England Business,* June 1, 1991, p. 52.

Sorkin, Andrew Ross, "Cendant Expected to Spin Off Wright Express, a Fleet Manager," *New York Times,* November 23, 2004, p. C2.

Welles, Edward O., "The View From the Front," *Inc.,* January 1995, p. 59.

Wickenheiser, Matt, "Portland-Based Fleet Management Services Firm Wright Express Goes Public," *Portland Press Herald,* February 17, 2005.

"Wright Express Evolves Into Universal Card," *National Petroleum News,* August 1994, p. 58.

"The Wright Stuff," *Credit Card Management,* February 1994, p. 10.

Index to Companies

Agusta S.p.A., **46** 66

AgustaWestland N.V., 75 18–20

Agway, Inc., 7 17–18; **21** 17–19 (upd.); **36** 440

Aherns Holding, **60** 100

AHI Building Products *see* Carter Holt Harvey Ltd.

AHL Services, Inc., 26 149; **27** 20–23; **45** 379

Ahlstrom Corporation, 53 22–25

Ahmanson *see* H.F. Ahmanson & Company.

AHMSA *see* Altos Hornos de México, S.A. de C.V.

Ahold *see* Koninklijke Ahold NV.

AHP *see* American Home Products Corporation.

AHS *see* American Hospital Supply Corporation.

AHSC Holdings Corp. *see* Alco Health Services Corporation.

Ahtna AGA Security, Inc., **14** 541

AI Automotive, **24** 204

AIC *see* Allied Import Company.

AICA, **16** 421; **43** 308

AICPA *see* The American Institute of Certified Public Accountants.

Aid Auto, **18** 144

Aida Corporation, **11** 504

AIG *see* American International Group, Inc.

AIG Global Real Estate Investment Corp., **54** 225

AIG Latin America Equity Partners, Ltda., **74** 48

AIG/Lincoln International L.L.C., **54** 225

Aigner *see* Etienne Aigner AG.

Aiken Stores, Inc., **14** 92

Aikenhead's Home Improvement Warehouse, **18** 240; **26** 306

AIL Technologies, **46** 160

AIM Create Co., Ltd. *see* Marui Co., Ltd.

AIM Management Group Inc., **65** 43–45

AIMCO *see* Apartment Investment and Management Company.

Ainsworth Gaming Technologies, **54** 15

Ainsworth National, **14** 528

AIP *see* American Industrial Properties; Amorim Investimentos e Participaço.

Air & Water Technologies Corporation, 6 441–42 *see also* Aqua Alliance Inc.

Air Berlin GmbH & Co. Luftverkehrs KG, 71 15–17

Air BP, **7** 141

Air By Pleasant, **62** 276

Air Canada, 6 60–62; **23** 9–12 (upd.); **29** 302; **36** 230; **59** 17–22 (upd.)

Air China, 46 9–11

Air Compak, **12** 182

Air de Cologne, **27** 474

Air Express International Corporation, 13 19–20; **40** 138; **46** 71

Air France *see* Groupe Air France; Societe Air France.

Air Global International, **55** 30

Air-India Limited, 6 63–64; **27** 24–26 (upd.)

Air Inter *see* Groupe Air France.

Air Inuit, **56** 38–39

Air Jamaica Limited, 54 3–6

Air La Carte Inc., **13** 48

Air Lanka Catering Services Ltd. *see* Thai Airways International.

Air Liberté, **6** 208

Air Liquide *see* L'Air Liquide SA.

Air London International, **36** 190

Air Mauritius Ltd., 63 17–19

Air Methods Corporation, 53 26–29

Air Midwest, Inc. *see* Mesa Air Group, Inc.

Air New Zealand Limited, 14 10–12; **24** 399–400; **27** 475; **38** 24–27 (upd.)

Air NorTerra Inc., **56** 39

Air Pacific Ltd., 70 7–9

Air Products and Chemicals, Inc., I 297–99; **10** 31–33 (upd.); **74** 6–9 (upd.)

Air Pub S.à.r.l., **64** 359

Air Russia, **24** 400

Air Sahara Limited, 65 14–16

Air Sea Broker AG, **47** 286–87

Air Southwest Co. *see* Southwest Airlines Co.

Air Taser, Inc. *see* Taser International, Inc.

Air Transport International LLC, **58** 43

Air Wisconsin Airlines Corporation, 55 10–12

Airborne Freight Corporation, 6 345–47; **13** 19; **14** 517; **18** 177; **34** 15–18 (upd.); **46** 72

Airbus Industrie *see* G.I.E. Airbus Industrie.

AirCal, **I** 91

Airco, **25** 81–82; **26** 94

Aircraft Modular Products, **30** 73

Aircraft Turbine Center, Inc., **28** 3

Airex Corporation, **16** 337

AirFoyle Ltd., **53** 50

Airgas, Inc., 54 7–10

Airguard Industries, Inc., **17** 104, 106; **61** 66

AirLib *see* Société d'Exploitation AOM.

Airline Interiors Inc., **41** 368–69

Airlines of Britain Holdings, **34** 398; **38** 105–06

Airlink Pty Ltd *see* Qantas Airways Ltd.

Airmark Plastics Corp., **18** 497–98

Airopak Corporation *see* PVC Container Corporation.

Airpax Electronics, Inc., **13** 398

Airport Leather Concessions LLC, **58** 369

Airrest S.A., **64** 359

Airshop Ltd., **25** 246

Airstream *see* Thor Industries, Inc.

AirTouch Communications, 11 10–12 *see also* Vodafone Group PLC.

Airtours Plc, 27 27–29, 90, 92

AirTran Holdings, Inc., 22 21–23; **28** 266; **33** 302; **34** 32; **55** 10–11

AirWair Ltd., **23** 399, 401–02

AirWays Corporation *see* AirTran Holdings, Inc.

Aisin Seiki Co., Ltd., III 415–16; **14** 64; **48** 3–5 (upd.)

AIT Worldwide, **47** 286–87

Aitchison & Colegrave *see* Bradford & Bingley PLC.

Aitken, Inc., **26** 433

AITS *see* American International Travel Service.

Aiuruoca, **25** 85

Aiwa Co., Ltd., 28 360; **30** 18–20

Ajinomoto Co., Inc., II 463–64, 475; **III** 705; **28** 9–11 (upd.)

AJS Auto Parts Inc., **15** 246

AK Steel Holding Corporation, 19 8–9; **41** 3–6 (upd.)

Akamai Technologies, Inc., 71 18–21

Akane Securities Co. Ltd., **II** 443

AKAY Flavours & Aromatics Ltd., **70** 56

Akbank TAS, 79 18–21

Akemi, **17** 310; **24** 160

Aker RGI, **32** 99

AKG Acoustics GmbH, 62 3–6

AKH Co. Inc., **20** 63

Akin, Gump, Strauss, Hauer & Feld, L.L.P., 18 366; **33** 23–25; **47** 140

Akorn, Inc., 32 22–24

Akro-Mills Inc., **19** 277–78

Akron Brass Manufacturing Co., **9** 419

Akron Extruders Inc., **53** 230

Akroyd & Smithers, **14** 419

Aktia Sparbank Abp, **69** 177, 179

Aktiebolaget Electrolux, 22 24–28 (upd.) *see also* Electrolux A.B.

Aktiebolaget SKF, III 622–25; **38** 28–33 (upd.)

Aktieselskabet Dampskibsselskabet Svendborg, **57** 3, 5

Akzo Nobel N.V., 13 21–23; **41** 7–10 (upd.)

Al-Amin Co. For Securities & Investment Funds *see* Dallah Albaraka Group.

Al Copeland Enterprises, Inc., **7** 26–28; **32** 13–15

Al-Tawfeek Co. For Investment Funds Ltd. *see* Dallah Albaraka Group.

Alaadin Middle East-Ersan, **IV** 564

Alabama Bancorp., **17** 152

Alabama Farmers Cooperative, Inc., 63 20–22

Alabama Gas Corporation, **21** 207–08

Alabama National BanCorporation, 75 21–23

Alabama Power Company, **38** 445, 447–48

Alabama Shipyards Inc., **21** 39–40

Aladdin Industries, **16** 487

Aladdin Mills Inc., **19** 276; **63** 300

Alagasco, **21** 207–08

Alagroup, **45** 337

Alain Afflelou SA, 53 30–32

Alain Manoukian *see* Groupe Alain Manoukian.

Alamac Knit Fabrics, Inc., **16** 533–34; **21** 192

Alamito Company, **6** 590

Alamo Engine Company, **8** 514

Alamo Group Inc., 32 25–28

Alamo Rent A Car, Inc., 6 348–50; **24** 9–12 (upd.); **25** 93; **26** 409

Alamo Water Refiners, Inc. *see* The Marmon Group, Inc.

Alania, **24** 88

ALANTEC Corporation, **25** 162

ALARIS Medical Systems, Inc., 65 17–20

Alarm Device Manufacturing Company, **9** 413–15

Alaron Inc., **16** 357

Alascom, Inc. *see* AT&T Corporation.

Alaska Air Group, Inc., 6 65–67; **11** 50; **29** 11–14 (upd.); **48** 219

Alaska Commercial Company, **12** 363

Alaska Junk Co., **19** 380

Alaska Native Wireless LLC, **60** 264

Alaska Railroad Corporation, 60 6–9

Alaska Steel Co., **19** 381

Alatas Mammoet, **26** 279

Alba Foods, **27** 197; **43** 218

Alba-Waldensian, Inc., 30 21–23

Albany Cheese, **23** 219

Albany International Corporation, 8 12–14; **51** 11–14 (upd.)

Albany Molecular Research, Inc., 77 9–12

Albaugh Inc., **62** 19

Albemarle Corporation, 59 23–25

Alberici Corporation, 76 12–14

Albert E. Reed & Co. Ltd. *see* Reed International PLC.

The Albert Fisher Group plc, 41 11–13

Albert Heijn NV, **II** 641–42; **38** 200, 202

Albert Nipon, Inc., **8** 323

Albert Willcox & Co., **14** 278

Albert's Organics, Inc. *see* United Natural Foods, Inc.

Alberta Energy Company Ltd., 16 10–12; **43** 3–6 (upd.)

Alberta Gas Trunk Line Company, Ltd. *see* Nova Corporation of Alberta.

Alberto-Culver Company, II 641–42; **8** 15–17; **36** 23–27 (upd.); **60** 258

Albertson's, Inc., II 601–03; **7** 19–22 (upd.); **30** 24–28 (upd.); **65** 21–26 (upd.)

Albion Industries, Inc., **16** 357

Albright & Wilson Ltd., **12** 351; **16** 461; **38** 378, 380; **50** 282; **59** 25

Albuquerque Gas & Electric Company *see* Public Service Company of New Mexico.

Albuquerque Gas, Electric Light and Power Company, **6** 561–62

Alcan Aluminium Limited, IV 9–13; **31** 7–12 (upd.); **45** 337

Alcan Inc., **60** 338

Alcatel S.A., 9 9–11; **36** 28–31 (upd.)

Alchem Capital Corp., **8** 141, 143

Alchem Plastics *see* Spartech Corporation.

Alco Capital Group, Inc., **27** 288

Alco Health Services Corporation, III 9–10 *see also* AmeriSource Health Corporation.

Alco Office Products Inc., **24** 362

Alco Standard Corporation, I 412–13

ALCO Trade Show Services, **26** 102

Alcoa Inc., 56 7–11 (upd.)

Alcon Laboratories, **10** 46, 48; **30** 30–31

Alden Merrell Corporation, **23** 169

Alderwoods Group, Inc., 68 11–15 (upd.)

Aldi Group, 13 24–26

Aldila Inc., 46 12–14

Aldine Press, **10** 34

Aldiscon, **37** 232

Aldus Corporation, 10 34–36

Alenia, **7** 9, 11

Alert Centre Inc., **32** 373

Alert Management Systems Inc., **12** 380

Alessio Tubi, **IV** 228

Alestra, **19** 12

Alex & Ivy, **10** 166–68

Alex Lee Inc., 18 6–9; **44** 10–14 (upd.)

Alexander & Alexander Services Inc., 10 37–39; **13** 476

Alexander & Baldwin, Inc., 10 40–42; **29** 307; **40** 14–19 (upd.)

Alexander and Lord, **13** 482

Alexander Hamilton Life Insurance Co., **II** 420; **29** 256

Alexander Howden Group, **10** 38–39

Alexander-Schroder Lumber Company, **18** 514

Alexander Smith, Inc., **19** 275

Alexander's, Inc., 45 14–16

Alexandria Petroleum Co., **51** 113

Alexis Lichine, **III** 43

Alfa Corporation, 60 10–12

Alfa-Laval AB, III 417–21; **64** 13–18 (upd.)

Alfa Romeo, 13 27–29; **36** 32–35 (upd.)

Alfa, S.A. de C.V., 19 10–12

Alfa Trading Company, **23** 358

Alfalfa's Markets, **19** 500–02

alfi Zitzmann, **60** 364

Alfred A. Knopf, Inc., 13 428, 429; **31** 376–79

Alfred Bullows & Sons, Ltd., **21** 64

Alfred Dunhill Limited, **19** 369; **27** 487–89

Alfred Marks Bureau, Ltd. *see* Adia S.A.

Alfred McAlpine plc, **51** 138

Alfred Ritter GmbH & Co. KG, 58 3–7

Alfried Krupp von Bohlen und Halbach Foundation, **IV** 89

ALG *see* Arkla, Inc.

Alga, **24** 83

Algamar, S.A., **64** 91

Algemeen Burgerlijk Pensioenfonds, **26** 421

Algemeen Dagblad BV, **53** 273

Algemene Bank Nederland N.V., II 183–84, 185, 239, 527

Algerian Saudi Leasing Holding Co. *see* Dallah Albaraka Group.

Algo Group Inc., 24 13–15

Algoma Steel Corp., **8** 544–45

Algonquin Gas Transmission Company, **14** 124–26

ALI *see* Aeronautics Leasing, Inc.

Aliança Florestal-Sociedade para o Desenvolvimento Agro-Florestal, S.A., **60** 156

Alicia S.A. *see* Arcor S.A.I.C.

Alico, Inc., 63 23–25

Alidata SpA *see* Alitalia—Linee Aeree Italiana, S.P.A.

Aligro Inc., **II** 664

Alimenta (USA), Inc., **17** 207

Alimentation Couche-Tard Inc., 77 13–16

Alimentos Indal S.A., **66** 9

Alimondo, **17** 505

Alitalia–Linee Aeree Italiana, S.p.A., 6 68–69; **24** 311; **29** 15–17 (upd.)

Aljazeera Satellite Channel, 79 22–25

Alkor-Oerlikon Plastic GmbH, **7** 141

All American Airways *see* USAir Group, Inc.

All American Communications Inc., 20 3–7

All American Gourmet Co., **12** 178, 199

All American Sports Co., **22** 458–59

All British Escarpment Company LTD, **25** 430

All-Clad Metalcrafters Inc., **34** 493, 496–97

The All England Lawn Tennis & Croquet Club, 54 11–13

All-Glass Aquarium Co., Inc., **58** 60

All Nippon Airways Co., Ltd., I 106; **6** 70–71; **38** 34–37 (upd.)

All Seasons Vehicles, Inc. *see* ASV, Inc.

All Woods, Inc., **18** 514

Allami Biztosito, **III** 209; **15** 30

Allcom, **16** 392

Alldays plc, 49 16–19

Allders plc, 37 6–8

Alleanza Assicurazioni S.p.A., 65 27–29

Alleghany Corporation, 10 43–45; **19** 319; **22** 494; **60** 13–16 (upd.)

Allegheny Airlines *see* USAir Group, Inc.; US Airways Group, Inc.

Allegheny Beverage Corp., **7** 472–73

Allegheny Energy, Inc., 38 38–41 (upd.)

Allegheny International, Inc., **8** 545; **9** 484; **22** 3, 436

Allegheny Ludlum Corporation, 8 18–20; **9** 484; **21** 489

Allegheny Power System, Inc., V 543–45 *see also* Allegheny Energy, Inc.

Allegheny Steel and Iron Company, **9** 484

Allegheny Steel Distributors, Inc. *see* Reliance Steel & Aluminum Company.

Allegiance Life Insurance Company, **22** 268; **50** 122

Allegis, Inc. *see* United Airlines.

Allegretti & Co., **22** 26

Allen & Co., **12** 496; **13** 366; **25** 270

Allen & Ginter, **12** 108

Allen-Bradley Co., **I** 80; **III** 593; **11** 429–30; **17** 478; **22** 373; **23** 211

Allen Canning Company, 76 15–17

Allen-Edmonds Shoe Corporation, 61 20–23

Allen Foods, Inc., 60 17–19

Allen Group Inc. *see* TransPro, Inc.

Allen Organ Company, 33 26–29

Allen-Stuart Equipment Company, **49** 160

Allen Systems Group, Inc., 59 26–28

Allen Tank Ltd., **21** 499

Allen's Convenience Stores, Inc., **17** 170

Allerderm *see* Virbac Corporation.

American Cast Iron Pipe Company, 50 **17–20**

American Cellular Corporation, **63** 131–32

American Cellular Network, **7** 91; **24** 122

American Cement Co. *see* Giant Cement Holding, Inc.

American Chrome, **III** 699

American Civil Liberties Union (ACLU), **60 28–31**

American Classic Voyages Company, 22 340, **27 34–37**

American Clay Forming Company, **8** 178

American Clip Company, **7** 3

American Coin Merchandising, Inc., 28 **15–17; 74 13–16 (upd.)**

American Colloid Co., 13 32–35 *see* AMCOL International Corporation.

American Colonial Insurance Company, **44** 356

American Commercial Lines Inc., **22** 164, 166–67

American Commonwealths Power Corporation, **6** 579

American Community Grocers, **II** 670

American Computer Systems *see* American Software Inc.

American Construction Lending Services, Inc., **39** 380, 382

American Cotton Cooperative Association, **17** 207; **33** 85

American Cotton Growers Association, **57** 283

American Council on Education, **12** 141

American Courier Express, Inc., **24** 126

American Crayon Company, **12** 115

American Crystal Sugar Company, 7 377; **11 13–15; 32 29–33 (upd.)**

American Cyanamid, I 300–02; 8 24–26 **(upd.)**

American Dairy Queen Corporation, **10** 373

American Data Technology, Inc., **11** 111

American Digital Communications, Inc., **33** 329

American Diversified Foods, Inc., **14** 351

American Drew, Inc., **12** 301

American Drug Company, **13** 367

American Eagle Airlines, Inc., **28** 22

American Eagle Outfitters, Inc., 24 **26–28; 55 21–24 (upd.)**

American Ecology Corporation, 77 **36–39**

American Education Press, **10** 479

American Electric Company, **12** 193; **22** 10; **54** 371–73

American Electric Power Company, V **546–49; 6 524; 11 516; 45 17–21** **(upd.)**

American Emulsions Co., **8** 455

American Encaustic Tiling Co., **22** 170

American Energy Management Inc., **39** 261

American Envelope Co., **28** 251

American Equipment Co., **I** 571

American Express Company, II 395–99; **10 59–64 (upd.); 38 42–48 (upd.)**

American Factors, Ltd. *see* Amfac/JMB Hawaii L.L.C.

American Family Corporation, III **187–89** *see also* AFLAC Inc.

American Family Publishers, **23** 393–94

American Feldmühle Corp., **II** 51; **21** 330

American Financial Corporation, III **190–92,** 221; **8** 537; **9** 452; **18** 549

American Financial Group Inc., 48 **6–10 (upd.)**

American Fine Wire, Inc., **33** 248

American First National Supermarkets, **16** 313

American Fitness Centers, **25** 40

American Fitness Products, Inc., **47** 128

American Flange, **30** 397

American Flavor & Fragrance Company, **9** 154

American Flyer Trains, **16** 336–37

American Foods Group, 43 23–27

American Football League, **29** 346

American Foreign Insurance Association *see* AFIA.

American Freightways Corporation, **42** 141

American Fructose Corp., **14** 18–19

American Fur Company, **25** 220

American Furniture Company, Inc., 21 **32–34**

American Gaming and Electronics, Inc., **43** 461

American Gas & Electric *see* American Electric Power Company.

American General Capital Corp., **I** 614

American General Corporation, III **193–94; 10 65–67 (upd.); 11 16; 46** **20–23 (upd.); 47 15**

American General Finance Corp., 11 **16–17**

American Girl, Inc., 69 16–19 (upd)

American Golf Corporation, 45 22–24

American Gramaphone LLC, 52 18–20

American Graphics, **23** 100

American Greetings Corporation, 7 **23–25; 22 33–36 (upd.); 59 34–39** **(upd.)**

American Grinder and Manufacturing Company, **9** 26

American Hardware & Supply Company *see* TruServ Corporation.

American Hawaii Cruises, **27** 34

American Health & Life Insurance Company, **27** 47

American Healthcorp Inc., **48** 25

American Healthways, Inc., 65 40–42

American Heritage Savings, **II** 420

American Hoechst Corporation *see* Hoechst Celanese Corporation.

American Hoist & Derrick Co., **8** 544

American Home Mortgage Holdings, **Inc., 46 24–26**

American Home Patients Centers Inc., **46** 4

American Home Products, I 622–24; 10 **68–70 (upd.)** *see also* Wyeth.

American Home Publishing Co., Inc., **14** 460

American Home Shield *see* ServiceMaster Inc.

American Home Video, **9** 186

American Homestar Corporation, 18 **26–29; 41 17–20 (upd.)**

American Homeware Inc., **15** 501

American Hospital Association, **10** 159

American Hospital Supply Co., **III** 80; **11** 459, 486; **19** 103; **21** 118; **30** 496; **53** 345

American Hydron, **13** 366; **25** 55

American I.G. Chemical Corporation *see* GAF Corporation.

American Impacts Corporation, **8** 464

American Improved Cements *see* Giant Cement Holding, Inc.

American Independent Oil Co. *see* Aminoil, Inc.

American Industrial Properties *see* Developers Diversified Realty Corporation.

American Information Services, Inc., **11** 111

American Institute of Certified Public **Accountants (AICPA), 44 27–30**

American Institutional Products, Inc., **18** 246

American Instrument Co., **13** 233

American Insurance Group, Inc., **73** 351

American International Airways, Inc., **17** 318; **22** 311

American International Group, Inc., III **195–98; 15 15–19 (upd.); 47 13–19** **(upd.)**

American Isuzu Motors, Inc. *see* Isuzu Motors, Ltd.

American Italian Pasta Company, 27 **38–40; 76 18–21 (upd.)**

American Janitor Service, **25** 15

American Jet Industries, **7** 205

American Ka-Ro, **8** 476

American Kennel Club, Inc., 74 17–19

American Knitting Mills of Miami, Inc., **22** 213

American La-France, **10** 296

American Land Cruiser Company *see* Cruise America Inc.

American Lawyer Media Holdings, Inc., **32 34–37**

American Learning Corporation, **7** 168

American Light and Traction *see* MCN Corporation.

American Lightwave Systems, Inc., **10** 19

American Limousine Corp., **26** 62

American Linen Supply Company *see* Steiner Corporation.

American Locker Group Incorporated, **34 19–21**

American Lung Association, 48 11–14

American Machine and Foundry Co., **7** 211–13; **11** 397; **25** 197

American Machine and Metals, **9** 23

American Machine and Tool Co., Inc., **57** 160

American Machinery and Foundry, Inc., **57** 85

American Maize-Products Co., 14 **17–20; 23 464**

Automatic Coil Corp., **33** 359, 361
Automatic Data Processing, Inc., III
117–19; 9 48–51 (upd.); 47 35–39
(upd.)
Automatic Liquid Packaging, **50** 122
Automatic Manufacturing Corporation,
10 319
Automatic Payrolls, Inc. *see* Automatic
Data Processing, Inc.
Automatic Retailers of America, Inc., **II**
607; **13** 48
Automatic Sprinkler Corp. of America *see*
Figgie International, Inc.
Automatic Toll Systems, **19** 111
Automatic Voting Machine Corporation
see American Locker Group
Incorporated.
AutoMed Technologies, Inc., **64** 27
Automobiles Citroen, 7 35–38
Automobili Lamborghini Holding
S.p.A., 13 60–62; 34 55–58 (upd.)
Automotive Components Limited, **10**
325; **56** 158
Automotive Diagnostics, **10** 492
Automotive Group *see* Lear Seating
Corporation.
Automotive Industries Holding Inc., **16**
323
AutoNation, Inc., 41 239; **50 61–64**
Autonet, **6** 435
Autonom Computer, **47** 36
Autophon AG, **9** 32
Autoroutes du Sud de la France SA, 55
38–40
Autosite.com, **47** 34
Autotote Corporation, 20 47–49 *see also*
Scientific Games Corporation.
Autoweb.com, **47** 34
AUTOWORKS Holdings, Inc., **24** 205
AutoZone, Inc., 9 52–54; 26 348; **31**
35–38 (upd.); 36 364; **57 10–12**
AVA AG (Allgemeine
Handelsgesellschaft der Verbraucher
AG), **33 53–56**
Avado Brands, Inc., 31 39–42; 46 234
Avalon Correctional Services, Inc., 75
40–43
Avalon Publishing Group *see* Publishers
Group, Inc.
AvalonBay Communities, Inc., 58
11–13
Avantel, **27** 304
Avantium Technologies BV, 79 46–49
Avaya Inc., **41** 287, 289–90
Avco *see* Aviation Corp. of the Americas.
Avco Corp., **34** 433
Avco Financial Services Inc., 13 63–65
Avco National Bank, **II** 420
Avdel, **34** 433
Avecia Group PLC, 63 49–51
Avecor Cardiovascular Inc., **8** 347; **22** 360
Aveda Corporation, 24 55–57
Avedis Zildjian Co., 38 66–68
Avendt Group, Inc., **IV** 137
Avenor Inc., **25** 13
Aventis Pharmaceuticals, **34** 280, 283–84;
38 378, 380; **63** 232, 235
Avery Communications, Inc., **72** 39

Avery Dennison Corporation, IV
251–54; 17 27–31 (upd.); 49 34–40
(upd.)
AvestaPolarit, **49** 104
Avex Electronics Inc., **40** 68
Avfuel, **11** 538
Avgain Marine A/S, **7** 40; **41** 42
Avia Group International, Inc. *see* Reebok
International Ltd.
Aviacionny Nauchno-Tehnicheskii
Komplex im. A.N. Tupoleva, 24
58–60
AVIACO *see* Aviacion y Comercio.
Aviall, Inc., 73 42–45
Avianca Aerovías Nacionales de
Colombia SA, 36 52–55
Aviation Corp. of the Americas, **9**
497–99; **11** 261, 427; **12** 379, 383; **13**
64
Aviation Inventory Management Co., **28**
5
Aviation Power Supply, **II** 16
Aviation Sales Company, 41 37–39
Aviation Services West, Inc. *see* Scenic
Airlines, Inc.
Avid Technology Inc., 38 69–73
Avimo, **47** 7–8
Avion Coach Corporation, **11** 363
Avionics Specialties Inc. *see* Aerosonic
Corporation.
Avions Marcel Dassault-Breguet
Aviation, I 44–46 *see also* Groupe
Dassault Aviation SA.
Avis Group Holdings, Inc., 6 356–58;
22 54–57 (upd.); 75 44–49 (upd.)
Avista Corporation, 69 48–50 (upd.)
Avisun Corp., **IV** 371
Aviva PLC, 50 65–68 (upd.)
Avnet Inc., **9 55–57**
Avocent Corporation, 65 56–58
Avon Products, Inc., III 15–16; 19
26–29 (upd.); 46 43–46 (upd.)
Avon Rubber plc, **23** 146
Avondale Industries, Inc., 7 39–41; 41
40–43 (upd.)
Avondale Mills, Inc., **8** 558–60; **9** 466
Avonmore Foods Plc, **59** 205
Avril Alimentaire SNC, **51** 54
Avro *see* A.V. Roe & Company.
Avstar, **38** 72
Avtech Corp., **36** 159
AVTOVAZ Joint Stock Company, 65
59–62
AVX Corporation, 21 329, 331; **67**
21–22; 41–43
AW Bruna Uitgevers BV, **53** 273
AW North Carolina Inc., **48** 5
AWA *see* America West Holdings
Corporation.
AWA Defence Industries (AWADI) *see*
British Aerospace Defence Industries.
AwardTrack, Inc., **49** 423
AWB Ltd., **56 25–27**
Awesome Transportation, Inc., **22** 549
Awrey Bakeries, Inc., 56 28–30
AXA Colonia Konzern AG, III 210–12;
49 41–45 (upd.)
AXA Financial, Inc., **63** 26–27

AXA Private Equity *see* Camaïeu S.A.
AXA UK plc, **64** 173
Axe-Houghton Associates Inc., **41** 208
Axel Johnson Group, I 553–55
Axel Springer Verlag AG, IV 589–91; 20
50–53 (upd.)
Axon Systems Inc., **7** 336
Ayala Corporation, **70** 182
Ayala Plans, Inc., **58** 20
Aydin Corp., 19 30–32
Aynsley China Ltd. *see* Belleek Pottery
Ltd.
Ayr-Way Stores, **27** 452
Ayres, Lewis, Norris & May, Inc., **54** 184
AYS *see* Alternative Youth Services, Inc.
AZA Immobilien AG, **51** 196
Azcon Corporation, 23 34–36
Azerbaijan Airlines, 77 46–49
Azerty, **25** 13
Azienda Generale Italiana Petroli *see* ENI
S.p.A.
AZL Resources, **7** 538
Azlan Group Limited, **74** 338
Aznar International, **14** 225
Azon Limited, **22** 282
AZP Group Inc., **6** 546
Aztar Corporation, 13 66–68; 71 41–45
(upd.)
Azteca, **18** 211, 213

B

B&D *see* Barker & Dobson.
B&G Foods, Inc., 40 51–54
B&J Music Ltd. *see* Kaman Music
Corporation.
B & K Steel Fabrications, Inc., **26** 432
B & L Insurance, Ltd., **51** 38
B&M Baked Beans, **40** 53
B & O *see* Baltimore and Ohio Railroad.
B&Q plc *see* Kingfisher plc.
B&S *see* Binney & Smith Inc.
B.A.T. Industries PLC, 22 70–73 (upd.)
see also Brown & Williamson Tobacco
Corporation
B. B. & R. Knight Brothers, **8** 200; **25**
164
B.B. Foods, **13** 244
B-Bar-B Corp., **16** 340
B.C. Rail Telecommunications, **6** 311
B.C. Sugar, **II** 664
B.C. Ziegler and Co. *see* The Ziegler
Companies, Inc.
B. Dalton Bookseller Inc., 25 29–31
B-E Holdings, **17** 60
B/E Aerospace, Inc., 30 72–74
B.F. Goodrich Co. *see* The BFGoodrich
Company.
B.F. Walker, Inc., **11** 354
B.I.C. America, **17** 15, 17
B.J.'s Wholesale, **12** 335
B.J. Alan Co., Inc., 67 44–46
The B. Manischewitz Company, LLC,
31 43–46
B. Perini & Sons, Inc., **8** 418
B Ticino, **21** 350
B.V. Tabak Export & Import Compagnie,
12 109
BA *see* British Airways.

Banco Comercial, **19** 188

Banco Comercial de Puerto Rico, **41** 311

Banco Comercial Português, SA, 50 69–72

Banco Credito y Ahorro Ponceno, **41** 312

Banco da América, **19** 34

Banco de Chile, 69 55–57

Banco de Comercio, S.A. *see* Grupo Financiero BBVA Bancomer S.A.

Banco de Credito Local, **48** 51

Banco de Credito y Servicio, **51** 151

Banco de Galicia y Buenos Aires, S.A., **63** 178–80

Banco de Londres, Mexico y Sudamerica *see* Grupo Financiero Serfin, S.A.

Banco de Madrid, **40** 147

Banco de Mexico, **19** 189

Banco de Ponce, **41** 313

Banco del Centro S.A., **51** 150

Banco del Norte, **19** 189

Banco di Roma, **II**, 257, 271

Banco di Santo Spirito, **I** 467

Banco di Sicilia S.p.A., **65** 86, 88

Banco do Brasil S.A., II 199–200

Banco Español de Credito, **II** 198

Banco Espírito Santo e Comercial de Lisboa S.A., 15 38–40 *see also* Espírito Santo Financial Group S.A.

Banco Federal de Crédito *see* Banco Itaú.

Banco Frances y Brasiliero, **19** 34

Banco Industrial de Monterrey, **19** 189

Banco Itaú S.A., 19 33–35

Banco Mercantil del Norte, S.A., **51** 149

Banco Nacional de Mexico, **9** 333; **19** 188, 193

Banco Opportunity, **57** 67, 69

Banco Pinto de Mahalhães, **19** 34

Banco Popolar *see* Popular, Inc.

Banco Português do Brasil S.A., **19** 34

Banco Santander Central Hispano S.A., 36 61–64 **(upd.); 42** 349; **63** 179

Banco Santander-Chile, **71** 143

Banco Serfin, **34** 82

Banco Sul Americano S.A., **19** 34

Banco União Comercial, **19** 34

BancOhio National Bank in Columbus, **9** 475

Bancomer S.A. *see* Grupo Financiero BBVA Bancomer S.A.

Bancorp Leasing, Inc., **14** 529

BancorpSouth, Inc., **14** 40–41

Bancrecer *see* Banco de Credito y Servicio.

BancSystems Association Inc., **9** 475, 476

Bandag, Inc., 19 36–38, 454–56

Bandai Co., Ltd., 55 44–48

Bando McGlocklin Small Business Lending Corporation, **53** 222–24

Banesto *see* Banco Español de Credito.

Banfi Products Corp., 36 65–67

Banfield, The Pet Hospital *see* Medical Management International, Inc.

Bang & Olufsen Holding A/S, 37 25–28

Bangkok Airport Hotel *see* Thai Airways International.

Bangkok Aviation Fuel Services Ltd. *see* Thai Airways International.

Bangladesh Krishi Bank, **31** 220

Bangor and Aroostook Railroad Company, **8** 33

Bangor Mills, **13** 169

Bangor Punta Alegre Sugar Corp., **30** 425

Banister Continental Corp. *see* BFC Construction Corporation.

Bank Austria AG, 23 37–39; 59 239

Bank Brussels Lambert, II 201–03, 295, 407

Bank Central Asia, **18** 181; **62** 96, 98

Bank du Louvre, **27** 423

Bank für Elektrische Unternehmungen *see* Elektrowatt AG.

Bank Hapoalim B.M., II 204–06; 54 33–37 **(upd.)**

Bank Hofmann, **21** 146–47

Bank Leumi le-Israel B.M., 60 48–51

Bank of America Corporation, 46 47–54 **(upd.)**

The Bank of Bishop and Co., Ltd., **11** 114

Bank of Boston Corporation, II 207–09 *see also* FleetBoston Financial Corporation.

Bank of Britain, **14** 46–47

Bank of China, 63 55–57

Bank of Delaware, **25** 542

Bank of East Asia Ltd., 63 58–60

Bank of England, **10** 8, 336; **14** 45–46; **47** 227

Bank of Hawaii Corporation, 73 53–56

Bank of Ireland, 50 73–76

Bank of Italy, **III** 209, 347; **8** 45

The Bank of Jacksonville, **9** 58

Bank of Lee County, **14** 40

Bank of Mexico Ltd., **19** 188

The Bank of Milwaukee, **14** 529

Bank of Mississippi, Inc., 14 40–41

Bank of Montreal, II 210–12, 231, 375; **26** 304; **46** 55–58 **(upd.)**

Bank of Nettleton, **14** 40

Bank of New England Corporation, II 213–15; 9 229

Bank of New Orleans, **11** 106

Bank of New South Wales *see* Westpac Banking Corporation.

Bank of New York Company, Inc., II 216–19, 247; **34** 82; **46** 59–63 **(upd.)**

Bank of North Mississippi, **14** 41

The Bank of Nova Scotia, II 220–23, 345; **59** 70–76 **(upd.)**

Bank of Oklahoma, **22** 4

The Bank of Scotland *see* The Governor and Company of the Bank of Scotland.

Bank of Sherman, **14** 40

Bank of the Ohio Valley, **13** 221

Bank of the Philippine Islands, 58 18–20

Bank of Tokyo-Mitsubishi Ltd., II 224–25; 15 41–43 **(upd.)**

Bank of Tupelo, **14** 40

Bank of Wales, **10** 336, 338

Bank One Corporation, 36 68–75 (upd.)

Bank-R Systems Inc., **18** 517

BankAmerica Corporation, II 226–28 *see also* Bank of America.

BankAtlantic Bancorp., Inc., **66** 273

BankBoston *see* FleetBoston Financial Corporation.

BankCard America, Inc., **24** 394

Bankers and Shippers Insurance Co., III 389

Bankers Corporation, **14** 473

Bankers Life and Casualty Co., **10** 247; **16** 207; **33** 110

Bankers Life Association *see* Principal Mutual Life Insurance Company.

Bankers National Life Insurance Co., **10** 246

Bankers Trust Co., **38** 411

Bankers Trust New York Corporation, II 229–31

Bankhaus August Lenz AG, **65** 230, 232

Banknorth Group, Inc., 55 49–53

Bankruptcy Services LLC, **56** 112

Banksia Wines Ltd., **54** 227, 229

BankWatch, **37** 143, 145

Banner Aerospace, Inc., 14 42–44; 37 29–32 **(upd.)**

Banner International, **13** 20

Banner Life Insurance Company, **III** 273; **24** 284

Banorte *see* Grupo Financiero Banorte, S.A. de C.V.

Banpais *see* Grupo Financiero Asemex-Banpais S.A.

BanPonce Corporation, **41** 312

Banque Bruxelles Lambert *see* Bank Brussels Lambert.

Banque de Bruxelles *see* Bank Brussels Lambert.

Banque de France, **14** 45–46

Banque de la Société Générale de Belgique *see* Generale Bank.

Banque de Paris et des Pays-Bas, **10** 346; **19** 188–89; **33** 179

Banque Indosuez, **II** 429; **52** 361–62

Banque Internationale de Luxembourg, **42** 111

Banque Lambert *see* Bank Brussels Lambert.

Banque Nationale de Paris S.A., II 232–34, 239; **III** 201, 392–94; **9** 148; **13** 203; **15** 309; **19** 51; **33** 119; **49** 382 *see also* BNP Paribas Group.

Banque Paribas *see* BNP Paribas Group.

Banque Sanpaolo of France, **50** 410

La Banque Suisse et Française *see* Crédit Commercial de France.

Banque Worms, **27** 514

Banta Corporation, 12 24–26; 32 73–77 (upd.); 79 50–56 (upd.)

Bantam Ball Bearing Company, **13** 522

Bantam Doubleday Dell Publishing Group, **IV** 594; **13** 429; **15** 51; **27** 222; **31** 375–76, 378

Banyan Systems Inc., 25 50–52

Banyu Pharmaceutical Co., **11** 290; **34** 283

Baoshan Iron and Steel, **19** 220

Baosteel Group International Trade Corporation *see* Baosteel Group International Trade Corporation.

BAP of New York, Inc., **15** 246

Bar-S Foods Company, 76 39–41

Bishop & Co. Savings Bank, **11** 114
Bishop National Bank of Hawaii, **11** 114
BISSELL, Inc., 9 70–72; **30** 75–78 **(upd.)**
Bisset Gold Mining Company, **63** 182–83
The BISYS Group, Inc., 73 63–65
Bit LLC, **59** 303
Bit Software, Inc., **12** 62
Bitco Corporation, **58** 258
Bits & Pieces, **26** 439
Bitumen & Oil Refineries (Australia) Ltd. *see* Boral Limited.
Bituminous Casualty Corporation, **58** 258–59
Bivac International, **55** 79
BIW *see* Bath Iron Works.
BIZ Enterprises, **23** 390
Bizarro e Milho, Lda., **64** 91
BizBuyer.com, **39** 25
Bizimgaz Ticaret Ve Sanayi A.S., **55** 346
Bizmark, **13** 176
BizMart, **6** 244–45; **8** 404–05
BJ Services Company, 15 534, 536; **25** 73–75
BJ's Pizza & Grill, **44** 85
BJ's Restaurant & Brewhouse, **44** 85
BJ's Wholesale Club, **12** 221; **13** 547–49; **33** 198
BJK&E *see* Bozell Worldwide Inc.
BK Tag, **28** 157
BK Vision AG, **52** 357
BL Systems *see* AT&T Istel Ltd.
BL Universal PLC, **47** 168
The Black & Decker Corporation, III 435–37; **20** 64–68 **(upd.); 67** 65–70 **(upd.)**
Black & Veatch LLP, 22 87–90
Black Box Corporation, 20 69–71
Black Clawson Company, **24** 478
Black Diamond Equipment, Ltd., 62 34–37
Black Entertainment Television *see* BET Holdings, Inc.
Black Hawk Broadcasting Group, **10** 29; **38** 17
Black Hills Corporation, 20 72–74
Black Pearl Software, Inc., **39** 396
BlackBerry *see* Research in Motion Ltd.
Blackfoot Telecommunications Group, 60 59–62
Blackhawk Holdings, Inc. *see* PW Eagle Inc.
Blackhorse Agencies, **II** 309; **47** 227
BlackRock, Inc., 79 66–69
Blacks Leisure Group plc, 39 58–60
Blackstone Dredging Partners LP, **69** 197
The Blackstone Group, L.P., **II** 434, 444; **IV** 718; **11** 177, 179; **13** 170; **17** 238, 443; **22** 404, 416; **26** 408; **37** 309, 311; **61** 208; **69** 101, 103; **75** 378
Blackstone Hotel Acquisition Co., **24** 195
Blackwater USA, 76 70–73, 193
Blackwell Publishing (Holdings) Ltd., 78 34–37
Blaine Construction Company *see* The Yates Companies, Inc.
Blair Corporation, 25 76–78; **31** 53–55

Blakeman's Floor Care Parts & Equipment *see* Tacony Corporation.
Blandburgh Ltd., **63** 77
Blanes, S.A. de C.V., **34** 197
BLC Insurance Co., **III** 330
BLD Europe, **16** 168
Blendax, **III** 53; **8** 434; **26** 384
Blessings Corp., 14 550; **19** 59–61
Blimpie International, Inc., 15 55–57; **49** 60–64 **(upd.)**
Bliss Manufacturing Co., **17** 234–35
Blitz-Weinhart Brewing, **18** 71–72; **50** 112, 114
Blizzard Entertainment, 78 38–42
Bloch & Guggenheimer, Inc., **40** 51–52
Block Drug Company, Inc., 8 62–64; **27** 67–70 **(upd.)**
Block Financial Corporation, **17** 265; **29** 227
Block Management, **29** 226
Block Medical, Inc., **10** 351
Blockbuster Inc., 9 73–75; **31** 56–60 **(upd.); 76** 74–78 **(upd.)**
Blockson Chemical, **I** 380; **13** 379
Blodgett Holdings, Inc., 61 34–37 **(upd.)**
Blohm Maschinenbau GmbH, **60** 193
Blonder Tongue Laboratories, Inc., 48 52–55
Bloomberg L.P., 18 24; **21** 67–71; **63** 326
Bloomingdale's Inc., 12 36–38
Blount International, Inc., 12 39–41; **24** 78; **26** 117, 119, 363; **48** 56–60 **(upd.)**
Blow-ko Ltd., **60** 372
BLP Group Companies *see* Boron, LePore & Associates, Inc.
BLT Ventures, **25** 270
Blue, **62** 115
Blue Arrow PLC, **9** 327; **30** 300
Blue Bell Creameries L.P., 30 79–81
Blue Bell, Inc., **V** 390–91; **12** 205; **17** 512
Blue Bell Mattress Company, **58** 63
Blue Bird Corporation, 35 63–66
Blue Bunny Ice Cream *see* Wells' Dairy, Inc.
Blue Byte, **41** 409
Blue Chip Stamps, **30** 412
Blue Circle Industries PLC, III 669–71, 702 *see also* Lafarge Cement UK.
Blue Cross and Blue Shield Association, 10 159–61; **14** 84
Blue Cross and Blue Shield Mutual of Northern Ohio, **12** 176
Blue Cross and Blue Shield of Colorado, **11** 175
Blue Cross and Blue Shield of Greater New York, **III** 245–46
Blue Cross and Blue Shield of Minnesota, **65** 41–42
Blue Cross and Blue Shield of Ohio, **15** 114
Blue Cross Blue Shield of Michigan, **12** 22
Blue Cross of California, **25** 525

Blue Cross of Northeastern New York, **III** 245–46
Blue Diamond Growers, 28 56–58
Blue Dot Services, **37** 280, 283
Blue Line Distributing, **7** 278–79
Blue Martini Software, Inc., 59 77–80
Blue Mountain Arts, Inc., 29 63–66
Blue Mountain Springs Ltd., **48** 97
Blue Nile Inc., 61 38–40
Blue Rhino Corporation, 56 34–37
Blue Ribbon Packing Company, **57** 57
Blue Ribbon Sports *see* Nike, Inc.
Blue Ridge Lumber Ltd., **16** 11
Blue Shield of California, **25** 527
Blue Square Israel Ltd., 41 56–58
Blue Tee Corporation, **23** 34, 36
Blue Water Food Service, **13** 244
Bluebird Inc., **10** 443
Bluefly, Inc., 60 63–65
Bluegreen Corporation, 80 29–32
BlueScope Steel Limited, **62** 55
Bluewin AG, **58** 337
Blumberg Communications Inc., **24** 96
Blundstone Pty Ltd., 76 79–81
Blyth, Inc., 18 67–69; **74** 35–38 **(upd.)**
Blyth Industries, Inc., 18 67–69
BM-Telecom, **59** 303
BMB Specialty Co., **74** 202
BMC Forestry Corporation, **58** 23
BMC Industries, Inc., 17 48–51; **59** 81–86 **(upd.)**
BMC Real Estate, Inc., **62** 55
BMC Software, Inc., 14 391; **55** 64–67; **58** 295
bmd wireless AG, **63** 204
BMG/Music *see* Bertelsmann AG.
BMHC *see* Building Materials Holding Corporation.
BMI *see* Broadcast Music Inc.
BMI Systems Inc., **12** 174
BMML, Confecçoes, Lda., **64** 91
BMO Corp., **III** 209
BMO Nesbitt Burns, **46** 55
BMS Laboratories Ltd., **59** 168
BMW *see* Bayerische Motoren Werke.
BNA *see* Banca Nazionale dell'Agricoltura; Bureau of National Affairs, Inc.
BNCI *see* Banque Nationale Pour le Commerce et l'Industrie.
BNE *see* Bank of New England Corp.
BNE Land & Development, **68** 54, 56
BNG, Inc., **19** 487
BNL *see* Banca Nazionale del Lavoro S.p.A.
BNP Paribas Group, 36 94–97 **(upd.); 42** 349
BNS Acquisitions, **26** 247
Boa Shoe Company, **42** 325
Oy Board International AB, **56** 255
Boart Longyear Company, 26 39–42, 69
Boatmen's Bancshares Inc., 15 58–60
BoatsDirect.com, **37** 398
Bob Evans Farms, Inc., 9 76–79; **63** 67–72 **(upd.)**
Bob's Red Mill Natural Foods, Inc., 63 73–75
Bobbie Brooks Inc., **17** 384
Bobbs-Merrill, **11** 198

Bobit Publishing Company, **55** 68–70

Bobro Products *see* BWP Distributors.

Bobs Candies, Inc., 70 23–25

BOC Group plc, I 314–16; **25** 79–82 (upd.); **78** 43–49 (upd.)

Boca Resorts, Inc., 37 33–36

BOCAP Corp., **37** 372

Bock Bearing Co., **8** 530

BOCM Fish Feed Group, **56** 257

BOCOM International, **71** 366, 368

Boddie-Noell Enterprises, Inc., 68 54–56

Boddington, **21** 247

Bodegas y Vinedos Penaflor S.A. *see* Penaflor S.A.

Bodeker Drug Company, **16** 399

Bodum Design Group AG, 47 57–59

The Body Shop International plc, 11 40–42; **53** 69–72 (upd.)

Bodycote International PLC, 63 76–78

Boehringer Gastro Profi, **60** 364

Boehringer Ingelheim GmbH *see* C.H. Boehringer Sohn.

Boehringer Mannheim Companies, **37** 111–12

The Boeing Company, I 47–49; **10** 162–65 (upd.); **32** 81–87 (upd.); **36** 122, 190; **38** 372; **48** 218–20; **50** 367

Bofors Nobel Inc., **9** 380–81; **13** 22

Bogen Communications International, Inc., 62 38–41

Bohemia, Inc., 13 99–101

BÖHLER-UDDEHOLM AG, 73 66–69

Bohm-Allen Jewelry, **12** 112

Bohn Aluminum & Brass, **10** 439

Boiron S.A., 73 70–72

Boise Cascade Corporation, IV 255–56; **8** 65–67 (upd.); **32** 88–92 (upd.)

Bokma Distillateurs BV, **74** 41

Bolands Ltd., **II** 649

Bolar Pharmaceutical Co., **16** 529

Boley G.m.b.H., **21** 123

Boliden AB, 80 33–36

Bolles & Houghton, **10** 355

Bollinger Shipyards, Inc., 61 41–43

Bollore, S.A., **65** 266–67

Bols Distilleries NV, 74 39–42

Bolsa Mexicana de Valores, S.A. de C.V., 80 37–40

BolsWessanen N.V. *see* Koninklijke Wessanen nv.

Bolt, Beranek & Newman Inc., **26** 520

Bolt Security, **32** 373

Bolthouse Farms, Inc., **54** 257

BOMAG, **8** 544, 546

Bombadier Defence Services UK, **41** 412

Bombardier Aerospace Group, **36** 190–91

Bombardier, Inc., 42 41–46 (upd.)

The Bombay Company, Inc., 10 166–68; **71** 60–64 (upd.)

Bon Appetit Holding AG, II 656; **48** 61–63

Bon Dente International Inc., **39** 320

The Bon Marché, Inc., 23 58–60

Bon Secours Health System, Inc., 24 68–71

The Bon-Ton Stores, Inc., 16 60–62; **50** 106–10 (upd.)

Bonanza, **7** 336; **10** 331; **15** 361–63

Bonanza Steakhouse, **17** 320

Bonaventura, **IV** 611

Bond Brewing International, **23** 405

Bond Corporation Holdings Limited, 10 169–71

Bondex International, **8** 456

Bonduel Pickling Co. Inc., **25** 517

Bonduelle SA, 51 52–54

Bongard *see* Aga Foodservice Group PLC.

Bongrain SA, 19 50; **23** 217, 219; **25** 83–85

Bonhams 1793 Ltd., 72 40–42

Boni & Liveright, **13** 428

Bonifiche Siele, **II** 272

Bonimart, **II** 649

Bonneville International Corporation, 29 67–70; **30** 15

Bonneville Power Administration, 50 102–05

Bonnie Plant Farm, **63** 21

Bonnier AB, 52 49–52

Bontrager Bicycles, **16** 495

Bonwit Teller, **13** 43; **17** 43; **54** 304–05

Book-Mart Press, Inc., **41** 111

Book-of-the-Month Club, Inc., 13 105–07

Booker plc, 13 102–04; **31** 61–64 (upd.)

Booker Cash & Carry Ltd., 68 57–61 (upd.)

Booker Tate, **13** 102

Booklink Technologies, **26** 19

Bookmasters, **10** 136

Books-A-Million, Inc., 14 61–62; **41** 59–62 (upd.)

Books Are Fun, Ltd. *see* The Reader's Digest Association, Inc.

Bookstop, **10** 136

Boole & Babbage, Inc., 25 86–88

Booth Bay, Ltd., **16** 37

Booth Creek Ski Holdings, Inc., 31 65–67

Booth, Inc., **II** 420

Bootprint Entertainment, **31** 240

The Boots Company PLC, V 17–19; **24** 72–76 (upd.)

Boots & Coots International Well Control, Inc., 79 70–73

Booz Allen & Hamilton Inc., 10 172–75

Boplan Ingénierie S.A.S. *see* SNC-Lavalin Group Inc.

Boral Limited, III 672–74; **43** 72–76 (upd.)

Borden Cabinet Corporation, **12** 296

Borden, Inc., II 470–73; **22** 91–96 (upd.)

Border Fine Arts, **11** 95

Border Television, **41** 352

Borders Group, Inc., 15 61–62; **43** 77–79 (upd.)

Borders, Perrin and Norrander, **23** 480

Borealis A/S, **30** 205; **45** 8; **61** 346

Borealis Industrier, A.B., **71** 193

Borg Instruments, **23** 494

Borg-Warner Australia, **47** 280

Borg-Warner Automotive, Inc., 14 63–66; **32** 93–97 (upd.)

Borg-Warner Corporation, III 438–41 *see also* Burns International.

Borland International, Inc., 9 80–82

Borman's, Inc., **II** 638; **16** 249

Borneo Airways *see* Malaysian Airlines System BHD.

Boron, LePore & Associates, Inc., 45 43–45

Borregaard Osterreich AG, **18** 395

Borror Corporation *see* Dominion Homes, Inc.

Borsheim's, **III** 215; **18** 60

Borun Bros., **12** 477

Bosch *see* Robert Bosch GmbH.

Boscov's Department Store, Inc., 31 68–70

Bose Corporation, 13 108–10; **36** 98–101 (upd.)

Bosendorfer, L., Klavierfabrik, A.G., **12** 297

Bosert Industrial Supply *see* W.W. Grainger, Inc.

Bossa, **55** 188

Bost Sports Clubs *see* Town Sports International, Inc.

Boston Acoustics, Inc., 22 97–99

Boston and Maine Corporation, **16** 350

The Boston Beer Company, Inc., 18 70–73; **50** 111–15 (upd.)

Boston Celtics Limited Partnership, 14 67–69

Boston Chicken, Inc., 12 42–44; **23** 266; **29** 170, 172 *see also* Boston Market Corporation.

The Boston Consulting Group, 9 343; **18** 70; **22** 193; **58** 32–35

Boston Corp., **25** 66

Boston Distributors, **9** 453

Boston Edison Company, 12 45–47

Boston Educational Research, **27** 373

Boston Garden Arena Corporation, **14** 67

Boston Gas Company *see* Eastern Enterprises.

Boston Globe, **7** 13–16

Boston Herald, **7** 15

Boston Market Corporation, 48 64–67 (upd.); **63** 280, 284–85

Boston National Bank, **13** 465

Boston Popcorn Co., **27** 197–98; **43** 218

Boston Professional Hockey Association Inc., 39 61–63

Boston Properties, Inc., 22 100–02

Boston Scientific Corporation, 37 37–40; **77** 58–63 (upd.)

Boston Technology, **43** 117

Boston Ventures Management, Inc., **17** 444; **27** 41, 393; **54** 334, 337; **65** 374

Boston Whaler, Inc. *see* Reebok International Ltd.

Bostrom Seating, **23** 306

BOTAS *see* Türkiye Petrolleri Anonim Ortakli;akgi.

Boticas Fasa S.A., **72** 128

Botswana General Insurance Company, **22** 495

Bott SA, **72** 221

Burberry Ltd., **17** 66–68; **41** 74–76
   (upd.)
Burda Holding GmbH. & Co., 20 53;
   23 85–89
Burdines, Inc., 9 209; **31** 192; **60** 70–73
Bureau de Recherches de Pétrole, **7**
   481–83; **21** 203–04
The Bureau of National Affairs, Inc., 23
   90–93
Bureau Veritas SA, 55 77–79
Burelle S.A., 23 94–96
Burger and Aschenbrenner, **16** 486
Burger Boy Food-A-Rama, **8** 564
Burger King Corporation, II 613–15;
   17 69–72 (upd.); **56** 44–48 (upd.)
Burgess, Anderson & Tate Inc., **25** 500
Burgundy Ltd., **68** 53
Bürhle, **17** 36; **50** 78
Burhmann-Tetterode, **22** 154
Buriot International, Inc., **53** 236
Burke Mills, Inc., 66 41–43
Burke Scaffolding Co., **9** 512
BURLE Industries Inc., **11** 444
Burlington Coat Factory Warehouse
   Corporation, 10 188–89; **60** 74–76
   (upd.)
Burlington Homes of New England, **14**
   138
Burlington Industries, Inc., V 354–55;
   17 73–76 (upd.)
Burlington Mills Corporation, **12** 117–18
Burlington Motor Holdings, **30** 114
Burlington Northern Santa Fe
   Corporation, V 425–28; **10** 190–91;
   11 315; **12** 145, 278; **27** 82–89
   (upd.); **28** 495
Burlington Resources Inc., 10 190–92;
   11 135; **12** 144; **47** 238
Burmah Castrol PLC, IV 381–84; **15**
   246; **30** 86–91 (upd.)
Burnards, **II** 677
Burndy, **19** 166
Burney Mountain Power, **64** 95
Burns & Ricker, Inc., **40** 51, 53
Burns & Wilcox Ltd., **6** 290
Burns-Alton Corp., **21** 154–55
Burns Companies, **III** 569; **20** 360
Burns International Security Services,
   III 440; **13** 123–25; **42** 338 *see also*
   Securitas AB.
Burns International Services
   Corporation, 41 77–80 (upd.)
Burns Lumber Company, Inc., **61** 254,
   256
Burns, Philp & Company Ltd., 63
   83–86
Burnup & Sims, Inc., **19** 254; **26** 324
Burpee & Co. *see* W. Atlee Burpee & Co.
Burr-Brown Corporation, 19 66–68
Burris Industries, **14** 303; **50** 311
Burroughs Corp. *see* Unisys Corporation.
Burroughs Mfg. Co., **16** 321
Burrups Ltd., **18** 331, 333; **47** 243
Burry, **II** 560; **12** 410
Burt's Bees, Inc., 58 47–50
The Burton Group plc, V 20–22 *see also*
   Arcadia Group plc.
Burton Rubber Processing, **8** 347

Burton Snowboards Inc., 22 118–20,
   460
Burtons Gold Medal Biscuits Limited, **II**
   466; **13** 53
Burwell Brick, **14** 248
Busch Entertainment Corporation, 73
   73–75
Bush Boake Allen Inc., 30 92–94; **38**
   247
Bush Brothers & Company, 45 71–73
Bush Hog, **21** 20–22
Bush Industries, Inc., 20 98–100
Bush Terminal Company, **15** 138
Business Communications Group, Inc. *see*
   Caribiner International, Inc.
The Business Depot, Ltd., **10** 498; **55**
   353
Business Expansion Capital Corp., **12** 42
Business Express Airlines, Inc., **28** 22
Business Information Technology, Inc., **18**
   112
Business Men's Assurance Company of
   America, III 209; **13** 476; **14** 83–85;
   15 30
Business Objects S.A., 25 95–97
Business Post Group plc, 46 71–73
Business Resources Corp., **23** 489, 491
Business Science Computing, **14** 36
Business Software Association, **10** 35
Business Software Technology, **10** 394
Business Wire, **25** 240
Businessland Inc., **III** 153; **6** 267; **10** 235;
   13 175–76, 277, 482
Busse Broadcasting Corporation, **7** 200;
   24 199
Buster Brown & Company *see* Brown
   Shoe Company, Inc.
BUT S.A., **24** 266, 270
Butler Bros., **21** 96
Butler Cox PLC, **6** 229
Butler Group, Inc., **30** 310–11
Butler Manufacturing Company, 12
   51–53; **43** 130; **62** 52–56 (upd.)
Butler Shoes, **16** 560
Butterfield & Butterfield *see* eBay Inc.
Butterfield & Swire *see* Swire Pacific Ltd.
Butterick Co., Inc., 23 97–99
Buttrey Food & Drug Stores Co., 18
   89–91
Butzbacher Weichenbau GmbH & Co.
   KG, **53** 352
Buxton, **23** 21
buy.com, Inc., 46 74–77
Buzzard Electrical & Plumbing Supply, **9**
   399; **16** 186
BVA Investment Corp., **11** 446–47
BWAY Corporation, 24 91–93
BWP Distributors, **29** 86, 88
Byerly's, Inc. *see* Lund Food Holdings,
   Inc.
Byron Weston Company, **26** 105

C

C&A, 40 74–77 (upd.)
C&A Brenninkmeyer KG, V 23–24
C&D *see* Church & Dwight Co., Inc.
C&E Software, **10** 507
C&G *see* Cheltenham & Gloucester PLC.

C & G Systems, **19** 442
C & H Distributors, Inc., **27** 177
C&J Clark International Ltd., 52 56–59
C&K Aluminio S.A., **74** 11
C & O *see* Chesapeake and Ohio Railway.
C&R Clothiers, **17** 313
C&S Bank, **10** 425–26
C&S Co., Ltd., **49** 425, 427
C&S/Sovran Corporation, **10** 425–27; **18**
   518; **26** 453; **46** 52
C & S Wholesale Grocers, Inc., 55
   80–83
C&W *see* Cable and Wireless plc.
C-COR.net Corp., 38 118–21
C-Cube Microsystems, Inc., 37 50–54;
   43 221–22
C-Mold *see* Moldflow Corporation.
C.A. Delaney Capital Management Ltd.,
   32 437
C.A. La Electricidad de Caracas, **53** 18
C.A. Muer Corporation, **65** 205
C.A.S. Sports Agency Inc., **22** 460, 462
C.A. Swanson & Sons *see* Vlasic Foods
   International Inc.
C Corp. Inc. *see* Alimentation
   Couche-Tard Inc.
C.D. Haupt, **IV** 296; **19** 226
C.E. Chappell & Sons, Inc., **16** 61–62;
   50 107
C.E.T. *see* Club Européen du Tourisme.
C.F. Burns and Son, Inc., **21** 154
C.F. Hathaway Company, **12** 522
C.F. Martin & Co., Inc., 42 55–58; **48**
   231
C.F. Mueller Co., **12** 332; **47** 234
C.F. Orvis Company *see* The Orvis
   Company, Inc.
C.G. Conn, **7** 286
C. Hoare & Co., 77 76–79
C.H. Boehringer Sohn, 39 70–73
C.H. Heist Corporation, 24 111–13
C.H. Masland & Sons *see* Masland
   Corporation.
C.H. Musselman Co., **7** 429
C.H. Robinson, Inc., 8 379–80; **11**
   43–44; **23** 357
C.H. Robinson Worldwide, Inc., 40
   78–81 (upd.)
C.I. Traders Limited, 61 44–46
C. Itoh & Co., I 431–33 *see also*
   ITOCHU Corporation.
C.J. Lawrence, Morgan Grenfell Inc., **II**
   429
C.J. Smith and Sons, **11** 3
C.M. Aikman & Co., **13** 168
C.M. Armstrong, Inc., **14** 17
C.M. Barnes Company, **10** 135
C.M. Life Insurance Company, **53** 213
C.M. Page, **14** 112
C-MAC Industries Inc., **48** 369
C.O.M.B. Company, **18** 131–33
C. Of Eko-Elda A.B.E.E., **64** 177
C/P Utility Services Company, **14** 138
C.P.T. Holding B.V., **56** 152
C.P.U., Inc., **18** 111–12
C.R. Anthony Company, **24** 458
C.R. Bard, Inc., 9 96–98; **65** 81–85
   (upd.)

Clef, **IV** 125

Clemente Capital Inc., **25** 542

Clements Energy, Inc., **7** 376

Cleo Inc., **12** 207–09; **35** 131

Le Clerc, **21** 225–26

Clessidra SGR, **76** 326

Cleve-Co Jig Boring Co., **23** 82

Cleveland and Western Coal Company, **7** 369

Cleveland-Cliffs Inc., 13 156–58; **62** 71–75 **(upd.)**

Cleveland Cotton Products Co., **37** 393

Cleveland Electric Illuminating Company *see* Centerior Energy Theodor.

Cleveland Fabric Centers, Inc. *see* Fabri-Centers of America Inc.

Cleveland Grinding Machine Co., **23** 82

Cleveland Indians Baseball Company, Inc., 37 92–94

Cleveland Iron Mining Company *see* Cleveland-Cliffs Inc.

Cleveland Pneumatic Co., **III** 512

Cleveland Precision Instruments, Inc., **23** 82

Cleveland Range Ltd. *see* Enodis plc.

Cleveland Twist Drill Company *see* Acme-Cleveland Corp.

Clevepak Corporation, **8** 229; **13** 442; **59** 349

Clevite Corporation, **14** 207

CLF Research, **16** 202; **43** 170

Click Messenger Service, Inc., **24** 126

Click Trips, Inc., **74** 169

Click Wine Group, 68 86–88

ClickAgents.com, Inc., **49** 433

ClientLogic Corporation *see* Onex Corporation.

Clif Bar Inc., 50 141–43

Clifford & Wills, **12** 280–81

Clifford Chance LLP, 38 136–39

Cliffs Corporation, **13** 157; **27** 224

Climaveneta Deutschland GmbH *see* De'Longhi S.p.A.

Clinical Partners, Inc., **26** 74

Clinical Pathology Facility, Inc., **26** 391

Clinical Science Research Ltd., **10** 106

Clinique Laboratories, Inc., **30** 191

Clinton Cards plc, 39 86–88; **70** 20–21

Clipper Group, **12** 439

Clipper, Inc., **IV** 597

Clipper Manufacturing Company, **7** 3

La Cloche d'Or, **25** 85

Cloetta Fazer AB, 70 58–60

Clopay Corp., **34** 195

The Clorox Company, III 20–22; **22** 145–48 **(upd.)**

Close Brothers Group plc, 39 89–92

Clothesline Corporation, **60** 65

The Clothestime, Inc., 20 141–44

Clougherty Packing Company, 72 72–74

Clouterie et Tréfilerie des Flandres, **IV** 25–26

Clover Club, **44** 348

Clovis Water Co., **6** 580

Clow Water Systems Co., **55** 266

CLRP *see* City of London Real Property Company Ltd.

CLSI Inc., **15** 372; **43** 182

Club Aurrera, **8** 556

Club Corporation of America, **26** 27

Club de Hockey Canadien Inc., **26** 305

Club Méditerranée S.A., 6 206–08; **21** 125–28 **(upd.)**; **27** 10

Club Monaco Inc., **62** 284

ClubCorp, Inc., 33 101–04

Cluett Corporation, **22** 133

Cluett, Peabody & Co., Inc., **8** 567–68

Cluster Consulting, **51** 98

Clyde Iron Works, **8** 545

Clydesdale Group, **19** 390

CM&M Equilease, **7** 344

CM&P *see* Cresap, McCormick and Paget.

CMAC Investment Corporation *see* Radian Group Inc.

CMB Acier, **IV** 228

CMB Packaging SA, **8** 477; **49** 295

CMC *see* Commercial Metals Company.

CME *see* Campbell-Mithun-Esty, Inc.; Central European Media Enterprises Ltd.; Chicago Mercantile Exchange Inc.

CMGI, Inc., 76 99–101

CMI International, Inc., **27** 202, 204

CMIH *see* China Merchants International Holdings Co., Ltd.

CML Group, Inc., 10 215–18

CMO *see* Chi Mei Optoelectronics Corporation.

CMP Media Inc., 26 76–80; **28** 504

CMP Properties Inc., **15** 122

CMS Energy Corporation, IV 23; **V** 577–79; **8** 466; **14** 114–16 **(upd.)**

CMS Healthcare, **29** 412

CMT Enterprises, Inc., **22** 249

CN *see* Canadian National Railway Company.

CNA Financial Corporation, III 228–32; **38** 140–46 **(upd.)**

CNB Bancshares Inc., **31** 207

CNBC, Inc., **28** 298

CNC Holding Corp. *see* Cole National Corporation.

CNCA *see* Caisse National de Crédit Agricole.

CNEP *see* Comptoir National d'Escompte de Paris.

CNET Networks, Inc., 47 77–80

CNF Transportation *see* Consolidated Freightways, Inc.

CNG *see* Consolidated Natural Gas Company.

CNH Global N.V., 38 147–56 **(upd.)**; **67** 9

CNI *see* Community Networks Inc.

CNN *see* Cable News Network.

CNP *see* Compagnie Nationale à Portefeuille.

CNPC *see* China National Petroleum Corporation.

CNS, Inc., 20 145–47

CNTS *see* Ceska Nezavisla Televizni Spolecnost.

Co-Counsel, Inc., **29** 364

Co-Op Blue Square Consumer Cooperative Society, **41** 56–58

Co-operative Group (CWS) Ltd., 51 86–89

Co-operative Insurance Society Ltd., **51** 89

Co-Steel International Ltd., **8** 523–24; **13** 142–43; **24** 144

Coach and Car Equipment Corp., **41** 369

Coach, Inc., 45 111–15 **(upd.)**; **54** 325–26

Coach Leatherware, **10** 219–21; **12** 559

Coach Specialties Co. *see* Fleetwood Enterprises, Inc.

Coach USA, Inc., 24 117–19; **55** 103–06 **(upd.)**

Coachmen Industries, Inc., 77 104–107

Coal India Ltd., IV 48–50; **44** 100–03 **(upd.)**

Coalport, **12** 528

Coast American Corporation, **13** 216

Coast Consolidators, Inc., **14** 505

Coast to Coast Hardware *see* TruServ Corporation.

Coast-to-Coast Stores, **12** 8

Coastal Coca-Cola Bottling Co., **10** 223

Coastal Container Line Inc., **30** 318

Coastal Corporation, IV 394–95; **7** 553–54; **31** 118–21 **(upd.)**

Coastal Lumber, S.A., **18** 514

Coastal States Corporation, **11** 481

Coastal States Life Insurance Company, **11** 482

CoastAmerica Corp., **13** 176

Coastline Distribution, Inc., **52** 399

Coates/Lorilleux, **14** 308

Coats plc, V 356–58; **44** 104–07 **(upd.)**

CoBank *see* National Bank for Cooperatives.

Cobb & Branham, **14** 257

COBE Cardiovascular, Inc., 61 68–72

COBE Laboratories, Inc., 13 159–61; **22** 360; **49** 156; **61** 70

Coberco *see* Friesland Coberco Dairy Foods Holding N.V.

Cobham plc, 30 129–32

Coborn's, Inc., 30 133–35

Cobra Electronics Corporation, 14 117–19; **60** 137

Cobra Golf Inc., 16 108–10

Cobra Ventilation Products, **22** 229

Coburn Vision Care, **III** 727

Coca-Cola Bottling Co. Consolidated, 10 222–24; **15** 299

Coca-Cola Bottling Company of Northern New England, Inc., **21** 319

The Coca-Cola Company, I 232–35; **10** 225–28 **(upd.)**; **32** 111–16 **(upd.)**; **67** 111–17 **(upd.)**

Coca-Cola Enterprises, Inc., 10 223; **13** 162–64; **23** 455–57; **32** 115

Cochlear Ltd., 77 108–111

Cochrane Corporation, **8** 135

Cochrane Foil Co., **15** 128

Cockburn & Campbell Ltd., **38** 501

Cockburn-Adelaide Cement, **31** 398, 400

Cockerill Sambre Group, IV 51–53; **22** 44; **26** 81–84 **(upd.)**; **42** 416

Coco's, **27** 16, 19

Cub Foods, II 669–70; **14** 411; **17** 302; **18** 505; **22** 327; **50** 455

Cuban American Oil Company, **8** 348

Cubic Corporation, 19 109–11

CUC International Inc., **16** 144–46 *see also* Cendant Corporation.

Cudahy Corp., **12** 199

Cuisinart Corporation, 24 129–32

Culbro Corporation, 14 19; **15** 137–39 *see also* General Cigar Holdings, Inc.

Culinar Inc., **59** 364

Culinary Foods, Inc., **14** 516; **50** 493

Cullen/Frost Bankers, Inc., 25 113–16

Culligan Water Technologies, Inc., 12 87–88; **38** 168–70 (upd.)

Cullinet Software Corporation, **14** 390; **15** 108

Cullman Bros. *see* Culbro Corporation.

Culp, Inc., 29 138–40

Culter Industries, Inc., **22** 353

Culver Franchising System, Inc., 58 79–81

Cumberland Farms, Inc., 17 120–22; **26** 450

Cumberland Federal Bancorporation, **13** 223; **31** 206

Cumberland Newspapers, **7** 389

Cumberland Packing Corporation, 26 107–09

Cummings-Moore Graphite Company *see* Asbury Carbons, Inc.

Cummins Cogeneration Co. *see* Cogeneration Development Corp.

Cummins Engine Co., Inc., I 146–48; **12** 89–92 (upd.); **40** 131–35 (upd.); **42** 387

Cummins Utility Supply, **58** 334

Cumo Sports, **16** 109

Cumulus Media Inc., 37 103–05

CUNA Mutual Group, 11 495; **62** 84–87

Cunard Line Ltd., 23 159–62

CUNO Incorporated, 57 85–89

CurranCare, LLC, **50** 122

Current, Inc., 37 106–09

Currys Group PLC *see* Dixons Group PLC.

Curtas Technologie SA, **58** 221

Curtice-Burns Foods, Inc., 7 17–18, **104–06; 21** 18, **154–57** (upd.) *see also* Birds Eye Foods, Inc.

Curtin & Pease/Peneco, **27** 361

Curtis Circulation Co., **IV** 619

Curtis Homes, **22** 127

Curtis Industries, **13** 165; **76** 107

Curtis 1000 Inc. *see* American Business Products, Inc.

Curtis Restaurant Supply, **60** 160

Curtis Squire Inc., **18** 455; **70** 262

Curtiss-Wright Corporation, 10 260–63; **35** 132–37 (upd.)

Curver-Rubbermaid *see* Newell Rubbermaid.

Curves International, Inc., 54 80–82

Cushman & Wakefield Inc., **58** 303

Cussons *see* PZ Cussons plc.

Custom Academic Publishing Company, **12** 174

Custom Building Products of California, Inc., **53** 176

Custom Chrome, Inc., 16 147–49; **74** 92–95 (upd.)

Custom Electronics, Inc., **9** 120

Custom Expressions, Inc., **7** 24; **22** 35

Custom Hoists, Inc., **17** 458

Custom, Ltd., **46** 197

Custom Organics, **8** 464

Custom Primers, **17** 288

Custom Publishing Group, **27** 361

Custom Technologies Corp., **19** 152

Custom Thermoform, **24** 512

Custom Tool and Manufacturing Company, **41** 366

Custom Transportation Services, Inc., **26** 62

Custom Woodwork & Plastics Inc., **36** 159

Customized Transportation Inc., **22** 164, 167

AB Custos, **25** 464

Cutisin, **55** 123

Cutler-Hammer Inc., **63** 401

Cutter & Buck Inc., 27 112–14

Cutter Precision Metals, Inc., **25** 7

CVC Capital Partners Limited, **49** 451; **54** 207

CVE Corporation, Inc., **24** 395

CVG Aviation, **34** 118

CVI Incorporated, **21** 108

CVN Companies, **9** 218

CVPS *see* Central Vermont Public Service Corporation.

CVRD *see* Companhia Vale do Rio Doce Ltd.

CVS Corporation, 32 166, 170; **34** 285; **45** 133–38 (upd.); **63** 335–36

CWA *see* City of Westminster Assurance Company Ltd.

CWM *see* Chemical Waste Management, Inc.

CWP *see* Custom Woodwork & Plastics Inc.

CWT Farms International Inc., **13** 103

CXT Inc., **33** 257

Cyber Communications Inc., **16** 168

CyberCash Inc., **18** 541, 543; **76** 370

Cybermedia, Inc., 25 117–19

Cybernet Electronics Corp., **II** 51; **21** 330

Cybernex, **10** 463

Cyberonics, Inc., 79 128–131

Cybershield, Inc., **52** 103, 105

CyberSource Corp., **26** 441

CYBERTEK Corporation, **11** 395

CyberTrust Solutions Inc., **42** 24–25

Cybex International, Inc., 49 106–09

Cycle & Carriage Ltd., **20** 313; **56** 285

Cycle Video Inc., **7** 590

Cyclops Corporation, **10** 45; **13** 157

Cydsa *see* Grupo Cydsa, S.A. de C.V.

Cygna Energy Services, **13** 367

Cygne Designs, Inc., 25 120–23; **37** 14

Cygnus Business Media, Inc., 56 73–77

Cymbal Co., Ltd. *see* Nagasakiya Co., Ltd.

Cymer, Inc., 77 125–128

Cynosure Inc., **11** 88

Cypress Amax Minerals Co., **13** 158; **22** 285–86

Cypress Insurance Co., **III** 214

Cypress Management Services, Inc., **64** 311

Cypress Semiconductor Corporation, 20 174–76; **48** 125–29 (upd.)

Cyprus Amax Minerals Company, 21 158–61

Cyprus Minerals Company, 7 107–09

Cyrix Corporation *see* National Semiconductor Corporation.

Cyrk Inc., 19 112–14; **21** 516; **33** 416

Cytec Industries Inc., 27 115–17

Cytyc Corporation, 69 112–14

Czarnikow-Rionda Company, Inc., 32 128–30

D

D&B *see* Dun & Bradstreet Corporation.

D&D Enterprises, Inc., **24** 96

D&F Industries, Inc., **17** 227; **41** 204

D&K Wholesale Drug, Inc., 14 146–48

D&N Systems, Inc., **10** 505

D&O Inc., **17** 363

D&W Computer Stores, **13** 176

D & W Food Stores, Inc., **8** 482; **27** 314

D Green (Electronics) Limited, **65** 141

D.B. Kaplan's, **26** 263

D.C. Heath & Co., **36** 273; **38** 374

D.C. National Bancorp, **10** 426

D. de Ricci-G. Selnet et Associes, **28** 141

d.e.m.o., **28** 345

D.E. Shaw & Co., **25** 17; **38** 269

D.E. Winebrenner Co., **7** 429

D.G. Calhoun, **12** 112

D.G. Yuengling & Son, Inc., 38 171–73

D.H. Holmes Company, Limited *see* Dillard's Inc.

D.I. Manufacturing Inc., **37** 351

D.K. Gold, **17** 138

D.L. Rogers Group, **37** 363

D.L. Saslow Co., **19** 290

D.M. Nacional, **23** 170

D.R. Horton, Inc., 58 82–84

D.W. Mikesell Co. *see* Mike-Sell's Inc.

Da Gama Textiles Company, **24** 450

D'Addario & Company, Inc. *see* J. D'Addario & Company, Inc.

Dade Behring Holdings Inc., 71 120–22

Dade Reagents Inc., **19** 103

DADG *see* Deutsch-Australische Dampfschiffs-Gesellschaft.

DAEDUK Techno Valley Company Ltd., **62** 174

Daewoo Group, III 457–59, 749; **18** 123–27 (upd.); **30** 185; **57** 90–94 (upd.)

DAF, **7** 566–67

Daffy's Inc., 26 110–12

NV Dagblad De Telegraaf *see* N.V. Holdingmaatschappij De Telegraaf.

D'Agostino Supermarkets Inc., 19 115–17

Dagsbladunie, **IV** 611

DAH *see* DeCrane Aircraft Holdings Inc.

Dahill Industries *see* Global Imaging Systems, Inc.

Dart Industries *see* Premark International Inc.

Dart Transit Co., **13** 550

Dartex, **18** 434

Darty S.A., 27 118–20

Darvel Realty Trust, **14** 126

Darya-Varia Laboratoria, **18** 182

DASA *see* Daimler-Benz Aerospace AG; Deutsche Aerospace Airbus.

Dashwood Industries, **19** 446

DASS Die andere SystementsorgungsGesellschaft mbH, **58** 28

Dassault Aviation SA, **21** 11

Dassault-Breguet *see* Avions Marcel Dassault-Breguet Aviation.

Dassault Systèmes S.A., 25 132–34; 26 179 *see also* Groupe Dassault Aviation SA.

Dassler, **14** 6

Dastek Inc., **10** 464; **11** 234–35

DAT GmbH, **10** 514

Data Acquisition Systems, Inc., **16** 300

Data Architects, **14** 318

Data Base Management Inc., **11** 19

Data-Beam Corp., **25** 301

Data Broadcasting Corporation, 31 147–50

Data Card Corporation, **IV** 680; **58** 340

Data Force Inc., **11** 65

Data General Corporation, 8 137–40

Data One Corporation, **11** 111

Data Preparation, Inc., **11** 112

Data Printer, Inc., **18** 435

Data Specialties Inc. *see* Zebra Technologies Corporation.

Data Structures Inc., **11** 65

Data Systems Technology, **11** 57; **38** 375

Data Technology Corp., **18** 510

Data 3 Systems, **9** 36

Datac plc, **18** 140

Datachecker Systems, **III** 164; **11** 150

Datacraft Asia Limited, **69** 127

Datacraft Corp., **II** 38

DataFocus, Inc., **18** 112

DataPath Systems, **64** 246

Datapoint Corporation, 11 67–70

Dataquest Inc., **10** 558; **21** 235, 237; **22** 51; **25** 347

Datas Incorporated *see* Delta Air Lines, Inc.

Datascope Corporation, 39 112–14

Dataset Communications Inc., **23** 100

Datastream International Ltd., **10** 89; **13** 417

Datatec Ltd., **67** 392–94

DataTimes Corporation, **29** 58

Datavision Inc., **11** 444

Datec, **22** 17

Datek Online Holdings Corp., 32 144–46; **48** 225–27

Datran, **11** 468

Datsun *see* Nissan Motor Company, Ltd.

Datura Corp., **14** 391

Dauphin Deposit Corporation, 14 152–54

Dauphin Distribution Services *see* Exel Logistics Ltd.

Daut + Rietz and Connectors Pontarlier, **19** 166

Dave & Buster's, Inc., 33 126–29

Davenport Mammoet Heavy Transport Inc., **26** 280

The Davey Tree Expert Company, 11 71–73

David & Charles Group *see* F&W Publications, Inc.

The David and Lucile Packard Foundation, 41 117–19

David B. Smith & Company, **13** 243

David Berg & Co., **14** 537

David Brown & Son *see* Brown & Sharpe Manufacturing Co.

David Brown, Ltd., **10** 380

David Clark, **30** 357

David Crystal, Inc., **9** 156

David Hafler Company, **43** 323

The David J. Joseph Company, 14 155–56; **76** 128–30 (upd.)

David Jones Ltd., 60 100–02

David Kelley Design *see* IDEO Inc.

David L. Babson & Company Inc., **53** 213

David Lloyd Leisure Ltd., **52** 412, 415–16

David Oppenheimer & Co. *see* Oppenheimer Group.

David S. Smith Ltd. *see* DS Smith Plc.

David Wilson Homes Ltd., **45** 442–43

David's Bridal, Inc., 33 130–32; 46 288

David's Supermarkets, **17** 180

Davide Campari-Milano S.p.A., 57 104–06

Davids *see* Metcash Trading Ltd.

Davidson & Associates, **16** 146

Davidson & Leigh, **21** 94

Davidson Brothers Co., **19** 510

Davis & Geck, **27** 115

Davis Manufacturing Company, **10** 380

Davis Polk & Wardwell, 36 151–54

Davis Service Group PLC, 45 139–41; **49** 374, 377

Davis-Standard Company, **9** 154; **36** 144

Davis Vision, Inc., **27** 209

Davis Wholesale Company, **9** 20

DaVita Inc., 73 102–05

Davlyn Industries, Inc., **22** 487

Davox Corporation, **18** 31

Davy Bamag GmbH, **IV** 142

Davy McKee AG, **IV** 142

DAW Technologies, Inc., 25 135–37

Dawe's Laboratories, Inc., **12** 3

Dawn Food Products, Inc., 17 126–28

Dawson Holdings PLC, 43 132–34

Day & Zimmermann Inc., 6 579; 9 162–64; **31** 151–55 (upd.)

Day Brite Lighting, **II** 19

Day-Glo Color Corp., **8** 456

Day International, **8** 347

Day-N-Nite, **II** 620

Day Runner, Inc., 14 157–58; 41 120–23 (upd.)

Day-Timers, Inc., **51** 9

Daybridge Learning Centers, **13** 49, 299

Dayco Products, **7** 297

Daylin Corporation, **46** 271

Days Inns of America, Inc., **III** 344; **11** 178; **13** 362, 364; **21** 362

Daystar International Inc., **11** 44

Daytex, Inc., **II** 669; **18** 505; **50** 455

Dayton Engineering Laboratories, **9** 416

Dayton Hudson Corporation, V 43–44; **18** 135–37 (upd.) *see also* Target Corporation.

Dayton Power & Light Company, **6** 467, 480–82

Daytron Mortgage Systems, **11** 485

Dazey Corp., **16** 384; **43** 289

DB *see* Deutsche Bundesbahn.

DB Group, **59** 59–60

DB Reise & Touristik AG, **37** 250

DBA Holdings, Inc., **18** 24

dba Luftfahrtgesellschaft mbH, 76 131–33

DBMS Inc., **14** 390

DBS Transit Inc. *see* Stabler Companies Inc.

DBT Online Inc. *see* ChoicePoint Inc.

DC Comics Inc., 25 138–41

DC Shoes, Inc., 60 103–05

DCA Advertising, **16** 168

DCA Food Industries, **27** 258–60, 299

DCE Consultants, **51** 17

DCL BioMedical, Inc., **11** 333

DCMS Holdings Inc., **7** 114; **25** 125

DCN S.A., 75 125–27

DDB Worldwide Communications, 14 159–61 *see also* Omnicom Group Inc.

DDD Energy, Inc., **47** 348, 350

DDI Corporation, 7 118–20; 13 482; **21** 330–31

DDJ Capital, **68** 345

NV De Beer and Partners, **45** 386

De Beers Consolidated Mines Limited / **De Beers Centenary AG, IV 64–68; 7** 121–26 (upd.); **28** 88–94 (upd.)

De Bono Industries, **24** 443

De Dietrich & Cie., 31 156–59

De Grenswisselkantoren NV, **III** 201

de Havilland Aircraft Co. *see* Bombardier Inc.

de Havilland Holdings, Ltd., **24** 85–86

De La Rue plc, 10 267–69; 34 138–43 (upd.); **46** 251

De Leuw, Cather & Company, **8** 416

De Paepe, **45** 386

De Streekkrant-De Weekkrantgroep NV, **48** 347

De Tomaso Industries, **11** 104; **50** 197

De Trey Gesellschaft, **10** 271

De Vito/Verdi, **26** 111

DEA Group, **23** 83

Dead Sea Works Ltd., **55** 229

Dealer Equipment and Services, **10** 492

Dealers Wholesale Inc., **56** 230

Dean & Barry Co., **8** 455

Dean & DeLuca, Inc., 36 155–57

Dean Foods Company, 7 127–29; 21 165–68 (upd.); **73** 106–15 (upd.)

Dean Witter, Discover & Co., 7 213; 12 96–98; **21** 97; **22** 405–07 *see also* Morgan Stanley Dean Witter & Company.

FSA Corporation, **25** 349
FSI International, Inc., 17 192–94 *see also* FlightSafety International, Inc.
FSP *see* Frank Schaffer Publications.
FT Freeport Indonesia, **57** 145
FTD *see* Florists Transworld Delivery, Inc.
FTI Consulting, Inc., 77 160–163
FTP Software, Inc., 20 236–38
Fubu, 29 207–09
Fuddruckers, **27** 480–82
Fuel Pipeline Transportation Ltd. *see* Thai Airways International.
Fuel Resources Development Co., **6** 558–59
Fuel Resources Inc., **6** 457
FuelCell Energy, Inc., 75 150–53
FuelMaker Corporation, **6** 569
Fuji Bank, Ltd., II 291–93
Fuji Electric Co., Ltd., II 22–23; **48** 180–82 (upd.)
Fuji Gen-Gakki, **16** 202; **43** 171
Fuji Heavy Industries, **I** 207; **9** 294; **12** 400; **13** 499–501; **23** 290; **36** 240, 243; **64** 151
Fuji Kaolin Co. *see* English China Clays Ltd.
Fuji Photo Film Co., Ltd., III 486–89; **18** 183–87 (upd.); **79** 177–184 (upd.)
Fuji Seito, **I** 511
Fuji Television, **7** 249; **9** 29
Fuji Xerox. *see* Xerox Corporation.
Fujian Hualong Carburetor, **13** 555
Fujisawa Pharmaceutical Company, Ltd., I 635–36; **58** 132–34 (upd.)
Fujitsu-ICL Systems Inc., 11 150–51
Fujitsu Limited, III 139–41; **16** 224–27 (upd.); **40** 145–50 (upd.)
Fujitsu Takamisawa, **28** 131
Fukuoka Mitsukoshi Ltd., **56** 242
Fukuoka Paper Co., Ltd., **IV** 285
Fukutake Publishing Co., Ltd., **13** 91, 93
Ful-O-Pep, **10** 250
Fulbright & Jaworski L.L.P., 22 4; **47** 138–41
Fulcrum Communications, **10** 19
The Fulfillment Corporation of America, **21** 37
Fulham Brothers, **13** 244
Fullbright & Jaworski, **28** 48
Fuller Company *see* FLSmidth and Co. A/S.
Fuller Smith & Turner P.L.C., 38 193–95
Fulton Bank, **14** 40
Fulton Co., **III** 569; **20** 361
Fulton Manufacturing Co., **11** 535
Fulton Performance Products, Inc., **11** 535
Funai Electric Company Ltd., 62 148–50
Funco, Inc., 20 239–41 *see also* GameStop Corp.
Fund American Companies *see* White Mountains Insurance Group, Ltd.
Fundimensions, **16** 337
Funk & Wagnalls, **22** 441
Funnel Cake Factory, **24** 241
Funtastic Limited, **52** 193

Fuqua Enterprises, Inc., 17 195–98
Fuqua Industries Inc., I 445–47; **8** 545; **12** 251; **14** 86; **37** 62; **57** 376–77
Furnishings International Inc., **20** 359, 363; **39** 267
Furniture Brands International, Inc., 39 170–75 (upd.)
The Furniture Center, Inc., **14** 236
Furon Company, 28 149–51
Furr's Restaurant Group, Inc., 53 145–48
Furr's Supermarkets, Inc., II 601; **28** 152–54
Furst Group, **17** 106
Furukawa Electric Co., Ltd., III 490–92; **15** 514; **22** 44
Futronix Corporation, **17** 276
Future Diagnostics, Inc., **25** 384
Future Graphics, **18** 387
Future Now, Inc., 6 245; **12** 183–85
Future Shop Ltd., 62 151–53; **63** 63
FutureCare, **50** 123
Futurestep, Inc., **34** 247, 249
Fuyo Group, **72** 249
FWD Corporation, **7** 513
FX Coughlin Inc., **51** 130
Fyffes Plc, 38 196–99, 201
Fytek, S.A. de C.V., **66** 42

G

G&G Shops, Inc., **8** 425–26
G&K Services, Inc., 16 228–30; **21** 115
G&L Inc., **16** 202; **43** 170
G&O Manufacturing Company, Inc. *see* TransPro, Inc.
G&R Pasta Co., Inc., **II** 512
G.B. Lewis Company, **8** 359
G. Bruss GmbH and Co. KG, **26** 141
G.C. Industries, **52** 186
G.C. Murphy Company, **9** 21
G.C. Smith, **I** 423
G.D. Searle & Co., I 686–89; **12** 186–89 (upd.); **34** 177–82 (upd.)
G. Felsenthal & Sons, **17** 106
G.H. Bass & Co., **15** 406; **24** 383
G.H. Besselaar Associates, **30** 151
G.H. Rinck NV, **V** 49; **19** 122–23; **49** 111
G. Heileman Brewing Co., I 253–55; **10** 169–70
G.I.E. Airbus Industrie, I 41–43; **12** 190–92 (upd.)
G.I. Joe's, Inc., 30 221–23
G-III Apparel Group, Ltd., 22 222–24
G.J. Coles & Coy. Ltd., **20** 155
G.J. Hopkins, Inc. *see* The Branch Group, Inc.
G.L. Kelty & Co., **13** 168
G.L. Rexroth GmbH, **III** 566; **38** 298, 300
G. Leblanc Corporation, 55 149–52
G.M. Pfaff AG, **30** 419–20
G.P. Group, **12** 358
G.R. Foods, Inc. *see* Ground Round, Inc.
G.R. Herberger's Department Stores, **19** 324–25; **41** 343–44
G.S. Blodgett Corporation, 15 183–85; **22** 350 *see also* Blodgett Holdings, Inc.

GABA Holding AG *see* Colgate-Palmolive Company.
Gabelli Asset Management Inc., 13 561; **30** 211–14 *see also* Lynch Corporation.
Gables Residential Trust, 49 147–49
GAC *see* The Goodyear Tire & Rubber Company.
GAC Holdings L.P., **7** 204; **28** 164
Gadzooks, Inc., 18 188–90; **33** 203
GAF, I 337–40; **22** 225–29 (upd.)
Gage Marketing Group, 26 147–49; **27** 21
Gaggenau Hausgeräte GmbH, **67** 81
Gagliardi Brothers, **13** 383
Gagnon & Associates, **74** 258
Gaiam, Inc., 41 174–77
Gain Technology, Inc., **10** 505
Gaines Furniture Manufacturing, Inc., **43** 315
Gainsco, Inc., 22 230–32
GalaGen Inc., **65** 216
Galardi Group, Inc., 72 145–47
Galas Harland, S.A., **17** 266, 268
Galavision, Inc., **24** 515–17; **54** 72
Galaxy Aerospace Co. L.P., **69** 216
Galaxy Carpet Mills Inc., **19** 276; **63** 300
Galaxy Energies Inc., **11** 28
Galaxy Nutritional Foods, Inc., 58 135–37
Galbreath Escott, **16** 474
Gale Research Co., *see* The Thomson Corporation
Galen Health Care, **15** 112; **35** 215–16
Galen Laboratories, **13** 160
Galerías Preciados, **26** 130
Galeries Lafayette S.A., V 57–59; **23** 220–23 (upd.)
Galey & Lord, Inc., 20 242–45; **66** 131–34 (upd.)
Gallaher Group Plc, 49 150–54 (upd.)
Gallaher Limited, V 398–400; **19** 168–71 (upd.); **29** 195
Gallatin Steel Company, **18** 380; **24** 144
Galleria Shooting Team, **62** 174
Gallo Winery *see* E. & J. Gallo Winery.
Gallop Johnson & Neuman, L.C., **26** 348
The Gallup Organization, 37 153–56; **41** 196–97
Galoob Toys *see* Lewis Galoob Toys Inc.
GALP, **48** 117, 119
Galveston Daily News, **10** 3
GALVSTAR, L.P., **26** 530
Galway Irish Crystal Ltd. *see* Belleek Pottery Ltd.
Galyan's Trading Company, Inc., 47 142–44
Gamax Holding, **65** 230, 232
Gamble-Skogmo Inc., **13** 169; **25** 535
The Gambrinus Company, 29 219; **40** 188–90
Gambro AB, 49 155–57
The GAME Group plc, 80 126–129
Gamebusters, **41** 409
Gamesa Corporacion Tecnologica S.A., **19** 192; **73** 374–75
GameStop Corp., 69 185–89 (upd.)
GameTime, Inc., **19** 387; **27** 370–71

Halliburton Company, III 497–500; **25** 188–92 (upd.); **55** 190–95 (upd.)

Hallmark Cards, Inc., IV 620–21; **16** 255–57 (upd.); **40** 228–32 (upd.)

Hallmark Chemical Corp., **8** 386

Hallmark Holdings, Inc., **51** 190

Hallmark Investment Corp., **21** 92

Hallmark Residential Group, Inc., **45** 221

Halo Lighting, **30** 266

Haloid Company *see* Xerox Corporation.

Halsam Company, **25** 380

Halstead Industries, **26** 4; **52** 258

Halter Marine, **22** 276

Hambrecht & Quist Group, **10** 463, 504; **26** 66; **27** 447; **31** 349

Hambro American Bank & Trust Co., **11** 109

Hambro Countrywide Security, **32** 374

Hambros Bank, **16** 14; **27** 474; **43** 7

Hamburg-Amerikanische-Packetfahrt-Actien-Gesellschaft *see* Hapag-Lloyd AG.

Hamburgische Electricitaets-Werke AG, **57** 395, 397

Hamelin Group, Inc. *see* Spartech Corporation.

Hamer Hammer Service, Inc., **11** 523

Hamersley Holdings, IV 59–61

Hamil Textiles Ltd. *see* Algo Group Inc.

Hamilton Beach/Proctor-Silex Inc., **17** 213–15

Hamilton Group Limited, **15** 478

Hamilton Industries, Inc., **25** 261

Hamilton/Hall-Mark, **19** 313

Hamilton National Bank, **13** 465

Hamilton Oil Corp., IV 47; **22** 107

Hamilton Standard, **9** 417

Hamilton Sundstrand, **76** 319

Hamish Hamilton, IV 659; **8** 526

Hammacher Schlemmer & Company Inc., **21** 268–70; **72** 160–62 (upd.)

Hammarplast, **13** 493

Hammermill Paper Co., **23** 48–49

Hammers Plastic Recycling, **6** 441

Hammerson plc, IV 696–98; **26** 420; **40** 233–35

Hammery Furniture Company, **14** 302–03

Hammes Co., **38** 482

Hamming-Whitman Publishing Co., **13** 559

Hampton Affiliates, Inc., **77** 175–179

Hampton Industries, Inc., **20** 280–82

Hampton Inns, **9** 425–26

Hampton Roads Food, Inc., **25** 389

Hamworthy Engineering Ltd., **31** 367, 369

Han Comm Inc., **62** 174

Han-Fa Electrification Co. Ltd., **76** 139

Hancock Fabrics, Inc., **18** 222–24

Hancock Holding Company, **15** 207–09

Hancock Jaffe Laboratories, **11** 460

Hancock Park Associates *see* Leslie's Poolmart, Inc.

Hancock Textile Co., Inc., **27** 291

Handleman Company, **15** 210–12

Handspring Inc., **49** 183–86

Handy & Harman, **23** 249–52

Handy Andy Home Improvement Centers, Inc., **16** 210; **26** 160–61

Hanes Corp., **8** 202, 288; **25** 166

Hanes Holding Company, **11** 256; **48** 267

Hang Chong, **18** 114

Hang Seng Bank Ltd., **60** 161–63

Hanger Orthopedic Group, Inc., **41** 192–95

Haniel & Cie. GmbH, **27** 175

Hanjin Group *see* Korean Ail Lines Co. Ltd.

Hanjin Shipping Co., Ltd., **50** 217–21

Hankook Tyre Manufacturing Company, V 255–56; **19** 508

Hankuk Glass Industry Co., III 715

Hankyu Corporation, V 454–56; **23** 253–56 (upd.)

Hankyu Department Stores, Inc., V 70–71; **62** 168–71 (upd.)

Hanley Brick, **14** 250

Hanmi Financial Corporation, **66** 169–71

Hanna Andersson Corp., **49** 187–90

Hanna-Barbera Cartoons Inc., **23** 257–59, 387

Hanna Mining Co., **8** 346–47

Hanna Ore Mining Company, **12** 352

Hannaford Bros. Co., **12** 220–22

Hannen Brauerei GmbH, **9** 100

Hannifin Corporation *see* Parker Hannifin Corporation.

HANNOVER International AG für Industrieversicherungen, **53** 162

Hannover Papier, **49** 353

Hanover Bank *see* Manufacturers Hanover Corporation.

Hanover Compressor Company, **59** 215–17

Hanover Direct, Inc., **36** 262–65

Hanover Foods Corporation, **35** 211–14

Hanover House, Inc., **24** 154

Hanover Insurance Company, **63** 29

Hansa Linie, **26** 279–80

Hansen Natural Corporation, **31** 242–45; **76** 171–74 (upd.)

Hansgrohe AG, **56** 149–52

Hansol Paper Co., **63** 315–16

Hanson Building Materials America Inc., **60** 164–66

Hanson Industries, **44** 257

Hanson PLC, III 501–03; **7** 207–10 (upd.); **30** 228–32 (upd.)

Hansvedt Industries Inc., **25** 195

Hanwha Group, **62** 172–75

Hapag-Lloyd AG, **6** 397–99; **42** 283

Happy Air Exchangers Ltd., **21** 499

Happy Kids Inc., **30** 233–35

Haralambos Beverage Corporation, **11** 451

Harbert Corporation, **13** 98; **14** 222–23

HARBIN Samick Corp., **56** 300

Harbison-Walker Refractories Company, **24** 207–09

Harbor Group, **41** 262–63

Harborlite Corporation, **10** 45; **60** 16

Harbour Group, **24** 16

Harco, Inc., **37** 31

Harcourt Brace and Co., **12** 223–26

Harcourt Brace Jovanovich, Inc., IV 622–24

Harcourt General, Inc., **20** 283–87 (upd.)

Harcros Investment Trust Ltd. *see* Harrisons & Crosfield PLC.

Hard E Beverage Co., **75** 166

Hard Rock Cafe International, Inc., **12** 227–29; **32** 241–45 (upd.)

Hardee's Food Systems Inc., II 679; **7** 430; **8** 564; **9** 178; **15** 345; **16** 95; **19** 93; **23** 505; **27** 16–18; **46** 98

Hardin Stockton, **21** 96

Harding Lawson Associates Group, Inc., **16** 258–60

Hardinge Inc., **25** 193–95

Hardman Inc., III 699

Hardware Wholesalers Inc. *see* Do it Best Corporation.

Hardy Oil & Gas, **34** 75

HARIBO GmbH & Co. KG, **44** 216–19

Harima Shipbuilding & Engineering Co., Ltd., I 511; III 533

Harken Energy Corporation, **17** 169–70

Harland and Wolff Holdings plc, **19** 197–200

Harlem Globetrotters International, Inc., **7** 199, 335; **61** 122–24

Harlequin Enterprises Limited, IV 587, 590, 617, 619, 672; **19** 405; **29** 470–71, 473; **52** 153–56

Harley-Davidson, Inc., **7** 211–14; **25** 196–200 (upd.)

Harleysville Group Inc., **37** 183–86

Harman International Industries Inc., **15** 213–15

Harman Oilgear Ltd. *see* The Oilgear Company.

Harmon Industries, Inc., **25** 201–04

Harmon Publishing Company, **12** 231

Harmonic Inc., **43** 221–23

Harmony Gold Mining Company Limited, **63** 182–85

Harmsworth Brothers, **17** 396

Harmsworth Publishing, **19** 118, 120

Harnischfeger Industries, Inc., **8** 241–44; **38** 224–28 (upd.)

Harold's Stores, Inc., **22** 248–50

Harp Lager Ltd., **15** 442; **35** 395, 397

Harper Group Inc., **17** 216–19

Harper House, Inc. *see* Day Runner, Inc.

Harper Robinson and Company, **17** 163

HarperCollins Publishers, **14** 555–56; **15** 216–18; **23** 156, 210; **24** 546; **46** 196

Harpers, Inc., **12** 298; **48** 245

Harpo Inc., **28** 173–75; **30** 270; **66** 172–75 (upd.)

Harrah's Entertainment, Inc., **16** 261–63; **43** 224–28 (upd.)

Harrell Construction Group, LLC, **75** 346

Harris & Harris Group, **59** 12

Harris Adacom Corporation B.V., **21** 239

Harris Bancorp, **46** 55

Harris Corporation, II 37–39; **20** 288–92 (upd.); **78** 142–148 (upd.)

Houston, Effler & Partners Inc., **9** 135

Houston Electric Light & Power Company, **44** 368

Houston Industries Incorporated, V 641–44 *see also* Reliant Energy Inc.

Houston International Teleport, Inc., **11** 184

Houston Oil & Minerals Corp., **11** 440–41

Houston Pipe Line Company, **45** 21

Hoveringham Group, **III** 753; **28** 450

Hoving Corp., **14** 501

Hovnanian Enterprises, Inc., 29 243–45

Howard B. Stark Candy Co., **15** 325

Howard Flint Ink Company, **13** 227

Howard H. Sweet & Son, Inc., **14** 502

Howard Hughes Corporation, **63** 341

Howard Hughes Medical Institute, 39 221–24

Howard Hughes Properties, Ltd., **17** 317

Howard Humphreys, **13** 119

Howard Johnson International, Inc., 17 236–39; 72 182–86 (upd.)

Howard Research and Development Corporation, **15** 412, 414

Howard Schultz & Associates, Inc., **73** 266

Howard, Smith & Levin, **40** 126

Howden *see* Alexander Howden Group.

Howdy Company, **9** 177

Howe & Fant, Inc., **23** 82

Howe Sound Co., **12** 253

Howmedica, **29** 455

Howmet Corporation, 12 IV 253–55; 22 506

Hoyle Products, **62** 384

Hoyt Archery Company, **10** 216

HP *see* Hewlett-Packard Company.

HPI Health Care Services, **49** 307–08

HQ Global Workplaces, Inc., **47** 331

HQ Office International, **8** 405; **23** 364

HRB Business Services, **29** 227

Hrubitz Oil Company, **12** 244

HSBC Holdings plc, 12 256–58; 26 199–204 (upd.); 80 155–163 (upd.)

HSG *see* Helikopter Services Group AS.

Hsiang-Li Investment Corp., **51** 123

HSN, 64 181–85 (upd.)

HSS Hire Service Group PLC, **45** 139–41

HTH, **12** 464

HTM Goedkoop, **26** 278–79; **55** 200

H2O Plus, **11** 41

Hua Bei Oxygen, **25** 82

Hua Yang Printing Holdings Co. Ltd., **60** 372

Hub Group, Inc., 26 533; 38 233–35

Hub Services, Inc., **18** 366

Hubbard Air Transport, **10** 162

Hubbard, Baker & Rice, **10** 126

Hubbard Broadcasting Inc., 24 226–28; 79 207–212 (upd.)

Hubbard Construction Co., **23** 332

Hubbell Inc., 9 286–87; 31 257–59 (upd.); 76 183–86 (upd.)

Huck Manufacturing Company, **22** 506

Hudepohl-Schoenling Brewing Co., **18** 72; **50** 114

Hudson Automobile Company, **18** 492

The Hudson Bay Mining and Smelting Company, Limited, 12 259–61

Hudson Foods Inc., 13 270–72

Hudson Housewares Corp., **16** 389

Hudson I.C.S., **58** 53

Hudson Pharmaceutical Corp., **31** 347

Hudson River Bancorp, Inc., 41 210–13

Hudson Software, **13** 481

Hudson's *see* Target Corporation.

Hudson's Bay Company, V 79–81; 25 219–22 (upd.)

Hue International, **8** 324

Hueppe Duscha, **III** 571; **20** 362

Huf-North America, **73** 325

Huffman Manufacturing Company, **7** 225–26

Huffy Bicycles Co., **19** 383

Huffy Corporation, 7 225–27; 26 184, 412; **30 239–42 (upd.)**

Hugerot, **19** 50

Hugh O'Neill Auto Co., **12** 309

Hughes Air West, **25** 421

Hughes Aircraft Corporation, **7** 426–27; **9** 409; **10** 327; **13** 356, 398; **15** 528, 530; **21** 201; **23** 134; **24** 442; **25** 86, 223; **30** 175 *see also* GM Hughes Electronics Corporation.

Hughes Communications, Inc., **13** 398; **18** 211

Hughes Corp., **18** 535

Hughes Electronics Corporation, 25 223–25

Hughes Helicopter, **26** 431; **46** 65

Hughes Hubbard & Reed LLP, 44 230–32

Hughes Markets, Inc., 22 271–73

Hughes Network Systems Inc., **21** 239

Hughes Properties, Inc., **17** 317

Hughes Space and Communications Company, **33** 47–48

Hughes Supply, Inc., 14 246–47; 39 360

Hughes Television Network, **11** 184

Hughes Tool Co. *see* Baker Hughes Incorporated.

Hugo Boss AG, 48 206–09

Hugo Neu Corporation, **19** 381–82

Hugo Stinnes GmbH, **8** 69, 494–95; **50** 168

Huhtamäki Oyj, 30 396, 398; 64 186–88

HUK-Coburg, 58 169–73

The Hull Group, L.L.C., **51** 148

Hulman & Company, 44 233–36; 46 245

Hüls A.G., I 349–50 *see also* Degussa-Hüls AG.

Hulsbeck and Furst GmbH, **73** 325

Hulton, **17** 397

Hulton Getty, **31** 216–17

Human Services Computing, Inc. *see* Epic Systems Corporation.

Humana Inc., III 81–83; 24 229–32 (upd.)

The Humane Society of the United States, 54 170–73

Humanetics Corporation, **29** 213

Humanities Software, **39** 341

Humberside Sea & Land Services, **31** 367

Humble Oil & Refining Company *see* Exxon.

Hummel International A/S, 68 199–201

Hummel Lanolin Corporation, **45** 126

Hummel-Reise, **44** 432

Hummer, Winblad Venture Partners, **36** 157; **69** 265; **74** 168

Hummingbird, **18** 313

Humongous Entertainment, Inc., 31 238–40

Humps' n Horns, **55** 312

Hunco Ltd., **IV** 640; **26** 273

Hungarian-Soviet Civil Air Transport Joint Stock Company *see* Mal&aacutev Plc.

Hungarian Telephone and Cable Corp., 75 193–95

Hungry Howie's Pizza and Subs, Inc., 25 226–28

Hungry Minds, Inc. *see* John Wiley & Sons, Inc.

Hunt Consolidated, Inc., 7 228–30; 27 215–18 (upd.)

Hunt Manufacturing Company, 12 262–64

Hunt-Wesson, Inc., 17 240–42

Hunter-Douglas, **8** 235

Hunter Fan Company, 13 273–75

Hunting plc, 78 163–166

Huntingdon Life Sciences Group plc, 42 182–85

Huntington Bancshares Inc., 11 180–82

Huntington Learning Centers, Inc., 55 212–14

Huntleigh Technology PLC, 77 199–202

Hunton & Williams, 35 223–26

Huntsman Chemical Corporation, 8 261–63; 9 305

Huntstown Power Company Ltd., **64** 404

Hupp Motor Car Company, **8** 74; **10** 261

Hurd & Houghton, **10** 355

Huron Steel Company, Inc., **16** 357

Hurricane Hydrocarbons Ltd., 54 174–77

Huse Food Group, **14** 352

Husky Energy Inc., 47 179–82; 49 203

Husky Oil Ltd., **IV** 695; **18** 253–54; **19** 159

Husqvarna AB, **53** 126–27

Husqvarna Forest & Garden Company, **13** 564

Hussmann Corporation, **I** 457–58; **7** 429–30; **10** 554; **13** 268; **22** 353–54; **67** 299

Hutcheson & Grundy, **29** 286

Hutchinson-Mapa, **IV** 560

Hutchinson Technology Incorporated, 18 248–51; 63 190–94 (upd.)

Hutchison Microtel, **11** 548

Hutchison Whampoa Limited, 18 252–55; 49 199–204 (upd.)

Huth Inc., **56** 230

Huth Manufacturing Corporation, **10** 414

Hüttenwerke Kayser AG, **62** 253

Huttepain, **61** 155

Huttig Building Products, Inc., 73 180–83

HVB Group, 59 237–44 (upd.)

Inland Pollution Control, **9** 110
Inland Steel Industries, Inc., **IV** 113–16;
  19 216–20 (upd.)
Inland Valley, **23** 321
Inmac, Inc., **16** 373
Inmobiliaria e Inversiones Aconcagua S.A.,
  71 143
Inmos Ltd., **11** 307; **29** 323
Inmotel Inversiones, **71** 338
InnCOGEN Limited, **35** 480
The Inner-Tec Group, **64** 198
InnerCity Foods Joint Venture Company,
  16 97
Inno-BM, **26** 158, 161
Inno-France *see* Societe des Grandes
  Entreprises de Distribution,
  Inno-France.
Innova International Corporation, **26** 333
Innovacom, **25** 96
Innovation, **26** 158
Innovative Marketing Systems *see*
  Bloomberg L.P.
Innovative Pork Concepts, **7** 82
Innovative Products & Peripherals
  Corporation, **14** 379
Innovative Software Inc., **10** 362
Innovative Sports Systems, Inc., **15** 396
Innovative Valve Technologies Inc., **33**
  167
Innovex Ltd. *see* Quintiles Transnational
  Corporation.
Inovoject do Brasil Ltda., **72** 108
Inpaco, **16** 340
Inpacsa, **19** 226
Inprise/Borland Corporation, **33** 115; **76**
  123–24
Input/Output, Inc., **73** 184–87
INS *see* International News Service.
Insa, **55** 189
Insalaco Markets Inc., **13** 394
Inserra Supermarkets, **25** 234–36
Insight Enterprises, Inc., **18** 259–61
Insight Marques SARL IMS SA, **48** 224
Insignia Financial Group, Inc. *see* CB
  Richard Ellis Group, Inc.
Insilco Corporation, **16** 281–83
Insley Manufacturing Co., **8** 545
Inso Corporation, **26** 215–19; **36** 273
Inspiration Resources Corporation, **12**
  260; **13** 502–03
Inspirations PLC, **22** 129
Insta-Care Holdings Inc., **16** 59
Insta-Care Pharmacy Services, **9** 186
Instant Auto Insurance, **33** 3, 5
Instant Interiors Corporation, **26** 102
Instapak Corporation, **14** 429
Instinet Corporation, **34** 225–27; **48**
  227–28
Institute de Development Industriel, **19**
  87
Institute for Professional Development, **24**
  40
Institute for Scientific Information, **8** 525,
  528
Institution Food House *see* Alex Lee Inc.
Institutional Financing Services, **23** 491
Instituto Bancario San Paolo di Torino, **50**
  407

Instituto Nacional de Industria, **I**
  459–61
Instromet International, **22** 65
Instrument Systems Corp. *see* Griffon
  Corporation.
Instrumentarium Corp., **13** 328; **25** 82;
  71 349
Instrumentation Laboratory Inc., **III**
  511–12; **22** 75
Instrumentation Scientifique de
  Laboratoire, S.A., **15** 404; **50** 394
Insul 8 Corporation, **76** 139
Insurance Auto Auctions, Inc., **23**
  285–87
Insurance Company of North America *see*
  CIGNA Corporation.
Insurance Company of the Southeast,
  Ltd., **56** 165
Insurance Partners L.P., **15** 257
InsurMark, **72** 149
InSync Communications, **42** 425
Intabex Holdings Worldwide, S.A., **27**
  126
Intalco Aluminum Corp., **12** 254
Intamin, **17** 443
Intarsia Corp., **38** 187
Intat Precision Inc., **48** 5
Integra-A Hotel and Restaurant Company,
  13 473
Integral Corporation, **14** 381; **23** 446; **33**
  331
Integrated Business Information Services,
  13 5
Integrated Computer Systems *see* Learning
  Tree International Inc.
Integrated Defense Technologies,
Integrated Defense Technologies, Inc.,
  44 423; **54** 178–80
Integrated Genetics, **8** 210; **13** 239; **38**
  204, 206
Integrated Health Services, Inc., **11** 282
Integrated Medical Systems Inc., **12** 333;
  47 236
Integrated Resources, Inc., **11** 483; **16** 54;
  19 393
Integrated Silicon Solutions, Inc., **18** 20;
  43 17; **47** 384
Integrated Software Systems Corporation,
  11 469
Integrated Systems Engineering, Inc., **51**
  382
Integrated Systems Operations *see* Xerox
  Corporation.
Integrated Systems Solutions Corp., **9**
  284; **11** 395; **17** 264
Integrated Telecom Technologies, **14** 417
Integris Europe, **49** 382, 384
Integrity Inc., **44** 241–43
Integrity Life Insurance, **III** 249
Intel Corporation, **II** 44–46; **10** 365–67
  (upd.); **36** 284–88 (upd.); **75**
  196–201 (upd.)
Intelcom Support Services, Inc., **14** 334
Intelicom Solutions Corp., **6** 229
Intelig, **57** 67, 69
IntelliCorp, Inc., **9** 310; **31** 298; **45**
  205–07

Intelligent Electronics, Inc., **6** 243–45;
  12 184; **13** 176, 277
Intelligent Interactions Corp., **49** 421
Intelligent Software Ltd., **26** 275
Intelligraphics Inc., **33** 44
Intellimetrics Instrument Corporation, **16**
  93
Intellisys, **48** 257
Inter American Aviation, Inc. *see* SkyWest,
  Inc.
Inter-American Satellite Television
  Network, **7** 391
Inter-City Gas Ltd., **19** 159
Inter-City Products Corporation, **52** 399
Inter-City Wholesale Electric Inc., **15** 385
Inter-Comm Telephone, Inc., **8** 310
Inter-Continental Hotels and Resorts, **38**
  77
Inter-Europa Bank in Hungary, **50** 410
Inter-Island Airways, Ltd., **22** 251; **24** 20
Inter-Island Steam Navigation Co. *see*
  Hawaiian Airlines.
Inter Island Telephone *see* Pacific Telecom,
  Inc.
Inter Link Foods PLC, **61** 132–34
Inter-Ocean Corporation, **16** 103; **44** 90
Inter Parfums Inc., **35** 235–38
Inter-Regional Financial Group, Inc., **15**
  231–33 *see also* Dain Rauscher
  Corporation.
Inter Techniek, **16** 421
Inter-Urban, Inc., **74** 370
Interactive Computer Design, Inc., **23**
  489, 491
InterActive Corporation, **71** 136–37
Interactive Media CCSP AG, **61** 350
Interactive Search Holding *see* Ask Jeeves,
  Inc.
Interactive Systems, **7** 500
InterAd Holdings Ltd., **49** 422
Interamericana de Talleras SA de CV, **10**
  415
Interbake Foods, **II** 631
InterBold, **7** 146; **11** 151
Interbrand Corporation, **70** 131–33
Interbrás, **IV** 503
Interbrew S.A., **17** 256–58; **50** 274–79
  (upd.)
Interceramic *see* Internacional de
  Ceramica, S.A. de C.V.
Interchemical Corp., **13** 460
Intercity Food Services, Inc., **II** 663
Interco Incorporated, **III** 528–31 *see also*
  Furniture Brands International, Inc.
Intercontessa AG, **35** 401; **36** 294
Intercontinental Apparel, **8** 249
Intercontinental Electronics Corp. *see* IEC
  Electronics Corp.
Intercontinental Mortgage Company, **8**
  436
Intercontinentale, **III** 404
Intercord, **22** 194
Intercorp Excelle Foods Inc., **64**
  199–201
Intercostal Steel Corp., **13** 97
Interdesign, **16** 421
**InterDigital Communications
  Corporation**, **61** 135–37

Manufacturers Hanover Corporation, II 312–14 *see also* Chemical Bank.

Manufacturers National Bank of Detroit, 40 116

Manufacturing Management Inc., 19 381

Manutan International S.A., 72 219–21

Manville Corporation, III 706–09; 7 291–95 (upd.) *see also* Johns Manville Corporation.

Manweb plc, 19 389–90; 49 363–64

Maola Milk and Ice Cream *see* Maryland & Virginia Milk Producers Cooperative Association, Inc.

MAP *see* Marathon Ashland Petroleum LLC.

MAPCO Inc., IV 458–59; 26 234; 31 469, 471

Mapelli Brothers Food Distribution Co., 13 350

MAPICS, Inc., 55 256–58

Maple Grove Farms of Vermont, Inc., 40 51–52

Maple Leaf Foods Inc., 41 249–53

Maple Leaf Mills, 41 252

Maple Leaf Sports & Entertainment Ltd., 61 188–90

MAPP *see* Mid-Continent Area Power Planner.

Mapra Industria e Comercio Ltda., 32 40

MAR Associates, 48 54

Mar-O-Bar Company, 7 299

Marantha! Music, 14 499

Marantz Co., 14 118

Marathon Ashland Petroleum LLC, 49 329–30; 50 49

Marathon Insurance Co., 26 486

Marathon Oil Co., 13 458; 49 328, 330 *see also* United States Steel Corp.

Marauder Company, 26 433

Marblehead Communications, Inc., 23 101

Marbodal, 12 464

Marboro Books, Inc., 10 136

Marbro Lamp Co., III 571; 20 362

Marc's Big Boy *see* The Marcus Corporation.

Marcade Group *see* Aris Industries, Inc.

Marcam Coporation *see* MAPICS, Inc.

Marceau Investments, II 356

March-Davis Bicycle Company, 19 383

March of Dimes, 31 322–25

March Plasma Systems, Inc., 48 299

Marchand, 13 27

Marchands Ro-Na Inc. *see* RONA, Inc.

Marchesi Antinori SRL, 42 245–48

Marchex, Inc., 72 222–24

marchFIRST, Inc., 34 261–64

Marchland Holdings Ltd., II 649

Marchon Eyewear, 22 123

Marciano Investments, Inc., 24 157

Marcillat, 19 49

Marco Acquisition Corporation, 62 268

Marco Business Products, Inc., 75 244–46

Marcolin S.p.A., 61 191–94; 62 100

Marcon Coating, Inc., 22 347

Marconi plc, 33 286–90 (upd.)

Marcopolo S.A., 79 247–250

The Marcus Corporation, 21 359–63

Marcy Fitness Products, Inc., 19 142, 144

Maremont Corporation, 8 39–40

Margarete Steiff GmbH, 23 334–37

Marge Carson, Inc., III 571; 20 362

Margo's La Mode, 10 281–82; 45 15

Marian LLC *see* Charisma Brands LLC.

Marico Acquisition Corporation, 8 448, 450

Marie Brizard & Roger International S.A., 22 342–44

Marie Callender's Restaurant & Bakery, Inc., 13 66; 28 257–59

Marina Mortgage Company, 46 25

Marine Bank and Trust Co., 11 105

Marine Computer Systems, 6 242

Marine Harvest, 13 103; 56 257

Marine Manufacturing Corporation, 52 406

Marine Midland Corp., 9 475–76; 11 108; 17 325

Marine Products Corporation, 75 247–49

Marine Transport Lines, Inc., 59 323

Marine United Inc., 42 361

Marinela, 19 192–93

MarineMax, Inc., 30 303–05; 37 396

Marinette Marine Corporation, 59 274, 278

Marion Brick, 14 249

Marion Foods, Inc., 17 434; 60 268

Marion Laboratories Inc., I 648–49

Marion Manufacturing, 9 72

Marion Merrell Dow, Inc., 9 328–29 (upd.)

Marionet Corp., IV 680–81

Marionnaud Parfumeries SA, 51 233–35; 54 265–66

Marisa Christina, Inc., 15 290–92

Maritime Electric Company, Limited, 15 182; 47 136–37

Maritz Inc., 38 302–05

Mark Controls Corporation, 30 157

Mark Cross, Inc., 17 4–5

Mark Goldston, 8 305

Mark IV Industries, Inc., 7 296–98; 28 260–64 (upd.)

The Mark Travel Corporation, 80 232–235

Mark Trouser, Inc., 17 338

Mark's Work Wearhouse Ltd. *see* Canadian Tire Corporation, Limited.

Markborough Properties, V 81; 8 525; 25 221

Market Development Corporation *see* Spartan Stores Inc.

Market Growth Resources, 23 480

Market National Bank, 13 465

Marketing Data Systems, Inc., 18 24

Marketing Equities International, 26 136

MarketSpan Corp. *see* KeySpan Energy Co.

Märklin Holding GmbH, 70 163–66

Marks and Spencer p.l.c., V 124–26; 24 313–17 (upd.)

Marks-Baer Inc., 11 64

Marks Brothers Jewelers, Inc., 24 318–20

Marlene Industries Corp., 16 36–37

Marley Co., 19 360

Marley Holdings, L.P., 19 246

Oy Marli Ab, 56 103

Marman Products Company, 16 8

The Marmon Group, Inc., IV 135–38; 16 354–57 (upd.); 70 167–72 (upd.)

The Marmon Group,

Marmon-Perry Light Company, 6 508

Marolf Dakota Farms, Inc., 18 14–15

Marotte, 21 438

Marpac Industries Inc. *see* PVC Container Corporation.

Marquam Commercial Brokerage Company, 21 257

Marquette Electronics, Inc., 13 326–28

Marquis Who's Who, 17 398

Marr S.p.A., 57 82–84

Marriner Group, 13 175

Marriot Inc., 29 442

Marriot Management Services, 29 444

Marriott International, Inc., III 102–03; 21 364–67 (upd.)

Mars, Incorporated, 7 299–301; 22 298, 528; 40 302–05 (upd.)

Marsh & McLennan Companies, Inc., III 282–84; 45 263–67 (upd.)

Marsh Supermarkets, Inc., 17 300–02; 76 255–58 (upd.)

Marshall & Ilsley Corporation, 56 217–20

Marshall Amplification plc, 62 239–42

Marshall Die Casting, 13 225

Marshall Field's, 8 33; 9 213; 12 283; 15 86; 18 488; 22 72; 50 117, 119; 61 394, 396; 63 242, 244, 254–63 *see also* Target Corporation.

Marshall Industries, 19 311

Marshalls Incorporated, 13 329–31; 14 62

Marship Tankers (Holdings) Ltd., 52 329

Marstellar, 13 204

Marstons, 57 412–13

The Mart, 9 120

Martank Shipping Holdings Ltd., 52 329

Martek Biosciences Corporation, 65 218–20

Marten Transport, 27 404

Martha Lane Adams, 27 428

Martha Stewart Living Omnimedia, Inc., 24 321–23; 73 219–22 (upd.)

Martin & Pagenstecher GMBH, 24 208

Martin-Baker Aircraft Company Limited, 61 195–97

Martin Band Instrument Company, 55 149, 151

Martin Bros. Tobacco Co., 14 19

Martin Collet, 19 50

Martin Dunitz, 44 416

Martin Franchises, Inc., 80 236–239

Martin Gillet Co., 55 96, 98

Martin Guitar Company *see* C.F. Martin & Co., Inc.

Martin Hilti Foundation, 53 167

Martin Industries, Inc., 44 274–77

Martin Marietta Corporation, I 67–69 *see also* Lockheed Martin Corporation.

Martin Mathys, 8 456

Merchants Bank & Trust Co., **21** 524

Merchants Distributors Inc. *see* Alex Lee Inc.

Merchants Home Delivery Service, **6** 414

Merchants National Bank, **9** 228; **14** 528; **17** 135

Mercian Corporation, 77 261–264

Merck & Co., Inc., I 650–52; 11 289–91 (upd.); 34 280–85 (upd.)

Mercury Air Group, Inc., 20 371–73

Mercury Asset Management (MAM), **14** 420; **40** 313

Mercury Communications, Ltd., 7 332–34

Mercury Drug Corporation, 70 181–83

Mercury General Corporation, 25 323–25

Mercury, Inc., **8** 311

Mercury Interactive Corporation, 59 293–95

Mercury International Ltd., **51** 130

Mercury Mail, Inc., **22** 519, 522

Mercury Marine Group, 68 247–51

Mercury Records, **13** 397; **23** 389, 391

Mercury Telecommunications Limited, **15** 67, 69

Mercy Air Service, Inc., **53** 29

Meredith Corporation, 11 292–94; 23 393; 29 316–19 (upd.); 74 189–93 (upd.)

Merfin International, **42** 53

Merial, **34** 284

Meriam Instrument *see* Scott Fetzer.

Merico, Inc., **36** 161–64

Merida, **50** 445, 447

Meridian Bancorp, Inc., 11 295–97

Meridian Emerging Markets Ltd., **25** 509

Meridian Gold, Incorporated, 47 238–40

Meridian Healthcare Ltd., **18** 197; **59** 168

Meridian Industrial Trust Inc., **57** 301

Meridian Investment and Development Corp., **22** 189

Meridian Oil Inc., **10** 190–91

Meridian Publishing, Inc., **28** 254

Merillat Industries, LLC, 13 338–39; 69 253–55 (upd.)

Merisant Worldwide, Inc., 70 184–86

Merisel, Inc., 12 334–36

Merit Distribution Services, **13** 333

Merit Medical Systems, Inc., 29 320–22; 36 497

Merit Tank Testing, Inc., **IV** 411

Merita/Cotton's Bakeries, **38** 251

Meritage Corporation, 26 289–92; 62 327

MeritaNordbanken, **40** 336

Meritor Automotive Inc. *see* ArvinMeritor Inc.

Merix Corporation, 36 329–31; 75 257–60 (upd.)

Merkur Direktwerbegesellschaft, **29** 152

Merlin Gérin, **19** 165

Merpati Nusantara Airlines *see* Garuda Indonesia.

Merrell, **22** 173

Merrell Dow, **16** 438

Merriam-Webster Inc., 70 187–91

Merrill Corporation, 18 331–34; 47 241–44 (upd.)

Merrill Gas Company, **9** 554

Merrill Lynch & Co., Inc., II 424–26; 13 340–43 (upd.); 40 310–15 (upd.)

Merrill Lynch Capital Partners, **47** 363

Merrill Lynch Investment Managers *see* BlackRock, Inc.

Merrill, Pickard, Anderson & Eyre IV, **11** 490

Merrill Publishing, **IV** 643; **7** 312; **9** 63; **29** 57

Merrimack Services Corp., **37** 303

Merry-Go-Round Enterprises, Inc., 8 362–64; 24 27

Merry Group *see* Boral Limited.

Merry Maids *see* ServiceMaster Inc.

Merryhill Schools, Inc., **37** 279

The Mersey Docks and Harbour Company, 30 318–20

Mervyn's California, 10 409–10; 39 269–71 (upd.) *see also* Target Corporation.

Merz + Co., **52** 135

Mesa Air Group, Inc., 11 298–300; 32 334–37 (upd.); 77 265–270 (upd.)

Mesa Petroleum, **11** 441; **27** 217

Mesaba Holdings, Inc., 28 265–67

Messerschmitt-Bölkow-Blohm GmbH., I 73–75

Messner, Vetere, Berger, Carey, Schmetterer, **13** 204

Mesta Machine Co., **22** 415

Mestek, Inc., 10 411–13

Met Food Corp. *see* White Rose Food Corp.

Met-Mex Penoles *see* Industrias Penoles, S.A. de C.V.

META Group, Inc., **37** 147

Metaframe Corp., **25** 312

Metal Box plc, I 604–06 *see also* Novar plc.

Metal-Cal *see* Avery Dennison Corporation.

Metal Casting Technology, Inc., **23** 267, 269

Metal Office Furniture Company, **7** 493

AB Metal Pty Ltd, **62** 331

Metalcorp Ltd, **62** 331

Metales y Contactos, **29** 461–62

Metaleurop S.A., 21 368–71

MetalExchange, **26** 530

Metall Mining Corp., **27** 456

Metallgesellschaft AG, IV 139–42; 16 361–66 (upd.)

MetalOptics Inc., **19** 212

Metalúrgica Gerdau *see* Gerdau S.A.

Metalurgica Mexicana Penoles, S.A. *see* Industrias Penoles, S.A. de C.V.

Metaphase Technology, Inc., **10** 257

Metatec International, Inc., 47 245–48

Metcalf & Eddy Companies, Inc., **6** 441; **32** 52

Metcash Trading Ltd., 58 226–28

Meteor Film Productions, **23** 391

Meteor Industries Inc., 33 295–97

Methane Development Corporation, **6** 457

Methanex Corporation, 12 365; 19 155–56; 40 316–19

Methode Electronics, Inc., 13 344–46

MetLife *see* Metropolitan Life Insurance Company.

MetMor Financial, Inc., **III** 293; **52** 239–40

Meto AG, **39** 79

MetPath, Inc., **III** 684; **26** 390

Metra Corporation *see* Wärtsilä Corporation.

Metra Steel, **19** 381

Metragaz, **69** 191

Metrastock Ltd., **34** 5

Metric Constructors, Inc., **16** 286

Metric Systems Corporation, **18** 513; **44** 420

Metris Companies Inc., 56 224–27

Metro AG, 23 311; **50 335–39**

Metro Distributors Inc., **14** 545

Metro-Goldwyn-Mayer Inc., 25 326–30 (upd.)

Metro Holding AG, **38** 266

Métro Inc., 77 271–275

Metro Information Services, Inc., 36 332–34

Metro International SA, **36** 335

Metro-Mark Integrated Systems Inc., **11** 469

Metro-North Commuter Railroad Company, **35** 292

Metro Pacific, **18** 180, 182

Metro-Richelieu Inc., **II** 653

Metro Southwest Construction *see* CRSS Inc.

Metro Support Services, Inc., **48** 171

Metrocall, Inc., 18 77; **39** 25; **41 265–68**

Metrol Security Services, Inc., **32** 373

Metroland Printing, Publishing and Distributing Ltd., **29** 471

Metromail Corp., **IV** 661; **18** 170; **38** 370

Metromedia Companies, 7 91, **335–37; 14 298–300**

Metromedia Company, 61 210–14 (upd.)

Metronic AG, **64** 226

Metroplex, LLC, **51** 206

Métropole Télévision S.A., 76 272–74 (upd.)

Metropolis Intercom, **67** 137–38

Metropolitan Baseball Club Inc., 39 272–75

Metropolitan Broadcasting Corporation, **7** 335

Metropolitan Clothing Co., **19** 362

Metropolitan Distributors, **9** 283

Metropolitan Edison Company, **27** 182

Metropolitan Financial Corporation, 12 165; **13 347–49**

Metropolitan Furniture Leasing, **14** 4

Metropolitan Life Insurance Company, III 290–94; 52 235–41 (upd.)

The Metropolitan Museum of Art, 55 267–70

Metropolitan Opera Association, Inc., 40 320–23

Metropolitan Reference Laboratories Inc., **26** 391

Metropolitan Tobacco Co., **15** 138

Metropolitan Transportation Authority, **35** 290–92

MetroRed, **57** 67, 69

Metrostar Management, **59** 199

METSA, Inc., **15** 363

Metsä-Serla Oy, **IV** 314–16 *see also* M-real Oyj.

Metsec plc, **57** 402

Metso Corporation, **30** 321–25 (upd.)

Mettler-Toledo International Inc., **30** 326–28

Mettler United States Inc., **9** 441

Metwest, **26** 391

Metz Baking Company, **36** 164

Metzdorf Advertising Agency, **30** 80

Metzeler Kautschuk, **15** 354

Mexican Metal Co. *see* Industrias Penoles, S.A. de C.V.

Mexican Restaurants, Inc., **41** 269–71

Meyer Brothers Drug Company, **16** 212

Meyer Corporation, **27** 288

Meyerland Company, **19** 366

Meyers Motor Supply, **26** 347

Meyers Parking, **18** 104

The Meyne Company, **55** 74

Meyr Melnhof Karton AG, **41** 325–27

M4 Data (Holdings) Ltd., **62** 293

M40 Trains Ltd., **51** 173

MFS Communications Company, Inc., **11** 301–03; **14** 253; **27** 301, 307

MG&E *see* Madison Gas & Electric.

MG Holdings *see* Mayflower Group Inc.

MG Ltd., **IV** 141

MGD Graphics Systems *see* Goss Holdings, Inc.

MGIC Investment Corp., **45** 320; **52** 242–44

MGM *see* McKesson General Medical.

MGM Grand Inc., **17** 316–19

MGM Mirage *see* Mirage Resorts, Incorporated.

MGM Studios, **50** 125

MGM/UA Communications Company, **II** 146–50 *see also* Metro-Goldwyn-Mayer Inc.

MGN *see* Mirror Group Newspapers Ltd.

MGT Services Inc. *see* The Midland Company.

MH Alshaya Group, **28** 96

MH Media Monitoring Limited, **26** 270

MHI Group, Inc., **13** 356; **16** 344

MHS Holding Corp., **26** 101

MHT *see* Manufacturers Hanover Trust Co.

MI *see* Masco Corporation.

MI S.A., **66** 244

Mi-Tech Steel Inc., **63** 359–60

Miami Computer Supply Corporation *see* MCSi, Inc.

Miami Power Corporation *see* Cincinnati Gas & Electric Company.

Miami Subs Corp., **29** 342, 344

Micamold Electronics Manufacturing Corporation, **10** 319

Mich-Wis *see* Michigan Wisconsin Pipe Line.

Michael Anthony Jewelers, Inc., **24** 334–36

Michael Baker Corporation, **14** 333–35; **51** 245–48 (upd.)

MICHAEL Business Systems Plc, **10** 257

Michael C. Fina Co., Inc., **52** 245–47

Michael Foods, Inc., **25** 331–34

Michael Joseph, **IV** 659

Michael Page International plc, **45** 272–74; **52** 317–18

Michael's Fair-Mart Food Stores, Inc., **19** 479

Michaels Stores, Inc., **17** 320–22; **71** 226–30 (upd.)

MichCon *see* MCN Corporation.

Michelin *see* Compagnie Générale des Établissements Michelin.

Michie Co., **33** 264–65

Michigan Automotive Compressor, Inc., **III** 638–39

Michigan Automotive Research Corporation, **23** 183

Michigan Bell Telephone Co., **14** 336–38; **18** 30

Michigan Carpet Sweeper Company, **9** 70

Michigan Consolidated Gas Company *see* MCN Corporation.

Michigan International Speedway *see* Penske Corporation.

Michigan Livestock Exchange, **36** 442

Michigan Motor Freight Lines, **14** 567

Michigan National Corporation, **11** 304–06; **18** 517

Michigan Oil Company, **18** 494

Michigan Packaging Company *see* Greif Inc.

Michigan Seamless Tube Company *see* Quanex Corporation.

Michigan Shoe Makers *see* Wolverine World Wide Inc.

Michigan Sporting Goods Distributors, Inc., **72** 228–30

Michigan Spring Company, **17** 106

Michigan Steel Corporation, **12** 352

Michigan Tag Company, **9** 72

Michigan Wisconsin Pipe Line, **39** 260

Mick's Inc., **30** 329

Mickey Shorr Mobile Electronics, **10** 9–11

Micrel, Incorporated, **77** 276–279

Micro Contract Manufacturing Inc., **44** 441

Micro-Controle, **71** 248

Micro D, Inc., **11** 194

Micro Decisionware, Inc., **10** 506

Micro Focus Inc., **27** 491

Micro Magic, Inc., **43** 254

Micro Metallics Corporation, **64** 297

Micro Peripherals, Inc., **18** 138

Micro Power Systems Inc., **14** 183

Micro Switch, **14** 284

Micro/Vest, **13** 175

Micro Warehouse, Inc., **16** 371–73

MicroAge, Inc., **16** 367–70; **29** 414

Microamerica, **12** 334

Microban Products Company, **27** 288

MicroBilt Corporation, **11** 112

Microcar SA, **55** 54, 56

MicroClean Inc., **50** 49

Microcom, Inc., **26** 93; **50** 227

Microcomputer Asset Management Services, **9** 168

Microcomputer Systems, **22** 389

Microdot Inc., **8** 365–68, 545

Microfral, **14** 216

MicroFridge, **44** 273

Micromass Ltd., **43** 455

Micromedex, **19** 268

Micron Technology, Inc., **11** 307–09; **29** 323–26 (upd.)

Micropolis Corp., **10** 403, 458, 463

MicroPro International Corp. *see* The Learning Company Inc.

Microprocessor Systems, **13** 235

Microprose Inc., **24** 538

Micros Systems, Inc., **18** 335–38

Microsensor Systems Inc., **43** 366

Microsoft Corporation, **6** 257–60; **27** 319–23 (upd.); **63** 64, 293–97 (upd.); **64** 78

Microtek, Inc., **22** 413

MicroUnity Systems Engineering Inc., **50** 53

Microware Surgical Instruments Corp., **IV** 137

Microwave Communications, Inc. *see* MCI Telecom.

Mid-America Capital Resources, Inc., **6** 508

Mid-America Dairymen, Inc., **7** 338–40; **11** 24; **22** 95; **26** 448

Mid-America Interpool Network, **6** 602

Mid-America Packaging, Inc., **8** 203

Mid-America Tag & Label, **8** 360

Mid Bus Inc., **33** 107

Mid-Central Fish and Frozen Foods Inc., **II** 675

Mid-Continent Computer Services, **11** 111

Mid-Continent Life Insurance Co., **23** 200

Mid-Continent Telephone Corporation *see* Alltel Corporation.

Mid-Georgia Gas Company, **6** 448

Mid-Illinois Gas Co., **6** 529

Mid-Michigan Music Co., **60** 84

Mid-Pacific Airlines, **9** 271; **24** 21–22

Mid-Packaging Group Inc., **19** 78

Mid-South Towing, **6** 583

Mid-States Development, Inc., **18** 405

Mid-Valley Dairy, **14** 397

MidAmerican Communications Corporation, **8** 311

Midas Inc., **56** 228–31 (upd.)

Midas International Corporation, **10** 414–15

MIDCO, **III** 340

Middle East Airlines - Air Liban S.A.L., **79** 251–254

Middle East Broadcasting Centre, Ltd., **25** 506, 508

Middle East Tube Co. Ltd., **25** 266

Middle South Utilities *see* Entergy Corporation.

Nevada Natural Gas Pipe Line Co., **19** 411

Nevada Power Company, 11 342–44; **12** 265

Nevada Savings and Loan Association, **19** 412

Nevada Southern Gas Company, **19** 411

Nevada State Bank, **53** 378

Neversink Dyeing Company, **9** 153

Nevex Software Technologies, **42** 24, 26

New Access Communications, **43** 252

New America Publishing Inc., **10** 288

New Asahi Co., **I** 221

New Balance Athletic Shoe, Inc., 25 350–52; **68** 267–70 (upd.)

New Bauhinia Limited, **53** 333

New Bedford Gas & Edison Light Co., **14** 124–25

New Belgium Brewing Company, Inc., 68 271–74

New Brunswick Scientific Co., Inc., 45 285–87

New Century Energies, **73** 384

New Century Equity Holdings Corporation, **72** 39

New Century Network, **13** 180; **19** 204, 285

New City Releasing, Inc., **25** 269

New CORT Holdings Corporation *see* CORT Business Services Corporation.

New Daido Steel Co., Ltd., **IV** 62–63

New Dana Perfumes Company, 37 269–71

New Departure, **9** 17

New Dimension Software, Inc., **55** 67

New England Audio Company, Inc. *see* Tweeter Home Entertainment Group, Inc.

New England Business Service, Inc., 18 361–64; **78** 237–242 (upd.)

New England Confectionery Co., 15 323–25

New England CRInc, **8** 562

New England Electric System, V 662–64 *see also* National Grid USA.

New England Gas & Electric Association, **14** 124–25

New England Life Insurance Co., **III** 261

New England Motor Freight, Inc., **53** 250

New England Mutual Life Insurance Co., III 312–14

New England Network, Inc., **12** 31

New England Paper Tube Co., **54** 58

New England Power Association *see* National Grid USA.

New Flyer Industries Inc., 78 243–246

New Found Industries, Inc., **9** 465

New Galveston Company, Inc., **25** 116

New Hampshire Gas & Electric Co., **14** 124

New Hampton Goldfields Ltd., **63** 182, 184

New Hampton, Inc., **27** 429

New Haven District Telephone Company *see* Southern New England Telecommunications Corporation.

New Haven Electric Co., **21** 512

New Holland N.V., 22 379–81 *see also* CNH Global N.V.

New Horizon Manufactured Homes, Ltd., **17** 83

New Hotel Showboat, Inc. *see* Showboat, Inc.

New Impriver NV *see* Punch International N.V.

New Jersey Bell, **9** 321

New Jersey Educational Music Company *see* National Educational Music Co. Ltd.

New Jersey Resources Corporation, 54 259–61

New Jersey Shale, **14** 250

New Jersey Tobacco Co., **15** 138

New Laoshan Brewery, **49** 418

New Line Cinema, Inc., 47 271–74; **57** 35

New London City National Bank, **13** 467

New Look Group plc, 35 308–10

New Market Development Company *see* Cousins Properties Inc.

New Materials Ltd., **48** 344

New Mather Metals, **III** 582

New Mitsui Bussan, **III** 296

New Orleans Canal and Banking Company, **11** 105

New Orleans Saints LP, 58 255–57

The New Piper Aircraft, Inc., 44 307–10

New Plan Realty Trust, 11 345–47

New Process Company, **25** 76–77

New Seasons Market, 75 272–74

New South Wales Health System, **16** 94

New Street Capital Inc., 8 388–90 **(upd.)** *see also* Drexel Burnham Lambert Incorporated.

New Sulzer Diesel, **III** 633

New Times, Inc., 45 288–90

New Toyo Group, **19** 227

New Trading Company *see* SBC Warburg.

New UPI Inc., **25** 507

New Valley Corporation, 17 345–47

New Vanden Borre, **24** 266–70

New Ventures Realty Corporation, **58** 272

New World Coffee-Manhattan Bagel, Inc., **32** 15

New World Communications Group, **22** 442; **28** 248

New World Development Company Limited, IV 717–19; **38** 318–22 **(upd.)**

New World Entertainment, **17** 149

New World Hotel (Holdings) Ltd., **13** 66

New World Pasta Company, 53 241–44

New World Restaurant Group, Inc., 44 311–14

New York Air, **I** 103, 118, 129

New York Capital Bank, **41** 312

New York Central Railroad Company, **9** 228; **10** 43–44, 71–73; **17** 496

New York City Health and Hospitals Corporation, 60 214–17

New York City Off-Track Betting Corporation, 51 267–70

New York City Transit Authority, **8** 75

New York Community Bancorp, Inc., 78 247–250

New York Daily News, 32 357–60

New York Electric Corporation *see* New York State Electric and Gas.

New York Envelope Co., **32** 346

New York Evening Enquirer, **10** 287

New York Eye and Ear Infirmary *see* Continuum Health Partners, Inc.

New York Fabrics and Crafts, **16** 197

New York Gas Light Company *see* Consolidated Edison Company of New York.

New York Health Care, Inc., 72 237–39

New York Life Insurance Company, III 315–17; **45** 291–95 **(upd.)**; **63** 14

New York Magazine Co., **12** 359

New York Marine and Gotham Insurance, **41** 284

New York Philharmonic *see* Philharmonic-Symphony Society of New York, Inc.

New York Presbyterian Hospital *see* NewYork-Presbyterian Hospital.

New York Quotation Company, **9** 370

New York Restaurant Group, Inc., 32 361–63

New York Sports Clubs *see* Town Sports International, Inc.

New York State Electric and Gas Corporation, 6 534–36

New York Stock Exchange, Inc., 9 369–72; **10** 416–17; **34** 254; **39** 296–300 **(upd.)**; **54** 242

New York Telephone Co., **9** 321

The New York Times Company, IV 647–49; **19** 283–85 **(upd.)**; **61** 239–43 **(upd.)**

New York Zoological Society *see* Wildlife Conservation Society.

New York's Bankers Trust Co., *see* Bankers Trust Co.

New Zealand Aluminum Smelters, *see* Rio Tinto.

New Zealand Countrywide Banking Corporation, **10** 336

Newa Insurance Co. Ltd., **64** 280

Neways, Inc., 78 251–254

Newark Electronics Co., **9** 420

Newbridge & Gilbert, **56** 285

Newco Waste Systems *see* Browning-Ferris Industries, Inc.

Newcor, Inc., 40 332–35

Newcrest Mining Ltd., **IV** 47; **22** 107

Newell Rubbermaid Inc., emphasis n="2">9 373–76; **52** 261–71 **(upd.)**; **53** 37, 40; **62** 231

Newfield Exploration Company, 65 260–62

Newfoundland Brewery, **26** 304

Newfoundland Energy, Ltd., **17** 121

Newfoundland Light & Power Co. *see* Fortis, Inc.

Newfoundland Processing Ltd. *see* Newfoundland Energy, Ltd.

Newhall Land and Farming Company, 14 348–50

Newly Weds Foods, Inc., 74 201–03

Norrell Corporation, 25 356–59
Norris Cylinder Company, 11 535
Norris Grain Co., 14 537
Norris Oil Company, 47 52
Norshield Corp., 51 81
Norsk Aller A/S, 72 62
Norsk Helikopter AS *see* Bristow
 Helicopters Ltd.
Norsk Hydro ASA, 10 437–40; 35
 315–19 (upd.)
Norsk Rengjorings Selskap a.s., 49 221
Norske Skog do Brasil Ltda., 73 205
Norske Skogindustrier ASA, 63 314–16
Norstan, Inc., 16 392–94
Norstar Bancorp, 9 229
Nortek, Inc., 14 482; 22 4; 26 101; 34
 308–12; 37 331
Nortel Inversora S.A., 63 375–77
Nortel Networks Corporation, 36
 349–54 (upd.); 50 130; 72 129–31
Nortex International, 7 96; 19 338
North African Petroleum Ltd., IV 455
North American Aviation, 7 520; 9 16;
 11 278, 427
North American Carbon, 19 499
North American Cellular Network, 9 322
North American Coal Corporation, 7
 369–71
North American Company, 6 552–53,
 601–02
North American Dräger, 13 328
North American Energy Conservation,
 Inc., 35 480
North American InTeleCom, Inc., IV 411
North American Light & Power
 Company, 12 541
North American Medical Management
 Company, Inc., 36 366
North American Mogul Products Co. *see*
 Mogul Corp.
North American Nutrition Companies
 Inc. (NANCO) *see* Provimi
North American Philips Corporation, 19
 393; 21 520
North American Plastics, Inc., 61 112
North American Printing Ink Company,
 13 228
North American Rockwell Corp., 10 173
North American Site Developers, Inc., 69
 197
North American Systems, 14 230
North American Training Corporation *see*
 Rollerblade, Inc.
North American Van Lines *see* Allied
 Worldwide, Inc.
North American Watch Company *see*
 Movado Group, Inc.
North Atlantic Energy Corporation, 21
 411
North Atlantic Laboratories, Inc., 62 391
North Atlantic Packing, 13 243
North Atlantic Trading Company Inc.,
 65 266–68
North British Rubber Company, 20 258
North Broken Hill Peko, IV 61
North Carolina Motor Speedway, Inc., 19
 294

North Carolina National Bank
 Corporation *see* NCNB Corporation.
North Carolina Natural Gas Corporation,
 6 578
North Carolina Shipbuilding Co., 13 373
North Central Financial Corp., 9 475
North Central Utilities, Inc., 18 405
North East Insurance Company, 44 356
North Eastern Bricks, 14 249
The North Face, Inc., 18 375–77; 78
 258–261 (upd.)
North Fork Bancorporation, Inc., 46
 314–17
North New York Savings Bank, 10 91
North of Scotland Hydro-Electric Board,
 19 389
North Pacific Group, Inc., 61 254–57
North Pacific Paper Corp., IV 298
North Ridge Securities Corporation, 72
 149–50
North Sea Ferries, 26 241, 243
North Sea Oil and Gas, 10 337
North Shore Gas Company, 6 543–44
North Shore Land Co., 17 357
North Star Communications Group Inc.,
 73 59
North Star Container, Inc., 59 290
North Star Egg Case Company, 12 376
North Star Marketing Cooperative, 7 338
North Star Mill, 12 376
North Star Steel Company, 13 138; 18
 378–81; 19 380; 40 87
North Star Transport Inc., 49 402
North Star Tubes, 54 391, 393
North Star Universal, Inc., 25 331, 333
North State Supply Company, 57 9
North Supply, 27 364
The North West Company, Inc., 12
 361–63
North-West Telecommunications *see*
 Pacific Telecom, Inc.
North West Water Group plc, 11
 359–62 *see also* United Utilities PLC.
Northbridge Financial Corp., 57 137
Northbrook Corporation, 24 32
Northbrook Holdings, Inc., 22 495
Northcliffe Newspapers, 19 118
Northeast Federal Corp., 13 468
Northeast Petroleum Industries, Inc., 11
 194; 14 461
Northeast Savings Bank, 12 31; 13
 467–68
Northeast Utilities, V 668–69; 13
 182–84; 21 408, 411; 48 303–06
 (upd.); 55 313, 316
Northeastern New York Medical Service,
 Inc., III 246
Northern Animal Hospital Inc., 58 355
Northern Arizona Light & Power Co., 6
 545
Northern California Savings, 10 340
Northern Dairies, 10 441
Northern Drug Company, 14 147
Northern Electric Company *see* Northern
 Telecom Limited.
Northern Energy Resources Company *see*
 NERCO, Inc.

Northern Engineering Industries Plc *see*
 Rolls-Royce Group PLC.
Northern Fibre Products Co., I 202
Northern Foods plc, 10 441–43; 61
 258–62 (upd.)
Northern Illinois Gas Co., 6 529–31
Northern Indiana Power Company, 6 556
Northern Indiana Public Service
 Company, 6 532–33
Northern Infrastructure Maintenance
 Company, 39 238
Northern Leisure, 40 296–98
Northern Light Electric Company, 18
 402–03
Northern National Bank, 14 90
Northern Natural Gas Co. *see* Enron
 Corporation.
Northern Pacific Corp., 15 274
Northern Pacific Railroad, 14 168; 26
 451
Northern Paper, I 614
Northern Pipeline Construction Co., 19
 410, 412
Northern Rock plc, 33 318–21
Northern Star Co., 25 332
Northern States Power Company, V
 670–72; 18 404; 20 391–95 (upd.) *see
 also* Xcel Energy Inc.
Northern Stores, Inc., 12 362
Northern Sugar Company, 11 13
Northern Telecom Limited, V 308–10
 see also Nortel Networks Corporation.
Northern Trust Company, 9 387–89
Northfield Metal Products, 11 256
Northgate Computer Corp., 17 196
Northland *see* Scott Fetzer Company.
Northland Cranberries, Inc., 38 332–34
Northland Publishing, 19 231
NorthPrint International, 22 356
Northrop Grumman Corporation, I
 76–77; 11 363–65 (upd.); 45 304–12
 (upd.)
NorthStar Computers, 10 313
Northwest Airlines Corporation, I
 112–14; 6 103–05 (upd.); 26 337–40
 (upd.); 74 204–08 (upd.)
Northwest Engineering Co. *see* Terex
 Corporation.
Northwest Express *see* Bear Creek
 Corporation.
Northwest Industries *see* Chicago and
 North Western Holdings Corporation.
Northwest Instruments, 8 519
Northwest Linen Co., 16 228
Northwest Natural Gas Company, 45
 313–15
Northwest Outdoor, 27 280
Northwest Paper Company, 8 430
Northwest Steel Rolling Mills Inc., 13 97
Northwest Telecommunications Inc., 6
 598
NorthWestern Corporation, 37 280–83
Northwestern Engraving, 12 25
Northwestern Financial Corporation, 11
 29
Northwestern Flavors LLC, 58 379
Northwestern Manufacturing Company, 8
 133

Richard R. Dostie, Inc. *see* Toll Brothers Inc.

Richards & O'Neil LLP, **43** 70

The Richards Group, Inc., 58 300–02

Richardson Company, **36** 147

Richardson Electronics, Ltd., 17 405–07

Richardson Industries, Inc., 62 298–301

Richardson-Vicks Company *see* The Procter & Gamble Company

Richardson's, **21** 246

Richfood Holdings, Inc., 7 450–51; **50** 458

Richland Co-op Creamery Company, **7** 592

Richland Gas Company, **8** 349

Richman Gordman Half Price Stores, Inc. *see* Gordmans, Inc.

Richmond American Homes of Florida, Inc., **11** 258

Richmond Carousel Corporation, **9** 120

Richmond Cedar Works Manufacturing Co., **12** 109; **19** 360

Richmond Corp., **15** 129

Richmond Paperboard Corp., **19** 78

Richmond Pulp and Paper Company, **17** 281

Richton International Corporation, 39 344–46

Richtree Inc., 63 328–30

Richway, **10** 515

Richwood Building Products, Inc., **12** 397

Richwood Sewell Coal Co., **17** 357

Rickards, Roloson & Company, **22** 427

Rickel Home Centers, **II** 673

Ricky Shaw's Oriental Express, **25** 181

Ricoh Company, Ltd., III 159–61; **36** 389–93 (upd.)

Ricola Ltd., 62 302–04

Ricolino, **19** 192

Riddarhyttan Resources AB *see* Agnico-Eagle Mines Limited.

Riddell Inc., **33** 467

Riddell Sports Inc., 22 457–59; **23** 449

Ridder Publications *see* Knight-Ridder, Inc.

Ride, Inc., 22 460–63

Ridge Tool Co., **II** 19

Ridgewell's Inc., **15** 87

Ridgewood Properties Inc., **12** 394

Ridgway Co., **23** 98

Ridgway Color, **13** 227–28

Ridley Corporation Ltd., 62 305–07

Riedel-de Haën AG, **22** 32; **36** 431

Rieke Corp., **III** 569; **11** 535; **20** 361

The Riese Organization, 38 385–88

Rieter Holding AG, 42 315–17

Riggin & Robbins, **13** 244

Riggs National Corporation, 13 438–40

Right Associates, **27** 21; **44** 156

Right Management Consultants, Inc., 42 318–21

Right Source, Inc., **24** 96

RightPoint, Inc., **49** 124

RightSide Up, Inc., **27** 21

Rijnhaave Information Systems, **25** 21

Rike's, **10** 282

Riken Corp., **10** 493

Riken Kagaku Co. Ltd., **48** 250

Riklis Family Corp., 9 447–50; **12** 87; **13** 453; **38** 169; **43** 355

Rinascente S.p.A., 71 308–10

Ring King Visibles, Inc., **13** 269

Ring Ltd., **43** 99

Ringier America, **19** 333

Ringköpkedjan, **II** 640

Ringling Bros., Barnum & Bailey Circus, **25** 312–13

Ringnes Bryggeri, **18** 396

Rini-Rego Supermarkets Inc., **13** 238

Rini Supermarkets, **9** 451; **13** 237

Rinker Group Ltd., 65 298–301

Rio de Janeiro Refrescos S.A., **71** 140

Rio Grande Industries, Inc., **12** 18–19

Rio Grande Servaas, S.A. de C.V., **23** 145

Rio Sportswear Inc., **42** 269

Rio Sul Airlines *see* Varig, SA.

Rio Tinto plc, IV 58–61, 189–91, 380; **19** 349–53 (upd.) **50** 380–85 (upd.)

Riocell S.A. *see* Klabin S.A.

Riordan Freeman & Spogli, **13** 406

Riordan Holdings Ltd., **10** 554; **67** 298

Ripley Entertainment, Inc., 74 273–76

Ripotot, **68** 143

Riser Foods, Inc., 9 451–54; **13** 237–38

Risk Management Partners Ltd., **35** 36

Risk Planners, **II** 669

Ritchie Bros. Auctioneers Inc., 41 331–34

Rite Aid Corporation, V 174–76; **19** 354–57 (upd.); **63** 331–37 (upd.)

Rite-Way Department Store, **II** 649

Riteway Distributor, **26** 183

Rittenhouse Financial Services, **22** 495

Ritter Co. *see* Sybron Corp.

Ritter Sport *see* Alfred Ritter GmbH & Co. KG.

Ritter's Frozen Custard *see* RFC Franchising LLC.

Ritz Camera Centers, 18 186; **34** 375–77

The Ritz-Carlton Hotel Company, L.L.C., 9 455–57; **29** 403–06 (upd.); **71** 311–16 (upd.)

Ritz Firma, **13** 512

Riunione Adriatica di Sicurtà SpA, III 345–48

Riva Group Plc, **53** 46

The Rival Company, 19 358–60

Rivarossi, **16** 337

Rivaud Group, **29** 370

River Boat Casino, **9** 425–26

River City Broadcasting, **25** 418

River Metals Recycling LLC, **76** 130

River North Studios *see* Platinum Entertainment, Inc.

River Oaks Furniture, Inc., 43 314–16

River Ranch Fresh Foods—Salinas, Inc., **41** 11

River Thames Insurance Co., Ltd., **26** 487

Riverdeep Group plc, **41** 137

Riverside Chemical Company, **13** 502

Riverside Furniture, **19** 455

Riverside Insurance Co. of America, **26** 487

Riverside Iron Works, Ltd., **8** 544

Riverside National Bank of Buffalo, **11** 108

Riverside Press, **10** 355–56

Riverside Publishing Company, **36** 272

Riverwood International Corporation, 7 294; **11** 420–23; **48** 340–44 (upd.)

Riviana Foods, 27 388–91

Riviera Holdings Corporation, 75 340–43

Riyadh Armed Forces Hospital, **16** 94

Rizzoli Publishing, **23** 88

RJMJ, Inc., **16** 37

RJR Nabisco Holdings Corp., V 408–10 *see also* R.J Reynolds Tobacco Holdings Inc., Nabisco Brands, Inc.; R.J. Reynolds Industries, Inc.

RK Rose + Krieger GmbH & Co. KG, **61** 286–87

RKO *see* Radio-Keith-Orpheum.

RKO-General, Inc., **8** 207

RLA Polymers, **9** 92

RMC Group p.l.c., III 737–40; **34** 378–83 (upd.)

RMH Teleservices, Inc., 42 322–24

RMP International, Limited, **8** 417

Roadhouse Grill, Inc., 22 464–66; **57** 84

Roadmaster Industries, Inc., 16 430–33

Roadmaster Transport Company, **18** 27; **41** 18

RoadOne *see* Miller Industries, Inc.

Roadstone-Wood Group, **64** 98

Roadway Express, Inc., V 502–03; **25** 395–98 (upd.)

Roanoke Capital Ltd., **27** 113–14

Roanoke Electric Steel Corporation, 45 368–70

Roanoke Fashions Group, **13** 532

Robb Engineering Works, **8** 544

Robbins & Myers Inc., 13 273; **15** 388–90

Robeco Group, **26** 419–20

Roberds Inc., 19 361–63

Robert Allen Companies, **III** 571; **20** 362

Robert Benson, Lonsdale & Co. Ltd. *see* Dresdner Kleinwort Wasserstein.

Robert Bosch GmbH, I 392–93; **16** 434–37 (upd.); **43** 317–21 (upd.)

Robert E. McKee Corporation, **6** 150

Robert Fleming Holdings Ltd., **I** 471; **11** 495

Robert Gair Co., **15** 128

Robert Garrett & Sons, Inc., **9** 363

Robert Half International Inc., 18 461–63; **70** 281–84 (upd.)

Robert Hall Clothes, Inc., **13** 535

Robert Hansen Trucking Inc., **49** 402

Robert Johnson, **8** 281–82

Robert McLane Company *see* McLane Company, Inc.

Robert McNish & Company Limited, **14** 141

Robert Mondavi Corporation, 15 391–94; **39** 45; **50** 386–90 (upd.); **54** 343

Robert Skeels & Company, **33** 467

Robert Stigwood Organization Ltd., **23** 390

Safeguard Scientifics, Inc., **10** 232–34, 473–75; **27** 338

Safelite Glass Corp., **19** 371–73

Safer, Inc., **21** 385–86

Safeskin Corporation, 18 467–70

Safety Components International, Inc., **63** 342–44

Safety 1st, Inc., **24** 412–15; **46** 192; **59** 164

Safety-Kleen Corp., **8** 462–65

Safety Rehab, **11** 486

Safety Savings and Loan, **10** 339

Safeway Inc., II 654–56; **24** 273, 416–19 (upd.)

Safeway PLC, **50** 401–06 (upd.)

Saffa SpA, **41** 325–26

Saffery Champness, **80** 324–327

Saffil Ltd. *see* Dyson Group PLC.

Safilo SpA, **40** 155–56; **54** 319–21

SAFR *see* Société Anonyme des Fermiers Reúnis.

Saga *see* Sociedad Andina de Grandes Almeneces.

Saga Communications, Inc., **27** 392–94

Saga Petroleum ASA, **35** 318

Sagami Optical Co., Ltd., **48** 295

Sagamore Insurance Company, **51** 37–39

The Sage Group, **43** 343–46

Sagebrush Sales, Inc., **12** 397

Sagebrush Steakhouse, **29** 201

SAGEM S.A., **37** 346–48

Saginaw Dock & Terminal Co., **17** 357

Sagitta Arzneimittel, **18** 51; **50** 90

Sahara Casino Partners L.P., **19** 379

Sahara Las Vegas Corp. *see* Archon Corporation.

SAI *see* Stamos Associates Inc.

Sai Baba, **12** 228

Saia Motor Freight Line, Inc., **6** 421–23; **45** 448

Saibu Gas, IV 518–19

SAIC *see* Science Applications International Corporation.

SAIC Velcorex, **12** 153; **27** 188

Saiccor, IV 92; **49** 353

SalesLink Corporation *see* CMGI, Inc.

Sainco *see* Sociedad Anonima de Instalaciones de Control.

Sainrapt et Brice, **9** 9

Sainsbury's *see* J Sainsbury PLC.

St. Alban Boissons S.A., **22** 515

St. Andrews Insurance, III 397

Saint-Gobain *see* Compagnie de Saint Gobain S.A.

Saint-Gobain Weber *see* Weber et Broutin France.

St. Ives Laboratories Inc., **36** 26

St Ives plc, **34** 393–95

St. James Associates, **32** 362–63

St. James's Place Capital, plc, **71** 324–26

The St. Joe Company, **31** 422–25

St. Joe Corporation, **59** 185

St. Joe Gold, **23** 40

St. Joe Minerals Corp., **8** 192

St. Joe Paper Company, **8** 485–88

St. John Knits, Inc., **14** 466–68

St. JON Laboratories, Inc., **74** 381

St. Jude Medical, Inc., **11** 458–61; **43** 347–52 (upd.)

St. Laurent Paperboard Inc., **30** 119

St. Lawrence Cement Inc., III 702; **8** 258–59

Saint Louis Bread Company, **18** 35, 37; **44** 327

St. Louis Concessions Inc., **21** 39

St. Louis Music, Inc., **48** 351–54

St. Louis Post-Dispatch LLC, **58** 283

St. Luke's-Roosevelt Hospital Center *see* Continuum Health Partners, Inc.

St. Martin's Press, **25** 484–85; **35** 452

St. Mary Land & Exploration Company, **60** 189; **63** 345–47

St. Michel-Grellier S.A., **44** 40

St. Paul Bank for Cooperatives, **8** 489–90

St. Paul Book and Stationery, Inc., **47** 90

St. Paul Fire and Marine Insurance Co. *see* The St. Paul Companies, Inc.

The St. Paul Travelers Companies, Inc., III 355–57; **22** 154, 492–95 (upd.); **79** 362–369 (upd.)

St. Paul Venture Capital Inc., **34** 405–06

St. Regis Paper Co., **10** 265; **12** 377

salesforce.com, Inc., **79** 370–373

Saipem S.p.A. *see* ENI S.p.A.

SAirGroup, **29** 376; **33** 268, 271; **37** 241; **46** 398; **47** 287

SAirLogistics, **49** 80–81

Saison Group, V 184–85, 187–89; **36** 417–18, 420; **42** 340–41

Sakae Printing Co., Ltd., **64** 261

Sako Ltd., **39** 151

Saks Fifth Avenue, **15** 291; **18** 372; **21** 302; **22** 72; **25** 205; **27** 329; **50** 117–19; **57** 179–80

Saks Holdings, Inc., **24** 420–23

Saks Inc., **41** 342–45 (upd.)

Sakura Bank *see* Sumitomo Mitsui Banking Corporation.

Salant Corporation, **12** 430–32; **27** 445; **51** 318–21 (upd.)

Sale Knitting Company *see* Tultex Corporation.

Salem Broadcasting, **25** 508

Salem Carpet Mills, Inc., **9** 467

Salem Sportswear, **25** 167

Salick Health Care, Inc., **21** 544, 546; **50** 58; **53** 290–92

Salient Partners & Pinnacle Trust Co., **70** 287

Salim Group, **18** 180–81

Salinas Equipment Distributors, Inc., **33** 364

Sallie Mae *see* SLM Holding Corp.; Student Loan Marketing Association.

Sally Beauty Company, Inc., **8** 15–17; **36** 23–26; **60** 258–60

Salmon River Power & Light Company, **12** 265

Salomon Brothers Inc., **28** 164

Salomon Inc., II 447–49; **13** 447–50 (upd.)

Salomon Smith Barney, **30** 124

Salomon Worldwide, **20** 458–60 *see also* adidas-Salomon AG.

Salon Cielo and Spa *see* Ratner Companies.

Salon Plaza *see* Ratner Companies.

Salt River Project, **19** 374–76

Salton, Inc., **30** 402–04

Salvagnini Company, **22** 6

The Salvation Army USA, **15** 510–11; **32** 390–93

Salvatore Ferragamo Italia S.p.A., **62** 311–13

Salzgitter AG, IV 200–01

SAM *see* Sociedad Aeronáutica de Medellín, S.A.

Sam & Libby Inc., **30** 311

Sam Ash Music Corporation, **30** 405–07

Sam Goody, **9** 360–61; **63** 65

Sam Levin Inc., **80** 328–331

Sam's Club, **40** 385–87

Samancor Ltd., IV 92–93

Samaritan Senior Services Inc., **25** 503

Samas-Groep N.V., **47** 91

Sambo's, **12** 510

Samcor Glass *see* Corning Inc.

Samedan Oil Corporation, **11** 353

Sames, S.A., **21** 65–66

Samick Musical Instruments Co., Ltd., **56** 297–300

Samim, IV 422

Sammy Corp., **54** 16; **73** 291

Samna Corp., **6** 256; **25** 300

Sampoerna PT, **62** 96–97

Sampson's, **12** 220–21

Samson Technologies Corp., **30** 406

Samsonite Corporation, **13** 451–53; **43** 353–57 (upd.)

Samsung-Calex, **17** 483

Samsung Display Co., Ltd., **59** 81

Samsung Electronics Co., Ltd., **14** 416–18; **18** 139, 260; **41** 346–49 (upd.)

Samsung Group, I 515–17; **13** 387; **29** 207–08; **62** 68–69

Samuel Austin & Son Company, **8** 41

Samuel Cabot Inc., **53** 293–95

Samuel Meisel & Company, Inc., **11** 80–81; **29** 509, 511

Samuel, Son & Co. Ltd., **24** 144

Samuels Jewelers Incorporated, **30** 408–10

San Antonio Public Service Company *see* City Public Service.

San Diego Gas & Electric Company, V 711–14 *see also* Sempra Energy.

San Diego Padres Baseball Club L.P., **78** 324–327

San Francisco Baseball Associates, L.P., **55** 340–43

San Francisco Maillots, **62** 228

San Francisco Mines of Mexico Ltd., **22** 285

San Gabriel Light & Power Company, **16** 496; **50** 496

San Giorgio Macaroni Inc., **53** 242

San Jose Water Company *see* SJW Corporation.

San Miguel Corporation, **15** 428–30; **23** 379; **57** 303–08 (upd.); **63** 227

San Paolo IMI S.p.A., **63** 52–53

Seifu Co. Ltd., **48** 250
Seigle's Home and Building Centers, Inc., 41 353–55
Seihoku Packaging Company *see* JSP Corporation.
Seiko Corporation, III 619–21; **17** 428–31 (upd.); **72** 314–18 (upd.)
Seiko Instruments USA Inc., **23** 210
Seikosha Co., **64** 261
Seimi Chemical Co. Ltd., **48** 41
Seino Transportation Company, Ltd., 6 427–29
Seirt SAU, **76** 326–27
Seismograph Service Limited, **11** 413; **17** 419
Seita, **23** 424–27 *see also* Altadis S.A.
Seitel, Inc., 47 348–50
The Seiyu, Ltd., V 187–89; **36** 417–21 (upd.); **63** 427, 431
Seizo-sha, **12** 483
Sekisui Chemical Co., Ltd., III 741–43; **72** 319–22 (upd.)
Selat Marine Services, **22** 276
Selby Shoe Company, **48** 69
Select Comfort Corporation, 34 405–08
Select Energy, Inc., **48** 305
Select-Line Industries, **9** 543
Select Medical Corporation, 65 306–08
Select Theatres Corp. *see* Shubert Organization Inc.
Selection Trust, **IV** 380, 565
Selectour SA, 53 299–301
Selectronics Inc., **23** 210
Selectrons Ltd., **41** 367
Selena Coffee Inc., **39** 409
Selenia, **I** 467; **38** 374
Self Auto, **23** 232
The Self-Locking Carton Company, **14** 163
Self-Service Drive Thru, Inc., **25** 389
Self Service Restaurants, **II** 613
Selfix, Inc. *see* Home Products International, Inc.
Selfridges Plc, 34 409–11
Selig Chemical Industries, **54** 252, 254
Seligman & Latz, **18** 455
Selkirk Communications Ltd., **26** 273
Sells-Floto, **32** 186
The Selmer Company, Inc., 19 392–94, 426, 428; **55** 113
Seltel International Inc., **35** 246
Sema plc, **59** 370
Semarca, **11** 523
Sematech, **18** 384, 481
SembCorp Logistics Ltd., **53** 199, 203
Sembler Company, **11** 346
SEMCO Energy, Inc., 44 379–82
Semi-Tech Global, **30** 419–20
Seminis, Inc., 21 413; **29** 435–37
Seminole Electric Cooperative, **6** 583
Seminole Fertilizer, **7** 537–38
Seminole National Bank, **41** 312
Semitic, Inc., **33** 248
Semitool, Inc., 18 480–82; **79** 379–382 (upd.)
Sempra Energy, 25 413–16 (upd.)
Semrau and Sons, **II** 601
Semtech Corporation, 32 410–13

Sencel Aero Engineering Corporation, **16** 483
Seneca Foods Corporation, 17 432–34; **60** 265–68 (upd.)
Senega, **63** 365
Sengstacke Enterprises *see* Real Times LLC.
Senior Corp., **11** 261
Sennheiser Electronic GmbH & Co. KG, 66 285–89
Sensi, Inc., **22** 173
Sensient Technologies Corporation, 52 303–08 (upd.)
Sensormatic Electronics Corp., 11 443–45; **39** 77–79
Sensory Science Corporation, 37 353–56
Sentinel Foam & Envelope Corporation, **14** 430
Sentinel Savings and Loan, **10** 339
Sentry, **II** 624
Sentry Insurance Company, **10** 210
La Senza Corporation, 66 205–07
Sepal, Ltd., **39** 152, 154
AB Separator *see* Alfa-Laval AB
SEPECAT, **24** 86
Sephora SA, **51** 234–35; **54** 265–67
SEPI *see* Sociedad Estatal de Participaciones Industriales.
Sepracor Inc., 45 380–83
Sept, **IV** 325
Sequa Corporation, 13 460–63; **54** 328–32 (upd.)
Sequana Capital, 78 338–342 (upd.)
Sequel Corporation, **41** 193
Sequent Computer Systems Inc., **10** 363
Sequoia Athletic Company, **25** 450
Sequoia Pharmacy Group, **13** 150
Sera-Tec Biologicals, Inc. *see* Rite Aid Corporation.
Seragen Inc., **47** 223
Serco Group plc, 47 351–53
Sereg Valves, S.A., **17** 147
Serewatt AG, **6** 491
Serologicals Corporation, 63 351–53
Serono S.A., 47 354–57
Serta, Inc., 28 416–18
Serval Marketing, **18** 393
Servam Corp., **7** 471–73
Service and Systems Solutions Ltd., **64** 404
Service America Corp., 7 471–73; **27** 480–81
Service Co., Ltd., **48** 182
Service Control Corp. *see* Angelica Corporation.
Service Corporation International, 6 293–95; **51** 329–33 (upd.)
Service Corporation of America, **17** 552
Service Games Company, **10** 482
Service Master L.P., **34** 153
Service Merchandise Company, Inc., V 190–92; **6** 287; **9** 400; **19** 395–99 (upd.)
Service Products Buildings, Inc. *see* Turner Construction Company.
Service Q. General Service Co., **I** 109

The ServiceMaster Company, 6 44–46; **23** 428–31 (upd.); **68** 338–42 (upd.)
Services Maritimes des Messageries Impériales *see* Compagnie des Messageries Maritimes.
ServiceWare, Inc., **25** 118
Servicios de Corte y Confeccion, S.A. de C.V., **64** 142
Servicios Financieros Quadrum S.A., **14** 156; **76** 129
Servisair Plc, **49** 320
Servisco, **II** 608
ServiStar Coast to Coast Corporation *see* TruServ Corporation.
ServoChem A.B., **I** 387
Servomation Corporation, **7** 472–73
Servomation Wilbur *see* Service America Corp.
Servoplan, S.A., **8** 272
SES Staffing Solutions, **27** 21
Sesame Street Book Club, **13** 560
Sesamee Mexicana, **48** 142
Sessler Inc., **19** 381
Setagaya Industry Co., Ltd., **48** 295
SETCAR, **14** 458
Seton Scholl *see* SSL International plc.
Seven Arts Limited, **25** 328
7-Eleven, Inc., 32 414–18 (upd.); **36** 358
Seven-Eleven Japan Co. *see* Ito-Yokado Co., Ltd.
Seven Generation, Inc., **41** 177
Seven Hills Paperboard, LLC, **59** 350
Seven Network Limited, **25** 329
Seven-Up Co., **18** 418
SevenOne Media, **54** 297
Sevenson Environmental Services, Inc., 42 344–46
Seventh Generation, Inc., 73 294–96
Seventh Street Corporation, **60** 130
Severn Trent PLC, 12 441–43; **38** 425–29 (upd.)
Severonickel Combine, **48** 300
Seversky Aircraft Corporation, **9** 205
Severstal Joint Stock Company, 65 309–12
Sewell Plastics, Inc., **10** 222
Sextant In-Flight Systems, LLC, **30** 74
Seymour Electric Light Co., **13** 182
Seymour International Press Distributor Ltd., **IV** 619
Seymour Press, **IV** 619
Seymour Trust Co., **13** 467
SF Bio, **52** 51
SF Recycling & Disposal, Inc., **60** 224
SFI Group plc, 51 334–36
SFIC Holdings (Cayman) Inc., **38** 422
SFIM Industries, **37** 348
SFNGR *see* Nouvelles Galeries Réunies.
SFS Bancorp Inc., **41** 212
SFX Broadcasting Inc., **24** 107
SFX Entertainment, Inc., 36 422–25
SG Cowen Securities Corporation, **75** 186–87
SG Racing, Inc., **64** 346
SGC *see* Supermarkets General Corporation.
SGE *see* Vinci.

Shoppers World Stores, Inc. *see* LOT$OFF Corporation.

ShopRite *see* Foodarama Supermarkets, Inc.

Shopwell/Food Emporium, **II** 638; **16** 247, 249

ShopWise.com Inc., **53** 13

Shore Manufacturing, **13** 165

Shorewood Packaging Corporation, **28** 419–21; **47** 189

Shorouk Airways, **68** 227

Short Brothers, **24** 85

Shoseido Co., **17** 110

Shotton Paper Co. Ltd., **IV** 350

Showa Aluminum Corporation, **8** 374

Showa Denko, **IV** 61

Showa Marutsutsu Co. Ltd., **8** 477

Showa Products Company, **8** 476

Showa Shell Sekiyu K.K., **IV** 542–43; **59** 372–75 (upd.)

ShowBiz Pizza Time, Inc., **13** 472–74 *see also* CEC Entertainment, Inc.

Showboat, Inc., **19** 400–02; **43** 227

Showcase of Fine Fabrics, **16** 197

Showco, Inc., **35** 436

Showscan Entertainment Inc., **34** 230

Showscan Film Corporation, **28** 206

Showtime Networks, Inc., **78** 343–347

Shred-It Canada Corporation, **56** 319–21

Shreve and Company, **12** 312

Shreveport Refrigeration, **16** 74

Shriners Hospitals for Children, **69** 318–20

Shu Uemura, **III** 43

Shubert Organization Inc., **24** 437–39

Shubrooks International Ltd., **11** 65

Shuffle Master Inc., **51** 337–40

Shuford Mills, Inc., **14** 430

Shugart Associates, **8** 466; **22** 189

Shulman Transport Enterprises Inc., **27** 473

Shure Inc., **60** 273–76

Shurfine International, **60** 302

Shurgard Storage Centers, Inc., **21** 476; **52** 293, **309–11**

Shuttleworth Brothers Company *see* Mohawk Industries, Inc.

Shuwa Corp., **22** 101; **36** 292

SHV Holdings N.V., **55** 344–47

SI Holdings Inc., **10** 481; **29** 425

The Siam Cement Public Company Limited, **56** 322–25

Siam Makro, **62** 63

SIAS, **19** 192

SIATA S.p.A., **26** 363

SIB Financial Services, **39** 382

Sibco Universal, S.A., **14** 429

Sibel, **48** 350

Siberian Moloko, **48** 438

Sibneft *see* OAO Siberian Oil Company.

Siboney Shoe Corp., **22** 213

SiCAP AG, **58** 338

SICC *see* Univision Communications Inc.

Sichuan Changhong Electric Co. Ltd., **63** 36

Sichuan Station Wagon Factory, **38** 462

Sick's Brewery, **26** 304

Siclet, **25** 84

Sicma Aero Seat, **36** 529

Sideco Americana S.A., **67** 346–48

Sidel *see* Groupe Sidel S.A.

Siderar S.A.I.C., **66** 293–95

Siderca S.A.I.C., **41** 405–06

Sidley Austin Brown & Wood, **40** 400–03 Sidmar N. V. *see* Arcelor Gent

Sidney Frank Importing Co., Inc., **69** 321–23

Siebe plc *see* BTR Siebe plc.

Siebel Group, **13** 544–45

Siebel Marketing Group, **27** 195

Siebel Systems, Inc., **38** 430–34

Siebert Financial Corp., **32** 423–25

Siegel & Gale, **64** 350–52

Siemens AG, **II** 97–100; **14** 444–47 (upd.); **57** 318–23 (upd.)

Siemens Solar Industries L.P., **44** 182

The Sierra Club, **28** 422–24

Sierra Designs, Inc., **10** 215–16

Sierra Health Services, Inc., **15** 451–53

Sierra Leone External Telegraph Limited, **25** 100

Sierra Nevada Brewing Company, **70** 291–93

Sierra On-Line, Inc., **15** 454–56; **41** 361–64 (upd.)

Sierra Pacific Industries, **22** 489–91

Sierra Precision, **52** 187

Sierrita Resources, Inc., **6** 590

Siete Oil and Gas Co., **63** 346

SIFCO Industries, Inc., **41**

Sifo Group AB *see* Observer AB.

SIG plc, **71** 334–36

Sight & Sound Entertainment, **35** 21

Sigma-Aldrich Corporation, **I** 690–91; **36** 429–32 (upd.)

Sigma Alimentos, S.A. de C.V., **19** 11–12

Sigma Network Systems, **11** 464

Signal Companies, Inc. *see* AlliedSignal Inc.

Signal Corporation, **54** 395–96

Signal Galaxies, **13** 127

Signal Oil & Gas Inc., **7** 537; **11** 278; **19** 175

Signal Pharmaceutical Inc. *see* Celgene Corporation.

Signalite, Inc., **10** 319

SignalSoft, **63** 202

Signature Bank, **54** 36

Signature Brands USA Inc., **28** 135; **30** 139

Signature Corporation, **22** 412–13

Signature Flight Support Services Corporation, **47** 450

Signature Health Care Corp., **25** 504

Signet Banking Corporation, **11** 446–48

Signet Communications Corp., **16** 195

Signet Group PLC, **61** 326–28

Signetics Co., **11** 56; **18** 383; **44** 127

Signode Industries, **III** 519; **22** 282

Sika Finanz AG, **28** 195

Sikes Corporation, **III** 612

Sikorsky Aircraft Corporation, **24** 440–43

SIL&P *see* Southern Illinois Light & Power Company.

SILA *see* Swedish Intercontinental Airlines.

Silband Sports Corp., **33** 102

Silenka B.V., **III** 733; **22** 436

Silex *see* Hamilton Beach/Proctor-Silex Inc.

Silgan Holdings Inc., **26** 59

Silhouette Brands, Inc., **55** 348–50

Silicon Beach Software, **10** 35

Silicon Compiler Systems, **11** 285

Silicon Energy Corporation, **64** 205

Silicon Engineering, **18** 20; **43** 17

Silicon Graphics Inc., **9** 471–73 *see also* SGI.

Silicon Light Machines Corporation, **48** 128

Silicon Magnetic Systems, **48** 128

Silicon Microstructures, Inc., **14** 183

Siliconware Precision Industries Ltd., **73** 300–02

Silit, **60** 364

Silk-Epil S.A., **51** 58

Silkies, **55** 196

Silknet Software Inc., **51** 181

Silo Electronics, **16** 73, 75

Silo Holdings, **9** 65; **23** 52

Silo Inc., **V** 50; **10** 306, 468; **19** 123; **49** 112

Silver Burdett Co., **IV** 672, 675; **7** 528; **19** 405

Silver Cinemas Inc., **71** 256

Silver City Airways *see* British World Airlines Ltd.

Silver City Casino *see* Circus Circus Enterprises, Inc.

Silver Dollar City Corporation *see* Herschend Family Entertainment Corporation.

Silver Dollar Mining Company, **20** 149

Silver Dolphin, **34** 3, 5

Silver Furniture Co., Inc., **15** 102, 104

Silver King Communications, **25** 213

Silver Screen Partners, **II** 174

Silverado Banking, **9** 199

Silverado Partners Acquisition Corp., **22** 80

Silverline, Inc., **16** 33

Silvermans Menswear, Inc., **24** 26

SilverPlatter Information Inc., **23** 440–43

Silvershoe Partners, **17** 245

Silverstar Ltd. S.p.A., **10** 113; **50** 42

Silverstein Properties, Inc., **47** 358–60; **48** 320

Simco S.A., **37** 357–59

Sime Darby Berhad, **14** 448–50; **36** 433–36 (upd.)

Simeira Comercio e Industria Ltda., **22** 320

SIMEL S.A., **14** 27

Simer Pump Company, **19** 360

SIMEST, **24** 311

Simi Winery, Inc., **34** 89

Simicon Co., **26** 153

Simkins Industries, Inc., **8** 174–75

Simmons Company, **34** 407; **47** 361–64

Simon & Schuster Inc., **IV** 671–72; **19** 403–05 (upd.)

Simon de Wit, **II** 641

SOMABRI, **12** 152
SOMACA, **12** 152
Somali Bank, **31** 220
Someal, **27** 513, 515
Somerfield plc, 47 365–69 (upd.)
Somerville Electric Light Company, **12** 45
Somerville Packaging Group, **28** 420
Sommer-Allibert S.A., 19 406–09
Sommers Drug Stores, **9** 186
Sonat Exploration Company, **63** 366
Sonat, Inc., 6 577–78; **22** 68
Sonatrach, 65 313–17 (upd.)
Sonecor Systems, **6** 340
Sonera Corporation, 50 441–44 *see also*
TeliaSonera AB.
Sonergy, Inc., **49** 280
Sonesta International Hotels
Corporation, 44 389–91
Sonet Media AB, **23** 390
SONI Ltd., **64** 404
Sonic Automotive, Inc., 77 396–399
Sonic Corp., 14 451–53; **37** 360–63
(upd.)
Sonic Duo, **48** 419
Sonic Innovations Inc., 56 336–38
Sonic Restaurants, **31** 279
Sonnen Basserman, **II** 475
SonnenBraune, **22** 460
Sonoco Products Company, 8 475–77
Sonofon *see* Telenor ASA.
The Sonoma Group, **25** 246
Sonor GmbH, **53** 216
SonoSite, Inc., 56 339–41
Sony Corporation, II 101–03; **12**
453–56 (upd.); **40** 404–10 (upd.)
Sony Ericsson Mobile Communications
AB, **61** 137
Soo Line Corporation *see* Canadian Pacific
Ltd.
Soo Line Mills, **II** 631
Sooner Trailer Manufacturing Co., **29** 367
Soparind, **25** 83–85
Sope Creek, **30** 457
Sophus Berendsen A/S, 49 374–77
SOPORCEL, **34** 38–39
Soporcel-Sociedade Portuguesa de Papel,
S.A., **60** 156
Sorbee International Ltd., 74 309–11
Sorbents Products Co. Inc., **31** 20
Sorbus, **6** 242
Soreal, **8** 344
Sorenson Research Company, **36** 496
Sorg Paper Company *see* Mosinee Paper
Corporation.
Soriana *see* Organización Soriana, S.A. de
C.V.
Sorin S.p.A., **61** 70, 72
Soros Fund Management LLC, 27 198;
28 432–34; **43** 218
Sorrento, Inc., 19 51; **24** 444–46; **26**
505
SOS Staffing Services, 25 432–35
Sosa, Bromley, Aguilar & Associates *see*
D'Arcy Masius Benton & Bowles, Inc.
Soterra, Inc., **15** 188
Sotetsu Rosen, **72** 301

Sotheby's Holdings, Inc., **11** 452–54; **15**
98–100; **29** 445–48 (upd.); **32** 164;
39 81–84; **49** 325
Soufflet SA *see* Groupe Soufflet SA.
Sound Advice, Inc., 41 379–82
Sound of Music Inc. *see* Best Buy Co.,
Inc.
Sound Trek, **16** 74
Sound Video Unlimited, **16** 46; **43** 60
Sound Warehouse, **9** 75
Souplantation Incorporated *see* Garden
Fresh Restaurant Corporation.
The Source Enterprises, Inc., 65 318–21
Source Interlink Companies, Inc., 75
350–53
Source One Mortgage Services Corp., **12**
79
Source Perrier, **7** 383; **24** 444
Sourdough Bread Factory *see* Matt
Prentice Restaurant Group.
Souriau, **19** 166
South African Airways Ltd., **27** 132 *see*
also Transnet Ltd.
The South African Breweries Limited, I
287–89; **24** 447–51 (upd.) *see also*
SABMiller plc.
South African Transport Services *see*
Transnet Ltd.
South Asia Tyres, **20** 263
South Australian Brewing Company, **54**
228, 341
South Beach Beverage Company, Inc.,
73 316–19
South Bend Toy Manufacturing Company,
25 380
South Carolina Electric & Gas Company
see SCANA Corporation.
South Carolina National Corporation, **16**
523, 526
South Carolina Power Company, **38**
446–47
South Central Bell Telephone Co. *see*
BellSouth Corporation.
South Central Railroad Co., **14** 325
South Coast Gas Compression Company,
Inc., **11** 523
South Coast Terminals, Inc., **16** 475
South Dakota Public Service Company, **6**
524
South Florida Neonatology Associates, **61**
284
South Fulton Light & Power Company, **6**
514
South Jersey Industries, Inc., 42 352–55
South of Scotland Electricity Board, **19**
389–90
South Overseas Fashion Ltd., **53** 344
South Sea Textile, **III** 705
South Wales Electric Company, **34** 219
South West Water Plc *see* Pennon Group
Plc.
South Western Electricity plc, **38** 448; **41**
316
South-Western Publishing Co., **8** 526–28
Southam Inc., 7 486–89; **15** 265; **24**
223; **36** 374
Southco, **II** 602–03; **7** 20–21; **30** 26
Southcorp Holdings Ltd., **17** 373; **22** 350

Southcorp Limited, 54 341–44
Southdown, Inc., 14 454–56; **59** 114–15
Southdown Press *see* PMP Ltd.
Southeast Bank of Florida, **11** 112
Southeast Public Service Company, **8** 536
Southeastern Freight Lines, Inc., **53** 249
Southeastern Personnel *see* Norrell
Corporation.
Southern and Phillips Gas Ltd., **13** 485
Southern Australia Airlines, **24** 396
Southern Bank, **10** 426
Southern Bearings Co., **13** 78
Southern Bell, **10** 202
Southern Blvd. Supermarkets, Inc., **22**
549
Southern Box Corp., **13** 441
Southern California Edison Co. *see* Edison
International.
Southern California Financial
Corporation, **27** 46
Southern California Fruit Growers
Exchange *see* Sunkist Growers, Inc.
Southern California Gas Co., **25** 413–14,
416
Southern Casualty Insurance Co., **III** 214
The Southern Company, V 721–23; **38**
445–49 (upd.)
Southern Cooker Limited Partnership, **51**
85
Southern Corrections Systems, Inc. *see*
Avalon Correctional Services, Inc.
Southern Cotton Co., **24** 488
Southern Cross Paints, **38** 98
Southern Discount Company of Atlanta,
9 229
Southern Electric PLC, 13 484–86 *see*
also Scottish and Southern Energy plc.
Southern Electric Supply Co., **15** 386
Southern Electronics Corp. *see* SED
International Holdings, Inc.
Southern Equipment & Supply Co., **19**
344
Southern Financial Bancorp, Inc., 56
342–44
Southern Foods Group, L.P. *see* Dean
Foods Company.
Southern Forest Products, Inc., **6** 577
Southern Gage, **III** 519; **22** 282
Southern Graphic Arts, **13** 405
Southern Guaranty Cos., **III** 404
Southern Idaho Water Power Company,
12 265
Southern Indiana Gas and Electric
Company, 13 487–89
Southern Lumber Company, **8** 430
Southern Manufacturing Company, **8** 458
Southern Minnesota Beet Sugar
Cooperative, **32** 29
Southern National Bankshares of Atlanta,
II 337; **10** 425
Southern National Corporation *see* BB&T
Corporation
Southern Natural Gas Co., **6** 577
Southern Nevada Power Company, **11**
343
Southern Nevada Telephone Company, **11**
343

Steger Furniture Manufacturing Co., **18** 493

Steiff *see* Margarete Steiff GmbH.

Steil, Inc., **8** 271

Steilman Group *see* Klaus Steilmann GmbH & Co. KG.

Stein Mart Inc., 19 423–25; **72** 337–39 **(upd.)**

Stein Printing Company, **25** 183

Stein Robaire Helm, **22** 173

Steinbach Inc., **14** 427

Steinbach Stores, Inc., **19** 108

Steinberg Incorporated, II 652–53, **662–65**

Steinberger, **16** 239

Steiner Corporation (Alsco), 53 308–11

Steinheil Optronik GmbH, **24** 87

Steinmüller Verwaltungsgesellschaft *see* Vereinigte Elektrizitaswerke Westfalen AG

Steinway & Sons, **16** 201; **43** 170

Steinway Musical Properties, Inc., 19 426–29

Stelco Inc., IV 208–10; 24 144; **51 349–52 (upd.)**

Stella Bella Corporation, **19** 436

Stella D'Oro Company, **7** 367

Stellar Systems, Inc., **14** 542

Stelmar Shipping Ltd., 52 329–31

Stelux Manufacturing Company, **13** 121; **41** 71

Stelwire Ltd., **51** 352

Stena AB, **25** 105; **29** 429–30

Stena Line AB, **38** 345

Stena-Sealink, **37** 137

Stens Corporation, **48** 34

Stentor Canadian Network Management, **6** 310

Stenval Sud, **19** 50

Stepan Company, 30 437–39

The Stephan Company, 60 285–88

Stephen F. Whitman & Son, Inc., **7** 429

Stephens Inc., **67** 129–30

Stephenson Clarke and Company, **31** 368–69

Sterchi Bros. Co., **14** 236

Steria SA, 49 382–85

Stericycle, Inc., 33 380–82; 74 316–18 (upd.)

STERIS Corporation, 29 449–52

Sterling Capital Partners, **57** 56–57

Sterling Chemicals, Inc., 16 460–63; **78 356–361 (upd.)**

Sterling Drug Inc., I 698–700

Sterling Electronics Corp., 18 496–98; **19** 311

Sterling Engineered Products, **III** 640, 642; **16** 9

Sterling European Airlines A/S, 70 300–02

Sterling Forest Corp., **III** 264

Sterling House Corp., **42** 4

Sterling Inc., **61** 326–27

Sterling Industries, **13** 166

Sterling Manhattan, **7** 63

Sterling Organics Ltd., **12** 351; **50** 282

Sterling Software, Inc., 11 468–70; **31** 296

Sterling Stores Co. Inc., **24** 148

Sterling Winthrop, **7** 164; **36** 174; **49** 351

Stern & Stern Textiles, **11** 261

Stern Bros. Investment Bank, **19** 359

Stern Bros., LLC, **37** 224

Stern Publishing, **38** 478

Stern's, **9** 209

Sternco Industries, **12** 230–31

Sterner Lighting, **76** 185

STET *see* Società Finanziaria Telefonica per Azioni.

Stet Hellas, **63** 378–79

Steuben Glass *see* Corning Inc.

Stevcoknit Fabrics Company, **8** 141–43

Steve's Ice Cream, **16** 54–55

Stevedoring Services of America Inc., 28 435–37; 50 209–10

Steven Madden, Ltd., 37 371–73

Stevens Linen Associates, Inc., **8** 272

Stevens Sound Proofing Co., **7** 291

Stevens, Thompson & Runyan, Inc. *see* CRSS Inc.

Stevens Water Monitoring Systems, **52** 226

Stew Leonard's, 56 349–51

Stewart and Richey Construction Co., **51** 170

Stewart & Stevenson Services Inc., 11 471–73

Stewart Enterprises, Inc., 20 481–83

Stewart Information Services Corporation, 78 362–365

Stewart Systems, Inc., **22** 352–53

Stewart, Tabori & Chang, **58** 155

Stewart's Beverages, 39 383–86

Stewart's Shops Corporation, 80 360–363

Steyr Walzlager, **III** 625

Stichting Continuiteit AMEV, **III** 202

Stickley *see* L. and J.G. Stickley, Inc.

Stieber Rollkupplung GmbH, **14** 63

Stihl *see* Andreas Stihl AG & Co. KG.

Stilecraft, **24** 16

Stillwater Mining Company, 47 380–82

Stilwell Financial Inc. *see* Janus Capital Group Inc.

Stimson & Valentine, **8** 552

Stimson Lumber Company Inc., 78 366–369

Stimsonite Corporation, **49** 38

Stinnes AG, **8** 68–69, 494–97; **23** 68–70, 451–54 (upd.); **33** 195; **59** 387–92 (upd.)

Stirling Group plc, 62 342–44

STM Systems Corp., **11** 485

STMicroelectronics NV, 52 332–35

Stock Clearing Corporation, **9** 370

Stock Yards Packing Co., Inc., 37 374–76

Stockholder Systems Inc., **11** 485

Stockpack Ltd., **44** 318

Stoddard International plc, 72 340–43

Stoelting Brothers Company, **10** 371

Stokely Van Camp, **II** 560, 575; **12** 411; **22** 338

Stokvis/De Nederlandsche Kroon Rijwiefabrieken, **13** 499

Stoll-Moss Theatres Ltd., 34 420–22

Stollwerck AG, 53 312–15

Stolt-Nielsen S.A., 42 356–59; **54** 349–50

Stolt Sea Farm Holdings PLC, 54 349–51

Stone & Webster, Inc., 13 495–98; **64** 368–72 (upd.)

Stone Container Corporation, IV 332–34 *see also* Smurfit-Stone Container Corporation.

Stone Manufacturing Company, 14 469–71; **43** 392–96 (upd.)

Stonega Coke & Coal Co. *see* Westmoreland Coal Company.

Stoner Associates *see* Severn Trent PLC.

Stonington Partners, **19** 318

StonyBrook Services Inc., **24** 49

Stonyfield Farm, 55 357–60

Stoody Co., **19** 440

Stoof, **26** 278–79

Stoomvaart Maatschappij Nederland *see* Koninklijke Nedlloyd N.V.

The Stop & Shop Supermarket Company, II 666–67; **24** 460–62 **(upd.); 68** 350–53 (upd.)

Stop N Go, **7** 373; **25** 126

Stoppenbauch Inc., **23** 202

Stora Enso Oyj, 36 128, 447–55 (upd.)

Stora Kopparbergs Bergslags AB, IV 335–37, 340; **12** 464; **28** 445–46 *see also* Stora Enso Oyj.

Storage Dimensions Inc., **10** 404

Storage Technology Corporation, 6 275–77

Storage USA, Inc., 21 475–77

Storebor Brux Company, **52** 406

Storehouse PLC, 16 464–66 *see also* Mothercare plc.

Storer Communications, **7** 91–92, 200–1; **24** 122

Storm Technology, **28** 245

Storybook, Inc., **70** 52

Storz Instruments Co., **25** 56; **27** 115

Stouffer Corp., 8 498–501

Stow Mills, Inc., **76** 360, 362

Stowe Machine Co., Inc., **30** 283

STP, **19** 223; **26** 349

STRAAM Engineers *see* CRSS Inc.

Straits Steamship Co. *see* Malaysian Airlines System.

Stran, **8** 546

StrataCom, Inc., 16 467–69

Stratagene Corporation, 70 303–06

Stratasys, Inc., 67 361–63

Strategic Implications International, Inc., **45** 44

Strategix Solutions, **43** 309

StrategyOne, **62** 115

Stratford Corporation, **15** 103; **26** 100

Stratos Boat Co., Ltd., **III** 600

Strattec Security Corporation, 73 324–27

Stratton Oakmont Inc., **37** 372–73; **46** 282

Stratton Ski Corporation, **15** 235

Stratus Computer, Inc., 10 499–501

Straumann Holding AG, 79 396–399

Svenska Aeroplan Aktiebolaget *see* Saab-Scania AB.

Svenska Aller AB, **72** 62

Svenska Cellulosa Aktiebolaget SCA, IV 338–40; 28 443–46 (upd.)

Svenska Handelsbanken AB, II 365–67; 50 460–63 (upd.)

Svenska Kullagerfabriken A.B. *see* AB Volvo.

Svenska Stålpressnings AB, **26** 11

Sverdrup Corporation, 14 475–78

SVF *see* Société des Vins de France.

SVIDO, 17 250

SWA *see* Southwest Airlines.

SWALEC *see* Scottish and Southern Energy plc.

Swales & Associates, Inc., 69 336–38

Swallow Airplane Company, **8** 49; **27** 98

Swallow Sidecar and Coach Building Company, **13** 285

Swan, **10** 170

Swank Inc., 17 464–66

Swarovski International Holding AG, 40 422–25

The Swatch Group SA, 26 479–81

Swearingen Aircraft Company, **9** 207; **48** 169

Swedish Ericsson Group, **17** 353

Swedish Match AB, 12 462–64; 39 387–90 (upd.)

Swedish Ordnance-FFV/Bofors AB, **9** 381–82

Swedish Telecom, V 331–33

SwedishAmerican Health System, 51 363–66

Sweedor, **12** 464

Sweeney Specialty Restaurants, **14** 131

Sweeney's, **16** 559

Sweet & Maxwell, **8** 527

Sweet Candy Company, 60 295–97

Sweet Life Foods Inc., **18** 507; **50** 457

Sweet Stripes, Inc. *see* Bobs Candies, Inc.

Sweet Traditions LLC, **21** 323

Sweetheart Cup Company, Inc., 36 460–64

Swenson Granite Company, Inc., **37** 331

Swett & Crawford Group, **III** 357; **22** 494

SWH Corporation, 70 307–09

Swift & Company, 55 364–67

Swift Adhesives, **10** 467

Swift Denim Group, **66** 134

Swift Energy Company, 63 364–66

Swift Independent Packing Co., **13** 350, 352; **42** 92

Swift Textiles, Inc., **12** 118; **15** 247

Swift Transportation Co., Inc., 26 533; **33** 468; **42 363–66; 64** 218

Swinerton Inc., 43 397–400

Swing-N-Slide, Inc. *see* PlayCore, Inc.

Swingline, Inc., **7** 3–5

Swire Pacific Ltd., I 521–22; 16 479–81 (upd.); 57 348–53 (upd.)

Swisher International Group Inc., 14 17–19; **23 463–65; 27** 139

Swiss Air Transport Company Ltd., I 121–22

Swiss Army Brands, Inc. *see* Victorinox AG.

Swiss Banca de Gottardo, **26** 456

Swiss Bank Corporation, II 368–70, 378–79; **14** 419–20; **52** 354 *see also* UBS AG.

Swiss Barry Callebaut AG, **53** 315

Swiss Broadcasting Corporation, **53** 325

Swiss Federal Railways (Schweizerische Bundesbahnen), V 519–22

Swiss International Air Lines Ltd., 48 379–81

Swiss Life, **52** 357–58

Swiss Reinsurance Company (Schweizerische Rückversicherungs-Gesellschaft), III 375–78; 15 13; **21** 146; **45** 110; **46 380–84 (upd.)**

Swiss Saurer AG, **39** 39, 41

Swiss Telecom PTT *see* Swisscom AG.

Swiss Time Australia Pty Ltd, **25** 461

Swiss Volksbank, **21** 146–47

Swissair Associated Co., **34** 397–98; **36** 426

Swissair Group, **47** 286–87; **49** 80–81

SwissCargo, **49** 81

Swisscom AG, 58 336–39

Swissport International Ltd., 70 310–12

Switchboard Inc., **25** 52

SXI Limited, **17** 458

Sybase, Inc., 10 504–06; 27 447–50 (upd.)

SyberVision, **10** 216

Sybra, Inc., **19** 466–68

Sybron International Corp., 14 479–81; **19** 289–90

Sycamore Networks, Inc., 45 388–91

SyCom Services, Inc., **18** 363; **74** 22

Sydney Electricity, **12** 443

Sydney FM Facilities Pty. Limited, **58** 359

SYDOOG, **64** 160

Sydsvenska Kemi AB, **51** 289

Sykes Enterprises, Inc., 45 392–95

Syllogic B.V., **29** 376

Sylvan, Inc., 22 496–99

Sylvan Lake Telephone Company, **6** 334

Sylvan Learning Systems, Inc., 35 408–11

Sylvania Companies, **7** 161; **8** 157; **11** 197; **13** 402; **23** 181; **50** 299

Symantec Corporation, 10 507–09

Symbian Ltd., **45** 346, 348

Symbios Logic Inc., **19** 312; **31** 5

Symbiosis Corp., **10** 70; **50** 538

Symbol Technologies, Inc., 10 363, 523–24; **15 482–84**

Symphony International, **14** 224

Syms Corporation, 29 456–58; 74 327–30 (upd.)

Symtron Systems Inc., **37** 399–400

Symtronix Corporation, **18** 515

Symyx Technologies, Inc., 77 420–423

Syn-Optics, Inc., **29** 454

Synavant Inc. *see* Dendrite International, Inc.

Synbiotics Corporation, **23** 284

Syncordia Corp., **15** 69

Syncro Ltd., **51** 89

Syncrocom, Inc., **10** 513

Syncrude Canada Limited, **25** 232

Synercom Technology Inc., **14** 319

Synercon Corporation, **25** 538

Synergen Inc., **13** 241

Synergy Dataworks, Inc., **11** 285

Synergy Software Inc., **31** 131

Synetic, Inc., **16** 59

Synfloor SA, **25** 464

SYNNEX Corporation, 73 328–30

Synopsys, Inc., 11 489–92; 69 339–43 (upd.)

SynOptics Communications, Inc., 10 510–12

Synovus Financial Corp., 12 465–67; 52 336–40 (upd.)

Synrad, Inc. *see* Excel Technology, Inc.

Syntex Corporation, I 701–03; III 53; **8** 216–17, 434, 548; **10** 53; **12** 322; **26** 384; **50** 321

Syntex Pharmaceuticals Ltd., **21** 425

Synthecolor S.A., **8** 347

Synthetic Blood Corp., **15** 380

Synthetic Pillows, Inc., **19** 304

Synthomer *see* Yule Catto & Company plc.

Syntron, Inc., **18** 513–15

SyQuest Technology, Inc., 18 509–12

Syracuse China, **8** 510

Syratech Corp., 14 482–84; 27 288

Syroco, **14** 483–84

SYSCO Corporation, II 675–76; 24 470–72 (upd.); 75 357–60 (upd.)

SYSCO Security Systems, Inc., **51** 81

Syscon Corporation, **38** 227

Sysorex Information Systems, **11** 62

SysScan, **V** 339

Systech Environmental Corporation, **28** 228–29

System Designers plc *see* SD-Scicon plc.

System Fuels, Inc., **11** 194

System Parking West, **25** 16

System Software Associates, Inc., 10 513–14

Systematic Business Services, Inc., **48** 256–57

Systematics Inc., **6** 301; **11** 131

Systemax, Inc., 52 341–44

Systembolaget, **31** 459–60

Systems & Computer Technology Corp., 19 437–39

Systems and Services Company *see* SYSCO Corporation.

Systems Center, Inc., **11** 469

Systems Construction Ltd., **II** 649

Systems Development Corp., **25** 117

Systems Engineering and Manufacturing Company, **11** 225

Systems Engineering Labs (SEL), **11** 45; **13** 201

Systems Exploration Inc., **10** 547

Systems Marketing Inc., **12** 78

Systron Donner Corp. *see* BEI Technologies, Inc.

Systronics, **13** 235

Sytner Group plc, 45 396–98

Syufy Enterprises *see* Century Theatres, Inc.

Totino's Finer Foods, **26** 436

TOTO LTD., III 755–56; **28** 464–66 (**upd.**)

Touch America Inc., **37** 127; **44** 288

Touch-It Corp., **22** 413

Touche Remnant Holdings Ltd., **II** 356

Touche Ross *see* Deloitte Touche Tohmatsu International.

Touchstone Films *see* The Walt Disney Company.

Toupargel-Agrigel S.A., 76 354–56

Le Touquet's, SA, **48** 197

Tourang Limited, **7** 253

Touristik Union International GmbH. and Company K.G., II 163–65; **46** 460 *see also* Preussag AG.

Tourtime America, **56** 223

TOUSA *see* Technical Olympic USA, Inc.

Toval Japon, **IV** 680

Towa Optical Manufacturing Company, **41** 261–63

Tower Air, Inc., 28 467–69

Tower Automotive, Inc., 24 498–500

Tower Records, **9** 361; **10** 335; **11** 558; **30** 224 *see also* MTS Inc.

Towers, **II** 649

Towers Perrin, 32 458–60

Towle Manufacturing Co., **14** 482–83; **18** 69

Town & Country Corporation, 19 451–53

Town Sports International, Inc., 46 430–33

Towngas *see* Hong Kong and China Gas Company Ltd.

Townsend Hook, **IV** 296, 650, 652; **19** 226

Townsends, Inc., 64 385–87

Toxicol Laboratories, Ltd., **21** 424

The Toxicology Group, LLC *see* NOF Corporation.

Toy Biz, Inc., 18 519–21 *see also* Marvel Entertainment, Inc.

Toy Liquidators, **13** 541–43; **50** 99

Toy Park, **16** 390

Toyad Corp., **7** 296

Toymax International, Inc., 29 474–76; **52** 193

Toyo Ink Manufacturing, **26** 213

Toyo Kogyo, **II** 361

Toyo Microsystems Corporation, **11** 464

Toyo Pulp Co., **IV** 322

Toyo Rayon *see* Toray Industries, Inc.

Toyo Sash Co., Ltd., III 757–58

Toyo Seikan Kaisha Ltd., I 615–16

Toyo Soda Manufacturing Co *see* Tosoh Corporation.

Toyo Tire & Rubber Co., **V** 255–56; **9** 248

Toyo Toki Co., Ltd. *see* Toto.

Toyo Trust and Banking Co., **17** 349

Toyoda Automatic Loom Works, Ltd., III 636–39

Toyota Industrial Equipment, **27** 294, 296

Toyota Motor Corporation, I 203–05; **11** 528–31 (**upd.**); **38** 458–62 (**upd.**)

Toyota Tsusho America, Inc., **13** 371

Toys 'R Us, Inc., V 203–06; **18** 522–25 (**upd.**); **57** 370–75 (**upd.**)

TP Transportation, **39** 377

TPA *see* Aloha Airlines Incorporated.

TPCR Corporation *see* The Price Company.

TPG N.V., 64 388–91 (**upd.**)

TPS SNC, **76** 274

Trac Inc., **44** 355

Trace International Holdings, Inc., **17** 182–83; **26** 502

Tracinda Corporation, **25** 329–30

Tracker Marine *see* Bass Pro Shops, Inc.

Tracker Services, Inc., **9** 110

Traco International N.V., **8** 250; **32** 249

Tracor Inc., 17 490–92

Tractebel S.A., 20 491–93 *see also* Suez Lyonnaise des Eaux.

Tractor Supply Company, 57 376–78

Tradax, **II** 617; **13** 137

Trade Development Bank, **11** 415–17

Trade Secret Development Corp. *see* Regis Corporation.

Trade Source International, **44** 132

Trade Waste Incineration, Inc., **9** 109

Trade-Winds Environmental Restoration, Inc., **62** 389

Trademark Metals Recycling LLC, **76** 130

Trader Classified Media N.V., 57 379–82

Trader Joe's Company, 13 525–27; **50** 487–90 (**upd.**)

Trader Media Group, **53** 152

Trader Publications, Inc., **IV** 597

Trader Publishing Company, **12** 302

Traders Group Ltd., **11** 258

Trading Cove Associates *see* Kerzner International Limited.

Trading Post Group Pty Ltd., **57** 381

The Trading Service, **10** 278

Tradition Financial Services *see* Viel & Cie.

Traex Corporation, **8** 359

Trafalgar House Investments Ltd., **IV** 259, 711; **20** 313; **23** 161; **24** 88; **36** 322

Trafalgar House PLC, **47** 178

TrafficLeader *see* Marchex, Inc.

Traffix, Inc., 61 374–76

Trafford Park Printers, **53** 152

Trafiroad NV, **39** 239

Trailer Bridge, Inc., 41 397–99

Trailways Lines, Inc., **I** 450; **9** 425; **32** 230

Trak Auto Corporation, **16** 159–62

TRAK Communications Inc., **44** 420

TRAK Microwave Corporation, **18** 497, 513

Trammell Crow Company, 8 532–34; **57** 383–87 (**upd.**)

Trane, 78 402–405

Trans-Canada Air Lines *see* Air Canada.

Trans Colorado, **11** 299

Trans-Continental Leaf Tobacco Company, (TCLTC), **13** 491

Trans Continental Records, **52** 430

Trans Freight Lines, **27** 473–74

Trans International Airlines, **41** 402

Trans Louisiana Gas Company, **43** 56–57

Trans-Lux Corporation, 51 380–83

Trans-Mex, Inc. S.A. de C.V., **42** 365

Trans-Natal Coal Corp., **IV** 93

Trans Ocean Products, **8** 510

Trans-Pacific Airlines *see* Aloha Airlines Incorporated.

Trans-Resources Inc., **13** 299

Trans Tech Electric Inc. *see* Quanta Services, Inc.

Trans Thai-Malaysia, **56** 290

Trans Union Corp., **IV** 137; **6** 25; **28** 119

Trans Western Publishing, **25** 496

Trans World Airlines, Inc., I 125–27; **12** 487–90 (**upd.**); **35** 424–29 (**upd.**)

Trans-World Corp., **19** 456; **47** 231

Trans World Entertainment Corporation, 24 501–03; **68** 374–77 (**upd.**)

Trans World International, **18** 262–63

Trans World Life Insurance Company, **27** 46–47

Trans World Music, **9** 361

Trans World Seafood, Inc., **13** 244

Transaction Systems Architects, Inc., 29 477–79

Transaction Technology, **12** 334

TransAlta Utilities Corporation, 6 585–87

Transamerica—An AEGON Company, 41 400–03 (**upd.**)

Transamerica Corporation, I 536–38; **13** 528–30 (**upd.**) *see also* TIG Holdings, Inc.

Transamerica Pawn Holdings *see* EZCORP Inc.

Transamerica Retirement Services, **63** 176

TransAmerican Waste Industries Inc., **41** 414

Transat *see* Compagnie Générale Transatlantique (Transat).

Transatlantic Holdings, Inc., III 198; **11** 532–33; **15** 18

Transatlantische Gruppe, **III** 404

Transax, **63** 102

TransBrasil S/A Linhas Aéreas, 31 443–45; **46** 398

TransCanada PipeLines Limited, V 737–38

Transco Energy Company, V 739–40; **18** 366 *see also* The Williams Companies.

Transcontinental and Western Air Lines, **9** 416; **12** 487

Transcontinental Gas Pipe Line Corporation *see* Transco Energy Company.

Transcontinental Services Group N.V., **16** 207; **76** 149

TransCor America, Inc., **23** 154

Transelco, Inc., **8** 178

Transfer Drivers, Inc., **46** 301

Transfracht, **6** 426

Transiciel SA, 48 400–02

Transit Homes of America, Inc., **46** 301

Transit Mix Concrete and Materials Company, **7** 541

Transitions Optical Inc., **21** 221, 223

Transitron, **16** 332

Ultra Mart, **16** 250

Ultra Pac, Inc., 24 512–14

Ultra Petroleum Corporation, 71
369–71

UltraCam *see* Ultrak Inc.

UltraCare Products, **18** 148

Ultrak Inc., 24 508–11

Ultralar, **13** 544

Ultralife Batteries, Inc., 58 345–48

Ultramar Diamond Shamrock
Corporation, IV 565–68; **31** 453–57
(upd.)

Ultrametl Mfg. Co., **17** 234

ULVAC, Inc., 80 388–391

Umacs of Canada Inc., **9** 513

Umberto's of New Hyde Park Pizzeria, **16**
447

Umbro Holdings Ltd. *see* Stone
Manufacturing Company.

UMC *see* United Microelectronics Corp.

UMG *see* Universal Music Group.

UMI Company, **29** 58

NV Umicore SA, 47 411–13

Umpqua River Navigation Company, **13**
100

Unadulterated Food Products, Inc., **11**
449

UNAT, **III** 197–98

Unbrako Socket Screw Company Ltd., **30**
429

Uncas-Merchants National Bank, **13** 467

UNCF *see* United Negro College Fund,
Inc.

Uncle Ben's Inc., 22 528–30

Under Armour Performance Apparel, 61
381–83

Underwood, **24** 269

Underwriter for the Professions Insurance
Company, **55** 128

Underwriters Laboratories, Inc., 30
467–70

Underwriters Reinsurance Co., **10** 45

Unefon, S.A., **39** 194, 196

UNELCO *see* Union Electrica de Canarias
S.A.

Unelec, Inc., **13** 398

UNG *see* United National Group, Ltd.

Ungaro SA, **62** 313

Uni-Cast *see* Sturm, Ruger & Company,
Inc.

Uni Europe, **III** 211

Uni-Marts, Inc., 17 499–502

Uni-President Group, **49** 460

Unibail SA, 40 444–46

Unibanco Holdings S.A., 73 350–53

Unibank, **40** 336; **50** 149–50

Unic *see* GIB Group.

Unica Corporation, 77 450–454

Unicapital, Inc., **15** 281

Unicare Health Facilities, **6** 182; **25** 525

Unicco Security Services, **27** 22

Unice, **56** 335

UNICEF *see* United Nations International
Children's Emergency Fund
(UNICEF).

Unicel *see* Rural Cellular Corporation.

Unicer, **9** 100

Unichem, **25** 73

Unichema International, **13** 228

Unicom Corporation, 29 486–90 (upd.)
see also Exelon Corporation.

Unicon Producing Co., **10** 191

Unicoolait, **19** 51

UNICOR *see* Federal Prison Industries,
Inc.

Unicord Company, **24** 115; **64** 60

UniCorp, **8** 228

UniCredito Italiano, **50** 410

Uniden, **14** 117

Unidrive, **47** 280

UniDynamics Corporation, **8** 135

Uniface Holding B.V., **10** 245; **30** 142

Unifi, Inc., 12 501–03; 62 372–76
(upd.)

Unified Energy System of Russia *see* RAO
Unified Energy System of Russia.

Unified Western Grocers, **31** 25

UniFirst Corporation, 21 505–07

Uniflex Corporation, **53** 236

Uniforce Services Inc., **40** 119

Unigate PLC, II 586–87; **28** 488–91
(upd.); 29 150 *see also* Uniq Plc.

Unigesco Inc., **II** 653

Uniglory, **13** 211

Unigro *see* Laurus N.V.

Unigroup, **15** 50

UniHealth America, **11** 378–79

Unijoh Sdn, Bhd, **47** 255

Unik S.A., **23** 170–171

Unilab Corp., **26** 391

Unilever PLC/Unilever N.V., II 588–91;
7 542–45 **(upd.); 32** 472–78 **(upd.)**

Unilife Assurance Group, **III** 273

UniLife Insurance Co., **22** 149

Unilog SA, 42 401–03

Uniloy Milacron Inc., **53** 230

UniMac Companies, **11** 413

Unimetal, **30** 252

Uninsa, **I** 460

Union Aéromaritime de Transport *see*
UTA.

Union Bag–Camp Paper Corp. *see* Union
Camp Corporation.

Union Bank *see* State Street Boston
Corporation.

Union Bank of California, 16 496–98
see also UnionBanCal Corporation.

Union Bank of New York, **9** 229

Union Bank of Scotland, **10** 337

Union Bank of Switzerland, II 378–79;
21 146 *see also* UBS AG.

Union Bay Sportswear, **17** 460

Union Biscuits *see* Leroux S.A.S.

Union Camp Corporation, IV 344–46

Union Carbide Corporation, I 399–401;
9 516–20 **(upd.); 74** 358–63 **(upd.)**

Union Cervecera, **9** 100

Union Colliery Company *see* Union
Electric Company.

Union Commerce Corporation, **11** 181

Union Commerciale, **19** 98

Union Corporation *see* Gencor Ltd.

Union des Assurances de Paris, II 234;
III 201, 391–94

Union des Coopératives Bressor, **25** 85

Union des Cooperatives Laitières *see*
Unicoolait.

Union des Mines, **52** 362

Union des Transports Aériens *see* UTA.

Union Electric Company, V 741–43; **26**
451 *see also* Ameren Corporation.

Unión Electrica Fenosa *see* Unión Fenosa
S.A.

Union Equity Co-Operative Exchange, **7**
175

Unión Fenosa, S.A., 51 387–90

Union Financiera, **19** 189

Union Financière de France Banque SA,
52 360–62

Union Fork & Hoe Company *see* Acorn
Products, Inc.

Union Gas & Electric Co., **6** 529

l'Union Générale des Pétroles, **IV** 560

Union Hardware, **22** 115

Union Laitière Normande *see* Compagnie
Laitière Européenne.

Union Levantina de Seguros, **III** 179

Union Light, Heat & Power Company *see*
Cincinnati Gas & Electric Company.

Union Minière *see* NV Umicore SA.

Union Mutual Life Insurance Company
see UNUM Corp.

Union National Bank of Wilmington, **25**
540

Union of European Football Association,
27 150

Union of Food Co-ops, **II** 622

Union Oil Co., **9** 266

Union Oil Co. of California *see* Unocal
Corporation.

Union Pacific Corporation, V 529–32;
28 492–500 **(upd.)** ; **79** 435–446
(upd.)

Union Pacific Resources Group, **52** 30

Union Pacific Tea Co., **7** 202

Union Paper & Co. AS, **63** 315

Union Planters Corporation, 54 387–90

Union Power Company, **12** 541

Union Power Construction Co. *see*
Quanta Services, Inc.

Union Pub Company, **57** 411, 413

Union Savings and Loan Association of
Phoenix, **19** 412

Union Savings Bank, **9** 173

Union Savings Bank and Trust Company,
13 221

Union Steamship Co. of New Zealand
Ltd., **27** 473

Union Sugar, **II** 573

Union Suisse des Coopératives de
Consommation *see* Coop Schweiz.

Union Tank Car Co., **IV** 137

Union Telecard Alliance, LLC, **34** 223

Union Telephone Company, **14** 258

Union Texas Petroleum Holdings, Inc.,
7 379; **9 521–23**

Union Trust Co., **9** 228; **13** 222

The Union Underwear Company, **8**
200–01; **25** 164–66

Union Verwaltungsgesellschaft mbH, **66**
123

Unionamerica, Inc., **III** 243; **16** 497; **50**
497

Index to Industries

Automotive

Beverages

Bio-Technology

Howard Hughes Medical Institute, 39
Huntingdon Life Sciences Group plc, 42
IDEXX Laboratories, Inc., 23
ImClone Systems Inc., 58
Immunex Corporation, 14; 50 (upd.)
IMPATH Inc., 45
Incyte Genomics, Inc., 52
Inverness Medical Innovations, Inc., 63
Invitrogen Corporation, 52
The Judge Group, Inc., 51
Life Technologies, Inc., 17
LifeCell Corporation, 77
Lonza Group Ltd., 73
Martek Biosciences Corporation, 65
Medtronic, Inc., 30 (upd.)
Millipore Corporation, 25
Minntech Corporation, 22
Mycogen Corporation, 21
New Brunswick Scientific Co., Inc., 45
Qiagen N.V., 39
Quintiles Transnational Corporation, 21
Seminis, Inc., 29
Serologicals Corporation, 63
Sigma-Aldrich Corporation, 36 (upd.)
Starkey Laboratories, Inc., 52
STERIS Corporation, 29
Stratagene Corporation, 70
Tanox, Inc., 77
TECHNE Corporation, 52
TriPath Imaging, Inc., 77
Waters Corporation, 43
Whatman plc, 46
Wisconsin Alumni Research Foundation, 65
Wyeth, 50 (upd.)

Chemicals

A. Schulman, Inc., 8
Aceto Corp., 38
Air Products and Chemicals, Inc., I; 10 (upd.); 74 (upd.)
Airgas, Inc., 54
Akzo Nobel N.V., 13
Albemarle Corporation, 59
AlliedSignal Inc., 22 (upd.)
American Cyanamid, I; 8 (upd.)
American Vanguard Corporation, 47
Arch Chemicals Inc. 78
ARCO Chemical Company, 10
Asahi Denka Kogyo KK, 64
Atanor S.A., 62
Atochem S.A., I
Avantium Technologies BV, 79
Avecia Group PLC, 63
Baker Hughes Incorporated, 22 (upd.); 57 (upd.)
Balchem Corporation, 42
BASF Aktiengesellschaft, I; 18 (upd.); 50 (upd.)
Bayer A.G., I; 13 (upd.); 41 (upd.)
Betz Laboratories, Inc., I; 10 (upd.)
The BFGoodrich Company, 19 (upd.)
BOC Group plc, I; 25 (upd.); 78 (upd.)
Brenntag AG, 8; 23 (upd.)
Burmah Castrol PLC, 30 (upd.)
Cabot Corporation, 8; 29 (upd.)
Calgon Carbon Corporation, 73
Caliper Life Sciences, Inc., 70

Cambrex Corporation, 16
Catalytica Energy Systems, Inc., 44
Celanese Corporation, I
Celanese Mexicana, S.A. de C.V., 54
Chemcentral Corporation, 8
Chemi-Trol Chemical Co., 16
Church & Dwight Co., Inc., 29
Ciba-Geigy Ltd., I; 8 (upd.)
The Clorox Company, 22 (upd.)
Croda International Plc, 45
Crompton Corporation, 9; 36 (upd.)
Cytec Industries Inc., 27
Degussa-Hüls AG, 32 (upd.)
DeKalb Genetics Corporation, 17
The Dexter Corporation, I; 12 (upd.)
Dionex Corporation, 46
The Dow Chemical Company, I; 8 (upd.); 50 (upd.)
DSM N.V., I; 56 (upd.)
Dynaction S.A., 67
E.I. du Pont de Nemours & Company, I; 8 (upd.); 26 (upd.)
Eastman Chemical Company, 14; 38 (upd.)
Ecolab Inc., I; 13 (upd.); 34 (upd.)
Elementis plc, 40 (upd.)
Engelhard Corporation, 72 (upd.)
English China Clays Ltd., 15 (upd.); 40 (upd.)
Enterprise Rent-A-Car Company, 69 (upd.)
Equistar Chemicals, LP, 71
Ercros S.A., 80
ERLY Industries Inc., 17
Ethyl Corporation, I; 10 (upd.)
Ferro Corporation, 8; 56 (upd.)
Firmenich International S.A., 60
First Mississippi Corporation, 8
Formosa Plastics Corporation, 14; 58 (upd.)
Fort James Corporation, 22 (upd.)
G.A.F., I
The General Chemical Group Inc., 37
Georgia Gulf Corporation, 9; 61 (upd.)
Givaudan SA, 43
Great Lakes Chemical Corporation, I; 14 (upd.)
Guerbet Group, 46
H.B. Fuller Company, 32 (upd.); 75 (upd.)
Hauser, Inc., 46
Hawkins Chemical, Inc., 16
Henkel KGaA, 34 (upd.)
Hercules Inc., I; 22 (upd.); 66 (upd.)
Hoechst A.G., I; 18 (upd.)
Hoechst Celanese Corporation, 13
Huls A.G., I
Huntsman Chemical Corporation, 8
IMC Fertilizer Group, Inc., 8
Imperial Chemical Industries PLC, I; 50 (upd.)
International Flavors & Fragrances Inc., 9; 38 (upd.)
Israel Chemicals Ltd., 55
Kemira Oyj, 70
Koppers Industries, Inc., I; 26 (upd.)
L'Air Liquide SA, I; 47 (upd.)
Lawter International Inc., 14

LeaRonal, Inc., 23
Loctite Corporation, 30 (upd.)
Lonza Group Ltd., 73
Lubrizol Corporation, I; 30 (upd.)
Lyondell Chemical Company, 45 (upd.)
M.A. Hanna Company, 8
MacDermid Incorporated, 32
Mallinckrodt Group Inc., 19
MBC Holding Company, 40
Melamine Chemicals, Inc., 27
Methanex Corporation, 40
Minerals Technologies Inc., 52 (upd.)
Mississippi Chemical Corporation, 39
Mitsubishi Chemical Corporation, I; 56 (upd.)
Mitsui Petrochemical Industries, Ltd., 9
Monsanto Company, I; 9 (upd.); 29 (upd.)
Montedison SpA, I
Morton International Inc., I; 9 (upd.); 80 (upd.)
Nagase & Company, Ltd., 8
Nalco Chemical Corporation, I; 12 (upd.)
National Distillers and Chemical Corporation, I
National Sanitary Supply Co., 16
National Starch and Chemical Company, 49
NCH Corporation, 8
Nisshin Seifun Group Inc., 66 (upd.)
NL Industries, Inc., 10
Nobel Industries AB, 9
NOF Corporation, 72
Norsk Hydro ASA, 35 (upd.)
Novacor Chemicals Ltd., 12
NutraSweet Company, 8
Occidental Petroleum Corporation, 71 (upd.)
Olin Corporation, I; 13 (upd.); 78 (upd.)
OM Group, Inc., 17; 78 (upd.)
OMNOVA Solutions Inc., 59
Penford Corporation, 55
Pennwalt Corporation, I
Perstorp AB, I; 51 (upd.)
Petrolite Corporation, 15
Pfizer Inc., 79 (upd.)
Pioneer Hi-Bred International, Inc., 41 (upd.)
Praxair, Inc., 11
Quantum Chemical Corporation, 8
Reichhold Chemicals, Inc., 10
Renner Herrmann S.A., 79
Rhodia SA, 38
Rhône-Poulenc S.A., I; 10 (upd.)
Robertet SA, 39
Rohm and Haas Company, I; 26 (upd.); 77 (upd.)
Roussel Uclaf, I; 8 (upd.)
RPM, Inc., 36 (upd.)
RWE AG, 50 (upd.)
The Scotts Company, 22
SCP Pool Corporation, 39
Sequa Corp., 13
Shanghai Petrochemical Co., Ltd., 18
Sigma-Aldrich Corporation, 36 (upd.)
Solutia Inc., 52
Solvay S.A., I; 21 (upd.); 61 (upd.)
Stepan Company, 30

Conglomerates

Construction

Electrical & Electronics

Engineering & Management Services

Financial Services: Excluding Banks

Food Products

Food Services & Retailers

Health & Personal Care Products

Health Care Services

Insurance

Legal Services

Manufacturing

Mining & Metals

Paper & Forestry

Personal Services

Publishing & Printing

Harold's Stores, Inc., 22
Harrods Holdings, 47
Harry Winston Inc., 45
Harvey Norman Holdings Ltd., 56
Hasbro, Inc., 43 (upd.)
Haverty Furniture Companies, Inc., 31
Hechinger Company, 12
Heilig-Meyers Company, 14; 40 (upd.)
Helzberg Diamonds, 40
Hennes & Mauritz AB, 29
Henry Modell & Company Inc., 32
Hensley & Company, 64
Hertie Waren- und Kaufhaus GmbH, V
Hibbett Sporting Goods, Inc., 26; 70 (upd.)
Highsmith Inc., 60
Hills Stores Company, 13
Hines Horticulture, Inc., 49
HMV Group plc, 59
Hobby Lobby Stores Inc., 80
The Hockey Company, 34
Holiday RV Superstores, Incorporated, 26
Holt's Cigar Holdings, Inc., 42
The Home Depot, Inc., V; 18 (upd.)
Home Hardware Stores Ltd., 62
Home Interiors & Gifts, Inc., 55
Home Shopping Network, Inc., V; 25 (upd.)
HomeBase, Inc., 33 (upd.)
Hot Topic, Inc., 33
House of Fabrics, Inc., 21
House of Fraser PLC, 45
HSN, 64 (upd.)
Hudson's Bay Company, V; 25 (upd.)
Huttig Building Products, Inc., 73
Ihr Platz GmbH + Company KG, 77
IKEA International A/S, V; 26 (upd.)
InaCom Corporation, 13
Indigo Books & Music Inc., 58
Insight Enterprises, Inc., 18
International Airline Support Group, Inc., 55
Intimate Brands, Inc., 24
Isetan Company Limited, V; 36 (upd.)
Ito-Yokado Co., Ltd., V; 42 (upd.)
J&R Electronics Inc., 26
J. Baker, Inc., 31
The J. Jill Group, Inc., 35
J.C. Penney Company, Inc., V; 18 (upd.); 43 (upd.)
J.L. Hammett Company, 72
Jack Schwartz Shoes, Inc., 18
Jacobson Stores Inc., 21
Jalate Inc., 25
James Beattie plc, 43
Jay Jacobs, Inc., 15
Jennifer Convertibles, Inc., 31
Jetro Cash & Carry Enterprises Inc., 38
JG Industries, Inc., 15
JJB Sports plc, 32
Jo-Ann Stores, Inc., 72 (upd.)
John Lewis Partnership plc, V; 42 (upd.)
JUSCO Co., Ltd., V
Just For Feet, Inc., 19
K & B Inc., 12
K & G Men's Center, Inc., 21
K-tel International, Inc., 21
Karstadt Aktiengesellschaft, V; 19 (upd.)

Kash n' Karry Food Stores, Inc., 20
Kasper A.S.L., Ltd., 40
kate spade LLC, 68
Kaufhof Warenhaus AG, V; 23 (upd.)
Kaufring AG, 35
Kay-Bee Toy Stores, 15
Kiabi Europe, 66
Kiehl's Since 1851, Inc., 52
Kingfisher plc, V; 24 (upd.)
Kinney Shoe Corp., 14
Kmart Corporation, V; 18 (upd.); 47 (upd.)
Knoll Group Inc., 14
Kohl's Corporation, 9; 30 (upd.); 77 (upd.)
Koninklijke Vendex KBB N.V. (Royal Vendex KBB N.V.), 62 (upd.)
Kotobukiya Co., Ltd., V; 56 (upd.)
Krause's Furniture, Inc., 27
Krispy Kreme Doughnuts, Inc., 61 (upd.)
L. and J.G. Stickley, Inc., 50
L. Luria & Son, Inc., 19
L.A. T Sportswear, Inc., 26
L.L. Bean, Inc., 38 (upd.)
La Senza Corporation, 66
La-Z-Boy Incorporated, 14; 50 (upd.)
Lamonts Apparel, Inc., 15
Lands' End, Inc., 9; 29 (upd.)
Lane Bryant, Inc., 64
Lanier Worldwide, Inc., 75
Lanoga Corporation, 62
Laura Ashley Holdings plc, 37 (upd.)
Lazare Kaplan International Inc., 21
Le Chateau Inc., 63
Lechmere Inc., 10
Lechters, Inc., 11; 39 (upd.)
LensCrafters Inc., 23; 76 (upd.)
Leroy Merlin SA, 54
Les Boutiques San Francisco, Inc., 62
Lesco Inc., 19
Leslie's Poolmart, Inc., 18
Leupold & Stevens, Inc., 52
Levenger Company, 63
Levitz Furniture Inc., 15
Lewis Galoob Toys Inc., 16
Li & Fung Limited, 59
Life is Good, Inc., 80
Lifetime Brands, Inc., 27; 73 (upd.)
The Limited, Inc., V; 20 (upd.)
Linens 'n Things, Inc., 24; 75 (upd.)
Little Switzerland, Inc., 60
Littlewoods plc, V; 42 (upd.)
Liz Claiborne, Inc., 25 (upd.)
LKQ Corporation, 71
Loehmann's Inc., 24
Lojas Americanas S.A., 77
Lojas Arapuã S.A., 22; 61 (upd.)
London Drugs Ltd., 46
Longs Drug Stores Corporation, V; 25 (upd.)
Lookers plc, 71
Lost Arrow Inc., 22
LOT$OFF Corporation, 24
Love's Travel Stops & Country Stores, Inc., 71
Lowe's Companies, Inc., V; 21 (upd.)
Luxottica SpA, 52 (upd.)
Mac Frugal's Bargains - Closeouts Inc., 17

Mac-Gray Corporation, 44
Manutan International S.A., 72
MarineMax, Inc., 30
Marionnaud Parfumeries SA, 51
Marks and Spencer p.l.c., V; 24 (upd.)
Marks Brothers Jewelers, Inc., 24
Marshall Field's, 63
Marshalls Incorporated, 13
Marui Company Ltd., V; 62 (upd.)
Maruzen Co., Limited, 18
Mary Kay, Inc., 30 (upd.)
Matalan PLC, 49
Matsuzakaya Company Ltd., V; 64 (upd.)
Maus Frères SA, 48
The Maxim Group, 25
The May Department Stores Company, V; 19 (upd.); 46 (upd.)
Mayor's Jewelers, Inc., 41
Mazel Stores, Inc., 29
McCoy Corporation, 58
McJunkin Corporation, 63
McKesson Corporation, 47 (upd.)
McLane Company, Inc., 13
MCSi, Inc., 41
Media Arts Group, Inc., 42
Meier & Frank Co., 23
Meijer Incorporated, 27 (upd.)
Melville Corporation, V
The Men's Wearhouse, Inc., 17; 48 (upd.)
Menard, Inc., 34
Mercantile Stores Company, Inc., V; 19 (upd.)
Mercury Drug Corporation, 70
Merry-Go-Round Enterprises, Inc., 8
Mervyn's California, 10; 39 (upd.)
Metro AG, 50
Michael C. Fina Co., Inc., 52
Michaels Stores, Inc., 17; 71 (upd.)
Michigan Sporting Goods Distributors, Inc., 72
Micro Warehouse, Inc., 16
MicroAge, Inc., 16
Migros-Genossenschafts-Bund, 68
Mitsukoshi Ltd., V; 56 (upd.)
MNS, Ltd., 65
Monrovia Nursery Company, 70
Monsoon plc, 39
Montgomery Ward & Co., Incorporated, V; 20 (upd.)
Moore-Handley, Inc., 39
Morse Shoe Inc., 13
Moss Bros Group plc, 51
Mothercare plc, 78 (upd.)
Mothers Work, Inc., 18
Moto Photo, Inc., 45
Mr. Bricolage S.A., 37
MSC Industrial Direct Co., Inc., 71
MTS Inc., 37
Mulberry Group PLC, 71
Musicland Stores Corporation, 9; 38 (upd.)
MWI Veterinary Supply, Inc., 80
Nagasakiya Co., Ltd., V; 69 (upd.)
Nash Finch Company, 65 (upd.)
National Educational Music Co. Ltd., 47
National Home Centers, Inc., 44
National Intergroup, Inc., V
National Record Mart, Inc., 29

Textiles & Apparel

Tobacco

Philip Morris Companies Inc., V; 18 (upd.)

R.J. Reynolds Tobacco Holdings, Inc., 30 (upd.)

RJR Nabisco Holdings Corp., V

Rothmans UK Holdings Limited, V; 19 (upd.)

Seita, 23

Souza Cruz S.A., 65

Standard Commercial Corporation, 13; 62 (upd.)

Swisher International Group Inc., 23

Tabacalera, S.A., V; 17 (upd.)

Taiwan Tobacco & Liquor Corporation, 75

Universal Corporation, V; 48 (upd.)

UST Inc., 9; 50 (upd.)

Vector Group Ltd., 35 (upd.)

Transport Services

Abertis Infraestructuras, S.A., 65

Aéroports de Paris, 33

Air Express International Corporation, 13

Airborne Freight Corporation, 6; 34 (upd.)

Alamo Rent A Car, Inc., 6; 24 (upd.)

Alaska Railroad Corporation, 60

Alexander & Baldwin, Inc., 10

Allied Worldwide, Inc., 49

AMCOL International Corporation, 59 (upd.)

Amerco, 6

AMERCO, 67 (upd.)

American Classic Voyages Company, 27

American President Companies Ltd., 6

Anderson Trucking Service, Inc., 75

Anschutz Corp., 12

APL Limited, 61 (upd.)

Aqua Alliance Inc., 32 (upd.)

Arriva PLC, 69

Atlas Van Lines, Inc., 14

Attica Enterprises S.A., 64

Avis Group Holdings, Inc., 75 (upd.)

Avis Rent A Car, Inc., 6; 22 (upd.)

BAA plc, 10

Bekins Company, 15

Berliner Verkehrsbetriebe (BVG), 58

Bollinger Shipyards, Inc., 61

Boyd Bros. Transportation Inc., 39

Brambles Industries Limited, 42

The Brink's Company, 58 (upd.)

British Railways Board, V

Broken Hill Proprietary Company Ltd., 22 (upd.)

Buckeye Partners, L.P., 70

Budget Group, Inc., 25

Budget Rent a Car Corporation, 9

Burlington Northern Santa Fe Corporation, V; 27 (upd.)

C.H. Robinson Worldwide, Inc., 40 (upd.)

Canadian National Railway Company, 71 (upd.)

Canadian National Railway System, 6

Canadian Pacific Railway Limited, V; 45 (upd.)

Cannon Express, Inc., 53

Carey International, Inc., 26

Carlson Companies, Inc., 6

Carolina Freight Corporation, 6

Celadon Group Inc., 30

Central Japan Railway Company, 43

Chargeurs, 6

CHC Helicopter Corporation, 67

CHEP Pty. Ltd., 80

Chicago and North Western Holdings Corporation, 6

Christian Salvesen Plc, 45

Coach USA, Inc., 24; 55 (upd.)

Coles Express Inc., 15

Compagnie Générale Maritime et Financière, 6

Consolidated Delivery & Logistics, Inc., 24

Consolidated Freightways Corporation, V; 21 (upd.); 48 (upd.)

Consolidated Rail Corporation, V

CR England, Inc., 63

Crowley Maritime Corporation, 6; 28 (upd.)

CSX Corporation, V; 22 (upd.); 79 (upd.)

Danzas Group, V; 40 (upd.)

Dart Group PLC, 77

Deutsche Bahn AG, V; 46 (upd.)

DHL Worldwide Network S.A./N.V., 6; 24 (upd.); 69 (upd.)

Dollar Thrifty Automotive Group, Inc., 25

Dot Foods, Inc., 69

East Japan Railway Company, V; 66 (upd.)

EGL, Inc., 59

Emery Air Freight Corporation, 6

Emery Worldwide Airlines, Inc., 25 (upd.)

Enterprise Rent-A-Car Company, 6

Eurotunnel Group, 37 (upd.)

EVA Airways Corporation, 51

Evergreen International Aviation, Inc., 53

Evergreen Marine Corporation (Taiwan) Ltd., 13; 50 (upd.)

Executive Jet, Inc., 36

Exel plc, 51 (upd.)

Expeditors International of Washington Inc., 17; 78 (upd.)

Federal Express Corporation, V

FedEx Corporation, 18 (upd.); 42 (upd.)

Forward Air Corporation, 75

Fritz Companies, Inc., 12

Frontline Ltd., 45

Frozen Food Express Industries, Inc., 20

Garuda Indonesia, 58 (upd.)

GATX Corporation, 6; 25 (upd.)

GE Capital Aviation Services, 36

Gefco SA, 54

General Maritime Corporation, 59

Genesee & Wyoming Inc., 27

Geodis S.A., 67

The Go-Ahead Group Plc, 28

The Greenbrier Companies, 19

Greyhound Lines, Inc., 32 (upd.)

Groupe Bourbon S.A., 60

Grupo TMM, S.A. de C.V., 50

Grupo Transportación Ferroviaria Mexicana, S.A. de C.V., 47

Gulf Agency Company Ltd. 78

GulfMark Offshore, Inc., 49

Hanjin Shipping Co., Ltd., 50

Hankyu Corporation, V; 23 (upd.)

Hapag-Lloyd AG, 6

Harland and Wolff Holdings plc, 19

Harper Group Inc., 17

Heartland Express, Inc., 18

The Hertz Corporation, 9

Holberg Industries, Inc., 36

Hospitality Worldwide Services, Inc., 26

Hub Group, Inc., 38

Hvide Marine Incorporated, 22

Illinois Central Corporation, 11

International Shipholding Corporation, Inc., 27

J.B. Hunt Transport Services Inc., 12

John Menzies plc, 39

Kansas City Southern Industries, Inc., 6; 26 (upd.)

Kawasaki Kisen Kaisha, Ltd., V; 56 (upd.)

Keio Teito Electric Railway Company, V

Keolis SA, 51

Kinki Nippon Railway Company Ltd., V

Kirby Corporation, 18; 66 (upd.)

Knight Transportation, Inc., 64

Koninklijke Nedlloyd Groep N.V., 6

Kuehne & Nagel International AG, V; 53 (upd.)

La Poste, V; 47 (upd.)

Laidlaw International, Inc., 80

Landstar System, Inc., 63

Leaseway Transportation Corp., 12

London Regional Transport, 6

The Long Island Rail Road Company, 68

Maine Central Railroad Company, 16

Mammoet Transport B.V., 26

Martz Group, 56

Mayflower Group Inc., 6

Mercury Air Group, Inc., 20

The Mersey Docks and Harbour Company, 30

Metropolitan Transportation Authority, 35

Miller Industries, Inc., 26

Mitsui O.S.K. Lines, Ltd., V

Moran Towing Corporation, Inc., 15

The Morgan Group, Inc., 46

Morris Travel Services L.L.C., 26

Motor Cargo Industries, Inc., 35

National Car Rental System, Inc., 10

National Express Group PLC, 50

National Railroad Passenger Corporation (Amtrak), 22; 66 (upd.)

Neptune Orient Lines Limited, 47

NFC plc, 6

Nippon Express Company, Ltd., V; 64 (upd.)

Nippon Yusen Kabushiki Kaisha (NYK), V; 72 (upd.)

Norfolk Southern Corporation, V; 29 (upd.); 75 (upd.)

Oak Harbor Freight Lines, Inc., 53

Ocean Group plc, 6

Odakyu Electric Railway Co., Ltd., V; 68 (upd.)

Oglebay Norton Company, 17

Old Dominion Freight Line, Inc., 57

OMI Corporation, 59

The Oppenheimer Group, 76

Österreichische Bundesbahnen GmbH, 6

Utilities

Gulf States Utilities Company, 6
Hawaiian Electric Industries, Inc., 9
Hokkaido Electric Power Company Inc. (HEPCO), V; 58 (upd.)
Hokuriku Electric Power Company, V
Hong Kong and China Gas Company Ltd., 73
Hongkong Electric Holdings Ltd., 6; 23 (upd.)
Houston Industries Incorporated, V
Hyder plc, 34
Hydro-Québec, 6; 32 (upd.)
Iberdrola, S.A., 49
Idaho Power Company, 12
Illinois Bell Telephone Company, 14
Illinois Power Company, 6
Indiana Energy, Inc., 27
International Power PLC, 50 (upd.)
IPALCO Enterprises, Inc., 6
ITC Holdings Corp., 75
The Kansai Electric Power Company, Inc., V; 62 (upd.)
Kansas City Power & Light Company, 6
Kelda Group plc, 45
Kenetech Corporation, 11
Kentucky Utilities Company, 6
KeySpan Energy Co., 27
Korea Electric Power Corporation (Kepco), 56
KU Energy Corporation, 11
Kyushu Electric Power Company Inc., V
LG&E Energy Corporation, 6; 51 (upd.)
Long Island Lighting Company, V
Lyonnaise des Eaux-Dumez, V
Madison Gas and Electric Company, 39
Magma Power Company, 11
Maine & Maritimes Corporation, 56
Manila Electric Company (Meralco), 56
MCN Corporation, 6
MDU Resources Group, Inc., 7; 42 (upd.)
Middlesex Water Company, 45
Midwest Resources Inc., 6
Minnesota Power, Inc., 11; 34 (upd.)
The Montana Power Company, 11; 44 (upd.)
National Fuel Gas Company, 6
National Grid USA, 51 (upd.)
National Power PLC, 12
Nebraska Public Power District, 29
N.V. Nederlandse Gasunie, V
Nevada Power Company, 11
New England Electric System, V
New Jersey Resources Corporation, 54
New York State Electric and Gas, 6
Neyveli Lignite Corporation Ltd., 65
Niagara Mohawk Holdings Inc., V; 45 (upd.)
NICOR Inc., 6
NIPSCO Industries, Inc., 6
North West Water Group plc, 11
Northeast Utilities, V; 48 (upd.)
Northern States Power Company, V; 20 (upd.)
Northwest Natural Gas Company, 45
NorthWestern Corporation, 37
Nova Corporation of Alberta, V
NRG Energy, Inc., 79
Oglethorpe Power Corporation, 6

Ohio Edison Company, V
Oklahoma Gas and Electric Company, 6
ONEOK Inc., 7
Ontario Hydro Services Company, 6; 32 (upd.)
Osaka Gas Company, Ltd., V; 60 (upd.)
Otter Tail Power Company, 18
Pacific Enterprises, V
Pacific Gas and Electric Company, V
PacifiCorp, V; 26 (upd.)
Panhandle Eastern Corporation, V
PECO Energy Company, 11
Pennon Group Plc, 45
Pennsylvania Power & Light Company, V
Peoples Energy Corporation, 6
PG&E Corporation, 26 (upd.)
Philadelphia Electric Company, V
Philadelphia Suburban Corporation, 39
Piedmont Natural Gas Company, Inc., 27
Pinnacle West Capital Corporation, 6; 54 (upd.)
PNM Resources Inc., 51 (upd.)
Portland General Corporation, 6
Potomac Electric Power Company, 6
Power-One, Inc., 79
Powergen PLC, 11; 50 (upd.)
PPL Corporation, 41 (upd.)
PreussenElektra Aktiengesellschaft, V
Progress Energy, Inc., 74
PSI Resources, 6
Public Service Company of Colorado, 6
Public Service Company of New Hampshire, 21; 55 (upd.)
Public Service Company of New Mexico, 6
Public Service Enterprise Group Inc., V; 44 (upd.)
Puerto Rico Electric Power Authority, 47
Puget Sound Energy Inc., 6; 50 (upd.)
Questar Corporation, 6; 26 (upd.)
RAO Unified Energy System of Russia, 45
Reliant Energy Inc., 44 (upd.)
Rochester Gas and Electric Corporation, 6
Ruhrgas AG, V; 38 (upd.)
RWE AG, V; 50 (upd.)
Salt River Project, 19
San Diego Gas & Electric Company, V
SCANA Corporation, 6; 56 (upd.)
Scarborough Public Utilities Commission, 9
SCEcorp, V
Scottish and Southern Energy plc, 66 (upd.)
Scottish Hydro-Electric PLC, 13
Scottish Power plc, 19; 49 (upd.)
Seattle City Light, 50
SEMCO Energy, Inc., 44
Sempra Energy, 25 (upd.)
Severn Trent PLC, 12; 38 (upd.)
Shikoku Electric Power Company, Inc., V; 60 (upd.)
SJW Corporation, 70
Sonat, Inc., 6
South Jersey Industries, Inc., 42
The Southern Company, V; 38 (upd.)
Southern Electric PLC, 13
Southern Indiana Gas and Electric Company, 13

Southern Union Company, 27
Southwest Gas Corporation, 19
Southwest Water Company, 47
Southwestern Electric Power Co., 21
Southwestern Public Service Company, 6
Suez Lyonnaise des Eaux, 36 (upd.)
TECO Energy, Inc., 6
Tennessee Valley Authority, 50
Tennet BV 78
Texas Utilities Company, V; 25 (upd.)
Thames Water plc, 11
Tohoku Electric Power Company, Inc., V
The Tokyo Electric Power Company, 74 (upd.)
The Tokyo Electric Power Company, Incorporated, V
Tokyo Gas Co., Ltd., V; 55 (upd.)
TransAlta Utilities Corporation, 6
TransCanada PipeLines Limited, V
Transco Energy Company, V
Trigen Energy Corporation, 42
Tucson Electric Power Company, 6
UGI Corporation, 12
Unicom Corporation, 29 (upd.)
Union Electric Company, V
The United Illuminating Company, 21
United Utilities PLC, 52 (upd.)
United Water Resources, Inc., 40
Unitil Corporation, 37
Utah Power and Light Company, 27
UtiliCorp United Inc., 6
Vattenfall AB, 57
Vereinigte Elektrizitätswerke Westfalen AG, V
VEW AG, 39
Viridian Group plc, 64
Warwick Valley Telephone Company, 55
Washington Gas Light Company, 19
Washington Natural Gas Company, 9
Washington Water Power Company, 6
Westar Energy, Inc., 57 (upd.)
Western Resources, Inc., 12
Wheelabrator Technologies, Inc., 6
Wisconsin Energy Corporation, 6; 54 (upd.)
Wisconsin Public Service Corporation, 9
WPL Holdings, Inc., 6
WPS Resources Corporation, 53 (upd.)
Xcel Energy Inc., 73 (upd.)

Waste Services

Allied Waste Industries, Inc., 50
Allwaste, Inc., 18
American Ecology Corporation, 77
Appliance Recycling Centers of America, Inc., 42
Azcon Corporation, 23
Berliner Stadtreinigungsbetriebe, 58
Brambles Industries Limited, 42
Browning-Ferris Industries, Inc., V; 20 (upd.)
Chemical Waste Management, Inc., 9
Clean Harbors, Inc., 73
Copart Inc., 23
E.On AG, 50 (upd.)
Ecology and Environment, Inc., 39
Industrial Services of America, Inc., 46
Ionics, Incorporated, 52

Geographic Index

Shimano Inc., 64
Shionogi & Co., Ltd., III; 17 (upd.)
Shiseido Company, Limited, III; 22 (upd.)
Shochiku Company Ltd., 74
Showa Shell Sekiyu K.K., IV; 59 (upd.)
Snow Brand Milk Products Company,
   Ltd., II; 48 (upd.)
Softbank Corp., 13; 38 (upd.)
Sony Corporation, II; 12 (upd.); 40
   (upd.)
The Sumitomo Bank, Limited, II; 26
   (upd.)
Sumitomo Chemical Company Ltd., I
Sumitomo Corporation, I; 11 (upd.)
Sumitomo Electric Industries, Ltd., II
Sumitomo Heavy Industries, Ltd., III; 42
   (upd.)
Sumitomo Life Insurance Company, III;
   60 (upd.)
The Sumitomo Marine and Fire Insurance
   Company, Limited, III
Sumitomo Metal Industries, Ltd., IV
Sumitomo Metal Mining Co., Ltd., IV
Sumitomo Mitsui Banking Corporation,
   51 (upd.)
Sumitomo Realty & Development Co.,
   Ltd., IV
Sumitomo Rubber Industries, Ltd., V
The Sumitomo Trust & Banking
   Company, Ltd., II; 53 (upd.)
Suntory Ltd., 65
Suzuki Motor Corporation, 9; 23 (upd.);
   59 (upd.)
Taiheiyo Cement Corporation, 60 (upd.)
Taiyo Fishery Company, Limited, II
The Taiyo Kobe Bank, Ltd., II
Takara Holdings Inc., 62
Takashimaya Company, Limited, V; 47
   (upd.)
Takeda Chemical Industries, Ltd., I; 46
   (upd.)
TDK Corporation, II; 17 (upd.); 49
   (upd.)
TEAC Corporation 78
Teijin Limited, V; 61 (upd.)
Terumo Corporation, 48
Tobu Railway Co Ltd, 6
Toho Co., Ltd., 28
Tohoku Electric Power Company, Inc., V
The Tokai Bank, Limited, II; 15 (upd.)
The Tokio Marine and Fire Insurance Co.,
   Ltd., III
The Tokyo Electric Power Company, 74
   (upd.)
The Tokyo Electric Power Company,
   Incorporated, V
Tokyo Gas Co., Ltd., V; 55 (upd.)
Tokyu Corporation, V; 47 (upd.)
Tokyu Department Store Co., Ltd., V; 32
   (upd.)
Tokyu Land Corporation, IV
Tomen Corporation, IV; 24 (upd.)
Tomy Company Ltd., 65
TonenGeneral Sekiyu K.K., IV; 16 (upd.);
   54 (upd.)
Toppan Printing Co., Ltd., IV; 58 (upd.)
Toray Industries, Inc., V; 51 (upd.)

Toshiba Corporation, I; 12 (upd.); 40
   (upd.)
Tosoh Corporation, 70
TOTO LTD., III; 28 (upd.)
Toyo Sash Co., Ltd., III
Toyo Seikan Kaisha, Ltd., I
Toyoda Automatic Loom Works, Ltd., III
Toyota Motor Corporation, I; 11 (upd.);
   38 (upd.)
Ube Industries, Ltd., III; 38 (upd.)
ULVAC, Inc., 80
Unitika Ltd., V; 53 (upd.)
Uny Co., Ltd., V; 49 (upd.)
Victor Company of Japan, Limited, II; 26
   (upd.)
Wacoal Corp., 25
Yamaha Corporation, III; 16 (upd.); 40
   (upd.)
Yamaichi Securities Company, Limited, II
Yamato Transport Co. Ltd., V; 49 (upd.)
Yamazaki Baking Co., Ltd., 58
The Yasuda Fire and Marine Insurance
   Company, Limited, III
The Yasuda Mutual Life Insurance
   Company, III; 39 (upd.)
The Yasuda Trust and Banking Company,
   Ltd., II; 17 (upd.)
The Yokohama Rubber Co., Ltd., V; 19
   (upd.)

Kuwait
Kuwait Airways Corporation, 68
Kuwait Petroleum Corporation, IV; 55
   (upd.)

Latvia
A/S Air Baltic Corporation, 71

Lebanon
Middle East Airlines - Air Liban S.A.L. 79

Libya
National Oil Corporation, IV; 66 (upd.)

Liechtenstein
Hilti AG, 53

Luxembourg
ARBED S.A., IV; 22 (upd.)
Cargolux Airlines International S.A., 49
Esp[00ed]rito Santo Financial Group
   S.A. 79 (upd.)
Gemplus International S.A., 64
RTL Group SA, 44
Société Luxembourgeoise de Navigation
   Aérienne S.A., 64
Tenaris SA, 63

Malaysia
Berjaya Group Bhd., 67
Genting Bhd., 65
Malayan Banking Berhad, 72
Malaysian Airlines System Berhad, 6; 29
   (upd.)
Perusahaan Otomobil Nasional Bhd., 62
Petroliam Nasional Bhd (Petronas), IV; 56
   (upd.)

PPB Group Berhad, 57
Sime Darby Berhad, 14; 36 (upd.)
Telekom Malaysia Bhd, 76
Yeo Hiap Seng Malaysia Bhd., 75

Mauritius
Air Mauritius Ltd., 63

Mexico
Alfa, S.A. de C.V., 19
Altos Hornos de México, S.A. de C.V., 42
América Móvil, S.A. de C.V., 80
Apasco S.A. de C.V., 51
Bolsa Mexicana de Valores, S.A. de C.V.,
   80
Bufete Industrial, S.A. de C.V., 34
Casa Cuervo, S.A. de C.V., 31
Celanese Mexicana, S.A. de C.V., 54
CEMEX S.A. de C.V., 20; 59 (upd.)
Cifra, S.A. de C.V., 12
Consorcio ARA, S.A. de C.V. 79
Consorcio G Grupo Dina, S.A. de C.V.,
   36
Controladora Comercial Mexicana, S.A.
   de C.V., 36
Corporación Internacional de Aviación,
   S.A. de C.V. (Cintra), 20
Desc, S.A. de C.V., 23
Editorial Television, S.A. de C.V., 57
Empresas ICA Sociedad Controladora,
   S.A. de C.V., 41
Ford Motor Company, S.A. de C.V., 20
Gruma, S.A. de C.V., 31
Grupo Aeropuerto del Sureste, S.A. de
   C.V., 48
Grupo Carso, S.A. de C.V., 21
Grupo Casa Saba, S.A. de C.V., 39
Grupo Cydsa, S.A. de C.V., 39
Grupo Elektra, S.A. de C.V., 39
Grupo Financiero Banamex S.A., 54
Grupo Financiero Banorte, S.A. de C.V.,
   51
Grupo Financiero BBVA Bancomer S.A.,
   54
Grupo Financiero Serfin, S.A., 19
Grupo Gigante, S.A. de C.V., 34
Grupo Herdez, S.A. de C.V., 35
Grupo IMSA, S.A. de C.V., 44
Grupo Industrial Bimbo, 19
Grupo Industrial Durango, S.A. de C.V.,
   37
Grupo Industrial Saltillo, S.A. de C.V., 54
Grupo Mexico, S.A. de C.V., 40
Grupo Modelo, S.A. de C.V., 29
Grupo Posadas, S.A. de C.V., 57
Grupo Televisa, S.A., 18; 54 (upd.)
Grupo TMM, S.A. de C.V., 50
Grupo Transportación Ferroviaria
   Mexicana, S.A. de C.V., 47
Hylsamex, S.A. de C.V., 39
Industrias Bachoco, S.A. de C.V., 39
Industrias Penoles, S.A. de C.V., 22
Internacional de Ceramica, S.A. de C.V.,
   53
Kimberly-Clark de México, S.A. de C.V.,
   54
Organización Soriana, S.A. de C.V., 35

United States

Empi, Inc., 26
Empire Blue Cross and Blue Shield, III
The Empire District Electric Company, 77
Empire Resorts, Inc., 72
Employee Solutions, Inc., 18
ENCAD, Incorporated, 25
Encompass Services Corporation, 33
Encore Acquisition Company, 73
Encore Computer Corporation, 13; 74 (upd.)
Encyclopaedia Britannica, Inc., 7; 39 (upd.)
Endo Pharmaceuticals Holdings Inc., 71
Energen Corporation, 21
Energizer Holdings, Inc., 32
Energy Conversion Devices, Inc., 75
Enesco Corporation, 11
Engelhard Corporation, IV; 21 (upd.); 72 (upd.)
Engineered Support Systems, Inc., 59
Engle Homes, Inc., 46
Engraph, Inc., 12
Ennis Business Forms, Inc., 21
Enquirer/Star Group, Inc., 10
Enrich International, Inc., 33
Enron Corporation, V, 19; 46 (upd.)
ENSCO International Incorporated, 57
Ensearch Corporation, V
Entercom Communications Corporation, 58
Entergy Corporation, V; 45 (upd.)
Enterprise Rent-A-Car Company, 6; 69 (upd.)
Entravision Communications Corporation, 41
Envirodyne Industries, Inc., 17
Environmental Industries, Inc., 31
Environmental Power Corporation, 68
Environmental Systems Research Institute Inc. (ESRI), 62
Enzo Biochem, Inc., 41
Eon Labs, Inc., 67
Epic Systems Corporation, 62
EPIQ Systems, Inc., 56
Equifax Inc., 6; 28 (upd.)
Equistar Chemicals, LP, 71
Equitable Life Assurance Society of the United States, III
Equitable Resources, Inc., 6; 54 (upd.)
Equity Marketing, Inc., 26
Equity Office Properties Trust, 54
Equity Residential, 49
Equus Computer Systems, Inc., 49
Erickson Retirement Communities, 57
Erie Indemnity Company, 35
ERLY Industries Inc., 17
Ernie Ball, Inc., 56
Ernst & Young, 9; 29 (upd.)
Escalade, Incorporated, 19
Eschelon Telecom, Inc., 72
Eskimo Pie Corporation, 21
ESPN, Inc., 56
Esprit de Corp., 8; 29 (upd.)
ESS Technology, Inc., 22
Essef Corporation, 18
Esselte, 64
Esselte Pendaflex Corporation, 11

Essence Communications, Inc., 24
The Estée Lauder Companies Inc., 9; 30 (upd.)
Esterline Technologies Corp., 15
Eternal Word Television Network, Inc., 57
Ethan Allen Interiors, Inc., 12; 39 (upd.)
Ethicon, Inc., 23
Ethyl Corporation, I; 10 (upd.)
EToys, Inc., 37
The Eureka Company, 12
Euromarket Designs Inc., 31 (upd.)
Europe Through the Back Door Inc., 65
Evans and Sutherland Computer Company 19; 78 (upd.)
Evans, Inc., 30
Everex Systems, Inc., 16
Evergreen International Aviation, Inc., 53
Everlast Worldwide Inc., 47
Exabyte Corporation, 12; 40 (upd.)
Exar Corp., 14
EXCEL Communications Inc., 18
Excel Technology, Inc., 65
Executive Jet, Inc., 36
Executone Information Systems, Inc., 13
Exelon Corporation, 48 (upd.)
Exide Electronics Group, Inc., 20
Expedia, Inc., 58
Expeditors International of Washington Inc., 17; 78 (upd.)
Experian Information Solutions Inc., 45
Express Scripts Inc., 17; 44 (upd.)
Extended Stay America, Inc., 41
EXX Inc., 65
Exxon Corporation, IV; 7 (upd.); 32 (upd.)
Exxon Mobil Corporation, 67 (upd.)
Eye Care Centers of America, Inc., 69
EZCORP Inc., 43
F&W Publications, Inc., 71
The F. Dohmen Co., 77
F. Korbel & Bros. Inc., 68
Fab Industries, Inc., 27
Fabri-Centers of America Inc., 16
FactSet Research Systems Inc., 73
Fair Grounds Corporation, 44
Fair, Isaac and Company, 18
Fairchild Aircraft, Inc., 9
Fairfield Communities, Inc., 36
Falcon Products, Inc., 33
Fallon McElligott Inc., 22
Fallon Worldwide, 71 (upd.)
Family Christian Stores, Inc., 51
Family Dollar Stores, Inc., 13; 62 (upd.)
Family Golf Centers, Inc., 29
Famous Dave's of America, Inc., 40
Fannie Mae, 45 (upd.)
Fannie May Confections Brands, Inc., 80
Fansteel Inc., 19
FAO Schwarz, 46
Farah Incorporated, 24
Farley Northwest Industries, Inc., I
Farley's & Sathers Candy Company, Inc., 62
Farm Family Holdings, Inc., 39
Farm Journal Corporation, 42
Farmer Bros. Co., 52
Farmer Jack Supermarkets 78

Farmers Insurance Group of Companies, 25
Farmland Foods, Inc., 7
Farmland Industries, Inc., 48
Farouk Systems Inc. 78
Farrar, Straus and Giroux Inc., 15
Fastenal Company, 14; 42 (upd.)
Fatburger Corporation, 64
Faultless Starch/Bon Ami Company, 55
Fay's Inc., 17
Faygo Beverages Inc., 55
Fazoli's Management, Inc., 76 (upd.)
Fazoli's Systems, Inc., 27
Featherlite Inc., 28
Fedders Corporation, 18; 43 (upd.)
Federal Agricultural Mortgage Corporation, 75
Federal Express Corporation, V
Federal National Mortgage Association, II
Federal Paper Board Company, Inc., 8
Federal Prison Industries, Inc., 34
Federal Signal Corp., 10
Federal-Mogul Corporation, I; 10 (upd.); 26 (upd.)
Federated Department Stores Inc., 9; 31 (upd.)
FedEx Corporation, 18 (upd.); 42 (upd.)
Feed The Children, Inc., 68
FEI Company 79
Feld Entertainment, Inc., 32 (upd.)
Fellowes Manufacturing Company, 28
Fender Musical Instruments Company, 16; 43 (upd.)
Fenwick & West LLP, 34
Ferolito, Vultaggio & Sons, 27
Ferrellgas Partners, L.P., 35
Ferro Corporation, 8; 56 (upd.)
F5 Networks, Inc., 72
FHP International Corporation, 6
FiberMark, Inc., 37
Fibreboard Corporation, 16
Fidelity Investments Inc., II; 14 (upd.)
Fidelity National Financial Inc., 54
Fieldale Farms Corporation, 23
Fieldcrest Cannon, Inc., 9; 31 (upd.)
Fifth Third Bancorp, 13; 31 (upd.)
Figgie International Inc., 7
Fiji Water LLC, 74
FileNet Corporation, 62
Fili Enterprises, Inc., 70
Film Roman, Inc., 58
FINA, Inc., 7
Fingerhut Companies, Inc., 9; 36 (upd.)
The Finish Line, Inc., 29; 68 (upd.)
FinishMaster, Inc., 24
Finlay Enterprises, Inc., 16; 76 (upd.)
Firearms Training Systems, Inc., 27
Fireman's Fund Insurance Company, III
First Albany Companies Inc., 37
First Alert, Inc., 28
The First American Corporation, The 52
First Aviation Services Inc., 49
First Bank System Inc., 12
First Brands Corporation, 8
First Cash Financial Services, Inc., 57
First Chicago Corporation, II
First Commerce Bancshares, Inc., 15
First Commerce Corporation, 11